Writer's Guide to Book Editors, Publishers, and Literary Agents

1998–1999

JEFF HERMAN

edited by

JAMIE M. FORBES

PRIMA PUBLISHING

PRIMA PUBLISHING and colophon are registered trademarks of Prima Communications, Inc.

ISBN: 0-7615-1012-5
ISSN: 1089-3369

97 98 99 00 01 BB 10 9 8 7 6 5 4 3 2 1
Printed in the United States of America

How to Order

Single copies may be ordered from Prima Publishing, P.O. Box 1260BK, Rocklin, CA 95677; telephone (916) 632-4400. Quantity discounts are also available. On your letterhead, include information concerning the intended use of the books and the number of books you wish to purchase.

Visit us online at www.primapublishing.com

This work is dedicated to anyone who wants to succeed and wants to see everyone else succeed as well.

—*Jeff Herman*

The power to publish is the power to destroy as well as to create. It is not for the publishers to issue the call; that is determined by a source beyond them. By merits granted or earned, some will be chosen. The gates should therefore never be sealed, and those with the power to publish revealed.

—*An Anonymous Literary Agent*

About the Author

Jeff Herman is founder of The Jeff Herman Literary Agency, Inc., in New York City. One of the youngest and most innovative agents in the book business, he represents more than 100 writers and has sold more than 300 titles. Herman has been extensively written and talked about in numerous print publications and broadcast programs.

Herman is the coauthor with Deborah Levine Herman of *Write the Perfect Book Proposal*.

About the Editor

Jamie M. Forbes works with award-winning creators in celebrity and journalistic non-fiction; business and communications; psychology and behavioral science; performing arts; kitchen arts; narrative and literary arts in print, theater, film, video, and electronic multimedia.

Contributors

Deborah Levine Herman is a vice president of The Jeff Herman Agency and coauthor of *Write the Perfect Book Proposal: 10 Proposals That Sold and Why* (John Wiley & Sons).

Gene Busnar is an author, collaborator, ghostwriter, and publishing consultant with dozens of books to his credit.

William Hamilton is the publisher at University of Hawaii Press.

Greg Ioannou is director of the Editorial Centre in Toronto, Ontario, Canada.

Jamie M. Forbes is a publishing and media consultant based in New York.

Contents

Acknowledgments

A huge project like this requires the dedication and wisdom of many players. In no particular order, they include:

Jamie Forbes, editorial director, contributor, and consultant to this *Writer's Guide*.

Debby Herman, my wife, who never lets me lose sight of worthy endeavors.

My publisher, Ben Dominitz, who has the guts and vision of a true entrepreneur. And his very patient and intelligent editors, Georgia Hughes, Susan Silva, and Brenda Nichols.

My staff of wonderful people: Meredith Browne, Lillian Moon Lee, Sarah Ward, and Pam Howard. I appreciate all the work they do.

Introduction

If you're a veteran consumer of this annual book, welcome home once again. If this is your first visit, your career is likely to receive a major boost.

The publishing business is a mysterious place, even for veteran players. But this book will help you to break the code, unmask false wizards, and empower you to challenge the obstacles.

Always recall the obvious: Growth and success cannot be known by those who give up or fail to even try.

I'm happy to learn from your experiences.

Sincerely,

Jeffrey H. Herman

Jeffrey H. Herman

The Jeff Herman Literary Agency, Inc.
140 Charles Street, Suite 15A
New York, NY 10014
212-941-0540

PART ONE

Writer's Directory of Book Publishers and Editors

United States Publishers

ABBEVILLE PUBLISHING GROUP

488 Madison Avenue
New York, NY 10022
212-888-1969
fax: 212-644-5085
800-278-2665 (800-ARTBOOK)

Abbeville is renowned for finely produced award-winning volumes in the areas of fine arts, art history, architecture, graphic arts, design, lifestyle, cuisine, handicrafts, nature, collectibles, popular culture, sports, and illustrated historical works. Abbeville also produces calendars, stationery items, pop-up children's books, artists' portfolios, and titles in biography, letters, literature, and humor. Abbeville issues hardcover and trade paperback editions—all published with attention to quality in design, illustration, and production standards.

Abbeville Publishing Group includes: Abbeville Press, Abbeville Kids, Artabras, Canopy Books, and Cross River Press. Abbeville Kids is the house's children's imprint (see subentry below). Tiny Folios is a line of small, handsome, reasonably priced gift volumes. The Cross River Press imprint offers titles with a worldwide cultural horizon, often with classic graphics and a literary bent to the text. Editions Abbeville is the house's enterprising French imprint. Aerospace Publishing offers a short list of aeronautical specialty titles. Artabras is a house imprimatur for specially priced promotional/premium volumes.

Abbeville Publishing Group is an international firm with offices in New York and Paris. Abbeville upholds a tradition of bookmaking established by the publisher Harry N. Abrams, who with his son Robert E. Abrams started Abbeville Press (in 1977) subsequent to the purchase of the eponymous publishing house Harry N. Abrams, Inc. by the Times Mirror Company (see entry for Abrams in this directory).

Representing the Abbeville list: *Perfect Country Rooms* by Emma-Louise O'Reilly; *Italian Frescoes: The Early Renaissance, 1400–1470* by Dr. Steffi Roettgen (photographs by Antonio Quattrone); *Curried Favors: Family Recipes from South India* by Maya Kaimal MacMillan; *The Private World of The Duke and Duchess of Windsor* by Hugh Vickers; *The Civil Rights Movement: A Photographic History, 1954–68* by Steven Kasher; *Color Style: How to Identify the Colors That Are Right for Your Home* by Carolyn Warrender; *The Bathroom* by Diane Berger (photographs by Fritz von der

Schulenburg); *St. Petersburg: Architecture of the Tsars* (photographs by Alex Orloff; text by Dmitri Shvidkovsky); *The Devil's Mischief: In Which His Own Story Is Told, in Words and Pictures* by Ed Marquand; *Hieroglyphics: The Writings of Ancient Egypt* by Maria Carmelo Betró; *Back to Mandalay: Burmese Life, Past and Present* by Norman Lewis (photography by Bruno Barbey and Steve McCurry); *Creating a Family Garden: Magical Outdoor Spaces for All Ages* by Bunny Guinness; *Elvis: Treasures of Graceland* by Todd Morgan.

The Wisdom Of . . . is an Abbeville series that presents the essence of the world's great religions and cultures in the words of the sages and the images of master artists and photographers. This ambitious list (edited by John O'Toole) includes titles on: Ancient Greece, Ancient Rome, Judaism, Jesus, Islam, Tao, Buddha, and Zen.

Tiny Folios accents miniature books—for those who love gifts that come in small packages. Series titles: *Treasures of the Museum of Fine Arts, Boston* (chapter introductions by Gillian Wohlauer); *Edgar Degas* by George T. M. Shackelford; *Treasures of the Hermitage* (introduction by Vitaly A. Suslov); *The Life of Christ* by Nancy Grubb; *Treasures of the National Gallery, London* by Erika Langmuir.

Titles from Cross River Press: *Western Furniture: 1350 to the Present Day* (edited by Christopher Wilk); *Harrods: A Palace in Knightsbridge* by Tim Dale (photographs by Fritz von der Schulenburg); *Trinity: A Church, a Parish, a People* (photographs by David Finn; text by Dena Merriam); *Contemporary Botanical Artists: The Shirley Sherwood Collection* by Shirley Sherwood.

Artabras (quality books at bargain prices) titles: *Norman Rockwell's Faith of America* (illustrated by Norman Rockwell; text by Fred Bauer); *The Life of Christ in Art* by Nancy Grubb.

Abbeville's colleagues at Paris-based Flammarion publish a vigorous list with international appeal. The Flammarion program includes: *Dressed to Kill: James Bond, the Suited Hero* by Jay McInerney, Nicholas Foulkes, Neil Norman, and Nick Sullivan; *The Violin* by Yehudi Menuhin; *City of Ambition: Artists and New York, 1900–1960* by Elizabeth Sussman and John G. Hanhardt; *Messengers of Modernism: American Studio Jewelry* by Toni Greenbaum; *A History of Mountain Climbing* by Roger Frison-Roche and Sylvain Jouty; *Impressions of Arabia: Architecture and Frescoes of the Asir Region* by Thierry Mauger; *Beat Culture and the New America: 1950–1965* (copublished with the Whitney Museum of American Art; prologue by Allen Ginsberg; lead essay by Lisa Phillips); *The Book of Chocolate* (preface by Jeanne Bourin).

Abbeville Press distributes its own books throughout the United States, and also distributes for Flammarion; international distribution is handled by regional representatives, including John Murray Ltd. for the United Kingdom.

ABBEVILLE KIDS

Abbeville Kids produces a lineup designed to introduce younger folk to the world of art and design—as well as to hone the tastes of younger artists and connoisseurs. Abbeville Kids offers breakthrough series of interactive, inquiry-based books designed to teach children about art by looking at the world, and about the world by looking at art.

Abbeville Kids also offers books with a broader scope that cover the finer pleasures of living and life.

Titles from Abbeville Kids: *Felix Activity Book* by Leslie Moseley and Marc Tyler Nobleman; *Monkey and the Moon* by John Randall (illustrated by Jim Edmiston); *Stories From the Sea* (compiled by James Riordan, illustrated by Amanda Hall); *Heroines: Great Women Through the Ages* by Rebecca Hazell (illustrated by the author); *Mother and Daughter Tales* (retold by Josephine Evetts-Secker; illustrated by Helen Cann); *Stories From the Stars: Greek Myths of the Zodiac* by Juliet Sharman-Burke (illustrated by Jackie Morris); *Where's the Cat* by Stella Blackstone (illustrated by Debbie Harter).

How Artists See . . . is a series from Abbeville Kids with such titles as *How Artists See the Weather*, *How Artists See the Elements*, *How Artists See People*, and *How Artists See Animals* (all by Colleen Carroll).

Query letters and SASEs should be directed to:

Susan Costello, Editorial Director
Gardening, nature, folk art.

Jackie Decter, Senior Editor
Russian interest, general.

Nancy Grubb, Executive Editor
Fine arts, women's interests.

ABC-CLIO

130 Cremora Drive
P.O. Box 1911
Santa Barbara, CA 93116-1911
812-357-8011

Acquisitions department:
50 South Steele Street, Suite 805
Denver, CO 80209

ABC-CLIO produces high-quality reference books and serial publications in the fields of history, social sciences, political science, humanities, bibliographical reference, art bibliographies, subject bibliographies, directories, guides, and handbooks. ABC-CLIO also produces video guides, CD-ROMs, and serials for professionals. ABC-CLIO is an independent house geared toward the educational market (including curriculum-support materials and references).

The main market for ABC-CLIO books covers school, public and academic libraries, with single books and series keyed to a variety of subjects, including history, politics, social issues, ethics and philosophy, women's studies, mythology, literature, and anthropology. Almost all ABC-CLIO publications are in hardcover; the house actively pursues subrights and foreign rights (with paperback reprint sales going to such houses as Oxford University Press and W. W. Norton).

ABC-CLIO also offers the following series: ABC-CLIO Contemporary World Issues; ABC-CLIO Literary Companions; ABC-CLIO American Leaders; ABC-CLIO Global Studies; ABC-CLIO American History Companions; ABC-CLIO World History Companions; Contemporary Legal Issues; ABC-CLIO's Contemporary World Issues.

ABC-CLIO Literary Companions are developed as definitive reference guides for students and lovers of literature. Titles: *Encyclopedia of Frontier Literature*, *Encyclopedia of Southern Literature*, and *Encyclopedia of Satirical Literature* by Mary Ellen Snodgrass; *Encyclopedia of Literary Epics* by Guida M. Jackson; *Encyclopedia of Allegorical Literature* by David Adams Leeming and Kathleen Morgan Drowne; *Encyclopedia of Apocalyptic Literature* by Valerie P. Zimbaro.

The Encyclopedias of the Human Experience are an exciting series of reference books that cover topics relevant to human behavior, culture, and society—topics of such universal interest as relationships, communication, growing up, and growing old. Titles: *Health and Illness: A Cross-Cultural Encyclopedia* by David Levinson and Laura Gaccione; *Religion: A Cross-Cultural Encyclopedia* by David Levinson; *The Global Village Companion: An A-to-Z Guide to Understanding Current World Affairs* by David Levinson and Karen Christensen; *Encyclopedia of North American Eating and Drinking Traditions, Customs, and Rituals* by Kathlyn Gay and Martin K. Gay.

ABC-CLIO's Contemporary Ethical Issues series present unbiased, up-to-date information on the most prominent ethical topics in today's society. Titles: *The Environment: A Reference Handbook* by Clare Palmer; *Law Enforcement Ethics: A Reference Handbook* by Joseph P. Hester; *Journalism Ethics: A Reference Handbook* by Elliot D. Cohen and Deni Elliott; *Medical Ethics: A Reference Handbook* by Lawrence H. Berlow; *Business Ethics: A Reference Handbook* by John W. Dienhart and Jordan Curnutt; *Encyclopedia of Values and Ethics* by Joseph P. Hester.

Representing the scope of the ABC-CLIO program: *Encyclopedia of Women and Sports* by Victoria Sherrow; *Native Americans: A Reference Guide* (volumes I and II) by Barry Pritzker; *Encyclopedia of Native American Sacred Ceremonies* and *Encyclopedia of Native American Healing* by William S. Lyon; *Encyclopedia of Sacred Places* by Norbert C. Brockman; *Heavens, Hells, and Other Worlds: An Encyclopedia of the Afterlife* by Lionel Rothkrug and Richard P. Taylor; *Spirits, Fairies, Gnomes, and Goblins: An Encyclopedia of the Little People* by Carol Rose; *The Encyclopedia of Capital Punishment* by Mark Grossman; *Encyclopedia of Conflict Resolution* by Heidi Burgess and Guy M. Burgess; *Encyclopedia of Modern American Social Issues* by Michael Kronenwetter; *Encyclopedia of Endangered America: Toxic Waste Sites* by Mark Crawford; *From Talking Drums to the Internet: An Encyclopedia of Communications Technology, Devices, Methods, and Systems* by Robert Gardner and Dennis Shortelle.

ABC-CLIO produces *Exegy*, an electronic encyclopedia of current world information.

Publishing opportunities are open for practitioners and researchers in all branches of the social sciences and humanities; ABC-CLIO welcomes proposals from authors working on projects that fit the publishing program. Writer guidelines are available from the publisher.

ABC-CLIO (founded in 1946) instituted its publishing program with a series of abstracts and indexes in 1955; the house launched its book program in 1967.

ABC-CLIO handles its own distribution.
Query letters and SASEs should be directed to:

Henry Rasof, Senior Acquisitions Editor

ABINGDON PRESS

(See Directory of Religious, Spiritual, and Inspirational Publishers)

ABRAMS

100 Fifth Avenue
New York, NY 10011
212-206-7715

Abrams publishes in the fields of fine art, architecture, design; anthropology, archeology, ethnology and culture; gardening and the home; literary and art criticism; world history; travel and the natural sciences; creative use of technology and new media.

The Abrams list accents fine illustrated volumes, mainly in hardcover, with some trade paperback editions and series, as well as a selection of works in electronic format. Many Abrams books are published in cooperation with institutions such as museums, foundations, or art galleries; these works bring together top-quality illustrative materials and expert text. Abrams publishes a strong seasonal list of new titles and maintains an extensive backlist.

Abrams was founded in 1950 as an independent house (then known as Harry N. Abrams, Inc.) and has been a subsidiary of the Times Mirror Company since 1977. From its inception, the firm has been among the leaders in the field of fine bookmaking in the areas of art, design, and illustrated works.

From Abrams: *Amazing Gems: An Illustrated Guide to the World's Most Dazzling Costume Jewelry* by Deanna Farneti Cera; *American Art Pottery: From the Collection of Everson Museum of Art* by Barbara Perry (photographs by Courtney Frisse); *Babies: History, Art, and Folklore* by Béatrice Fontanel and Claire d'Harcourt; *Max Beckman in Exile* (a Guggenheim Museum publication; writings by Max Beckman; essays by Barbara Stehlé-Akhtar, Reinhard Spieler, and others); *Manuel Alvarez Bravo* (photography) by Susan Kismaric (a Museum of Modern Art book); *Henry Ford Museum: An ABC of American Innovation* by Wes Hardin; *Gardens of Delight: A Pop-Up Anthology of Romantic Verse and Paper Flowers* (illustrations by Robert Nicholls); *Jewish Art* by Gabrielle Sed-Rajna; *The Maya Textile Tradition* (photographs by Jeffrey Jay Foxx; edited by Margot Blum Schevill; foreword by Linda Schele); *The Necklace: From Antiquity to the Present* by Daniela Mascetti and Amanda Triossi; *The Rothschild Gardens* by Miriam Rothschild, Kate Garon, and Lionel de Rothschild (photographs by Andrew Lawson and Lionel de Rothschild); *The Sonoran Desert* (photographs by Jack W. Dykinga; text by Charles Bowden); *The Upland Bird Art of Maynard Reece* by

Maynard Reece (introduction by Roger Tory Peterson); *Virtual Archeology: Re-Creating Ancient Worlds* (edited by Maurizio Forte and Alberto Siliotti; foreword by Colin Renfrew).

Abrams trade paperback lines include Cameo Books: Great Modern Masters (volumes about individual artists); Perspectives (keyed to arts of specific periods or styles); and Discoveries (books covering history, archeology, natural history, culture and the arts over the full range of house subject areas of interest).

Titles here: *Francis Bacon: Painter of a Dark Vision* by Christopher Domino; *Lewis Carroll in Wonderland: The Life and Times of Alice and her Creator* by Stephanie Lovett Stoffel; *Cleopatra: The Life and Death of a Pharaoh* by Edith Flamarion; *Heraldry: An Introduction to a Noble Tradition* by Michael Pastoureau; *Voodoo: Search for the Spirit* by Laënnec Hurbon; *Renaissance Florence: The Invention of a New Art* by A. Richard Turner.

Electronic products: *Escher Interactive: Exploring the Art of the Infinite* (CD-ROM); *Splendors of Imperial China: Treasures from the National Palace Museum, Taipei* (an electronic catalog on CD-ROM).

It should be noted that Abrams is a specialist house and acquires projects on a highly selective basis that gives particular weight to such factors as the national or international renown and credentials of participant artists, photographers, and writers.

Abrams distributes its own books in the United States, and utilizes regional representatives worldwide. Abrams also has a European subsidiary headquartered in the Netherlands as well as a Japanese branch with offices in Tokyo.

Query letters and SASEs should be directed to:

Margaret Chase, Managing Editor

ACADEMY CHICAGO PUBLISHERS

363 West Erie Street
7th Floor East
Chicago, IL 60610
312-751-7300
fax: 312-751-7306
800-248-7323
academy363@aol.com (e-mail)

Academy Chicago publishes general nonfiction, art, history, and gender and cultural studies as well as fiction (including mysteries). The house also offers a line of classic reprints. Academy Chicago Publishers (established in 1975), a small press with an inspired list, is a major player in American letters.

Nonfiction from Academy Chicago includes popular works with an emphasis on contemporary culture, current events, and historical interpretation. Titles here: *I Wish Someone Had Told Me: A Realistic Guide to Early Motherhood* by Nina Barrett; *Ireland: A Concise History from the Twelfth Century to the Present Day* by Paul Johnson; *One Family's Letters from Prague: 1939–1941* (compiled by Raya Czerner

Schapiro and Helga Czerner Weinberg); *The Methuselah Factors: Learning from the World's Longest-Living People* by Dan Georgakas.

The Academy Chicago program in fiction and letters encompasses English-language originals, often with a historical or cultural hook; a solid number of these titles feature the mystery and suspense modes. Academy Chicago also publishes a variety of contemporary and vintage novels in translation, many of which bear the Plover Press imprint.

Frontlist fiction includes: *The Notorious Abbess* by Vera Chapman; *The Monkey's Paw and Other Tales of Mystery and the Macabre* by W. W. Jacobs, edited by Gary Hoppenstand; *The Green Man* by Kingsley Amis.

Representing the range of Academy Chicago fiction and literary works: *The Fat Woman's Joke* by Fay Weldon; *The Life and Times of Deacon A. L. Wiley* by Gregory Alan-Williams (drama/African-American studies); *The Perfect Murder* by H. R. F. Keating. Academy Chicago is the American publisher of the successful British series of humorous and profound Miss Read novels, including *Fresh from the Country*.

Fiction from Plover Press: *Gambusino* by Carlos Montemayor (translated by John Copeland); *On the Seventh Day: Portrait of the Artist as a Creative Writer* by John Mitchell.

Academy Chicago handles its own distribution.

Query letters and SASEs should be directed to:

Anita Miller, Senior Editor

Jordan Miller, Vice President and Editor

ADAMS MEDIA CORPORATION

Adams Publishing
260 Center Street
Holbrook, MA 02343
617-767-8100
fax: 617-767-0994
http://www.adamsonline.com (World Wide Web)

The Adams list accents business and careers, popular psychology, self-improvement and awareness, pets, parenting and the family, lifestyle, cooking and cuisine, sports and games, humor, and gift items (including a line of annotated datebooks). Series include Knock 'Em Dead (career books), JobBank, Adams Business Advisors, Everything books. Adams publishes hardcover and trade paperback editions, and produces a line of titles in electronic format.

The publisher's extensive backlist is particularly strong in the fields of sales how-to, professional-exam preparation, job hunting, and personal finance.

Adams Media Corporation was begun in 1980 as Bob Adams, Inc., Publishers. The current corporate name reflects the increased diversity, continued growth, and marketing success that the enterprise has earned over the years.

Among the fastest-growing book publishers in the United States, Adams is recognized throughout the industry for aggressive promotion. The house is on the lookout for outstanding new nonfiction book proposals in a number of broad trade nonfiction categories, including areas in which the house has met with particular success: personal finance, business, and careers; lifestyle and cuisine; entertainment, sports, and recreation; regional and local interest; interpersonal relationships; and women's issues—as well as book/software packages that fit with the house's core interests.

From Adams: *The New Living Heart* (revised and updated edition of the classic bestseller *The Living Heart*) by Michael E. DeBakey, M.D. and Antonio M. Gotto, Jr., M.D.; *The New Professional Image: From Corporate Casual to the Ultimate Power Look—How to Tailor Your Appearance for Success in Today's Workplace* by Susan Bixler with Nancy Nix-Rice; *Small Miracles: Extraordinary Coincidences from Everyday Life* by Yitta Halberstam and Judith Leventhal (preface by Bernie Siegel); *Marketing Magic* by Don Debelak; *Golf Is a Woman's Game: 25 Simple Techniques for Building a Better Game* by Jane Horn; *Test Your Cat's Mental Health* by Missy Dizick; *Weird History 101: My Dinner with Attila the Hun, "I Started World War I," Watching Custer's Last Stand and Other Tales of Intrigue, Mayhem, and Outrageous Behavior* by John Richard Stephens; *How I Sold a Million Copies of My Software . . . and How You Can, Too!* by Herbert R. Kraft; *The Everything Backyard Book* by Tracy Will (part of the Everything series); *Healing Mind, Body, and Spirit: Take Control of Your Health and Well-Being* by M. J. Abadie; *Really Reading! 10 Simple and Effective Methods to Develop Your Child's Love for Reading!* by Janet Gardner and Lora Myers.

Topical interest, popular biography, and backlist favorites include: *Old Soldiers Never Die: The Life of Douglas MacArthur* by Geoffrey Perret; *Happy Days Were Here Again: Reflections of a Libertarian Journalist* by William F. Buckley Jr.; *Life, Liberty, and the Pursuit of Happiness* by Peggy Noonan; *Famous Friends of the Wolf Cookbook* by Nancy Reid and Sheila Liermann (photographs by Jim Brandenburg and Jim Dutcher); *Josephine: The Josephine Baker Story* by Jean-Claude Baker and Chris Chase; *I Fall to Pieces: The Music and the Life of Patsy Cline* by Mark Bego; *The Lost Lennon Interviews* by Geoffrey and Brenda Giuliano; *365 Excuses for Being Late to Work* by Andy Sharpe; *You Know You're Drinking Too Much Coffee When . . .* by Aviv and Davide Ilan; *Just Do It: The Nike Spirit in the Corporate World* by Donald Katz.

Among its successful series, the Adams program has featured Knock 'Em Dead career books by Martin Yate, which detail techniques in résumé writing and employment interviews. The ongoing JobBank series profiles employment opportunities in regionally keyed directories.

The innovative Streetwise line offers a heavily illustrated approach and hundreds of concise entries for practical presentation of on-target information. Titles here: *Streetwise Selling* by Nancy J. Stephens; *Streetwise Consulting* by David Kintler; *Streetwise Small Business Start-Up* by Bob Adams.

Adams Business Advisors are books designed to help new and growing private enterprises start right, solve problems, and endure successfully. Titles here: *The Small Business Legal Kit* (including companion software) by J. W. Dicks; *Winning the Entrepreneur's Game* by David E. Rye; *Managing People* by Darien McWhirter. How to Incorporate and Start a Business is a series by J. W. Dicks geared to individual states.

Representative of Adams books geared to children and the family: *101 Reasons Why Cats Make Great Kids* by Allia Zobel (illustrated by Nicole Hollander); *The Everything*

Baby Names Book by Lisa Shaw; *The Museum of Science Activities for Kids* by Tanya Gregoire, Joan Wilcox, and Boston's Museum of Science; *365 TV-Free Activities You Can Do with Your Child* and *365 Outdoor Activities You Can Do with Your Child* (both by Steve and Ruth Bennett).

Adams orchestrates its own worldwide distribution network. In the United States, Adams distributes directly to bookstore chains and independents, and also operates through wholesalers and jobbers; in the United Kingdom and elsewhere in the world, the publisher distributes via overseas distributors. The house also sells its products to the gift trade, the office trade, and the computer software trade.

Query letters and SASEs should be directed to:

Pam Altschul Liflander, Editor

Commercial nonfiction consistent with house list. Special areas: health, New Age, spirituality, humor, biography, and women's issues. Projects include: *Small Miracles*; *The New Living Heart* (with Dr. Michael DeBakey); books in the EVERYTHING series—covering backyards, bicycles, cats, college survival, pasta, home improvement, wine, golf, dreams, and more.

Edward Walters, Editor in Chief

Acquires in a wide range of commercial nonfiction categories. Especially interested in: humor, investing, personal finance, popular reference, relationships, science, small business, and sports. Projects include: *Good Families Don't Just Happen*; *You Know You're Drinking Too Much Coffee When . . .* ; *The Psychologist's Book of Career Self-Tests*; *Selling Microsoft*; The New York Public Library's *Around the American Table*; *King of the Cowboys*; The Museum of Science's *Book of Answers & Questions*; *Sally Edwards' Heart Zone Training*.

Ann Weaver, Editor

Women's issues, self-help, parenting, and education. Projects include: *Really Reading: 10 Steps for Developing Your Child's Reading*; *Don't Stop at Green Lights*; and *Changing Positions: Women Speak Out on Sex and Desire*.

ADDISON WESLEY LONGMAN PUBLISHING COMPANY

One Jacob Way
Route 128
Reading, MA 01867-3999
617-944-3700

School Publishing Group

2725 Sand Hill Road
Menlo Park, CA 94025

Addison Wesley Longman Publishing Group publishes in hardcover and paperback with a trade focus on business, health, parenting, psychology, and science. The three primary acquisitions programs of the General Publishing Group are designated Business, Science, and Lifelong Learning. Other special areas include business management, general business, and computer books. Addison Wesley Longman also hones an established educational and textbook program.

Addison Wesley Longman is not currently acquiring general-interest trade nonfiction outside its core speciality program.

The Addison Wesley Longman trade division incorporates a number of imprints and subsidiaries with varied specialties. Addison Wesley imprints and divisions include Merloyd Lawrence Books (serious commercial books), Peachpit Press (computer books), Helix Books (titles in the sciences), and Planet Dexter (children's books).

Addison Wesley Longman offers a full range of computer books. For the most part, titles on the Developers Press imprint are directed toward programmers and the technical end. The house's trade computer books are geared to such areas as business computing, graphics, and database management, covering the Apple and Windows realms. In late 1994 Addison Wesley acquired consumer-computer book specialist Peachpit Press, thus increasing house presence in this burgeoning arena. (Please see separate main entry in this section for Peachpit Press.)

Trade nonfiction from Addison Wesley Longman: *Race Rules: Navigating the Color Line* by Michael Eric Dyson; *Walking Possession: Essays and Reviews, 1968–1993* by Ian Hamilton; *A Life in School: What the Teacher Is Learning* by Jane Tompkins; *Catholics in Crisis: An American Parish Fights for Its Soul* by Jim Naughton; *The Controversy of Zion: Jewish Nationalism, the Jewish State, and the Unresolved Jewish Dilemma* by Geoffrey Wheatcroft; *The Nature of Massachusetts: Massachusetts Audubon Society* by Christopher Leahy, John Hanson Mitchell, and Thomas Conuel (illustrated by Lars Jonsson); *Yellow Fever, Black Goddess: The Coevolution of People and Plagues* by Christopher Wills; *Alvin Ailey: A Life in Dance* by Jennifer Dunning; *Jewish Power: Inside the American Jewish Establishment* by J. J. Goldberg; *Bad Boy: The Life and Politics of Lee Atwater* by John Brady; *Hitler's Thirty Days to Power: January 1933* by Henry Ashby Turner, Jr.; *The Cruelty of Depression* by Jacques Hassoun, Ph.D.; *Venus Revealed: A New Look Below the Clouds of Our Mysterious Twin Planet* by David H. Grinspoon; and *The Growth of the Mind: And the Endangered Origins of Intelligence* by Stanley I. Greenspan, M.D. with Beryl Lieff Benderly.

On the list in business, economics, finance, and careers: *Customers Mean Business: How World-Class Companies Build Relationships That Last* by James A. Unruh (Chairman and CEO, Unisys Corporation); *The Microsoft Way: The Real Story of How the Company Outsmarts Its Competition* by Randall E. Stross; *The Feminine Economy and Economic Man: A Radical Proposal* by Shirley P. Burggraf, Ph.D.; *Creative Collaboration: Leading Groups to Greatness* by Warren Bennis and Patricia Ward Biederman; *The Health-Care Revolution: Who Wins, Who Loses in the Transformation of America's Largest Service Industry* by Regina Herzlinger, Harvard Business School; *Reinventing Your Government: Strategies, Tools, and Tactics for Transforming the Public Sector* by David Osborne and Peter Plastrik; *Mining the Sky: Untold Riches from the Asteroids, Comets, and Planets* by John S. Lewis.

Addison Wesley Longman handles distribution for its list, as well as for its subsidiaries and imprints.

Query letters and SASEs should be directed to:

John Bell, Editor
Health, parenting, psychology.

Nick Philipson, Executive Editor
Business.

Jeff Robbins, Editor in Chief, Helix Books
The sciences; popular works.

Beth Wolfensberger, Planet Dexter
Children's activity books.

John Wait, Editor, Computer Books Division
Computer books.

MERLOYD LAWRENCE BOOKS
ADDISON WESLEY LONGMAN

Boston office:
102 Chestnut Street
Boston, MA 02108
617-523-5895

Merloyd Lawrence Books produces a list with areas of focus in issues of contemporary interest, child development, psychology, and education. The imprint is home to the Radcliffe Biography Series, a collection of historical biographies of notable women.

From the Merloyd Lawrence list: *The Challenging Child: How to Understand, Raise, and Enjoy Your "Difficult" Child* by Stanley I. Greenspan with Jacqueline Salmon; *Bonding: Building the Foundations of Secure Attachment and Independence* by Marshall H. Klaus, John H. Kennell, and Phyllis H. Klaus; *Dr. Susan Love's Breast Book* by Susan Love with Karen Lindsey.

Query letters and SASEs should be directed to:

(Ms.) Merloyd Lawrence, President and Publisher

ADDISON WESLEY LONGMAN

New York office:
1185 Avenue of the Americas
New York, NY 10036
212-782-3300

Query letters and SASEs should be directed to:

Henning Gutmann, Senior Editor
Politics, history, business and economics, current events.

ALGONQUIN BOOKS OF CHAPEL HILL
(See Workman Publishing Company)

ALYSON PUBLICATIONS

6922 Hollywood Boulevard, Suite 1000
Los Angeles, CA 90028
213-871-1225

Alyson Publications is geared to topnotch expressions of the gay and lesbian cultural arenas. Alyson also catalogs a list with multicultural, bisexual, and transgender appeal, as well as crossover titles of mainstream interest and social import. Alyson offers a select seasonal list of trade nonfiction and commercial fiction, published in hardcover, trade paperback, and mass-market paperbacks. The press tends a heady backlist.

Alyson accents both issues and lifestyle in such nonfiction categories as current affairs, history, biography and memoirs, games and puzzles, cartoon collections, and popular reference (including books of anecdotes and lists). Fiction keynotes both mainstream narratives and genre titles. Works of literary note are offered in all areas.

Alyson Publications was founded in 1977 by Sasha Alyson (reputedly with an initial outlay of $500) and was headquartered in Boston for its first decade and a half, during which the house released many prominent titles in the lesbian-and-gay publishing arena. In 1995 Alyson Publications was purchased by the publishers of *The Advocate* magazine, and its editorial offices relocated from the east coast to the west coast.

Indicative of Alyson trade nonfiction: *Lesbians Raising Sons* (edited by Jess Wells); *School's Out: The Impact of Gay and Lesbian Issues on America's Schools* by Dan Woog; *The Lesbian Sex Book: A Guide for Women Who Love Women* by Wendy Caster; *A Lotus of Another Color: An Unfolding of the South Asian Gay and Lesbian Experience* (edited by Rakesh Ratti); *Bi Any Other Name* (edited by Loraine Hutchins and Lani Kaahumanu).

Fiction and literary works embrace novels and story collections, literary memoirs, essays, and category-keyed anthologies. Titles here: *If Only for One Nite* (fiction) by James Earl Hardy; *Resident Alien* (commentary and memoir) by Quentin Crisp; *The Hadra* (lesbian fantasy adventure) by Diana Rivers; *The Femme Mystique* (collection edited by Lesléa Newman); *Rattler!* (part of the Dakota series of Westerns) by Cap Iverson; *Rapture and the Second Coming* (suspense) by Wendy Borgstrom; *My First Time: Gay Men Describe Their First Same-Sex Experience* (edited by Jack Hart); *Macho Sluts* (pansexual erotica) by Pat Califia; *Embracing the Dark* (tales of horror; edited by Eric Garber); *Dykescapes* (literary anthology; edited by Tina Portillo); *Below the Belt and Other Stories* by Phil Andros; *Amnesty* (literary writing) by Louise A. Blum.

An uninhibited poetry slam is presented in print through the pages of *Gents, Bad Boys, and Barbarians* (edited by Rudy Kikel).

Educational and younger-readers' titles: *Daddy's Roommate* by Michael Willhoite; *Heather Has Two Mommies* by Lesléa Newman (illustrated by Diana Souza); *Two Teenagers in Twenty: Writings by Gay and Lesbian Youth* (edited by Ann Heron).

Alyson Publications distributes through Consortium.

Query letters and SASEs should be directed to:

Greg Constante, Publisher

Gerry Kroll, Editor in Chief

AMACOM

American Management Association
1601 Broadway
New York, NY 10019-7420
212-586-8100
fax: 212-903-8083

AMACOM publishes business and management books, primarily for a professional readership. AMACOM trade nonfiction lines include works that cover the fields of accounting and finance, career, customer services, management issues, general business and management, human resources, management skills, international business, manufacturing, personal development, quality, reference books, personal finance, project management, marketing and advertising, personal development, small business, supervision, sales and sales management, and training. The house also offers a special series on successful office skills.

Managers in large and small companies are encouraged to use AMACOM books as an inexpensive and effective way to energize their staff, explain new concepts, teach specific skills, and inspire employees at all levels. AMACOM challenges companies to empower employees at all levels to teach themselves!

Titles from AMACOM: *The 8 Practices of Exceptional Companies* by Jac Fitz-enz; *Beyond the Looking Glass* by Alan Downs; *Delivering Knock-Your-Socks-Off Service* by Kristin Anderson and Ron Zemke; *Get It Together by 30* by Richard D. Thau and Jay S. Heflin; *Technical Analysis of Stock Trends* by Robert D. Edwards and John Magee; *Silent Sabotage: Rescuing Our Careers, Our Companies, and Our Lives from the Creeping Paralysis of Anger and Bitterness* by William J. Morin; *The Northbound Train: Finding the Purpose, Setting the Direction, Shaping the Destiny of Your Organization* by Karl Albrecht; *Cybercorp* by James Martin; *Crisis Management for Corporate Self-Defense: How to Protect Your Organization in a Crisis . . . How to Stop a Crisis Before It Starts* by Steve Albrecht; *Beyond Race and Gender: Unleashing the Power of Your Total Work Force by Managing Diversity* by R. Roosevelt Thomas, Jr.; *Preventing Violence in the Workplace* by Charles E. Labig; *Why This Horse Won't Drink: How to Win and Keep Employee Commitment* by Ken Matejka; *Business Buzzwords: Everything You Need to Know to Speak the Lingo of the 90's* by Charles B. Wendel and Elaine Svennson; *The Time Trap: The New Version of the 20-Year Classic on Time Management* by Alex Mackenzie; *Computer Desktop Encyclopedia* by Alex Freedman; *Cybermarketing* by Len L. Keller.

Prospective writers might keep in mind the AMACOM readership profile (not to typecast, but rather to offer guidelines): AMACOM readers are definitely not mass-market consumers; they want specialized materials and information on business issues that concern them most. AMACOM bookbuyers want more than a quick fix. They crave in-depth ideas and practical approaches they can try out on the job. They like to be on the leading edge and get a jump on the competition. They do not want second-hand information. They want to go straight to the source. AMACOM readers appreciate value and a good deal.

AMACOM distributes its own products through multiple marketing channels, including retail trade, direct marketing, special sales, and international sales (through McGraw-Hill).

Query letters and SASEs should be directed to:

Adrienne Hickey, Senior Acquisitions Editor
General and human resource management.

Ellen Kadin, Senior Acquisitions Editor
Career skills, sales and marketing, customer service, self-development.

AMERICAN BAR ASSOCIATION BOOK PUBLISHING

750 North Lake Shore Drive
Chicago, IL 60611
312-988-5000

The American Bar Association publishes a variety of resources for wide categories of specialty legal fields. The publishing division offers books, periodicals, pamphlets, and videotapes.

The American Bar Association is the national organization of the legal profession. The Association is committed to keeping its members and the general public informed of the latest developments in law and law-related fields. To accomplish this goal, it publishes numerous books and pamphlets and, on a regular basis, a variety of magazines, journals, and newsletters.

The prospective writer should note that American Bar Association publishes for the professional market, and each ABA division publishes its own line of books. Please inquire as to which divisional line your project fits before querying. For general-interest professional-legal projects, query letters and SASEs may be directed to:

Joseph Weintraub, Director of Publications, Planning, and Marketing

Kerry Klumpy, Managing Editor

AMERICAN FEDERATION OF ASTROLOGERS

(See Directory of Religious, Spiritual, and Inspirational Publishers)

AMERICAN MEDICAL ASSOCIATION
AMA BOOKS

515 North State Street
Chicago, IL 60610
312-464-5983

American Medical Association books cover areas of professional information and reference in the healthcare field, as well as a growing concentration in patient-information and related materials intended for a popular general readership.

American Medical Association (founded in 1847), in addition to being a preeminent professional organization in the field of medicine, is the world's largest medical publisher. The focus of this organization's publishing program is professional information and reference. In addition, the house has expanded its line of publications for the commercial trade market.

Books that bear the AMA logo (based on the serpent staff of Aesculapius) satisfy rigorous editorial and professional standards. In addition to medical-specialist works, AMA Books considers proposals from qualified authors on topics of interest to the broad and diversified patient market. AMA looks for materials that are supported by sound medical research and that can withstand the demands of AMA's review process; these works should also be user friendly, aimed at an audience with no formal medical training.

For particular trade-oriented projects, AMA functions as copublisher; these titles are marketed and distributed through the offices of the partner publishers or independent trade-distribution specialists. For example, AMA has combined with Random House on several selected titles (including *AMA Pocket Guide to Back Pain* and *AMA Pocket Guide to Calcium*); these books are catalogued and marketed with the Random House list.

Query letters and SASEs should be directed to:

Gail L. Cassel, Manager, Product Line Development

AMERICAN PSYCHIATRIC PRESS, INC.

1400 K Street, NW
Washington, DC 20005
202-682-6268
fax: 202-682-6341
800-368-5777
http://www.appi.org (World Wide Web)

American Psychiatric Press (founded in 1981) publishes professional, reference, and trade books, as well as college textbooks. The press's spheres of interest include the behavioral and social sciences, psychiatry, and medicine. The house publishes a midsized booklist in hardcover and trade paper, and also produces a number of professional journals; selected reference works are issued in electronic formats (including diskettes and CD-ROM).

Although by far the major portion of the American Psychiatric list is geared toward the professional and academic markets, the house catalogs a number of books in the areas of patient information and books for the general public, among which are selected titles marketed through trade channels.

Representative of the American Psychiatric popular-interest list: *The Broken Connection: On Death and the Continuity of Life* by Robert Jay Lifton; *Wrestle with*

Demons: A Psychiatrist Struggles to Understand His Patients and Himself by Keith Russell Ablow; *Lies! Lies! Lies! The Psychology of Deceit* by Charles V. Ford; *Bad Men Do What Good Men Dream* by Robert I. Simon; *Talking About Sex* by Derek C. Polonsky, *How to Help Your Child Overcome Your Divorce* by Elissa P. Benedek and Catherine F. Brown; *Surviving Childhood Cancer: A Guide for Families* by Margot Joan Fromer; and *The Preteen's First Book About Love, Sex, and AIDS* by Michelle Harrison (illustrated by Lynn Beckstrom).

New professional titles from American Psychiatric: *Comprehensive Review of Geriatric Psychiatry* (second edition) (edited by Joel Sadavoy, M.D., Lawrence W. Lazarus, M.D., Lissy F. Jarvik, M.D., Ph.D., and George T. Grossberg, M.D.); *The American Psychiatric Press Textbook of Consultation-Liaison Psychiatry* (edited by James R. Rundell, M.D. and Michael G. Wise, M.D.); *Textbook of Homosexuality and Mental Health* (edited by Robert P. Cabaj, M.D. and Terry S. Stein, M.D.); *American Psychiatric Association Practice Guidelines* by the American Psychiatric Association; *Impulsivity and Compulsivity* (edited by John M. Oldham, M.D., Eric Hollander, M.D., and Andrew E. Skokdol, M.D.); *Long-Term Treatments of Anxiety Disorders* (edited by Matig R. Mavissakalian, M.D. and Robert F. Prien, Ph.D.); *Psychopharmacology and Women: Sex, Gender, and Hormones* (edited by Margaret F. Jensvold, M.D., Uriel Halbreich, M.D., and Jean A. Hamilton, M.D.); *Sexual Harassment in the Workplace and Academia: Psychiatric Issues* (Clinical Practice 38) (edited by Diane K. Shrier, M.D.); *Do They Grow Out of It? Long-Term Outcomes of Childhood Disorders* (edited by Lily Hechtman, M.D.); *The Selfish Brain: Learning from Addiction* by Robert L. DuPont, M.D.; *The Dilemma of Ritual Abuse: Cautions and Guides for Therapists* (edited by George A. Fraser, M.D.).

American Psychiatric Press is the publisher of the psychiatric profession's accredited clinical guidebook: *Diagnostic and Statistical Manual of Mental Disorders* (fourth edition), also known as *DSM-IV*.

American Psychiatric Press distributes through several regional distribution services.

Query letters and SASEs should be directed to:

Carol C. Nadelson, M.D., President and Chief Executive Officer, Editor in Chief

Claire Reinburg, Editorial Director

AMERICAN PSYCHOLOGICAL ASSOCIATION, INC.

750 First Street, NE
Washington, DC 20002-4242
202-336-5793

Areas of American Psychological Association publishing interest include virtually all aspects of the field of psychology: methodology, history, student aids, teaching, health, business strategies, violence, personality, and clinical issues. APA publications include books, journals, publishing resources, continuing-education/home-study programs, audiotapes, videotapes, and databases.

The information resources produced by APA are grounded in a long publishing tradition of scholarly and professional works that encompass diverse topics and applications in the arena of human behavior, from basic research to practical therapies, including the teaching curriculum of psychology as well as the contributions of psychology to progressive education, from personality disorders to implications for psychology of public policies. American Psychological Association (founded in 1892) is the major psychological organization in the United States.

On the APA list: *Manual of Diagnosis and Professional Practice in Mental Retardation* (edited by John W. Jacobson and James A. Mulick); *Stereotyped Movements: Brain and Behavior Relationships* (edited by Robert L. Sprague and Karl M. Newell); *Exploring Sport and Exercise Psychology* (edited by July L. Van Raalte and Britton W. Brewer); *School-Based Prevention for Children at Risk: The Primary Mental Health Project* by Emory L. Cowen, A. Kirk Hightower, Joanne L. Pedro-Carroll, William C. Work, and Peter A. Wyman with William G. Haffey; *Religion and the Clinical Practice of Psychology* (edited by Edward Shafranske); *Heart and Mind: The Practice of Cardiac Psychology* (edited by Robert Allan and Stephen Scheidt); *Casebook of Clinical Hypnosis* (edited by Steven Jay Lynn, Irving Kirsch, and Judith W. Rhue); *Why We Eat What We Eat: The Psychology of Eating* (edited by Elizabeth D. Capaldi); *Neuropsychology for Clinical Practice: Etiology, Assessment, and Treatment of Common Neurological Disorders* (edited by Russell L. Adams, Oscar A. Parsons, Jan L. Culbertson, and Sara Jo Nixon); *Measuring Self-Concept Across the Life Span: Issues and Instrumentation* by Barbara M. Byrne; *Men in Groups: Insights, Interventions, and Psychoeducational Work* (edited by Michael P. Andronico); *Answering Your Questions About AIDS* by Seth C. Kalachman; *Body Image, Eating Disorders, and Obesity: An Integrative Guide for Assessment and Treatment* (edited by J. Kevin Thompson); *Adaptation to Chronic Childhood Illness* by Robert J. Thompson, Jr., and Kathryn E. Gustafson; *Stereotype Accuracy: Toward Appreciating Group Differences* (edited by Yueh-Ting Lee, Lee J. Jussim, and Clark R. McCauley); *Ethnocultural Aspects of Posttraumatic Stress Disorder: Issues, Research, and Clinical Applications* (edited by Anthony J. Marsella, Matthew J. Friedman, Ellen T. Gerrity, and Raymond M. Scurfield); *Psychosocial Treatments for Child and Adolescent Disorders: Empirically Based Strategies for Clinical Practice* (edited by Euthymia D. Hibbs and Peter S. Jensen); *Converging Operations in the Study of Visual Selective Attention* (edited by Arthur F. Kramer, Gordon D. Logon, and Michael G. H. Coles); *Diet–Behavior Relationships: Focus on Depression* by Larry Christenson.

A publication of American Psychological Association that has wide influence in all areas of scholarly publishing, especially the social and behavioral sciences, is *Publication Manual of the American Psychological Association* (now in its fourth edition), a resource that guides writers and editors through manuscript preparation and production.

APA handles its own distribution.

Query letters and SASEs should be directed to:

Julia Frank-McNeil, Director, APA Books

AMERICAN SOCIETY FOR TRAINING AND DEVELOPMENT (ASTD)
ASTD BOOKS

1640 King Street
P.O. Box 1443
Alexandria, VA 22313-2043
703-683-8100

American Society for Training and Development (ASTD) Books is a business-information specialist. Among ASTD's major categories are customer service, sales and marketing, quality, training basics, performance appraisals and improvement, multicultural and women's issues, America and the new economy, workforce issues, consulting, teamwork, technology, games, and problem solving and creativity. In addition to books, ASTD offers training kits, diagnostic tools, presentation materials, games and simulations, videos, audiotapes, and computer software.

ASTD Books (founded in 1944) is the book-publishing wing of American Society for Training and Development, a nonprofit membership organization. The house's professional books cover such areas as employee education, training, and development; human resource development; organization management; and career development. Within this business arena, ASTD strives to put forth a list that represents the most current topics, the most innovative techniques, and the most gifted authors in the field. ASTD publishes selected titles in conjunction with other business-oriented houses, such as Irwin Professional Publications, Jossey-Bass, and McGraw-Hill.

Books listed in the ASTD catalog are reviewed and selected by a distinguished and professional peer group.

Titles from ASTD: *ASTD Models for Human Performance Improvement: Roles, Competencies, and Outputs* by William J. Rothwell; *Elements of Competency for Diversity Work* by The ASTD Multicultural Forum, in collaboration with the Disabilities Awareness Forum, Women's Forum, and Sexual Orientation Issues in the Workplace; *Strategic Thinking: A Guide to Identifying and Solving Problems* by Roger Kaufman; *The Standup Trainer: Technique from the Theater and the Comedy Club to Help Your Students Laugh, Stay Awake, and Learn Something Useful* by Ellen Dowling; *ASTD's Guide to Learning Organization Assessment Instruments.*

The ASTD Trainer's Sourcebook Series by Richard L. Roe, Senior Editor, was developed by ASTD in partnership with McGraw-Hill. The new series is written by known experts in each topic. The sourcebooks feature an overview of the subject, experiential learning activities, role plays, handouts, assessment instruments, discussion questions. Also included are full-day, half-day, one-hour, and 30-minute training designs that can be customized to meet individual needs.

Writers: If you are working on a book targeted to trainers that you think ASTD might like to publish, please contact Nancy Olson, Vice President for Publications (703-683-8131). Guidelines for submitting a book proposal are available upon request.

ASTD Books distributes its own list via an in-house easy-ordering program; selected ASTD books are available through other publishing houses, for which ASTD returns the favor by cataloging business titles from a variety of other publishers—not limited to business specialists: John Wiley; Random House; Scott, Foresman; and Van Nostrand Reinhold.

Query letters and SASEs should be directed to:

Nancy Olson, Vice President for Publications

ANDREWS AND MCMEEL

4520 Main Street
Kansas City, MO 64111-7701
816-932-6700
fax: 816-932-6749

Andrews and McMeel (founded in 1970) is a Universal Press Syndicate company that publishes a wide assortment of general trade nonfiction books and consumer references, children's nonfiction, humor (including cartoon books), and calendars. Areas of interest include journalism and current affairs, popular culture and lifestyles, politics, psychology and self-help, health and medicine, business, sports and fitness, travel, biography, new age and inspiration, women's issues, nature, gift books (including highly illustrated and full-color titles), children's interactive and book-plus products. Andrews and McMeel publishes over 100 calendars each year in day-to-day, wall, and desk-diary format.

Titles from Andrews and McMeel trade: *Mary Engelbreit: The Art and the Artist* by Mary Engelbreit and Patrick Regan; *It's a Magical World: A Calvin and Hobbes Collection* by Bill Watterson; *Fugitive from the Cubicle Police: A Dilbert Book* by Scott Adams; *Last Chapter and Worse: A Far Side Collection* by Gary Larson; *Virtual Doonesbury* by G. B. Trudeau; *Meditations for Toddlers Who Do Too Much* by Sarah Gillespie and Nancy Parent; *Ernie: Out of Control* by Bud Grace; *The PSI Factor: Chronicles of the Paranormal* (edited by Dan Aykroyd); *Modern-Day Miracles: How Ordinary People Experience Supernatural Acts of God* by Paul Rather; *John F. Kennedy Jr.: A Life in the Spotlight* by Montague Druitt; *Never Drink Coffee from Your Saucer . . . and Other Tips on Socially Correct Dining* by Sheila M. Long; *Everything You Need to Know About College Sports Recruiting: A Guide for Players and Parents* by Jim Walsh with Richard Trubo; *The Lost History of the Canine Race: Our 15,000-Year Love Affair with Dogs* by Mary Elizabeth Thurston; *Good Nights: How to Stop Sleep Deprivation, Overcome Insomnia, and Get the Sleep You Need* by Gary Zammit, M.D.

Also of note from Andrews and McMeel: *Protect Your Achilles Heel: Crafting Armor for the New Age at Work* by Wess Roberts, Ph.D.; *The Man Who Loved God* by William X. Kienzle; *Re-Create Your Life: Transforming Yourself and Your World Through the Decision Maker Process* by Morty Lefkoe; *The Dog Ate My Homework: Personal Responsibility—How We Avoid It and What to Do About It* by Vincent Barry; *The Kinship of Women: A Celebration of Enduring Friendship* by Pat Ross; *When the Bough Breaks: Forever After the Death of a Son or Daughter* by Judith R. Bernstein, Ph.D.; *Pregnant Fathers: Challenges and Discoveries on the Road to Being a Father* by Jack Heinowitz, Ph.D.; *Naturally Slim and Powerful: The Natural Way to Boost*

Serotonin Levels Without Drugs . . . Lose Weight Without Losing Your Mind by Dr. Philip Lipetz and Monika Pichler; *Golf Ching: Golf Guidance and Wisdom from the I Ching* by Terrence MacClure; *Bedtime Stories for Cats* by Leigh Anne Jasheway; *The Most Important Thing I Know: Life Lessons from Colin Powell, Stephen Covey, Maya Angelou, and 100 Other Eminent Individuals* (edited by Lorne Adrain); *Keep Talking: A Mother–Daughter Guide to the Pre-Teen Years* by Lynda Madison, Ph.D.; *How to Be the Perfect Mother-In-Law* by Camille Russo with Michael Shain; *Politically Correct Old Testament Stories* by Robert Martin Walker; *Naughty Shakespeare: The Lascivious Lines, Cuckolded Characters, and Politically Incorrect Notions of the Baddest Bard of All* by Michael Macrone; *Dave Barry's Book of Bad Songs* by Dave Barry; *Tall Blondes: A Book about Giraffes* by Lynn Sherr; *The Union Station Massacre: The Making of J. Edgar Hoover's FBI* by Robert Unger.

Tiny Tomes are tiny, of course—as well as topical, traditional, tactile, tempting, and targeted. These teeny books from Andrews and McMeel are less than half the size of their little gift books—the tactile allure of these palm-size volumes is said to be irresistible. Titles include: *Friendship*; *Love*; *For Mother with Love*; *For Father with Love*; *Brides*; *Babies*; *Faith & Inspiration*.

Each volume in the Cader Unstamped Books line presents 16 sheets of exquisitely designed and printed stamps. Use them to personalize and decorate correspondence, collect them, or frame them. Titles here include: *Nature Unstamped*; *Holidays Unstamped*; *Angels Unstamped*.

Andrews and McMeel distributes its own list, which is handled by regional sales representatives. Andrews and McMeel also distributes for Cumberland House Publishing and Greenwich Workshop. The house copublishes Cader Books.

Agents, please query. No unsolicited manuscripts are accepted. Query letters and SASEs should be directed to:

Christine Schillig, Vice President and Editorial Director
General nonfiction, all categories.

Dorothy O'Brien, Executive Managing Editor
Humor and general nonfiction.

Jean Lowe, Executive Editor
Psychology, self-help, new age, inspiration.

Jake Morrissey, Senior Editor and Director, Newspaper Publishing
Journalism and current affairs, politics, general nonfiction.

Patty Rice, Associate Editor
Child care, parenting, careers.

Polly Blair, Editorial
General nonfiction.

THE ANONYMOUS PRESS, INC.

332 Bleecker Street F36
New York, NY 10014
888-2WRITE2 (888-297-4832)

The Anonymous Press specializes in high-velocity projects that tap the current cultural pulse. The house is on the lookout for commercial, inherently marketable nonfiction in such areas as investigative and journalistic accounts; issues-oriented human-interest stories; celebrity biographies and memoirs; ultimate conspiracies, exposés, and scandalous affairs; and popular reference works (including high-interest single-volume encyclopedias, personal and professional how-to, and awareness).

The Anonymous Press, Inc. (founded in 1996) is an independent publisher dedicated to open expression and individual liberty. This is viewed as an activist mission, not a statement of guaranteed privilege. People must take it upon themselves to carry the ongoing fight for their personal right to pursue the life that's best for them. The press publishes in recognition of the primary designs of the book-buying public: looking good, feeling good, making money.

The Anonymous Press featured as its initial release *Sleeping with the President: My Intimate Years with Bill Clinton* by Gennifer Flowers—a powerful personal memoir written as a riveting political love story.

Another Anonymous hit: *The Elvis Cover-Up* by Gail Brewer-Giorgio explores the secret lives of Elvis Presley, his connection to United States government law-enforcement agencies and his involvement with a deep-cover sting operation; Elvis may have hoaxed his own death to lead a new life underground. This brand-new investigatory biography follows the author's *Is Elvis Alive?* (multimillion-copy *New York Times* best-seller); several highly rated, syndicated television specials and video documentaries; and *Orion* (best-selling pop-cultural fiction; dramatic story of a mercurial musical performer).

Anonymous wishes to break through old barriers to create new publishing frontiers; the house is open to a wide variety of creative projects that will inspire the publisher's marketing vision. It is essential that submitted materials be imaginatively conceived and in professional book-proposal format. Authors must demonstrate expertise in the chosen topic area, and must offer thorough and credible documentation.

Do not send materials via registered mail, overnight express delivery, or any other means requiring a recipient's signature. Please query first.

Query letters and SASEs should be directed to:

(Mr.) Gilchrist (Chris) Bonner, Acquisitions

THE APEX PRESS
THE BOOTSTRAP PRESS
Council on International and Public Affairs
777 United Nations Plaza, Suite 3C
New York, NY 10017

Branch office:
Box 337
Croton-on-Hudson, NY 10520
914-271-6500

Apex accents nonfiction titles in such fields as corporate accountability, grassroots and worker participation, and intercultural understanding. One special publishing focus is on economic and social justice, human rights, and the impact of technology on contemporary society.

The Apex Press (introduced in 1990) is an imprint of the nonprofit research, education, and publishing group Council on International and Public Affairs (CIPA). Apex publishes hardcover and paperback books that provide critical analyses of and new approaches to significant economic, social, and political issues in the United States, other industrialized nations, and the Third World.

The Apex publishing program has a special focus on economic and social justice, human rights, and the impact of technology on contemporary society. The Council on International and Public Affairs was founded in 1954 and is a nonprofit research, education, and publishing group. The Council seeks to further the study and public understanding of problems and affairs of the peoples of the United States and other nations of the world through conferences, research, seminars and workshops, publications, and other means.

From Apex Press: *The Underbelly of the U.S. Economy: Joblessness and Pauperization of Work* by David Dembo and Ward Morehouse; *Economics, Culture and Society—Alternative Approaches: Dissenting Views from Economic Orthodoxy* (edited by Oscar Nudler and Mark A. Lutz); *Human Rights: The Universal Declaration of Human Rights* by Winin Pereira; *Nuclear Weapons Are Illegal: The Opinions and Story Behind the Historic Decision of the World Court* (edited by Ann Fagan Giner); *Nurtured by Knowledge: Learning by Doing Participatory Action-Research* (edited by Susan E. Smith and Dennis G. Willms with Nancy A. Johnson); *Washington's New Poor Law: Welfare Reform and Jobs Illusion* by Sheila D. Collins and Gertrude Schaffner Goldberg; *Greenwash: The Reality Behind Corporate Environmentalism* by Jed Greer and Kenny Bruno.

The Apex Press handles its own distribution; the house catalog includes books and additional resources (including videos) from a number of publishers worldwide.

THE BOOTSTRAP PRESS

Intermediate Technology Development Group of North America
777 United Nations Plaza Suite 3C
New York, NY 10017
914-271-6500

Bootstrap's publishing interest focuses on social economics and community economic change; the house covers small-scale and intermediate-scale or appropriate technology in both industrialized and emerging countries, with an aim to promote more just and sustainable societies. Its books explore business and industry theory and how-to, gardening and agriculture, building and construction, and communications.

The Bootstrap Press (inaugurated in 1988) is an imprint of Intermediate Technology Development Group of North America (ITDG/North America) in cooperation with Council on International and Public Affairs.

Titles from Bootstrap: *Greening Cities: Building Just and Sustainable Communities* by Joan Reolofs; *Building Sustainable Communities: Tools and Concepts for Self-Reliant Economic Change* by C. George Benello, Robert Swann, and Shann Turnbull; *Gross National Waste Product* by Larry Martin; *Chicken Little, Tomato Sauce and Agriculture: Who Will Produce Tomorrow's Food?* by Joan Dye Gussow.

Titles of Intermediate Technology Publications (London), previously distributed by the Bootstrap Press, are now available through Women, Ink.

Bootstrap publications are distributed with those of sibling operation The Apex Press.

Query letters and SASEs should be directed to:

Ward Morehouse, President

Judi Rizzi, Publications Manager

APPLAUSE THEATRE BOOK PUBLISHERS

211 West 71st Street
New York, NY 10023
212-496-7511

Applause Theatre Book Publishers (established in 1983) produces a list geared to fields of stage, cinema, and the entertainment arts. Applause produces collections, compendiums, biographies, histories, resource books, reference works, and guides keyed to the needs of the house's wide readership of seasoned pros, rookies, and aficionados.

The Applause program covers hardback and paperback editions, among them a number of generously illustrated and well-produced works. Applause issues stage plays and screenplays (many in translation and many in professional working-script format) that run the gamut from the classical repertory, to contemporary works in drama, comedy, and musicals. Applause also offers audio works and a video library. The publisher's backlist is comprehensive.

Special-production volumes encompass works that detail the background and history behind the creation of works for stage and screen in addition to containing complete scripts.

Titles from Applause: *The Life and Death of Peter Sellers* by Roger Lewis; *The Encyclopedia of Fantastic Film: Ali Baba to Zombies* by R. G. Young; *Theatre for Young Audiences: Around the World in Twenty-One Plays* by Lowell Swortzell; *The Ghost and the Darkness: The Screenplay* by William Goldman; *Chaos as Usual: Conversations About Rainer Werner Fassbinder* (edited by Juliane Lorenz; translated by Christa Armstrong and Maria Pelikan); *The Collected Words of Harold Clurman: Six Decades of Commentary on Theatre, Dance, Music, Film, Art, Letters, and Politics* (edited by Marjorie Loggia and Glenn Young); *Meyerhold at Work* (edited and translated by Paul Schmidt); *Mad About Theatre* by Richard Hornby; *Alarums and Excursions: Our Theatres in the 90s* by Charles Marotwitz.

For theatrical professionals and students as well, Applause offers: *Acting in Film* (from the Applause Acting Series) by Michael Caine; *Telling Moments: 15 Gay*

Monologues by Robert C. Reinhart, *The Actor and the Text* by Cicely Berry, and *The Secret of Theatrical Space* by Josef Svoboda.

Applause Annuals include *Applause/Best Plays Theater Yearbook*, *The Best American Short Plays*, *Screen World*, and *Theatre World*. Also periodically revised and updated are *Applause: New York's Guide to the Performing Arts* and *Applause: The Los Angeles Guide to the Performing Arts*.

Applause Theatre Books is distributed by R. R. Donnelley & Sons.

Query letters and SASEs should be directed to:

Glenn Young, President and Publisher

ARCADE PUBLISHING

141 Fifth Avenue
New York, NY 10010
212-475-2633

Arcade Publishing (founded in 1988 by Jeannette and Richard Seaver) produces commercial and literary nonfiction and fiction, as well as selected poetry. Nonfiction standouts include issues-oriented titles, contemporary human-interest stories, and cultural historical works. Arcade's fiction list includes entrants in such categories as mystery, suspense, and thrillers. Arcade's program leans toward learned and enlightened reading.

From Arcade nonfiction: *Prohibition: Thirteen Years That Changed America* by Edward Behr; *Christian Dior: The Man Who Made the World Look New* by Marie-France Pochna (translated from the French by Joanna Savill); *The Jimi Hendrix Experience* by Jerry Hopkins; *Saatchi & Saatchi: The Inside Story* by Alison Fendley; *Katharine Hepburn: An Independent Woman* by Ronald Bergan; *Voices from the Century Before: The Odyssey of a Nineteenth-Century Kentucky Family* by Mary Clay Berry; *Journey to My Father, Isaac Bashevis Singer* by Israel Zamir (translated from the Hebrew by Barbara Harshav).

Arcade fiction and literature: *The Three-Arched Bridge* by Ismail Kadare (translated from the Albanian by John Hodgson); *In the Manner of the Island Women: A Novel of Cuba* by Zoe Valdes (translated from the Spanish by Sabina Cienfuegos); *Famine* by Todd Komarnicki; *Private Confessions* by Ingmar Bergman (translated from the Swedish by Joan Tate); *The Death and Life of Miguel de Cervantes: A Novel* by Stephen Marlowe; *The Lost Brother* by Rick Bennet; *Trying to Save Peggy Sneed* by John Irving; *Our Lady of Babylon* by John Rechy; *The Ego Makers* by Donald Everett Axinn.

Arcade Publishing is distributed by Little, Brown.

Prospective authors please note that Arcade does not accept unsolicited submissions. Query letters and SASEs should be directed to:

Calvert Barksdale, Senior Editor
All areas of house interest.

Timothy Bent, Senior Editor
All areas of house interest.

Jeannette Seaver, Executive Editor
Fiction: literary. Nonfiction: history, politics, literary criticism, cookbooks, illustrated books.

Richard Seaver, President
Fiction: literary. Nonfiction: history, politics, literary criticism, illustrated books.

JASON ARONSON INC., PUBLISHERS

230 Livingston Street
Northvale, NJ 07647
201-767-4093
http://www.aronson.com (World Wide Web)

Jason Aronson Inc., Publishers, marks two main sectors of publishing concentration: One Aronson line comprises psychotherapy, offering professional books (as well as some trade-oriented titles) in psychiatry, psychoanalysis, counseling (including pastoral care), and the behavioral sciences. The other Aronson publishing arena is Judaica, covering contemporary thought as well as traditional works. (Please see Aronson listing in Directory of Religious, Spiritual, and Inspirational Publishers). Aronson's strong backlist encompasses a wide range of publications well regarded in the field of psychotherapy.

Among Aronson highlights in psychotherapy: *Creating the Capacity for Attachment: Treating Addictions and the Alienated Self* by Karen B. Walant; *Winning Cooperation from Your Child! A Comprehensive Method to Stop Defiant and Aggressive Behavior in Children* by Kenneth Winning; *Dancing with Fear: Overcoming Anxiety in a World of Stress and Uncertainty* by Paul Foxman; *Cognitive Therapy: Basic Principles and Applications* by Robert Leahy; *Sons, Lovers, and Fathers: Understanding Male Sexuality* by Didier Dumas; *Psychic Deadness* by Michael Eigen; *The Adolescent Journey: Development, Identity Formation, and Psychotherapy* by Marsha Levy-Warren; *Using DSM-IV: A Clinician's Guide to Psychiatric Diagnosis* by Anthony L. LaBruzza and José Méndez-Villarrubia; *A Curious Calling: Unconscious Motivations for Practicing Psychotherapy* by Michael R. Sussman.

Jason Aronson Inc., Publishers (started in 1965) oversees a distribution network that utilizes its own in-house services as well as independent trade-fulfillment services. Aronson also features a direct-mail catalog that includes special-interest titles from other presses.

Query letters and SASEs should be directed to:

Michael Moskowitz, Publisher

ARTE PÚBLICO PRESS

University of Houston
Houston, TX 77204-2090
713-743-2841

Arte Público Press (founded in 1979) publishes books of fiction, poetry, drama, literary criticism, reference works, and children's literature by and about Americans with roots in Mexico, Cuba, Puerto Rico, and the American Southwest, as well as other American Latino writers. In addition, the press has a particular focus on women's literature. Arte Público is the oldest and largest publisher of Spanish-American writing of the United States.

The house publishes works in both the English and Spanish languages, as well as in bilingual editions. Arte Público's Piñata Books imprint is devoted to books for children and young adults that address the United States Hispanic experience. Arte Público issues a full roster of new titles each season and maintains a steadfast backlist.

Arte Público was the original publisher of *The House on Mango Street* by Sandra Cisneros (in 1985), and has published *The Last of the Menu Girls* by Denise Chavez, as well as the works of Victor Villaseñor, Rolando Hinojosa, and Luis Valdez.

On the Arte Público list: *Little Havana Blues: A Cuban-American Literature Anthology* (edited by Virgil Suárez and Delia Poey); *History and Legends of the Alamo and Other Missions in and Around San Antonio* by Adina de Zavala (edited by Richard Flores); *Recovering the U.S. Hispanic Literary Heritage* (Volume 2) (edited by Erlinda Gonzales-Berry and Chuck Tatum); *The Twins, the Dream: Two Voices* by Ursula LeGuin and Diana Bellessi (poetry); *A Shot in the Cathedral* (novel) by Mario Bencastro (translated by Susan Giersbach Rascón); *Cactus Blood* by Lucha Corpi; *A Fire in the Earth* by Marcos McPeek Villatoro; *Handbook of Hispanic Cultures of the United States* by Nicolás Kanellos and Claudio Esteva Fabregat.

Arte Público handles its own distribution and distributes Hispanic literature for smaller presses, in addition to publishing *The Americas Review* literary journal.

PIÑATA BOOKS

Piñata Books publishes books for children and young adults that deal with the United States Hispanic experience. The list is selected with the intention to promote writing that will thrill and inspire.

Piñata Books is the first imprint devoted to providing materials for children that authentically and realistically portray themes, characters, and customs unique to U.S. Hispanic culture.

Titles from Piñata: *Jumping Off to Freedom* by Anilú Bernardo (novel); *The Gift of the Poinsettia* by Pat Mora and Charles Ramírez Berg (illustrated by Daniel Lechón) (children's picture book); *Walking Stars* by Victor Villeseñor (memoir); *Mexican Ghost Tales of the Southwest* by Alfred Avila (compiled by Kat Avila) (short fiction); *Aplanso! Hispanic Children's Theater* (edited by Joe Rosenberg).

Query letters and SASEs should be directed to:

Nicolás Kanellos, Publisher

ASTD BOOKS
(See American Society for Training and Development [ASTD])

ATHENEUM PUBLISHERS
(See Simon & Schuster)

ATLANTIC MONTHLY PRESS
(See Grove/Atlantic, Inc.)

AUGSBURG FORTRESS PUBLISHING
(See Directory of Religious, Spiritual, and Inspirational Publishers)

AUGUST HOUSE
P.O. Box 3223
Little Rock, AR 72203
501-372-5450

Areas of August House interest include narrative tales and fiction, cooking and entertaining, family, humor, regionally keyed themes, trade titles of mainstream interest, as well as some titles that target a younger readership. A major August House focus is on storytelling and folklore. August House publishes books in hardcover and trade paperback, maintains a solid backlist, and issues several series of storytelling and regional music on its August House Audio list.

August House (founded in 1979) is a medium-sized publisher with a concise catalog strong in its core areas; the house publishes selectively outside this central theme arena. Much of the August House list is, by nature, of rich local flavor—and many titles exhibit literary depth.

August House produces the American Folklore series among a number of lines that are directed on a subscription basis toward libraries, educators, and institutions. Silver Moon Press is an imprint that bridges the gap between schoolwork and pleasure reading.

At August House, entrepreneurial publishing means selecting exciting projects, working with authors to create engaging and spirited manuscripts, adding inviting illustration and design, insisting on archival-quality paper and sewn bindings, marketing creatively, and delivering on time.

August House storytelling and folkways titles: *Fair Is Fair: World Folktales of Justice* by Sharon Creeden; *Buried Treasures of California* by W. C. Jameson; *Best Stories from the Texas Folktelling Festival* (edited by Finley Stewart); *Through a Ruby Window: A Martha's Vineyard Childhood* by Susan Klein; *Still Catholic (After All These Fears)* by Ed Stivender; *Queen of the Cold-Blooded Tales* by Roberta Simpson Brown.

On the list for younger readers: *Wildlife Challenge* (text by Lucy Moreland and illustrations by Robin D'Alanno); *Race with the Buffalo and Other Native American Stories for Young Readers* (collected by Richard and Judy Dockrey Young). Silver Moon Press addresses home and library markets with books targeted for readers in grades 5 to 8: *Family Gatherings*; *The Public Life*; *The Written Word*.

August House distributes its own books to the trade and also uses the services of a number of regional sales representatives.

Query letters and SASEs should be directed to:

Liz Smith Parkhurst, Editor in Chief

AUTONOMEDIA/ SEMIOTEXT(E)

P.O. Box 568 Williamsburgh Station
55 South Eleventh Street
Brooklyn, NY 11211
718-387-6471

Autonomedia/Semiotext(e) accents art and music; gender and ethnicity; fiction and belles lettres; and contemporary, futurist, and historical criticism. The two divisional imprints overlap in their respective areas of interest; however, Autonomedia and Semiotext(e) remain distinctive entities with regard to editorial approach and featured series lines.

Although Autonomedia/Semiotext(e) publications are not intended for specialist market sectors, individual titles are of particular appeal to media buffs, political watchers, pop-culture hounds, and aficionados of the arts, as well as artistic practitioners; the publishing scope also includes works that speak distinctly to an academic audience.

Autonomedia/Semiotext(e) is a publisher with a vision and a mission. Begun in 1983, this double-barreled house produces a powerful list of what is portrayed as movement literature. Whatever the designation—traditional book-publishing labels simply do not stick—Autonomedia and Semiotext(e) describe their role as that of anti-authoritarian publishers; they show a bent literature that "examines culture from a perspective that is against work and all forms of exploitation, and promotes actively the abolition thereof."

The house oversees its own distribution.

AUTONOMEDIA

Autonomedia emphasizes cultural theory and criticism. The house features original artistic and literary expression on topics that radiate from perspectives of ethnicity and race (black radicalism), notions of gender and sexuality (gay, lesbian, feminist), and spirited renditions of personalized philosophical viewpoints. Autonomedia produces a gamut of creative thought that, though perhaps implicitly active in political arenas, is essentially unfettered by conventional notions of partisanship.

Indicative of the Autonomedia list: *Arcane of Reproduction: Housework, Prostitution, Labor and Capital* by Leopoldina Fortunati; *TAZ: The Temporary Autonomous Zone, Ontological Anarchy, Poetic Terrorism* (essays) by Hakim Bey; *The Damned Universe of Charles Fort* by Louis Kaplan; *Wiggling Wishbone: Stories of Patasexual Speculation* by Bart Plantegna; *Cassette Mythos: The New Music Underground* (edited by Robin James); *Magpie Reveries* by James Koehnline; *The New Fuck You: Adventures in Lesbian Reading* (edited by Eileen Myles and Liz Kotz); *About Face: Race in Postmodern America* by Maliqalim Simone; *Columbus and Other Cannibals* by Jack Forbes; *Horsexe: Essay on Transsexuality* by Catherine Millot; *Radiotext(e)* (edited by Neil Strauss and Dave Mandl); *File Under Popular: Theoretical and Critical Writings on Music* by Chris Cutler; *Sounding Off: Music as Subversion/ Resistance/Revolution* by Ron Sakolsky and Fred Wei-Han Ho.

New Autonomy is a series of anarchist and antihierarchical works in the areas of literature, politics, and culture. Bob Black (author of the successful title *Friendly Fire*) and Tad Kepley are coeditors of *ZeroWork: The Anti-Work Anthology*—a collection of writings that in large measure epitomizes the publisher's primary stance.

Query letters and SASEs should be directed to:

Jim Fleming, Editor

Peter Lamborn Wilson, Editor

SEMIOTEXT(E)

The Semiotext(e) lineup features series keyed to such fields as radical European continental philosophy (including works by Jean Beaudrillard, Pierre Clastres, and Michel Foucault); social and cultural theory; gender expression and sexuality (including fiction, essay, and memoir); artistic and political affairs; and native Asian feminist and gay literature (including fiction and poetry).

Representative titles from Semiotext(e): *Assassination Rhapsody* by Derek Pell; *The Cutmouth Lady* by Romy Ashby; *Whore Carnival* by Shannon Bell; *I Shot Mussolini* by Eldon Garnet; *Madame Realism Comples* by Lynne Tillman; *Unholy Bible: Hebrew Literature of the Kingdom Period* by Jacob Rabinowitz; *Sick Burn Cut* by Deran Ludd; *Hannibal Lecter, My Father* by Kathy Acker; *If You're a Girl* by Ann Rower; *Polysexuality* (edited by François Peraldi); *Semiotext(e): Architecture* (edited by Hraztan Zeitlian); *Semiotext(e) USA* (edited by Jim Fleming and Peter Lamborn Wilson); *Semiotext(e) SF* (edited by Rudy Rucker, Robert Anton Wilson, and Peter Lamborn Wilson); *Semiotext(e) Canadas* (edited by Jordan Zinovich); *Speed and Politics* by Paul Virilio.

Special Semiotext(e) production: *¡Zapatistas! Documents of the New Mexican* by the Emiliano Zapata Liberation Army—features the insider lowdown on the world's first postmodern revolution, fresh from the jungles of Chiapas in their own words.

Query letters and SASEs should be directed to:

Jim Fleming, Editor

Sylvere Lotringer, Editor

AVALON BOOKS

401 Lafayette Street
New York, NY 10003
212-598-0222

Avalon Books produces fiction lines primarily for distribution to library and institutional markets on a subscriber basis. Avalon editions are wholesome, family stories in the following categories: traditional mysteries; mainstream romance; career romance; traditional genre Westerns. Avalon produces a line of literary classics in reprint (on the Airmont Classics imprint).

Avalon Books (a subsidiary of Thomas Bouregy & Company, founded in 1950) publishes a primarily hardcover fiction list. The house emphasis on new original novels caters to the tastes and preferences of the all-important library readership; stories should consist of those likely to be of high interest to the patrons of this core market.

Distribution is primarily through library sales.

Query letters and SASEs should be directed to:

Marcia Markland, Publisher

AVERY PUBLISHING GROUP

120 Old Broadway
Garden City Park, NY 11040
516-741-2155
fax: 516-742-1892
800-548-5757

Avery's publishing scope includes a broad range of topical nonfiction, accenting such areas as health and nutrition, parenting, spirituality, science and technology, business, education, gardening, government, and history.

Avery Publishing Group produces a freewheeling list of high-interest commercial nonfiction in hardcover and trade paperback. Avery also catalogs fantasy-theme art from Paper Tiger Books, as well as college textbooks and professional reference works. Avery is the publisher of the West Point Military History series.

Avery books are designed to take readers back to where they've been, mirror who they are today, and show what they can aspire to be. Avery's authors and conceptual hooks often lead with an alternative edge or reach out to challenge with fresh views on current readership and cultural trends.

When Avery Publishing began (founded in 1976), their mission was simple: to produce good books and succeed as a business. As the house has matured, Avery's mission has remained the same. The publisher attributes this success to several factors: a commitment to quality; a passion for doing what they do; a curiosity about how things work; an able staff that gets things done; and a growing circle of authors that has provided them with solid manuscripts.

From health care to child care, from cookbooks to nutrition, Avery Publishing offers books readers can enjoy reading as much as Avery enjoys publishing them.

Health and nutrition titles: *Sharks Still Don't Get Cancer: The Continuing Story of Shark Cartilage Therapy* by I. William Lane and Linda Comac; *Chromium Picolinate: Everything You Need to Know* by Gary Evans; *The Shopper's Guide to Fat in Your Food* by Karen J. Bellerson; *From Fatigued to Fantastic! A Manual for Moving Beyond Chronic Fatigue and Fibromyalgia* by Jacob Teitelbaum; *Healing Teas: How to Prepare and Use Teas to Maximize Your Health* by Marie Nadine Antol; *Performance Nutrition for Athletes: A Complete Nutritional Guide for Peak Sports Performance* by Daniel Gastelu and Fred Hatfield; *Secrets of Lactose-Free Cooking* by Arlene Burlant; *Positive Cooking: Cooking for People Living with HIV* by Janet Brauer, Lisa McMillan, and Jill Jarvie; *Simply Delicious Recipes for Diabetics* by Christine Roberts, Jennifer McDonald, and Margaret Cox.

Avery general-interest works: *Your Guide to Retiring to Mexico, Costa Rica and Beyond: Finding the Good Life on a Fixed Income* by Shelley Emling; *Coping with Colorblindness: Sound Helpful Strategies and Advice to Those Who Must Deal with Colorblindness Every Day* by Odeda Rosenthal and Robert H. Phillips; *The Coming Energy Revolution: The Search for Free Energy* by Jeane Manning.

Avery Publishing is distributed to the trade by Publishers Group West. Avery titles are also available through Ingram, Baker & Taylor, and Bookazine. Avery uses traditional trade bookseller channels as well as health food and nutritional-store outlets within a network that includes Whole Health Books.

Query letters and SASEs should be directed to:

Rudy Shur, Managing Editor

Joanne Abrams, Editorial Coordinator

AVON BOOKS
(See the Hearst Book Group)

BAEN PUBLISHING ENTERPRISES
Baen Books
P.O. Box 1403
Riverdale, NY 10471
212-532-4111

Baen publishes science fiction and fantasy writing. The house's new releases are generally published in mass-market paperback format, with targeted lead titles produced in special trade paper and hardcover editions. Baen is a prominent publisher of series in science fiction and fantasy, and also publishes a notable lineup of collections and anthologies geared to various subgenre traditions and the works of individual writers. The Baen program aims a significant portion of its list toward a younger readership.

Baen Publishing Enterprises (founded in 1984) concentrates its concise list on its proven categories of publishing strength. Baen's roster of writers includes Poul and Karen Anderson, Piers Anthony, Margaret Ball, Marion Zimmer Bradley, Lois McMaster Bujold, John Dalmas, Robert A. Heinlein, Mercedes Lackey, Anne McCaffrey, Frederik Pohl, Spider and Jeanne Robinson, and Melissa Scott.

From Baen: *Nanodreams* (edited by Elton Elliot); *Doc Sidhe* by Aaron Allston; *Proteus in the Underworld* by Charles Sheffield; *The Magnificent Wilf* by Gordon R. Dickson; *The Printer's Devil* by Chico Kidd; *Mall, Mayhem, and Magic* by Holly Lisle and Chris Guin; *1945* by Newt Gingrich and William R. Forstchen; *Allies and Aliens* by Roger McBride Allen; *The Shattered Oath* by Josepha Sherman; *Winning Colors* by Elizabeth Moon.

Baen Books is distributed by Simon & Schuster.

Query letters and SASEs should be directed to:

Toni Weisskopf, Executive Editor

BALLANTINE
DEL REY
FAWCETT
COLUMBINE
IVY
(See Random House)

BANTAM DOUBLEDAY DELL PUBLISHING GROUP
BANTAM BOOKS
DOUBLEDAY & COMPANY
DELL PUBLISHING
DELACORTE PRESS BROADWAY BOOKS
1540 Broadway
New York, NY 10036
212-354-6500

Bantam Doubleday Dell Publishing Group addresses the entire mainstream book-publishing spectrum from frontlist commercial products to specialty nonfiction titles and genre fiction; the house issues titles published in hardcover, trade paperback, and mass-market paperback rack editions. Bantam Doubleday Dell publishes for adult and children's markets and catalogs an audio-publishing specialty list (BDD Audio). Bantam Doubleday Dell Books for Young Readers hosts the house's children's program. (Please see subentries.)

Bantam Doubleday Dell is a colossal enterprise that comprises under one canopy several formerly independent major houses (primarily Bantam, Doubleday, and Dell/Delacorte) plus new lines (such as Broadway Books). Bantam Doubleday Dell is itself owned by the German-based communications conglomerate Bertelsmann Publishing Group International.

Broadway Books is a dynamic trade division that accents highly marketable nonfiction projects, as well as selected titles in fiction. (Please see subentry below for Broadway Books).

WaterBrook Press is a new venture in Christian publishing, an autonomous subsidiary of BDD located in Oregon (see WaterBrook Press in Directory of Religious, Spiritual, and Inspirational Publishers).

Bantam Doubleday Dell Publishing Group handles its own distribution.

BANTAM BOOKS

Bantam is active in virtually every nonfiction area and fiction genre, including frontlist commercial categories and literary works. The fighting-cock logo of Bantam Books (founded in 1945) was for decades synonymous with paperbacks in mass-market editions. Bantam currently publishes hardcover and paperback originals, while carrying on its stalwart mass-market tradition (in both originals and reprints). Special Bantam frontlist titles enjoy simultaneous release on BDD Audio.

Bantam nonfiction: *Embraced by the Light* by Betty J. Eadie with Curtis Taylor; *Notes from an Incomplete Revolution: Real Life Since Feminism* by Meredith Moran; *Worth the Wait: My Lifelong Journey to the World Series* (autobiography) by Joe Torres with Tom Verducci; *Diet 911: Food Cop to the Rescue with 265 New Low-Fat Recipes* by Yolanda Bergman with Daryn Eller; *Strong Women Stay Young* by Miriam E. Nelson, Ph.D. with Sarah Wernick, Ph.D.; *The Fine Art of Erotic Talk: How to Entice, Excite, and Enchant Your Lover with Words* by Bonnie Gabriel; *Sex, Power, and Boundaries: Understanding and Preventing Sexual Harassment* by Peter Rutter; *Loving Each One Best: A Caring and Practical Approach to Raising Siblings* by Nancy Samalin with Catherine Whitney, *'Scuse Me While I Kiss the Sky: The Life of Jimi Hendrix* by David Henderson, *Red Hot Mamas: Coming into Our Own at Fifty* by Colette Dowling; *Family Secrets: The Path to Self-Acceptance and Reunion* by John Bradshaw.

Bantam fiction encompasses commercial novels; mysteries, suspense, and thrillers; science fiction and fantasy; romance and women's fiction; and select literary works. Crime Line is a Bantam imprint that accents topnotch suspense and detective fiction.

Titles here: *A Thin Dark Line* by Tami Hoag (author of *Guilty as Sin*); *The Clinic* by Jonathan Kellerman; *The Ugly Duckling* by Iris Johansen; *God Save the Queen!* by Dorothy Cannell; *Walking to Mercury* by Starhawk; *Jane and the Man of the Cloth:*

Being the Second Jane Austen Mystery by Stephanie Barron (author of *Unpleasantness at Scargrave Manor: Being the First Jane Austen Mystery*); *Death and the Language of Happiness* by John Straley; *Tallgrass: A Novel of the Great Plains* by Don Coldsmith; *Riding Shotgun* by Rita Mae Brown; *Brothers* by Ben Bova. A commercial approach to popular verse is exemplified by *The Book of Birth Poetry* (edited by Charlotte Otten).

Query letters and SASEs should be directed to:

(Ms.) Toni Burbank, Executive Editor
New Age, addiction/recovery, health.

Cassie Goddard, Associate Editor
Women's fiction; mysteries, suspense, and thrillers. Commercial nonfiction, popular culture. Works with Beth de Guzman.

Anne Lesley Groell, Editor
Works with Patrick Lobrutto (please see). Fiction: Bantam Spectra science fiction/fantasy imprint.

Beth de Guzman, Senior Editor
Romance, general fiction, suspense, women's fiction.

Katie Hall, Editor
Wide range of interests consistent with the house list.

Ann Harris, Executive Editor
Nonfiction interests consistent with the house list.

Emily Heckman, Senior Editor
Popular reference and general nonfiction.

Stephanie Kip, Associate Editor
Women's fiction. Commercial nonfiction, popular culture.

Beverly Lewis, Senior Editor
Broad interests consistent with the house list.

Patrick Lobrutto, Senior Editor
Fiction: Science fiction. Acquires for the Bantam Spectra science fiction/fantasy imprint.

Wendy McCurdy, Senior Editor
Women's fiction, romance. Commercial nonfiction, popular culture.

Kate Burke Miciak, Associate Publisher, Crime Line
Mysteries, thrillers, true crime.

Elisa Petrini, Senior Editor
Varied nonfiction interests, especially popular science and women's issues. Popular fiction, especially mysteries and thrillers.

Brian Tart, Editor
New Age, spirituality, popular religion, inspiration, health/fitness.

Nita Taublib, Deputy Publisher
Projects consistent with the Bantam list.

DOUBLEDAY & COMPANY, INC.
ANCHOR BOOKS

Doubleday (founded in 1897) is one of America's cherished publishing names; the house's emblematic colophon (a dolphin entwined round a ship's anchor) is equally beloved among bookbuyers, booksellers, and critics. Doubleday & Company is known for its potent commercial list in fiction and nonfiction, with major concentration in mainstream popular nonfiction and genre fiction (Double D Westerns, Perfect Crime, Loveswept), as well as works of literary note.

Doubleday publishes hardcover and paperback editions. The Anchor imprint features original nonfiction and fiction in hardcover and trade paper, as well as paperback reprints. Doubleday/Currency produces a list of high-interest books in business, finance, management, and human relations. Doubleday Equestrian Library publishes top-of-the-line titles in the art and sport of horsemanship. Doubleday is also the home of Nan A. Talese's personalized trade imprint (see separate subentry below).

Doubleday spins off many of its lead titles on BDD Audio.

Indicative of Doubleday fiction and popular literature: *Meg* (a "Jurassic shark" thriller) by Steve Alten; *Some Love, Some Pain, Sometime* (stories) by J. California Cooper; *Parsley, Sage, Rosemary, and Crime: A Pennsylvania Dutch Mystery with Recipes* by Tamar Myers; *The War Trail North: A New Novel of the Cherokee People* by Robert J. Conley; *Wilderness of Mirrors* by Linda Davies; *Pandora's Clock* by John J. Nance; *St. Famous* by Jonathan Dee.

Doubleday is the publisher of *The Partner* by John Grisham, as well as his earlier works in the legal-thriller field (*The Firm*; *The Pelican Brief*; *The Client*; *The Chamber*; *The Rainmaker*; *The Runaway Jury*). Doubleday hosts a notable lineup by the 1988 winner of the Nobel Prize for literature, Naguib Mahfouz, which includes *The Cairo Trilogy*: (I) *Palace Walk*; (II) *Palace of Desire*; and (III) *Sugar Street*.

Representing Doubleday nonfiction: *Animalogies* (humor) by Michael Macrone; *Racial Healing: Confronting the Fear Between Blacks and Whites* by Harlon L. Dalton; *The '21' Cookbook: Recipes and Lore from New York's Fabled Restaurant* by Michael Lomonaco with Donna Forsman; *The Last Word on Power: Reinvention for Executives Who Want to Change Their World* by Tracy Goss (edited by Betty Sue Flowers); *The Sixth Extinction: Patterns of Life and the Future of Humankind* by Richard Leakey and Roger Lewin; *The Way of Woman: Awakening the Perennial Feminine* by Helen Luke.

On the **Anchor Books** list: *The Book of Ruth* (dramatic fiction with a domestic-violence theme) by Jane Hamilton; *Into the Wild* (nonfiction account of a fateful wilderness trek) by Jon Krakauer; *Virtual Equality: The Mainstreaming of Gay and Lesbian Liberation* by Urvashi Vaid; *Dark Carnival: The Secret World of Tod Browning—Hollywood's Master of the Macabre* by David J. Skal and Elias Savada; *Sister to Sister: Women Write About the Unbreakable Bond* (edited by Patricia Foster); *Nine Poets of Desire: The Hidden World of Islamic Women* by Geraldine Brooks.

Query letters and SASEs should be directed to:

Sean Coyne, Senior Editor, Doubleday
Commercial fiction and nonfiction. Some specialties: mysteries, psychological suspense, sports, crime and investigative stories, popular culture.

Mark Frety, Senior Editor, Religious Publishing
Scholarly and popular works on religion and spirituality.

Jackie Gill, Editor, Doubleday Books for Young Readers
Fiction and nonfiction for children to age 10; seeking primarily illustrated volumes.

Janet Hill, Senior Editor, Doubleday
African-American studies, commercial fiction and nonfiction.

Frances Jones, Editor, Main Street Books
Practical nonfiction.

Judith Kern, Senior Editor
Fiction: quality commercial, historical romance. Nonfiction: cookbooks, diet books, self-help and how-to, illustrated.

Elizabeth Lerner, Executive Editor
Fiction: literary and women's. Nonfiction: popular psychology, social/cultural history, anthropology.

Martha Levin, Publisher and Senior Vice President, Anchor Books
Fiction: quality prose and poetry. Nonfiction: upscale, academically oriented titles in human behavior, biography, history, and contemporary issues. Also reprints.

Eric Major, Director, Religious Publishing
Scholarly and popular works on religion and spirituality; titles likely to provoke religious controversy; books covering a wide range of religious thought, including Hinduism and Buddhism; Judaica.

Rob McQuilken, Editor, Anchor Books
Literary fiction and nonfiction.

(Ms.) Pat Mulcahy, Vice President and Editor in Chief, Doubleday
Commercial and literary fiction. Does a lot of suspense, thriller, and mystery fiction. General nonfiction; special interests include music and other popular culture.

Trace Murphy, Editor, Religious Publishing
Scholarly and popular works on religion and spirituality.

Harriet Rubin, Publisher, Currency
Acquires business-oriented titles for Currency imprint.

Roger Scholl, Senior Editor, Anchor Books
Current affairs, history, literary fiction and nonfiction, popular science, sociology.

Bill Thomas, Senior Editor
General nonfiction, politics, current affairs.

Bruce Tracy, Executive Editor, Main Street Books
Practical nonfiction (health, psychology, fitness), how-to, popular culture, humor. General trade nonfiction, some quality fiction.

NAN A. TALESE BOOKS

The personalized imprint of Nan A. Talese promotes topical issues of widespread interest addressed through commercial nonfiction and selected fiction. The Talese roster is particularly strong in works that tie in with contemporary cultural themes.

Representative of the Talese list: *Alias Grace* (fiction) by Margaret Atwood; *What Falls Away* (memoir) by Mia Farrow; *The Voyage* (fiction) by Robert MacNeil; *Beach Music* (fiction) by Pat Conroy; *Choices* (a novel) by Mary Lee Settle; *Milton in America* (speculative fiction) by Peter Ackroyd; *How the Irish Saved Civilization: The Untold Story of Ireland's Historic Role from the Fall of Rome to the Rise of Medieval Europe* by Thomas Cahill; *"Feminism Is Not the Story of My Life": How Today's Feminist Elite Has Lost Touch with the Real Concerns of Women* by Elizabeth Fox-Genovese; *Skin Deep: Black Women and White Women Write About Race* (edited by Marita Golden and Susan Richards Shreve).

Talese does not wish to receive unagented/unsolicited submissions. Query letters and SASEs should be directed to:

Nan A. Talese, Publisher

Jesse Cohen, Editor

Fiction: literary (particularly women authors on a variety of female issues); occasional commercial works. Nonfiction: biographies of fine and performing artists, essays, subjects of popular or contemporary cultural interest.

BANTAM DOUBLEDAY DELL NEW MEDIA

Computer-based works including multimedia properties.

Query letters and SASEs should be directed to:

Jonathan Guttenberg, Senior Editor

DELL PUBLISHING
DELACORTE PRESS
THE DIAL PRESS
DTP TRADE PAPERBACKS
LAUREL

The Dell/Delacorte wing spans commercial nonfiction and popular fiction, including mainstream titles as well as mystery, suspense, and thrillers. Dell/Delacorte has a strong presence in hardcover, trade paperback, and mass-market areas.

Dell Publishing produces trade and mass-market paperbacks in virtually all fiction and nonfiction categories, along with selected hardcover originals. Dell (founded in 1921) upholds a traditional position as one of the major players in paperback publishing. The DTP imprint covers practical and inspirational nonfiction in trade paperback. Delta Trade Paperbacks include serious (and fun) contemporary fiction, narrative

Turkeyfoot Reading Center
Confluence, PA

nonfiction, popular culture, popular science, and issues-oriented psychology. The Laurel imprint includes literary and reference titles in trade paper and mass-market paperback. Dell mass-market paperbacks feature reprints of Delacorte hardcovers, mass-market editions of hardcover originals from other BDD divisions, and a raft of paperback originals.

Delacorte Press concentrates on hardcover frontlist releases. Among Delacorte's nonfiction areas of interest are popular psychology, self-help, child care, humor, politics, true crime, and current issues and events. Delacorte trade fiction includes commercial novels, mystery, romance, historical sagas, and futurist works. A good number of Delacorte's frontlist titles are presented with simultaneous release on BDD Audio Cassette.

Delacorte Press nonfiction and popular works: *Tricks in the Wilderness of Dreaming: Exploring Interior Landscape Through Practical Dreamwork* by Robert Bosnak; *Men Like Women Who Like Themselves (and Other Secrets That the Smartest Women Know)* by Steven Carter and Julia Sokol; *In Sickness and Health: Sex, Love, and Chronic Illness* by Lucille Carlton; *Wild Steps of Heaven* by Victor Villaseñor; *Rush Limbaugh Is a Big Fat Idiot (and Other Observations)* by Al Franken; *Bad As I Wanna Be* by Dennis Rodman with Tim Keown.

Delacorte commercial fiction and literary works: *Drums of Autumn* by Diana Gabaldon; *Evening Class* by Maeve Binchy; *Five Days in Paris* by Danielle Steel; *Buzz Cut* by James W. Hall; *Promises* by Belva Plain; *The Last Sanctuary* by Craig Holden; *Sudden Exposure* (a Jill Smith mystery) by Susan Dunlap; *Riding the Rap* by Elmore Leonard; *The Horse Whisperer* by Nicholas Evans; the Carlotta Carlyle mysteries by Linda Barnes; *Women on the Case* (introduced and edited by Sara Paretsky); *Murder for Love* (edited by Otto Penzler). Delacorte publishes Sara Paretsky's series of V. I. Warshawski detective fiction.

The Dial Press is a revived presence in the Dell Publishing division of Bantam Doubleday Dell Publishing Group. Dial offers a short, selective commercial-literary list (fiction and serious nonfiction) published primarily in hardcover editions under its own lion-and-cupid logo.

The Dial Press literary purview in fiction: *The Giant's House: A Romance* by Elizabeth McCracken; *Fast Greens* by Turk Pipkin; *Veronica* by Nicholas Christopher. Creative nonfiction from Dial: *Drinking: A Love Story* by Caroline Knapp; *Light Fantastic: Adventures in Theatre* by John Lahr.

DTP Trade Paperbacks presents up-to-the-minute trends in a principally mainline nonfiction list that also hits specialty sectors such as humor and puzzles. The DTP nonfiction program covers: *I Am the Walrus: Confessions of a Blue-Collar Golfer* by Craig Stadler with John Andrisani; *Rock the Casbah: The Ultimate Guide to Hosting Your Own Theme Party* by Ellen Hoffman (illustrations by Louise Farrell); *White Moon, Red Dragon* (science fiction) by David Wingrove; *Seven Weeks to Better Sex* by Domeena Renshaw; *I Am Not a Corpse! and Other Quotes Never Actually Said* (humor) by Mark Katz.

Delta trade paperbacks embrace both originals and reprints in mainstream nonfiction and in popular and cutting-edge fiction. Representing the Delta line: *When Elephants Weep: The Emotional Lives of Animals* by Jeffrey Moussieff Masson and Susan

McCarthy; *Blown Sideways Through Life: A Hilarious Tour de Résumé* (autobiography) by Claudia Shear; *Letters from Motherless Daughters: Words of Courage, Grief, and Healing* (edited by Hope Edelman); *M31: A Family Romance* by Stephen Wright; *A Day in the Life: The Music and Artistry of the Beatles* by Mark Hertsgaard; *Rolling Stone's Alt-Rock-a-Rama: An Outrageous Compendium of Fact, Fiction, Trivia and Critiques on Alternative Rock* by Scott Schinder and the Editors of Rolling Stone Press; *The Paperboy* (fiction) by Pete Dexter.

Laurel publishes the writing and editing reference *The 21st Century Manual of Style* (edited by the Princeton Language Institute) on a primarily reprint trade-paper and mass-market list.

Query letters and SASEs should be directed to:

(Ms.) Jackie Cantor, Executive Editor, Delacorte Press
Fiction: women's fiction, mysteries, historical romance, and quality/literary fiction.

Laura Cifelli, Editor, Dell
Romance fiction. Nonfiction: women's issues, general self-help.

(Ms.) Jackie Farber, Executive Editor, Delacorte Press
Quality/literary fiction. Mysteries and suspense.

Jacob Hoye, Editor
Commercial nonfiction. Popular and literary fiction, including mainstream novels, mysteries, suspense, thrillers.

Kathleen Jayes, Associate Editor, Dell
Commercial and popular projects in fiction and nonfiction. From new writers: a fresh voice, unique point of view, personal style with something new to say.

Susan Kamil, Vice President and Executive Editor, Delacorte; Editorial Director, Dial Press
Quality nonfiction. Literary fiction.

Mary Ellen O'Neill, Senior Editor, Dell
Projects consistent with house interest.

Brooke Rogers, Editor
Commercial nonfiction, literary and commercial fiction for Dell and Delacorte.

Michael Shohl, Editor
Commercial nonfiction, literary and commercial fiction.

Leslie Schnur, Vice President and Editor in Chief, Dell Publishing/Delacorte Press
Strong projects consistent with the house list.

BDD AUDIO PUBLISHING
BANTAM DOUBLEDAY DELL AUDIO PUBLISHING

The audio-publishing division of Bantam Doubleday Dell acquires projects primarily through licensing audio rights for big fiction and nonfiction book titles. Audio adaptations are usually published simultaneously with the book release, so the publisher needs to see and consider materials as early as possible.

(Ms.) Traci Cothran, Acquisitions Editor

Jenny Frost, President and Publisher

BANTAM DOUBLEDAY DELL
BOOKS FOR YOUNG READERS

Bantam Doubleday Dell Books for Young Readers publishes for the preschool through young-adult markets. This division encompasses numerous lines and imprints, including Doubleday Books for Young Readers, Bank Street (Ready-to-Read Books and Museum Books), Audubon One Earth Books, Delacorte Press Middle Readers, Skylark, Delacorte Press Young Adult, Starfire, Laurel, Little Rooster, Rooster, and Yearling. This division issues books in hardcover, trade paperback, and economically priced paper editions.

Representative projects: *Yo, Hungry Wolf* by David Vozar (illustrated by Betsy Lewin); *Weird on the Outside* by Shelley Stoehr; *Sweet Valley High* by Francine Pascal (series plus spin-off on television); *Music in the Wood* by Cornelia Cornelissen (photographs by John MacLachlan); *Camp Dracula* by Tom B. Stone; *Big David, Little David* by S. E. Hinton (illustrated by Alan Daniel); *Thwonk* by Jon Bauer; *A Season for Goodbye* by Lurlene McDaniel.

Query letters and SASEs should be directed to:

Lawrence David, Assistant Editor

Kim French, Assistant Editor

Laura Hornik, Editor

Beverly Horowitz, Editor in Chief, Vice President, Deputy Publisher

Wendy Loggia, Editor

Karen Meyers, Assistant Editor

Michelle Poploff, Editorial Director

Karen Wojtyla, Senior Editor

BROADWAY BOOKS

Broadway generates commercial nonfiction in celebrity autobiography and biography; historical, political, and cultural biography and memoirs; politics and current affairs; multicultural topics; popular culture; cookbooks, diet, and nutrition; consumer reference, business, and personal finance; popular psychology, spirituality, and women's issues. The house also provides selective commercial/literary frontlist fiction, primarily by established and/or highly promotable authors.

Broadway's emporium strategy involves publishing unique, marketable books of the highest editorial quality by authors who are authorities in their field and who use their credibility and expertise to promote their work.

Broadway Books began operation in mid-1995, with a mission to publish high-quality nonfiction hardcovers and trade paperbacks. William M. Shinker was named president and publisher of the Broadway Books adult trade division in late 1994, joined by John Sterling as Editor in Chief, and Janet Goldstein as the wing's executive editor.

The publishing house's namesake street and logo (a diagonally bisected letter B) are emblematic of the publisher's mandate. Broadway is New York's oldest thoroughfare, and runs obliquely through the diversity of Manhattan's multicultural neighborhoods, from the original harbor and the financial district, along the city's centers of government, literature, music, theater, communications, retail shops, and educational and medical institutions.

Broadway frontlist nonfiction: *The Kingdom of Shivas Irons* by Michael Murphy (author of *Golf in the Kingdom*); *What It Means to Be a Libertarian: A Personal Interpretation* by Charles Murray (coauthor of *The Bell Curve*); *How to Retire Rich* by James O'Shaughnessy; *Bare Knuckles and Back Rooms: My Life in American Politics* by Ed Rollins and Tom DeFrank; *Hard Questions, Heart Answers* by Bernice A. King; *The Fourth Turning: An American Prophecy* by William Strauss and Neil Lowe; *Revenue Management: Hard-Core Tactics for Market Domination* by Robert G. Cross; *The Corner: A Year in the Life of an Inner-City Neighborhood* by David Simon and Edward Burns; *Heaven in a Chip: Fuzzy Visions of Science and Society in the Digital Age* by Bart Kosko; *Killer Instinct: How Two Beginners Took on Hollywood and Made the Most Controversial Film of the Decade* by Jane Hamsher; *Webonomics: Nine Essential Principles for Growing Your Business on the World Wide Web* by Evan I. Schwartz.

Also on tap: a memoir from Bob Costas (written with Pulitzer Prize–winner H. G. "Buzz" Bissinger); another book from Bernice King (youngest daughter of Martin Luther King, Jr., and Coretta Scott King); a narrative nonfiction account of one student's heroic effort to leave the inner-city by Pulitzer Prize–winner Ron Suskind (who also reports for *The Wall Street Journal*).

Broadway's general nonfiction program includes kitchen-arts and lifestyle; relationships, parenting, and the family; popular business; popular issues; humor; and popular psychology, inspirational, and self-help/self-awareness works.

Sample projects here: *Eat Your Way Across the U.S.A.* by Jane and Michael Stern; *A Fresh Taste of Italy* by Michele Scicolone; *Bake and Freeze Chocolate Desserts* by Elinor Klivans; *Polenta* by Michele Anna Jordan; *The Simple Living Guide* by Janet Luhrs; *Becoming the Parent You Want to Be* by Laura Davis and Janis Keyser; *The Roller Coaster Years* by Charlene Canape Giannetti and Margaret Sagarese; *A Family Like Any Other* (a work on stepfamilies in America) by James Bray; *Big Bertha and Me* by Ely Callaway (founder of Callaway Golf); *It's Here Now (Are You?)* by Bhagavan Das; *With God on Our Side: The Rise of the Religious Right in America* by William Martin; *Picture This: A Visual Diary* by Tipper Gore; *Let's Pave the Stupid Rainforests & Give School Teachers Stun Guns and Other Ways to Save America* by Ed Anger; *The Unshredded Files of Hillary and Bill Clinton* by Henry Beard and John Boswell; *The Wise Woman's Guide to Erotic Videos* by Angela Cohen and Sarah Gardner Fox.

On Broadway's preferred fiction list: *As Francesca*, a first novel from Martha Baer (executive editor for the online magazine *HotWired*, former features editor for *Wired* magazine; founding member of the V-Girls performance group), an erotic work serialized as a work-in-progress on the Internet; *A Face at the Window* by Pulitzer

Prize–winning novelist Dennis McFarland (described as a literary ghost story); *Eat Me* (a down-under sensation) from Sydney-based author Linda Jaivin, as well as Linda's new work, *Rock 'n' Roll Babes from Outer Space*; a new crime/suspense novel from Richard Price (author of *Clockers*, as well as *The Wanderers* and *Bloodbrothers*).

Please query the house's acquisition stance prior to submitting projects—Broadway wishes to receive no unsolicited manuscripts; only agented works will be considered. Query letters and SASEs may be directed to:

Harriet Bell, Executive Editor
Cookbooks and the kitchen arts.

Charles Conrad, Vice President and Executive Editor
New nonfiction projects: popular culture, social history, literary nonfiction. Contemporary literary and quality fiction. In charge of trade-paperback reprints.

Janet Goldstein, Vice President and Executive Editor; Editorial Director for Trade Paperbacks
Women's and feminist issues; relationships and popular psychology; social trends, parenting, and family issues.

John Sterling, Vice President and Editor in Chief
Literary fiction and nonfiction.

Lauren Marino, Editor
Nonfiction, especially popular culture, entertainment, humor, spirituality.

Suzanne Oaks, Editor
Commercial nonfiction, investigative and other business stories.

BARRICADE BOOKS INC.

1530 Palisade Avenue
Fort Lee, NJ 07020
201-592-0926

Editorial offices:
150 Fifth Avenue, Suite 700
New York, NY 10011
212-627-7000

Barricade's publishing interest includes arts and entertainment; cookbooks; fiction (including topflight mainstream novels, genre anthologies, and tales of mystery and suspense); how-to/self-help; biography, history, politics, and current events; humor; natural sciences; new age, occult, and religion; psychology, health, and sexuality; recreation; and true crime.

Barricade Books was founded in 1991 by Carole Stuart and Lyle Stuart (formerly of the publishing house Lyle Stuart, which is now a component of Carol Publishing Group). Barricade Books was launched in order to continue the tradition begun in 1956 when Lyle Stuart became a publisher—to specialize in books other publishers might hesitate to publish because they were too controversial.

Barricade publisher Carole Stuart is the author of a number of successful books including *I'll Never Be Fat Again* and *Why Was I Adopted?* She has worked in book publishing her entire adult life. Lyle Stuart is a former newspaper reporter who launched his career as a book publisher with $8,000 that he won in a libel action against Walter Winchell. Stuart sold that company three decades later for $12 million.

The Barricade catalog expands this tradition with a roster of freethinking writers that is perhaps unrivaled in the international commercial-publishing arena. Barricade's list is exemplary of publishing courage in action.

From Barricade: *The King of Clubs: The Story of Scores—the Famed Topless Club—and the Lurid Life Behind the Glitter* by Jay Bildstein (as told to Jery Schmetter); *Killer Kids, Bad Law: Tales of the Juvenile Court System* by Peter Reinharz; *The Complete Book of Devils and Demons* by Leonard R. N. Ashley; *Hollywood Lesbians* by Boze Hadleigh; *My Struggle: The Explosive Views of Russia's Most Controversial Political Figure* by Vladimir Zhirnovsky; *Jokes for Your John: The Full Bathroom Reader* by Omri Bar-Lev and Joe Weis; *Injustice for All: How Our Adversary System of Law Victimizes Us and Subverts True Justice* by Anne Strick; *Mark It with a Stone: A Moving Account of a Young Boy's Struggle to Survive the Nazi Death Camps* by Joseph Horn; *Great Big Beautiful Doll: The Anna Nicole Smith Story* by Eric and D'Eva Redding.

Indicative of the Barricade tradition in fiction and the literary arts: *Gasp! A Novel of Revenge* by Frank Freudberg; *The Best Japanese Science Fiction Stories* (edited by John Apostolou and Martin Greenberg); *Orion: The Story of a Rape* by Ralph Graves; *Norman Corwin's Letters* (edited by A. J. Langguth); *The George Seldes Reader* (edited by Randolph T. Holhut).

Notable Barricade projects: *L. Ron Hubbard: Messiah or Madman?—The Book That Survived Every Attempt to Suppress Its Publication* (revised and updated version) by Brent Corydon; *The Anarchist Cookbook* by William Powell—a radical classic now into well over three dozen printings with more than two million volumes sold; a trade edition of the underground epic (and political hot potato) *The Turner Diaries* by Andrew MacDonald.

Barricade Books manages its own sales and distribution services.

Query letters and SASEs should be directed to:

(Ms.) Carole Stuart, Publisher

BARRON'S
BARRON'S EDUCATIONAL SERIES, INC.

250 Wireless Boulevard
Hauppauge, NY 11788
516-434-3311

Barron's hosts a broad publishing operation that encompasses books in business and finance, gift books, titles in cooking, family and health, gardening, nature, pets, and retirement lifestyle, as well as selected titles in arts, crafts, and hobbying. Barron's produces computer books and software. The house highlights a children's line.

Barron's (founded in 1945) was originally known for its comprehensive line of study notes and test-preparation guides in business, literature, and languages, and standardized tests in individual subject and professional fields. The house offers a number of practical business series, retirement and parenting keys, programs on skills development in foreign languages (as well as in English), and specialty reference titles in allied areas of interest.

Barron's cookbooks address international cuisines as well as areas of concentration such as chocolate, pasta, and ice cream. Family and health books cover home nursing, first aid, baby care, and dictionaries of health-related terms, as well as general-interest works. Under the rubric of special-interest titles, Barron's produces series on arts and crafts techniques, biographies of well-known artists, fashion traditions and trends, and home and garden. Books on pets and pet care include numerous titles keyed to particular breeds and species of birds, fish, dogs, and cats.

Children's and young-adult books and books of family interest include series on pets, nature and the environment, dinosaurs, sports, fantasy, adventure, and humor. Many of these are picture storybooks, illustrated works, and popular reference titles of general interest.

Barron's offers an extensive general-interest series lineup of interest to students and educators: Journey Through History Series, Five Senses Series, Four Elements Series, Discover My World Series, Famous Artists Series, Let's Discover Series, Let's Investigate Series, and Science Magic Series. Barron's also offers children's books in bilingual as well as foreign-language editions (for example, in French and Spanish).

Barron's Study Guides subjects include: book notes, college review, easy-way series, English language arts, EZ-101 Study Keys, foreign language, law, literature, mathematics, philosophy/religion, science, social studies, study tips/reference, and test preparation.

From Barron's (tradelist titles and backlist reference stalwarts): *Double-Vision: Artists Face-to-Face* by Antoine (illustrated by Jonniaux); *The Fortune Telling Kit* by Morgan; *The Great American Bake Sale* by Boteler; *Keys to Parenting Your Anxious Child* by Manassis; *Once Upon a Potty* by Frankel; *1100 Words You Need to Know* by Bronberg and Gordon; *Profiles of American Colleges: Descriptions of Colleges and Index of College Majors* (21st edition) by Barrons's College Division; *Dictionary of Finance and Investment Terms* by Downes and Goodman; *Algebra the Easy Way* (third edition) by Downing; *501 French Verbs* and *501 Spanish Verbs* by Kendris; *ACT—How to Prepare for the American College Testing Program Assessment* (10th edition) by Ehrenhaft, Lehrman, Obrecht, and Mundsack; *CLEP—College Level Exam Program* (seventh edition) by Doster, Ward, Poitras, Bjork, Hockett, and Capozzoli Ingui; *The Complete Book of Dog Breeding* by Rice; *Labrador Retrievers* by Kern.

Barron's handles its own distribution.

Query letters and SASEs should be directed to:

Grace Freedson, Acquisitions Manager

BASICBOOKS
(See HarperCollins)

BASKERVILLE PUBLISHERS
7616 LBJ Freeway, Suite 510
Dallas, TX 75251-1008
214-934-3451
fax: 214-516-1471

Baskerville publishes literary fiction and trade nonfiction, in hardcover and paperback editions. Baskerville series include Great Voices (biographies of vocalists) and Basset Books (trade paperbacks).

Baskerville Publishers (first list, 1992) presents individualist writing voices that sing in the American idiom. Story concepts derived from mainstream or popular culture set Baskerville's fiction writers apart. Often unexpectedly laced with humor, Baskerville's storytellers present tales that emerge from a dark-tinged web.

Fiction from Baskerville includes: *Manny* by Isaac Rosen; *Over There* by Kyle Jarrard; *Watching Vanessa* by Patricia M. Tiffin; *The Hotel in the Jungle* by Albert J. Guerard; *Fata Morgana* by Lynn Stegner; *Graveyard Working* by Gerald Duff; *Moon People* by Sondra Shulman; *Opportunities in Alabama Agriculture* by Tito Perdue; *Skirts* by Mimi Albert; *The Crawlspace Conspiracy* by Thomas Keech; *The Raven* by Stephen Landesman.

Great Voices series titles: *Corelli: The Man, The Voice* by Marina Boagno with Gilberto Starone (translated from Italian); *Galli-Curci: Her Life* by Kathryn H. Brown.

Baskerville handles its own distribution through major wholesalers.

Query letters and SASEs should be directed to:

Jane Howle, Publisher

BEACON PRESS
25 Beacon Street
Boston, MA 02108
617-742-2110

Beacon is primarily a publisher of nonfiction works (along with a limited list of literary fiction and poetry). Beacon's areas of publishing interest include contemporary affairs; gender, ethnic, and cultural studies; the life of the mind and spirit; history; science; and the spectrum of global and environmental concerns. The publisher also hosts a short, strong list of titles in fiction, literary essays, and poetry. The house no longer publishes children's titles. Beacon Press tenders an extensive backlist.

Beacon Press has been a light of independent American publishing since 1854, when the house was established by the Unitarian Universalist Church. The Beacon Press list is presented as a complement to corporate publishing's rapt attention to commercially correct topics and as a publishing platform for those whose search for meaning draws them to fresh points of view. Indeed, the house's estimable reputation thrives on the diversity and divergence of the ideas and stances advanced by Beacon authors.

Emblematic of the Beacon list: *A Fire in the Bones: Reflections on African-American Religious History* by Albert J. Raboteau; *Beyond Pro-Life and Pro-Choice: Moral Diversity in the Abortion Debate* by Kathy Rudy; *Fist Stick Knife Gun: A Personal History of Violence in America* by Geoffrey Canada; *Meeting the Great Bliss Queen: Buddhists, Feminists, and the Art of the Self* by Anne Carolyn Klein; *Queer Spirits: A Gay Men's Myth Book* (edited by Will Roscoe); *Remembering the Bone House: An Erotics of Place and Space* by Nancy Mairs; *Seeing and Believing: Religion and Values in the Movies* by Margaret R. Miles; *Tasting Food, Tasting Freedom: Excursions into Eating, Culture, and the Past* by Sidney W. Mintz; *Transgender Warriors: Making History from Joan of Arc to RuPaul* by Leslie Feinberg; *Women in the Trees: U.S. Women's Short Stories of Battering and Resistance, 1839–1994* (edited by Susan Koppelman).

Scholarly highlight: Beacon's edition of the seventeenth-century classic *Lieutenant Nun: Memoir of a Transvestite in the New World* by Catalina de Erauso (translated by Michele Stepto and Gabriele Stepto; foreword by Marjorie Garber).

Writers, please note these Beacon titles that address themes in the writing life: *Ruined by Reading: A Life in Books* by Lynne Sharon Schwartz; *Facing the Lion: Writers on Life and Craft* (edited by Kurt Brown); *Talking to Angels: A Life Spent at High Latitudes* by Robert Perkins.

Beacon Press is distributed to the trade by Ballantine Books, a division of Random House.

Query letters and SASEs should be directed to:

Deborah Chasman, Editorial Director
Gay/lesbian studies; African American, Jewish, and native American studies.

Andrew Hrycyna, Editor
Philosophy, politics, education.

Deanne Urmy, Executive Editor
Environmental and nature studies, family issues.

Marya Van't Hul, Editor
Science and society; women's studies; Asian-American studies.

Susan Worst, Editor
Religion, guidance.

BEAR & COMPANY PUBLISHING
(See Directory of Religious, Spiritual, and Inspirational Publishers)

PETER BEDRICK BOOKS

2112 Broadway, Suite 318
New York, NY 10023
212-496-0751
fax: 212-496-1158
bedrick@panix.com (e-mail)

Bedrick's list focuses on popular reference works in history, folklore and mythology, and women's studies; the Bedrick children's list accents highly illustrated nonfiction, including several ongoing series in world history and cultures, and numerous educational titles. Bedrick also issues a line of children's books in cooperation with Blackie & Sons under the Bedrick/Blackie imprint.

Peter Bedrick Books was established in 1983, following the founder's long and successful association with Schocken Books. Today a midsized publishing house with a fetching swan logo, Bedrick still has a personal touch—evident from the first Bedrick list, which featured adult and children's books, and introduced the initial three titles in the Library of the World's Myths and Legends, which remain in print in both hardcover and paperback editions.

Special from Bedrick: *The World of the Medieval Knight* by Christopher Gravett (illustrated by Brett Breckon); *The World of Castles and Forts* by Malcolm Day; *Chagall from A to Z* by Marie Sellier; *Corot from A to Z* by Caroline Larroche.

The Inside Story series offers titles filled with full-color cutaway illustrations and informative text. Notable entrants here: *The Roman Colosseum* by Fiona Macdonald (illustrated by Mark Bergin); *A Renaissance Town* by Jacqueline Morley (illustrated by Mark Peppe).

First Facts Series titles: *First Facts About the American Frontier* and *First Facts About the Ancient Romans* by Fiona Macdonald; *First Facts About the Ancient Egyptians* by Jacqueline Morley.

Peter Bedrick Books are distributed by Publishers Group West.

Query letters and SASEs should be directed to:

Peter Bedrick, President and Publisher

MATTHEW BENDER AND COMPANY

2 Park Avenue
New York, NY 10010
212-448-2000
fax: 212-224-3188
http://www.bender.com (World Wide Web)

Bender produces works in the fields of law, accounting, banking, insurance, and related professions. Areas of Bender concentration include general accounting, administrative law, admiralty, civil rights law, computer law, employment/labor, environmental, estate and financial planning, government, health care, immigration, insurance, intellectual property, law-office management, personal injury/medico-legal, products liability, real estate, securities, taxation, and worker's compensation.

Matthew Bender (founded in 1887), a subsidiary of Times Mirror, is a specialist publisher of professional information in print and electronic format. Bender publishes general references as well as state-specific works. Bender produces treatises, textbooks, manuals, and form books, as well as newsletters and periodicals. Many Matthew Bender publications are available in the CD-ROM format.

Matthew Bender has served professionals for more than 108 years and has achieved its unique status as a specialty publisher in diverse areas of the law. Matthew Bender combines in-house editorial talent and publishing ties with the foremost experts in the legal profession to produce a product that will fit their customers' needs. Matthew Bender is one of the world's leading publishers of legal analysis and case law and pours this experience and expertise into more than 500 publications in print and electronic formats and serves professionals in more than 160 countries.

Over the past two years, sweeping changes have taken place at Matthew Bender, including pricing initiatives aimed at providing customers with more information at less cost, streamlined operations, and a renewed commitment to customer service. What remains consistent is Bender's goal of providing the highest quality, state-of-the-art legal resources.

Representative titles from Matthew Bender: *Business Organizations with Tax Planning* by Zolman Cavitch; *Employment Discrimination* by Lex K. Larson; *Moore's Federal Practice* by James William Moore and the Moore's Editorial Board; *Immigration Law and Procedure* by Charles Gordon, Stanley Mailman, and Stephen Yale-Loehr; *Responsibilities of Insurance Agents and Brokers* by Bertram Harnett; *World Patent Law and Practice: Patent Statutes, Regulations and Treaties* by John P. Sinnott and William Joseph Cotreau.

Bender now issues a catalog of publications devoted exclusively to environmental law. Like the environment itself, the field of environmental law touches almost every aspect of society. It is concerned with cleaning and preserving natural resources and regulating the disposal of waste material. Its impact can be felt in the simplest real estate transaction to the most complex personal-injury case. Titles: *Environmental Law Practice Guide* by Michael B. Berrard (general editor); *Insurance Coverage for Environmental Claims* by Mitchell L. Lathrop; *Environmental Law in Real Estate and Business Transactions* by David R. Berz and Stanley M. Spracker; *Treatise on Environmental Law* by Frank P. Grad; *A Guide to Toxic Torts* by Margie Tyler Searcy (editor in chief).

Matthew Bender handles its own distribution.

Query letters and SASEs should be directed to:

Ken Halajian, Vice President, Professional Relations

BERKLEY PUBLISHING GROUP

(See Putnam Berkley Publishing Group)

BERRETT-KOEHLER PUBLISHERS

155 Montgomery Street
San Francisco, CA 94104-4109
415-288-0260
bkpub@aol.com (e-mail)

Berrett-Koehler's nonfiction program accents the areas of work and the workplace, business, management, leadership, career development, entrepreneurship, human resources, and global sustainability. Berrett-Koehler Publishers (instituted in 1992) is an independent press that produces books, periodicals, journals, newsletters, and audiocassettes.

The Berrett-Koehler booklist is produced in well-crafted, ecologically aware hardcover and paperback editions.

Berrett-Koehler stands for a commitment to produce publications that support the movement toward a more enlightened world of work and more free, open, humane, effective, and globally sustainable organizations. They are committed to do publications that challenge conventional views of work and management, that create new lenses for understanding organizations, that pioneer new purposes and values in business, and that open up new sources of guidance for today's complex work world.

Another basic commitment is to apply the concepts of stewardship and partnership to create more open, collaborative, and egalitarian relationships with authors and others with whom we work than is the norm in publishing. The Berrett-Koehler approach features innovative guidance, thought, and technique. Five of the six books announced in a 1997 catalog are by authors of previous bestselling books (James Autry, Geoffrey Bellman, Ken Blanchard, John Miner, and Meg Wheatley), and 13 successful authors have already chosen to do second books with B-K. As a result of discussions with about 60 B-K customers, authors, and others, several grass-roots volunteer initiatives are being organized, including forming groups of readers interested in particular publications, developing a B-K reader network, and exploration of a possible nonprofit organization for activities beyond the scope of our publishing program.

Titles: *A Simpler Way* by Margaret J. Wheatley and Myron Kellner-Rogers; *Confessions of an Accidental Businessman: It Takes a Lifetime to Find Wisdom* by James A. Autry; *Your Signature Path: Gaining New Perspectives on Life and Work* by Geoffrey M. Bellman; *How to Get Ideas* by Jack Foster, illustrated by Larry Corby; *The 4 Routes to Entrepreneurial Success* by John B. Miner; *Managing by Values* by Ken Blanchard and Michael O'Connor.

Berrett-Koehler tends its own multichanneled distribution, through bookstores, direct-mail brochures, catalogs, a toll-free telephone-order number, book clubs, association book services, and special sales to business, government, and nonprofit organizations; the house is distributed to the trade via Publishers Group West.

Query letters and SASEs should be directed to:

Steven Piersanti, President and Publisher

BETHANY HOUSE PUBLISHERS

(See Directory of Religious, Spiritual, and Inspirational Publishers)

Betterway Books

(See Writer's Digest Books)

Birch Lane Press

(See Carol Publishing Group)

Black Sparrow Press

24 Tenth Street
Santa Rosa, CA 95401
707-579-4011

Black Sparrow publishes original poetry and prose, literary reprints, scholarly bibliography, and literary criticism. The press offers a succinct list of new seasonal titles and maintains a full backlist.

Black Sparrow Press (begun in 1966) is a small house with a purview that encompasses ethereal literary zones. The house catalogs some dazzling and visionary writing, featuring works by some of the most distinguished modern and contemporary authors. Many Black Sparrow productions are of academic and cultural importance—and are not necessarily scholastic in tone: The house focus is anything but narrow.

From Black Sparrow Press: *According to Her Contours* (stories and poems) by Nancy Boultier; *African Sleeping Sickness* (poetry and stories) by Wanda Coleman; *Betting on the Muse: Poems & Stories* by Charles Bukowski; *Bitches Ride Alone* (stories) by Laura Chester; *Enchanted Men* (stories) by Thaisa Frank; *Mythologies of the Heart* (poems) by Gerard Malanga; *The Emerald City of Las Vegas* (epic poetry) by Diane Wakoski.

On culture and criticism, these representative works, not necessarily traditional in form: *Junkets on a Sad Planet: Scenes from the Life of John Keats* by Tom Clark; *Chekov* (a biography in verse) by Edward Sanders; *Prodigious Thrust* (memoir) by William Everson; *Maxfield Parrish: Early and New Poems* by Eileen Myles.

Black Sparrow Press handles its own distribution.

The publisher concentrates first and foremost on its established roster of authors; Black Sparrow does not wish to receive unsolicited manuscripts. Query letters and SASEs should be directed to:

John Martin, President

Blast Books

P.O. Box 51 Cooper Station
New York, NY 10276

Blast Books publishes an eclectic list featuring offbeat nonfiction. Whatever categories Blast titles fall into—or through—the house remains on the lookout for perversely compelling properties. Blast founder Ken Sweezy formerly partnered Amok Press with Adam Parfrey (now of Feral House; see separate entry). Blast Books (established in 1989) is a small independent press with an extremely select group of new seasonal offerings; the house holds a full backlist.

On the Blast list: *Alone with the President* by John Strausbaugh (comprising a canny selection of celebrity photographs with United States presidents, along with accompanying documentation); *Grace Beats Karma: Letters from Prison 1958–1960* by Neal Cassady (with foreword by Carolyn Cassady); *Guillotine: Its Legend and Lore* by Daniel Gerould; *Mr. Arashi's Amazing Freak Show: A Graphic Novel* by Suehiro Maruo; *Venus in Furs and Selected Letters* by Leopold von Sacher-Masoch (a Literary Guild pick; features correspondence between author Sacher-Masoch and Emilie Mataja; translated by Uwe Moeller and Laura Lindgren).

Generally, Blast acquires new books through networking and personal contact with the authors; the publisher cannot recall ever having acquired a book through an unsolicited submission. In addition, Blast traditionally has not bought works through agents—primarily on account of the publisher's relatively low advances, which naturally serves to lessen an agent's interest. However, in order to stem the tide of unsolicited manuscripts and unwanted queries, the house's stance is to accept agented manuscripts only (this means no unagented submissions) when there does not already exist a previous relationship.

Potential Blast authors should note: If you believe you must get this publisher's attention, pay careful attention to the publisher's list and preferences, and then definitely query via *letter* and SASE *only*—rather than sending a complete manuscript or even a proposal. Though Blast has published fictional works (primarily in reprint), the house does not wish to receive fiction submissions.

Blast Books is distributed by Publishers Group West.

Query letters and SASEs should be directed to:

Ken Sweezy, Publisher

BLOOMBERG PRESS

100 Business Park Drive
P.O. Box 888
Princeton, NJ 08542-0888
609-279-3000
fax: 609-683-7523
800-388-2749

Bloomberg publishes books in finance, personal finance, business, economics, management, investments, insurance, and works within related categories. House imprints and specialty lines include: Bloomberg Professional Library (primarily for financial professionals), Bloomberg Personal Bookshelf (consumer-oriented personal-finance titles), and Bloomberg Small Business (small businesses and entrepreneurship).

Bloomberg Press (founded in 1996) is part of Bloomberg L.P., a global, multimedia-based information service that combines news, data, and analysis for financial markets and businesses. The company runs a real-time financial-information network, as well as a number of periodicals (newsletters, journals, magazines), news-service operations (supplying news and stories to, among other clients, reporters, editors, and news bureaus), and radio and television enterprises (Bloomberg Information Radio, Bloomberg Business News, Bloomberg Small Business).

Bloomberg Press books have a distinctive look and feel; befitting their compact format, the books are concentrated and practical—for demanding and busy people—and deliver a lot of specific and useful information: tips, dos and don'ts, rules of thumb, step-by-step procedures. These books are intended to be to-the-point and to equip readers to take action.

Bloomberg Professional Library publishes compact books for brokers, traders, portfolio managers, analysts, money managers, CEOs, CFOs, bankers, and other financial professionals, as well as for small-business people, consultants, and sophisticated investors worldwide. Subject areas include: investment intelligence, portfolio management, markets, financial analytics, economic analysis of use to traders and other financial professionals:

Representative titles: *A Guide to Trading in the Energy Markets* by Ian Vlarke; *Convertible Bonds: An Option-Based Modeling Approach* by Eric Berger and David Klein; *How to Trade in Electricity: New Strategies for the Era of Deregulation* by Albert Bassano; *Best Practices for Financial Advisors* by Mary Rowland; *Best Practices for Nonprofit Boards: Managing Finances and Investments* by Robert W. Casey; *An Introduction to Option-Adjusted Spread Analysis* by Tom Windas; *Swap Literacy: A Comprehensible Guide* by Elizabeth Ungar.

Bloomberg Personal Bookshelf publishes concise books for consumers, business people, and professionals. Categories include: investing; managing personal wealth; choosing products and services, including insurance, health care, banking services, and real estate; personal-finance reference, education, use of personal computers for investment decisions, and online information; balancing personal and professional lives, managing careers and households; other topics, from a personal-finance angle, such as credit, taxes, and estate planning.

Titles include: *How to Invest in Emerging Markets* by Ted Mertz; *Wisdom of the 50 Best Money Managers* by Mary Rowland; *A Trade for All Seasons: An Encyclopedia of Trading Strategies* by Christopher Graja and Elizabeth Ungar; *Industry-by-Industry Guide to Company Analysis* by the Bloomberg Equity Department; *The Investigative Investor: How to Get Valuable Company Information* by the Reporters and Editors of Bloomberg Business News and other organizations; *Where to Go When the Bank Says No: Alternative Financing for Businesses* by David R. Evanson; *A Commonsense Guide to Your 401(k)* by Mary Rowland; *Smartest Questions to Ask Your Financial Advisers* by Lynn Brenner; *Blue-Chip Drips: How to Build a Portfolio Using Bloomberg's 100 Best Dividend Reinvestment Plans* by Jonathan M. Heller; *Choosing and Using an HMO* by Ellyn Spragins; *Small-Cap Stocks: How to Invest in the Fast-Growing Small Companies Wall Street Can't Touch* by Christopher Graja and Elizabeth Ungar; *Smarter Insurance Solutions* by Janet Bamford; *A Commonsense Guide to Mutual Funds* by Mary Rowland.

Bloomberg Small Business is a recent addition to the Bloomberg Press family of imprints—a line sure to synergize with the Bloomberg TV show of the same name.

Bloomberg markets its products and services internationally, through a creative variety of outlets including traditional print venues as well as electronic distribution. Bloomberg Press is distributed by Irwin Professional Publishing.

Query letters and SASEs should be directed to:

Michael Bloomberg, Publisher

Jared Kieling, Editorial Director

BLUE MOON BOOKS

61 Fourth Avenue
New York, NY 10003
212-505-6880
bluoff@aol.com (e-mail)
http://www.bluemoonbooks.com (World Wide Web)
Blue Moon's Web site contains a complete listing of available books, cover art, the Blue Notes newsletter, ordering information, writer's guidelines, and snippets of erotica.

Blue Moon's erotica includes some of the finest novels and stories in the field. Blue Moon Books also publishes selected trade fiction and nonfiction. The North Star Line offers a discriminating literary list.

Blue Moon Books was established in 1987 by Barney Rosset, the trailblazing publisher who earlier founded Grove Press and developed that enterprise into a house of international literary, cultural, and commercial renown.

Blue Moon/North Star highlights: *Goa Freaks: My Hippie Years in India* by Cleo Odzer; *Brazen* by Ghislaine Dunant (translated by Rosette Lamont); *The Mad Club* (in a new edition) by Michael McClure; and *Seventeen (The Political Being)* and *J (The Sexual Being)* (two novellas) by Kenzaburo Oe.

Blue Moon erotica: *The Encounter* by Maria Madison; *Romance of Lust* by Anonymous; *Mariska* by Olga Tergora; *Shogun's Agent* by Akahige Namban; *Sundancer* by Briony Shilton; *Ironwood Revisited* by Don Winslow; *Shadow Lane III: The Romance of Discipline* by Eve Howard; *Souvenirs from a Boarding School* by Anonymous; *The Pearl* by Anonymous; *Julia* by Elaine Rice; *Carousel* by Daniel Vian; *Our Scene* by Wilma Kauffen; *The Captive III* by Anonymous; *My Secret Life* by Anonymous; *Laura* by Patrick Hendren; *The Reckoning* by Anonymous; and *Ellen's Story* by Anonymous.

In addition to fervid classical romances, Blue Moon offers erotic works with such contemporary themes as psychosexual suspense thrillers; the house offers a significant listing of erotic fiction by women.

Blue Moon Books oversees its own distribution.

NORTH STAR LINE

The North Star Line features fine writing in both hardcover and paperback. North Star hosts literary anthologies, poetic works, shorter and longer fiction, as well as general trade titles.

On the North Star list: *Stirrings Still* by Samuel Beckett; *The Man Sitting in the Corridor* (fiction) by Marguerite Duras; *The Correct Sadist* (novel) by Terence Sellers; *Lament: A Novel About How the West Was Blown* by David (Sunset) Carson; *The Ghost Ship* (poetry) by Henry Hart; *Trangulation from a Known Point* (poetry) by Ruth Danon; *New and Selected Poems 1930–1990* by Richard Eberhart; *The Colors of Infinity* (poetry) by Donald E. Axinn; and *Two Dogs and Freedom: The Open School in Soweto* (schoolchildren from South Africa's Open School speak out).

North Star Line has republished a number of classic literary compilations: *The Olympia Reader* and *The New Olympia Reader* (edited by Maurice Girodias) are filled with ribald and erotic writings first published in Paris by the germinal publisher of Olympia Press Maurice Girodias; these volumes feature the work of such authors as Jean Genet, Henry Miller, Chester Himes, Lawrence Durrell, William S. Burroughs, Gregory Corso, George Bataille, John Cleland, Pauline Réage, Samuel Beckett, and the Marquis de Sade. Blue Moon publisher Barney Rosset, along with associates, has edited *Evergreen Review Reader 1957–1966*, featuring selections from *Evergreen*, America's fabled journal of literary provocateurism.

Query letters and SASEs should be directed to:

Barney Rosset, President

Margarita Shalina, Publisher's Assistant

BONUS BOOKS, INC.

160 East Illinois Street
Chicago, IL 60611
312-467-0580

Bonus publishes general nonfiction, accenting titles in automotive, broadcasting, business and careers, collectibles, consumer, legal, self-help, humor and nostalgia, health and fitness, cooking, autobiography and biography, books of regional interest (including the Chicago area), sports, gambling, and current affairs. Titles from the Precept Press imprint are written by and for fund-raising professionals and physicians.

Bonus Books, Inc. (founded in 1985) had an original focus on sports titles and grew quickly into a trade book publisher with nationwide prominence. Strong Bonus growth categories have been sports books and gambling books. As remarked in a letter to booksellers from Bonus publisher Aaron Cohodes: "I don't know what this says about our society, but perhaps that's just as well."

Bonus highlights include: *Buttermilk Cookbook: The Rest of the Carton* by Susan Costello and Anna Heller; *Selling Your Valuables* by Jeanne Siegel; *Sampras: A Legend in the Works* by H. A. Branham; *Do Well by Doing Good* by Keith E. Gregg; *Woulda, Coulda, Shoulda* (new expanded edition) by Dave Feldman with Frank Sugano; *Silver Linings* by Herschell Gordon Lewis; *Handbook of Commonly Used Chemotherapy Regimens* (edited by F. Anthony Greco).

Bonus's watershed title, *Ditka: An Autobiography* by Mike Ditka with Don Pierson, remains in print on a sturdy backlist. Other Bonus backlist favorites: *101 Ways to Make*

Money in the Trading-Card Market Right Now! by Paul Green and Kit Kiefer; *Best Blackjack* by Frank Scoblete; *Break the One-Armed Bandits: How to Come Out When You Play the Slots* by Frank Scoblete; *Overlay: How to Bet Horses Like a Pro* by Bill Heller; *Quarterblack: Shattering the NFL Myth* by Doug Williams with Bruce Hunter. *Settle It Yourself: When You Need a Lawyer—and When You Don't* by Fred Benjamin and Dorothea Kaplan.

Bonus Books distributes its own list and utilizes a number of national sales representatives.

Query letters and SASEs should be directed to:

Aaron Cohodes, President and Publisher

Aili Bresnahow, Assistant Editor

Deborah Flapow, Managing Editor

THE BOOTSTRAP PRESS
(See listing for The Apex Press)

MARION BOYARS PUBLISHING
237 East 39th Street
New York, NY 10016
212-697-1599

The Marion Boyars publishing program gives preeminence to fine writing and is open to considering the highest level of expression in virtually any category. Areas of particular Marion Boyars accomplishment are in the fields of fiction, poetry, belles lettres, memoirs, literary criticism, biography, music, theater, sociology, and travel.

Marion Boyars Publishing (founded in 1978) has achieved international renown and commercial presence in letters with an individualist precision and personalized disposition. Marion Boyars releases a moderate-sized seasonal list; the house tends a strong backlist.

Though not technically a United States publishing house (projects emanate editorially from the London base), Boyars presents writers whose works may have more an international appeal than a strictly commercial-American flavor. The publisher acquires on the basis of enthusiasm for a given work—and is not necessarily based on projections of huge initial sales. Indeed, Marion Boyars herself has remarked that overlooked books and translations are often the house's jewels.

A representative coup is the English-language publication of *Nip the Buds, Shoot the Kids* by Nobel laureate Kenzaburo Oe.

On the Marion Boyars list: *Gents* by Warwick Collins; *Asher* by Mark Fyfe; *The Ministry of Hope* by Roy Heath; *Four Black Revolutionary Plays* by Amiri Baraka; *Creativity and Disease* by Dr. Philip Sandblom.

Marion Boyars Publishing is distributed by Rizzoli International; books are also available to the trade through the LPC Group.

Query letters and SASEs should be directed to:

(Ms.) Marion Boyars, President, Editor in Chief
Marion Boyars Publishing
24 Lacy Road
London SW15 INL, England, U.K.

BOYDS MILLS PRESS

815 Church Street
Honesdale, PA 18431
717-253-1164
fax: 717-253-0179
800-949-7777

Boyds Mills produces storybooks, picture books, rhyming books, craft books, game-books, posters, and poetry—nonsensical verse as well as more serious fare. The press promotes a solid seasonal list of new titles and hosts a hefty backlist. Boyds Mills Press (founded in 1990) is a subsidiary of Highlights for Children. From its headquarters in the mountains of Pennsylvania, this house issues books for children of all ages.

Boyds Mills wants books that challenge, books that inspire, and books that entertain young people the world over. Boyds Mills has published such international best-sellers as *Dougal Dixon's Dinosaurs* (over a dozen editions in ten languages, plus multi-volume spinoffs).

Boyds Mills releases: *Dinosaur Worlds: New Dinosaurs—New Discoveries* by Don Lessem (founder of The Dinosaur Society); *Harvest Year* by Cris Peterson (photographs by Alvis Upitis); *O Christmas Tree* (a Christmas story from the West Indies) by Vashanti Rahaman (illustrated by Frané Lessac); *I Am The Ice Worm* (lost in the Arctic, a girl learns the meaning of hardship and survival) by Mary Ann Easley; *From Anne to Zach: A My Name Is Anne, Z My Name Is Zach* by Mary Jane Martin; *Summer Tunes: A Martha's Vineyard Vacation* by Patricia McMahon (photographs by Peter Simon); *The Sun Is Up: A Child's Year of Poems* (verses compiled by William Jay Smith and Carol Ra); *New Moon* by Pegi Deitz Shea; *175 Easy-to-Do Christmas Crafts* (edited by Sharon Dunn Umnik); *175 Easy-to-Do Thanksgiving Crafts* (edited by Sharon Dunn Umnik); *Sun Through the Window: Poems for Children* by Marci Ridlon (foreword by Shelley Harwayne); *The Sky Is Not So Far Away: Night Poems for Children* by Margaret Hillert (illustrated by Tom Werner); *Mother Hubbard's Christmas* (retold and illustrated by John O'Brien); *The Jade Horse: The Cricket and the Peach Stone* by Ann Tompert (illustrated by Winson Trang); *Deck the Halls: An Old Welsh Carol* (illustrated by Iris Van Rynbach); *The Faraway Drawer* by Harriett Diller (illustrated by Andrea Shine); *If Dogs Had Wings* by Larry Dane Brimmer (illustrated by Chris L. Demarest);

Mr. Lincoln's Whiskers: The True Story of the Girl Who Wrote to Abraham Lincoln by Karen B. Winnick (illustrated by the author).

Among featured Boyds Mills authors is award-winning Jane Yolen, who checks in with *Sing Noel* (Christmas carols selected by Jane Yolen; musical arrangements by Adam Stemple; illustrations by Nancy Sippel Carpenter). Additional Jane Yolen books from Boyds Mills include *Sleep Rhymes Around the World* and *An Invitation to the Butterfly Ball*.

Boyds Mills Press handles its own distribution.

Query letters and SASEs should be directed to:

Kent L. Brown, Jr., Publisher

Clay Winters, President

GEORGE BRAZILLER, INC.

171 Madison Avenue
New York, NY 10016
212-889-0909

George Braziller accents fine editions in art and design, architecture, and art movements and history. The house also publishes selected literary titles, as well as philosophy, science, history, criticism, and biographical works. The house hosts a solid backlist.

George Braziller, Inc. (founded in 1955) is perhaps most widely known for original fine books in the fields of art and architecture. Much of Braziller's fiction and poetry is foreign literature in translation, although the publisher does publish original literary novels (such as works by Janet Frame), and works in the English language that have received initial publication elsewhere.

Braziller also has a strong interest in literary criticism and writing relating to the arts, in addition to a small selection of contemporary and modern poetry. Essential Readings in Black Literature is a Braziller series that features world-class writers from around the globe. Other Braziller series include Library of Far Eastern Art and New Directions in Architecture.

From Braziller: *Annibale Carracci: The Farnese Palace, Rome* by Charles Dempsey; *Celtic Goddesses: Warriors, Virgins, and Mothers* by Miranda Green; *Constructivism: Origins and Evolution* by George Rickey; *Georgia O'Keefe: Canyon Suite* by Barbara J. Bloeink; *Multiples: From Duchamp to the Present* (edited by Zdenek Felix); *Samuel Beckett* (photographs by John Minihan; introduction by Aidan Higgins); *The Future Eaters: An Ecological History of the Australasian Lands and People* by Timothy Flannery.

Braziller fiction and literary works: *Poetry of the American Renaissance* (edited by Paul Kane); *The First Century After Beatrice* (novel) by Amin Malouf; *The Game in Reverse: Poems and Essays* by Taslima Nasrin; *Papa's Suitcase* (a comic tale) by Gerhard Köpf.

Braziller handles its own distribution, as well as that of Persea Books and Persea's imprint Ontario Review Press.

Query letters and SASEs should be directed to:

Adrienne Baxter, Fine Arts Editor
Fine arts.

George Braziller, Publisher
All areas consistent with publisher description.

BROADMAN PRESS

(See Directory of Religious, Spiritual, and Inspirational Publishers)

BRUNNER/MAZEL

19 Union Square West
New York, NY 10003
212-924-3344

Brunner/Mazel publishes a nonfiction list, with titles in psychology, psychiatry, psychotherapy, psychoanalysis, neurology, social work, special education, child development, couples, marriage, family therapy, and group therapy. Brunner/Mazel produces a juveniles line that highlights the publisher's pertinent topic areas, as well as a limited number of gift books. The house maintains a comprehensive backlist.

Brunner/Mazel (instituted in 1945) publishes primarily for a professional market. The house also offers titles with appeal toward general readers.

The publishing program at Brunner/Mazel keeps abreast of developments in this active professional sector; the house has frontlisted titles in fields of family therapy, child sexual abuse, sex therapy, self-psychology, stress and trauma, substance abuse, eating disorders, hypnosis, art therapy, and parenting.

Representative Brunner/Mazel projects: *Acting for Real: Drama Therapy Process, Technique, and Performance* by Renee Emunha; *Aging into the 21st Century: The Exploration of Aspirations and Values* by Rachelle A. Dorfman; *Eating Disorders and Marriage: The Couple in Focus* by D. Blake Woodside, Lorie Shekter-Wolfson, Jack S. Brandes, and Jan B. Lackstrom; *Family Therapy: Fundamentals of Theory and Practice* by William A. Griffin; *Magazine Photo Collage: A Multicultural Assessment and Treatment Technique* by Helen B. Landgarten; *Self-Hypnosis: The Complete Manual for Health and Self-Change* by Brian M. Alman and Peter D. Lambrou; *Sex, Priests, and Power: Anatomy of a Crisis* by A. W. Richard Sipe; *The Illustrated Manual of Sex Therapy* by Helen Singer Kaplan; *Therapists Who Have Sex with Their Patients* by Herbert S. Strean; *Vampires, Werewolves, and Demons: Twentieth-Century Reports in the Psychiatric Literature* by Richard Noll.

Magination Press is an imprint for books that help parents help their children. Titles: *Luna and the Big Blur: A Story for Children Who Wear Glasses* by Shirley Day (illustrated by Don Morris); *You Can Call Me Willy: A Story for Children About AIDS* by Joan C. Verniero (illustrated by Verdon Flory); *Proud of Our Feelings* by Lindsay Leghorn.

Brunner/Mazel oversees its own distribution services, including a strong mail-order operation directed toward the professional market; the publisher's books my also be ordered through Publishers Group West.

Query letters and SASEs should be directed to:

Marc Tracten, President
Psychology, behavioral sciences, hypnosis, family therapy, psychoanalysis, psychiatry, child and adolescent development, eating disorders, marriage and family therapy, sex therapy, and related fields.

BULFINCH PRESS
(See Little, Brown)

BUSINESS ONE IRWIN
(See Irwin Professional Publishing)

BUTTERWORTH-HEINEMANN
(See listing for Heinemann)

CAMBRIDGE UNIVERSITY PRESS
(See Directory of University Presses)

CAPRA PRESS
P.O. Box 2068
Santa Barbara, CA 93210
805-966-4590
fax: 805-965-8020

Capra presents cultivated nonfiction and contemporary literary fiction in trade formats. Capra's specialties include books in the categories of art and architecture, letters, travel and American regional, natural history, mystery fiction, and merchandise such as post-card series.

Capra Press (founded in 1970) is a small house with a highly select catalogue geared to the general trade. Capra's respected mountain goat colophon mascot was initially associated with fine books on the American West. The Capra interest has since expanded, and the current backlist features a solid assortment of the house's own originals as well as literary works in reprint.

From the Capra list: *Eating and Drinking in Spanish* by Andy Herbach and Michael Dillon; *Bad Girl* by Leslie Hall; *Wine and Dine: California Fine Wines Matched with Gourmet Recipes* by Ron Breitstein and Hendrick Van Leuven; *Men Down West* by Kenneth Lincoln; *Tides in Time* by Douglas Isaac Busch; *Charles Hillinger's America* (foreword by Charles Kuralt; photographs by the author); *The Book of Days: Wisdom Through the Seasons* (edited by Elizabeth Pepper and John Wilcock); *Short Cuts on Wine: Everything the Wine Lover Needs to Know* by Edmond Masciana; *The Witches' Almanac: The Complete Guide to Lunar Harmony* by Elizabeth Pepper and John Wilcock; *In the Presence of Elephants* by Peter Beagle (photographs by Genaro Molina; introduction by Pat Derby).

The Capra imprint Perseverance Press focuses on mystery and suspense fiction, often with a West Coast twist; the Capra Western Classics line offers fiction with a Western theme. Capra also publishes cat books, crossword puzzle collections, and books of Santa Barbara regional focus.

As Capra rounds the bend into its 27th year, the publisher expresses this view of publishing in the 1990s: "Independent publishers and booksellers, besieged as they are by the roughshod centralization of the superstores and superpublishers, are nevertheless bringing out a greater diversity of books than ever before in direct response to America's insatiable need to hear voices in the crowd. The strength of our culture comes not from our unity, but from our very salmagundi. We thrive in tolerance not single-mindedness and that's where the midlist books live. The publishers with Consortium represent a microcosm of what books in America are all about."

Capra Press titles are distributed to the book trade by Consortium Book Sales and Distribution. Titles are also available to individuals via mail order.

Query letters and SASEs should be directed to:

Noel Young, President

CAREER PRESS

3 Tice Road
P.O. Box 687
Franklin Lakes, NJ 07417
201-848-0310

Career Press is established as a hard-driving, entrepreneurial business and financial publisher. The house offers a wide variety of titles in such fields as business and financial how-to, books for owners of small businesses, financial planning, retirement, and general nonfiction (where the list includes lifestyle, recreation, parenting, and popular reference). The publisher also produces specialty educational titles (including study series). Career tends a select, fast-moving backlist.

The resolute Career Press product line is no accident. The publisher promotes aggressively and resourcefully—and stocks booksellers with titles geared to receive major review attention; national print, radio, and TV exposure, including radio phone-in shows nationwide.

Career Press (founded in 1985) originally secured a publishing niche for its career-related titles with a short list of practical business books for the professional market (career planning, job search, how-to résumé and interview books).

Today, Career Press is dedicated to publishing accessible, practical books for business people, educators, and students—as well as assuming a commercial presence in mainstream nonfiction. The Career Press mission is simple—publishing books that help improve life. Career Press has established a copublishing agreement with Successories, an organization known as an innovative and specialty retailer and mail-order company that designs and markets motivational products.

From Career Press (including general trade titles, as well as books in business, career, and finance): *Breaking the Rules: Last-Ditch Tactics for Landing the Man of Your Dreams* (a parody by Laura Banks and Janette Barber); *Motivational Minutes: Insightful Ideas for Improving the Quality of Your Life* by Don Essig; *Think Out of the Box* by Mike Vance and Diane Deacon; *Bootstrapper's Success Secrets: 151 Tactics for Building Your Business on a Shoestring Budget* by Kimberly Stansell; *Management Mess-Ups: 57 Pitfalls You Can Avoid (and Stories of Those Who Didn't)* by Mark Eppler; *Diane Warner's Complete Book of Wedding Toasts: Hundreds of Ways to Say "Congratulations!"* by Diane Warner; *Secrets of Breakthrough Leadership* by Peter Capezio and Debra Morehouse; *Taking Your Business Global: Your Small Business Guide to Successful International Trade* by James Wilfong and Toni Seger; *Insider's Guide to Medical School Admissions* by R. Stephen Toyos, M.D.; *Start-Up Financing: Hundreds of Ways to Get the Cash You Need to Start or Expand Your Business* by William J. Stolze.

Great Little Book series titles: *Great Little Book on Universal Laws of Success*; *Great Little Book on Personal Achievement*; *Great Little Book on Successful Selling* (all by Brian Tracy).

In the Great Quotes series (powerful thoughts from powerful people): *Great Quotes from Great Leaders*; *Great Quotes from Great Sports Heroes*; *Great Quotes from Great Women*; *Great Quotes from Zig Ziglar*.

One of Career's perennial sellers is a two-volume hardback edition of the United States government's reference tome *Dictionary of Occupational Titles*—produced by Career as a professional business resource.

Career Press distributes its own list.

Query letters and SASEs should be directed to:

Ronald Fry, President

Carol Publishing Group

120 Enterprise Avenue
Secaucus, NJ 07094
201-866-0490

Carol Publishing accents trade nonfiction books; the Carol list, incorporating the Birch Lane and Citadel imprints, covers essentially all popular categories. Among the several Carol imprints, Birch Lane Press highlights commercial nonfiction (and occasional lead fiction), and Citadel Press accents popular culture, titles in awareness and improvement, and titles with media-related or celebrity themes in film, music, and other mass-entertainment fields. The Carol Publishing Group publishes hardcover books, trade paperbacks, and mass-market paperback editions.

Carol is a large independent publisher incorporating several lines, with Birch Lane Press the featured frontlist imprint. Many Carol/Birch Lane books veer toward the provocative—some are intentionally controversial—and authors with a publicity edge are prime candidates for publication opportunities.

Carol Publishing Group was established in 1989 when Steven Schragis acquired several formerly independent presses, including Citadel Press, University Books, and the publishing house Lyle Stuart.

Citadel was (and remains) the second largest publisher of entertainment books in the country. The Lyle Stuart list earned a reputation for hard-hitting, serious commercial vehicles with lively sales potential in areas of topical interest eminently appropriate for talk-show debate, a tradition in which Carol participates. Citadel Stars is an imprint created for books that tap into mass-media trends and personalities.

Though Carol has successfully produced commercial fiction—often featuring hot-button topics or tied in with a celebrity-author—at this juncture Carol publishes fiction only on a specialty basis.

Representing the Carol list in trade nonfiction: *Do We Need Another Baby? Helping Your Child Welcome a New Arrival—with Love and Illustrations* by Cynthia MacGregor (illustrated by David Roth); *The Hispanic Cookbook: Traditional and Modern Recipes in English and Spanish* by Nilda Luz Rexach; *The Titanic Conspiracy: Cover-Ups and Mysteries of the World's Most Famous Sea Disaster* by Robin Gardiner and Dan Van Der Vat; *The Psychedelic Experience: A Manual Based on the Tibetan Book of the Dead* by Timothy Leary, Ralph Metzner, and Richard Alpert.

Entrants in the arena of contemporary culture and celebrity: *Total Exposure: The Movie Buff's Guide to Celebrity Nude Scenes* by Jami Bernard; *Liz: An Intimate Biography of Elizabeth Taylor* by C. David Heymann; *Little Girl Lost: The Troubled Childhood of Princess Diana by the Woman Who Raised Her* by Mary Clark; *Jodie Foster: A Life On Screen* by Philippa Kennedy; *The Woman in the White House: The Remarkable Story of Hillary Rodham Clinton* by Norman King; *Wannabe: A Would-Be Player's Misadventures in Hollywood* by Everett Weinberger; *The Man in the Red Velvet Dress: Inside the World of Cross-Dressing* by J. J. Allen.

From Carol's select lineup in fiction: *Continue Laughing* (a novel) by Carl Reiner.

Carol Publishing Group distributes its own list domestically, as well as handling titles from Dr. Who, Gambling Times Books, High-Top Sports Audio, the National Hemlock Society, and Virgin Publishing; international sales are handled by a worldwide network of regional representatives.

Project submissions from agents, as well as query letters and SASEs, may be directed to the Carol editors (please use the New Jersey address for queries). All Carol editors acquire in the following areas: popular culture, business, current events, biography, history, controversial subjects, entertainment. Listed below are editors with specific or additional individual interests:

Hillel Black, Editor in Chief
General nonfiction, celebrity fiction, current affairs, history, biography, popular culture, music, film.

Carrie Cantor, Editor

Jim Ellison, Senior Editor
Entertainment, celebrity biography, bridge and gambling, humor, Judaica, New Age and occult, travel, specialty cookbooks.

Lisa Kaufman, Senior Editor
Current events, popular culture, film, entertainment, history, biography.

Mike Lewis, Editor

Alan Wilson, Executive Editor
Fiction: mainstream. Nonfiction: biography, books about film.

CARROLL & GRAF PUBLISHERS, INC.

19 West 21st Street, Suite 601
New York, NY 10010-6805
212-889-8772

Carroll & Graf publishes commercial trade nonfiction and literary and commercial fiction (including a strong list in mystery and suspense). Carroll & Graf (founded in 1983) is a compact house with a catalog as select and well targeted as it is diverse. In addition to its original titles, Carroll & Graf reprints American classics and genre works, and foreign literature in translation. The house issues a full raft of genre-specific anthologies, and offers a topflight lineup of erotic literature. Carroll & Graf produces hardcover, trade paper, and mass-market paperback editions.

Carroll & Graf nonfiction emphasizes contemporary culture, current events, and issues-oriented perspectives (including investigative accounts, political and historical works, and top-end true crime); business, finance, and economics; self-improvement, relationships, how-to; humor and games; and high-interest topical reference.

Nonfiction from Carroll & Graf: *Rosie: Rosie O'Donnell's Biography* by James Robert Parish; *The Inspired Executive: The Art of Leadership in the Age of Knowledge* by Granville Toogood; *101 Reasons Why He Didn't Call You Back* by Hillary Jacobs and Audrey Thompson; *The Pocket Guide to Sensational Sex* by Jane Hertford; *Prisoner 1167: The Madman Who Was Jack the Ripper* by J. C. H. Tully; *Homosexuals in History* by A. L. Rowse; *Notes to Myself: A Creative Guide to Journal Writing* (creative writing/self-help) by Anne H. Aldritch; *The Last Will and Testament of Jacqueline Kennedy Onassis* (collector's edition with handsome binding, gold-tipped pages, and specially designed endpapers; authentic reproduction of document and signature); *Genius and Lust: The Creative and Sexual Lives of Cole Porter and Noel Coward* by Joseph Morella and George Mazzei; *Love at Second Sight: Strange Romantic Encounters* by Paul McLaughlin; *The Machiavellian's Guide to Womanizing* by Nick Casanova; *Outposts: A Catalog of Rare and Disturbing Information* by Russ Kick.

In fiction and the literary arts, Carroll & Graf produces mainstream novels, tales of the supernatural, fantasy, science fiction, and is particularly adventuresome in suspense categories, publishing an array of titles that runs from traditional mysteries to future-horror crime thrillers with a literary bent.

Highlights in fiction and literature from Carroll & Graf: *The Drive-In: A Double-Feature Omnibus* by Joe R. Lansdale; *Wild Women* (prose and poetry anthology; edited by Melissa Mia Hall); *Lady with a Laptop* by D. M. Thomas (author of *The White Hotel*); *The Rage of Angels* (literary fiction) by Alan Fisher; *Love Kills* (mystery anthology, edited by Ed Gorman and Martin H. Greenberg); *Wild Strawberries* (a Barsetshire novel) by Angela Thirkell; *Traitor's Purse* by Margery Allingham (author of the Albert Campion series); *The Red Right Hand* (suspense classic) by Joel Townsley Rogers; *Illusions* by Bill Pronzini (creator of *Sentinels* and other Nameless Detective mysteries); *Prelude to a Scream* by Jim Nisbet; *The Nightmare Factory* (stories) by Thomas Ligotti; *Grave Doubt* by Michael Allegretto; *Bad Dreams* by Kim Newman; *Louisiana Purchase* by A. E. Hotchner; *A Dead Man in Deptford* by Anthony Burgess; *Black Hornet* by James Sallis (author of *Long-Legged Fly* and *Moth*).

Works with an amatory inclination: *Confessions d'Amour* by Anne-Marie Villefranche; *His Mistress's Voice* by G. C. Scott; *Skin: Sensual Tales* (short fiction) by Catharine Hiller; *Sweet Friction* by Marcus Van Heller; *Erotica: An Illustrated Anthology of Sexual Art and Literature* (multivolume series; edited by Charlotte Hill and William Wallace); *Love's Theater* (edited by Esther Selsden); *Slow Dancing* by Joan Elizabeth Lloyd (author of *The Pleasures of Jessicalynn* and *Black Satin*); *Tart Tales: Elegant Erotic Stories* by Carolyn Banks.

Mammoth Books is a line from Carroll & Graf that accents quantity as well as quality: the Mammoth list includes literary anthologies, works of topical appeal, and specialist interests. Titles here: *The Mammoth Book of Chess* by Graham Burgess; *The Mammoth Book of Carnival Puzzles* by David J. Bodycombe; *The Mammoth Book of Fortune Telling* by Celestine; *The Mammoth Book of Kings and Queens of England* by Mike Ashley; *The Mammoth Book of Gay Short Stories* (edited by Peter Burton); *The*

Mammoth Book of Pulp Fiction (edited by Maxim Jakubowski); *The Mammoth Book of Dracula* (edited by Stephen Jones).

Carroll & Graf books are distributed to the trade by Publishers Group West (which owns 20% of Carroll & Graf).

Query letters and SASEs should be directed to:

Kent Carroll, Publisher and Executive Editor

CATBIRD PRESS
GARRIGUE BOOKS

16 Windsor Road
North Haven, CT 06473
800-360-2391
fax: 203-230-8029
catbird@pipeline.com (e-mail)

Catbird Press (founded in 1987), along with its Garrigue Books imprint, is a small publisher with concentration in the areas of citizen-action reference, American fiction, general humor, travel humor, legal humor, and Central European literature. Series include Legal Humor That Stays Within the Law, Fiction from the New Czech Republic, Corporate and Other Nightmares, and Humor for Grownups.

Fiction, humor, and titles with a literary appeal: *The Breath of an Unfee'd Lawyer: Shakespeare on Lawyers and the Law* (edited by Edward J. Bander; illustrated by Jerry Warshaw); *Daylight in Nightclub Inferno: Czech Fiction from the Post-Kundera Generation* (edited by Elena Lappin); *Human Resources: A Corporate Nightmare* (fiction) by Floyd Kemske; *Was That a Tax Lawyer Who Just Flew Over? From Outside the Offices of Fairweather, Winters & Sommers* (fiction/humor) by Arnold B. Kanter; *Trials and Tribulations: Appealing Legal Humor* (edited by Daniel R. White).

General nonfiction includes: *Jewish Voices, German Words: Growing Up Jewish in Postwar Germany and Austria* (edited by Elena Lapin); *Talks with T. G. Masaryk* (biography) by Karel Capek (translated and edited by Michael Henry Heim); and *The Giver's Guide: Making Your Charity Dollars Count* by Philip English Mackey.

Catbird epitomizes small-press savvy in its continuing success in garnering industry publicity and promotion: Catbird was among the first presses to post selected works-in-progress via the electronic Online Bookstore.

Catbird Press and Garrigue Books are distributed to the trade by Independent Publishers Group.

Query letters and SASEs should be directed to:

Robert Wechsler, Publisher

Christine C. Schmitt, Promotion and Marketing Director

CCC PUBLICATIONS

1111 Rancho Conejo Boulevard, Suites 411 & 412
Newbury Park, CA 91320
805-375-7700
fax: 805-375-7707
800-248-LAFF (orders only)

CCC Publications accents nonfiction trade books in crisply targeted categories: relationships, self-help/how-to, humor, inspiration, humorous inspirational titles, age-related and over-the-hill titles, games and puzzles, party books, cartoon books, gift books and merchandise, gag and blank books—and a group of titles mischievously cataloged as On the Edge. CCC publishes a number of books by bestselling author Jan King.

CCC produces primarily trade paperbacks, smaller gift-size editions, accessories (such as bags and bookmarks), and a line of audio works (including collections of answering-machine messages and sound effects).

On the CCC list: *Smart Comebacks to Stupid Questions* by Richard Porteus (illustrated by Charles Goll); *The Book of White Trash* by Laraine Shape; *The Art of Mooning* by Scott Wilson; *Sexy Crotchword Puzzles* by Don Grant; *Retirement: The Get Even Years* by Fred Sahner (illustrated by Lennie Peterson); *Getting Old Sucks—But It Sure Beats the Alternative!* by Ed Strand; *The Total Bastard's Guide to Golf* (written and drawn by Jed Pascoe); *Technology Bytes!* by Randy Glasbergen; *Cat Love: 150 Wonderful Things You Can Do for Your Cat* by Jill Kramer; *How to Survive a Jewish Mother: A Guilt-Ridden Guide* by Steven Arnold; *Red-Hot Monogamy in Just 60 Seconds a Day* by Patrick T. Hunt, M.D.; *50 Ways to Hustle Your Friends* by Jim Karol.

From On the Edge: *Men Are Pigs, Women Are Bitches* by Jerry King; *The Definitive Fart Book* by Desmond Mullan; *The Very Very Sexy Adult Dot-to-Dot Book* by Tony Goffe; *The Complete Wimp's Guide to Sex* by Jed Pascoe.

Jan King books: *Ladies, Start Your Engines: The Secrets for Restoring Romance, Passion and Great Sex in Your Relationship; Why Men Don't Have a Clue; Hormones from Hell; Killer Bras (and Other Hazards of the 50's).*

CCC (founded in 1983) orchestrates its own distribution.

Query letters and SASEs should be directed to:

Cliff Carle, Editorial Director

Mark Chutnick, Publisher

CELESTIAL ARTS

(See Ten Speed Press/Celestial Arts)

CHAPMAN AND HALL

115 Fifth Avenue
New York, NY 10003
212-254-3232

Chapman and Hall is an academic-science publisher that produces professional, techni-cal, and reference titles in a variety of fields, as well as books slated for the educational arena. Chapman and Hall subject areas include: business and economics, medicine, life sciences, chemistry, earth science, food science and technology, statistics, mathematics, computer science, new media, and engineering. Chapman and Hall is part of Thomson Science and Professional.

A former division of the publishing firm Routledge and Chapman and Hall, this house is currently an independent enterprise. (Please see entry for Routledge, Inc. in this directory.)

Chapman and Hall handles its own distribution.

Query letters and SASEs should be directed to:

Joe Marcelle, President
Medical.

Margaret Cummins, Acquisitions Editor
Engineering.

Henry Flesh, Projects Editor
Life sciences.

Dean Smith, Publisher, New Business and Media

Joanna Turtletaub, Associate Editor
Food science and technology.

CHAPTERS PUBLISHING

2031 Shelburne Road
Shelburne, VT 05482
802-985-8700

Chapters specializes in books on cooking and nutrition, health and fitness, gardening, nature, country living, and home and family (including a series of weekend-projects books). The house offers a line of calendars with themes linked to its overall publishing interests. Chapters productions are recognized for their excellent book design, and fea-ture top-quality paper and binding.

Chapters Publishing (founded in 1991) publishes a select number of new titles each season and tends toward larger print runs; many Chapters titles enjoy sales through es-tablished book clubs. Chapters' evolution as a small commercial press has been markedly winning; and writers might note that the publisher's advances are generally comparable with those expected of large houses.

On the Chapters list: *The Artful Pie: Unforgettable Recipes for Creative Cooks* by Lisa Cherkasky and Renée Comet; *Sea of Slaughter: A Chronicle of the Destruction of Animal Life in the North Atlantic* by Farley Mowat; *American Favorites: Streamlined and Updated Renditions of the Recipes We Love* by Betty Rosbottom (photographs by Louis B. Wallach); *The Light Touch Cookbook: All-Time Favorite Recipes Made Healthful and Delicious* by Marie Simmons; *Storage Projects You Can Build* by David and Jeanie Stiles; *The Conscientious Marine Aquarist: A Commonsense Handbook for Successful Saltwater Hobbyists* by Robert M. Fenner; *Natural Reef Aquariums: Simplified Approaches to Creating Living Saltwater Microcosms* by John H. Tullock; *Passing Strange: True Tales of New England Hauntings and Horrors* by Joseph A. Citro (illustrated by David Dias); *Cooking Under Cover: One-Pot Wonders—A Treasury of Soups, Stews, Braises and Casseroles* by Linda and Fred Griffith (photographs by Alan Richardson); *Eating Thin for Life: Food Secrets and Recipes from People Who Have Lost Weight and Kept It Off* by Anne M. Fletcher.

Among Chapters series: Simply Healthful Cookbooks (recipes for tasty, healthful dishes without a lot of fuss and bother); How to Spot . . . (books written by professional naturalists that give a thorough description of a specific animal's habitat, range, diet, and breeding habits to increase amateur naturalists enjoyment of animal watching).

The Curious Naturalist Series promotes works (in handsome trade paperback editions) from some of North America's finest naturalist writers, such as Peter Mathiessen, R. D. Lawrence, Adrian Forsyth, and Sy Montgomery. Titles here include: *A Natural History of Sex: The Ecology and Evolution of Mating Behavior* by Adrian Forsyth; *Birds of Tropical America* by Steven J. Hilty; *Nature's Everyday Mysteries: A Field Guide to the World in Your Backyard* by Sy Montgomery; *Shark! Nature's Masterpiece* by R. D. Lawrence; *The Wind Birds: Shorebirds of North America* by Peter Mathiessen.

Chapters is distributed in the United States by W. W. Norton; Canadian distribution is handled by Key Porter Books.

Query letters and SASEs should be directed to:

James Lawrence, Publisher

Barry Estabrook, Editor in Chief

Russ Martin, Senior Editor

Sandy Taylor, Consulting Editor

Cristen Brooks, Acquisitions Editor

CHELSEA GREEN PUBLISHING COMPANY

205 Gates-Briggs Building
P.O. Box 428
White River Junction, VT 05001
802-295-6300

Chelsea Green publishes trade nonfiction in natural gardening and food, energy and shelter, nature and the environment, and regional books (including travel, social issues, history and culture). Chelsea Green projects include a publishing co-venture with Real

Goods Trading Company, designated by the imprimatur Real Goods Independent Living Book. Chelsea Green also issues titles geared to children's activities.

Chelsea Green Publishing Company (founded in 1984) is a compact, independent firm of individualistic spirit; the house continues to hone its publishing program through a small number of new seasonal releases (in hardcover and trade paper formats) and a hardy backlist.

On the Chelsea Green list: *Baba á Louis Bakery Bread Book: The Secret Book of the Bread* by John McLure; *The Safari Companion: A Guide to Watching African Mammals* by Richard D. Estes (illustrated by Daniel Otte); *In the Northern Forest* by David Dobbs and Richard Ober; *A Patch of Eden: America's Inner-City Gardeners* by H. Patricia Hynes; *The Rammed Earth House: Rediscovering the Most Ancient Building Material* by David Easton (photographs by Cynthia Wright); *Beyond the Limits: Confronting Global Collapse, Envisioning a Sustainable Future* by Donella H. Meadows, Dennis L. Meadows, and Jørgen Randers.

Chelsea Green handles its own distribution, and distributes for a number of other small, innovative independent presses such as Orwell Cove, OttoGraphics, Ecological Design Press, Harmonious Press, and Seed Savers Exchange. Chelsea Green catalogs products from the Canadian publisher Nimbus (books and calendars), Real Goods Trading Company, and NatureSound Studios (environmental booklet/audiocassette packets).

Query letters and SASEs should be directed to:

Ian Baldwin, Jr., President, Cofounder

Stephen Morris, Publisher

Jim Schley, Editor in Chief

Donella Meadows, Consulting Editor

Noel Perrin, Consulting Editor

Michael Potts, Consulting Editor

Joni Praded, Consulting Editor

Ben Watson, Consulting Editor

CHELSEA HOUSE PUBLISHERS

1974 Sproul Road, Suite 400
Broomall, PA 19008-0914
610-353-5166
fax: 610-359-1439
800-848-2665
http://www.chelseahouse.com (World Wide Web) The entire Chelsea House catalog is available on the Internet's World Wide Web.

Chelsea House produces books for older children and young adults. The Chelsea House program accents the educational and institutional market in history, young-adult fiction and nonfiction, reference works, and literary criticism, as well as some works of broader appeal. Books on the Chelsea House list are most often produced in library-bound hardcover volumes, with some titles offered in trade paperback editions.

The editorial focus is on biography, culture, and history (American and worldwide). Broad interest areas include multicultural studies, social studies, literary criticism/ English, general biography, gender studies, mythology, sports, science, health/drug education, art, parenting, Spanish-language books, economics/business and personal finance, and law.

This approach is underscored by developmental marketing of such series as the Asian-American Experience, Folk Tales and Fables, the Immigrant Experience, Issues in Gay and Lesbian Life, Lives of the Physically Challenged, Milestones in Black American History, Mysterious Places, Pop Culture Legends, Science Discoveries, Sports Legends, and different series of theme-oriented fiction.

Chelsea House Publishers was originally instituted (founded in 1967) as a small press (then located in New York City) devoted to trade and reference titles on American history and popular culture. The company was bought in 1983 by Main Line Book Company, a library distributor based in suburban Philadelphia—whereupon the house's emphasis turned toward nonfiction for a young-adult readership.

Chelsea House series and highlights:

Milestones in Black American History: *The Gathering Storm: From the Framing of the Constitution to Walker's Appeal (1787–1829)*; *Bound for Glory: From the Great Migration to the Harlem Renaissance (1910–1930)*; *Struggle and Love: From the Gary Convention to the Present (1972–)*.

Great Achievers: Lives of the Physically Challenged: *Ludwig van Beethoven*; *Bob Dole*; *Ernest Hemingway*; *Mary Tyler Moore*; *Christopher Reeve*.

African American Achievers: *The Black Cowboys*; *Jimi Hendrix—Musician*; *Whitney Houston—Singer/Actress*; *Bob Marley—Musician*.

Race Car Legends: *Crashes and Collisions*; *Drag Racing*; *Formula One Racing*; *Jeff Gordon*; *Motorcycles*; *Women in Racing*.

Pop Culture Legends: *The Grateful Dead*; *David Letterman*; *Steven Spielberg*.

Bloom's Notes (comprehensive research and study guides) edited by Harold Bloom.

Life In America 100 Years Ago (illustrated books on turn-of-the-century lifestyles): *Communication*; *Education*; *Government and Politics*; *Industry and Business*; *Manners and Customs*.

Chelsea House distributes its own books and is particularly strong in the library and institutional market.

Chelsea House is moving through a transitional phase, and editorial address and contacts should be checked before submitting publishing projects for consideration. Administrative and warehousing facilities are currently located in the Philadelphia area.

Query letters and SASEs should be directed to:

Jim Gallagher, Editor in Chief

CHILTON BOOK COMPANY

One Chilton Way
Radnor, PA 19089-0230
610-964-4743

Chilton—"the world's most trusted automotive manuals." Chilton Book Company accents automotive titles: for professionals, for collectors, for practical repair and personal interest. Successful series include: TOTAL CAR CARE, TOTAL SERVICE, COLLECTOR'S EDITION REPAIR MANUALS, and REPAIR AND TUNE-UP GUIDES.

Chilton Book Company (founded in 1968) is a subsidiary of Capital Cities/ABC. By early 1997 Krause Publications had acquired the non-automotive divisions of the Chilton Book Company, including an array of titles in antiques, collecting, and sewing and crafts. (For these lines, please see Krause Publications.)

Chilton's TOTAL CAR CARE series was created because the cars of today are a world apart from the cars of a generation ago. The manuals are model-specific repair manuals and provide the amateur mechanic in-depth information on all systems and complete, easy-to-follow, illustrated procedural directions for removal and replacement.

Chilton's TOTAL SERVICE manuals provide the most complete up-to-date information for all automotive and related repair maintenance and service procedures. The new user-friendly format is designed with the do-it-yourselfer in mind to bring even the most complex system servicing into reach.

Chilton's COLLECTOR'S EDITION REPAIR MANUALS offer comprehensive coverage for older automobiles, both American and imported. Chilton's REPAIR AND TUNE-UP GUIDES offer repair and tune-up guidance designed for the weekend mechanic, covering basic maintenance and troubleshooting.

Chilton also offers Spanish-language repair manuals.

Chilton Book Company distributes its own list via a network of regional sales representatives.

Query letters and SASEs should be directed to:

Kerry Freeman, Publisher and Editor in Chief, Automotive Division

---

CHRONICLE BOOKS
PHAIDON

85 Second Street
Sixth Floor
San Francisco, CA 94105
415-777-7240
415-777-8467 (customer service)
800-722-6657 (catalogs and orders)
fax: 800-858-7787 (for catalog requests and orders)
http://www.chronbooks.com (World Wide Web)

Chronicle's areas of interest include architecture and fine arts, design, photography, history and popular culture, travel and the outdoors (including regional guides—California and nationwide), lifestyle (cuisine, pets, travel, home, and family), business and finance, and sports; the house issues a separate catalog for its children's books and for the GiftWorks list. Phaidon is a Chronicle division with core interests in the arts and its own editorial and production approach (see separate subentry below).

Chronicle Books (founded in 1966) was initially best known for its glossy hardcover series of illustrated theme cookbooks. Since that era, Chronicle has gradually ventured further afield and currently publishes general nonfiction in both hardback and paperback. Chronicle Books also publishes selected fiction and literary works.

The Chronicle program features many selections of California regional interest (food, architecture, outdoors), with focus on San Francisco and the Bay Area in particular (on both frontlist and backlist). The publisher has expanded its regional scope: Chronicle is open to an increasing variety of titles keyed to areas and travel destinations worldwide. Chronicle scored major bestseller hits with Nick Bantock's Griffin & Sabine fiction trilogy: *Griffin & Sabine*, *Sabine's Notebook*, and *The Golden Mean*.

Representative Chronicle titles: *Aperitif: Recipes for Simple Pleasures in the French Style* by Georgeanne Brennan (photographs by Kathryn Kleinman); *Face Forward: Young African American Men in a Critical Age* by Julian C. R. Okwu; *Teach Yourself to Dream: A Practical Guide to Unleashing the Power of the Subconscious Mind* by David Fontana, Ph.D.; *The Vegetarian Bistro: 250 Authentic French Regional Recipes* by Marlene Spieler; *Rock and Roll Hall of Fame + Museum Summer of Love* (edited by James Henke; essays by Charles Perry and Barry Miles); *What Cats Are* (photographs by Sharon Beals); *Treading the Maze: An Artist's Journey Through Breast Cancer* by Susan E. King; *Behind Adobe Walls: The Hidden Homes and Gardens of Santa Fe and Taos* by Landt Dennis (photographs by Lisl Dennis); *The Paranoid's Pocket Guide* by Cameron Tuttle; *The Starlore Handbook: An Essential Guide to the Night Sky* by Geofrey Cornelius.

Chronicle produces a traditionally strong roster of titles keyed regionally to California and environs. As the house trade tag says: The best books on California from the publisher who knows California best. Representative titles here: *Wine Country Bike Rides: The Best Tours in Sonoma, Napa, and Mendocino Counties* by Lena Emmery; *Mendocino: The Ultimate Wine & Food Lover's Guide* by Heidi Hughy Cusic (photographs by Richard Gillette); *Napa Valley: The Ultimate Winery Guide* by Antonia Allegra (photographs by Richard Gillette); *Fun Places to Go with Children in Southern California* by Stephanie Kegan; *Fun Places to Go with Children in Northern California* by Elizabeth Pomada; *The Earth Shook, the Sky Burned: A Photographic Record of the 1906 San Francisco Earthquake and Fire* by William Bronson; *The Best of San Francisco* by Don and Betty Martin.

Literary projects include: *Dancer with Bruised Knees* (novel) by Lynne McFall; *Lies of the Saints* (stories) by Erin McGraw; *Texas Stories: Tales from the Lone Star State* (edited by John and Kirsten Miller); *White Rabbit: A Psychedelic Reader* (edited by John Miller and Randall Koral).

PHAIDON

Phaidon focus is on fine arts, music, design, decorative arts, architecture, and photography. Series include: Art & Ideas, 20th-Century Composers, and Architecture in Detail. Phaidon produces finely illustrated publications in hardcover and trade-paperback editions.

Phaidon was previously corporate sibling to Universe Publishing (as part of a firm then known as Phaidon Universe). Universe has since become an affiliated property of Rizzoli International; Phaidon is a primary part of the Chronicle program.

On the list from Phaidon: *From Suffragettes to She-Devils* (design) by Liz McQuiston; *Gothic Revival* by Megan Aldrich; *Art Deco Style* by Bevis Hillier and Stephen Escritt; *The Art Book Mini Edition* (portable version of Phaidon's bestselling alphabetical guide to artists).

Art & Ideas is a line of introductory books in art history. These works are clearly written, up-to-date, and richly illustrated—intended to be essential for the student and irresistible for the general reader. Titles here include: *Islamic Arts* by Jonathan Bloom and Sheila Blair; *Early Christian and Byzantine Art* by John Lowden.

20th-Century Composers covers modern and contemporary musicians in an ongoing series of single-volume works: *Giacomo Puccini* by Conrad Wilson; *Carl Nielsen* by Jack Lawson.

Sample titles from Architecture in Detail: *Unity Temple: Oak Park, Illinois, 1905—Frank Lloyd Wright* by Robert McCarter; *Venice: The City and Its Architecture* by Richard Goy.

Annie Barrows, Senior Editor
All publisher's described areas, with special interest in art, illustrated, and photography books.

Christine Carswell, Executive Editor and Associate Publisher
All publisher's described areas.

Caroline Herter, Associate Publisher
Illustrated and visual books. GiftWorks.

Bill LeBlond, Senior Editor and Cookbook Editor
Acquires in all publisher's described areas, with special interest in cookbooks and design books (all book types).

(Mr.) Nion McEvoy, Editor in Chief and Associate Publisher
All publisher's described areas, with special interest in New Age, business, and multimedia books.

Leslie Oonath, Editor
Gardening, lifestyle, cookbooks.

Jay Schaefer, Senior Editor, Fiction
Send complete manuscript, synopsis, and SASE. No queries, please.

Jeffrey Schulte, Editor
Popular culture—all areas.

Karen Silver, Editor
All publisher's described areas, with special interest in regional books.

CHRONICLE CHILDREN'S BOOKS

Chronicle's children's lineup has a reputation for high quality and innovation in traditional and not-so-traditional formats. From the Chronicle children's list: *Hush Little*

Baby by Sylvia Long; *If I Had a Horse* by Jonathan London (illustrated by Brooke Scudder); *Desert Dwellers: Native People of the American Southwest* by Scott Warren; *The Clubhouse Crew's Joker's Bag of Tricks* by Anne Civardi and Ruth Thomson (illustrated by Mark Oliver); *The Merchant of Marvels and the Peddler of Dreams* by Frederick Clement; *Beneath the Sea in 3-D* by Mark Blum; *Star Wars*™, *The Empire Strikes Back*™, and *Return of the Jedi*™ by John Whitman (illustrated by Brandon McKinney); *A Rainbow at Night: The World in Words and Pictures by Navajo Children* by Bruce Hucko.

Chronicle handles its own distribution.

Query letters and SASEs should be directed to:

Victoria Rock, Director, Children's Books, and Associate Publisher
Children's Books.

CHRONIMED PUBLISHING

Ridgedale Office Center, Suite 250
13911 Ridgedale Drive
Minnetonka, MN 55305
612-541-0239

Chronimed covers the areas of nutrition, healthful cookbooks, health, parenting, general health, chronic health challenges, transplants, psychology, fitness, diabetes, and health resources and professional needs. The publisher also offers health-education videos, slides, and cassettes.

Chronimed Publishing (formerly known as DCI Publishing) was founded in 1985 as a publishing division of Diabetes Institute, Inc. The house trade banner runs: "The best in health, wellness, and nutrition." Chronimed Publishing is dedicated to new life-enhancing, breakthrough titles on a wealth of health topics—from self-improvement to fitness to healthy eating to coping with a chronic illness.

Chronimed titles: *The American Dietetic Association's Complete Food and Nutrition Guide: The Most Comprehensive and Up-to-Date Resource on Healthy Food Choices from the World's Foremost Experts* by The American Dietetic Association; *Walk This Way: A Fun and Easy Walking Exercise Program That Anyone Can Do to Help Reduce Weight and Stress and Increase Energy and Health* by John Ratzenberger; *Taste vs. Fat: Rating the Low-Fat and Fat-Free Foods* by Elaine Moquette-Magee; *A Cancer Survivor's Almanac: Charting Your Journey* (edited by Barbara Hoffman, J.D.); *The Healthy Heart Formula: The Powerful, New Commonsense Approach to Preventing and Reversing Heart Disease* by Frank Berry, M.D. with Bridget Swinney; *The Orchestra Conductor's Secret to Health and Long Life: Conducting and Other Easy Things to Do to Feel Better, Keep Fit, Lose Weight, Increase Energy and Live Longer* by Dale L. Anderson, M.D.

The publisher offers a series of publications (including a particularly strong line of patient-information books and pamphlets) from the International Diabetes Center and the Joslin Diabetes Center.

Chronimed Publishers distributes its own list.
Query letters and SASEs should be directed to:

Cheryl Kimball, Associate Publisher

CIRCLET PRESS

P.O. Box 15143
Boston, MA 02215
circlet-info@apocalypse.org (e-mail)

Circlet specializes in imaginative approaches to the erotic arts. The house produces narrative fiction; photography, illustration, and artwork; and creative literary forms in combination with visual art. One of the house's trade tags is: Experience the sensual universe of Circlet Press.

Circlet Press presents a noteworthy line of short stories and anthologies in erotic science fiction and fantasy, a genre field in which Circlet is clearly among the pioneers. The publisher catalogs its own products as well as works from a number of alternate sources: novels, books on sadomasochism, erotic fantasy, graphic novels, and a selection of cutting-edge portfolios and books in art and photography.

Anthologies and collections from Circlet: *Blood Kiss* (vampire erotica); *The Beast Within* (wolf and werewolf—lust transforms . . .); *Feline Fetishes* (for those who meow and claw); *TechnoSex* (cyberage pastimes); *SexMagick* (power to the fullest potential).

Special Circlet editions: *Vampire Dreams* (edited by S. G. Johnson); *Beauty's Punishment* by Anne Rice; *SM 101* by Jay Wiseman; *Sexual Portraits* by Michael Rosen.

Circlet (founded in 1992) sees to its own distribution.
Query letters and SASEs should be directed to:

Cecilia Tan, Publisher and Editor

CITY LIGHTS PUBLISHERS

261 Columbus Avenue
San Francisco, CA 94133
415-362-1901

City Lights publishes literary essays and criticism, biography, philosophy, literary fiction (including first novels), and poetry, as well as artistically ecumenical volumes featuring both words and visual images.

City Lights Booksellers and Publishers (founded in 1953 by the poet-publisher Lawrence Ferlinghetti) is a San Francisco treasure, its bookstore a North Beach landmark, and above all else a resolute cultural institution and self-embodied tradition. City Lights initially featured the Pocket Poets series, which introduced such writers as

Gregory Corso, Allen Ginsberg, Jack Kerouac, and other Beats to a wider audience. Since then, as successive literary generations have commenced and terminated, City Lights remains most assuredly commercially viable.

Highlights from City Lights: *Blackshirts and Reds: Rational Fascism and the Overthrow of Communism* by Michael Parenti; *The Beat Generation in New York: A Walking Tour of Jack Kerouac's City* by Bill Morgan; *Tracking the Serpent: Journeys to Four Continents* by Janine Pommy Vega; *Ploughing the Clouds: The Soma Ceremony in Ancient Ireland* by Peter Lamborn Wilson; *A Little Matter of Genocide: Holocaust and Denial in the Americas, 1492 to the Present* by Ward Churchill; *City of Memory and Other Poems* by José Emilio Pacheco (translated by Cynthia Steele and David Lauer); *Bed of Sphinxes: Selected Poems* by Philip Lamantia; *Anthology of Black Humor* by André Breton (translated from the French by Mark Polizzotti).

The City Lights backlist embraces many of this publishing house's classic publications, such as *Howl and Other Poems* by Allen Ginsberg (available in the original Pocket Poets format as well as lavish trade-paper reprint); *Gasoline* (poetry) by Gregory Corso; *Scripture of the Golden Eternity* (literary writings) by Jack Kerouac; William S. Burroughs's *Yage Letters* (creative essays and imaginative correspondence with Allen Ginsberg); and *Shock Treatment* (monologues from performance artist Karen Finley). Each fall, the publisher issues *City Lights Review: Annual Journal of Literature and Politics*, which brims with original poetry, essays, and fiction.

City Lights is distributed by the Subterranean Company of Monroe, Oregon, and has its own in-house mail-order fulfillment department.

Query letters and SASEs should be directed to:

Nancy J. Peters, Executive Editor

CLEIS PRESS

P.O. 8933
Pittsburgh, PA 15221
412-937-1555

Branch office:

Cleis West
P.O. Box 14684
San Francisco, CA 94114
415-864-3385

Cleis Press publishes books in sexual politics and self-help, lesbian and gay studies and culture, feminism, fiction, erotica, humor, and translations of world-class women's literature. Cleis titles cross-market from niches of gender and sexuality to reach the widest possible audiences.

Projects from Cleis Press (founded in 1980) garner numerous awards and reviews—and include many bestselling books. The house is committed to publishing the most original, creative, and provocative works by women (and a few men) in the United States and Canada.

From the Cleis list: *Body Alchemy: Transsexual Portraits* (photoessay) by Loren Cameron; *The Good Vibrations Guide to Sex* by Cathy Winks and Anne Semans; *Good Sex: Real Stories from Real People* by Julia Hutton; *Public Sex: The Culture of Radical Sex* by Pat Califia; *Sexual Reality* and *Susie Bright's Sexwise* by Susie Bright (billed as America's Favorite X-Rated Intellectual); *Dyke Strippers: Lesbian Cartoonists A to Z* (edited by Roz Warren).

Trade nonfiction: *Different Daughters: A Book by Mothers of Lesbians* (edited by Louise Rafkin); *I Am My Own Woman: The Outlaw Life of Charlotte von Mahlsdorf, Berlin's Most Distinguished Transvestite* by Charlotte von Mahlsdorf (translated by Jean Hollander); *1 in 3: Women with Cancer Confront an Epidemic* (edited by Judith Brady).

Cleis fiction includes: *Only Lawyers Dancing* (literary thriller) by Jan McKemmish; *A Ghost in the Closet* (mystery featuring Nancy Clue and the Hardly Boys) by Mabel Maney; *Best Gay Erotica* (published annually; edited by Michael Ford; selected and introduced by Scott Heim); *Best Lesbian Erotica* (published annually; edited by Tristan Taormino; selected and introduced by Heather Lewis); *Dark Angels: Lesbian Vampire Stories* (edited by Pam Keesey; a sequel to the popular *Daughters of Darkness: Lesbian Vampire Stories*); *Half a Revolution: Contemporary Fiction by Russian Women* (edited by Masha Green); *Switch Hitters: Lesbians Write Gay Male Erotica and Gay Men Write Lesbian Erotica* (edited by Carol Queen and Lawrence Schimel).

Cleis Books is represented to the book trade by Publishers Group West.

Query letters and SASEs should be directed to:

Frederique Delacoste, Acquisitions Editor (San Francisco)

Felice Newman, Publisher and Marketing (Pittsburgh)

CLEVELAND STATE UNIVERSITY POETRY CENTER
(See Directory of University Presses)

COBBLEHILL BOOKS
(See Penguin USA)

COFFEE HOUSE PRESS
27 North Fourth Street, Suite 400
Minneapolis, MN 55401
612-338-0125
fax: 612-338-4004

Coffee House produces contemporary poetry, short fiction, and novels. The press is a source of contemporary writing that is challenging and thought-provoking, funny and furious, wildly diverse, even downright wacky, vibrant, and lyrical.

Coffee House Press is a nonprofit publisher dedicated to presenting visionary books of contemporary literature by diverse authors. The mission of Coffee House Press is to promote exciting, vital, and enduring authors of our time; to delight and inspire readers; to increase awareness of and appreciation for the traditional book arts; to enrich our literary heritage; and to contribute to the cultural life of our community. Coffee House Press publishes books that advance the craft of writing; books that present the dreams and ambitions of people who have been underrepresented in published literature; books that help build a sense of community; and books that help to shape our national consciousness.

Coffee House descends from what was originally (in the 1970s) a letterpress specialty firm, with a small list and an intimate circle of readers. The publisher then introduced titles geared toward an expanded readership; happily, conviviality and craft remain in strong evidence. Coffee House Press (established in 1984) is a publisher of trade titles and fine editions in a program that features a creative approach to the publishing arts. The house colophon is a steaming book, which is chosen to let the reader know (as the Coffee House motto runs) "where good books are brewing."

From Coffee House: *Foreign Devil* by Wang Ping; *Flickering Shadows* by Kwadwo Agymah Kamau; *Paul Metcalf: Collected Works 1956–1976* (introduction by Guy Davenport); *Glass Houses* (stories) by George Rabasa; *Certain People* (short-short stories) by Roberta Allen; *Lovis Book II* (poems) by Anne Waldman; *Millennium Fever* (poems) by Jack Marshall.

Coffee House books are printed on acid-free paper stock and have sewn bindings for long life and comfortable reading—as well they might, for the house features a comprehensive and enduring backlist.

Coffee House Press oversees its own marketing and sales network with the assistance of regional representatives; trade distribution is handled by Consortium.

Query letters and SASEs should be directed to:

Chris Fischbach, Editorial Assistant

Allan Kornblum, Editor and Publisher

COLUMBIA UNIVERSITY PRESS
(See Directory of University Presses)

COLLECTOR BOOKS
5801 Kentucky Dam Road
Paducah, KY 42001
502-898-6211

Mailing address:
P.O. Box 3009
Paducah, KY 42002
800-626-5420

Collector Books produces books for collectors in such fields as depression glass, glassware, pottery, pottery and porcelain, china and dinnerware, cookie jars and salt shakers, stoneware, paper collectibles, Barbie dolls, dolls, toys, quilts, tools and weapons, jewelry and accessories, furniture, advertising memorabilia, bottles, Christmas collectibles, cigarette lighters, decoys, doorstops, and gas station memorabilia.

Collector Books (founded in 1969) is a division of Schroeder Publishing Company. Collector Books is dedicated to bringing the most up-to-date information and values to collectors in an attractive, high-quality format. Books are designed to be practical, easy-to-use tools that assist dealers and collectors in their pursuit of antiques and collectibles. Collector's publications are liberally illustrated editions, generally filled with histories, production facts and lore, research sources, and identification information. Collector Books also produces inventory ledgers for professional dealers and avid collectors.

The house produces a midsized list of new offerings each year and maintains a sizable backlist. Springing from its original principles of offering quality products, customer satisfaction, giving customers the most for their dollar, and one-day sudden service, Collector Books has grown from one title on fruit jars to over 500 titles, and from a firm of two employees to over 60. Fueled by strong customer support, the publisher's list of new releases continues its recent growth.

Every August, Collector publishes *Schroeder's Antiques Price Guide*, which features more than 50,000 listings and hundred of photographs for identification and current values as well as background and historical information.

Sample titles: *B. J. Summers' Guide to Coca-Cola®* by B. J. Summers; *World of Beer Memorabilia* by Herb and Helen Haydock; *Collector's Guide to Electric Fans* by John M. Witt; *A Decade of Barbie Dolls and Collectibles, 1981–1991* by Beth Summers; *Elegant Glassware of the Depression Era* (seventh edition); *Pocket Guide to Depression Glass and More* (1920s–1960s) (tenth edition); *Very Rare Glassware of the Depression Years* (fifth edition); *Stemware Identification Featuring Cordials with Values, 1920s–1960s* by Gene Florence; *McCoy Pottery: Collector's Reference and Value Guide* by Bob Hanson, Craig Nissen, and Margaret Hanson; *Fostoria Volume II: Identification and Value Guide to Etched, Carved and Cut Designs* by Ann Kerr; *Figural Nodders: Identification and Value Guide—Includes Bobbin' Heads and Swayers* by Hilma R. Irtz; *Antique and Collectible Buttons: Identification and Values* by Debra J. Wisniewski; *Antique and Vintage Clothing: A Guide to Dating and Valuation of Women's Clothing, 1850–1940* by Diane Snyder-Haug; *Collector's Guide to Antique Radios* (fourth edition) by Marty and Sue Bunis; *The Standard Knife Collector's Guide* (third edition) by Roy Ritchie and Ron Stewart.

Collector Books looks for its authors to be knowledgeable people considered experts within their fields. Writers who feel there is a real need for a book on their collectible subject and have available a large comprehensive collection are invited to contact the publisher at the house's mailing address.

Collector Books distributes its own list, targeting particularly bookstore buyers and antiques-trade professionals. Collector operates an especially strong mail-order program and purveys selected works from other publishers, including out-of-print titles in the collectibles and antiques field.

Query letters and SASEs should be directed to:

Bill Schroeder, Publisher
Lisa Stroup, Editor

CompCare Publishers

(See listing for Hazelden Publishing Group in Directory of Religious, Spiritual, and Inspirational Publishers)

Compute Books

Compute Books (a computer-book specialist founded in 1979) is no longer doing business.

Computer Science Press

(See W. H. Freeman and Company)

Conari Press

2550 Ninth Street, Suite 101
Berkeley, CA 94710
510-649-7183

Conari Press (founded in 1987) accents works in relationships, self awareness, spirituality, and the family. In addition to books, Conari produces a select line of audiotapes, project packets, buttons, and posters. The house began as a small press, and has grown step by step, expanding cogently on its strong backlist base. Conari is one of the most successful regional independent publishers.

Conari titles: *Wild Women in the White House: The Formidable Females Behind the Throne, on the Phone, and (Sometimes) Under the Bed* by Autumn Stephens; *Simple Pleasures: Soothing Suggestions and Small Comforts for Living Well Year Round* by Robert Taylor, Susannah Seton, and David Greer; *Honor Thy Children: One Family's Journey to Wholeness* by Molly Fumia; *No Mountain High Enough: Secrets of Successful African American Women* by Dorothy Ehrhart-Morrison, Ph.D.; *The Woman's Book of Confidence: Meditations for Strength and Inspiration* by Sue Patton

Thoele; *House as a Mirror of Self: Exploring the Deeper Meaning of Home* by Clare Cooper Marcus; *Blessed Expectations: Nine Months of Wonder, Reflection, and Sweet Anticipation* by Judy Ford; *Chore Wars: How Households Can Share the Work and Keep the Peace* by James Thornton; *Uppity Women of Medieval Times* by Vicki Leon; *Communication Miracles for Couples: Easy and Effective Tools to Create More Love and Less Conflict* by Jonathan Robinson; *Positive Aging: Every Woman's Quest for Wisdom and Beauty* by Karen Kaigler-Walker, Ph.D.; *The Heart of Synchronicity: Stories from the Marvelous World of Meaningful Coincidence* by Phil Cousineau.

The Barnard Biography Series for Young Women is produced in conjunction with Barnard College: "Expanding the universe of heroic women." Titles: *Beryl Markham: Never Turn Back* by Catherine Gourley; *Elizabeth Blackwell: A Doctor's Triumph* by Nancy Kline.

Conari Press seeks to be a catalyst for profound change by providing enlightening books on topics that range from spirituality and women's issues to sexuality, relationships, and personal growth. Conari values integrity, process, compassion, and receptivity, in publishing projects as well as the house's internal workings.

Conari is distributed to the trade by Publishers Group West; gift store distribution is handled through Sourcebooks, Inc.

Query letters and SASEs should be directed to:

Mary Jane Ryan, Acquisitions

CONSUMER REPORTS BOOKS
101 Truman Avenue
Yonkers, NY 10703
914-378-2000

Consumer Reports Books is active in a number of consumer-information spheres. Among them: product-buying guides and consumer reference; automotive; children and teenagers; consumer issues; food, cooking, and nutrition (including cookbooks); general interest; health and fitness; home and environment; law for consumers; personal finance; and travel.

Consumer Reports Books is the book-publishing wing of the Consumers Union (founded in 1936), which publishes *Consumer Reports* magazine. Consumer Reports Books specializes in nonfiction works (most of them in trade paperback format, along with a few hardcovers) designed as guides for consumers as they make purchasing decisions or participate in the demands of certain sectors of contemporary corporate and commercial society—especially healthcare, personal finance, and the law. Some Consumer Reports titles hone a controversial edge.

The publisher typically offers a small number of new books each season (plus periodically revised editions of some of the house's more popular and important works). Consumer Reports maintains a steadfast backlist.

Many Consumer Reports titles originate in house and are researched and written by Consumer Reports editors; however, the house acquires and produces a limited number of works from independent authors.

Representative guides (often in updated editions): *Guide to Personal Computers*; *New Car Buying Guide*; *Used Car Buying Guide*; *Home Appliance Buying Guide*; *Audio/Video Buying Guide*; *Yard and Garden Equipment Buying Guide*; *Homeowner's Legal Guide*; *Consumer Reports Best Travel Deals*; *Travel Buying Guide*; *Consumer Reports Buying Guide* (an extensive, single-volume general reference).

Featured Consumer Reports trade titles: *How to Clean Practically Anything*; *How to Buy a House, Condo, or Co-op*; *How to Avoid Auto Repair Rip-offs*; *Easy Lawn and Garden Care*; *Complete Book of Bathroom Design*; *Mind/Body Medicine*; *Health Schemes, Scams and Frauds*; *101 Health Questions*; *AIDS: Trading Fears for Facts*; *Women's Sexual Health*; *Sumptuous Desserts*; *Consumer Reports Money Book: How to Get It, Save It, and Spend It Wisely*; *Below the Line: Living Poor in America*.

Consumer Reports Books distributes to the trade through St. Martin's Press.

Query letters and SASEs should be directed to:

Will Michalopoulos, Executive Editor

CONTEMPORARY BOOKS

(Please see under NTC/Contemporary Publishing Company)

CONTINUUM PUBLISHING GROUP

370 Lexington Avenue
New York, NY 10017
212-953-5858
fax: 212-953-5944
contin@tiac.net (e-mail)
http://www.continuum-books.com (World Wide Web) Continuum's Web site contains details on forthcoming, current, and previously published titles as well as links to Chiron Publications, Spring Publications, and Paragon House.

Continuum publishes general trade books, texts, scholarly monographs, and reference words in the areas of literature and the arts, psychology, history and social thought, women's studies, and religion. Continuum offers more than 100 new publications a year, as well as 700 established backlist titles.

Continuum's broad focus integrates the fields of literature and criticism, psychology and counseling, women's studies, and social issues of contemporary public interest. The house is known for its select line of books in popular and scholarly approaches to religion and philosophy. The Frederick Ungar imprint specializes in literature, film, and the performing arts.

Continuum and Crossroad Publishing Company were editorially independent components of the Crossroad/Continuum Publishing Group from 1980 into the early 1990s, since which time Continuum has pursued its own independent publishing trajectory. (For Crossroad Publishing, see entry in Directory of Religious, Spiritual, and Inspirational Publishers.)

From the Continuum trade list: *Encyclopedia of German Resistance to the Nazi Movement* (edited by Wolfgang Benz and Walter H. Pehle); *Against All Hope: Resistance in the Nazi Concentration Camps 1938–1945* by Hermann Langbein; *Shakespeare, in Fact* by Irvin Leigh Matus; *Women and Sexuality in China* by Harriet Evans; *Working with Images: The Theoretical Base of Archetypal Psychology* (edited by Benjamin Sells); *Young Carl Jung* by Robert Brockway; *Psyche and Family: Jungian Applications to Family Therapy* (edited by Laura Dodson and Terrill Gibson); *Naked and Erect: Male Sexuality and Feeling* by Joel Ryce-Menuhin; *Men, Power, and Myths: The Quest for Male Identity* and *The Incredible Fascination of Violence: Ideas on Dealing with Aggression and Brutality Among Children* by Allan Guggenbühl; *The Mermaid in the Pond: An Erotic Fairy Tale for Adults* by Verena Kast; *Are the Gods Pushing Marriage?* (edited by James Hillman); *Mythanalysis* by Pierre Solié; *Socrates Among the Corybantes: Dionysian Spirituality and the Philosophy of Plato* by Carl Levenson; *Aesthetics and Experience: An Introduction to the Philosophy of Aesthetics* by Gordon Graham.

Spirituality/religion titles: *The Soul of Shamanism* by Daniel C. Noel; *The Jews in Christian Art: An Illustrated History* by Heinz Schreckenberg; *Encyclopedia of Women in Religious Art* by Dian Apostolos-Cappadona; *A New History of Christianity* by Vivian Green; *Beyond the Threshold: A Life in Opus Dei* by Maria del Carmen Tapia; *Que(e)rying Religious Studies: A Critical Anthology* (edited by Gary David Comstock and Susan E. Henking); *Redeeming the Time: A Political Theology of the Environment* by Stephen Bede Scharper; *Lyrics for Re-Creation: Language for the Music of the Universe* by James A. Conlon; *Psalms for Praying: An Invitation to Wholeness* by Nan C. Merrill; *Early Christian Art and Architecture: An Introduction* by Guntram Koch; *How to Read the Prophets* by Jean-Pierre Prévost; *How to Understand the Virgin Mary* by Jacques Bur; *Transforming Grace: Christian Tradition and Women's Experience* by Ann E. Carr; *Veiled Desire: Augustine on Women* by Kim Power; *Naming Grace: Preaching and the Sacramental Imagination* by Mary Catherine Hilkert; *Setting the Gospel Free: Experiential Faith and Contemplative Practice* by Brian C. Taylor; *The Silent Dialogue: Zen Letters to A Trappist Abbot* by David G. Hackett; *And I, Francis: The Life of Francis of Assisi in Word and Image* by Lauren Glen Dunlap and Kathleen Frugé-Brown; *A Friar's Joy: Magic Moments from Real Life* (edited by Kevin M. Cronin); *Removing Anti-Judaism from the Pulpit* (edited by Howard Clark Kee and Irwin J. Borowsky); *History and Contemporary Issues: Studies in Moral Theology* by Charles E. Curran; *The Radiance of Being: Complexity, Chaos and the Evolution of Consciousness* by Allan Combs.

Special Continuum projects: *Modern American Literature (Volume 6: Third Supplement to the Fourth Edition)* (general editor, Martin Tucker) completes the highly praised reference set on 20th-century American authors. This volume is one of the internationally renowned volumes in A Library of Literary Criticism.

Continuum Hollywood-related titles: *Robert Altman: Hollywood Survivor* by Daniel O'Brien; *The Cinema of Oliver Stone* by Norman Kagan; *The Cinema of Stanley Kubrick* by Norman Kagan; *Steven Spielberg: The Man, His Movies, and Their Meaning* by Philip M. Taylor.

Continuum is distributed through Publisher Resources Inc. Continuum also distributes the distinguished publishing programs of Chiron Publications, Spring Publications, Paragon House, and the Templeton Foundation.

Query letters and SASEs should be directed to:

(Mr.) Evander Lomke, Managing Editor
Psychological counseling, history and the arts, literary criticism, current affairs, women's studies.

Justus George Lawler, Associate Editor
Literary criticism, religion.

Frank Oveis, Publishing Director
Academic religious and biblical studies, world religions, spirituality.

John Heidenry, Associate Editor
Social research.

DAVID C. COOK PUBLISHING COMPANY
(See Directory of Religious, Spiritual, and Inspirational Publishers)

COPPER CANYON PRESS
P.O. Box 271
Port Townsend, WA 98368
360-385-4925

The Copper Canyon mission is to publish poetry distinguished in both content and design, within the context of belief that the publisher's art—like the poet's—is sacramental. Copper Canyon Press (founded in 1973) publishes a literary list in hardcover and paperback as well as special fine editions.

Copper Canyon's commitment is demonstrated through its program to further the exposure of and enthusiasm for contemporary poetry. Copper Canyon also offers selected belletristic offerings that include essays, critiques, and forays into diverse fictional forms.

Within this ambitious vision, there are limitations; Copper Canyon generally does not sign many new writers. The house assigns its resources to furthering its established roster. The publisher's success in its aim is proven through abundant and continuing recognition of its authors via honors, awards, grants, and fellowships.

Copper Canyon Press publishes a list that teems with such titles as these: *Resurrection Update: Collected Poems, 1975–1997* by James Galvin; *The Landlady in*

Bangkok by Karen Swenson; *Armored Hearts* by David Bottoms; *August Zero* by Jane Miller; *Collected Longer Poems* by Hayden Carruth; *Lethal Frequencies* by James Galvin; *Infanta* by Erin Belieu; *My Town* by David Lee; *Sappho's Gymnasium* by Olga Broumas and T Begley; *Soul Make a Path Through Shouting* by Cyrus Cassells; *The Book of Light* by Lucille Clifton; *The Second Four Books of Poems* by W. S. Merwin.

Copper Canyon distributes to the trade via Consortium.

Query letters and SASEs should be directed to:

Sam Hamill, Editor

CORNELL UNIVERSITY PRESS
(See Directory of University Presses)

CRAIN BOOKS
(See NTC Publishing Group)

CRISP PUBLICATIONS
1200 Hamilton Court
Menlo Park, CA 94025
415-949-4988

Crisp Publications produces nonfiction business books and media packages; topic areas include: management, personal improvement, human resources and wellness, communications and creativity, customer service, sales, small businesses, financial planning, adult literacy and learning, careers, and retirement and life planning. The house is known for a number of successful lines: 50-Minute Book, series in small-business ventures, and business titles keyed to use of technology and new media.

Crisp Publications (founded in 1985) is a specialist in target business publishing, and is equally expert at marketing the resultant product. Crisp offers an extensive selection of training programs (including self-study formats) that incorporate books, manuals, and audiovisual materials. The house's aim is to provide high-quality cost-effective books and videos that can help business organizations succeed in competitive times. Crisp also offers a specialized speaker/trainer referral service.

The 50-Minute Book is Crisp's signature designation for books produced with the concept of being concise, easily read, and readily understood through personal involvement with exercises, activities, and assessments. Other Crisp lines are the Quick Read Series, the Small Business and Entrepreneurship Series, and Crisp Computer Series. A significant portion of the Crisp list is available in Spanish-language editions.

Highlights from Crisp: *Organizing Your Workspace* by Odette Pollar; *Measure and Manage Stress* by Herbert Kindler and Marilyn Ginsburg; *Motivating at Work:*

Empowering Employees to Give Their Best by Twyla Dell; *Preventing Job Burnout* by Beverly A. Potter; *Preventing Workplace Violence* by Marianne Minor; *The Art of Communicating* by Bert Decker; *The New Supervisor* by Elwood N. Chapman; *Training Managers to Train* by Brother Herman Zaccarelli; *A Legal Guide for Small Business* by Charles Lickson; *Writing Fitness: Practical Exercises for Better Business Writing* by Jack Swenson.

Crisp Publications distributes through National Book Network, and also catalogs on a title-selective basis for several other business-related publishing houses.

Query letters and SASEs should be directed to:

Michael G. Crisp, Publisher

THE CROSSING PRESS

P.O. Box 1048
Freedom, CA 95019
408-722-0711

Crossing Press accents cooking and cuisine, alternative healthcare (special focus on herbalism), awareness and illumination, relationships, spiritualism, art and photography, poetry, multicultural and gender studies, women's and feminist literature and general nonfiction (including a focus on the lesbian arena), and men's studies and the men's movement (including titles of gay orientation).

The Crossing Press produces a range of hardcover and trade paperback editions, as well as merchandise items such as notecards, postcards, calendars, and journals.

The Crossing Press was established in upstate New York in 1972 as a modest house, indeed a veritable cottage press run from the farmhouse of the founders, Elaine Goldman-Gill and John Gill, who were at the time teaching at Cornell University. Relocated to the central California coastal region and with a new office building adjacent to the warehouse, the expanded scope of Crossing Press nevertheless retains its personalized editorial touch and small-press savvy.

The Crossing Press has particular commercial success with its distinguished series of recipe books; the house is well known for its anthologies and collections (including fiction and essays) relevant to those fields in which it specializes. Crossing Press hosts a selected list of new seasonal titles and nurtures a solid backlist.

Crossing Press general nonfiction: *An Astrological Herbal for Women* by Elisabeth Brooke; *Natural Healing for Babies and Children* by Aviva Jill Romm; *Psychic Healing with Spirit Guides and Angels* by Diane Stein; *Reach for Joy: How to Find the Right Therapist and Therapy for You* by Lynne D. Finney; *Revolutionary Laughter: The World of Women Comics* (edited by Roz Warren); *Breaking Convention with Intercultural Romances* (edited by Dianne Dicks); *Nudes* (photography) by Amy Sibiga; *A Loving Testimony: Remembering Loved Ones Lost to AIDS* (edited by Lesléa Newman); *Transsexuals: Candid Answers to Private Questions* by Gerald Ramsey; *The Wiccan Path: A Guide for the Solitary Practitioner* by Rae Beth.

Titles in the kitchen arts: *Good Food: The Complete Guide to Eating Well* by Margaret M. Wittenberg; *Jungle Feasts & Dangerous Dining: Adventures and Recipes from a Culinary Rogue* by Richard Sterling; *Meltdown! The Official Fiery Foods Show Cookbook and Chilehead Resource Guide* by Dave DeWitt and Mary Jane Wilan; *New Vegetarian Classics: Entrées* by Mary F. Taylor; *Pocket Guide to Good Food: A Shopper's Resource* by Margaret M. Wittenberg; *The Hot Sauce Bible* by Dave DeWitt and Chuck Evans; *Traveling Jamaica with Knife, Fork & Spoon: A Righteous Guide to Jamaican Cooking* by Robb Walsh and Jay McCarthy.

Calendars and posters from Crossing: *The Black Woman's Perpetual Calendar: Our Names Are Many* (edited by Terri Jewell); *The Chilehead Art Calendar* by Ron Genta (along with a Chilehead line of poster art); *The Goddess Book of Days: A Perpetual 366-Day Engagement Calendar* by Diane Stein; *Women Writers Engagement Calendar* (edited by Dena Taylor).

Fiction and literature from Crossing has run the spectrum of traditional categories. Current activity in this arena is limited, though the house tends a solid backlist in science fiction and fantasy, mystery, poetry, and special-interest anthologies. A title here is *Poems of Passion, Poems of Love* (edited by Elaine Goldman-Gill and John Gill). Other fiction and literary works: *When Warhol Was Alive* by Margaret McMullan; *Hog Heaven: Erotic Lesbian Stories* by Caressa French; *Breaking Up Is Hard to Do: Stories by Women* (edited by Amber Coverdale Sumrall).

Crossing Press distributes to the trade through a group of regional services and a network of independent sales representatives.

Query letters and SASEs should be directed to:

Elaine Gill, Publisher and Editor

CROSSROAD PUBLISHING COMPANY
(See Directory of Religious, Spiritual, and Inspirational Publishers)

CROWN PUBLISHING GROUP
(See Random House)

DALKEY ARCHIVE PRESS (DAP)
Illinois State University Box 4241
Normal, IL 61790
309-438-7555
800-338-BOOK (800-338-2665) (orders)

Dalkey Archive Press accents art, literature, media arts, architecture, photography, and popular culture. The house's production forte is finely designed, innovatively conceived paperback editions as well as selected deluxe hardcover publications.

Dalkey Archive (founded in 1984) is dedicated to breakthrough artistic expression in fiction and creative voices in all fields of letters. Dalkey's writers are among the most influential stylists on the printed page, and their designers and artists represent the finest quality in the trade. Dalkey Archive Press (DAP) is a division of the Review of Contemporary Fiction.

From the Dalkey Archive list: *My Face for the World to See: The Diaries of Candy Darling* (edited by Hardy Marks); *Documenta X: The Book* by Cantz; *Island People* by Coleman Dowell; *New York Girls* (photography by Richard Kern; introduction by Lydia Lunch); *Palinuro of Mexico* by Fernando del Paso (translated by Elisabeth Plaister); *Pierced Hearts and True Love: A Century of Drawings for Tattoos* (graphics and essays in conjoint publication with the Drawing Center, New York); *Sabbatical* by John Barth; *Storytown* by Susan Daitch; *The Poor Mouth: A Bad Story About the Hard Life* by Flann O'Brien (translated by Patrick C. Power; illustrated by Ralph Steadman); *The Red Shoes and Other Tattered Tales* by Karen Elizabeth Gordon.

Dalkey Archive distributes through Chicago Distribution Center.

Query letters and SASEs should be directed to:

Angela Weaser, Marketing Director

John O'Brien, Publisher

THE DARTNELL CORPORATION

4660 North Ravenswood Avenue
Chicago, IL 60640
773-561-4000

Dartnell is a business-specialist house that publishes practical books, handbooks, manuals, periodicals, planners, and business how-to and education programs, including audiocassettes, films, videotapes, and computer software. Dartnell's major publishing concentration is in the areas of sales, marketing, and office administration and management.

The Dartnell Corporation (established in 1917) is a privately owned, international business-information and training publisher dedicated to supplying diverse business audiences with instructional and motivational materials. The Dartnell bannerline reads: "Helping You Compete Through Better Training."

Dartnell takes pride in its ability to reach corporate audiences at all levels in a variety of businesses and industries with products that target members of the business community from factory line workers to executive officers. Topical highlights of the Dartnell list include sales skills, sales motivation, sales management, leadership, communication, team building and teamwork, customer service, quality, general motivation, influence and persuasion, and sexual harassment and gender-based issues.

Dartnell's approach encompasses not only the production and publication of their varied media products; the publisher is also a service organization. Dartnell invites corporate and business clients to contact the house representatives and determine what promotions, programs, or training tools can be worked into a customized package that will best serve that particular client's needs.

Dartnell's list reflects a simple, steadfast commitment to how-to, results-oriented training, and accents publications that often incorporate components within a number of different media formats.

Representative Dartnell titles: *A Team of Eagles* by Mike Singletary; *How Leaders Lead: The Essential Skills for Career and Personal Success* by Ken Blanchard and Brian Tracy; *How to Negotiate Anything with Anyone Anywhere in the World* by Frank L. Acuff; *Take Charge of Your Life* by Les Brown; *Connecting with Your Customers* by Bill Bethel; *Winning with Promotion Power* by Frank Caci and Donna Howard; *Super Selling Skills* by Tony Alessandra; *Cracking New Accounts* by Terry L. Booton; *Creative Training and Presentation Techniques* by Robert Pike; *Psyched to Sell* by Art Mortell.

Dartnell distributes its own books and other media products.

Query letters and SASEs should be directed to:

Scott B. Pemberton, Vice President of Editorial Division

DAW BOOKS, INC.

375 Hudson Street
New York, NY 10014
212-366-2096

DAW Books publishes science fiction, fantasy, science fantasy, future fiction and future fantasy, dark suspense, and horror. DAW publishes mass-market paperbound originals and reprints, as well as hardcovers and trade paperbacks.

The DAW line includes masterful genre-keyed anthologies that showcase some of the most respected writers in their respective literary provinces. DAW typically produces a medium-sized seasonal list of new titles. The DAW backlist is replete with successful individual titles, along with a host of perennially selling series.

DAW Books (founded in 1971) is at the forefront of the literary categories and genres in which it specializes. The house is affiliated with Penguin USA.

From DAW Books: *Death Watch* by Elizabeth Forrest; *Fire in the Sky* by Jo Clayton; *Murder at the Galactic Writers' Society* by Janet Asimov; *Northlight* by Deborah Wheeler; *The Winds of Darkover* by Marion Zimmer Bradley; *Vampire Detectives* (edited by Martin H. Greenberg).

DAW distribution is through an affiliation with Penguin USA.

Query letters and SASEs should be directed to:

Elizabeth Wollheim, Publisher

Sheila Gilbert, Publisher

Peter Stampfel, Submissions Editor

DCI PUBLISHING

(See Chronimed Publishing)

DEACONESS PRESS
(See Fairview Press)

DEARBORN PUBLISHING GROUP, INC.

155 North Wacker Drive
Chicago, IL 60606-1719
312-836-4400

Dearborn is a diverse business-oriented house with a number of imprints and affiliates that include Dearborn Trade, Commodity Trend Service, Dearborn R&R Newkirk, Upstart Publishing, Real Estate Education Company, and Vernon Publishing.

Founded in 1982 as Longman Financial Services Publishing, and subsequently operating as Dearborn Financial Publishing, Inc., this house has grown and metamorphosed into Dearborn Publishing Group, Inc.

After 35 years at its earlier location, Dearborn moved into enhanced corporate digs in late 1994. Upstart Publishing Company was acquired in full and moved to Chicago, after having been an editorially independent affiliate with a New Hampshire base for the previous few years. At the new, more expansive headquarters, Dearborn is actively developing audio, CD-ROM, video, and software products in addition to its print publishing program.

DEARBORN TRADE
DEARBORN FINANCIAL PUBLISHING, INC.

Dearborn Trade and Dearborn Financial Publishing, Inc. produce trade and professional books and training materials in the areas of entrepreneurship, real estate, financial planning, investments, personal finance, insurance, management, careers, small business, and banking. Dearborn offers titles intended for corporate and institutional markets in addition to books aimed primarily toward the individual bookbuyer. Dearborn also produces career and college guides, reference books, and regional real estate guides.

Entrepreneurship receives special Dearborn emphasis, with titles catalogued for the emerging entrepreneur, the growing business, the maturing business, and the established entrepreneur. The Upstart imprint specializes in entrepreneurship and small-business management.

Through its Real Estate Education Company division, Dearborn offers a wealth of practical training materials including books, audio, video, and computer-based training products. These items cover such fields as real estate licensing, property management, new homes and renovation, advertising and marketing, and sales skills.

From Dearborn: *365 Ways to Simplify Your Work Life* by Odette Pollar; *Wealth on Minimal Wage: Living Well on Less* by James W. Steamer; *Money Mastery in Just Minutes a Day* by Fred E. Waddell; *Finding Your Financial Freedom: Every Woman's*

Guide to Success by Joyce Ward; *Toastmaster's International® Guide To Successful Speaking* by Jeff Slutsky and Michael Aun; *The Home Buying Game: A Quick and Easy Way to Get the Best Home for Your Money* by Julie Garton-Good; *Buying Your Vacation Home: For Fun and Profit* by Ruth Rejnis and Claire Walter; *Century 21® Guide to Selling Your Home: 50 Insider Secrets for a Top Dollar Sale* by Century 21®; *The Will Kit* and *Beating the Paycheck-to-Paycheck Blues* by John Ventura; *Point & Click Investor* and *Point & Click Business Builder* by Seth Godin; *The Complete Guide to Consulting Success* (third edition) by Howard Shenson, Ted Nicholas, and consulting editor Paul Franklin.

The Dearborn Multimedia imprint offers personal-productivity book/CD-ROM packages of bestselling titles in small business, personal finance/investments, home ownership/real estate, and careers. Sample titles: *Starting a Home-Based Business*; *How to Form Your Own Corporation Without a Lawyer for Under $75*; *The Budget Kit*; *The Mortgage Kit*; and *The Credit Repair Kit*.

Dearborn distributes its own list, as well as books by a number of smaller business-oriented houses.

Upstart Publishing Company

The Upstart imprint specializes in entrepreneurship and small-business management.

Upstart Publishing (incorporated in 1979) became an independent division of Dearborn Publishing Group in 1991. In early 1995, Upstart's editorial operations were transferred from its original New Hampshire habitat to the expanded Dearborn corporate environs in Chicago.

"A small business is one where you can bring your dog to work." This philosophical statement is from the bestselling Upstart book, *The Business Planning Guide* by David H. Bangs, founder of Upstart and author of the Planning Guide Series. Other Upstart series are Small Business Basics and Common Sense (with the editors of *Common Sense*).

Representative Upstart titles: *Restaurant Planning Guide* by Peter Rainsford and David H. Bangs Jr.; *From Kitchen to Market: Selling Your Gourmet Food Specialty* by Stephen F. Hall; *On Your Own: A Woman's Guide to Building a Business* by Laurie B. Zuckerman; *100 Best Retirement Businesses* by Lisa Agnowski Rogak and David H. Bangs Jr.; *The Entrepreneur's Guide to Going Public* by James B. Arkebauer and Ron Schultz; *The Complete Guide to Selling Your Business* by Paul S. Sperry and Beatrice H. Mitchell; *Media Power: How Your Business Can Profit from the Media* by Peter G. Miller; *Sit and Grow Rich: Petsitting and Housesitting for Profit* by Patricia A. Doyle; *The Language of Small Business* (a dictionary of business usage) by Carl O. Trautmann.

Query letters and SASEs should be directed to:

Cynthia Zigmund, Executive Editor
Finance.

Danielle Egan-Miller, Acquisitions Editor
Consumer real estate, small business.

DELACORTE PRESS
(See Bantam Doubleday Dell)

DELL BOOKS
(See Bantam Doubleday Dell)

DIGITAL PRESS
(See Heinemann)

DISNEY PRESS
(See Hyperion)

DOUBLEDAY
(See Bantam Doubleday Dell)

DOVE BOOKS
DOVE ENTERTAINMENT
8955 Beverly Boulevard
West Hollywood, CA 90048
310-786-1600
fax: 310-777-7667

Dove Books is centrally located as a major player in publication of high-interest topical titles that tie in with current events, celebrities, and popular culture. Dove currently issues a select fiction list. The house also offers a line of children's titles (on the Dove Kids imprint). Dove Audio features a popular lineup of audio books.

Dove titles: *Primary Whites, A Novel Look at Right-Wing Politics: A Parody* as told to Cathy Crimmins and Tom Maeder; *Worse Than He Says He Is: White Girls Don't Bounce* by Anicka Bakes Rodman (ex-wife of literary luminary and professional basketball player Dennis Rodman); *Foetal Attraction* (fiction) by Kathy Lette; *Newt Gingrich's Bedtime Stories for Orphans* by Cathy Crimmins and Tom Maeder; *Inside the NRA* by Jack Anderson; *The Phoenix Solution: Getting Serious About Solving America's Drug War* by Vincent Bugliosi; and *Jackson Family Values* by Margaret Maldonado Jackson.

Backlist favorites: *You'll Never Make Love in This Town Again* by Robin, Liza, Linda, and Tiffany (as told to Joanne Parrent); *Nicole Brown Simpson: The Private Diary of a Life Interrupted* by Faye D. Resnick; *Fatal Subtraction: The Inside Story of Buchwald vs. Paramount* by Pierce O'Donnell and Dennis McDougal (introduction by Art Buchwald).

Dove Books is distributed by Penguin Putnam, Inc.

DOVE KIDS

Deborah Raffin, President of Dove Kids, states that the goal of Dove Kids is to publish the highest quality "edutainment" for young children—books that in many instances will also be enjoyed by the adults in their households.

Dove Kids strives to make its products affordable works that show strong moral and educational concerns. Dove Kids is proud to be the home of Marva Collins, among the most outstanding educators of children in America today.

Frontlist titles feature a noteworthy array of celebrity writers on a list geared toward a youthful readership. Dove Kids has discovered the hidden talents of versatile stars who can cross over successfully to a new medium: Sidney Sheldon, Cheryl Ladd, Jack Lemmon, Eric Idle, Erica Jong, and Sharon Stone.

Representative works: *The Adventures of Drippy the Runaway Raindrop* by Sidney Sheldon and Mary Sheldon (illustrated by Alexandra Sheldon); *The Adventures of Little Nettie Windship* by Cheryl Ladd and Brian Russell (illustrated by Ezra Tucker and Nancy Krause) (this is the first title in a series of picture books designed to promote good values in children from renowned actress Cheryl Ladd, her partner Brian Russel, and two award-winning illustrators); *Megan's Two Houses* by Erica Jong (illustrated by Freya Tanz); *The Quite Remarkable Adventures of the Owl and the Pussycat* by Eric Idle (illustrated by Edward Lear and Wesla Weller); *An Off-the-Wall Fairy Tale: Snow White and the Seven Dwarfs* by Richard Hack (illustrated by Tuko Fujisaki); *The Long Journey of the Little Seed* by Annie Reiner (illustrated by the author).

Query letters and SASEs should be directed to:

Michael Viner, Publisher

Beth Lieberman, Acquisitions

Michelle Ozols, Acquisitions

DRAMATIC PUBLISHING

P.O. Box 129
311 Washington Street
Woodstock, IL 60098
815-338-7170
fax: 815-338-8981

Dramatic Publishing is one of the leading publishers of plays and musicals in the United States. Dramatic offers full-length plays, one-act plays, plays and musicals for young audiences, holiday plays and musicals, musicals, useful books on the theatre, short non-royalty plays, play posters, as well as stage sounds, audition tapes, and sound effects tapes.

Dramatic publishes more than 1,000 plays, musicals, and theatre books, and represents the works of more than 800 writers. Their catalogs are sent to more than 50,000 schools, universities, and amateur and stock theatres each year. Additionally, the house has active representation in the United Kingdom and Australia.

Charles H. Sergel, at the age of 24, founded The Dramatic Publishing Company in Chicago in 1885—and his catalog featured four plays. The firm was incorporated in 1887 and, by the turn of the century, Sergel's small company offered dramatic works by Ibsen, Strindberg, Ostrovsky, and Maeterlinck. Dramatic Publishing is still owned and operated by the Sergel family. Today the catalog includes such authors as Edward Bond, John Osborne, Arthur Miller, Eugene O'Neill, Timberlake Wertenbaker, David Mamet, Brian Friel, C. P. Taylor, Josefina Lopez, Eduardo de Filippo, Langston Hughes, Steve Allen, Jean Cocteau, and Suzan Zeder.

Dramatic has been a leader in bringing contemporary works by prominent Russian, Australian, and British playwrights to the U.S. market. The publisher's goal is to carry the Dramatic Publishing tradition well into the next century by continuing to broaden their selection of high-quality plays and musicals and by expanding their alliance with authors and producers so that, together, they can go about creating great theatre.

Books on the Dramatic trade list: *Acting Up: An Innovative Approach to Creative Drama for Older Adults* by Marcie Telander, Flora Quinlan, and Karol Verson; *New Monologues for Mature Actors* (compiled and edited by Ann McDonough); *Stage Dialects* and *More Stage Dialects* by Jerry Blunt; *The Play Book: Complete Guide to Quality Productions for Christian Schools and Churches* by Dwight Swanson and Travis Tyre; *Duet Scenes for Competitions* (Volume I) and *Monologues for Competitions,* (Volume I) by Travis Tyre; *Journey Through Drama* by Holly Lamb, Hollie Bedford, Stephen Taylor, and Ann Sims.

Dramatic also offers useful books on theatre: *An Audition Handbook of Great Speeches* by Jerry Blunt; *How to Make It in Showbiz: A Survival Kit* by June Walker Rogers; *How Not to Write A Play* by Walter Kerr; *How to Produce the Play* by John Wray Young and Margaret Mary Young; *How to Direct the High School Play* by Leon C. Miller; *So You Want to Be a Professional Actor* by H. T. Laughlin; *Comedy Is a Serious Business* by Harry Ruskin; *Do's and Don'ts of Drama* a collection by Jean Lee Latham; *Impromptu Entertainments* by Bill Majeski; *Audition Scenes for Students* by John Wray Young; *How to Audition* by Gordon Hunt; *Street Mime* by Joames W. Gousseff; *Stagecraft I: A Complete Guide to Backstage Work* by William H. Lord; *Fairy Tales for Theater* by Lev Ustinov; *Hisses, Boos and Cheers: A Practical Guide to the Production and Presentation of Old-Time Melodramas* by Charles H. Randall and Joan LeGro Bushnell.

Representative full-length play titles: *Indiscretions* (a comedy) by Jean Cocteau (translated by Jeremy Sams); *Truth on Trial: The Ballad of Sojourner Truth* (drama with music) by Dr. Douglas W. Larche; *I Ain't Yo' Uncle (The New Jack Revisionist Uncle Tom's Cabin)* (comedy/drama) by Robert Alexander; *The Death of the Black Jesus* (drama) by David Barr; *Angel in the Night* (drama) by Joanna H. Kraus; *Confessions of Women from East L.A.* (comedy) by Josefina López; *The Wake* (drama/comedy) by Steve Allen; *Do Not Go Gentle* (comedy/drama) by Suzan L. Zeder; *The Death and Sale of Alexander Goland* (absurdist comedy) by Nikki Harmon; *John Lennon and Me* (comedy/drama by Cherie Bennet); *Never Come Morning* (drama based on the novel by Nelson Algren; adapted by Paul Peditto).

Query letters and SASEs may be directed to:

Linda Habjan, Acquisitions Editor

DUTTON

(See Penguin USA)

THE ECCO PRESS

100 West Broad Street
Hopewell, NJ 08525
609-466-4748
fax: 609-466-4706

The Ecco list presents literary fiction, general nonfiction, poetry, and essays, as well as selected imaginative and practical works on travel, food, culture, and sports. The Ecco Press (founded in 1970) is a small, distinguished publisher of trade books (many in special fine editions).

Stalwarts on Ecco's roster of poets include Louise Glück, Robert Hass, Zbigniew Herbert, Carolyn Kizer, Czeslaw Milosz, Robert Pinsky, and Charles Simic. The house also offers classic reprints in the Essential Poets series. In addition, Ecco publishes the literary journal *Antæus*.

Ecco's original mandate remains in effect—to publish significant books of enduring quality.

Popular features from Ecco: *The Gardener's Son,* a never-before-published screenplay from Cormac McCarthy; *Sun Under Wood*, the long-awaited new book of poems from U.S. Poet Laureate Robert Hass; two first novels: *Hallucinating Foucault* by Patricia Duncker and *Blue Italian* by Rita Ciresi; newest volume in Essential Poets Series, *The Essential Dickinson* (edited by Joyce Carol Oates); *Kiki's Memoirs (*bold and sassy autobiography of the model who became the reigning queen of 1920s Montparnasse, banned by U.S. Customs in 1929 and only now published in America for the first time) (edited and annotated by Billy Klüver and Julie Martin; with an introduction by Ernest Hemingway).

Fiction and literary works: *The Tenor Saxophonist's Story* (novel) by Josef Skvorecky; *Continent* (novel) by Jim Crace; *The American Kitchen* (cooking) by Judie Geise; *The Marriage in the Trees* (poems) by Stanley Plumly; *The Quest for Corvo* (biography/literature) by A. J. A. Symons; *The Nature Reader* (nature/science) by

Daniel Halpern and Dan Frank; *Bloom and Blossom* (gardening/literature) by Mary Swander; *Plays in One Act* (drama) by Daniel Halpern; *Open Water* (novel) by Maria Flook.

Favorites from the Ecco catalog: *First Love* by Joyce Carol Oates; *Meadowlands* by Louise Glück; *The Roaring Stream: A New Zen Reader* (edited by Nelson Foster and Jack Shoemaker; foreword by Robert Aitken); *The Paper Wife* by Linda Spalding; *A Child's Anthology of Poetry* (edited by Elizabeth Hauge Sward with Victoria McCarthy; illustrated by Tom Pohrt); *A Drop of Patience* by William Melvin Kelley; and *The First Book of Jazz* by Langston Hughes.

Books of the Ecco Press are distributed by W. W. Norton.

Query letters and SASEs should be directed to:

Daniel Halpern, President and Editor in Chief

WILLIAM B. EERDMANS PUBLISHING COMPANY
(See Directory of Religious, Spiritual, and Inspirational Publishers)

M. EVANS AND COMPANY
216 East 49th Street
New York, NY 10017
212-688-2810

The M. Evans frontlist features high-profile offerings in topical issues; investigative stories in politics, business, and entertainment; and popular biography. The core Evans program accents popular nonfiction books in the areas of health and fitness, human relationships, business and finance, and lifestyle and cuisine. Evans also issues a small list in popular fiction (including Westerns), and a line of books for children. The house tends a strong and varied backlist.

M. Evans and Company (founded in 1963) thrives as a selective trade publisher (in hardcover and trade paperback) with a clear, constantly honed commercial focus in its favored market niches.

Evans nonfiction includes: *Dr. Atkins' New Carbohydrate Gram Counter* by Robert C. Atkins, M.D.; *Horrors of War: Historical Reality and Philosophy* by Franjo Tudjman; *The Brain Workout Book* by Snowden Parlette III; *Welcome to the End of the World: Prophecy, Rage, and the New Age* by Teresa Kennedy; *The Muscle Memory Method: Easy All Day Fitness for a Stronger, Firmer, Younger Body* by Marjorie Jaffe with Jo Sgammato; *The Randle Report: UFOs in the 90's* by Kevin Randle; *Natural Acts: Reconnecting with Nature to Recover Community, Spirit, and Self* by Amy E. Dean; *Ablaze! A Study of Spontaneous Human Combustion* by Larry E. Arnold; *Lost Gold and Buried Treasure: A Treasure Hunter's Guide to 100 Fortunes Waiting to Be Found* by Kevin D. Randle; *The Artist in the Marketplace: Making Your Living in the Fine Arts* by James Adams and Patricia Frischer; *Prospero's Kitchen: Mediterranean*

Cooking of the Ionian Islands from Corfu to Kythera by Diana Farr Louis and June Marinos.

Evans fiction is exemplified by: *Down the Common* by Ann Baer; *First Victim* by Douglas MacKinnon; *A Fine Italian Hand* (a Shifty Lou Anderson mystery) by William Murray. Evans novels of the West include *The Sons of Grady Rourke* by Douglas Savage; *Buckskinner* by R. C. House; *Wolfer* by Mac McKee.

M. Evans is the distributor for the Masters Press list; M. Evans books are distributed to the trade via National Book Network and Kampmann.

Query letters and SASEs should be directed to:

George C. de Kay, President
Popular psychology, health, cookbooks.

F&W Publications
(See Writer's Digest Books)

Faber and Faber, Inc.
53 Shore Road
Winchester, MA 01890
617-721-1427

Faber and Faber publishes trade nonfiction and selected titles in fiction and literature. Nonfiction strengths include history, biography, health, women's interest, gay and lesbian issues, popular science, music, film, and drama. Much of the Faber fiction list has a distinguished literary bent.

Faber and Faber, Inc. (instituted in 1976) is the American subsidiary of the British publisher Faber and Faber Ltd. In addition to producing original books by American authors, FF also handles North American distribution for its parent company.

Nonfiction from Faber and Faber: *Counterpoint* by Paul Brodeur; *Demand and Get the Best Health Care for You: An Eminent Doctor's Practical Advice* by Curtis Prout, M.D.; *The Faber Book of Madness* (edited by Roy Porter); *Savoring the East: Feasts and Stories from Istanbul to Bali* by David Burton; *Tourists: How the Fastest Growing Industry Is Changing the World* by Larry Krotz.

On the Faber fiction and literary list: *Duplex Planet: Everybody's Asking Who I Was* by David Greenburger; *Bailey's Beads* by Terry Wolverton; *Empire Under Glass* by Julian Anderson; *Ladies, Start Your Engines* (edited by Elinor Nauen); *The Tempest of Clemenza* by Glenda Adams; *The Life Stone of Singing Bird* by Melodie Stevenson; *Twilight at the Equator* by Jaime Manrique; *His 2: More Brilliant New Fiction by Gay Writers* and *Hers 2: More Brilliant New Fiction by Lesbian Writers* (the second set of paired anthologies; edited by Robert Drake and Terry Wolverton; the first *His* volume was nominated for a Lambda Literary Award).

Performance—whether stage and screen or in the musical arena—represents one of Faber and Faber's strongest areas. FF publishes an array of accessible titles on film actors and directors, music producers and performers, and life in the theater—as well as a topnotch selection of plays and screenplays. Titles here: *Fargo* by the Coen brothers (Joel and Ethan Coen); *Leaving Las Vegas* by Mike Figgis; *The General from America* by Richard Nelson; *Impersonating Elvis* by Leslie Rubinkowski; *Knowing Hepburn* by Jim Prideaux (about the later years of Katharine Hepburn's life); *A Year with Swollen Appendices* by Brian Eno; *Magic Hour: The Life of a Cameraman* by Jack Cardiff; and titles in the Projections series, including *Projections 7* (edited by John Boorman and Walter Donohue).

Although a number of children's books and volumes of poetry are published by Faber and Faber, these titles are by and large acquired through the London office.

Faber and Faber orchestrates its own distributional network worldwide; the house utilizes a number of independent regional sales representatives in the U.S.

Unsolicited queries should be two pages long. Do not include SASE—the publisher will contact the author if interested in the project. Query letters should be directed to:

Dan Weaver, Editor in Chief

Valerie Cimino, Senior Editor

FACTS ON FILE

11 Penn Plaza, 15th Floor
New York, NY 10001-2006
212-967-8800
fax: 800-678-3633
800-322-8755

Facts On File specializes in reference and information titles in a broad popular range, including business, popular culture, art and architecture, design, sports, health, history, current affairs and politics, the environment, and young adult lines—in addition to general reference works. Facts On File offers a broad selection of historical and cultural atlases, dictionaries, and encyclopedias geared toward professional as well as popular interests and is one of the pioneers of the CD-ROM multimedia-publishing frontier.

Facts On File (founded in 1940) is a dynamic popular-reference publisher. The house has a full skein of award-winning titles to its credit, and many Facts On File publications feature an innovative production approach. The publisher is extremely well tuned to specific category markets, which it targets with marked commercial consistency.

Beverly A. Balaz, President, joined Facts On File in January 1996. The following paraphrases the publisher's outlook during a transitional phase: Facts On File is undergoing a thrilling metamorphosis. The house is now changing its product, its image, and its vision to not just accommodate, but truly embrace the exciting transitions in store for all Facts On File readers. Customers will find that the publisher has created, or is in the process of developing, everything needed to bring a library, classroom, bookstore, or special program into the 21st century: cutting-edge print and electronic titles, plus tried-and-true reference books designed to cover 100 percent of the customer's needs.

Now, more than ever, Facts On File is about growth. As a result of emerging technologies, new curriculum standards, and educational trends, the typical customer needs and wants demand an innovative product. Facts On File responds to these changes as quickly as possible . . . with new enthusiasm, spirit, and sparkle.

The publisher's message urges customers to consider Facts On File as "partners for success" in education—a source for rich content and up-to-date, accurate information. Facts On File has a list that is growing to boast perfect symmetry; its breadth and depth make it truly one of a kind, providing consumers with an impressive variety and well-balanced selection of titles.

Metamorphic! Facts On File transforms with emerging technologies, changing curricula, and cutting-edge research developments. Check out Facts On File for reference titles of all stripes.

Business books include guides to telecommunications, franchising, and the business aspects of the health care industry, as well as business history and biography.

Young adult books cover cultural history worldwide—with emphasis on United States and ethnic heritage—as well as series in science and technology, the natural environment, and space exploration.

Sample titles: *The Elder Law Handbook for Caregivers and Seniors: A Legal and Financial Survival Guide for the '90s* by Peter J. Strauss and Nancy M. Lederman; *Cops, Crooks, and Criminologists: An International Biographical Dictionary of Law Enforcement* by Alex Axelrod and Charles Phillips; *Career Opportunities in Advertising and Public Relations* (revised edition) by Shelly Field; *Free Money for College: A Guide to More Than 1,000 Grants and Scholarships for Undergraduate Schools* and *Free Money for Graduate School: A Guide to More Than 1,000 Grants and Scholarships for Graduate Study* by Laurie Blum; *Straight Talk About Post-Traumatic Stress Disorder: Coping with the Aftermath of Trauma* by Kay Marie Porterfield; *The Young Gaia Atlas of Earthcare* by Miles Litvinoff; *Night of the Cruel Moon: Cherokee Removal and the Trail of Tears* by Stanley Hoig; *100 Years of Children's Books in America: Decade by Decade* by Marjorie N. Allen.

On File is an award-winning collection of reference materials. Spanning virtually every subject in the middle and high school curricula, each On File contains hundreds of images that visually depict complex subjects in a way that will both engage and inform young people. Even students at the elementary and college levels will find the material useful. Filled with hundreds of exciting hands-on activities, projects, exercises, and experiments, On File volumes encourage critical thinking and allow students to actively participate in their educational process.

Facts On File utilizes individualized marketing and distribution programs that are particularly strong in the areas of corporate, institutional, and library sales.

Query letters and SASEs should be directed to:

Laurie Likoff, Project Editor
Science, music, history.

Drew Silver, Associate Editor
Reference books: entertainment subjects, TV, movies, Broadway, sports.

Hilary Poole, Associate Editor
Reference books: entertainment subjects, TV, movies, Broadway, sports.

Nicole Bowen, Senior Editor
Nonfiction young-adult reference books about military history, sports, American culture and history, music.

FAIRVIEW PRESS

2450 Riverside Avenue South
Minneapolis, MN 55454
612-672-4228
fax: 612-672-4980
800-544-8207
http://www.Press.Fairview.org (World Wide Web)

Fairview Press publishes books on issues that affect adults, families, children, and the communities in which they live. These issues include relationships, parenting, domestic violence, divorce, family activities, aging, health, self-esteem, social issues, and addictions.

Fairview's commitment to its customers is that the materials Fairview publishes will offer the advice and support that individuals and families need to face stressful situations, difficult choices, and the trials and changes of everyday life. In addition, Fairview Press books are tools to help families enjoy and appreciate each other and strengthen family bonds. Fairview usually offers several special series especially for kids.

Fairview Press (formerly Deaconess Press; founded in 1988) is a service of Fairview Health System and a division of Fairview Riverside Medical Center.

On the Fairview list: *Good Morning, Captain: Fifty Wonderful Years with Bob Keeshan, TV's Captain Kangaroo* by Bob Keeshan; *The Joy of Imperfection* by Enid Howard and Jan Tras; *Live Long, Die Fast: Add Years to Your Life and Life to Your Years* by John H. Bland, M.D.; *Painted Diaries: A Mother and Daughter's Experience through Alzheimer's* by Kim Howes Zabbia; *Of Work and Men: How Men Can Become More Than Their Careers* by Harvey Deutschendorf; *Taking Back Our Neighborhoods: Building Communities That Work* by Mary I. Wachter and Cynthia Tinsley; *Solo Parenting: Raising Strong and Happy Families* by Diane Chambers; *Grandloving: Making Memories with Your Grandchildren* by Sue Johnson and Julie Carlson (illustrated by Ronnie Walter Shipman).

Slim Goodbody, award-winning star of children's public TV, celebrates "Wonderful You" in a unique series—*The Body, The Mind,* and *The Spirit* by Slim Goodbody (illustrated by Terry Boles). Slim Goodbody, developed over 20 years ago, is the creation of performer John Burnstein.

Woodland Press Children Can Cope Series (illustrated by children) is a line of workbooks developed to help children work through feelings about traumatic events and changes. Titles include: *When Someone Very Special Dies; When Mom and Dad Separate; When Someone Has a Very Serious Illness.*

Fairview Press, a specialist publisher and distributor, operates through a variety of sales venues; the press is distributed to the trade through the National Book Network.

Query letters and SASEs should be directed to:

Edward A. Wedman, Publisher

Jessica Thorson, Children's Editor

Lane Stiles, Senior Editor

FANTAGRAPHICS BOOKS

7563 Lake City Way NE
Seattle, WA 98115
206-524-1967

Fantagraphics produces comics and comic art. The house accents a list of mainstream, classic, and borderline offerings in this specialty arena, and also purveys a strong line of erotic comics and books. Fantagraphics Books (inaugurated in 1976) produces trade paperbacks, hardbound editions, and quality fine-art album editions of graphic productions, in addition to comic books, comics-related magazines, and a line of gift items dedicated to this most accessible literary form.

The Fantagraphics catalog lists, in addition to its own lines, products from additional publishers of comics and books, as well as audio, video, and multimedia works.

The Fantagraphics roster features some of the finest cartoonists of America and around the world—underground masters, political satirists, artists in the realms of science fiction and fantasy, and reprints of classic newspaper comic-strip series—as well as works from the emerging young turks in the field.

Comics creators cataloged by Fantagraphics include Peter Bagge, Vaughn Bode, Daniel Clowes, Guido Crepax, Robert Crumb, Dame Darcy, Kim Deitch, Julie Doucet, Jules Feiffer, Frank Frazetta, Drew Friedman, Rick Geary, Los Bros. Hernandez, Peter Kuper, Terry LeBan, Douglas Michael, Joe Sacco, Gilbert Shelton, Art Spiegelman, Ralph Steadman, Basil Wolverton, and Wallace Wood.

Fantagraphics projects: *The Book on the Edge of Forever* by Christopher Priest; *Diary of a Dominatrix* by Molly Kiely; *As Naughty As She Wants to Be* (part of the *A Bitch Is Born* series) by Roberta Gregory; *Invasion of the Mind Sappers* by Carol Swain; *Grit Bath* by Renée French; *Omaha the Cat Dancer* (series anthologies) by Reed Waller and Kate Worley; *Yummy Fur: Fuck & Matthew* (classic series) by Chester Brown; *Trailer Trash* by Roy Tompkins; *Primitive Cretin* by Henriette Valium; *Peepshow* by Joe Matt, *Real Stuff* by Dennis Eichhorn, and *The New American Splendor Anthology* by Harvey Pekar.

Fantagraphics also offers Burne Hogarth's set of art-instruction books.

Fantagraphics distributes its own list and catalogs selections from a number of other comics- and graphics-oriented publishers, in addition to audio CDs, computer CD-ROMs, videotapes, and books, posters, and calendars.

Query letters (accompanied by short, carefully selected samples) and SASEs should be directed to:

Ezra Mark, Submissions Editor

FARRAR STRAUS & GIROUX
HILL AND WANG
NORTH POINT PRESS
FARRAR STRAUS & GIROUX BOOKS FOR YOUNG READERS

19 Union Square West
New York, NY 10003
212-741-6900

Farrar Straus & Giroux is a trade house that produces a wide range of general-interest and specialist nonfiction as well as top-of-the-line fiction and literature. FS&G is known for its commercial list of finely designed hardcover and trade paperback editions.

Among FS&G divisions and imprints are Hill and Wang and North Point Press (see separate subentries below); the primarily trade-paperback imprints are Noonday Press for adult titles and Sunburst Books for young readers. FS&G tends a solid backlist and issues a line of classic works in reprint.

Long a mainstay among independently owned American publishing houses, Farrar Straus & Giroux (founded in 1946) was bought by Verlagsgruppe Georg von Holtzbrinck. In this multinational corporate phase, FS&G retains an affluent spirit that seeks to represent writing at its commercial-literary best, presented under the esteemed and widely recognized FS&G logo of three abstract fish.

In an era when there is great market leverage obtained from a publisher's offer of full-spectrum publishing packages for high-interest projects, FS&G's absence in the mass-market paperback arena proved a hitch in acquiring certain prime properties. Farrar Straus therefore employs combination hardcover/paperback acquisition deals, with paperback-reprint rights slotted to the mass-market paperback programs of other United States–based Holtzbrinck properties, such as Henry Holt and Company and St. Martin's Press.

FS&G nonfiction offerings cover topical issues and current events; popular and fine arts; contemporary culture; popular history, biography, and memoir; popular science; family, relationships, and awareness; lifestyle, travel, and cuisine.

Representative nonfiction: *From the Beast to the Blonde: On Fairy Tales and Their Tellers* by Marina Warner; *Utopia Parkway: The Life and Work of Joseph Cornell* by Deborah Solomon; *End Game: The Betrayal and Fall of Srebrenica: Europe's Worst Massacre Since the Holocaust* by David Rohde; and *The Snarling Citizen* (commentary) by Barbara Ehrenreich.

FS&G interest in literature and the arts encompasses novels, short stories, drama (and other theatrical works), history, essays and criticism, biography, memoirs, and poetry. In this area, the house's offerings often feature an adventuresome approach to both form and content. FS&G has published such diverse writers as Joseph Brodsky, Carlos

Fuentes, John McPhee, Philip Roth, Aleksandr Solzhenitsyn, Calvin Trillin, Scott Turow, Mario Vargas Llosa, Tom Wolfe, and Susan Sontag. In addition to the FS&G roster of established and marketable literary talent, the house is alert to hitherto lesser-appreciated literary voices primed for the commercial spotlight.

Farrar Straus & Giroux fiction, literature, and criticism: *The Autobiography of My Mother* by Jamaica Kincaid; *The Golden Plough* (thriller) by James Buchan; *Galatea 2.2* by Richard Powers; *Panama* (historical international thriller) by Eric Zencey; *Hunters and Gatherers* (satire of the sexes) by Francine Prose; *Flesh and Blood* (literary family saga) by Michael Cunningham; *The Chess Garden or the Twilight Letters of Gustav Uyterhoeven* by Brooks Hansen; *A Little Too Much Is Enough* by Kathleen Tyau; *Lytton Strachey: The New Biography* by Michael Holroyd.

Poetry from FS&G: *The Man with Night Sweats* by Thom Gunn; *Red Sauce, Whiskey, and Snow* by August Kleinzahler; *Chickamauga* by Charles Wright; *Gilgamesh: A New Rendering in English Verse* by David Ferry; *Madoc: A Mystery* by Paul Muldoon.

Trade distribution for FS&G is handled by the Putnam Publishing Group, while FS&G's catalog and promotional endeavors include services for a number of smaller houses with literary orientations, such as Beacon and Soho.

Query letters and SASEs should be directed to:

Elisabeth Dyssegaard, Executive Editor, Noonday Press
Fiction: literary, German and Scandinavian translations. Nonfiction: open to many areas.

Paul Elie, Editor
Literary nonfiction, music, religion.

Jonathan Galassi, Editor in Chief
Acquires in areas consistent with house description.

John Glusman, Executive Editor
Literary fiction, biography, science, politics, current events.

Rebecca Kurson, Editor, Noonday Press
Interests consistent with house list.

Elisabeth Sifton, Vice President and Senior Editor
History, politics, current events and issues. Literary fiction. Oversees the Hill & Wang program (see subentry).

FARRAR STRAUS & GIROUX BOOKS FOR YOUNG READERS

Farrar Straus & Giroux Books for Young Readers publishes for a wide-ranging audience under several individualized imprints: Sunburst Books for younger and middle readers, Aerial Fiction for teenagers, and Mirasol *libros juveniles* (children's books in Spanish). Among FS&G children's authors are William Steig, Maurice Sendak, and Madeleine L'Engle.

Titles here: *The Library* by Sarah Stewart (illustrated by David Small); *Carl's Birthday* by Alexandra Day; *Troubling a Star* by Madeleine L'Engle; *Falling into Glory* (young-adult novel) by Robert Westall; *Brainstorm! The Stories of Twenty Kid Inventors* by Tom Tucker (pictures by Richard Loehle); *Saturday Sancocho* by Leyla Torres; *Lost Summer* by Elizabeth Feuer; *Paper Dinosaurs* (a cut-out book) by Satoshi

Kitamura; *Dear Elijah* (a Passover story) by Miriam Bat-Ami; *In the Back Seat* by Deborah Durland Desaix.

Query letters and SASEs should be directed to:

Wes Adams, Senior Editor

Margaret Ferguson, Editorial Director

Frances Foster, Publisher, Frances Foster Books

Beverly Reingold, Executive Editor

HILL AND WANG

Hill and Wang highlights trade nonfiction as well as selected titles in drama as literature. Otherwise (and traditionally) viewed as part of the scholarly academic publishing scene, the Hill and Wang program is increasingly active commercially with an eclectic and lively list that features titles keyed to popular interests and cultural themes as well as current issues. Hill and Wang is established as a leader in academic and trade topics in the humanities and the sciences.

From Hill and Wang: *Cracking Up: The Work of Unconscious Experience* by Christopher Bollas; *The Organic Machine* by Richard White; *Village Journey: The Report of the Alaska Native Review Commission* (new edition) by Thomas R. Berger; *Abandoned in the Wasteland: Children, Television, and the First Amendment* by Newton Minow and Craig LaMay; *Going All the Way: Teenager Girls' Tales of Sex, Romance, and Pregnancy* by Sharon Thompson; *Manifest Destiny: American Expansionism and the Empire of Right* by Anders Stephanson.

Query letters and SASEs should be directed to:

Elisabeth Sifton, Publisher, Hill and Wang
History, politics, current events and issues. Literary fiction.

Lauren Osborne, Editor

NORTH POINT PRESS

North Point Press features a list that accents trade and literary nonfiction. Strong North Point categories include: nature writing and natural history; literary, food, travel, and sports writing; Asian literature; books about spirituality and religion; biographies, memoirs, and essays.

On the North Point list are such authors and projects as: Robert Aitken (*Taking the Path of Zen*); Wendell Berry (*What Are People For?*; *The Gift of the Good Land*); M. F. K. Fischer (*The Gastronomical Me*; *How to Cook a Wolf*); Beryl Markham (*West with the Night*); Gary Snyder (*Practice of the Wild*; *Riprap and Cold Mountain Poems*); *But Beautiful: A Book About Jazz* by Geoff Dyer; and *Caught Inside: A Surfer's Year on the Californica Coast* by Doug Duane.

Founded in Berkeley, California, in 1980, North Point Press is now a division of Farrar Straus & Giroux.

Query letters and SASEs should be directed to:

Ethan Nosowsky, Editor

FELDHEIM PUBLISHERS/FELDHEIM BOOKS
(See Directory of Religious, Spiritual, and Inspirational Publishers)

THE FEMINIST PRESS AT THE CITY UNIVERSITY OF NEW YORK
(See Directory of University Presses)

FERAL HOUSE
P.O. Box 3466
Portland, OR 97208-3466
310-822-0905
fax: 310-822-1288
feralhouse@aol.com (e-mail)
http://www.buzzcut.com/central/feralhouse (World Wide Web) The Feral House Web
site features sample chapters from Feral House books, periodically updated with fascinating new articles and photos.

Feral House publishes individualistic trade nonfiction, including such assertive genres
as all-encompassing cultural critiques, mordant essays, penetrating investigative and
journalistic accounts, and quirky popular reference works. A special house focus is on
armageddon and apocalypse studies.

The press publishes a variety of carefully designed and produced hardcover and
trade paperback formats, including limited-edition signed clothbound volumes and illustrated paperbound books, in addition to a select audio library. Feral House typically
issues several new titles per season and maintains a heady backlist.

Feral House (founded in 1988) surveys a brainscape of expression (and its attendant
readership market) that traditional media have hitherto been slow—or fearful—to address. Feral House has time and again proved the commercial viability of its creators'
visions with a slate of successful releases.

Feral founder Adam Parfrey formerly fronted the celebrated Amok Press (now de-
funct) in tandem with Ken Sweezy (publisher of Blast Books; please see separate Blast
Books entry in this directory).

Wild cubs from Feral House: *The Octopus: The Life and Death of Danny Casolaro*
by Kenn Thomas and Jim Keith; *The Bomb* by Frank Harris; *Killer Fiction* by G. J.
Schaefer; *Rollerderby: The Book* by Lisa Crystal Carver; *Cold-Blooded: The Saga of
Charles Schmid, The Notorious "Pied Piper of Tucson"* by John Gilmore; *Death
Scenes: A Homicide Detective's Scrapbook* (edited and designed by Sean Tejaratchi;
text by Katherine Dunn); *Meditations on the Peaks* by Julius Evola (translated by
Guido Stucco); *Grossed-Out Surgeon Vomits Inside Patient: An Insider's Look at the
Supermarket Tabloids* by Jim Hogshire; *The Making of a Serial Killer: The Story of the*

Gainesville Student Murders in the Killer's Own Words by Danny Rolling and Sondra London; *Influencing Minds: A Reader in Quotations* (edited by Leonard Roy Frank).

More picks of the Feral House litter: *Cad: A Handbook for Heels* (edited by Charles Schneider); *Kooks: A Guide to the Outer Limits of Human Belief* by Donna Kossy; *Crying Wolf: Hate Crime Hoaxes in America* by Laird Wilcox; *I Cried, You Didn't Listen: A Survivor's Exposé of the California Youth Authority* by Dwight Edgar Abbott with Jack Carter; *Kooks: A Guide to the Outer Limits of Human Belief* by Donna Kossy; *Loser: The Real Seattle Music Story* by Clark Humphrey (coffee-table edition, designed by Art Chantry); *Secret and Suppressed: Banned Ideas and Hidden History* (edited by Jim Keith); *Tortures and Torments of the Christian Martyrs: Illuminated by Contemporary Artists & Loathsome Criminals* by Antonio Gallonio; a series of works by and about Anton LaVey (founder of the Church of Satan); and the sumptuous retrospective volume *Cosmic Retribution: The Infernal Art of Joe Coleman.*

On the all-important subsidiary-rights front: Feral's *Nightmare of Ecstasy: The Life and Art of Edward D. Wood, Jr.* by Rudolph Gray was the basis for the Academy Award–winning film *Ed Wood* (directed by Tim Burton). Feral House has rescued Josh Alan Friedman's *Tales of Times Square*, produced in an affordable photo-illustrated edition (after the original version was killed through neglect by a major mainstream trade publisher).

Feral's own homegrown tome, *Cult Rapture: Revelations of the Cosmic Mind* by Adam Parfrey, was published as an instant classic; this work is a worthy follow-up to the renowned *Apocalypse Culture* (edited by Adam Parfrey), which has earned an enlarged and revised edition.

Potential Feral authors should note the following, and direct their queries accordingly: This house is very selective. The published materials may seem weird, wild, and extreme; the topics may indeed cover the more unusual aspects of popular culture, crime, the occult, film, and music. Yet, for this very reason, the writing has to be thoughtful and accomplished. The house seeks manuscripts for its new imprint Funeral Home, which is devoted to rock music and popular culture.

The Feral House list is distributed to the book trade exclusively through Publishers Group West. Feral House titles are also available through regional and specialty distributors: See Hear, Subterranean, and Last Gasp.

Query letters and SASEs should be directed to:

Adam Parfrey, President

FICTION COLLECTIVE TWO (FC2)

Publications Center
Box 494
University of Colorado
Boulder, CO 80309
303-492-8947

Fiction Collective Two publishes innovative works of fiction; the house is among the most renowned small literary operations in the nation. Fiction Collective Two (FC2) considers finely honed projects that feature stylistic experimentation and challenging subject material. FC2 imprints and lines include Black Ice Books, On the Edge, and New Women's Fiction.

Samples: *Aviary Slag* by Jacques Servin; *Anarcho-Hindu* by Curtis White; *Chick Lit: Postfeminist Fiction* (edited by Cris Mazza and Jeffrey De Shell); *Five Days of Bleeding* by Ricardo Cortez Cruz; *Degenerative Prose* (edited by Mark Amerika and Ronald Sukenick).

Fiction Collective Two (founded in 1974) is the successor to the Fiction Collective, which originally gained renown for its line of highly stylized literary works.

Fiction Collective Two oversees its own distributional network, including regional and national trade representation.

Query letters and SASEs should be directed to:

Ronald Sukenick, Director

Curtis White, Director

DONALD I. FINE, INC.
(See under listings for Penguin USA)

FIREBRAND BOOKS
141 The Commons
Ithaca, NY 14850
607-272-0000

Firebrand publishes award-winning titles in feminist and lesbian literature. The house is known for its venturesome list in popular nonfiction (including informational works, personal tales, historical and cultural studies); far-reaching fiction (including most popular genre categories, short stories, and literary novels); exuberant poetry; and wholehearted humor. Among Firebrand's strong suits is writing from an ethnic or cultural perspective, including African American, American Indian, Latina, Italian American, Jewish, and the American South.

Firebrand Books (founded in 1984 by Nancy K. Bereano) is eminently inventive in its pursuit of new avenues for marketing and sales; the house holds fast to a solid backlist and issues a well-tuned list of new titles each season.

Frontlist releases from Firebrand: *Cookin' with Honey: What Literary Lesbians Eat* (edited by Amy Scholder); *The Rooms We Make Our Own* by Toni Mirosevich; *Love and Death, and Other Disasters: Stories 1987–1995* by Jenifer Levin; *Breathless* (erotica) by Kitty Tsui; *Exile in the Promised Land* (memoir) by Marcia Freedman;

Metamorphosis: Reflections on Recovery by Judith McDaniel; *Restoring the Color of Roses* by Barrie Jean Borich; *Eight Bullets: One Woman's Story of Surviving Anti-Gay Violence* by Claudia Brenner with Hannah Ashley; *My Mama's Dead Squirrel: Lesbian Essays on Southern Culture* by Mab Segrest; *Politics of the Heart: A Lesbian Parenting Anthology* (edited by Sandra Pollack and Jeanne Vaughn); *Skin: Talking About Sex, Class and Literature* by Dorothy Allison (author of *Bastard Out of Carolina* and *Trash*).

Firebrand fiction and literary works: *Free Ride* by Marilyn Gayle; *Good Enough to Eat* by Lesléa Newman; *Letting in the Night* by Joan Lindau (Alden); *Running Fiercely Toward a High Thin Sound* by Judith Katz; *Scuttlebutt* by Jana Williams; *Shoulders* by Georgia Cotrell; *Sister Safety Pin* by Lorrie Sprecher; *Stone Butch Blues* by Leslie Feinberg; *Legal Tender* (mystery) by Marion Foster; *A Gathering of Spirit: A Collection by North American Indian Women* (edited by Beth Brant); *The Gilda Stories* (time-traveling African-American vampire account) by Jewelle Gomez; *Moll Cutpurse* (an Elizabethan picaresque) by Ellen Galford.

On Firebrand's poetry list: *Artemis in Echo Park* by Eloise Klein Healy; *Beneath My Heart* by Janice Gould; *The Black Back-Ups* by Kate Rushin, *Crime Against Nature* by Minnie Bruce Pratt; *Humid Pitch* (narrative poetry) by Cheryl Clarke; *Jonestown and Other Madness* by Pat Parker; *Now Poof She Is Gone* by Wendy Rose.

Firebrand is the publisher of the renowned *Lesbian (Out)law: Survival Under the Rule of Law* by Ruthann Robson, and the cultural classic *Diamonds Are a Dyke's Best Friend* by Yvonne Zipter (an in-depth look at the lesbian national pastime of baseball).

Firebrand publishes the writer's resource guide *Words to the Wise: A Writer's Guide to Feminist and Lesbian Periodicals & Publishers* by Andrea Fleck Clardy.

Humor on Firebrand's list features the *Dykes to Watch Out For* cartoon series by Alison Bechdel.

Firebrand is strong in direct-mail marketing and offers a toll-free number for credit-card orders. Firebrand titles are distributed to the trade by LPC/InBook.

Query letters and SASEs should be directed to:

Nancy K. Bereano, Editor and Publisher

FIRST GLANCE BOOKS, INC.
11990 Loch Lomond Road
Middletown, CA 95461
707-928-1994
fax: 707-928-1995

Mailing address:
P.O. Box 960
Cobb, CA 95426

First Glance Books accents self-help in the following areas: health and healing, sexuality and relationships, self-help spirituality, psychological self-help, financial self-help, cookbooks, parenting, and career success.

First Glance (founded in 1991) began as a remainder house, selling publishers' out-of-print stocks. In 1995 First Glance added frontlist publishing to their enterprise with *Italian Immigrant Cooking*. First Glance achieved this success with editorial quality, promotional savvy, and through well-developed distribution channels. First Glance cofounder Neil Panico previously established Atrium distribution services; cofounder Rodney Grisso has partnered Neil Panico in several successful business ventures.

First Glance acquisitions editor Bill Gottlieb was formerly Editor in Chief and senior vice president at Rodale Books. (Bill Gottlieb is also currently editorial director of Dawn Horse Press, the publishing house of his spiritual community.)

First Glance Books, Inc. oversees its own distribution.

Query letters and SASEs should be directed to:

Bill Gottlieb, Acquisitions Editor

FOCAL PRESS
(See Heinemann)

FOUR WALLS EIGHT WINDOWS
39 West 14th Street, Suite 503
New York, NY 10011
212-206-8965
fax: 212-206-8799
http://users.aol.com/specpress/fourwalls.htm (World Wide Web)

Four Walls Eight Windows offers a select seasonal list in creative nonfiction and literary fiction oriented toward topical issues and current culture. The house is known for journalistic forays into progressive politics; experimental fiction that features a stylistic and intellectual edge (including illustrated narrative); American and world culture expressed and portrayed through the essay; penetrating literary and critical studies; and individualistic poetry.

This is a publisher with a list far from the norm: Four Walls Eight Windows catalogs cultural artifacts in book form. The house hosts a healthy backlist laden with critically acclaimed, accomplished sellers, as well as an array of literary reprints.

Four Walls Eight Windows (established in 1986) was dubbed descriptively—for the initial editorial environs—by founders John Oakes and Daniel Simon. Repeat: Contrary to speculation, when Dan Simon split to found the independent press Seven Stories (in early 1996; see separate entry for Seven Stories in this directory), John Oakes *did not even contemplate* a name change to Two Walls Four Windows.

Entrants in the Four Walls nonfiction arena: *Birds of Prey, Boeing vs. Airbus: A Battle for the Skies* by Matthew Lynn; *A Day in Part 15: Law & Order in Family Court* by Judge Richard Ross; *Gandhi: Lifelines* by Mahatma Gandhi (illustrated and edited by Béatrice Tanaka); *O My Land, My Friends: The Selected Letters of Hart Crane* (edited by Langdon Hammer and Brom Weber); *Simple Annals: Two Centuries of an American Family* by Robert H. Allen; *Fermat's Last Theorem: Unlocking the Secret of an Ancient Mathematical Problem* by Amir D. Aczel; *The Last, Great Pennsylvania Station* by Lorraine B. Diehl; *The Red Mafia: The Eastern European Mob* by Werner Raith (translated by Edna McCown).

Frontlist fiction and pictorial narratives include: *Lovesong for the Giant Contessa* by Steven Tye Culbert; *The Quigmans: Tunnel of Just Friends* by Buddy Hickerson (syndicated cartoon); *The Book of Candy* by Susan Dworkin; *American Splendor Presents: Bob & Harv's Comics* (by Harvey Pekar; illustrated by R. Crumb); *In the Season of the Daisies* by Thomas Phelan; *The Award* by Lydia Salayre (translated by Jane Davey).

Four Walls Eight Windows is proud to publish Gordon Lish's entire body of work, beginning this fall with a new novel, *Epigraph*, and two reissues, *Dear Mr. Capote* and *What I Know So Far*.

Additional fiction, literary works, and creative publishing ventures from Four Walls Eight Windows: *Ribofunk* (interconnected short stories) by Paul Di Filippo (author of *The Steampunk Trilogy*); *Eluthéria* (dramatic work) by Samuel Beckett; *Illuminated Poems* by Allen Ginsberg (illustrations by Eric Drooker); *American Poets Say Goodbye to the Twentieth Century* (edited by Andrei Codrescu and Laura Rosenthal).

Among Four Walls Eight Windows nonfiction favorites: *Blood Season: Mike Tyson and the World of Boxing* by Phil Berger.

Four Walls Eight Windows books are distributed to the trade by Publishers Group West; foreign rights are administered by Writers House.

Query letters and SASEs should be directed to:

John Oakes, Publisher

FREE SPIRIT PUBLISHING

400 First Avenue North, Suite 616
Minneapolis, MN 55401-1724
612-338-2068

Free Spirit Publishing produces trade nonfiction arenas keyed to parenting, human development, the family, education, and relationships. Areas of special concentration: self-help for kids; gifted and talented education, learning differences (LD), creative learning, parenting and teaching, the free-spirited classroom, school success. Free Spirit Publishing offers creative learning materials that enrich the lives of children and teens.

Free Spirit publications include education guides for students, educators, parents, and mental health professionals, as well as self-help for parents, educators, children, and teens. The publisher (founded in 1983) has been particularly successful with its Self-Help for Kids line of books and educational materials. Free Spirit also catalogs posters and other creative learning wares.

Free Spirit highlights: *Growing Good Kids: 28 Activities to Enhance Self Awareness, Compassion, and Leadership* by Deb Delisle and Jim Delisle; *Totally Private and Personal: Journaling Ideas for Girls and Young Women* by Jessica Wilber; *Teach to Reach: Over 300 Strategies, Tips, and Helpful Hints for Teachers of All Grades* by

Craig Mitchell with Pamela Espeland; *How to Help Your Child with Homework: Every Caring Parent's Guide to Encouraging Good Study Habits and Ending the Homework Wars* (revised and updated edition) by Marguerite C. Radencich, Ph.D. and Jeanne Shay Schumm, Ph.D.; *How to Do Homework Without Throwing Up* by Trevor Romain; *Succeeding with LD: 20 True Stories About Real People with LD (Learning Differences)* by Jill Lauren; *Teaching Kids with Learning Difficulties in the Regular Classroom: Strategies and Techniques Every Teacher Can Use to Challenge & Motivate Struggling Students* by Susan Winebrenner; *The Gifted Kids' Survival Guide: A Teen Handbook* (revised, expanded, and updated edition) by Judy Galbraith and Jim Delisle, Ph.D.; *Alphabet Antics: Hundreds of Activities to Challenge and Enrich Letter Learners of All Ages* by Ken Vinton.

Free Spirit's distribution has been primarily in the educational arena; the house is expanding into the broader book-trade market.

Query letters and SASEs should be directed to:

Judy Galbraith, Publisher

W. H. FREEMAN AND COMPANY PUBLISHERS
SCIENTIFIC AMERICAN BOOKS
COMPUTER SCIENCE PRESS

41 Madison Avenue
New York, NY 10010
212-576-9400

W. H. Freeman accents mathematics and the sciences; the house roster features trade titles of general interest, textbooks, and professional books. Areas of trade interest include anthropology, astronomy, current issues, nature and the environment, health and medicine, life sciences, parenting, and psychology.

W. H. Freeman represents a tradition of outstanding and innovative publishing in the sciences. Freeman books—especially the popular works—often display superb graphics and fine design. W. H. Freeman and Company (established in 1946) is a subsidiary of Scientific American, Inc. The house logs a trusty backlist.

From Freeman: *Privileged Hands* by Geerat Vermeij; *Politics on the Nets: Wiring the Political Process* by Wayne Rash, Jr.; *Why People Believe Weird Things: Pseudoscience, Superstition, & Other Confusions of Our Time* by Michaael Shermer (foreword by Stephen Jay Gould); *Age of Propaganda: The Everyday Use and Abuse of Persuasion* (revised edition) by Anthony Pratkins and Elliot Aronson; *Overcoming Infertility: A Compassionate Resource for Getting Pregnant* by Robert Jansen, M.D.; *Galileo's Commandment: An Anthology of Great Science Writing* (edited by Edmund Blair Bolles); *Cultures of Healing: Correcting the Image of American Health Care* by Robert T. Francher; *Strong Shadows: Scenes from an Inner City AIDS Clinic* by Abigail Zuger, M.D.; *Between Therapist and Client: The New Relationship* (revised edition) by Michael Kahn; and *Shadow of a Star: The Neutrino Story of Supernova 1987A* by Alfred K. Mann.

From Scientific American Library, a line of trade-oriented books authored by celebrated scientists, come titles geared to particular fields in addition to works of general-readership appeal. Sample titles: *Mathematics: The Science of Patterns—the Search for Order in Life, Mind, and the Universe* by Keith Devlin; *The Evolving Coast* by Richard A. Davis, Jr.; and *The Elusive Neutrino: A Subatomic Detective Story* by Nickolas Solomey.

A special coproduction of Infon, Inc., Scientific American, and W. H. Freeman is *Molecular Cell Biology* (CD-ROM).

W. H. Freeman oversees its own distribution.

Query letters and SASEs should be directed to:

Deborah Allen, Acquisitions Editor
Biology, biochemistry.

Richard Bonacci, Acquisitions Editor
Mathematics.

Susan Brennan, Acquisitions Editor
Psychology.

Jonathan Cobb, Acquisitions Editor
Trade Scientific American Library series.

Holly Hodder, Acquisitions Editor
Astronomy, anthropology, geosciences, physics, statistics.

Michelle Julet, Acquisitions Editor
Chemistry.

John Michael, Acquisitions Editor
Trade areas of house interest.

COMPUTER SCIENCE PRESS

Computer Science Press publishes in computer science and information technology, with an eye on emerging areas within these quick-moving fields. The house offers introductory- to advanced-level college texts in computer sciences, telecommunications, and computer mathematics, as well as related areas. Computer Science Press, founded in 1974, became an imprint of W. H. Freeman in 1988.

Query letters and SASEs should be directed to:

Richard Bonacci, Publisher

FRIENDSHIP PRESS

(See Directory of Religious, Spiritual, and Inspirational Publishers)

FROMM INTERNATIONAL PUBLISHING CORPORATION

560 Lexington Avenue
New York, NY 10022
212-308-4010

Fromm International is a small-size house with a strong literary nonfiction list. Originally known for modern and contemporary fiction from around the globe (originals and reprints), Fromm now publishes primarily a line of diverse and high-quality writings in such nonfiction categories as history, biography, memoirs, belles lettres, essays, cultural and performing arts, analytical psychology, and issues of contemporary interest. The house produces hardcovers, trade paperbacks, and special fine editions.

Fromm International (founded in 1982) has branch offices in Germany and Switzerland.

From Fromm: *Art Carney: A Biography* by Michael Seth Starr; *The Story of Britain* by Roy Strong; *André Malraux: A Biography* by Curtis Cate; *The Two-Million-Year-Old Self* by Anthony Stevens; *Unfinished Journey: Twenty Years Later* by Yehudi Menuhin; *Bauhaus: Crucible of Modernism* by Elaine S. Hochman; *From Atlantis to the Sphinx: Recovering the Lost Wisdom of the Ancient World* by Colin Wilson; *Hermann Hesse: Pilgrim of Crisis* by Ralph Freedman; *Treasure Hunt: A New York Times Reporter Tracks the Quedlinburg Hoard* by William H. Honan; *Charles Laughton: A Difficult Actor* by Simon Callow; *Handsome Is: Adventures with Saul Bellow* by Harriet Wasserman.

Fromm orchestrates its own distributional schemes.

Query letters and SASEs should be directed to:

Leo V. Fromm, President

Fred Jordan, Executive Director

FULCRUM PUBLISHING

350 Indiana Street, Suite 350
Golden, CO 80401-5093
303-277-1623

Fulcrum publishes general trade nonfiction books, with emphasis in gardening, nature and the outdoors; food; travel guides; business and the environment; Colorado and the Rockies; parenting; health; humor; and American history, world history, and cultural history.

Fulcrum imprints and lines include the Library of Congress series of Americana, educational books (for children and adults), and the Starwood line of books and calendars; the house also issues selected audiocassettes on the Fulcrum Audio Book imprint. Native American writers and subjects are a vital part of the Fulcrum program.

Fulcrum Publishing (founded in 1984) is a growing firm with an ambitious list. It is the Fulcrum vision to produce works that provide a link to the experiences and wisdom of the past. This image fits in neatly with the publisher's characterization of the editorial relationship:

In his autobiography, Anthony Trollope wrote, "Of all the needs that a book has, the chief need is that it be readable." When that happens, it is due to excellent writers and professional and understanding editors. It is difficult and sometimes lonely being a writer, but a good editor is a supporter, a confidant, a representative of the reader and often can assist the writer in producing a book far better than the writer is capable of creating alone. Sometimes the changes are obvious, sometimes subtle, but always aimed at making the book readable. Bob Baron, Publisher, would like to praise and thank Fulcrum dedicated editors who have made all of their 250 books possible and who have tried to achieve the standards of Trollope.

This is good news for Fulcrum readers, and good news for writers too. Fulcrum supports a hefty backlist.

Special Fulcrum projects: *The Book in American* by Richard Clement, which used the vast resources in the Library of Congress to trace the history of the American book. *All the World's a Stage*, a volume that combines writing from William Shakespeare with the calligraphy and full-color illustrations of Dorothy Boux. Fulcrum is working with colleagues in England to celebrate the building of the new Globe Theatre in London. *Faces of a Nation: The Rise and Fall of the Soviet Union, 1917–1991* is a photoessay featuring Dmitri Daltermants, Russia's most famous photographer, with text by noted historian Theodore H. Von Laue.

General nonfiction on the Fulcrum list: *Roots of Survival: Native American Storytelling and the Sacred* by Joseph Bruchac; *Celebration of American Food: Four Centuries in the Melting Pot* by Gerry Schremp; *The Wit and Wisdom of Politics* by Chuck Henning; *Stifled Laughter: One Woman's Story About Fighting Censorship* by Claudia Johnson; *America's Botanical Beauty* by James L. Reveal; *Weeder's Digest: The Best of Green Prints* (edited by Pat Stone); *The Joy of Jazz: Swing Era, 1935–1947* by Tom Scanlan; *Walking for Health, Fitness and Sport* by Bob Carlson; *God Is Red: A Native View of Religion* by Vine Deloria, Jr.; *Keepers of Life: Discovering Plants Through Native American Stories and Earth Activities for Children* by Michael J. Caduto and Joseph Bruhac (illustrated book; accompanying set of audiocassettes).

Travel titles: *Seasonal Guide to the Natural Year: North Carolina, South Carolina and Tennessee* by John Rucker; *Seasonal Guide to the Natural Year: Florida with Georgia and Alabama Coasts* by M. Timothy O'Keefe; *New Mexico's Best* by Richard Mahler; *The West Less Traveled: The Best (and Lesser Known) Parks, Monuments and Natural Areas* by Jan Bannan; *Rocky Mountain Skiing* (second edition) by Claire Walter.

Fulcrum Publishing handles its own distribution.

Query letters and SASEs should be directed to:

T. J. Baker, Acquisitions Editor
Projects consistent with the house list.

Suzanne I. Barchers, Editor, Fulcrum Kids and Fulcrum Resources
Or send prospective projects in care of **Submissions Department**.

GALE

835 Penobscot Building
Detroit, MI 48226
313-961-2242

Gale catalogs professional and popular reference and information works; major fields of interest include technological innovation, international business, environmental issues, literature and author biographies, multicultural studies, and women's studies. Gale also produces titles in arts and entertainment, religion and occultism, education, careers, business, nation and world, government and law, science and medicine, the electronic information industry, publishing and information science, general reference, and sports.

Gale is a stalwart specialist in reference products, including books and databases for businesses, consumers, students, and general information seekers. Gale's list embraces directories, biographical works, specialty dictionaries, and series in literary and cultural criticism. The house catalog includes products from such imprints and subsidiaries as Visible Ink Press, St. James Press, and the Taft Group. Gale (formerly Gale Research) was begun in 1954; the firm is currently a subsidiary of the Thomson Corporation.

As an information publisher, Gale constantly courts new topic arenas and information-delivery systems to address the ever-widening range of reader requests and needs as well as to take advantage of the burgeoning reservoir of information sources. Gale titles are available through on-line delivery services, on diskette, magnetic tape, CD-ROM, and the Internet.

From Gale: *Worldwide Government Directory*; *The Vampire Book: The Encyclopedia of the Undead*; *The Student Contact Book*; *Statistical Record of Religion in America*; *Pop Culture Landmarks*; *National Housing Directory for People with Disabilities*; *European Wholesalers and Distributors Directory*; *Encyclopedia of College Basketball*; *Divorce Help Sourcebook*; *Chronology of Native North American History*; *Cemeteries of the U.S.*; *Major 20th-Century Writers*; and *Directory of Online Databases*.

Gale oversees its own trade and library distribution, as well as its own electronic distribution; the house catalog includes products from Visible Ink Press, St. James Press, the Taft Group, and UXL.

Query letters and SASEs should be directed to:

Dedria Bryfonski, President and Chief Operating Officer

GALLAUDET UNIVERSITY PRESS
(See Directory of University Presses)

THE GAMMON PRESS
P.O. Box 294
Arlington, MA 02174
617-641-2091
fax: 617-641-2660

Gammon publishes works that deal with games of skill and chance, primarily backgammon, poker, blackjack, and video poker. The press also offers additional titles in areas such as hyper-backgammon, theory of gambling, sports betting, horse racing, and (very occasionally) chess. The Gammon Press emphasizes practical instruction, strategy, and game improvement; the house also publishes profiles of players, match analyses, and techniques of the masters.

The Gammon Press is a specialty house that produces a select number of new products each year. In addition to books, Gammon offers backgammon sets and supplies, precision dice, calendars, periodicals (including *Inside Backgammon*), computer software and CD-ROMs, and videotapes. Gammon's goal is to make the customer a better player by publishing the best advice from the best players. The house maintains a hardy backlist.

Gammon Press Ratings: As an aid to the customer, Gammon rates all books according to the skill level of their intended audience —either beginner, intermediate, or advanced.

Gammon catalogs a strong core backgammon list that includes: *The Backgammon Handbook* by Enno Heyken and Martin Fischer; *Hyper-Backgammon: Game of Lightning Speed* by Hugh Sconyers; *How to Play Tournament Backgammon* and *New Ideas in Backgammon* by Kit Woolsey; *In the Game Until the End: Winning in Ace-Point Endgames* by Bob Wachtel; *Learning from the Machine: Robertie vs. TD-Gammon* by Bill Robertie.

Also from Gammon: *Basics of Sports Betting* by Avery Cardoza; *Poker Essays* by Mason Malmuth; *Winning Poker* by David Slansky; *Basics of Horse Racing* by Whitney Cobb; *MatchQuiz: Annotated Matches on Computer Diskettes* (compiled by Hal Heinrich; commentary by Kit Woolsey).

In addition to producing original new works, the Gammon Press actively searches for quality out-of-print books from the heyday of backgammon publishing in the 1970s. In particular, the house attempts to stock books by the following authors: Magriel, Cooke, Deyong, Dwek, and Martyn.

Inside Backgammon is a bimonthly magazine full of problems, advice, and analysis, and presents some of the best backgammon writing anywhere. The magazine emphasizes clear, lucid explanation, with games and problems geared not only for the advanced player, but also geared toward the aspiring intermediate.

The Gammon Press handles its own distribution.

Query letters and SASEs should be directed to:

William Robertie, President

GARRETT PUBLISHING

384 South Military Trail
Deerfield Beach, FL 33442
954-480-8543

Garrett's focus is on books in business, finance, law, and personal finance. Garrett books are practical, often featuring a self-help/how-to approach that highlights sample forms, ready-to-use templates, checklists, instructions, resources, and informative examples. A major Garrett imprint is E•Z Legal Books.

Garrett Publishing (founded in 1990) is on the lookout for authors with marketable projects: authors who are expert in their fields and know how to get their point across clearly and enthusiastically. Garrett's marketing department is staffed with professionals skilled in publicity, promotions, advertising, and editorial services. Garrett promotes its authors' books through print advertising, television appearances, and radio spots. The house offers competitive advances and royalties.

With sales representatives located strategically across the United States, Garrett's books are available in the giant trade bookseller chains and are obtainable from major wholesalers and distributors. Over the past several seasons, the publisher has expanded its retail distribution.

Representative of the Garrett program: *Asset Protection Secrets*; *The Family Limited Partnership Book*; *Mind Over Pain Relief Program*; *Don't Put Me in a Nursing Home!*; *Guaranteed Credit*; *The Business Doctor*; *How to Settle with the IRS . . . for Pennies on the Dollar*; *How to Protect Your Money Offshore*; *Offshore Havens*; *How I Made Millions with Just a Few Simple Ideas*; *Buying and Selling a Business*.

Garrett Publishing distributes through its own house operation as well as via such outlets as Quality Book Distributors, Ingram, and Baker and Taylor.

Query letters and SASEs should be directed to:

Arnold Goldstein, Editor/Owner

GENERAL PUBLISHING GROUP

2701 Ocean Park Boulevard, Suite 140
Santa Monica, CA 90405
310-314-4000
800-745-9000

General Publishing produces commercial nonfiction in high-interest areas, including the world of film, television, music, popular culture; global issues, history, politics; personalities, popular inspiration; self-improvement, fitness, and sports; and humor. General publishes in hardcover, quality trade paper, and mass-market paperback editions, in addition to a selection of illustrated gift books.

General Publishing Group (founded in 1991) accents entertainment and the media; General Publishing projects by and large share an emphasis on instantly recognizable, celebrity- and media-oriented topics and subjects in the news (including tie-in publications).

Sample General titles: *As the World Turns: The Complete Family Scrapbook* by Julie Poll; *How to Be a Hollywood Superstar* by Barry Dutter and Rich Hoover; *Jacqueline Kennedy Onassis: The Making of a First Lady* by James Lowe (introduction by Letitia Baldridge); *Nips and Tucks: Everything You Must Know Before Having Cosmetic Surgery* by Diana Barry; *Pamela Anderson in Pictures* (photographed by Stephen Wayda; text by Bibi Jordan); *The Simpson Trial in Black and White* by Tom Elias and Dennis Schatzman.

Among the house's initial successes were a lavish biography of Hugh Hefner and *The Bettie Page Book*. Daytime television drama is featured in *General Hospital* and *All My Children* (both by Gary Warner). Big hits from the General list include *Frank*

Sinatra by Nancy Sinatra (in editions featuring a lineup of collector's CD recordings); *100 Greatest Moments in Olympic History* by Bud Greenspan; *Top 40 Years of Rock & Roll* by Casey Kasem.

General Publishing Group oversees its own distribution.

Query letters and SASEs should be directed to:

Peter Hoffman, Editorial Director

GLENEIDA PUBLISHING GROUP

(See Baker Book House and Liguori Publications, both listed in Directory of Religious, Spiritual, and Inspirational Publishers)

THE GLOBE PEQUOT PRESS

6 Business Park Road
Old Saybrook, CT 06475
203-395-0440

Mailing address:
P.O. Box 833
Old Saybrook, CT 06475

Globe Pequot is a specialist in travel and outdoor recreation, with additional interest in cooking, personal finance, and home-based business. The publisher accents titles marketed to both trade and specialty market slots.

Within this program, Globe Pequot looks for works in a number of important categories: travel books—regional and special-interest travel guides; family adventure guides; travel annuals, accommodations guides, itinerary-format guides, and travel how-tos; outdoor recreation—any outdoor sport; how-to and where-to guides; home-based business—authors should have firsthand experience running the featured home-based business; source books—almanac-style books that combine informational essay with source information on specific avocations and areas of interest.

In the travel arena, Globe Pequot is well regarded for several bestselling series and also distributes for a number of travel-specialist houses. Among Globe Pequot lines: Discover Historic America; Quick Escapes (weekend and day trips keyed to metropolitan areas or regions); Recommended Country Inns; the Bed & Breakfast guidebook series; Family Adventure Guides; Cadogan Guides to destinations worldwide for the discriminating traveler; Karen Brown Travel Press personalized guides; and the popular Off-the-Beaten-Path series. Globe Pequot also updates a variety of annuals, among them *Europe by Eurail*. Globe Pequot's regionally keyed books also cover such interest areas as biking, hiking, mountaineering, skiing, and family activities in wilderness and on the beach.

Globe Pequot catalogs the following representative titles: *Beautiful Easy Lawns and Landscapes* by Laurence Sombke; *Enduring Harvests: Native American Foods and Festivals for Every Season* by E. Barrie Kavasch; *Family Adventure Guide: Illinois* by Lori Meek Schuldt; *Getting the Most for Your Travel Dollar* by Herbert Teison and Nancy Dunnan; *Guide to Ancient Native American Sites* by Michael Durham; *Kayaking Made Easy: A Manual for Beginners with Tips for the Experienced* by Dennis O. Stuhaug; *Pirates & Patriots of the Revolution: An Illustrated Encyclopedia of Colonial Seamanship* by C. Keith Wilbur; *Stepping Lightly on Australia: A Traveler's Guide to Ecotourism* by Shirly LaPlanche; *The 100 Best Honeymoon Resorts of the World* by Katharine D. Dyson.

The Globe Pequot Press (originated in 1947) operates from publishing and warehouse headquarters in Old Saybrook. The press distributes its own list through its home-office facilities as well as a network of regional sales representatives. The house handles distribution for such houses as Appalachian Mountain Club Books, Berlitz Publishing, Karen Brown Travel Press, Cadogan Guides, Corkscrew Press, and Moorland Publishing.

Globe Pequot was purchased in early 1997 by Morris Communications Corporation, a privately held company (founded in 1795) with nationwide, diversified holdings in newspaper and magazine publishing, radio, outdoor advertising, and computer services.

Query letters and SASEs should be directed to:

Laura Strom, Acquisitions Editor

Linda Kennedy, President and Publisher

DAVID R. GODINE, PUBLISHER, INC.

Box 9103
9 Lewis Street
Lincoln, MA 01773
614-259-0700
fax: 617-259-9198

Godine publishes trade nonfiction in such areas as history and criticism, typography and graphic arts, art and architecture, horticulture, cooking, Americana, and regional-interest books. The house also publishes fiction (including mysteries), literature and essays, and poetry, as well as children's books. Godine offers a line of classic works in reprint as well as works in translation.

The Godine program is committed to quality. Godine specializes in attentively produced hardcover and trade paperback editions. The house issues a small catalog of new titles each year while maintaining an active backlist. Godine's imprints include Country Classics, Double Detectives, and Nonpareil Books.

David R. Godine, Publisher (founded in 1969) was started in an abandoned cow barn, where David R. Godine both worked and lived; the expanding operation later moved to Boston. Now relocated to Lincoln, Massachusetts, Godine has an increasingly successful distribution arrangement and a stronger concentration on titles with backlist potential (particularly nonfiction).

Godine has intentionally kept itself small, the list eclectic, and the quality consistently high. The house maintains its fortunate position of being able to ask: What do we really believe is superior rather than what are we confident will sell? The editors at Godine have learned to trust their instincts. By staying small, this house is lucky enough to have kept most of their goals attainable. They do not need to sell 10,000 copies of a book to make money. They do not need to put authors on tour, or to indulge in massive hype. Good books, like water, find their own levels. It sometimes takes years, but it is inevitable.

In short, David R. Godine, Publisher remains what it was 25 years ago: a true cottage industry, surviving on a very small budget, and doing what it does and what it *knows* best: publishing books that matter for people who care.

General trade nonfiction from Godine: *Tyranny of the Normal: Essays on Bioethics, Theology, and Myth* by Leslie Fiedler; *Great Camps of the Adirondacks* by Harvey H. Kaiser (now back in print); *The Grand Resort Hotels of the White Mountains: A Vanishing Architectural Legacy* by Bryant F. Tolles, Jr.; *Schola Illustris: The Roxbury Latin School, 1645–1995* by F. Washington Jarvis; *Crowning Glory: Silver Torah Ornaments of the Jewish Museum, New York* by Rafi Grafman (edited by Vivian B. Mann); *Bright Starts, Dark Trees, Clear Water: Natural Writing from North of the Border* (edited by Wayne Grady).

Representative of Godine special-interest nonfiction: *The Art of the Printed Book, 1455–1955* by Joseph Blumenthal; *Into Print: Selected Writings on Printing History, Typography, and Book Production* by John Dreyfus; *Calligraphic Flourishing: A New Approach to an Ancient Art* by Bill Hildebrandt; *Giving Up the Gun: Japan's Reversion to the Sword, 1545–1879* by Noel Perrin.

On the Godine fiction list: *The Disobedience of Water* (stories) by Sena Jeter Naslund; *Last Trolley from Beethovenstraat* by Grete Weil (translated from the German by John Barrett); *Life: A User's Manual* by Georges Perec (translated from the French by David Ellos); *In the Heart of the Heart of the Country* by William H. Gass; *Disappearances* by Howard Frank Mosher.

Mystery and suspense titles include: *The Man Who Liked Slow Tomatoes* by K. C. Constantine; *The Woman in Black* by Susan Hill.

Godine's children's-books backlist includes: *We Didn't Mean to Go to the Sea* by Arthur Ransome and *Crime and Puzzlement: 24 Solve-Them-Yourself Picture Mysteries* by Lawrence Treat (illustrated by Leslie Cabarga).

Godine distributes through National Book Network; the house distributes for Eridanos Press, which publishes foreign literature in translation.

Query letters and SASEs should be directed to:

Mark Polizzotti, Editorial Director

GOODFELLOW PRESS

16625 Redmond Way, Suite M20
Redmond, WA 98052
206-868-7323

Goodfellow publishes character-driven mainstream trade paperback fiction of all kinds. Categories and genres include love stories and romances, mysteries and suspense novels, and strong contemporary stories with mainstream-readership appeal.

The house publishes a short, selective list of new seasonal titles and maintains a reasonable backlist.

Goodfellow Press distribution is primarily through mail-order and library markets.

Writer guidelines are available from the publisher. Please query first. Query letters and SASEs should be directed to:

Sally Astridge, Acquisitions Editor

Pamela R. Goodfellow, Editorial Director

Kay Morison, Acquisitions Editor

Sharon Plowman, Acquisitions Editor

C. J. Wycoff, Acquisitions Editor

GRAYWOLF PRESS

2402 University Avenue, Suite 203
Saint Paul, MN 55114
612-641-0077
fax: 612-641-0036

Graywolf publishes poetry, fiction, and belletristic nonfiction and essays. Graywolf produces works by writers past and present, with particular emphasis on the scene of contemporary international letters as well as a line of literary anthologies and reissues. The Graywolf Discovery series focuses on reprint gems in paperback. Graywolf hosts a solid backlist of featured titles.

About the Graywolf Press trade motto: *Creative writing for creative reading.* This distinctive approach to publishing signifies Graywolf Press as an independent, not-for-profit literary publisher dedicated to the publication of contemporary literature of outstanding quality.

Graywolf backs up its authors and its literary claims with publishing prowess: the Graywolves have been successful in finding an audience for their works, and the Graywolf Press list has been augmented, confirming the achievement of a program that runs contrary to the stream of contemporary commercial publishing.

Begun in 1974, Graywolf Press exemplifies the small-scale independent American literary house. The publisher's wolfpack logo marks a list rippling with award-winners and critical endorsement.

The *Graywolf Forum* series is launched with the publication of *Graywolf Forum One: Tolstoy's Dictaphone: Technology and the Muse*, a collection of new essays edited by Sven Birkerts (author of the hotly debated *Gutenberg Elegies*).

General-interest trade books include: *A Song of Love and Death: The Meaning of Opera* by Peter Conrad; *Diary of a Left-Handed Birdwatcher* by Leonard Nathan; *North Enough: AIDS and Other Clear-Cuts* by Jan Zita Grover.

Graywolf fiction and literary works: *The Apprentice* by Lewis Libby; *Frenzy* by Percival Everett; *Places in the World a Woman Could Walk* by Janet Kauffman; *Beachcombing for a Shipwrecked God* by Joe Coomer; *Wise Poison* (poems) by David Rivard; *The Owl in the Mask of the Dreamer: Collected Poems of John Haines* by John Haines; *Otherwise: New and Selected Poems* by Jane Kenyon.

Graywolf Press utilizes a network of regional sales representatives; books are proffered to the trade through Consortium Book Sales and Distribution.

Query letters and SASEs should be directed to:

Fiona McCrae, Publisher and Editor

Anne Czarniecki, Managing Editor

GREENWOOD PUBLISHING GROUP
AUBURN HOUSE
BERGIN & GARVEY
GREENWOOD PRESS
PRAEGER PUBLISHERS
QUORUM BOOKS

88 Post Road West
P.O. Box 5007
Westport, CT 06881-5007
203-226-3571
fax: 203-222-1502
http://www.greenwood.com (World Wide Web)

The Greenwood publishing program encompasses general trade nonfiction, along with a traditional emphasis on professional, academic, and reference books in economics, business, social sciences and humanities, law enforcement, business, law, and current affairs, as well as special series of reference works. In addition, Greenwood produces reprints of scholarly monographs and journals. The house issues editions in hardcover and trade paperback.

Greenwood Publishing Group (instituted in 1967) comprises a number of imprints and divisions that include Auburn House, Bergin & Garvey, Greenwood Press, Quorum Books, and Praeger Publishers. (See separate subentries below.) Greenwood imprints generally maintain extensive backlists.

Greenwood Publishing Group orchestrates its own distribution. A major portion of Greenwood's sales are aimed at the library, institutional, and corporate markets.

Greenwood Academic and Trade Publishing:
Auburn House
Bergin & Garvey
Praeger Publishers

Greenwood Publishing Group's general nonfiction trade books and academic works are published under the imprints Auburn House, Bergin & Garvey, and Praeger Publishers. Each imprint has its own individual publishing orbit and distinct editorial approach.

Auburn House emphasizes professional and academic works in economics, business, health care, labor relations, and public policy.

Bergin & Garvey concentrates on scholarly monographs in the social sciences and humanities, as well as general nonfiction works in a similar subject range geared toward a popular audience.

Praeger Publishers promotes a vigorous approach to trade nonfiction and areas of scholarly specialist attention. Categories of publishing interest include history (including cultural history), military studies (including history, espionage, and military operations), political science and international relations, women's studies, business and economics, psychology, and urban affairs.

Sample works in the social and behavioral sciences (political science, history, economics, sociology, anthropology, education, psychology, health and medicine, and science and computers): *A Lost Cause: Bill Clinton's Campaign for National Health Insurance* by Nicholas Laham; *Jimmy Carter as Peacemaker: A Post-Presidential Biography* by Rod Troester; *Russian Foreign Policy After the Cold War* by Leszek Buszynski; *Identity, Interest, and Ideology: An Introduction to Politics* by Martin C. Needler; *Prominent Sisters: Mary Lamb, Dorothy Wordsworth, and Sarah Disraeli* by Michael Polowetzky; *The American Civil War: A Handbook of Literature and Research* (edited by Steven E. Woodworth); *The Cost of Being Female* by Sue Headlee and Margery Elfin; *Warriors and Wildmen: Men, Masculinity, and Gender* by Stephen Wicks; *365 Ways . . . Retirees' Resource Guide for Productive Lifestyles* (edited by Helen K. Kerschner and John E. Hansan); *S/He Brain: Science, Sexual Politics, and the Myths of Feminism* by Robert L. Nadeau; *Procrastination and Blocking: A Novel, Practical Approach* by Robert Boice; *Bachelors: The Psychology of Men Who Haven't Married* by Charles A. Waehler.

Representing the humanities (literature, music, theatre and drama, religion, philosophy, popular culture, communication and mass media, library and information science, and art and architecture): *The Critical Response to Tennessee Williams* (edited by George W. Crandell); *Thomas K. Beecher: Minister to a Changing America, 1824–1900* by Myra C. Glenn; *The Meaning of Mind: Language, Morality, and Neuroscience* by Thomas Szasz; *Everybody Is Sitting on the Curb: How and Why America's Heroes Disappeared* by Alan Edelstein; *Crashing the Old Boys' Network: The Tragedies and Triumphs of Girls and Women in Sports* by David F. Salter; *George Burns and Gracie Allen: A Bio-Bibliography* by Cynthia Clements and Sandra Weber; *The Use of Arthurian Legend in Hollywood Film: From Connecticut Yankees to Fisher Kings* by Rebecca A. Umland and Samuel J. Umland; *Harvesting Minds: How TV Commercials Control Kids* by Roy E. Fox; *The Message Is the Medium: Online All the*

Time for Everyone by Tom Koch; *For Sex Education, See Librarian: A Guide to Issues and Resources* by Martha Cornog and Timothy Perper.

Query letters and SASEs should be directed to:

James Dunton, Publisher

Lynn Taylor, Assistant Vice President for Editorial

James Ice, Editor
Business, Economics.

Alan Sturmer, Editor
Textbooks.

Daniel Eades, Senior Editor
Political science, history, and military studies.

Elizabeth Murphy, Editor
Anthropology, education, women's studies, ethnic studies.

Nick Street, Editor
Sociology and psychology.

Nina Pearlstein, Editor
Humanities.

GREENWOOD REFERENCE PUBLISHING

The Greenwood Reference Publishing imprint offers popular, educational, scholarly, and professional reference works. The house counts among its specialty areas library and information sciences; social sciences, humanities, the arts, and works covering contemporary trends in cultural studies and criticism.

Greenwood reference series are diverse and comprehensive, and are authored and edited primarily by academics working in the respective fields of concentration. Series include: Music Reference Collection, Bio-Bibliographies in Music, Contributions in Economics and Economic History, Contributions in Women's Studies, Contributions to the Study of Science Fiction and Fantasy, and Contributions to the Study of World History. (Some individual series titles are cited in the listing above for Greenwood Academic and Trade division.)

Query letters and SASEs should be directed to:

Cynthia Harris, Executive Editor

Alicia Merrit, Acquisitions Editor
Humanities.

Barbara Rader, Senior Editor
School and public library reference.

Nita Romer, Editor
Social and behavioral science.

George Butler, Associate Editor
Library and information science.

Emily Michic, Assistant Editor
School and Public Library Reference.

GREENWOOD BUSINESS AND PROFESSIONAL PUBLISHING QUORUM BOOKS

At Greenwood Business and Professional Publishing the accent is on titles keyed to areas of topical interest, including timely issues in business, finance, and law. Sectors of this division's scope are management trends; business ethics; international business and economics; business, law, and public policy; environment and energy; information and corporate communications; human resource management; organizational behavior and development; finance, investment, and banking; accounting and taxation; marketing, advertising, and sales; and public and not-for-profit management.

Quorum Books is a dedicated imprint for professional and scholarly books in business, business-related law, and applied economics. Quorum scholarly studies recount findings and hypotheses derived from significant academic research and offer well-reasoned analysis, interpretations, and opinions.

Quorum professional books are more applied in scope and presentation. These works are intended for people who are skilled in their work, rising in their organizations, and who have urgent need for highly technical, timely, and specialized knowledge. These books thus provide readers with a blend of theory and practice not easily found or produced; it is significant that among Quorum readers are also many Quorum authors.

Titles here include: *The Muted Conscience: Moral Silence and the Practice of Ethics in Business* by Frederick Bruce Bird; *Leadership and the Job of the Executive* by Jeffrey A. Barach and D. Reed Eckhardt; *Scaling the Ivory Tower: Stories from Women in Business School Faculties* (edited by Dianne Cyr and Blaize Horner Reich); *Toxic Leaders: When Organizations Go Bad* by Marcia Lynn Whicker; *Virtual Reality Systems for Business* by Robert J. Thierauf; *Cross-Cultural Business Negotiations* by Donald W. Hendon, Rebecca Angeles Hendon, and Paul Herbig; *Measuring the Employment Effects of Regulations: Where Did the Jobs Go?* by Neal S. Zank; *The Future of the Space Industry: Private Enterprise and Public Policy* by Roger Handberg; *Reflexive Communication in the Culturally Diverse Workplace* by John E. Kikoski and Catherine Kano Kikoski; *Business Decisions, Human Choices: Restoring the Partnership Between People and Their Organizations* by Lloyd C. Williams; *Selling Sin: The Marketing of Socially Unacceptable Products* by D. Kirk Davidson.

Query letters and SASEs should be directed to:

Eric Valentine, Publisher, Quorum Books

GROLIER CHILDREN'S PUBLISHING
GROLIER INCORPORATED
CHILDREN'S PRESS
ORCHARD BOOKS
FRANKLIN WATTS

Grolier Incorporated is a subsidiary of the Matra Hachette international multimedia communications empire. Grolier Children's Publishing is the umbrella under which the separate book-publishing houses Franklin Watts and Orchard Books, as well as the Children's Press division, operate their independent, distinctive lists geared to children's and young-adult markets. (See separate subentries below.)

FRANKLIN WATTS

Sherman Turnpike
Danbury, CT 06816
203-797-3500

Franklin Watts produces a comprehensive array of school and library books for grades 4–12, and offers a line of Spanish-language titles. Emphasis at Franklin Watts is on historical and contemporary biography, nature and the environment, social issues, health and the human body, science and technology, and language arts. Many Franklin Watts books are issued through the house's numerous successful series projects.

Franklin Watts (founded in 1942) publishes a few general trade books, in addition to its core concentration on scholarly and educational titles for a school-age readership, as well as a select reference list.

Franklin Watts series for ages eight and up include The African-American Experience; Amateur Science; The Changing Family; Cincinnati Zoo Books; Country Topics for Craft Projects; First Books (series provides basic facts about subjects in the social studies, the sciences, sports, and practical and fine arts); Holiday Craft Books; How Would You Survive?; Impact Biographies; The Lesbian and Gay Experience; Projects for Young Scientists; Places and People; Speak Out, Write On!; Try This; Timelines; Venture Books; A Very Peculiar History; Women Then—Women Now; Worldwise; X-Ray Picture Books.

From the African-American Experience lineup: *African Americans and Jewish Americans: A History of Struggle* by Hedda Garza; *Jazz: The Great American Art* by Gene Seymour; *The House on Fire: The Story of the Blues* by Craig Awmiller.

First Books series titles: *Alexander the Great*; *Cleopatra*; *Herod the Great*; and *Tutankhamun* by Robert Green.

How Would You Survive? titles: *How Would You Survive as an Ancient Egyptian?* by Jacqueline Morley; *How Would You Survive as an Ancient Greek?* by Fiona Macdonald; *How Would You Survive as an Ancient Roman?* by Anita Ganeri.

The Speak Out, Write On! series includes: *How to Write a News Article* by Michael Kronenwetter; *How to Write a Poem* by Margaret Ryan; *How to Write a Story* by Kathleen C. Phillips.

Women Then—Women Now series titles: *Barred from the Bar: A History of Women and the Legal Professional* and *Women in Medicine* by Hesdda Garza.

Franklin Watts handles its own distribution.

Franklin Watts does not consider fiction or adult titles. Query letters and SASEs should be directed to:

Melissa Stewart, Editor
Science.

Scott Prentzas, Senior Editor
Young-adult nonfiction.

Russell Prim, Executive Editor, Director
All other areas of house interest.

ORCHARD BOOKS
CHILDREN'S PRESS

95 Madison Avenue
New York, NY 10016
212-951-2649

Orchard Books produces mainstream trade-oriented fiction and nonfiction books for children, many of them copiously illustrated works—and here again award-winning titles and authors abound. Storybooks and picture books for children are among areas of particular house emphasis; Orchard also publishes ancillary merchandise such as card sets. Children's Press concentrates on special series projects.

Orchard emphasizes individual trade titles and series. Representative titles: *The Cats of Mrs. Calamari* by John Stadler; *Matilda the Moocher* by Diana Cain Blumenthal; *A Is for Asia* by Cynthia Chin-Lee (illustrated by Yumi Heo); *1,000 Miles in 12 Days: Pro Cyclists on Tour* by David Hautzig; *Counting Our Way to Maine* by Maggie Smith; *Griffin's Castle* by Jenny Nimmo; *The Moonglow Roll-O-Rama* by Dav Pilkey; *Homeless* (written and photographed by Bernard Wolf).

Children's Press series for ages three and up include: Bear and Alligator Tales; Childhood Fantasies & Fears; Circle the Year with Holidays; Cornerstones of Freedom; Extraordinary People; First Science; From Sea to Shining Sea; Get Set . . . Go!; Getting to Know the World's Greatest Artists; Getting to Know the World's Greatest Composers; Holiday Collection; Just One More; I Can Be; Learning About Horses; Little Brown Bear; Many Voices, One Song; Math Counts; My First Holiday Books; My First Reader; New True Books; People of Distinction; Picture-Story Biographies; Rookie Biographies; Rookie Read-About Science; Rookie Read-About Science Big Books; Rookie Readers; A World of Difference; Walkabout; Start-Off Stories.

Cornerstones of Freedom series titles: *African-Americans in the Thirteen Colonies* and *The Disability Rights Movement* by Deborah Kent; *The Transcontinental Railroad* by Peter Anderson; *The Liberty Bell* by Gail Sakurai; *Building the Capital City* by Marlene Targ Brill.

Little Brown Bear series titles: *Little Brown Bear Dresses Himself*; *Little Brown Bear Helps His Mama*; *Little Brown Bear Is Going on a Trip*; *Little Brown Bear Takes a Bath*.

New True Books is a series that seeks to provide answers to many basic questions children may have about animals, the environment, the human body, space, sports, and the like.

Children's Press also publishes selected series in Spanish: Sea to Shining Sea; Holiday Books; My First Reader; Rookie Read-About®; Rookie Readers®.

Grolier All-Pro Biographies represents a new series targeted to ages 9–12. Perseverance, courage, and the personal will to succeed are the qualities that bind the athletes profiled in this new series of sports biographies. Selected titles include *Cedrick Ceballos*; *John Elway*; *Dan Marino*; *Orlando Merced*; *Hakeem Olajuwon*; *Lyn St. James*; *Steve Young*.

Query letters and SASEs should be directed to:

Neal Porter, President and Publisher

Maggie Herold, Executive Editor

GROVE/ATLANTIC, INC.

841 Broadway
New York, NY 10003
212-614-7850

Grove/Atlantic publishes trade nonfiction and fiction; these works often display a contemporary cultural bent or an issues-oriented edge. Grove Press and Atlantic Monthly Press, two previously independent houses, are united under the Grove/Atlantic, Inc. corporate crest. Grove/Atlantic operates from the former Grove headquarters on Broadway, (with Atlantic having relocated from its previous digs at nearby Union Square West). Grove/Atlantic operates essentially as one house while maintaining the distinction of two major imprints. (See separate subentries below for both Atlantic Monthly Press and Grove Press.)

Grove Press/Atlantic holds a tradition of publishing arresting literature—from the writing of Samuel Beckett and William S. Burroughs to Jean Genet and Marguerite Duras, from John Kennedy Toole and J. P. Donleavy to Henry Miller and Jeanette Winterson. The house initiated an aggressive program to repackage these modern classics as well as to return to print the work of such celebrated writers as Terry Southern, Robert Coover, Jerzy Kosinski, Frederick Barthelme, Patricia Highsmith, Aharon Appelfeld, Barry Hannah, and Kenzaburo Oe. In a marketplace it sees as increasingly dominated by ephemera, Grove/Atlantic is committed to publishing serious books that last and to introducing classic books to a new generation of readers.

Subsequent to the above-noted Grove–Atlantic merger—with Atlantic most decidedly the major partner—speculation was that Atlantic had bought Grove essentially for Grove's extensive, internationally renowned backlist; Atlantic would presumably vampirize Grove's backlist, then cast aside the dry husk of Grove Press to any interested bidders. Happily, such tiresome prognostications have not come to pass; the publishing image of Grove/Atlantic is, if anything, more finely honed under the auspices of the umbrella house. (See separate subentries below.)

Grove/Atlantic books are distributed by Publishers Group West.

ATLANTIC MONTHLY PRESS

Atlantic Monthly Press paces the spectrum of commercial categories, publishing hardcover and trade paperback editions in memoirs, belles lettres, history, social sciences, current affairs, natural history, ethnology, lifestyle, fashion, and cuisine, in addition to literary and popular fiction. AMP authors have over the years garnered an enormous wealth of recognition for their work, including Pulitzers, Nobels, and National Book Awards. The AMP Traveler series encompasses nonfiction works that offer unstinting looks at nations, cultures, and peoples of the world.

Atlantic Monthly Press has long been representative of the highest aims of American publishing—with a list that features quality writing, fine production, and strong commercial presence. Atlantic Monthly Press was inaugurated originally (in 1917) to be primarily a book-publishing vehicle for writers associated with *Atlantic Monthly* magazine. From 1925 through 1984 the press was an imprint of Boston's Little, Brown. Atlantic Monthly Press was bought by Carl Navarre in 1985, and under current owner-publisher Morgan Entrekin (who bought out Navarre in 1991), AMP (now in consort with Grove) continues as a leading force in American letters.

Representing Atlantic nonfiction: *Within the Context of No Context* by George W. S. Trow; *Merrill Markoe's Guide to Love* (humor) by Merrill Markoe; *The Lucifer Principle: A Scientific Expedition into the Forces of History* by Howard Bloom; *United Nations: The First Fifty Years* by Stanley Meisler; *Twilight of the Habsburgs: The Life and Times of Emperor Francis Joseph* by Alan Palmer; *The Price of Experience: Money, Power, Image, and Murder in Los Angeles* by Randall Sullivan; *The Enemies List* by P. J. O'Rourke (with contributions from the readers of *The American Spectator* magazine); *Yakuza Diary: Doing Time in the Japanese Underworld* by Christopher Seymour; *A Flyfisher's World* by Nick Lyons (drawings by Mari Lyons); and *The Little Book of Weddings: Anthology* (a keepsake/gift book) (edited by Will Balliett).

Fiction and literature from AMP: *On the Couch: Great American Stories About Therapy* (edited by Erica Kates); *A Stolen Tongue* by Sheri Holman; *Sewer, Gas & Electric: The Public Works Trilogy* by Matt Ruff; *The Ordinary Seaman* by Francisco Goldman; *Grey Area* by Will Self; *Worst Fears* by Fay Weldon; *Dead Folks* (a Detective Sergeant Mulheisen mystery) by Jon A. Jackson.

GROVE PRESS

Grove Press accents trade nonfiction and fiction with a sharp cultural consciousness and literary flair. The house continues to expand on its powerful backlist base by engaging at the forefront of publishing trends: Grove publishes a line of feature-film screenplays and has instituted a new poetry series.

Grove Press was founded in 1952 by literary trailblazer Barney Rosset, who established a tradition of enterprising lists that featured some of the finest and most fearless writing from around the globe. This literary institution was purchased by Ann Getty in 1985; in league with the British-based house of Weidenfeld & Nicholson, the publisher (briefly) operated under the sobriquet Grove Weidenfeld. With the early retreat of the Weidenfeld interests, the fate of Grove was a popular topic of publishing tattle—rumored by some to be perpetually on the block, both prior and subsequent to the house's merger with Atlantic Monthly Press.

Throughout these corporate shifts, Grove nevertheless extended its distinguished reputation, with a masterly mix of backlist offerings as well as commercially successful and stimulating new titles—as befits the Grove tradition.

The Grove nonfiction list covers biography and memoirs, popular culture worldwide, literary criticism, history and politics, fine crafts and art, and cuisine.

Titles here include: *How I Became Hettie Jones* by Hettie Jones; *Che Guevara: A Revolutionary Life* by Jon Lee Anderson; *Reviving the Spirit: A Generation of African Americans Goes Home to Church* by Beverly Hall Lawrence; *Please Kill Me: The Uncensored History of Punk* by Legs McNeil and Gillian McCain, *Bound and Gagged: Pornography and the Politics of Fantasy in America* by Laura Kipnis, *ClitNotes: A Sapphic Sampler* (memoir) by Holly Hughes, *New Orleans: Behind the Masks of America's Most Exotic City* by Carol Flake, and *The Language of Vision: Meditations on Myth and Metaphor* by Jamake Highwater.

In fiction, Grove owns a historic commitment to literature that explodes boundaries, having published such authors as Kathy Acker, William S. Burroughs, Robert Coover, Thulani Davis, Jack Kerouac, Milan Kundera, Henry Miller, Bharati Mukherjee, Hubert Selby Jr., and Diane Williams. Grove publishes a wide variety of world literature in translation, has a strong drama list, and produces a significant poetry list.

Indicative of Grove fiction and literary works: *Pussy, King of the Pirates* by Kathy Acker (which ties in with the independently produced grunge/punk musical version on CD, featuring author Acker and the Mekons music group, with graphics by S. Clay Wilson); *Leaving Las Vegas* by John O'Brien; *Wild at Heart* by Barry Gifford; *Bongwater* by Michael Hornburg; *The Dream Police* by Dennis Cooper; *99 Poems in Translation* (selected by Harold Pinter, Geoffrey Godbert, and Anthony Astbury); *Briar Rose* and *Pinocchio in Venice* by Robert Coover; *Elvisey* and *Ambient* by Jack Womack; *Paradise Overdose* by Brian Antoni; *Meeting the Master* by Elissa Wald; *The Ages of Lulu* by Almudena Grandes; *Behind Closed Doors* and *The Butcher and Other Erotica* by Alina Reyes (both volumes translated from the French by David Watson); *The Water Buddha Drinks* by Banana Yoshimoto (translated from the Japanese by Ann Sherif); *Remnants of the First Earth* and *Black Eagle Child: The Facepaint Narratives* by Ray A. Young Bear; *The Shadow Catcher* and *Self-Portrait with Woman* by Andrzej Szczypiorski (translated from the Polish by John Johnston); *Chairman Mao Would Not Be Amused: Fiction from Today's China* (edited by Howard Goldblatt).

Backlist literary classics include the freshly designed reissue of major works (including collections) authored by the Marquis de Sade: *The 120 Days of Sodom and Other Writings*; *Juliette*; *Justine*; *Philosophy in the Bedroom and Other Writings*.

Grove/Atlantic Monthly editors acquire in all areas consistent with house description. Prospective authors please note that Grove/Atlantic no longer accepts unsolicited material. However, you may still send a query or (occasionally) talk directly with an editor before sending a manuscript. Query letters and SASEs should be directed to:

Morgan Entrekin, Publisher

Joan Bingham, Editor

Jim Moser, Executive Editor

Anton Muller, Senior Editor

GULF PUBLISHING COMPANY

P.O. Box 2608
Houston, TX 77252-2608
713-520-4444
fax: 713-520-4438
http://www.gulfpub.com/business.html (World Wide Web)

Gulf Publishing Company (founded in 1916) is a leading publisher in the areas of recreation and travel, business and management, training and adult education, and science and technology. As a large and varied media enterprise, Gulf also produces audiotapes, videotapes, and computer software.

Gulf Publishing's regional-interest list covers North America in general as well as the Gulf Coast belt and Texas; a house specialty line offers regional business and legal guides that supplement a strong selection of travel, recreational, and historical works.

In addition, Gulf publishes selectively throughout the gamut of general trade categories, with seasonal lists that include current affairs, political stories, lifestyle and cuisine, some children's books for kids ages nine and up, and occasional fiction. Gulf offers a robust backlist, and a significant portion of Gulf's travel-guide titles are released in periodically updated versions.

Gulf's imprints include Pisces Books (diving and snorkeling guides, as well as titles in history); and Mariner's Atlas Series (maps, charts, and cartographic guides to cruising waters for mariners, anglers, and divers); Texas Monthly Guidebooks and the Texas Monthly Field Guides; Ray Miller's Eyes of Texas historical travel guides. Gulf Publishing also offers a software catalog, videotape training programs, and professional reference books in engineering.

Invitation to authors, editors, organizations, and professional societies: Gulf Publishing Company is recognized across the country and internationally as a leading publisher of quality books on science and technology, recreation and travel, regional-interest subjects, business and management, and training and adult education. Gulf Publishing is always on the lookout for new manuscripts in its areas of interest. Write to (enclose an SASE): William J. Lowe, Editor in Chief, Book Publishing Division, P.O. Box 2608, Houston, TX 77252-2608.

On the Gulf trade list: *America's Regional Cookbook* by Betty Evans; *Contemporary Mexican Cooking* by Anne Lindsay Greer; *More Texas Sayings Than You Can Shake a*

Stick At by Anne Dingus; *Introduction to Space Sciences and Spacecraft Applications* by Bruce A. Campbell and Samuel Walter McCandless, Jr.; *Best Practice Benchmarking* by Sylvia Codling; *Teams: Who Needs Them and Why?* by Ronald J. Recardo, David Wade, Charles A. Mention III, and Jennifer A. Jolly.

Backlist items: *The Denver Chronicle: From a Golden Past to a Mile-High Future* by David Kent Ballast; *Backroads of New England* by Bob Howells; *International Business Case Studies for the Multicultural Marketplace* (edited by Robert T. Moran, David Braaten, and John Walsh); *Solution Selling* by Robert R. Blake and Rachel Kelly McKee; and the children's title *Hank the Cowdog: The Case of the Double Bumblebee Sting* by John R. Erickson.

Gulf Publishing Company's customer-service team manages regional, national, and international sales and distribution, both in-house and through a network of regional sales representatives.

Query letters and SASEs should be directed to:

William J. Lowe, Editor in Chief, Book Publishing Division

HARCOURT BRACE & COMPANY

San Diego office:
525 B Street, Suite 1900
San Diego, CA 92101-4495
619-699-6769; 619-699-6816

New York office:
15 East 26th Street
New York, NY 10010
212-592-1000; 212-592-1120

The Harcourt Brace trade division publishes the gamut of nonfiction categories, as well as some serious and commercial fiction, in hardcover and paperback editions. Special lines include HB's Judaica backlist, literary works in translation, the Harvest imprint (which accents American and international literature and culture in trade paper originals and reprints), Gulliver Books (popular works in hardcover and trade paper for readers of all ages), and HB Miller Accounting Publications.

Harcourt Brace & Company (founded in 1919) has through the decades evolved into a publishing house of prodigious reach. HB's multidimensional sprawl encompasses offices in such diverse locations as Chicago, Orlando, San Diego, Toronto, and New York. Although the trade-publishing program was trimmed markedly through the late 1980s into the early 1990s, Harcourt Brace (formerly Harcourt Brace Jovanovich) remains particularly potent in the arena of educational materials and texts, as well as professional reference.

Among HB subsidiaries are Academic Press, HB Legal and Professional Publications, Johnson Reprint (scholarly and special-interest titles), W. B. Saunders (professional and academic medical publications), and Holt, Rinehart, & Winston (focusing on the educational market from elementary through university levels).

On the Harcourt Brace nonfiction trade list: *Turning Stones: My Days and Nights with Children at Risk* by Marc Parent; *The Grapes of Ralph: Wine According to Ralph Steadman* by Ralph Steadman; *Gardener's Art Through the Ages* by Richard G. Tansey and Fred S. Kleiner; *The Odyssey of a Manchurian* by Belle Yang; *Byrne's Wonderful World of Pool and Billiards: A Cornucopia of Instruction, Strategy, Anecdote, and Colorful Characters* by Robert Byrne; *Ben-Gurion and the Holocaust* by Shabtai Teveth; *Defining Vision: The Battle for the Future of Television* by Joel Brinkley; *Men on Divorce: The Other Side of the Story* (edited by Penny Kaganoff and Susan Spano).

Harcourt Brace fiction and literary works: *Nearer the Moon: From a Journal of Love—The Unexpurgated Diary of Anaïs Nin, 1937–1939* by Anaïs Nin; *Uncertainty* by Michael Larson (translated from the Danish by Lone Thygesen Blecher and George Blecher); *A Book of Luminous Things: An International Anthology of Poetry* (edited by Czeslaw Milosz); *Don't Call It Night* by Amos Oz (translated from the Hebrew by Nicholas de Lange); *The Wall of the Sky, the Wall of the Eye* (science fiction) by Jonathan Lethem; *Pig* by Andrew Cowan; *The Name of a Bullfighter* by Luis Sepúlveda (translated from the Spanish by Suzanne Ruta); *Walking the Black Cat* (poetry) by Charles Simic; *Imaginings of Sand* by André Brink; *Matisse: A Portrait* by Hayden Herrera; *Homosexuality in History* by Colin Spencer; *Nebula Awards: SFWA's Choices for the Best Science Fiction and Fantasy of the Year* (new edition annually; edited by Pamela Sargent).

Harcourt Brace handles its own distribution.

HARVEST BOOKS

Harvest Books, the trade paperback imprint of Harcourt Brace, offers the best from HB's illustrious 77-year publishing history as well as from its distinguished present. The Harvest in Translation Series publishes some of the world's finest literature, many from the distinguished Helen and Kurt Wolff imprint.

Harvest Books publishes fiction, nonfiction, and poetry by some of the most exciting writers and celebrities. Many Harcourt Brace hardcovers are published simultaneously in paperback by Harvest Books.

The Wilderness Experience series (Harvest originals) volumes are written by top nature writers, who act as guides, selecting pieces on a chosen theme from the best writers, environmentalists, and naturalists.

New Wilderness titles: *Echoes from the Summit* (edited by Paul Schullery); *Call of the River* (edited by Page Stegner); *Lure of the Sea* (edited by Joseph E. Brown).

Although Harcourt Brace has greatly reduced its acquisitions of commercially oriented titles, the house is still active in the trade arena. Query letters and SASEs should be directed to:

Daniel H. Farley, Vice President and Publisher (New York and San Diego)
Adult trade books.

Walter Bode, Editor (New York)

Candace Hodges, Assistant Editor (San Diego)

Christa Malone, Editor (San Diego)

(Ms.) Drenka Willen, Editor (New York)
Literary fiction, translations; some poetry.

Vick Austin-Smith, Senior Editor (San Diego)
Serious and general fiction and nonfiction in hardcover and paperback, with emphasis on backlist titles. Some humor.

Diane Sterling, Senior Editor (San Diego)
Translations. Test-preparation books.

Yoji Yamaguchi, Associate Editor (New York)

Jane Isay, Executive Editor (New York)
Nonfiction books; hardcover originals; also works intended for the Harvest trade paper line.

HARCOURT BRACE CHILDREN'S BOOKS

Harcourt Brace children's categories include picture books, easy readers, nonfiction, fiction, poetry, big books, older readers, and reference books.

Harcourt Brace produces a full offering of children's books in hardcover and paperback. Many HB titles are presented as books for all ages—intended to embrace a wide readership range.

The house features several distinct imprints for young readers. Among them: Jane Yolen Books, Gulliver Books, Gulliver Green, Gulliver Books in Paperback, Browndeer Press, Red Wagon Books, Magic Carpet Books, HB Big Books, HB Creative Curriculum Connections, and the paperback lines Odyssey and Voyager Books—along with a lineup of author videos. Libros Viajeros is the Voyager line of Spanish-language books.

On the HB children's list: *Hobby: The Young Merlin Trilogy* by Jane Yolen; *Bright and Early Thursday Evening: A Tangled Tale* (dreamed by Audrey Wood; imagined by Don Wood); *Moonbathing* by Liz Rosenberg (illustrated by Stephen Lambert); *Dig Hole, Soft Mole* by Carolyn Lesser (illustrated by Laura Regan); *Hilda Hen's Scary Night* by Mary Wormell; *Puppies, Dogs, and Blue Northers: Reflections on Being Raised by a Pack of Sled Dogs* by Gary Paulsen (illustrated by Ruth Wright Paulsen); *Cecil Bunions and the Midnight Train* by Betty Paraskevas (illustrated by Michael Paraskevas); *And the Earth Trembled: The Creation of Adam and Eve* by Shulamith Levey Oppenheim (illustrated by Neil Waldman).

Unsolicited manuscripts are no longer accepted. Editors now work exclusively through literary agents. Query letters and SASEs should be directed to:

Diane D'Andrade, Senior Editor (San Diego)

Allyn Johnson, Senior Editor (San Diego)

Karen Grove, Editor (San Diego)

HARCOURT BRACE LEGAL AND PROFESSIONAL PUBLISHING DIVISION

Harcourt Brace's Legal and Professional division is based in Chicago, Illinois. This division specializes in publications for lawyers and law students. There are more than 850,000 lawyers in the United States, and experts predict that by the year 2000 the number will exceed one million. The lawyer market is one of the largest professional markets in the world—it outnumbers all doctors and accountants combined!

Sample legal titles: *Proceed with Caution: A Diary of the First Year at One of America's Largest, Most Prestigious Law Firms* by William Formon; *The 100 Best Law Firms to Work for in America* by Kim Alayne Walton; *What Lawyers Earn: Getting Paid What You're Worth* by Edward Clough; *Checkerboard Careers: How Surprisingly Successful Attorneys Got to the Top . . . and How You Can, Too!* by William Wise.

HARLEQUIN BOOKS
SILHOUETTE BOOKS

300 East 42nd Street 6th Floor
New York, NY 10017
212-682-6080

Harlequin and Silhouette publish romance novels, love stories, and women's fiction. With commanding emphasis on these interrelated categories, the publisher is always experimenting with inventive, distinctive lines that explore new approaches to the age-old tradition of tales of amour.

The Harlequin Books New York office issues several Harlequin series; the rest of the list is published from the Harlequin Enterprises base in Ontario, Canada (please see directory of Canadian publishers and editors) and the house's United Kingdom branch (contact information for which is listed under the Harlequin listing in the Canadian section). Silhouette Books (a division of Harlequin with editorial offices in New York) is profiled here in a separate subentry below.

Both Harlequin and Silhouette provide editorial guidelines for writers who wish to submit manuscripts for publishing consideration. Included in these materials are series requirements—including tips for authors regarding plot and character (some of which are applicable to other fiction-genre areas), as well as nuts-and-bolts advice pertaining to the preferred physical properties of manuscripts they review.

HARLEQUIN BOOKS

Harlequin Books is an innovator—not only in the romance category field, but in defining and refining the market for women's fiction in general. The Harlequin enterprise continues to access that important market sector through venues that range from direct marketing to discount-department-store wire racks to the woodgrained shelves of major book-chain superstores.

A précis of the Harlequin Books American lines follows.

Harlequin American Romance is an exciting series of passionate and emotional love stories—contemporary, engrossing, and uniquely American. These are longer, satisfying novels of conflict and challenge, stories of modern men and women dealing with life and love in today's changing world. Harlequin American Romance offers a lineup of contemporary, upbeat, action-packed novels, set in a world where everything is possible—not problem-based or introspective. These stories feature a characteristically self-assured, perceptive American woman as heroine. The hero is a dynamic American man who is irresistible, whether he's rough around the edges, earthy, slick, or sophisticated. Sizzling repartee and one-upmanship are hallmarks of the characters' attraction.

Harlequin Intrigue offers something unique in the world of romance fiction: a compelling blend of romance, action, and suspense. These are complex mysteries, full of twists and turns, combined with thrilling contemporary romances in the finest Harlequin tradition. Intrigue . . . because romance can be quite an adventure. Harlequin Intrigue may be seen as an exciting presentation of contemporary romance within such genre formats as mystery, suspense, espionage, woman-in-jeopardy, adventure, and puzzles. The love story is central to the mystery at the level of the novel's premise. The heroine and her hero must be indispensable in solving the mystery or completing whatever adventure they undertake. Their lives are on the line, as are their hearts.

Harlequin Historicals are tales of yesterday written for today's women. This distinctly different line delivers a compelling and quickly paced love story with all the scope of a traditional historical novel. Passionate romance and historical richness combined to give Harlequin Historicals a unique flavor. Harlequin Historicals are conceived as sweeping period romances and range from Medieval sagas to lighthearted Westerns and everything in between. These romance titles should be authentically detailed and realistic (to provide atmosphere, rather than a history lesson). Heroes and heroines are equally strong willed, with their relationship the focus of the story. The writing should be rich and evocative, with the characters bringing the material alive so that the reader may connect with and appreciate the attributes of the historical setting. The story focus is on the heroine and how one man changes her life forever; the stories must have depth and complexity: subplots and important secondary characters are necessary items here.

Length of manuscript and level of sensuality vary from series to series; contact Harlequin for detailed editorial guidelines.

Harlequin is distributed to the book trade by Simon & Schuster.

When corresponding with Harlequin, please specify the series for which your manuscript is intended. Query letters and SASEs should be directed to:

Debra Matteucci, Senior Editor and Editorial Coordinator
Harlequin American Romance and Harlequin Intrigue.

Tracy Farrell, Senior Editor
Harlequin Historicals.

Margaret O'Neill Marbury, Associate Editor
Harlequin Historicals.

Karen Kosztolnyik, Associate Editor
Harlequin Historicals.

Denise O'Sullivan, Editor
Harlequin American Romance and Harlequin Intrigue.

(Ms.) Huntley Fitzpatrick, Associate Editor
Harlequin American Romance and Harlequin Intrigue.

SILHOUETTE BOOKS
300 East 42nd Street
New York, NY 10017
212-682-6080

Silhouette Books publishes adult category romances set in a contemporary milieu. Authors must indicate with their submissions for which series their work is intended. Silhouette Books was previously a major competitor of Harlequin Enterprises, its current parent company. A summary of the Silhouette romance lines follows.

Silhouette Romance is the house's original line of romance fiction. Silhouette Romance tales are contemporary stories of change and challenge, often in exotic settings. They focus on women who must choose between their desire for the man they love and their ideal of romantic love. Exotic settings provide lush background for joyful lovers. Although the hero and heroine do not make love unless married, continuing sexual tension keeps the reader engaged. Silhouette encourages writers to come up with new twists, and new writers are welcome.

Silhouette Desire is an exciting series with a strong emotional impact. Built on believable situations about how two people grow and develop, the plots explore the emotional and physical aspects of love that create a meaningful relationship between two people. Silhouette Desire accents the sensuous side of romance. These books are written for today's woman, whether innocent or experienced. The conflict should be emotional, springing naturally from within the characters. The characters do not have to be married to make love, but lovemaking is not taken lightly. New slants on tried-and-true formulas are welcome. Secondary characters and subplots must blend with the core story.

Silhouette Special Edition romances are substantial contemporary tales that probe deeply into their characters. The depth of the characters heightens the drama of the plot—the issues that are important to the characters should be important to the reader. Sensuality may be sizzling or subtle. The plot can run the gamut from the wildly innovative to the comfortably traditional. The novel's depth and emotional vividness should contribute to the overall effect of a very special romance. Silhouette Special Editions are longer, sophisticated novels with more complex plots and fully developed characters. The contemporary situations follow the romantic tension that develops between the hero and heroine as they overcome real-life problems facing their relationship.

Silhouette Intimate Moments features characters swept into a magical world larger than life. These works explore new directions by setting the romantic fiction within the framework of today's mainstream novels: glamour, melodrama, suspense, and adventure. Let your imagination be your guide. Silhouette Intimate Moments is the most sensual Silhouette line. These exciting stories of quest, romance, and fantasy take place in exotic, glamorous settings. They are stories that whisk the reader away into a special world where passions are larger than life.

Silhouette Yours Truly are romances for the 1990s—modern, upbeat, and very sexy! The hero and heroine meet, directly or indirectly, through a form of written communication. They are stories that are fun, flirtatious, and entertaining. Silhouette Yours Truly features short, sassy tales with a contemporary, modern tone; the story opens with some form of written communication, such as a personal ad, invitation, or letter—leading unexpectedly to meeting, dating . . . and marrying Mr. Right.

Manuscript length and other series requirements vary; detailed editorial guidelines are available from the publisher.

Silhouette is distributed through Simon & Schuster.

When querying, please specify the series for which your work is intended. Query letters and SASEs should be directed to:

Isabel Swift, Editorial Director

Leslie Wainger, Senior Editor and Editorial Coordinator
Silhouette Intimate Moments and Silhouette Yours Truly.

Tara Gavin, Senior Editor and Editorial Coordinator
Silhouette Special Edition and Silhouette Steeple Hill (new imprint; write for guidelines).

Joan Marlowe Golan, Senior Editor
Silhouette Romance.

Melissa Senate, Senior Editor
Silhouette Desire.

Marcia Book Adirim, Editor
Silhouette contact for Love and Laughter (published through Harlequin Canadian offices).

Gail Chasan, Editor

Christine Grace, Editor

Mary Theresa Hussey, Editor

Melissa Jeglinski, Editor

Karen Taylor Richman, Editor

Lynda Curnyn, Associate Editor

Ann Leslie Tuttle, Assistant Editor
Silhouette Desire.

Debra Robertson, Assistant Editor

HARMONY BOOKS
(See Crown Publishing Group under Random House)

HARPERCOLLINS PUBLISHERS
HARPERBUSINESS
HARPERPRISM
REGANBOOKS
HARPERCOLLINS CHILDREN'S BOOKS
HARPERCOLLINS SAN FRANCISCO
WESTVIEW PRESS

New York offices:
10 East 53rd Street
New York, NY 10022-5299
212-207-7000

HarperCollins Publishers offers a program that spans a full spectrum of commercial, trade, professional, and academic interest within a number of interlocked divisions (located on both the east and west coasts, as well as in the Rockies). HarperCollins projects are released in hardcover and paperback, as well as multimedia editions.

Among the HarperCollins east-coast American components are HarperPerennial (trade paper originals and reprints), HarperPaperback (mass-market), and BasicBooks (scholarly and professional academic with significant commercial trade crossover). A special high-concept HarperCollins program is the ReganBooks imprint.

HarperLibros publishes a wide range of works in the Spanish language. Harper-Collins is home to a number of children's-book and reference divisions. (See separate subentries below.)

The HarperCollins San Francisco wing features the Harper San Francisco division, with its special emphasis on trade titles in spirituality, awareness, and healing (please see Harper San Francisco entry in directory of Religious, Spiritual, and Inspirational publishers).

Westview Press accents scholarly and academic works, with some trade crossover. HarperCollins also owns Hazelden Publishing Group and Zondervan (see entries for Hazelden and Zondervan in directory of Religious, Spiritual, and Inspirational publishers).

HarperCollins Publishers is the current corporate embodiment of the venerable firm (founded in 1817) previously known as Harper & Row. HarperCollins is part of Rupert Murdoch's transnational communications empire, which includes the New York *Post* newspaper and Twentieth Century Fox. For all its international divisions, imprints, and subsidiaries, HarperCollins is a publishing colossus with a well-defined image: The house's flaming-torch logo signifies a reputation for superior editorial quality and mighty commercial carriage.

George Craig, President and Chief Executive Officer, HarperCollins Publishers, issued a corporate mandate: HarperCollins intends to meet the unprecedented challenges that face the publishing industry and is committed to being an organization that leads in those behaviors and practices critical to shared success. In order to achieve this goal, HarperCollins has embarked on an initiative called Vision & Values. At the core of this initiative is our Vision Statement:

> Our Goal is to be the world's best publisher, a growth company with excellence in products, customer service, and financial performance. We will treat each other, our authors, customers, and business partners with care, integrity, and respect. We will attract and retain the best people by creating an environment where managers act as leaders and coaches and all employees are encouraged to develop and excel. We will face reality and embrace change in all aspects of our business life.

Within months of these 1996 declarations George Craig was replaced. To engage corporate challenges head on, Anthea Disney, President and Chief Executive Officer HarperCollins, announced realignment of the trade-publishing wing as well as elimination of former HarperCollins divisions HarperReference and BasicBooks (including the firing of all HarperReference and BasicBooks editors). HarperCollins then announced cancellation of a major portion of its list, in order to concentrate on the books most worthy of editorial and marketing resources.

The trade group was synthesized into three primary divisions, each with its own entrepreneurial mission: HarperCollins Trade (commercial nonfiction and fiction); HarperBusiness (top-of-the-list nonfiction in business and finance); HarperPrism (thrillers, suspense fiction). Selected nonfiction titles may be stamped with the BasicBooks imprint, though that house is otherwise suspended.

HarperCollins handles its own distribution.

HARPERCOLLINS TRADE DIVISION

HarperCollins produces adult hardcover books, trade paperbacks, and mass-market paperback editions that cover the breadth of trade publishing categories, including feature biographies (celebrity, sports, and historical), business books, mysteries and thrillers, popular culture, humor, inspiration, and how-to (including cookbooks and health), in addition to works across most popular reference categories. HarperStyle specializes in illustrated works keyed to contemporary lifestyle, design, and culture. Many HarperCollins frontlist titles are also available on HarperAudio.

Representing HarperCollins general nonfiction and popular titles: *The Plain Truth of Things* (edited by Colin Greer and Herbert Kohl); *Natural Woman, Natural Menopause* by Marcus Laux, N.D., and Christine Conrad; *Super Sexual Orgasm: A Woman's Guide to Ultimate Pleasure* by Barbara Keesling, Ph.D.; *Shelter for the Spirit: How to Make Your Home a Haven in a Hectic World* by Victoria Moran; *Manifest Your Destiny: The Nine Spiritual Principles for Getting Everything You Want* by Dr. Wayne Dyer; *How To Raise a Child with a High E.Q.: A Parent's Guide to Emotional Intelligence* by Lawrence E. Shapiro, Ph.D.; *Love Beyond Life: The Healing Power of After-Death Communications* by Joel Martin and Patricia Romanowski; *The Blues Ain't Nothing but a Good Woman Feeling Bad: Healing the Hidden Depression of Black Women* by Charlotte Watson Sherman; *Bouncing Back: How to Survive Anything . . . and I Mean Anything* by Joan Rivers; *The Three-Day Energy Fast* by Pamela Serure; *The Circle of Simplicity* by Cecile Andrews; *Maye and Faye's Building and Loan* by Maye Smith and Faye Hudson with Leslie Whitaker; *When a Parent Has Cancer: A Guide to Caring for Your Children* by Wendy S. Harpham, M.D.; *The Confidence Course: Seven Steps to Self-Fulfillment* by Walter Anderson; *True Love: Real-Life Stories* by Robert Fulghum; *Triangles: What You Need to Know About Affairs* by Lana Stahell, Ph.D.; *The Secret School: Preparation for Contact* by Whitley Strieber; *Color-Blind: Seeing Beyond Race in a Race-Obsessed World* by Ellis Cose; *A Return to Love: Reflections on the Principles of a Course in Miracles* by Marianne Williamson.

HarperCollins offers fiction and literary works on a diversified program that includes commercial novels and standout category titles, in addition to select literary works. HarperCollins has published such authors as Anne Rivers Siddons, Ursula K. Le Guin, Sue Miller, Len Deighton, Allen Ginsberg, Barbara Taylor Bradford, Oscar Hijuelos, Tony Hillerman, Leon Uris, and William Lashner. HarperPrism is the imprint designation for selected high-concept titles in science fiction, fantasy, horror, and thrillers.

Fiction from HarperCollins: *The Fallen Man* by Tony Hillerman; *Charity: A Bernard Samson Novel* by Len Deighton; *A Woman's Place* by Barbara Delinsky; *The Price of Blood* by Chuck Logan; *Trading Reality* by Michael Ridpath; *The Measured Man* by Howard Owen; *Deal on Ice* by Les Standiford; *Monkey King* by Patricia Chao; *Mommy and the Money* by Nancy Goldstone; *The Dancing Floor* by Barbara Michaels; *The Right Man for the Job* by Mike Magnuson; *Earl in the Yellow Shirt* by Janice Daugharty; *The Escape Artist* by Diane Chamberlain; *Illusions* by Janet Dailey.

Further representative of the HarperCollins program in the popular literary arts: *The Trouble with a Bad Fit: A Novel of Food, Fashion, and Mystery* by Camilla T. Crespi; *Stainless* by Todd Grimson (HarperPrism); *The Only World* (poems) by Lynda Hull (edited by David Wojahn); *Heat Wave* by Penelope Lively; *What Keeps Me Here* (stories) by Rebecca Brown.

Paperback original titles from HarperPerennial: *3rd Rock from the Sun: The Official Tie-In* by Bonnie and Terry Turner; *The Darden Dilemma: 12 Black Writers on Justice and Race Relations in America* (edited by Ellis Cose); *Tonics: 200 Recipes That Improve the Body & the Mind* by Robert A. Barnett; *Get Your Rear in Gear: Firming, Toning, and Shaping Your Butt* by Harry Hanson with Robin K. Levinson; *The Complete Book of Shoulders and Arms* by Kurt Brungardt; *The Green Kitchen Handbook: The Simple, Sensible Guide to Keeping the Most Important Room in Your Home Healthy* by Annie Berthold-Bond and Mothers & Others for a Livable Planet (foreword by Meryl Streep).

The HarperPaperbacks program includes a strong lineup in mystery, suspense, and thrillers (primarily reprints, along with a few originals). HarperPaperbacks also publishes a select number of mass-market true crime titles, as well as a few hardcover originals in commercial fiction genres. HarperMonogram is a mass-market imprint that specializes in women's fiction, including historical romances, time-travel, and commercial contemporaries.

HARPERPRISM

HarperPrism concentrates on commercial, high-concept thrillers and hones the leading edge in frontlist suspense fiction. HarperPrism has produced a limited selection of popular nonfiction with a contemporary-to-futurist bent. HarperPrism fiction and literary works cover a select group of suspense and thriller categories and modes: fantasy and science fiction, technical thrillers, medical thrillers, action tales and adventure novels, military fiction, mystery and suspense fiction, occasional outstanding horror. Nonfiction areas of interest include: popular science, history and future of science and technology, topical commentary, unexplained phenomena (including UFOs and the like).

HARPERBUSINESS

HarperBusiness heralds the latest trends of thought in such fields as management, finance, and international business. Business books from HarperCollins are most often (but not always) presented under the HarperBusiness banner. The HarperCollins business list is distinguished by gifted, individualistic author voices geared to attract a wide popular readership in addition to interested business professionals. HarperCollins also releases comprehensive and specifically targeted professional reference works and career how-tos.

On the HarperCollins business list: *The Yankelovich Report on Generational Marketing: Reaching America's Three Consumer Generations* by J. Walker Smith, Ph.D., and Ann S. Clurman; *The Agile Investor: Profiting from the End of Buy and Hold* by Stephen Leeb with Roger Conrad; *Unbridled Power: What Every Citizen Should Know About the IRS* by Shelley L. David; *Intellectual Capital: Realizing Your Company's True Value by Finding Its Hidden Brainpower* by Leif Edvinsson and Michael S. Malone; *From Mind to Market: The Definitive Guide to Retailing in the New Millennium* by Roger D. Blackwell; *The Individualized Corporation: A New Doctrine for Managing People* by Sumantra Ghoshal and Christopher A. Bartlett.

Query letters and SASEs should be directed to:

HarperCollins Trade Division

Query letters and SASEs should be directed to:

Lawrence Ashmead, Executive Editor
Fiction: mysteries, thrillers. Nonfiction: biographies and autobiographies, gardening, general self-help.

Cynthia Barrett, Editor
Fiction: literary and commercial. Nonfiction: biographies and memoirs, military and general history, nutrition, medicine, celebrity stories, popular culture, true crime, sports, current events, business. Works with Gladys Justin Carr (see below).

(Mr.) Cass Canfield, Jr., Publisher, Icon Editions
Nonfiction: history; social and intellectual issues; gardening; foods, wine, and cookery; art, design, and architecture. Fiction: Latin American translations.

Gladys Justin Carr, Associate Publisher
Fiction: literary and commercial. Nonfiction: biographies and memoirs, military and general history, nutrition, medicine, celebrity stories, popular culture, true crime, sports, current events, business.

Linda Cunningham, Vice President and Publishing Director, HarperAudio
General and popular reference: how-to/self-help, popular culture, college and career, family resources, sports, hobbies and recreation, consumer, business, specialized dictionaries. Acquires audio projects for the HarperAudio program.

Joelle Delbourgo, Senior Vice President, Associate Publisher, and Editor in Chief
Oversees hardcover program and also acquires quality paperbacks.

(Mr.) Eamon Dolan, Senior Editor
Fiction: literary and suspense. Nonfiction: science, social issues, cyberculture, health, humor, ethnic interest.

Susan Friedland, Senior Editor
Food, cookbooks, literary history.

Robert Jones, Executive Editor, HarperPerennial
Quality literary fiction. Nonfiction: social issues, current affairs, psychology.

(Ms.) Terry Karten, Executive Editor
Quality literary fiction. Nonfiction: biographies and autobiographies, history, current issues, women's issues.

(Ms.) Trena Keating, Associate Editor
Fiction: literary and commercial, women's; especially interested in contemporary western American settings. Nonfiction: contemporary issues, inspirational, spiritual, self-improvement, memoir.

Diane Reverand, Publisher and Editor in Chief, Reverand Books
Personalized approach to highly commercial works in trade nonfiction as well as breakthrough fiction.

Eric Steel, Senior Editor
Select fiction. Nonfiction: current issues, politics, culture, history, memoirs, biographies.

Mauro DiPreta, Senior Editor
Nonfiction: pop-culture, humor, commercial nonfiction.

Laureen Connelly Rowland, Editor
Humor/pop culture, business, literary fiction, self-help, and spirituality. Looking for projects written by and geared specifically toward the twentysomething audience.

Peternelle Van Arsdale, Senior Editor, HarperPerennial
Fiction: literary and commercial. Nonfiction: African-American and multicultural studies, gender studies, current issues, women's issues.

Hugh Van Dusen, Executive Editor, HarperPerennial
History, biography, spirituality, self-help. Fiction and nonfiction reprints and originals in quality paperback.

Buz Wyeth, Executive Editor
Fiction: commercial and literary. Nonfiction: biography, history, inspiration, human interest, popular reference, nature and outdoor activities, military affairs.

HarperBusiness

Query letters and SASEs should be directed to:

(Mr.) Adrian Zackheim, Senior Vice President and Publisher
Business books; general nonfiction.

David Conti, Executive Editor
Investment subjects, nonfiction business stories.

HarperPrism

Query letters and SASEs should be directed to:

John Silbersack, Senior Vice President and Publishing Director, HarperPrism
Science fiction/fantasy, some horror.

John R. Douglas, Senior Editor, HarperPrism and HarperCollins
Fiction: science fiction, adventure, military, mystery, horror. Nonfiction: UFOs, history.

HarperPaperbacks

Query letters and SASEs should be directed to:

Abigail Kamen Holland, Editor, HarperPaperbacks
Mass-market fiction: women's stories in mystery and suspense, romances, Westerns.

Jessica Lichtenstein, Senior Editor, HarperPaperbacks
Wide range of interests in fiction and nonfiction. Commercial nonfiction, including true crime originals. Young-adult fiction is a specialty. Fiction also includes mysteries and commercial women's fiction.

Carolyn Marino, Editor in Chief, Editorial Director, HarperPaperbacks
Mass-market fiction: women's stories in mysteries, suspense, historical romances; some Westerns.

Sharon Morey, Assistant Editor, HarperPaperbacks
Women's fiction, romances.

REGANBOOKS

10 East 53rd Street
New York, NY 10022
212-207-7400

ReganBooks hosts a selective list of general nonfiction and commercial fiction. The house scouts properties with bestseller and high commercial promise. Nonfiction tends to be tailored toward celebrity, personality, and topical issues. In fiction, the house accents extremely commercial big-concept works, especially projects with entertainment- and performance-rights potential.

Nonfiction from Regan: *Mastering the Zone: The Art of Achieving SuperHealth* by Barry Sears, Ph.D., with Mary Goodbody; *The Solution: The Six Causes and Six Cures of Weight Problems* by Laurel Mellin, M.A., R.D.; *Whores of the Court: The Fraud of Psychiatric Testimony and the Rape of American Justice* by Margaret A. Hagen, Ph.D.; *7 Paths to Purity: Spiritual Solutions to Everyday Problems* by Bishop Phillip H. Porter, Jr., with W. Terry Whalin; *Safe, Not Sorry: Keeping Yourself and Your Family Safe in a Violent Age* by Tanya K. Metaksa; *Simple Social Graces: Recapturing the Joys of Victorian Life* by Linda S. Lichter.

Popular works include: *In Contempt* by Christopher Darden with Jess Walter; *Enter Whining* by Fran Drescher; *Slouching Towards Gomorrah: Modern Liberalism and American Decline* by Robert H. Bork.

Regan fiction: *Veritas* (legal thriller) by William Lashner; *Vendetta: Lucky's Revenge* by Jackie Collins; *Microserfs* by Douglas Coupland (author of *Generation X*).

Publishing virtuoso Judith Regan has set the literary world alight with a set of extraordinarily popular titles from such contemporary cultural icons as Howard Stern, Rush Limbaugh, Dennis Rodman, and Beavis and Butthead. HarperCollins launched the ReganBooks enterprise to fully realize Regan's manifold talents. Thus another publishing star is born.

Query letters and SASEs should be directed to:

Judith Regan, President and Publisher

(Ms.) Caron K, Vice President, the Regan Company, and Senior Editor, ReganBooks Acquires books; also develops film projects for the Regan Company.

David Craig, Editor

HARPERCOLLINS CHILDREN'S BOOKS

HarperCollins Children's Books produces hardcovers, trade paperbacks, and mass-market titles in fiction and nonfiction for all readership levels, from preschool through young adult. The HarperFestival and HarperTrophy lines issue primarily novelty publications and paperbacks.

HarperCollins Children's is interested in hardcover picture books, fiction, nonfiction, and poetry, as well as novelty projects. The Harper Arco Iris program of books in the Spanish language covers a wide range of products aimed at children and young adults.

HarperCollins children's titles include: *The Official Carmen Sandiego Clue Book* by Rusel DeMaria; *From Cover to Cover: Evaluating and Reviewing Children's Books* by Kathleen T. Horning.

Favorites from the backlist: *Falling Up* (poems and drawings) by Shel Silverstein; *Falcons Nest on Skyscrapers* by Priscilla Belz Jenkins (illustrated by Megan Lloyd); *Street Music: City Poems* by Arnold Adoff (pictures by Karen Barbour); *Making Music: 6 Instruments You Can Create* by Eddie Herschel Oates (pictures by Michael Koelsch).

Query letters and SASEs should be directed to:

Kate Morgan Jackson, Vice President, Associate Publisher, and Editor in Chief

Stephanie Spinner, Vice President and Editorial Director, HarperTrophy

Mary Alice Moore, Editorial Director, HarperFestival

Sally Doherty, Executive Editor

Robert Warren, Executive Editor

Joanna Cotler, Editorial Director, Joanna Cotler Books

Michael DiCapra, Editorial Director, Michael DiCapra Books

Laura Geringer, Editorial Director, Laura Geringer Books

Phoebe Yeh, Executive Editor

Donz"a Bush, Editor

HARPERCOLLINS SAN FRANCISCO

1160 Battery Street
San Francisco, CA 94111
415-477-4400

HarperCollins San Francisco incorporates several California-based divisions. Harper-Collins San Francisco International Editions publishes imported original titles and reprints originating from HarperCollins divisions outside the U.S. sphere (Australia, New Zealand, South Africa, Canada, and the United Kingdom).

The former imprint Collins Publishers San Francisco moved in the fall of 1996 to New York and combined with HarperStyle to form the illustrated division of HarperCollins Trade.

Harper San Francisco (please see Directory of Religious, Spiritual, and Inspirational Publishers) is a general publishing house with a list that accents books that inspire the mind, body, and spirit, as well as trends in world culture.

WESTVIEW PRESS

5500 Central Avenue
Boulder, CO 80301-2877
303-444-3541
fax: 303-449-3356
westview@harpercollins.com (e-mail)
http://www.harpercollins.com (World Wide Web)
http://www.hcacademic.com (World Wide Web)

Westview's publishing interests include works of nonfiction for the general trade readership in addition to the hefty Westview list in college texts, reference materials, professional academic publications, and scientific symposia. Westview is known for its scholarly lines in social sciences and applied natural sciences, international relations, area studies, domestic and international development, military affairs, political science, history, anthropology, sociology, psychology, government, economics, philosophy, religion, communication, criminology, law, health sciences, environment, energy, agriculture, earth sciences, and biology.

Westview Press is a specialist division of HarperCollins Publishers accenting scientific, scholarly, and academic works for professionals, and works in related topics geared for a popular readership. Westview catalogs numerous mainstream-interest titles in current affairs and popular culture. In addition to its Colorado operation, the Westview enterprise (founded in 1975 as a subsidiary of SCS Communications) includes a vast United Kingdom division and additional offices in San Francisco.

Industry news had Westview on the sales block by the end of 1996; HarperCollins, it was widely reported, sought to integrate their primarily mainstream program by trimming Westview's list, with its individualized distribution and marketing requirements.

Titles from Westview: *American Winescapes: The Cultural Landscapes of America's Wine Country* by Gary L. Peters; *Bloom's Morning: Toothpaste, Toasters, and the Secret Meaning of Everyday Life* by Arthur Asa Berger; *In Search of Elvis: Music, Race, Art, Religion* (edited by Vernon Chadwick); *Same Sex, Different Cultures: Exploring Gay and Lesbian Lives* by Gilbert Herdt; *Opera in the Flesh: Sexuality in Operatic Performance* by Sam Abel; *Eros of the Impossible: The History of Psychoanalysis in Russia* by Alexander Etkind; *Eros: The Myth of Ancient Greek Sexuality* by Bruce S. Thornton; *Palestine and the Palestinians* by Samih K. Farsoun and Christian Zacharia; *Joseph Perl's Revealer of Secrets: The First Hebrew Novel* (translated by Dov Taylor); *Planet Dora: A Memoir of the Holocaust and the Birth of the Space Age* by Yves Beon; *Jesus at 2000* (edited by Marcus J. Borg); *Latin Looks: Latino Images in the Media* (edited by Clara E. Rodriguez); *Dressing in Feathers: The Construction of "The Indian" in American Popular Culture* (edited by S. Elizabeth Bird); *Guide to Native Americans of the Southwest: The Serious Traveler's Guide to People and Places* by Zdenek and Joy M. Salzmann; *Betrayed: A History of Presidential Failure to Protect Black Lives* by Earl Ofari Hutchinson; *Scarlet Memorial: Tales of Cannibalism in Modern China* by Zheng Yi (edited and translated by T. P. Sym); *Leadership: Quotations from History's Greatest Motivators* (edited by Robert A. Fitton); *Nightwatch over Nature: Peoples, Nature, Politics* by Alexander Cockburn.

Query letters and SASEs should be directed to:

Dean Birkenkamp, Editorial Director

Spencer Carr, Editorial Director

Jennifer Knerr, Senior Acquisitions Editor

Susan McEachern, Senior Acquisitions Editor

HARPER SAN FRANCISCO
(See Directory of Religious, Spiritual, and Inspirational Publishers)

HARVARD BUSINESS SCHOOL PRESS
(See Directory of University Presses)

THE HARVARD COMMON PRESS

535 Albany Street
Boston, MA 02118
617-423-5803
fax: 617-695-9794

Harvard Common accents trade nonfiction in the areas of home and the family, small-business guides, travel, cuisine, and lifestyle, and in addition offers a select list of children's books.

The Harvard Common Press (founded in 1976) is a smaller house devoted to the publication of general nonfiction books in hardcover and trade paperback; the press maintains a solid backlist. The company colophon features a representation of a classical javelin thrower on the run—emblematic of the house's athletic publishing vigor.

Harvard Common issues the Best Places to Stay series as part of its travel line; the Gambit Books imprint covers how-to business titles geared to starting up and operating enterprises such as small restaurants, small newspapers, and small theaters, as well as alternative careers for teachers.

Parenting and the family are sectors where Harvard Common shows particular traditional success. Titles: *Getting to Dry: How to Help Your Child Overcome Bedwetting* by Max Maizels, M.D., Diane Rosenbaum, Ph.D., and Barbara Keating, R.N.; *Nursing Mother, Working Mother: The Essential Guide for Breastfeeding and Staying Close to Your Baby After You Return to Work* by Gale Pryor; *The Birth Partner: Everything You Need to Know to Help a Woman Through Childbirth* by Penny Simkin; *Adopting the Older Child* by Claudia Jewett; *Crying Baby, Sleepless Nights: Why Your Baby Is Crying and What You Can Do About It* by Sandy Jones.

Titles in the kitchen arts: *Vegetarian Planet* by Didi Emmons; *Paul Kirk's Championship Barbecue Sauces: 150 Make-Your-Own Sauces, Marinades, Dry Rubs, Wet Rubs, Mops, and Salsas* by Paul Kirk; *Norman Van Aken's Feast of Sunlight* by Norman Van Aken; *The Sugar Mill Caribbean Cookbook: Casual and Elegant Recipes Inspired by the Islands* by Jinx and Jefferson Morgan; *Smoke & Spice: Cooking with Smoke—The Real Way to Barbecue* and *Sublime Smoke: Bold New Flavors Inspired by the Old Art of Barbecue* by Cheryl Alters Jamison and Bill Jamison; *The Gas Grill Gourmet: Great Grilled Food for Everyday Meals and Fantastic Feasts* by A. Cort Sinnes with John Puscheck; *Cold Soups* by Linda Ziedrich.

Representative Harvard Common titles in lifestyle and travel: *The Best Things in New York Are Free* by Marian Hamilton; *Where to Eat in Canada* by Anne Hardy; *A Guide to Public Art in Greater Boston* by Marty Carlock; *Travel Writer's Markets: Where to Sell Your Travel Articles and Place Your Press Releases* by Elaine O'Gara; *Buller's Professional Course in Bartending for Home Study* by Jon Buller.

The Harvard Common Press is represented to the trade by National Book Network.

Query letters and SASEs should be directed to:

Dan Rosenberg, Managing Editor

Bruce Shaw, President

HARVARD UNIVERSITY PRESS
(See Directory of University Presses)

HAZELDEN PUBLISHING GROUP/
HAZELDEN EDUCATIONAL MATERIALS
(See Directory of Religious, Spiritual, and Inspirational Publishers)

HEALTH COMMUNICATIONS, INC.
3201 Southwest 15th Street
Deerfield Beach, FL 33442
954-360-0909
fax: 954-360-0034

Health Communications features nonfiction trade titles in relationships, finance, spirituality, health, empowerment, esteem, and social issues. The publisher has achieved notable success with topical approaches to personal growth, women's issues, addiction and other compulsive behaviors, abuse and trauma, family relationships, and healing.

Health Communications (founded in 1976) publishes with the intent to provide direction for the journey of living. The publisher's issues-orientation is apparent in a list that addresses a family spectrum of interest, encompassing books geared to be read by early reader through adult, as well as targeted market interest segments. Health Communications publishes books in affordable hardcover and trade paperback editions and also produces a line of audiobooks.

Health Communications operates in tandem with sister companies U.S. Journal, U.S. Journal Training, A & D Publications, and Children Are People Too! The program brings together professional caregivers and the broader community in a publishing forum that embraces books, journals, pamphlets, and conferences.

Exemplifying the Health Communications list: *The Little Book of Wisdom* (complied by Richard Torregrossa; illustrated by the author); *The New Beverly Hills Diet: A 35-Day Program for Lifelong Slimhood* by Judy Mazel; *Bradshaw On: The Family, Revised Edition: A New Way of Creating Solid Self-Esteem* by John Bradshaw; *The Sound of the Soul: Discovering the Power of Your Voice* by Arthur Samuel Joseph; *Putting Your Talent to Work: Identifying, Cultivating and Marketing Your Natural Talents* by Lucia Capacchione, Ph.D., and Peggy Van Peit, Ph.D.; *Gifts of the Heart: Stories That Celebrate Life's Defining Moments* by Bettie B. Youngs, Ph.D.; *The Tomorrow Trap: Unlocking the Secrets of the Procrastination-Protection Syndrome* by Karen E. Peterson, Ph.D.; *Online Friendship, Chat-Room Romance and Cybersex: Your Guide to Affairs of the Net* by Michael Adamse, Ph.D., and Sheree Motta, Psy.D.; *Instant Insight: 200 Ways to Create the Life You Really Want* by Jonathan Robinson;

Golden Eggs: Spiritual Wisdom for Birthing Our Lives by Gay Lynn Williamson and David Williamson, D. Min.; *Lasting Purpose: A Mindset for Success* by Sid E. Williams; *Bloom Where You're Planted: Daily Adventures in Self-Inspiration* by Jacques Weisel; *The Daily Journal of Kindness: A Year-Long Guide for Creating Your Own Kindness Revolution* by Meladee McCarty and Hanoch McCarty, Ed.D.

Health Communications published *Chicken Soup for the Soul: 101 Stories to Open the Heart and Rekindle the Spirit* (written and compiled by Jack Canfield and Mark Victor Hansen), an entertaining, uplifting work that features selections from a wide variety of writers. As this book goes to press, the original *Chicken Soup* has been an international bestseller for several years. This book has spawned a number of successful *Chicken Soup* collections. Indeed, if imitation is the sincerest form of flattery, the number of works with allied themes that currently appear under other publishers' imprints is a genuine tribute from the industry to this popular genre originated by the authors and Health Communications.

More titles in this series: *Chicken Soup for the Women's Soul: 101 Stories to Open the Hearts and Rekindle the Spirits of Women* by Jack Canfield, Mark Victor Hansen, Jennifer Read Hawthorne, and Marci Shimoff; *Condensed Chicken Soup for the Soul* by Jack Canfield, Mark Victor Hansen, and Patty Hansen; *A Cup of Chicken Soup for the Soul* by Jack Canfield, Mark Victor Hansen, and Barry Spilchuk; *Chicken Soup for the Soul at Work: 101 Stories of Courage, Compassion & Creativity in the Workplace* by Jack Canfield, Mark Victor Hansen, Martin Rutte, Maida Rogerson, and Tim Clauss.

Backlist titles from Health Communications include: *Garden of the Soul: Lessons on Living in Peace, Happiness and Harmony* by Sri Chinmoy; *Living Simply: Timeless Thoughts for a Balanced Life* by Sara Orem and Larry Demarest; *Reclaiming Pride: Daily Reflections on Gay and Lesbian Life* by Joseph H. Neisen; *The Myth of the Maiden: On Being a Woman* by Joan E. Childs.

Health Communications distributes its own list, as well as those of its sister companies U.S. Journal, Children Are People Too!, U.S. Journal Training, and A&D Publications.

Query letters and SASEs should be directed to:

Christine Belleris, Editorial Director

Mark Colucci, Editorial Assistant

Matthew Diener, Acquisitions Editor

THE HEARST BOOK GROUP
WILLIAM MORROW & COMPANY, INC.
MORROW CHILDREN'S BOOKS
ROB WEISBACH BOOKS
AVON BOOKS
AVON CAMELOT AND AVON FLARE

1350 Avenue of the Americas
New York, NY 10019
212-261-6500

William Morrow & Company and Avon Books are the two primary book-publishing wings of the privately held Hearst Corporation media company. This large publishing operation features multiple imprints that run the spectrum of mainstream commercial trade publishing in nonfiction and fiction, as well as children's books. The house publishes hardcover, trade paper, and mass-market paperback editions. Morrow & Company and Avon Books are distinct divisions with their own extensive individual programs. (Please see separate subentries below.)

WILLIAM MORROW & COMPANY

1350 Avenue of the Americas
New York, NY 10019
212-261-6500

Morrow excels in commercial nonfiction and frontlist fiction covering the full gamut of trade categories. William Morrow & Company (founded in 1926) upholds the tradition established in earlier (and smaller) days, as a publisher of books selected attentively and promoted with care, so that individual titles achieve maximum market potential.

Morrow imprints include Hearst Books, Hearst Marine Books, Fielding Travel Books, Quill (trade paperbacks), and AvoNova (science fiction and fantasy published conjointly with Avon), and a children's division that encompasses Morrow Junior Books, Tambourine Books, Mulberry Books, Beech Tree Books, Greenwillow Books, and Lothrop, Lee & Shepard Books (please see subentries below for Avon Books, Morrow children's lines, and for Avon's Camelot and Flare juveniles imprints).

Rob Weisbach gained acclaim as an editor with uncommon commercial savvy who, during his stint at Bantam, produced a number of celebrity-driven titles that shot straight up the bestseller charts. Weisbach arrived at Morrow as head of his own publishing regime, the imprint known as **Rob Weisbach Books**, with an eye cocked toward high-edge projects including celebrity biographies, popular culture, and juicy investigative scenarios.

Rob Weisbach Books features *It All Begins with Whoopi* by Whoopi Goldberg; *Openly Bob* by Bob Smith; *From Mine Eyes* by Attallah Shabazz. Fiction and the literary arts from Weisbach: *The Melancholy Death of Oyster Boy* by Tim Burton; *Joe and Me* by James Prosek; *Rent* by Jonathan Larson (tie-in with the stage musical); and *The Tenth Justice* by Brad Meltzer.

Exemplifying the popular eclecticism of Morrow's trade nonfiction program: *Don't Know Much About the Civil War: Everything You Need to Know About America's Greatest Conflict But Never Learned* by Kenneth C. Davis; *Tragic Failure: Racial Integration in America* by Tom Wicker; *Humanity's Descent: An Ecological Epic* by Rick Potts; *Fit over Forty: A Revolutionary Plan to Achieve Lifelong Physical and Spiritual Health and Well-Being* by James M. Rippe; *Louisiana Real and Rustic* by Emeril Lagasse and Marcelle Bienvenu (photographs by Brian Smale); *Savoring Spices and Herbs: Recipe Secrets of Flavor, Aroma, and Color* by Julie Sahni; *Phil Simms on Passing: Fundamentals of Throwing the Football* by Phil Simms with Rick Meier.

Morrow fiction is selective and dramatically frontlist. In addition to popular contemporary literature, the house hits heavily through the major mainstream categories of mystery and suspense, science fiction and fantasy, and women's lead fiction. Morrow's fiction roster has featured such authors as Kathleen E. Woodiwiss, Trevor Barnes, Lynda La Plante, Faye Kellerman, Ken Follett, Ed McBain, Kinky Friedman, Piers Anthony, Sidney Sheldon, and John Irving.

Reflecting Morrow's vigorous fiction list: *Darkness, Take My Hand* by Dennis Lehane; *The Boat Ramp* by Andrew Holleran; *Final Victim* by Stephen J. Cannell; *Let the Drum Speak: A Novel of Ancient America* by Linda Lay Shuler; *Simple Simon* by Ryne Douglas Pearson; *Sister* by A. Manette Ansay; *Tumbling* by Diane McKinney Whetstone; *The Vipers' Club* by John H. Richardson.

William Morrow & Company distributes for all its imprints.

Query letters and SASEs should be directed to:

Paul Bresnick, Senior Editor
Nonfiction: humor, show business, sociology, popular biography and autobiography, cartoons, cultural ephemera.

Doris Cooper, Editor
Popular culture, current events, how-to/self-help, topical nonfiction.

Joann Davis, Senior Vice President and Editor in Chief, Eagle Brook
Hardcover and paperback originals; commercial fiction and nonfiction. Initial imprint list accents spirituality, healing, inspiration.

Jacqueline Deval, Associate Publisher, Hearst Books
Tie-ins with magazines and periodicals; projects with topical media appeal—popular personalities, contemporary trends.

Colin Dickerman, Editor, Rob Weisbach Books
Media and other celebrity books. Topical nonfiction; outstanding commercial fiction.

Henry Ferris, Senior Editor
Politics, current events, social issues.

Paul Fedorko, Senior Vice President and Publisher

Pam Hoenig, Executive Editor
Presides over cookbook-publishing program.

Betty Nichols Kelly, Vice President and Editor in Chief

Ben Schafer, Editor
Biography, nonfiction. Literary and cultural history; current culture.

Zachary Schisgal, Editor
Commercial and literary fiction and nonfiction.

(Ms.) Toni Sciarra, Senior Editor
Psychology, health, science, women's issues, relationships, social trends, spirituality.

Rob Weisbach, Publisher, Rob Weisbach Books
Personality and celebrity titles. Frontlist commercial fiction and nonfiction.

MORROW CHILDREN'S BOOKS:
MORROW JUNIOR BOOKS
BEECH TREE BOOKS
GREENWILLOW BOOKS
LOTHROP, LEE & SHEPARD BOOKS
MULBERRY BOOKS
TAMBOURINE BOOKS

The children's book divisions of William Morrow include Morrow Junior Books, which publishes fiction and nonfiction for all ages from the youngest readers through young adult, as well as picture books primarily for children in the middle grades. Morrow's other children's imprints are editorially independent and include Beech Tree Books, Greenwillow Books, Lothrop, Lee & Shepard Books, Mulberry Books, and Tambourine Books.

Morrow Junior Books publishes titles throughout the range of children's and young-adult categories. From the Morrow Junior list: *Engelbert Joins the Circus* by Tom Paxton (illustrated by Roberta Wilson); *Lightning* by Seymour Simon; *African Animals* by Caroline Arnold; *Shark in the Sea* by Joanne Ryder (illustrated by Michael Rothman); *The Never-Ending Greenness* by Neil Waldman.

The **Beech Tree** line accents fiction and nonfiction paperbacks (often reprints) for 8- to 14-year-old readers. "Paperback books for kids who love to read." Popular titles: *Yours Till Banana Splits: 201 Autograph Rhymes* by Joanna Cole and Stephanie Calmenson (illustrated by Alan Tiegren); *Shadow Play* by Bernie Zubrowski (illustrated by Roy Doty); *Lanyard: Having Fun with Plastic Lace* by Camilla Gryski; *Gertie's Green Thumb* by Catherine Dexter.

Greenwillow Books produces picture-and-story editions for a younger readership. On the Greenwillow list: *Heat Wave and Mud Flat* by James Stevenson; *Westminster West* by Jessie Haas; *Jorah's Journal* by Judith Coseley.

Lothrop, Lee & Shepard publishes picture books, pop-up specialties, and fiction and nonfiction for middle and older readers. Titles: *Gathering the Sun: An Alphabet in Spanish and English* by Alma Flor Ada (illustrated by Simón Silva); *Chameleons on Location* by Kathy Darling (photography by Fara Darling); *Mayeros: A Yucatan Mayan Family* by George Ancona; *Enchantment in the Garden* by Shirley Hughes; *Waterman's Child* by Barbara Mitchell and Daniel San Souci.

Mulberry Books specializes in popular-priced picture books in paperback. Representative Mulberry titles: *Whose Hat?* by Margaret Miller; *The Big Sneeze* by Ruth Brown; *Jack's Garden* by Henry Cole.

Tambourine Books addresses a primarily preschooler readership with a lively, illustrated line. Tambourine titles: *Coconut Mon* by Linda Milstein (pictures by Cheryl Munro Taylor); *Do Angels Sing the Blues?* by A. C. LeMieux; *I Pretend* by Heidi Goennel.

Query letters and SASEs should be directed to:

Paula Kaufman, Editor in Chief, Mulberry Books and Beech Tree Books

Leonard Hort, Senior Editor, Mulberry Books and Beech Tree Books

Golda Laurena, Art Director, Mulberry Books and Beech Tree Books

Andrea Schneeman, Editor, Morrow Junior Books

Elizabeth Shub, Senior Editor, Greenwillow Books
Juvenile to young adult.

Susan Pearson, Editor in Chief, Lothrop, Lee & Shepard Books
Books for juveniles.

Melanie Donovan, Senior Editor, Lothrop, Lee & Shepard Books

AVON BOOKS

1350 Avenue of the Americas
New York, NY 10019
212-261-6800

Avon's trade approach includes practical and inspirational nonfiction, with particular emphasis on history, business, health, parenting, how-to, multicultural subjects, memoir, psychology, popular science, gender studies, and light reference. The house also hosts a mix of belletristic and commercial fiction, including category works in suspense, science fiction, and romance.

Avon is part of the privately held Hearst Corporation, which also owns the book-publishing firm William Morrow & Company. Avon Books began as a mass-market paperback reprint house in 1941; since then, Avon has branched out to encompass original fiction and nonfiction in trade paperback and mass-market rack-size editions, as well as reprints. Fall of 1996 witnessed the kickoff of Avon's hardcover line. (For Avon young readers' division, please see subentry below for Camelot and Flare lines.) In Fall of 1996, Avon announced plans for a new imprint, tentatively titled Tartikoff Books, in partnership with film and television producer Brandon Tartikoff; projected are 30 commercial fiction and nonfiction titles developed over three years.

Avon purveys an extensive nonfiction list that covers celebrity and historical biography, self-help and awareness, popular psychology, inspirational works, new age, business, humor, lifestyles, sports, current issues, and occasional high-interest true crime.

Nonfiction from Avon: *Writing Your Life: Putting Your Past on Paper* by Lou Willett Stanek, Ph.D.; *Fitronics for Life* by Marilyn Diamond and Dr. Donald Burton Schnell; *The True Work of Dying: A Practical and Compassionate Guide to Easing the Dying Process* by Jan Selliken Bernard, R.N., N.D., and Miriam Schneider; *Boys Like Us: Gay Writers Tell Their Coming-Out Stories* (edited by Patrick Merta); *Tao Te Ching: A New Approach, Backward Down the Path* by Jerry O. Dalton; *The X-Factor: David Duchovny* by Chris Nickson; *Get It Done: A Guide to Motivation, Determination & Achievement* by Ian McMahan, Ph.D.; *More Prophecies for the Coming Millennium* by Shawn Robbins and Edward Susman; *Raising Safe Kids in an Unsafe World: 30 Simple Ways to Prevent Your Child from Becoming Lost, Abducted or Abused* by Jan Wagner; *Is Greenland Really Green?* by Laurence Moore; *After Death: A New Future for Human Consciousness* by Darryl Reanney; *The Neanderthal Enigma: Solving the Mystery of Modern Human Origins* by James Shreeve; *The Art of the Possible: The Path from Perfectionism to Balance and Freedom* by Alexandra Stoddard.

The Confident Collector series offers identification and price guides for the serious collector and dealer—covering everything from bottles and quilts to comic books and baseball cards.

Avon fiction encompasses commercial titles as well as selected high-concept literary works, and sweeps the gamut of popular genres: adventure, romance, Westerns, suspense, thrillers, mysteries, science fiction and fantasy, and horror. Avon mass-market releases include many category originals and a heavy-hitting reprint list of hardcover successes. Avon fiction authors include Patricia Cornwell, Raymond Feist, J. A. Jance, Johanna Lindsey, Elizabeth Lowell, Alison Lurie, Colleen McCullough, and Roger Zelazny. AvoNova is Avon's imprint for premiere science, futurist, and fantasy fiction.

Representing Avon fiction: *A Creed for the Third Millennium* by Colleen McCullough; *Recipes from the Dump* by Abigail Stone; *Ashes in the Wind* by Kathleen E. Woodiwiss; *Bloodsucking Fiends: A Love Story* by Christopher Moore; *Fool Me Twice* by Paul Levine; *Hostile Witness* by Richard Berman; *The Kiss* by Kathryn Reines; *The List of 7* by Mark Frost; *Past Imperative: Round One of the Great Game* (science fiction) by Dave Duncan; *Moonrise* (science fiction) by Ben Bova; *Quicker Than the Eye* (science fiction) by Ray Bradbury; *The Magic of You* by Joanna Lindsey; *Love Wild and Fair* by Bertrice Small; *Like a Lamb to Slaughter* (mystery) by Lawrence Block; *The Legend of Bagger Vance: A Novel of Golf and the Game of Life* by Steven Pressfield; *Memoir from Antproof Case* by Mark Helprin; *The Living End* and *Mrs. Ted Bliss* by Stanley Elkin; *Come and Go, Molly Snow* by Mary Ann Taylor-Hall; *Tex and Mollie in the Afterlife* by Richard Grant; *Blood: A Southern Fantasy* by Michael Moorcock.

A special Avon project is Neon Lit, a series conceived by Bob Callahan and Art Spiegelman (author of *Maus*), which combines the best of modern crime literature with graphic illustrations. Series titles include Paul Auster's *City of Glass* and Barry Gifford's *Perdita Durango*.

Avon handles its own distribution.

Query letters and SASEs should be directed to:

Charlotte Abbott, Editor of Trade Paperbacks
Nonfiction: women's studies, history, popular culture, reference, nature. Literary fiction.

Lou Aronica, Senior Vice President and Publisher
Oversees the Avon program.

Chris Condry, Associate Editor

Lisa Considine, Editor of Trade Paperbacks
Nonfiction: psychology, health and childcare, nature, multicultural books, Confident Collector series.

Ellen Edwards, Executive Editor, Romance
Fiction: historical and contemporary romance, women's suspense, general women's fiction.

(Ms.) Carrie Feron, Executive Editor
Fiction: mystery, romance, women's suspense, general women's fiction. Nonfiction: spirituality, health, childcare, pet care.

Trish Lande Grader, Executive Editor
Wide interests in commercial nonfiction and fiction, including mysteries and suspense.

Jennifer Hershey, Executive Editor
Wide range of trade interests in fiction and nonfiction. Atmospheric mysteries with emphasis on character and narrative voice.

Lyssa Keusch, Associate Editor
Fiction: romance, mystery. Nonfiction: Self-help.

Rachel Klayman, Editorial Director of Trade Paperbacks
Nonfiction: women's studies, history, popular reference, psychology, popular science.

Micki Nuding, Assistant Editor
Fiction: historical and contemporary romance, women's suspense, general women's fiction. Commercial nonfiction.

Stephen S. Power, Senior Editor
Mass-market: true crime, mysteries, thrillers. Trade: humor, business.

Ann McKay Thoroman, Assistant Editor
Fiction: mystery, romance, women's suspense, commercial and literary women's fiction. Nonfiction: spirituality, health, psychology, inspirational, parenting, pet care.

Christine Zika, Associate Editor
Fiction: romance. Nonfiction: health, relationships.

AVON CAMELOT AND AVON FLARE

The Avon Camelot imprint produces paperback children's titles (middle readers, ages 8–12), and the Avon Flare line is directed toward the young-adult readership (ages 12 and up); both lists feature topnotch fiction, and otherwise selectively cover the gamut of children's nonfiction categories. Avon addresses the educational-sales market through Avon Paperbacks for Schools and Libraries.

Avon Camelot covers general fiction, including family, peer, and school-related stories.

Titles from Camelot: *Going to the Net: A Girl's Guide to Cyberspace* by Marian Salzman and Robert Pondiscio; *Kwanzaa: A Family Affair* by Mildren Pitts Walter; *Breaking Free* by Louann Gaeddert; *The Drummer Boy* (fiction) by Larry Weinberg; *The Ghost Ship* (fiction) by Don Whittington; *Looking for Juliette* (fiction) by Janet Taylor Lisle; *Merry Christmas, Amelia Bedelia* (young adult) by Peggy Parish.

Avon Flare publishes general fiction (coming of age, family, and peer stories), as well as historical novels, horror, and suspense titles. Romance can be a strong story element, but Flare does not publish genre romance as such.

From Avon Flare: *Cry Baby* by Phyllis Karras; *The Dark Charm* by Don Whittington; *Heart of the Hills* by Shelly Ritthaler; *Only Child* by Jesse Osburn; *Sister of the Bride* by Beverly Cleary; *Teen Angels No. 6: Love Without End* by Cherie Bennett and Jeff Gottesfeld; *The Unified Field* by Mark Leon; *Crash Landing* by Nicole Davidson.

Query letters and SASEs should be directed to:

Gwen Montgomery, Editorial Director

Stephanie Siegel, Assistant Editor

HEINEMANN
BUTTERWORTH-HEINEMANN
BOYNTON/COOK
FOCAL PRESS
DIGITAL PRESS
NEWNES

361 Hanover Street
Portsmouth, NH 03801-3912
800-541-2086
http://www.heinemann.com (World Wide Web)

Legal-publishing office:
8 Industrial, Unit C
Salem, NH 03079

Heinemann offers a varied general-interest primarily nonfiction trade list, with selected fiction and literary works. Frontlist offerings accent titles in drama and the performing arts, education, creative writing, and the humanities. Heinemann (founded in 1976) is a wing of the internationally based Reed Elsevier Group.

This publisher's books are offered under such logos as Heinemann and Butterworth, as well as Butterworth-Heinemann. In addition, the house comprises several specialist subsidiaries and imprints that produce professional titles in architecture; business management and operations, technique, and theory; computer technology; state and regional law books and periodicals; and medical, scientific, and security books and journals.

Butterworth-Heinemann continues to publish in such traditional strongholds as electronics (many of these titles are now under the Newnes imprint), engineering, security, and science, as well as an ever-broadening list of computer and business titles.

Many of the house's corporate subsidiaries operate primarily through editorial offices based outside North America. The subentries for Focal Press and Digital Press below are keyed to imprints with acquisitions functions centered in the United States. The core trade list—usually catalogued to booksellers as Heinemann and Butterworth-Heinemann books—often includes selections from the internationally based general trade and specialty imprints.

Reed Trade offers choice CD guides and craft titles conceived, developed, and promoted to become classics in the field.

From Heinemann: *Mosaic of Thought: Teaching Comprehension in a Reader's Workshop* by Ellen Oliver Keene and Susan Zimmermann; *Moon Journals: Writing, Art, and Inquiry Through Focused Nature Study* by Joni Chancer and Gina Rester-Zodrow; *What's a Schwa Sound Anyway? A Holistic Guide to Phonetics, Phonics, and Spelling* by Sandra Wilde; *Teaching Reading and Writing in Spanish in the Bilingual Classroom* by Yvonne S. Freeman and David E. Freeman; *Keepsakes: Using Family Stories in Elementary Classrooms* by Linda Winston; *Developing Judgment: Assessing Children's Work in Mathematics* by Jean Moon; *Rethinking the Education of Deaf Students: Theory and Practice from a Teacher's Perspective* by Sue Livingston; *The Magical Classroom: Exploring Science, Language, and Perception with Children* by Michael J. Strauss;

Achieving Scientific Literacy: From Purposes to Practices by Rodger W. Bybee; *Living with Uncertainty: The Messy Reality of Classroom Practice* by Curt Dudley-Marling; *A Teacher's Project Guide to the Internet* by Kevin R. Crotchett.

Heinemann distributes the lists of its various components via an international network of book trade representatives and distribution offices.

NEWNES

Butterworth-Heinemann has announced the launch of the Newnes imprint, which is planned eventually to encompass all electronics titles. For years readers have known Newnes for its successful and well-received line of pocket books and Butterworth-Heinemann for its line of professional and technical reference books. The Newnes imprint is intended to epitomize the most innovative information products for electronics professionals and hobbyists.

From Newnes: *Cellular Telephones and Pagers: An Overview* by Stephen W. Gibson; *Securing Home and Business: A Guide to the Electronic Security Industry* by Simon Hakim and Erwin A. Blackstone; *Build Your Own Multimedia PC: A Complete Guide to Renovating and Constructing Personal Computers* by Ian Sinclair.

BOYNTON/COOK PUBLISHERS

361 Hanover Street
Portsmouth, NH 03801-3912

A member of the Reed Elsevier Group, Boynton/Cook publishes books for English teaching, secondary and college. Boynton/Cook publishes a strong line of books in the following subject areas: secondary school English and language arts, college composition, English as a second language, creative writing, student texts for high school and college writing.

A note from Peter Stillman, the publisher at Boynton/Cook:

> Nobody has teaching figured out, mainly because nobody has humans figured out, and when I come across a teacher or a book that argues otherwise, it gives me the willies. Boynton/Cook doesn't publish books that one can flip through and find a sure-fire game plan for next Monday's classes. None of our titles are dogmatic, closed to possibilities beyond itself. This doesn't mean our books are short on strategies for Monday—quite the opposite—but that they're derivative of thorough research and an informed curiosity about where ethical and intellectual concepts of English education should compel us.

On the Boynton/Cook list: *Meeting the Challenges: Stories from Today's Classroom* (edited by Maureen Barbieri and Carol Tateishi); *Where to Begin: A Guide to Teaching Secondary English* by Jane Kearns; *Keywords in Composition Studies* (edited by Paul Heilker and Peter Vandenberg); *Sharing Pedagogies: Students and Teachers Write About Dialogic Practices* (edited by Gail Tayko and John Tassoni); *Language and Literacy: Studying Discourse in Communities and Classrooms* by Eleanor Kutz; *For*

All Time: A Complete Guide to Writing Your Family History by Charley Kempthorne; *Breathing In, Breathing Out: Keeping a Writer's Notebook* by Ralph Fletcher; *More Than the Truth: Teaching Nonfiction Writing Through Journalism* (edited by Dennie Palmer Wolf and Julie Craven with Dana Balick).

More works especially for writers (and their fans) from Boynton/Cook: *Writing Outside the Lines: Developing Partnerships for Writers* by Candida Gillis; *From Disk to Hard Copy: Teaching Writing with Computers* by James Strickland; *Deciding to Lead: The English Teacher As Reformer* by Denny Wolfe and Joseph Antinarella; *Making Conversation: Collaborating with Colleagues for Change* by Mark Larson; *Latina and Latino Voices in Literature for Children and Teenagers* by Frances Ann Day; *Turns of Thought: Teaching Composition as Reflexive Inquiry* by Donna Qualley; *Elements of Alternative Style: Essays on Writing and Revision* (edited by Wendy Bishop); *The Spiritual Side of Writing: Releasing the Learner's Whole Potential* (edited by Regina Foehr and Susan S. Schiller).

For Boynton/Cook, query letters and SASEs should be directed to:

Peter Stillman, Publisher, Boynton/Cook

BUTTERWORTH-HEINEMANN

313 Washington Street
Newton, MA 02158-1626

Butterworth-Heinemann's U.S. Business line publishes ground-breaking management, written and endorsed by the best in the field today—books the publisher promotes to achieve a wisdom that will keep them selling for years to come.

U.S. business titles: *Leading from the Heart: Choosing Courage over Fear in the Workplace* by Kay Gilley; *Power Partnering: A Strategy for Business Excellence in the 21st Century* by Sean Gadman; *Leadership in a Challenging World: A Sacred Journey* by Barbara Shipka; *Business and the Feminine Principle: The Untapped Resource* by Carol R. Frenier; *Beyond Time Management: Business with Purpose* by Robert A. Wright; *Getting a Grip on Tomorrow: An Executive's Guide to Survival and Success in the Changed World of Work* by Mike Johnson.

Representative of the Heinemann trade list: *The Audition Process: A Guide for Actors* by Bob Funk; *Hi Concept–Lo Tech: Theatre for Everyone in Any Place* by Barbara Carlisle and Don Drapeau; *Fight Directing for the Theatre* by J. Allen Suddeth; *The Last Closet: The Real Lives of Lesbian and Gay Teachers* by Rita Kissen, *The Career Novelist: A Literary Agent Offers Strategies for Success* by Donald Maass. Heinemann series include African Studies, Caribbean Writers, African Writers, and Creative Sparks (titles about the creative process).

FOCAL PRESS

225 Wildwood Avenue
Woburn, MA 01801
617-928-2500

Focal Press publishes professional titles and textbooks in such fields as communications, cinematography, photography, and television. The house has been publishing works geared to the media arts since its inception in 1938.

The Focal house intends its titles to make a difference in the lives and careers of their readers by keeping them in the forefront of technological and creative innovation in the arenas of photography, broadcast, audio, film, video, computer media, and theater. The press looks for outstanding new book and audiovisual projects that help media professionals and students achieve their potential. A number of Focal handbooks and manuals are classics in their fields and head a potent backlist.

Focal Press has always displayed a strong commitment to the latest and best information in film, video, photography, broadcast, audio and lighting. Focal titles cover the gamut from guides for beginners to reference works for professionals, as well as the popular *Variety Movie Guide*—a book for everyone.

Focal Press highlights: *Writing for Multimedia: Entertainment, Education, Training, Advertising, and the World Wide Web* by Timothy Garrand; *Holography for Photographers* by John Iovine; *Videotape Editing: A Post Production Primer* by Steven E. Browne; *Working in Commercials: A Complete Sourcebook for Adult and Child Actors* by Elaine Keller Beardsley; *Film Production Management* by Bastian Cleve; *Playwriting: The First Workshop* by Kathleen E. George, *Photography and the Performing Arts* by Gerry Kopelow; *Electronic Media Criticism: Applied Perspectives* by Peter B. Orlick; *Corporate Video Directing* by Howard Hall.

For Butterworth-Heinemann and Focal Press, all query letters and SASEs should be directed to:

Karen M. Speerstra, Publishing Director

Marie Lee, Editor

DIGITAL PRESS

313 Washington Street
Newton, MA 02158
617-928-2500

Digital Press publishes books for the information-technology community, from absolute beginner to seasoned pro. Among the press's titles are those that relate directly to Digital products and services, whereas the major portion of the list addresses broader interests. The company strives to provide its readership with the latest technical information—presented in readable and useful formats—and is on the lookout for projects that reflect imminent advances in the computer universe.

Digital catalogs titles in the areas of networking and data communications, windowing, artificial intelligence, policy and strategy, organizational design, software development, computer technology, and Alpha/VAX/VMS operating systems. In addition, Digital Press marketing services handle computing titles published under the auspices of the umbrella company.

Digital Press, the former book-publishing group of Digital Equipment Corporation, is now part of the Butterworth-Heinemann division of the Reed Elsevier Group.

On the Digital Press list: *Working with Microsoft Exchange* by Tony Redmond; *Tune Up Your PC for Windows 95: A Practical Guide* by Mike Tooley; *High Performance Cluster Configuration System Management* by James Gursha; *Exploring Workstation Applications with CDE and Motif* by Katherine Haramandanis.

Query letters and SASEs should be directed to:

Mike Cash, Editor

HI JINX PRESS

203 F Street, Suite A
P.O. Box 1814
Davis, CA 95616
916-759-8514

Hi Jinx Press (founded in 1995) is expert in publishing and marketing inventive fiction and literary works. The house looks for projects that are offbeat, somewhat hip; most of the list consists of quick reads—the sort of books that pair up well with what are often characterized as alternative markets and sold at emporiums of popular culture as well as via the traditional book trade.

From Hi Jinx: *Working Stiff* by John Richards; *Sacred Hearts* by Greg Boyd; *Jackdog Summer* by Geoffrey Clark; *Confessions of a Polish Used-Car Salesman* by Mark Wisniewski; *Foreigners* by Joel Martin; *Man on Stage* (stories) by Stephen Dixon.

Hi Jinx handles its own distribution, orchestrating in-house services with regional representation, wholesalers, and jobbers. Hi Jinx hits such venues as Tower Records & Books, Borders, major independent booksellers, and shops that may also stock such items as fashionable apparel, magazines, and CDs.

Query letters and SASEs should be directed to:

Greg Boyd, Acquisitions

Phillippa Savage, Editor

HIPPOCRENE BOOKS

171 Madison Avenue
New York, NY 10016
212-685-4371
fax: 212-779-9338

Hippocrene accents history, military science, international literature, music, travel, cuisine, and scholarly Judaica and Polonica. The house offers selected works in the areas of current affairs and popular culture, in addition to comprehensive lines of foreign-language dictionaries, maps, and atlases—the house publishes dictionaries and instruction books in over 100 languages. Hippocrene Books (founded in 1971) publishes hardcovers and trade paperbacks. The house also produces a line of audiobooks.

Hippocrene has undertaken publication of the works of Polish writer Henryk Sienkiewicz (1905 Nobel laureate in literature) in English translation.

Hippocrene titles for the general trade: *Uncertain Glory: Robert E. Lee at War* by John D. McKenzie; *The Enigma of General Blaskowitz* by Dr. Richard Giziowski; *Monsieur Venus* by Rachilde; *The Daedalus Book of French Horror: The 19th Century* (edited by Terry Hale); *Who's Who in Polish America*; *Polish Customs, Traditions, and Folklore* by Sophie Hodorowicz Knab; *Hippocrene Insider's Guide to the World's Most Exciting Cruises* by Lea Lane and Shirley Linde; *A View of the World* by Norman Lewis.

Hippocrene Books prides itself on being the foremost United States publisher of international cookbooks and foreign language dictionaries.

International cookbook titles: *Art of South American Cookery* by Myra Waldo; *Good Food from Sweden* by Inga Norberg; *Old Polish Traditions in the Kitchen and at the Table*; *Traditional Recipes of Old England*; *Traditional South African Cookery* by Hilegonda Duckitt; *Traditional Food From Scotland: The Edinburgh Book of Plain Cookery Recipes*.

Hippocrene's Bilingual series introduces the Treasury of Love Stories, with initial offerings in French, Polish, and Spanish. Each volume will contain selections from classic literature, and the foreign text will be side-by-side with its English translation. The Bilingual Series also includes Bilingual Love Poetry, which provides a glimpse of each culture's unique approach to affairs of the heart. Readings of the selections, performed by native speakers, are available on cassette as an accompaniment to each volume.

Hippocrene offers practical and concise dictionaries as well as unabridged and comprehensive dictionaries, specialty dictionaries, proverbs dictionaries, and standard dictionaries in over 100 languages.

The Compact Dictionary is a new Hippocrene series that features portable, lightweight, flexible dictionaries that are small enough for travelers or students to carry in their pocket. Among available languages are Slovak, Bosnian, Armenian, Ukrainian, and Polish.

Mastering Advanced . . . guides make up a line that offers the student reasonably priced, contemporary foreign-language instruction. The Hippocrene Beginner's series is designed for students with little or no background in a foreign language. The goal of each volume is to provide readers with a basic knowledge to travel independently, speak and understand, and read and write essential words.

Hippocrene distributes its own list.

Query letters and SASEs should be directed to:

George Blagowidow, President and Editorial Director

HOLIDAY HOUSE

425 Madison Avenue
New York, NY 10017
212-688-0085

Holiday House specializes in children's and young-adult books in a program that encompasses quality trade hardcover picture books, short-chapter books, and middle-grade readers, as well as selected novels for young adults. Holiday House publishes general nonfiction works for all age levels, ethnic stories and nonfiction, fast-paced adventure stories, historical fiction, boys' books, humorous stories, folktales, fairy tales, poetry, and fantasy for ages 8 to 12.

Holiday House (established in 1935) is a smaller independent publisher with a large and varied backlist of fiction and nonfiction children's books. The publisher is open to inspired, well-written, new ideas—and is on the alert for writers who have developed keenly original projects.

Sample picture-book titles: *The Magic Dreidels: A Hanukkah Story* by Eric A. Kimmel (illustrated by Katya Krenina); *The Christmas Story* (adapted from the Bible; illustrated by Kay Chroao); *Too Many Pumpkins* by Linda White (illustrated by Megan Lloyd); *Fraction Fun* by David A. Adler (illustrated by Nancy Tobin); *Cats* and *Deserts* by Gail Gibbons (illustrated by the author); *An Alcott Family Christmas* by Alexandra Wallner (illustrated by the author); *Tailypo: A Newfangled Tall Tale* (retold by Angela Shelf Medearis; illustrated by Sterling Brown); *The Log Cabin Quilt* by Ellen Howard (illustrated by Ronald Himler); *Prairies* by Dorothy Hinshaw Patent (photographs by William Muñoz); *Haunts: Five Hair-Raising Tales* by Angela Shelf Medearis (drawings by Trina Schart Hyman); *The Cheyennes: A First Americans Book* by Virginia Driving Hawk Sneve (illustrated by Ronald Himler); *Celebrating Hanukkah* by Diane Hoyt-Goldsmith (photographs by Lawrence Migdale).

Further representative of the Holiday House list: *The Shooting Star: A Novel about Annie Oakley* by Sheila Solomon Klass; *Hey Dad, Get a Life!* by Todd Strasser; *The Ghost by the Seal* by Eileen Dunlop; *What I Believe: Kids Talk About Faith* by Debbie Holsclaw Birdseye and Tom Birdseye (photographs by Robert Crum); *Rosie No-Name and the Forest of Forgetting* by Gareth Owen; *Pictures in the Dark* by Gillian Cross; *The Golem* (a version by Barbara Rogasky; illustrated by Trina Schart Hyman).

From the Picture Book Biographies line: *A Picture Book of Thomas Alva Edison* by David A. Adler (illustrated by John and Alexandra Wallner). Mr. Adler has written 23 other Picture Book Biographies including: *A Picture Book of John F. Kennedy*; *A Picture Book of Martin Luther King, Jr.*; *A Picture Book of Eleanor Roosevelt*; *A Picture Book of Paul Revere*; *A Picture Book of Florence Nightingale*.

Holiday House's authors' guidelines contain concise advice all authors of children's books would do well to follow; contact the publisher for detailed information regarding manuscript submissions.

Holiday House handles its own distribution.

Query letters and SASEs should be directed to:

Regina Griffin, Editor in Chief

Alison Cunningham, Assistant Editor

HOLLOWAY HOUSE PUBLISHING GROUP

8060 Melrose Avenue
Los Angeles, CA 90046-7082
213-653-8060
fax: 213-655-9452

Holloway House publishes fiction and nonfiction within its areas of publishing interest, including African American, American Indian, and Hispanic literature, as well as selected titles in games and gambling. Holloway House (founded in 1960) is the world's largest publisher of paperbacks representing the American Black experience.

The publisher is noted for hard-hitting novels, historical anthologies and biographical series (including the Educator's Library), and selected public-interest nonfiction. The house is also known for reprint editions of classic works by such authors as Donald Goines and Iceberg Slim. Among Holloway House imprints are Avanti, Heartline Romances, Mankind, and Melrose Square. Holloway also produces calendars, postcard books, and posters. The publisher typically publishes a midsized list of new titles each year and maintains a strong backlist.

On the Holloway House fiction list: *The Listening Sky* by Bernice Anderson Poole; *The Revenge of June Daley* by Rina Keaton; *Buffalo Soldier* by C. R. Goodman; *Shack Town* by Glen T. Brock; *Black Bait* by Leo Guild; *Daddy Must Die* by William O. Brown; *Coming of Age* by Lorri Hewett; *Black Cheyenne* by Charles R. Goodman.

Nonfiction includes: *Arthur Ashe* by Ed Weissberg; *B. B. King* by J. Nazel; *Bill Cosby* by M. Ruuth; *Billie Holiday* by Bud Kliment; *James Baldwin* by Lisa Rosset; *Jackie Robinson* by Richard Scott; *Jesse Owens* by Tony Gentry; *Muhammad Ali* by C. Riccella; *Oprah Winfrey* by M. Ruuth; *Women in History* by D. L. Shepherd; *To Kill a Black Man* (dual biography of Martin Luther King and Malcolm X) by Louis E. Lomax; *Dizzy Gillespie* by Tony Gentry; *Kathleen Dunham* by Darlene Donloe.

The Holloway House list is handled by All America Distributors Corporation.

Query letters and SASEs should be directed to:

Ray Locke, Senior Editor

HENRY HOLT AND COMPANY
METROPOLITAN BOOKS
JOHN MACRAE BOOKS
MARIAN WOOD BOOKS
OWL BOOKS
HENRY HOLT AND COMPANY BOOKS FOR YOUNG READERS
MIS: PRESS/M & T BOOKS

115 West 18th Street
New York, NY 10011
212-886-9200

Henry Holt and Company publishes a full range of trade nonfiction, as well as a strong complement of fiction and literary works. In addition, Holt maintains a number of individualized imprints and divisions. Holt emphasizes hardcover and trade paperback editions.

Metropolitan Books is an imprint that features an international lineup of topical-interest nonfiction and literary fiction; Metropolitan is open to different genres, unconventional points of view, controversial opinions, and perhaps a few new voices in fiction. Other Holt trade hardcover imprints include John Macrae Books and Marian Wood Books. Owl Books is host to the house line of trade paperbacks. (See subentry below.)

Computer titles are the specialty at Holt subsidiaries MIS: Press, Inc. and M & T Books (please see subentry for MIS: Press/M & T Books).

The house presents several fine children's and young-adult lines under the aegis of Henry Holt's Books for Young Readers (please see subentry below).

Henry Holt offers a solid popular and scholarly reference list that, rather than being collected under a separate reference-division umbrella, is cataloged under the house's respective imprints. Henry Holt and Company nurtures a healthy backlist.

Henry Holt and Company (founded in 1866) is part of the German-based international Verlagsgruppe Georg von Holtzbrinck. Holt was previously a thriving independent publisher, subsequent to the sale of former umbrella operation Holt Rinehart & Winston's textbook division to Harcourt Brace in 1987.

Henry Holt's offerings come stamped with the house's bookish owl colophon (a symbol of the wise goddess Athena), one of the most respected mascot logos in book publishing.

The Henry Holt nonfiction scope spans the trade spectrum. Areas of interest include politics and current events; contemporary issues and popular culture; cuisine, travel, and lifestyle; nature and ecology; art and design; antiques and collectibles; literary commentary; popular and scholarly biography and memoir; business, personal finance, and career; psychology and medicine; health, exercise, and nutrition; spirituality and awareness; reference works keyed to popular, academic, and professional topics.

From the Holt nonfiction list: *The Famine Ships: The Irish Exodus to America* by Edward Laxton; *Paint: Choosing, Mixing, and Decorating with Water-Based Paints* by John Sutcliffe; *Sacred Journeys: An Illustrated Guide to Pilgrimages Around the World* by Jennifer Westwood; *A Commotion in the Blood: A Century of Using the Immune System to Battle Cancer and Other Diseases* by Stephen S. Hall; *Achilles in the Quantum Universe: The Definitive History of Infinity* by Richard Morris; *Maria Tallchief: America's Prima Ballerina* by Maria Tallchief with Larry Kaplan; *The Return of the Wolf to Yellowstone* by Thomas McNamee; *American Heirloom Vegetables: A Master Gardener's Guide to Planting, Seed-Saving, and Cultural History* by William Woys Weaver (foreword by Peter Hatch); *The Adirondacks: A History of America's First Wilderness* by Paul Schneider; *Penelope Hobhouse's Garden Designs* by Penelope Hobhouse; *Invisible Republic: Bob Dylan's Basement Tapes* by Greil Marcus; *Les Bon Mots: How to Amaze Tout le Monde with Everyday French* by Eugene Ehrlich; *Blue Rooms: Ripples, Rivers, Pools, and Other Waters* by John Jerome; *A Spider for Loco Shoat* by Douglas C. Jones; *Idiom Savant: Slang As It Is Slung* by Jerry Dunn; *Every Man Will Do His Duty: The Story of the Age of Nelson in Firsthand Accounts* (edited by Dean King with John B. Hattendorf, Ph.D.) *Quinceañera!: The Essential Guide to Planning the Perfect Sweet Fifteen Celebration* by Michele Salcedo; *The Classical Roman Reader: New Encounters with Ancient Rome* (edited by Kenneth J. Atchity); *Man of the Century: The Life and Times of Pope John Paul II* by Jonathan Kwitny; *Jumping the Broom* by Harriette Cole; *Blood Rites: Origins and History of the Passions of War* by Barbara Ehrenreich.

Henry Holt fiction includes frontlist commercial novels and literary works, as well as topflight mystery and suspense fiction. Representative titles here: *Mason & Dixon* by Thomas Pynchon; *No Brakes* by Lois Gould; *Blessed Is the Fruit* by Robert Antoni; *Esau* by Philip Kerr; *Mrs. Horenstein* by Fredrica Wagman; *Benjamin's Crossing* by Jay Parini; *Out of the Sun* by Robert Goddard; *The Story of the Night* by Colm Tóibín.

Backlist features (including Owl trade-paper reprints of recent Holt hardcover originals): *Edisto Revisited* by Padgett Powell; *The Debt to Pleasure* by John Lanchester; *Amnesiascope* by Steve Erickson; *The Death of Frank Sinatra* by Michael Ventura; *Sandra Nichols Found Dead* (a Jerry Kennedy novel) by George V. Higgins; *Angel Maker: The Collected Short Stories of Sara Maitland* by Sara Maitland; *Go the Way Your Blood Beats: An Anthology of Gay and Lesbian Literary Writings by African Americans* (edited by Shawn Stewart Ruff).

Holt also features John Harvey's Charlie Resnick mysteries, John Lutz's Fred Carver mysteries, Collin Wilcox's San Francisco police procedurals, and Sue Grafton's alphabetically titled Kinsey Millhone detective series.

Henry Holt and Company handles its own distribution.

Query letters and SASEs should be directed to:

Sara Bershtel, Associate Publisher, Metropolitan Books
Individualistic nonfiction and literary fiction.

Tom Engelhardt, Consulting Editor, Metropolitan Books
Expressive, inventive, and creative nonfiction and literary fiction.

Stephen Hubbell, Senior Editor, Metropolitan Books
International fiction and affairs, politics, biography, literary memoir, travel essays.

Jack Macrae, Editorial Director, John Macrae Books
American history and biography, scientific inquiry, travel and nature.

Allen Peacock, Senior Editor
Literary fiction.

Ray Roberts, Senior Editor
Gardening, design, biography; literary detective fiction.

William Strachan, Editor in Chief, Associate Publisher
History, current events, natural history, biography.

(Ms.) Marian Wood, Associate Publisher, Marian Wood Books
History, biography, travel essays, nature, military subjects, Judaica. Literary fiction.

William Patrick, Senior Executive Editor (Henry Holt)
Popular nonfiction; narrative or creative approaches to science, medicine, technology, current events. Operates out of Boston-area home office; query through New York office.

OWL BOOKS

Owl Books publishes a wide range of nonfiction (commercial, popular, and literary) and literary fiction. Owl is a Holt division recognized for its trade-paperback program in both originals and reprints.

Owl is expanding its nonfiction program with more books in more areas of interest to trade-paperback readers. Owl areas include: topical issues and popular culture; cuisine and lifestyle; travel and nature; art and design; antiques and collectibles; literary essay; biography and memoir; business, personal finance, and career; popular psychology, health and nutrition, and awareness; popular and scholarly reference.

Owl has also opened a distinctive fiction line that features reprints of novels and stories from some of the most celebrated contemporary writers: Irene Dische, John Lanchester, Paul Beatty, Salman Rushdie, Tom De Haven, Padgett Powell, Alison Lurie, Robert Olmstead, Steve Erickson, Tibor Fischer, Alexander Theroux, George V. Higgins, and Hilary Mantel.

Though an established imprint at Holt, the premiere Owl Books catalog was issued for the spring and summer of 1997—the Year of the Owl.

Owl nonfiction originals: *The Louisville Slugger Ultimate Book of Hitting* by John Monteleone and Mark Gola; *Nature Walks of Central Park* by Dennis Burton; *Coping with Lyme Disease: A Practical Guide to Dealing with Diagnosis and Treatment* (revised edition) by Denise Lang with Joseph Territo, M.D.; *The Medicinal Garden: How to Grow and Use Your Own Medicinal Herbs* by Annie McIntyre; *Photomosaics: Magic Techniques with Photographs* (created by Robert Silvers; edited by Michael Hawley); *The National Wildlife Federation Book of Family Nature Activities: 50 Simple Projects and Activities in the Natural World* by Page Chichester; *The Illustrated Encyclopedia of Civil War Collectibles* by Charles Lawliss; *First-Job Survival Guide* by Andrea J. Sutcliffe; *Frugal Indulgents: How to Cultivate Decadence When Your Age and Salary Are Under 30* by Kera Bolonik and Jennifer Griffin; *The World on a String: How to Become a Successful Freelance Foreign Correspondent* by Alan Goodman and John Pollack; *The Writer's Home Companion: An Anthology of the World's Best Writing Advice, From Keats to Kunitz* (collected and edited by Joan Bolker, Ph.D.); *Yoga Journal's Yoga Basics: The Essential Beginner's Guide to Yoga for a Lifetime of Health and Fitness* by Mara Carrico and the Staff of Yoga Journal; *The Queerest Places: A National Guide to Gay and Lesbian Historic Sites* by Paula Martinac; *Secrets of Successful Telephone Selling* by Robert W. Bly; *Sea of Words: A Lexicon and Companion for Patrick O'Brian's Seafaring Tales* (by Dean King with John B. Hattendorf and John Worth Estes); *David Carradine's Introduction to Chi Kung: The Beginner's Program for Physical, Emotional, and Spiritual Well-Being* by David Carradine and David Nakahara; *Feeling Smart: How to Raise Your Emotional IQ* by Jeanne Segal, Ph.D.; *The Book of Zines: Readings from the Fringe* (edited by Chip Rowe).

Owl fiction and popular literature: *Father and Son* by Larry Brown; *Tabloid Dreams* by Robert Olen Butler; *The Bear Went Over the Mountain* by William Kotzwinkle; *The Pope's Rhinoceros* by Lawrence Norfolk; *The Enchantment of Lily Dahl* by Siri Hustvedt; John Harvey's Charlie Resnick series.

Query letters and SASEs should be directed to:

Alessandra Bocco, Assistant Editor, Owl Books
Literary fiction, bold and memorable female protagonists; any work that illustrates a uniquely American experience. U.S. history, especially Southern and old New York; Caribbean and American voodoo; Native American history/religion; rock and roll.

(Mr.) Tracy Brown, Executive Editor, Owl Books
Literary fiction. Serious nonfiction, including current issues, business, politics, history, biography, literary memoir, popular science, nature writing, travel essays.

Elizabeth Crossman, Editor at Large
Specializes in the culinary area: food, wine, gardening. Some crafts.

Jonathan Landreth, Associate Editor, Owl Books
Nonfiction: the Pacific Rim and Asia, the environment, outdoor pursuits, popular culture.

Amy Rosenthal, Editorial Assistant, Owl Books
Nonfiction in women's issues, health, psychology, multicultural culture, social history, religion, business, politics. Selected literary fiction. Works with Theresa Burns.

Amelia Sheldon, Editor, Owl Books
Wide range of commercial nonfiction: parenting, relationships, popular psychology, self-help, spirituality, health, nutrition, alternative health, personal finance, pop culture, women's issues, home, garden, pets, travel, leisure activities. Literary nonfiction.

(Ms.) Tracy Sherrod, Editor
Serious nonfiction and literary fiction written by and/or for African-Americans and lesbians and gays; women's issues.

David Sobel, Senior Editor
Science, natural history, popular reference, health, history, sports, the outdoors, business, personal finance, multicultural subjects, popular culture.

Darcy Tromanhauser, Associate Editor, Owl Books
Literary fiction and nonfiction. American history and culture, natural history, women's issues, travel, international topics.

Cynthia Vartan, Editor at Large
Nonfiction in health, parenting, family, relationships, psychology, writing, biography, popular business; practical how-to books.

HENRY HOLT AND COMPANY BOOKS FOR YOUNG READERS

Henry Holt and Company Books for Young Readers publishes in categories that range from the youngest readers through young-adult. The list includes illustrated storybooks, specialty items and kits, fiction, reference books, and nonfiction volumes of popular educational appeal.

Imprints, series, and specialty lines include Books by Michael Hague, Books by Bill Martin Jr. and John Archambault, W5 (Who What Where When Why) Reference, Edge Books, Redfeather Books, and Owlet Paperbacks. The hardcover young-adult Edge imprint features themes keyed to contemporary culture and multicultural titles from around the world. Among Holt productions in the children's arena are those issued in finely crafted, elegantly understated editions.

Representative of the Holt Books for Young Readers list: *In the Wild* by Nora Leigh Ryder; *Who Said That? Famous Americans Speak* by Robert Burleigh (illustrated by David Catrow); *Life on Mars* by David Getz (illustrated by Peter McCarty); *Whistle Me Home* by Barbara Wersba; *Earth Explained: A Beginner's Guide to Our Planet* by Barbara Taylor; *Fish Faces* by Norbert Wu.

From the Edge Books imprint: *Hit the Nerve: New Voices of the American Theater* (edited by Stephen Brennan); *The Beautiful Days of My Youth: My Six Months in Auschwitz and Plaszow* by Ana Novac.

Query letters and SASEs should be directed to:

Laura Godwin, Senior Editor

MIS: PRESS, INC.
M & T BOOKS

115 West 18th Street
New York, NY 10011
212-886-9200

Offerings from MIS: Press, Inc. and M & T Books constitute the main computer-book list for Henry Holt and Company. The house goal in publishing computer books is to inspire confidence while building competence. Achievement and continued growth comes from the combined efforts of talented authors, editors, a strong sales and marketing team, and customer support.

MIS: Press, Inc. (established in 1980) is a subsidiary of Henry Holt and Company. The press offers a carefully crafted list of books that appeal to every major segment of the computer market. MIS is recognized for books that offer complete, accurate, and easy-to-understand information (including packages with accompanying diskettes), particularly geared to some of the most popular computer hardware and software. Expanded areas of MIS interest include CD-ROM, multimedia, and PC sound. Noteworthy MIS series include Welcome to . . . and Teach Yourself . . . , with many of the house's titles geared to proprietary products.

M & T Books (founded in 1984 as a division of M & T Publishing) was acquired by MIS: Press in April of 1993. After transition from its former California location, the house is at home in its New York abode, out of which all titles are produced, edited, and marketed. M & T is a publisher of high-quality books for the serious computer user. M & T has traditionally supported its publishing program via aggressive advertising campaigns directed at driving the consumer into the bookstore to buy M & T titles—a success that in part derives from the house's association with some of the most potent computer magazines.

M & T offers a complete line of titles for technical professionals as well as advanced end users. The list has focused on emerging developments in such areas as multimedia, artificial life and intelligence, networking, programming languages, graphics programming, and desktop publishing.

MIS: Press and M & T Books are distributed through the parent organization Henry Holt and Company. MIS: Press books combine with those of sibling imprint M & T Books to qualify for bookseller discount.

Query letters and SASEs should be directed to:

Paul Farrell, Vice President and Associate Publisher, Computer Book Group

Rebecca Young, Editor

THE JOHNS HOPKINS UNIVERSITY PRESS
(See Directory of University Presses)

HORIZON PUBLISHERS
(See Directory of Religious, Spiritual, and Inspirational Publishers)

HOUGHTON MIFFLIN COMPANY

Boston office:
222 Berkeley Street
Boston, MA 02116-3764
617-351-5000

New York office:
215 Park Avenue South
New York, NY 10003
212-420-5800
http://www.hmco.com/trade (World Wide Web)

Houghton Mifflin produces general trade nonfiction and fiction in hardcover and paperback, as well as a strong general-reference list. Mariner is a trade-paperback imprint covering house interests in fiction and nonfiction. Children's divisions include Houghton Mifflin Books for Children, and the editorially independent juveniles imprint Clarion Books (see subentries below). Houghton Mifflin personalized imprints include Peter Davison Books and Marc Jaffe Books. The backlist of formerly independent Ticknor & Fields has been incorporated into the core Houghton Mifflin catalog.

Houghton Mifflin (founded in 1832) is one of the grand names of American publishing tradition. The house's renowned leaping-dolphin emblem embellishes a distinguished list.

Houghton Mifflin nonfiction encompasses mainstream titles in such areas as current events, international affairs, business, journalism, lifestyle and travel, and natural history.

Reference works from Houghton include: *American Heritage Dictionary of the English Language* (an excellent resource for American writers); *The Columbia Encyclopedia* (copublished with Columbia University): *Cannon's Concise Guide to Rules of Order*.

Also on the Houghton Mifflin list are travel and nature series that include the Apa Insight Guides, Peterson Field Guides, and Best Places to Stay Guides.

Popular Houghton Mifflin nonfiction: *Ancestors: A Beginner's Guide to Family History and Genealogy* by Jim and Terry Willard with Jane Wilson (tie-in with the PBS television series); *A Who's Who of Sports Champions: Their Stories and Their Records* by Ralph Hickok; *Listening to America: Twenty-Five Years in the Life of a Nation as Told to National Public Radio* (edited by Linda Wertheimer); *The Good Marriage: How and Why Love Lasts* by Judith S. Wallerstein and Sandra Blakeslee; *Headache Help: A Complete Guide to Understanding Headaches and the Medicines that Relieve Them* by Lawrence Robbins and Susan S. Lang; *Guerrilla Marketing Online: The Entrepreneur's Guide to Earning Profits on the Internet* by Jay Conrad and Charles Rubin; *Tasha Tudor's Engagement Calendar* (photographs by Richard W. Brown; text by Tovah Martin).

Fiction and works with literary and cultural scope: *Arkansas: Three Novellas* by David Leavitt; *Family Terrorists: Seven Stories and a Novella* by Antonya Nelson; *In the Loyal Mountains: Stories* by Rick Bass; *Slippage: Previously Uncollected, Precariously Poised Stories* by Harlan Ellison; *The Love Letter* (fiction) by Cathleen Schine; *Split Horizon* (novel) by Thomas Lux; *Clockers* (modern classic crime novel) by Richard Price; *Gringa Latina: A Woman of Two Worlds* (literary reflections) by Gabriella De Ferrari; *Evelyn Waugh: A Biography* by Selina Hastings; *Inventing the Truth: The Art and Craft of Memoir* (edited by William Zinsser).

The publisher also issues selected works of poetry, including: *Time & Money: New Poems* by William Matthews; *Nature: Poems Old and New* by May Swenson.

Houghton Mifflin distributes its own list.

Query letters and SASEs should be directed to:

Alan Andres, Editor (Boston)
Travel guides. Oversees the Insight travel guides.

Marnie Patterson Cochran, Guidebook Editor (New York)
Practical nonfiction. Oversees Guerrilla Marketing and Covert Bailey books.

Peter Davison, Peter Davison Books (Boston)
Poetry, biography, literary nonfiction.

Harry L. Foster, Jr., Senior Editor (Boston)
Nature and history. Oversees Peterson Field Guides.

Steve Fraser, Executive Editor
Nonfiction, social history, economic issues, political commentary.

Holly Hartman, Assistant Editor
General reference works.

Wendy Holt, Associate Editor
Women's issues, social history, literary fiction and nonfiction by young writers.

Marc Jaffe, Marc Jaffe Books (New York)
Books with a Western orientation, Jewish issues, fiction.

William Lung, Editorial (New York)
Literary fiction; nonfiction consistent with the house list.

John Radziewicz, Senior Editor and Director of Mariner Trade Paperbacks
Fiction, nonfiction, and poetry: Projects consistent with the house list.

Dawn Seferian, Executive Editor (New York)
Literary fiction and nonfiction; African American, Asian American, Latino, gay and lesbian fiction and nonfiction. Literary criticism and biography.

Janet Silver, Executive Editor (Boston)
Literary nonfiction and fiction. Nonfiction: biographies, arts and culture, women's issues. Focus on developing writers.

Frances Tenenbaum, Editor (Boston)
Gardening books. Oversees Taylor gardening guides and Tasha Tudor books.

HOUGHTON MIFFLIN BOOKS FOR CHILDREN

The Houghton Mifflin children's-book division stands out with a broad list that addresses topics of wide import; at all reading levels, the Houghton program accents works of thematic complexity and emotional depth. Imprints and lines include Walter Lorraine Books (illustrated and novelty titles) and Sandpiper Paperbacks.

Houghton Mifflin Books for Children publishes hardcover and paperback titles from picture books for the youngest readers to fiction for young adults, audio products, foldout books, board books, lift-the-flap books—and the house showcases a brace of successful authors as well. Caldecott and Newbery medallions abound in the tradition of Houghton Mifflin Books for Children.

Representing the Houghton Mifflin approach: *Baby Buggy, Buggy Baby* by Harriet Ziefert (illustrated by Richard Brown); *Curious George: A Pop-Up Book* (written and illustrated by H. A. Ray); *Under the Cherry Blossom Tree: An Old Japanese Tale* (retold and illustrated by Allen Say); *Secrets of Animal Flight* (written and illustrated by Nic Bishop); *Mist over the Mountains: Appalachia and Its People* (written and illustrated by Raymond Bial); *Shoes: Their History in Words and Pictures* (written and illustrated by Charlotte and David Yue; bibliography and index included).

Sandpiper Paperbacks include: *Table, Chair, Bear: A Book in Many Languages* (written and illustrated by Jane Feder); *Turtle Time* by Sandol Stoddard (illustrated by Lynn Munsinger); *Nights of the Pufflings* (written and illustrated by Bruce McMillan); *The Haunting of Cassie Palmer* by Vivien Alcock.

Query letters and SASEs should be directed to:

Ann Rider, Senior Editor

Margaret Kaymo, Senior Editor

Eden Edwards, Paperback Editor (Boston)

CLARION BOOKS
HOUGHTON MIFFLIN

215 Park Avenue South
New York, NY 10003
212-420-5800

Clarion publishes books, audiocassettes, and videos geared for the youngest readers up through the early teen years. Clarion's fiction includes serious, topical works and timeless classics. Clarion Books is an award-winning children's book division that is editorially independent of Houghton Mifflin's other lines.

On Clarion's list in fiction and picture books: *P. J. & Puppy* (written and illustrated by Cathryn Falwell); *The Polar Bear Son: An Inuit Tale* (retold and illustrated by Lydia Dabcovich); *The Great Frog Race and Other Poems* by Kristine O'Connell George (illustrated by Kate Kiesler; introduction by Myra Cohn Livingston); *Breath of the Dragon* by Gail Giles (illustrated by June Otani); *Danger Along the Ohio* by Patricia Willis; *Spider Boy* by Ralph Fletcher.

Nonfiction titles: *Stone Age Farmers Beside the Sea: Scotland's Prehistoric Village of Skara Brae* by Caroline Arnold (photographs by Arthur P. Arnold); *Gandhi, Great Soul* by John B. Severance; *Out of Darkness: The Story of Louis Braille* by Russell Freedman (illustrated by Kate Kiesler).

Query letters and SASEs should be directed to:

Dorothy Briley, Editor in Chief and Publisher

HOWARD UNIVERSITY PRESS
(See Directory of University Presses)

HRD PRESS
HUMAN RESOURCE DEVELOPMENT PRESS

22 Amherst Road
Amherst, MA 01002
413-253-3488
fax: 413-253-3490
800-822-2801
http://www.hrdpress.com (World Wide Web)

HRD Press (also known as Human Resource Development Press) is a business-publishing specialist. HRD category emphasis encompasses training-resource books, management, professional interest, and finance. HRD topic areas include customer service, tools for trainers, teams, change and problem solving, Situational Leadership, leadership and empowerment, performance-skills series, performance, interviewing, games and activities, sexual harassment, interpersonal skills, ethics, management and supervision, strategic planning, employee selection, and diversity.

From the HRD list: *The MbM Questionnaire: Managing by Motivation* (third edition), *The Visionary Leader: Leader Behavior Questionnaire*, and *Conflict Style Inventory* by Dr. Marshall Sashkin; *The New Fieldbook for Training: Tips, Tools, and Techniques* by John E. Jones, Ph.D., William L. Bearley, Ph.D., and Douglas C. Watsabaugh; *The HR Handbook* (edited by Elaine Biech and John E. Jones); *Self-Directed On-the-Job Learning Workshop* by William J. Rothwell, Ph.D.; *Establishing the Value of Training: Practical Tools and Techniques for Calculating Training Costs and Returns* by Sharon G. Fisher and Barbara J. Ruffino; *The Project Manager's*

Partner: A Step-by-Step Guide to Project Management by Michael Greer; *Flex Style Negotiating* by Alexander Watson Hiam.

HRD Press distributes to the trade through National Book Network.

Query letters and SASEs should be directed to:

Robert Carkhuff, President

HUMANICS PUBLISHING GROUP

1482 Mecaslin Street NW
Atlanta, GA 30309
404-874-2176
fax: 404-874-1976
800-874-8844

The Humanics publishing program covers the categories of self-help, how-to, psychology, human relations, health and nutrition, creative expression (in art, crafts, literature), education, humor, and spirituality. Special emphasis is on subjects such as personal growth, love and relationships, environment and peace, and Taoism. Market areas of concentration include elementary child and child development, teachers' resource books, childcare, and the family.

Humanics produces children's books under the Humanics Children's House imprint. The Humanics line of teachers' resource books and materials in child development are directed in part to colleges and institutional markets; popular works in this arena are published under the Humanics Learning imprint.

Humanics Publishing Group (founded in 1976) publishes a small- to medium-sized list of paperback trade books, a line of special fine editions, and audiocassettes.

Humanics titles: *The Magic of Zen* by Inez D. Stein; *The I Ching of Management* by William Sadler; *Many Paths, One Truth: The Common Thread* by Carole Addlestone; *While You Are Expecting: Your Prenatal Classroom* by F. Rene Van DeCarr and Marc Lehrer, M.D.; *The Creative Tao* by Pamela Metz; *Grief the Healer* by Jim McGregor; *A Goddess in My Shoes: Seven Steps to Peace* by Rickie Moore; *Balance of Body, Balance of Mind: A Rolfer's Vision of Buddhist Practice in the West* by Will Johnson; *Shades of Love: A Collection of Poetry* by JoAnne Berkow; *The Best Chance Diet* by Joe D. Goldstritch; *Working and Managing in a New Age* by Ron Garland.

The Humanics Tao series offers a variety of titles: *The Tao of Women* by Pamela Meets and Jacqueline Tobin; *The Tao De Ching: A New Approach—Backward Down the Path* by Jerry Dalton; *The Tao of Being: A Think and Do Workbook* and *The Tao of Relationships: A Balancing of Man and Woman* by Ray Grigg; *The Tao of Management: An Age-Old Study for New Age Managers* by Bob Messing.

Humanics oversees its own distribution.

Query letters and SASEs should be directed to:

Arthur Bligh, Acquisitions Editor
Adult trade books.

Humanics Children's House
Humanics Learning

The accent at Humanics Children's House is on original stories and tales targeted for younger readers, in a program geared primarily toward illustrated works. The Fun E. Friends series is one of the house's successful lines. Humanics produces guides for caregivers and educators under the Humanics Learning logo.

On the Children's House list: *Cambio Chameleon* by Mauro Magellan; *The Planet of the Dinosaurs* by Barbara Carr (illustrated by Alice Bear); *The Adventure of Paz in the Land of Numbers* by Miriam Bowden; *Giggle E. Goose, Fibber E. Frog, Fraid E. Cat*, and *Greb E. Dog* by Al Newman (illustrated by Jim Doody).

Titles for teachers and caregivers under the Humanics Learning imprint: *Parental Classroom: A Parent's Guide for Teaching Your Baby in the Womb* by Rene Van De Carr and Marc Lehrer; *Teaching Terrific Twos* by Terry Graham and Linda Camp; *The Infant and Toddler Handbook* by Kathryn Castle; *Toddlers Learn by Doing* by Rita Schrank.

Query letters and SASEs should be directed to:

Arthur Bligh, Humanics Children's House

Human Kinetics

1607 North Market Street
P.O. Box 5076
Champaign, IL 61820
217-351-5076
fax: 217-351-1549
800-747-4457 (orders)
http://www.humankinetics.com (World Wide Web)

Human Kinetics produces works in recreational and competitive sports, physical education, sports medicine, and fitness. Human Kinetics (founded in 1974) offers a list of trade and academic works (including college textbooks) that cover a wide range of athletic pursuits, with books geared for professional-level coaches, trainers, and participants, in addition to serious leisure-time athletes. Human Kinetics has established the Human Kinetics Foundation to issue grants promoting youth sports and school physical education.

A notable HK imprint is YMCA of America Books. Human Kinetics books are issued primarily in trade paperback editions, with special editions in hardcover. The press also publishes a number of periodicals in its areas of interest. Human Kinetics bills itself as the premier publisher for sports and fitness.

Frontlist titles: *Building Strength and Stamina: New Nautilus Training for Total Fitness* by Wayne Westcott, Ph.D./Nautilus International; *Strength Basics: Your Guide to Resistance Training for Health and Optimal Performance* by Brian B. Cook and

Gordon W. Stewart; *Training for Young Distance Runners* by Larry Greene and Russ Pate; *Hockey Drills for Puck Control* by Vern Stenlund; *AFCA's Defensive Football Drills* by the American Football Coaches Association; *Tennis Tactics: Winning Patterns of Play* by the United States Tennis Association; *Coaching Soccer Successfully* by Roy Rees and Cor van der Meer; *Playing the Post: Basketball Skills and Drills* by Burrall Paye; *Coaching Cheerleading Successfully* by Linda Rae Chappell.

The Fitness Spectrum series offers books that take the guesswork out of working out. Each book is packed with easy-to-use, color-coded workouts that add variety and produce results. Titles here: *Fitness Aquatics* by LeAnne Case; *Fitness Stepping* by Debi Pillarella and Scott O. Roberts.

Outdoor Pursuits is a series that emphasizes safety, environmental responsibility, and outdoor activity. Some titles: *Orienteering* by Tom Renfrew; *Rock Climbing* by Phil Watts; *Snowshoeing* by Sally Edwards and Melissa McKenzie.

Steps to Success Activity books represent a line designed to serve as primary resources for beginners in a variety of sports and activities. Readers learn to perform basic skills quickly and easily. Representative titles: *Archery* by Kathleen M. Haywood and Catherine F. Lewis; *Team Handball* by Reita E. Clanton and Mary Phyl Dwight; *Social Dance* by Judy Patterson Wright, Ph.D.

Backlist favorites: *Better Runs: 25 Years' Worth of Lessons for Running Faster and Farther* by Joe Henderson; *Basketball for Women: Becoming a Complete Player* by Nancy Lieberman-Cline and Robin Roberts; *Winning Racquetball: Drills, Skills, Strategies* by Ed Turner and Woody Clouse; *Your Child's Fitness: Practical Advice for Parents* by Susan Kalish; *Ice Skating: Steps to Success* by Karin Künzle-Watson and Steve DeArmond; *Offensive Baseball Drills* by Rod Delmonico.

Human Kinetics oversees its own distribution.

Query letters and SASEs should be directed to:

Rainer Martens, Publisher and President

HYPERION
HYPERION BOOKS FOR CHILDREN
DISNEY PRESS
MIRAMAX BOOKS

114 Fifth Avenue
New York, NY 10011-5690
212-633-4400

Hyperion (founded in 1991) publishes commercial fiction and literary works, and frontlist nonfiction in the areas of popular culture, international affairs, current topical interest, popular psychology and self-help, and humor. The house publishes books in hardcover, trade-paperback, and mass-market paperback formats. Hyperion operates a strong children's program that encompasses Hyperion Books for Children and Disney

Press. (See separate subentry below.) Miramax Books (see separate subentry below) concentrates on projects that tie in with the world of film.

Hyperion is part of Disney—the transnational corporate entity noted for its bountiful theme parks, hotels, and resorts, as well as its considerable ledger of film and television enterprises (including ABC, ESPN, Touchstone, Miramax, and Disney studios). Disney launched Hyperion as a full-fledged, well-funded book-publishing division, and the house's top-of-the-line reputation commenced with its initial well-chosen list.

Exemplifying the arrangements available for coveted properties via major media enterprises, Hyperion acquired publishing rights to *Takedown: The Pursuit and Capture of America's Most Wanted Computer Criminal* by cybersleuth Tsutomu Shinomura and journalist John Markoff (of *The New York Times*); Miramax Films simultaneously consummated a contract for dramatic (stage and screen) rights, as well as CD-ROM/interactive (computer game) rights to the project.

Representing Hyperion nonfiction: *Make the Connection* by Bob Greene and Oprah Winfrey; *The Path: Creating Your Mission Statement for Work and for Life* by Laurie Beth Jones; *A Separate Creation: The Search for the Biological Origins of Sexual Orientation* by Chandler Burr; *In Heaven As on Earth: A Vision of the Afterlife* by M. Scott Peck; *Disney's Family Cookbook: Irresistible Recipes That Make Mealtime Fun* by Deanna Cook and the Experts at Family Fun Magazine; *Living the Simple Life: 100 Steps to Scaling Down and Enjoying More* by Elaine St. James; *Foxworthy* by Jeff Foxworthy; *Lucille's Car Care: Everything You Need to Know from Under the Hood— by America's Most Trusted Mechanic* by Lucille Treganowan with Gina Catanzarite; *My Road to the Sundance: One Man's Journey into Native Spirituality* by Manny Twofeathers; *Think Yourself Thin: The Visualization Technique That Will Make You Lose Weight Without Exercise or Diet* by Debbie Johnson; *The Inner Elvis: A Psychological Biography of Elvis Aaron Presley* by Peter O. Whitmer.

More media-related hits include: *Go, Cat, Go! The Life and Times of Carl Perkins, the King of Rockabilly* by Carl Perkins and David McGee; *Knee Deep in Paradise* (memoir) by Brett Butler; *I'm Only One Man* by Regis Philbin with Bill Zehme; *I Am Spock* by Leonard Nimoy; *Spike, Mike, Slackers and Dykes: A Guided Tour Through a Decade of American Cinema* by John Pierson; *We Played the Game: 65 Players Remember Baseball's Greatest Era, 1947–1964* (edited by Danny Peary); *Ismail Merchant's Passionate Meals: The New Indian Cuisine for Fearless Cooks and Adventurous Eaters* by Ismail Merchant.

Emblematic of Hyperion fiction and literary works (including mystery, suspense, and thrillers): *Chain of Evidence* by Ridley Pearson; *Sunset Express* (an Elvis Cole novel) by Robert Crais; *The Free Fall of Webster Cummings* by Tom Bodett; *The Gettin Place* by Susan Straight; *Going Local* (mystery) by Jamie Harrison; *The Triggerman's Dance* by T. Jefferson Parker; *Crows over a Wheatfield* by Paula Sharp; *Cadillac Jukebox* by James Lee Burke.

Other notable projects have included *Myst: The Book of Atrus* (based on the bestselling CD-ROM game) by Robyn and Rand Miller; *Act of Betrayal* by Edna Buchanan; *Tropical Depression* by Laurence Shames; *Arise and Walk* by Barry Gifford.

Hyperion hardcover and trade paperback books are distributed to the trade by Little, Brown; Warner Books handles special sales as well as the mass-market paperback list.

The Hyperion editors listed (unless otherwise noted) acquire fiction and nonfiction titles consistent with the house description. Query letters and SASEs should be directed to:

Laurie Abkemeier, Senior Editor
Nonfiction concentration; no fiction.

Jennifer Barth, Editor

David Cashion, Associate Editor

Brian DeFiore, Editor in Chief

Lisa Hudson, Editor

Wendy Lefkon, Executive Editor
Disney-related projects.

Maureen O'Brien, Senior Editor
Major nonfiction: popular culture, current affairs, the media.

Will Schwalbe, Senior Editor

Gretchen Young, Editor

HYPERION BOOKS FOR CHILDREN
HYPERION PAPERBACKS FOR CHILDREN
DISNEY PRESS

The children's book division of Hyperion publishes titles for younger readers through young adult via a number of series, imprints, and lines. On the Hyperion children's division list are volumes that are finely designed and luxuriously produced in hardcover and paperback.

Hyperion Books for Children produces illustrated fairy tales, picture storybooks, poetry, illustrated fiction, calendars, and activity books—many of which are lavish, inventively presented works. Disney Press concentrates on illustrated works that tie in with Disney children's cinema classics, old and new—including series novelizations and books with cinematically conceived formats.

From Hyperion Books for Children: *William Wegman's Mother Goose* (retold by William Wegman; illustrated by the author); *Ten Bears Go Marching: A Pop-Up Counting Book* (by John Richardson, illustrated by the author); *The Sleepy Men* (by Margaret Wise Brown; illustrated by Robert Rayevsky); *Here Is the Westland* (by Madeleine Dunphy, illustrated by Wayne McLoughlin); *Lucky's 24-Hour Garage* (by Daniel Kirk, illustrated by the author); *The Wise Washerman: A Folktale from Burma* (retold by Deborah Froese; illustrated by Wang Kui); *Sea Sums* (by Joy N. Hulme; illustrated by Carol Schwartz); *Bonjour, Lonnie* (by Faith Ringgold; illustrated by the author; Caldecott Honor Award recipient); *Skeleton Closet: A Spooky Pop-Up Book* (by Steven Guarnaccia; illustrated by the author); *Klutz* (by Henrick Drescher; illustrated by the author); *American Fairy Tales from Rip Van Winkle to the Rootabaga Stories* (compiled by Neil Philip; illustrated by Michael McCurdy); *Sees Behind Trees* by Michael Dorris.

Other noteworthy titles: *Tim Burton's Vincent* (by Tim Burton; illustrated by the author; his first picture book, which he wrote and illustrated, was *The Nightmare Before Christmas*); *Anastasia's Album* (by Shelley Tanaka; edited by Hugh Brewster; the true story of the youngest daughter of Czar Nicholas II of Russia and her incredible life told through her own snapshots, diaries, and letters); *On Board the Titanic: An I Was There Book* (by Shelly Tanaka; illustrated by Ken Marschall; true-story account of the famous ocean liner's fate told through the eyes of two young survivors).

Hyperion is the publisher of bestselling author and radio host Garrison Keillor's first novel for children: *The Sandy Bottom Orchestra* by Garrison Keillor and Jenny Lind Nilsson (wife of Garrison Keillor).

Fiendly Corners by E. W. Leroe is a new Hyperion series that features paperback originals with eye-popping die-cut covers: *Fiendly Corners No. 1: Monster Vision*; *Fiendly Corners No. 2: Pizza Zombies*; *Fiendly Corners No. 3: Revenge of the Hairy Horror*; *Fiendly Corners No. 4: Nasty the Snowman*.

Hyperion is proud to announce an ongoing series of FamilyPC books designed to grow as families grow. The FamilyPC book series is intended as the absolute best option for parents who want to get the most productivity and fun out of their home computers—in tandem with the editors of award-winning *FamilyPC* magazine. Titles: *The FamilyPC Guide to Homework* by Gregg Keizer and the Editors of Family PC; *The FamilyPC Software Buyer's Guide* by Kurt Carlson, Valle Dwight, and the Editors of FamilyPC; *The FamilyPC Guide to Cool PC Projects* by Sam Mea and the Editors of Family PC.

Disney Press produces a lineup that includes picture books, board books, pop-up books, novels, and activity books. Many of these works are derived from such successful Disney cinematic productions as *101 Dalmatians*, *The Hunchback of Notre Dame*, *The Lion King*, *Beauty and the Beast*, *James and the Giant Peach*, *Aladdin*, *Pocahontas*, *Lady and the Tramp*, *Bambi*, *The Mighty Ducks*, and *The Little Mermaid*.

Special Hyperion project: *Since the World Began: Walt Disney World's First 25 Years* by Jeff Kurtti. This work celebrates the twenty-fifth anniversary of the Disney World theme park. The book is a lavish, entertaining, and absolutely unique history of Walt's city of dreams—and the world's most popular tourist destination.

Hyperion Books for Children and products from Disney Press are distributed to the trade by Little, Brown.

Query letters and SASEs should be directed to:

Andrea Cascardi, Associate Publisher

Lisa Holton, Vice President and Publisher

Ken Geist, Associate Publisher

Gretchen Young, Editor

Also works with core Hyperion adult-trade list.

Miramax Books

Miramax Books accents titles keyed to cinema—as a profession, industry, lifestyle, or avocation. The Miramax imprint develops a wide range of markets within this interest area. The Miramax list includes select original fiction (usually with a high-concept media link, or at least a halfway-celebrity author), reprints of novels that serve as the basis for films, and other movie tie-in projects.

From Miramax Books: *From Dusk Till Dawn* (a script by Quentin Tarantino); *The Last of the High Kings* (novel keyed to a film project) by Ferdia MacAnna; a currently untitled dark-comic novel by David Lipsky (author of *The Pallbearer*); *The Piano* (a script by Jane Campion); *The Postman* (a script by Antonio Skarmeta); *Jane Eyre* by Charlotte Brontë (classic fiction produced in a film tie-in reprint edition); *Pulp Fiction* (a script by Quentin Tarantino and Roger Avary).

Query letters and SASEs should be directed to:

Susan Dalsimer, Vice President of Publishing
Film-related projects.

David Cashion, Associate Editor
Books with media tie-ins, especially to film. Also works with core Hyperion trade list.

IDG BOOKS WORLDWIDE

919 East Hillsdale Boulevard, Fourth Floor
Foster City, CA 94404
415-655-3000
800-762-2974 (catalog requests)
http://www.idgbooks.com (World Wide Web)
http://www.dummies.com (World Wide Web)

IDG Books produces titles for the computer user and general nonfiction reader that cover a broad range of popular topics. The IDG computer list is keyed primarily to proprietary applications software and operating systems, and the house produces several prominent series in this vein.

IDG has well over 50 selections in the popular . . . FOR DUMMIES series; Hot . . . Secrets titles accent such areas as Windows, DOS, and network security; Macworld Books concentrates on the universe of Apple users; PC World handbooks are hands-on tutorial reference works. Many IDG books come packaged with bonus software that features some of the best in shareware, freeware, and macros.

IDG Books Worldwide (founded in 1990) is a subsidiary of International Data Group. Expanding beyond its original sphere of computer titles, IDG is interested in authors and/or potential projects that are appropriate for series in all areas of business and general reference. IDG takes pride in issuing books chock full of information and valuable advice the reader is not likely to encounter anywhere else—brought together with attention to quality, selection, value, and convenience.

Representative general computing titles from IDG Books Worldwide: *Discover Office 97* by S. O'Hara, D. Vega, and J. Kelley; *Caligari trueSpace Bible* by Peter Plantec; *Macworld Mac SECRETS* by David Pogue and Joe Schorr; *Windows 95 Simplified* by Maran Graphics.

On the expanding and highly successful . . . For Dummies list: *Windows 95 for Dummies* by Andy Rathbone; *The Internet for Dummies* by John Levine and Carol Baroudi; *Macs for Dummies* by David Pogue; *DOS for Dummies* by Dan Gookin. General interest titles: *Golf for Dummies* by Gary McCord with John Huggan; *Gardening for Dummies* by Michael MacCaskey and the Editors of the National Gardening Association; *Cooking for Dummies* by Bryan Miller and Marie Rama; *Wine for Dummies* by Mary Ewing-Mulligan and Ed McCarthy; *Fitness for Dummies* by Suzanne Schlosberg and Liz Neporent; *Dogs for Dummies* by Gina Spadafori; *Home Buying for Dummies* by Eric Tyson and Ray Brown; *Sex for Dummies* by Dr. Ruth Westheimer; *Selling for Dummies* by Tom Hopkins; *Job Hunting for Dummies* by Max Messmer; *Investing for Dummies* by Eric Tyson.

Backlist hits: *Windows for Dummies* by Andy Rathbone; *The Internet for Dummies* by John Levine and Carol Baroudi; *Macs for Dummies* by David Pogue; *DOS for Dummies* by Dan Gookin.

IDG Books Worldwide directs its own distribution services.

Query letters and SASEs should be directed to:

Mimi Sells, Public Relations Director

Brenda McLaughlin, Senior Vice President and Publisher, Technology

Kathleen A. Welton, Vice President and Publisher (Chicago)
Business and general reference books (does not do computer titles).
645 North Michigan Avenue
Chicago, IL 60611
312-482-8460

INDIANA UNIVERSITY PRESS
(See Directory of University Presses)

INDUSTRIAL PRESS
200 Madison Avenue
New York, NY 10016
212-889-6330
fax: 212-545-8327
INDUSPRESS@aol.com (e-mail)

Industrial Press produces scientific works, technical handbooks, professional guides, and reference books in the areas of engineering and the law, manufacturing processes and materials, design engineering, and quality control. The house offers a line of works designed for plant and industrial engineering interface with management and logistics. In addition to advanced professional books, Industrial Press produces basic references in its fields of interest.

Industrial Press (founded in 1883) is a leading specialist house in the professional, scientific, and scholarly publishing arenas. The publisher typically offers several hand-picked new titles a year in addition to its ongoing backlist of established sellers.

Industrial Press continues to offer its classic *Machinery's Handbook* by Erik Oberg, Franklin D. Jones, Holbrook L. Horton, and Henry H. Ryffel (elaborated from the Green–McCauley original), along with a companion guidebook (in fully revised formats).

Representative of the Industrial Press list: *Engineering Formulas, Conversions, Definitions, and Tables* by Frank Sims; *CNC Machining Handbook* by James Madison; *Setup Reduction Through Effective Workholding* by Edward G. Hoffman; *Blueprint Reading Basics* (second edition) by Warren Hammer; *Assembly Automation: A Management Handbook* (second edition) by Frank J. Riley; *Statistical Process Control* (second edition) by Leonard A. Doty; *Plastic Component Design* by Paul Campbell; *Why Systems Fail: And How to Make Sure Yours Doesn't* by David A. Turbide; *Purchasing for Manufacturing* by Harry E. Hough; *Lubrication for Industry* by Kenneth E. Bannister; and *Managing Factory Maintenance* by Joel Levitt; *Microbiologically Influenced Corrosion Handbook* by Susan Watkins Borenstein, *Fundamentals of Product Liability Law for Engineers* by Linda K. Enghagen, and *Pipefitter's Handbook* by Forrest R. Lindsey.

Industrial Press handles its own distribution.

Query letters and SASEs should be directed to:

John F. Carleo, Editorial Director

INNER TRADITIONS INTERNATIONAL
(See Directory of Religious, Spiritual, and Inspirational Publishers)

INTERVARSITY PRESS
(See Directory of Religious, Spiritual, and Inspirational Publishers)

IRWIN PROFESSIONAL PUBLISHING
1333 Burr Ridge Parkway
Burr Ridge, IL 60521
708-789-4000
800-634-3966

Irwin Professional produces a comprehensive lineup of business and professional publications. Areas within the Irwin scope include accounting, banking, corporate finance, employee benefits, entrepreneurship, financial advising, futures and options, general business, healthcare management, individual investing, institutional investing, management, manufacturing, marketing, quality, and sales.

Irwin slots such topical niches as business economics, international trade, real estate, small business, personal finance, fixed income, lending and retail banking, global investing, mutual funds, stocks, portfolio management, business strategy, communication, customer satisfaction, diversity, global management, executive management, sales management, operations, auditing, compliance, human resources, fraud prevention/ security, insurance, leadership, teams, and training.

Irwin Professional Publishing (part of McGraw-Hill) is the single largest publisher devoted to business publishing in the United States. Irwin strives constantly to create unique, innovative products tailored to meet the information demands of today's busiest people. The publisher produces an array of books, video seminars, and other media products of interest to seasoned corporate veterans as well as to rookie recruits—keyed to professional business markets worldwide.

Irwin Professional Publishing has a strong sales focus on the corporate and institutional market (featuring quantity discounts); of particular interest is the house's customer advisory service that involves working with individual companies to develop specially tailored in-house training programs that feature Irwin Professional Publishing products. In addition, Irwin Professional Publishing has a section that specializes in custom-published and copublished corporate projects.

ASQC Quality Press and Irwin Professional Publishing have a conjoint arrangement; the fruits of this endeavor include the Malcolm Baldridge National Quality Award Series as well as a line that focuses on issues of quality.

Irwin Professional (founded in 1965) went by the name of Dow Jones–Irwin until Dow Jones sold its interest in 1990; for several years subsequently the house published under the Business One Irwin imprint. Irwin merged with formerly independent Probus Publishing Company in late 1994.

Prior to its acquisition by Irwin Professional, Probus Publishing Company (founded in 1984) was a privately held house specializing in trade and professional books for investors, business professionals, and entrepreneurs. Combining the complementary strengths of Irwin and Probus creates a market leader with increased publishing savvy and financial strength—of potential benefit to authors and booksellers alike. The plan goes forward with a large and varied publishing program dedicated to the development and marketing of business and financial books—as well as other information of significance to professionals around the world.

A subsidiary of Times Mirror International Publishers/Times Mirror Company, Irwin Professional Publishing is part of the McGraw-Hill group of specialty publishers.

Titles: *Fraud: Bringing Light to the Dark Side of Business* by W. Steve Albrecht, Gerald Wernz, and Timothy L. Williams; *The Banking Revolution: Positioning Your Bank in the New Financial Services Marketplace* by Tom Harvey; *Getting the Money You Need: Solutions for Financing Your Small Business* by Gibson Heath; *Healthcare Marketing in Transition: Practical Answers to Pressing Questions* by Terrence J. Rynne; *Soros: The Life, Times, and Trading Secrets of the World's Greatest Investor* by Robert Slater; *Stocks for the Long Run: A Guide to Selecting Markets for Long-Term*

Growth by Jeremy J. Siegel; *Bogle on Mutual Funds: New Perspectives for the Intelligent Investor* by John C. Bogle; *The WOW Factory: Creating a Customer Focus Revolution in Your Business* by Paul Levesque; *Riding the Waves of Culture: Understanding Diversity in Global Business* by Fons Trompenaars; *The New Science of Marketing* by Vithala R. Rao and Joel W. Steckel; *The Ultimate Guide to Sport Event Management and Marketing* by Stedman Graham, Joe Jeff Goldblatt, and Lisa Delpy; *ISO 14000: A Guide to the New Environmental Management Standards* by Tom Tibor with Ira Feldman; *The Paradox Principles: How High-Performance Companies Manage Chaos, Complexity, and Contradiction to Achieve Superior Results* by Price Waterhouse Change Integration Team.

Irwin Professional Publishing handles its own distribution.

Query letters and SASEs should be directed to:

Jeffrey A. Krames, Associate Publisher and Editor in Chief
Individual investing, personal finance, management, sales and marketing management, employee benefits.

Kevin Commons, Editor
Finance and investment.

ISLAND PRESS

1718 Connecticut Avenue NW, Suite 300
Washington, DC 20009
202-232-7933
800-828-1302

West Coast operations:
P.O. Box 7
Covelo, CA 95428
707-983-6432
fax: 707-983-6414
http://www.islandpress.org

Island Press issues books for resource conservation professionals and activists. The Island Press list is keyed to topics and issues in ecology, conservation, nature, regional studies, science (including biology and natural sciences), landscape architecture, land use, education, policy and planning, economics, and reference. Island publishes hardcover and trade-paperback editions. The Shearwater Books imprint accents books of mainstream trade appeal and topical interest in hardbound and trade paper.

Island Press (founded in 1979; a subsidiary of Center for Resource Economics) pronounces itself: "the environmental publisher." Many Island Press books are authored in association with research groups, funds, and institutes with environmental focus.

From Island Press: *Nature's Services: Societal Dependence on Natural Ecosystems* (edited by Gretchen C. Daily; forewords by John Peterson Myers and Joshua S. Reichert); *The Next West: Public Lands, Community, and Economy in the American*

West (edited by John A. Baden and Donald Snow); *Conservation Through Cultural Survival: Indigenous Peoples and Protected Areas* by Stan Stevens; *The SCA Guide to Graduate Environmental Programs* by the Student Conservation Association (foreword by Scott D. Izzo).

Titles from Shearwater: *Fishcamp: Life on an Alaskan Shore* by Nancy Lord (illustrations by Laura Simonds Southworth); *Kinship to Mastery: Biophilia in Human Evolution and Development* by Stephen R. Kellert; *The Value of Life: Biological Diversity and Human Society* by Stephen R. Kellert; *The Others: How Animals Made Us Human* by Paul Shepard.

Island Press handles its own distribution.

Acquisitions are made primarily through the Washington office. Initial contact names and locations should be confirmed prior to any query. Query letters and SASEs should be directed to:

Barbara Dean, Executive Editor

Joe Ingram, Editor in Chief

JEWISH LIGHTS PUBLISHING

(See Directory of Religious, Spiritual, and Inspirational Publishers)

THE JEWISH PUBLICATION SOCIETY

(See Directory of Religious, Spiritual, and Inspirational Publishers)

KENSINGTON PUBLISHING CORPORATION
ZEBRA BOOKS
PINNACLE BOOKS

850 Third Avenue 16th Floor
New York, NY 10022-6222
212-407-1500
http://kensingtonbooks.com (World Wide Web)

The Kensington, Zebra, and Pinnacle programs cover all major categories of commercial and popular trade nonfiction and fiction. Kensington nonfiction is strong in issues-oriented investigatory works of topical interest, humor, health, self-help and awareness, true crime, and popular biography. Areas of fiction concentration include romance fiction (historical and contemporary), horror, mystery and suspense, thrillers, and women's fiction.

Kensington is one of the largest independently owned book publishers. Kensington Publishing Corporation is home to such divisional imprints as Kensington Books (primarily hardcover and trade paperback originals), along with Zebra and Pinnacle (mainly mass-market paperback editions, as well as selected hardcovers). Long a leader in the paperback category arena, the house has expanded its publishing emphasis along the commercial spectrum; under the Kensington and Zebra/Pinnacle banners, the house is a vital hardcover presence.

The Kensington mass-market imprint publishes quality and commercial fiction and nonfiction, both original titles and reprints.

Zebra Books (founded in 1975) and its sibling house Pinnacle Books (acquired in 1987) publish a colossal list of mass-market paperback originals that span the spectrum of mainstream and genre categories. Zebra and Pinnacle also produce mass-market reprints of hardcover originals, as well as fiction and nonfiction in trade paper, and designated high-profile titles in original hardcover editions.

The paperback-originals division of the house maintains a firm backlist of books—however, in keeping with mass-market rack tradition, titles that don't move are soon gone.

Kensington continues its romance program under such imprints, series, and lines as Lovegram Romance, Regency Romance, Historical Romance, and Arabesque (a line of multicultural romances).

Sample Kensington titles: *The Unauthorized X-Files Challenge: Everything You Ever Wanted to Know About TV's Most Incredible Show!* by James Hatfield and George "Doc" Burt; *The Official Bewitched Cookbook* by Kasey Rogers with Mark Wood; *Wake Up to Murder* (mystery) by Steve Allen.

Representative Zebra titles: *An Angel's Touch* by Heather Graham; *Obsession* by Wendy Morgan; *Enchant the Dream* by Kathleen Morgan; *Savannah Scarlett* by Becky Lee Weyrich; *Wings of Love* by Teresa George.

From Pinnacle: *Enchanted Fire* by Roberta Gellis; *Winter Woman* (western fiction) by F. M. Parker; *Evil Secrets* (nonfiction/true crime) by Kathy Braidhill; *American Presidents* (reference) by John Holmes; *Roll Over, Rover* (humor) by Richard Dommers.

Also on the house roster within the various fiction genres and categories are these backlist successes: *Vegas Heat* by Fern Michaels; *Murder Among Friends* (a Kate Austen mystery) by Jonnie Jacobs (from Partners in Crime); *Back\Slash: A Cyber Thriller* by William H. Lovejoy; *Pig Town* by William Caunitz.

Kensington oversees its own distributional operations.

All listed Kensington editors have a wide range of interests in fiction and nonfiction; some of their personal specialties are noted below. Query letters and SASEs should be directed to:

Tracy Bernstein, Executive Editor, Kensington (trade paper)
Nonfiction; mysteries/suspense, mainstream commercial fiction.

Paul Dinas, Editor in Chief
Supervises all hardcover trade and mass-market titles, as well as the Zebra and Pinnacle imprints. Specialties: true crime, nonfiction.

Kate Duffy, Senior Editor
Commercial fiction; women's stories, romance—especially Regencies, mysteries. Nonfiction.

Karen Haas, Consulting Editor
Commercial women's fiction, including romance.

Monica Harris, Editor
Romance, women's fiction, Arabesque.

Lee Heiman, Consulting Editor
Alternative-health companion.

Ann LaFarge, Executive Editor, Zebra
Women's fiction.

Carin Cohen Ritter, Consulting Editor
Commercial women's fiction, including romance.

John Scognamiglio, Senior Editor
Horror, psychological suspense, mysteries, romance.

MICHAEL KESEND PUBLISHING, LTD.

1025 Fifth Avenue
New York, NY 10028
212-249-5150
fax: 212-249-2129

Kesend's publishing scope is focused on travel, leisure, animals, pets, nature, the outdoors, hiking, nature, health, and sports. The house also produces a line of belles lettres and biographies (often with themes related to the core house interest areas). Kesend in addition publishes occasional serious new fiction as well as classic literary reprints, along with some general trade nonfiction (especially in healthcare issues).

Michael Kesend Publishing (begun in 1979) is an intimate house that offers personalized attention to the authors and books on its choice list. Kesend intends to pursue its program of publishing books with lasting quality that appeal to a broad readership.

Michael Kesend Publishing, Ltd. is now in its third decade. The publishing successes of recent years—primarily national and regional travel guidebooks—has resulted in numerous updated editions. The house typically releases a small number of new hardcover and trade paperback titles each year and maintains a backlist featuring the publisher's many perennial sellers.

Representing the Kesend list in travel, leisure, and the outdoors: *Art on Site: Country Artwalks from Maine to Maryland* by Marina Harrison and Lucy D. Rosenfeld; *A Guide to the Sculpture Parks and Gardens of America* by Jane McCarthy and Laurily K. Epstein; *Walks in Welcoming Places: Outings in the Northeast for Strollers of All Ages and the Disabled* by Marina Harrison and Lucy D. Rosenfeld; *The Essential Guide to Wilderness Camping and Backpacking in the United States* by Charles Cook; *Mountainsigns/Mountain Life* (in the illustrated Pocket Nature Guidebook series) by

Gerald Cox; *Care of the Wild, Feathered and Furred: Treating and Feeding Injured Birds and Animals* by Mae Hickman and Maxine Guy (with foreword by Cleveland Amory).

A novel with a travel theme is *Season of the Migration to the North* by Tayeb Salih (translated from the Arabic by Denys Johnson-Davies). Literary travel writing includes a reprint of the classic *A Poet's Bazaar: A Journey to Greece, Turkey, and Up the Danube* by Hans Christian Andersen.

Kesend books in sports and athletics: *The Historical Dictionary of Golfing Terms: From 1500 to the Present* by Peter Davies; *Swee'pea and Other Playground Legends: Tales of Drugs, Violence and Basketball* by John Valenti with Ron Naclerio; *Butch Beard's Basic Baseball: The Complete Player* by Butch Beard with Glenn Popowitz and David Samson (with foreword by Julius Erving).

Health and popular medicine from Kesend: *Hysterectomy: Learning the Facts, Coping with the Feelings, Facing the Future* by Wanda Wigfall-Williams; *Understanding Pacemakers* by David Sonnenburg, Michael Birnbaum, and Emil A. Naclerio.

Michael Kesend Publishing handles its own distribution.

Query letters and SASEs should be directed to:

Michael Kesend, Publisher

KITCHEN SINK PRESS

320 Riverside Drive
Northampton, MA 01060
413-582-7107

Kitchen Sink Press (founded in 1969) publishes graphic novels, collections of contemporary comic masters, and classic reprints in editions that encompass hardcover and paperback books, magazines, and comic books. The house also sells T-shirts, posters, serigraphs, portfolios, postcards, mugs, cloisonné pins, neckties, beach towels, satin jackets, finger puppets, statuettes, and other merchandise—all related to pictorial literary forms.

Along with such publishers as Fantagraphics and Last Gasp (please see separate entries in this directory), KSP is at the forefront of the movement to generate increased marketing of comics-related works (especially graphics novels and hardcover or trade paper collections) via traditional publishing-trade venues (independent bookstores as well as chain outlets) in addition to comics specialty shops. After Kitchen Sink acquired Tundra, another comics publisher, KSP relocated to Massachusetts from its previous Wisconsin headquarters.

Trade projects from Kitchen Sink: *A Century of Women Cartoonists* (edited by Trina Robbins); *Comics and Sequential Art* by Will Eisner; *Understanding Comics* by Scott McCloud; *The Comic Strip Art of Lyonel Feininger* (edited by Bill Blackbeard).

Narrative graphics and other pictorial literature: *Blab* (edited by Monte Beauchamp); *Black Hole* by Charles Burns; *Cherry Collection* by Larry Welz; *Introducing Kafka* by Robert Crumb and David Zane Mairowitz; *New York* by Will Eisner ("Father of the

Graphic Novel"); *Now, Endsville* by Carol Lay; *The Collected Crow* by James O'Barr; *Twisted Sisters* (edited by Diane Noomin); *Waiting for Food* by Robert Crumb; *Voodoo Child: The Illustrated Legend of Jimi Hendrix* (written by Martin I. Green; painted by Bill Seinkiewicz; bonus music CD: *Jimi by Himself*).

Kitchen Sink Press distributes its own products; the house also maintains distribution arrangements with mass-market and trade book establishments such as Berkley Books.

Query letters (with samples) and SASEs should be directed to:

Denis Kitchen, Publisher

Kivakí Press

P.O. Box 1053
Skyland, NC 28776
704-684-1988
fax: 704-684-7372

Kivakí Press is a small house with a focus on three editorial areas: environmental restoration; community renewal and education; and personal and holistic healing. Kivakí exists to provide people with practical strategies for restoring their ecosystems, for reconnecting with their places and local cultures, and for renewing their bodies holistically. Kivakí addresses academic, holistic health, and environmental book markets. Located in the mountains of North Carolina, the press produces a small number of new titles on a seasonal basis to add to a strong backlist.

Indicative of Kivakí interest: *A Wilder Life: Essays from Home* by Ken Wright; *The Company of Others: Essays in Celebration of Paul Shepard* (edited by Max Oelschlaeger); *Look to the Mountain: An Ecology of Indigenous Education* by Gregory Cajete; *Seasons of Change: Growing Through Pregnancy and Birth* by Suzanne Arms; *Restoration Forestry: An International Guide to Sustainable Forestry Practices* (edited by Michael Pilarski); *Flora of the San Juans: A Field Guide to the Mountain Plants of Southwestern Colorado* by Sue Komarek; *Sacred Land Sacred Sex: Rapture of the Deep—Concerning Deep Ecology and Celebrating Life* by Dolores LaChapelle; *Neuropathic Handbook of Herbal Formulas: A Practical and Concise Herb User's Guide* (revised edition) by Richard Scalzo.

Kivakí oversees its own distribution, including direct mail-order, and a trade distribution network that utilizes the facilities of several national fulfillment and distribution firms.

Query letters and SASEs should be directed to:

Fred Gray, Publisher

Knopf Publishing Group/Alfred A. Knopf

(See Random House)

KODANSHA AMERICA
KODANSHA INTERNATIONAL

114 Fifth Avenue
New York, NY 10011
212-727-6460

Kodansha America produces hardcover and trade paperback books in English by a variety of authors in a diverse array of subject areas. Interests include autobiography and biography, business and psychology, garden and design, health and lifestyle, parenting, self-help, history and sociology, natural history, world culture, religion and spirituality, and women's studies.

Kodansha America is the wholly owned United States subsidiary of Kodansha Ltd., Japan's largest publishing company (started in 1963 and headquartered in Tokyo). Kodansha America maintains the Kodansha Globe Trade Paperbacks imprint, and also acts as distributor and marketing representative for its sister company, Kodansha International. Kodansha America offers a strong seasonal list and tends a solid backlist.

The house list, including distribution/marketing clients Kodansha International and Japan Publications, has a sizable selection of individual works relating to Japanese cultural tradition.

Kodansha America's nonfiction includes: *Living Color: Master Lin Yun's Guide to Feng Shui and the Art of Color* by Sarah Rossbach and Lin Yun; *Ground Rules: What I learned My Daughter's Fifteenth Year* by Sherril Jaffe; *A Diary of the Century* by Edward Robb Ellis; *Niagara: A History of the Falls* by Pierre Berton; *One Life: The Autobiography of an African-American Actress* by Ellen Holly; *Baseball Letters: A Fan's Correspondence with His Heroes* by Seth Swirsky; *The Way We Are: The Astonishing Anthropology of Everyday Life* by Margaret Visser; *Bold New World: The Essential Roadmap to the Twenty-First Century* by William Knoke; *Not for America Alone: The Triumph of Democracy and the Fall of Communism* by George F. Mitchell; *The Roads to Sata: A 2000-Mile Walk Through Japan* by Alan Booth; *Like Hidden Fire: The Plot to Bring Down the British Empire* by Peter Hopkirk; *Moscow Days: Life and Hard Times in the New Russia* by Galina Dutkina; *Owning It: Zen and the Art of Facing Life* by Perle Besserman.

Kodansha fiction and literary writing (all of it translations from the Japanese) includes works from such authors as Kobo Abe, Sawako Ariyoshi, Takeshi Kaiko, Saiichi Maruya, Yukio Mishima, and Nobel laureate Kenzaburo Oe; the house also publishes critical works in art, culture, and letters from writers worldwide. Titles: *The Smoky Mountain Cage Bird Society and Other Magical Tales from Everyday Life* by John Skoyles; *On Kissing: Travels in an Intimate Landscape* by Adrianne Blue; *A Cultural History of Intoxicants in Society* by Richard Rudgley; *Coin Locker Babies* by Ryu Murakami; *A Healing Family* by Kenzaburo Oe; *The Art of Peter Voulkos* by Rose Slivka and Karen Tsujimoto; *Trash* by Amy Yamada.

Books on the Japan Publications list accent the interrelationship of physical and mental well-being in the contexts of health and fitness, cuisine and nutrition, and lifestyle.

Kodansha is distributed in the United States by OUP.

Query letters and SASEs should be directed to:

Philip Turner, Editor in Chief

History, exploration and adventure, memoir, animal behavior, sports, popular reference.

Deborah Baker, Executive Editor

Women's issues, autobiography, personal growth and development, health, cross-cultural narratives.

Nancy Cooperman, Senior Editor

Health and lifestyle, self-improvement, science, parenting, natural history, cross-cultural narratives, and popular reference in both narrative and how-to formats.

Joseph Sitaer, Assistant Editor

Popular culture, technology, self-improvement, Asia, memoir.

H. J. KRAMER INC.

(See Directory of Religious, Spiritual, and Inspirational Publishers)

KRAUSE PUBLICATIONS

700 East State Street
Iola, WI 54945
888-457-2873

Krause is a large publisher of trade nonfiction, with a concentration in antiques, collectibles, sewing, ceramics, and crafts and hobbies, as well as technical and professional topics (in such areas as engineering). Series include Contemporary Quilting, Creative Machine Arts, and a full lineup of consumer/trade titles that list current market values for a wide range of antiques and collectibles (usually in periodically updated editions).

Krause Publications has acquired the non-automotive titles of the Chilton Book Company, including all antique and collecting and sewing and craft lines. (For automotive titles, see entry for Chilton Book Company.)

Representative of the list: *Mom Always Said, "Don't Play Ball in the House," ... and Other Stuff We Learned from TV* by David and Joe Borgenicht; *Life Is Not a Dress Size: Rita Farro's Guide to Attitude, Style, and a New You* by Rita Farro; *The Art and Craft of Paper Sculpture: A Step-by-Step Guide to Creating 20 Outstanding and Original Paper Projects* by Paul Jackson; *Fruits, Vegetables and Berries—An Arranger's Guide* by Kally Ellis and Ercole Moroni; *StampCraft: Dozens of Creative Ideas for Stamping on Cards, Clothing, Furniture, and More* by Cari Haysom; *The Irresistible Bead: Designing and Creating Exquisite Beadwork Jewelry* by Linda Fry Kenzie;

Contemporary Decoupage: Fresh Ideas for Gifts, Keepsakes, and Home Furnishings by Linda Barker; *The Art of Manipulating Fabric* by Colette Wolff; *Outdoor Projects* by the editors of *Workbench*; *Rolling Bearings Handbook and Troubleshooting Guide* by Raymond A. Guyer, Jr.; *Warman's Coins & Currency* (in updated editions) by Allen G. Berman and Alex G. Malloy; *Collectors' Information Bureau's Collectibles Market Guide & Price Index* (in updated editions); *Coykendall's Complete Guide to Sporting Collectibles* by Ralph Coykendall, Jr.; *The Doulton Figure Collectors Handbook* (in updated editions).

Query letters and SASEs should be directed to:

Deb Faupel, Editor, Book Division

Don Johnson, Vice President of Publishing
Magazines and periodicals.

KTAV PUBLISHING HOUSE INC.
(See Directory of Religious, Spiritual, and Inspirational Publishers)

LAST GASP ECO-FUNNIES, INC.
LAST GASP OF SAN FRANCISCO

777 Florida Street
San Francisco, CA 94110
415-824-6636
http://www.lastgasp.com (World Wide Web)

Last Gasp covers the fields of popular and cult comics, underground comics, punk rock (recordings and print publications), popular and diverse subcultures, and marijuana literature. In addition to trade paperbacks and comics folios, the house produces an array of goods that relate to the world of illustrative art. Imprints include Gentzer & Gonif.

Last Gasp catalogs its own items, as well as publications from other houses and such diverse merchandise as poster art, decorative and illustrated cards, T-shirts and other apparel, and audio, visual, and multimedia works.

From Last Gasp: *The Binky Brown Sampler* by Justin Green; *She Comics: An Anthology of Big Bitch* by Spain; *Spots* by S. Clay Wilson; *Zap Comix* (entire series in reissue); *Complete Dirty Laundry Comics* by Aline Kominsky-Crumb.

Last Gasp Eco-Funnies, Inc. (founded in 1970) is distributed to the trade through Publishers Group West; the house shows heavy catalog sales through direct marketing.

Query letters and SASEs should be directed to:

Ronald E. Turner, Publisher

Gerald Kelleher, Editor

LATIN AMERICAN LITERARY REVIEW PRESS

121 Edgewood Avenue
Pittsburgh, PA 15218
412-371-9023

Latin American Literary Review Press produces reference books, trade books, and specialty publications in Latin American interest and studies. The press produces books in art, architecture, literature, and poetry; history, biography, and natural science; country studies, Spain, Europe, United States, Latin America; and children's books.

Latin American Literary Review Press (founded in 1980) is an independent house that is particularly vigorous in such fields as Latin American literature in English translation, Spanish-language art books, and literary criticism in Spanish. The press also publishes the journal *Latin American Literary Review*.

Representative titles in fiction and literature: *A Bag of Stories* (short stories) by Edla Van Steen (translated from the Portuguese by David George); *Bazaar of the Idiots* (stories) by Gustavo Alvarez Gardeazábal (translated by Jonathan Titler and Susan F. Hill); *Beatle Dreams and Other Stories* by Guillermo Samperio (translated by Russell M. Cluff and L. Howard Quackenbush); *Borinqueña: Puerto Rico in the Sixties* (fiction) by Flora Becker; *The Pink Rosary* (novel) by Ricardo Means Ybarra; *When New Flowers Bloomed: Short Stories by Women Writers from Costa Rica and Panama* (edited and with a prologue by Enrique Jaramillo Levi).

Nonfiction and critical works: *XVIII Century Spanish Music Villancicos of Juan Francés de Iribarren* by Marta Sánchez; *Mexican American Theater: Legacy and Reality* by Nicolás Kanellos; *The Art of Mariano Azuela* by Eliud Martínez.

Latin American Literary Review Press has its own in-house distribution operation; in addition, the house markets through direct-mail catalog dissemination, and utilizes a variety of national and regional distribution houses. Major markets include public libraries, trade booksellers, and university and college libraries. Latin American Literary Review Press handles distribution for a number of domestic and international presses.

Query letters and SASEs should be directed to:

Connie Matthews, Assistant to the Editor

Yvette E. Miller, President and Editor

Kathleen Ballew, Editorial Assistant

LEISURE BOOKS

276 Fifth Avenue, Suite 1008
New York, NY 10001
212-725-8811

Leisure's publishing program centers on mass-market paperback originals in fiction and nonfiction, with a short list of hardcover reprints. Leisure's category fiction embraces contemporary women's fiction, horror, mysteries and detective fiction, suspense, thrillers, and Westerns.

Leisure hosts a fine list from established genre writers, and also offers works from newer authors; the house publishes several brand-name category series and issues a notable number of deluxe double editions. The innovative Love Spell line has defined new market territory with experimental marketing slates in contemporary, historical, futuristic, and time-travel romance. Leisure Books (founded in 1970) is a division of Dorchester Publishing Company.

Indicative of Leisure Books interest: *Feather in the Wind* by Madeline Baker; *The Cowboys: Jake* by Leigh Greenwood; *Love's Ambush* by Theresa Scott; *Savage Longings* by Cassie Edwards; *Flame* by Connie Mason; *A Fire in the Blood* by Shirl Henke; *Fancy* by Norah Hess; *Sheik's Promise* by Carole Howey; *The Outlaw Viking* by Sandra Hill; *Timbal Gulch Trail* by Max Brand; *Renegade Nation* by Judd Cole; *Captive Legacy* by Theresa Scott.

Love Spell offers titles in Angel's Touch Romance, Faerie Tale Romance, Time-Travel Romance, Futuristic Romance, Paranormal Romance, Contemporary Romance, and Historical Romance.

Leisure Books handles its own distribution.

Query letters and SASEs should be directed to:

Alicia Condon, Editorial Director

Joanna Cagan, Editor

Don D'Auria, Editor
Westerns and technothrillers; horror.

Mira Son, Editorial Assistant

(Mr.) Chris Keeslar, Assistant Editor

LEXINGTON BOOKS
(See Jossey-Bass under Simon & Schuster listing)

LITTLE, BROWN AND COMPANY
(See Time Life Books)

LODESTAR BOOKS
(Imprint of Dutton/NAL; see Penguin USA)

LONELY PLANET PUBLICATIONS

155 Filbert Street, Suite 251
Oakland, CA 94607
510-893-8955
fax: 510-893-8563
info@lonelyplanet.com (e-mail)
http://www.lonelyplanet.com (World Wide Web) Lonely Planet's Web site includes up-to-date, down-to-earth travel information.

Lonely Planet specializes in travel guides and phrasebooks for the practical traveler, city guides, walking guides, and guides for those on a shoestring budget. Lonely Planet's list offers travel survival kits that provide in-depth coverage of a single country or group of countries with travel options for a range of budgets and styles. Lonely Planet also offers a line of literary travel narratives.

Lonely Planet Travel Atlas series comprise detailed full-color maps in a sturdy atlas format with comprehensive road and rail details and countrywide introductory sections. City Guides offer the best of the world's great cities in a pocket-sized format. Walking Guides offer informative and reliable route descriptions, easy-to-follow maps and advice on preparation, equipment, and supplies for some of the world's most exciting trekking routes. Phrasebooks are handy, pocket-sized books covering essential words and phrases for almost every travel situation.

Lonely Planet Journeys is a series that delves into the world's hidden places, capturing the spirit of a place and the nature of travel. These are books to read while you are planning a trip, while you are on the road, or while you are at home in your favorite armchair.

Lonely Planet Publications also offers audio packs that include unique language recordings to help travelers learn essential words and phrases and their correct pronunciation by participating in realistic travel situations. Lonely Planet videos offer original footage of today's most interesting destinations. These videos (as seen on the cable television Travel Channel) offer the same approach to travel as Lonely Planet guidebooks—get off the beaten track, be informed about where you are going, get to know the locals and have fun!

Recent titles: *Antarctica: Travel Survival Kit* by Jeff Rubin; *Full Circle: A South American Journey* by Luis Sepulveda; *Trekking in the Karakoram & Hindukush.*

The people at Lonely Planet (founded in 1975) strongly believe that travelers can make a positive contribution to the countries they visit, both through their appreciation of the countries' culture, wildlife, and natural features, and through the money they spend. In addition, Lonely Planet makes a direct contribution to the countries and regions it covers. Since 1986 a percentage of the income from each book has been donated to ventures such as famine relief in Africa; aid projects in India, agricultural projects in Central America, Greenpeace's efforts to halt French nuclear testing in the Pacific; and Amnesty International.

As the publisher's message suggests: "I hope we send the people out with the right attitude about travel. You realize when you travel that there are many different perspectives about the world, so we hope these books will make people more interested in what they see. These are guidebooks, but you can't really guide people. All you can do is point them in the right direction."

Lonely Planet produces an anecdotal and informative travel newsletter and distributes its own list in America through its United States office. The Lonely Planet Publications editorial division is located in Australia—though manuscripts and proposals are given preliminary consideration at the stateside contact address.

Query letters and SASEs should be directed to:

Eric Kettunen, U.S. Manager (at United States office)

LONGMEADOW PRESS

Longmeadow Press, begun in 1984, is no longer operating as a publisher. The house was a proprietary publishing division of the powerful retail-bookstore chain WaldenBooks.

LONGSTREET PRESS

2140 Newmarket Parkway, Suite 122
Marietta, GA 30067
770-980-1488
800-927-1488

Longstreet publishes general nonfiction (often with a Southern regional accent), travel and lifestyle, cooking and the kitchen arts, gardening, sports, inspiration, health, humor, photography and art, gift books, calendars, and selected fiction. Longstreet produces a series of books published in conjunction with the Arthritis Foundation.

Longstreet nonfiction: *The Millionaire Next Door* (analysis of wealthy Americans) by Thomas J. Stanley and William D. Danko (*New York Times* bestseller); *Dragons of God: A Journey Through Far-Right America* by Vincent Coppola; *The Spa Life at Home* by Margaret Pierpont and Diane Tegmeyer (photography by Jill Uris); *Somewhere in a Small Town* by T. Stacy Hamilton (photography by Cayce Callaway); *No More Bad Hair Days: A Woman's Journey Through Cancer, Chemotherapy, and Coping* by Susan Sturges Hyde; *Thelma's Treasures: Secret Recipes from One of the South's Finest Cooks* by Susanna Thomas with Thelma Linton; *Stressed Is Just Desserts Spelled Backwards: A Collection of Great American Desserts* by Sheryl Meddin and Bennett Frisch; *The BBQ Digest Glovebox Guide to Barbecue* (three volumes thus far: Alabama, Georgia, South Carolina) (edited by BBQ Digest); *The Dean Smith Photo Album: A Portrait of the Winningest Coach in NCAA Basketball History* by Phillip L. Ben; *1001 More Facts Somebody Screwed Up* by Deane Jordan; *The Americana Coca-Cola Calendar* (paintings by Jim Harrison); *Jeff Foxworthy's Laugh-a-Day Calendar* by Jeff Foxworthy (illustrated by David Boyd).

Fiction and literary works: *Jenny Dorset* (novel) by Philip Lee Williams; *Too Blue to Fly* (novel) by Judith Richards.

With the Arthritis Foundation: *250 Tips for Making Life with Arthritis Easier; Your Personal Guide to Living Well with Fibromyalgia; Arthritis 101: Answers to Your Questions About Arthritis* (all volumes by the Arthritis Foundation).

For children: *The Zoo Garden: 40 Animal-Named Plants Kids Can Grow Themselves* by Chris Hastings (illustrations by Janet Hamlin); *Old Missus Milliwhistle's Book of Beneficial Beasties* by Ron and Val Lindahn; *Super Science Secrets: Exploring Nature Through Games, Puzzles and Activities* by Sandra Markle.

Longstreet oversees its own distribution.

Query letters and SASEs should be directed to:

John Yow, Senior Editor

Chuck Perry, President and Editor

Suzanne Comer-Bell, Editor

LOOMPANICS UNLIMITED

Box 1197
Port Townsend, WA 98368

Loompanics Unlimited produces books of nonfiction trade interest in addition to professional and special-interest nonfiction. The Loompanics list accents practical self-help and how-to, contemporary and historical culture, and sociopolitical and issues-oriented works. The house offers a selective fiction list (primarily reprints of hitherto overlooked masterworks).

Loompanics offers books in such categories as underground economy, tax "avoision," money-making opportunities, individual privacy, fake identification, Big Brother is watching you, conducting investigations, crime and police science, locks and locksmithing, self-defense, revenge, guns, weapons, bombs and explosives, guerrilla warfare, murder and torture, survival, self-sufficiency, head for the hills, gimme shelter, health and life extension, paralegal skills, sex, drugs, rock and roll, intelligence increase, science and technology, heresy/weird ideas, anarchism and egoism, work, mass media, censorship, reality creation, self-publishing—and an enigmatic category of works classified solely as miscellaneous.

Since its foundation in 1973, Loompanics titles have been among the most controversial and unusual publications available, and the publishing program (which includes books, audiotapes, and videocassettes) has produced recognized classics in a number of fields.

Many Loompanics publications test the edge of the free-speech envelope—and often do so with humorous subversiveness and literary zest; some of the more treacherous materials are clearly intended exclusively for amusement, informational, or scholarly reference purposes.

Loompanics features: *The Outlaw's Bible* by E. X. Boozhie; *Natural Law: Or Don't Put a Rubber on Your Willy* by Robert Anton Wilson; *Take No Prisoners: Destroying Enemies with Dirty and Malicious Tricks* by Mack Nasty; *Gaslighting: How to Drive Your Enemies Crazy* by Victor Santoro; *Poison Pen Letters* by Keith Wade; *Getting Started in the Underground Economy* by Adam Cask; *Anarchic Harmony: The Spirituality of Social Disobedience* by William J. Murray; *Principia Discordia: Or How I Found the Goddess and What I Did to Her When I Found Her* by Malaclypse the Younger; *How to Sneak into the Movies* by Dan Zamudio; *Practical LSD Manufacture* by Uncle Fester; *Secondhand Success: How to Turn Discards into Dollars* by Jordan L. Cooper; *The Hitchhiker's Handbook* by James MacLaren; *The Politics of Consciousness: A Practical Guide to Personal Freedom* by Steve Kubby; *Stoned Free: How to Get High Without Drugs* by Patrick Wells with Douglas Rushkoff; *You Are Going to Prison* (a survival guide) by Jim Hogshire.

From the arena of literary fiction: *Freak Show* (a classic literary novel in reprint) by Jacquin Sanders; *The Gas* (another classic literary work in reissue) by Charles Platt.

Some backlist Loompanics hits: *Bad Girls Do It! An Encyclopedia of Female Murderers* by Michael Newton (author of *Serial Slaughter: What's Behind America's Murder Epidemic?*; *Hunting Humans: An Encyclopedia of Modern Serial Killers*); *Psychedelic Shamanism* by Jim DeKorne; *Secrets of a Superhacker* by an incognito information superhighwayman known as the Knightmare; *Shadow Merchants: Successful Retailing Without a Storefront* by Jordan L. Cooper; *The Art & Science of Dumpster Diving* by John Hoffman (with original comix by Ace Backwords); *The Emperor Wears No Clothes—Hemp and the Marijuana Conspiracy* by Jack Herer; *Community Technology* by Karl Hess; *Free Space: Real Alternatives for Reaching Outer Space* by B. Alexander Howerton; *How to Obtain a Second Passport and Citizenship and Why You Want To* by Adam Starchild; *The Rape of the American Constitution* by Chuck Shiver; *The Wild and Free Cookbook* by Tom Squire; *Travel-Trailer Homesteading Under $5,000* by Brian D. Kelly; *Screw the Bitch: Divorce Tactics for Men* by Dick Hart.

Special Loompanics compilations: *Loompanics' Greatest Hits: Articles and Features from the Best Book Catalog in the World* (edited by Michael Hoy); *Loompanics Unlimited Live! in Las Vegas* (edited by Michael Hoy).

Loompanics Unlimited is editorially a reclusive house. Writers who wish to work with Loompanics should note that their business is the printed word, and potential authors should approach Loompanics through the printed word (via mail—do not telephone). The publisher also notes that the press tends toward small advances and works through literary agents only on occasion.

The Loompanics Unlimited direct-order catalog (emblazoned with the publisher's freebooter-spaceship colophon) depicts a wealth of titles from its own list as well as select offerings from other houses in a luscious newsprint format that includes graphics, essays, and short fiction, as well as blurbs from reviewers and satisfied customers testifying to the potency of the house's list and the efficacy of the Loompanics distribution and fulfillment services.

Query letters and SASEs should be directed to:

Michael Hoy, President

Dennis Eichhorn, Editorial Director

LOTHROP, LEE & SHEPARD BOOKS

(See William Morrow & Company, Inc. under The Hearst Book Group)

LOUISIANA STATE UNIVERSITY PRESS

(See Directory of University Presses)

LOWELL HOUSE

2020 Avenue of the Stars, Suite 300
Los Angeles, CA 90067
310-552-7555
fax: 310-552-7573

Lowell House is dedicated to publishing quality nonfiction in such fields as medicine and health, self-help and improvement, cuisine, parenting, and areas of women's interest. The press also hosts a flourishing children's-publishing division. Lowell House specialty imprints include Anodyne, Extension Press, Global Gourmet, Legacy Press, and Woman to Woman. Lowell House (established in 1988) is a division of RGA Publishing Group.

The **Anodyne** line addresses contemporary health and medical issues and concerns; Anodyne offers titles with an overall emphasis on innovative approaches in prevention, acceptance, and action.

Extension Press helps those who want to help themselves; the Extension list accents entertaining and practical works to help readers master the skills that make life interesting.

Global Gourmet purveys a line of cookbooks—most of which feature healthy low-fat fare; the imprint concentrates on unusual recipes from creative cooks featuring the world's cuisines so that the reader may indulge in gourmet without guilt.

Legacy Press addresses concerned parents who have an interest in raising the healthy family through books that exemplify the human side of parenting—top-quality advice by experts in the field.

The **Woman to Woman** imprint issues titles primarily authored by women (as well as by an occasional qualified man). These works are directed toward women readers and are about such concerns as career, health, and relationships; the imprint embodies a veritable support group between book covers.

Titles from the **Lowell House** imprint include general trade books that address topics both timely and timeless.

Representative of the Lowell House list: *The Reagan Years A to Z* by Kenneth Kurz, Ph.D.; *The 50 Most Influential Women in Law* by Dawn Bradley Berry, J.D.; *The Plastic Surgery Sourcebook* by Kimberly Henry, M.D., and Penny Heckaman; *The Thyroid*

Sourcebook: Everything You Need to Know by M. Sara Rosenthal; *The Eating Disorder Sourcebook: Everything You Need to Know* by Carolyn Costin; *The Teacher's Almanac: The Professional Teacher's Handbook* by Pat Woodward; *The Writer's Sourcebook: From Writing Blocks to Writing Blockbusters* by Rachel Ballon; *The Dram Sourcebook Journal: A Bedside Companion* by Phyllis Koch-Sheras, Ph.D., Peter Sheras, and Amy Lemley; *The Men's Health Sourcebook: Everything You Need to Know* by Alfred Dashe, M.D.; *Three Generations of Chilean Cuisine* by Mirtha Umaña-Murray; *The Breast Sourcebook: Everything You Need to Know About Cancer Prevention, Treatment, and Politics* by M. Sara Rosenthal; *Making The Radiation Therapy Decision* by David J. Brenner, Ph.D., and Eric J. Hall.

Lowell House titles are distributed through Contemporary Books; special sales are handled by the Lowell House/RGA Publishing Group home office.

Query letters and SASEs should be directed to:

Bud Sperry, Editor in Chief
All described areas.

LOWELL HOUSE JUVENILE

The Lowell House Juvenile division issues well-designed books in a number of distinct lines geared to appeal to youthful readers. Beanstalk Books make learning fun through the vehicle of high-quality illustrated and photographic titles—picture books, board books, and activity books for kids ages 2 to 6. FRESH stands for *f*riendly, *r*eal, *e*steem-building, *s*mart, and *h*onest; the FRESH line of nonfiction books explores topical issues that affect today's young females. Gifted & Talented books are designed by experts in the field of early childhood education to bring out every child's gifts via workbooks, beginning readers, picture books, and reference works. Periscope Press brings the mysteries and wonders of the natural world into sharp focus for readers ages 5 to 13; in addition to science titles, Periscope offers reference works in language arts, writing, and more.

Introducing a brand-new series of novels from the creators of the Scary Stories for Sleep-Overs. Each bone-chilling novel in this all-new series is a surefire fright. Representative titles: *The Living Ghost* and *Lost in Horror Valley* by Allen B. Ury.

Titles for the age range from 8 to 12: *Gross Goodies: Sickening Sweets That Look Detestable But Taste Delectable* by Tina Vilicich-Solomon; *Martial Arts Masters* by Ngo Vinh-Hoi; *Aliens: Terrifying Extraterrestrial Tales* by Don Wulffson; *The 25 Scariest Hauntings in the World* (story by Mary Batten; illustrations by Brian W. Dow); *Scary Stories from 1313 Wicked Way* by Craig Strickland.

Gifted & Talented series titles: *Gifted & Talented Reading Comprehension: A Workbook for Ages 6–8* (text by Martha Cheney; illustrated by Leo Abbet); *Gifted & Talented: More Questions & Answers for Ages 4–6* (text by Bailey Kennedy; illustrated by Larry Nolte); *Gifted & Talented Reading Puzzles & Games: A Workbook for Ages 4–6* (text by Martha Cheney; illustrated by Kerry Manwaring). *Gifted & Talented Math Puzzles & Games: A Workbook for Ages 4–6* (text by Martha Cheney, illustrated by Larry Nolte).

The Wordshop Workbooks are designed to build children's knowledge and understanding of the alphabet as well as to develop their ability to use the dictionary as a reference guide. Titles: *Word and Dictionary Workbook: Kindergarten*; *Word and Dictionary Workbook: First Grade*; *Word and Dictionary Puzzles & Games: Kindergarten–First Grade* (volumes written by Kaye Furlong, illustrated by Rick Detorie).

Query letters and SASEs should be directed to:

Brenda Pope Ostrow, Children's Editor

LYONS & BURFORD PUBLISHERS

31 West 21st Street
New York, NY 10010
212-620-9580
fax: 212-929-1836
800-836-0510 (orders)

Lyons & Burford produces trade nonfiction, especially books on the outdoors, natural history, and outdoor recreation and sports; the house also produces works aimed at regional interests worldwide, selected literary fiction and essays, and reference. A successful Lyons & Burford line is the Cook's Classic Library, featuring reprints of books on food and cooking.

The company logo shows a leaping cetacean poised gracefully midair over the publisher's ingenuous L&B colophon. Lyons & Burford produces a midsize seasonal roster of new titles and keeps a substantial backlist.

From Lyons & Burford: *Spy on the Roof of the World* (Himalayan espionage chronicle) by Sydney Wignall; *Equinox: Life, Love, and Birds of Prey* by Dan O'Brien; *Furniture by Design* by Graham Blackburn; *Classic and Antique Fly-Fishing Tackle: A Guide for Collectors and Anglers* by A. J. Campbell; *Too Soon to Panic* (insider account of professional tennis) by Gordon Forbes; *Water Workouts* by Steve Tarpinian and Brian Awbrey, M.D.; *The Foraging Gourmet* by Katie Letcher Lyle; *The Master of Putting* by George Low with Al Barkow; *The Juggling Book* by Peter Owen.

Fiction and literature: *Dry Rain* (stories) by Pete Fromm; *Travers Corners* (stories about the Lake Wobegon of fly fishing) by Scott Waldie.

Lyons & Burford (independent publishers since 1984) handles its own distribution.

Query letters and SASEs should be directed to:

Nick Lyons, President

Peter Burford, Publisher

Lilly Golden, Editor

M & T BOOKS

(See Henry Holt and Company)

MACMILLAN PUBLISHING GROUP

(See Simon & Schuster)

MANIC D PRESS

1853 Stockton
San Francisco, CA 94133
415-788-6459

Manic D Press (founded in 1984) produces a short list of contemporary fiction, poetry, literary works, and creative nonfiction. Emphasis is on innovative styles and nontraditional writers and artists. The house publishes primarily in trade paperback editions, and offers a line of recordings.

Featured on the Manic D list: *Alibi School* by Jeffrey McDaniel; *King of the Road-kills* by Bucky Sinister; *The Rise and Fall of Third Leg* by Jon Longhi; *Signs of Life: Channel Surfing Through the 90s Culture* (edited by Jennifer Joseph and Lisa Taplin); *The Underground Guide to San Francisco* (edited by Jennifer Joseph).

Manic D Press distributes through Publishers Group West.

Query letters and SASEs should be directed to:

Jennifer Joseph, Publisher

MARLOWE & THUNDER'S MOUTH
MARLOWE & COMPANY
THUNDER'S MOUTH PRESS

632 Broadway
New York, NY 10012
212-780-0380

Marlowe & Thunder's Mouth emphasizes trade nonfiction in current events, contemporary culture, biography/personality, the arts, and popular reference. Marlowe & Thunder's Mouth combines two previously independent firms, Thunder's Mouth Press and Marlowe & Company, each with overlapping fields of concentration and its own distinct publishing persona.

Thunder's Mouth Press (founded in 1980) upholds a tradition of producing high-interest nonfiction (as well as selected fiction with media/cultural cross-publicity potential). Thunder's Mouth is known for works of quirky ambiance and decidedly popular appeal. An overview of the Thunder's Mouth nonfiction program provides a list particularly strong in the areas of topical issues, popular culture, and specialty reference. In fiction, Thunder's Mouth spouts modern and contemporary literary writing in addition to classic genre fiction, poetry, and works for stage and screen, with additional focus on the African American tradition, works from the Beat generation, and hitherto underappreciated women authors (many of these works published in reprint editions).

During early 1995, Thunder's Mouth initiated a radical restructuring. Thunder's Mouth publisher Neil Ortenberg announced that substantially all assets of the house had been acquired by Avalon Publishing Group, an affiliate of Publishers Group West (the distribution house with an East Coast office located conveniently adjacent to the Thunder's Mouth digs). The Thunder's Mouth program was downsized dramatically—everyone was fired, leaving Ortenberg the sole crew. The house was poised for consolidation and regrowth, with a projected scenario reminiscent of that at Grove/Atlantic.

Thunder's Mouth merged with Marlowe & Company, a new, independent house headed by John Webber. Marlowe was previously part of Universal Sales and Marketing, a promotional and remaindering operation; the new Marlowe operation purchased the Paragon Publishing backlist. In tandem with the Thunder's Mouth literary resources, this evolving publishing entity (known corporately as Marlowe & Thunder's Mouth) features two main imprints (Marlowe and Thunder's Mouth) and covers the publishing spectrum from commercial to controversial.

Please note: The overall house focus and imprint identities are currently believed to be in transition.

Representative general nonfiction: *Synchronicity: Science, Myth, and the Trickster* by Allan Combs and Mark Holland; *Hot Copy: Behind the Scenes at the Daily News* by Theo Wilson; *Murder in Memphis: The FBI and the Martin Luther King Assassination* by Mark Lane and Dick Gregory; *Judgment at the Smithsonian: The Bombing of Hiroshima and Nagasaki* by Philip Nobile; *The Big White Lie: The Inside Story of the Deep Cover Sting Operation That Exposes the Drug War* by Michael Levine with Laura Kavanau-Levine; *Information Warfare: Chaos on the Electronic Superhighway* by Winn Schwartau; *The Canary Syndrome: The Complete Guide for Diagnosing, Treating, and Preventing Environmental Illness* by Dana Godbout Laake and Cindy Sharon Spitzer; *Doctors Are Gods: Corruption and Unethical Practices in the Medical Profession* by David Jacobsen and Eric D. Jacobsen; *The Baby Name Countdown: Meanings and Popularity Ratings for 50,000 Names* by Janet Schwegel.

Works with a cultural/personality tilt: *Captain Trips: A Biography of Jerry Garcia* by Sandy Troy; *Fear and Loathing: The Strange and Terrible Saga of Hunter S. Thompson* by Paul Percy; *John Lennon: In My Life* by Pete Shotton with Nicholas Shaffner; *To Be, or Not . . . tgo Bop: Memoirs—the Autobiography of Dizzy Gillespie* by Dizzy Gillespie and Al Fraser; *The Velvet Years, 1965–1967: Warhol's Factory* (photography, graphics, and essay) by Stephen Shore and Lynne Tillman.

Sample fiction and literary works: *A Treasury of African Folklore* (edited, retold, and with commentary by Harold Courlander); *Life Is Hot in Cracktown* by Buddy Giovinazzo; *Goodbye, Sweetwater: New and Selected Stories* by Henry Dumas; *City of Light* by Cyrus Colter; *Panther* by Melvin Van Peebles (who authored the screenplay for the film of the same name, directed by his son Mario Van Peebles—whose first movie appearance was as a kid in Melvin's own classic *Sweet Sweetback's Baadasssss Song*).

Another event of media interest was the publication of *Marita* (memoir) by Marita Lorenz, Fidel Castro's former mistress. In a related development, Thunder's Mouth publisher Ortenberg was wed to Lorenz's daughter, the internationally known cultural luminary Monica Mercedes.

Meanwhile: What has the name Thunder's Mouth got to do with all this? William Shakespeare's *King John* provides the source: "O that my tongue were in the thunder's mouth! Then with a passion would I shake the world."

Marlowe & Thunder's Mouth Press is distributed by Publishers Group West.

Query letters and SASEs should be directed to:

Neil Ortenberg, Senior Editor and Publisher, Thunder's Mouth

John Webber, Publisher, Marlowe

Masquerade Books

801 Second Avenue
New York, NY 10017
212-661-7878
fax: 212-986-7355
800-375-2356 (orders)
MaqBks@aol.com (e-mail)

Masquerade Books (founded in 1989) is dedicated to vanguard publishing in a number of breakthrough literary sectors: dark romance, erotica, futurist fiction, horror, and crime, as well as creative/niche high-interest nonfiction and literary works. Masquerade is known for writers with original voices issued through mass-market paperback originals as well as hardcovers and trade paperbacks.

Masquerade Books lets this be known: Send a manuscript in; if we like it, we'll want to publish it. Areas of potential interest are open, as is format: Hardcover, trade paper, mass-market paperback. "If we can make money on it, we'll publish it."

Masquerade imprints include Badboy, Hard Candy, Rhinoc*Eros*, a Richard Kasak Book, and Rosebud. Writers who wish to submit works to the house should request a set of guidelines (include SASE with your guideline query).

Here's an overview of some of Masquerade's special-imprint series (primarily mass-market paperback releases, with some trade-paper editions and occasional hardcovers).

Masquerade: Straight erotica, usually with an SM bent. Includes Victorian titles.

Badboy: Erotica for gay men.

Rosebud: Erotica for gay women. Includes the Leatherwomen series.

Hard Candy: Literary works by gay men and women with a strong emphasis on sexuality and sexual themes.

Rhinoc*Eros*: Pansexual literary works with a strong emphasis on sexuality and sexual themes. Includes the Marketplace series.

A Richard Kasak Book is an imprint designation given to many of the house's more mainstream trade projects.

Selected titles: *Albrick's Gold* (medical thriller) by Simon LeVay; *Lust, Inc.* by Erica Bronte; *Bound to the Past* by Amanda Ware; *The Ties That Bind* by Vanessa Duriés;

The Darker Passions: The Picture of Dorian Gray by Amarantha Knight; *The Parlor* by N. T. Morley; *Passion in Tokyo* by Sachi Mizuno; *The Captivity of Celia* by M. S. Valentine; *The Best of Paul Little* by Paul Little; *Come Quickly: For Couples on the Go* (edited by Julian Anthony Guerra); *Once upon a Time: Erotic Fairy Tales for Woman* (edited by Michael Ford); *Backstage Passes: An Anthology of Rock-and-Roll Erotica from the Pages of Blue Blood Magazine* (edited by Amelia G).

Samples from the heralded backlist: *Ask Isadora* by Isadora Alman; *The Repentance of Lorraine* by Andrei Codrescu; *Flesh* by Philip José Farmer, *Chains* by Larry Townsend; *The Sexpert* by Pat Califia; *F/32* by Eurydice; *Dryland's End* by Felice Picano; *Unnatural Acts* by Lucy Taylor; *The Motion of Light in Water* by Samuel R. Delany.

Masquerade also publishes a bi-monthly erotic newsletter.

Masquerade orchestrates its own sales and distribution; orders are handled in house as well as through a network of regional distributors and wholesalers.

Query letters and SASEs should be directed to:

Richard Kasak, Publisher

Jennifer Reut, Managing Editor

Kiri Blakeley, Editor

McGraw-Hill Publishing Group
Business McGraw-Hill
Osborne/McGraw-Hill
TAB Books
Ragged Mountain Press

New York offices:
11 West 19th Street
New York, NY 10011
212-512-2000

McGraw-Hill operates specialty programs in a variety of professional, business, and educational fields, such as law, healthcare, high-tech industries, and college textbooks. The house produces books for professional, institutional, and trade markets; journals keyed to core areas of interest; seminar and group workshop materials; and issues a selection of electronic products (including CD-ROM).

McGraw-Hill officially disbanded its adult general trade book-publishing operation in 1989; since then, the house's lineup of professional and reference book divisions has continued to thrive. Still geared primarily toward business and professional titles, McGraw-Hill is again venturing into the broader range of commercial trade arenas. In the United States, this international house publishes titles in business, trades and technical fields, computing, architecture, engineering/electronics, science, and leisure. (See subentries below.)

An area of particular McGraw-Hill presence encompasses the interface of business, personal computing, and computer science; many of these titles are published from within the McGraw-Hill list and that of the Osborne/McGraw-Hill subsidiary. (See separate subentries below.)

McGraw-Hill distributes for all its divisions.

BUSINESS MCGRAW-HILL

Business McGraw-Hill produces trade and professional titles in business, finance, entrepreneurship, marketing, training, human resources, investing, management, advertising, sales, self-help, and communication.

Indicative of the Business McGraw-Hill list: *The Power of Management Capital: Reconnecting the Disconnected Corporation* by Armand Feigenbaum; *The Culture of Success: Building a Competitive Advantage by Keeping Your Corporate Vision in Sight* by John Zimmerman and Ben Tregge; *Creativity Boosters: Provoking Creativity in Individuals and Organizations* by H. James Harrington; *Virtual Learning: A Paradoxical Approach to Building the High Performance Organization* by Roger Schank; *Great Personal Letters for Busy People: 300 Ready-to-Use Letters for Every Occasion* by Dianna Booher; *WOW! Résumés for Creative Jobs* by Matthew J. DeLuca and Nanette F. DeLuca; *7 Secrets of Successful Women* by Donna Brooks and Lynn Brooks; *Jenrette: The Contrarian Manager* by Richard Jenrette; *Reflections for the Workplace: A Collection of Wisdom and Inspiration for Working People Everywhere* by Bruce Hyland and Merle Yost; *The Articulate Executive: Learn to Look, Act, and Sound Like a Leader* by Granville N. Toogood.

Query letters and SASEs should be directed to:

Susan Barry, Editorial Director
Management, current events, investing.

Betsy Brown, Senior Editor
Career, self-help, executive skills, communications.

Barbara Gilson, Editorial Director, Schaum
Popular reference, educational reference, guidance, careers, self-help.

Mary E. Glenn, Editor
Management and management theory, self-help with a business focus, some marketing and sales; topical books with global appeal that can cross over into serious nonfiction.

Richard Narramore, Senior Editor
Training and development, organizational development, management.

Philip Ruppel, Publisher
All areas indicated in house description, including marketing, management, quality, human resources, training, operations management.

COMPUTING MCGRAW-HILL

Computing McGraw-Hill is the trade designation (used widely in advertising and promotional venues) for titles in computing that emerge from the various McGraw-Hill divisions, including a number of projects acquired through the trade/business wing as well as some from the Osborne/McGraw-Hill subsidiary (please see separate subentry below).

Computing titles from McGraw-Hill: *Hands-On ATM* by David McDysan and Darren Spohn; *The Complete Guide to Java Database Programming* by Ken North; *Public Key Infrastructure* by the CommerceNet PKI Task Force; *Webmaster Engineer Certification Handbook* by Net Guru Technologies, Inc.; *Web Objects* by Ron Ben-Natan; *Internet Explorer 4.0: Browsing and Beyond* by Dave Johnson.

OSBORNE/MCGRAW-HILL

2600 Tenth Street
Berkeley, CA 94710
510-549-6600

Osborne/McGraw-Hill targets the hands-on user approach to computer software, hardware, and systems, with many titles geared toward specific types of projects or proprietary systems and programs. Many titles on the Osborne/McGraw-Hill list are book/software packages.

Primary areas of Osborne/McGraw-Hill interest include spreadsheets, accounting, integrated software, graphics, word processing, desktop publishing, computer-aided design, telecommunications, networking, operating systems, hardware, programming languages, databanks, and business applications, as well as games and entertainment. The house also frontlists select titles with broader appeal for a wide range of computer-friendly readers.

Sample titles: *The Internet Kids and Family Yellow Pages* by Jean Armour Polly; *Great American Websites: An Almanac of All Things American* by Edward J. Renehan, Jr.; *The Webmaster's Toolkit* by Michael Erwin; *Windows 95 Programming from the Ground Up* by Herbert Schildt; *The McGraw-Hill Encyclopedia of Networking* by Tom Sheldon.

Osborne/McGraw-Hill distributes its titles via the order-services center shared with and operated through TAB/McGraw-Hill.

Query letters and SASEs should be directed to:

Larry Levitsky, Editor in Chief

MCGRAW-HILL, INC./TAB BOOKS/ RAGGED MOUNTAIN PRESS

13311 Monterey Lane
Blue Ridge Summit, PA 17294
717-794-2191

This division of McGraw-Hill publishes books in a growing number of specialty areas—notably aviation, boating, business, professional design and architecture, electronics, residential construction, science, travel and recreation. Among this McGraw-Hill division's imprints are the outdoorsy Ragged Mountain Press, Design Press, International Marine, and the Aero series (aeronautics).

Representative of the McGraw-Hill/TAB division's list: *The Art of Architectural Illustration* by Gordon Grice; *Complete Interior Designs* by Stanley Abercrombie; *Good Cruising: The Illustrated Essentials* by Zora and David Aiken; *Why Didn't I Think of That? 1,198 Hints from 222 Cruisers on 120 Boats from 9 Countries* by John and Susan Roberts; *Chicago in and Around the Loop: Walking Tours of Architecture and History* by Gerard R. Wolfe; *Everyday Math for Contractors: A Timesaving Field Guide* by James Gerhart; *Lasers, Ray Guns, and Light Cannons! Projects from the Wizard's Workbench* by Gordon McComb; *Encyclopedia of Electronic Circuits* by Rudolf F. Graf and William Sheets.

Ragged Mountain Press is dedicated to "books that take you off the beaten path," and for every unit sold, a contribution is made to an environmental cause. Subjects here are travel, sport, recreation, the environment and nature, and outdoor discovery.

From Ragged Mountain: *The Ragged Mountain Press Guide to Outdoor Sports: Skills and Knowledge for the Whole Outdoors* by Jonathan and Roseann Hanson; *The Dayhiker's Handbook: An All-Terrain, All-Season Guide* by John Long; *The Art of Trolling: A Complete Guide to Freshwater Methods* by Ken Schultz; *Adventure New England: An Outdoor Vacation Guide* by Diane Bair and Pamela Wright.

McGraw-Hill handles distribution through its own order-services operation.

Query letters and SASEs should be directed to:

Jon Eaton, Editor
International Marine Books series.

Larry Hager, Editor
Electrical, mechanical, and civil engineering.

Roland Phelps, Editor
Electronics, adult-level science.

Jennifer DiGiovanna, Editor
Computer books.

April Nolan, Editor
Trades and technical.

Brad Schepp, Senior Editor
Computer books.

Kim Tabor, Editor in Chief
General science (K–12).

Shelley Chevalier, Editor
Aviation.

MEADOWBROOK PRESS

18318 Minnetonka Boulevard
Deerhaven, MN 55391
612-473-5400
fax: 612-475-0736

Meadowbrook publishes books with a family outlook, encompassing the areas of pregnancy and childcare, parenting, health, the environment, business, travel, cooking, reference, party-planning, children's-activity books, and humor. Meadowbrook Press (established in 1975) is a small trade-oriented house that has particular success pinpointing such specialty markets as baby names, family humor, and the facts of life.

Frontlist releases: *Bruce Lansky's Poetry Party* by Bruce Lansky (illustrated by Stephen Carpenter); *Sweet Dreams* by Bruce Lansky (illustrated by Vicki Wehrman); *Girls to the Rescue, Book II* by Bruce Lansky; *Kids' Party Cookbook* by Penny Warner; *Free Stuff for Kids* (in periodically updated editions) by The Free Stuff Editors.

From the Meadowbrook backlist: *The Very Best Baby Name Book in the Whole Wide World* by Bruce Lansky; *Eating Expectantly* by Bridget Swinney; *Feed Me! I'm Yours* by Vicki Lansky; *First-Year Baby Care* (edited by Paula Kelly); *The Joy of Grandparenting* by Audrey Sherins and Joan Holleman; *Baby and Child Emergency First Aid Handbook* by Mitchell J. Enzig; *The Working Woman's Guide to Breastfeeding* by Nancy Dana and Anne Price; *The Joy of Marriage* by Monica and Bill Dodds; *Birth Partner's Handbook* by Carl Jones; *The Baby Journal* by Matthew Bennett (illustrated by Breck Wilson).

Meadowbrook Press is distributed by Simon & Schuster.

Query letters and SASEs should be addressed to:

Bruce Lansky, President and Publisher

MECKLERMEDIA CORPORATION

Mecklermedia (founded in 1971; earlier known as Meckler Publishing) is no longer publishing. The house was a specialist publisher with emphasis on informational books, directories, and databases keyed to a wide range of subjects and applications.

MERCURY HOUSE, INC.

201 Filbert Street Suite 400
San Francisco, CA 94133
415-433-7042
fax: 415-392-3041
800-998-2129

Mercury House produces a list strong in contemporary fiction, world literature in translation, literary classics, Asian literature and philosophy, cultural studies, film and performing arts, current affairs, nature and environment, and general nonfiction. The press issues hardcovers and trade paperbacks.

Mercury House (a nonprofit corporation founded in 1984) is a publisher guided by literary values; categories of house interest encompass quality fiction; biographies and autobiographies; history and narrative nonfiction; multiethnic and cross-cultural literary expression (including essays and true-life narratives, as well as fiction); arts and entertainment; literary travel. The Mercury House logo is a graphic representation of a winged manuscript scroll in flight.

From Mercury House: *Dirty Bird Blues* (novel) by Clarence Major; *Red Diaper Baby* (comic literary novel) by Josh Kornbluth; *Work and the Life of the Spirit* (careers and inspiration; edited by Douglas Thorpe; foreword by Thomas Moore); *Tantra* (awareness and relationships) by Charles Muir and Caroline Muir; *Road to Heaven* (literary travel in China) by Bill Porter; *Flesh and Blood* (sex, violence, and censorship; edited by Peter Keough); *They Went Thataway* (genre film criticism; edited by Richard Jameson).

Mercury House issues the journal *Artes: An International Reader of Literature, Art and Music* (new editions released periodically; edited by Bengst Jangfeldt and Gunnar Harding).

Mercury House distributes through Consortium.

Query letters and SASEs should be directed to:

William M. Brinton, Publisher

Thomas Christensen, Executive Editor

P. O. Bronson, Associate Publisher

MESORAH PUBLICATIONS
(See Directory of Religious, Spiritual, and Inspirational Publishers)

MICROSOFT PRESS
One Microsoft Way
Redmond, WA 98052-6399
206-882-8080
800-677-7377

Microsoft Press specializes in solution-oriented computer books—especially those relating to the corpus of Microsoft products, the Microsoft operating system, and selected titles pertaining to the Apple Macintosh world. Microsoft Press lists titles in general personal-computer applications, programming, and general-interest computing areas. The house brochure features books, book-and-software packages (including diskettes and CD-ROMs), and training videos. Microsoft Press (founded in 1983) is a division of the Microsoft Corporation.

Microsoft Press titles are constantly updated and released in newly revised versions in order to anticipate advances in hardware and software systems as well as the underlying technology to which they pertain. The house aims to produce information that is reliable, timely, and easy to use so that readers can get their work done faster and without frustration.

Series from Microsoft Press include Step by Step (self-paced training); Running (in-depth reference and inside tips from the software experts); Field Guide (quick, easy answers); WYSIWYG (What You See Is What You Get—books for beginners); Best Practices (candid accounts of the new movement in software development—highly readable accounts of what works in the real world); Microsoft Professional Editions (technical information straight from the source); Microsoft Programming (the foundations of software development); Solution Developer (expert development strategies for creating custom business solutions).

The Mastering series is a line of CD-ROM–based interactive training titles created to help intermediate and advanced developers master tasks and concepts for writing sophisticated solutions with Microsoft tools.

A representative general reference work is *Microsoft Press Computer Dictionary*.

Microsoft Press distributes its own books; the list is also available through electronic mail via CompuServe.

Query letters and SASEs should be directed to:

Jennifer Brown, Acquisitions Coordinator

MILKWEED EDITIONS

430 First Avenue North, Suite 400
Minneapolis, MN 55401-1743
612-332-3192
fax: 612-332-6248
800-520-6455 (orders)

Milkweed publishes fiction, essays and literature, images and words, poetry anthologies, poetry, and art volumes, as well as nonfiction works that address social and cultural issues. Milkweeds for Young Readers is the house's children's line. Milkweed Editions (instituted in 1984) presents a personalized small-house approach that accents high standards of content and production.

Milkweed was founded as a nonprofit literary arts organization (in 1979) with the philosophy that literature is a transformative art uniquely able to convey the essential experiences of the human heart and spirit. The house presents distinctive voices of literary merit in handsomely designed, visually dynamic books, exploring the ethical, cultural, and esthetic issues that free societies must continually address.

Under Emilie Buchwald (Publisher/CEO), the house maintains its position to make a humane impact on society. Milkweed Editions offers an award-winning list of distinctive literary voices, with a line of handsomely designed, visually dynamic volumes that address ethical, cultural, and esthetic issues.

Milkweed publishes diverse, nonhomogenous literary books that take artistic and financial risks and that give readers access to the richness, aliveness, and possibilities afforded by the written word. Milkweed exists to publish, promote, and keep alive this important literature for readers today and in the future.

The company's continued marketing success augments the publisher's stance in support of exceptional books with appeal to discerning readers. Milkweed Editions hosts a substantial backlist of hardcovers, paperbacks, and chapbooks.

Poetry: *Invisible Horses* by Patricia Goedicke; *The Long Experience of Love* (poems) by Jim Moore; *Firekeeper: New and Selected Poems* by Pattiann Rogers; *The Phoenix Gone, the Terrace Empty* (poems) by Marilyn Chin; *Drive, They Said: Poems About Americans and Their Cars* (edited by Kurt Brown).

Culture and criticism: *Changing the Bully Who Rules the World: Reading and Thinking About Ethics* (edited by Carol Bly); *Transforming a Rape Culture* (sociocultural anthology; edited by Emilie Buchwald, Pamela Fletcher, and Martha Roth); *Basic Needs: A Year with Street Kids in a City School* by Julie Landsman; *A Male Grief: Notes on Pornography and Addition* by David Mura; *What Makes Pornography "Sexy"?* by John Stoltenberg.

General nonfiction: *Chasing Hellhounds: A Teacher Learns from His Students* by Marvin Hoffman; *Sacred Ground: Writings About Home* (edited by Barbara Bonner).

Milkweed is the publisher of Susan Straight's acclaimed *Aquaboogie: A Novel in Stories* (among a number of novels-in-stories projects); *The Historian: Six Fantasies of the American Experience* by Eugene K. Garber (with paintings by Kathryn Nobbe); and *Minnesota Gothic* (in the Seeing Double series of collaborative books; poetry by Mark Vinz; photography by Wayne Gudmundson).

Contact the editorial department for information pertaining to the Milkweed Prize for Children's Literature and the Milkweed National Fiction Prize.

Books from Milkweed Editions are available via direct order from the publisher; the house's titles are distributed to the trade through Publishers Group West.

MILKWEEDS FOR YOUNG READERS

Milkweeds for Young Readers produces children's books of literary merit that embody humane values. Books that ask the most of young readers, the publisher maintains, have the staying power to influence them for a lifetime. Milkweed also produces a series of teaching guides.

Titles from Milkweed's children's program: *A Bride for Anna's Papa* by Isabel Marvin; *I Am Lavina Cumming: A Novel for Young Readers* by Susan Lowell; *Gildaen: The Heroic Adventures of a Most Unusual Rabbit* by Emilie Buchwald (illustrations by Barbara Flynn).

Query letters and SASEs should be directed to:

Elisabeth Fitz, First Reader

Emilie Buchwald, Publisher

MIS: PRESS, INC.

(See Henry Holt and Company)

THE MIT PRESS
(See Directory of University Presses)

WILLIAM MORROW & COMPANY, INC.
(See The Hearst Book Group)

THE MOUNTAINEERS BOOKS
1001 Southwest Klickitat Way, Suite 201
Seattle, WA 98134
206-223-6303
fax: 206-284-4977
800-284-8554 (orders)
bookstore@mountaineers.org (e-mail)

The Mountaineers produces adventure narratives; mountaineering histories and guides; books on bicycling, kayaking/canoeing, hiking, and rock climbing; instructional guides to the outdoors and winter trekking; maps; historical works related to the house themes; natural history guides, and works on environmental conservation.

The Mountaineers (founded in 1906) is a conservation and outdoor-activity group with a mission to explore, study, preserve, and enjoy the natural beauty of the outdoors.

The Mountaineers Books was founded in 1961 as a nonprofit publishing program of the club. The Mountaineers sponsors the Barbara Savage/Miles From Nowhere Memorial Award competition for outstanding unpublished nonfiction adventure-narrative manuscripts. The initial title offered by Mountaineers Books, *Mountaineering: The Freedom of the Hills* is still in print in a fully revised edition. The press now offers a new edition of the classic *100 Hikes in Washington's North Cascades: Glacier Peak Region*.

Series from Mountaineers: Best Hikes with Children (guides to day hikes and overnighters for families); Let's Discover (children's activity books for ages 6–11); Hikes In (fully detailed, bestselling mountain hiking guides).

Mountaineers titles: *Himalaya Alpine-Style* by Andy Fanshawe and Stephen Venables; *Ice World* by Jeff Lowe; *The Mont Blanc Massif: The 100 Finest Routes* by Gaston Rebuffat; *K-2: The Story of the Savage Mountain* by Jim Curran; *Best Hikes with Children in San Francisco's North Bay* by Bill McMillon; *Bicycle Touring in Australia* by Leigh Hemmings; *Camp Four: Recollections of Yosemite Rockclimber* by Steve Roper; *Cascade Alpine Guide: Climbing and High Routes* by Fred Beckey; *Columbia River Gorge: A Complete Guide* (edited by Philip Jones); *Exploring Colorado's Wild Areas* by Scott Warren; *GPS Made Easy: Global Positioning Systems in the Outdoors* by Lawrence Letham; *Heroic Climbs* (edited by Chris Bonnington); *Hold the Heights: The Foundations of Mountaineering* by Walt Unsworth; *Mexico's*

Volcanoes: A Climbing Guide by R. J. Secor; *Photography Outdoors: A Field Guide for Travel and Adventure Photographers* by Mark Gardner and Art Wolfe; *The Crystal Horizon: Everest—the First Solo Ascent* by Reinhold Messner; and *Trekking in Nepal: A Traveler's Guide* by Stephen Bezruchka.

A winner of the Barbara Savage/Miles From Nowhere competition: *Himalayan Passage: Seven Months in the High Country of Tibet, Nepal, China, India, and Pakistan* by Jeremy Schmidt (with photographs by Patrick Morrow).

The Mountaineers Books distributes its list via direct orders and also utilizes the services of regional and national wholesalers and trade representatives.

Query letters and SASEs should be directed to:

Virginia Felton, Executive Director

Margaret Foster, Editor in Chief

Cindy Bohn, Managing Editor

MOYER BELL LIMITED

Kymbolde Way
Wakefield, RI 02879
401-789-0074
fax: 401-789-3793
moyerbell@genie.geis.com (e-mail)

Moyer Bell Limited specializes in literary works, reference works, and books in art and design. Many general-interest nonfiction works from this smaller house evidence a high-interest cultural or public-issues slant. Within this specialty arena, Moyer Bell produces original titles, reprints, and translations The house also maintains a strong commitment to poetry. The Asphodel Press imprint was founded as a nonprofit organization in 1990 and concentrates on fine literary titles.

Moyer Bell Limited was established in 1984 by Jennifer Moyer and Britt Bell; this notably independent house (with a U.K. base in London in addition to its U.S. operations) has received worldwide accolades for its roster of fine writers and stylish product.

Moyer Bell nonfiction: *World Enough and Time: A Political Chronicle* by Jonathan Schell; *The Art of Lucien Pissarro* by Lora Urbanelli; *Don't Look Back: A Memoir* by Patrick O'Connor; *Walking to LaMilpa: Living in Guatemala with Armies, Demons, Abrazos, and Death* by Marcos McPeek Villatoro; *The New Genetics: Challenges for Science, Faith, and Politics* by Roger L. Shinn; *In the Wake of Death: Surviving the Loss of a Child* by Mark Cosman; *Rebirth of Thought: Light from the East* by Ruth Nanda Anshen; *The Elixirs of Nostradamus: Nostradamus' Original Recipes for Elixirs, Scented Water, Beauty Potions and Sweetmeats* by Knut Boeser (illustrated by Leonhard Fuchs); *A Trifle, a Coddle, a Fry: An Irish Literary Cookbook* by Veronica Jane O'Mara and Fionnuala O'Reilly.

Fiction and literary titles: *The Only Piece of Furniture in the House* by Diana Glancy; *The Orchard on Fire* by Shene Mackay; *The Raven: With the Philosophy of*

Composition by Edgar Allan Poe (poetry and essay; illustrated by Alan James Robinson); *Peace Breaks Out*; *Private Enterprise*; and *The Demon in the House* by Angela Thirkell (granddaughter of Edward Burne-Jones and a cousin of Rudyard Kipling); *Peony* by Pearl S. Buck.

On Moyer Bell's reference-book list are the periodically revised *Grant Seekers Guide* by James McGrath Morris and Laura Adler, and *Directory of American Poetry Books* from Poets House.

From Asphodel Press: *Directory of Literary Magazines* (updated annually) by The Council of Literary Magazines and Presses.

Moyer Bell Limited books are distributed to the trade by Publishers Group West.

Query letters and SASEs should be directed to:

Jennifer Moyer, Editor and Publisher

Britt Bell, Editor and Publisher

JOHN MUIR PUBLICATIONS

P.O. Box 613
Santa Fe, NM 87504
505-982-4078
fax: 505-988-1680
800-285-4078

John Muir Publications is known for its outstanding list in three primary areas: travel, children's, and automotive books. Founded in 1969, the house produces titles in areas that include adventure and trekking; art, crafts, and style; parenting and the family; books for young readers; aeronautics, space, and automotive interest; ski tech; and education.

John Muir's program features a high percentage of titles that remain in print indefinitely and/or are reissued in updated editions. Among Muir's long-lasting works are *The People's Guide to Mexico* along with the companion volume *The People's Guide to RV Camping in Mexico* by Carl Franz with Steve Rogers (edited by Lorena Havens). Another backlist stalwart is the classic *How to Keep Your Volkswagen Alive: A Manual of Step-by-Step Procedures for the Compleat Idiot* by John Muir himself (illustrated by Peter Aschwanden; over 2.3 million copies sold).

City Smart Guidebooks target the great midsized cities (such as Nashville, Cleveland, Denver, Portland, Tampa/St. Petersburg, and Minneapolis/St. Paul). This new series, written by authors/residents of the cities they write about, is a boon for visitors, new transplants, and longtime residents alike. A portion of the profits of these books is used to purchase trees for each city's parks and streets.

Series produced by John Muir Publications include: Unique Travel Guides (entertaining exploration of the location, climate, topography, and demographics that give states their individual personalities); 2 to 22 Days Itinerary Planners (advice to the traveler about how to plan an itinerary that encompasses creative destinations and pursuits); The Visitor's Guide to the Birds of the National Parks; Natural Destination (for the ecologically oriented traveler).

From the Muir travel list: *Gene Kilgore's Ranch Vacations: The Complete Guide to Guest and Resort, Fly-Fishing, and Cross-Country Skiing Ranches* by Gene Kilgore; *Saddle Up! A Guide to Planning the Perfect Horseback Vacation* by Ute Haker; *The Florida Gulf Coast Travel Smart Trip Planner* by Jan Kirby; *Northern California Travel Smart Trip Planner* by Paul Otteson; *The Birder's Guide to Bed and Breakfasts: United States and Canada* by Peggy van Hulsteyn; *The World Awaits: A Comprehensive Guide to Extended Backpack Travel* by Paul Otteson; *California Public Gardens: A Visitor's Guide* by Eric Sigg; *Watch It Made in the U.S.A.: A Visitor's Guide to the Companies That Make Your Favorite Products* by Bruce Brumberg and Karen Axelrod; *A Foreign Visitor's Survival Guide to America* by Shauna Singh Baldwin and Marilyn M. Levine.

From the prolific Rick Steves (and cohorts): *Rick Steves' Europe Through the Back Door: The Travel Skills Handbook for Independent Travelers* and *Rick Steves' European Country Guides* and *Rick Steves' Phrase Guides* by Rick Steves; *Europe 101: History and Art for the Traveler* and *Mona Winks: Self-Guided Tours of Europe's Top Museums* by Rick Steves and Gene Openshaw.

In addition to the aforementioned classic *How to Keep Your Volkswagen Alive*, John Muir publishes a number of offbeat automotive works: *How to Keep Your Subaru Alive: A Manual of Step-by-Step Procedures for the Compleat Idiot* by Larry Owens; *How to Keep Your Datsun/Nissan Alive: A Manual of Step-by-Step Procedures for the Compleat Idiot* by Colin Messer (illustrated by Peter Ashwanden); *How to Keep Your Toyota Pickup Alive: A Manual of Step-by-Step Procedures for the Compleat Idiot* by Larry Owens; *The Greaseless Guide to Car Care* by Mary Jackson; *Off-Road Emergency Repair and Survival* by James Ristow. A representative title in ski tech is *Ski Tech's Guide to Equipment, Skiwear, and Accessories* (edited by Bill Tanler).

JOHN MUIR KIDS BOOKS

John Muir publishes a strong children's list, including a hefty skein of successful series: Kids Go! (keeps kids occupied and entertained while exploring vacation destinations or even their own hometowns); Extremely Weird (helps kids discover that few things of the imagination are as amazing or weird as real life); Masters of Motion (the reader controls powerful, fast-moving vehicles); X-Ray Vision (answers perplexing questions and investigates the basics of science); Rough & Ready (explores the lives of the groups who evoke the spirit of the Old West—cowboys, outlaws, lawmen); Bizarre & Beautiful (spirited investigation into the mysteries of the five senses in the world of animals); American Origins (introduces young readers to their own and others' roots, as well as the cultural heritages that different ethnic groups brought with them to America); Rainbow Warrior Artists (introduces young readers to creative individuals from all over the world and inspires them to unleash their own creativity).

In the Kids Explore series, each book is written by elementary school students in the Westridge Young Writers Workshop. The Workshop is made up of elementary school students from across the county, and the Workshop promotes appreciation for the many different cultures in America through writing and research.

Another kids' title from John Muir includes: *The Butterfly Book: A Kid's Guide to Attracting, Raising, and Keeping Butterflies* by Kersten Hamilton.

John Muir Publications is distributed to the trade by Publishers Group West; the house distributes its books worldwide through the offices of a number of regional services.

Query letters and SASEs should be directed to:

Steven Cary, President

MULTNOMAH PRESS

(See listing for Questar in Directory of Religious, Spiritual, and Inspirational Publishers)

MUSTANG PUBLISHING COMPANY

P.O. Box 3004
Memphis, TN 38173
901-521-1406
fax: 901-521-1412
MustangPub@aol.com (e-mail)

Mustang produces trade nonfiction books in hardcover and paperback. Mustang is especially successful with its lines of specialty how-tos, and titles in the fields of humor, games, outdoor recreation, sports, travel, and careers. Mustang Publishing Company (founded in 1983) is a modest-sized house with a concise publishing vision and compactly tailored list.

Representative frontlist titles: *Dear Elvis: Graffiti from Graceland* by Daniel Wright; *Lucky Pants and Other Golf Myths* by Joe Kohl; *The Complete Book of Golf Games* by Scott Johnston; *How to Be a Way Cool Grandfather* by Verne Steen.

Mustang's specialty books include those geared to expansive lifestyles. Titles here: *Paintball! Strategies and Tactics* by Bill Barnes with Peter Wrenn, *Bet on It! The Ultimate Guide to Nevada* by Mary Jane and Greg Edwards, and *The Hangover Handbook: 101 Cures for Humanity's Oldest Malady* by Nic van Oudtshoorn. There's also the immensely popular *The Complete Book of Beer Drinking Games* by Andy Griscom, Ben Rand, and Scott Johnson—as well as *Beer Games II: The Exploitative Sequel.*

The "For Free" series is a godsend for people scared by the high cost of travel and everyone who loves a bargain. Each book describes hundreds of terrific things to do and see, and nothing costs one single penny, lire, franc, or pfennig. Titles: *Europe for Free, London for Free,* and *DC for Free* by Brian Butler; *The Southwest for Free* by Mary Jane and Greg Edwards; *Hawaii for Free* by Frances Carter; *Paris for Free (Or Extremely Cheap)* by Mark Beffart.

The touring and travel list also includes: *Festival Europe! Fairs and Celebrations Throughout Europe* by Margaret M. Johnson; *The Nepal Trekker's Handbook* by Amy

R. Kaplan with Michael Keller; *Europe on 10 Salads a Day* by Mary Jane and Greg Edwards; plus the hilariously revised and expanded edition of *Let's Blow Thru Europe: How to Have a Blast on Your Whirlwind Trip Through Europe* by Thomas Neenan and Greg Hancock.

A solid group of Mustang books targets a higher-education-bound audience, including series for students and graduate-school applicants, often geared toward particular professional curricula: *The One Hour College Applicant* by Lois Rochester and Judy Mandell; *Medical School Admissions: The Insider's Guide* by John A. Zebala and Daniel B. Jones.

The Essays That Worked series inspires thousands of students to write the best essays they can. There's also lots of practical advice on the application process. Titles: *Essays That Worked for College Applicants* and *Essays That Worked for Business Schools* (edited by Boykin Curry and Brian Kasbar); *Essays That Worked for Law Schools* (edited by Boykin Curry).

Representative career title: *Working in T.V. News: The Insider's Guide* by Carl Filoreto with Lynn Setzer.

Mustang also offers Alan and Theresa von Altendorf's general reference *ISMs: A Compendium of Concepts and Beliefs from Abolitionism to Zygodactylism.*

Writers should note that Mustang welcomes book proposals on almost any nonfiction topic. The publisher prefers to see an outline and two to three sample chapters—and urges authors to be sure to enclose a self-addressed stamped envelope (the ubiquitous SASE) with each submission. No phone calls, please.

Mustang's books are distributed through National Book Network.

Query letters and SASEs should be directed to:

Rollin A. Riggs, President and Publisher

THE MYSTERIOUS PRESS
(See Warner Books)

THE NAIAD PRESS
P.O. Box 10543
Tallahassee, FL 32302
904-539-5965
fax: 904-539-9731

Naiad publishes lesbian and feminist fiction, essays, poetry, short stories, humor, translations, and bibliographies. The Naiad emphasis in category fiction includes stylish and traditional mysteries, espionage thrillers, adventure yarns, science fiction, fantasy, romances, historical fiction, erotica, and Westerns. Naiad Press (established in 1973) is the oldest and largest lesbian publishing company in the world.

Naiad has been particularly innovative among book-publishing operations in the development of specialized target-marketing techniques. The house has expanded its media presence to become active in the wider arena of audio books, videos, and theatrical film. The romantic fiction *Claire of the Moon* by Nicole Conn (writer and director of the feature film of the same name) represents a groundbreaking Naiad project that embraces documentary, music, and storytelling in cinema, video, audiocassette, CD, and print. Naiad Books maintains a comprehensive backlist.

On Naiad's roster of authors: Jane Rule, Lee Lynch, Diane Salvatore, Denise Ohio, Sarah Aldridge, Amanda Kyle Williams, Gertrude Stein, and Patricia Highsmith (writing as Claire Morgan).

Nonfiction from Naiad: *Sex Variant Women in Literature* by Jeannette H. Foster; *For Love and for Life: Intimate Portraits of Lesbian Couples* by Susan Johnson; *Woman Plus Woman* by Dolores Klaich; *There's Something I've Been Meaning to Tell You: An Anthology About Lesbians and Gay Men Coming Out to Their Children* (edited by Loralee MacPike); *The Lesbian Periodicals Index* by Claire Potter; *Sapphistry: The Book of Lesbian Sexuality* by Pat Califia.

Sample Naiad fiction and belles lettres: *Love or Money* by Jackie Calhoun; *Laurel* by Isabel Miller (pen name of Alma Routsong); *The Erotic Naiad: Love Stories by Naiad Press Authors*; *The Mysterious Naiad: Love Stories by Naiad Press Authors*; *The Romantic Naiad: Love Stores by Naiad Press Authors* (series edited by Barbara Grier); *Bar Girls* by Lauran Hoffman; *The Price of Salt* by Claire Morgan (AKA Patricia Highsmith); *Double Bluff: 7th Detective Inspector Carol Ashton Mystery* by Clair McNab; *Murder at Red Rook Ranch* by Dorothy Tell; *Old Dyke Tales* by Lee Lynch; *Say Jesus and Come to Me* by Ann Allen Shockley.

On January 1, 1997, Naiad Press celebrated its 24th birthday, remaining joyously the oldest and largest lesbian publishing company in the world. In those years, they went from one title to being the publisher of over 350 books.

The women of Naiad Press continue in pursuit of their essential goal—which is to make sure that someday, any woman, anyplace, can recognize her lesbianism and be able to walk into a bookstore and pick up a book that says to her: "Yes, you are a lesbian and you are wonderful." With that aim in mind, Naiad has adopted the following slogan for use in its potent mailing-list campaigns: Lesbians always know; if it's a book by Naiad Press, it's a book you want to own.

Naiad Press books are available directly from the publisher via a toll-free telephone-order number and from the following distributors as well: Bookpeople, Borders, Ingram.

Query letters and SASEs should be directed to:

Barbara Grier, Chief Executive Officer

NATIONAL TEXTBOOK COMPANY
(See NTC Publishing Group)

NAVAL INSTITUTE PRESS
(See Directory of University Presses)

THOMAS NELSON

(See Directory of Religious, Spiritual, and Inspirational Publishers)

NELSON-HALL PUBLISHERS

111 North Canal Street, Suite 399
Chicago, IL 60606
312-930-9446

Nelson-Hall publishes titles in business, criminology, psychology, journalism, history, political science, sociology, educational travel, African American studies, how-to, and self-help. Nelson-Hall Publishers (founded in 1909) produces educational, scholarly, and professional books; college textbooks; and a line of general-interest nonfiction trade crossovers.

Samples from the Nelson-Hall list: *Blind Mazes: A Study of Love* by George W. Kelling; *Food Power: A Doctor's Guide to Common Sense Nutrition* by L. Earle Arnow; *Personal Valuing: An Introduction* by Dale D. Simmons; *Philosophers Look at Science Fiction* (edited by Nicholas D. Smith); *The Classic Clitoris: Historic Contributions to Scientific Sexuality* (edited by Thomas Power Lowry); *The Decision-Making Process in Journalism* by Carl Hausman; *What Handwriting Tells You—About Yourself, Your Friends, and Famous People* by M. N. Bunker; *The Arts in Therapy* by Bob Fleshman and Jerry L. Fryrear.

Nelson-Hall Publishers handles its own distribution.

Query letters and SASEs should be directed to:

Richard Meade, Senior Editor

NEW AMERICAN LIBRARY/NAL

(See Penguin USA)

NEW AMSTERDAM BOOKS

101 Main Street
P.O. Box C
Franklin, NY 13775
212-685-6005

New Amsterdam publishing scope encompasses art and art history, literature and fiction, biography and letters, food and drink, drama and performing arts, travel, photography, architecture, design, archaeology, Islamic studies, publishing, and design.

New Amsterdam Books (begun in 1987) is a small house that publishes a preferred list of trade titles in targeted fiction and nonfiction topic areas. Featured on the New

Amsterdam list are books of an eclectic European cultural viewpoint, as well as American editions of European books. New Amsterdam editions are produced in paperback and clothbound formats. The press typically issues a few new original works seasonally, acquires selected reprint rights from overseas publishers, and maintains a comprehensive backlist.

Characteristic of New Amsterdam general trade titles: *Anarchism and Anarchists* by George Woodcock; *Life and Food in the Caribbean* by Cristine Mackie; *Alastair Sawday's Guide to French Bed & Breakfast* (updated edition by arrangement with Alastair Sawday Publishing); *The Whiskies of Scotland* by R. J. S. McDowell; *The Great Fire at Hampton Court* by Michael Fishlock (with foreword by HRH, the Prince of Wales).

Literary and critical works, the fine and popular arts, and culturally themed projects: *Killing the Mandaris* (popular multicultural fiction) by Juan Alonso; *The Three-Arched Bridge* (literary novel) by Albanian writer Ismail Kildare; *Tennyson: An Illustrated Life* by Norman Page; *Walt Whitman's New York: From Manhattan to Montauk* (edited by Henry M. Christman); *Victorian Theatre: The Theatre of Its Time* (edited by Russell Jackson); *British Landscape Watercolors, 1750–1850* by Jane Munro; *The Story of Western Furniture* by Phyllis Bennett Oates (illustrated by Mary Seymour); *Typefaces for Books* by James Sutton and Alan Bartram; *Mrs. Delany, Her Life and Her Flowers* by Ruth Hayden.

New Amsterdam issues the illustrated historical series Manuscripts in the British Library.

New Amsterdam Books handles its own distribution.

Query letters and SASEs should be directed to:

Emile Capouya, Managing Director

NEW HORIZON PRESS

34 Church Street
Liberty Corners, NJ 07938
908-604-6311
fax: 908-604-6330

Mailing address:
P.O. Box 669
Far Hills, NJ 07931

New Horizon Press: Real people . . . incredible stories. That's right. The New Horizon list accents true-life events with narrative nonfiction accounts told by actual participants. In its broader program, the house addresses topics of social concern, including corporate and professional responsibility, behavioral diversity, and politics, as well as personal self-help, how-to, and mainstream business books.

New Horizon Press (established in 1983) was originally an imprint of Horizon Press; now a separate publishing entity, New Horizon Press is remarkable for its pinpoint commercial vision in the arena of nonfiction stories of courageous individuals. These incredible tales of real people display an intense human-interest appeal and often embody an investigative journalistic stance that probes related public issues. The house maintains a solid backlist that is particularly strong in self-help titles.

New Horizon is configured as a small press: Projects are often initiated with restrained author advances; more money accrues to the writer through subsequent sales. The publisher has had conspicuous success in expanding the scope of its projects via targeted promotion, advertising, touring, and subsidiary rights, both in print via bookclub selections and in the electronic arena in the form of related television docudramas, talkshow appearances by authors, and feature items on television journals.

From the New Horizon list: *Legal Beagle: Diary of a Canine Counselor* by Linda A. Cawley; *How Far Do You Wanna Go? The Man Who Turned Sixteen Inner City Kids into a Team of Champions—a True Story* by Ramon "Tru" Dixon and David Aromatorio; *Porphyria: The Woman Who Has "The Vampire Disease"* by Tammy Evans; *Smoldering Embers: The True Story of a Serial Murderer and Three Courageous Women* by Joy Wellman, Lisa McVey, and Susan Replogle; *Mountain Madness: A True Story of Murder, Guilt, and Innocence* by Jimmy Dale Taylor and Donald G. Bross; *Undying Love: The True Story of a Passion That Defied Death* by Ben Harrison; *Gifts: Two Hospice Professionals Reveal Messages from Those Passing On* by Anne Wallace Sharp and Susan Handle Terbay; *60 Second Chronic Pain Relief: The Quickest Way to Soften the Throb, Cool the Burn, Ease the Ache* by Peter G. Lehndorff, M.D. and Brian Tarcy; *Fatal Analysis: A True Story of Therapeutic Privilege and Serial Murder* by Martin Obler, Ph.D. and Thomas Clavin; *Elder Care: What to Look For . . . What to Look Out For* by Thomas M. Cassidy; *Cutoffs: How Families Who Sever Relationships Can Reconnect* by Carol Netzer; *Telemedicine: What the Future Holds When You're Ill* by Mariann Karinch.

SMALL HORIZONS

Small Horizons is an imprint offering self-help books for children written by teachers and mental-health professionals. From Small Horizons: *The Boy Who Sat by the Window* by Chris Loftus (art by Catherine Gallagher); *The Special Raccoon: Helping a Child Learn About Handicaps and Love* by Kim Carlisle; *Up and Down the Mountain: Helping Children Cope with Parental Alcoholism* by Pamela Leib Higgins (art by Gail Zawacki).

New Horizon Press is distributed by National Book Network, Inc.

Query letters and SASEs should be directed to:

Joan S. Dunphy, Editor in Chief

NEWMARKET PRESS

18 East 48th Street
New York, NY 10017
212-832-3575
fax: 212-832-3629
800-669-3903

Newmarket concentrates on general nonfiction, accenting such categories as contemporary issues, history and biography, humor, psychology, parenting, health, nutrition, cooking, personal finance, and business. A major Newmarket program salutes classic literary figures, other media and performing arts, featuring titles in film (including shooting scripts) and music. Newmarket also issues a small number of children's titles (Newmarket Medallion imprint) as well as occasional works of high-interest fiction (the house was the original publisher of the hardcover edition of Michael Blake's novel *Dances with Wolves*).

Newmarket Press (founded in 1981) is a division of Newmarket Publishing and Communications Company. The house produces books in hardcover, trade paper, and mass-market paperback editions.

General trade titles: *Grandparenting in a Changing World* by Eda LeShan; *The Twenty Vision Steps to Wisdom* by Jennifer James; *The Antioxidant Save-Your-Life Cookbook: 150 Nutritious High-Fiber, Low-Fat Recipes to Protect Yourself Against the Damaging Effects of Free Radicals* by Jane Kinderlehrer; *Gifting to People You Love: An Intergenerational Financial Guide* by Adriane G. Berg; *Love Is a Happy Cat* by Michael W. Fox (illustrated by Harry Gans); *Discovering Great Music: A Listener's Guide to the Top Composers and Their Master Works* by Roy Hemming.

Special Newmarket editions: *The Words of Gandhi* (selected and introduced by Sir Richard Attenborough); *The Words of Albert Schweitzer* (selected and introduced by Norman Cousins); *The Words of Martin Luther King, Jr.* (selected and introduced by Coretta Scott King).

Film-related books: *The Proprietor: The Screenplay and Story Behind the Film* by Ismail Merchant; *Fly Away Home: The Novelization and Story Behind the Film* by Shelley Tanaka (from the screenplay by Robert Rodat and Vince McKewin). Shooting-script titles: *The Ice Storm: The Shooting Script* (screenplay by James Schamus; introduction by Ang Lee); *Dead Man Walking: The Shooting Script* (screenplay and notes by Tim Robbins); *The People vs. Larry Flynt: The Shooting Script* (screenplay and notes by Scott Alexander and Larry Karaszewski); *Out of Africa: The Shooting Script* (screenplay by Kurt Luedtki).

Newmarket distributes its list through Random House and maintains a network that utilizes a number of regional sales representatives.

Query letters and SASEs should be sent to:

Esther Margolis, President and Publisher

THE NEW PRESS

450 West 41st Street
New York, NY 10036
212-629-8802

The New Press accents cultural criticism, American politics, history, education, social policy, the arts, and world literature. House highlights include topical issues in sex and gender, ethnicity, the law, the healthcare industry, political and economic questions, investigative accounts, popular history and science, and lifestyle works with cultural themes. The New Press mission promotes a full-scale not-for-profit forum for publishing hardcover and trade paperback books and other materials.

The New Press (founded in 1992) is an independent publisher in the most absolute sense. Established in the face of increasing corporate control of commercial publishing, the New Press is committed to publishing, in innovative ways, works of educational, cultural, and community value. The press operates in the public interest rather than for private gain; works from the New Press inform public debate and reach out to audiences that are not generally priority markets for mainstream publishing firms.

The New Press program is tempered toward contemporary issues, and courts the controversial. Indeed, plans for the inception of the press are said to have been engendered by director André Schiffrin immediately upon his resignation as head of Pantheon Books in response to what was interpreted as the Random House ownership's plan to redirect Pantheon's emphasis toward the commercial mainstream.

The New Press does have its own brand of commercial prescience as well as attendant market niche. The house is blessed with legendary small-press savvy, as well as personnel with solid corporate backgrounds and extensive industry contacts. Studs Terkel led off a heavy-hitting initial list with the bestselling *Race: How Blacks & Whites Think & Feel About the American Obsession*; other New Press authors have followed suit and achieved high-profile media recognition and substantial sales.

Among New Press nonfiction features: *The Unreal America: Architecture and Illusion* by Ada Louise Huxtable; *The Romantics: England in a Revolutionary Age* by E. P. Thompson; *One Hundred Years of Socialism: The West European Left in the Twentieth Century* by Donald Sassoon; *Not Only for Myself: Identity Politics and the Law* by Martha Minow; *Ellis Island: A Reader and Resource Guide* by Virginia Yans-McLaughlin and Marjorie Lightman (with the Statue of Liberty–Ellis Island Foundation); *The Sex Side of Life: Mary Ware Dennett's Pioneering Battle for Birth Control and Sex Education* by Constance Chen; *Recipe of Memory: Five Generations of Mexican Cuisine* by Victor M. Valle and Mary Lau Valle (foreword by Elena Poniatowska); *The Vampire State and Other Myths and Fallacies About the U.S. Economy* by Fred Block; *China Pop: How Soap Operas, Tabloids, and Bestsellers Are Transforming a Culture* by Jianying Zha; *The Art of Ancient Egypt: A Portfolio—Masterpieces from the Brooklyn Museum* by the Brooklyn Museum.

New Press expression in fiction and literature: *Anita and Me* (novel) by Meera Syal; *Pig Tales: A Novel of Lust and Transformation* by Marie Darrieussecq (translated from the French by Linda Coverdale); *Big Blondes* (novel) by Jean Echenoz (translated from the French by Marl Polizzotti); *Lines of Fate* (novel) by Mark Kharitonov (translated from the Russian by Helena Goscilo); *If I Could Write This in Fire: An Anthology of Literature from the Caribbean* (edited by Pamela Maria Smorkaloff); *Coming of Age in America: A Multicultural Anthology* (edited by Mary Frosch).

Special project: *May It Please the Court: Live Recordings and Transcripts of the Oral Arguments Made Before the Supreme Court in Sixteen Key First Amendment Cases* edited by Peter Irons. This hardcover item is produced in a boxed-set edition that includes accompanying audiocassettes.

The New Press distributes to the trade through W. W. Norton.

Query letters and SASEs should be directed to:

André Schiffrin, Director

Joe Wood, Editor

NEW YORK UNIVERSITY PRESS
(See Directory of University Presses)

THE NOBLE PRESS

The Noble Press, a Chicago-based firm (founded in 1988) with an issues-oriented trade list, is not doing business as this volume goes to press.

NOLO PRESS
950 Parker Street
Berkeley, CA 94710
510-549-1976
http://www.nolo.com (World Wide Web)

Nolo Press presents a glittering array of self-help titles in law and business. The house also promotes a related list in lifestyle, recreation, travel, and retirement. Nolo also produces law-form kits, legal software, electronic books, and videotapes.

Nolo's consumerist perspective encompasses homeowners, landlords, and tenants; going to court; money matters; estate planning and probate; business; legal reform; patents, copyrights, and trademarks; employee rights and the workplace; family matters; immigration; research and reference; older Americans; and humor titles.

Nolo Press is the pioneer publisher of self-help legal books and software. The house (started in 1971) was founded by two Legal Aid lawyers who were fed up with the public's lack of access to affordable legal information and advice. Convinced that with good, reliable information Americans could handle routine legal problems without hiring an attorney, they began writing plain-English law books for the general readership.

Nolo led off its first list with *How to Do Your Own Divorce in California* and has been going strong since with a steady stream of titles addressing consumer needs in a wide range of general and specialist areas. Whereas lawyers have historically sold information only to the few who can afford their services, Nolo aims to provide comprehensive low-cost information to the public at large.

Nolo News is a newsletter (and catalog) published quarterly to keep readers up to date on law changes that affect Nolo products and to provide practical legal information (and a little humor) to their readers. Like all their products, *Nolo News* strives to give readers information they can use in everyday life.

Many Nolo publications are regularly revised and are issued in updated editions, and the publisher maintains a hardy backlist. Most Nolo titles are written by practicing attorneys who are specialists in their fields of authorship. A major portion of the Nolo list exhibits a national orientation, while some titles are specifically geared to regional markets.

Representative titles: *Get Mad at Your Lawyer: What to Do When You're Overcharged, Ignored, Betrayed, or a Victim of Malpractice* by Attorney Tanya Starnes; *Child Custody: Building Agreements That Work* (revised edition) by Mimi E. Lyster; *Patent It Yourself* (revised edition) by Attorney David Pressman; *Your Rights in the Workplace* (revised edition) by Attorney Barbara Kate Repa; *How to Win Your Personal Injury Claim* (revised edition) by Attorney Joseph Matthews; *How to Sue for Up to $25,000—and Win!* by Judge Roderic Duncan.

Social, community, career, lifestyle, and issues-oriented titles: *Trouble-Free Travel . . . and What to Do When Things Go Wrong* by Attorneys Stephen Colwell and Ann Shulman; *Get a Life: You Don't Need a Million to Retire Well* by Ralph Warner; *The Copyright Handbook: How to Protect and Use Written Works* by Stephen Fishman; *How to Buy a House in California* by Attorney Ralph Warner, Ira Serkes, and George Devine; *Stand Up to the IRS* by Frederick W. Daily; *Dog Law* by Mary Randolph; *Neighbor Law: Fences, Trees, Boundaries & Noise* by Cora Jordan; *A Legal Guide for Lesbian and Gay Couples* by Hayden Curry, Denis Clifford, and Robin Leonard; *The Independent Paralegal's Handbook* (revised edition) by Attorney Ralph Warner; *How to Mediate Your Dispute: Find a Solution You Can Live with Quickly and Cheaply Outside the Courtroom* by Peter Lovenheim.

Some humor!: *29 Reasons Not to Go to Law School* by Ralph Warner, Toni Ihara, and Barbara Kate Repa; *Poetic Justice: The Funniest, Meanest Things Ever Said About Lawyers* (edited by Jonathan and Andrew Roth); *The Devil's Advocates: The Unnatural History of Lawyers* by Andrew and Jonathan Roth.

Nolo Press distributes its own books to the trade (along with selected titles from other publishers) and also utilizes several distribution services; in addition, Nolo sells to consumers via direct mail and operates its own bookstore in Berkeley.

Query letters and SASEs should be sent to:

Barbara Repa, Senior Editor

W. W. NORTON AND COMPANY, INC.
FOUL PLAY BOOKS
COUNTRYMAN PRESS

500 Fifth Avenue
New York, NY 10110
212-354-5500

Norton publishes trade nonfiction, commercial fiction and belles lettres, and works for professional and academic markets. W. W. Norton (founded in 1923) offers prime-caliber publications in all areas of its trade program; the house is equally esteemed for its line of college texts and professional reference titles.

W. W. Norton produces hardcover and trade paperback editions under its celebrated gliding-seagull colophon as well as through a variety of imprints including Liveright and Countryman. Norton nourishes a comprehensive backlist of books in all areas of its publishing interest.

Norton nonfiction accents trade titles in topics of current interest, with a range of works featuring the popular as well as scholarly approach to fields including cultural criticism, biography, psychology, history, economics, politics, natural history, the sciences, fine arts and design, photography, and lifestyle. Norton also offers a line of books for enthusiasts of sailing and publishes Blue Guide travel books.

Nonfiction from Norton: *Car: Making the #1 Automobile in America* by Mary Walton; *Glenn Gould: The Ecstasy and Tragedy of Genius* by Peter Ostwald; *Pleasure Wars: The Bourgeois Experience—Victoria to Freud* by Peter Gay; *Jane Brody's Allergy Fighter* by Jane Brody; *The Talking Brain: The Co-Evolution of Language and the Human Brain* by Terrence Deacon; *Words for the Taking: The Hunt for a Plagiarist* by Neal Bowers; *The Analects of Confucius* by Confucius (translation and notes by Simon Leys); *Ways of War and Peace: Realism, Liberalism, and Socialism* by Michael Doyle; *Mathematics: From the Birth of Numbers* by Jan Gullberg; *Mind ←→ Body Deceptions: The Psychosomatics of Everyday Life* by Steven L. Dubrovsky, M.D.; *War by Other Means: Economic Espionage in America* by John J. Fialka; *Passionate Marriage: Sex, Love, and Intimacy in Emotionally Committed Relationships* by David Schnarch; *Germs and Steel: Investigations in the Science of Human History* by Jared Diamond; *The Virgin Homeowner: The Essential Guide to Owning, Maintaining, and Surviving Your First Home* by Janice Papolos; *Fundamentals of Sailing, Cruising, and Racing* by Stephen Colgate.

In fiction and literary writing Norton publishes novels, poetry (including the Norton Anthologies series), and short story collections—from established, distinguished scribes and from a select few marketable new voices. In addition, the house publishes critical essays, biographies, and literary histories. The Norton fiction list covers classical, modern, contemporary, and experimental styles, as well as novels showing a mainstream commercial profile; the Norton program also encompasses mystery and suspense fiction.

Examples from the Norton fiction list: *The Players* by Stephanie Cowell; *Mexican Hat* by Michael McGarrity; *About Yvonne* by Donna Masini; *Busted Scotch* by James Kelman; *Suspicion* by Robert McCrum; *No New Jokes* by Steven Bloom; *The Secrets of a Fire King* by Kim Edwards; *Growing Through the Ugly* by Diego Vazquez, Jr.; *Hope Mills* by Constance Pierce; *Lava* by Pamela Ball; *Letting Loose the Hounds* by Brady Udall; *Love Warps the Mind a Little* by John Dufresne; *Bag Men* by John Flood; *The Commodore* by Patrick O'Brian; *Always Outnumbered, Always Outgunned* by Walter Mosley; *Seduction Theory* (stories) by Thomas Beller.

Norton poetry includes: *The Country Without a Post Office* by Agha Shahid Ali; *Glare* by A. R. Ammons; *Collected Poems* by Audre Lorde; *Loosestrife* by Stephen

Dunn; *Singularity* by Greg Glazner; *Woman Police Officer in Elevator* by James Lasdun; *Mother Love* by Rita Dove; *My Father Was a Toltec and Selected Poems* by Ana Castillo; *Poetry in Motion: 100 Poems from the Subways and Buses* (edited by Elise Paschen, Molly Peacock, and Neil Neches).

Works of speculative literary configuration: *The Coral Sea* (poetry, fiction, and essay) by Patti Smith; *In Short: A Collection of Brief Creative Nonfiction* (edited by Judith Kitchen and Mary Paumier Jones); *Sudden Fiction (Continued): 60 New Short-Short Stories* (edited by Robert Shepard and James Thomas); *When the Air Hits Your Brain: Tales of Neurosurgery* by Frank Vertosick; *Wise Women: Over 2,000 Years of Spiritual Writing by Women* (edited by Susan Cahill); *Holy Land: A Suburban Memoir* by D. J. Waldie.

W. W. Norton distributes its own list and handles distribution for its subsidiaries and imprints, as well as a number of other publishers. Norton's distribution network includes: Chapters Publishing, Countryman Press, Ecco Press, Liveright Publishing Corporation, New Directions Books, The New Press, Pushcart Press, The Taunton Press, Thames and Hudson, Verso.

Query letters and SASEs should be directed to:

Edwin Barber, Vice Chairman
Acquires for the full range of house interests.

Jill Bialosky, Associate Editor
Literary fiction. Biographies, memoirs. Some poetry.

(Ms.) Amy Cherry, Editor
History, biography, women's issues, African-American, health.

(Ms.) Carol Houck Smith, Editor at Large
Literary fiction, travel memoirs, behavioral sciences, nature.

(Mr.) Gerald Howard, Editor and Vice President
Acquires nonfiction and literary fiction for the trade.

(Mr.) Starling Lawrence, Editor in Chief
Acquires for the full range of house interests.

Angela von der Lippe, Senior Editor
Trade nonfiction. Serious works in behavioral sciences, earth sciences, astronomy, neuroscience, education.

Jim Mairs, Vice President
History, biography, illustrated books.

(Ms.) Alane Mason, Editor
Serious nonfiction for a general audience, particularly cultural and intellectual history, some illustrated books. Literary fiction and memoir.

(Mr.) W. Drake McFeely, President
Nonfiction of all kinds, particularly science and social science.

FOUL PLAY PRESS

500 Fifth Avenue
New York, NY 10110

Foul Play is heavy on traditional mystery and suspense fiction, including classic reprints, United States editions of British originals, and a short list of homegrown originals. Foul Play Press was until 1996 part of Countryman Press, which developed the Foul Play imprint with careful small-press attention and independent-press savvy.

From Foul Play: *Slaughter Music* by Russell James; *Penance* (a Holland Taylor mystery) by David Housewright; *Astride a Grave* by Bill James; *Fête Fatale* by Robert Barnard; *Family Business* by Michael Z. Lewin.

Query letters and SASEs should be directed to:

Candace Watt, Editor (New York)

COUNTRYMAN PRESS/ BACKCOUNTRY PUBLICATIONS

New England office:
P.O. Box 748
Woodstock, VT 05091
802-457-4826; 802-457-1049
800-245-4151 (orders)

Countryman specializes in regional history, recreation, travel, gardening, nature, environment, how-to, regional hiking, walking, bicycling, fishing, cross-country skiing and canoeing guides. Imprints include Countryman Press and Backcountry Publications. Previously developers and proprietors of the Foul Play line, the house has a successful heritage in mystery and suspense fiction.

Countryman (founded in 1973) has been on the cusp of the small, regional press initiative that has enriched the North American publishing scope through editorial acumen and niche-marketing panache. Now affiliated with W. W. Norton, Countryman remains editorially independent.

Representative Countryman titles: *Alaska on Foot: Wilderness Techniques for the Far North* by Erik Molvar; *The Lake Champlain Corridor: Touring Historic Battle Sites from Saratoga to Quebec* by Howard Coffin and Will and Jane Curtis; *Covered Bridges of Vermont* by Ed Barna; *The Maze: A Desert Journey* (literary travel fiction) by Lucy Rees; *The Architecture of the Shakers* by Julie Nicoletta (photographs by Bret Morgan).

Backcountry Publications: *Walks and Rambles in Ohio's Western Reserve: Discovering Nature and History in the Northeastern Corner* by Jay Abercrombie; *25 Mountain Bike Tours in the Hudson Valley* by Peter Kick; *50 Hikes in Connecticut: From the Berkshires to the Coast* by David, Sue, and Gerry Hardy.

Sales and distribution for Countryman are handled by the parent corporation, W. W. Norton.

Query letters and SASEs should be directed to:

Helen Whybrow, Editor in Chief (New England)

NTC/Contemporary Publishing Company
NTC Publishing Group
National Textbook Company
NTC Business Books
VGM Career Horizons
Passport Books
Contemporary Books

4255 West Touhy Avenue
Lincolnwood, IL 60646-1975
847-679-5500
fax: 847-679-2494
800-323-4900 (orders)
ntcpub2@aol.com (e-mail)

New York offices:
712 Fifth Avenue
New York, NY 10019
212-903-3840

California offices:
9752 Keeneland Row
La Jolla, CA 92037
619-587-6775

NTC Publishing Group and Contemporary Books merged in early 1997. The new operation is known as NTC/Contemporary Publishing Company, which combines NTC's tradition of standout business and travel reference lines with Contemporary's broad trade nonfiction emphasis. The house has editorial offices in the Chicago area, New York, and the San Diego environs.

NTC Publishing Group
National Textbook Company

NTC Publishing Group (founded in 1982 as National Textbook Company) boasts comprehensive offerings in the areas of business and career, professional how-to, and travel titles, as well as books of general nonfiction interest and reference works of broad appeal.

The structure of NTC Publishing Group (stamped with the staunch emblem of an eagle perched in profile) embraces business and professional divisions that incorporate the formerly independent Crain Books, as well as NTC Business Books and VGM Career Horizons. The trade logo of Passport Books is a globe in an open book, which covers titles in travel-related fields; Passport also functions as a crossover imprint for some of NTC's books in the area of international business culture. General reference works are issued under the rubric of National Textbook Company.

Focal points of the NTC imprints, divisions, and specialty lines: Passport Books (travel, languages, juveniles); National Textbook Company (English language and literature references); Teach Yourself (language, study guides, leisure); VGM Career Horizons (career information for students and adults); NTC Business Books (expertise and innovation in business); The Quilt Digest Press (quilts, quilts, quilts).

NTC books in the reference arena include foreign-language references, phrase books, and dictionaries (French, Italian, German, Polish, Russian); resources in the English language (*NTC's Thesaurus of Everyday American English* and *Essentials of English Grammar*); and general-interest works such as *NTC's Dictionary of Shakespeare*.

National Textbook Company titles: *12 Easy Steps to Successful Research Papers* by Nell W. Meriwether; *Writing for Magazines: A Beginner's Guide* by Cheryl Sloan Wray; *Who's Who in Classical Mythology* by Adrian Room; *Slang Through the Ages* by Jonathon Green; *NTC's Dictionary of Commonplace Words in Real-Life Contexts* by Anne Bertram.

NTC introduces the Artful Wordsmith Series: A Reference Shelf for Writers. Titles here: *Slang American Style and Straight from the Horse's Mouth* by Richard A. Spears; *In Other Words* by Anne Bertram; *Short Cuts: The Dictionary of Useful Abbreviations* by Steven Racek Kleinedler (edited by Richard A. Spears); *Aw Shucks! The Dictionary of Country Jawing* by Anne Bertram (edited by Richard A. Spears); *Taking Care of Business: The Dictionary of Contemporary Business Terms* by Donald Caruth and Steven Austin Stovall.

Teach Yourself books include guides to teach yourself a foreign language (Polish, Swahili, Turkish, Portuguese, Chinese, Japanese); study guides (women's studies, politics, algebra); religious guides (old testament, new testament, Christianity); leisure guides (weather, mythology, better chess); writing guides (creative writing, screenwriting, copywriting, writing poetry); health (healthy eating for babies and children, understanding medicine); alternative health (aromatherapy, reflexology, astrology).

From The Quilt Digest Press: *Treasures in Cross-Stitch: 50 Projects Inspired by Antique Needlework* by Jane Greenoff; *In a Patchwork Garden* by Janet Bolton; *Threads & Ties That Bind: Exquisite Quilts from Tie Fabrics* by Jean Johnson; *Star Quilts* by Mary Elizabeth Johnson; *Quiltmakers of Australia: Celebrating the Traditions* by Karen Fail.

NTC Publishing Group handles its own distribution.

NTC BUSINESS BOOKS
VGM CAREER HORIZONS

NTC Business Books accents business how-to, advertising, promotion, and marketing, as well as extensive interest in the fields of international business, media planning and use, and general business reference. Formerly a part of the Crain family publishing empire, Crain Books was acquired by NTC and its backlist folded into the NTC Business Books imprint.

NTC Business titles: *Selling on the Net: The Complete Guide* by Herschell Gordon Lewis and Robert Lewis; *The Complete Guide to Infomercial Marketing* by Timothy R. Hawthorne; *Strategies for Effective Customer Education* by Peter Honebein; *Marketing*

Strategies for Growth in Uncertain Times by Allan J. Magrath; *Write on Target: The Direct Marketer's Copywriting Handbook* by Donna Baier Stein and Floyd Kemske; *Beyond 2000: The Future of Direct Marketing* by Jerry I. Reitman; *How to Develop Successful New Products* by Jerry Patrick; *Guide to Writing for the Business Press* by Patrick Clinton.

NTC Business Books Passport line of intercultural guides to the global marketplace are keyed to a number of geographic locales, including China, Germany, Mexico, and Japan.

VGM Career Horizons are resources and how-tos covering a variety of professional and career opportunities and specialties. VGM Career titles: *Career Portraits: Science* by Jane Kelsey; *Careers for Music Lovers & Other Tuneful Types* by Jeff Johnson; *Real People Working in Communications* by Blythe Camenson and Jan Goldberg; *Career Success for People with Physical Disabilities* by Sharon F. Kissane, Ph.D.; *Great Jobs for Sociology Majors* by Stephen Lambert; *Up Your Grades! Proven Strategies for Academic Success* by Ann Hunt Tufariello; *How to Run Your Own Home Business* by Coralee Smith Kern; *Beating Job Burnout: How to Turn Your Work into Your Passion* by Paul Stevens.

Query letters and SASEs should be directed to:

Mark R. Pattis, President

Richard Hagle, Editor, Business Books.

Ann Knudson, Senior Editor, The Quilt Digest Press
Quilting and other crafts.

Betsy Lancefield, Editor, VGM Career Horizons
Careers and related titles.

John T. Nolan, Editorial Director, NTC/Contemporary Publishing Company
Projects consistent with the house list.

Richard Spears, Executive Editor, NTC/National Textbook Company
Dictionaries and general reference.

PASSPORT BOOKS

Passport Books is known as a publisher of titles in the field of travel. Series from Passport include Essential Travel Guides, Trip Planner, Footprint Handbooks, Regional Guides of Italy, Illustrated Travel Guides from Thomas Cook, and a set of food-and-wine travel guides.

Footprint Handbooks is the new name for the series of guidebooks previously called Passport's Handbooks of the World. The flagship of the series is the *South American Handbook* (73rd edition; published annually since 1924), the longest running guide-book in the English language, and a living legend in guidebook publishing.

Examples from the various Passport lines: *101 Great Choices: New York City* by Jan Aaron; *Traveller's Literary Companion: Caribbean* by James Ferguson; *Scottish Highlands & Islands* by John Baxter, David Winpenny, Pat and Charles Athie; *Essential Normandy* by Robert Kane; *Zimbabwe* by Paul Tingay; *Toronto's Best-Kept*

Secrets (and New Views of Old Favorites) by Mike Michaelson; *Essential Travel Guide to Orlando and Disney World.*

Query letters and SASEs should be directed to:

John Nolan, Executive Editor, Passport Books

CONTEMPORARY BOOKS

Contemporary offers a general nonfiction lineup that accents the areas of self-improvement, personal finance, self-awareness, health, popular biography, and life-style. The list is particularly strong in sports, parenting, cooking, pets, new age, relationships, and personality and historical profiles. Jamestown Publishing is a line that accents the educational market. Contemporary Books also has a major concentration in materials for adult education.

Contemporary Books (established in 1947) is part of the Tribune New Media organization, and an imprint of NTC/Contemporary Publishing Company. Contemporary has branched out from a former emphasis on sports titles to a program broad in scope that includes hardcover and trade paperback editions.

From Contemporary: *Real Family Values: The Ten Steps to Incorporating Meaningful Ethics into Everyday Life* by Mel Krantzler, Ph.D. and Patricia B. Krantzler, M.A.; *How To Make Anyone Fall in Love with You* by Leil Lowndes; *The Time-Out Prescription: A Parent's Guide to Positive and Loving Discipline* by Donna G. Corwin; *Game Plans for Success: Winning Strategies for Business and Life from 10 Top NFL Head Coaches* (edited by Ray Didinger); *Shape Training: The 8-Week Total Body Makeover* by Robert Kennedy and Maggie Greenwood-Robinson; *Terrain Skiing: How to Master Tough Skiing Like the Experts* by Seth Masia; *Jodie: A Biography* by Louis Chunovic; *101 Ways to Spoil Your Grandchild* by Vicki Lansky; *Marketing Your Services: For People Who Hate to Sell* by Rick Crandall, Ph.D.; *Feng Shui: The Book of Cures—150 Easy Solutions for Creating a Healthier and Happier Home or Office* by Nancilee Wydra; *Restoring Balance to a Mother's Busy Life* by Beth Wilson Saavedra; *Bobby Sherman: Still Remembering You* by Bobby Sherman and Dena Hill; *Better Golf the Sam Snead Way: The Lessons I've Learned* by Sam Snead with Don Wade; *Daley: Power and Presidential Politics* by F. Richard Ciccone; *Lou Ferrigno's Guide to Personal Power, Bodybuilding, and Fitness* by Lou Ferrigno; *The Reagan Years A to Z* by Kenneth Kurz, Ph.D.; *The Baywatch Cookbook* by Frankie Diamond.

Contemporary's Buying Retail Is Stupid! discount guides is a series geared toward buying everything at up to 80% off retail; works include information on all aspects of discount shopping (mail order, outlets, resale stores, auctions, government surplus sales).

Contemporary is also on the lookout for titles of topical cultural interest, including works with an investigative or issues-oriented edge. Sample: *Camilla: The King's Mistress—a Love Story* by Caroline Graham.

Contemporary Books handles its own distribution and also distributes books for American Diabetes Association, Chicago Home Books, FASA, Health Plus, IMG Publishing, Lowell House, Marlor Press, The Sporting News, and VeloPress.

JAMESTOWN PUBLISHERS

Jamestown Publishers targets their books to the educational community to help lay a foundation for learning success. Their series are targeted from elementary school to the high school graduate, as well as the college student. Jamestown books build reading skills, help to improve basic English skills, pique the interest of reluctant readers, help to improve reading rate, build reading comprehension skills, help to improve writing skills, foster love of good literature, build vocabulary, and develop basic math concepts.

Jamestown series include: Attention Span Stories, Adult Learner Series, Six-Way Paragraphs, Skimming and Scanning, Beginning Writer Series, Best-Selling Chapters, Best Short Stories, Beyond Basics, Breakthroughs, Jamestown Classics, Single Skills Series.

Contemporary also offers GED (high school equivalency examination) preparation texts. Feature titles: *GED: How to Prepare for the High School Equivalency Examination*; *Essential GED: A Complete and Compact Review for the High School Equivalency Exam*; *The GED Math Problem Solver: Reasoning Skills to Pass the Test*; *The GED Essay: Writing Skills to Pass the Test*.

Query letters and SASEs should be directed to:

Linda Gray, Senior Editor, Contemporary Books and Passport (Illinois)
General trade and travel. Popular culture, popular psychology, entertainment, humor, cookbooks, fun/game books.

Susan Schwartz, Senior Editor, Contemporary Books (New York)
Reference and general commercial nonfiction.

Matthew Carnicelli, Senior Editor, Contemporary Books (New York)
General trade nonfiction, popular business.
712 Fifth Avenue
New York, NY 10019
212-903-3840

Kara Leverte, Senior Editor (California)
General trade nonfiction. Health and fitness, child care, self-help.
kleverte@tribune.com (e-mail)
9752 Keeneland Row
La Jolla, CA 92037
619-587-6775

OHIO UNIVERSITY PRESS

(See Directory of University Presses)

ORCHARD BOOKS
(See Grolier Children's Publishing)

ORYX PRESS
4041 North Central at Indian School Road, Suite 700
Phoenix, AZ 85012-3397
602-265-2651
info@oryxpress.com (e-mail)
http://www.oryxpress.com (World Wide Web) The Oryx Web site includes sample chapters from selected books, online versions of Oryx Press catalogs, book reviews, and author biographies.

Oryx covers reference and informational publications in such fields as business and careers, medicine and consumer health, popular culture, popular science (including nature and environment), technical science, sports, elderly population and services, social services, education, human growth and development, gender studies, multicultural studies, international government and politics, and regional or period American history.

Oryx Press (founded in 1975) targets the informational marketplace, specializing in directories, databases, CD-ROMs, periodicals, looseleaf services, library and information science readers, and educational texts, as well as general reference works. Many Oryx releases are geared toward the library, corporate, institutional, educational, academic, and technical research arenas. The press issues special catalogs for the school market and for series in higher education.

Yes, Oryx is a specialist press—one with a broad range of interest. This independent, innovative house is on the lookout for books with greater high-profile trade potential. Oryx wants books that can carry high prices, stay in print for long periods of time, and deliver royalties consistently.

Oryx Press introduces a new line: Oryx American Family Tree. This series is the first to explain the how-tos of genealogical research in simple, jargon-free language. The series explores how to research family history for 12 different ethnic groups: African American, British American, Japanese American, Polish American, German American, Scandinavian American, Italian American, Native American, Chinese American, Jewish American, and Mexican American.

From the Oryx list: *Multicultural Folktales for the Feltboard and Readers' Theater* by Judy Sierra; *Holidays of the World Cookbook for Students* by Lois Sinaiko Webb; *Distinguished African American Scientists of the 20th Century* by James H. Kessler, J. S. Kidd, Renée A. Kidd, and Katherine A. Morin; *Job Skills for the 21st Century* by Lawrence K. Jones; *The Contemporary Thesaurus of Social Science Terms and Synonyms: A Guide for Natural Language Computer Searching* (compiled and edited by Sara K. Knapp); *Directory of College Cooperative Education Programs* by the National Commission for Cooperative Education; *Dictionary of Multicultural Education* by Carl A. Grant and Gloria Ladson-Billings; *Dictionary and Reference Guide to Learning Disabilities* by Kathleen McLane; *Prime Time Religion: An Encyclopedia of Religious Broadcasting* by J. Gordon Melton, Phillip Charles Lucas, and Jon R. Stone; *Homelessness in America* (edited by Jim Baumohl, for the National Coalition for the Homeless); *The Reference Guide to the World's Famous Landmarks: Bridges, Tunnels, Dams, Roads, and Other Structures* by Lawrence H. Berlow; *Understanding the Census: A Guide for Marketers, Planners, Grant Writers, and Other Data Users* by Michael R. Lavin; *Statistical Handbook on Violence in America* by Adam Dobrin, Brian Wiersema, Colin Loftin, and David McDowall.

The Oryx Press handles its own distribution.

Editors listed below acquire in all areas consistent with publisher description. Query letters and SASEs should be directed to:

Phyllis Steckler, President

Art Stickney, Director of Acquisitions

Mary Jo Godwin, Director of Marketing, Sales, and Promotional Services

---

THE OVERLOOK PRESS

368 West Broadway
New York, NY 10012
212-477-7162

Overlook focuses on general nonfiction, and offers a respected line in fiction, belles lettres, and poetry. The nonfiction purview encompasses biography, crafts, how-to, fine arts, architecture and design, Hudson Valley regionals, cookbooks, and natural history. The house releases a limited number of titles directed toward the young reader.

The Overlook Press was founded in 1971 by Peter Mayer (until recently also chief executive of the Worldwide Penguin Group) and his father. Overlook is a smaller publisher with a diverse and select list. Under its enigmatic logo (a mythical beast in cartouche that calls to mind winged elephantine species), Overlook produces books in special fine editions, hardcover, and trade paperback. The house nurtures a thriving backlist that features such titles as the business–martial arts classic *Book of Five Rings* (by Miyamoto Musashi; translated by Victor Harris); *The Gormenghast Trilogy* by Mervyn Peake; and *Tiny Houses* by Lester Walker.

Overlook was founded with the intent to publish against the grain. Here was a new publishing company that did not exactly imitate the policies of large companies. The editors did not pursue bestsellers; they wanted good-sellers. And they believed in the backlist. They did not want to be a niche publisher; just a small general publisher. They wanted to publish books that very likely had been "overlooked" by larger houses—although the Overlook name actually came from a mountain in Woodstock, New York.

Overlook made a name by publishing useful books in areas where none existed. They published the first book on wood stoves in the early 1970s, anticipating a major trend; when they produced the first book on Kendo published in the United States

(*A Book of Five Rings*)—who knew it would become famous as a metaphor for business strategy!

In 1977 Overlook launched the Ivory Press to publish unusual books in the visual arts, joining Tusk paperbacks in the Overlook family of imprints.

Overlook's authors roster is one of the finest in the land. Fiction: Paul West, Geoff Nicholson, Steve Weiner, Richard Foreman, Robert Schneider, David Shapiro, and Paul Auster. Film Books: Howard Koch, Peter Bogdanovich, Ian McKellen, Derek Jarman, Ang Lee, Guin Turner, Rose Troche, Michael Ritchie, Cyril Collard, and Bruce Robinson. Nonfiction: Buckminster Fuller, Erving Goffman, Martin Esslin, Armond White, and Howard Jacobson. Design: Milton Glaser, Raymond Loewy, Terence Conran, Osborne & Little, Judith Miller, and Caroline Wrey.

Overlook nonfiction titles: *Derek Jarman's Garden* by Derek Jarman (photographs by Howard Sooley); *Food of the Sun: A Fresh Look at Mediterranean Cooking* by Alastair Littel and Richard Whittington; *The Craft and Art of Clay: A Complete Potter's Handbook* by Susan Peterson; *The Complete Guide to Conservatory Plants* by Ann Bonar; *The Cistercians: Monks and Monasteries of Europe* by Stephen Tobin; *A Woman's Guide to Martial Arts: How to Choose a Discipline and Get Started* by Monica McCabe-Cardoza; *Vivienne Westwood: Fashion, Perversity and the Sixties Laid Bare* by Fred Vermorel; *Terence Conran on Design* by Terence Conran, with Elizabeth Wilhide; *Woody: Movies from Manhattan* by Julian Fox; *Andy Warhol Nudes* (text by Linda Nochlin).

Indicative of the Overlook backlist: *Chanel: The Couturière at Work* by Amy De La Haye and Shelley Tobin; *100 Great Albums of the Sixties* by John Tobler; *Diagnosis for Disaster: The Devastating Truth About False Memory Syndrome and Its Impact on Accusers and Families* by Claudette Wassil-Grimm; *Walk Aerobics* by Les Snowdon and Maggie Humphreys; *The Zen of Cooking: Creative Cooking With and Without Recipes* by Claire Hyman and Lucille Naimer.

Overlook's literary emphasis is on vanguard fiction, poetry, biography, memoirs, travel, and criticism. Fiction from Overlook: *Egg Dancing* by Liz Jensen; *In the Flesh* by Anne Schmidt; *The Photographer's Sweethearts* by Diane Hartog; *The Rose Crossing* by Nicholas Jose; *Ali and Nino* by Kurban Said; *No-Body: A Novel in Parts* by Richard Foreman (the first work of fiction by America's leading avant-garde playwright); *Footsucker* by Geoff Nicholson; *The Gods Are Thirsty* by Tanith Lee; *Sporting with Amaryllis* by Paul West. Further highlights: *Kafka's Prague: A Literary Tour of the City That Fed the Vivid, Nightmarish Imagination of Franz Kafka* by Klaus Wagenbach; *Boyopolis: Essays from Gay Eastern Europe* by Stan Persky.

Backlist entrants here include *X-Ray: The Unauthorized Autobiography* by Ray Davies; *The Ukimwi Road: From Kenya to Zimbabwe* by Dervla Murphy; *In Catskill Country: Collected Essays on Mountain History, Life and Lore* by Alf Evers; *Chroma* by Derek Jarman; *Nico: The End* by James Young.

Overlook Press is distributed by Penguin USA.

Query letters and SASEs should be directed to:

(Ms.) Tracy Karns, Editor

Peter Mayer, Publisher

OXFORD UNIVERSITY PRESS

(See Directory of University Presses)

OXMOOR HOUSE

P.O. Box 2262
Birmingham, AL 35201
205-877-6560
fax: 205-877-6504
800-366-4712
OxmoorCS@aol.com (e-mail)

Oxmoor's book-publishing interest covers cooking, gardening, decorating, home improvement, crafts, art, sports, hobbies, travel, how-to, and personal finance. Many Oxmoor titles are issued in tandem with how-to videos, and the house also produces software products. Leisure Arts is an Oxmoor imprint that produces a line of attractive, reasonably priced volumes covering roughly the same domain as Oxmoor's program.

Oxmoor House (started in 1968) is a subsidiary of Southern Progress Corporation, which is a division of Sunset Publishing Corporation, a part of the Time Warner communications conglomerate. Within this corporate domain, Oxmoor House remains essentially a smaller publisher of general adult nonfiction.

Most Oxmoor titles are originated in house, with a large percentage of its titles representing the book-publishing incarnation of several massively circulated and specialist magazines including *Money*, *Sports Illustrated*, *Southern Living*, *Sunset*, *People*, and *Time*.

Authors please note: Oxmoor is not a likely home for an original trade-book publishing project; it may be a worthwhile place for writers to investigate when spelunking for freelance assignments.

Sample titles: *Southern Living Best Recipes Made Lighter*; *Cooking Light Five-Star Recipes*; *Eatright: Seven Simple Steps to Lose Weight*; *More Quick Rotary Cutter Quilts*; *Fishes of Alabama and the Mobile Basin*; *The Cookie Jar*; *Alma-Lynne's Cross-Stitch for Special Occasions*.

Oxmoor House is distributed to the retail trade by Leisure Arts, Inc.

Query letters and SASEs should be directed to:

Nancy Fitzpatrick, Vice President and Editor in Chief
Crafts, including cross-stitch, quilting, bazaar crafts.

Ann Harvey, Editor
Special publications.

Susan Payne, Senior Food Editor
Cookbooks.

PALADIN PRESS

Box 1307
Boulder, CO 80306
303-443-7250
fax: 303-442-8741
pala@rmii.com (e-mail)
http://www.paladin-press.com (World Wide Web)

Paladin issues new titles and reprints in such categories as new identity and personal freedom, espionage and investigation, explosives and demolitions, weapons, military science, ninjutsu, revenge and humor, special forces, survival, martial arts, action careers, sniping, knives and knife fighting, locksmithing, self-defense, police science, terrorism, silencers, and history and culture relating to the above fields, as well as selected general-interest books. Paladin also purveys a video library. Paladin Press (established in 1970) is a division of Paladin Enterprises.

Certain Paladin titles exhibit a markedly subversive approach, and are intended as high-edge, satiric amusement. It should be further noted that particular works on the Paladin list contain material that may be restricted in some jurisdictions and are sold for academic, research, or informational reference purposes only.

Frontlist catalog entrants: *The Encyclopedia of Dim-Mak: The Main Meridians* by Erle Montaigue and Wally Simpson; *Renaissance Swordsmanship: The Illustrated Use of Rapiers and Cut-and-Thrust Swords* by John L. Clements; *1,001 Street Fighting Secrets: The Principles of Contemporary Fighting Arts* by Sammy France; *Do-It-Yourself Medicine: How to Find and Use the Most Effective Antibiotics, Painkillers, Anesthetics, and Other Miracle Drugs . . . Without Costly Doctors' Prescriptions or Hospitals* by Ragnar Benson; *Heckler & Koch's Handguns* by Duncan Long.

Highlights from the backlist (including all-time Paladin hits): *Hard-Won Wisdom from the School of Hard Knocks: How to Avoid a Fight and Things to Do When You Can't or Don't Want To* by Alain Burrese; *Protect Your Assets: How to Avoid Falling Victim to the Government's Forfeiture Laws* by Adam Starchild; *Running a Ring of Spies: Spycraft and Black Operations in the Real World of Espionage* by Jefferson Mack; *Fighting Power: How to Develop Explosive Punches, Kicks, Blocks, and Grappling* by Loren Christensen; *SWAT Battle Tactics: How to Organize, Train, and Equip a SWAT Team for Law Enforcement or Self-Defense* by Pat Cascio and John McSweeney; *Silencer History and Performance (Volume 1): Sporting and Tactical Silencers* by Alan C. Paulson; *Mega-Marketing for the Private Investigator: How to Drastically Increase Your Agency Business with Effective Mega-Marketing Techniques* by Ralph D. Thomas; *Body for Sale: An Inside Look at Medical Research, Drug Testing, and Organ Transplants and How You Can Profit from Them* by Ed Brassard; *How to Investigate by Computer* by Ralph D. Thomas; *Secrets of Successful Process Serving: How to Start a Successful Service of Process Business and Make It Grow* by Nelson Tucker; *Zips, Pipes, and Pens: Arsenal of Improvised Weapons* by J. David Truby.

Paladin's Web site contains information on the lawsuit against Paladin Press and the press's fight to preserve the integrity of the First Amendment. (A noted antigun lawyer vows to put Paladin Press out of business; a federal district court in Maryland has already dismissed a lawsuit that would have held Paladin Press liable for a brutal contract killing during the investigation of which Paladin Press publications are alleged to have been discovered in a context that indicated they were among the possessions of the accused.) No matter how controversial Paladin books and videos may seem to some, the publisher believes it is the responsibility of us all to recognize and defend unequivocally the fact that if all ideas were safe and mainstream, there would be no need for a First Amendment.

Paladin Press looks for original manuscripts on combat shooting, firearms and exotic weapons, personal and financial freedom, military science, and other action topics. For more information, call or write the publisher for a copy of the *Author Style Guide* and *Insider Newsletter*.

Paladin Press distributes its own list and in addition services individual orders via toll-free ordering numbers.

Query letters and SASEs should be directed to:

Jon Ford, Editorial Director

PARAGON HOUSE PUBLISHERS

2700 University Avenue West, Suite 47
St. Paul, MN 55114-1016
612-644-3087; 612-644-0997

Paragon House publishes books that feature an interdisciplinary approach to philosophy, critical thought, and religious culture. The Paragon line is further typified by categories such as ethics and morality; philosophy and society; world religions; religion and society; spirituality (including new-age approaches); and reference works.

On the Paragon House roster are general trade books in popular areas related to the house's core interests. Many Paragon House titles in philosophy and religion are distributed primarily in the academic and scholarly market. Paragon House (founded in 1982) publishes trade paperback and hardcover editions and maintains a solid backlist.

The Paragon House operations base has moved to St. Paul, Minnesota, from its former location in New York.

From Paragon: *First Person Mortal* by Lucy Bregman and Sara Thiermann; *Nature's Web: Rethinking Our Place on Earth* by Peter Marshall; *The Soul: An Owner's Manual* by George Jaidar; *Path of the Kabbalah* by David Sheinkin; *Enemies Without Guns: The Catholic Church in China* by James T. Myers; *Through the Moral Maze: Searching for Absolute Values in a Pluralistic World* by Robert Hilary Kane; *From Behind the Wall: Commentary on Crime, Punishment, Race, and the Underclass by a Prison Inmate* by Mansfield B. Frazier; *Work and Employment* (edited by David Marsland); *Critical Theory: The Essential Readings* (edited by David Ingram and Julia Simon-Ingram).

Paragon House distributes through Continuum Publishing Group, in care of Publisher Resources (800-937-5557).

Query letters and SASEs should be directed to:

Laureen Enright, Acquisitions Editor

Gordon Anderson, Executive Director

PARAMOUNT COMMUNICATIONS
PARAMOUNT PUBLISHING
(See Simon & Schuster)

PASSPORT BOOKS
(See NTC Publishing Group)

PATHFINDER PRESS
410 West Street
New York, NY 10014
212-741-0690
fax: 212-727-0150
pathfinder@igc.apc.org (e-mail)

The Pathfinder program catalogs such fields as black and African studies; women's rights; the Cuban revolution in world politics; revolutionaries and working-class fighters; fascism, big business, and the labor movement; Russia, Eastern Europe, and the Balkans; scientific views of politics and economics; trade unions: past, present, and future; United States history and political issues; Latin America and the Caribbean; the Middle East and China; and art, culture, and politics. Pathfinder titles often suggest such streams of thought as populism, internationalism, utopianism, socialism, and communism.

Pathfinder Press (established in 1940) issues books, booklets, pamphlets, posters, and postcards keyed to issues affecting working people worldwide. Pathfinder produces titles in English, Spanish, French, Swedish, Farsi, Greek, Icelandic, and Russian. Pathfinder publishes the journal *New International*.

The Pathfinder Mural that once adorned the company's editorial and manufacturing digs in Manhattan's Far West Village featured a depiction of a gargantuan printing press in action as well as portraits of revolutionary leaders whose writings and speeches are published by Pathfinder; this community cultural represented the work of more than 80 artists from 20 countries.

Representative Pathfinder books: *Episodes of the Cuban Revolutionary War, 1956–58* by Ernesto Che Guevara (firsthand account of the military campaigns and political events that culminated in the January 1959 popular insurrection that overthrew the U.S.–backed dictatorship in Cuba); *Lenin's Final Fight: Speeches and Writings, 1922–23* by V. I. Lenin; *In Defense of Marxism: The Social and Political Contradictions of the Soviet Union* by Leon Trotsky; *The Second Declaration of Havana*.

On Pathfinder's staunch backlist: *Bolivian Diary* by Ernesto (Che) Guevara (in a new translation by Inti Peredo); *Peru's Shining Path: Anatomy of a Reactionary Sect* by Martín Koppel; *Lenny Bruce: The Comedian as Social Critic and Secular Moralist* by Frank Kofsky; *The Revolution Betrayed: What Is the Soviet Union and Where Is It Going?* by Leon Trotsky; *The History of American Trotskyism: Report of a Participant,*

1928–38 by James P. Cannon; *The Politics of Chicano Liberation* (edited by Olga Rodriguez); *Polemics in Marxist Philosophy* by George Novack; *The Communist Manifesto* by Karl Marx and Frederick Engels; *Cuba's Internationalist Foreign Policy, 1975–80* by Fidel Castro; *Marxism and Terrorism* by Leon Trotsky; *To Speak the Truth: Why Washington's "Cold War" Against Cuba Doesn't End* by Fidel Castro and Che Guevara; *How Far We Slaves Have Come! South Africa and Cuba in Today's World* by Nelson Mandela, Fidel Castro; *Che Guevara: Economics and Politics in the Transition to Socialism* by Carlos Tablada; *The History of the Russian Revolution* by Leon Trotsky.

Pathfinder's *New International* is a magazine of Marxist politics and theory. Many of the articles that appear in *New International* are available in Spanish, French, and Swedish. The magazine is a numbered series in trade paperback format.

Special Pathfinder series include Malcolm X: Speeches and Writings, as well as written works and spoken words from James P. Cannon, Eugene V. Debs, Farrell Dobbs, Carlos Fonseca, Mother Jones, Rosa Luxemburg, Nelson Mandela, Fidel Castro, and Ernesto (Che) Guevara; the house also publishes the works of Karl Marx, Frederick Engels, V. I. Lenin, and Leon Trotsky.

Pathfinder runs a number of bookstores around the world and offers membership in a readers' club for an annual fee (entitling members to enjoy special discounts); individual orders are payable via Visa and Mastercard. Pathfinder Press distributes its own publications in the United States and worldwide primarily through its own fulfillment centers.

Query letters and SASEs should be directed to:

Greg McCartan, Editorial Director
Projects consistent with the Pathfinder list.

PAULIST PRESS
(See Directory of Religious, Spiritual, and Inspirational Publishers)

PEACHPIT PRESS
2414 Sixth Street
Berkeley, CA 94710
510-548-4393
fax: 510-548-5991
800-283-9444 (orders)
http://www.peachpit.com (World Wide Web)

Peachpit is a specialist computer-publishing house with a list in personal computing and desktop publishing for business and recreational users. Peachpit publishes books and book/software packages (including CD-ROM products) that tackle basic practical tasks and troubleshooting, as well as advanced applications.

Peachpit covers a number of categories: general introductory works on computing, general works about the Macintosh computer system, Macintosh Bible series, Visual QuickStart series, desktop publishing, graphics, Windows and Windows applications, word processing, and related topics. Many Peachpit releases are keyed to particular proprietary products.

Visual QuickStart Guides provide exactly what the title implies: a fast, simple way to get up and running with a new program—which is perhaps the secret to the popularity of this successful line.

Peachpit's editorial approach is to make the computing world relevant, make it dramatic, make it fun. Peachpit authors are at the forefront of ongoing technological developments and trends in computer hardware and software development, and masterful at teasing out the nuances of end-user potential in print.

In this connection, Peachpit Press has published its first fiction title: *Chat* by Nancy McCarthy (a tale about love online).

Publisher's statement: Peachpit is not only in the book business, and not only a player on the computer-business stage; Peachpit is also in the teaching business. In addition to trade bookstores and computer venues, Peachpit hits a variety of market sectors such as schools and educational enterprises (including evening classes and adult education); library, institutional and corporate consumers; and end-user and professional groups.

Peachpit Press (founded in 1986) was acquired by Addison-Wesley in late 1994 and the house is now a division of Addison Wesley Longman. Within this corporate structure, Peachpit maintains its independent editorial stance and gains financial and distributional leverage from the new ownership to the benefit of Peachpit's worthy list.

Titles from Peachpit: *Beyond "The Mac Is Not a Typewriter"* by Robin Williams; *Digital Image Creation* by Hisaka Kojima; *The Photographer's Digital Studio* by Joe Farace; *Start with a Scan* by Janet Ashford and John Odam; *Shocking the Web: Mac Edition*, and *Shocking the Web: Windows Edition* by Lee Swearingen, David K. Anderson, and Cathy Clarke; *Windows 95 Is Driving Me Crazy!* by Kay Yarborough Nelson; *The Little Quicken Book* by Lawrence J. Magid and Louis G. Fortis.

Peachpit Press is distributed through the parent Addison-Wesley Publishing Company.

To suggest a book idea or submit a book proposal, contact **Roslyn Bullas** (510-548-4393) or e-mail (roslyn@peachpit.com). Query letters and SASEs should be directed to:

Nancy Ruenzel, Publisher

PEACHTREE PUBLISHERS, LTD.
494 Armour Circle NE
Atlanta, GA 30324-4088
404-876-8761
fax: 404-875-2578

Peachtree publishes general trade nonfiction and commercial literary fiction, and offers a substantial and growing children's list. Peachtree has a concentration in markedly innovative books in self-help, self-awareness, and self-improvement, as well as parenting, cooking and gardening, humor. A special area of Peachtree publishing interest encompasses regional topics, including the American South in general and the state of Georgia in particular. Peachtree is also known for its storytelling series.

Peachtree Publishers (established in 1978) is a midsize house that produces books in hardcover and trade paperback editions, and offers selected works in electronic recorded formats. Peachtree hosts a hardy backlist.

From Peachtree: *Cheap Psychological Tricks: What to Do When Hard Work, Honesty, and Perseverance Fail!* by Perry Buffington (illustrated by Mitzi Cartee); *Food Gifts for All Seasons* by Anne Byrne (illustrated by Anne Hathaway); *Archival Atlanta: Electric Street Dummies, the Great Stonehenge Explosion, Nerve Tonics and Bovine Laws* by Perry Buffington and Kim Underwood; *The Hiking Trails of North Georgia* by Tim Homan with the Georgia Conservancy; *Margaret Mitchell & John Marsh: The Love Story Behind Gone with the Wind* by Marianne Walker; *Cooking in the New South: A Modern Approach to Traditional Southern Fare* by Anne Byrne; *Master Switch* (fiction) by William H. Stender, Jr.; *The Single Mother's Book: A Practical Guide to Managing Your Children, Career, Home, Finances, and Everything Else* by Joan Anderson.

Standout Peachtree projects: *Over What Hill? Notes from the Pasture* by Effie Leland Wilder (illustrated by Laurie Klein) is a humorous and perceptive coming-of-age tale for older adults. *Growing Up Cuban in Decatur, Georgia* by Carmen Agra Deedy combines the rich traditions of her southern upbringing and her Latin American culture in a blend of delightful stories, many of which have been heard on National Public Radio's "All Things Considered." *The New Austerities* by Tito Perdue features a dramatic antimodernist approach to going-home-to-Alabama fiction.

Peachtree distributes its own list to the trade with the assistance of regional sales representatives.

PEACHTREE CHILDREN'S BOOKS

Children's editions from Peachtree encompass award-winning frontlist illustrated storybooks for younger readers as well as a select group of works directed toward parents. Peachtree Jr. is a line of chapter books targeted for ages 8 years and up. The AllStar SportStory series combines contemporary tales with sports history and statistics.

Titles here: *Wishing* by Ruth Tiller (illustrated by Debrah Santini); *Curious Kids Go to Preschool: Another Big Book of Words* and *Curious Kids Go on Vacation: Another Big Book of Words* by Heloise Antoine (illustrated by Ingrid Godon); *Tulips* by Jay O'Callahan (illustrated by Debrah Santini); *Teaching Your Child the Language of Social Success* by Marshall Duke, Stephen Nowicki, Jr., and Elizabeth Martin; *Herman & Marguerite* (an environmental story) by Jay O'Callahan (illustrated by Laura O'Callahan); *Kishina: A True Story of Gorilla Survival* by Maxine Rock; *T. J.'s Secret Pitch* and *Playoff Dreams* (in the AllStar SportStory series) by Fred Bowen (illustrated by Jim Thorpe); *Once upon a Child: Writing Your Child's Special Story* by Debbie McChesney (illustrated by Sarah Carter); *Orange Cheeks* (written by Jay O'Callahan and illustrated by Patricia Raine; issued along with a line of audios from storyteller Jay).

Query letters and SASEs should be directed to:

Margaret M. Quinlin, President and Publisher

PELICAN PUBLISHING COMPANY

1101 Monroe Street
Gretna, LA 70053
504-368-1175
fax: 504-368-1195
800-843-1724 (orders)

Mailing address:
P.O. Box 3110
Gretna, LA 70054
sales@pelicanpub.com (e-mail)
http://www.pelicanpub.com (World Wide Web)

Pelican Publishing Company (founded in 1926) produces a general trade list with special interests in travel and lifestyle guides, Americana, cookbooks, art and architecture, photography, humor, sports, motivational and inspirational titles. Many Pelican titles offer a regional or cultural perspective in such areas as the American South, Civil War history, Louisiana and the New Orleans environs, and Scottish American heritage. Pelican produces a short menu of children's books, and offers a select group of fiction works, many of which have a regional or historical twist.

Pelican's travel series include the Maverick Guides (for the independent traveler—these guides include history, customs, language, and attractions, as well as current prices and recommendations for accommodations, dining spots, etc.); The Marmac Guides (up-to-date information on population, services, recreation, accommodations, restaurants on various American cities); At Cost Travel Guide series (for the value-conscious traveler), the Pelican Guide series (designed to give the discriminating traveler insight into some of the most interesting locations with the U.S.).

Other Pelican series include the Majesty Architecture series, the New Orleans Architecture series, the Best Editorial Cartoons of the Year series, the Editorial Cartoonists series, the Cruising Guides series, and the Clovis Crawfish Series for Cajun kids.

From Pelican: *In Search of Your True Self: 21 Incredible Insights That Will Revitalize Your Body, Mind and Spirit* by Walter Staples; *With Wings, There Are No Barriers: A Woman's Guide to a Life of Magnificent Possibilities* by Sue Augustine; *The Secret to Conquering Fear* by Mike Hernacki; *One Potato, Two Potato: The Potato Cookbook* by Janet Reeves; *Florida Scams* by Victor M. Knight; *Golfing in Ireland: The Most Complete and Comprehensive Guide for Adventurous Golfers* by Rob Armstrong; *Travel Guide to Jewish Germany* by Peter Hirsch and Billie Ann Lopez; *Stories from the Hearts of Two Grandmas* by Ibbie Ledford and Johnnie Countess; *Holly Day's Café and Other Christmas Stories* by Gerald R. Toner; *Ezra Jack Keats: A Bibliography and Catalogue* by Brian Alderson; *Cajun Heart and Humor* by Tommy Joe Breaux (illustrated by Dominicus Maters); *The Majesty of Williamsburg* by Peter Beney.

Pelican's Top-30 list includes: *See You at the Top* and *Confessions of a Happy Christian* by Zig Ziglar; *The Justin Wilson Cook Book*, *The Justin Wilson Gourmet and Gourmand Cookbook*, and *Justin Wilson's Outdoor Cooking with Inside Help* by Justin Wilson; *Cooking with Country Music Stars* by Country Music Foundation.

Representing the Pelican's children's list favorites: *Toby Belfer's Seder: A Passover Story Retold* by Gloria Teles Pushker (illustrated by Judith Hierstein); *Eyr the Hunter: A Story of Ice-Age America* by Margaret Zehmer Searcy (illustrated by Joyce Haynes); *Little Freddie at the Kentucky Derby* by Kathryn Cocquyt (illustrated by Sylvia Corbett).

Pelican Publishing Company handles its own distribution.

Query letters and SASEs should be sent to:

Milburn Calhoun, President and Publisher

Nina Kooij, Editor

Penguin USA
Viking
Dutton
Penguin Studio
Donald I. Fine Books
Penguin USA Children's Divisions

375 Hudson Street
New York, NY 10014
212-366-2000

Penguin USA is a major component of Penguin Putnam, Inc. Beneath the spread of its two primary branches—Viking Penguin and Dutton Signet—Penguin USA offers a wealth of distinctive and distinguished lines and imprints. The house produces books in hardcover, trade paper, and mass-market paperback editions.

In early 1997 Penguin USA and the Putnam Berkley Group—two huge book-publishing enterprises—merged to form Penguin Putnam, Inc. Within this expansive domain, Penguin USA remains an imposing publishing group, one of North America's leading houses.

Penguin earns an admirable industry presence through a diverse program that includes a solid seasonal list of new commercial titles as well as a select group of imprints featuring some of publishing's classic lines in poetry, belles-lettres, and literary fiction (established backlist sellers, newer reprints, and originals). The Viking Penguin division incorporates such imprints as Viking, Penguin, and Penguin Studio. The Dutton Signet division includes Dutton, Mentor, New American Library, Obelisk, Onyx, Plume, Roc, Signet, and Topaz.

In the Penguin USA lineup are a number of children's-book divisions, among them Cobblehill, Dial Books for Young Readers, Dutton Children's Books, Lodestar, Puffin, and Viking Children's Books (please see subentry below for Penguin USA Children's Divisions).

Penguin USA is also home to the Frederick Warne imprint, Arkana, Virago Modern Classics, and the autonomous imprint Truman M. Talley Books, as well as the subsidiary Stephen Greene Press. The previously independent publishing house Donald I. Fine is part of the Penguin operation (please see subentry below for Donald I. Fine/Dutton).

Mass-market paperback originals are published under a group of Dutton specialty imprints, including Signet, New American Library, Mentor, Obelisk, Onyx, Roc, Topaz, and the affiliated DAW Books (please see the subentry below for Dutton, as well as separate DAW main entry). These imprints produce a selection of mass-market category novels in such areas as historical romances, horror, science fiction and fantasy, mystery and suspense, thrillers, and Westerns.

Penguin Putnam distributes for all its divisions and imprints; Penguin also handles distribution for books published by a variety of houses, including Sports Illustrated, DAW, Dove Books, Overlook Press, Hamish Hamilton, and Michael Joseph.

The Viking Penguin program informs us that it does not accept unsolicited manuscripts *or queries*. Any materials sent to the house with SASE is returned *unread*. Anything without SASE is recycled. The house accepts only agented or otherwise solicited work. *The acquisitions contacts listed below are for information and reference purposes.*

VIKING

Viking covers the trade spectrum in nonfiction and fiction. Nonfiction areas include current events, popular and academic history, personal finance, cooking and food, lifestyle and design, travel, health, music, popular philosophy, self-help, women's studies, history, general reference, essays, biography and autobiography, and literary criticism. Viking fiction hits all the popular categories, including popular literature, thrillers, mystery, and suspense. Viking's output includes books for young readers (please see below under Penguin USA children's divisions).

Viking produces primarily hardcover trade editions under its captivating, illustrious logo of a seafaring dragon ship. Viking's publishing program spins off many of its originals into paper editions via the Penguin and Dutton reprint lists.

Acquisition contacts (agented only):

Barbara Grossman, Publisher
Wide-ranging nonfiction interests; some fiction.

Carolyn Carlson, Senior Editor
Narrative nonfiction, cultural history, biography, women's issues, commercial nonfiction, commercial and literary fiction, mysteries.

Courtney Hodell, Senior Editor
Wide range of interests.

Pamela Dorman, Executive Editor
Commercial fiction, especially women's fiction and suspense. Nonfiction interests include self-help and psychology, investigative stories and narrative nonfiction, popular inspiration, popular reference, and women's issues.

Dawn Drzal, Senior Editor
Food, cooking, and wine; science, mathematics, and technology; nature and environment.

Susan Hans O'Connor, Associate Editor
Commercial and literary fiction, mysteries, dance/theater/arts.

Al Silverman, Editor at Large
Mysteries and thrillers, American history (political, literary, social), 20th-century biography, military history, current events, sports.

Wendy Weil, Senior Editor
Nonfiction, especially music, culture, humor.

Mindy Werner, Executive Editor
Women's issues, Judaism, contemporary issues, health, true crime, and parenting. Literary and commercial fiction.

PENGUIN

Penguin (founded in 1935) is an imprint of the Viking Penguin division of Penguin Putnam. Penguin's original publishing vision was to make great books available—and affordable—to a broad audience. Publishing under the widely recognized imprint of its emblematic penguin cartouche, the house retains a paperback orientation and operates a program that encompasses both originals and reprints. Many Viking hardcover books are reprinted in Penguin paperback editions.

In addition to the celebrated Penguin Classics line, the imprint features the Viking Portable series, the Viking Critical Library, the Penguin Nature Classics, the Penguin Travel Library, and Penguin Twentieth-Century Classsics. Penguin offers an acclaimed assortment of poetry that accents contemporary voices (including titles in the Penguin Poets line). The Arkana imprint is devoted to spirituality and philosophy. Penguin is always on the lookout for strong original trade-paperback titles.

In 1996, Penguin launched Penguin Ediciones, a paperback line of books written in Spanish; authors include Carlos Fuentes, Gabriel Garcia Marques, and Manuel Puig.

Representative Viking Penguin nonfiction: *The Money Diet* by Ginger Applegarth; *Speaking with the Devil: A Dialogue with Evil* by Carl Goldberg; *Ms. Miller's Etiquitte for Cats* by Melissa Miller; *Lost and Found: The 9,000 Treasures of Tros—Heinrich Schliemann and the Gold That Got Away* by Caroline Moorehead; *How to Find the Work You Love* by Laurence C. Boldt; *Going Global: Four Entrepreneurs Map the New World Marketplace* by William C. Taylor and Alan M. Webber; *From Paperclips to Printers* (cost-cutting home-office how-to) by Dean and Jessica King; *Daniel Johnnes's Top 200 Wines* by Daniel Johnnes; *The Budget Gardener* by Maureen Gilmer; *Combat Golf: The Competitor's Field Manual for Winning against Any Opponent* by Captain Bruce Warren Ollstein.

Viking Penguin fiction and literary highlights: *A Boy Named Phyllis: A Suburban Memoir* by Frank DeCaro; *Because We Are Here* by Chuck Wachtel; *Biggest Elvis* by P. F. Kluge; *How Stella Got Her Groove Back* by Terry McMillan; *Keith Haring: Journals* by Keith Haring; *My First White Friend: Confessions on Race, Love, and Forgiveness* by Patricia Raybon; *Nice Girls Finish Last* (a Robin Hudson Mystery) by Sparkle Hayter; *Soultown* (a Whitney Logan mystery) by Mercedes Lambert; *The Frog* by John Hawkes; *The Penguin Book of Erotic Stories by Women* (edited by Richard

Glynn Jones and A. Susan Williams); *The Possessions of a Lady* by Jonathan Gash; *The Serpent Garden* by Judith Merkle Riley; *The Woman Who Walked into Doors* by Roddy Doyle; *Trail of Secrets* by Eileen Goudge; *Volcano and Miracle: A Selection of Fiction and Nonfiction from the Journal Written at Night* (edited by Gustaw Herling).

The house has success with a roster of best-selling novels from popular authors: *Felicia's Journey* by William Trevor, *The Cunning Man* by Robertson Davies, *Redeye* by Clyde Edgerton, *Songs in Ordinary Time* by Mary McGarry Morris, *Rose Madder* by Stephen King, *Speaking in Tongues* by Jeffrey Deaver, and *At Home in Mitford* by Jan Karon.

Acquisition contacts (agented only):

Kathryn Court, Publisher
Literary and commercial fiction, including Third World and European fiction. Non-fiction interests include humor, travel writing, biography, current affairs, business, nature, women's issues, and true crime.

Robert Dreeson, Senior Editor
Literature, history, science, literary criticism.

Michael Millman, Senior Editor
Oversees the Penguin Classics and Twentieth-Century Classics, the Viking Portable Library, and the Penguin Nature Classics series.

Kristine Puopolo, Editor
Trade paperback originals, reprint fiction and nonfiction, literature, narrative history, social and cultural studies, psychology, women's lives, Penguin Classics.

David Stanford, Senior Editor
Nonfiction paperback originals with backlist potential in several areas: popular culture, music, humor, current events, environment. Also hardcover and/or paperback originals for the Arkana imprint, which publishes spiritual literature in areas including mythology, Zen, Tibetan Buddhism, women's spirituality, and Western traditions. Oversees Penguin Poets, which publishes six original poetry works per year.

Jane von Mehren, Executive Editor
Health and social issues, self-help, child care and parenting, nature, popular culture, and personal stories, as well as contemporary and historical commercial fiction.

Caroline White, Editor
Literary fiction, women's issues, memoirs, sociology, religion, film and television, popular culture, Penguin Classics.

PENGUIN STUDIO

Penguin Studio publishes commercial, illustrated publications (primarily books, as well as such related merchandise as calendars) for adults in all subject categories and in all price ranges. Studio titles tend toward high-interest frontlist offerings in art and culture, fashion and design, lifestyle, and sports, with interests that cross over into such arenas as health and nutrition, popular psychology and inspiration, humor, works with social and historical themes, and literary writing.

Representing the Studio lineup: *The Complete Book of Irish Country Cooking: Traditional and Wholesome Recipes from Ireland* by Darina Allen; *The Healing Bath: Holistic Bubbles and Soothing Soaks* by Maribeth Riggs (paintings by Sir Lawrence Alma-Tadema); *Glorious American Quilts: The Quilt Collection of the Museum of American Folk Art* by Elizabeth V. Warren and Sharon L. Eisenstat; *Kitchens for Cooks: Planning Your Perfect Kitchen* by Deborah Krasner; *The Blue Dog Art Calendar* by George Rodrigue; *The Complete Home Office* by Alvin Rosenbaum; *The Romanov Legacy* by Zoia Belyakova; *Amen: A Gathering of Forty Prayers and Blessings from Around the World* by Emily Gwathmey and Suzanne Slesin; and *Mud Hens and Mavericks: The Illustrated Travel Guide to the Minor Leagues* by Judith Blahnik and Philip S. Schulz.

Acquisition contacts (agented only):

Michael Fragnito, Publisher
Music, history, sports, nostalgia, social issues and current events, science and technology, humor, and how-to.

Christopher Sweet, Executive Director
Popular culture, sports, art, photography, humor, music, history.

Cyril Nelson, Senior Editor
Folk art and crafts, gardening, quilting, collecting, antiques, and architecture.

Sarah Scheffel, Editor
Health; food and cooking; decorating and design; illustrated fiction.

Marie Timell, Senior Editor
Occult, astrology, new age, reference, recovery, psychology, medicine.

DUTTON

Dutton spans the spectrum of trade categories in fiction and nonfiction. Dutton is a major player in popular nonfiction areas, covering personality and celebrity books, topical interest, current events, biography and memoirs, business and careers, parenting and the family, psychology and inspiration, cultural studies, history, science, and reference. The house produces a substantial list in contemporary fiction, with an emphasis in top-rank suspense and mystery novels, science fiction and fantasy, Westerns, and popular literary works.

The Dutton division of Penguin USA is a corporate incarnation of the former E. P. Dutton. Under the Dutton umbrella are a number of imprints, including Signet, Onyx, Topaz, Truman M. Talley Books, and the William Abrahams line.

Dutton Signet's mass-market paperback originals come out under such imprints as Mentor, New American Library, Obelisk, Onyx, Roc, Signet, Topaz, and the affiliated DAW Books (see separate DAW main entry). These imprints address popular nonfiction (how-to, self-improvement, topical stories) and produce category fiction lineups in mystery and suspense, thrillers, romance, science fiction and fantasy, horror, and Westerns.

New American Library is a designation given to a portion of the Signet/NAL mass-market rack-size paperback list covering broad categories in nonfiction and fiction.

Plume publishes primarily trade paperback nonfiction and fiction, original titles as well as reprints. Plume accents commercial nonfiction and selected high-interest contemporary fiction, as well as classics and literary works. Plume also produces a variety of television and film tie-ins and a strong line of popular nutrition, health, and self-improvement titles.

Indicative of the Dutton program in fiction, literary works, and letters: *The World on Blood* by Jonathan Nasaw; *Millionaires Row* by Norman Katkov; *Gossip* by Christopher Bram; *Touched* by Carolyn Haines; *Streets of Fire* by Soledad Santiago; *Fearful Symmetry* by Greg Bills; *Infamous* by Joan Collins; *No Use Dying over Spilled Milk: A Pennsylvania Dutch Mystery with Recipes* by Tamar Myers; *Bad Angel* by Helen Benedict; and *First Cases: First Appearances of Classic Private Eyes* (edited by Robert J. Randisi).

Dutton has published such authors as Nancy Taylor Rosenberg, Helena Maria Viramontes, Lisa Appignanesi, Lisa Alther, Dorothy Allison, Joyce Carol Oates, Julia Alvarez, Max Allan Collins, Joan Hess, Lawrence Block, and Christopher Bram.

Representative Dutton nonfiction: *What Women Want* by Patricia Ireland; *Harriet Roth's Deliciously Healthy Jewish Cooking: 350 New Low-Fat, Low-Cholesterol, Low-Sodium Recipes for Holidays and Every Day* by Harriet Roth; *Facing the Wolf: Inside the Process of Deep Feeling Therapy* by Theresa Sheppard Alexander; *The Directory of Saints: A Concise Guide to Patron Saints* by Annette Sandoval; *Howard Hughes: The Untold Story* by Peter Harry Brown and Pat H. Broeske; *Behind Blue Eyes: The Life of Pete Townshend* by Geoffrey Giuliano; *Split Image: The Life of Anthony Perkins* by Charles Winecoff; *Growing Myself: A Spiritual Journey Through Gardening* by Judith Handelsman; *Faith of Our Fathers: African-American Men Reflect on Fatherhood* (edited by Andre Willis); *Mama's Boy: The True Story of a Serial Killer and His Mother* by Richard T. Pienciak; and *Orion's Legacy: A Cultural History of Man As Hunter* by Charles Bergman.

Acquisition contacts (agented only):

Rosemary Ahern, Senior Editor
Scholarly/academic books. Literary fiction.

Deb Brody, Senior Editor
Self-help and popular psychology.

Hamilton Cain, Senior Editor
Narrative nonfiction, business, politics/current affairs, literary fiction.

Carole DeSanti, Vice President, Editor at Large
Women's issues, literary fiction, cookbooks, health.

Arnold Dolin, Senior Vice President and Associate Publisher
General nonfiction ranging from business to psychology, contemporary political and social issues, theater, and the entertainment media. Literary fiction. Acquires for Dutton, Plume, and Signet.

Laura Ann Gilman, Executive Editor
Acquires for Roc science fiction and fantasy line; mysteries.

(Ms.) Michaela Hamilton, Vice President, Editor in Chief, Signet and Onyx; Associate Publisher, Dutton
True crime. Commercial fiction.

Todd Keithley, Senior Editor
Thrillers, mysteries (contemporary and historical), Westerns. Popular nonfiction.

Audrey LaFehr, Executive Editor, Dutton Signet; Editorial Director, Topaz
Commercial fiction, romance, suspense.

Lori Lipsky, Vice President, Associate Publisher, Editor in Chief, Adult Trade
Commercial fiction, thrillers, suspense; general nonfiction, cookbooks, novelty books. Presides over Dutton hardcover.

Jennifer Moore, Associate Editor
Health, self-help, African-American studies, cookbooks, serious nonfiction.

Dierdre Mullane, Executive Editor
Narrative nonfiction, science, spirituality, multicultural literary fiction.

Kari Paschall, Associate Manuscript Editor

Danielle Perez, Senior Editor; Manager, Film and Television Publishing, Dutton Signet
Commercial fiction, mysteries, thrillers, and suspense. General nonfiction, spirituality, novelty books, movie tie-ins.

Joseph Pitman, Senior Editor
Thrillers, mysteries, commercial fiction, horror, celebrity.

Hugh Rawson, Editorial Director, Penguin Reference
Reference, general nonfiction.

(Ms.) Hillary Ross, Associate Executive Editor
Women's fiction, romance, suspense, thrillers, commercial fiction, general nonfiction.

Jennifer Sawyer-Fisher, Senior Editor, Dutton Signet
Romance, commercial women's fiction, suspense; would consider a truly outstanding concept in horror. Looking for writers who show freshness and an edge.

Julia Serebinsky, Associate Editor
Journalism, psychology, film, novelty books, cookbooks, literary fiction.

Al Silverman, Senior Vice President, Editor at Large
Thrillers, sports, fiction. (See also this editor's listing under Viking.)

Truman M. Talley, Publisher, Truman M. Talley Books
Business, general history, biography.

Donald I. Fine Books/Dutton

Dutton's Fine imprint (formerly the independent house Donald I. Fine, Inc.) hosts a topflight genre list in the fiction categories of mysteries, technothrillers, suspense, and science fiction, along with a selection of high-interest nonfiction.

Donald I. Fine, founder and former publisher of Arbor House, created Donald I. Fine, Inc. in 1983. The company grew to become a medium-sized producer of hardcover and trade paperback books with a discriminating list of adult fiction and nonfiction works. The Fine persona was among the elect group of publishers with an editorial sense that exhibited both literary depth and commercial appeal. With the acquisition by Penguin USA (in late 1995), the imprint maintains a considerable brace of successful volumes on an extensive backlist.

Fiction from Fine includes *Grand Jury* by Philip Friedman; *The Geezer Factory Murders* by Corinne Holt Sawyer; *The Third Sister* (a sequel to Jane Austen's *Sense and Sensibility*) by Julia Barrett; *True Confessions: The Novel* by Mary Bringle; *Green Lake* by S. K. Epperson; and *The Devil's Menagerie* by Louis Charbonneau.

From the Fine nonfiction portfolio: *La Moreau: A Biography of Jeanne Moreau* by Marianne Gray; *Nimitz: The Man and His Wars* by Randall Brink; *The Huntress: The True Saga of Dottie and Brandi Thorson, Modern Day Bounty Hunters* by Christopher Keane with Dottie Thorson; and *Seasons in Hell: With Billy Martin, Whitey Herzog, and "the Worst Baseball Teams in History," the 1973–1975 Texas Rangers* by Mike Shropshire.

The Primus imprint issues a line of original paperbacks as well as reprints, including the Primus Library of Contemporary Americana. Titles here are *A Sistermony* by Richard Stern; *Bardot: An Intimate Portrait* by Jeffrey Robinson; *In the Place of Fallen Leaves* by Tim Pears; *Widow's Walk: One Woman's Spiritual and Emotional Journey to a New Life* by Anne Hoasansky; and *How to Give Good Phone* by Lisa Collier Cool.

Donald I. Fine, Editor in Chief

Jason Poston, Editor

PENGUIN USA CHILDREN'S DIVISIONS

The Penguin children's book-publishing operations offer a panoply of distinctive divisions, imprints, and affiliates of Penguin's component houses, including Cobblehill Books, Dial Books for Young Readers, Dutton Children's Books, Lodestar Books, Puffin Books, and Viking Children's Books. Each imprint publishes a wide range of titles in a variety of formats, and each children's house is a recognized name in the industry; taken together, this Penguin lineup represents a powerhouse in the young-reader arena.

The **Cobblehill Books** affiliate accents picture books with stories to tell, as well as nonfiction for the range of youthful readership. Among Cobblehill titles: *When the Wolves Return* (photoessay) by Ron Hirschi (photography by Thomas D. Mangelsen); *Kids In and Out of Trouble* by Margaret O. Hyde; *The Chicks' Trick* (written and illustrated by Jeni Bassett); *Emeka's Gift: An African Counting Story* (written and photographed by Ifeoma Onyefulu); and *The Haunting of Holroyd Hill* by Brenda Seabrooke.

Dial Books for Young Readers is a division that publishes the spectrum from preschoolers through older readers. On the Dial list: *Boundless Grace* by Mary Hoffman; *It's a Spoon, Not a Shovel* by Caralyn Buehner (pictures by Mark Buehner); *Titanic Crossing* by Barbara Williams; *The Secret Code Book* (with press-out code-busters) by Helen Huckle; and *Do the Whales Still Sing?* by Dianne Hofmeyr (pictures by Jude Daly).

The **Dutton Children's Books** program includes humorous and serious titles for the youngest readers through young adult. Indicative of the Dutton list are *Jeremy Kooloo* by Tim Mahurin; *Dinner at Magritte's* (written and illustrated by Michael Garland); *Jimmy, the Pickpocket of the Palace* by Donna Jo Napoli (illustrated by Judith Byron Schachner); and *It's for You: An Amazing Picture-Puzzle Book* by John Talbot.

Lodestar Books offers a vigorous approach to fiction and nonfiction for all age groups, as well as an innovative line of activity books and specialty items. Lodestar fiction and nonfiction titles often have a social-issue edge and deal with such phenomena as ethnic experience, gender relations, art and culture, and sexual preference.

Representative Lodestar titles are *For Home and Country: A Civil War Scrapbook* by Norma Bolotin and Angela Herb; *Toads and Diamonds* (retold and illustrated by Robert Bender); *Paco and the Witch: A Puerto Rican Folktale* (retold by Felix Pitre; illustrations by Christy Hale; also available in Spanish as *Paco y la Bruja*, translated by Osvaldo Blanco); and *Earth, Sky, and Beyond: A Journey Through Space* by Jean-Pierre Verdet (illustrations by Pierre Bon).

Puffin Books is a division that produces the gamut of mainstream children's categories with emphasis on popular-priced paperback picture-book editions for the youngest readers and novels and nonfiction for the older group. Sample Puffin entrants: *Glasses—Who Needs 'Em?* by Lane Smith; *The Day the Goose Got Loose* by Reeve Lindbergh (illustrated by Steven Kellogg); *Springtime* by Ann Schweninger; *Cats in the Sun* by Lesley Ann Ivory; and *The Sea Lion* by Ken Kesey (illustrated by Neil Waldman). Puffin Classics issues a line of traditional children's works in new editions. The house also produces Spanish-language books.

F. Warne & Company concentrates on reissues of works by such historic masters as Beatrix Potter and Cicely Mary Barker.

Viking Children's Books publishes a well-rounded list that includes picture books for the youngest readers as well as works aimed toward middle and older readership in fiction and nonfiction (some keyed to high-interest contemporary topics); the house also produces a respected reference line. Titles here are *Taking Flight: My Story* by Vicki Van Meter with Dan Gutman; *Two's Company* by Amanda Benjamin; *Dinosaurs: The Fastest, the Fiercest, the Most Amazing* by Elizabeth McLeod (illustrated by Gordon Sauvé); *The Encyclopedia of Native America* (edited by Trudy Griffin-Pierce); and *Undone! More Mad Endings* by Paul Jennings.

Query letters and SASEs should be directed to:

Jo Ann Daly, Editorial Director, Cobblehill Books

Rosanne Lauer, Executive Editor, Cobblehill Books

Virginia Buckley, Editorial Director, Lodestar Books

Phyllis Fogelman, Publisher, Dial Books for Young Readers

Cindy Kane, Executive Editor, Dial Books for Young Readers

Toby Sherry, Senior Editor, Dial Books for Young Readers

Tracy Tang, Publisher, Puffin Books

Regina Hayes, Publisher, Viking Children's Books

Deborah Brodie, Executive Editor, Viking Children's Books

PENTLAND PRESS, INC.

5124 Bur Oak Circle
Raleigh, NC 27612
919-782-0281
fax: 919-781-9042
800-948-2786

Pentland publishes general fiction and nonfiction, with a diverse catalog that accents such areas as history, military, mystery, religion, science fiction, short stories, Westerns, autobiography, memoirs, music, poetry, romance, self-help, philosophy, and psychology.

Pentland Press, formed in 1982 in Edinburgh, Scotland, as Pentland Press, Ltd., has subsequently established offices in Cambridge and Durham, England, in addition to its American offices (opened in 1993). Pentland is not known for grandiose advances; publishing contracts may involve cooperative investment or subsidization commitment from the author.

Samples from the Pentland list: *Inner Journeys to Sacred Places* by David Roomy; *Come Walk with Me* by Reverend Bob Allen; *The Weekend Golfer* by Bill Mace; *Understanding Liberalism: A History and Analysis of the Politics of the Last Half-Century* by Virgil Cowart; *Wheelchair Around the World* by Patrick Simpson; *The Doodledipper Works* (children's stories) by Stan Larke; *East of Tucson* (Western novel) by Walter Andrea; *Sweet'ning Relationships* (popular family psychology) by Thomas A. Gregg; *Maria* (historical women's fiction) by Margaret Haswell; *The Saga of Phil and the Red Piece of Meat* (narrative poetry) by David Lindamood.

Pentland Press is a member of COSMEP: The International Association of Independent Publishers, Publishers Association of the South, and Southeast Booksellers Association. Pentland's wholesale representation is through Baker and Taylor.

Query letters and SASEs should be directed to:

Ronda J. Swaney, Managing Editor

Arlene Calhoun, Editorial Director

THE PERMANENT PRESS/SECOND CHANCE PRESS

4170 Noyac Road
Sag Harbor, NY 11963
fax: 516-725-1101

Founded in 1978 by copublishers Judith and Martin Shepard, the Permanent Press produces expressive, vital, and exciting nongenre fiction. The sine qua non here for titles is that they be artfully written. The Permanent Press publishes twelve books a year in cloth editions only. Selected out-of-print books are released in reprint under the Second Chance Press imprint.

Judith and Martin Shepard have endeavored to bring out quality writing, primarily fiction, without regard to authors' reputations or track records. The publisher presents a handpicked list in which they firmly believe. Such dedication is not without payoff: Permanent Press titles generate considerable and favorable word of mouth among readers and booksellers, and reap the kinds of reviews that pique wide interest (particularly in the realm of subsidiary rights).

While publishing only twelve books a year, Permanent Press has, since 1986, gained 49 literary awards for its titles (including an American Book Award and a National Book Award finalist). The press has launched the careers of such novelists as Bill Albert, Larry Duberstein, David Galef, Andrew Klavan, Howard Owen, Sandra Scofield, and William Browning Spencer. Permanent has published a Nobel prize winner (Halldor Laxness) and a Nobel Prize Nominee (Berry Fleming). This is the house that gave a fresh start to Clifford Irving after his misadventures involving the Howard Hughes "autobiography," by publishing Irving's account of that episode (*The Hoax*).

To celebrate Permanent's twentieth year, the list presents twenty titles (eight more than they have ever done before) selected from the over 8,000 submissions received: 16 novels, 3 works of nonfiction, and a short-story collection.

Fiction on the Permanent Press list: *Marginalia* by Doran Larsen; *Natural Bridges* by Debbie Lynn McCampbell; *The Trap* by Rink van der Velde (originally published in The Netherlands in 1966); *Licking Our Wounds* by Elise D'Haene; *Geometry of Love* by Joan Fay Cuccio; *Up, Down, & Sideways* and *Life Between Wars* by Robert H. Patton; *The Deer Mouse* by Ken Grant; *As I Walked Out One Evening* by Donald Wetzel; *The Speed of Light* by Susan Pashman; *Change of Partners* by David Margolis; *Bending Time* by Stephen Minot (short stories); *Queen of the Silver Dollar* by Edward Hower; *Attic Light* by Carol Burnham; *Apology for Big Rod* by Charles Holdefer; *They Don't Play Stickball in Milwaukee* by Reed Farrel Coleman; *Going to Chicago* by Rob Levandoski.

Nonfiction titles: *So's Your Old Man: A Curmudgeon's Words to His Son* by Peter Cross; *Fishing in the Stars: The Education of Namory Keita* by Donald Lawder; *Home to India* by Jacqueline Singh (originally published in New Delhi by Penguin, India).

News from the sub-rights front: *Résumé with Monsters* (science fiction) by William Browning Spencer has garnered foreign rights in at least two countries—Germany and Italy. The film option for *An Occasional Hell* (mystery) by Randall Silvis became an official purchase when the cameras started to roll.

The house has also brought back all the original works (and some new ones) by Marco Vassi—works that gained Vassi a reputation as the best erotic writer of his generation. The Vassi Collection is a ten-volume offering of erotic fiction that has hitherto been long out of print and generally unavailable. Titles in the Vassi Collection: *The Stoned Apocalypse*; *Mind Blower*; *The Gentle Degenerate*; *The Saline Solution*; *Contours of Darkness*; *Tackling the Team*; *In Touch*; *The Devil's Sperm Is Cold*; *The Sensual Mirror*; *Slave Lover*. More from Vassi: *A Driving Passion*; *The Erotic Comedies*; *The Other Hand Clapping*.

Permanent Press handles its own distribution.

Query letters and SASEs should be directed to:

Judith Shepard, Editor and Copublisher

PERSEA BOOKS, INC.

171 Madison Avenue
New York, NY 10016
212-779-7668

Persea produces a discriminating list in trade and reference nonfiction, fiction and belles lettres, and poetry. Persea's categories include essays, memoirs, literary criticism, novels and stories, fine arts and art history, scholarly works, social sciences, and gender and cultural studies.

Persea Books (founded by Michael Braziller in 1975) is an independently owned press. The house's titles in the arts are brought out in handsomely designed and produced editions. Persea's contemporary literature has an international cast of eminent writers. Ontario Review Press is a Persea imprint that focuses on fiction and literary works.

Entrants from the Persea program: *Beyond Telling: Stories* by Jewel Mogan; *Paper Dance: 55 Latino Poets* (edited by Victor Hernández Cruz, Leroy V. Quintana, and Virgil Suarez); *Rhapsodies of a Repeat Offender: Poems* by Wayne Koestenbaum; *Show Me a Hero: Great Contemporary Stories About Sports* (edited by Jeanne Schinto); *The Heart Knows Something Different: Teenage Voices from the Foster Care System* by Youth Communication (edited by Al Desetta); *The Shovel and the Loom* (novel) by Carl Friedman (translated from the Dutch by Jeannette Ringold); *Things Shaped in Passing: More "Poets of Life" Writing from the AIDS Pandemic* (edited by Michael Klein and Richard McCann).

From Ontario Review Press: *Women, Animals, and Vegetables: Essays and Stories* by Maxine Kumin; and *Doris Lessing: Conversations* (edited by Earl G. Ingersoll).

Persea shares office space with and is distributed by George Braziller.

Query letters and SASEs should be sent to:

Karen Braziller, Editorial Director

PETERSON'S

P.O. Box 2123
202 Carnegie Center
Princeton, NJ 08543-2123
609-243-9111

Peterson's is a leading publisher of educational and career resource and reference materials. Peterson's runs the gamut in the arena of college admissions, standardized-test preparation, graduate and professional studies, educational administration, job hunting and career opportunities, executive education, educational travel and adventure, and continuing education.

Peterson's initially specialized in guides to colleges and graduate schools; currently the house offers a broad selection of specialty reference works (many updated annually) and publishes information in a wide arena.

Peterson's broader areas of interest currently include international work and study opportunities, as well as general resources for kids, teenagers, and families. Peterson's markets strongly to libraries and institutions, as well as to the corporate arena. Peterson's (founded in 1966) produces books, data services, and computer software (including CD-ROM).

From Peterson's: *Peterson's Guide to Distance Learning: The Complete Sourcebook on Accredited Educational Programs Delivered Electronically; Virtual College—a Quick Guide to How You Can Get the Degree You Want with Computer, TV, Video, Audio, and Other Distance Learning Tools* by Pam Dixon; *Writing a Winning College Application Essay* by Wilma Davidson and Susan McCloskey; *Financing Graduate School* by Patricia McWade; *50 Ways to Bring Out the Smarts in Your Kid: How to Provide Inspiration and Guidance That Enhances Children's Learning in Every Way* by Marge Kennedy; *The Working Parents Help Book* by Susan Crites Price and Tom Price; *Why Change Doesn't Work: Why Initiatives Go Wrong and How to Try Again, and Succeed* by Harvey Robbins, Ph.D. and Michael Finley; *Fat Free Meetings: How to Keep Them Fast, Focused, and Fun* by Burt Albert.

Peterson's/Pacesetter is an imprint that covers "thinking books for thinking business-people." On the Pacesetter roster: *Why Teams Don't Work: What Went Wrong and How to Make It Right* by Harvey Robbins and Michael Finley; *Getting It Done: The Transforming Power of Self-Discipline* by Andrew J. DuBrin, Ph.D.; *Small Business, Big Politics: What Entrepreneurs Need to Know to Use Their Growing Political Power* by Charles A. Riley II; *The IdeaFisher: How to Land That Big Idea and Other Secrets of Creativity in Business* by Marsh Fisher.

The Peterson's program highlights the bestselling *Guide to Four-Year Colleges* (updated annually; packaged with College Application Planner software). Also of note: *TOEFL Success* (Test of English as a Foreign Language); *MCAT Success* (Medical College Admission Test); *GRE Success* (Graduate Record Exam).

Peterson's handles its own distribution.

Query letters and SASEs should be directed to:

Carol Hupping, Executive Editor
Education, careers, family.

Ian Gallagher, Senior Editor, Test Preparation

Eileen Fiore, Executive Assistant, Research & Editorial Development
Interests consistent with house list.

PFEIFFER & COMPANY
(See listing with Jossey-Bass under Simon & Schuster)

PFEIFFER-HAMILTON PUBLISHERS

210 West Michigan Street
Duluth, MN 55802-1908
218-727-0500
fax: 218-727-0505
800-247-6789

Pfeiffer-Hamilton produces publications in self-awareness, motivation, and improvement; inspirational works; books on peace and healing; and select children's titles. Additional Pfeiffer-Hamilton focus is on gift books and books that celebrate the special beauty and unique lifestyle of the North Country.

This house offers books that awaken your senses, excite your imagination, make you laugh, make you cry, touch your heart, and give you hope; books that inspire creativity, critical thinking, inner change, and personal growth.

Pfeiffer-Hamilton Publishers (founded in 1985), along with its sibling company Whole Person Associates, develops a noteworthy lineup of stress-management and wellness training materials, including books, audiotapes, and videotapes. The house has achieved increasing market penetration. P-H's marketing strategy is to concentrate promotional efforts regionally prior to inaugurating national campaigns.

On the Pfeiffer-Hamilton list: *Not Now—I'm Having a No-Hair Day: Humor and Healing for People with Cancer* by Christine Clifford (illustrated by Jack Lindstrom); *Grandmothers' Alphabet* by Eve Shaw (illustrated by the author); *Sharing the Wonder of Birds with Kids* by Laura Erickson (illustrated by Kathryn MarsaLa); *Journey of the Heart: Spiritual Insights on the Road to a Transplant* by Beth Bartlett; *Kicking Your Holiday Stress Habits* by Donald A. Tubesing and Nancy Loving Tubesing; *Canoe Country Flora: Plants and Trees of the North Woods and Boundary Waters* by Mark Stensaas (illustrated by Jeff Sonstegard).

On the Whole Person Associates imprint are books targeted for educators, counselors, therapists, trainers, and group leaders. Also available keyed to these books are complete teaching instructions and supplemental materials along with extra resources for reference. Titles here: *Sleep Secrets for Shift Workers & People with Off-Beat Schedules* by David Morgan; *Don't Get Mad, Get Funny!: A Light-Hearted Approach to Stress Management* by Leigh Anne Jasheway (illustrated by Geoffrey M. Welles); *Working with Groups to Explore Food & Body Connections* by Sandy Stewart Christian; *Working with Groups to Overcome Panic, Anxiety, & Phobias: Structured Exercises in Healing* by Shirley Babior and Carol Goldman.

Whole Person Associates also offers a wide variety of relaxation and healing audiotapes as well as videotapes on achieving healthy lifestyles and managing job stress. On the video list: *Team Esteem Overview*; *Building Communication in the Workplace*; *Empowerment and Wellness in the Workplace*; *Developing a Specialized and Unique Team*; *Developing Mission and Purpose*; *Putting Team Esteem to Work*.

Pfeiffer-Hamilton Publishers oversees its own distribution.

Query letters and SASEs should be directed to:

Donald Tubesing, President

Carlene Sippola, Publisher

PINNACLE BOOKS

(See Kensington Publishing Corporation)

PLENUM PUBLISHING GROUP
DA CAPO PRESS
INSIGHT BOOKS
PLENUM PUBLISHING CORPORATION

233 Spring Street
New York, NY 10013-1578
212-620-8000
fax: 212-463-0742
http://www.plenum.com (World Wide Web)

Plenum Publishing comprises three primary lines under the auspices of a single publisher. The individual lists of Da Capo Press, Plenum Publishing Corporation, and Insight Books each stake claim to an identifiable primary domain. The press overall encompasses popular, scholarly, and academic works in the areas of art, music, and culture (Da Capo's emphasis); medicine, science, and technology (the Plenum arena); and public-interest issues, psychology, and self-awareness (under the Insight aegis).

Plenum Publishing Group handles its own distribution via a network of regional sales and distribution services.

DA CAPO PRESS

Da Capo emphasis is on classical music; jazz, blues, and popular music; dance; theater; film and television; photography; art and architecture; crafts and antiques; literature; African American studies; the American Civil War; history; true crime; science and technology; popular culture; and sports. Da Capo produces primarily reprints in trade paperback, with an occasional new title.

Da Capo nonfiction reprint editions are trade paper; the imprint specializes in making out-of-print and hard-to-find books available again. Many Da Capo books are first-hand accounts by artists, musicians, and historical figures and are often revised editions of classic writings in their fields. Though much of Da Capo's list has a learned slant, these works are by no means of strictly academic appeal; included among these are a deck of popular reference works in education, health, history, and literature.

Representative Da Capo titles: *The Gershwin Years: George and Ira* by Edward Jablonski and Lawrence D. Stewart; *Pennies from Heaven: The American Popular Music Business in the Twentieth Century* by Russell Sanjek and updated by David Sanjek; *Remembering Buddy: The Definitive Biography of Buddy Holly* by John Goldrosen and John Beecher; *The Theater Essays of Arthur Miller* (revised and expanded) (edited by Robert A. Martin and Steven R. Centola; foreword by Arthur

Miller); *The Story of My Life* by Clarence Darrow; *Stranger on the Earth: A Psychological Biography of Vincent van Gogh* by Dr. Albert J. Lubin; *The American Cinema: Directors and Directions, 1929–1968* by Andrew Sarris; *Dr. Seuss and Mr. Geisel: A Biography* by Judith and Neil Morgan; *The Bowie Companion* (edited by Elizabeth Thomson and David Gutman); *Up and Down with The Rolling Stones* by Tony Sanchez; *The Patton Papers, 1940–1945* by Martin Blumenson; *Faces in the Crowd: Musicians, Writers, Actors and Filmmakers* by Gary Giddins.

Query letters and SASEs should be directed to:

Yuval Taylor, Senior Editor, Da Capo Press
All Da Capo subject areas.

Michael Dorr, Editor, Da Capo Press
All Da Capo subject areas.

PLENUM PUBLISHING CORPORATION
PLENUM TRADE

Plenum trade-publishing scope includes popular biography, criminology, health, and popular renditions of vanguard scientific theory. Plenum remains a potent producer of journals in the fields of biosciences (including biology and medicine) and environmental sciences.

Plenum Publishing Corporation (trade motto: "the language of science") was originally established as a publisher of professional, scholarly, and academic works—including a noteworthy line of journals and monographs that provided western academia with a window into the former Soviet Union–dominated scientific and scholarly scene. The house currently has a broad base of interest that includes related commercial veins of its traditional subject areas,

From the Plenum Trade frontlist: *The Decline and Fall of the American Empire: Corruption, Decadence, and the American Dream* by Tony Bouza; *Asteroid: Earth Destroyer or New Frontier?* by Patricia Barnes-Svarney; *Millennium Rage: Survivalists, White Supremacists, and the Doomsday Prophecy* by Philip Lamy; *Mathematical Mysteries: The Beauty and Magic of Numbers* by Calvin C. Clawson; *A Sexual Odyssey: From Forbidden Fruit to Cybersex* by Kenneth Maxwell; *The Ulcer Story: The Authoritative Guide to Ulcers, Dyspepsia, and Heartburn* by W. Grant Thompson, M.D.

Query letters and SASEs should be directed to:

Mariclaire Cloutier, Editor, Plenum
Medicine.

Erika Goldman, Editor, Plenum Trade
General trade nonfiction; popular and social sciences; natural sciences and ecology; child care, medicine, public health; computers and society; practical psychology, criminology, and the law; business; travel; women's studies. Projects include issues-oriented, information-oriented works, as well as theoretical and reflective approaches.

Michael Kennelly, Editor, Plenum
Biology.

Amelia McNamara, Senior Editor, Plenum
Physical sciences.

Lucien S. Marchand, Senior Editor, Plenum
Engineering, mathematics, computer science.

Linda Greenspan Regan, Executive Editor, Plenum Trade
Nonfiction in popular science, social science, criminology, mathematics, anthropology.

Eliot Werner, Executive Editor, Plenum
Social sciences.

INSIGHT BOOKS

The publishing outlook of Insight Books (a trade imprint of Plenum Publishing Corporation) exemplifies a comprehensive popular- and professional-market approach to social and interpersonal psychology, self-improvement, current events, relationships, gender studies, and issues that reflect currents of thought in behavioral science. Insight publishes most titles solely in hardcover at a length of approximately 300 pages (about 90,000–100,000 words). No phone calls.

On the Insight list: *Hallowed Ground: Rediscovering Our Spiritual Roots* by Stephen Burgard; *The Rebellious Body: Reclaim Your Life from Environmental Illness or Chronic Fatigue Syndrome* by Janice Strubbe Wittenberg, R.N.; *AIDS and HIV-Related Diseases: An Educational Guide for Professionals and the Public* by John Powell; *The Tough-on-Crime Myth: Real Solutions to Cut Crime* by Peter T. Elikann; *Body and Soul: Sexuality on the Brink of Change* by Anne Stirling Hastings; *Can We Talk? The Power and Influence of Talk Shows* by Gini Graham Scott; *The Power Struggle: How It Enhances or Destroys Our Lives* by William T. Shannon.

Query letters and SASEs should be directed to:

Frank K. Darmstadt, Editor, Insight Books
Popular psychology, gay and lesbian concerns, ethics, religion, communications, lifestyle issues, contemporary sociology, marriage and family situations.

POCKET BOOKS
(See Simon & Schuster)

POMEGRANATE PUBLICATIONS
POMEGRANATE ARTBOOKS, INC.
Box 6099
Rohnert Park, CA 94927
707-586-5500
fax: 707-586-5518
800-227-1428

Pomegranate publishes an attractive array of graphically lavish books and specialty items geared to popular interests such as nature and the outdoors, travel, cuisine, lifestyle, culture and the arts, crafts, home and the family. Pomegranate is among the premier publishers of calendars of all types and stripes, posters and poster art, notecards, games and puzzles, specialty sets, and popular topical card decks.

Pomegranate is an independent house and operates its own distributional network, including foreign representation worldwide.

Query letters and SASEs should be directed to:

Thomas F. Burke, President and Publisher

CLARKSON POTTER
(See Crown Publishing Group under Random House)

PRAEGER PUBLISHERS
(See Greenwood Publishing Group)

PRENTICE HALL
(See Simon & Schuster)

PRESIDIO PRESS
505B San Marin Drive, Suite 300
Novato, CA 94945-1340
415-898-1081
fax: 415-898-0383

Presidio is known for works in such areas as general military history, American history, aviation, biography and memoirs, World Wars, Korean War, Vietnam, African-American studies, military theory, and professional studies. Presidio also issues a small number of superior fiction titles (often on the Lyford Books imprint) that favor a military-historical or action-adventure milieu.

Presidio Press (founded in 1974) is among America's foremost trade publishers of works in the military-services arena. The house emphasizes both popular and scholarly works, especially those with potential for backlist endurance. Presidio publishes in hardcover and quality paperback editions.

Nonfiction from Presidio: *Honor by Fire: Japanese Americans at War in Europe and the Pacific* by Lyn Crost; *Covert Warrior: Fighting the CIA's Secret War in Southeast*

Asia and China, 1965–1967 (Vietnam War memoir by Warner Smith); *Easy Target: The Long, Strange Trip of a Scout Pilot in Vietnam* (memoir by Tom Smith); *When the Odds Were Even: The Vosges Mountains Campaign, October 1944–January 1945* by Keith E. Bonn; *The Biographical Dictionary of World War II* by Mark M. Boatner III; *Platoon Leader* (memoir by James McDonough); *Destroyer Skipper: A Memoir of Command at Sea* by Don Sheppard; *Phantom over Vietnam: Fighter Pilot, USMC* (memoir by John Trotti); *Operation Dragoon: The Allied Invasion of the South of France* by William B. Breuer; *What They Didn't Teach You About the Civil War* by Mike Wright; *Spec Ops: Case Studies in Special Operations Warfare—Theory and Practice* by William H. McRaven; *Ten Corps in Korea, 1950* by Shelby L. Stanton; *They Had a Dream: The Story of African-American Astronauts* by J. Alfred Phelps; *Elvis in the Army: The King of Rock 'n' Roll As Seen by an Officer Who Served with Him* by William J. Taylor, Jr.

Presidio's Gulf War memoir, *She Went to War: The Rhonda Cornum Story* by flight surgeon Rhonda Cornum as told to Peter Copeland, garnered considerable subsidiary-rights interest—including a high-profile television-movie.

Fiction includes: *Blood Tells* by Ray Saunders; *A Once Perfect Place* (a Jake Eaton mystery) by Larry Maness; *Fenwick Travers and the Panama Canal: An Entertainment* by Raymond M. Saunders; *A Murder of Crows* by Steve Shepard; *1901* (a what-if alternative history novel) by Robert Conroy; *Cut-Out* (contemporary thriller) by Bob Mayer.

Presidio Press titles, as well as those of associated imprints (such as British military publisher Greenhill Books and books of the Lyford Press), are distributed to the book trade in the United States and Canada through National Book Network.

Query letters and SASEs should be directed to:

(Mr.) E. J. McCarthy, Executive Editor

PRICE STERN SLOAN

(See Putnam Berkley Publishing Group)

PRIMA PUBLISHING

3875 Atherton Road, Suite 98
Rocklin, CA 95765
916-632-4400
fax: 916-632-4405
http://www.primapublishing.com (World Wide Web)

Prima Publishing (founded in 1984) is an independent trade publisher with three divisions—Entertainment, Computer Products Division (CPD), and Lifestyles. Prima is among the fastest growing independent publishers in North America, with a fluid and innovative list.

Prima Publishing: Books for the way we live, work, and play. The Prima editorial operation embraces popular culture, current affairs and international events, parenting and education, business and entrepreneurship, careers, legal topics, biography, computer books (business and professional as well as games and edutainment), fiction, inspiration, natural history, psychology and self-help, sports, travel, environmental issues, and writing and reference.

The world's leader in electronic entertainment publishing, Prima's Entertainment Division focuses on computer and game strategy guides. Select titles include: *Myst, Star Wars: Shadows of the Empire, Doom 64, Tomb Raider, Diablo,* and *Warcraft 2: The Dark Saga.*

The Computer Products Division publishes basic tutorials for the layperson on popular software applications. Prima's bestselling *Fast & Easy* series consists of easy-to-follow visual learning guides with titles such as *Word 97, Office 97,* and *Windows 95.* Other titles include: *Windows NT Server 4: Administrator's Guide* and *Internet Information Server 3: Administrator's Guide.*

The company's Lifestyles Division specializes in general trade books. Representative titles include: the bestselling *Wave 3* and *Wave 3 Way* books by Richard Poe; *The Wealthy Barber* by David Chilton; the *Lean and Luscious* series of cookbooks by Bobbie Hinman and Millie Snyder; *Fat Free* and *Fat Free 2* by Doris Cross; *Family* by Samantha Glen and Mary Pesaresi; *Corporate Espionage* by Ira Winkler; *The Compassion of Animals* by Kristin von Kreisler; *Beat Depression with St. John's Wort* by Steven Bratman, M.D.; *Scully X-Posed* and *Xena X-Posed* by Nadine Crenshaw; *The Arthritis Solution* by Joseph Kandel, M.D., and David B. Sudderth, M.D.; *Cubicle Warfare* by Blaine Pardoe; *Safer Than Phen-Fen!* by Michael Anchors, M.D., Ph.D.; *If You're Writing, Let's Talk* by Joel Saltzman; *Regional Foods of Northern Italy* by Marlena de Blasi; *Journey from Anxiety to Freedom* by Mani Feniger; *writers.net* by Gary Gach; *The Homeschooling Handbook* by Mary Griffith; *Astrological Secrets for the New Millennium* by Laurie Baum; *Mother's Who Drive Their Daughters Crazy* by Susan and Ed Cohen; *Sales for the Self-Employed* and *Marketing for the Self-Employed* by Martin Edic; *From Book Idea to Bestseller* by Michael Snell, Kim Baker, and Sunny Baker; *Homeopathic Self-Care* by Robert Ullman, N.D., and Judyth Reichenberg-Ullman, N.D.; *Herbal Remedies for Women* by Amanda McQuade Crawford; *The Stay-at-Home Mom's Guide to Making Money* by Liz Folger. Prima is also the publisher of the book you are now reading, *Writer's Guide to Book Editors, Publishers, and Literary Agents* by Jeff Herman.

Forum, Prima's serious nonfiction imprint, covers topics such as current affairs, public policy, libertarian/conservative thought, high-level management, individual empowerment, and historical biography. Recent titles include: *Churchill on Leadership* by Steven F. Hayward; *Character Is Destiny* by Russell W. Gough; *God: The Evidence* by Patrick Glynn; *PBS: Behind the Screen* by Laurence Jarvik; *Break These Chains* by Daniel McGroarty; and *The Race Card* edited by Peter Collier and David Horowitz.

Prima has its own national sales force and is distributed to the trade by Random House Distribution Center.

Query letters and SASEs should be directed to:

Deborah F. Abshier, Acquisitions Editor, Computer Products Division

Matthew H. Carleson, Publisher, Computer Products Division

Debra Kempker, Publisher, Entertainment Division

Paula Munier Lee, Associate Publisher, Lifestyles Division
Steven K. Martin, Forum, Managing Editor, Lifestyles Division
Jamie Miller, Associate Acquisitions Editor, Lifestyles Division
Stacy Mollsen, Acquisitions Editor, Entertainment Division
Amy Raynor, Acquisitions Editor, Entertainment Division
Susan Silva, Acquisitions Editor, Lifestyles Division
Jenny Watson, Acquisitions Editor, Computer Products Division

PRINCETON UNIVERSITY PRESS

(See Directory of University Presses)

PROBUS PUBLISHING COMPANY

(See Irwin Professional Publishing)

PROFESSIONAL PUBLICATIONS, INC.

1250 Fifth Avenue
Belmont, CA 94002
415-593-9119
http://www.ppi2pass.com (World Wide Web)

Professional Publications accents titles in engineering, accounting, and architecture, as well as works aimed toward the broader business and professional trade arena. The house produces books and educational aids (such as flashcards, audiocassettes, videos, software, and study guides) for the professional market.

Professional Publications (established in 1981) earned initial success with examination-preparation packages (reference manual, ancillary workbooks, flashcards, sample questions) for the professional engineering license examination given to applicants in the major engineering disciplines. Once this niche market was secured, the house branched into wider publishing territory.

On the Professional Publications list: *Engineering Your Writing Success: How Engineers Can Master Effective On-the-Job Communication Skills* by James E. Vincler and Nancy Horlick Vincler; *Standard Handbook for Civil Engineers* (edited by Frederick S. Merritt); *High-Technology Degree Alternatives: Earning a High-Tech Degree While Working Full Time* by Joel Butler; *345 Solved Seismic Design Problems* by Majid Baradar; *Intellectual Property Protection: A Guide for Engineers* by Virginia Shaw Medlen; *The Expert Witness Handbook: A Guide for Engineers* by D. G. Sunar.

Professional Publications oversees its own distribution; selected titles are offered to the trade through Harcourt Brace.

Query letters and SASEs should be directed to:

Gerry Galbo, Acquisitions Editor

PROMETHEUS BOOKS

59 John Glenn Drive
Amherst, NY 14228-2197
716-691-0133
fax: 716-564-2711
800-421-0351 (orders)
Pbooks6205@aol.com (e-mail)

Prometheus catalogs works with challenging stances on contemporary issues. The house is particularly strong in popular science, science and the paranormal, biblical criticism, religion and politics, politics and current events, consumer health and fitness, philosophy, humanism, free thought, sports, human sexuality and sexual autobiography, literature and literary history, popular culture, creation vs. evolution, religion, and education, as well as reference works in allied fields, and occasional works of fiction. Prometheus also publishes books for young readers, a line of titles on human aging, and serves the educational market with several series of modestly priced classics in reprint (including Great Books in Philosophy, Literary Classics, and Great Minds). The house offers select works in electronic format.

Prometheus Books (established in 1969) produces an ambitious frontlist that embraces a wide range of perennially popular nonfiction topics; more enduring titles are backlisted indefinitely.

Prometheus also publishes the following periodicals: *Nutrition Forum* (bimonthly newsletter on the frontline of the anti–health-fraud movement); *Journal for Higher Education Management* (journal of the American Association of University Administrators; deals with issues in education for colleges and universities); *The Journal for the Critical Study of Religion, Ethics, and Society* (articles in the area of religious studies and scholarly assessments of society, ethics, and culture that have a bearing on the understanding of religion; seeks to promote a broadly humanistic understanding of culture).

On the Prometheus list: *All-American Monster: The Unauthorized Biography of Timothy McVeigh* by Brandon M. Stickney; *Gilda's Disease: Sharing Personal Experiences and a Medical Perspective on Ovarian Cancer* by M. Steven Piver, M.D. with Gene Wilder; *But Seriously . . . Steve Allen Speaks His Mind* by Steve Allen; *The Case Against School Vouchers* by Edd Doerr, Albert J. Menendez, and John M. Swomley; *Evangelicals at the Ballot Box* by Albert J. Menendez; *Add a Dash of Pity and Other*

Short Stories by Peter Ustinov; *Weird Water and Fuzzy Logic: More Notes of a Fringe Watcher* by Martin Gardner; *Without a Prayer: Religious Expression in Public Schools* by Robert S. Alley; *The X-Rated Videotape Guide VI* by Patrick Riley; *The Gay Agenda: Talking Back to the Fundamentalists* by Jack Nichols; *What's Wrong with Grandma?: A Family's Experience with Alzheimer's* by Margaret Shawver (illustrated by Jeffrey K. Bagby); *Doomsday Asteroid: Can We Survive?* by Donald W. Cox, Ed.D. and James H. Chestek; *The Truth About Everything: An Irreverent History of Philosophy, with Illustrations* by Matthew Stewart, D.Phil.; *The Big Domino in the Sky and Other Atheistic Tales* by Michael Martin; *Deception and Self-Deception: Investigating Psychics* by Richard Wiseman, Ph.D.

Prometheus Books introduces the Literary Classics line. This series of attractive, moderately priced paperback editions of classic authors (in both poetry and prose) whose works embody free inquiry and free thought. Titles here: *The Turn of the Screw: The Lesson of the Master* by Henry James; *The Awakening* by Kate Chopin; *Main Street* by Sinclair Lewis; *The Confidence Man* by Herman Melville.

Please note: Though known primarily as a house that operates on an advance/royalty arrangement, Prometheus has on occasion offered agreements to authors through which the author invests cooperatively in the costs and thus subsidizes publication.

Prometheus distributes its own list.

Query letters and SASEs should be directed to:

Steven L. Mitchell, Editorial Director

Mark Hall, Ph.D., Managing Editor

PUSHCART PRESS

Box 380
Wainscott, NY 11975
516-324-9300

Pushcart Press (established in 1973) is a small, personalized house that is emblematic of the mission to provide useful as well as entertaining trade books and reference volumes directed primarily toward writers, editors, small publishers, and literary aficionados; Pushcart Press is also a dedicated forum for fiction and nonfiction works of literary merit, and the house list includes many award-winning volumes.

Pushcart is known as the house that issues the established annual literary anthology *The Pushcart Prize: Best of the Small Presses*, in addition to the classic *The Publish-It-Yourself Handbook: Literary Tradition and How-To Without Commercial or Vanity Publishers* (both works edited by Pushcart publisher Bill Henderson). *The Pushcart Book of Essays* (edited by Anthony Brandt) expands the house's line of exemplary writing collections.

Ongoing Pushcart Press publishing projects include the Literary Companion series, the Editors' Book Award series, and Pushcart Rediscovery.

Titles from Pushcart: *To a Violent Grave: An Oral Biography of Jackson Pollock* by Jeffrey Potter; *Put That Quill Back in the Goose!* (edited by James Charlton); *Yeshua:*

The Gospel of St. Thomas by Alan Decker McNary; *Garden State: A Novel* by Rick Moody; *Imagine a Great White Light* by Sheila Schwartz; *Writing for Your Life* by Sybil Steinberg; the anonymous *Autobiography of an Elderly Woman* (with an afterword by Doris Grumbach); and *The Tale of the Ring: A Kaddish* by Frank Stiffel.

Pushcart Press is distributed by W. W. Norton.

Query letters and SASEs should be directed to:

Bill Henderson, President

THE PUTNAM BERKLEY GROUP
PUTNAM
BERKLEY
BOULEVARD
PERIGEE BOOKS
RIVERHEAD BOOKS
PRICE STERN SLOAN
TARCHER
PUTNAM & GROSSET
HP BOOKS

200 Madison Avenue
New York, NY 10016
212-951-8400

The Putnam Berkley Group is part of Penguin Putnam, Inc. Founded in 1838 and subsequently known as G. P. Putnam's Sons, this house achieved renown as one of America's principal publishers. Over the past several decades the company has expanded dramatically. In 1965 Putnam acquired Berkley Books, and in 1975 the augmented enterprise was acquired by the communications conglomerate MCA, itself now part of the Seagram's Corporation wing that also incorporates Universal Studios.

The group's primary trade paper imprint, Perigee Books, was established in 1979, and since then additional divisions have been instituted, including the children's houses Philomel Books and Grosset & Dunlap (see under Putnam & Grosset subentry below). During the early 1990s, two formerly independent entities, Jeremy P. Tarcher and Price Stern Sloan (please see subentries), have been brought under the corporate shield. Riverhead Books, created in the mid-1990s, features fiction and nonfiction with a contemporary cultural slant.

In early 1997 Seagram's/MCA divested itself of the entire Putnam Berkley Group. Putnam Berkley merged with Penguin USA (home of the Viking, Penguin, and Dutton programs) to form Penguin Putnam, Inc. This mammoth book-publishing eminence combines what had been two of North America's grandest trade-publishing establishments into a single powerful marketing force.

The Putnam Publishing Group assumes a profile at once streamlined and eclectic—this division's mission is to launch top-of-the-charts titles across the board. Thus the relentlessly commercial Putnam frontlist, during a given season, can accent any and all popular fiction and nonfiction areas.

The Berkley Publishing Group—which comprises such lines as Berkley, Jove, Ace, and Boulevard—publishes trade and mass-market paperback reprints and originals in nonfiction and fiction, as well as selected hardcover originals.

The nomenclature and categorization of Putnam Berkley lists is flexible; designated projects can assume many different formats and experimental imprints—as in, for instance, hardcover genre-fiction releases bearing the Ace/Putnam stamp, Riverhead titles catalogued under both Putnam (for hardcovers) and Berkley (trade paper originals and reprints), and trade titles in business, finance, and topical spirituality interest released as Tarcher/Putnam books.

Putnam New Media was initiated to ride the multimedia tide; for a rash of corporate reasons, during 1995, this division's assets were shifted under the umbrella of another of MCA's media enterprises.

Penguin Putnam distributes its own list as well as providing services for a number of other houses including Farrar Straus & Giroux.

THE PUTNAM PUBLISHING GROUP

200 Madison Avenue
New York, NY 10016
212-951-8400

The Putnam Publishing Group produces fiction and nonfiction hardcover trade books. Putnam fiction highlights commercially bankable novels, popular literary fare, and top-of-the-list entrants in category fiction including mystery, science fiction, suspense, and historical novels. Putnam nonfiction covers the range of topical, popular, and commercial interest.

Putnam trade books are published primarily under the G. P. Putnam's Sons imprint. Putnam from time to time combines with other Putnam Berkley imprints for special projects issued under such banners as Ace/Putnam (frontlist category novels), and Tarcher/Putnam (business and professional; awareness; current issues and trends).

Putnam fiction offers a star-studded lineup of authors, including such works as *That Camden Summer* by LaVyrle Spencer; *McNally's Puzzle* by Lawrence Sanders; *The Dark Room* by Minette Walters; *Man O' War* by William Shatner; *Seduced: The Life and Times of a One-Hit Wonder* by Nelson George; *Honky Tonk Kat* by Karen Kijewski; *Killing Critics* by Carol O'Connell; *Firestorm* by Nevada Barr; *Sudden Prey* by John Sandford; *Cold Fall* by John Gardner; *Drink with the Devil* by Jack Higgins; *Cause of Death* by Patricia Cornwell; and *Rosehaven* by Catherine Coulter.

Putnam produces spectacular omnibus fiction anthologies featuring such power-house authors as Tom Clancy, W. E. B. Griffin, Lilian Jackson Braun, Dean Koontz, and LaVyrle Spencer.

The Putnam nonfiction list includes *The Achievement Zone: 8 Skills for Winning All the Time from the Playing Field to the Boardroom* by Shane Murphy; *The Way of the Explorer: An Apollo Astronaut's Journey Through the Material and Mystical Worlds* by

Edgar Mitchell with Dwight Williams; *Extraordinary Golf: The Art of the Possible* by Fred Shoemaker with Pete Shoemaker; *The Maria Paradox: How Latinas Can Merge Old World Traditions with New World Self-Esteem* by Rosa Maria Gil and Carmen Inoa Vazquez; *The Alchemy of Love and Lust: Discovering Our Sex Hormones and How They Determine Who We Love, When We Love, and How Often We Love* by Theresa L. Crenshaw; and *Smart Money Moves for African Americans* by Kelvin Boston.

Putnam distributes its own list to the trade.

Query letters and SASEs should be directed to:

Stacy Creamer, Vice President and Senior Editor
Fiction: thrillers, crime and detective novels, horror, medical themes. Nonfiction: true crime.

Liza Dawson, Executive Editor
Commercial fiction and nonfiction. Fiction: mysteries, women-oriented. Nonfiction: wide interests, especially parenting and psychology.

John Duff, Vice President and Senior Editor
Nonfiction, self-help, popular reference. (See also listing for John Duff under Perigee Books.)

David Highfill, Senior Editor
Fiction: mysteries and mainstream novels, commercial nonfiction.

Neil Nyren, Publisher, G. P. Putnam's Sons
Serious and commercial fiction and nonfiction.

Christine Pepe, Senior Editor
Fiction: mysteries, thrillers, horror. Nonfiction: business, health, celebrity stories.

Faith Sale, Executive Editor
Serious fiction and nonfiction.

The Berkley Publishing Group
Boulevard
Jove
Ace
Prime Crime

200 Madison Avenue
New York, NY 10016
212-951-8800

The Berkley Publishing Group produces a solid commercial list of fiction and nonfiction, including frontlist titles in trade paper and hardcover editions; the house also accents a mass-market paperback list. Berkley fiction encompasses such categories as romance and women's fiction, action adventure, Westerns, mysteries, science fiction, and fantasy. Nonfiction interests run the gamut of commercial categories. Berkley publishes reprints (many of them originally on the Putnam list) as well as original fiction and nonfiction under the Berkley, Jove, and Ace imprints.

Berkley's nonfiction range includes self-help and awareness, business, true crime, popular culture, and parenting. **Boulevard** is a media-oriented imprint with an accent on popular culture. **Perigee Books** concentrates on commercial nonfiction in trade paperback.

Nonfiction titles from Berkley include *Dare to Win* by Jack Canfield and Mark Victor Hansen; *Mo' Yo' Mama* by Snap C. Pop and Kid Rank; *Do-It-Yourself . . . or Not?* by Katie and Gene Hamilton; *The Practically Meatless Gourmet* by Cornelia Carlson; *Generals in Muddy Boots: A Concise Encyclopedia of Combat Commanders* by Dan Cragg (edited by Walter J. Boyne); *Eyes of the Sphinx: The Newest Evidence of Alien Contact in Ancient Cultures* by Erich von Daniken; *The Dull Knives of Pine Ridge: A Lakota Odyssey* by Joe Starita; *The Good Nanny Book: How to Find, Hire, and Keep the Perfect Nanny for Your Child* by P. Michelle Riffin; *Diamond in the Rough: The Secret to Finding Your Own Value and Making Your Own Success* by Barry J. Farber; and *A Different Angle: Fly Fishing Stories by Women*, edited by Holly Morris.

Berkley Group fiction authors include Tom Clancy, John Sandford, and LaVyrle Spencer; a significant portion of the list crosses over from Putnam hardcover originals into Berkley paperback reprint editions. Prime Crime is an imprint that emphasizes original frontlist mysteries and suspense fiction. The Berkley romance line includes such bestselling writers as Nora Roberts, Kathleen Sutcliff, Laura Kinsale, and Mary Balogh.

Features from **Berkley Prime Crime** include *The Death of a Dancing Fool* by Carole Berry; *Murder Among the Angels* by Stefanie Matteson; *She Came by the Book* by Mary Wings; and *Most Likely to Die* by Jacqueline Girdner.

The **Ace Books** list denotes the forefront of science fiction and fantasy, including original titles as well as reprints. On the Ace list: *The Dragon and the Djinn* by Gordon R. Dickson; *Looking for the Mahdi* by N. Lee Wood; *The Tranquillity Alternative* by Allen Steele; and *Cradle of Splendor* by Patricia Anthony.

Jove produces a primarily mass-market fiction list, including originals and reprints in romance, historical romance, suspense, action adventure, mysteries, and Westerns.

Query letters and SASEs should be directed to:

Susan Allison, Vice President, Editor in Chief, Ace Books
Science fiction, fantasy, horror.

Ginjer Buchanan, Executive Editor, Ace Books
Horror, science fiction, fantasy, mysteries, psychological suspense.

Louise Burke, Executive Director, Trade Paperbacks, Senior Vice President, and Deputy Publisher
Responsible for all trade paperbacks, including Riverhead.

(Ms.) Hillary Cige, Senior Editor
Commercial nonfiction; business subjects.

Tom Colgan, Senior Editor
Wide range of commercial nonfiction and fiction. Nonfiction: history, business, inspiration, biography. Fiction: suspense, mysteries, thrillers; adventure, police, espionage.

Jessica Faust, Assistant Editor

Gail Fortune, Editor
Women's fiction, romance, mystery.

Leslie Gelbman, Publisher, Senior Vice President, and Editor in Chief for Berkley; Executive Editor, Putnam
Wide range of projects in commercial fiction and nonfiction. Works with such authors as Nora Roberts, Laura Kinsale, Erich Segal.

Natalie Rosenstein, Vice President, Senior Executive Editor
General fiction, mystery.

Denise Silvestro, Editor
Women's fiction and nonfiction, health, self-help, pop culture, inspirational and New Age books.

Judith Palais, Senior Editor
Women's fiction, general fiction, commercial/literary works, romance.

Elizabeth Beier, Senior Editor, Director of Boulevard Books
Movie tie-in books, general nonfiction.

PERIGEE BOOKS

Perigee Books is Penguin Putnam Inc.'s mainline Berkley trade paperback imprint. Perigee acquires originals and reprints in all of the principal Putnam nonfiction categories.

Query letters and SASEs should be directed to:

John Duff, Publisher, Perigee Books
Wide range of commercial nonfiction, cookbooks, popular reference, self-help/how-to, family and parenting issues.

Sheila Curry, Senior Editor, Perigee Books
Spirituality, general nonfiction.

Suzanne Bober, Editor, Perigee Books
Nonfiction, self-help, relationships.

RIVERHEAD BOOKS

Riverhead publishes fiction and nonfiction hardcover and trade paperback originals and reprints. Riverhead fiction and literary works cover an array of serious, lively, and imaginative arenas; explore the frontiers of expression; and resound with the variety and depth of cultural experience. Nonfiction at Riverhead embraces psychology, history, popular culture, and sports; the house is also on the lookout for strong, creative works in religious and spiritual thought.

The Riverhead name was chosen because of its variety of metaphorical themes. *River* expresses the power of moving water to nurture, terrorize, creep, or inundate; *head* resounds with images of authority and unity.

On Riverhead's nonfiction list: *The Color of Water: A Black Man's Tribute to His White Mother* by James McBride; *Brutal Bosses and Their Prey* by Harvey A. Hornstein; *Sex Death Enlightenment: A True Story* by Mark Matousek; *The Cloister Walk* by Kathleen Norris; *Journey into Motherhood: Writing Your Way to Self-Discovery* by Leslie Kirk Campbell; and *Ethics for the Next Millennium* by His Holiness the Dalai Lama and Alexander Norman.

Fiction and literary works from Riverhead: *Going Down* by Jennifer Belle; *The Woman Who Walked on Water* by Lily Tuck; *Depth Takes a Holiday: Essays from Lesser Los Angeles* by Sandra Tsing Loh; *Violette's Embrace* by Michelle Zackheim; *The Romance Reader* (novel) by Pearl Abraham; *High Fidelity* by Nick Hornsby; and *Loving Edith* by Mary Tannen.

Query letters and SASEs should be directed to:

Susan J. Petersen, Publisher

Julie Grau, Senior Editor

Amy Hertz, Senior Editor

Mary South, Senior Hardcover Editor; Editor in Chief for Trade Paperbacks

Celina (Cindy) Spiegel, Senior Editor

Wendy Carlton, Associate Editor

PRICE STERN SLOAN

200 Madison Avenue
New York, NY 10016
212-951-8800

Price Stern Sloan produces nonfiction titles in crafts, cookery, business, popular psychology, health, gardening, photography, sports, and humor. The house is known for a particularly strong selection of calendars. Price Stern Sloan also produces titles for children and young adults, featuring activity books, craft kits, pop-ups, audiocassettes, and other specialty publications. (See description of overall Putnam children's program below under the Putnam & Grosset Book Group subentry.)

Price Stern Sloan was founded as an independent in 1964; since 1993 PSS has been a part of the Putnam Publishing Group. As PSS assumes its role within the Putnam operation, its publishing categories and focus continues to evolve. The house was moved from its previous Los Angeles offices to New York in mid-1997.

Query letters and SASEs should be directed to:

Lara Bergen, Editorial Director, Price Stern Sloan

TARCHER

200 Madison Avenue
New York, NY 10016
212-951-8800

Tarcher's emphasis is on high-profile commercial titles in popular psychology, healing, self-help/awareness, sexuality, unconventional business books, new directions in scientific thought, and current social issues in such topical areas as gender and health care. The Tarcher imprint is the corporate banner of the formerly independent Jeremy P. Tarcher, Inc. (founded in 1964), which grew from a small West Coast house to a midsize publisher of hardcover and trade paperback titles in adult trade nonfiction, along with a line of innovative philosophical science fiction. Subsequent to Tarcher's acquisition by the Putnam Publishing Group (in 1994), the operation was relocated from its Los Angeles base to Putnam Berkley's New York offices.

On the Tarcher list: *Poetic Medicines* by John Fox; the Working from Home series by Paul and Sarah Edwards; *Son of Man* by Andrew Harvey; *Sweat Your Prayers* by Gabrielle Roth; *Seven Years in Tibet* by Heinrich Harrer; *Tarot Handbook* by Angeles Arrien; *Working Out/Working Within* by Jerry Lynch and Chunliang Al Huang; *Your Life As Story: Writing the New Autobiography* by Tristine Rainer; *Rumi: In the Arms of the Beloved* by Jonathan Star.

Tarcher publishes works of Julia Cameron, including: *The Artist's Way: A Spiritual Path to Higher Creativity*, *Vein of Gold: A Journey to Your Creative Heart*, and *Heart Steps*.

Query letters and SASEs should be directed to:

Irene Prokop, Editor in Chief

THE PUTNAM & GROSSET BOOK GROUP

200 Madison Avenue
New York, NY 10016
212-951-8800

The Putnam & Grosset Book Group produces children's books under such imprints as G. P. Putnam's Sons, Philomel Books, Sandcastle Books, Grosset & Dunlap, and Platt & Munk. Children's books from the Price Stern Sloan division are coordinated with the Putnam & Grosset program. The list ranges from picture books for toddlers to novels for young adults, ranging over the full spectrum of nonfiction and fiction areas, board books, first reading books, novelty books, miniature editions, foreign-language books, and holiday books.

Titles include *Goodnight, Gorilla* by Peggy Rathmann; *The Ghost of Elvis and Other Celebrity Spirits* by Daniel Cohen; *Mountain Valor* by Gloria Houston (illustrated by Thomas B. Allen); *Nora's Surprise* by Satomi Ichikawa; *The Very Hungry Caterpillar Board Book* by Eric Carle; and *Spot's Big Book of Colors, Shapes, and Numbers* by Eric Hill.

Query letters and SASEs should be directed to:

Lara Bergen, Editorial Director, Price Stern Sloan

Jane O'Connor, President, Grosset & Dunlap

Patricia Lee Gauch, Publisher, Philomel Books

Nancy Paulsen, Publisher, G. P. Putnam's Sons

QUE CORPORATION

(See Macmillan Computer Publishing under Simon & Schuster listing)

RANDOM HOUSE
RANDOM HOUSE REFERENCE AND INFORMATION PUBLISHING
RANDOM HOUSE BOOKS FOR YOUNG READERS
RANDOM HOUSE VALUE PUBLISHING
BALLANTINE PUBLISHING GROUP
CROWN PUBLISHING GROUP
KNOPF PUBLISHING GROUP
ALFRED A. KNOPF BOOKS FOR YOUNG READERS
CROWN BOOKS FOR YOUNG READERS
CLARKSON POTTER JUVENILE BOOKS
PANTHEON BOOKS
SCHOCKEN BOOKS
TIMES BOOKS
VILLARD BOOKS
VINTAGE BOOKS

201 East 50th Street
New York, NY 10022
212-751-2600
http://www.randomhouse.com (World Wide Web)

Random House (founded in 1925) is among the celebrated names of the American book trade. As a major domain of the Newhouse publishing empire, Random House has evolved into an intricate commonwealth of publishing groups, divisions, and imprints with a far-flung web of interests and diverse specialties in virtually all categories of commercial fiction and nonfiction. Random House publishes books in hardcover, trade paperback, and mass-market rack editions.

The house's breadth is indicated by the central trade group that encompasses the mainstream sweep of Random House adult trade books; the resolute commercial orientation of the Villard hardcover imprint; the discriminating trade-paper scheme of Vintage Books; and the Modern Library Classics series. Random House publishing entities include Ballantine Publishing Group, Crown Publishing Group, Knopf Publishing Group/Alfred A. Knopf, Pantheon, Schocken, and Times Books. Random House publishing groups also produce an equally fine medley of lines for young readers. (Please see separate subentries below.)

Random House distributes for itself and its subsidiaries, as well as for a raft of other publishers, including National Geographic Books, Prima Publishing, Shambhala Publications, and Sierra Club Books.

RANDOM HOUSE TRADE DIVISION

Assuming a mainstream commercial profile, Random House presents a preferred list of trade fiction and nonfiction titles within its wide-ranging adult trade hardcover lineup.

Random House nonfiction presents topics of popular interest in current events; history, biography, and memoirs; investigative stories and narrative nonfiction; lifestyle and the arts; and popular science. Fiction accents frontlist novels; outstanding mysteries, suspense tales, and thrillers; and commercial literary works.

Random House also publishes large-print editions, audiobooks, electronic/computer-related works, offers a home-video catalog, and produces a series of reference books covering business, law, and literary areas. The evocative Random House logo of a rambling home is a recognized symbol of unstinting standards in bookmaking.

Random House nonfiction encompasses *Guilty* by Harold Rothwax; *The Best 499 Public Golf Courses in the United States, Canada, Mexico and the Caribbean* by Robert McCord; *The Private Life of Chairman Mao* by Li Zhisui with Anne F. Thurston; *Ross Perot and Third-Party Politics* by Gerald Posner; *Ghost of a Chance* by Peter Duchin; *The Rogers and Gray Italian Country Cookbook* by Ruth Rogers and Rose Gray; *Massage for Pain Relief* by Peijian Shen; *Man-to-Man* by Michael Korda; *Mr. Truman's War* by J. Robert Moskin; and *Civil War Battlefields and Landmarks* (edited by Frank E. Vandriver).

The Princeton Review line of college directories, academic how-to, and test-preparation guides are popular and valuable items among university students and college-bound readers. Random House hosts the Paris Review belles-lettres product line.

The Random House list in fiction and letters includes *Neanderthal* by John Darnton; *Primary Colors* (satirical political thriller) by Anonymous; *Murder at the National Gallery* by Margaret Truman; *Women Writers at Work* (edited by George Plimpton); *The Shadow Man* by Mary Gordon; *Rose* by Martin Cruz Smith; *The Falconer* by Elaine Clark McCarthy; *Babel Tower* by A. S. Byatt; *Ants on the Melon* by Virginia Adair; *Dance for the Dead* by Thomas Perry; *And Still I Rise* by Maya Angelou; *The Devil Soldier* by Caleb Carr; *Oswald's Tale* by Norman Mailer; and *The City and the Pillar and Seven Early Stories* by Gore Vidal.

Query letters and SASEs should be directed to:

Deb Futter, Vice President and Executive Editor
Wide range of interests consistent with the house list.

Ann Godoff, Executive Editor
Nonfiction: contemporary issues. Commercial and literary fiction.

Ian Jackman, Managing Director, Modern Library
Classics and reprints in paperback; some originals.

Jonathan Karp, Editor
Current events, politics, popular culture, fiction.

Robert D. Loomis, Executive Editor
Military and U.S. history, current events, politics, biography. Commercial and literary fiction.

Kate Medina, Executive Editor
Commercial fiction, women's fiction.

David Rosenthal, Executive Editor
Literary and commercial fiction. Nonfiction: current events, politics, contemporary biographies.

RANDOM HOUSE REFERENCE AND INFORMATION PUBLISHING

Random House Reference and Information Publishing offers a tight, well-developed list that accents traditional works alongside new high-profile books.

Random House reference titles include: *The Order of Things* by Barbara Ann Kipfer; *Random House Book of Jokes and Anecdotes* by Joe Claro; *Spy Book* by Norman Polmar and Thomas B. Allen; *The Most Challenging Quiz Book Ever* by Louis Phillips. In the perennially strong standard-reference arena, with a new twist or two, are *Random House Compact Unabridged Dictionary* (book and CD-ROM), and a revised version of the hardy desktop stand-by *Random House Webster's College Dictionary*.

Query letters and SASEs should be directed to:

Charles Levine, Publisher and Editorial Director
Reference titles.

RANDOM HOUSE BOOKS FOR YOUNG READERS

Random House Books for Young Readers publishes books for preschoolers through young adults, with a preponderance of its highly commercial list slated for the younger audience.

Established Random House lines include Babar the Elephant productions, Dr. Seuss titles, Boy Talk, the Betsy Books, and the Sesame Street series. The Pictureback Readers, which appear in English as well as in bilingual Spanish/English editions, are designed to exemplify the type of works that younger readers want to read on their own.

Other Random series include readers geared to specific reader levels and age ranges, as well as a reference line. The house engages in a variety of formats, including peek-a-board books, pop-up books, chunky-shaped books, cuddle-cloth books, scratch-'n'-sniff books, books with phosphorescent ink, mini-storybooks, kits, and book-and-cassette packages.

This division no longer accepts unsolicited manuscripts directly from authors; all projects go through agents. Query letters and SASEs should be directed to:

Kate Klimo, Publisher

RANDOM HOUSE VALUE PUBLISHING

Random House Value Publishing continues the tradition of quality category publishing. By publishing a wide variety of titles in many categories, Random House Value Publishing has the ability to offer a fantastic selection at incredible prices.

Wings Books is well known for its bestselling omnibus and cookbook programs, along with hardcover originals and reprints.

Gramercy Books focuses on literature and reference titles, while also offering beautiful original gift books.

By reaching out to publishers worldwide, **Crescent Books** produces lavishly illustrated volumes of art, travel, gardening, and the like—along with a variety of original titles.

Glorya Hale Books offers beautiful original gift titles.

Derrydale, **Children's Classics**, and **Jellybean Press**, all of them juvenile imprints, offer high-quality titles for children of all ages.

The **Gramercy Park** line features Anything Blank Books of all sizes and styles, plus specialty journals for juveniles and adults.

Query letters and SASEs should be directed to:

Susanne Jaffe, Vice President and Editor in Chief

Nancy Davis, Editor

Greg Suriano, Editor

Donna Lee Lurker, Editor

THE BALLANTINE PUBLISHING GROUP
BALLANTINE
DEL REY
FAWCETT
COLUMBINE
HOUSE OF COLLECTIBLES
ONE WORLD
IVY BOOKS

201 East 50th Street
New York, NY 10022
212-751-2600

The Ballantine Publishing Group is a Random House division that produces trade paperbacks and hardcovers, in addition to its traditionally commanding presence in mass-market paperbacks. The house is active in a full range of commercial fiction and nonfiction areas—originals as well as reprints. Hardcover originals bear the Ballantine or Fawcett logo; general trade paperbacks are likewise released under these two stamps. The other imprints in this division are typified by their respective specialist lines (see below). Ballantine is also home to a number of imprints geared to young-reader interest.

Ballantine and Fawcett fiction accents novels with a popular orientation, including mainstream, literary, and category works, with particular emphasis in mysteries, suspense, and thrillers. Representative titles: *The Kindness of Strangers* by Julie Smith, *The Lethal Partner* by Jake Page, *Imagine Love* by Katherine Stone, *A Shred of Evidence* by Jill McGown, *That Day the Rabbi Left Town* by Harry Kemelman, *Pentecost Alley* by Anne Perry, *My Lover Is a Woman: Contemporary Lesbian Love Poems* (edited by Lesléa Newman), and *Buck Naked* by Joyce Burditt.

Ballantine and Fawcett nonfiction plays to the high-interest commercial arena. Titles include *Creating from the Spirit: Living Each Day As a Creative Act* by Dan Wakefield, *Without Child: Challenging the Stigma of Childlessness* by Laurie Lisle, *The 5-Day Miracle Diet* by Adele Puhn, and *Sun Pin: The Art of Warfare* (translated, with an introduction and commentary by D. C. Lau and Roger T. Ames).

Del Rey publishes science fiction and fantasy titles (originals and reprints) in hardcover, trade paper, and mass-market paperback formats, including major series offerings. Titles here are *The Crystal Singer Trilogy* by Anne McCaffrey; *The Ringworld Throne* by Larry Niven; *First King of Shannara* by Terry Brooks; *The Warrior Returns* (an epic fantasy of the Anteros) by Allan Cole; and *Slow River* by Nicola Griffith.

House of Collectibles produces comprehensive reference works in such fields as fine arts, numismatics, music, Hollywood memorabilia, arrowheads, antique jewelry, and garden accessories.

One World is a distinguished imprint that presents commercial and literary writing from authors representing a variety of world cultures. One World books include *Getting Good Loving: How Black Men and Women Can Make Love Work* by Audrey B. Chapman, *Low-Fat Soul* by Jonell Nash, *Messengers of the Wind: Native American Women Tell Their Life Stories* (edited by Jane Katz), *Crossing Over Jordan* by Linda Beatrice Brown, *Brotherman: The Odyssey of Black Men in America—an Anthology* (edited by Herb Boyd and Robert L. Allen), and *Native Wisdom for White Minds: Daily Reflections Inspired by the Native Peoples of the World* by Anne Wilson Schaef.

Ivy Books is a mass-market paperback imprint that covers a wide range of fiction and nonfiction.

Query letters and SASEs should be directed to:

Joe Blades, Executive Editor and Associate Publisher
Fiction: hardcover and mass-market originals; mysteries, suspense, espionage.

Judith Curr, Editor in Chief
Oversees entire hardcover and mass-market programs. Wide range of how-to/self-help nonfiction titles. Frontlist fiction.

Virginia Faber, Senior Editor
Psychology, spiritual subjects, serious nonfiction.

Owen Lock, Editor at Large
Military history.

Leona Nevler, Editorial Director
Commercial fiction.

Maureen O'Neal, Editorial Director for Trade Paperbacks
Upscale, commercial nonfiction. Literary and commercial fiction. In charge of trade paperback program.

Susan Randol, Senior Editor
Nonfiction: popular reference, infotainment, how-to/self-improvement.

Amy Scheibe, Editor at Large
Acquires a broad, eclectic range of nonfiction and fiction projects; works with all Random House trade divisions.

Elisa Wares, Senior Editor
Fiction: commercial women's; Regency romances, some historicals.

Cheryl Woodruff, Senior Editor
Spirituality, religion, new age. One World Books (multicultural imprint).

Joanne Wyckoff, Senior Editor

Nonfiction: history, women's issues, biography, current events. Some literary fiction.

Elizabeth Zack, Editor

Fiction: frontlist commercial. Nonfiction: popular reference, self-help, inspirational.

CROWN PUBLISHING GROUP
CROWN BOOKS
THREE RIVERS PRESS
CLARKSON POTTER/PUBLISHERS
HARMONY BOOKS

201 East 50th Street
New York, NY 10022
212-751-2600

Crown publishes a variety of trade-oriented fiction and nonfiction titles in hardcover and paperback. Crown (acquired by Random House in 1988) incorporates a number of Random House imprints and acquisitions that together make up Crown Publishing Group. Crown imprints include Harmony Books (known for commercial versatility, as well as commitment to quality fiction and nonfiction), Crown Arts and Letters, Clarkson Potter/Publishers, Living Language, Bell Tower, and Prince Paperbacks, as well as Fodor's Travel Publications.

Three Rivers Press is a new designation for what was formerly Crown Trade Paperbacks.

Crown's fiction includes commercial novels across the trade spectrum, including mystery and suspense; Harmony Books embraces a typically more vanguard literary tone.

The group's fiction list and works of cultural and literary interest are exemplified by *Spring Collection* by Judith Krantz, *Red Moon Passage* by Bonnie Horrigan, *The Island of the Mapmaker's Wife and Other Tales* by Marilyn Sides, *Poemcrazy* by Susan Wooldridge, *Blood Lines* by Ruth Rendell, *Beauty* by Susan Wilson, *Sister Feelgood* by Donna Marie Williams, *The Piano Man's Daughter* by Timothy Findlay, and *The Information* by Martin Amis.

Crown nonfiction encompasses popular titles in biography, history, art, antiques and collectibles, contemporary culture, crime, sports, travel, languages, cookbooks, and self-help/how-to, as well as popular-reference works.

Cuisine and lifestyle are areas of Harmony and Clarkson Potter emphasis. Releases here include Martha Stewart's coffee-table editions and Lee Bailey's effusive line of savory kitchen-cum-culture excursions.

From Crown nonfiction: *Revised American History* by Edward P. Moser, *Radical Golf* by Michael Laughlin, *A Queer Geography* by Brank Browning, *The Flavors of Sicily* by Anna Tasca Lanza, *The Spiritual Traditions of Sex* by Richard Craze, *Barking at Prozac* by Buck (as told to Tom McNichol), *Perfect Weight* by Deepak Chopra, *Lesbianism Made Easy* by Helen Eisenbach, *Miss Manners Rescues Civilization* by

Judith Martin, *Good Girls Don't Eat Dessert* by Rosalyn Meadow and Lillie Weiss, *Chicken Breasts* by Diane Rozas, and *Keeping Kids Reading* by Mary Leonhardt.
    Query letters and SASEs should be directed to:

Sue Carswell, Executive Editor

P. J. Dempsey, Senior Editor
Commercial projects, including a wide range of serious and popular nonfiction.

Kristin Kiser, Editor

Ayesha Pande, Associate Editor

Ann Patty, Vice President and Executive Editor

Betty Prashker, Executive Vice President and Editor at Large

Karen Rinaldi, Senior Editor
Broad range of nonfiction interests. Commercial fiction.

Steve Ross, Vice President and Editorial Director
Upscale, commercial nonfiction. Literary and commercial fiction.

Carol Taylor, Editor
Commercial and popular nonfiction. Commercial fiction; multicultural stories.

CLARKSON POTTER/PUBLISHERS

Roy Finamore, Editor, Special Projects
Cooking and food, design and architecture, special projects, style and decorating, biography, popular culture.

Annetta Hanna, Senior Editor
Design, gardening, biography, popular culture, how-to style and decorating books.

Pam Krauss, Executive Editor
Cooking and food, self-help, craft, health and fitness, how-to style and decorating books.

Lauren Shakely, Vice President and Editorial Director
How-to style and decorating books, art books, gardening, biography.

Katie Workman, Senior Editor
Cooking and food, popular culture, how-to style and decorating books.

HARMONY BOOKS

Shaye Areheart, Executive Editor
Literary fiction, biographies, humor. Wide general nonfiction interests.

Peter Guzzardi, Senior Editor
Specialties: Southern writers, scholarly works accessible to a general audience.

Toinette Lippe, Editorial Director, Bell Tower
Spirituality and inspiration (*not* reincarnation, astrology, crystals, and the like).

(Ms.) Leslie Meredith, Vice President and Editorial Director
Holistic and alternative healing and wellness, spirituality, Buddhism, relationships and erotica, and pop culture. Literary and quirky fiction.

Sherri Rifkin, Editor
Wide range of commercial and serious nonfiction.
Pop culture, business, humor, women's issues, sex/relationships, alternative health.

Dina Siciliano, Assistant Editor
Wide interests, including popular culture, fiction from contemporary writers.

KNOPF PUBLISHING GROUP
ALFRED A. KNOPF

201 East 50th Street
New York, NY 10022
212-751-2600

The publishing firm of Alfred A. Knopf was long associated with fine bookmaking and the literary tradition. The regime of publisher Sonny Mehta (begun in 1990) has seen a bestselling radiance to the house, now astutely positioned in the arena of commercial contemporary letters in its corporate incarnation as Knopf Publishing Group, which, in addition to the Alfred A. Knopf imprint, covers Vintage, Pantheon, and Schocken (see separate Random House subentries). Knopf Books for Young Readers stakes a solid claim in the kids' books domain. Random House corporate marketing and promotion support combines with Knopf editorial and publishing tradition to make for a truly formidable house.

The Knopf roster of eminent authors includes major voices worldwide in virtually every field of fiction and nonfiction. Regardless of the category or genre affiliation or lack thereof, these books are Knopf: The volumes are consummately designed products, and Knopf's running-dog colophon—the illustrious Borzoi—can in and of itself signal a potential reviewer's priorities.

Knopf fiction and literary works express established traditions as well as new domains in popular contemporary writing, including provocatively styled mysteries and suspense fiction, inventive approaches in nonfiction, and literary writing in travel, food, and lifestyle. Knopf has published such writers as Ann Beattie, John le Carré, Sandra Cisneros, Michael Crichton, Brett Easton Ellis, James Ellroy, Carl Hiaasen, P. D. James, Dean R. Koontz, Peter Maass, Cormac McCarthy, Susanna Moore, Toni Morrison, Anne Rice, Donna Tartt, John Updike, and Andrew Vachss.

Titles here include *Intensity* by Dean Koontz, *Servant of the Bones* by Anne Rice, *The Dangerous Old Woman* by Clarissa Pinkola Estés, *The Last Thing He Wanted* by Joan Didion, *My Dark Places* by James Ellroy, *I Was Amelia Earhart* by Jane Mendelsohn, *A Regular Guy* by Mona Simpson, *In the Beginning* by Karen Armstrong, *Tales from Watership Down* by Richard Adams, *Golf Dreams: Writings on Golf* by John Updike, *Selected Stories* by Alice Munro, *Art Objects: Essays on Ecstasy and Effrontery* by Jeanette Winterson, and *Santa Evita* by Tomás Eloy Martínez.

Knopf lists a notable array of poetry, including *The Vixen* by W. S. Merwin, *A Silence Opens* by Amy Clampitt, *Sunday Skaters* by Mary Jo Salter, *Tesserae* by John Hollander, *Collected Poems* by John Updike, *Fire Lyric* by Cynthia Zarin, and *Hotel Lautréamont* by John Ashbery.

Knopf nonfiction accents contemporary culture, issues of public interest, art and architecture, biography and memoir, and titles in health, fitness, and lifestyle; otherwise, Knopf titles roam virtually anywhere across the reaches of the mainstream publishing emporium, including popular reference and humor.

The Knopf list in nonfiction and popular works is represented by *Clint Eastwood: A Biography* by Richard Schickel, *David Brinkley's Homilies* by David Brinkley, *Hitler's Willing Executioners* by Daniel Jonah Goldhagen, *American Foreign Policy* by George W. Bush and Brent Scowcroft, *Nancy Lancaster: Her Life, Her World, Her Art* by Robert Becker, *The Dictionary of Global Culture* by Kwame Anthony Appiah and Henry Louis Gates, Jr., *The Florida Cookbook: 200 Recipes—from Gulf Coast Gumbo to Key Lime Pie* by Jeanne Voltz and Caroline Stuart, *The Book of Jewish Food: An Odyssey from Samarkand to New York* by Claudia Roden, *The Quotable Feline* (an illustrated work) by Jim Dratfield and Paul Coughin, and *Chic Simple Work Clothes* by Kim Johnson Gross and Jeff Stone.

Knopf is home to the National Audubon Society Pocket Guides (field guides) series; the Knopf Guides series includes regionally keyed handbooks to such areas of travel interest as Ireland and the Route of the Mayas; Chic Simple books highlight ingenious approaches to the good life.

Query letters and SASEs should be directed to:

Ann Close, Editor
Fiction: contemporary themes; especially interested in Southern or Western settings. Nonfiction: art books.

Robin Desser, Editor
Contemporary fiction; works with international/multicultural outlook; narrative nonfiction, including literary travel.

Gary Fisketjon, Editor at Large
Literary fiction. Varied serious nonfiction interests.

Harry Ford, Senior Editor
Poetry.

Jane Garrett, Editor
United States history, some European and Middle Eastern history, craft and hobby books.

Judith Jones, Senior Editor and Vice President
Literary fiction, cookbooks, cultural history, the arts.

Edward Kastenmeier, Senior Editor
Acquires in all areas covered in publisher description.

Susan Ralston, Editor
Biography, cultural history, the arts, contemporary events and issues.

Ken Schneider, Assistant Editor
Contemporary fiction. Nonfiction: cultural history, the arts (drama, music, ballet). Works with Judith Jones.

Jonathan Segal, Senior Editor
Twentieth-century history, contemporary events and issues.

Victoria Wilson, Senior Editor
Nonfiction: biography and memoir; cultural and social history; performing and creative arts, including film. Literary fiction.

ALFRED A. KNOPF BOOKS FOR YOUNG READERS
CROWN BOOKS FOR YOUNG READERS
CLARKSON POTTER JUVENILE BOOKS

The Knopf and Crown programs for young readers, including the Clarkson Potter line, provide works geared to all age ranges in hardcover and paperback formats. This division produces trade reference and entertainment titles, as well as works for the educational market. Knopf, Crown, and Potter together cover a broad range that includes picture books, reference books, readers, fiction and nonfiction, novelty and gift productions, and numerous series.

Crown encompasses the imprints Crown Books for Young Readers and Clarkson Potter Juvenile Books. Crown's children's list is distinguished by illustrated works in hardcover and paperback, mainly for kids between the ages of 3 and 12; the program offers a few nonfiction titles for older grade-school readers including the cutting-edge series Face to Face With Science. Crown has a special emphasis in science fiction and fantasy titles.

The Knopf children's book program produces a hardy list of picture books, books for middle readers, and young adult fiction and nonfiction, along with a slate of special-interest reference series.

The Eyewitness Juniors series, designed for very young naturalists, produces titles geared to special species and interest areas such as snakes and reptiles, frogs and toads, cats, dogs, and amazing poisonous animals. Eyewitness Books, lavishly illustrated volumes on such topics as ancient Egypt and Rome, automobiles, and airplanes are designed for readers aged 10 and up.

Knopf Paperbacks for Kids includes Dragonfly Books (for the very young), Bullseye Books (for middle-grade readers), and Borzoi Sprinters (middle-grade and young adult readers). Umbrella Books offers affordable hardcover picture books.

This division prefers submissions that go through agents. Unsolicited manuscripts are no longer accepted or considered. Query letters and SASEs from authors should be directed to **Editorial Department**; agented submissions may sent to:

Simon Boughton, Publishing Director

Tracy Gates, Senior Editor

PANTHEON BOOKS

201 East 50th Street
New York, NY 10022
212-751-2600

Pantheon accents nonfiction books in current events, international affairs, contemporary culture, literary criticism and the arts, popular business, psychology, travel, nature, science, and history. The house also has a strong list in contemporary fiction, poetry, and drama. Pantheon also offers Fairytale and Folktale Library.

Pantheon Books was founded in 1942 by German Jewish émigrés and, from its U.S. base, forged an international reputation as a publisher of exemplary titles in fiction and nonfiction while remaining a viable business entity. Pantheon was bought by Random House in 1990, subsequent to which occurred the famous and abrupt departure of director André Schiffrin, followed by the resignation of members of the editorial staff and the shift of major authors to other houses. Although awestruck literary commentators were quick to offer epitaphs, Pantheon regrouped along a profile similar to that previously pursued; the house continues its product success with seasonally vigorous lists and refined editorial eye.

Pantheon books include: *Bad Land* by Jonathan Raban; *All Over but the Shoutin'* by Rick Bragg; *Texaco* by Patrick Chamoisseau; *Cosí Fan Tutti* by Michael Dibdin; *Secret Muses* by Julie Kavanaugh; *All Soul's Rising* by Madison Smartt Bell; *The Moor's Last Sigh* by Salman Rushdie; *Breaking the News* by James Fallows; *A Tour of the Calculus* by David Berlinski; *Mr. Wilson's Cabinet of Wonder* by Lawrence Weschler; *Murder in the Temple of Love: The Story of Yahweh Ben Yahweh* by Sydney P. Freedberg; *A Match to the Heart: One Woman's Story of Being Struck by Lightning* by Gretel Ehrlich; *Let 'Em Eat Cake* (novel) by Susan Jedren; *Art, Dialogue, and Outrage: Essays on Literature and Culture* by Wole Soyinka; *Entries* (poetry) by Wendell Berry.

Query letters and SASEs should be directed to:

Daniel Frank, Vice President and Editorial Director, Pantheon Books
Nonfiction: serious subjects, history, science, current issues. Literary fiction.

Erroll McDonald, Executive Editor, Pantheon Books
Literary fiction. Nonfiction: politics, current issues and contemporary culture.

Claudine O'Hearn, Editor, Pantheon Books

Shelley Wanger, Senior Editor, Pantheon Books
Picture, illustrated books, biography, film, culture.

SCHOCKEN BOOKS

201 East 50th Street
New York, NY 10022
212-751-2600

With strong footholds in both academic and commercial publishing, Schocken produces titles in cultural, religious, and women's studies; Judaica; literature; science and health; and the social sciences.

Schocken Books was founded in Germany in 1933 by Salman Schocken, a noted bibliophile, Zionist, and department-store kingpin. The house's German division was shut down after Kristallnacht (the formal institution of the full brunt of the Nazi pogram on November 9, 1938), but much of Schocken's holdings had been moved to

Jerusalem and Tel Aviv by that time. In 1945 Schocken opened New York offices and flourished as an independent until acquired by Pantheon division in 1987.

Under the Random House restructuring, Schocken assumed the stature of an imprint within an imprint, with a lowered profile and restricted publishing operation, giving the impression that the house was viewed primarily as a source of revenue accruing from its classic backlist. Schocken controls the world rights to the works of Franz Kafka, and otherwise includes works by Jean-Paul Sartre, Claude Lévi-Strauss, Susannah Heschel, Gershom Scholem, Elie Wiesel, Primo Levi, and Harold Kushner.

Schocken (under editorial director Arthur Samuelson, a former editor who has, in between Schocken stints, worked at Summit Books and Paragon House) is a major player in the Random House publishing partnership. A strong line of redesigned reissues of Schocken's backlist bestsellers is in full swing; the house has staked new claims in the field of Judaica; and likewise the house has adopted a robust approach across the contemporary cultural horizon.

Schocken's list sports a logo based on the Bauhaus-style S that was emblematic of Salman Schocken's business enterprises in Germany earlier in the century.

On the Schocken list: *The Five Books of Moses*, a riveting translation by Everett Fox, is the first volume of a four-volume Bible-translation project in progress: the *Schocken Bible*. Also of note: *The Sunflower: On the Possibilities of Forgiveness* by Simon Wiesenthal; *Madame Blavatsky's Baboon* by Peter Washington.

Literary writing from Schocken includes new translations of Kafka's *The Castle* and *The Trial*; *The Schocken Book of Contemporary Jewish Fiction* (edited by Ted Solartoff and Nessa Rapoport); *All the Rivers Flow to the Sea* (autobiography) by Elie Wiesel; *A Book That Was Lost and Other Stories* by S. Y. Agnon.

Judaica from Schocken:, *The Jewish Holiday Baker* by Joan Nathan; *Choosing a Jewish Life: A Handbook for People Converting to Judaism and for Their Family and Friends* (edited by Jack Riemer).

Query letters and SASEs should be directed to:

Arthur Samuelson, Editorial Director

Cecelia Cancellaro, Editor

TIMES BOOKS

201 East 50th Street
New York, NY 10022
212-751-2600

Times Books publishes general trade nonfiction across the gamut of commercial areas including business and career, finance, current affairs, social issues, science, how-to, cooking, education, travel, humor, reference, and puzzles and games. Times is particularly strong in the crossword-puzzle publishing arena.

The Times Business imprint incorporates titles in such areas as magagement, practical career boosters, business biography, business journalism, and investigative business stories into a finely honed and well-directed publishing program. Times Books is the distributor for Kiplinger Books.

Times Books (founded in 1959 by the New York *Times* newspaper) is among the houses acquired by Random House during the latter 1980s.

On the Times Books list: *The Crossword Answer Book* by Stanley Newman and Daniel Stark; *Living Faith* by Jimmy Carter; *The Edison Trait* by Lucy Jo Palladino, Ph.D.; *Man Without a Face* by Markus Wolf; *Forced Exit* by Wesley J. Smith; *American Catholic* by Charles R. Morris; *The Fiske Guide to Colleges* by Edward B. Fiske; *The American Bar Association Guide to Family Law* (edited by the ABA).

From Times Business: *Real Change Leaders* by Jon R. Katzenbach; *Everything You've Heard about Investing Is Wrong!* by William H. Gross; *Stress for Success* by James E. Loehr; *The Witch Doctors* by John Mickelthwaite and Adrian Wooldridge; *The Complete Job Search Organizer* by Jack O'Brien; *The Young Entrepreneur's Guide to Starting and Running a Businesss* by Steve Mariotti.

Query letters and SASEs should be directed to

John Mahaney, Executive Editor, Times Business
Special interest in general business, management, marketing, business reference, economics.

Stanley Newman, Managing Director, Puzzles & Games
Puzzles, games; popular culture.

Elizabeth Rapoport, Senior Editor
Popular science, health, and medicine.

(Ms.) Tracy Smith, Editor in Chief
Technology and business.

Karl Weber, Managing Director, Times Business
General business titles.

VILLARD BOOKS

201 East 50th Street
New York, NY 10022
212-751-2600

Villard leads with titles of high commercial interest in nonfiction and frontlist fiction. Villard nonfiction covers areas such as food, popular psychology, self-enlightenment, humor, inspiration, popular topics in medicine, health, fitness, and sports, as well as true crime and general reference books. Villard's fiction roster presents mainstream commercial fare as well as mysteries, thrillers, and works of literary interest.

From Villard nonfiction: *Wake Up and Smell the Coffee* by Ann Landers; *Beyond Ritalin* by Stephen W. Garber, Marianne Daniels Garber, and Robyn Freedman Spizman; *George Foreman's Knock-Out-the-Fat Barbecue and Grilling Cookbook* by George Foreman and Cherie Calhoun; *Politically Incorrect's Greatest Hits* by Bill Maher; and *From Beginning to End* by Robert Fulghum.

Villard fiction and works of literary interest: *High and Tight* by Bud Klapisch, *Maiden Voyage* by Cynthia Bass, *Turnaway* by Jesse Browner, *I'm Losing You* by Bruce Wagner, and *Who in Hell* by Sean Kelly and Rosemary Rogers.

Query letters and SASEs should be directed to:

Craig Nelson, Executive Editor

David Rosenthal, Publisher

Annik LaFarge, Associate Publisher

VINTAGE BOOKS

201 East 50th Street
New York, NY 10022
212-751-2600

Vintage trade paperbacks are renowned for high style in design and production standards as well as their substantial content. Vintage accents new titles in the fields of contemporary global and American literature and current-interest nonfiction along with its preponderance of reprints in trade fiction and nonfiction. Among Vintage series are Vintage International, Vintage Contemporaries, Vintage Departures, Vintage Books/ The Library of America, Vintage Classics, Alfaguara/Vintage Español, and Vintage/ Black Lizard Crime.

Indicative of the Vintage list: *The Collected Works of Billy the Kid* by Michael Ondaatje, *Cuba and the Night* by Paco Ayer, *Making Movies* by Sidney Lumet, *My Lead Dog Was a Lesbian* by Brian Patrick O'Donohue, *The Quantity Theory of Insanity* by Will Self, *Walt Whitman's America* by David S. Reynolds, *Jaguars Ripped My Flesh* by Tom Cahill, *Krik? Krak!* by Edwidge Danticat, *Miami Purity* by Vicki Hendricks, *American Dreams* by Sapphire, *The Origin of Satan* by Elaine Pagels, and *The Vintage Book of Contemporary World Poetry* (edited by J. D. McClatchby).

Query letters and SASEs should be directed to:

Lu Ann Walther, Vice President
All areas consistent with publisher description.

Martin Asher, Editor in Chief

READER'S DIGEST GENERAL BOOKS

260 Madison Avenue
New York, NY 10016
212-953-0030

Reader's Digest General Books accents how-to/do-it-yourself and self-help in topics that cover home maintenance and repair, gardening, crafts and hobbies, cooking, and health. Reader's Digest also produces reference books in law, medicine, money management, English-language usage and vocabulary, history and geography, science and nature, religion and archaeology, travel, and general reference.

Reader's Digest Books (founded in 1961) is a publisher of general nonfiction, most of which is conceptualized and commissioned editorially. Author credit on many of the house's books is given as the Editors of Reader's Digest; indeed, most titles are originated in-house and are written by consulting writers. Reader's Digest General, thus, is not a likely home for an original publishing project, but when prospecting assignments, the house might be worth a try for well-qualified freelance writers.

On the Reader's Digest General list: *The Ehrman Needlepoint Book* by Hugh Ehrman; *Calligraphy School: A Step-by-Step Guide to the Fine Art of Lettering* by Anna Ravenscroft and Gaynor Goffe; *Garden Design: How to Be Your Own Landscape Architect* by Robin Williams; *The Art of Watercolor* by Ray Campbell Smith.

Among house-authored titles are: *Deluxe Tapestry Sewing Basket*; *Complete Book of Embroidery*; *The Calligrapher's Studio*; *Decorating for Christmas*; *Papercraft School*; *The Rolling Tool Box*; *Heartland Cooking Breads*; *Professionals' Guide to Patient Drug Facts*; *Guide to Medical Cures and Treatments*; *The Bible Through the Ages*; *A Journey Down Route 66*; *America's First Ladies*; *Gift Wraps, Baskets & Bows Book*.

Reader's Digest General Books directs a wide marketing and distribution team.

Query letters and SASEs should be directed to:

David Palmer, General Books Editor

REED PUBLISHING (USA)
REED TRADE PUBLISHING
REED REFERENCE PUBLISHING

Reed Trade Publishing:
225 Wildwood Avenue
Woburn, MA 01801
800-366-2665

Reed Reference Publishing:
121 Chanlon Road
New Providence, NJ 07974
908-464-6800

Reed Publishing (USA), along with Reed Reference Publishing, constitutes one of the leading houses in the arena of biographical, bibliographical, and business reference materials. Reed's professional titles cover virtually the entire reference spectrum, from law, medicine, and science to education, history, and the performing arts. Reed is also a leader in electronic publishing, with many titles currently available on CD-ROM.

Reed Reference is a division of Reed Publishing (USA), an international publisher of reference works and directories for trade, institutional, corporate, and library markets that is a wing of the Reed Elsevier Group. RRP imprints include R. R. Bowker (publisher of *Literary Market Place*; *Books in Print*), Congressional Information Service, Martindale Hubbell (law directories), Marquis Who's Who, National Register Publishing, K. G. Sauer, Bowker-Sauer, and D. W. Thorpe.

Reed Elsevier also owns Heinemann (see separate main entry for Heinemann, along with its Digital Press and Focal Press divisions).

Reed is exploring the acquisition of new trade books that dovetail with their existing product lines. Fields of special publishing emphasis are self-help, how-to, and other directory/reference works, particularly in the business, legal, and healthcare fields. Catalog areas cover epic adventure, satire, and photography; fantasy, family health, and biography; thrillers, literary works, and popular science; travel, lifestyle, psychology, and inspiration; and popular history and reference.

For prospective trade projects: Please query publisher beforehand, as this is an experimental line and is therefore subject to reorganization (not to mention complete downsizing) at any given instant.

Representative Reed trade titles: *Kalashnikovs and Zombie Cucumbers* by Nick Middleton; *Positive Parenting* by Elizabeth Hartley-Brewer; *Mind, Body, and Immunity* by Rachel Charles; *The Magistrate's Tale* by Nora Naish; *The Celibate* by Michael Arditti; *Literary Guide to Dublin* by Vivien Igoe; *Claudia Schiffer* by Karl Lagerfeld; *Bulimia* by David Haslam; *Beating the Blues* by Xandia Williams.

Distribution is overseen by Reed's in-house team via book-trade channels, direct-ordering facilities, and international marketing via Reed subsidiary facilities. RRP delivers its information worldwide in a variety of formats—books, CD-ROM, microfiche, tape leasing, and through on-line accessing of RRP databases.

Query letters and SASEs should be directed to:

Peter Simon, Vice President (New Jersey)

REGNERY PUBLISHING, INC.

422 First Street SE, Suite 300
Washington, DC 20003
202-546-5005
800-462-6420

Areas of Regnery publishing interest include contemporary politics, current events, public issues, the media, biography, history, and humor; the house is open to projects with broad trade appeal along the gamut of nonfiction categories.

Regnery Publishing Inc. (formerly Regnery Gateway, founded in 1947) is a growing, midsize house that produces primarily nonfiction projects in hardcover and quality paper editions. Regnery Gateway was acquired by Phillips Publishing International and is part of Phillips's Eagle Publishing subsidiary, which produces public-policy periodicals and operates the Conservative Book Club. A major accent of Regnery's program is to feature books that offer an inside-the-Beltway Washington-insider purview. The house is also traditionally strong in paperbound reprints for the college market. Regnery Publishing supports a strong backlist.

The Phillips corporate connection enables Regnery to promote titles through such venues as Phillips's *Human Events* newspaper and to take advantage of the parent company's expertise in direct-mail and special-market sales.

Tumbleweed Press is an imprint that highlights narratives of the American frontier. Gateway Editions offers reprints of classics from historic cultures worldwide, as well as contemporary works of international scope in literature, politics, and religion.

From the Regnery Publishing trade list: *Murder in Brentwood* by Mark Fuhrman (foreword by Vincent Bugliosi); *Unlimited Access: An FBI Agent Inside the Clinton White House* by Gary Aldrich; *Confessions of a White House Ghost: Five Presidents and Other Political Adventures* by James Humes (foreword by Julie Nixon Eisenhower); *The Future of Homeschooling: A New Direction for Christian Home Education* by Michael Farris; *Where the Water Buffalo Roam: The Assault on Free Speech on America's Campuses* by Alan Charles Kors and Harvey Silvergate; *Goldwater: The Man Who Made a Revolution* by Lee Edwards; *Hoover's FBI: The Inside Story by Hoover's Trusted Lieutenant* by Cartha D. "Deke" DeLoach; *Inventing the AIDS Virus* by Peter Duesberg and Bryan Ellison; *Prelude to Leadership: The European Diary of John F. Kennedy, Summer 1945* by John F. Kennedy (introduction by Hugh Sidney; edited by Deirdre Henderson).

Representative of the Tumbleweed Press imprint (which targets readers with works in the Western and Frontier genres): *Tackett and the Saloon Keeper* (the third novel of the Tackett Trilogy) by Lyn Nofziger.

Indicative of this house's heritage is founder Henry Regnery's choice of his publisher's mark—the gateway that serves as colophon for books published by Regnery. This gateway is a graphic representation of the *Porta Nigra* in Trier, Germany, a Roman gate constructed about 300 AD when Trier was a colonial capital city of the Roman Empire. As such, the gateway symbolizes the passage from barbarous realms into the world of civilization.

Regnery Publishing is distributed to the trade by National Book Network.

Query letters and SASEs should be directed to:

Alfred Regnery, Publisher

Richard Vigilante, Vice President and Executive Editor

RENAISSANCE BOOKS

175 Fifth Avenue
New York, NY 10010
212-674-5151 (extensions: 586; 591)
fax: 212-995-2488

California offices:
4338 Gentry Avenue, Suite 1
Studio City, CA 91604-1764
818-753-9455
fax: 818-505-6509
audiojoe@worldnet.att.net (e-mail)

Renaissance Books is a nonfiction trade publisher dedicated to an editorial mix of popular culture and serious inquiry. Subjects and categories include: self-help, motivation, business, how-to, entertainment, current trends—and popular reference works in related topics. The house produces trade nonfiction packages as well as trivia books, coffee-table books, and pictorial volumes. Renaissance publishes in hardcover and paperback.

Rennaissance Books (founded in 1997) is the book-publishing imprint sibling to Audio Renaissance, a company known for marketing innovation in audio publishing. Through the company's book imprint, headquartered in Manhattan's historic Flatiron Building, Renaissance has transferred its program in the fields of self-help, motivation, and business from audio publishing into print. Renaissance Books remains dedicated to the company's historic roots and at the same time looks for projects that will expand the vision: works that reveal popular tastes and culture, ride the crest of a coming wave, and are well written, perceptive, and entertaining in and of themselves.

Bill Hartley, President and Publisher, Audio Renaissance and Renaissance Books, proffers the following outlook: Renaissance Books is an exciting new step for the company—one that is expected to mirror the philosophy that has guided the enterprise's growth as an audio publisher. The publisher projects a well-balanced mixture of nonfiction, including books on personal and spiritual growth, self-help, and motivation. The house plans an extensive program of books on popular culture, show business, and entertainment.

Representative titles: *Powerful Prayers* by Larry King with the Rabbi Irwin Katsof; *Instant Guts: Take a Risk and Win in Every Area of Your Life* by Joan Gale Frank.

With Renaissance plans including titles in celebrity biography and autobiography, TV show guides, and entertainment reference books, the house is committed to appearing on the bestseller lists as well as building a strong backlist.

Authors and agents are requested to inquire as to the address to which prospective projects should be sent, particularly during the start-up and transitional phases of the Renaissance Books operation.

Renaissance Books is distributed by St. Martin's Press.

Query letters and SASEs should be directed to:

Joe McNeely, Director of Acquisitions
Self-help, motivation, business, celebrity and show-business books.

Michael Levine, Editor
Business, sales, motivation, promotion, public relations, celebrity titles.

Richard F. X. O'Connor, Editor (California)
Popular trade nonfiction; self-help, inspiration, how-to, New Age topics; personal and spiritual growth; business and marketing.

James Robert Parrish, Editor (California)
Performing arts and pop culture; biography and autobiography; entertainment and show-business stories.

AUDIO RENAISSANCE

5858 Wilshire Boulevard, Suite 2000
Los Angeles, CA 90036
213-939-1840
fax: 213-939-6436

Audio Renaissance produces audio products in a variety of nonfiction subjects. the house is a major presence in the areas of personal and spiritual growth, self-help, business, and motivation.

For the past 10 years, Audio Renaissance has been one of the leading independent audio publishers in America, publishing over 450 titles in that time. Among them: *How to Argue and Win Every Time* by Gerry Spence, *James Herriot's Favorite Dog Stories*; *Emotional Intelligence* by Daniel Goleman; *You Can Negotiate Anything* by Herb Cohen; *Psycho-Cybernetics* by Maxwell Maltz; *How to Meditate* by Laurence LeShan; *Think and Grow Rich* by Napoleon Hill.

Audio Renaissance typically acquires projects by licensing audio rights to works originally created in other media, primarily books.

Queries (with SASE):

Joe McNeely, Director of Acquisitions.

RE/SEARCH PUBLICATIONS
V/SEARCH
JUNO BOOKS

180 Varick Street, Tenth Floor
New York, NY 10014
212-807-7300
fax: 212-807-7355

RE/Search Publications focuses on media and the arts; cultural studies; word art and graphics; biography and memoir; erotic interfaces of all natures. RE/Search and V/Search productions are often published in oversize trade-paperback journal formats. Juno Books is a personalized trade-paperback book imprint. The press publishes a short list of new titles per year and hosts a comprehensive backlist.

A number of works from this house have achieved classic status virtually instantaneously upon release. Areas of renown include cultures of the mind and body, general mischief, literature in reprint, popular music, and film studies.

From **RE/Search**: *The Confessions of Wanda von Sacher-Masoch* (edited by Andrea Juno and V. Vale); *William Burroughs, Brion Gysin, Throbbing Gristle* (edited by Andrea Juno and V. Vale); *Freaks: We Who Are Not As Others* by Daniel P. Mannix; *Incredibly Strange Films* (edited by Andrea Juno and V. Vale); *Incredibly Strange Music* (2 volumes; edited by Andrea Juno and V. Vale); *The Atrocity Exhibition* by J. G. Ballard; *J. G. Ballard* (literary-critical studies; edited by Andrea Juno and V. Vale).

The **V/Search** list includes: *Pranks!* (edited by Andrea Juno and V. Vale); *Industrial Culture Handbook* (edited by Andrea Juno and V. Vale); *Memoirs of a Sword Swallower* by Daniel P. Mannix; *Zines! Incendiary Interviews with Independent Publishers* (2 volumes; edited by Andrea Juno and V. Vale); *Modern Primitives* (edited by Andrea Juno and V. Vale); *Search and Destroy: An Authoritative Guide to Punk History* (edited by Andrea Juno and V. Vale).

On the **Juno Books** imprint: *Concrete Jungle* (examination of pop media by collaborative artists, theorists, and scientists; edited by Alexis Rockman and Mark Dion); *Angry Women* (edited by Andrea Juno); *Bob Flanagan: Super Masochist* (edited by Andrea Juno and V. Vale); *Angry Women in Rock* (2 volumes; edited by Andrea Juno and V. Vale); *The RE/Search Guide to Bodily Fluids* by Paul Spinrad; *The Torture Garden* by Octave Mirabeau (reprint of 1899 classic).

RE/Search, V/Search, and Juno Books distribute to the trade through Consortium; direct marketing for selected titles is handled through a number of independent catalogers, including Fantagraphics.

Query letters and SASEs should be directed to:

Andrea Juno, Executive and Editorial Director

FLEMING H. REVELL COMPANY

(See under Baker Book House in Directory of Religious, Spiritual, and Inspirational Publishers)

RIZZOLI INTERNATIONAL PUBLICATIONS

300 Park Avenue South
New York, NY 10010-5399
212-982-2300

Rizzoli catalogs titles in fine arts, architecture, crafts, culinary arts, decorative arts, design, fashion, the home, gardens, landscaping, travel, and photography. Rizzoli also offers selected titles in sports and the performing arts, as well as a line of children's books.

Rizzoli International (founded in 1976) is one of the exclusive set of cosmopolitan publishers renowned for finesse in the bookmaking craft. The house interest embraces artistic realms worldwide, throughout history as well as the contemporary arena.

Rizzoli's consummately produced volumes feature graphics of the highest quality and are offered in hardback and trade paperback editions. Rizzoli's products also include wall calendars, desk diaries, and journals. The house works closely with the editors of such associated presses as Assouline, PBC International, Villegas Editores, and the Universe Publishing affiliate. (Please see entry for Universe Publishing.)

Titles from Rizzoli: *Creating Privacy in the Garden* by Chuck Crandall and Barbara Crandall; *Pleasures of the Porch* by Daria Price Bowman and Maureen LaMarca; *Picasso Bon Vivant* by Ermine Herscher; *Unseen Warhol* by John O'Connor and Benjamin Liu; *What My Heart Has Seen* by Tony Bennett; *Classic Fabrics* by Lady Henrietta Spencer-Churchill (photographs by Andreas von Einsiedel); *The Dome of the Rock* (photographs and essay by Said Nuseibeh); *Richard Meier Houses* (introduction by Paul Goldberger); *The Cooking of Parma* by Richard Camillo Sidoli; *New Swedish Style* by Sasha Waddell (photographs by Pai Tryde); *Making the Most of Bathrooms* by

Catherine Haig; *The Vegetable Book: A Detailed Guide to Identifying, Using and Cooking over 100 Vegetables* by Colin Spencer (photographs by Linda Brugess).

From Assouline: *Coty: Parfumeur and Visionary* by Elisabeth Barille (photographs by Keiichi Tahara); *Haute Couture: Tradesmen's Entrance* by Olivier Seguret (photographs by Keiichi Tahara); *L'Espirit Serge Lutens: The Spirit of Beauty* by Serge Lutens; *Panama: A Legendary Hat* by Martine Buchet (photographs by Laziz Hamani); *Symbols of Judaism* by Marc-Alain Ouaknin; *The Taste of Provence: The Columbe D'Or at Saint Paul de Vence* by Martine Buchet (photographs by Prosper Assouline).

PBC International titles: *Pleasure Paradises: International Clubs & Resorts 2* by John P. Radulski and William Weathersby, Jr.; *Restaurant Style* by Charles Morris Mount; *Interior Details: The Designers' Style* by Noel Jeffrey; *New Modern: Creative Living Spaces* by Carla Breeze; *The New Office: Designs for Corporations, People & Technology* by Karin Tetlow; *Lifestyle Stores* by Martin Pegler; *Shops & Boutiques* by Grant Kirkpatrick (foreword by Giorgio Armani); *School of Visual Arts Gold: Fifty Years of Creative Graphic Design* by the School of Visual Arts; *American Typeplay* by Steven Heller and Gail Anderson; *Food Warp: Food & Drink Packaging Graphics* by Steven Heller and Anne Fink.

Rizzoli International Publications is distributed to the trade in the United States by St. Martin's Press; Canadian distribution is handled through McClelland & Stewart. The Rizzoli catalog offers titles from additional publishers in the arts and literary arena, including Artemis, Assouline, Guggenheim Museum Publications, Gustavo Gili, Marion Boyars, Moyer Bell Limited, PBC International, Scala Books, Solveig Williams Foreign Editions, Sotheby's, Villegas Editores, and Zwemmer.

The house acquires new projects only on an extremely selective basis.

RIZZOLI CHILDREN'S LIBRARY

Rizzoli Children's Library produces books and activity packages with themes and in subject areas congruent with the overall Rizzoli house interest. The titles entertain in ways that engage cultural and artistic appreciation, stretch the mind, and entertain—with little heed paid to the currently popular gooey and goofy trends.

Rizzoli Children's Library presents: *Carnevalia! African-Brazilian Folklore and Crafts* by Liza Papi; *Edward Lear's Nonsense* (illustrated by James Wines); *The Nightingale and the Wind* (story by Paul Mandelstein; illustrations by Pamela Silin-Palmer); *The Will and the Way: Paul R. Williams, Architect* by Karen E. Hudson.

A representative Rizzoli series is A Weekend with the Artist, visually commanding volumes keyed to individual artists and their worlds. Titles here: *A Weekend with Winslow Homer*; *A Weekend with Picasso*; *A Weekend with Renoir*.

Query letters and SASEs should be directed to:

Barbara Einzig, Senior Editor
Art and general trade books.

David Morton, Senior Editor
Architecture.

RODALE PRESS

33 East Minor Street
Emmaus, PA 18098-0099
610-967-5171

Rodale Press (founded in 1932) specializes in books in nutrition and healthy cooking, health and fitness, gardening and the home, environment, crafts (including quilting, sewing, and woodworking), practical spirituality, self-improvement, lifestyle, and selected titles in general reference. Rodale produces hardcover and paperback editions as well as some video and audio products.

Rodale publishes among its magazines: *Prevention, Organic Gardening, Runner's World, American Woodworker, Men's Health, Shape, Heart and Soul* (a health magazine for African-American women), *Quilter's Newsletter, Bicycling, Scuba Diver,* and *Backpacker.*

Rodale imprints include: Prevention Magazine Health Books, Fitness Books, and Cookbooks; Men's Health Books; and Rodale Garden Books, Craft Books, Quilt Books, Woodworking Books, and Nature Books. Daybreak Books is the house's new trade imprint.

Rodale Press engages tremendous marketing energy; in addition to sales through the bookstore trade, Rodale is highly attuned to the venue of direct marketing. The press itself operates a number of specialty book clubs, among them Prevention Book Club, Successful Sewing Club, Men's Health Book Service, Organic Gardening Book Club, Nature Book Society, and the National Wildlife Federation Book Club. Rodale is among the leaders in addressing the Spanish-language and Latino markets. The company's database contains in the neighborhood of 25 million names.

Another Rodale strength is editorial quality and developmental expertise. Rodale does not produce books on a hunch—Rodale researches the market to find out what readers want and gives it to them. The house is an established leader in its field; as such, Rodale always aims to give readers more than they want, more than they ever thought to ask for, more than they knew they wanted, with products that offer practical value in every sentence. The house's mission statement runs thus: To inspire or enable people to improve their lives and the world around them. Many of Rodale's titles are agented or packaged; others are created by Rodale's in-house staff.

From Rodale: *Christmas with Jinny Beyer: Decorate Your Home for the Holidays with Beautiful Quilts, Wreaths, Arrangements, Ornaments, and More* by Jinny Beyer; *Prevention's Healing with Vitamins: The Most Effective Vitamins and Mineral Treatments for Everyday Health Problems and Serious Disease—from Allergies and Arthritis to Water Retention and Wrinkles* by the editors of Prevention Magazine Health Books; *Herbs for Health and Healing: A Drug-Free Guide to Prevention and Cure* by Kathi Keville with Peter Korn; *Healthy Favorites from America's Community Cookbooks* by the Food Editors of Prevention Magazine Health Books; *Never Pay Retail: How to Save 20% to 80% on Everything You Buy* by Sid Kirchheimer; *Easy Machine Quilting: 12 Lessons from the Pros, Plus a Dozen Projects to Machine Quilt* (edited by Jane Townswick); *The Female Body: An Owner's Manual* by the Editors of

Prevention Magazine Health Books; *Router Magic: Jigs, Fixtures, and Tricks to Unleash Your Router's FULL Potential* by Bill Hylton; *The Male Body: An Owner's Manual* by K. Winston Caine, Perry Garfinkel, and the Editors of Men's Health Books; *No Time to Sew: Fast & Fabulous Tips & Techniques for Sewing a Figure-Flattering Wardrobe* by Sandra Betzina; *Natural Medicine for Allergies: The Best Alternative Methods for Quick Relief* and *Natural Medicine for Arthritis: The Best Alternative Methods for Relieving Pain and Stiffness* by Glenn S. Rothfeld, M.D. and Susan LeVert; *High-Fashion Sewing Secrets from the World's Best Designers* by Claire B. Shaeffer; *Natural Landscaping* by Sally Roth; *Nick Engler's Woodworking Wisdom* by Nick Engler; *The Thimbleberries Book of Quilts* by Lynette Jensen.

Rodale Press distributes its books directly to readers through such routes as mailing lists and its numerous book clubs; St. Martin's Press distributes Rodale titles to the bookstore trade.

Query letters and SASEs should be directed to:

Maggie Lydie, Editorial Director, Rodale Gardening Books; Executive Editor, Rodale Crafts & Quilting Books
Books for the home and garden; hobbies and crafts.

Sally Reith, Assistant Acquisitions Editor
Projects consistent with Rodale interest.

Zora Yost, Editorial Director, Prevention Magazine Health Books
Health and fitness books.

YANKEE BOOKS

Yankee Books creates how-to books with the kind of folksy, practical homespun wisdom that New Englanders are famous for. Subject areas include home and garden hints, money-saving ideas, personal finance, outdoor activities, pets, and travel. Yankee Books projects are produced primarily in collaboration with the publisher of *Yankee* magazine and the annual *The Old Farmer's Almanac*.

Sample Yankee titles: *Earl Proulx's Yankee Home Hints;* Yankee *Magazine's Make It Last;* Yankee *Magazine's Practical Problem Solver;* Yankee *Magazine's Practical Problem Solver for Pets*.

Formerly an independent regional specialist house (begun in 1966), Yankee Books is distributed nationally via the marketing division of its parent company, Rodale Press. Trade distribution for Yankee is through St. Martin's.

Query letters and SASEs should be directed to:

Jeff Bredenberg, Senior Editor

DAYBREAK BOOKS

733 Third Avenue
New York, NY 10017

Daybreak Books is a new trade imprint of Rodale Books. Daybreak publishes in such areas as spirituality, health, and inspiration. With a nondenominational perspective, the

Daybreak program presents books that help people have a greater understanding of their spiritual nature and how they can apply spirituality in everyday life. Daybreak is *not* a religious publisher.

Titles here include: *Gift of Life: A Spiritual Companion for the Mother-to-Be* by Joan Swirsky, R.N.; *The 12 Lessons on Life I Learned from My Garden* by Vivian Elisabeth Glyck; *Self-Esteem Through Spirituality* by Adele Wilcox; *Prayer: Language of the Soul* by Philip Dunn; *Love Yourself Thin: A Revolutionary Spiritual Approach to Weight Loss* by Victoria Moran; *20/20 Insight: Tap the Power of the Mind's Eye and Achieve Extraordinary Success in Life and Relationships* by Randy Gibbs; *The Daily Word: Love, Inspiration, and Guidance for Everyone* (collected by the editors of the Daily Word magazine); *Christmas in Calico: An American Fable* (fiction) by Jack Curtis.

Daybreak is distributed to the trade through St. Martin's Press.

Query letters and SASEs should be directed to:

Karen Kelly, Editorial Director, Daybreak Books
Health and spirituality. Celebrity stories, how-to, inspiration.

ROUTLEDGE, INC.

29 West 35th Street
New York, NY 10001-2299
212-244-3336
fax: 212-564-7854
800-265-8504 (orders)
http://www.routledge.com/routledge.html (World Wide Web) Updated biweekly, the Routledge Online database of 6,000 backlist and 800 frontlist titles can be searched by title, author, ISBN, keyword, or topic.

Routledge accents current events, communications and media, cultural studies, education, self-improvement and psychology, world political and cultural studies, philosophical thought, economics, feminist theory, gender studies, history, and literary criticism. The house produces trade nonfiction and academic works.

Routledge produces adult nonfiction in the humanities and sciences. Routledge specialties include projects that give a vanguard twist to topical issues. Routledge imprints include Theatre Arts Books and Routledge/Thoemmes Press.

Founded as Methuen Inc. (in 1977), and then as part of Routledge and Chapman and Hall (as a subsidiary of International Thompson Organization), the house held to the overall profile of a commercial publisher, abreast of trends in scholarship and general public interest, as it issued strong lines of trade and academic books. Routledge (with a concentration in the contemporary trade arena) and Chapman and Hall are today separate publishing companies. (Please see Chapman and Hall entry in this directory).

Routledge titles: *Excitable Speech: Contemporary Scenes of Politics* by Judith Butler; *Reel to Real: Race, Sex, and Class at the Movies* by bell hooks; *Elvis After Elvis: The Posthumous Career of a Living Legend* by Gilbert B. Rodman; *Three Plays by Mae West: Sex, The Drag, and Pleasure Man* (edited by Lillian Schlissel);

Modest_Witness@Second_Millennium.Female/Man.©Meets_OncoMouse: Feminism and Technoscience by Donna J. Haraway (with paintings by Lynn Randolph); *White Trash: Race and Class in America* (edited by Annalee Newitz and Matt Wray); *Remembering Anna O: A Century of Mystification* by Mikkel Borch-Jacobsen; *Whores and Other Feminists* (edited by Jill Nagle); *The Talking Cure: TV Talk Shows and Women* by Jane Shattuc; *How the Irish Became White* by Noel Ignatiev; *Transcending the Talented Tenth: Black Leaders and American Intellectualism* by Joy James; *The Conquest of Assyria: Excavations in an Antique Land* by Mogens Trolle Larsen; *Animal Acts: Configuring the Human in Western History* (edited by Jennifer Ham and Matthew Senior); *Twentieth Century Political Theory: A Reader* (edited by Stephen Eric Bronner); *The Second Wave: A Reader in Feminist Theory* (edited by Linda Nicholson); *African American Religion: Interpretive Essays in History and Culture* (edited by Timothy E. Fulop and Albert J. Raboteau).

Routledge handles its own distribution and also distributes for the U.K. publishing house, Verso.

Query letters and SASEs should be directed to:

Paul Mooney, Editor
Education and sociology.

William Germeno, Editorial Director
Literary and cultural studies, film, communications, theater, classics.

Amy Lee, Editor
Philosophy and psychoanalysis.

RUNNING PRESS BOOK PUBLISHERS
125 South 22nd Street
Philadelphia, PA 19103-4399
215-567-5080
fax: 215-568-2919
800-310-4145

Running Press shows flair in the areas of popular culture and arts, lifestyle, popular science, hobby how-to, and popular-interest reference titles. Running Press produces a singular line of specialty items that include bookstore-counter impulse-sales wares, striking free-standing exhibition units for kids' books, and a gleaming array of display and promotional titles (especially on the Courage Books imprint).

Running Press Book Publishers (founded in 1972) publishes hardcover and paperback trade books in general nonfiction. The house, in addition, issues audiocassettes, stylized journals, diaries, calendars, datebooks, bookplates, Miniature Editions, generously appointed educational-entertainment kits, and postcard books. Running Press products are associated with sleek production, as well as a sometimes humorous or insouciant air. Running Press maintains a solid backlist.

Running Press Miniature Edition books are delightful little books that fit in the palm of your hand. The list covers an astonishing range of subjects: *The Nutcracker*; *Bytes of Wisdom: A User's Guide to the World*; *Happy Holidays!*; *I Love You!*; *The Joys of Christmas: A Treasury of Seasonal Smiles*; *The Button Book* by Diana Epstein; *Moose-wood Cookbook Classics* by Mollie Katzen; *The Rolling Stone Book of Love* and *The Rolling Stone Book of Respect: Wisdom from Women in Rock* (compiled by the editors of Rolling Stone Press); *Sunflowers: A Little Treasury of Joy*.

Courage Books is the promotional imprint of Running Press, producing eye-catching volumes that can be advertised by booksellers as attractive, reasonably priced items. Sample Courage titles: *The Brain Pack: An Interactive, Three-Dimensional Exploration of the Mysteries of the Mind* (created by Ron Van der Meer; text by Ad Dudink); *Among the Amish* by Keith Bowen (illustrated by the author); *Fortune-Telling: A New Guide to Palm Reading and the Tarot* by Dennis Fairchild and Julie Paschkis; *The Dragon's Tooth: An Ancient Manuscript on the Secret History of the Dragon and the Unicorn* by Michael Green; *Men Are Lunatics! Women Are Nuts!* (compiled by Ronald Schwartz).

Running Press participates in a joint publishing program with M. Shanken Communications, Inc., publishers of *Wine Spectator* and *Cigar Aficionado* magazines. Titles available: *California Wine: A Comprehensive Guide to the Wineries, Wines, Vintages and Vineyards of America's Premier Winegrowing State* by James Laube; *Ultimate Guide to Buying Wine*; *Guide to Great Wine Values $10 and Under*; *Buying Guide to Premium Cigars*.

Running Press distributes its own list.

RUNNING PRESS BOOKS FOR CHILDREN

Running Press Books for Children features finely engineered pop-up books, foldouts, small-format editions, kits, coloring books, and how-tos—in stand-alone editions and numerous series.

Running Press created the Fit-A-Shape series (books for preschoolers that teaches basic concepts using three-dimensional objects that fit matching shapes); the Gem series (captivating, fact-filled titles, each with vast amounts of information in a handy format); Five-Minute Mysteries (that test your powers of observation and deductive reasoning); Treasure Chests (expeditions into ancient cultures); Action Books (informative texts and components for exploring science and creating projects); Discovery Kits (read about a specific subject, such as a radio, then build your own); Book Buddy created by Penny Dann (each title in this series features a die-cut corner where a soft-fabric Book Buddy lives); Start Collecting (each title includes a guide that explains the history of the category, famous specimens, a poster, and tips on how to begin collecting).

Query letters and SASEs should be directed to:

Stuart Treacher, President and Publisher

Nancy Steele, Director of Acquisitions

Brian Perrin, Editorial Director

ST. MARTIN'S PRESS
PICADOR USA
STONEWALL INN EDITIONS
BUZZ BOOKS
ST. MARTIN'S GRIFFIN
A THOMAS DUNNE BOOK FOR ST. MARTIN'S PRESS
A WYATT BOOK FOR ST. MARTIN'S PRESS
ST. MARTIN'S SCHOLARLY AND REFERENCE BOOKS

175 Fifth Avenue
New York, NY 10010
212-674-5151

St. Martin's publishes across the spectrum of trade nonfiction and hosts a wide range of popular and literary fiction. The house is particularly strong in a number of special areas, some with associated lines and imprints (including popular culture, international arts and letters, relationships, multicultural topics, science, business and professional). St. Martin's is known for a strong list of scholarly and reference titles, and offers a solid lineup of college textbooks. St. Martin's produces hardcover, trade paperback, and mass-market paper editions, and also offers a line of calendars. The press produces a few works for younger readers.

St. Martin's Press is an international publisher with a broad and comprehensive program. St. Martin's is part of the German-based international communications conglomerate Verlagsgruppe Georg von Holtzbrinck. Within this framework, St. Martin's enjoys its long-standing tradition of editorial independence as it operates from its historic environs in Manhattan's famed Flatiron Building.

St. Martin's Press is home to an array of divisions and imprints, including Picador USA, Stonewall Inn Editions, Buzz Books, St. Martin's Griffin, A Thomas Dunne Book for St. Martin's Press, A Wyatt Book for St. Martin's Press, and St. Martin's Scholarly and Reference Books.

Picador USA is a St. Martin's imprint geared to the international literary and cultural scene. Picador publishes both originals and reprints. (Please see separate Picador USA subentry below.)

St. Martin's was among the first commercial houses to highlight topflight entrants in the arena of lesbian, gay, and gender issues and interest. The house publishes noteworthy mainstream fiction and nonfiction in this vein, as well as works with a literary approach. (Please see the subentry below for Stonewall Inn Editions.)

Buzz Books hooks into the current of contemporary culture. St. Martin's Griffin speaks to timely nonfiction and fiction titles in trade paperback. (Please see separate subentries below.)

A Thomas Dunne Book for St. Martin's Press and A Wyatt Book for St. Martin's Press represent two imprints with a personalized editorial dimension. (Please see separate subentries below.)

St. Martin's distributes its own books as well as those of such houses as Academy Editions, Amistad Press, Audio Renaissance and Renaissance Books, Boyds Mills

Press, Consumer Reports Books, Rodale Press, Tor Books/Forge, Universe Publishing, and World Almanac.

ST. MARTIN'S PRESS TRADE

St. Martin's (founded in 1952) publishes within all major trade and popular reference categories. Combined with the house's enterprising commercial spirit, St. Martin's shows remarkable depth and strength across its entire program. The house issues a hefty seasonal frontlist and maintains a strong backlist.

Areas of St. Martin's nonfiction interest include current events, popular culture, true crime, cookbooks, business, sports, biography, self-awareness and self-improvement, popular science and psychology, travel and the outdoors, and gardening. St. Martin's instituted a collaborative editorial operation with West Coast–based *Buzz* magazine to develop high-interest titles in the contemporary current-culture arena.

In fiction and literature, St. Martin's publishes top-of-the-line commercial works and is a leader in such genres as mysteries, thrillers, suspense titles, and historical works, as well as selected science fiction and fantasy, along with some contemporary Westerns (most often in the action-adventure or suspense modes). (For more information regarding category fiction, especially science fiction, fantasy, futurist adventure, horror, and Westerns, please see separate main entry for the St. Martin's affiliate Tor Books.) The publisher's roster embraces cultural biographies and criticism, as well as poetic works and short-story collections.

Nonfiction from St. Martin's: *Concrete Confidence: A 30-Day Program for an Unshakable Foundation of Self-Assurance* by Sam Horn; *The Synergy Myth: And Other Ailments of Business Today* by Harold Geneen with Brent Bowers; *Trust No One: The Glamorous Life and Bizarre Death of Doris Duke* by Ted Schwarz with Tom Rybak; *Eden Renewed: The Public and Private Life of John Milton* by Peter Levi; *The Arthritis Cure* by Jason Theodosakis, M.D., Barry Fox, and Brenda Adderly; *Once a Dancer* (autobiography) by Allegra Kent; *Jules Verne: An Exploratory Biography* by Herbert R. Lottman; *Will: The Autobiography of G. Gordon Liddy* by G. Gordon Liddy; *Meatless Mexican Home Cooking* by Nancy Zaslavsky; *An Original Man: The Life and Times of Elijah Muhammad* by Claude Clegg; *The Power to Get In: A Step-by-Step System to Get in Anyone's Door Faster, More Effectively, and with Less Expense* by Michael A. Boylan; *The Mythology of Dogs: Canine Fables, Legend, and Lore Through the Ages* by Gerald Hausman and Loretta Hausman; *Kiss Your Stockbroker Goodbye: A Guide to Independent Investing* by John G. Wells, CFA; *American Aurora: The Suppressed History of Our Nation's Beginnings and the Heroic Newspaper That Tried to Report It* by Richard Rosenfeld; *Twilight Warriors: Inside the World's Special Forces* by Martin C. Arostegui; *Attracting Terrific People: How to Find, and Keep, the People Who Bring Your Life Joy* by Lillian Glass, Ph.D.; *Song of the Phoenix: Voices of Comfort and Healing from the Afterlife* by Lily Fairchilde; *Good Girls Go To Heaven, Bad Girls Go Everywhere: How to Break the Rules and Get What You Want from Your Job, Your Family, and Your Relationship* by Eve Ehrhardt (translated by Margot Dembo); *The Alarming History of Famous and Difficult Patients: Amusing Medical Anecdotes from Typhoid Mary to FDR* by Richard Gordon; *To Your Health: Exploring the Healing Properties of Alcohol* by Barry Fox; *What Are We Fighting For? Sex, Race, Class, and the Future of Feminism* by Joanna Russ.

St. Martin's frontlist fiction and popular literature: *Tryin' to Sleep in the Bed You Made* by Virginia DeBerry and Donna Grant; *The Boy Who Went Away* by Eli Gottlieb; *Harvest Moon* by Judith Saxton; *Far From Home* by Charlotte Hardy; *All We Know of Heaven* by Anna Tuttle Villegas; *Carry Me Back* by Laura Watt; *The Honeymakers* by Diana Saville; *Dead Things* by Richard Calder; *Death in Equality* by Lucinda Ebersole; *Snowboarding to Nirvana* by Frederick Lenz; *An Army of Angels: A Novel of Joan of Arc* by Pamela Marcantel; *The Bell Witch: An American Haunting* by Brent Monahan; *Getting Off Clean* by Timothy Murphy; *Angels of the Universe* by Einar Mar Gudmundsson; *The Set-Up* by Paul Erdman; *Bad Vibes* by Alberto Fuguet (translated by Kristina Cordero); *Highway and Dancehalls* by Diana Atkinson; *The Romance: Being the Fifth Volume of The Daughters of Mannerling* by Marion Chesney.

St. Martin's presents a rich and varied lineup in the arena of mystery, suspense, and thrillers. The list features stand-alone works as well as ongoing series, published in hardcover and trade paper. Dead Letter is St. Martin's sobriquet for an adventurous, eclectic, commercial mass-market paperback list of mystery and suspense, including reprints of successful hardcover titles.

Titles from St. Martin's list in mysteries, suspense fiction, and thrillers: *A Letter of Mary* by Laurie R. King; *The Hoydens and Mr. Dickens: The Strange Affair of the Feminist Phantom* by William J. Palmer; *Beyond the Beyond* by Lee Goldberg; *The Cold Heart of Capricorn* by Martha C. Lawrence; *Notches: A Montana Mystery Featuring Gabriel Du Pré* by Peter Bowen; *Asking Questions* (an Inspector Ghote mystery) by H. R. F. Keating; *Dirge for a Doge* by Elizabeth Eyre; *An Image to Die For* (a Sam Dean mystery) by Mike Phillips; *The Garden Plot* by J. S. Borthwick; *The Fred Astaire and Ginger Rogers Murder Case* by George Baxt; *A Touch of Mortality* (a Mitchell and Markby Village whodunit) by Ann Granger; *The Hour of Our Death* (a Sister Agnes mystery) by Alison Joseph.

PICADOR USA

St. Martin's Press initiated the Picador USA imprint during the last part of 1994, and the house was an immediate industry presence with an array of titles featuring an international cast of world-class writers. Picador USA (along with its sibling Picador United Kingdom imprint) publishes in hardcover and trade paperback editions, and highlights original titles as well as reprints.

Picador marketing support encompasses dynamic full-scale promotion and advertising campaigns, author publicity, exposure via major book and literary reviews, and radio spots.

Representative Picador nonfiction: *Blue Windows: A Christian Science Childhood* by Barbara Wilson; *The Cocktail: The Influence of Spirits on the American Psyche* by Joseph Lanza.

From the Picador fiction portfolio: *In the Deep Midwinter* by Robert Clark; *Archangel* by Paul Watkins; *Little* by David Treuer; *The Mystery Roast* by Peter Gadol; *Blackwater* by Kerstin Ekman; *Behind the Scenes at the Museum* by Kate Atkinson;

Winterkill by Craig Lesley; *The Book of Secrets* by M. G. Vassanji; *Electricity* by Victoria Glendinning; *Dreamhouse* by Alison Habens; *The Smell of Apples* by Mark Behr; *Emerald City* by Jennifer Egan.

Backlist favorites: *The Romantic Movement: Sex, Shopping and the Novel* by Alain de Botton; *Rotten: No Irish, No Blacks, No Dogs* by John Lydon (with Keith and Kent Zimmerman); *The Dog with the Chip in His Neck: Essays from NPR and Elsewhere* by Andrei Codrescu; *Voodoo Dreams: A Novel of Marie Laveau* by Jewell Parker Rhodes; *Four Hands: A Novel* by Paco Ignacio Taibo II (translated by Laura C. Dail); *Elevator Music: A Surreal History of Muzak, Easy-Listening, and Other Moodsong* by Joseph Lanza.

STONEWALL INN EDITIONS

Stonewall Inn Editions publishes works with a lesbian and gay cultural slant in hardcover and paperback editions. The house addresses such trade areas as current events and public interest, reference works, cultural affairs, literary anthologies, Stonewall Inn Studio Books (featuring graphically lavish and luxuriously produced gift volumes), and the Stonewall Inn Mysteries line. The scope of St. Martin's lesbian- and gay-interest list is not limited to works issued under the Stonewall Inn imprint.

Featured Stonewall Inn authors have included such lights as Quentin Crisp, Larry Kramer, Paul Monette, Ethan Mordden, Denise Ohio, Randy Shilts, Edmund White, and Mark Richard Zubro.

Popular titles from Stonewall Inn: *The Violet Quill Reader: The Emergence of Gay Writing After Stonewall* (edited by David Bergman); *Sportsdykes: Stories from On and Off the Field* by Susan Fox Rogers; *Dark Wind: A True Account of Hurricane Gloria's Assault on Fire Island* by John Jiler; *Another Dead Teenager* (a Paul Turner mystery) by Mark Richard Zubro; *Sacred Lips of the Bronx* (a love story) by Douglas Sadonick; *End of the Empire* (visionary romance-adventure) by Denise Ohio.

BUZZ BOOKS

Productions from St. Martin's Buzz Books imprint often share the West Coast ambiance of copublisher *Buzz* magazine. Areas include: autobiography/biography, music, current culture, fiction.

ST. MARTIN'S GRIFFIN

St. Martin's Griffin publishes exclusively trade paperbacks, with a strong emphasis in crafts, cooking, nutrition and fitness, modern and contemporary fiction, current culture, biography, and travel. Griffin authors include Douglas Coupland, Studs Terkel, Doris Kearns-Goodwin, Vincent Scully, James Baldwin, and Bob Dylan. Griffin reprints a preferred selection of St. Martin's hardcover originals in trade-paper editions.

Titles from Griffin: *Bread Machine Magic* by Linda Rehberg and Lois Conway; *The Cancer Prevention Diet* by Michio Kushi; *Critical Path* by R. Buckminster Fuller;

Nancy Drew Scrapbook by Karen Plunkett-Powell; *England's Dreaming* by Jon Savage; *Generation X* by Douglas Coupland; *Route 66* by Michael Wallis; *Vurt* by Jeff Noon; *The World's Most Famous Math Problem* by Marilyn Vos Savant.

Travel titles include the Let's Go Series, with some twenty-four new, updated, and revised titles a year plus six map guides.

A THOMAS DUNNE BOOK FOR ST. MARTIN'S PRESS

In Thomas Dunne's more than 25 years at St. Martin's Press, he has published virtually every kind of book, from runaway bestsellers such as *The Shell Seekers* by Rosamunde Pilcher and *River God* by Wilbur Smith to the critically acclaimed nonfiction of Robert Kaplan and Juliet Barker. The Thomas Dunne imprint produces roughly 150 titles per year and covers a wide array of interests that include: commercial fiction, mysteries, military histories, biographies, divination systems, politics, philosophy, humor, literary fiction, and current events.

Titles from Thomas Dunne: *The Story of the Gun* by Ian V. Hogg; *Italia: The Art of Living Italian Style* by Edmund Howard (photographs by Oliver Benn); *Vodka, Tears and Lenin's Angel: My Adventures in the Wild and Wooly FSU (Former Soviet Union)* by Jennifer Gould; *Ireland: A Photographic Portrait* by Michael O'Mara; *The Sylvan Path: A Journey Through America's Forests* by Gary Ferguson; *A Life of Matthew Arnold* by Nicholas Murray; *Another America: Native American Maps and the History of Our Land* by Mark Warhus; *Crimes of the Scene: A Guide to Mystery Novels Set in the Countries You'll Visit* by Nina King, with Robin Winks and Others; *The It-Doesn't-Matter-Suit* by Sylvia Plath.

From the Thomas Dunne line of mystery, suspense, and thriller titles: *Death of an Angel* (a Sister Mary Helen mystery) by Sister Carol Anne O'Marie; *Simon Said* by Sarah R. Shaber; *An Accidental Shroud* (an Inspector Mayo mystery) by Marjorie Eccles; *Murder of a Dead Man* by Katherine John; *All That Glitters* by Jerry Kennealy; *The Dead of Winter* by Patricia Hall; *Close Quarters* (a Thames Valley mystery) by Claire Curzon; *Malarkey* by Sheila Simonson; *Privileged to Kill* by Steven F. Havill.

A WYATT BOOK FOR ST. MARTIN'S PRESS

Robert B. Wyatt's imprint is characterized by an enviable editorial eye. Within a vision that encompasses commercial clarity and deeply personalized writing, A Wyatt Book for St. Martin's Press produces topnotch fiction from authors new and established. Robert Wyatt is an editor and publisher whose celebrated career has included stints with Avon and Ballantine.

From Wyatt Books for St. Martin's Press: *Renaissance Moon* by Linda Nevins; *Naming the New World* by Calvin Baker; *The Reconstruction* by Claudia Casper; *Wizard of the Wind* by Don Keith; *Here, Kitty, Kitty* by Winifred Elze; *Cowkind* by Ray Peterson; *Lorien Lost* by Michael King; *The Virgin Knows* by Christine Palamidessi Moore.

St. Martin's Scholarly and Reference Division

St. Martin's Scholarly and Reference Division publishes works pertinent to particular professional and academic fields and disciplines, as well as a select group of titles with mainstream-crossover potential keyed to areas of the house's core publishing program.

Areas of St. Martin's Scholarly and Reference publishing scope include: arts and humanities, the sciences, history, biography, politics and economics, regional studies and travel, essay and commentary.

Some titles here: *Pilgrimage for Peace: A Secretary General's Memoir* by Javier Peréz de Cuéllar; *The Arabs: Myth and Reality* by Gerald Butt; *Digital Delirium* (edited by Arthur Kroker and Marilouise Kroker); *Channel Surfing: Race Talk and the Destruction of American Youth* by Henry A. Giroux; *Money: A History* (edited by Jonathan Williams); *Telltale Hearts: The Origins and Impact of the Vietnam Antiwar Movement* by Adam Garfinkle; *Chateux of the Loire* by Thorsten Droste and Axel M. Mosler; *Pursued by Furies: A Life of Malcolm Lowry* by Gordon Bowker.

Query letters and SASEs should be directed to:

(Ms.) Dana Albarella, Editor
Wide range of nonfiction interests: biography, music, current culture; distinctive fiction. Works with James Fitzgerald (Buzz Books imprint).

Sally Richardson, President and Publisher Trade Division; President, Mass Market Division

Matthew J. Shear, Vice President and Publisher, Mass-Market Division
All mass-market categories in fiction and nonfiction.

Reagan Arthur, Editor
Contemporary fiction, mysteries, media-related nonfiction. Works with the Picador USA imprint. Projects include *I Killed Hemingway* by William McCranor Henderson; *The Lost Diaries of Frans Hals* by Michael Kernan; *The Ballad of Rocky Ruiz* by Manuel Ramos.

Ruth Cavin, Senior Editor; Associate Publisher, A Thomas Dunne Book for St. Martin's Press
Crime fiction, contemporary fiction, anecdotal science and medicine novelties (quotation books). Titles include *The Beekeeper's Apprentice* by Laurie R. King; *Whoever Fights Monsters* by Robert Ressler; *Four Hands* by Paco Ignacio Taibo II.

Hope Dellon, Senior Editor
Fiction: mysteries, serious historical novels. Nonfiction: parenting, women's issues, psychology, biography. Titles include *Mary Queen of Scotland and the Isles* by Margaret George; *The Sculptress* by Minette Walters; *Beyond Jennifer and Jason* by Linda Rosenkrantz & Pamela Redmond Satran.

Michael Denneny, Senior Editor
Literary nonfiction and fiction. Gay and lesbian subjects.

Thomas L. Dunne, Vice President, Executive Editor; Publisher, A Thomas Dunne Book for St. Martin's Press
Eclectic interests; projects have covered commercial women's fiction, mysteries, military histories, biographies, divination systems, politics, philosophy, humor, literary

fiction, current events. Titles include *The Shell Seekers* by Rosamunde Pilcher, *The Book of Runes* by Ralph H. Blum, and *Balkan Ghosts* by Robert Kaplan.

Jennifer Enderlin, Senior Editor
Women's fiction, psychological suspense, general commercial fiction. Commercial nonfiction (sex, relationships, psychology). Projects include *To Build the Life You Want, Create the Work You Love* by Marsha Sinetar; *End the Struggle and Dance with Life* by Susan Jeffers; *Just between Us Girls* by Sydney Biddle Barrows.

James Fitzgerald, Executive Editor
Autobiography/biography, music, current culture, fiction. Titles include *Leni Riefenstahl* by Leni Riefenstahl; *Generation X* by Douglas Coupland; *Rotten* by John Lydon. Responsibilities include overseeing the Buzz Books imprint (featuring primarily a West Coast purview).

Heather Jackson, Editor
Commercial nonfiction of all stripes: health, nutrition, parenting, childcare, popular reference, popular culture, psychology/self-help. Titles include *The Ten Commandments of Pleasure* by Susan Block, *The Kitchen Klutz* by Colleen Johnson, and *Secrets of Serotonin* by Carol Hart.

Keith Kahla, Editor
Gay and lesbian interest, mystery and suspense, literary fiction, cartoon books, anthologies. Projects include *Murder on the Appian Way* by Steven Saylor; *Pawn to Queen Four* by Louis Eighner; *Beyond Acceptance: Parents of Lesbians and Gays Talk About Their Experiences* by Caroline Griffin, Marian Wirth, and Arthur G. Wirth.

(Ms.) Marian Lizzi, Associate Editor
Nonfiction: pop culture, women's issues, popular history, self-improvement, and an occasional cookbook. Titles include *Funk: The Music, the People, and the Rhythm of the One* by Rickey Vincent; *Welcome to the Jungle* by Geoffrey Holtz; *The Greek Vegetarian* by Diane Kochilas; *The Vinegar Jar* by Berlie Doherty.

John Sargent, Chairman, Editorial Director
Best-seller fiction, controversial current affairs.

Shannon McKenna, Assistant Editor
Commercial nonfiction: popular how-to/self-help; popular science; sex, relationships, psychology. Women's fiction, psychological suspense, general commercial fiction. Works with Jennifer Enderlin.

Calvert D. Morgan, Jr., Editor
Nonfiction: American culture and history; biography; books on music and film; essays. Fiction: Exceptional voices in American fiction, both literary and commercial. Titles include *King of Comedy: The Life and Art of Jerry Lewis* by Shawn Levy; *Blues and Trouble* (short stories) by Tom Piazza; *The Florence King Reader.*

Kelley Ragland, Associate Editor
Commercial and serious nonfiction. Literary nonfiction, especially related to women's or racial issues, also including parenting, psychology, biography; essays. Popular and literary fiction: mysteries—wide range, thrillers, suspense. Serious contemporary or

historical women's fiction. Open to new writers: Attracted to the quality and craft of the writing; looks for standout characters and unique voice.

Anne Savarese, Editor
Practical and popular nonfiction, travel, women's issues, mystery and contemporary fiction. Projects include *The Country Music Lover's Guide to the U.S.A.* by Janet Byron; *Keep Still* (a Marti MacAlister mystery) by Eleanor Taylor Bland; *Daughters of Feminists* by Rose L. Glickman.

Charles Spicer, Senior Editor
Commercial fiction: crime, suspense, mysteries. Nonfiction: true crime, biography, history. Titles include *The Other Mrs. Kennedy* by Jerry Oppenheimer; *Topping from Below* by Laura Reese; *The Rise and Fall of the British Empire* by Lawrence James.

Gordon Van Gelder, Editor
Science fiction, popular culture, mystery/horror, books on writing. Titles include *The Encyclopedia of Science Fiction* by John Clute and Peter Nicholls; *The Psychotronic Video Guide* by Michael J. Weldon; *The Big Blowdown* by George P. Pelicanos.

Joe Veltre, Editor
Commercial fiction and nonfiction. Thrillers, mysteries, memoirs, "literary" fiction, and the like. Edits the Dead Letter mass-market paperback mystery imprint.

Robert Weil, Senior Editor
Nonfiction, biography, popular culture, literary fiction. Projects include *Mercy of a Rude Stream* by Henry Roth, *More Than Words* by Mario Cuomo, and *Mankiller* by Wilma Mankiller.

Jennifer Weis, Executive Editor
Commercial fiction: women's, thrillers, romance. Commercial nonfiction: people books, narrative nonfiction, cookbooks, self-help, health and parenting, humor, popular culture. Projects include *Aaron Spelling: A Prime-Time Life* by Aaron Spelling; *Are You Normal?* by Bernice Kanner; *Innocence Undone* by Kat Martin.

George Witte, Director, Picador USA and Editor, St. Martin's Press
For Picador: Quality literary fiction and nonfiction of literary or intellectual interest. Titles include *Farewell, I'm Bound to Leave You* by Fred Chappell, *In the Deep Midwinter* by Robert Clark; *The River Beyond the World* by Janet Peery. For St. Martin's: commercial fiction, business, sports, politics, contemporary issues. Titles include *Dumbing Down Our Kids* by Charles Sykes; *Sweepers* by P. T. Deutermann; *The Power to Get In* by Michael Boylan.

Peter Wolverton, Senior Editor and Associate Publisher, A Thomas Dunne Book for St. Martin's Press
Fiction: Commercial and popular literature, genre mysteries. Nonfiction: Wide range consistent with the Thomas Dunne list; sports—golf, football.

Robert B. Wyatt, President, A Wyatt Book for St. Martin's Press
Commercial fiction, especially original, new, high-caliber writing. Projects include *Tully* by Paullina Simons; *Saudade* by Katherine Vaz; *Jennie* by Douglas Preston.

SASQUATCH BOOKS

615 Second Avenue, Suite 260
Seattle, WA 98101
206-467-4300
fax: 206-467-4301
800-775-0817 (orders)
books@sasquatchbooks.com (e-mail)
http://www.sasquatchbooks.com (World Wide Web)

Sasquatch specializes in books on travel, regional interest, gardening, guidebooks, nature, the outdoors, and food and wine. Sasquatch is broadening its Pacific Northwest regional concentration and intends to build its children's list. Additional areas of Sasquatch interest include literary nonfiction, especially in subject areas related·to the house's core interests.

Sasquatch Books (founded in 1979) is known for a string of small-press successes. Among these: the Best Places travel series (*Northwest Best Places*; *Northern California Best Places*), the Cascadia Gardening series, and the Northwest Mythic Landscape series.

Books from Sasquatch: *This Place on Earth: Home and the Practice of Permanence* by Alan Thein Durning; *Northwest Garden Style: Ideas, Designs, and Methods for the Creative Gardener* by Jane Kowalczewski Whitner (photography by L. Quartman Younker); *Alaska on My Mind: 20 Voices from Above the 54th Parallel* (edited by Susan Fox Rogers); *Overstory: Zero, Real Life in Timer Country* (literary narrative) by Robert Leo Heilman; *Wild Life: The Guide to Unusual Oregon* by Mark Christensen; *Voyage of a Summer Sun: Canoeing the Columbia River* by Robin Cody; *Red Hot Peppers* (a book-audiocassette-jump rope pack) by Bob and Diane Boardman; *O Is for Orca* (photographs by Art Wolfe; text by Andrea Helman).

Titles in the Best Places series: *Best Places Restaurant Guide: Seattle* (edited by Nancy Leson); *The NorthWest Best Places Cookbook: Recipes from the Outstanding Restaurants and Inns of Washington, Oregon, and British Columbia* by Cynthia Nims and Lori McKean.

Sasquatch Books is distributed through a network of regional sales representatives.

Query letters and SASEs should be directed to:

Chad Haight, President

Gary Luke, Editorial Director

SCHOLASTIC, INC.

555 Broadway
New York, NY 10012
212-343-6100

Scholastic publishes titles for younger readers. Scholastic produces an embracing array of age-range-targeted narrative fiction and general-interest nonfiction, as well as instructional materials for use from early childhood through high school.

The house publishes trade and educational lines in hardcover and paperback editions, and owns a solid niche in electronic publishing. A portion of Scholastic's trade list is intended to appeal to young adults and younger readers alike. In addition, Scholastic, Inc. (founded in 1920) issues magazines, operates classroom book clubs, and offers computer software.

Scholastic offers a wide array of books in series, among them Big Books (picture books), lift-the-flap books, board books, gift sets, ESL (English as a second language) titles, easy readers, middle-grade readers, and a panoply of readers and professional materials for teachers. Scholastic's current enterprise encompasses Spanish-language and bilingual Spanish/English items. Scholastic is home to a distinguished roster of writers and illustrators.

Sample Scholastic projects and imprints are Blue Sky Press, Cartwheel Books, Nightmare Hall, Time Quest Books, The Baby-Sitters Club, Mariposa, and Scholastic Reference. The incredibly successful Goosebumps series of scary stories by R. L. Stine has engendered a line of spin-offs and tie-ins including collectors' novelty items.

Scholastic created the Literacy Place and Solares lines: These two core-curriculum reading and language-arts programs are for English and Spanish languages. Scholastic spent six years developing these programs because they believe teachers and children need and deserve a coherent plan of skills development (including phonics), better assessment, and, of course, the best children's literature.

Wiggleworks and Wiggleworks-español for grades K–2 (a complete early literacy system) are geared to raise reading scores. These programs use books and other educational technology that help emerging readers develop fluency, confidence, and control by reading, writing, listening, and speaking.

Solares is an innovative K–6 reading and language program in Spanish. Children read a wide variety of quality fiction that includes works originally written in Spanish, as well as classics translated from English and other languages. Solares provides a solid foundation for literacy through a program of explicit, intentional skills instruction that includes phonics.

Scholastic handles its own distribution.

The editors at Scholastic wish to emphasize that the house accepts *no* unsolicited manuscripts, and that the acquisitions personnel deal only with agented material. Query letters and SASEs should be directed to:

Diane Hess, Executive Editor

Grace Maccarone, Executive Editor, Cartwheel Books

Ann Reit, Executive Editor

SEAL PRESS

3131 Western Avenue, Suite 410
Seattle, WA 98121-1041
206-283-7844
sealprss@scn.org (e-mail)
http://www.seanet.com/~sealpress (World Wide Web)

Seal Press is dedicated to promoting the work of women writers. In addition to its several successful mystery series, Seal publishes a wide range of fiction, poetry, titles in women's studies and lesbian studies, sports and the outdoors, popular culture, parenting, self-help, awareness, and health.

Seal Press books enjoy a reputation for high literary quality, and the list often features finely designed, well-produced editions in hardcover and trade paperback. Seal Press supports a hardy backlist.

Seal Press (founded in 1976) is a smaller house that has leapt into its third decade of publishing with the same enthusiasm and mission that inspired the first book to bear the Seal name. Some 150 books later, the publishing business as well as the cultural climate around feminism have changed considerably. Seal remains editorially agile and responsive to the industry's current challenges. Recent Seal books evidence the shifting signposts of feminism and an ever-expanding range of women's interests.

A new series was launched in 1995 by *Listen Up: Voices from the Next Feminist Generation*. This line provides a forum for young women to wield fresh brands of feminism, to acknowledge their lives as different from their mothers', and to apply their realities to an established, yet necessarily fluid movement for social change.

Seal fiction is known for offbeat approaches to genre and gender, in addition to such mystery series as Barbara Wilson's Cassandra Reilly series and Pam Nilsen mysteries; Elisabeth Bowers's Meg Lacey series; Jean Taylor's Maggie Garrett series, and Ellen Hart's Jane Lawless mysteries.

Nonfiction from Seal: *SurferGrrrls: Look, Ethel! An Internet Guide for Us!* by Laurel Gilbert and Crystal Kile; *Everyday Acts Against Racism: Raising Children in a Multiracial World* (edited by Maureen T. Reddy); *Dharma Girl: A Road Trip Across the American Generations* by Chelsea Cain; *She's a Rebel: The History of Women in Rock & Roll* by Gillian G. Gaar (preface by Yoko Ono); and *A Vindication of the Rights of Whores* (edited by Gail Phetersen; preface by Margo St. James).

Seal fiction and popular literature includes: *Robber's Wine* (a Jane Lawless mystery) by Ellen Hart; *If You Had a Family* by Barbara Wilson; *Where the Oceans Meet* by Bhargavi C. Mandava; *Night Bites: Vampire Stories by Women* (edited by Victoria A. Brownworth); *The Dyke and the Dybbuk* by Ellen Galford; *Another America / otra America* (poetry) by Barbara Kingsolver (with Spanish translations by Rebeca Cartes).

Adventura Books is a Seal imprint that captures women's outdoor and travel experiences with some of the finest writing of its kind. Adventura blazes a literary trail and encourages the spirit of adventure in every woman. Some Adventura series titles: *Season of Adventure: Off the Beaten Track with Women Over Fifty* (edited by Jean Gould). Backlist Adventura titles: *Uncommon Waters: Women Write About Fishing* (edited by Holly Morris); *Leading Out: Women Climbers Reaching for the Top* (edited by Rachel da Silva); *Water's Edge: Women Who Push the Limits in Rowing, Kayaking and Canoeing* by Linda Lewis.

Special Seal titles in self-help and recovery: *Getting Free: You Can End Abuse and Take Back Your Life* by Ginny NiCarthy; *Dating Violence: Young Women in Danger* (edited by Barrie Levy); *New Beginnings: A Creative Writing Guide for Women Who Have Left Abusive Partners* by Sharon Doane; *Nating the Violence: Speaking Out About Lesbian Battering* (edited by Kerry Lobel); *The Obsidian Mirror: An Adult*

Healing from Incest and *The Mother I Carry: A Memoir of Healing from Emotional Abuse* by Louise M. Wisechild; *You Don't Have to Take It! A Women's Guide to Confronting Emotional Abuse at Work* by Ginny NiCarthy, Naomi Gottlieb, and Sandra Coffman; *She Who Was Lost Is Remembered: Healing from Incest Through Creativity* (edited by Louise M. Wisechild).

Seal Press is distributed to the trade by Publishers Group West.

Query letters and SASEs should be directed to:

Faith Conlon, Publisher

Holly Morris, Editorial Director

SELF-COUNSEL PRESS

1704 North State Street
Bellingham, WA 98225
360-676-4530
fax: 360-676-4549

Vancouver editorial office:

1481 Charlotte Road
North Vancouver, BC Canada V7J 1H1
604-986-3366

Self-Counsel produces business how-to, legal reference, self-help, and practical popular psychology. Topical areas include entrepreneurship, the legal system and you, business training, the family, and human resources development and management. The house also produces titles geared to lifestyles and business and legal issues in Florida, Oregon, and Washington.

Self-Counsel Press (founded in 1977) is a smaller house dedicated to providing well-researched up-to-date books (primarily trade paperbacks) as well as cassettes and work kits. The company's trade motto is "Our business is helping business people succeed." Self-Counsel's expertly written books do not just tell people what to do; they show them—step by step—how to do it. Kick Start Guides is a lineup of pocket-size titles designed for business travelers. The Start and Run list shows how to start and run a number of different kinds of small-business ventures.

Self-Counsel books cover everything from business to finance, legal matters to family matters, in language that everyone can understand. Self-Counsel prides itself on delivering concise, easy-to-understand books and audio offering the practical information you need, whether it is for helpful legal tips, succeeding in business, or personal self-help issues.

Self-Counsel also offers legal books covering national issues as well as books covering legal matters in Florida, Oregon, and Washington. Other topics include retirement, personal self-help, and lifestyles.

From Self-Counsel: *So You Wanna Buy a Car . . . Insider Tips for Saving Money and Your Sanity* by Bruce Fuller and Tony Whitney; *Start and Run a Profitable Mail-Order*

Business by Robert W. Bly; *Start and Run a Profitable Tour Guiding Business* by Barbara Braidwood, Susan Boyce, and Richard Cropp; *First-Time Sales Rep: Sound Like a Pro, Act Like a Pro, Sell Like a Pro!* by Wayne Vanwyck; *Study Smarter, Not Harder: Your Guide to Successful Learning and Studying in Any Situation* and *The Complete Guide to Canadian Universities: How to Select a University and Succeed When You Get There* by Kevin Paul; *Cut Your Losses! A Smart Retailer's Guide to Loss Prevention* by Keith O'Brien; *A Small Business Guide to Doing Big Business on the Internet* by Brian Hurley and Peter Birkwood.

Kick Start Guides is a series of handy, pocket-size guides developed for the business traveler. Each guide is written for a specific country and is designed to help readers kick-start themselves into action as soon as they arrive at their destination. The Guides are also helpful tools for entrepreneurs on the lookout for overseas business opportunities.

The Start and Run series offers step-by-step business plans and shows how to set up shop, sell products or services, hire employees, get financing, design marketing strategies, and identify legal considerations for a variety of different enterprises. The Start and Run Series includes titles keyed to bed-and-breakfast, the crafts business, freelance writing, secondhand bookstores, student-run businesses, and the gift-basket business.

Self-Counsel Press operates its own distributional services.

Query letters and SASEs should be directed to:

Diana R. Douglas, President (Vancouver Office)

Ruth Wilson, Managing Editor (Vancouver Office)

SERPENT'S TAIL/HIGH RISK

Serpent's Tail (founded in 1986) is known for innovative original works and sharp acquisition of reprint titles. Based in the United Kingdom, Serpent's Tail operated a downtown New York office for a few years during the late 1980s to middle 1990s; the U.S. office closed down in late 1996. For reference, here is the U.K. contact information:

Query letters and SASEs should be directed to:

Pete Ayrton, Publisher
Serpent's Tail
4 Blackstock Mews
London, N4 2BT
171 354-1949
fax: 171 704-6467

SEVEN STORIES PRESS

632 Broadway 7th Floor
New York, NY 10012
212-995-0908

Seven Stories publishes trade nonfiction, commercial literature, and popular reference works. The house's signature is a provocative edge in current events, contemporary culture, biography/personality and memoirs, and inventive writing of all stripes (including classic reprints).

Seven Stories Press was founded by publisher Dan Simon in 1996. Simon was previously cofounder (with John Oakes) of Four Walls Eight Windows (see separate main entry). Seven Stories's publishing assets include backlist properties formerly catalogued by Four Walls.

From Seven Stories: *Harnessing Anger: The Way of an American Fencer* by Peter Westbrook with Tej Hazarika; *Nonconformity: Writing on Writing* by Nelson Algren; *Exteriors* by Annie Ernaux (translated by Tanya Leslie); *A Frozen Woman* by Annie Ernaux (translated by Linda Coverdale); *Lovely Me: The Life of Jacqueline Susann* by Barbara Seaman; *Healing Your Body Naturally: Alternative Treatments to Illness* and *The Woman's Encyclopedia of Natural Healing* by Dr. Gary Null; *The House of Moses All-Stars* by Charley Rosen; *Surviving the Americans: The Continued Struggle of the Jews After Liberation* by Robert L. Hilliard, Ph.D.; *Trips: Hallucinogens in the '90s, How They Work in Your Brain* by Cheryl Pellerin (heavily illustrated by R. Crumb and Ellen Seefelt); *Marilyn: Story of a Woman* (a novel in graphics form) by Kathryn Hyatt; *Censored: The News That Didn't Make the News and Why: The Project Censored Yearbook* by Carl Jensen and Project Censored (introduction by Walter Cronkite); *The Winner of the Slow Bicycle Race: Satirical Writings* by Paul Krassner.

Distribution to the trade for Seven Stories is handled by Publishers Group West.

Query letters and SASEs should be directed to:

Dan Simon, Publisher

SHAMBHALA PUBLICATIONS

(See Directory of Religious, Spiritual, and Inspirational Publishers)

M. E. SHARPE

80 Business Park Drive
Armonk, NY 10504
914-273-1800
fax: 914-273-2106
800-541-6563 (orders)

Sharpe publishes across the range of social and political sciences, including law, literature and literary criticism, area studies, women's studies, multicultural studies, business, comparative politics, and international and developmental economics. Special Sharpe focus is on Asian studies, business (international and domestic), Latin American studies, economics, political science, history, sociology, comparative public-policy analysis, and studies of the formerly Soviet area and Eastern Europe.

M. E. Sharpe (founded in 1959) is a privately held company that produces trade books, reference books, scholarly and academic works, business books, and professional books in hardcover and paperback.

M. E. Sharpe has long been known for its area studies program covering Russia, Eastern Europe, and Asia. Expanding on that excellent publishing tradition, Sharpe has inaugurated programs in Latin American studies, American studies, African studies, and European studies, as well as related disciplines of comparative studies, women's studies, and literature, to provide a comprehensive understanding of today's world.

M. E. Sharpe chooses titles and authors that will define future debates about the political, economic, and social issues faced by various global regions and their peoples. Titles are selected by the editors to represent the most innovative and critical thinking in their respective disciplines.

Along with the primarily scholarly works, M. E. Sharpe publishes major single and multivolume reference works under the Sharpe Reference imprint; books aimed at the professional market are generally under the Sharpe Professional stamp.

North Castle Books is an imprint designed to bring the global sweep of knowledge and the literary arts to a broad general audience, principally through trade bookstore distribution. North Castle emphasizes works with artistic and cultural significance issued in trade paperback editions. In this arena, Sharpe's list features works by a number of Nobel laureates, including Wasily Leontief, Vaclav Havel, and Kenzaburo Oe.

The Sharpe list thus encompasses original research, policy studies, translations, reference compendiums, popular literature and classic reprints, and books that lend themselves to slots in the trade market. Sharpe started as a publisher of academic and professional journals and, by the late 1970s, had begun expansion into book publishing.

Books from Sharpe: *An Enquiry Concerning the Intellectual and Moral Faculties, and Literature of Negroes* by Henri Grégoire; *The Ethnic Moment: The Search for Equality in the American Experience* (edited by Philip L. Fetzer); *Double Exposure: Poverty & Race in America* (edited by Chester Hartman); *Asia in Western and World History: A Guide for Teaching* (edited by Ainslie T. Embree and Carol Gluck); *The Empire of Schools: Japan's Universities and the Molding of a National Power Elite* by Robert L. Cutts; *The Haunting Past: Politics, Economics and Race in Caribbean Life* by Alvin O. Thompson; *Politics and Society in Modern Israel: Myths and Realities* by Adam Garfinkle; *Revolution and Change in Central and Eastern Europe: Political, Economic, and Social Challenges* by Minton F. Goldman; *Women in Russian History: From the Tenth to the Twentieth Century* by Natalia Pushkareva; *The Politics of Abortion in the United States and Canada: A Comparative Study* by Raymond Tatalovich; *The History Highway: A Guide to Internet Resources* by Dennis A. Trinkle, Dorothy Auchter, Scott A. Merriman, and Todd E. Larson.

The Writers' Worlds line is devoted to interdisciplinary studies of world writers and the fictional universes they create. The series spans Africa, Anglo-American, Asian, East and West European, Latin American, and Middle Eastern cultural traditions. First in the series is *The Explosive World of Tatyana N. Tolstaya's Fiction* by Helena Goscilo. Proposals are welcomed by the series editor: Vladimir Padunov, 1421A Cathedral of Learning, University of Pittsburgh, Pittsburgh, PA 15260.

Sharpe wants to highlight titles of the practical how-to variety on its professional, technical, and reference lists. Sharpe sells and promotes its titles both nationally and internationally; the house is a recognized industry leader in worldwide distribution. A large part of Sharpe's sales come from direct marketing; in addition, the house pursues a variety of means to sell its list—such as libraries, universities, trade and institutional bookstores, and catalogs. First and foremost, Sharpe projects must have the potential to work as direct-mail items.

M. E. Sharpe orchestrates its own distributional network, including stateside regional sales representatives, library-market specialists, and international wholesalers and reps.

Query letters and SASEs should be directed to:

Peter Coveney, Executive Editor
American history, religion, philosophy, sociology.

Stephen Dalphin, Executive Editor
Textbooks/economics. Latin America studies, world history.

Patricia A. Kolb, Executive Editor
Books about Europe and the former Soviet Union.

Olivia Lane, Executive Editor
Professional business books.

Doug Merwin, Executive Editor
Asian studies.

Vladimir Padunov, Series Editor, Writers's Worlds
Interdisciplinary, multicultural accounts of writers and their fictional worlds. Write (with SASE): Vladimir Padunov, 1421A Cathedral of Learning, University of Pittsburgh, Pittsburgh, PA 15260.

SHEEP MEADOW PRESS

P.O. Box 1345
Riverdale, NY 10471
718-548-5547
800-972-4491 (orders)

Sheep Meadow publishes a literary list that accents poetry, the shorter prose fictional forms, and the essay, as well as selected nonfiction. Sheep Meadow has on occasion ventured into mainstream trade venues, as with the lifestyle title *Dean Cuisine: The Liberated Man's Guide to Fine Cooking* by Jack Greenberg and James Vorenberg.

Sheep Meadow Press (inaugurated in 1976) sports an international cast of renowned authors and offers small-press dedication to expressive, meaningful writing and fine bookmaking.

From the Sheep Meadow poetry list: *The Ice Lizard* by Judith Johnson; *The Center for Cold Weather* by Cleopatra Mathis; *Collected Poems (1935–1990)* by F. T. Prince; *The Landscape Is Behind the Door* by Pierre Martory (translated by John Ashbery); *Selected Poems* by Diana Der-Hovanessian; *The Past Keeps Changing* by Chana Bloch.

Indicative of Sheep Meadow's other interests: *Cape Discovery: The Provincetown Fine Arts Work Center Anthology* (edited by Bruce Smith and Catherine Gammon); *Interviews and Encounters* by Stanley Kunitz; *Kabbalah and Consciousness* by Allen Afterman; *No Success Like Failure: The American Love of Self-Destruction, Self-Aggrandizement and Breaking Even* by Ivan Solotaroff; *The Stories and Recollections of Umberto Saba* (translated by Estelle Gilson).

Sheep Meadow titles are available directly from the publisher (call 800-972-4491); and through a variety of trade and library wholesalers, including Inland, Small Press Distribution, Yankee Book Peddler, and Blackwell North American.

All manuscripts must be accompanied by SASEs (reporting time is six months). Projects should be directed to:

Stanley Moss, President and Publisher

SIERRA CLUB BOOKS

85 Second Street, Second Floor
San Francisco, CA 94105
415-977-5500
fax: 415-291-1602
http://www.sierraclub.org/books (World Wide Web)

Sierra Club publishes works in the categories of nature, appropriate technology, outdoor activities, mountaineering, health, gardening, natural history, travel, and environmental issues. Sierra Club series include the Adventure Travel Guides, Sierra Club Totebooks, Naturalist's Guides, Natural Traveler, the John Muir Library, and Guides to the Natural Areas of the United States. Sierra Club Books has a strong division that publishes works geared to children and young adults (see separate subentry below).

Founded in 1892 by John Muir, the membership of the Sierra Club has for over a century stood in the forefront of the study and protection of the earth's scenic, environmental, and ecological resources; Sierra Club Books is part of the nonprofit effort the club carries on as a public trust. The house publishes hardcover and paperback books, many of them finely illustrated.

Sierra Club Books has the proud tradition of publishing books that are worldwide messengers for the Sierra Club mission: "To explore, enjoy and protect the wild places of the Earth; to practice and promote the responsible use of the Earth's ecosystems and resources; to educate and enlist humanity to protect and store the quality of the natural and human environment; and to use all lawful means to carry out these objectives."

The books represent the finest in outdoor photographic artistry; fervent and thought-provoking discussions of ecological issues; literary masterworks by the highest-caliber naturalist authors; authoritative handbooks to the best recreational activities the natural world can offer. Today, the need to protect and expand John Muir's legacy is greater than ever—to help stop the relentless abuse of irreplaceable wilderness lands, save endangered species, and protect the global environment.

On the Sierra Club list: *Women in the Material World* by Faith D'Aluisio and Peter Menzel; *How Flowers Changed the World* by Loren Eiseley; *The Art of Adventure* by Galen Rowell; *The Case Against the Global Economy* by Jerry Mander and Edward Goldsmith; *Resist Much, Obey Little: Remembering Ed Abbey* (edited by James R. Hepworth and Gregory McNamee); *Mark of the Bear: Legend and Lore of an American Icon* (edited by Paul Schullery); *Orca: Visions of the Killer Whale* by Peter Knudtson; *The Great House of Birds: Classic Writings About Birds* (edited by John Hay); *People of Legend* by John Annerino.

The Lost Gospel of the Earth by Tom Hayden (founder of SDS, member of the Chicago Seven, and longtime California Legislator) presents a passionate eco-spiritual manifesto calling for a return to the ancient belief in nature as a sacred source of wisdom.

Pictorial works: *Wetlands: The Web of Life* by Paul Rezendes and Paulette Ray; *The Sierra Club Guide to 35mm Landscape Photography* by Tim Fitzharris (revised edition).

Fiction from Sierra: *A Condor Brings The Sun: A Novel of Peru's Ancient Runa Culture* by Jerry McGahan.

Sierra Club Pathstone Editions are inspirational words by visionary authors in inexpensive, elegantly designed gift editions: *Creative Energy: Bearing Witness for the Earth* by Thomas Berry; *All the World Over: Notes from Alaska* by John Muir.

Sierra Club Books Adventure Travel Guides (newly published or up-to-date revised editions): *Adventuring in Hawaii* by Richard McMahon; *Adventuring in British Columbia* by Isobel Nanton and Mary Simpson; *Adventuring in The Caribbean* by Carrol B. Fleming; *Adventuring in Arizona* by John Annerino; *Adventuring in The Pacific* by Susanne Margolis.

Sierra Club Books are distributed to the book trade by Random House.

Query letters and SASEs should be directed to:

James Kohee, Senior Editor
Areas consistent with house list.

Carl Pope, Executive Director
Nature writing; environmental issues; nonfiction literary works dealing with nature, environment, cultural anthropology, history, travel, and geography. Fiction and poetry that is clearly related to natural or environmental themes.

SIERRA CLUB BOOKS FOR CHILDREN AND YOUNG ADULTS

Sierra Club Books for Children and Young Adults publishes primarily nonfiction, along with selected fiction keyed to subject areas that generally reflect the overall Sierra Club house emphasis.

Titles here: *Desert Trip* by Barbara A. Steiner (illustrated by Ronald Himler); *The Empty Lot* by Dale H. Fife (illustrated by Jim Arnosky); *The Seal Oil Lamp* (retold by Dale DeArmond); *The Snow Whale* by Caroline Pitcher (illustrated by Jackie Morris); *Squishy, Misty, Damp & Muddy: The In-Between World of Wetlands* by Molly Cone; *Wild in the City* by Jan Thornhill (illustrated by the author); *Animals You Never Even*

Heard Of by Patricia Curtis; *Buffalo Sunrise: The Story of a North American Giant* by Diane Swanson; *In Good Hands* by Stephan R. Swinburne; *Wolf of Shadows* by Whitley Streiber.

Author-artist Barbara Bash has written and illustrated six celebrated children's titles for Sierra Club Books, including *In the Heart of the Village: The World of the Indian Banyan Tree*, the latest book in her award-winning Tree Tales series.

Sierra Club Books for Children and Young Adults is distributed to the trade by Little, Brown.

Query letters and SASEs should be directed to:

Helen Sweetland, Editor in Chief, Sierra Club Children's Book Division

---

SILHOUETTE BOOKS
(See Harlequin Books)

SIMON & SCHUSTER
PARAMOUNT COMMUNICATIONS
POCKET BOOKS
SCRIBNER
THE FREE PRESS
MACMILLAN PUBLISHING USA
BRASSEY'S (U.S.)
JOSSEY-BASS
PRENTICE HALL
SIMON & SCHUSTER CHILDREN'S PUBLISHING DIVISION

New York offices:
1230 Avenue of the Americas
New York, NY 10020
212-698-7000
http://www.SimonSays.com (World Wide Web)

Simon & Schuster is a leader in consumer books, educational and academic works, business and professional publishing, and reference lines. Simon & Schuster represents an elaborate network of divisions, imprints, and publishing groups that together address virtually all publishing categories and market niches. This powerhouse of publishing operates primarily from editorial environs at several New York addresses, as well offices in New Jersey, Virginia, San Francisco, and other United States locations.

S&S imprints and divisions include Simon & Schuster Trade Publishing, Simon & Schuster Children's Publishing Division, Simon & Schuster Interactive, Pocket Books, Scribner, The Free Press, Brassey's (U.S.), Jossey-Bass, The New Lexington Press,

Pfeiffer & Company, Prentice Hall, Silver Burdett Ginn, Allyn & Bacon, Computer Curriculum Corporation, Educational Management Group, and Macmillan Publishing USA.

Simon & Schuster Trade imprints, along with Scribner and Pocket Books programs and books from the Free Press, cover the commercial trade spectrum. In addition to its own trade lineup, Pocket Books maintains a traditional mass-market publishing concentration. Macmillan and Prentice Hall have commanding presence in professional, business, and academic publishing. Simon & Schuster Children's Publishing Division is a strapping domain of books for young readers.

The Simon & Schuster Trade Division is first and foremost a publisher of popular works, with a vast list that includes such imprints as Simon & Schuster, Touchstone, and Fireside.

Pocket Books publishes commercial works in fiction and nonfiction in hardcover, trade paperback, and mass-market paperback editions, and offers movie and television tie-ins on the Tundra imprint.

Simon & Schuster operates divisions (many under the Macmillan and Prentice Hall designations) devoted primarily to business, professional, computer publishing, and educational offerings, books in the arena of hobbies, horticulture, and travel, as well as personal development, lifestyle how-to, and general reference.

Simon & Schuster is the book-publishing flagship of Viacom-owned Paramount Communications. Viacom Inc. is an enormous communications colossus that straddles the media worlds of film, radio, television, video, electronics, and print.

Simon & Schuster (founded in 1924) was among America's largest publishing houses by the time it was acquired by Gulf + Western in 1975. Subsequent to the S&S acquisition, G+W transformed its own corporate tag to Paramount Communications, under which name it operated a megamedia conglomerate that encompassed film and television-broadcast and cable interests, videos, music, and electronic as well as print publishing enterprises.

In 1984 Simon & Schuster acquired Prentice Hall, itself a publisher of mammoth size and proven reputation for hitting exceedingly well-targeted professional and educational markets.

The 1994 acquisition by Paramount of the extensive remnants of the Macmillan Publishing Group fit nicely into a corporate tradition of multifaceted change and growth. The former trade-publishing wing of Macmillan was realigned (along with other S&S properties) under the Scribner imprint in 1994; by the middle of 1995, a new trade division emerged, bearing a refreshed Macmillan logo, to concentrate on practical nonfiction, business, and popular reference.

The Paramount Publishing designation was inaugurated in 1993 to cover all Simon & Schuster and Prentice Hall divisions, as well as the operations embraced in the Paramount buyout of Macmillan Publishing Group. Many Paramount Publishing lines continued to be issued under their historic imprints. In light of established trade-name recognition and publishing tradition, in May 1994 the name of the book-publishing umbrella reverted to what it had been—and thus the house of Simon & Schuster endures.

Simon & Schuster distributes its many constituent imprints and divisions (please see separate subentries below); S&S also handles distribution services for a number of smaller and midsize houses.

SIMON & SCHUSTER TRADE DIVISION

The Simon & Schuster logo (an iconic rendition of Jean François Millet's famous sower) signals hardcover and trade paperback books in a wide range of commercial nonfiction and fiction areas, generally selected for potential appeal to the broadest possible spectrum of mainstream and special-interest readerships.

In nonfiction, Simon & Schuster is ever a major player in such topical arenas as popular history and current affairs, popular culture, business, health, self-awareness and improvement, and popular biography and memoirs.

Nonfiction from S&S: *Apocalypse Now: Tales for a New (or at Least Very Low Mileage) Millennium* by James Finn Garner; *The Language of Names: What We Call Ourselves and Why It Matters* by Justin Kaplan and Anne Bernays; *Gods of Death: Around the World, Behind Closed Doors, Operates an Ultra Secret Business of Sex and Death, One Man Hunts the Truth About Snuff Films* by Yaron Svoray with Thomas Hughes; *The Heart of Parenting: Raising an Emotionally Intelligent Child* by John Gottman with Joan DeClaire; *The Road Less Traveled and Beyond* by M. Scott Peck; *Unlimited Power: A Black Choice* by Anthony Robbins and Joseph McClendon III; *The Maverick Mindset: Finding the Courage to Journey from Fear to Freedom* by Doug Hall with David Wecker; *The Dream Messenger: How Dreams of the Departed Bring Healing Gifts* by Patricia Garfield, Ph.D.; *Everywoman's Guide to Sexual Fulfillment* by Susan Quilliam; *The Assault on Parenthood: How Our Culture Undermines the Family* by Dana Mack; *John Wayne's America: The Politics of Celebrity* by Garry Wills; *You Can Make It Happen: A Nine-Step Plan for Success* by Stedman Graham; *Confessions of a Late-Night Talk-Show Host: The Autobiography of Larry Sanders* by Garry Shandling and David Rensin; *Susie Bright's Sexual State of the Union* by Susie Bright; *Spiritual Serendipity: Cultivating the Art of the Unexpected* by Richard Eyre; *Dreammaker: A Biography of Steven Spielberg* by Joseph McBride; *Jack Nicklaus: My Story* by Jack Nicklaus with Ken Bowden; *Rising Tide: The Great Mississippi Flood of 1927 and How It Changed America* by John M. Barry; *The Whole Shebang: The State-of-the-Universe Report* by Timothy Ferris; *Virtual Power: Living, Learning, Loving, and Positively Thriving with Your Personal Computer* by Mark Bunting; *Ben & Jerry's Double-Dip Capitalism: Lead with Your Values and Make Money Too* by Ben Cohen and Jerry Greenfield; *The Defense is Ready: Life in the Trenches of Criminal Law* by Leslie Abramson with Richard Flaste; *What Losing Taught Me About Winning: The Complete Book for Success in Small Business* by Fran Tarkenton.

Simon & Schuster's roster of popular fiction and literary writing include works of cultural note. Among Simon & Schuster's fiction authors are such popular and critically respected writers as Maxine Chernoff, Mary Higgins Clark, Jackie Collins, Andrei Codrescu, John Hawkes, Larry McMurtry, and Roxanne Pulitzer.

As a group these books address the mainstream popular readership; S&S titles are usually in the commercial frontlist mode, with topnotch representatives in mystery and suspense, Westerns, women's romances and family sagas, and adventure and espionage thrillers. S&S also produces literary history, biography, and memoirs; investigative narrative nonfiction; and literary inspirational works.

Fiction titles include: *Tycoon* by Harold Robbins; *The Killer's Game* by Jay Bonansinga; *Change of Heart* by Tracy Stern; *Triple Feature* by Louise Bagshawe;

Last Rites by Philip Shelby; *Fall on Your Knees* by Ann-Marie MacDonald; *Pretend You Don't See Her* by Mary Higgins Clark; *Charity* by Paulette Callen; *Hocus: An Irene Kelly Mystery* by Jan Burke; *One, Two, Buckle My Shoe* by Jessie Hunter.

Simon & Schuster Editions (series of deluxe editions of American short-novel classics): *Bartleby the Scrivener: A Story of Wall Street* by Herman Melville; *The Country of the Pointed Firs* by Sarah Orne Jewett; *Cruddy* by Lynda Barry.

Query letters and SASEs should be directed to:

Charles F. Adams, Senior Editor
Commercial fiction and nonfiction. Titles include *No Regrets* by Caroline Seebohm, *Armadillos & Old Lace* by Kinky Freidman, *Ray Had an Idea about Love* by Eddie Lewis, and *Off Stage* by Betty Comden.

Dominick Anfuso, Senior Editor
General nonfiction and literary fiction. Titles include *Dance with the Devil* by Susan Powter; *The Golf of Your Dreams* by Bob Rotella; *Off the Road: A Walk Down the Pilgrim's Route into Spain* by Jack Hitt; *The Blood Countess: A Novel* by Andrei Codrescu.

Robert Bender, Senior Editor
Popular psychology, natural history, health and fitness, literary biography; wide commercial interests (excluding new age and celebrity stories). Titles include *Sophia Loren* by Warren G. Harris; *Curing Cancer* by Michael Waldholtz; *The Science of Desire: The Search for the Gay Gene and the Biology of Behavior* by Dean Hamer and Peter Copeland.

Laurie Bernstein, Senior Editor
Commercial fiction and nonfiction. Projects include *Women Make the Best Friends* by Lois Wyse; *Shed 10 Years in 10 Weeks* by Julian Whitaker and Carol Colman; *Divided Lives: The Public and Private Struggles of Three Accomplished Women* by Elsa Walsh; *Trunk Show* by Alison Glen.

Laurie Chittenden, Senior Editor
Popular and commercial works in nonfiction. Occasional fiction. Specialty works: acquired the best-selling novelty book *The Xmas Box*. Also: *The Letter* by Richard Paul Evans.

Frederic W. Hills, Vice President and Senior Editor
General nonfiction, including biography and memoirs, modern history, business subjects, health and fitness, self-improvement. Titles include *The Language of Names* by Justin Kaplan and Anne Bernays; *Global Bargain Hunting* by Burton Malkiel and Mei Jianping; *Bitter Harvest* by Ann Rule; *When Your Doctor Doesn't Know Best* by Richard N. Podell, M.D., and William Proctor; *Imperfect Control* by Judith Viorst; *The Slightly Older Guy* by Bruce Jay Freidman.

Michael Korda, Editor in Chief
Commercial fiction and nonfiction. *Flood Tide* by Clive Cussler; *Comanche Moon* by Larry McMurtry. With **Charles Adams** (see separate entry above): *Climbing the Mountain* by Kirk Douglas; *Footnotes* by Tommy Tune.

Elizabeth C. Mackey, Executive Editor, S&S Audio
Audio projects.

Alice Mayhew, Editorial Director, Simon & Schuster Trade Division
Politics, current events, contemporary biographies and memoirs. Projects include *Making the Most of Your Money* by Jane Bryant Quinn; *Pillar of Fire* by Taylor Branch; *In Love with Daylight* by Wilfrid Sheed; *Taking Charge* by Michael Bechloss; *Darwin's Dangerous Idea* by Daniel C. Dennett.

Marion Maneker, Senior Editor
Serious nonfiction.

Bob Mecoy, Editor
Commercial fiction. Nonfiction in psychology, science, and technology. Titles include *You Have More Than You Think* by Tom Gardner and David Gardner; *Ring Game* by Pete Hautman; *Into the Twilight, Endlessly Grousing* by Patrick F. McManus; *One Must Wait* by Penny Micklebury.

Mary Ann Naples, Senior Editor
Quality fiction. Nonfiction: cultural issues, psychology, celebrity, music, pop culture, biography, and spiritual books. Projects include *Courtney Love* by Poppy Brite; *Illuminated Prayers* by Marianne Williamson; *Beyond Dreams and Beasts: Computers and the Culture of Simulation* by Sherry Turkle.

Jeff Neuman, Senior Editor
Sports stories and biographies; humor. Titles include *Year of the Cat* by Scott Fowler and Charles Chandler; *Under the Lone Star Flagstick* by Melanie Hauser; *Postcard from Hell* by Rex Dancer.

Rick Richter, President and Publisher
Commercial projects in nonfiction and fiction.

Bill Rosen, Simon & Schuster Editions; Vice President and Associate Publisher for Illustrated Books for the Simon & Schuster Group
In charge of illustrated books and special projects.

Rebecca Saletan, Senior Editor
Psychology, popular science, journalism, women's issues, fiction. Titles include *Right-Brained Children in a Left-Brained World* by Jennrey Freed and Laurie Parsons; *Cuisine of the Water Gods* by Patricia Quintana, *Fire Your Shrink!* by Michele Weiner-Davis.

SIMON & SCHUSTER TRADE PAPERBACKS
FIRESIDE BOOKS
TOUCHSTONE BOOKS
SCRIBNER PAPERBACK FICTION
FREE PRESS PAPERBACKS

1230 Avenue of the Americas
New York, NY 10020
212-698-7000

Editors at Simon & Schuster Trade Paperbacks division can acquire for the following imprints: Fireside, Touchstone, Scribner Paperback Fiction, and Free Press Paperbacks; editors also acquire hardcover for Simon & Schuster, Scribner, and Free Press.

Fireside, Simon & Schuster's principal trade paperback imprint, covers the entire slate of commercial nonfiction categories. House emphasis includes current affairs, popular culture, business and finance, fitness and health, sports, games (including crossword puzzles), lifestyle and hobbies, and parenting.

Fireside Books concentrates on original nonfiction (mainly in trade paper with some hardcover) and trade paperback reprints covering the mainstream commercial field.

Simon & Schuster's Touchstone Books imprint emphasizes popular nonfiction in trade paper and mass-market reprint editions, many of which have been originally published in hardcover by Simon & Schuster. Touchstone also issues selected original titles.

Selected titles from Simon & Schuster Trade Paperbacks (Touchstone, Scribner Paperback Fiction, Free Press Paperbacks): *Tumbling* (fiction) by Diane McKinney-Whetstone; *Undaunted Courage: Meriwether Lewis, Thomas Jefferson, and the Opening of the American West* by Stephen E. Ambrose; *Megatrends Asia: Eight Asian Megatrends That Are Reshaping Our World* by John Naisbitt; *The End of Alice* (fiction) by A. M. Homes; *Management of the Absurd: Paradoxes in Leadership* by Richard Farson (foreword by Michael Crichton); *Beachcombing for a Shipwrecked God* (fiction) by Joe Coomer; *The Song of the Dodo: Island Biogeography in an Age of Extinctions* by David Quammen; *Time and Again* (fiction) by Jack Finney.

More from Simon & Schuster Trade Paperbacks (Fireside, Kaplan Interactive, Simon & Schuster Libros en Español): *Living Lean, The Larry North Program: It's Not About Perfection, It's About Progress* by Larry North; *1001 Reasons to Think Positive: Special Insights to Achieve a Better Attitude Towards Life* by Ella Patterson; *God Wants You To Be Rich: How and Why Everyone Can Enjoy Material and Spiritual Wealth in Our Abundant World* by Paul Zane Pilzer; *The Healing Choice: Your Guide to Emotional Recovery After an Abortion* by Candace De Puy, Ph.D. and Dana Dovitch, Ph.D.; *Italian So Fat, Low Fat, No Fat* by Betty Rohde; *Guests Without Grief: Entertaining Made Easy for the Hesitant Host* by Paul Jhung; *Timeless Healing: The Power and Biology of Belief* by Herbert Benson, M.D. with Marg Stark.

Query letters and SASEs should be directed to:

Trish Todd, Vice President and Editor in Chief
Areas consistent with the house description, particularly popular and commercial works in the areas of psychology, sociology, social history, biography, and self-help.

Sarah Baker, Associate Editor
Political issues, current events, psychology/self-help, music, women's subjects, fiction. Projects include *A Voice of Her Own* by Marlene Schiwy, *Dancing at the Rascal Fair* by Ivan Doig, and *Having an Abortion* by K. Kaufmann.

Becky Cabaza, Senior Editor
General self-help, popular reference, health and fitness, humor, and fiction. Projects include *Maternal Fitness: Preparing for a Healthy Pregnancy, The Homebrewer's Recipe Guide, and Selena's Secret: The Real Story Behind Her Tragic Death*. Fiction titles include *A Place Where the Sea Remembers* by Sandra Benitez (winner of the Barnes & Noble Discover Award) and *The Shipping News* by E. Annie Proulx (winner of the Pulitzer Prize and National Book Award). Looking for projects for the Simon & Schuster Aguilar Libros en Español list.

Dawn M. Daniels, Editor
Black, Latino, and Asian studies, literary fiction, health and fitness, career-oriented books, and self-help/motivation topics. Also works with Simon & Schuster Aguilar Libros en Español. Projects include *Acts of Faith: Daily Meditations for People of Color* by Iyanla Vanzant, *About My Sister's Business: The Black Woman's Road Map to Successful Entrepreneurship, Flyy Girl* (fiction) by Omar Tyree, and *To Do, Doing, Done: A Simple Process for Creating Results and Finishing Everything You Start.*

Penny Kaganoff, Senior Editor
Fiction, religion, women's studies, Judaica, history, politics, personal memoir, archaeology, anthropology, film, fitness, and cooking. Titles include *Lies my Teacher Told Me* by James Loewen, *The World of Jewish Cooking* by Gil Marks, *The Concise Conservative Encyclopedia* (edited by Brad Miner), and *Scribner's Best of the Fiction Workshops* (edited by John Kulka and Natalie Danford).

Sydny Weinberg Miner, Executive Editor
Women's issues, family and childcare, education, health, psychology and self-help, inspiration, multicultural projects, food and cooking, science, nature, and fishing. Titles include *The Firefighter's Cookbook* by John Sineno, *A Penny Saved: Teaching Your Children the Values and Life Skills They Will Need to Live in the Real World* by Neale Godfrey, *The Third Force: A Novel of the Gadget* by Mark Laidwal, and *Re-Envisioning the Earth: A Guide to Opening the Healing Channels between Mind and Nature* by Paul Devereux.

Sarah W. Pinckney, Editor
Humor/pop culture, business, literary fiction, self-help, and spirituality. Open to projects written by and geared specifically toward the youthful adult audience.

Betsy Radin Herman, Editor
Psychology/self-help, fiction, humor, parenting, pop reference, pet and gift books, and "merch." Titles include *Poems for Life* by the Nightingale-Bradford School, *Exorcising Your Ex: How to Get Rid of Demons from Relationships Past* by Elizabeth Kuster, and *Difficult Questions Kids Ask (and Are Afraid to Ask) About Divorce* by Meg Scheider and Joan Zuckerberg. Fiction includes *Winter Birds* by Jim Grimsley and *Water from the Well* by Myra McLarey.

Caroline Sutton, Senior Editor
Focus on new age/spirituality, alternative medicine, and psychology. Also interested in serious fiction, narrative nonfiction—especially personal journeys. Would like to do the right cat book. Projects include *Touching Spirit, Mortally Wounded,* and *Beauty* (a first novel) by Susan Wilson.

POCKET BOOKS
WASHINGTON SQUARE PRESS

1230 Avenue of the Americas
New York, NY 10020
212-698-7000

The Pocket Books division of Simon & Schuster produces commercial fiction and non-fiction in hardcover and trade paperback editions while maintaining its tradition of mammoth mass-market paperback presence. Pocket Books is currently structured into three separate units: adult fiction and nonfiction; Star Trek Books; and Pocket Books for Young Adults.

Nonfiction from Pocket hits all sectors of the popular spectrum, including current issues, contemporary culture, health and fitness, relationships, self-awareness, personal finance, celebrity-based stories, humor, games and puzzles, and popular reference.

Pocket Books maintains a powerful category-fiction list that includes originals and reprints in such genres as thrillers and suspense, romance, science fiction (including the Star Trek series), fantasy, action adventure, and horror; in addition, the house produces original commercial and literary fiction (with many of the literary works issued under the **Washington Square Press** imprint).

Pocket Books offers a line of books for young adults, including a number of solid fiction and nonfiction series.

Nonfiction and popular works from the Pocket Books list: *Renovating Woman: A Guide to Home Repair, Maintenance, and Real Men* by Allegra Bennett; *Pimps, Whores, and Welfare Brats: The Reformation of a Welfare Queen* by Star Parker; *"Children of the Troubles": Our Lives in the Crossfire of Northern Ireland* by Laurel Holliday; *Wings of Fury: From Vietnam to the Gulf War—the Astonishing, True Stories of America's Elite Fighter Pilots* by Robert Wilcox; *The Day After Roswell* by Colonel Philip J. Corso with William J. Birnes; *Heart and Soul: A Psychological and Spiritual Guide to Preventing and Healing Heart Disease* by Bruno Cortis, M.D.; *The Gods of Golf* by David L. Smith and John P. Holms; *Leadership Secrets of the Rogue Warrior* (and others in the series) by Richard Marchinko; *Let's Be Heard: The Uncensored Views of the Nations' Most Controversial Broadcaster—with a New Chapter About the Cost of Free Speech!* by Bob Grant; *A Dog in Heat Is a Hot Dog and Other Rules to Live By* by E. Jean Carroll.

Pocket Books fiction, literary writing, and cultural chronicles: *She's Come Undone* by Wally Lamb; *Dark Homecoming* by Eric Lustbader; *Audrey Hepburn's Neck* by Alan Brown; *Avenger* by William Shatner (part of the Star Trek line); *I Still Miss My Man, But My Aim Is Getting Better* by Sarah Shankman; *Jackson Street and Other Soldier Stories* by John A. Miller; *Hidden Latitudes* by Alison Anderson; *Hoopi Shoopi Donna* by Suzanne Strempek Shea; *Guinevere: The True Story of One Woman's Quest for Her Past Life Identity and the Healing of Her Eternal Soul* by Laurel Phelan; *Hiding My Candy* by the Lady Chablis with Theodore Bouloukos II; *Lord of the Dead* by Tom Holland; *Tarnished Gold* by V. C. Andrews; *Knights* by Linda Lael Miller; *Defiance County* by Jay Brandon; *The Journal of Callie Wade* by Dawn Miller.

From Paradox Graphic Mysteries: *A History of Violence* (written by John Wagner; illustrated by Vince Locke); *Green Candles* (written by Tom DeHaven; illustrated by Robin Smith).

Pocket Books (founded in 1937) was America's first publisher to specialize in customized drugstore/newsstand rack-size paperback editions. Today, the house excels in both original titles and reprint lines brought out under its well-known reading-kangaroo logo (what better animal to convey the notion of a pouch-size edition?).

Query letters and SASEs should be directed to:

Emily Bestler, Vice President and Editorial Director
Varied nonfiction including health, family, parenting, inspirational, popular science, lifestyle. Commercial fiction: thrillers, mysteries.

Jane Cavolina, Senior Editor
Wide range of interests in commercial nonfiction and popular fiction. Celebrity bios; topical interest; self-improvement. Frontlist fiction, mysteries, thrillers, suspense.

Tristram Coburn, Associate Editor
Military and political nonfiction. Action-adventure fiction; military and espionage stories. Works with Paul McCarthy.

Gary Goldstein, Senior Editor

Mitchell Ivers, Senior Editor

Greer Kessel, Associate Editor, Pocket Books and Washington Square Press
Popular nonfiction. Health, sports, popular culture, some humor. Literary fiction from established as well as emerging voices.

Nancy Miller, Senior Editor, Pocket Books and Washington Square Press
Popular nonfiction. Health, sports, popular culture, some humor. Literary fiction: established as well as emerging voices. Washington Square Press publishes a strong line of nonfiction and fiction reprints.

Amy Pierpont, Assistant Editor

Julie Rubenstein, Executive Editor
Commercial fiction, women's nonfiction. Narrative nonfiction: women's interest, health. Does a lot of reprints.

Dan Slater, Editorial Assistant
Media tie-ins. High-edge fiction.

Dave Stern, Senior Editor
Wide range of commercial nonfiction. Men's fiction: adventures, mysteries, thrillers. Special area: cyberfiction; nonfiction pertaining to the internet and new technology.

Caroline Tolley, Senior Editor
Historical romances.

POCKET BOOKS STAR TREK BOOKS

Query letters and SASEs should be directed to:

Kara Welsh, Vice President and Associate Publisher

Kevin Ryan, Editorial Director

John Ordover, Editor

POCKET BOOKS FOR YOUNG ADULTS

Query letters and SASEs should be directed to:

Patricia MacDonald, Vice President and Editorial Director

Nancy Pines, Vice President and Associate Publisher

Ruth Ashby, Editor

Lisa Clancy, Editor

SCRIBNER

1230 Avenue of the Americas
New York, NY 10020
212-698-7000

Scribner publishes trade fiction and nonfiction, with much of the list devoted to authoritative and accomplished writing. Scribner nonfiction covers current events, cultural history, biography, criticism, science, true crime, and popular reference. Scribner is home to Lisa Drew Books, a feature line with an especially hard-hitting commercial approach to frontlist publishing. The Rawson Associates imprint concentrates on self-awareness, health, and business books. Fiction from Scribner embraces the range of commercial literary interests and tastes; the house is particularly strong (and admired) in crime fiction, and hosts a number of ongoing mystery series.

Scribner often acquires hard/soft with other S&S divisions, including Touchstone, Fireside, and the Scribner Paperback Fiction imprint, as well as with Pocket Books.

The Scribner list bears the name as well as the midnight-reader's oil-lamp logo of the former Charles Scribner's Sons, Publishers, originally an independent firm (founded in 1846). The house subsequently became part of Macmillan; following the acquisition of Macmillan by Simon & Schuster, much of the Macmillan trade operation was taken over by the Scribner program. In addition, remnants of the former Atheneum imprint were added to the Scribner lineup.

Nonfiction titles from Scribner: *Translating History: Thirty Years on the Front Lines of Diplomacy with a Top Russian Interpreter* by Igor Korchilov; *The Riverkeepers: Two Activists Fight to Reclaim Our Environment As a Basic Human Right* by John Cronin and Robert F. Kennedy, Jr.; *The Wheel of Life: A Memoir of Living and Dying* by Elisabeth Kübler-Ross, M.D.; *Timeshare on the River Styx: Waking Up Screaming from the American Dream* by Bob Garfield; *Make a Difference: Henry W. Foster, M.D., Founder of the "I Have a Future" Program, Shares His Vision for Young America* (with Alice Greenwood); *Tee Times: On the Road with the Ladies' Professional Golf Tour* by Jim Burnett; *Colleen Dewhurst: Her Autobiography* (written with and supplemented by Tom Viola); *The ADDed Dimension: Everyday Advice for Adults with ADD* by Kate Kelly, Peggy Ramundo, and Steven Ledingham; *The Art of Fact: An Historical Anthology of Literary Journalism* by Kevin Kerrane and Ben Yagoda; *Molecules of Emotion: Why You Feel the Way You Feel* by Candace B. Pert, Ph.D.; *Second Act: A Personal and Practical Guide to Life After Colostomy* by Barbara Barrie; *Does the World Need the Jews? Rethinking Chosenness and American Jewish Identity* by Daniel Grodis; *Should You Leave? A Psychiatrist Explores Intimacy and Autonomy—and the Nature of Advice* by Peter Kramer, M.D.

Of popular note: *Coyote Medicine: Lessons from Native American Healing* by Lewis Mehl-Madrona; *Dog Eat Dog: A Very Human Book About Dogs and Dog Shows* by Jane and Michael Stern; *Don't Stand Here: Single Mothers and the Myth of the Welfare Queen* by David Zucchino; *Awakening to Zen Teachings* by Roshi Philip Kapleau;

Letitia Baldrige's More Than Manners: Raising Today's Kids to Have Good Manners & Kind Hearts by Letitia Baldrige; *Bill James' Guide to Baseball Managers: From 1870 to Present* by Bill James; *Serious Business: Cartoons in America from Betty Boop to Toy Story* by Stefan Kanfer; *The Trouble with Testosterone, and Other Essays on the Biology of the Human Predicament* by Robert M. Sapolsky; *Money: Who Has How Much and Why* by Andrew Hacker; *Jimmy Carter: A Comprehensive Biography from Plains to Post-Presidency* by Peter G. Bourne; *Prescription for Profits: How the Pharmaceutical Industry Bankrolled the Unholy Marriage Between Science and Business* by Linda Marsa.

Scribner fiction and literary writing includes: *The Falling Boy* by David Long; *Time on My Hands: A Novel with Photographs* by Peter Delacorte; *Accordion Crimes* (novel) by E. Annie Proulx, *The Luckiest Girl in the World* by Steven Levenkron; *Sanctuary: A Tale of Life in the Woods* by Paul Monette (illustrated by Vivienne Flesher); *The Dogs of Winter* by Kem Nunn; *Go Now* (novel) by Richard Hell; *Off the Face of the Earth* by Aljean Harmetz; *The Rescue of Memory* by Cheryl Sucher; *Terrestrials: A Novel of Aviation* by Paul West.

Mystery, suspense, and crime fiction from Scribner (no alibis will hold if you maintain these genres are in all ways literary): *Likely to Die* by Linda Fairstein; *A Deadly Vineyard Holiday* (a Martha's Vineyard mystery) by Philip R. Craig; *Life Before Death* by Abby Frucht; *Foamers: A Novel of Suspense* by Jon Berson; *Giotto's Hand* (a Jonathan Argyll mystery) by Iain Pears; *Three to Get Deadly* (a Stephanie Plum novel) by Janet Evanovich; *Doubled in Spades* (a Cassandra Swann mystery) by Susan Moody; *Past Tense* (a John Marshall Tanner novel) by Stephen Greenleaf; *Caught in a Rundown* (a novel introducing Jewel Averick and Dee Sweet) by Lisa Saxton; *Full Frontal Murder* (a mystery with Marian Larch) by Barbara Paul; *Hard Bargain* (a Cat Marsala mystery) by Barbara D'Amato.

Lisa Drew Books hones a select list in the area of current events and high-interest nonfiction, along with some popular fiction. From Lisa Drew: *Quest for Perfection: The Engineering of Human Beings* by Gina Maranto; *Napoleon and Josephine: An Improbable Marriage* by Evangeline Bruce; *Wasteland* (crime novel) by Peter McCabe.

Query letters and SASEs should be directed to:

Gillian Blake, Editor
Commercial and literary fiction and nonfiction consistent with the Scribner list. Projects include *For Colored Girls Who Have Considered Suicide/When the Rainbow Is Enuf* by Ntozake Shange; *Nixon's Ten Commandments of Statecraft: Commentary and Lessons from History* by James Hume; *Clement Greenburg: A Life* by Florence Rubenfeld.

Lisa Drew, Publisher, Lisa Drew Books
Commercial nonfiction, including high-interest history, celebrity biographies, and current affairs. Popular fiction. Titles include *George Bush: The Life of a Lone Star Yankee* by Herbert S. Parmet; *Michael and Natasha: The Life and Love of Michael II, the Last of the Romanov Tsars* by Rosemary and Donald Crawford; *A History of American Life* (abridged and revised by Mark C. Carnes and Arthur M. Schlesinger, Jr.).

Nan Graham, Vice President and Editor in Chief
American literary fiction; fiction about clashing cultures—Third World and European. Nonfiction interests include contemporary social and political issues, women's studies,

historical and literary biography, and biographies of artists. Projects include *Underworld* by Don DeLillo; *Love in a Blue Time* by Hanif Kureishi; *Accordion Crimes* by E. Annie Proulx.

Maria Guarnaschelli, Senior Editor
Literary biographies, popular science, cookbooks. Wide range of trade interests, including fiction. Projects include *The Joy of Cooking* by Irma S. Rombauer, Marion Rombauer Becker, and Ethan Becker; *The Chimera* by Sebastiano Vasalli.

Leigh Haber, Senior Editor
Literary fiction. Nonfiction consistent with house description. Projects include *The Year of Reading Proust* by Phyllis Rose; *The Skull of Charlotte Corday and Other Stories* by Leslie Dick; *Eating Chinese Food Naked* by Mei Ng; *Go Now* by Richard Hell.

Susanne Kirk, Senior Editor
Mystery and suspense fiction. Titles include *Déjà Dead* by Kathy Reichs; *Dreaming of the Bones* by Deborah Crombie; *Tequila Mockingbird* by Paul Bishop; *Final Jeopardy* by Linda Fairstein; *Death on a Vineyard Beach* by Philip R. Craig.

Susan Moldow, Publisher
Areas consistent with house interest. Projects include *The Illusionist* by Dinitia Smith; *The Color Code* by Taylor Hartman, Ph.D.; *Three Gospels* by Reynolds Price.

Scott Moyers, Editor
Commercial and literary fiction and nonfiction consistent with the house list. Projects include *Prospecting Your Way to Sales Success* by Bill Good; *Lost Laysen* by Margaret Mitchell (author of *Gone with the Wind*).

Bill Rosen, Simon & Schuster Editions; Vice President and Associate Publisher for Illustrated Books for the Simon & Schuster Group
Projects include *The Woven Figure* by George F. Will; *The Middle East* by Bernard Lewis.

Jane Rosenman, Senior Editor
Literary fiction, commercial nonfiction. Projects include *Good Meat* by Bruce Aidelis and Denis Kelly; *Name-Dropping* by Alan King; *There's a Word for It!* by Charles Harrington Elster.

RAWSON ASSOCIATES

1230 Avenue of the Americas
New York, NY 10020
212-698-7000

Rawson Associates produces selected books in health and diet, self-help, popular psychology, and business how-to. Representative Rawson projects: *Filling the Void: Six Steps from Loss to Fulfillment* by Dorothy Bullitt; *Healing the Child: A Mother's Story* by Nancy Cain; *Rejecting Mothers, Wounded Daughters* by Ann Symonds.

Query letters and SASEs should be directed to:

Eleanor Rawson, Publisher

THE FREE PRESS

1230 Avenue of the Americas
New York, NY 10020
212-698-7000

The Free Press produces trade nonfiction titles with emphasis on business, biography, psychology, history, and current affairs; the division also presents general-interest works that address popular contemporary themes. The Free Press also publishes professional and academic books in the social sciences and humanities.

New Republic Books is a Free Press imprint (published in association with *New Republic* magazine) that specializes in works that explore contemporary social and political issues.

Popular titles from the Free Press list: *The Diversity Machine* by Frederick R. Lynch; *The Coming Russian Boom* by Richard Layard and John Parker; *The Patriot: An Exhortation to Liberate America from the Barbarians* by Gary Hart; *When Someone You Love Is Depressed* by Laura Epstein Rosen and Xavier F. Amador; *Taking Judaism Personally* by Judy Petsonk; *The Landmark Thucydides* (edited by Robert B. Strassler); *The Idea of Decline in Western History* by Arthur Herman.

Query letters and SASEs should be directed to:

Susan Arellano, Senior Editor
Psychology and behavioral sciences.

Adam Bellow, Vice President and Editorial Director
Politics, history, current affairs.

Janet Coleman, Senior Editor
General nonfiction; business and management topics.

Mitch Horowitz, Senior Editor
Politics and current affairs.

Bruce Nichols, Senior Editor
History, economics, military history.

Robert Wallace, Vice President and Senior Editor
Business and economics (not popular or how-to topics).

SIMON & SCHUSTER REFERENCE DIVISIONS

The reference division of Simon & Schuster, Macmillan Publishing USA covers books in the areas of general, popular, business, professional, and library reference. A number of individual imprints appear, each staking claim to a piece of the house's diverse reference-publishing turf.

Major lines and imprints include Macmillan General Reference, Macmillan Computer Publishing, and Macmillan Library Reference. Additional imprints and lines include Audel, Howell Book House, and Schirmer Books.

Subsequent to the Macmillan buyout, the trade designations as well as the organization of the company's reference divisions underwent dramatic changes. The names and components of the divisions profiled below are therefore subject to change, though it is anticipated that their established publishing programs will continue by whatever appellation they are known.

MACMILLAN PUBLISHING USA
MACMILLAN GENERAL REFERENCE USA
MACMILLAN BOOKS
MACMILLAN TRAVEL
MACMILLAN BRANDS
HOWELL BOOK HOUSE
ALPHA BOOKS
ARCO
AUDEL
SCHIRMER BOOKS
LASSERS
WEBSTERS

1633 Broadway, 7th Floor
New York, NY 10019
212-654-1000; 212-654-8500
fax: 212-654-4850

Macmillan Publishing hosts trade reference, library reference, and special-interest as well as general trade lines. The reference divisions of the Macmillan General Reference umbrella offer specialized as well as general lines, including commercial trade nonfiction, popular and consumer reference, business and professional reference, and titles slated for the institutional market.

Macmillan General Reference publishes a gamut of categories under the following inprints: Macmillan Books, Macmillan Travel, Macmillan Brands, Howell Book House.

Macmillan Books (Natalie Chapman, publisher): Popular reference, cookbooks, sports, health, business, illustrated reference, atlases, general-interest nonfiction. Representative titles: *The New York Yankee Encyclopedia; How to Get Out of the Hospital Alive; The New York Public Library American History Desk Reference; Family Pride: The Complete Guide to Tracing African-American Genealogy.*

Macmillan Travel (Michael Spring, publisher): Frommer's travel guides, Baedeker Guides; Travel & Leisure Guides, and Unofficial Guides.

Macmillan Brands (Susan Clarey, publisher) Weight Watchers; Betty Crocker; Burpee Books.

Alpha Books (Lloyd Short, publisher): hooks into traditional how-to/self-help areas with an accent on awareness and inspiration, careers and personal finance, lifestyle, and humor; Complete Idiot's Guides on a wide variety of practical and lifestyle subjects (see subentry).

The **Audel** series is made up of reference books on home repair that provide practical information in such areas as plumbing, house wiring, and pumps, listing titles such as *Questions and Answers for Electricians' Examinations* revised by Paul Rosenberg and *Professional Tiling* by Edwin M. Field and Selma G. Field.

Howell Book House (Sean Frawley, publisher) is an imprint that specializes in pet care and training books (including dogs, cats, horses, and other animals), as well as equestrian titles. On the Howell list: *Pet Owner's Guide to the Shetland Sheepdog* by Mary Davis; *Practical Dressage* by Jane Kidd; *The Less-Than-Perfect Rider* by Lesley Bayley and Caroline Davis; a line of pet-care works by Tim Hawcroft (titles include: *First Aid for Birds*; *First Aid for Cats*; and *First Aid for Dogs*).

Arco (Kevin Umeh, publisher): Test-preparation and career guides.

Lassers (Kevin Umeh, publisher): Tax guides.

Schirmer Books produces books in the area of music, including references, cultural histories, biography and memoir, and illustrated works. Representative of the Schirmer list: *More Opening Nights on Broadway: A Critical Quote Book of the Musical Theatre, 1965–1981* by Steven Suskin; *Frank Zappa Companion: Four Decades of Commentary* (edited by Richard Kostelanetz); *Blank Generation Revisited: Early Days of Punk Rock* (photographs by Roberta Bayley, Stephanie Chernikowski, George Du Bose, Gadlis, Bob Gruen, and Ebet Roberts; foreword by Glenn O'Brien; introduction by Lenny Kaye); *Road Stories and Recipes* by Don Nix; *Chopin* by Jim Samson (in the Master Musicians series).

Websters (Marie Butler-Knight, publisher): Dictionaries, language guides.

Macmillan General Reference

Natalie Chapman, Publisher, Macmillan Books
General nonfiction, illustrated reference, popular reference, historical and popular atlases.

Ken Samelson, Editor, Macmillan books
Sports reference and instructional.

Betsy Thorpe, Editor, Macmillan Books
Health, popular reference.

Jennifer Griffin, Editor
Cookbooks.

Michael Spring, Publisher, Macmillan Travel
Travel guides.

Kevin Umeh, Publisher, Consumer Information Group
Test preparation, career, self-help, business.

Marie Butler-Knight, Publisher, Websters
Dictionaries, language guides.

Sean Frawley, Publisher, Howell Book House
Pet care and training books.

Madelyn Larsen, Senior Editor, Howell Book House
Equestrian books.

Macmillan Library Reference

Geoff Golson, Publisher, Single-Volume Reference
Encyclopedias, companions, geographic atlases, academic atlases.

Karen Day, Publisher, Charles Scribners Sons
Multivolume reference books in the areas of world literature and world history for school, public, and college libraries.

Elly Dickason, Publisher, Macmillan Reference
Multivolume reference books in the areas of world literature and world history for school, public, and college libraries.

MACMILLAN COMPUTER PUBLISHING

David Israel, Vice President and Publisher
Query via New York office (see subentry for Macmillan Computer Publishing).

ARCO

Linda Bernbach, Editorial Director, Arco
Test prep, careers, study aids.

Eve Steinberg, Senior Editor
Study guides, education-reference materials, self-help, popular reference.

ALPHA BOOKS

Alpha Books and its highly successful Complete Idiot's Guide series takes the intimidation out of a wide range of complex subjects—from cooking to car repair to philosophy to yoga. This user-friendly series, known for its staple humorous sidebars and cartoon art, has recently ventured into the realms of pop culture (*The Complete Idiot's Guide to Elvis*), new age (*The Complete Idiot's Guide to Astrology*), and sports (*The Complete Idiot's Guide to Understanding Football Like a Pro*). Among the house's best-selling titles are: *The Complete Idiot's Guide to Dating* and *The Complete Idiot's Guide to Wall Street*. Prospective authors: Please query first for author guidelines.

   Query letters and SASEs should be directed to:

Gary Krebs, Executive Editor, Alpha Books
The Complete Idiot's Guide series; topical and humorous general reference.

Nancy Mikhail, Acquisitions Editor, Alpha Books
Lifestyles, sports, careers, education, relationships, general self-help. Oversees Complete Idiot's line of titles.

Lloyd Short, Publisher, Alpha Books

FIVE STAR ROMANCE
A DIVISION OF MACMILLAN PUBLISHING USA

P.O. Box 403
Unity, ME 04988
800-223-1244 (orders)

Five Star is a division of Macmillan Publishing USA that produces a line of category romance fiction. Five Star Romances feature bestselling romance authors produced in editions designed for and sold to the library market, primarily on a subscription basis. Five Star books are library-bound hardcover volumes, guaranteed to survive the rigors of this high-interest patronage.

Samples: *Wish List* by Fern Michaels; *The Fulfillment* by LaVyrle Spencer; *Valentine* by Jane Feather; *Fast Courting* by Barbara Delinsky; *The Rebel Bride* by Catherine Coulter.

The Five Star Romance list is focused on high-recognition author names in reprint editions. Publishers, editors, agents, or subsidiary-rights persons who are interested in purveying reprint rights to works by established authors of romance fiction should initiate contact with inquiry through the Macmillan Publishing USA offices in New York.

PRENTICE HALL DIRECT
PRENTICE HALL CAREER AND PERSONAL DEVELOPMENT
PRENTICE HALL BUSINESS, TRAINING & HEALTHCARE GROUP

240 Frisch Court
Paramus, NJ 07652
201-909-6415

Prentice Hall produces an extensive trade list in hardcover and trade paperback that accents books keyed to diverse career and business orientations, as well as noteworthy lines in such areas as health, fitness, and lifestyle—geared for direct-mail audiences.

Prentice Hall is a respected publisher in the educational arena; the educational and textbook divisions of Prentice Hall produce series in all subject and curricula areas for the youngest students through postgraduates, along with professional reference works in such fields as law and engineering.

This house is not known for strong distribution to the trade; it specializes in direct marketing and sales to the individual, corporate, and institutional markets. The business and professional division is widely known for the targeted mailing lists it compiles; some of these lists contain more than a million names and addresses.

Sample titles: *Winning! Using Lawyers' Courtroom Techniques to Get Your Way in Everyday Situations* by Noelle C. Nelson; *60-Minute Financial Planner* by Dana Shilling; *Double Your Brainpower* by Jean Marie Stein; *Reflexology Remedies* by Richard Leviton and Judith Lewis; *Speak and Grow Rich* by Dottie Walters and Lilly Walters; *Dive Right In—The Sharks Won't Bite* by Jane Weisman; *Naked Marketing: The Bare Essentials* by Robert Stede; *Break the Weight-Loss Barrier* by Jim Meschino, M.D. and Barry Simon, M.D.; *Heinerman's Encyclopedia of Healing Juices* by John Heinerman; *Doing Business in the New Vietnam* by Christopher Engholm; *Paralegal Practices and Procedure* by Deborah Larbalestrier; *The Broker's Edge* by Steven Drosdeck and Karl Gretz; *Violence at Work: How to Make Your Company Safer for Employees and Customers* by Joseph A. Kinney.

Query letters and SASEs should be directed to:

Eugene F. Brissie, Vice President and Editorial Director, Business and Self-Improvement
Business, management, health, and self-improvement.

Ellen Schneid Coleman, Executive Editor
Professional and personal finance, accounting.

Luis Gonzales, Senior Editor
All areas of business.

Douglas Corcoran, Editor
Health and fitness books, with emphasis on natural healing.

Karen Hansen, Senior Editor
Human resources, training, marketing, advertising, sales, secretarial skills, personal self-improvement.

Susan McDermott, Editor
Plant and operations management, environmental management, existing law books.

Tom Power, Senior Editor
General how-to business titles, management, career, spoken and written communications.

PRENTICE HALL PROFESSIONAL TECHNICAL REFERENCE DIVISION

240 Frisch Court
Paramus, NJ 07652
201-909-6415; 201-816-4110

Query letters and SASEs should be directed to:

Stephen G. Guty, Executive Editor
Computer operating systems; software development tools.

MACMILLAN COMPUTER PUBLISHING

Macmillan Computer Publishing comprises several imprints and subsidiaries from around the Simon & Schuster publishing domain. These programs produce titles rated all along the beginner–intermediate–advanced-user spectrum. As a group, these houses address such areas as accounting and finance, audio, computer-aided design (CAD), children's games, databases and integrated systems, desktop publishing, graphics, multimedia, hardware and utilities, Macintosh, networking and communications, operating systems, professional reference, programming, spreadsheets, and word processing.

The several imprints herein all publish computer books—some of them exclusively. The editorial orientation of each imprint seeks to define its own specialized market niche. However, there is some overlap, and interested authors (in addition to consulting the publishers' current catalogs) might therefore find it advisable to query more than one imprint simultaneously and separately with regard to proposed computer-book projects.

On the Macmillan Computer Publishing list: *New Riders' Official InterNet Yellow Pages*; *Andrew Tobias' Managing Your Money*; *Advanced Digital Audio*; *AutoCAD for Beginners*; *Alpha-Bytes Fun with Computers*; *Introduction to Databases*; *Quick and Dirty Harvard Graphics Presentations*; *IBM Personal Computer Troubleshooting & Repair*; *Cool Mac Clip Art Plus!*; *Workgroup Computing with Windows*; *Using Assembly Language*; *Introduction to Programming*.

MACMILLAN COMPUTER PUBLISHING USA
BRADY BOOKS
BradyGAMES
HAYDEN BOOKS
NEW RIDERS PUBLISHING/NRP
QUE
SAMS PUBLISHING
SAMS.NET
WAITE GROUP PRESS
ZIFF-DAVIS PRESS

201 West 103rd Street
Indianapolis, IN 46290
317-581-3500

This parcel of specialist publishers—ranging from former independents to freshly minted imprints—covers a vast domain of trade computer publishing within the corporate structure and marketing arm of Macmillan Computer Publishing.

Macmillan Computer Publishing imprints: Brady Books, BradyGAMES, Hayden Books, New Riders, Que, Sams Publishing, Sams.net, Waite Group Press, Ziff-Davis Press.

The **Brady Books** subsidiary produces authoritative works from experts such as Peter Norton, Jim Seymour, and Winn L. Rosch. Brady also represents alliances between Brady and the computer industry leaders exemplified by the lines of titles on imprints such as Symantec Books, Lotus Books, Brady Programming Library, and Peter Norton Computing. **BradyGAMES** is one of the leading publishers of game books, providing players with all the inside tips, tricks, strategies, and secret codes on the hottest video games.

Hayden Books is the premier publisher of innovative Macintosh hardware, software, and desktop-design books. **Adobe Press**, which publishes books in conjunction with Hayden, has earned the respect of designers with its official guides to Adobe products. Hayden Books believes that computing does not have to be boring. A major focus here is on electronic publishing, with increasing emphasis in the areas of computer sound, graphics, and animation.

New Riders is the world's leading AutoCAD and NetWare publisher and provides users of all skill levels with expert advice on a variety of topics, such as networking, using multimedia products, and system design. New Riders Publishing/NRP books accent titles keyed to specific operating systems, proprietary computer-aided design packages, Windows-based graphics, networking, and new technology (such as online communications and electronic publishing).

Que provides superior coverage of all major applications for a wide audience. Que is the current incarnation of Que Corporation (former division of Macmillan). Que computer books deliver comprehensive, high-quality products to every segment of the computer book publishing market. Que was one of the first computer book publishers and now holds an enviable position of market leadership in customer satisfaction for books that address the interests and needs of professional users and programmers in such application areas as business, data processing, and desktop publishing and graphics.

Sams Publishing has over 45 years of expertise in publishing titles in technical training; Sams produces some of the most widely used professional references available for programmers and developers. Sams Publishing lineage incorporates the former independent Howard W. Sams, Inc.—a house known for computer and technical books, including guides to popular video games. Sams computer books provide information and instruction on programming languages, operating environments, networking systems, and related topic areas. **Sams.net** is the premier publisher of internet-related technology books.

Waite Group Press is the newest addition to the Macmillan Computer Publishing team. Waite Group Press publishes unique cutting-edge titles on programming languages and emerging technologies.

Ziff-Davis Press (founded in 1990 as a division of Ziff Communications) is a recent addition to Macmillan Computer Publishing. Ziff-Davis specializes in computer books and book/software products. The house issues an assortment of up-to-date guides keyed to particular proprietary computer products, as well as selected titles for children. With several highly successful and popular book lines, Ziff-Davis Press has a solid reputation among computer users, both novice and enthusiast. As of this printing, Ziff-Davis is operating from its California base (see contact address in editor listings below).

Titles from Macmillan Computer Publishing imprints: *Easy Access for Windows 95* by Jeffrey Byrne; *Every Family's Guide to Computers* by Winston Steward; *Year 2000: Will Your Information Systems Survive?* by Ed McPherson and Coopers & Lybrand; *The Complete Idiot's Guide to Upgrading Your PC* by Jennifer Fulton; *Freehand Graphic Studio Skills* by William Harley, Don Parsons, and Sebastian Hassinger; *10 Minute Guide to Lotus Notes Mail* by Jane Calabria; *The America Online Money Guide* by Gus Venditto; *Strategic Internet Marketing* by Tom Vassos; *Advertising on the Web: Planning and Design Strategies* by the Hayden Development Team; *Bats and Other Internet Beasties* by Joseph Williams; *Web Site Administrator's Survival Guide* by Jerry Alban and Scott Yanoff; *How Intranets Work* by Preston Gralla; *Apache Server Survival Guide* by Manuel Alberto Ricart; *Teach Yourself Active X Programming in 21 Days* by Sams.net Development Team; *Teach Yourself WWW Database Programming with Java in 21 Days* by Scridhar Mudduri and Jack Stefani; *Building and Maintaining an Intranet with the Macintosh* by Tobin Anthony.

Query letters and SASEs should be directed to:

Tracy Turgeson, Senior Acquisitions Editor, New Riders Publishing

Steve Poland, Acquisitions Editor, Alpha Books

Karen Whitehouse, Acquisitions Editor, Hayden Books

Rick Ranucci, Acquisitions Editor, Que

Gregg Bushyeager, Acquisitions Editor, Sams Publishing

ZIFF-DAVIS PRESS

5903 Christie Avenue
Emeryville, CA 94608
510-801-2000

Query letters and SASEs should be directed to:

Cheryl Applewood, Publishing Director

Juliette Langley, Associate Publisher

BRASSEY'S (U.S.), INC.

22883 Quicksilver Drive, Suite 100
Dulles, VA 20166
703-260-0602
fax: 703-260-0701

Brassey's (U.S.) is a leading publisher in foreign policy, defense, and national and international affairs. The house emphasizes military history, contemporary military culture, and military reference, as well some titles in sports, a few titles in business and management, and selected trade nonfiction for the mainstream. Brassey's also publishes occasional fictional works featuring a military or historical milieu.

From the Brassey's list: *The U.S. Military Online: A Directory for Internet Access to the Department of Defense* by William E. Arkin; *War in the Mediterranean: A World War II Pictorial History* (by Center of Military History); *Fifty Years at the Front: The Life of War Correspondent Frederick Palmer* by Nathan Haverstock; *The Vietnam War: The Story and Photographs* by Donald M. Goldstein, Katherine V. Dillon, and J. Michael Wenger; *Wellington's Army* by Ian Fletcher (in the History of Uniforms series); *While the Cannons Roared: The Civil War Behind the Lines* by John M. Taylor; *Touchdown! The Favorite Football Stories of Great Coaches* by Larry S. Roseberry and Ted Royal; *The International Jewish Sports Hall of Fame* by Joseph M. Siegman; *The Court of Blue Shadows* (novel set in the aftermath of WW II) by Maynard Allington.

Query letters and SASEs should be directed to:

Don McKeon, Associate Director of Publishing

JOSSEY-BASS, INC., PUBLISHERS
THE NEW LEXINGTON PRESS
PFEIFFER & COMPANY

350 Sansome Street
San Francisco, CA 94104-1310
415-433-1740

Jossey-Bass, Inc., Publishers (established in 1967) produces nonfiction in professional and advanced trade categories covering business, management, and administration in public and nonprofit sectors, as well as issues in psychology, social and health sciences, and education. Major Jossey-Bass divisions include The New Lexington Press and Pfeiffer & Company. The house sustains an extensive backlist and publishes specialist journals in fields allied to the house's areas of book-publishing scope.

The New Lexington Press (formerly Lexington Books, a division of D.C. Heath & Co.; later part of Macmillan, and recently a component of Simon & Schuster's Free Press imprint) publishes trade, professional and academic works in the areas of business, economics, international relations, political affairs, and popular lifestyle, psychology, and social concerns.

Pfeiffer & Company is a formerly independent business-and-workplace specialist press acquired by Jossey-Bass in 1996 (see separate entry below).

Jossey-Bass has an editorial commitment to provide useful, leading-edge resources grounded in research and proven in practice. These works present substantive ideas that will help individuals and organizations to learn, develop, and improve their effectiveness.

The Jossey-Bass publishing niche accents theory-to-practice books for thinking professionals, often in larger corporations, who are progressive and curious in their thinking, and who are in a position to influence their organizations. Most J-B books are grounded in primary research by the authors, and are aimed at the twin concerns of development of the organization as a whole as well as the individuals within the organization.

Jossey-Bass sells via a half-dozen channels; about 20 to 25 percent of J-B business and management titles get general-market trade-bookstore distribution, while the balance are sold through direct mail, direct to corporations, via catalog companies, through agency bookstore accounts (mostly large, independent professional booksellers), and for use in college-level courses.

Titles: *Customer Loyalty: How to Earn It, How to Keep It* by Jill Griffin; *The Divorce Mediation Handbook: Everything You Need to Know* by Paula James; *Leading Corporate Transformation: A Blueprint for Business Renewal* by Robert H. Miles; *Fatal Extraction: Kimberly Bergalis, The Centers for Disease Control, Health Care Workers, and HIV* by Mark Carl Rom; *Losing Your Job, Reclaiming Your Soul: Stories of Resilience, Renewal, and Hope* by Mary Lynn Pulley; *Never the Same Again: How Travel Can Change Your Life* by Jeffrey A. Kottler; *Daughters of Thunder: Black Women Preachers and Their Sermons, 1850–1978* by Bettye Collier-Thomas; *The Courage to Teach* by Parker Palmer; *Practicing Our Faith: A Way of Life for a Searching People* by Dorothy Bass.

A representative Drucker Foundation Future series book: *The Leader of the Future: New Visions, Strategies, and Practices for the Next Era* (edited by Frances Hesselbein, Marshall Goldsmith, and Richard Beckhard; foreword by Peter F. Drucker). This Drucker Foundation Future Series book asks the leaders of today to imagine the leadership of tomorrow.

Books from Warren Bennis Executive Briefing series: *The 21st Century Organization: Reinventing Through Reengineering* by Warren Bennis and Michael Mische; *Why Leaders Can't Lead: The Unconscious Conspiracy Continues* by Warren Bennis;

Fabled Service: Ordinary Acts, Extraordinary Outcomes by Betsy Sanders; *The Absolutes of Leadership* by Philip B. Crosby.

Bill Hicks, Publisher and Senior Editor, The New Lexington Press
Management science.

Leslie Berriman, Senior Editor, The New Lexington Press
Psychology.

Catherine Mallon, Editorial Assistant, The New Lexington Press

PFEIFFER & COMPANY

350 Sansome Street, Fifth Floor
San Francisco, CA 94104
415-433-1740

Pfeiffer's trade business list targets such areas as career/personal development and general business/management. Pfeiffer also produces a dynamic array of training games, simulation/experiential-learning leader's manuals, computer software/CD-ROM, and audio- and videocassettes.

Pfeiffer & Company is an international house that specializes in business topics directed particularly toward trainers, consultants, and managers; with offices is Amsterdam, Johannesburg, London, Sydney, and Toronto, in addition to its former United States home in San Diego, the Pfeiffer & Company scope is adamantly global. As an imprint of Jossey-Bass Inc., Publishers, Pfeiffer & Company offers innovative products for Human Resource Development.

From Pfeiffer & Company: *Getting Together: Icebreakers and Group Energizers* by Lorraine L. Ukens; *Feeding the Zircon Gorilla and Other Team Building Activities* by Sam Sikes; *Team Players and Teamwork: The New Competitive Business Strategy* by Glenn M. Parker; *The Skilled Facilitator: Practical Wisdom for Developing Effective Groups* by Roger M. Schwarz; *Leading with Soul: An Uncommon Journey of Spirit* by Lee G. Bolman and Terrence E. Deal; *Empowerment Takes More Than a Minute* by Ken Blanchard, John P. Carlos, and Alan Randolph.

Query letters and SASEs for Pfeiffer should be directed to:

Susan Rachmeller, Associate Editor
Business titles consistent with Pfeiffer list: management, careers, training.

Cheryl Greenway, Assistant Editor
Business management.

Rachel Livesy, Associate Editor
Nonprofit sector, religion, and religion-in-practice.

Katie Levine, Assistant Editor
Health.

Cedric Crocker, Editor
Business and management.

(Ms.) Gale Erlandson, Senior Editor
Higher and adult education.

Larry Alexander, Senior Editor
Business and management.

(Ms.) Lesley Iura, Senior Editor
Education.

Andy Pasternak, Editor
Health/social and behavioral sciences.

Sarah Polster, Editor
Religion-in-practice.

Alan Rinzler, Senior Editor
Social and behavioral sciences.

Alan Schrader, Senior Editor
Public administration and nonprofit sector.

SIMON & SCHUSTER CHILDREN'S PUBLISHING DIVISION
SIMON & SCHUSTER BOOKS FOR YOUNG READERS
ATHENEUM BOOKS FOR YOUNG READERS
MARGARET K. MCELDERRY BOOKS
ALADDIN PAPERBACKS
LITTLE SIMON
NICKELODEON BOOKS AND NICK JR.
RABBIT EARS BOOK AND AUDIO

1230 Avenue of the Americas
New York, NY 10020
212-698-7000

The Simon & Schuster Children's Publishing Division features a robust lineup of nonfiction, fiction, and poetry in all age ranges, plus a rich array of picture books and specialty publications. S&S publishes books for the Spanish-language market under the Libros Colibrí imprint. Rabbit Ears Book and Audio concentrates on book-and-audio packages. The new Nickelodeon Books operation includes television show tie-in titles and general publishing projects under the Nick imprint.

The division was created subsequent to Paramount's acquisition of Macmillan. The Macmillan enterprise had itself been a major force in children's publishing. The newly forged Simon & Schuster Children's Publishing Division has cohered into a powerful performance sphere, with numerous award-winning and bestselling titles.

The **Simon & Schuster Books for Young Readers** imprint is a primarily hardcover publisher that aims to create high-quality books that sell to both libraries and bookstores and become backlist staples. The house publishes fiction and nonfiction for all readership groups, from preschoolers through young adults. About half the list is made up of picture books (but not board books or novelty books), nonfiction, and storybooks for older readers. The rest of the list features novels, photoessays, and poetry collections for middle-grade readers and young adults.

Representing the Simon & Schuster Books for Young Readers list: *Don't Leave an Elephant to Go and Chase a Bird* (by James Berry; illustrated by Ann Grifalconi); *Duppy Talk: West Indian Tales of Mystery and Magic* by Gerald Hausman; *Forever* by Judy Blume; *How I Changed My Life* by Todd Strasser; *Summerspell* by Jean Thesman; *Myths and Legends from Around the World* by Sandy Shepherd; *Past Forgiving* by Gloria D. Miklowitz; *Running Out of Time* by Margaret Peterson Haddix; *Sitti's Secret* by Naomi Shihab Nye; *The Faithful Friend* (by Robert D. San Souci; illustrated by Brian Pinckney); *Under the Domim Tree* by Gila Almagor; *Zin! Zin! Zin! a Violin* (by Lloyd Moss; illustrated by Marjorie Priceman). Series include: Animal Peek and Pops (by Sadie Fields with illustrations by David Hawcock); Teeny-Popper Books (by B. J. Johnson); Talking with Artists (edited by Pat Cummings); the S&S Reference line; and Nature Adventure Books.

Atheneum Books for Young Readers produces picture books, fiction, and non-fiction that covers the spectrum of reader-age ranges in all genres (except for board books and novelty books). Atheneum books are often richly produced hardcover editions; works that feature illustration and photography are often packaged with fine-art quality graphics. About a third of the list consists of picture books; however, Atheneum is renowned for topnotch titles in fiction and nonfiction. Produced under Atheneum auspices are Jean Karl Books, Anne Schwartz Books, and the Libros Colibrí Spanish-language line.

From Atheneum: *Virginia's General* by Albert Marrin; *The Conjure Woman* (by William Miller; illustrated by Terea Shaffer); *The Absolutely True Story . . .* by Willo Davis Roberts; *Tears of a Tiger* by Sharon Draper; *Parallel Journeys* by Eleanor H. Ayer; *Mary Wolf* by Cynthia D. Grant; *I See the Moon* by C. B. Christiansen; *Emperor Mage* by Tamora Pierce; *Black Swan/White Crow* (by J. Patrick Lewis; illustrated by Chris Manson); *Abigail Adams: Witness to a Revolution* by Natalie S. Bober; *A Place to Call Home* by Jackie French Koller; *A Gaggle of Geese* (written and illustrated by Philippa-Alys Browne).

Margaret K. McElderry Books publishes original hardcover trade books for children. The McElderry list encompasses picture books, easy-to-read series, fiction and nonfiction for 8- to 12-year-olds, science fiction and fantasy, and young adult fiction and nonfiction. McElderry titles: *Yolanda's Genius* by Carol Fenner; *Dog Friday* by Hilary McKay; *A Sound of Leaves* (by Lenore Blegvad; illustrated by Erik Blegvad).

Aladdin Paperbacks primarily produces reprints of Simon & Schuster Publishing Division hardcover originals. The Aladdin scope covers preschoolers through young adult, including picture books, paperback reprints, novelty books, and fiction and mysteries for kids to the age of 12. Aladdin originals include selective series and media tie-ins.

Little Simon is a line devoted to novelty books and book-related merchandise. The Little Simon addresses a range from birth through eight years. Popular formats include pop-up books, board books, cloth books, bath books, sticker books, and book-and-audiocassette sets.

Nickelodeon Books and Nick Jr. is queued to Nickelodeon cable-channel programming. This line creates books and other products that cross-promote with co-licensees in the arenas of toys, home videos, CD-ROM, and party goods.

Rabbit Ears is an award-winning entertainment company that produces children's videos. The Simon & Schuster Rabbit Ears Book and Audio lineup concentrates on a slate of tales based on the videos, retold and illustrated in high-profile new editions, accompanied by audiocassettes replete with surround-sound design and musical scores for a discerning audience. Representative performing artists involved are Rubén Blades, Holly Hunter, John Hurt, Garrison Keillor, Jack Nicholson, Meg Ryan, and Kathleen Turner; musicians include Mickey Hart, Mark Isham, Tangerine Dream, and Bobby McPherrin.

Query letters and SASEs should be directed to:

Rick Richter President and Publisher, Simon & Schuster Children's Publishing Division

Stephanie Owens Lurie, Associate Publisher and Editorial Director, Simon & Schuster Books for Young Readers
Picture books, chapter books, middle-grade and young-adult fiction, and nonfiction for all age groups. Looks for picture-book manuscripts with a strong story line, middle-grade fiction with an extra sparkle of humor and imagination, and young-adult fiction that is multilayered and sophisticated in both plot and characterization. Likes to publish nonfiction that is as compelling as a good novel and as attractive as the best picture books. Also interested in Judaica.

Virginia Duncan, Executive Editor, Simon & Schuster Books for Young Readers
Picture books (both short texts for younger readers and longer texts for older readers), interesting and fresh nonfiction for all age groups, and middle-grade novels with a distinctive voice. Likes books that are innovative, appealing to children, and built around a strong plot.

David Gale, Senior Editor, Simon & Schuster Books for Young Readers
Middle-grade and young-adult novels, primarily. Looks for sharp writing and fresh voices. Does not want to consider standard young-adult problem novels or romances, but is interested in more unusual, hardhitting, and literary young-adult novels.

Andrea Davis Pinkney, Editor, Simon & Schuster Books for Young Readers
Picture-book manuscripts that explore significant yet lesser-known nonfiction topics in an exciting way. Likes to see stories about people from different cultures around the world, and fiction that is based on real-life events.

Rebecca Davis, Editor, Simon & Schuster Books for Young Readers
Picture books, middle-grade and young-adult fiction, and unusual nonfiction projects. Particularly fond of poetry, multicultural stories, and historical fiction—tales with distinctive characters and a strong sense of time and place.

Jonathan Lanman, Vice President and Editorial Director, Atheneum Books for Young Readers

Marcia Marshall, Executive Editor, Atheneum Books for Young Readers

Jean Karl, Field Editor, Jean Karl Books, an imprint of Atheneum Books for Young Readers

Ana Cerro, Associate Editor, Atheneum Books for Young Readers

Margaret K. McElderry, Vice President and Publisher, Margaret K. McElderry Books

Emma K. Dryden, Editor, Margaret K. McElderry Books

Ellen Krieger, Vice President and Editorial Director, Aladdin Paperbacks

Ruth Katcher, Senior Editor, Aladdin Paperbacks

Julia Sibert, Editor, Aladdin Paperbacks

Robin Corey, Vice President and Editorial Director, Little Simon; Vice President and Editorial Director, Rabbit Ears

Alison Weir, Senior Editor, Little Simon

Laura Hunt, Editor, Little Simon; Editor, Rabbit Ears

Amy Bartram, Production Editor, Little Simon

GIBBS SMITH, PUBLISHER
PEREGRINE SMITH BOOKS

P.O. Box 667
Layton, UT 84041
801-544-9800
800-748-5439
www.gibbs-smith.com (e-mail)

Gibbs Smith publishes general trade nonfiction, including cuisine and lifestyle, architecture, art and collectibles, photography, gardening, nature, travel, decorating, and poetry. Gibbs Smith also produces a solid lineup in children's literature and family reading. The house has a strong emphasis on literature of the Western United States, including cowboy humor and poetry. The publisher's architecture program features a series of titles about Frank Lloyd Wright by Thomas A. Heinz.

The house produces books on the Gibbs Smith and Peregrine Smith Books imprints, in fine hardcover and trade paper editions, and offers distinctive lines of gift books keyed to the publisher's interest areas.

Gibbs Smith also publishes the hardback version of the underground classic *The Lazy Man's Guide to Enlightenment* by Thaddeus Golas (first published in 1972).

Gibbs Smith, Publisher (founded in 1969) is a house with a resourceful spirit. Company mission statement: To create books that contribute to the positive unfolding and evolution of the world's culture with style, wit, intelligence, and taste. Gibbs Smith looks for new projects that contribute to and refresh this spirit, and considers these questions: What makes good writing? What makes good publishing? Gibbs Smith believes that the single most important quality for both writer and publisher is passion: a sense of great purpose; an unusually heightened interest in the subject matter and in the task—whether it be writing or publishing. As Gibbs M. Smith writes: "It is a great privilege to work from our old barn office in the Rocky Mountains and have our books enter the literary bloodstream of the world."

High on the Gibbs Smith list: *Headin' for the Sweet Heat: Fruit and Fire Spice Cooking* by Landeen Jacqueline; *The First Gift of Christmas* by Richard Paul Evans (New York *Times* bestselling author); *Rocky Mountain Home: Spirited Western Hideaways* by Elizabeth Clair Flood (photographs by Peter Woloszynki); *Fishing Camps* by Ralph Kylloe; *The Beautiful Necessity: Decorating with Arts and Crafts* by Bruce Smith and Yoshiko Yamamoto; *Journal to the Soul: The Art of Sacred Journal Keeping* by Rose Offner; *MailBox, U.S.A—Stories of Mailbox Owners and Makes: A Celebration of Mailbox Art in America* by Rachel Epstein; *On Your Anniversary* and *Tenth Anniversary Wishes* (edited by Catherine Kouts and Laura Cavaluzzo; photographs by Elisabeth Fall); *Blue* and *Red* by Belinda Recio; *Seven Habits for Highly Happy People* by Bix Bender; *Don't Whiz on a 'lectric Fence: Grandpa's Country Wisdom* by Roy English; *Cow Chips Aren't for Dippin': A Guide to Life in the New Wild West* by Coke Newell (illustrated by Ben DeSoto); *Perfect Hell* by H. L. Hix; *Faces of Utah: A Portrait* (edited by Shannon R. Hoskins).

A representative Gibbs Smith seasonal-holiday sampler: *Countdown to Christmas* by Charlotte Argyle and Taff Davidson; *Christmas Waltz* by Buck Ramsey (illustrations by Janet Hurley); *A Cat's Night Before Christmas* and *A Dog's Night Before Christmas* and *A Teacher's Night Before Christmas* by Sue Carabine (illustrated by Shauna Mooney Kawasaki); *A Trucker's Night Before Christmas* by Dawn Valentine Hadlock (illustrated by Brad Taere); *A Golfer's Night Before Christmas* by Jody Feldman (illustrated by Shauna Mooney Kawasaki); *Fisherman's Night Before Christmas* by Stephen Stovall and Jody Feldman (illustrated by Shauna Mooney Kawasaki); *Gargoyles' Christmas* by Louisa Campbell (illustrated by Bridget Starr Taylor).

Of interest to children and family: *I Know What You Do When I Go to School* by Ann Edwards Cannon (illustrated by Jennifer Mazzucco); *You Don't Always Get What You Hope For* by Rick Walton (illustrated by Heidi Stetson Mario); *The Naturalist's Handbook: Activities for Young Explorers* by Lynn Kuntz (illustrated by Michael Moran).

A Gibbs Smith vignette: Mackey Hedges, a cowboy in his mid-50s, walked in with the typescript of a work based on the author's experiences as a working cowboy over the last 30 years. With a unique prose style that evokes that of Jack Kerouac, this proved to be a major literary achievement and makes its debut on the Gibbs Smith list as *Last Buckaroo*.

Gibbs Smith, Publisher distributes its own list and utilizes a network of regional sales representatives.

Query letters and SASEs should be directed to:

Madge Baird, Editorial Director
Humor, Western.

Gail Yngve, Editor
Poetry, literature, home/design, New Age.

Caroll Shreeve, Editor
Gardening, cookbooks, craft, architecture.

Theresa Desmond, Editor
Children's.

Linda Nimori, Editor

Soho Press

853 Broadway
New York, NY 10003
212-260-1900

Soho publishes trade nonfiction and historical works. Nonfiction covers areas such as investigative stories, international affairs, and historical works. This compact house is also distinguished for its formidable list of contemporary fiction (often with a literary bent), which includes mysteries and historical reprints. The Soho train of interest also verges into travel, autobiography, and the social sciences.

Soho Press (founded in 1986) publishes a superior roster of hardcover and softcover trade books. Many of the house's titles have achieved marked critical and commercial success.

Soho nonfiction includes: *A Woman in Amber: Healing the Trauma of War and Exile* by Agate Nesaule; *Vietnamerica: The War Comes Home* by Thomas A. Bass; *The Manhattan Family Guide to Private Schools* by Catherine Hausman and Victoria Goldman; *The Other Mother: A Woman's Love for the Child She Gave Up for Adoption* by Carol Shaefer.

Fiction and the literary arts from Soho: *Pagan's Father* by Michael Arditti; *The Handmaid of Desire* by John L'Heureux; *Tree of Heaven* by R. C. Binstock; *The Sixteen Pleasures* by Robert Hellenga; *The Body Is Water* by Julie Schumacher; *Pleasure of Believing* by Anastasia Hobbett; *Dizzy Z: The Confessions of a Meteoric Rocker Contemplating Re-Entry* by Matthew Holland; *The Liar* by Stephen Fry; *Krik? Krak! Stories* by Edwidge Danticat; *Antonia Saw the Oryx First* by Maria Thomas.

Soho mysteries: *The Blond Baboon* and *The Maine Massacre* by Janwillem van de Wetering (a former Zen Buddhist monk, Amsterdam detective, and world traveler, the author has written 14 mysteries in the Amsterdam Cop Series; the latest is *The Hollow Eyed Angel*); *The Whispering Wall* and *The Souvenir* by Patricia Carlon; *Steal Away* by Timothy Watts. Other titles in crime and suspense fiction: *What's a Girl Gotta Do?* by Sparkle Hayter; *The Kiss Off* by Jim Cirni; *Jade Lady Burning* by Martin Limón; *Her Monster* by Jeff Collignon.

The Hera Series presents works of historical fiction that feature strong female characters. Hera series titles: *Lady of the Reeds* by Pauline Gedge; *Reich Angel* by Anita Mason; *Stealing Heaven: The Love Story of Heloise and Abelard* by Marion Meade.

Soho Press books are distributed to the trade by Farrar Straus & Giroux.

Query letters and SASEs should be directed to:

Laura Hruska, Associate Publisher

Juris Jurjevics, Publisher

The Sporting News Publishing Company

10176 Corporate Square Drive, Suite 200
St. Louis, MO 63132
314-997-7111

The Sporting News Publishing Company (founded in 1886) is a subsidiary of Times Mirror. This publisher issues the periodical *The Sporting News* and produces a short list of books that includes annual digests of sports facts, statistical compilations, team registers, and media guides under the rubric of the Sporting News Library.

The house also publishes a select list of feature titles, especially a line dealing with the history and culture of the game of baseball. Virtually all of the books published by the Sporting News are put together by the editorial staff or are specially commissioned works arising in-house rather than proposed by independent authors.

Sample titles: *College Basketball Yearbook*; *Official NBA Rules*; *The Complete Hockey Book*; *Pro Football Guide*; *Fantasy Baseball Owners Manual*; *Official Baseball Rules*; *Baseball's Golden Age: The Photographs of Charles M. Conlon* by Neal McCabe and Constance McCabe.

Distribution for the Sporting News list of books is handled by its parent company; books may also be ordered directly or through Contemporary Books.

Query letters and SASEs should be directed to:

Gary Brinker, Director of Information Development

SPRINGER-VERLAG
BIRKHÄUSER
COPERNICUS
TELOS/THE ELECTRONIC LIBRARY OF SCIENCE
175 Fifth Avenue
New York, NY 10010
800-SPRINGE(R) (800-777-4643)

Springer-Verlag publishes along the scientific spectrum in such subject areas and disciplines as: architecture, astronomy, biology, biosciences, chemistry, computer science, computers, ecology, economics/business, engineering, geosciences, mathematics (theoretical and applied; statistics), medicine, philosophy, physics, and psychiatry/psychology.

Springer-Verlag offers a wide-ranging collection of works for scientists, researchers, students, and interested general readers. Among Springer-Verlag divisions and imprints, several have strong academic and/or trade identities: Birkhäuser (biology, physical sciences, architecture, mathematics); Copernicus (frontlist nonfiction, books for the general trade); TELOS (The Electronic Library of Science; books/electronics packages).

Throughout the medical and scientific world, Springer-Verlag is established as a publisher of outstanding books and journals. Since 1842, when Julius Springer expanded his Berlin bookstore to publish books his customers needed, Springer-Verlag has been actively involved in the marketplace. Springer published volumes of poetry, philosophical writings, children's books, and practical guides, as well as works of German literary authors, including Jeremias Gotthelf and Theodor Fontane—a multi-faceted reflection of the era.

By late in the 19th century, Springer-Verlag had become preeminent internationally in the scientific-publishing field, with successive generations of Springers involved in the development of the firm. During the Third Reich, the Springers were forced to relinquish their positions because of their Jewish ancestry, but the publishing house (by this time greatly expanded) survived—if just barely—and the Springers resumed their offices after the war to rebuild their shattered company.

Springer-Verlag began publishing an increasing number of books and journals in the English language; combined with the concentration of contacts with scientists worldwide and the establishment of Springer-Verlag New York (in 1964), the firm's share of the international market has grown profusely through recent decades.

Springer-Verlag is today an international house with offices in New York, Berlin, Heidelberg, Vienna, London, Paris, Tokyo, Hong Kong, Barcelona, Budapest, and Singapore. Springer-Verlag is among the largest privately owned science publishing houses. With its worldwide network of publishing and marketing centers, Springer-Verlag distributes books and journals virtually everywhere. Anywhere scientific advances are made, Springer-Verlag is nearby to report them.

Yes, it has been said among professionals in the world scientific community: "If Springer-Verlag hasn't published it, no one has."

Titles from Springer-Verlag: *Human Mummies: A Global Survey of Their Status and the Techniques of Conservation* by Konrad Spindler; *Business in the Information Age: Heading for New Processes* by H. Österle; *An Introduction to Difference Equations* by Saber Elaydi; *Mental Health Computing* by Marvin J. Miller, M.D., Kenric W. Hamilton, M.D., and Matthew J. Hile, Ph.D.; *Particle Physics at the New Millennium* by Byron P. Roe; *Seeing Between the Pixels: Pictures in Interactive Systems* by Thomas Strothotte and Christine Strothotte.

Springer-Verlag oversees an international distribution system.

BIRKHÄUSER

675 Massachussets Avenue
Cambridge, MA 02139
617-876-2333

Birkhäuser publishes in a variety of biological and physical sciences, and is a leading world publisher of works in architecture and mathematics. Birkhäuser publications are in the U.S. generally cataloged along with the core Springer-Verlag list.

Birkhäuser was founded in 1879 by Emile Birkhäuser, a printer in Basel, Switzerland. After publishing *Chronicles of Christian Wurstein* (in 1883), the house produced books in history, art, and culture, as a pivotal player in the development of Basel as a European publishing center.

Birkhäuser Boston was established in 1979; Springer-Verlag purchased Birkhäuser in 1985. Birkhäuser has retained its specialty concentrations and editorial autonomy.

Query letters and SASEs should be directed to:

(Ms.) Alla Margolina-Litvin, Ph.D., Editor of Biomedical Sciences

Wayne Yuhasz, Executive Editor of Computational Sciences and Engineering

Anne Kostant, Senior Editor of Mathematical Sciences

COPERNICUS

175 Fifth Avenue
New York, NY 10010
800-SPRINGE(R) (800-777-4643)

Copernicus covers commercial and professional titles in topical areas that range from science, physics, and mathematics to medicine, philosophy, and the relationship between science and art. Copernicus extends Springer-Verlag's commanding presence in scientific publishing into the popular sphere.

Copernicus books stand out for their accessible presentations of difficult topics and ideas. Some Copernicus books are lighthearted and fun; others are more serious and demanding of the reader's involvement—all titles under this imprint strive to present the kinds of imagination and insight that make them a pleasure to read.

The historical personage known as Copernicus (Mikolaj Kopernik, 1473–1543) is perhaps best known for his contributions to astronomy. The Copernican description of the arrangement of the solar system signaled the birth of a new era in modern science. Far more than being known as an astronomer, Copernicus and the Renaissance have become symbols for innovative thought.

From Copernicus: *The Call of the Distant Mammoths: Why the Ice Age Mammals Disappeared* by Peter Ward; *Beyond Calculation: The Next Fifty Years of Computing* (edited by Peter Denning and Robert Metcalfe); *Slanted Truths: Essays on Gaia, Symbiosis and Evolution* by Lynn Margulis and Dorion Sagan; *Hubble: A New Window to the Universe* by Daniel Fischer and Hilmar Duerbeck; *Insights of Genius: Imagery and Creativity in Science and Art* by Arthur I. Miller; *The Universe in a Handkerchief: Lewis Carroll's Mathematical Recreations, Games, Puzzles, and Word Plays* by Martin Gardner; *Our Molecular Nature: What We're Made of and How It Works* by David Goodsell; *Einstein Atomized: Cartoons on Science* by Sidney Harris; *A History of Astronomy: From 1890 to the Present* by David Leverington; *Out of Their Minds: The Lives and Discoveries of 15 Great Computer Scientists* by Dennis Shasha and Cathy Lazere.

Query letters and SASEs should be directed to:

William Frucht, Senior Editor

TELOS/THE ELECTRONIC LIBRARY OF SCIENCE

3600 Pruneridge Avenue, Suite 200
Santa Clara, CA 95051
408-249-0314
fax: 408-249-2595
info@TELOSpub.com
http://www.telospub.com (World Wide Web)

TELOS (The Electronic Library of Science) is an imprint of Springer-Verlag New York with publishing facilities in Santa Clara, California. The TELOS program encompasses the natural and physical sciences, computer science, mathematics, and engineering. All TELOS publications have a computational orientation, as TELOS's primary publishing strategy is to wed the traditional print medium with emerging electronic media in order to provide the reader with a truly interactive multimedia information environment.

Every TELOS publication delivered on paper has an associated electronic component: book/diskette combinations, book/CD-ROM packages, books delivered via networks, electronic journals, newsletters. TELOS is not committed to any single technology—any delivery medium is a possible TELOS venue.

The range of TELOS publications extends from research-level reference works through textbook materials for the higher-education audience, practical handbooks for working professionals, as well as broadly accessible science, computer science, and high-technology trade publications. Many TELOS publications are interdisciplinary, and most are targeted for individual buyers.

Of the numerous alternate definitions for the Greek word *telos*, the one perhaps most representative of this division's publishing philosophy is "to turn," or "turning point." The establishment of TELOS is a significant step toward attainment of a new plateau of information packaging and dissemination in the interactive learning environment.

Representative TELOS projects: *The Microprocessor: A Biography* by Michael S. Malone (book/CD-ROM); *The Web Empowerment Book* by Ralph Abraham, Frank Jas, and Will Russell (book/freeware and shareware); *Webmaster: An Introduction to Electronic Publishing on the Global Internet* by Dennis Woo (book/downloadable software, text, and graphics components); *Seeing Numbers: Visual Data Analysis for Scientists and Engineers* by Brand Fortner (book/cross-platform CD-ROM); *Introduction to Symbolic Computation: Computers in Pure and Applied Mathematics* by Ilan Vardi (book/diskette).

Query letters and SASEs should be directed to:

Allan Wylde, Publisher

STACKPOLE BOOKS

5067 Ritter Road
Mechanicsburg, PA 17055
717-796-0411
fax: 717-796-0412
800-732-3669

Stackpole specializes in nature and the outdoors, crafts and hobbies, fly fishing, gardening, cooking, sporting literature, carving and woodworking, history (especially military history), military reference, and works geared to the Pennsylvania region.

Stackpole Books publishes editions that are created lovingly, with striking design. When selecting projects to produce, the publisher determines what readers need and how these needs will be met through a proposed project's fresh perspective. Stackpole signs expert authors, juggles production schedules, and commits the personalized verve to make the dream real. Stackpole believes in perfectionism and care—when focused upon the practical—as keys to successful publishing.

Stackpole Books was established in 1933 as Stackpole Sons, a small family-owned publishing enterprise. The house acquired Military Service Publishing Company in 1935 and has continued to grow into additional publishing areas while remaining attuned to its original publishing vision.

On the Stackpole list: *Cook and Peary: The Polar Controversy, Resolved* by Robert M. Bryce; *Selling Nature Photographs* by Norbert Wu; *Birds of Forest, Yard, and Thicket* by John Eastman; *From Winchester to Cedar Creek: The Shenandoah Campaign* by Jeffry D. Wert; *Accessible Gardening: Tips and Techniques for Seniors and the Disabled* by Joann Woy; *Carving and Painting a Black-Capped Chickadee with Ernest Muehlmatt* by Curtis Badger; *Fishing Atlantic Salmon: The Flies and the Patterns* by Joseph D. Bates, Jr., and Pamela Bates Richards; *Saltwater Fish Cookbook* by A. D. Livingston; *West of Key West* (edited and compiled by John Cole); *Reliving the Civil War: A Reenactor's Handbook* by R. Lee Hadden; *To Everest via Antarctica: Climbing Solo on the Highest Peak on Each of the World's Seven Continents* by Robert Mads Anderson.

Additional areas of Stackpole interest are represented by *How to Produce a Successful Crafts Show* by Kathryn Caputo; *How to Start and Run Your Own Bed & Breakfast Inn* by Ripley Hotch and Carl Glassman.

Stackpole distributes its own books, as well as a list of titles in military history from United Kingdom publishers Greenhill and Osprey; the house utilizes the services of regional distribution houses and sales representatives.

Query letters and SASEs should be directed to:

Judith Schnell, Editorial Director
Fly fishing, carving, nature, woodworking.

Mark Allison, Editor
Outdoor sports.

William C. Davis, Editor
History.

Ed Skender, Editor
Military reference.

STERLING PUBLISHING COMPANY

387 Park Avenue South
New York, NY 10016
212-532-7160

Sterling emphasizes general popular reference and information books, science, nature, arts and crafts, architecture, home improvement, history, humor, health, self-help, wine and food, gardening, business and careers, social sciences, sports, pets, hobbies, drama and music, psychology, occult, and military-science books. Sterling also publishes games, puzzles, calendars, and children's books.

The current scope of the Sterling Publishing Company program includes a wide range of nonfiction practical approaches, including informative how-to books in gardening, crafts, and woodworking; books on military history; art and reference titles; and activity and puzzle books for the kids. The house (founded in 1949) hosts a formidable backlist.

Representative Sterling titles: *Aztec Astrology: An Introduction* by Michael Colmer; *Celtic Key Patterns* by Ian Bain; *Irish Toasts, Curses, and Blessings* by Padraic O'Farrell; *Keep Your Bonsai Alive and Well* by Herb L. Gustafson; *Nature Crafts with a Microwave: Over 80 Projects* by Dawn Cusick; *New and Traditional Styles of Chip Carving: From Classic to Positive Imaging* by Wayne Barton; *The Art of Italian Regional Cooking* by Francesco Antonucci, Marta Pulini, and Gianni Salvaterra; *The Healing Touch of Massage* by Carlo De Paoli; *Time Travel: Fact, Fiction, and Possibility* by Jenny Randles; *Wreaths from the Garden: 75 Fresh and Dried Floral Wreaths to Make* by Leslie Dierks; *Easy Card Tricks* by Bob Longe; *World's Most Incredible Puzzles* by Charles Barry Townsend.

On the Sterling children's-book list: *101 Science Surprises: Exciting Experiments with Everyday Materials* by Roy Richards; *Rainforest Animals Dot-to-Dot* by Susan Baumgart (illustrated by Richard Salvucci); *Five Minute Frights* (short fiction) by William A. Walker, Jr. (illustrated by Will Suckow and Martin Charlot).

Sterling handles its own distribution.

Query letters and SASEs should be directed to:

Sheila Barry, Acquisitions Manager

STEWART, TABORI & CHANG

575 Broadway
New York, NY 10012
212-941-2929
fax: 212-941-2982

Stewart, Tabori, & Chang publishes luxuriously produced titles in art, popular culture, design, home, cuisine, lifestyle, and collecting. The house offers topnotch specialty merchandise such as calendars, cards, journals, and engagement books. Terrail is an imprint in collaboration with Editions Terrail that publishes a line of art books at reasonable prices. The Essential Gardens library is a line accenting a wide range of topical-interest editions. The publisher offers a solid list of new seasonal titles and supports an impeccably select backlist.

Stewart, Tabori & Chang books are produced in hardcover and trade paperback editions. Booksellers especially appreciate the quality product signified by the publisher's prancing-bison trade logo—these books on display in a bookstore can draw significant point-of-purchase interest from customers. House trade motto: "The heart and soul of illustrated books."

Stewart, Tabori & Chang (founded in 1981 by Andy Stewart, Lena Tabori, and Nai Chang), recently part of the publishing stable of Peter Brant (owner of the magazines *Interview*, *Art in America*, and *Antiques*), is now a division of U.S. Media Holdings, Inc.

From Stewart, Tabori & Chang: *Tango* by Evelyne Pieiller (photographs by Isabel Muñoz); *Microcosmos: The Invisible World of Insects* by Claude Noridsany and Marie Perenou; *The Humongous Book of Dinosaurs* (editorial consultant David Norman); *Celebrating the Impressionist Table* by Pamela Todd (photographs by Laurie Evans); *Healthy Thai Cooking* by Sri Owen (photographs by James Murphy); *Famouz: Photographs 1976–88* by Anton Corbin; *Leaves: In Myth, Magic, & Medicine* by Alice Thomas Vitale; *Secrets from a Vegetarian Kitchen* by Nadine Abensur (photographs by Gus Filgate).

The Essential Garden Library series encompasses gardening titles covering a variety of subjects and formats. Each book in the series features Stewart, Tabori & Chang quality in writing, photography, and production. Numbered chronologically, these books are uniform in height and width to stand next to one another in the reader's garden library. Some titles: *Herbs* by George Carter (photographs by Marianne Marjerus); *Getting Ready for Winter and Other Fall Tasks* by Stephen Bradley.

Stewart, Tabori & Chang distributes to the trade via Publishers Resources; in addition, the house uses a network of independent regional sales representatives.

Query letters and SASEs should be directed to:

Linda Sunshine, Editorial Director

Mary Kalamaras, Editor

Alexandra Childs, Assistant Editor

THE SUMMIT PUBLISHING GROUP

One Arlington Centre
1112 East Copeland Road, Fifth Floor
Arlington, TX 76011
817-274-1821
fax: 217-274-1196
800-875-3346

Summit showcases general nonfiction, with a list that features contemporary biography, business, sports, how-to, self-help, education, politics and economics, children's activity books, religion, health and fitness, cookbooks, occasional fiction, gift books and merchandise, and humor. Summit series offerings include: You Can Do It! and Eye-D.

The Summit Publishing Group (founded in 1990; formerly Summit Publishing) began as an advertising agency, then moved progressively into its current focus as a publisher of books.

Summit's expertise shows in its support for lead titles. Publicity is among the strong points of the house's marketing strategy; word has it that Summit's salaried publicists earn commissions keyed to a book's outstanding performance. Significant marks have been notched by such novelty titles as *Barney Fife's Guide to Life, Love and Self-Defense*, *The Autobiography of Santa Claus: It's Better to Give*, and *Death at Sea* (a murder mystery that includes clues hidden in 3-D images).

Summit's You Can Do It! is a line of educational and interactive kits that include instructional books, props, and toys. Titles include those geared to: piano playing, face painting, card tricks, hula dancing, dog training.

The Eye-D series is both educational and fun. The Eye-D Picture Challenge uses every child's love of pictures to teach important facts about history, geography, science, math, language, and the arts.

On Summit's list: *The Dollar Crisis: A Blueprint to Help Rebuild the American Dream* by Ross Perot and Senator Paul Simon; *A Business Handbook: The Essential Elements of Success* by Ross Perot; *The Dallas Cowboys: The Authorized Pictorial History* by Jeff Guinn; *Market Maker: The Role and Impact of Alan Greenspan, Chairman of the Federal Reserve Board* by Mike Towle; *Love and War: 250 Years of Wartime Love Letters* by Susan Besze Wallace; *Arm & Hammer's Household Survival Guide: More Than 1000 Tips to Make the Home Sweet Home—With and Without Baking Soda* by the Arm & Hammer Development Staff; *Bargains! for the Home: Home Cheap Home* by Sue Goldstein; *Pediatric Primer: Answers to Questions Most Asked by Parents* by Charles Ginsburg, M.D.; *Popcorn King: How Orville Redenbacher Created One of America's Most Popular Brands* (based on the biography by Robert Topping); *Free Admission: A Foolproof Guide to Getting in Free to Concerts, Games and Special Events* by Scott Kerman; *The Gabby Cabby: Life on the Street from New York's Radio-Active Cabdriver* by Peter Franklin; *Women Are from Pluto, Men Are from Uranus: Why You Can't Get What You Want in Relationships* by Mike Nichols; *1001 Most Asked Texas Gardening Questions* by Neil Sperry; *Byron Nelson: The Little Black Book* (revised edition); *The Kissing Book: Everything You Ever Wanted to Know* by Tomima Edmark; *Bewitched Forever: The Immortal Companion to Television's Most Magical Supernatural Situation Comedy* by Herbie J. Pilato.

Summit Publishing Group distributes for the Millennium Publishing Group. Millennium presents three distinct imprints, one established and two new, of beautifully designed books with well-defined markets (Bon Vivant Press, Samuel Wachtman's Sons, and Millennium). The arrangement between Summit and Millennium provides exciting advantages in title development, production, marketing, and distribution.

Bon Vivant Press offers extensively researched cookbooks and guidebooks, featuring the secret recipes of America's finest chefs. Titles include: *Cooking Secrets for Healthy Living*; *The Gardener's Cookbook*; *The Great Vegetarian Cookbook*; *Pacific Northwest Cooking Secrets*; *San Francisco's Cooking Secrets*; *Monterey's Cooking Secrets*; *California Wine Country Cooking Secrets*; *The Great California Cookbook*; *New England's Cooking Secrets*; *Cape Cod's Cooking Secrets* by Kathleen DeVanna Fish.

Millennium Publications offers: *Tullio's Orange Tree—A Fable* by Ted Gerstl (illustrated by Jan Albertin).

Samuel Wachtman's Sons is a new Jewish imprint for this discriminating market. Titles include: *Jewish Cooking from Here and Far: Traditions & Memories from Our Mother's Kitchens* by the Congregation Beth Israel of the Monterey Peninsula; *How to Survive—and Profit from—Your Son's Bar Mitzvah!* By Marvin Shapiro.

Summit oversees its own distribution network.

Query letters and SASEs should be directed to:

Len Oszustowicz, President and Publisher

SUN & MOON PRESS

6026 Wilshire Boulevard
Los Angeles, CA 90036
213-857-1115
fax: 213-857-1043

Sun & Moon emphasizes international fiction, poetry, and drama; essays and criticism; selected journals, letters, biography, and memoirs. Sun & Moon series include American Theater Arts, New American Fiction, New American Poetry, and Sun & Moon Classics.

Sun & Moon (founded in 1978) is a program of the Contemporary Arts Educational Project, Inc. The press catalogs original fiction and nonfiction; foreign literature in translation; poetry and literary anthologies; journals; sidelines and gift books. The house aims toward distinguished editorial quality, an innovative and experimental list, and holds superb production and design standards in hardbound and trade paperback editions. The Sun & Moon colophon is a fulsome Sun overlapped by a slice of crescent Moon afloat in the ether.

Sun & Moon releases a midsize seasonal roster of new offerings and maintains a staunch backlist.

From Sun & Moon: *Nothing the Sun Could Not Explain: New Brazilian Poetry* (edited by Régis Bonvivino, Nelson Asher, and Michael Palmer); *The Poets' Calendar: For the Millennium* (edited by Douglas Messerli); *Puddingstone* (fiction) by Mark Mirsky; *J. P. Morgan Saves the Nation* (musical theater) by Jeffrey M. Jones; *Lotion Bullwhip Giraffe* (poetry) by Tan Lin; *Poe's Mother: Selected Drawings of Djuna Barnes* by Djuna Barnes; *From the Other Side of the Century: A New American Drama 1960–1995* (edited by Douglas Messerli and Mac Wellman); *May Skies: There's Always Tomorrow* (history and anthology of haiku in the World War II internment camps for Japanese American citizens; edited by Violet Kazue Matsuda de Cristoforo); *Seeking Air* (novel) by Barbara Guest; *Dancers Without Music, Without Dancers, Without Anything* (cultural essays and dance criticism) by Louis Ferdinand Céline; *Terror of Earth* (fables) by Tom La Farge.

Sun & Moon distributes through Consortium.

Query letters and SASEs should be directed to:

Douglas Messerli, Director

SURREY BOOKS

230 East Ohio Street, Suite 120
Chicago, IL 60611
312-751-7330

Surrey targets nonfiction areas of business and careers, self-improvement, education, the family, travel, cooking, nutrition, and health. Surrey Books (founded in 1982) is a small publishing house that successfully reaches special reader-interest markets. Surrey's numerous ongoing series (among them: the "Skinny" series, Free & Equal Cookbooks, How to Get a Job, Undiscovered Museums) provide a dependable quality baseline for booksellers and readers alike.

On the Surrey list: *Atomic Bodyslams to Chocolate Zorros: A Bartender's Guide for the 21st Century* by Adam Rocke; *1,001 Low-Fat Vegetarian Recipes* by Sue Spitzler with Linda Yoakam; *The Travel Writer's Handbook* (revised edition) by Louise Purwin Zobel.

From the Surrey "Skinny" series: *Skinny Comfort Foods* and *Skinny Mexican Cooking* by Sue Spitler; *Skinny Italian Cooking* by Ruth Glick and Nancy Baggett; *Skinny Sandwiches* by Desiree Witkowski.

The Free & Equal Cookbooks by Carole Kruppa accent the use of non-sugar sweetening. The How to Get a Job series is keyed to specific metropolitan and regional areas. The Undiscovered Museum series by Eloise Danto provides surprising and welcome tips for a variety of travel destinations.

Surrey Books oversees its own distribution services.

Query letters and SASEs should be directed to:

Susan H. Schwartz, Publisher

Sybex, Inc.

2021 Challenger Drive
Alameda, CA 94501
415-523-8233

Sybex produces educational and professional books geared toward personal computing for business, small business, and individual end users on introductory, intermediate, and advanced levels. The Sybex list offers timely, high-quality tutorials and reference works in areas ranging from desktop publishing to networking to games.

Sybex how-to products (including book-and-diskette packages) are geared to specific operating systems and proprietary programs. Areas of particular Sybex technical scope encompass assembly languages, database management, and creative utilization of spreadsheets. Sybex (founded in 1976) issues a solid block of state-of-the-art titles each year and supports a healthy backlist.

The Sybex catalog highlights the Up & Running computer-book series for beginners and intermediate computer users; the introductory lineup of Your First titles; and Novell Press books for users of Novell networks.

The Sybex product-classification roster offers titles in computer-assisted design (CAD), communications, compact guides, computer literacy, database management, desktop presentation, desktop publishing/PC, file utilities, financial management, fun and games, hardware, Macintosh, networking, operating systems, PostScript printing, sound, spreadsheets, technical, word processing, and virus protection.

From Sybex: *The Internet Voyeur* by Jim Howard; *The Musician's Guide to MIDI* by Christian Braut; *Corel Ventura Quick and Easy* by Robin Merrin; *Tom McDonald's PC Games Extravaganza!* by T. Liam McDonald; *The Visual FoxPro Codebook* by Yair Alan Griver; *Microsoft Word for Kids* by Peter Dublin.

Sybex handles its own distribution.

Query letters and SASEs should be directed to the developmental editor/product manager appropriate for the proposal. These are:

Guy Hart-Davis, Network Press
All networking.

Gary Masters
Operating systems, programming languages, PC hardware, utilities.

Richard Mills
Spreadsheets, financial management, CAD, general computer literacy.

Brenda Kienan
Internet, electronic mail, communications software, computers for children.

Damon Dean
Macintosh (except databases, spreadsheets, and word processing); desktop graphics and design (Macintosh); multimedia; alternative platforms; games.

Melanie Spiller
Databases; presentation software (windows).

James Sumser
Word processing, integrated packages.

Additional Sybex acquisitions contact:

Kristine Plachy, Acquisitions Manager (and general liaison with authors)
Maintains close contact with the developmental editors; any book or series idea may be directed to her. Also responsible for the areas of proprietary-related projects (including licensing arrangements), new product updates, nondisclosure agreements, software and evaluation copies.

TAB BOOKS
(See McGraw-Hill)

JEREMY P. TARCHER
(See Tarcher under The Putnam Berkley Group)

TAYLOR PUBLISHING COMPANY

1550 West Mockingbird Lane
Dallas, TX 75235
214-819-8501

Taylor presents frontlist trade books and targeted-interest practical titles in the areas of celebrity biography, health and fitness, gardening, home improvement, lifestyle, nature and the outdoors, parenting, popular culture, regional, sports, and coffee-table/gift books. TFB Commemorative Press is an imprint that specializes in titles keyed to university and professional sports teams and franchises. Taylor Publishing Company (founded in 1980) is an innovative house that is particularly adept at hitting specialty interest areas and international gift-book/display markets.

Titles from Taylor: *Reach Higher* by Scottie Pippen with Greg Brown (illustrated by Doug Keith); *Paul Newman* by Lawrence J. Quirk; *Jackie Chan: Inside the Dragon* by Clyde Gentry III; *The Golf Dictionary* by Michael Corcoran; *A Sense of the Sacred: Finding Our Spiritual Lives* by Adele Getty; *Rooted in the Spirit: Exploring Inspirational Gardens* by Maureen Gilmer (photography by Jerry Pavia).

Backlist hits: *Spielberg: The Man, the Movies, the Mythology* by Frank Santello; *Patty Sheehan on Golf* by Patty Sheehan and Betty Hicks; *White Trash Gardening* by Rufus T. Firefly as told to Mike Benton; *Bonnie Blair: A Winning Edge* by Bonnie Blair with Greg Brown (illustrated by Doug Keith); *Tom Cruise: The Unauthorized Biography* by Frank Sanello; *Never Give Up* by Cal Ripken, Jr.; *Nightwalkers: Gothic Horror Movies* by Bruce Lanier Wright; and *Living on Flood Plains and Wetlands: A Homeowner's Handbook* by Maureen Gilmer.

Taylor Publishing distributes its own list and handles distribution for a variety of other houses.

Query letters and SASEs should be directed to:

Maurice Dake, President

Lynn A. Brooks, Publisher and Editorial Director

TEN SPEED PRESS/CELESTIAL ARTS
TRICYCLE PRESS

P.O. Box 7123
Berkeley, CA 94707
510-559-1600
fax: 510-524-1052

Ten Speed/Celestial Arts publishes practical nonfiction in cooking, business and careers, women's issues, parenting, health, self-discovery, leisure and lifestyle, humor, outdoors, house crafts, and popular reference. Tricycle Press (please see separate subentry below) is Ten Speed/Celestial's children's division. Ten Speed Press/Celestial

Arts publishes hardcover and paperback titles; the house also offers audio literature and produces a line of posters and novelty items.

Ten Speed Press (founded in 1971) gained success with *Anybody's Bike Book* by Tom Cuthbertson—the first book the publisher produced; this classic work has been revised and updated several times and is emblematic of the type of reference book that Ten Speed Press publishes so well. With the acquisition of the Celestial Arts subsidiary (see separate subentry below), the house obtained the midsize status that set the platform for subsequent expansion of the list. Throughout this growth, Ten Speed has been renowned for its small press publishing savvy.

Ten Speed/Celestial is selective in acquiring new works, and procures in part on the basis of projected endurance: The hardy backlist and announcements of revised editions read as fresh and bright as many houses' new releases.

Ten Speed is noted for the individualist expression of the American culture as voiced by the house's authors. Many Ten Speed titles feature unconventional approaches to the subject matter at hand—making creativity an enduring Ten Speed/Celestial Arts hallmark. Among its perennial sellers, Ten Speed publishes *What Color Is Your Parachute?* and other career-related works by Richard Bolles; *The Moosewood Cookbook* by Mollie Katzen (along with several additional food titles by Ms. Katzen and the Moosewood Collective). *Barcelona: Jews, Transvestites, and an Olympic Season* is a literary travel piece by Richard Schweid (author of the esteemed culinary classics *Catfish and the Delta* and *Hot Peppers*).

Ten Speed titles: *Peppers of the World: An Identification Guide* by Dave DeWitt and Paul Bosland; *The Compleat Cockroach: A Comprehensive Guide to the Most Despised (and Least Understood) Creature on Earth* by David Gordon; *World Sourdoughs from Antiquity* by Ed Wood; *Diane Seed's Rome for All Seasons* by Diane Seed (illustrated by Marlene McLoughlin); *New Cooking from the Old West* by Greg Patent; *Tombstones: 80 Famous People and Their Final Resting Places* by Gregg Felsen; *Test Your Cat's Creative Intelligence* by Burton Silver; *Fishing Dogs* by Ray Coppinger; *How to Find Your Mission in Life* by Richard Nelson Bolles; *Asher's Bible of Executive Résumés and How to Write Them* by Donald Asher; *Great American Microbrewery Beer Book* by Jennifer Trainer Thompson; *Be Your Own Literary Agent: The Ultimate Insider's Guide to Getting Published* by Martin P. Levin.

Ten Speed Press/Celestial Arts handles its own distribution.

Query letters and SASEs should be directed to:

Philip Wood, President and Editorial Director

CELESTIAL ARTS

The Celestial Arts program homes toward titles in self-discovery, popular psychology, relationships and healing, pregnancy and parenting, gay and lesbian issues, practical how-to, kitchen arts, and general trade nonfiction.

Celestial Arts was founded as an independent house in 1966 and was acquired by Ten Speed Press in 1983. The house produces an individual line of hardcover and trade paperback books, along with calendars, maps, poster art, personal journals, and engagement books.

On the Celestial Arts roster: *Listen to Me: A Book for Women and Men About Father–Son Relationships* by Gerald G. Jampolsky, M.D., and Lee L. Jampolsky, Ph.D.; *Maui Onion Cookbook* by Barbara Santos; *Oats! A Tribute to Our Favorite Comfort Food* by Shirley Streshinsky and Maria Streshinsky; *The Totalled Roadkill Cookbook* by Buck Peterson; *Computers and Your Health: Problems, Prevention & Cures* by Joanna Bawa; *Eastern Body, Western Mind: Psychology and the Chakra System As a Path to the Self* by Anodea Judith; *Everyday Pediatrics for Parents* by Elmer R. Grossman, M.D.; *The Detox Diet: A How-to Guide for Cleaning the Body of Toxic Substances* by Elson M. Haas, M.D.

Celestial Arts is distributed by Ten Speed Press/Celestial Arts.

Query letters and SASEs should be directed to:

David Hines, Editorial Director

TRICYCLE PRESS

Tricycle is devoted to books, posters, and audiotapes for kids and their grown-ups. Tricycle Press was started in 1994 to unify and expand the house's children's list (previously divided between Ten Speed and Celestial). Tricycle Press, in addition to its own roster of originals, catalogs appropriate backlist selections from Ten Speed and Celestial Arts.

Tricycle is commited to publishing projects that reflect the creative spirit of the parent company, Ten Speed Press, and its publishing partner, Celestial Arts.

Titles from Tricycle: *Amelia Writes Again* by Marissa Moss; *Raptors, Fossils, Fins & Fangs: A Prehistoric Creature Feature* by Ray Troll and Brad Matsen (illustrated by Ray Troll); *Cody Coyote Cooks! A Southwest Cookbook for Kids* by Denice Skrepcinski, Melissa T. Stock, and Lois Bergthold (illustrated by Lois Bergthold).

Query letters and SASEs to Tricycle Press should be directed to:

Nicole Geiger, Managing Editor

TEXAS MONTHLY PRESS

(See Gulf Publishing)

THAMES AND HUDSON

500 Fifth Avenue
New York, NY 10110
212-354-3763
fax: 212-398-1252

Thames and Hudson publishes popular and scholarly works as well as college texts in the fine arts, archaeology, architecture, biography, crafts, history, mysticism, music, photography, and the sciences.

Thames and Hudson (founded in 1977) is an international producer of well-crafted nonfiction trade books in hardcover and trade paperback under its double-dolphin logo. Though a portion of the publisher's list is originated through the New York editorial office, the greater part of Thames and Hudson's titles are imports via the house's United Kingdom branch.

From Thames and Hudson: *France from the Air* by Claire Julliard (photographs by Daniel Philippe); *The Animated Alphabet* by Hughes Demeude; *Monuments and Masterpieces: Histories and Views of Public Sculpture in New York City* by Donald Martin Reynolds; *Rachel Whiteread* (edited by Fiona Bradley); *Paula Rego: A Retrospective* by Fiona Bradley, Judy Collins, Ruth Rosengarten, and Vic Willing; *The Cities of Ancient Mexico: Reconstructing a Lost World* by Jeremy A. Sabloff; *Inside Architecture: Interiors by Architects* by Susan Zevon (photographs by Judith Watts); *Stories in Stone: The Medieval Roof Carvings of Norwich Cathedral* by Martial Rose and Julia Hedgecoe; *Ancient Peoples of the American Southwest* by Stephen Plog; *Henri Cartier-Bresson: Mexican Notebooks* (text by Carlos Fuentes); *Balinese Gardens* (text by William Warren; photographs by Luca Invernizzi Tettoni); *The Splendor of Islamic Calligraphy* by Abdelkebir Khatibi and Mohammed Sijelmassi; *Significant Others: Creativity and Intimate Partnership* (edited by Whitney Chadwick and Isabelle de Courtivron); *The True History of Chocolate* by Sophie D. and Michael D. Coe; *Ports of Entry: William S. Burroughs and the Arts* by Robert A. Sobieszek (with the Los Angeles County Museum of Art).

Real Kids/Real Science is a series of children's books covering such areas as marine biology, entomology, and invertebrate zoology.

Thames and Hudson is distributed to the trade by W. W. Norton. The house also offers an 800 ordering number and has in-house fulfillment services for purchases by individual consumers.

Query letters and SASEs should be directed to:

Peter Warner, President

THEATRE COMMUNICATIONS GROUP

355 Lexington Avenue
New York, NY 10017
212-697-5230
fax: 212-983-4847

Theatre Communications Group publishes works in stage performance and the performing arts for professionals and a general readership. Areas of interest include plays published in book format; literary and critical works; stagewriting and stagecraft; biography and memoir; anthologies; reprints of popular and classic works; directories and references. The house issues hardcovers and trade paperbacks. Typically, Theatre Communications Group releases a small number of new seasonal titles while endorsing a solid backlist.

Theatre Communications Group (founded in 1961) proclaims the following trade motto: "Plays are literature."

On the Theatre Communications Group list: *Stage Writers Handbook: A Complete Business Guide for Playwrights, Composers, Lyricists and Librettists* by Dana Singer; *Testimonies: Five Plays* by Emily Mann; *Mad Forest: A Play from Romania* by Caryl Churchill; *Mojo* (drama) by Jez Butterworth; *Theatre Profiles: The Illustrated Guide to America's Nonprofit Professional Theatres* (updated biennially; edited by Steven Samuels).

Theatre Communications Group distributes to the trade through Consortium.

Query letters and SASEs should be directed to:

Steven Samuels, Editor

THUNDER'S MOUTH PRESS
(See Marlowe & Thunder's Mouth)

TIME WARNER BOOK GROUP
WARNER BOOKS
THE MYSTERIOUS PRESS
LITTLE, BROWN AND COMPANY
Time & Life Building
1271 Avenue of the Americas
New York, NY 10020
212-522-7200

Warner Books publishes trade nonfiction and commercial fiction. Warner produces mass-market, trade paperback, and hardcover originals as well as reprints. Among Warner's nonfiction categories are biography, business, cooking, current affairs, history, house and home, humor, popular culture, psychology, self-help, sports, games books and crosswords, and general reference. Warner fiction accents the popular approach and includes frontlist commercial novels and works in the categories of mystery and suspense, fantasy and science fiction, action thrillers, horror, and contemporary and historical romance.

Warner Aspect is an imprint that specializes in thrillers, suspense, action adventure, future fiction, science fiction, and fantasy. Warner Vision books are generally high-profile mass-market releases. Books on cassette are the domain of Time Warner AudioBooks. The formerly independent Mysterious Press publishes a distinguished list of mystery, suspense, and crime novels as well as selected crime nonfiction and reference (see separate subentry below).

Warner Books (founded in 1961) is a division of Time Warner Communications.

From the Warner nonfiction list: *My Sergei* by Ekaterina Gordeeva with E. M. Swift; *Simple Abundance* by Sarah Ban Breathnach; *The Rules* by Ellen Fein and Sherrie

Schneider; *Mountain, Get Out of My Way* by Montel Williams with David Paisner; *Victory of the Spirit: Meditations on Black Quotations* by Janet Cheatham Bell; *The Investment Club Book* by John F. Wasik; *Jump Start Your Brain* by Doug Hall with David Wecker; *Buns of Steel* by Leisa Hart; *Curries Without Worries: An Introduction to Indian Cuisine* by Sudha Koul.

Among major novelists who have appeared on the Warner imprint are Sidney Sheldon, Scott Turow, Rebecca Brandywyne, and Alexandra Ripley. Representative Warner fiction: *Total Control* by David Baldacci (author of *Absolute Power*); *The Notebook* by Nicholas Sparks; *The Grid* by Philip Kerr; *Hang Time* by Zev Chafets; *Iced* by Carol Higgins Clark (copublished with Dove); *The Tenth Insight* by James Redfield (author of *The Celestine Prophecy*); and novels of Robert James Waller (author of *The Bridges of Madison County*; *Slow Waltz at Cedar Bend*; *Border Music*; *Puerto Vallarta Squeeze*).

Warner Books handles its own distribution and distributes book products from other publishers.

Query letters and SASEs should be directed to:

Danielle Dayan, Assistant Editor
Women's fiction, romances.

Airié Dekidjiev, Associate Editor
Quality fiction, pop culture, Hispanic-market books.

Amye Dyer, Associate Editor, Warner Treasures
Humor, games, puzzles, novelty publications.

Maureen Egen, President and Publisher
Presides over the Warner Books program.

Amy Einhorn, Executive Editor, Warner Trade Paperbacks
Pop culture, business, fitness and self-help.

Rick Horgan, Vice President and Executive Editor
Biographies, pop culture, business, general nonfiction. Fiction: Thrillers.

Colleen Kapklein, Editor
Health, self-help, general commercial nonfiction. Literary fiction.

Caryn Karmatz, Editor
Women's fiction, multicultural books.

Rob McMahon, Assistant Editor

Betsy Mitchell, Editor
Science fiction.

Jessica Papin, Editorial Assistant
Commercial fiction, popular fiction. Commercial nonfiction, including popular science.

Mel Parker, Senior Vice President and Publisher
Presides over Warner paperbacks.

(Ms.) Jamie Raab, Executive Editor
General nonfiction. Commercial fiction.

Diane Stockwell, Associate Editor

Susan Sandler, Senior Editor
Commercial fiction and nonfiction.

Rick Wolff, Senior Editor
Business, sports.

Claire Zion, Executive Editor
Women's fiction, including romance.

THE MYSTERIOUS PRESS

The Mysterious Press features novels of crime and suspense, detective fiction, and thrillers, as well as anthologies within these fields. The house also produces literary criticism, some true crime, and reference works for writers and aficionados of mystery and detection. Mysterious Press issues titles in hardcover, trade paperback, and mass-market paper formats, and also releases opulent series of slipcased editions signed by the authors. The Mysterious Press was founded as an independent house in 1976.

Mysterious Press publishes works by such writers as Robert Campbell, Jerome Charyn, George C. Chesbro, Mary Higgins Clark, Janet Dailey, Aaron Elkins, Nicolas Freeling, Elmore Leonard, Charlotte MacLeod, Margaret Maron, Marcia Muller, Elizabeth Peters, Ellis Peters, Ruth Rendell, Julie Smith, David Stout, Donald E. Westlake, Teri White, and Margaret Yorke.

Indicative of Mysterious Press fiction: *Two Bear Mambo* by Joe R. Lansdale; *Smoke* by Donald E. Westlake; *Life Itself* by Paco Ignacio Taibo II; *Electric City* by K. K. Beck; *Double* by Marcia Muller and Bill Pronzini; *Death of a Charming Man* by M. C. Beaton.

Time Warner Electronic Publishing and Simultronics Corporation launched *Modus Operandi*, an on-line, multiplayer computer mystery game series, with interactive plots based on scenarios created by authors and editors of Mysterious Press.

The Mysterious Press list is distributed by Warner Books.

Query letters and SASEs should be directed to:

William Malloy, Editor in Chief

Sara Ann Freed, Executive Editor

LITTLE, BROWN AND COMPANY

New York office:
Time & Life Building
1271 Avenue of the Americas
New York, NY 10020
212-522-8700
fax: 212-522-2062

Boston office:
34 Beacon Street
Boston, MA 02108
617-227-0730
800-343-9204 (catalog requests)

Little, Brown publishes commercial trade nonfiction and fiction. Nonfiction interests encompass popular and literary biography, history, travel, art, medicine and allied health education, law, science, cuisine and lifestyle, reference, inspiration, and keepsake volumes/gift books. Little, Brown also produces commercial and literary fiction, essays, and memoirs; cultural, literary, and art criticism; and selected poetry. Little, Brown publishes in hardcover, trade paper, and mass-market paperback editions, and produces selected deluxe editions of bestselling works, coffee-table volumes, and a line of calendars.

Little, Brown and Company (founded in 1837) originated as an independent house with a Boston home base. Little, Brown earned renown as a publisher with a dynamic, commercially successful line as well as an outstanding literary list. Little, Brown, now a subsidiary of Time Warner, functions autonomously, primarily from within the Time & Life building (where its main trade offices reside), and releases titles under its stately colophon image of an eagle-topped column. Bulfinch Press (a division still based in Boston; see subentry below) is one of the leading houses to specialize in fine-arts publishing and illustrated volumes.

Back Bay Books is a Little, Brown trade paperback imprint that accents contemporary fiction; Back Bay titles are generally cataloged with the core Little, Brown list. Little, Brown and Company Books for Young Adults is among the strongest and most respected imprints in its field. (Please see separate subentry below.)

Little, Brown nonfiction and popular works: *The West: An Illustrated History* by Geoffrey C. Ward; *Emergency Room, Lives Saved and Lost: Doctors Tell Their Stories* (edited by Dan Sachs, M.D.); *How Good Do We Have To Be? A New Understanding of Guilt and Forgiveness* by Harold Kushner; *The Indebted Society: Anatomy of an Ongoing Disaster* by James Medoff and Andrew Harless (foreword by John Kenneth Galbraith); *I Want to Thank My Brain for Remembering Me: A Memoir* by Jimmy Breslin; *Hello, He Lied: And Other Truths from the Hollywood Trenches* by Lynda Obst; *Parenting the Fussy Baby and High-Need Child* by William Sears, M.D., and Martha Sears, R.N.; *The Best of Sports Illustrated* by the editors of *Sports Illustrated*; *Crazy Sexy Cool: The US Portfolio* by the editors of *US* Magazine and Rolling Stone Press; *The Cook's Bible: The Best of American Home Cooking* by Christopher Kimball; *A Civil War: Army vs. Navy—a Year Inside College Football's Purest Rivalry* by John Feinstein; *Mandela: An Illustrated Autobiography* by Nelson Mandela; *The Coming Race War in America: A Wake-Up Call* by Carl T. Rowan; *Leaving a Doll's House: A Memoir* by Claire Bloom; *Companion to the Cosmos* by John Gribbin; *The Watchman: The Twisted Life and Crimes of Serial Hacker Kevin Poulsen* by Jonathan Littman; *Nothing to Lose: Fitness for All Shapes and Sizes* by Dee Hakala and Michael D'Orso; *Virus-X: Tracking the New Killer Plagues—Out of the Present and into the Future* by Frank Ryan, M.D.; *Life Support: Three Nurses on the Front Lines* by Suzanne Gordon; *Five Against One: The Saga of Eddie Vedder and Pearl Jam* by Kim Neely; *Last Night in Paradise: Sex and Morals at the Century's End* by Katie Roiphe; *A World Without Jews: Is There a Future for Us?* by Alan Dershowitz.

Little, Brown fiction and belles lettres encompasses topnotch commercial novels and popular literature, as well as a high-profile selection of thrillers, suspense stories, and mysteries. Featured titles: *Dairy Queen Days* by Robin Inman; *Love and Longing in*

Bombay by Vikram Chandra; *Trunk Music* (a Harry Bosch novel) by Michael Connelly; *The Weight of Water* by Anita Shreve; *The Courts of Love* by Ellen Gilchrist; *The Hottest State* (novel) by Ethan Hawke; *Miracle on the 17th Green* (novelistic golf fable) by James Patterson and Peter deJonge; *Jack and Jill* (suspense) by James Patterson; *Infinite Jest* by David Foster Wallace; *On with the Story* (stories) by John Barth; *Let's Face the Music and Die* (a Lauren Laurano mystery) by Sandra Scoppettone; *The Seasons of Beento Blackbird* by Akosua Busia; *Best American Gay Fiction* (annual series; edited by Brian Bouldrey).

The Ansel Adams Publishing Program: Little, Brown is the sole authorized publisher of the Ansel Adams line of books, calendars, and posters, authorized by the Publishing Rights Trust established by Ansel Adams. Top-quality design and papers and meticulous attention to detail ensure the enduring legacy of America's great landscape photographer.

Little, Brown maintains an extensive backlist, which is especially strong in literary fiction and nonfiction. Little, Brown distributes its own titles as well as those of a changing list of other publishing houses both large and small, including Arcade Publishing, Bilingual Books, Food and Wine, Hyperion Books, and Miramax.

Please note: There are currently no Little, Brown adult-trade editors in Boston full-time. Query letters and SASEs should be directed to these New York editors:

Terry Adams, Director, Trade Paperbacks

Sarah Burnes, Editor
General nonfiction. Literary and serious commercial fiction.

Fredrica Friedman, Vice President, Associate Publisher, Editorial Director
Commercial fiction, celebrity books, and social history; general nonfiction. Projects have included: *The Day After Tomorrow* by Allan Folson; *Hide and Seek* by James Patterson; *Dream Makers, Dream Breakers* by Carl Rowan; *Tangled Vines* by Janet Dailey; *The Best Cat Ever* by Cleveland Amory; *New York Days* by Willie Morris; *Life of the Party* by Christopher Ogden; *Chutzpah* by Alan Dershowitz; and books with Henry Kissinger, Victoria Glendening, and Letty Cottin Pogrebin.

Paul Harrington, Senior Editor
Pop culture, music-related books; general commercial nonfiction; literary fiction.

Jennifer Josephy, Senior Editor
General nonfiction, cookbooks. Projects include: *Revolution from Within* by Gloria Steinhem; *Consciousness Explained* by Daniel Dennett; *A Different Mirror* by Ronald Takaki; *The Baby Book* by William Sears, M.D.; *Joan Lunden's Healthy Cooking* by Joan Lunden and Laura Morton; *The Cook's Bible* by Chrisotpher Kimball; *Colette's Cakes* by Colette Peters; *Handbook for the Soul* (edited by Richard Carlson, Ph.D., and Benjamin Shields, Ph.D.).

Geoffrey Kloske, Editor
General nonfiction; some fiction.

Rick Kot, Executive Editor
Commercial works in nonfiction; some fiction.

Amanda Murray, Assistant Editor

Eclectic interests in nonfiction and fiction. Young-women's stories with individualistic voices; appreciates dark humor.

William D. Phillips, Editor in Chief

General nonfiction; some literary fiction.

Michael Pietsch, Vice President and Executive Editor

Music-related books, pop culture, and literary fiction; general nonfiction. Projects have included *A Good Walk Spoiled: Days and Nights on the PGA Tour* by John Feinstein; *The Poet* by Michael Connelly; *Cobain* and *Garcia* by the editors of *Rolling Stone*; *Last Train to Memphis* by Peter Guralnick; *Faithfull* by Marianne Faithfull and David Dalton; *Hank Williams* by Colin Escott; and books by David Mamet, David Foster Wallace, Anita Shreve, Rick Moody, Tony Early, Peter Guralnick, and Brock Yates.

Bulfinch Press

Bulfinch Press is a Little, Brown and Company division (based in Boston) that specializes in fine arts, architecture, photography, and design, as well as finely produced collections of literary classics and illustrated volumes with a historical, cultural, or geographic accent. The house produces lush hardcover and paperback volumes, as well as merchandise lines including posters and calendars.

Representative of the Bulfinch list: *Children First: Voices and Images for the Invisible Homeless*; *Visions of Roses: Using Roses in over 30 Beautiful Gardens* (text by Peter Beales; photographs by Vivian Russell); *Decorative Designs: Over 100 Ideas for Painted Interiors, Furniture, and Decorated Objects* by Graham Rust; *The Bulfinch Guide to Art History: A Comprehensive Survey and Dictionary of Western Art and Architecture* (edited by Shearer West); *Glimpses Toward Infinity* by Gordon Parks; *Masterworks in Berlin: A City's Paintings Reunited* by Colin Eisler; *Where Masks Still Dance: New Guinea* by Chris Rainier; *Egypt: Antiquities from Above* by Marilyn Bridges; *Glorafilia: The Ultimate Needlepoint Collection* by Carole Lazarus and Jennifer Berman; *Paintings in the Vatican* by Carlo Pietrangeli; *The Bulfinch Anatomy of Antique Furniture: An Illustrated Guide to Identifying Period, Detail, and Design* by Paul Atterbury and Tim Forrest; *Hot Spots: America's Volcanic Landscape* (photographs by Diane Cook and Len Jenshel); *Life 60 Years: An Anniversary Celebration* by the Editors of *Life*; *Vanishing Songbirds, The Sixth Order: Wood Warblers and Other Passerine Birds* by Eliot Porter; *Batman Collected* (text by Chip Kidd; photographs by Geoff Spear).

A special Bulfinch project: *All Quiet on the Western Front: The Illustrated Edition* by Erich Maria Remarque. This classic war novel was first published by Little, Brown and Company in 1929, and is here illustrated for the first time with fascinating and moving historical photographs from World War I.

Query letters and SASEs should be directed to:

Carol Judy Leslie, Publisher (Bulfinch Press; Boston)

Illustrated gift/coffee-table books.

LITTLE, BROWN AND COMPANY BOOKS FOR CHILDREN AND YOUNG ADULTS

34 Beacon Street
Boston, MA 02108
617-227-0730
800-343-9204 (catalog requests)

Little, Brown's children's books division (headquartered in Boston) produces picture books, springboard books, flip books, book-and-toy packages, activity books and kits, pop-up editions, and general fiction and nonfiction titles for middle and young-adult readers.

This division also issues resource guides and reference titles in careers, social issues, and intellectual topics for higher grade levels and the college bound. The *Where's Waldo?* series has been an especially successful project. The house offers volumes in the Spanish language and in dual Spanish/English editions and is on the lookout for an increasing list in the multicultural arena.

Sample titles: *Fairy Wings* by Lauren Mills and Dennis Nolan; *The Jolly Pocket Postman* by Janet and Allen Ahlberg; *Monster's Lunch Box* by Marc Brown; *SLUGS: Pet Slug and Book* by David Greenberg; *The Kid Detective's Handbook and Scene-of-the-Crime Kit* by William Vivian Butler; *Papa Gatto* by Ruth Sanderson.

The house distributes Sierra Club Books for Children, a line of fine nature-theme picture books. Children's books from other publishers distributed by Little, Brown and Company include publications of Disney Press and Hyperion Books for Children.

Prospective authors please note: Little, Brown's children's division does not accept unsolicited manuscripts directly from authors. Manuscripts go through an agent to:

J. Scott Oberacker, Editorial Assistant (Boston)

TIMES BOOKS

(See Random House)

TOR BOOKS/FORGE BOOKS

175 Fifth Avenue, 14th Floor
New York, NY 10010
212-388-0100

Tor and Forge cover general trade nonfiction and commercial fiction. Tor publishes a list of mass-market and trade paperbacks, as well as trade hardcovers. Tor's mountain-top logo adorns standout titles in horror, science fiction and fantasy, mystery and suspense, and American historicals (including Westerns), as well as general commercial fiction and nonfiction. The Forge Books imprint (see subentry below) tends toward the center of the trade spectrum in fiction and nonfiction categories. In addition, Tor offers books for younger readers (some of which are intended for the educational market). Tor/Forge (founded in 1980) is a subsidiary of Tom Doherty Associates, an affiliate of St. Martin's Press.

From the Tor program: *The Girl Who Heard Dragons* by Anne McCaffrey. *The Furies* by Suzy McKee Charnas; *Steps to Midnight* by Richard Matheson; *Count Geiger's Blues* by Michael Bishop; *Bloodletter* by Warren Newton Beath; *Black Carousel* by Charles Grant; *Goodlow's Ghosts* by T. M. Wright; *Slow Funeral* by Rebecca Ore; *A Crown of Swords* by Robert Jordan.

Tor mass-market rack editions feature paperback books with foiled and embossed covers; the publisher provides eye-catching floor displays to booksellers for many of its major releases. Tor's list is distributed to the trade by St. Martin's Press.

FORGE BOOKS

The books that carry the Forge emblem (a stylized flaming anvil) run the gamut of commercial fiction and nonfiction. At Forge the various genres and categories are well represented (often with frontlist sensibility), and many titles honor mainstream conventions even as they exhibit their own individualistic bent.

Fiction from Forge: *Play It Again* (detective fiction) by Stephen Humphrey Bogart (author is son of Lauren Bacall and Humphrey Bogart); *Cat on a Blue Monday* (and other Midnight Louie mysteries) by Carole Nelson Douglas; *Steroid Blues* (suspense) by Richard La Plante (author of *Mantis* and *Leopard*); *The Cutting Hours* by Julia Grice; *Speak Daggers to Her* by Rosemary Edgehill; *Presumed Dead* by Hugh Holton; *False Promises* by Ralph Arnote.

Representing Forge nonfiction: *Zoo Book: The Evolution of Wildlife Conservation Centers* by Linda Koebner; *The October Twelve: Five Years of Yankee Glory* by Phil Rizzuto and Tom Horton; *Deke! My Thirty-Four Years in Space* by Donald K. Slayton with Michael Cassutt.

Query letters and SASEs should be directed to:

Natalia Aponte, Associate Editor
Women's fiction, romances, mysteries.

Greg Cox, Editor
Science fiction, fantasy, and horror.

Claire Eddy, Editor
Women's fiction, romances, mysteries.

David Hartwell, Senior Editor
Science fiction.

Patrick Nielsen Hayden, Senior Editor, Manager of Science Fiction
Science fiction, fantasy.

Beth Meacham, Executive Editor, Science Fiction

Melissa Ann Singer, Senior Editor
Women's fiction, romances, mysteries.

J. N. TOWNSEND

12 Greenleaf Drive
Exeter, NH 03833
603-778-9883
fax: 603-772-1980
800-333-9883
JNTOWN@aol.com (e-mail)

J. N. Townsend is a small publisher with a successful line of titles about living with an-imals. Townsend (founded in 1986) initially published in softcover format only, and is-sued its first hardcover title in 1994. The house has thrived on the basis of short press runs and by keeping titles alive on a full backlist.

From Townsend: *Two Perfectly Marvelous Cats: A True Story* by Rosamond M. Young; *Shunka: Life with an Arctic Wolf* by Marika Lumi Morgan; *Operation Pet Rescue: Animal Survivors of the Oakland, California Firestorm* by Gregory N. Zompolis; *Sharing a Robin's Life* by Linda Johns; *How Do You Spank a Porcupine?* by Ronald Rood; *Sasha's Tail: Lessons from a Life with Cats* by Jacqueline Damian; *Nana's Adoption Farm: The Story of Little Rachell* by Tryntje Horn (illustrated by Dana Lacroix).

J. N. Townsend Publishing presents the latest book by Era Zistel, *The Good Year,* who writes about her life with animals in the Catskill Mountains of New York. Other Zistel titles: *Gentle People*; *Wintertime Cat*; *Orphan*; *A Cat Called Christopher*; *A Gathering of Cats*; *Good Companions.*

Celebrating a third printing is *Separate Lifetimes: A Collection* by Irving Townsend (illustrated by Judith Roberts-Rondeau); this collection of essays is particularly cher-ished by readers who have suffered the loss of an animal companion. *Separate Lifetimes* was the first book published by the press in 1986 as a memorial to the pub-lisher's father.

J. N. Townsend handles its own distribution.

Query letters and SASEs should be directed to:

(Ms.) Jeremy N. Townsend, Publisher

TURNER PUBLISHING, INC.

1050 Techwood Drive NW
Atlanta, GA 30318
404-885-4114
fax: 404-885-4066

Turner publishes primarily popular nonfiction, with occasional, extremely selective, frontlist fiction. Turner Publishing, Inc. (instituted in 1989) was begun as a book-producing wing of the Turner Communications media conglomerate.

Turner Publishing projects have involved tie-ins to other Turner properties and enter-prises, such as film classics of MGM Studios and television programming, both broad-cast and cable. Turner Publishing products include lavishly produced items, profusely illustrated and with generous use of color. In addition to books, Turner's list includes calendars and pop-up volumes.

When Ted Turner sold Turner Communications to Time Warner in 1996, the dignitaries at the Time Warner Book Group (Warner Books; Little, Brown) declined the opportunity to incorporate the Turner book-publishing program, located in Atlanta, within Time Warner's primarily New York sphere. Acquisitions and other operations at Turner Publishing were for a time suspended indefinitely, with selected Turner book properties unofficially slated to appear under a Time Warner book imprint.

Last news as this book goes to press is that Turner publishing has survived as a separate entity, though corporate affiliations and other details are expected to evolve.

Titles from Turner: *Paul Newman: A Biography* by Eric Lax; *James Stewart: A Biography* by Donald Dewey; *Tex Avery: Artist, Animator, and Director from the Golden Age of Animated Cartoons* by John Canemaker; *Great Women Chefs: Marvelous Meals & Innovative Recipes from the Stars of American Cuisine* by Julie Stillman; *The Holy Bible: Family Edition* (with illustrations from the Vatican Library); *Cooking for Healthy Living* by Jane Fonda; *The Passion to Skate: An Intimate View of Figure Skating* by Sandra Bezic with David Hayes; *The Coolest Guys on Ice* by Jeff Z. Klein and Karl-Eric Reif; *Pirates: Terror on the High Seas from the Caribbean to the South China Sea* (David Cordingly, general editor); *The Intimate Couple: Reaching New Levels of Sexual Excitement Through Body Exercises and Relationship Renewal* by Jack L. Rosenberg, Ph.D. and Beverly Kitaen-Morse, Ph.D.; *Women Who Dare: Inspiring Stories from the Women Who Lived Them* by Katherine Martin.

Fiction features: *Outlaws* (suspense) by Tim Green (NFL analyst for Fox television and author of *Outlaws*; *Ruffians*; and *Titans*); *The Gris-Gris Man: A Voodoo Murder Mystery* by Don Davis; *The Last Wild River Ride* (fiction) by Richard Bangs; *Jeremiah: Terrorist Prophet* (thriller) by Michael A. Smith; *"That Kennedy Girl" A Biographical Novel* by Robert Demaria; *Tesla* by Tad Wise (based on the life of visionary inventor Nikola Tesla); *Natural Enemies* (ecological action novel) by Sara Cameron; *Necessary Risks* (inspirational drama) by Janet Keller.

Turner Publishing distributes to the trade through Andrews and McMeel.

Query letters and SASEs should be directed to:

Jim Davis, Director of Development

Katherine Buttler, Editor

2.13.61 PUBLICATIONS, INC.
TWO THIRTEEN SIXTY-ONE PUBLICATIONS

P.O. Box 1910
Los Angeles, CA 90078
213-969-8043 (information hotline)
213-969-8791

2.13.61 Publications offers new fiction and creative narratives, creative prose nonfiction, poetry, cultural events and critical works, photographic books, and audiovisual products. The house was founded in 1988.

Frontlist fandangos: *Fragile: Human Organs* (photographs) by Ross Halfin; *I Need More* by Iggy Pop; *Dear Dear Brenca: The Love Letters of Henry Miller to Brenda Venus* by Henry Miller (edited by Brenda Venus); *Totem of the Depraved* by Nick Zedd; *Attach God Inside* (poetry) by Tricia Warden; *No Forwarding Address* (fiction) by Natalie Jacobson; *King Ink II* by Nick Cave; *Not Wet Yet* by Ian Shoales.

Samples from the packrat backlist: *Eye Scream* by Henry Rollins; *Openers II—the Lyrics of Roky Erikson* by Roky Erikson; *Reach* by Don Bajema; *The Consumer* (short, dark fictions) by M. Gira; *Fuck You Heroes* by Glen E. Friedman (photographic excursion into skateboarder–hardcore punker–rap music culture—along with follow-up volume *Fuck You Too*); *Dream Baby Dream: Images from the Blank Generation* (historical photoessay) by Stephanie Chernikowski; *Rock and the Pop Narcotic* by Joe Carducci; *Letters to Rollins* by R. K. Overton.

Oh, incidentally: It's no big secret, but this operation is under the eye of none other than poet-rocker Henry Rollins himself. Want to start a contest? Guess what 2.13.61 means; offer a fancy facsimile of Henry Rollins's birth certificate to the winner.

2.13.61 Publications, Inc. distributes to the trade through Publishers Group West.

Query letters and SASEs should be directed to:

Carol Bua, Director

UNITED PUBLISHERS GROUP/UPG
ROSSET-MORGAN BOOKS
HASTINGS HOUSE
GATES & BRIDGES
JUDD PUBLISHING

50 Washington Street
South Norwalk, CT 06854
203-838-4083

United Publishers Group/UPG produces a number of trade nonfiction lines and selective fiction through several affiliated imprints. The group includes Hastings House (Daytrips travel guides); Gates & Bridges (works with multicultural/global themes); Judd Publishing (illustrated editions); Rosset-Morgan Books (books with a literary or cultural perspective).

United Publishers Group (founded in 1996) and its imprints conduct their programs from offices in several locations, including Connecticut; Washington, D.C.; and Manhattan. UPG is a subsidiary of the German-based Peter Leers Group, a privately held real-estate and insurance amalgamate.

Henno Lohmeyer (UPG publisher) opened the house in fine style, by acquiring several previously independent publishing firms, and by securing the United States rights to a number of international publishing properties. Plans are to build the publishing group through a number of robust boutique imprints, rather than by combining editorial operations.

From UPG: *Tom Cruise Unauthorized* by Wensley Clarkson; *Fifty Dead Men Walking* by Martin McGartland (investigatory piece on the Irish Republican Army); a showboat cookbook highlighting Southern cooking and Mississippi Breeze punch.

Gates & Bridges is a new imprint that features works that exemplify the essential image: "gates to new worlds . . . bridges between continents." From G&B: *Ascending Dragon/Rediscovering Vietnam* (photoessay).

United Publishers Group distributes through Publishers Group West.

Initial queries to UPG may be directed to the main-entry address. Query letters and SASEs should be directed to:

Ruina W. Judd, Editor in Chief, Judd Publishing
Illustrated books.

Hy Steirman, Editor in Chief, Hastings House
Presides over Hastings House (now featuring Daytrips travel guides).

Henno Lohmeyer, Publisher and Editor, Gates & Bridges
Works from an international perspective; regional markets; commercial and trade nonfiction.

ROSSET-MORGAN BOOKS

61 Fourth Avenue
New York, NY 10003
212-505-6880

The UPG imprint Rosset-Morgan Books accents literary writing in fiction and nonfiction. The house lineup includes Barney Rosset (founder of Grove Press and Blue Moon Books), the Foxrock line, and backlist titles by Marguerite Duras, Samuel Beckett, and Kenzaburo Oe.

Blue Moon Books (see separate main entry in this directory), another Rosset enterprise, continues to operate independently.

From Rosset-Morgan: *In Broken Wigwag* by Suchi Asano; *Watching* by John Fergus Ryan (author of *The Little Brothers of St. Mortimer*); *Power Game* by Perry Henzell (creator of the reggae cinema classic *The Harder They Come*).

Query letters and SASEs should be directed to:

Gabriel Morgan, Editor

Barney Rosset, Editor

UNIVERSE PUBLISHING

300 Park Avenue South
New York, NY 10010
212-982-2300

Universe produces books in art history and appreciation, architecture and design, photography, fashion, sports, alternative culture, and performing arts. Universe Publishing also takes on selected high-interest projects in literary writing and criticism, and the occasional human- or social-interest title in illustrated format. The Universe Publishing emphasis (through individual titles and a number of successful series) is on works of popular as well as scholarly interest in the arts worldwide, and the arts and artists of the Western and European tradition from prehistoric to contemporary times.

Universe Publishing (founded in 1956; formerly a wing of Phaidon Universe) is an affiliate division of Rizzoli International. Imprints and associated publishers include Universe, Children's Universe, Universe Calendars, Vendome, and Universe Publishing. Among Universe's products are illustrated gift books, children's books, children's paper products, calendars, address books, and diaries.

Universe titles: *A Growing Gardener* by Abbie Zabar; *Hollywood Handbook: The Chateau Marmont* (edited by André Balazs); *Rock Facts: Rock and Roll Hall of Fame and Museum* (edited by James Henke); *The Essential Book of Rural America: Down-to-Earth Buildings* by David Larkin; *Fly Fishing in America* by Tom Rosenbauer; *Traditional Country Style* by Elizabeth Wilhide; *What Is Beauty? New Definitions from the Fashion Vanguard* by Dorothy Schefer (foreword by Bruce Weber; introduction by Isabella Rossellini); *Stories of the People: Native American Voices* (from National Museum of the American Indian, Smithsonian Institution); *Davis Cup Yearbook* (with the International Tennis Federation); *Naked Men: Pioneering Male Nudes* by David Leddick; *Color Full Pain: Tattoos & Piercing* (photographs by Walter Kehr); *Ultra Lounge: The Lexicon of Easy Listening* by Dylan Jones.

Universe Publishing and Vendome Press combine on special series lines: Universe of Fashion; Universe of Design; Universe of Art. Beautifully printed and designed—and reasonably priced—these books are geared to appeal equally to novice and expert.

Universe of Fashion offerings are introduced by Grace Mirabella (of magazine fame); each volume deals with the works of great twentieth-century couturiers. These books connect the worlds of art, couture, and society with stories of legendary designers. Titles: *Coco Chanel* by Francois Baudot; *Dior* by Marie-France Pocha; *Yves Saint Laurent* by Pierre Bergé; *Valentino* by Bernadine Morris; *Versace* by Richard Martin.

From Universe of Design: *Ferrari and Pininfarina* by Lionel Froissard; *Cartier* by Philippe Trétiack.

The Universe of Art series features shifting, distinctive approaches. Some titles focus on an important facet in the work of an individual legendary master, generally a period or place that encapsulates the essence of a lifetime's work. Titles: *Matisse in Nice* by Xavier Girard; *Renoir's Nudes* by Isabelle Cahn; *Degas Backstage* by Richard Kendall; *Cézanne in Provence* by Denis Coutagne. Other titles in this series feature celebrity authors writing on celebrated artists: *Jasper Johns* by Leo Castelli; *Andy Warhol* by Bob Colacello.

From Vendome: *Paris Between the Wars: Artistic Life in the Twenties and Thirties* by Carol Mann; *Great Carpets of the World* by Valerie Berinstein and others; *Design and Color in Islamic Architecture* by Michael Barry (photographs by Roland and Sabrina Michaud); *Opera Houses of the World* by Thierry Beauvert (photographs by Jacques Moatti and Florian Kleinefern); *Bali Style* by Rio Helmi and Barbara Walker; *Haute Couture Embroidery: The Art of Lesage* by Palmer White; *The Fountains of Rome* by Mario Sanfilippo (photographs by Francesco Venturi); *Lisa Fonssagrives: A Portrait* (edited by David Seidner; essay by Martin Harrison).

CHILDREN'S UNIVERSE

Children's Universe produces a variety of inventive products, ranging from book-and-toy packages to story books, to hide-and-seek books (with moveable parts), cut-out puppets, posters, masks, and make-it-yourself gift boxes. These are finely designed books and are produced in sturdy editions to withstand carefree handling.

Books from Children's Universe: *Skateboard Monsters* by Daniel Kirk; *Ravita and the Land of Unknown Shadows* (story by Marietta and Peter Brill; illustrations by Laurie Smollett Kutscera); *Head Trips* by Sara Schwartz; *First Steps in Paint: A New and Simple Way to Learn How to Paint* by Tom Robb; *Dinosaur Cowboys Puppet Theatre* by Judy Lichtenstein; *The ABC's of Art* (with a wall frieze version) by National Gallery of Art, London (with flash cards by National Gallery of Art, Washington, DC).

Universe is distributed to the trade by St. Martin's.

Query letters and SASEs should be directed to:

Charles Miers, Publisher
Calendars, graphic products; Children's Universe projects.

James Stave, Senior Editor
Art, architecture, women's studies.

VAN NOSTRAND REINHOLD

115 Fifth Avenue
New York, NY 10003
212-780-6157

Van Nostrand Reinhold (founded in 1848) publishes professional reference and trade books. House specialties include the areas of business, finance, and careers; leadership and project management; business technology and internet business; communications and network management. Van Nostrand also produces periodicals, computer software, and graphic design. VNR is also known for professional and technical works in food and nutrition.

Representative titles from Van Nostrand Reinhold: *Lasting Change: Building the Shared Values That Make Companies Great* by Ron Lebow and William L. Simon; *Project Management: A Systems Approach to Planning, Scheduling and Controlling* (revised edition) by Harold Kerzner; *The Geek's Guide to Internet Business Success: The Definitive Business Blueprint for Internet Developers, Programmers, Consultants, Marketers, and Service Providers* by Bob Schmidt; *Cheryl Currid's Guide to Business Technology* by Cheryl Currid; *Global Connections: International Telecommunications Infrastructure and Policy* by Heather E. Hudson; *Graphic Design on the Desktop: A Guide for the Non-Designer* by Marcelle Lapow Toor.

Van Nostrand Reinhold overses its own distributional network.

Query letters and SASEs should be directed to:

Noah Schactman, Acquisitions Editor
Business and professional books; related trade nonfiction.

VERSO, INC.

180 Varick Street
New York, NY 10014
212-807-9680
Versoinc@aol.com (e-mail)

Verso accents trade nonfiction and literary fiction. Areas of Verso scope include contemporary issues and culture; history and biography; investigative works; world literature and thought in translation; continental, postmodernist, and deconstructivist philosophy and criticism; humor. Verso produces hardcover and trade paperback editions, as well as occasional special merchandise lines such as calendars and cards.

Verso, Inc. (founded in 1968) is an international house; the United Kingdom headquarters operates from London offices; the downtown New York wing is responsible for Stateside promotion, marketing, sales, and distribution; the major editorial acquisitions program is centered in the U.K.; over the past several seasons the U.S. list has gained increasing presence.

General nonfiction from Verso: *Secrets of Life and Death: Women and the Mafia* by Renate Siebert (translated by Liz Heron); *Red Dirt: Growing Up Okie* by Roxanne Dunbar-Ortiz; *Animal Geographies: Place, Politics; and Identity in the Nature-Culture Borderlands* (edited by Jennifer Wolch and Jody Emel); *The Way the Wind Blew: A History of the Weather Underground* by Ron Jacobs; *The Invention of the White Race (volume 2): The Origins of Racial Oppression in Anglo-America* (edited by Theodore W. Allen); *Dead Again: The Russian Intelligentsia After Communism* by Masha Gessen; *Motorcycle Diaries: A Journey Around South America* by Ernesto Che Guevara (translated by Ann Wright); *Mexican Postcards* by Carlos Monsalvos.

Works of popular and cultural note: *Hotel America: Scenes in the Lobby of the Fin de Siècle* by Lewis H. Lapham; *Power Misses: Essays Across (Un)Popular Culture* by David E. James; *Machos, Mistresses, Madonnas: Contesting the Power of Latin American Gender Imagery* (edited by Marit Melhuus and Kristi Anne Stølen); *NASA/ Trek: Popular Science and Sex in America* by Constance Penley; *The History of Forgetting: Los Angeles and the Erasure of Memory* by Norman M. Klein; *Washington Babylon* (investigatory reporting) by Alexander Cockburn and Ken Silverstein; *Shades of Noir* (essays on film; edited by Joan Copjec); *The Missionary Position: Mother Teresa in Theory and Practice* (exposé) by Christopher Hitchens.

Verso distributes to the trade through W. W. Norton (U.S.); Penguin Canada (Canada); and Marston Book Services (U.K. and the rest of the world).

Query letters and SASEs for the United States concerns and interests of Verso, Inc. should be directed to **Managing Editor** at the New York address:

Otherwise contact **U.K. offices:**

Verso/New Left Books

6 Meard Street
London W1V 3HR
0171.437.3546
fax: 0171.734.0059
100434.1414@compuserve.com (e-mail)

VIKING
(See Penguin USA)

WALKER AND COMPANY
435 Hudson Street
New York, NY 10014
212-727-8300
fax: 212-727-0984

Walker publishes trade nonfiction and fiction. Nonfiction emphasis includes science, sports, nature, self-help, business and entrepreneurship, travel, education and parenting, and marriage and family. Frontlist fiction accents mysteries and Westerns. Walker produces a list of large-print Judaica and Christian inspirational titles; books for children range from preschool picture books to books for young adults (please see separate subentry below for Walker and Company Books for Young Readers).

Walker and Company (established in 1959) is a concentrated powerhouse with a hardhitting, diverse list; especially strong are Walker's market niches in mysteries, Westerns, large-print religious and inspirational titles, and children's books chosen to complement a broad, carefully chosen selection of adult nonfiction titles.

Walker operates on the publishing credo that what often separates the success of one book from another is the ability to execute an effective marketing strategy; what then separates one house from another is the ability to execute many such strategies—often simultaneously—season upon season.

Walker and Company was founded by the intrepid Sam Walker, who expressed the view "there cannot be a surfeit of good taste." Such faith in editorial content remains at the heart of the firm today, under the current leadership of publisher George Gibson. Underlying the house's publishing strategy is a commitment to quality of product. This two-pronged assault on the marketplace thus relies on compositional and literary depth as well as the ability to capitalize on the potential appeal of such works.

Walker nonfiction titles: *Letting Go: Morrie's Reflections on Living While Dying* by Morrie Schwartz; *Hamilton's Blessing: The Extraordinary Life and Times of Our National Debt* by John Steele Gordon; *The Official Rules for Lawyers, Politicians . . . and Everyone They Torment* by Paul Dickson; *Phantom Islands of the Atlantic: The Mapping of Lands That Never Were* by Donald S. Johnson; *All the Presidents' Words: The Bully Pulpit and the Creation of the Virtual Presidency* by Carol Gelderman; *Popping the Question: Real Life Stories of Marriage Proposals, from the Romantic to the Bizarre* by Sheree Bykofsky and Laurie Viera; *Stress: 63 Ways to Relieve Tension and Stay Healthy* by Charles B. Inlander and Cynthia K. Moran; *Longitude: The True Story of a Lone Genius Who Solved the Greatest Scientific Problem of His Time* by Dava Sobel (a New York *Times* bestseller).

In fiction Walker is admired for its standout approach to category books (a significant number of which are first novels) in mysteries and Westerns. (Walker discontinued its lines in such genres as thrillers, romances, and adventure novels.) Walker also publishes standout mainstream novels.

Exemplifying Walker fiction: *When Well Horses Die* by Sandra West Prowell; *The Innocents* by Richard Barre; *The Devil on Horseback* by Lauran Paine; *The Last Free Range* by James A. Ritchie.

On the Walker list in mystery: *The Trouble in Town Hall* (a Dorothy Martin mystery) by Jeanne Dams; *Perilous Friends* (a Barbara Simons mystery) by Carole Epstein; *This Dog for Hire* (a Rachal Alexander and Dash mystery) by Carol Lea Benjamin; *The Late Town Cop* (a Carl Wilcox Mystery) by Harold Adams; *The Fatal Elixir* (a Lobo Blacke/Quinn Booker mystery) by William L. DeAndrea; *Curl Up and Die* (a Stella the Stargazer mystery) by Christine T. Jorgensen; *The Sound of the Trumpet* (an Evan Horne mystery) by Bill Moody; *Count Your Enemies* (a Bert Swain mystery) by Paul Nathan; *Deadly Partnership* (a Kate Kinsella mystery) by Christine Green; *The Water Cannibals* (a Lieutenant Abe Rainfinch mystery) by P. B. Shaw.

Walker's guidelines for manuscript submission to their genre lists include valuable hints for fiction authors in general and category writers in particular; the sheet for Walker mysteries notes such tips as the editorial view that the mystery novel is a game between author and reader, an entertaining puzzle to be savored and solved; the mystery must be primary (with such nuances as romantic interest secondary); the mystery-novel storyline must be rooted in the real world (and not imbued with supernatural overtones); and manuscripts should in general respect the conventions of the genre.

Because Walker does welcome unsolicited submissions, the publisher emphasizes the importance of including a stamped, self-addressed envelope as well as maintaining the other customary manuscript-related courtesies—contact the publisher for detailed submission guidelines. Authors please note: Materials submitted without a self-addressed stamped envelope (SASE) will *not* be returned.

Walker handles marketing, sales, and distribution for its own list.

Query letters and SASEs should be directed to:

George Gibson, Publisher
Nonfiction in all Walker areas, including science, nature, parenting, education, business, health, sourcebooks.

Jacqueline Johnson, Editor
Nonfiction.

Michael Seidman, Editor
Mysteries. No romantic suspense or horror stories.

WALKER AND COMPANY BOOKS FOR YOUNG READERS

Walker and Company Books for Young Readers maintains a backlist in addition to its seasonal offerings of new books. The house caters to a variety of young-reader markets from preschooler picture books to fiction and nonfiction for young adults.

Walker titles for young readers: *Meet the Monsters* by Jane Yolen and Heidi E.Y. Stemple (illustrated by Patricia Ludlow); *Scruffy: A Wolf Finds His Place in the Pack* by Jim Brandenburg; *Snow Day* by Moira Fain; *Police Patrol* by Katherine K. Winkleman (illustrated by John S. Winkleman); *Tabitha: The Fabulous Flying Feline* by Carol Ann Timmel (illustrated by Laura Kelly); *101 Questions and Answers About Backyard Wildlife* by Ann Squire (illustrated by Jennifer DiRubbio); *How to Babysit an Orangutan* (story and photographs by Tara and Kathy Darling).

Query letters and SASEs should be directed to:

Emily Easton, Editorial Director

Soyung Pak, Editor

Robin Ben-Joseph, Assistant Editor

The above three editors acquire children's books. Especially interested in young science, photoessays, historical fiction for middle grades, biographies, current affairs, and young-adult nonfiction.

WARNER BOOKS
THE MYSTERIOUS PRESS

(See Time Life Books)

WATSON-GUPTILL PUBLICATIONS

1515 Broadway
New York, NY 10036-8986
212-764-7300

Watson-Guptill produces titles in art instruction and technique, graphic design, fine arts, photography, crafts, environmental and interior design, architecture, music, theater, and film. Manuals and handbooks abound on the Watson-Guptill booklist, as do annual design reviews geared to these specialized fields.

Watson-Guptill's imprints include Whitney Library of Design, Amphoto, Billboard Books, Back Stage Books, and RAC Books. A significant portion of the Watson-Guptill list comprises reissues and reprints; the publisher maintains an extensive backlist and is a leading publisher in its areas of interest. Watson-Guptill Publications (founded in 1937) is a division of Billboard Publications.

The Watson-Guptill imprint addresses art instruction and graphic design. Whitney Library of Design issues titles in architecture, interior design, and planning. Amphoto produces instructional volumes from leading photographers. Billboard Books vends authoritative, up-to-the-minute books on every aspect of music and entertainment. Back Stage Books purveys informative reference and instruction books in the performing arts. RAC Books offers a complete line of titles for radio amateurs.

Watson-Guptill distributes its own list.

Query letters and SASEs should be directed to:

Candace Raney, Senior Acquisitions Editor
Graphic design and art instruction.

(Ms.) Robin Simmen, Senior Editor
Amphoto.

Bob Nirkind, Senior Editor
Billboard Books.

FRANKLIN WATTS INC.
(See Grolier Children's Publishing)

SAMUEL WEISER, INC.
(See Directory of Religious, Spiritual, and Inspirational Publishers)

WESTERN PUBLISHING COMPANY, INC.
GOLDEN BOOKS FAMILY ENTERTAINMENT
ADULT PUBLISHING GROUP
GOLDEN BOOKS CHILDREN'S PUBLISHING GROUP
850 Third Avenue
New York, NY 10022
212-753-8500

Western Publishing accents children's books and adult trade nonfiction plus some commercial fiction. The children's program includes illustrated color picture books, coloring books, activity books, gift books, and games and puzzles. Western also produces videocassettes, electronic books, related merchandise and toys; the house also has a line of promotional/display titles. Western Publishing's Golden Books Family Entertainment Adult Publishing Group publishes trade books with a family focus in nonfiction and fiction.

Western Publishing imprints include Artists & Writers Guild Books, Golden Books (for children), Goldencraft, Golden Press, Wave Books (paperbacks for teenagers), and Golden Books Family Entertainment Adult Publishing Group.

Western Publishing (founded in 1907) is a worldwide enterprise with offices in Wisconsin, Australia, Canada, and London. Western Publishing's colorfully illustrated Golden Books for children are popular with young readers all over the globe.

Western Publishing announced plans to expand presence in the adult trade when Richard Snyder took over the helm at Western in late 1995, subsequent to Snyder's departure from Simon & Schuster, where he had been chief executive officer.

Projects from Golden Books Family Entertainment Adult Publishing Group: *Energize Yourself: The Ten-Minute Solution* by Bradford Keeney (and *Energize Your*

Life); *Grace* (fictionalized family memoir) by Robert Ward (writer for television's *Hill Street Blues*); *It's NOT Just a Phase* by Susan Swedo, M.D. and Henrietta Leonard, M.D.; *Conscious Connections* by Dr. Ron Taffel with Melinda Blau; *Twice Chosen: Reviving the Arts of Courage and Commitment* by Wayne Brown.

Western Publishing orchestrates its own global distribution.

Query letters and SASEs should be directed to:

Robert Asahina, President and Publisher

Laura Yorke, Editor in Chief

WESTMINSTER/JOHN KNOX PRESS

(See Directory of Religious, Spiritual, and Inspirational Publishers)

WESTVIEW PRESS

(See listing for Westview Press under HarperCollins Publishers)

WHITE PINE PRESS

10 Village Square
Fredonia, NY 14083
716-672-5743

White Pine is a literary house with a focus on new fiction, short stories, and poetry; issues-oriented nonfiction; and literature in translation. White Pine series include Terra Incognito (voices from emerging nations of Eastern Europe); Secret Weavers (Latin American perspectives); works from winners of the White Pine Poetry Prize. White Pine (founded in 1973) produces a short list of new works each year and tends a full backlist.

From White Pine: *Four Questions of Melancholy: New and Selected Poems* by Tomaz Salamun (translated from the Slovenian by Christopher Merrill and Michael Biggins); *The Voice of Manush* (novel) by Victor Walter; *Zoo and Cathedral* (winner of the White Pine Poetry Prize) by Nancy Johnson; *Goldsmith's Return* (fiction) by Terry Richard Bazes ("a novel of unusual ability and imagination"—Joseph Heller); *Ashes of Revolt: Essays on Human Rights* by Marjorie Agosín.

White Pine announces a distinguished new literary competition: The White Pine Prize for a collection of short stories, sponsored by the Reba and Dave Williams Writing Center at Marymount Manhattan College. Contact: Lewis Burke FrumkIs, Director of the Writing Center, Marymount Manhattan College, 221 East 71st Street, New York, NY 10021 (212-734-4419).

White Pine distributes to the trade through Consortium.

Query letters and SASEs should be directed to:

Elaine LaMattina, Editor in Chief

Dennis Maloney, Publisher

JOHN WILEY & SONS

605 Third Avenue
New York, NY 10158-0012
212-850-6000
fax: 212-850-8641
800-225-5945
http://www.wiley.com (World Wide Web) Wiley's Web site has the latest information on new books, journals, and other publications along with special promotions and publicity.

Wiley is best known in the areas of architecture and design, business and management, careers, children's and young adult nonfiction, computers, current affairs, finance biography, history, hospitality, investment, nature, psychology, science, tax, and travel. The publisher maintains a reputation for publishing top-drawer professional and popular works, in addition to academically oriented works in business and the sciences. Wiley publishes in hardcover and trade paperback editions.

John Wiley & Sons (established in 1807) is a press with tradition. Through a sequence of partnership shifts and business incarnations over the years (Charles Wiley, Wiley & Halsted, Wiley & Long, Wiley & Putnam), the house has an historical involvement with the course of American letters: for example, as publishers of such writers as Edgar Allan Poe, Elizabeth Barrett Browning, and James Fenimore Cooper. Today, John Wiley & Sons is an independent house that produces books for the general trade as well as for specialized professional, scientific, and college markets.

From the Wiley trade list: *Bloomberg: The Message Is the Message* by Mike Bloomberg with Matthew Winkler; *Quiet Crisis in America: What Politicians Won't Tell You About Our Economy and Your Future* by Ravi Batra; *The Empire God Built: Inside Pat Robertson's Media Machine* by Alec Foege; *Wide-Angle Vision: Beat Your Competition by Focusing on Fringe Competitors, Lost Customers, and Rogue Employees* by Wayne Burkan; *Forbes Greatest Business Stories of All Time* by Dan Gross and the editors of *Forbes* Magazine; *Against the Gods: The Remarkable Story of Risk* by Peter L. Bernstein; *The Nordstrom Way: The Inside Story of America's No. 1 Customer Service Company* by Robert Spector and Patrick D. McCarthy; *Women of the Street: Making It on Wall Street, the World's Toughest Business* by Sue Herera; *The Drama of Leadership* by Patricia Pitcher; *Back from the Brink: The Greenspan Years* by Steven K. Beckner; *The Education of a Speculator* by Victor Niederhoffer; *Jacqueline Bouvier: An Intimate Memoir* by John H. Davis; *Jerusalem in the Twentieth Century* by Martin Gilbert; *Superchefs: Signature Recipes from America's New Royalty* by Karen Gantz Zahler; *Would-Be Worlds: Breaking the Complexity Barrier with the New*

Science of Simulation by John L. Casti; *Have No Fear: The Charles Evers Story* by Charles Evers and Andrew Szanton; *Sister Power: How Phenomenal Black Women Are Rising to the Top in a Race-Conscious Society* by Patricia Reid-Merritt; *Goodbye, Descartes: The End of Logic and the Search for a New Cosmology of the Mind* by Keith Devlin; *Modern Bride Complete Wedding Planner* by Cele Goldsmith Lalli and Stephanie H. Dahl; *The National Trust Guide to Art Deco in America* by David Gebhard.

John Wiley & Sons handles its own distribution.

WILEY CHILDREN'S BOOKS

Wiley Children's Books show the house motto: "Discovering the world up close." Wiley children's titles offer an in-depth approach to subjects at hand, be it the natural world, science and technology, or witty fun-and-game experimental projects. Branches in the Wiley children's family include the Earth-Friendly series, Janice VanCleave's science lines (including the Science for Every Kid series), Flying Start, and The House of Science.

Some titles: *Detective Science: 40 Crime-Solving, Case-Breaking, Crook-Catching Activities for Kids* by Jim Wiese; *Janice VanCleave's 202 Oozing, Bubbling, Dripping, and Bouncing Experiments* by Janice VanCleave; *Online Kids: A Young Surfer's Guide to Cyberspace* by Preston Gralia; *Student Science Opportunities: Your Guide to Over 300 Exciting National Programs, Competitions, Internships, and Scholarships* by Gail Grand.

Query letters and SASEs should be directed to:

Jim Bissent, Editor
General business and management topics.

Kate Bradford, Editor
Science, nature, children's nonfiction.

Jeff Brown, Senior Publisher
Accounting.

Deborah Englander, Editor
Financial and investment subjects.

Barbara Goldman, Executive Editor
Wide-range of interests.

Carole Hall, Associate Publisher and Editor in Chief, Professional and Trade Division

Mike Hamilton, Senior Editor
Career development, small businesses, real estate.

Gerard Helferich, Publisher
General Interest and Children's books.

Bob Ipsen, Publisher, Trade Computer Books
Computer books; technology-related topical nonfiction.

Emily Loose, Senior Editor
Economics, sociology, serious nonfiction.

Judith McCarthy, Editor
Parenting, health, popular reference, women's interest.

Joanne Miller, Executive Editor
Psychology, counseling.

Tom Miller, Senior Editor
Health, how-to, self-help, popular reference.

Ruth Mills, Editor
General business and management topics.

Myles Thompson, Executive Editor
Investing, banking, business reference.

WILLIAMSON PUBLISHING COMPANY

P.O. Box 185
Church Hill Road
Charlotte, VT 05445
802-425-2102

Williamson accents activity books for kids, and highlights topics within the subject areas of parenting and the family. Williamson also produces titles in the fields of business and career, education, travel, cooking, country living, and livestock husbandry. The house publishes primarily in trade-paperback format.

Williamson Publishing Company (founded in 1983) is known for a wide variety of works and viewpoints united through an enthusiastic, upbeat, purposeful how-to approach. Williamson typically produces a small list of new titles each year and commands a comprehensive backlist.

On the Williamson list in children's activity titles and entertainingly educational books: *Tales Alive! Ten Multicultural Folk Tales with Art, Craft, and Creative Experiences* by Susan Milord; *Super Science Concoctions: 50 Mysterious Mixtures for Fabulous Fun* by Jill Frankel Hauser; *Kids Make Music! Clapping and Tapping from Bach to Rock* by Avery Hart and Paul Mantell; *Stop, Look, and Listen: Exploring the World Around You* by Sarah A. Williamson; *SAT Preparatory Flash Cards: With 500 Math and Vocabulary Questions and Answers* by David Jaffe.

Titles in parenting and the family: *Parents Are Teachers, Too: Enriching Your Child's First Six Years* by Claudia Jones; *Doing Children's Museums: A Guide to 265 Hands-On Museums* by Joanne Cleaver.

Indicative of Williamson trade nonfiction, in general interest and specialist fields: *The Women's Job Search Handbook: With Issues and Insights into the Workplace* by Gerri Bloomberg and Margaret Holden; *Retirement Careers: Combining the Best of Work and Leisure* by DeLoss L. Marsh; *Dining on Deck: Fine Foods for Sailing and Boating* by Linda Vail; *Building a Multi-Use Barn: For Garage, Animals, Workshop, or Studio* by John Wagner; *The Sheep Raiser's Manual* by William K. Kruesi.

Williamson Publishing distributes its list, and works through a number of regional book sales representatives.

Query letters and SASEs should be directed to:

Jack Williamson, President

WORD PUBLISHING

(See Directory of Religious, Spiritual, and Inspirational Publishers)

WORKMAN PUBLISHING COMPANY
ARTISAN
GREENWICH WORKSHOP PRESS
ALGONQUIN BOOKS OF CHAPEL HILL

New York offices:
708 Broadway
New York, NY 10003
212-254-5900

Workman publishes commercial nonfiction with an accent on lifestyle areas of cooking, food and wine, health and exercise, how-to, sports, pregnancy and childcare, cats, and related popular reference. The house is known for a precisely targeted selection of games and puzzles, cartoon books, and specialty merchandise such as gift books, calendars, journals, and diaries. General trade nonfiction hits the high points of most how-to/self-help categories; business, careers, and personal finance; and quirky works that strike a contemporary note in the popular culture. Workman hosts an outstanding line of children's books.

Workman also lists titles in popular science, some science fiction and general fiction, satire and humor, self-discovery, fun and games, hobbies and handicrafts, gardening and the home, and travel. Workman produces electronic works, including software, multimedia, and interactive products; these projects are often copublished with or distributed for such firms as Turner Interactive and Swfte International.

Workman imprints and divisions include Artisan and Greenwich Workshop Press (which stress lifestyle, crafts, and design). In 1988 Workman acquired Algonquin Books of Chapel Hill, which specializes in American fiction and belletristic nonfiction. (See subentries.)

Workman Publishing Company (started in 1967) is adept at a marketing, sales, and promotional style that features such results as eye-catching counter displays for booksellers and racks devoted entirely to Workman lines.

Highlights from Workman: *USA Cookbook* by Sheila Lukins; *1001 Ways to Energize Employees* by Bob Nelson; *Fat-Proof Your Child* by Joseph S. Piscatella; *Fearless Frying Cookbook* by Hoppin' John Martin Taylor; *Welcome to Lumpy Gravy* (cartoons) by John Long; *100 English Roses for the American Garden* by Clair G. Martin III (photographs by Saxon Holt); *Thighs to Die For: Book & Custom Exercise Pouch* by Ann Piccirillo with Ruth Harris.

Calendars and diaries are often theme-keyed to other arenas of Workman publishing interest. Many calendar lines tie in with Workman's successful series in lifestyle, inspiration, nature, games and puzzles, humor, sports, cats and dogs.

Of interest to young readers and the family: *The First Things to Know About Ants* by Patricia Grossman (illustrated by John D. Dawson); *Learn-to-Read Treasure Hunt* by Steve Cohen; *97 Ways to Make a Baby Laugh* by Jack Moore.

Workman Publishing Company handles its own distribution.

ARTISAN
GREENWICH WORKSHOP PRESS

Workman's Artisan division specializes in lifestyle titles; the Artisan list includes titles from the Greenwich Workshop Press imprint (crafts and the arts), as well as calendars and other specialty merchandise. Artisan and Greenwich Workshop Press together accent crafts, home, garden, and design, each with its own distinctive editorial approach and publishing lines.

On the Artisan list: *Pierre Franey Cooks with His Friends* by Pierre Franey with Claudia Franey Jensen (photographs by Martin Brigdale and Jean Cazals); *French Tarts: 50 Savory and Sweet Recipes* by Linda Dannenberg (photographs by Guy Bouchet; illustrations by Vavro); *Portobello Cookbook* (mushroom recipes) by Jack Czarnecki (photographs by Alexandra Maldonado); *Fresh Cuts: Arrangements with Flowers, Leaves, Buds & Branches* by Edwina von Gal (photographs by John Hall; foreword by Ken Druse); *Picasso's One-Liners* (single-line drawings by Pablo Picasso); *Cowgirl Rising* (paintings by Donna Howell-Sickles; text by Peg Streep; introduction by Teresa Jordan); *The Glory of Flight: The Art of William S. Phillips* (paintings by William S. Phillips; text by Edwards Park; introduction by Stephen Coonts).

Artisan is the publisher of the Audubon Society's calendar line and distributes books for Eating Well Books (from *Eating Well* magazine).

Query letters and SASEs should be directed to:

Sally Kovalchick, Editor in Chief
Humor, quirky popular science and culture.

Suzanne Rafer, Editor
Cookbooks, humor, family issues. Children's activity books.

Peter Workman, President
Oversees entire program. Acquires in all areas consistent with list, including health.

ALGONQUIN BOOKS OF CHAPEL HILL
P.O. Box 2225
Chapel Hill, NC 27515

This division of Workman Publishing Company has a primarily literary orientation in commercial nonfiction and fiction. The house list represents the American tradition, ranging from the homespun to the avant-garde. Algonquin Books of Chapel Hill presents its titles in hardcover and trade paper editions with a look and feel befitting the publisher's emphasis on both the classical and contemporary—books designed to be comfortably handled when read. The Algonquin editorial organization operates from both the Chapel Hill and New York Workman offices.

Algonquin nonfiction includes: *Mrs. Whaley and Her Charleston Garden* by Emily Whaley in conversation with William Baldwin (with line drawings); *Pie Every Day: Recipes and Slices of Life* by Pat Willard (with line drawings); *My Life As a Boy: A Woman's Story* by Kim Chernin (author of *In My Father's Garden*); *The Road Home* (memoir) by Eliza Thomas.

Algonquin fiction and literary works: *Little Miss Strange* (novel) by Joanna Rose; *Normal* (stories) by Lucia Nevai; *Lightning Song* (fiction) by Lewis Nordan; *A Crime in the Neighborhood* (novel) by Suzanne Berne; *Meeting the Minotaur* by Carol Dawson; *Excuse Me for Asking* by Janis Arnold. Backlist favorites: *The Passion of Ellie O'Barr* (romance) by Cindy Bonner; *The Strange Death of Mistress Coffin* (mystery) by Robert J. Begiebing; *Omnivores* (contemporary sexual satire) by Lydia Millet.

Front Porch Paperbacks is a trade-paper line specializing in the work of respected literary voices as well as new writers. Front Porch reprints selected Algonquin hardcover titles.

Algonquin Books of Chapel Hill is distributed by the parent Workman Publishing Company.

Query letters and SASEs should be directed to:

Shannon Ravenel, Editorial Director

Elizabeth Scharlatt, Publisher

THE WRIGHT GROUP

19201 120th Avenue NE
Bothell, WA 98011
800-345-6073; 800-523-2371
http://www.wrightgroup.com (World Wide Web)

The Wright Group (founded in 1980) is a leading publisher of educational books for elementary school and junior high curricula. Wright series lines include SUNSHINE, Foundations, Heritage Readers, Woodland Mysteries, The Writing Project, Visions: African-American Experiences, The Evangeline Nichols Collection, Story Vine, and Primarily Health.

The Wright Group publishers believe that, after the parents' role, teachers are the most important person in the life of a child. The teacher who empowers a child to read fulfills the greatest purpose.

Wright educational tools feature the "whole language" approach to reading, and hosts a wide range of books in science and social studies, as well as professional books for educators. The house has a full slate of books geared to the Spanish-language market.

The SUNSHINE program is a core instructional reading program with over 1,000 books for children. SUNSHINE includes fiction, nonfiction, poetry, plays, collections, traditional tales, and more. SUNSHINE features a mix of talented authors and illustrators from cultures and countries around the world. SUNSHINE is also available in Spanish.

The Foundations program introduces a powerful intervention system for use by classroom teachers. Foundations offers immediate intervention for children that are having problems learning to read and write.

Heritage Readers is an integrated literature and language-arts program for K–8 students. Heritage Readers are illustrated by renowned artists from the past and present and feature stories from the classic literary legacies of many cultures.

Woodland Mysteries is a collection of 20 high-interest novels designed especially for discouraged readers and ESL students.

The Writing Project complements and extends any language-arts program. Using their own life experience, students structure their writing from authentic writing models that incorporate various styles, forms, and functions.

Visions: African-American Experiences is a guide–reading program for young students that brings together a collaborative team of African-American educators, authors, and illustrators.

The Evangeline Nichols Collection introduces students to rich multi-ethnic characters and true-to-life urban settings. Story Vine is a line that weaves tales of the American continent. These multicultural books include contemporary stories, traditional stories, and a memoir.

Primarily Health is a dynamic, hands-on health curriculum for grades K–3. Primarily Health was created by the Comprehensive Health Education Foundation with the input of children, nurses, educators, and national experts.

The Wright Group also offers professional books for teachers: *The Pippin Teacher's Library; Supporting Struggling Readers* by Barbara J. Walker; *Whole Learning: Whole Child* by Joy Cowley; *The Spelling Teacher's Book of Lists* and *Teaching Writing: The Nuts and Bolts of Running a Day-to-Day Writing Program* by Jo Phenix.

The Wright Group handles its own distribution.

Query letters and SASEs should be directed to:

Rebel Williams, Vice President, Project Development

THE WRITER, INC.

120 Boylston Street
Boston, MA 02116-4615
617-423-3157

The Writer, Inc. publishes a selection of books in hardcover and paperback on all phases of writing and selling that written work; these publications are written and edited by experienced and successful authors.

Since 1887, both aspiring and professional writers have looked to *The Writer* magazine ("the pioneer magazine for literary workers") as a practical guide to instruct, inform, and inspire them in their work. The Writer is renowned for the annually updated reference resource *The Writer's Handbook* (edited by Sylvia K. Burack). The house also publishes *Plays: The Drama Magazine for Young People* with an attendant list in books. (See separate subentry below.)

Frontlist offerings: *How to Write Your Novel* by Margaret Chittenden; *Write on Target* by Dennis E. Hensley and Holly G. Miller; *The Elements of Mystery Fiction* by William G. Tapply; *Writing & Revising Your Fiction* by Mark Wisniewski.

Reference books for writers: *The Writer's Handbook* (edited by Sylvia K. Burack); *The Thirty-Six Dramatic Situations* by Georges Polti; *Dictionary of Fictional Characters* by Martin Seymour-Smith; *Preparing Your Manuscript* by Elizabeth Preston; *The Writer's Rhyming Dictionary* by Langford Reed; *Writing Poetry: Where Poems Come From and How to Write Them* by David Kirby; *Preparing Your Manuscript* by Elizabeth Preston; *Guide to Fiction Writing* by Phyllis A. Whitney; *Writing Books for Young People* by James Cross Giblin; *Write and Sell Your Free-Lance Article* by Linda Buchanan Allen.

The Writer distributes its own books.

PLAYS, INC., PUBLISHERS

Plays, Inc., Publishers is a wing of the Writer that targets younger performers in theater. This imprint's list also includes a solid slate of resource materials of value to professionals who work in the theater with children.

From Plays, Inc.: *Great American Events on Stage*, *Thirty Plays from Favorite Stories*, and *The Big Book of Skits* (edited by Sylvia E. Kamerman); *Plays from African Tales* by Barbara Winther; *Costume: An Illustrated Survey from Ancient Times to the 20th Century* by Margot Lister; *The Puppet Book* by Claire Buchwald (illustrations by Audrey Jacubiszyn); *Mime: Basics for Beginners* by Cindie and Mathew Straub (photographs by Jeff Blanton); *Modern Educational Dance* by Valerie Preston-Dunlop.

Query letters and SASEs should be directed to:

Sylvia K. Burack, Editor

WRITER'S DIGEST BOOKS
F&W PUBLICATIONS
NORTH LIGHT BOOKS
BETTERWAY BOOKS
STORY PRESS

1507 Dana Avenue
Cincinnati, OH 45207
513-531-2222
fax: 513-531-4744

Writer's Digest/F&W produces books to help writers, poets, artists, songwriters, and photographers develop their talent, hone their professional skills, and—of course—sell their work. The publisher pursues this mission by issuing a list of guidebooks, how-to, reference, and professional titles in hardcover and paperback editions.

Writer's Digest Books (founded in 1919) is a division of F&W Publications, publisher of *Writer's Digest* magazine. Writer's Digest Books offers a classic and expansive list for the professional as well as aspiring writer. Story Press is an imprint geared to literary interest. North Light Books issues professional titles in fine arts and design. Betterway features a variety of topic-oriented titles in fields such as woodworking, genealogy, theater, and coaching guides. (See subentries.) Writer's Digest/F&W maintains a comprehensive backlist.

WRITER'S DIGEST BOOKS

The Writer's Digest list covers virtually all commercial writing fields; many of these works are high on the professional-writer's recommendation list. Writer's Digest Books features a series of annually updated resource guides including *Writer's Market*.

From Writer's Digest Books: *The Writer's Digest Dictionary of Concise Writing* by Robert Hartwell Fiske; *Writing and Selling Your Novel* by Jack M. Bickham; *Get That Novel Written!* by Donna Levin; *The Writer's Guide to Everyday Life in Renaissance England* by Kathy Lynn Emerson; *Body Trauma: A Writer's Guide to Wounds and Injuries* by David W. Page, M.D.; *Amateur Detectives: A Writer's Guide to How Private Citizens Solve Criminal Cases* by Elaine Raco Chase and Dr. Anne Wingate.

Writer's Digest offers the electronic (CD-ROM) version of their classic *Writer's Market: Where & How to Sell What You Write* (edited by Kirsten C. Holm).

Additional titles are keyed to writers' needs in comedy, horror, historical fiction, science fiction, Westerns, suspense fiction, popular songwriting, business writing, and children's/young-adult books. The Howdunit series has met with particular success, and features works geared for writers in the fields of mystery, suspense, and true crime.

Sample titles: *Malicious Intent: A Writer's Guide to How Criminals Think* by Sean P. Mactire; *Modus Operandi: A Writer's Guide to How Criminals Work* by Mauro V. Corvasce and Joseph R. Paglino; *Armed and Dangerous: A Writer's Guide to Weapons* by Michael Newton; *The Writer's Guide to Everyday Life in the Middle Ages* by Sherrilyn Kenyon; *Aliens and Alien Societies* by Stanley Schmidt.

The **Story Press** imprint features classic works for literary devotees (many of them in reprint) along with destined-to-be-classic new works. From Story Press: *The Joy of Writing Sex* by Elizabeth Benedict; *Maura B. Jacobson's New York Magazine Crossword Puzzles* by Maura B. Jacobson.

Bill Brohaugh does not wish to receive any unsolicited queries, proposals, or manuscripts at the Story Press imprint; all acquisitions for this line are editorially generated in house and activated through existing avenues.

Distribution for Writer's Digest Books is through the marketing network of corporate umbrella F&W publications.

Query letters and SASEs should be directed to:

Bill Brohaugh, Editorial Director, Writer's Digest Books
How-to books for writers, how-to books for photographers.

David Borcherding, Editor
How-to books for writers, how-to books for photographers.

NORTH LIGHT BOOKS

The North Light Books division of F&W Publications produces how-to books geared to the areas of drawing, painting, clip art, printing, desktop publishing, and graphic arts, along with a line of titles for young readers.

Representative North Light titles: *Painting Houses, Cottages and Towns on Rocks* by Lin Wellford; *Romantic Oil Painting Made Easy* by Robert Hagan; *Great Design Using Non-Traditional Materials* by Sheree Clark and Wendy Lyons; *How to Get Started Selling Your Art* by Carole Katchen; *How to Create Action, Fantasy and Adventure Comics* by Tom Alvarez; *Painting Baby Animals with Peggy Harris; The North Light Artist's Guide to Materials & Techniques* by Phil Metzger; *Capturing the Magic of Children in Your Paintings* by Jessica Zemsky; *Fake Your Own Antiques* by Peter Knott.

North Light Books is distributed by F&W Publications; the house also catalogs the lists of Coast to Coast Books and Rockport Publishers.

Query letters and SASEs should be directed to:

Rachel Wolf, Editor for Fine Arts
How-to books for fine artists, and graphic designers.

Lynn Haller, Editor
Graphic design.

BETTERWAY BOOKS

Betterway Books (founded in 1980) is a former independent that is now part of F&W Publications. Betterway is a midsized imprint in the interest areas of home-building and remodeling, resource guides and handbooks, small business and personal finance, self-help, theater crafts, collectibles, sports, and reference.

From Betterway: *The Doll Sourcebook for Collectors and Artists* (edited by Argie Manolis); *The Unpuzzling Your Past Workbook: Essential Forms and Letters for all Genealogists* by Emily Anne Croom; *Skiing on a Budget* by Claire Walter; *The Stagecraft Handbook* by Daniel A. Ionazzi; *Making Elegant Gifts from Wood* by Kerry Pierce; *100 Keys to Preventing and Fixing Woodworking Mistakes* and *100 Keys to Woodshop Safety* by Alan and Gill Bridgewater; *Getting the Very Best from Your Router* by Pat Warner.

Betterway Books is distributed through the network of F&W Publications, the parent company.

Query letters and SASEs should be directed to:

William Brohaugh, Editorial Director
How-to and reference books on sports, recreation, consumer information, weddings, theater, performing arts, genealogy.

David Borcherding, Editor
How-to books for writers, how-to books for photographers.

David Lewis, Editorial Director
How-to and reference books on home building and remodeling, small business and personal finance, hobbies, collectibles, and woodworking.

WYNWOOD PRESS

(See Baker Book House in Directory of Religious, Spiritual, and Inspirational Publishers)

YANKEE BOOKS

(See Rodale Press)

ZEBRA BOOKS

(See Kensington Publishing Corporation)

ZIFF-DAVIS PRESS

(See Macmillan Computer Publishing USA under Simon & Schuster)

ZOLAND BOOKS

384 Huron Avenue
Cambridge, MA 02138
617-864-6252
fax: 617-661-4998

Zoland Books produces fiction, poetry, and books of literary interest as well as literary and art criticism. A significant portion of the Zoland list accents the interrelationship between the written and visual arts. The house also issues audiotape renditions of selected works, especially poetry. Zoland nurtures a staunch backlist.

Zoland (founded in 1987) is a small independent house that publishes a small group of new titles from year to year, usually not geared to any particular seasonal business goals; projects are acquired on an extremely selective basis.

On the list from Zoland: *Letting Loose* by Christopher T. Leland; *Straight Man* by Sallie Bingham; *Billy in Love* by Norman Kotker; *Gas Station* by Joseph Torra; *Cross a Parted Sea* (poems) by Sam Cornish; *Seeing Eye* (short stories) by Michael Martone; *The Instinct for Bliss* (short stories) by Melissa Pritchard; *The Circles I Move In* (short stories) by Diane Lefer; *Talking Pictures: The Photography of Rudy Burckhardt, 1933–1988* by Rudy Burckhardt and Simon Pettet.

Zoland is distributed to the trade by National Book Network.

Query letters and SASEs should be directed to:

Roland F. Pease, Jr., Publisher and Editor

ZONDERVAN PUBLISHING HOUSE

(See Directory of Religious, Spiritual, and Inspirational Publishers)

University Presses

The University As Publisher
From Academic Press to Commercial Presence

WILLIAM HAMILTON

You nod as you glance at the ads in the book-reviews, you are aware of the spots you heard or saw on radio and late-night television, and you recognize the authors from television interviews and radio call-in shows. So you know today's university presses publish much more than scholarly monographs and academic tomes.

While the monograph is—and will always be—the bread and butter of the university press, several factors over the past quarter century have compelled university presses to look beyond their primary publishing mission of disseminating scholarship. The reductions in financial support from parent institutions, library-budget cutbacks by federal and local governments, and the increasing scarcity of grants to underwrite the costs of publishing monographs have put these presses under severe financial pressure. The watchword for university presses, even in the 1970s, was survival.

While university presses were fighting for their lives, their commercial counterparts were also experiencing difficult changes. The commercial sector responded by selling off unprofitable and incompatible lists or merging with other publishers; many houses were bought out by larger concerns. Publishers began to concentrate their editorial and marketing resources on a few new titles that would generate larger revenues. Books that commercial publishers now categorized as financial risks, the university presses saw as means of entry into new markets and opportunities to revive sagging publishing programs.

Take a look through one of the really good bookstores in your area. You'll find university press imprints on regional cookbooks, popular fiction, serious nonfiction, calendars, literature in translation, reference works, finely produced art books, and a considerable number of upper-division textbooks. Books and other items normally associated with commercial publishers are now a regular and important part of university press publishing.

There are approximately 100 university presses in North America, including United States branches of the venerable Oxford University Press and Cambridge University Press. Of the largest American university presses—California, Chicago, Columbia,

Harvard, MIT, Princeton, Texas, and Yale—each publishes well over 100 books per year. Many of these titles are trade books that are sold in retail outlets throughout the world.

The medium-sized university presses—approximately 20 fit this category—publish between 50 and 100 books a year. Presses such as Washington, Indiana, Cornell, North Carolina, Johns Hopkins, and Stanford are well established as publishers of important works worthy of broad circulation.

All but the smallest university presses have developed extensive channels of distribution, which ensure that their books will be widely available in bookstores and wherever serious books are sold. Small university presses usually retain larger university presses or commissioned sales firms to represent them.

UNIVERSITY PRESS TRADE PUBLISHING

The two most common trade areas in which university presses publish are (1) nonfiction titles that reflect the research interests of their parent universities and (2) regional titles.

For example, University of Hawaii Press publishes approximately 30 new books a year with Asian or Pacific Rim themes. Typically, 8 to 10 of these books are trade titles. Recent titles have included Japanese literature in translation, a lavishly illustrated book on Thai textiles, books on forms of Chinese architecture, and a historical guide to ancient Burmese temples. This is a typical university press trade list—a diverse, intellectually stimulating selection of books that will be read by a variety of well-informed, responsive general readers.

For projects with special trade potential, some of the major university presses enter into copublishing arrangements with commercial publishers—notably in the fields of art books and serious nonfiction with a current-issues slant—and there seems to be more of these high-profile projects lately.

Certain of the larger and medium-sized university presses have in the past few years hired editors with experience in commercial publishing in order to add extra dimensions and impact to the portion of their program with a trade orientation.

It's too early to know if these observations represent trends. Even if so, the repercussions remain to be seen. Obviously, with the publishing community as a whole going through a period of change, it pays to stay tuned to events.

UNIVERSITY PRESS AUTHORS

Where do university press authors come from? The majority of them are involved in one way or another with a university, research center, or public agency, or are experts in a particular academic field. Very few would list their primary occupation as author. Most of the books they write are the result of years of research or reflect years of experience in their fields.

The university press is not overly concerned about the number of academic degrees following its trade book authors' names. What matters is the author's thoroughness in addressing the topic, regardless of his or her residence, age, or amount of formal education. A rigorous evaluation of content and style determines whether the manuscript meets the university press's standards.

UNIVERSITY PRESS ACQUISITION PROCESS

Several of the other essays in this volume provide specific strategies for you to follow to ensure that your book idea receives consideration from your publisher of choice—but let me interject a cautionary note: The major commercial publishers are extremely difficult to approach unless you have an agent, and obtaining an agent can be more difficult than finding a publisher!

The commercial publishers are so overwhelmed by unsolicited manuscripts that you would be among the fortunate few if your proposal or manuscript even received a thorough reading. Your unagented proposal or manuscript will most likely be read by an editorial assistant, returned unread, or thrown on the slushpile unread and unreturned.

An alternative to the commercial publisher is the university press. Not only will the university press respond; the response will generally come from the decision maker—the acquisitions editor.

Before approaching any publisher, however, you must perform a personal assessment of your expectations for your book. If you are writing because you want your book to be on the bestseller list, go to a medium-to-large commercial press. If you are writing in order to make a financial killing, go to a large commercial publisher. If you are writing in the hope that your book will be a literary success, contribute to knowledge, be widely distributed, provide a modest royalty, and be in print for several years, you should consider a university press.

SHOULD A UNIVERSITY PRESS BE YOUR FIRST CHOICE?

That depends on the subject matter. It is very difficult to sell a commercial publisher on what appears on the surface to be a book with a limited market. For example, Tom Clancy was unable to sell *The Hunt for Red October* to a commercial publisher because the content was considered too technical for the average reader of action-adventure books. Clancy sent the manuscript to a university press that specialized in military-related topics. Naval Institute Press had the foresight to see the literary and commercial value of Clancy's work. As they say, the rest is history. Tom Clancy created the present-day technothriller genre and has accumulated royalties well into the millions of dollars. Once Clancy became a known quantity, the commercial publishers began courting him. All of his subsequent books have been published by commercial houses.

How do you find the university press that is suitable for you? You must research the university press industry. Start by finding out something about university presses. In addition to the listings in the directory of publishers and editors appearing in this book, most university presses are listed in *Literary Market Place*.

A far better and more complete source is *The Association of American University Presses Directory*. The AAUP directory offers a detailed description of each AAUP member press with a summary of its publishing program. The directory lists the names and responsibilities of each press's key staff, including the acquisitions editors. Each press states its editorial program—what it will consider for publication. A section on submitting manuscripts provides a detailed description of what the university press expects a proposal to contain. Another useful feature is the comprehensive subject grid, which identifies over 125 subject areas and lists the university presses that publish in each of them.

An updated edition of *The Association of American University Presses Directory* is published every fall, and is available for a nominal charge from the AAUP central offices in New York City or through its distributor, University of Chicago Press.

Most university presses are also regional publishers. They publish titles that reflect local interests and tastes and are intended for sale primarily in the university press's local region. For example, University of Hawaii Press has over 250 titles on Hawaii. The books—both trade and scholarly—cover practically every topic one can think of. Books on native birds, trees, marine life, local history, native culture, and an endless variety of other topics can be found in local stores, including the chain bookstores.

This regional pattern is repeated by university presses throughout the country. University of Washington Press publishes several titles each year on the Pacific Northwest and Alaska. Rutgers University Press publishes regional fiction. University of New Mexico Press publishes books on art and photography, most dealing with the desert Southwest. Louisiana State University Press publishes Southern history and literature. Nebraska publishes on the American West.

Almost all university presses publish important regional nonfiction. If your book naturally fits a particular region, you should do everything possible to get a university press located in that region to evaluate your manuscript.

Do not mistake the regional nature of the university press for an inability to sell books nationally—or globally. As mentioned earlier, most university presses have established channels of distribution and use the same resources that commercial publishers use for book distribution. The major difference is that the primary retail outlets for university press books tend to be bookstores associated with universities, smaller academic bookstores, specialized literary bookstores, and independent bookstores that carry a large number of titles.

Matching books to buyers is not as difficult as you might think. Most patrons of university press bookstores know these stores are likely to carry the books they want.

Traditionally, very few university press titles are sold through major chain bookstores outside their local region. Even so, this truism is subject to change. Some of the biggest bookstore chains are experimenting with university press sections in their large superstores.

What to Expect at a University Press

You should expect a personal reply from the acquisitions editor. If the acquisitions editor expresses interest, you can expect the evaluation process to take as long as 6 to 8 months. For reasons known only to editorial staffs—commercial as well as those of university presses—manuscripts sit and sit and sit. Then they go out for review, come back, and go out for review again!

Once a favorable evaluation is received, the editor must submit the book to the press's editorial board. It is not until the editorial board approves the manuscript for publication that a university press is authorized to publish the book under its imprint.

A word about editorial boards. The imprint of a university press is typically controlled by an editorial board appointed from the faculty. Each project presented to the editorial board is accompanied by a set of peer reviews, the acquisitions editor's summary of the reviews, and the author's replies to the reviews. The project is discussed with the press's management and voted upon.

Decisions from the editorial board range from approval, through conditional approval, to flat rejection. Most university presses present to the editorial board only those projects they feel stand a strong chance of acceptance—approximately 10% to 15% of the projects submitted annually. So if you have been told that your book is being submitted to the editorial board, there's a good chance that the book will be accepted.

Once a book has been accepted by the editorial board, the acquisitions editor is authorized to offer the author a publishing contract. The publishing contract of a university press is quite similar to a commercial publisher's contract. The majority of the paragraphs read the same. The difference is most apparent in two areas—submission of the manuscript and financial terms.

University presses view publishing schedules as very flexible. If the author needs an extra 6 to 12 months to polish the manuscript, the market is not going to be affected too much. If the author needs additional time to proofread the galleys or page proofs, the press is willing to go along.

Why? Because a university press is publishing for the long term. The book is going to be in print for several years. It is not unusual for a first printing of a university press title to be available for 10 or more years. Under normal circumstances the topic will be timeless, enduring, and therefore of lasting interest.

University presses go to great lengths to ensure that a book is as close to error-free as possible. The academic and stylistic integrity of the work is foremost in the editor's mind. Not only the content but the notes, references, bibliography, and index should be flawless—and all charts, graphs, maps, and other illustrations perfectly keyed.

It does not matter if the book is a limited-market monograph or serious nonfiction for a popular trade. The university press devotes the same amount of care to the editorial and production processes to ensure the book is as accurate and complete as possible. Which leads us to the second difference—the financial terms.

Commercial publishers follow the maxim that time is money. The goal of the organization is to maximize shareholder wealth. Often the decision to publish a book is based solely on financial considerations. If a book must be available for a specific season in order to meet its financial goals, pressure may be applied to editorial by marketing, and editorial in turn puts pressure on the author to meet the agreed-upon schedule. This pressure may result in mistakes, typos, and inaccuracies—but will also assure timely publication and provide the publisher with the opportunity to earn its expected profit. At the commercial publishing house, senior management is measured by its ability to meet annual financial goals.

University presses are not-for-profit organizations. Their basic mission is to publish books of high merit that contribute to universal knowledge. Financial considerations are secondary to what the author has to say. A thoroughly researched, meticulously documented, and clearly written book is more important than meeting a specific publication date. The university press market will accept the book when it appears.

Do not get the impression that university presses are entirely insensitive to schedules or market conditions. University presses are aware that certain books—primarily textbooks and topical trade titles—must be published at specific times of the year if sales are to be maximized. But less than 20% of any year's list would fall into such a category.

UNIVERSITY PRESSES AND AUTHOR REMUNERATION

What about advances? Royalties? Surely university presses offer these amenities—which is not to suggest they must be commensurate with the rates paid by commercial houses.

No and yes. No royalties are paid on a predetermined number of copies of scholarly monographs—usually 1,000 to 2,000.

A royalty is usually paid on textbooks and trade books. The royalty will be based on the title's sales revenue (net sales), and will usually be a sliding-scale royalty ranging from as low as 5% to as high as 15%.

As with commercial publishers, royalties are entirely negotiable. Do not be afraid or embarrassed to discuss them with your publisher. Just remember that university presses rarely have surplus funds to apply to generous advances or high royalty rates. However, the larger the university press, the more likely you are to get an advance for a trade book.

Never expect an advance for a monograph or supplemental textbook.

WHEN CONSIDERING A UNIVERSITY PRESS

When you're deciding where to submit your manuscript, keep the following in mind. University presses produce approximately 10% of the books published in the United States each year. University presses win approximately 20% of the annual major book awards. Yet university presses generate just 2% of the annual sales revenue.

So if you want to write a book that is taken seriously, that will be carefully reviewed and edited; if you want to be treated as an important part of the publishing process, and want your book to have a good chance to win an award; and if you are not too concerned about the financial rewards—then a university press may very well be the publisher for you.

ARTE PÚBLICO PRESS
(see Directory of United States Publishers)

CAMBRIDGE UNIVERSITY PRESS
40 West 20th Street
New York, NY 10011-4211
212-924-3900
800-872-7423

The Cambridge list includes hardcover and paperback titles of topical contemporary general interest as well as academic import in the fields of literature, art, music, religion, history, philosophy, economics, the classics, mathematics, and the behavioral, biological, physical, social, and computer sciences. One of publishing's old guard, Cambridge University Press (founded in 1534) is now a major international operation that holds fast to a long commitment to quality.

Cambridge University Press is the printing and publishing house of the University of Cambridge. It is a charitable enterprise required by University Statute to devote itself to printing and publishing in the furtherance of the acquisition, advancement, conservation and dissemination of knowledge in all subjects; to the advancement of education, religion, learning, and research; and to the advancement of literature and good letters.

Special imprints include Cambridge Film Classics and the popularly priced Canto line. Cambridge also produces some titles for young readers, and publishes a full range of academic and popular reference works. Cambridge is strong in the reprint area, offering editions of anthologies and compilations as well as individual classic works. The Cambridge United States office is editorially independent of the British home office.

From Cambridge: *Arguments About Aborigines: Australia and the Evolution of Social Anthropology* by L. R. Hiatt; *Space Is the Machine: A Configurational Theory of Architecture* by Bill Hillier; *The Crisis of Vision in Modern Economic Thought* by Robert Heilbroner and William Milberg; *Competitive Governments: An Economic Theory of Politics and Public Finance* by Albert Breton; *A Realistic Theory of Categories: An Essay on Ontology* by Roderick M. Chisholm; *The Sources of Moral Agency: Essay in Moral Psychology and Freudian Theory* by John Deigh; *The Psychology of Freedom* by Thomas Pink; *Individual Choice and the Structures of History: Alexis de Tocqueville As Historian Reappraised* by Harvey Mitchell; *The*

NOTE: Many university presses are participants in the Combined Online Catalogue Project of the Association of American University Presses (AAUP). Book descriptions from all participating publishers can be searched by author, title, and Library of Congress subject keyword. The site can be accessed at:
   http://www.press.uchicago.edu
   http://aaup.princeton.edu
   gopher://aaup.princeton.edu

History of Mental Symptoms: Descriptive Psychopathology Since the 19th Century by German E. Berrios; *Drug-Induced Infertility and Sexual Dysfunction* by Robert Forman, Susanna Gilmour-White, and Nathalie Forman; *Adults with Autism: A Guide to Theory and Practice* (edited by Hugh Morgan); *Psychotherapy, Psychological Treatments and the Addictions* (edited by Griffith Edwards and Christopher Dare); *The Search for Political Community: American Activists Reinventing Commitment* by Paul Lichterman; *Nationalism and Literature: The Politics of Culture in Canada and the United States* by Sarah M. Corse; *God's Just Vengeance: Crime, Violence and the Rhetoric of Salvation* by Timothy Gorringe; *Power, Gender and Christian Mysticism* by Grace M. Jantzen.

The house hosts a strong reference list, including *The Cambridge International Dictionary of English* (edited by Paul Procter).

Cambridge University Press handles its own distribution.

Query letters and SASEs should be directed to:

Barbara Colson, Director

Julia Hough, Editor
Psychology and computer science.

Lauren Cowles, Editor
Mathematics and computer science.

(Mr.) Terry Moore, Executive Editor
Philosophy and humanities.

Florence Padgett, Editor
Physical sciences.

Beatrice Rehl, Editor
Fine arts and media studies.

Mary Vaughn, Executive Editor
ESL (English as a second language) books.

Frank Smith, Executive Editor
History and social sciences.

CLEVELAND STATE UNIVERSITY POETRY CENTER

1983 East 24th Street
Cleveland, OH 44115-2440
216-687-3986

Cleveland State University Poetry Center was begun in 1962 at Fenn College (which became Cleveland State in 1964); the center initiated its book-publishing program in 1971. The press publishes poets of local, regional, and international reach, generally under the aegis of one or another of the center's ongoing series. Under its flying-unicorn logo, CSU Poetry Center most often publishes trade paper editions, and also offers some titles in hardbound. The press generally produces a limited number of new titles each year. In addition, the house maintains a full backlist.

CSU Poetry Center presents a variety of styles and viewpoints—some with evident sociopolitical bent, others with broadly inspirational themes, and others notable for their strong individualistic inflections. The Poetry Center sponsors the Poetry Forum workshop and presents programs of public readings.

The center sponsors an annual poetry contest; please contact the CSU Poetry Center for submissions guidelines.

The following winners were selected from 998 manuscripts submitted for the 1996 competition. The competition is extremely tough and the Poetry Center recommends that poets publish some individual poems in magazines and literary journals before submitting to this series. It is also recommended that prospective entrants review some of the work that the Poetry Center publishes.

Books from the Poetry Center: *Warscape, with Lovers* by Marilyn Krysl (winner of 1996 CSU Poetry Center Prize); *Fresh Kills* by David Breskin; *Out of Eden* by Frankie Paino.

Shorter volumes and chapbooks: *Mystery Hill* by Susan Grimm; *The Book of Snow* by Mary Moore; *As If Our Lives . . .* by Elizabeth Murawski; *The Pull of the Planet* by Steven Reese.

The full range of publications from CSU Poetry Center Press includes award-winning volumes from established bards and releases from accomplished new writers. On the CSU list: *Blood Stories* by Martha Ramsey; *Beastmorfs* by Leonard Trawick; *Order, or Disorder* by Amy Newman; *Hyena* by Jan Freeman; *Refinery* by Claudia Keelan; *Fugitive Colors* by Chrystos; and *Lives of the Saints and Everything* by Susan Firer; *The Long Turn Toward Light* by Cleveland poet and artist Barbara Tanner Angell; *At Redbones* by Thylias Moss; *The Sioux Dog Dance: shunk ah weh* by Red Hawk.

Poetry Center books are distributed through Bookslinger, Inland, and Spring Church Book Company.

The Poetry Center accepts unsolicited manuscripts *only from December 1 to March 1* in connection with the Center's annual competition ($15 entry fee; full manuscripts only). For complete guidelines send request plus SASE. Query letters and SASEs should be directed to:

Leonard Trawick, Editor

Neal Chandler, Editor

COLUMBIA UNIVERSITY PRESS

562 West 113th Street
New York, NY 10025
212-666-1000

Columbia hosts a roster of specialty titles, including distinguished lines in media studies, journalism, and film. Columbia's publishing interest also includes current events, public issues, popular culture and fine arts, gay and lesbian studies, history, the sciences, literature, and Asian studies. Columbia University Press (established in 1893) publishes a slate of general-interest titles in addition to its established list of scholarly, academic, and scientific works. Also on the roster are a number of standard reference works geared for the institutional and academic market. The press produces books in hardcover and trade paperback editions and nurtures a healthy backlist.

Among Columbia highlights: *Winning the Peace: America and World Order in the New Era* by John Gerard Ruggle; *Losing Control: The Decline of Sovereignty in an Age of Globalization* by Saskia Sassen; *Famous Lines: A Columbia Dictionary of Familiar Quotations* (edited by Robert Andrews); *Of the People, by the People, for the People: and Other Quotations from Abraham Lincoln* (edited by Gabor Boritt); *Straight News: Gays, Lesbians, and the News Media* by Edward Alwood; *Noel Coward and Radclyffe Hall: Kindred Spirits* by Terry Castle; *Render Me, Gender Me: Lesbians Talk Sex, Class, Color, Nation, Studmuffins . . .* by Kath Weston; *Hard to Imagine: Gay Male Eroticism in Photography and Film from Their Beginnings to Stonewall* by Thomas Waugh; *Writings on Psychoanalysis: Freud and Lacan* by Louis Althusser; *Playing Nice: Politics and Apologies in Women's Sports* by Mary Jo Festle; *The Erotic in Sports* by Allen Guttmann; *Creating GI Jane: Sexuality and Power in the Women's Army Corps During World War II* by Leisa D. Meyer; *The Art of Reflection: Women Artists' Self-Portraiture in the 19th Century* by Marsha Meskimmon; *Family Wisdom: The 2,000 Most Important Things Ever Said About Parenting, Children, and Family Life* (edited by Susan Ginsberg).

From Columbia reference: *The Columbia Anthology of American Poetry* (edited by Jay Parini); *The Columbia Guide to Standard American English* by Kenneth G. Wilson.

Columbia University Press distributes its own list and handles distribution for a number of other academically oriented publishers, including Free Association Books, East European Monographs, University of Tokyo Press, American University in Cairo Press, and Edinburgh University Press.

Query letters and SASEs should be directed to:

Jennifer Crewe, Publisher
Humanities.

Edward E. Lugenbeel, Executive Editor
Science.

Ann Miller, Associate Executive Editor
Gay and lesbian studies, art history, philosophy, journalism, media.

James Raines, Assistant Director, Reference

John Michel, Associate Executive Editor
Sociology, anthropology, psychology, psychiatry, social work.

Kate Wittenberg, Editor-in-Chief
Political science, international affairs, modern studies, history.

CORNELL UNIVERSITY PRESS

Sage House
512 East State Street
P.O. Box 250
Ithaca, NY 14851-0250
607-277-2338

Cornell publishes trade nonfiction and selected fiction, literary works, and poetry in addition to a wide berth of academic and scholarly titles. Cornell's list is anchored by strong interest in literary and art criticism, philosophy, classics, history, political science, agriculture, and science. The press's Comstock Books series continues a tradition of excellence in natural history. Cornell University Press (begun in 1869) is the oldest university press in the United States.

Representing the Cornell program: *National Diversity and Global Capitalism* by Suzanne Berger and Ronald Dore; *Medieval Death: Ritual and Representation* by Paul Binski; *The Real Life of Mary Ann Evans: George Eliot, Her Letters and Fiction* by Rosemarie Bodenheimer; *"The Cross and the Sickle" : Sergei Bulgakov and the Fate of Russian Religious Philosophy, 1890–1920* by Catherine Evtuhov; *The Republic of Letters: A Cultural History of the French Enlightenment* by Dena Goodman; *In the Mirror of the Third World: Capitalist Development in Modern Europe* by Sandra Halperin; *A Geological Companion to Greece and the Aegean* by Michael Denis Higgins and Reynold Higgins; *A Mighty Baptism: Race, Gender, and the Creation of American Protestantism* (edited by Susan Juster and Lisa MacFarlane); *Beauty and the Revolution in Science* by James W. McAllister.

Cornell University Press distributes its own list.

Query letters and SASEs should be directed to:

John Ackerman, Director

Peter A. Agree, Editor
United States history, law, agriculture, social sciences, rural sociology.

Roger Haydon, Editor
Studies of the former Soviet Union and Eastern Europe, philosophy, political history, history of science, documentary series in American social history, series in international political economy, immigration history, regional studies.

Bernard Kendler, Executive Editor
Literary criticism.

Peter Prescott, Editor
Science.

DUKE UNIVERSITY PRESS

Box 90660
Durham, NC 27708-0660
919-687-3600

Areas of Duke publishing scope include cultural studies; literary studies; Latin American and Caribbean studies; legal studies; history; East European, Soviet, and post-Soviet studies; German studies; environmental studies; and history of economics. Post-Contemporary Interventions is a series that features imaginative world-class thinkers on culture, media, and global society.

Duke University Press (founded in 1921) publishes scholarly, trade, and textbooks in hardcover and trade paperback editions and maintains a strong backlist. Duke also publishes a number of academic journals, including *MLQ: Modern Language Quarterly.*

On the Duke list: *Man-Made Medicine: Women's Health, Public Policy, and Reform* (edited by Kary L. Moss); *Science Wars* (edited by Andrew Ross); *Illuminations: Women's Writings on Photography from the 1850s to the Present* (edited by Liz Heron and Val Williams); *The Third and Only Way: Reflections on Staying Alive* by Helen Bevington; *Keeping An Open Door: Passages in a University Presidency* by Keith Brodie and Leslie Banner; *Borrowed Time* (photographs by Caroline Vaughan).

The C. Eric Lincoln Series on the Black Experience is designed to facilitate the effort to help the black experience know itself better, and to share what it knows in the common interest. Representative title: *In the Name of Elijah Muhammad: Louis Farrakhan and the Nation of Islam* by Mattias Gardell.

Of popular cultural note: *The Third Eye: Race, Cinema, and Ethnographic Spectacle* by Fatimah Tobing Rony; *Vampires, Mummies, and Liberals: Bram Stoker and the Politics of Popular Fiction* by David Glover; *Pop Out: Queer Warhol* (edited by Jennifer Doyle, Jonathan Flatley, and José Esteban Muñoz); *Guilty Pleasures: Feminist Camp from Mae West to Madonna* by Pamela Robertson; *Rhythm and Noise: An Aesthetics of Rock* by Theodore Gracyk.

Duke University Press oversees its own distribution.

Query letters and SASEs should be directed to:

Kenneth A. Wissoker, Editor in Chief

THE FEMINIST PRESS AT THE CITY UNIVERSITY OF NEW YORK

311 East 94th Street
New York, NY 10128-5684
212-360-5790

The publishing horizon at the Feminist Press includes biographies, cross-cultural studies, fiction, health and medicine, history/sociology, interdisciplinary texts, literary anthologies, art and music, resources and reference works, educational materials, children's books, and women's studies (including several notable series). The house hosts a reprint program as well as its renowned originals, and also supports several feminist journals. The Feminist Press publishes in hardcover and paperback editions and moves a backlist both heady and deep through special sales including holiday mailings.

The Feminist Press maintains its aim to express and celebrate differences within the cultural context of humanity; in so doing the house has held the publishing forefront with a series of important works that bring fresh dimensions to the attention of readers.

Founded in 1970 at the crest of the second wave of American feminism, the press led off with a list that concentrated on a program to reestablish hitherto overlooked women's literary classics, aligned with an additional focus on literature of United States working-class women. The house's agenda has expanded gradually to encompass such themes as growing up female, women artists, and the family, as well as the publication of academic and general-interest works with an international cast of authors in varied disciplines and literary forms.

Highlights from Feminist Press: *Among the White Moon Faces: An Asian-American Memoir of Homelands* by Shirley Geok-lin Lim; *The New Lesbian Studies: Into the 21st Century* (edited by Bonnie Zimmerman and Toni A. H. McNaron); *Sisterhood Is Global: The International Women's Movement Anthology* (edited by Robin Morgan); *China for Women: Travel and Culture* (combination travel/women's studies; edited by Feminist Press); *Black and White Sat Down Together: Reminiscences of an NAACP Founder* by Mary White Ovington; *Motherhood by Choice: Pioneers in Women's Health and Family Planning* by Perdita Huston; *Get Smart! What You Should Know (But Won't Learn in Class) About Sexual Harassment and Sex Discrimination* by Montana Katz and Veronica Vieland; *Women Composers: The Lost Tradition Found* by Diane Peacock Jezic.

In fiction and literature: *Paper Fish* by Tina De Rosa (first published in 1980 in a run of only 1,000 copies, it retained a loyal following among a handful of scholars of Italian-American literature); *Winter's Edge* by Valerie Miner (one of the few novels to center on the lives of older, working-class women); the African novel *Changes* by Ama Ata Aidoo; the Japanese-American story collection *Songs My Mother Taught Me* by Wakako Yamauchi; a collection of stories by Italian writers titled *Unspeakable Women* (edited and translated by Robin Pickering-Iazzi); a bilingual edition of *The Answer/La Repuesta* by "the first feminist of America," the Mexican Sor Juana Inéz de la Cruz; Maureen Brady's novel *Folly*, set among black and white women in a North Carolina mill town; and *What Did Miss Darrington See? An Anthology of Feminist Supernatural Fiction* (edited by Jessica Amanda Salmonson).

A noteworthy Feminist Press educational project is *Women of Color and the Multicultural Curriculum*, edited by Liza Fiol-Matta and Miriam K. Chamberlain, which includes essays and course outlines.

A special-production volume from Feminist Press is *Long Walks and Intimate Talks*, with stories and poems by Grace Paley and paintings by Vera B. Williams.

Feminist Press books may be ordered directly from the publisher; the list is distributed to the trade in the United States via Consortium Book Sales & Distribution.

Query letters and SASEs should be directed to:

Jean Casella, Senior Editor

Susan Cozzi, Executive Director

___

GALLAUDET UNIVERSITY PRESS

800 Florida Avenue NE
Washington, DC 20002-3695
202-651-5488

Gallaudet offers titles in categories such as communication, language arts, deaf culture and history, employment and law, audiology and speechreading, instructional materials, literature, parenting, and professional books, as well as a special concentration in sign language (including American Sign Language). The publisher maintains an extensive backlist.

Imprints of Gallaudet University Press include Clerc Books and Kendall Green Publications. Among areas of current publishing emphasis are audiology, sociolegal issues in special education, English as a second language (ESL), and signed children's books in English; the house also markets a line of videotapes.

The publishing program of Gallaudet University Press (founded in 1968) exemplifies the educational impulse of Gallaudet University through an accent on issues pertinent to deafness. Gallaudet University Press publishes scholarly, educational, and general-interest titles, as well as children's books, along with the magazine *Perspectives in Education and Deafness*.

Among Gallaudet features: *Multicultural Aspects of Sociolinguistics in Deaf Communities* (edited by Ceil Lucas); *A Journey into the Deaf-World* by Harlan Lane, Robert Hoffmeister, and Ben Behan; *Silent Poetry: Deafness, Sign, and Visual Culture in Modern France* by Nicholas Mirzoeff; *Deaf Heritage in Canada* by Clifton F. Carbin; *Silence of the Spheres: The Deaf Experience in the History of Science* by Harry G. Lang; *The New Language of Toys: Teaching Communication Skills to Children with Special Needs* by Sue Schwartz and Joan Heller Miller; *Toddler Talk: The First Signs of Intelligent Life* by Joseph Garcia; *The Politics of Deafness* by Owen Wrigley; *Deaf Persons in the Arts and Sciences* by Harry G. Lang and Bonnie Meath Lang; *Communication Therapy: An Integrated Approach to Aural Rehabilitation* (edited by Mary June Moseley and Scott Bally); *All About Deafness: Where to Turn for Answers to Questions About Hearing Loss* by Salvatore J. Parlato; *Signs in Judaism: A Resource for the Jewish Deaf Community* by Adele Kronick Shuart.

On the children's list from Gallaudet: *Signing Is Fun: A Child's Introduction to the Basics of Sign Language* by Mickey Flodin; *Handsigns: A Sign Language Alphabet* by Kathleen Fain; *Jake's the Name, Sixth Grade's the Game* by Deb Piper; *Gaps in Stone Walls* by John Newfeld; *A World of Knowing: A Story About Thomas Hopkins Gallaudet* by Andy Russell Bowen; *Cosmo Gets an Ear* by Gary Clemente; *Signs of Spring* by Patrick Quinn.

Representing the Gallaudet backlist: *The Week the World Heard Gallaudet* by Jack R. Gannon; *Deaf President Now!* by John B. Christiansen and Sharon N. Barnartt; *A Study of American Deaf Folklore* by Susan Rutherford; *Growing Up Sexually* by Angela Bednarczyk; *No Walls of Stone: An Anthology of Literature by Deaf and Hard of Hearing Writers* (edited by Jill Jepson); *Gopen's Guide to Closed Captioned Video* by Stuart Gopen.

Gallaudet University Press handles distribution for its own list; the Gallaudet University Bookstore catalogs additional titles in the deafness area from other publishers, as well as a line of gift items.

Query letters and SASEs should be directed to:

Ivey Wallace, Managing Editor

HARVARD BUSINESS SCHOOL PRESS

230 Western Avenue, Fourth Floor
Allston, MA 02134
617-495-6700

Harvard Business School Press publishes trade and professional books for the business and academic communities. Areas of publishing interest embrace organizational behavior/human-resource management, finance, marketing, production and operations management, accounting and control, business history, and managerial economics. Harvard Business publishes the Baker Library line of reference books and offers series on videocassette, as well as HBS Press Expanded Books on diskette; the press also issues the journal *Harvard Business Review* along with a line of books on the Harvard Business Review imprint.

Harvard Business School Press is the publishing division of Harvard University Business School. The press was founded in 1984 as an elaboration of the increasingly successful line of business titles published by Harvard University Press. With the established aim of influencing the way readers think and act, HBS Press has a mandate to publish books that represent the best of contemporary thinking and research in business and that advance the practice of management.

Among Harvard Business School Press books: *The Balanced Scorecard: Translating Strategy into Action* by Robert S. Kaplan and David P. Norton; *Leading Change: An Action Plan from the World's Foremost Expert on Business Leadership* by John P. Kotter; *Winning Through Innovation: A Practical Guide to Leading Organizational Change and Renewal* by Michael L. Tishman and Charles A. O'Reilly III; *Human Resource Champions: The Next Agenda for Adding Value and Delivering Results* by Dave Ulrich; *The Truth About the National Debt: Five Myths and One Reality* by Francis X. Cavanaugh; *Transforming the Bottom Line: Managing Performance with the Real Numbers* by Tony Hope and Jeremy Hope; *Generation to Generation: Life Cycles of the Family Business* by Kelin E. Gersick, John A. Davis, Marion McCollom Hampton, and Ivan Lansberg; *The Loyalty Effect: Creating Value Through Partnership* (edited by Frederick F. Reichheld); *The Development Factory: Unlocking the Potential of Process Innovation* by Gary P. Pisano; *Standing Room Only: Strategies for Marketing the Performing Arts* by Philip Kotler and Joanne Scheff.

Harvard Business School Press Operations Department oversees the house's publications distribution; the house list is also available to the trade through McGraw-Hill.

Query letters and SASEs should be directed to:

Carol Franco, Director

Marjorie Williams, Executive Editor

Kirsten D. Sandberg, Senior Editor

Nicola "Nikki" Sabin, Editor

HARVARD UNIVERSITY PRESS

79 Garden Street
Cambridge, MA 02138
617-495-2600

Harvard's publishing categories include current events, cultural affairs, the arts, history, psychology, literary studies (including selected poetry), the sciences, legal studies, and economics. Harvard special series have included such lines as The Twentieth Century Fund, the Global AIDS Policy Coalition, and the Developing Child series.

Harvard University Press (started in 1913) is currently the largest academic press in the United States. Harvard University Press produces a large number of trade-oriented general-interest books for an eclectic readership, while maintaining its core program to provide a balanced offering of scholarly works in a range of academic fields. Harvard's extensive list is published in hardcover and trade paperback editions.

Featured Harvard titles: *Sisters in Arms: Catholic Nuns Through Two Millennia* by Jo Ann Kay McNamara; *Inside the Vatican: The Politics and Organization of the Catholic Church* by Thomas J. Reese; *The Harvard Biographical Dictionary of Music* (edited by Don Michael Randel); *The Thermal Warriors: Strategies of Insect Survival* by Bernd Heinrich; *Invention by Design: How Engineers Get from Thought to Thing* by Henry Petroski; *The State of the Nation* by Derek Bok; *Miles to Go: A Personal History of Social Policy* by Daniel Patrick Moynihan; *Performing Rites: On the Value of Popular Music* by Simon Frith; *Graceland: Going Home with Elvis* by Karal Ann Marling; *Fevered Lives: Tuberculosis in American Culture Since 1870* by Katherine Ott; *Betrayal Trauma: The Logic of Forgetting Childhood Abuse* by Jennifer J. Freyd; *Harlem's Glory: Black Women Writing, 1900–1950* (edited by Lorraine Elena Roses and Ruth Elizabeth Randolph); *British Military Spectacle: From the Napoleonic Wars Through the Crimea* by Scott Hughes Myerly; *On or About December 1910: Early Bloomsbury and Its Intimate World* by Peter Stansky; *The Irony of Free Speech* by Owen M. Fiss; *Democracy and Disagreement* by Amy Gutmann and Dennis Thompson; *Violent Land: Single Men and Social Disorder from the Frontier to the Inner City* by David T. Courtwright; *Wild Beasts and Idle Humours: The Insanity Defense from Antiquity to the Present* by Daniel N. Robinson; *Cultural Psychology: A Once and Future Discipline* by Michael Cole; *Lessons from Privilege: The American Prep School Tradition* by Arthur G. Powell; *Integration or Separation? A Strategy for Racial Equality* by Roy L. Brooks.

Harvard University Press handles its own distribution.

The publisher will not consider unsolicited poetry or fiction. Query letters and SASEs should be directed to:

Michael A. Aronson, Senior Editor, Social Sciences
Economics, political science, sociology, law, some business.

Aida Donald, Assistant Director and Editor-in-Chief
History, sociology with historical emphasis, women's studies with historical emphasis.

Michael Fisher, Executive Editor for Science and Medicine
Medicine, science (except astronomy), neuroscience.

Margaretta Fulton, General Editor for the Humanities
Classics (including Loeb Classics), religion, music, art, Jewish studies, women's studies.

Elizabeth Suttell, Senior Editor
East Asian studies.

Elizabeth Knoll, Senior Editor for the Behavioral Sciences
Behavioral sciences, earth sciences, astronomy, neuroscience, education.

(Mr.) Lindsay Waters, Executive Editor for the Humanities
Literary criticism, philosophy, film studies, cultural studies.

Stephanie Gouse, Paperbacks and Foreign Rights

Joyce Seltzer, Senior Executive Editor
History, contemporary affairs.
contact Joyce Seltzer at:
150 Fifth Avenue, Suite 625
New York, NY 10011
212-337-0280

THE JOHNS HOPKINS UNIVERSITY PRESS

2715 North Charles Street
Baltimore, MD 21218-4319
410-516-6900

The Johns Hopkins University Press (founded in 1878) issues a strong list of contemporary-interest titles and fiction as well as academic, scholarly, technical, and professional works in such diverse academic areas as literary criticism, ancient studies, Jewish studies, economics, political science, and history of and current trends in medicine, science, and technology.

Johns Hopkins titles: *How the West Was Lost: The Transformation of Kentucky from Daniel Boone to Henry Clay* by Stephen Aron; *Our Common Affairs: Texts from Antebellum Southern Women* (edited by Joan E. Cashin); *Hollywood's High Noon: Moviemaking and Society Before Television* by Thomas Cripps; *Roman Literary Culture: From Cicero to Apuleius* by Elaine Fantham; *The Fate of Carmen* by Evelyn Gould; *The Art of Bargaining* by Richard Ned Lebow; *Emerging Agenda for Global Trade: High Stakes for Developing Countries* by Robert A. Lawrence, Dani Rodrik, and John Whalley; *From Blue Ridge to Barrier Islands: An Audubon Naturalist Reader* (edited by J. Kent Minichiello and Anthony M. White); *A Natural History of Homosexuality* by Francis Mark Mondimore, M.D.; *Building Resemblance: Analogical Imagery in the Early French Renaissance* by Michael Randall; *Sick, Not Dead: The Health of British Workingmen During the Mortality Decline* by James C. Riley; *An Architectural History of Harford County, Maryland* by Christopher Weeks.

The Johns Hopkins literary scope is illustrated by *I Am Dangerous* (stories) by Greg Johnson; *In the Crevice of Time: New and Collected Poems* by Josephine Jacobsen; *The Bad Infinity* (drama collection) by Mac Wellman; *Home at Last* (stories) by Jean

McGarry; *The Geographical History of America* by Gertrude Stein; *The Johns Hopkins Guide to Literary Theory and Criticism* (edited by Michael Groden and Martin Kreiswirth).

Johns Hopkins produces a number of specialty lines, such as the collection of works by microhistorian Carlo Ginzburg, the American Land Classics series of facsimile reprints, and Complete Roman Drama in Translation.

The Johns Hopkins University Press handles its own distribution with the support of regional sales representatives.

The press will not consider unsolicited poetry or fiction. Query letters and SASEs should be directed to:

Douglas Armato, Editor and Manager of Book Division
Classics and ancient studies, film studies, American studies, theatre.

Robert Brugger, History Editor
American history, history of science and technology, regional titles, documentary editions.

Wendy Harris, Medical Editor
Medicine (hard science for medical professionals), public health.

Ginger Berman, Science Editor
Sciences; especially mathematical sciences, earth, planetary and life sciences.

Willis Regier, Director
Humanities, literary theory and criticism.

George F. Thompson, Project Editor
Geography and environmental studies, Anabaptist studies, urban planning.

Henry Y. K. Tom, Executive Editor
Economics, development, European history.

Jacqueline C. Wehmueller, Acquisitions Editor
Trade medical books for an educated general audience; Caribbean studies; books in higher education; history of medicine; reference books.

HOWARD UNIVERSITY PRESS

1240 Randolph Street NE
Washington, DC 20017
202-806-4935

Customer service:
P.O. Box 50283
Baltimore, MD 21211
410-516-6947

A major sector of the Howard University Press publishing scope covers issues and traditions pertaining to Africa—including African-related cultural expressions worldwide, geopolitical topics, and historical studies, in addition to the African American purview. Howard University Press (founded in 1972) produces scholarly and general nonfiction works in the areas of history, biography, economics, sociology, political science, education, contemporary affairs, communications, the arts, and literature, and produces a strong line of general-reference books. HU Press generally publishes a select group of new titles per year in hardcover and trade paperback editions. The press maintains a diverse backlist.

Indicative of the Howard University Press publishing program: *The Jamaican Crime Scene: A Perspective* by Bernard Headley: *Pathways to Success* (edited by Lloyd Ren Sloan); *Basic Currents of Nigerian Foreign Policy* by Mae C. King; *We Paid Our Dues: Women Trade Union Leaders of the Caribbean* by A. Lynn Bolles; *African Americans and U.S. Policy Toward Africa* by Elliott P. Skinner; *Captain Paul Cuff's Logs and Letters, 1808–1817: A Black Quaker's Voice from Within the Veil* (edited by Rosalind Wiggins); *An African Victorian Feminist: The Life and Times of Adelaide Smith Casely Hayford, 1869–1960* by Adelaide Cromwell; *The Demography of America* by James Tarver; *Cocoa and Chaos in Ghana* by Gwendolyn Mikell; *One Third of a Nation* (edited by Lorenzo Morris and Jean Oyemade).

On the literary, cultural, and artistic front: *Social Rituals and the Verbal Art of Zora Neale Hurston* by Lynda Marion Hill; *The Dramatic Vision of August Wilson* by Sandra Shannon; *Ancient Songs Set Ablaze: The Theatre of Femi Osofisan* by Sandra L. Richards; *Black Drama in America* (edited by Darwin T. Turner); *Modern Negro Art* by James A. Porter; *The New Cavalcade: African American Writing from 1700 to the Present* (edited by Arthur P. Davis, J. Saunders Redding, and Joyce Ann Joyce).

Howard University Press handles distribution through its own in-house marketing department; fulfillment is handled through Johns Hopkins University Press.

Please note: Howard University Press suspended operations in August of 1996 in order to reorganize. Please contact the press prior to sending any correspondence, including queries.

Query letters and SASEs should be directed to:

Edwin Gordon, Director of the Press

INDIANA UNIVERSITY PRESS

601 North Morton Street
Bloomington, IN 47404-3797
812-855-4203

Indiana University Press (founded in 1950) publishes books of serious trade interest as well as titles directed toward scholarly and academic audiences. The press addresses such subjects as regional and cultural studies, military history, criminology, political science and international affairs, popular culture and the arts, semiotics, journalism, business and economics, science and technology, environmental issues and natural history, literary criticism, and gender studies. Indiana University Press also publishes short-story collections and fiction in translation. IUP produces hardcover and paperback editions.

Indiana University Press issues a number of prestigious series, among them Theories of Representation and Difference, Theories of Contemporary Culture, Blacks in the Diaspora, Arab and Islamic Studies, and Medical Ethics. The house is home to a variety of academic journals, including *The Middle East Journal*, *Discourse*, and a number of journals in feminist studies.

On the IUP list: *The Hostage Child: Sex Abuse Allegations in Custody Disputes* by Leora N. Rosen and Michelle Etlin; *The Hundred Thousand Fools of God: Musical Travels in Central Asia (and Queens, New York)* by Theodore Levin; *Sherman's Horsemen: Union Cavalry Operations in the Atlanta Campaign* by David Evans; *Drawn from Africa Dwellings* by Jean-Paul Bourdier and Trinh T. Minh-ha; *Germany 1945: Views of War and Violence* by Dagmar Barnouw; *Studebaker: The Life and Death of an American Corporation* by Donald T. Critchlow; *Perennials for the Lower Midwest* by Ezra Haggard; *Indiana from the Air* by Richard Fields and Hank Huffman; *Frontier Indiana* by Andrew R. L. Cayton; *New Ways of Making Babies: The Case of Egg Donation* (edited by Cynthia B. Cohen); *Choreography and Narrative: Ballet's Staging of Story and Desire* by Susan Leigh Foster; *Re-Viewing Reception: Television, Gender, and Postmodern Culture* by Lynne Joyrich; *Sexualities in Victorian Britain* (edited by Andrew H. Miller and James Eli Adams); *Fetishism and Curiosity* by Laura Mulvey; *The Domain-Matrix: Performing Lesbian at the End of Print Culture* by Sue-Ellen Case.

Indiana University Press publishes *Guidelines for Bias-Free Writing* by Marilyn Schwartz and the Task Force on Bias-Free Language of the Association of American University Presses. IUP also recommends to potential authors the popular writing-reference stylebook *The Handbook of Nonsexist Writing* by Casey Miller and Kate Swift.

Also of high cultural concern: *The Well-Tempered Announcer: A Pronunciation Guide to Classical Music* by Robert Friedkin.

Indiana University Press distributes its own list, as well as books produced by the Cleveland Museum of Art, the Indiana Historical Society, and the British Film Institute; IUP also serves as regional sales representative for several other university presses.

Query letters and SASEs should be directed to:

Joan Catapano, Senior Sponsoring Editor
Women's studies, film, folklore, black studies, literary theory, regional studies, cultural history and theory.

John Gallman, Director
All areas.

Janet Rabinowich, Senior Sponsoring Editor
Russian and East European studies, African studies, Middle Eastern and Judaic studies, philosophy, and art.

Robert Sloan, Sponsoring Editor
Science, business, medical ethics, history, drama and performance, religion, and political studies.

Jeff Ankrom, Editor and Music Sponsor
Music studies, studies in Russian music.

LOUISIANA STATE UNIVERSITY PRESS

P.O. Box 25053
Baton Rouge, LA 70894-5053
504-388-6294

Areas of Louisiana State University Press interest include Southern history, the American Civil War, African-American history, United States history, Latin American history, European history, philosophy and politics, art, architecture and design, photography, literary voices of the South, American literature, general criticism and European literature, music, natural history, and medicine. LSU offers a wide variety of regional books (not limited to Louisiana environs) as well as concentrations in contemporary fiction, poetry, and literary criticism. The house produces hardcover and trade paperback editions and maintains a solid backlist. Louisiana State University Press (founded in 1935) publishes a primarily academic and scholarly list, along with a good number of general-interest titles.

From LSU Press: *Art in the American South: Words from the Ogden Collection* by Randolph Delehanty; *YA/YA! Young New Orleans Artists and Their Storytelling Chairs (And How to YA/YA in Your Neighborhood)* by Claudia Barker; *Plants for American Landscapes* by Neil G. Odenwald, ASLA, Charles F. Fryling, Jr., ASLA, and Thomas E. Pope; *Pistols and Politics: The Dilemma of Democracy in Louisiana's Florida Parishes, 1810–1899* by Samuel C. Hyde, Jr.; *From George Wallace to Newt Gingrich: Race in the Conservative Counterrevolution, 1963–1994* by Dan T. Carter; *Six Years of Hell: Harpers Ferry During the Civil War* by Chester G. Hearn.

Fiction and poetry from LSU: *Sky and Island Light* (poems) by Brendan Galvin; *Long Gone* (poems) by Dabney Stuart; *Understanding Fiction: Poems, 1986–1996* by Henry Taylor; *Alive Together* (new and selected poems) by Lisel Mueller; *Trinity* (poems) by Susan Ludvigson; *Open Field, Understory* (new and selected poems) by James Seay; *It Is Time, Lord* (novel) by Fred Chappell; *An Evening Performance* (new and selected stories) by George Garrett; *The House on Coliseum Street* (novel) by Shirley Ann Grau.

Louisiana State University Press oversees a distributional network that utilizes the services of regional university presses and book-distribution companies as well as independent sales representatives.

Query letters and SASEs should be directed to:

Maureen G. Hewitt, Editor-in-Chief

THE MIT PRESS

55 Hayward Street
Cambridge, MA 02142
617-253-5646

The MIT Press publishes nonfiction trade and reference titles in the forefront of such fields as contemporary art, architectural studies, urban management and design, computer science and artificial intelligence, cognitive and neurological sciences, linguistics, and economic science and finance; as well as works attuned to more traditional approaches within the disciplines of philosophy, engineering, and the physical sciences. The house also produces scholarly and professional works, as well as advanced educational textbooks. The MIT Press was founded in 1961 as the publishing wing of the Massachusetts Institute of Technology.

Features from MIT: *Hal's Legacy: 2001's Computer As Dream and Reality* (edited by David G. Stork); *Moths to the Flame: The Seductions of Computer Technology* by Gregory J. E. Rawlins; *Internet Dreams: Archetypes, Myths, and Metaphors* by Mark Stefik; *Abstracting Craft: The Practiced Digital Hand* by Malcolm McCullough; *Somehow a Past: The Autobiography of Marsden Hartley* by Marsden Hartley (edited by Susan Elizabeth Ryan); *Taxing Ourselves: A Citizen's Guide to the Great Debate over Tax Reform* by Joel Slemrod and Jon Bakija; *The Politics of Denial* by Michael A. Milburn and Sheree D. Conrad; *Darwin's Dreampond: Drama in Lake Victoria* by Tijs Goldschmidt; *Wild China* by John MacKinnon (photographs by Nigel Hicks); *The U.S. Paper Industry and Sustainable Production: An Argument for Restructuring* by Maureen Smith; *The Discovery of Spoken Language* by Peter W. Jusczyk; *History and Overview of Solar Heat Technologies* (edited by Donald A. Beattie); *Can We Afford to Grow Older?* by Richard Disney; *Gateways to Knowledge: The Role of Academic Libraries in Teaching, Learning, and Research* (edited by Lawrence Dowler).

The MIT Press also produces educational lines and publishes a number of specialist journals such as *TDR The Drama Review: A Journal of Performance Studies*, *The Washington Quarterly*, and *October* (a journal of art and activist theory), as well as the October Book Series. Bradford Books accents titles representing the frontiers of such areas as cognitive science, philosophy, and linguistics.

The MIT Press distributes its own list and handles distribution for several other publishers (including houses that specialize in architecture and design).

Query letters and SASEs should be directed to:

Larry Cohen, Science Editor

Roger Conover, Architecture and Design Editor

Amy Pierce, Linguistics Editor and Bradford Books

Robert Prior, Computer Science Editor

Douglas Sehry, Computer Science Editor

Elizabeth Stanton, Cognitive Science Editor and Bradford Books Philosophy.

Henry Stanton, Cognitive Science Editor and Bradford Books

Fiona Stevens, Neuroscience Editor

Madeline Sunley, Environmental Sciences Editor

Terry Vaughn, Economics Editor

NAVAL INSTITUTE PRESS

118 Maryland Avenue
Annapolis, MD 21402-5035
410-268-6110

Naval Institute Press features trade books in addition to the house's targeted professional and reference titles. Areas of NIP interest include how-to books on boating and navigation, battle histories, and biographies, as well as occasional selected titles in fiction (typically with a nautical adventure orientation). Specific categories encompass such fields as seamanship, naval history and literature, the Age of Sail, aviation and aircraft, World War II naval history, World War II ships and aircraft, current naval affairs, naval science, and general naval resources and guidebooks. Bluejacket Books is a trade-paperback imprint that includes time-honored classics as well as original titles. Naval Institute Press also publishes a line of historical and contemporary photographs and poster art.

Naval Institute Press, situated on the grounds of the United States Naval Academy, is the book-publishing imprint of the United States Naval Institute, a private, independent, nonprofit professional society for members of the military services and civilians who share an interest in naval and maritime affairs. USNI was established in 1873 at the Naval Academy in Annapolis; the press inaugurated its publishing program in 1898 with a series of basic guides to United States naval practice.

Titles from Naval Institute Press: *Authors at Sea: Modern American Writers Remember Their Naval Service* (edited by Robert Shenk); *Winning My Wings: A Woman Airforce Service Pilot in World War II* by Marion Stegeman Hodgson; *Bold Endeavors: Lessons from Polar and Space Exploration* by Jack Stuster; *Sea of Grass: The Maritime Drug War, 1970–1990* by Charles M. Fuss, Jr.; *Quarterdeck and Bridge: Two Centuries of American Naval Leaders* (edited by James C. Bradford); *Forgotten Tragedy: The Sinking of HMT Rohna* by Carlton Jackson; *John Paul Jones: America's Sailor* by Clara Ann Simmons; *Pete Ellis: An Amphibious Warfare Prophet, 1880–1923* by Dirk Anthony Ballendorf and Merrill L. Bartlett; *Secret Weapon: U.S. High-Frequency Direction Finding in the Battle of the Atlantic* by Kathleen Broome Williams; *Underwater Warriors: Midget Submarine Operations in War* by Paul Kemp; *Nelson's Battles: The Art of Victory in the Age of Sail* by Nicholas Tracy; *At the Water's Edge: Defending Against the Modern Amphibious Assault* by Theodore L. Gatchel.

Fighter Squadron at Guadalcanal by Max Brand is a lost classic, published 50 years after the author's death. Now after more than 50 years and a string of fortunate coincidences, Brand's stirring firsthand account of the 212th Marine Fighter Squadron's operations at Guadalcanal in 1942 has been published.

The Naval Institute Guide to the Ships and Aircraft of the U.S. Fleet (16th edition) by Norman Polmar is indispensable to anyone needing technical data and program information on the contemporary U.S. Navy.

Bluejacket Books is an exciting series of fiction and nonfiction titles available in affordable paperback editions. Titles: *The Bridge at Dong Ha* by John Grider Miller; *The Fighting Liberty Ships: A Memoir* by A. A. Hoehling; *Lejeune: A Marine's Life,*

1867–1942 by Merrill L. Bartlett; *Life in Nelson's Navy* by Dudley Pope; *The Potemkin Mutiny* by Richard Hough; *Rocks & Shoals: Naval Discipline in the Age of Fighting Sail* by James E. Valle.

Naval Institute Press handles its own distribution.

Query letters and SASEs should be sent to:

Paul Wilderson, Executive Editor

Mark Gatlin, Senior Acquisitions Editor

NEW YORK UNIVERSITY PRESS

70 Washington Square South
New York, NY 10012
212-998-2575

New York University Press covers the fields of literature and literary criticism, gender studies, psychology, law and politics, history, American history, Jewish studies, Middle Eastern studies, business, finance, economics, and journalism, as well as popular culture, fine arts, and the decorative arts.

New York University Press (founded in 1916) offers a list laden with works of wide contemporary appeal for the general reader; NYU also maintains a strong presence in the scholarly and professional arena. Major series include titles catalogued under Fast Track (general-interest contemporary issues and affairs), International Library of Essays in Law & Legal Theory, Essential Papers in Psychoanalysis, and Cutting Edge: Lesbian Life and Literature. NYU publishes hardcover and paperback editions and supports a vigorous backlist.

From the NYU program: *A Practical Guide to Aging: What Everyone Needs to Know* (edited by Christine K. Cassel, M.D.); *Immigrants Out! The New Nativism and the Anti-Immigrant Impulse in the United States* (edited by Juan F. Perea); *Notes of a Racial Caste Baby: Colorblindness and the End of Affirmative Action* by Bryan K. Fair; *In Defense of Single-Parent Families* by Nancy E. Dowd; *Who Will Care for Us? Aging and Long-Term Care in Multicultural America* by Ronald J. Angel and Jacqueline L. Angel; *Please Don't Wish Me a Merry Christmas: A Critical History of the Separation of Church and State* by Stephen M. Feldman; *Medical Blunders: Amazing True Stories of Mad, Bad, and Dangerous Doctors* by Robert M. Youngson and Ian Schott; *Gangsters: Fifty Years of Madness, Drugs, and Death on the Streets of America* by Lewis Yablonsky; *Cyberfutures: Culture and Politics on the Information Superhighway* (edited by Ziauddin Sardar and Jerome R. Ravetz); *Jekyll on Trial: Multiple Personality Disorder & Criminal Law* by Elyn R. Saks with Stephen H. Behnke; *Evil and the Demonic: A New Theory of Monstrous Behavior* by Paul Oppenheimer; *Japanese Lessons: A Year in a Japanese School Through the Eyes of an American Anthropologist and Her Children* by Gail R. Benjamin.

New York University Press is now the exclusive North American distributor of Greenwich University Press, established in 1994 and located just outside of London. Greenwich titles have never before been distributed in the United States. Greenwich

University Press publishes in the area of sociology, anthropology, history, law, politics, psychology, economics, gender studies, and African American studies.

Literature, art, and cultural studies: *Freakery: Cultural Spectacles of the Extraordinary Body* (edited by Rosemarie Garland Thomson); *Sexual Investigations* by Alan Soble; *Girls! Girls! Girls! Critical Essays on Women and Music* (edited by Sarah Cooper); *Drag: A History of Female Impersonation in the Performing Arts* by Roger Baker; *Lesbian Erotics* (edited by Karla Jay); *Female Fetishism* by Lorraine Gamman and Merja Makinen; *Sodomy and the Pirate Tradition: English Sea Rovers in the Seventeenth-Century Caribbean* by B. R. Burg.

NYU Press also publishes *The Gay, Lesbian, and Bisexual Student's Guide to Colleges, Universities, and Graduate Schools* by Jan-Mitchell Sherrill and Craig Hardesty.

Bobst Literary Award winners include *Bird-Self Accumulated* (fiction) by Don Judson; *Crazy Water: Six Fictions* (short stories) by Lori Baker; *Rodent Angel* (poetry) by Debra Weinstein.

New York University Press handles distribution through its own sales office as well as a network of regional sales and marketing representatives.

Query letters and SASEs should be directed to:

Timothy Bartlett, Editor
Psychoanalysis, psychology, and literature.

Jennifer Hammer, Associate Editor

Niko Pfund, Editor-in-Chief
Economics, politics, Jewish and women's studies.

Eric Zinner, Editor
Literary criticism and cultural studies.

OHIO UNIVERSITY PRESS

Scott Quadrangle
Athens, OH 45701
614-593-1155

Ohio University Press areas of interest encompass biography, literary criticism, philosophy, African studies, history, economics, international regional and cultural studies, Western Americana, and natural history; the press also publishes fiction reprints and anthologies. Poetry issued through the Swallow Press imprint certifies the house's outstanding presence in this literary niche.

Ohio University Press (established in 1964) produces scholarly and academic works as well as a line of general-interest titles. OU Press publishes in hardcover and paperback. The house backlist is comprehensive.

On the OU Press list: *Eight Prison Camps: A Dutch Family in Japanese Java* by Dieuwke Wendelaar Bonga; *Robert Browning's Rondures Brave* by Michael Bright; *The Centennial Atlas of Athens County Ohio* (reprint of 1905 edition; compiled and edited by Fred W. Bush); *Shakespeare in Production: Whose History?* by H. R.

Coursen; *In Darkest Hollywood: Exploring the Jungles of Cinema's South Africa* by Peter Davis; *Recollections of Anais Nin by Her Contemporaries* (edited by Benjamin V. Franklin); *Romanticism and the Anglican Newman* by David Goslee; *Language, Ideology, and Power in Brunei Darussalam* by Geoffrey C. Gunn; *Religious Pluralism and the Nigerian State* by Simeon Olusegun Ilesanmi; *Panamanian Militarism: A Historical Interpretation* by Carlos Guevara Mann; *Trollope and Victorian Moral Philosophy* by Jane Nardin; *Theory in the Practice of the Nicaraguan Revolution* by Bruce E. Wright.

Ohio University Press oversees its own sales and distribution.

Query letters and SASEs should be directed to:

Gillian Berchowitz, Senior Editor

OXFORD UNIVERSITY PRESS

198 Madison Avenue
New York, NY 10016
212-726-6000

Oxford's list is especially prominent in the subject areas of current affairs, world history (both ancient and modern), and United States history. Popular and classical music constitute another area of Oxford focus; the house's books on jazz are especially well known. In addition, Oxford is strong in literary studies and historical and contemporary cultural expression.

Oxford University Press (founded in 1478) is an international publisher of trade, scholarly, professional, and reference titles in the humanities, the arts, science, medicine, and social studies in hardcover and paperback editions.

Oxford titles include: *Pigskin: The Early Years of Pro Football* by Robert W. Peterson; *In Hope of Liberty: Culture, Community and Protest Among Northern Free Blacks, 1700–1860* by James O. Horton and Lois E. Horton; *The Faces of the Goddess* by Lotte Motz; *Impact! The Threat of Comets and Asteroids* by Gerrit L. Verschuur; *Are We Not Men? Masculine Anxiety and the Problem of African-American Identity* by Phillip Brian Harper; *Nehru: A Tryst with Destiny* by Stanley Wolpert; *The Transplanted Executive: Managing in Different Cultures* by P. Christopher Earley and Miriam Erez; *The Cold War and Soviet Insecurity: the Stalin Years* by Vojtech Mastny; *The Paradox of Progress: Growing Pessimism in an Era of Expanding Opportunities* by Richard B. McKenzie; *The American Corporation Today* (edited by Carl Kaysen); *Revising Herself: Women's Identity from College to Midlife* by Ruthellen Josselson; *Sex and the Origins of Death* by William R. Clark; *Art and Affection: A Life of Virginia Woolf* by Panthea Reid; *Jancis Robinson's Guide to Wine Grapes* by Jancis Robinson; *A Book of Legal Lists: The Best and Worst in American Law with 150 Court and Judge Trivia Questions* by Bernard Schwartz; *The Mythology of Transgression: Homosexuality as Metaphor* by Jamake Highwater; *Sun Tzu and the Art of Business: Six Strategic Principles for Managers* by Mark R. McNeilly; *Knowledge, Trust, and Power: The Essential Keys to Effective Leadership* by Dale E. Zand. *Life Itself:*

Exploring the Realm of the Living Cell by Boyce Rensberger; *Neither Black Nor White Yet Both: Thematic Explorations of Interracial Literature* by Werner Sollors; *The Broken Mirror: Understanding and Treating Body Dysmorphic Disorder* by Katharine A. Phillips; *Holding My Own in No Man's Land: Men and Women and Film and Feminism* by Molly Haskell.

The Oxford line of dictionaries and general-reference works is among the most prominent in the field. Among them: *The Oxford English Dictionary* and *The Oxford Dictionary of the American Language*. Other reference titles: *The Oxford Guide to Contemporary Writing* (general editor John Sturrock); *The Oxford Dictionary and Thesaurus* (American edition; edited by Frank Abate); *The Oxford Companion to 20th Century Literature in English* (edited by Jenny Stringer); *The New Oxford Book of Children's Verse* (edited by Neil Philip); *Dictionary of the Bible* by W. R. F. Browning; *The Oxford History of World Cinema* (edited by Geoffrey Nowell-Smith); *The Oxford Companion to Christian Art and Architecture* by Peter Murray and Linda Murray.

Oxford also publishes college textbooks, Bibles, music, English as a second language (ESL) educational materials, and children's books, as well as a number of journals. The Twentieth Century Fund series accents works in the public interest that consider contemporary political, governmental, cultural, and international issues.

Oxford University Press presents *The Oxford Mark Twain* (series editor Shelley Fisher Fishkin). This 29-volume set collects the writings of Mark Twain, including all the original illustrations, some of which were drawn by Twain himself. Many of these works have not been readily available for decades.

Oxford's New York division is editorially independent of the British home office and handles distribution of its own list as well as titles originating from Oxford outposts worldwide.

Query letters and SASEs should be directed to:

Herbert Addison, Vice President, Executive Editor
Business and economics from academic and theoretical viewpoints; religion; Bibles.

Beth Kaufman Barry, Senior Editor
Clinical medicine.

Joyce Berry, Senior Editor
Medicine, science, geology, geography, art and architecture.

Joan Bossert, Editor
Psychology and medicine.

Claude Conyers, Editorial Director, Academic Reference

Peter Ginna, Executive Editor, Trade Department
Commercial nonfiction consistent with house list.

Jeff House, Vice President
Medicine.

Kirk Jensen, Senior Editor
Life sciences.

Donald Kraus, Senior Editor
Bibles.

Nancy Lane, Senior Editor
World history.

Elizabeth Maguire, Senior Editor
Comparative literature.

Helen McInnis, Vice President, Executive Editor
Humanities and social sciences.

Robert Miller, Senior Editor
Philosophy, classics.

Maribeth Payne, Executive Editor
Music.

Cynthia Read, Senior Editor
Religion, linguistics.

Robert Rogers, Senior Editor
Chemistry.

Nancy Toff, Executive Editor
Children's and young-adult books.

PRINCETON UNIVERSITY PRESS

41 William Street
Princeton, NJ 08540
609-258-4900

Princeton University Press has particularly strong focus in such areas as popular culture and fine arts, current affairs, literary biography, European history, political science, economics, and natural history. Princeton University Press (founded in 1905) publishes trade and general-interest books in addition to a list of scholarly and scientific works that span the academic spectrum. Popular Princeton lines include the Bollingen series and Princeton Science Library. Princeton publishes hardcover and paperback editions and hosts a comprehensive backlist.

Princeton titles: *T. Rex and the Crater of Doom* by Walter Alvarez; *Why Toast Lands Jelly-Side Down: Zen and the Art of Physics Demonstrations* by Robert Ehrlich; *Volcanoes* by Richard V. Fisher, Grant Heiken, and Jeffrey B. Hulen; *Molding Japanese Minds* by Sheldon Garon; *What's Happened to the Humanities?* (edited by Alvin Kiernan); *Baseball on the Border: A Tale of Two Laredos* by Alan M. Klein; *Cellblock Visions: Prison Art in America* by Phyllis Kornfeld; *Religions of Tibet in Practice* (edited by Donald S. Lopez); *George Grosz and the Communist Party* by Barbara McCloskey; *Conservatism: An Anthology of Social and Political Thought from David Hume to the Present* by Jerry Z. Muller; *A Tale of Two Continents: A Physicist's Life in an Turbulent World* by Abraham Pais; *The Fire Within the Eye: A Historical Essay on the Nature and Meaning of Light* by David Park; *The Era of the Individual* by Alain Renaut; *Trapped in the Net: The Unanticipated Consequences of Computerization* by Gene I. Rochlin; *A History of Heaven* by Jeffrey Burton Russell; *Believing in Opera* by Tom Sutcliffe; *Defining Russia Musically* by Richard Taruskin; *Art and Representation: New Principles in the Analysis of Pictures* by John Willats; *The Nature of Space and Time* by Stephen Hawking and Roger Penrose.

The Bollingen Series, established in 1941, is sponsored by the Bollingen Foundation and has been published by Princeton since 1967. Bollingen titles are works of original scholarship, translations, and new editions of classics. An ongoing Bollingen project is Mythos: The Princeton/Bollingen series in world mythology. Titles here: *Psychology of Kundalini Yoga* by C. G. Young; *On the Laws of the Poetic Art* by Anthony Hecht; *The Survival of the Pagan Gods: The Mythological Tradition and Its Place in Renaissance Humanism and Art* by Jean Seznec.

Books from the Princeton Science Library include *Infinity and the Mind* by Rudy Rucker, *A Natural History of Shells* by Geerat J. Vermeij, and *Total Eclipses of the Sun* by J. B. Zirker.

Princeton University Press handles distribution through the offices of California/Princeton Fulfillment Services, as well as regional sales representation worldwide.

Query letters and SASEs should be directed to:

Robert Brown, Editor
Poetry translations.

Malcolm Litchfield, Political Science Editor
Political science, international relations, law, cognitive science.

Peter Dougherty, Economics Editor
Economics; some sociology.

Walter Lippincott, Director
Political science, anthropology, opera.

Trevor Lipscomb, Physical Sciences Editor
Mathematics, physics, astronomy, computer science.

Mary Murrell, Sociology and Anthropology Editor
Sociology, anthropology; women's and gender studies, film studies.

Ann Wald, Editor
Philosophy, political theory, religion.

Emily Wilkinson, Editor-in-Chief
Life sciences and history of science.

William E. Woodcock, Editor-at-Large (West Coast editor; contact through New Jersey office)
Physical anthropology, paleoanthropology, archaeology, life sciences, earth sciences.

RUTGERS UNIVERSITY PRESS

Building 4161 Livingston Campus
Rutgers University
Joyce Kilmer Avenue
Rockefeller Road
Piscataway, NJ 08855
908-445-7762

Mailing address:
P.O. Box 5062
New Brunswick, NJ 08903

Rutgers subject areas include African studies, American history, anthropology, art and architecture, biography, communications, environment and ecology, European history, film, gay and gender studies, geography, health, history of medicine and science, humor, literature and literary criticism, New Jerseyana, peace studies, poetry, religion, and sociology. The press also issues selected fiction titles.

Rutgers University Press (founded in 1936) publishes a list of general-interest trade books in addition to scholarly titles in the humanities and social sciences, as well as books with a regional American bent.

Representing the nonfiction Rutgers list: *Does It Run in the Family? A Consumers' Guide to DNA Testing for Genetic Disorders* by Doris Teichler Zallen; *Subway City: Riding the Trains, Reading New York* by Michael W. Brooks; *Day of Jubilee: The Great Age of Public Celebrations in New York, 1788–1909* by Rooks McNamara; *Sisters on a Journey: Portraits of American Midwives* by Penfield Chester (photographs by Sarah Chester McKusick); *Skeptic in the House of God* by James Kelley; *The Politics of Research* (edited by E. Ann Kaplan and George Levine); *Reading in an Age of Theory* (edited by Bridget Gellert Lyons); *Between Resistance and Revolution: Cultural Politics and Social Protest* (edited by Richard G. Fox and Orin Starn); *Disquiet in the Land: Cultural Conflict in American Mennonite Communities* by Fred Kniss; *Real Heat: Gender and Race in the Urban Fire Service* by Carol Chetkovich; *Community Organizing and Community Building for Health* (edited by Meredith Minkler).

In the Rutgers literary and cultural scope: *Our Movie Heritage* by Tom McGreevey and Joanne Yeck; *Acting Now: Conversations on Craft and Career* by Edward Vilga; *Field of Sun and Grass: An Artists' Journal of the New Jersey Meadowlands* by John R. Quinn; *Flatlining on the Field of Dreams: Cultural Narratives in the Films of President Reagan's America* by Alan Nadel; *Jewish-American Artists and the Holocaust* by Matthew Baigell; *Media, Culture, and the Environment* by Alison Anderson; *Feminisms: An Anthology of Literary Theory and Criticism* (edited by Robyn R. Warhol and Diane Price Herndl); *The Other Side of the Sixties: Young Americans for Freedom and the Rise of Conservative Politics* by John Andrew; *Favored Strangers: Gertrude Stein and Her Family* by Linda Wagner-Martin; and volumes by such creative writers as Rachel Hadas and Alice Walker.

Rutgers features the Touring North America guidebook series that offers an accent on regional landscape. Titles: *Beyond the Great Divide: Denver to the Grand Canyon*; *Megalopolis: Washington, D.C. to Boston.*

New Jerseyana from Rutgers includes *Roadside New Jersey* by Peter Genovese; *Murdered in Jersey* by Gerald Tomlinson.

Rutgers University Press handles its own distribution.

Query letters and SASEs should be directed to:

Leslie Mitchner, Editor-in-Chief
Literature, film, communications.

Doreen Valentine, Science Editor
Sciences.

Martha Heller, Editor
Social sciences.

STANFORD UNIVERSITY PRESS

Stanford, CA 94305-2235
415-723-9598

Stanford produces a notable line of titles in the fields of new technology, the global political and natural environment, postmodern philosophy and psychology, gender studies, and international issues, as well as a number of books (many in translation) dealing with current cultural and literary theory. A major Stanford publishing concentration is in the Asian American and Pacific Rim fields of studies.

Stanford University Press (started in 1925) produces trade and scholarly books in literature, the social sciences, religion, history, political science, anthropology, and natural science in hardcover and paperback editions.

Highlights from Stanford: *Recollected Words of Abraham Lincoln* (compiled and edited by Don E. Fehrenbacher and Virginia Fehrenbacher); *Brotherhoods and Secret Societies in Early and Mid-Qing China: The Formation of a Tradition* by David Ownby; *Christianity in China: From the 18th Century to the Present* (edited by Daniel H. Bays); *The Temple of Memories: History, Power, and Morality in a Chinese Village* by Jun Jing; *An Anticlassical Political-Economic Analysis: A Vision for the Next Century* by Yasusuke Murakami (translated by Kozo Yamamura); *Unmasking Japan: Myths and Realities About the Emotions of the Japanese* by David Matsumoto; *Revolution and the Meanings of Freedom in the 19th Century* (edited by Isser Woloch); *Trade and Gunboats: The United States and Brazil in the Age of Empire* by Steven C. Topik; *Words That Matter: Linguistic Perception in Renaissance English* by Judith H. Anderson; *Virtue's Faults: Correspondences in 18th Century British and French Women's Fiction* by April Alliston; *Samuel Beckett and the End of Modernity* by Richard Begam; *Practicing Desire: Homosexual Sex in the Era of AIDS* by Gary W. Dowsett; *Language and Relation . . . That There Is Language* by Christopher Fynsk;

Bubonic Plague in 19th Century China by Carol Benedict; *The Making of an Enterprise: The Society of Jesus in Portugal, Its Empire, and Beyond, 1540–1750* by Dauril Alden; *The Insistence of History: Revolution in Burke, Wordsworth, Keats, and Baudelaire* by Geraldine Friedman.

Stanford University Press distributes its own books.

Query letters and SASEs should be directed to:

Muriel Bell, Senior Editor
Asian studies, political science, anthropology.

Norris Pope, Director
Latin American studies, history, Victorian studies, natural sciences.

Helen Tartar, Assistant Director
Philosophy, literary criticism and theory.

John Feneron, Managing Editor
Asian literature.

SYRACUSE UNIVERSITY PRESS

1600 Jamesville Avenue
Syracuse, NY 13244-5160
315-443-5534

Syracuse University Press (founded in 1943) hosts a publishing program that accents scholarly, general, and regional (New York and New England) nonfiction interests, as well as literature and criticism. Syracuse has particular presence in Irish studies, Iroquois studies, Middle Eastern studies, studies in peace and conflict resolution, history of the medieval period, and historical American utopianism and communitarianism.

On the Syracuse list: *Gen X TV: "The Brady Bunch" to "Melrose Place"* by Rob Owen; *Glory Bound: Black Athletes in a White America* by David K. Wiggins; *Finding the Trapdoor: Essays, Portraits, Travels* by Adam Hochschild; *Crossing Borders: An American Woman in the Middle East* by Judith Caesar; *Contested Terrain: A New History of Nature and People in the Adirondacks* by Philip G. Terrie; *The Best Adirondack Stories of Philander Deming* by Philander Deming; *Reflections from Canoe Country: Paddling the Waters of the Adirondacks and Canada* by Christopher Angus; *The Manufacture of Madness: A Comparative Study of the Inquisition and the Mental Health Movement* by Thomas Szasz; *Building Sisterhood: A Feminist History of the Sisters* by Sisters, Servants of the Immaculate Heart of Mary, Monroe, Michigan; *The Pulitzer Diaries: Inside America's Greatest Prize* by John Hohenberg; *Frankenstein's Daughter: Women Writing Science Fiction* by Jane Donawerth.

Syracuse presents the Sports and Entertainment series (Steven Riess, series editor). This series focuses on the history of sports and entertainment and provides readers with interdisciplinary books about the phenomenon of organized sports and entertainment in the popular culture of the United States. Titles: *The Fastest Kid on the Block: The Marty Glickman Story* by Marty Glickman with Stan Isaacs; *Silver Seasons: The Story of the Rochester Red Wings* by Jim Mandelaro and Scott Pitoniak; *They're Off! Horse Racing at Saratoga* by Edward Hotaling.

Syracuse University Press distributes its list via its own in-house offices and utilizes a variety of distribution services worldwide.

Syracuse University Press does not wish to receive unsolicited manuscripts. Query letters and SASEs should be directed to:

Cynthia Maude-Gembler, Executive Editor

TEXAS A&M UNIVERSITY PRESS

John H. Lindsey Building
Drawer C
College Station, TX 77843-4354
409-845-1436

Texas A&M University Press (founded in 1974) publishes scholarly nonfiction, regional studies, art, economics, government, history, environmental history, natural history, social science, United States–Mexican borderlands studies, veterinary medicine, women's studies, and military studies. A special portion of the Texas A&M list accents Texas photography, history, and literature.

Texas A&M nonfiction: *Bigmama Didn't Shop at Woolworth's* by Sunny Nash; *All Rise: Reynaldo G. Graza, the First Mexican American Federal Judge* by Louise Ann Fisch; *Empire Builder in the Texas Panhandle: William Henry Bush* by Paul H. Carlson; *Texas Wanderlust: The Adventures of Dutch Wurzbach* by Douglas V. Meed; *The Development of the Rudder: A Technological Tale* by Lawrence V. Mott; *The Alaska-Siberia Connection: The World War II Air Route* by Otis Hayes, Jr.; *Sideshow War: The Italian Campaign, 1943–1945* by George F. Botjer; *Beyond the Rhetorical Presidency* (edited by Martin J. Medhurst); *"King of the Wildcatters": The Life and Times of Tom Slick, 1883–1930* by Ray Miles; *Bless the Pure and Humble: Texas Lawyers and Oil Regulation, 1919–1936* by Nicholas George Malavis; *Tickling Catfish: A Texan Looks at Culture from Amarillo to Borneo* by Jerry Craven; *In Their Shoes: A White Woman's Journey Living As a Black, Navajo, and Mexican Illegal* by Grace Halsell; *The Alleys and Back Buildings of Galveston* by Ellen Beasley; *Tanglewood: Inside an Alzheimer's Unit* by Joyce Dyer.

Fiction from Texas A&M: *Brother Frank's Gospel Hour* (stories) by W. P. Kinsella; *Short-Term Losses* (stories) by Mark Lindensmith; *Willy Slater's Lane* (novel) by Mitch Wieland; *Circle View* (stories) by Brad Barkley; *Acceptable Losses* (novel) by Edra Ziesk; *The Woman in the Oil Field* (stories) by Tracy Daugherty; *Bitter Lake* (novel) by Ann Harleman; *Border Dance* (novel) by T. L. Toma.

Texas A&M University Press manages its own distribution network and handles distribution for several other regional academically oriented presses.

Query letters and SASEs should be directed to:

Noel Parsons, Editor-in-Chief

UNIVERSITY OF ARIZONA PRESS

1230 North Park Avenue, Suite 102
Tucson, AZ 85719
520-621-1441

University of Arizona Press (founded in 1959) publishes works of general as well as academic interest related primarily to the scholarly emphasis of the university's programs in Southwest regional culture and natural history. Fields of publishing concentration include general nonfiction about Arizona, the American West, and Mexico; wider categories encompass the American Indian and Latin America. The house also publishes individual and collected works of fiction and poetry—often with a regional, folkloric, or literary tone—as well as belletristic nonfiction.

From the Arizona program: *Indians and Anthropologists: Vine Deloria, Jr. and the Critique of Anthropology* (edited by Thomas Biolsi and Larry J. Zimmerman); *Native American Verbal Art: Texts and Contexts* by William Clements; *Bulls, Bullfighting, and Spanish Identities* by Carrie B. Douglass; *Coyotes I Have Known* by John Duncklee; *Re-Imaging the Modern American West: A Century of Fiction, History, and Art* by Richard Etulain; *Earthquake Weather: Poems* by Janice Gould; *Mexican Cinema/Mexican Women, 1940–1950* by Joanne Hershfield; *Healing with Plants in the American and Mexican West* by Margarita Artschwager Kay; *Mary Austin: Song of a Maverick* by Esther F. Lanigan; *Petrified Forest National Park: A Wilderness Bound in Time* by George M. Lubick; *Images and Conversations: Mexican Americans Recall a Southwestern Past* (edited by Patricia Preciado Martin); *Homicide, Race, and Justice in the American West, 1880–1920* by Clare V. McKanna; *The Desert Is No Lady: Southwestern Landscapes in Women's Writing and Art* (edited by Vera Norwood and Janice Monk); *The Mysterious Lands: A Naturalist Explores the Four Great Deserts of the Southwest* by Ann Zwinger.

University of Arizona Press handles its own distribution and also distributes titles originating from the publishing programs of such enterprises and institutions as Arizona Highways, the Phoenix Art Museum, and the Mexican American Studies and Research Center.

Query letters and SASEs should be directed for further routing to:

Stephan Cox, Director

Joanne O'Hare, Senior Editor

UNIVERSITY OF ARKANSAS PRESS

201 Ozark Avenue
Fayetteville, AR 72701
501-575-3246

University of Arkansas Press (begun in 1980) features titles in general humanities, biography, fiction, poetry, translation, literary criticism, history, business, regional studies, natural science, political science, and popular culture. The house issues a moderate list of new books each season (in hardcover and paperback editions) while tending a hardy backlist. University of Arkansas Press hosts an electronic-publishing program with a selection of software editions.

Indicative of the Arkansas list: *The Razorbacks: A Story of Arkansas Football* by Orville Henry and Jim Bailey; *Why Not the Best? The First Fifty Years* by Jimmy Carter; *From Slavery to Uncertain Freedom: The Freedmen's Bureau in Arkansas, 1865–1869* by Randy Finley; *Portraits of Conflict: A Photographic History of Georgia in the Civil War* by Anne J. Bailey and Walter J. Fraser, Jr.; *Meter in English: A Critical Engagement* (edited by David Baker); *Cattle on a Thousand Hills: A History of the Cattle Industry in Arkansas* by Connell J. Brown; *Our Own Sweet Sounds: A Celebration of Popular Music in Arkansas* by Robert Cochran.

The Arkansas program in literature and cultural studies: *Overgrown with Love* (stories) by Scott Ely; *Atomic Love: A Novella and Eight Stories* by Joe David Bellamy; *The Hero's Apprentice* (essays) by Laurence Gonzales; *The Best of Fisher: 28 Years of Editorial Cartoons from Faubus to Clinton* by George Fisher.

Poetry titles: *New and Selected Poems, 1956–1996* by Philip Appleman; *The Holy Surprise of Right Now* (selected and new poems) by Samuel Hazo; *Autumn Rhythm* (new and selected poems) by Leon Stokesbury.

In the area of folklore, Arkansas has produced *Roll Me in Your Arms* and *Blow the Candle Out* by Vance Randolph (edited by G. Legman) and *The Arkansas Folklore Sourcebook* (edited by W. K. McNeil and William M. Clements).

University of Arkansas Press supports the Arkansas Poetry Award (details of the competition are available from the press upon request). The Timelines catalogue features titles of wider interest in the areas of history and biography.

University of Arkansas Press distributes its own list.

Query letters and SASEs should be directed to:

Miller Williams, Director

Debbie Self, Managing Editor

Brian King, Assistant Managing Editor

Kevin Brock, Acquisitions Editor

UNIVERSITY OF CALIFORNIA PRESS

2120 Berkeley Way
Berkeley, CA 94720
510-642-4247

University of California Press (founded in 1893) publishes a solid general-interest list in addition to its substantial contribution in academic publishing; the house maintains a broad program that encompasses scholarly and classical studies, humanities and the arts, medicine and science, the environment, popular historical and contemporary culture and issues, and language and linguistics. The press has major concentrations in such specialty areas as California and the West, the Pacific Ocean region including the Pacific Rim, Asian studies, Oceania, and Latin America. University of California Press also produces literary fiction, letters, and poetry.

University of California titles include: *Benjamin Franklin and His Enemies* by Robert Middlekauff; *Lisa Meitner: A Life in Physics* by Ruth Lewin Sime; *The Day the Presses Stopped: A History of the Pentagon Papers Case* by David Rudenstine; *Drug War Politics: The Price of Denial* by Eva Bertram, Morris J. Blackman, Kenneth Sharpe, and Peter Andreas; *Storm over Mono: The Mono Lake Battle and the California Water Future* by John Hart; *Erotic Faculties* by Joanna Frueh; *Visionaries: The Spanish Republic and the Reign of Christ* by William A. Christian, Jr.; *The Future of the Book* (edited by Geoffrey Nunberg); *The Forgiving Air: Understanding Environmental Change* by Richard C. J. Somerville.

University of California Press distributes its own list.

Query letters and SASEs should be directed to:

Doug Abrams Arava, Editor
Religious studies.

Stephanie Fay, Editor
Fine arts.

Deborah Kirshman, Editor
Fine arts.

Doris Kretchmer, Editor
Natural history, biology.

Mary Lamprech, Editor
Classics.

Sheila Levine, Editorial Director
Asian studies and European studies.

Monica McCormick, Editor
African studies and American studies.

Linda Norton, Editor
Literature.

Naomi Schneider, Executive Editor
Sociology, politics, gender studies, ethnic studies, Latin American studies.

Lynne Withey, Editor
Music.

Los Angeles office:
1010 Westwood Boulevard, Suite 410
Los Angeles, CA 90024
310-794-8147

Edward Dimendberg, Editor
Philosophy, film.

Stan Holwitz, Assistant Director
Anthropology, Judaica, history.

UNIVERSITY OF CHICAGO PRESS

5801 South Ellis Avenue
Chicago, IL 60637
773-702-7700

University of Chicago Press (founded in 1891) specializes in the arts, humanities, and social sciences. Above all a scholarly and academic house, Chicago nonetheless has a noteworthy list of books intended for a wider readership. Major areas of Chicago publishing interest are history, regional Chicago and Illinois books, literary studies, philosophy and linguistics, anthropology, archaeology, art, architecture, music, religion, business and economics, media studies, political science, sociology, psychology, education, legal studies, gender studies, popular culture, and publishing, along with selected titles in the biological and physical sciences.

Titles from University of Chicago Press: *The Fourth Great Awakening: The Political Realignment of the 1990s and the Fate of Egalitarianism* by Robert W. Fogel; *The Scientific Revolution* by Steven Shapin; *The Long Affair: Thomas Jefferson and the French Revolution, 1785–1800* by Conor Cruise O'Brien; *Wittgenstein's Ladder: Poetic Language and the Strangeness of the Ordinary* by Marjorie Perloff; *The Last Happy Occasion* by Alan Shapiro; *The Solitary Self: Jean-Jacques Rousseau in Exile and Adversity* by Maurice Cranston; *More Than Victims: Battered Women, the Syndrome Society, and the Law* by Donald Alexander Downs; *In the Open: Diary of a Homeless Alcoholic* by Timothy Donahue; *The Future of Academic Freedom* (edited by Louis Menard); *Westerns: Making the Man in Fiction and Film* by Lee Clark Mitchell; *Contesting Tears: The Hollywood Melodrama of the Unknown Woman* by Stanley Cavell; *A Guide to America's Sex Laws* by Richard A. Posner and Katharine B. Silbaugh; *Maximum Security: The Culture of Violence in Inner-City Schools* by John Devine; *The Recovery of Unconscious Memories: Hyperamnesia and Reminiscence* by Matthew Hugh Erdelyi.

The press publishes the professional reference work *The Chicago Manual of Style* as well as the annually updated resource for academic writers *Association of American University Presses Directory*.

University of Chicago Press distributes its own list.

Query letters and SASEs should be directed to:

Susan Abrams, Editor
Biological science, history of science.

T. David Brent, Editor
Anthropology, philosophy, psychology.

Kathleen Hansell, Editor
Music.

Geoffrey Huck, Editor
Economics, linguistics.

Penelope Kaiserlian, Editor
Geography.

Douglas Mitchell, Editor
Sociology, history.

Alan Thomas, Editor
Literary criticism and theory, religious studies.

John Tryneski, Editor
Political science, law, education.

Susan Bielstein, Editor
Art, architecture, classics, women's studies.

University of Georgia Press

330 Research Drive
Athens, GA 30602-4901
706-369-6130

University of Georgia Press (established in 1938) publishes a solid list of mainstream-interest books in addition to its specialized roster of academic, scholarly, and scientific publications. Georgia trade-book titles accent fiction and literature, biography and memoirs, history, current affairs, and regional titles; the house academic emphasis overlaps these areas of concentration, in a program that features scholarly nonfiction, poetry, short fiction, regional studies, and novels. The press publishes hardcover and trade paperback editions.

Representative of the Georgia list: *Jimmy Carter, American Moralist* by Kenneth E. Morris; *The Potomac Chronicle: Public Policy and Civil Rights from Kennedy to Reagan* by Harold C. Fleming with Virginia Fleming; *Because I Remember Terror, Father, I Remember You* by Sue William Silverman; *In a Dark Wood: Personal Essays by Men on Middle Age* (edited by Steven Harvey); *The Trial of Stephen: The First Christian Martyr* by Alan Watson; *Melville and His Circle: The Last Years* by William B. Dillingham; *The Power of the Porch: The Storyteller's Craft in Zora Neale Hurston, Glorida Naylor, and Randall Kenan* by Trudier Harris.

Backlist favorites: *Classic Natchez: History, Homes, and Gardens* by Randolph Delehanty and Van Jones Martin; *American Plants for American Gardens: Plant Ecology—the Study of Plants in Relation to Their Environment* by Edith A. Roberts and Elsa Rehmann; *Jesus and the Law* by Alan Watson (the third volume of a provocative series that probes the historical roots of Jesus).

The New Georgia Guide is filled with essays, tours, maps, and other resources keyed to Georgia's heritage and culture.

University of Georgia Press sponsors the Flannery O'Connor Award for Short Fiction. (Please call or write for entry requirements and submission guidelines.)

University of Georgia Press oversees its own distribution.

Query letters and SASEs should be directed to:

Karen Orchard, Executive Editor and Director

UNIVERSITY OF HAWAII PRESS

2840 Kolowalu Street
Honolulu, HI 96822-1888
808-956-8255

Areas of University of Hawaii Press publishing interest include cultural history, economics, social history, travel, arts and crafts, costume, marine biology, natural history, botany, ecology, religion, law, political science, anthropology, religion, and general reference; particular UHP emphasis is on regional topics relating to Hawaii, East Asia, South and Southeast Asia, and Hawaii and the Pacific.

University of Hawaii Press (started in 1947) publishes books for the general trade as well as titles keyed to the academic market. UHP also issues a series of special-interest journals. The house maintains an established backlist.

On the University of Hawaii list: *The Backpackers Guide to Hawaii* by Stuart M. Ball, Jr.; *Shaping History: The Role of Newspapers in Hawaii* by Helen Geracimos Chapin; *Fire in the Sea: An Anthology of Poetry and Art* (compiled by Sue Cowing); *ABC (Alphabetically Based Computerized) Chinese-English Dictionary* (edited by John DeFrancis); *Another History: Essays on China from a European Perspective* by Mark Elvin; *Observations Made During a Voyage Round the World* by Johann Reinhold Forster; *Women and Children First: The Life and Times of Elsie Wilcox of Kauai* by Judith Dean Gething Hughes; *Breeding Anthuriums in Hawaii* by Haruyuki Kamenoto and Adelheid R. Kuehnle; *The Food of Paradise: Exploring Hawaii's Culinary Heritage* by Rachel Laudan; *Angkor Wat: Time, Space, and Kingship* by Eleanor Mannikka; *Unruly Gods: Divinity and Society in China* edited by Meir Shahar and Robert P. Weller.

A notable UHP series is Talanoa: Contemporary Pacific Literature, which makes writing of Pacific Islanders available to a wider audience. Sample titles here: *Deep River Talk: Collected Poems* by Hone Tuwhere; *Once Were Warriors* by Alan Duff; *Leaves of the Banyan Tree* by Albert Wendt.

The University of Hawaii Press handles its own distribution via a network that includes in-house fulfillment services as well as independent sales representatives.

Query letters and SASEs should be directed to:

William Hamilton, Director

UNIVERSITY OF ILLINOIS PRESS

1325 South Oak Street
Champaign, IL 61820
217-333-0950

University of Illinois Press (founded in 1918) publishes books of general and scholarly nonfiction, with strong emphasis on American studies (especially history, literature, music), communications, film studies, folklore, gender studies, African American studies, regional studies, ecology, law and political science, religion and philosophy, labor studies, and athletics. The press also publishes poetry and short fiction.

Representative of the University of Illinois program: *The Civil War in Books: An Analytical Bibliography* (edited by David J. Eicher); *A Voice of Thunder: The Civil War Letters of George E. Stephens* (edited by Donald Yacovone); *Unrepentant Leftist: A Lawyer's Memoir* by Victor Rabinowitz; *Affirmative Action and the Stalled Quest for Black Progress* by W. Avon Drake and Robert D. Holsworth; *In the Opinion of the Court* by William Domnarski; *Betrayal of the Spirit: My Life Behind the Headlines of the Hare Krishna Movement* by Nori J. Muster; *Last Cavalier: The Life and Times of John A. Lomax, 1867–1948* by Nolan Porterfield; *Go Cat Go! Rockabilly Music and Its Makers* by Craig Morrison; *The Occupation of Alcatraz Island: Indian Self-Determination and the Rise of Indian Activism* by Troy R. Johnson; *Calf's Head and Union Tale: Labor Yarns at Work and Play* by Archie Green; *Writing Mothers, Writing Daughters: Tracing the Maternal in Stories by American Jewish Women* by Janet Handler Burstein; *People of Prowess: Sport, Leisure, and Labor in Early Anglo-America* by Nancy L. Struna; *Forbidden Relatives: The American Myth of Cousin Marriage* by Martin Ottenheimer; *Choosing Who's to Live: Ethics and Aging* (edited by James W. Walters).

Celebrating 25 years of publishing poetry: For the past 11 years, the University of Illinois Press has been chosen as one of the publishers for the National Poetry Series. New poetry titles: *Walt Whitman Bathing* (poems) by David Wagoner; *To the Bone* (new and selected poems) by Sydney Lea; *The Tracks We Leave: Poems on Endangered Wildlife of North America* by Barbara Helfgott Hyett (illustrated by Robert W. Treanor); *The Broken World* (poems) by Marcus Cafagna; *Dance Script with Electric Ballerina* (poems) by Alice Fulton; *Bruised Paradise* (poems) by Kevin Stein; *Floating on Solitude* (three volumes of poetry) by Dave Smith.

Of literary note: *Taking It Home: Stories from the Neighborhood* by Tony Ardizzone; *Flights in the Heavenlies* (stories) by Ernest J. Finney; *The New World* (stories) by Russell Banks; *Walter Burley in America* (photographs and essay by Mati Maldre; essay, catalog, and selected bibliography by Paul Kruty).

University of Illinois Press distributes its own list as well as books from other university publishers, including Vanderbilt University Press.

Query letters and SASEs should be directed to:

Elizabeth G. Delany, Associate Director
Western Americana, religious studies, archaeology, anthropology.

Karen M. Hewitt, Associate Editor
Women's studies, environmental studies, film studies.

Ann Lowry, Journals Manager and Senior Editor
Literature.

Judith M. McCulloh, Executive Editor
Music, folklore, pop culture.

Richard J. Martin, Executive Editor
Political science, sociology, law, philosophy, architecture, economics.

Richard L. Wentworth, Director
American history, black history, communications, sports history, and regional books.

UNIVERSITY OF IOWA PRESS

University of Iowa
100 Kuhl House
Iowa City, IA 52242
319-335-2000

University of Iowa Press (established in 1938) produces a solid list in selected categories that include scholarly works, general-interest nonfiction, and regional titles in the areas of archaeology, anthropology, and history. The house also produces short stories, literary criticism, and poetry.

Iowa series include American Land and Life, Singular Lives: The Iowa Series in North American Autobiography, and publications from the annual Iowa Poetry Prize competition.

Iowa nonfiction: *China Dreams: Growing Up Jewish in Tientsin* by Isabelle Maynard; *My Ever Dear Daughter, My Own Dear Mother: The Correspondence of Julia Stone Towne and Mary Julia Towne, 1868–1882* (edited by Katherine Redington Morgan); *The Iowa Breeding Bird Atlas* by Laura Spess Jackson, Carola A. Thompson, and James J. Dinsmore; *Birds of an Iowa Dooryard* by Althea R. Sherman; *Places of Quiet Beauty: Parks, Preserves, and Environmentalism* by Rebecca Conard; *Broken Heartland: The Rise of America's Rural Ghetto* by Osha Gray Davidson; *Black The Homeless of Ironweed: Blossoms on the Crag* by Benedict Giamo.

Iowa fiction and literature: *Hints of His Mortality* by David Borofka; *Western Electric* by Don Zancanella; *Selected Poems, 1954–1983* by George Mackay Brown.

Literary criticism and the arts are areas in which Iowa has traditionally produced a strong list. Titles here: *Metafiction: Self-Consciousness in African American Literature* by Madelyn Jablon; *Notations of the Wild: Ecology in the Poetry of Wallace Stevens* by Gyorgyi Voros; *The Literary Biography: Problems and Solutions* (edited by Dale Salwak); *Emily Dickinson's Gothic: Goblin with a Gauge* by Daneen Wardrop; *Textual and Theatrical Shakespeare: Questions of Evidence* (edited by Edward Pechter).

Iowa offers *The Writing Path: An Annual of Poetry and Prose from Writers' Conferences*, a series edited by Michael Pettit. Winners of the Iowa Poetry Prize include *Furious Cooking* by Maureen Seaton and *Swamp Candles* by Ralph Burns.

University of Iowa Press oversees its own distributional services, including representation to the trade by Baker & Taylor.

Query letters and SASEs should be directed to:

Paul Zimmer, Director

Holly Carver, Associate Director and Editor

UNIVERSITY OF MICHIGAN PRESS

839 Greene Street
Box 1104
Ann Arbor, MI 48106-1104
313-764-4388

University of Michigan publishes trade nonfiction and works of scholarly and academic interest. Topic areas and categories include: African-American studies, anthropology, archaeology, Chinese studies, classical studies, criticism and theory, economics, education, German studies, history, human development, language and linguistics, law, literary biography, literature, mathematics and engineering, Michigan and the Great Lakes region, music, natural and physical sciences, philosophy and religion, poetry, political science, psychology, sociology, theater and drama, and women's studies.

University of Michigan Press (founded in 1930) executes a major program to publish an abundant list of textbooks, monographs, academic literature, and professionally oriented works primarily of scholarly interest. Subject areas here encompass disciplines within the behavioral and biological sciences as well as the humanities. University of Michigan Press publishes in hardcover and paperback editions. Ann Arbor Paperbacks is an imprint geared toward the general trade market.

From the Michigan list: *Lake Country* (literary essays) by Kathleen Stocking; *Let the Good Times Roll: The Story of Louis Jordan and His Music* by John Chilton; *Medical Malpractice and the American Jury* by Neil Vidmar; *The American Poet at the Movies: A Critical History* by Laurence Goldstein; *The Gay Critic* by Hubert Fichte; *Early French Cookery* by Eleanor D. Scully and Terence Scully; *The Spiral of Memory* (a literary work) by Joy Harjo; *Unsportsmanlike Conduct* by Walter Byers; *Wild Men in the Looking-Glass: The Mythic Origins of European Otherness* by Roger Bartra (translated by Carl T. Berrisford).

University of Michigan Press handles distribution through a worldwide network of independent sales representatives.

Query letters and SASEs should be directed to:

Ellen Bauerle, Editor
Classics, archaeology, history.

Colin Day, Director
Economics.

Mary Erwin, Assistant Director
ESL (English as a second language), regional.

LeAnn Fields, Executive Editor
Literature, theater, women's studies.

Heather Lengyel, Assistant Editor
Ann Arbor Paperbacks.

Charles Myers, Editor
Political science, law.

Susan Whitlock, Desk Editor
Anthropology, series.

UNIVERSITY OF MINNESOTA PRESS

111 Third Avenue South, Suite 290
Minneapolis, MN 55401-2520
612-627-1970

University of Minnesota Press (founded in 1927) focuses on scholarly, professional, and reference works; university-level textbooks; regional nonfiction; special fiction series; cultural theory, media studies, and literary theory; and gay and lesbian studies.

Minnesota general nonfiction: *Resisting State Violence: Radicalism, Gender, and Race in U.S. Culture* by Joy James; *The Rise and Fall of Palestine: A Personal Account of the Intifada Years* by Norman G. Finkelstein; *Patty's Journey: From Orphanage to Adoption and Reunion* by Donna Scott Norling; *The Boundary Water Wilderness Ecosystem* by Miron Heinselman; *Political Correctness: A Response from the Cultural Left* by Richard Feldstein; *The Self-Made Map: Cartographic Writing in Early Modern France* by Tom Conley; *Policing Space: Territoriality and the Los Angeles Police Department* by Steve Herbert.

Cultural and literary works: *Reclaiming the Heartland: Lesbian and Gay Voices from the Midwest* (edited by Karen Lee Osborne and William J. Spurlin); *Far from Tame: Reflections from the Heart of a Continent* by Laurie Allmann; *The Snow Lotus: Exploring the Eternal Moment* by Peter M. Leschak; *Ghostly Matters: Haunting and the Sociological Imagination* by Avery F. Gordon; *Reconstructing Architecture: Critical Discourses and Social Practices* (edited by Thomas A. Dutton and Lian Hurst Mann); *Too Much of a Good Thing: Mae West As a Cultural Icon* by Ramona Curry; *Queer Noises: Male and Female Homosexuality in Twentieth-Century Music* by John Gill; *Further Selections from the Prison Notebooks* by Antonio Gramsci (edited and translated by Derek Boothman); *A Concise Dictionary of Minnesota Ojibwe* by John D. Nichols and Earl Nyholm. A noteworthy Minnesota series is Emergent Literature.

University of Minnesota Press distributes through several independent services worldwide.

Query letters and SASEs should be directed to:

Micah Kleit, Acquisitions Editor

Carrie Mullen, Acquisitions Editor

Todd Orjala, Acquisitions Editor

UNIVERSITY OF MISSOURI PRESS

2910 LeMone Boulevard
Columbia, MO 65201
573-882-7641

University of Missouri Press accents scholarly books, general-interest trade titles, fiction, poetry, music, art, and regional works. Specific areas within the UMP publishing range include African American studies, cultural studies, economics, education, folklore, gender studies, intellectual history, journalism, and photography. University of Missouri Press (founded in 1958) publishes in hardback and trade paper editions.

Highlights of the Missouri line: *Shades of Blue and Gray: An Introductory Military History of the Civil War* by Herman Hattaway; *Confessions of a Depression Muralist* by Frank W. Long; *Zion in the Valley: The Jewish Comunity of St. Louis: Volume I, 1807–1907* by Walter Ehrlich; *The Making of Adolf Hitler: The Birth and Rise of Nazism* and *The Unmaking of Adolf Hitler* by Eugene Davidson; *The Chain Gang: One Newspaper versus the Gannett Empire* by Richard McCord; *Dancing to a Black Man's Tune: A Life of Scott Joplin* by Susan Curtis.

In the UMP literary arena: *Four Decades* (new and selected stories) by Gordon Weaver; *Quake* (stories) by Nance Van Winckel; *Hardship and Hope: Missouri Women Writing About Their Lives, 1820–1920* (edited and with an introduction by Carla Waal and Barbara Oliver Korner); *Second Sight: Poems for Paintings by Carol Cloar* by Dabney Stuart; *The Golden Labyrinth* (poems) by Maurya Simon; *Goodnight Silky Sullivan* (stories) by Laurie Alberts; *Writing the World* (belles lettres) by Kelly Cherry.

From the Give 'em Hell Harry series: *Off the Record: The Private Papers of Harry S. Truman* (edited by Robert H. Ferrell); *The Truman Scandals and the Politics of Morality* by Andrew J. Dunar.

Titles in the Missouri Heritage Readers series: *The Trail of Tears Across Missouri* by Joan Gilbert; *The Osage in Missouri* by Kristie C. Wolferman; *Orphan Trails to Missouri* by Michael D. Patrick and Evelyn Goodrich Trickel.

University of Missouri Press handles its own distributional services.

Query letters and SASEs should be directed to:

Beverly Jarrett, Director and Editor-in-Chief

(Mr.) Clair Willcox, Acquisitions Editor

UNIVERSITY OF NEBRASKA PRESS
312 North 14th Street
P.O. Box 880484
Lincoln, NE 68588-0484
402-472-3581

The program at University of Nebraska Press encompasses agriculture and natural resources, anthropology, history, literature and criticism, musicology, philosophy, psychology, wildlife and environment, and general reference works. The house further accents the literature and history of the Trans-Missouri West, the American Indian, contemporary and modern literary trends, sports, and the environment (especially emphasizing Western U.S. and American Indian tie-in topics).

University of Nebraska Press (founded in 1941) publishes general trade titles in hardcover and paperback, as well as selected fiction and scholarly nonfiction. Many UNP titles and subject areas overlap categories, and thus are provided wider marketing exposure. University of Nebraska Press has successfully established niches in each of its targeted market sectors; a solid showcase of Nebraska titles have garnered book-club sales in both mainstream and specialty venues.

The University of Nebraska literary horizon features leading-edge criticism and theory, works keyed to the American West and the American Indian, and historical as well as current writers worldwide, including Latin American, British and Scottish, European women, French feminist, and international literature of political and religious import; the house offers a strong selection of scholarly writings on the life and works of Willa Cather.

University of Nebraska Press produces the Books of the West series, which accents biography, autobiography, and memoirs; the Women in the West series; Western history and literature; art and photography; film; American Indian topics; and the great outdoors. Bison Books is Nebraska's imprint for popularly oriented trade titles featuring a line of Western classics in reprint.

Nebraska's American Indian studies include biography and memoirs, literature and legend, society and culture, and history, as well as a line of titles for young readers. Series listed in this area are American Indian Lives, Sources of American Indian Oral Literature, Studies in the Anthropology of North American Indians, Indians of the Southeast, and American Tribal Religions. The press offers the North American Indian Prose Award in conjunction with the Native American Studies Program at the University of California, Berkeley. (Detailed information is available from the publisher upon request.) A recent winner of this award is *Completing the Circle* by Virginia Driving Hawk Sneve.

Representative of the Nebraska publishing program: *Budapest Diary: In Search of the Motherbook* by Susan Rubin Suleiman; *Smart Jews: The Construction of the Image of Jewish Superior Intelligence* by Sander L. Gilman; *Your Name Is Hughes Hannibal Shanks: A Caregiver's Guide to Alzheimer's* by Lela Knox Shanks; *Son of Two Bloods* by Vincent L. Mendoza; *The Nebraska Sand Hills: The Human Landscape* by Charles Barron McIntosh; *Drawing the Line: Legislative Ethics in the States* by Alan Rosenthal.

The Thunder Moon series represents some of Max Brand's (pen name of Frederick Schiller Faust) best work, originally published in 1927–1928 as a series of interlocking stories. The University of Nebraska Press is now republishing these stories uncut and in the sequence Faust intended, with careful reference to the original typescripts. In order, the works appear in four volumes as: *The Legend of Thunder Moon*; *Red Wind and Thunder Moon*; *Thunder Moon and the Sky People*; *Farewell, Thunder Moon*. Also available: *The Bells of San Carlos and Other Stories* by Max Brand (edited by Jon Tuska).

Politics and Governments of the American States series (John Kincaid, general editor; Daniel J. Elazar, founding editor): The volumes in this series describe the unique political culture and history of each state, examine its political parties and interest groups, explain the institutional framework of the state's government, and place the state's politics within a federal context. Titles: *Illinois Politics and Government: The Expanding Metropolitan Frontier* by Samuel K. Gove and James D. Nowlan; *Nevada Politics and Government: Conservatism in an Open Society* by Don W. Driggs and

Leonard E. Goodall; *West Virginia Politics and Government* by Richard A. Brisbin, Jr., Robert Jay Dilger, Allan S. Hammock, and Christopher Z. Mooney.

Books with popular cultural hooks: *The Guitar in Jazz: An Anthology* (edited by James Sallis); *Basketball: Its Origin and Development* by James Naismith (introduction by William J. Baker); *The Man in the Dugout: Fifteen Big League Managers Speak Their Minds* by Donald Honig, *The Cubist Poets in Paris: An Anthology* (edited and translated by LeRoy C. Breunig).

University of Nebraska Press distributes its own list.

Query letters and SASEs should be directed to:

Dan Ross, Director

Doug Clayton, Editor-in-Chief

UNIVERSITY OF NEW MEXICO PRESS

1720 Lomas Boulevard NE
Albuquerque, NM 87131-1591
505-277-2346

University of New Mexico Press (begun in 1929) is a publisher of general, scholarly, and regional trade books in hardcover and paperback editions. Among areas of strong New Mexico interest are archaeology, folkways, literature, art and architecture, photography, crafts, biography, women's studies, travel, and the outdoors. New Mexico offers a robust list of books in subject areas pertinent to the American Southwest, including native Anasazi, Navajo, Hopi, Zuni, and Apache cultures, and Nuevo-mexicano (New Mexican) culture, the pre-Columbian Americas, and Latin American affairs. UNP also publishes works of regional fiction and belles lettres, both contemporary and classical. The press commands a staunch backlist.

Representative of the University of New Mexico Press list: *Wisdom Sits in Places: Landscape and Language Among the Western Apache* by Keith H. Basso; *Art and Anger: Essays on Politics and the Imagination* by Llan Stavans; *Navajo and Photography: A Critical History of the Representation of an American People* by James C. Faris; *The Amphibians and Reptiles of New Mexico* by William G. Degenhardt, Charles W. Painter, and Andrew W. Price; *Indian Uprising on the Rio Grande: The Pueblo Revolt of 1680* by Franklin Folsom; *Bert Geer Phillips and the Taos Art Colony* by Julie Schimmel and Robert R. White; *Ceramics and Ideology: Salado Polychrome Pottery* by Patricia L. Crown; *Washington Matthews: Studies of Navajo Culture, 1880–1894* (edited by Katherine Spencer Halpern and Susan Brown McGreevy); *The Fatal Confrontation: Historical Studies of Indians, Environment, and Historians* by Wilbur R. Jacobs; *National Parks and the Woman's Voice: A History* by Polly Welts Kaufman.

New Mexico literary horizons emphasize regional literary expression, as well as works in the broader areas of criticism and biography. Titles: *Beyond Bounds: Cross-Cultural Essays on Anglo, American Indian, and Chicano Literature* by Robert

Franklin Gish; *Hours: Conversations with Lawrence Block* by Lawrence Block and Ernie Bulow, *Broken Bars: New Perspectives from Mexican Women Writers* by Kay S. García; *Spud Johnson and Laughing Horse* by Sharyn Udall; *Lighting the Corners: On Art, Nature, and the Visionary* by Michael McClure; and *Poet-Chief: The Native American Poetics of Walt Whitman and Pablo Neruda* by James Nolan.

University of New Mexico Press is home to the literary journal *Blue Mesa Review*. The Pasó por Aquí series makes available texts from the Nuevomexicano literary heritage (many editions in bilingual format). Diálogos is a series in Latin American studies, specializing in books with crossover potential in both academic and general markets.

University of New Mexico Press handles distribution for its own list and also works through regional sales representatives.

Query letters and SASEs should be directed to:

Elizabeth Hadas, Director

Dianne Edwards, Assistant to the Director

David V. Holtby, Associate Director and Editor

Barbara Guth, Managing Editor

Dana Asbury, Editor

Larry Durwood Ball, Editor

Andrea Otañez, Editor-at-Large

UNIVERSITY OF NORTH CAROLINA PRESS

P.O. Box 2288
Chapel Hill, NC 27515-2288
919-966-3561

University of North Carolina Press publishing interest encompasses African American studies, American studies, British history, business history, Civil War, folklore, Latin American studies, lifestyle, literary studies, anthropology, world history, nature, political science, social issues, legal history, sports and sports history, and gender studies.

University of North Carolina Press (founded in 1922) publishes works of general nonfiction, scholarly titles, and regional books, as well as a selection of general-interest trade titles. The house has a broad array of books on a firm backlist.

North Carolina nonfiction: *Wings of Paradise: The Great Saturniid Moths* by John Cody; *The Woodwright's Apprentice: Twenty Favorite Projects from The Woodwright's Shop* by Roy Underhill; *A Guide to the Historic Architecture of Eastern North Carolina* by Catherine W. Bishir and Michael T. Southern; *Gender and Jim Crow: Women and the Politics of White Supremacy in North Carolina, 1896–1920* by Glenda Elizabeth Gilmore; *Good Wives, Nasty Wenches, and Anxious Patriarchs: Gender, Race, and Power in Colonial Virginia* by Kathleen M. Brown; *Historical Truth and Lies About the Past: Reflections on Dewey, Dreyfus, de Man, and Reagan* by Alan B. Spitzer;

Wilhelm II, Volume 2: Emperor and Exile, 1900–1941 by Lamar Cecil; *From People's War to People's Rule: Insurgency, Intervention, and the Lessons of Vietnam* by Timothy J. Lomperis; *Tonkin Gulf and the Escalation of the Vietnam War* by Edwin E. Moïse; *Kings and Queens of Europe: A Genealogical Chart of the Royal Houses of Great Britain and Europe* (compiled and designed by Anne Tauté; illustrated by Romilly Squire); *Genoa and the Genoese, 958–1528* by Steven A. Epstein; *Southern Pamphlets on Secession, November 1860–April 1861* (edited by Jon L. Wakelyn).

Representing the literary portion of the North Carolina list: *The Party at Jack's: A Novella* by Thomas Wolfe; *U.S. History as Women's History: New Feminist Essays* (edited by Linda K. Kerber, Alice Kessler-Harris, and Kathryn Kish Sklar).

University of North Carolina Press handles its own distribution with the assistance of regional sales representatives.

Query letters and SASEs should be directed to:

Lewis Bateman, Executive Editor
American and European history, legal and business history.

David Perry, Editor-in-Chief
Southern regional studies, Latin American studies.

Kate Torrey, Director
American studies, gender studies.

(Ms.) Sian Hunter White, Editor

UNIVERSITY OF OKLAHOMA PRESS

1005 Asp Avenue
Norman, OK 73019-0445
405-325-5111

University of Oklahoma Press highlights the fields of Americana, regional topics (especially the American West), anthropology, archaeology, history, military history, political science, literature, classical studies, and women's studies. University of Oklahoma Press series include the Western Frontier Library, the American Indian Literature and Critical Studies series, and the Bruce Alonzo Goff Series in Architecture.

University of Oklahoma Press (founded in 1928) publishes a wide range of scholarly nonfiction, with crossover trade titles primarily in popular history and the arts; the house's prowess is particularly renowned in the arena of the native cultures of North, Central, and South America—the extensive backlist as well as new and current offerings in these fields embrace a wellspring of over 250 titles.

On Oklahoma's nonfiction list: *The C-Span Revolution* by Stephen Frantzich and John Sullivan; *The Garter Snakes: Evolution and Ecology* by Douglas A. Rossman, Neil B. Ford, and Richard A. Seigel; *Encyclopedia of United States Army Insignia and Uniforms* by William K. Emerson; *Thomas Moran: The Field Sketches, 1856–1923* by Anne Morand; *A Song to the Creator: Traditional Arts of Native American Women of the Plateau* (edited by Lillian A. Ackerman); *An Archaeological Guide to Northern*

Central America: Belize, Guatemala, Honduras, and El Salvador by Joyce Kelly; *Game Without End: State Terror and the Politics of Justice* by Jaime Malamud-Goti; *Big Dams and Other Dreams: The Six Companies Story* by Donald E. Wolf; *Mexico's Sierra Marahumara: A Photohistory of the People of the Edge* by W. Dirk Raat and George R. Janecek; *Inside American Philanthropy: The Dramas of Donorship* by Waldemar A. Nielsen; *A Lower-Middle-Class Education* by Robert Murray Davis; *Ethics in Higher Education: Case Studies for Regents* by Alexander B. Holmes; *John Slocum and the Indian Shaker Church* by Robert H. Ruby and John A. Brown; *The Black Hills Journals of Colonel Richard Irving Dodge* (edited by Wayne R. Kime); *Necessary Fraud: Defective Law, Monopoly, and Utah Coal* by Nancy J. Taniguchi.

Works of special cultural note: *Triggernometry: A Gallery of Gunfighters* by Eugene Cunningham; *Running with Bonnie and Clyde: The Ten Fast Years of Ralph Fults* by John Neal Phillips; *The Life and Legacy of Annie Oakley* by Glenda Riley; *When Indians Became Cowboys: Native Peoples and Cattle Ranching in the American West* by Peter Iverson; *International Encyclopedia of Horse Breeds* by Bonnie L. Hendricks.

Fiction and literary titles: *Gerald Vizenor: Writing in the Oral Tradition* by Kimberly M. Blaeser; *Bone Game* by Louis Owens; *Smith and Other Events: Tales of the Chilcotin* by Paul St. Pierre; *Girl on a Pony* by LaVerne Hanners; *The WPA Oklahoma Slave Narratives* (edited by T. Lindsay Baker and Julie P. Baker). The Oklahoma program includes a roster of works in the American Indian Literature and Critical Studies series.

University of Oklahoma Press distributes its own books with the assistance of regional sales representatives.

Query letters and SASEs should be directed to:

John N. Drayton, Editor-in-Chief
Western history.

Ron Chrisman, Acquisitions Editor
Paperbacks.

Kimberley Wiar, Acquisitions Editor
Literary criticism, classics.

UNIVERSITY OF SOUTH CAROLINA PRESS

937 Assembly Street
Eighth Floor
Carolina Plaza
Columbia, SC 29208
803-777-5243
800-768-2500

University of South Carolina Press covers Southern studies, military history, contemporary and modern American literature, maritime history, international relations, religious studies, speech and communication, international business, and industrial relations.

University of South Carolina Press (founded in 1944) publishes a strong academic and scholarly list, with some crossover general trade titles. The press publishes in hardcover as well as trade paperback, and maintains an extensive backlist.

Indicative of the South Carolina program: *The Buildings of Charleston: A Guide to the City's Architecture* by Jonathan Poston; *The Secret Six: The True Tale of the Men Who Conspired with John Brown* by Edward J. Renehan, Jr.; *A Northern Woman in the Plantation South: Letters of Tryphena Blanche Holder Fox, 1856–1876* (edited by Wilma King-Hunter); *U.S. Army Patches: An Illustrated Encyclopedia of Cloth Unit Insignia* by Barry Jason Stein; *Civil Rights and Wrongs: A Memoir of Race and Politics, 1944–1996* (revised edition) by Harry S. Ashmore; *Charleston Furniture, 1700–1825* by E. Milby Burton; *The Endangered Atmosphere: Preserving a Global Commons* by Marvin S. Soroos.

On the South Carolina literary and cultural horizon: *"Struggling for Wings": The Art of James Dickey* (edited by Robert Kirschten); *Katherine Anne Porter's Poetry* (edited by Darlene Harbour Unrue); *Mamba's Daughters: A Novel of Old Charleston* by DuBose Heyward; *The Doctor to the Dead: Grotesque Legends and Folk Tales of Old Charleston* by John Bennett; *America's Greatest Game Bird: Archibald Rutledge's Turkey-Hunting Tales* (edited by Jim Casada); *The Falling Hills* by Perry Lentz (a novel based on the Civil War's Fort Pillow massacre).

From the James Dickey Contemporary Poetry series (edited by Richard Howard): *Error and Angels* (poems) by Maureen Bloomfield; *Portrait in a Spoon* (poems) by James Cummins.

University of South Carolina Press oversees its own distribution.

Query letters and SASEs should be directed to:

Fred Kameny, Editor and Chief

UNIVERSITY OF TENNESSEE PRESS

293 Communications Building
Knoxville, TN 37996-0325
423-974-3321

Areas addressed by the University of Tennessee Press include African-American studies, American government, American history, Appalachian studies, arts and culture, Civil War studies, constitutional studies, earth science, education, guidebooks, history of journalism, literary criticism, material culture, poetry studies, policy studies, political science, presidential studies, religion, Southern studies, Tennessee studies, vernacular architecture, and women's studies. University of Tennessee Press (established in 1940) specializes in carefully produced scholarly books and monographs, as well as exemplary general nonfiction, and popular works of regional interest. The house hosts a staunch backlist.

Representative Tennessee titles: *HomeWorks: A Book of Tennessee Writers* (edited by Phyllis Tickle and Alice Swanson); *New Old-Fashioned Ways: Holidays and*

Popular Culture by Jack Santino; *Haunting Memories: Echoes and Images of Tennessee's Past* by Wilma Dykeman (hand-tinted photographs by Christine P. Patterson); *Echoes from the Holocaust: A Memoir* by Mira Ryczke Kimmelman; *David E. Lilienthal: The Journey of an American Liberal* by Steven M. Neuse; *Families and Farmhouses in 19th Century America: Vernacular Design and Social Change* by Sally McMurry; *Wise As Serpents, Innocent As Doves: American Mennonites Engage Washington* by Keith Graber Miller; *A Colonial Woman's Bookshelf* by Kevin J. Hayes; *The Fear of Sinking: The American Success Formula in the Gilded Age* by Paulette D. Kilmer; *Re-Searching Black Music* by Jan Michael Spencer.

Voices of the Civil War (Frank L. Byrne, general editor) is a Tennessee series represented by: *A Very Violent Rebel: The Civil War Diary of Ellen Renshaw House* (edited by Daniel E. Stuerhland); *A Southern Boy in Blue: The Memoir of Marcus Woodcock, 9th Kentucky Infantry (U.S.A.)* (edited by Kenneth W. Noe); *From Huntsville to Appomattox: R. T. Coles's History of 4th Regiment, Alabama Volunteer Infantry, C.S.A., Army of Northern Virginia* (edited by Jeffrey D. Stocker); *Valleys of the Shadow: The Memoir of Confederate Captain Reuben G. Clark* (edited by Wilene B. Clark).

The Outdoor Tennessee series includes *From Ridgetops to Riverbottoms: A Celebration of the Outdoor Life in Tennessee* by Sam Venable; *Hiking Trails of the Great Smoky Mountains: A Comprehensive Guide* by Kenneth Wise; *Tennessee's Historic Landscapes* by Carroll Van West; *A Geologic Trip Across Tennessee by Interstate 40* by Harry L. Moore.

University of Tennessee Press is distributed via Chicago Distribution Center.

Query letters and SASEs should be directed to:

Joyce Harrison, Acquisitions Editor

UNIVERSITY OF TEXAS PRESS

P.O. Box 7819
Austin, TX 78713-7819
512-471-7233

Areas of University of Texas Press publishing scope include international politics and regional studies, gender studies, Latin America, American Southwest, Texana, Mesoamerica, linguistics, literature (including Latin American and Middle Eastern works in translation), the environment and nature, cuisine and lifestyle, art and architecture, film studies, social sciences, and humanities.

University of Texas Press (founded in 1950) is among the largest American university presses. UTP publishes in a wide range of general nonfiction fields, offering titles of popular interest and for scholarly and academic readers produced in hardcover and trade paperback.

On the UTP nonfiction list: *Howard Garrett's Plants for Texas* by Howard Garrett; *Butterflies of Houston and Southeast Texas* by John and Gloria Tveten; *Cycles of the*

Sun, Mysteries of the Moon: The Calendar in Mesoamerican Civilization by Vincent H. Malmstrom; *Dallas: The Making of a Modern City* by Patricia Evridge Hill; *The Great Texas Banking Crash: An Insider's Account* by Joseph M. Grant; *Mass Media and Free Trade: NAFTA and the Cultural Industries* (edited by Emile G. McAnany and Kenton T. Wilkinson); *Showing Off: The Geltung Hypothesis* by Philip L. Wagner; *Doin' Drugs: Patterns of African American Addiction* by William H. James and Stephen L. Johnson.

Literature, the arts, and cultural studies: *A Comprehensive Guide to Outdoor Sculpture in Texas* by Carol Morris Little; *A John Graves Reader* by John Graves; *The Sitwells and the Art of the 1920s and 1930s* by Sarah Bradford, Honor Clerk, Jonathan Fryer, Robin Gibson, and John Pearson; *Just As We Were: A Narrow Slice of Texas Womanhood* by Prudence Mackintosh; *The Dread of Difference: Gender and the Horror Film* (edited by Barry Keith Grant); *How Writing Came About* by Denise Schmandt-Besserat; *Women of Color: Mother-Daughter Relationships in 20th-Century Literature* (edited by Elizabeth Brown-Guillory); *Migrant Song: Politics and Process in Contemporary Chicano Literature* by Teresa McKenna; *Texan Jazz* by Dave Oliphant; *Covarrubias* by Adriana Williams.

University of Texas Press handles its own distribution; the house catalog includes books issued by the Menil Foundation, Menil Collection, and Rothko Chapel.

Query letters and SASEs should be directed to:

Theresa J. May, Assistant Director and Executive Editor
Social sciences, Latin American studies.

Joanna Hitchcock, Director
Humanities and classics.

Shannon Davies, Editor
Sciences.

UNIVERSITY OF WASHINGTON PRESS

Box 50096
Seattle, WA 98145-5096
206-543-4050

The program at University of Washington Press is particularly strong in some of the fields of the publisher's major academic concentrations, which encompasses fine arts (including a special interest in the arts of Asia), regional America (with an emphasis on Seattle and the Pacific Northwest), and Native American studies. University of Washington Press maintains a solid backlist.

University of Washington Press (established in 1920) is a midsized house with a primarily scholarly list that features select titles geared toward the general-interest trade market. The house produces books in hardcover and paperback (including reprint editions), and distributes adjunct visual resources (including videotapes, films, and filmstrips). University of Washington also handles a line of scholarly imports (primarily fine arts titles). UWP enters into joint-publication projects with a variety of museums and cultural foundations, and produces a large number of fine arts books and exhibition catalogues.

On the Washington list: *Their Day in the Sun: Women of the 1932 Olympics* by Doris H. Pieroth; *King: The Bullitts of Seattle and Their Communications Empire* by O. Casey Corr; *Doors to Madame Marie* by Odette Meyers; *Out of Inferno: Strindberg's Reawakening As an Artist* by Harry G. Carlson; *A Confederacy of Ambition: William Winlock Miller and the Making of Washington Territory* by William L. Lang; *Champion Trees of Washington State* by Robert Van Pelt; *A History of Ukraine* by Paul Robert Magocsi; *Women of Mongolia* by Martha Avery; *The Oriental Rug Lexicon* by Peter F. Stone; *People, Paths, and Purposes: Notations for a Participatory Envirotecture* by Philip Thiel.

The Native American and regional cultural arena is represented by: *Haida Art* by George F. MacDonald; *Where There Is No Name for Art: The Art of Tewa Pueblo Children* by Bruce Hucko (photographs by author); *Pilchuck: A Glass School* by Tina Oldknow; *Glass Art* by Peter Layton; *The Living Tradition of Yup'ik Masks: Agayuliyararput, Our Way of Making Prayer* by Ann Fienup-Riordan (translations by Marie Meade; photography by Barry McWayne); *A Legacy of Arctic Art* by Dorothy Jean Ray; *Inuit Women Artists* by Odette Leroux, Marion E. Jackson, and Minnie Aodla Freeman; *Haa Kusteeyí (Our Culture): Tlingit Life Stories* (edited by Nora Marks Dauenhauer and Richard Dauenhauer); *Seeing Seattle* by Roger Sale (photographs by Mary Randlett); *Shaping Seattle Architecture: A Historical Guide to the Architects* (edited by Jeffrey Karl Ochsner); *A Wealth of Thought: Franz Boaz on Native American Art* (edited by Aldona Jonaitis).

University of Washington Press handles its own distribution via its home office and a number of regional sales representatives, as well as distributes for a number of other specialist publishers and arts institutions, including the Tate Gallery, Asian Art Museum of San Francisco, Reaktion Books, the Columbus Museum of Art, National Portrait Gallery of the Smithsonian Institution, Exhibitions International, and the Idaho State Historical Society.

Query letters and SASEs should be directed to:

Naomi Pascal, Editor-in-Chief

UNIVERSITY OF WISCONSIN PRESS

114 North Murray Street
Madison, WI 53715-1199
608-262-4928

University of Wisconsin Press catalogues such fields as African studies, African American studies, agriculture, American studies, anthropology and folklore, biography, contemporary issues, economics, environmental studies, European studies, gay studies, geography, history, history of science, Latin American studies, law, literature and criticism, medicine, music, philosophy, poetry, political science, rhetoric, sociology, statistics, Wisconsin regional studies, and women's studies. The press hosts a steadfast backlist.

University of Wisconsin Press (founded in 1937) is a midsize house that specializes in nonfiction and scholarly books and journals, with a short list of crossover titles geared to mainstream trade interest.

Titles from the Wisconsin program: *Cultural Map of Wisconsin: A Cartographic Portrait of the State* by David Woodward, Robert C. Ostergren, Onno Brouwer, Steven Hoelscher, and Joshua Hane; *Why I Can't Read Wallace Stegner, and Other Essays: A Tribal Voice* by Elizabeth Cook-Lynn; *Farm Boys: Lives of Gay Men from the Rural Midwest* (edited by Will Fellows); *The Great American Blow-Up: Puffery in Advertising and Selling* by Ivan L. Preston; *Street Smarts and Critical Theory: Listening to the Vernacular* by Thomas McLaughlin; *The World According to Hollywood, 1918–1939* by Ruth Vasey; *Kenneth Burke in Greenwich Village: Conversing with the Moderns, 1915–1931* by Jack Selzer; *The Tongue Is Fire: South African Storytellers and Apartheid* by Harold Scheub; *Brief Landing on the Earth's Surface* by Juanita Brunk (poems).

A special Wisconsin series is the acclaimed Life Course Studies, which represents a broad interdisciplinary spectrum of inquiry into the nature of human timetables and biographies—the human biocultural life course.

Distribution for University of Wisconsin Press publications is through the house's customer service office; trade sales are garnered nationwide by the press's formidable lineup of regional field representatives.

Query letters and SASEs should be directed to:

Rosalie Robertson, Senior Acquisitions Editor

Mary Elizabeth Braun, Assistant Acquisitions Editor

UNIVERSITY PRESS OF NEW ENGLAND/ WESLEYAN UNIVERSITY PRESS

110 Mount Vernon Street
Middletown, CT 06459-0433
860-685-2420

The University Press of New England/Wesleyan University Press program is known for individualistic works that often exhibit an interdisciplinary focus, as well as titles keyed to particular scholarly fields. The house focuses on fiction and literature, public issues, poetry and the arts, history, biography, social sciences, gender studies, cultural studies, law and social policy, and southern Africa.

University Press of New England is a publishing consortium comprising a number of educational establishments. These include: Brandeis University, Dartmouth College, Middlebury College, the National Gallery of Art, Tufts University, University of Connecticut, University of New Hampshire, University of Rhode Island, Salzburg

Seminar, University of Vermont, and Wesleyan University. University Press of New England (started in 1970) and Wesleyan University Press (founded in 1957) share editorial offices.

From UPNE/Wesleyan: *Longer Views: Extended Essays* by Samuel R. Delany; *Postmodern Materialism and the Future of Marxist Theory: Essays in the Althusserian Tradition* (edited by Antonio Callari and David F. Ruccio); *Genealogies of Conflict: Class, Identity, and State in Palestine/Israel and South Africa* by Ran Greenstein; *Realm of Unknowing: Meditations on Art, Suicide, and Other Transformations* by Mark Rudman; *Children of Bondage: A Social History of the Slave Society at the Cape of Good Hope, 1652–1838* by Robert C.-H. Shell.

Additional important nonfiction: *A New Name for Peace: International Environmentalism, Sustainable Development, and Democracy* by Philip Shabecoff; *Up River: The Story of a Maine Fishing Community* (photographs and text by Olive Pierce; word pictures by Carolyn Chute); *The Heretic's Feast: A History of Vegetarianism* by Colin Spencer; *Looking for Heroes in Postwar France* by Neal Oxenhandler.

Fiction, literature, culture, and the arts play a large part in the UPNE/Wesleyan program. Titles here: *Moving Toward Life: Five Decades of Transformational Dance* by Ana Halprin (edited by Rachel Kaplan); *Musicage: Cage Muses on Words, Art, Music* (John Cage in conversation with Joan Retallack); *Club Cultures: Music, Media, and Subcultural Capital* by Sarah Thornton; *Voices in the Wilderness: American Nature Writing and Environmental Politics* by Daniel G. Payne; *So Fine a Prospect: Historic New England Gardens* by Alan Emmet; *No More Nice Girls: Countercultural Essays* by Ellen Willis; and *The Substance of Style: Perspectives on the American Arts and Crafts Movement* (edited by Bert Denker).

On the list in poetry: *The Front Matter, Dead Souls* (an experiment in literary form) by Leslie Scalpino; *The Spaces Between Birds* by Sandra McPherson; *The Tulip Sacrament* by 'annah Sobelman; *Disfortune* by Joe Wenderoth; *Rider* (poetry) by Mark Rudman (National Book Critics Circle award); *Neon Vernacular: New and Selected Poems* by Usef Komunyakaa (winner of the Pulitzer Prize for poetry); *The Empty Bed* by Rachel Hadas; *Edge Effect: Trails and Portrayals* by Sandra McPherson.

The dandelion logo signifies **A Hardscrabble Book,** an imprint that highlights imaginative New England literature. Sample titles: *Wherever That Great Heart May Be* (stories) by W. D. Wetherell; *J. Eden* (novel) by Kit Reed; *The Best Revenge* (stories) by Rebecca Rule; *The Hair of Harold Roux* (a National Book Award winner) by Thomas Williams; *Live Free or Die* (novel) by Ernest Herbert.

High-profile past selections from UPNE/Wesleyan include: *Atlantis* by Samuel R. Delany (a suite of novellas that dramatize the African American literary experience). Another headline-garnering project was Wesleyan's acquisition of the controversial final novel of Jean Genet, a pro-Palestinian homoerotic quasi-philosophical work called *Prisoner of Love.*

University Press of New England provides distribution services for all its associated imprints.

Query letters and SASEs should be directed to:

Tom Radko, Director of Wesleyan University Press

YALE UNIVERSITY PRESS

302 Temple Street
P.O. Box 209040
New Haven, CT 06520-9040
203-432-0960

The Yale publishing program offers both trade and academically oriented titles in the fields of the arts, the humanities, and the social sciences. Particular general-interest areas include contemporary issues, culture, and events; architecture, art criticism, and art history; history of America (with additional focus on the American West); literature and literary criticism; and political science, economics, and military studies. Yale produces hardcover and trade paper editions.

Yale University Press sponsors the annual Yale Younger Poets Competition and publishes the winning manuscript. Yale series include Composers of the Twentieth Century and Early Chinese Civilization.

Yale University Press (established in 1908) is at the forefront of university publishing. The house is one of the major academic houses, and Yale's commercial presence is evident in the catalogs of book clubs as well as on national, regional, and specialty bestseller lists.

On the nonfiction list at Yale: *The Strategy of Rhetoric: Campaigning for the American Constitution* by William H. Riker; *The Self After Postmodernity* by Calvin O. Schrag; *Freud's Dora: A Psychoanalytic, Historical, and Textual Study* by Patrick J. Mahony; *Like Subjects, Love Objects: Essays on Recognition and Sexual Difference* by Jessica Benjamin; *Handwriting in America: A Cultural History* by Tamara Plakins Thornton; *University Life in 18th Century Oxford* by Graham Midgley; *The Elements of Teaching* by James M. Banner, Jr. and Harold C. Cannon; *Invented Cities: The Creation of Landscape in Nineteenth-Century New York and Boston* by Mona Domosh; *Marihuana, the Forbidden Medicine* by Lester Grinspoon and James B. Bakalar; *Comrade Criminal: The Rise of the New Russian Mafiya* by Stephen Handelman.

Cultural criticism, literary works, and the arts: *Visionary Fictions: Apocalyptic Writings from Blake to the Modern Age* by Edward J. Ahearn; *Rethinking the Rhetorical Tradition: From Plato to Postmodernism* by James L. Kastely; *Dryden and the Problem of Freedom: The Republican Aftermath, 1649–1680* by David B. Haley; *The Sound of Virtue: Philip Sidney's Arcadia and Elizabethan Politics* by Blair Worden; *Recollections of a Tour of Scotland* by Dorothy Wordsworth (edited and illustrated by Carol Kyros Walker); *The Letters of Gertrude Stein and Thornton Wilder* (edited by Edward M. Burns and Ulla E. Dydo with William Rice); *The Emergence of the Modern American Theater, 1914–1929* by Ronald H. Wainscott; *Russia Through Women's Eyes: Autobiographies from Tsarist Russia* (edited by Toby W. Clyman and Judith Vowles); *Utamakura, Allusion, and Intertextuality in Traditional Japanese Poetry* by Edward Kamens; *English Poems, Life of Pico, The Last Things: The Yale Edition of the Complete Works of St. Thomas More* (volume I) (edited by Anthony S. G. Edwards, Katherine Gardiner Rodgers, and Clarence H. Miller); *Noah's Flood: The Genesis Story in Western Thought* by Norman Cohn.

Yale University Press handles its own distribution.
Query letters and SASEs should be directed to:

Jean E. Thomson Black, Editor
Science and medicine.

Jonathan Brent, Executive Editor
Classics, literature, philosophy, poetry.

John S. Covell, Senior Editor
Economics, law, political science.

Charles Grench, Editor-in-Chief
Anthropology, archaeology, history, Judaic studies, religion, women's studies.

Harry Haskell, Editor
Music and performing arts.

Judy Metro, Senior Editor
Art, art history, architecture and history of architecture, geography, landscape studies.

John G. Ryden, Director

Gladys Topkis, Senior Editor
Education, psychiatry, psychology, psychoanalysis, sociology.

Religious, Spiritual, and Inspirational Publishers

The Writer's Journey
Themes of the Spirit and Inspiration

Deborah Levine Herman

If you have decided to pursue writing as a career instead of as a longing or a dream, you might find yourself falling into a pattern of focusing on the goal instead of the process. When you have a great book idea, you may envision yourself on a book-signing tour or as a guest on *Oprah* before you've written a single word.

It's human nature to look into your own future, but too much projection can get in the way of what the writing experience is all about. The process of writing is like a wondrous journey that can help you cross a bridge to the treasures hidden within your own subconscious. Some people believe that it's a way for you to link with the collective or universal consciousness, the storehouse of all wisdom and truth, as it has existed since the beginning of time.

There are many methods of writing that bring their own rewards. Some people can produce exceptional prose by using their intellect and their mastery of the writing craft. They use research and analytical skills to help them produce works of great importance and merit.

Then there are those who have learned to tap into the wellspring from which all genius flows. They are the inspired ones who write with the intensity of an impassioned lover. They are the spiritual writers who write because they have to. They may not want to, they may not know how to, but something inside them is begging to be let out. It gnaws away at them until they find a way to set it free.

Although they may not realize it, spiritual writers are engaged in a larger spiritual journey toward ultimate self-mastery and unification with God.

Spiritual writers often feel as if they're taking dictation. It is as though their thoughts have a life of their own and the mind is merely a receiver. Some people refer to this as "channeling" and believe disembodied spirits take over and write through them. Although I sincerely doubt that Gandhi or other notables have authored as many channeled books as people have been claiming, truly spiritual writing does have an otherworldly feeling and can often teach the writer things he or she would otherwise not have known.

Writing opens you up to new perspectives, much like self-induced psychotherapy. Although journals are the most direct route for self-evaluation, fiction and nonfiction also serve as vehicles for a writer's growth. Writing helps the mind expand to the limits of the imagination.

Anyone can become a spiritual writer. There are many benefits from doing so, not the least of which is the development of your soul. On a more practical level, it is much less difficult to write with flow and fervor than it is to be bound by the limitations of logic and analysis. If you tap into the universal source, there is no end to your potential creativity.

The greatest barrier to becoming a spiritual writer is the human ego. We treat our words as if they were our children—only we tend to be neurotic parents. A child is not owned by a parent, but rather must be loved, guided, and nurtured until he or she can carry on, on his or her own.

The same is true for our words. If we try to own and control them like property, they will be limited by our vision for them. We will overprotect them and will not be able to see when we may be taking them into the wrong direction for their ultimate well-being.

Another ego problem that creates a barrier to creativity is our need for constant approval and our tendency toward perfectionism. We may feel the tug toward free expression, but will erect blockades to ensure appropriate style and structure. We write with a "schoolmarm" hanging over our shoulders waiting to tell us what we are doing wrong.

Style and structure are important to ultimate presentation, but that is what editing is for. Ideas and concepts need to flow like water through a running stream.

The best way to become a spiritual writer is to relax and have fun. If you are relaxed and are in a basically good mood, you'll be open to intuition. Writers tend to take themselves too seriously, which causes anxiety, which exacerbates fear, which causes insecurity, which diminishes our self-confidence and leads ultimately to mounds of crumpled papers and lost inspiration.

If you have faith in a Supreme Being, the best way to begin a spiritual writing session is with the following writer's prayer:

> Almighty God (Jesus, Allah, Great Spirit, etc.), Creator of the Universe, help me to become a vehicle for your wisdom so that what I write is of the highest purpose and will serve the greatest good. I humbly place my (pen/keyboard/Dictaphone) in your hands so that you may guide me.

Prayer helps to connect you to the universal source. It empties the mind of trash, noise, and potential writer's blocks. If you are not comfortable with formal prayer, a few minutes of meditation will serve the same purpose.

Spiritual writing as a process does not necessarily lead to a sale. The fact is that some people have more commercial potential than others, no matter how seemingly unimportant their message might be. Knowledge of the business of writing will help you make a career of it. If you combine this with the spiritual process, it can also bring you gratification and inner peace.

If you trust the process of writing and allow the journey to take you where it will, it may bring you benefits far beyond your expectations.

ABINGDON PRESS

201 Eighth Avenue South
P.O. Box 801
Nashville, TN 37202-0801
615-749-6290

Abingdon Press is the book-publishing division of the United Methodist Publishing House (founded in 1789). Abingdon produces hardcover, trade paperback, and mass-market paperback editions covering a wide range of religious specialty, religious trade, and popular markets. Areas of concentration include professional reference and resources for the clergy; academic and scholarly works in the fields of religious and biblical history and theory; inspirational and devotional books; and titles with contemporary spiritual and ethical themes intended for a wider readership. Abingdon's publishing presence includes software and works on CD-ROM.

Abingdon also issues several series of books for children, in addition to resources for Sunday school and general Christian education, as well as church supplies (posters, calendars, certificates, maps, buttons, music, and dramatic scripts). Dimensions for Living is an Abingdon imprint dedicated to titles with a popular orientation (see separate subentry below). Abingdon reprints a number of its bestselling titles in mass-market paperback editions and tends a formidable backlist.

On the Abingdon list: *In Ordinary Time: Healing the Wounds of the Heart* by Roberta C. Bondi; *The Jesus I Knew: Creative Portrayals of Gospel Characters* by Robert Martin Walker; *Entertainment Evangelism: Taking the Church Public* by Walt Kallestad; *Team Ministry: A Workbook for Getting Things Done* by Steve Schey and Walt Kallestad; *The Complete Ministry Audit: How to Measure 20 Principles for Growth* by William M. Easum; *The Interventionist* by Lyle E. Schaller; *White Soul: Country Music, the Church, and Working Americans* by Tex Sample; *The Downtown Church: The Heart of the City* by Howard Edington with Lyle E. Schaller; *Leading Your Ministry* by Alan E. Nelson; *Leading Edge: Leadership Strategies from the New Testament* by Robert D. Dale; *Be Filled: Sermons on the Beatitudes* by Arthur Lee McClanahan; *Preaching on the Brink: The Future of Homiletics* edited by Martha J. Simmons; *Wrestling with the Patriarchs: Retrieving Women's Voices in Preaching* by Lee McGee; *A Healing Homiletic: Preaching & Disability* by Kathy Black; *Embracing God: Praying with Teresa of Avila* by Dwight Judy; *Introducing the Bible* by William Barclay; *The Search for Meaning in the Workplace* by Thomas H. Naylor, William H. Willimon, and Rolf V. Osterberg.

The Grand Sweep series by J. Ellsworth Kalas is a Bible-study program that moves in canonical sequence based on Ellsworth Kalas's book *365 Days from Genesis Through Revelation*. Titles: *The Grand Sweep: Bible Study for Individuals and Groups*; *The Grand Sweep: Daily Response Book*; *The Grand Sweep: Guide for Group Study*; *The Grand Sweep: Sermon Ideas for 52 Weeks*.

Body & Soul: A Disciplined Approach to a Healthy Lifestyle is a series of programs for Christians seeking a healthy lifestyle. Body & Soul focuses on the spiritual, physical, mental, emotional, and social aspects of persons for a powerful approach to behavior change. Titles: *Health Yourself*; *Second Helpings*; *Wonderfully Healthy*; *Caring & Sharing*.

Serious trade books, scholarly reference, and academic and professional how-to books (as stand-alones or in sets) have long been mainstays of the Abingdon program. Academic and scholarly titles—some with crossover religious trade appeal—are represented by: *Faithful Change: The Personal and Public Challenges of Postmodern Life* by James W. Fowler; *Jews & Christians in Pursuit of Social Justice* by Randall M. Falk and Walter J. Harrelson; *Stewards of Life: Bioethics and Pastoral Care* by Sondra Ely Wheeler; *The Business Corporation & Productive Justice* by David A. Krueger with Donald W. Shriver, Jr. and Laura Nash; *Environmental Ethics and Christian Humanism* by Thomas S. Derr with James A. Nash and Richard John Neuhaus; *Listening In: A Multicultural Reading of the Psalms* by Stephen Breck Reid.

In addition to distributing its own books, Abingdon Press handles the lists of several other smaller religious publishers.

Query letters and SASEs should be directed to:

Mary Catherine Dean, Editor, Trade Books
Nonfiction books that "help families and individuals live Christian lives"; contemporary social themes of Christian relevance.

Jack Keller, Editor, Professional Books and Reference Books
Methodist doctrine and church practices for clergy and laity. Dictionaries and general reference guides relevant to Methodist history and policy.

Dr. Rex D. Matthews, Editor, Academic Books
Books for Sunday and parochial schools and seminaries.

DIMENSIONS FOR LIVING

Dimensions for Living is an Abingdon imprint devoted to general-interest religious trade books on practical Christian living. Dimensions for Living publishes in the popular categories of inspiration, devotion, self-help, home, and family, as well as gift volumes. The concept behind the Dimensions for Living imprint—"quality books that celebrate life"—was developed in response to market research. The editorial approach is to combine contemporary themes with mainstream Christian theology.

Titles from Dimensions for Living: *Christmas Gifts That Always Fit: Friendship, Encouragement, Kindness, Faith, Hope, Love* by James W. Moore; *Intimacy on the Run: Staying Close When So Much Keeps You Apart* by Robert H. Lauer and Jeanette C. Lauer; *365 Meditations for Mothers of Teens* (contributors: M. Garlinda Burton, Pamela Crosby, Lisa Flinn, Kay C. Gray, Margaret Anne Huffman, Pam Kidd, Anne Killinger, Marjorie L. Kimbrough, LaDonna Meinders, Mary Catharine Neal, Anne Wilcox, and Mary Zimmer); *365 Meditations for Teachers* by Anne Marie Drew, Joan Laney, Ellamarie Parkison, and Anne Wilcox.

Simple Pleasures books are designed to encourage, motivate, and enable individuals and families to simplify, to discover life's slower, more tranquil pace. Titles: *Simple*

Pleasures for Christmas; *Simple Pleasures for Busy Men*; *Simple Pleasures for Busy Women*; *Simple Pleasures for Busy Families*.

Query letters and SASEs should be directed to:

Sally Sharpe, Editor, Dimensions for Living

Quality books that celebrate life and affirm the Christian faith.

AMANA BOOKS

P.O. Box 678
Brattleboro, VT 05302
802-257-0872
fax: 802-254-5123

Amana Books (founded in 1984) publishes scholarly and religious titles with an editorial emphasis on topics of particular concern with respect to the Middle East geographic area. Amana categories include Middle Eastern studies, Islamic studies, and works of general interest. The house publishes a select number of new titles each year and maintains a solid backlist.

In Arabic, the word *Amana* signifies "that which is placed in trust"—meaning faith and commitment to humanitarian justice for all peoples in all lands. Amana Books supports this cause through the publication of books that provide analyses of political, historical, cultural, and religious issues and traditions. The publishing house seeks to explore the causes and effects of oppression, injustice, and misunderstanding, while offering original insights and possible solutions. By challenging established conceptions, works from Amana contribute vigorously to the public debate on social and political conditions throughout the world.

Representative Amana titles: *Princes & Emperors: International Terrorism in the Real World* by Noam Chomsky; *Taking Sides: America's Secret Relations with a Militant Israel* by Stephen Green; *Warriors at Suez: Eisenhower Takes America into the Middle East in 1956* by David Neff; *Through the Hebrew Looking Glass: Arab Stereotypes in Children's Literature* by Fouzi El-Asmar; *Islam, Christianity, and African Identity* by Sulayman S. Nyang; *Conversations with Contemporary Armenian Artists* by Jackie Abramiam; *Alfonsina Storni: Selected Poems* (translated by Dorothy Scott Loos); *Giving Up the Dream* (literary reflections) by Deborah Shea.

Amana publishes *The Qur'an: Translation and Commentary* by Thomas B. Irving in two editions: hardcover in both the Arabic and English languages, and paperback in the English language only.

Amana Books handles its own distribution.

Query letters and SASEs should be directed to:

S. A. Rabbo, Publisher

AMERICAN FEDERATION OF ASTROLOGERS

6535 South Rural Road
Box 22040
Tempe, AZ 85285-2040
602-838-1751
fax: 602-838-8293
AFA@msn.com (e-mail)

American Federation of Astrologers (founded in 1938) is a specialist publisher of books in professional astrology; the house also offers cassette tapes, astrological software, charts and other astrological aids.

As an organization, American Federation of Astrologers aims to further astrological education and research. AFA is the world's largest astrological membership organization, as well as a major publisher and distributor of astrological books and related supplies. AFA books are written by a variety of talented astrologers from all over the globe.

AFA encourages and promotes the science and art of astrology and advocates freedom of thought and speech in the astrological arena; the house offers a monthly membership bulletin and hosts periodic conventions. The organization's publishing program has generally produced a short list of new titles each year and supports an extensive publications backlist.

From American Federation of Astrologers: *Phases of the Moon* by Marilyn Busteed and Dorothy Wergin; *Midpoint Keys to Chiron* by Chris Brooks; *Stars over England* and *Horoscopes of the USA and Canada* by Marc Penfield; *How to Give an Astrological Health Reading* by Diane L. Cramer; *A New Age Conversation* by Doris Chase Doane and Earl Cramer, M.D.; *Let's Read a Horoscope* and *How Body Language Defines Character* by Doris Chase Doane.

Authors please note: American Federation of Astrologers wishes to consider for publication completed manuscripts only—and does not wish to consider queries, outlines, samples, or proposals. Manuscripts may be submitted along with copies on diskette (other than Macintosh). Subject matter should appeal only to the sophisticated astrologer; Sun-sign-oriented material geared to the amateur or popular audience is not suited for the house's publishing program.

American Federation of Astrologers distributes its own list as well as publications of other houses.

Complete manuscripts and/or diskettes (with SASEs) should be directed to:

Kris A. Riske, Publications Manager

JASON ARONSON INC., PUBLISHERS

230 Livingston Street
Northvale, NJ 07647
201-767-4093
http://www.aronson.com/ (World Wide Web)

Jason Aronson Inc., Publishers (founded in 1965) produces a strong list of works in the field of Jewish interest, covering contemporary currents of Jewish thought as well as traditional Judaica. The house interest embraces popular, scholarly, and literary works—original titles and reprints. The well-nurtured Aronson backlist includes a lineup of established classics. (For Aronson's program in psychotherapy, please see Directory of U.S. Publishers.)

Representative of the Aronson list: *Chosen Tales: Stories Told by Jewish Storytellers* (edited by Peninnah Schram); *The Encyclopedia of Jewish Prayer: Ashkenazic and Sephardic Rites* by Macy Nuluman; *Frumspeak: The First Dictionary of Yeshivish* by Chaim M. Weiser; *The Jewish Encyclopedia of Moral and Ethical Issues* by Nachum Amsel; *Jewish History in 100 Nutshells* by Naomi Pasachoff and Robert J. Littman; *Jewish Stories One Generation Tells Another* (retold by Peninnah Schram); *The Jewish Traveler: Hadassah Magazine's Guide to the World's Jewish Communities and Sights* (edited by Alan M. Tigay); *Learn Talmud: How to Use The Talmud* (The Steinsaltz Edition) by Judith Z. Abrams; *Night/Dawn/Day* by Elie Weisel; *On Being Free* by Adin Steinsaltz; *Shlomo's Stories: Selected Tales* by Shlomo Carlebach with Susan Yael Mesinai; *The Thirteen Petalled Rose* by Adin Steinsaltz; *To Be a Jewish Woman* by Lisa Aiken; *Understanding Judaism: The Basics of Deed and Creed* by Benjamin Blech.

Aronson supervises its own distribution, which, in addition to a network of regional and national trade-fulfillment services, features a direct-mail catalog operation. Aronson also oversees the operations of the Jewish Book Club.

Query letters and SASEs should be directed to:

Arthur Kurzweil, Publisher

AUGSBURG FORTRESS PUBLISHING

426 South Fifth Street
P.O. Box 1209
Minneapolis, MN 55440-1209
612-330-3300

Augsburg Fortress publishes titles in popular and professional religious categories. The Augsburg Fortress list accents works of interest to general readers in addition to books that appeal primarily to a mainstream religious readership, as well as a solid selection of works geared to professional clergy and practitioners of pastoral counseling.

Categories include theology and pastoral care, biblical and historical academic studies, the life and tradition of Martin Luther, self-improvement and recovery, and books for younger readers from nursery and preschoolers through young adult.

The Fortress Press imprint accents issues of contemporary cultural, theological, and political impact. In addition, Augsburg Fortress produces computer software, recordings, artwork, and gift items. Augsburg Fortress also vends a line of liturgical vestments and supplies. The house is widely known for its full range of Bibles, produced in a variety of edition styles.

Augsburg Fortress's ecumenical emphasis enables the house to address a broad range of issues and views within a diversified booklist. Augsburg Fortress Publishing (founded in 1890) is a subsidiary of the Publishing House of the Evangelical Lutheran Church in America.

Representative of the Augsburg list: *Nurturing Silence in a Noisy Heart: How to Find Inner Peace* by Wayne E. Oates; *Autumn Wisdom: Finding Meaning in Life's Later Years* by James E. Miller; *The Contemplative Pastor: Returning to the Art of Spiritual Direction* by Eugene Peterson; *The Jesus Prescription for a Healthy Life* by Leonard Sweet; *Grieving the Death of a Friend* by Harold Ivan Smith; *A Year of Prayer: 365 Reflections for Spiritual Growth* by Jeanne Hinton; *Soul Weavings: A Gathering of Women's Prayers* (edited by Lyn Klug); *Our Hope for Years to Come: The Search for Spiritual Sanctuary, Reflections and Photographs* (text by Martin Marty; photographs by Micah Marty); *I'm Thinking of You: Spiritual Letters of Hope and Healing* by Herbert F. Brokering; *Wrestling with Depression: A Spiritual Guide to Reclaiming Life* by William and Lucy Hulme; *The Book of God* by Walt Wangerin; *Streams of Living Water: Celebrating the Five Great Traditions of Christian Faith* by Richard J. Foster; *Love Letters from Cell 92* by Ruth-Alice von Bismarck and Ulrich Kabitz; *Dead Sea Scrolls Today* by James C. VanderKam; *The History of God: The 4,000 Year Quest of Judaism, Christianity, and Islam* by Karen Armstrong; *Breaking the Code: Understanding the Book of Revelation* by Bruce M. Metzger.

Children's selections include the line of Good News Explorers Sunday school curriculum series, the Rejoice series, and the Witness series, as well as individual titles. Samples here: *Swamped!* by Nathan Aaseng; *So I Can Read* by Dandi Mackall (illustrations by Deborah A. Kirkeeide); *Ms. Pollywog's Problem-Solving Service* by Ellen Javernick (illustrated by Meredith Johnson).

Authors should note: Augsburg Fortress prefers to receive a proposal rather than a completed manuscript; the house receives over 3,000 submissions per year—a finely honed book proposal may therefore be considered essential.

Augsburg Fortress has a potent distribution network with sales representatives operating via offices nationwide.

FORTRESS PRESS

Fortress Press focuses on the ever-changing religious worldview of the contemporary world. The Fortress list is keyed to issues of topical interest, tackled with vision and precision; these works address political and cultural issues, and are often on the cusp of current religious debate. The Fortress market orientation tilts toward both the general trade and the religious trade.

Titles from Fortress Press: *God Beyond Gender: Feminist Christian God Language* by Gail Ramshaw; *The Crucifixion of Jesus: History, Myth, Faith* by Gerard S. Sloyan; *The Paradoxical Vision: A Public Theology for the Twenty-First Century* by Robert Benne; *The Spirituality of African Peoples: The Search for a Common Moral Discourse* by Peter J. Paris; *Theology for a Scientific Age: Being and Becoming—Natural, Divine, and Human* by Arthur Peacocke; *Womanism and Afrocentrism in Theology* by Cheryl J. Sanders; *X-odus: An African-American Male Journey* by Garth Kasimu Baker-Fletcher.

Query letters and SASEs should be directed to:

Ronald Klug, Director of Publications

Robert Klausmeier, Senior Acquisitions Editor

AURORA PRESS

300 Catron Road, Suite B
Santa Fe, NM 87501
505-989-9804
fax: 505-982-8321

Mailing address:
P.O. Box 573
Santa Fe, NM 87504

Aurora titles specialize in astrology, health, metaphysical philosophies, and the emerging global consciousness. Aurora Press (founded in 1982) publishes works that catalyze personal growth, balance, and transformation. The press aims to make available to the book-buying public writings that promote an innovative synthesis of ancient wisdom and 20th-century resources, and thus integrate esoteric knowledge with daily life. Aurora Press typically issues a limited number of new titles each season; the house backlist includes many perennial sellers.

Aurora selects manuscripts for publication on the following basis: The information presented must be beneficial in a practical way, new to the general public, and helpful in exploring inner potential, expanding consciousness, or improving the quality of life.

The outstanding sales of Aurora's titles (including many foreign-language editions) has validated the Aurora publishing stance that it is possible to produce high-quality books without compromising personal ideals or values.

From the Aurora list: *The I Ching and the Genetic Code: The Hidden Key to Life* by Martin Shonberger; *Uninvited Guests: A Documented History of UFO Sightings, Alien Encounters, and Coverups* by Richard Hall; *The Sabian Symbols in Astrology: Illustrated by 1000 Horoscopes of Well Known People* by Marc Edmund Jones (revised edition); *Coming Home: A Guide to Dying at Home with Dignity* by Deborah Duda; *Silver Dental Fillings: The Toxic Time Bomb* by Sam Ziff.

Series from Aurora include works by Elisabeth Haitch (*Sexual Energy & Yoga*; *Wisdom of the Tarot*) and Dane Rudhyar (*The Planetarization of Consciousness*; *An Astrological Triptych*).

Aurora Press is distributed to the trade and individual customers via the Samuel Weiser fulfillment and distribution center.

Aurora Press does not accept unsolicited manuscripts. Query letters and SASEs should be directed to:

Barbara Somerfield, President

Michael King, Director

BAHÁ'Í PUBLISHING

Bahá'í National Center
1233 Central Street
Evanston, IL 60201
847-251-1854
800-999-9019 (catalog requests)

Bahá'í Publishing Trust (founded in 1902) is a subsidiary of the National Spiritual Assembly of the Bahá'ís of the United States. The house publishes books pertaining to the Bahá'í religion; interest areas include history, juveniles, scholarly works, and multimedia materials.

From Bahá'í Publishing: *Messages from the Universal House of Justice, 1963–1986: The Third Epoch of the Formative Age* (compiled by the Universal House of Justice); *Messages to the Bahá'í World, 1950–1957* by Shaoghi Effendi; *Heart of the Gospel* by George Townshend; *God of Buddha* by Jamshed Fozdar; *Pupil of the Eye: African Americans in the World Order of Baha'u'llah* (compiled by Bonnie J. Taylor); *Short History of the Bahá'í Faith* by Peter Smith; *Sacred Moments: Daily Meditations on the Virtues* by Linda Kavelin Popov; *Meditation* by Wendi Momen; *Law of Love Enshrined: Selected Essays* by John Hatcher and William Hatcher; *Toward the Most Great Justice: Elements of Justice in the New World Order* (edited by Charles O. Lerche); *My Pilgrimage to Haifa, November 1919* by Bahiyyih Winckler.

The house's Bahá'í Distribution Service wing handles trade and personal order fulfillment.

Query letters and SASEs should be directed to:

Dale Spenner, General Manager

BAKER BOOK HOUSE
FLEMING H. REVELL
CHOSEN BOOKS
SPIRE BOOKS
WYNWOOD BOOKS

Twin Brooks Industrial Park
6030 East Fulton Road
Ada, MI 49301
616-676-9185
fax: 616-676-9573

Mailing address:
P.O. Box 6287
Grand Rapids, MI 49516-6287
http://www.bakerbooks.com (World Wide Web)

Baker Book House (founded in 1939) produces works across the spectrum of general religious subject areas (from Protestant and ecumenical perspectives). Baker Book House is a preeminent distributor in the religious-publishing field; in addition to books, Baker carries audiovisual materials.

Baker Book House distributes its own list (including its diverse imprints) and catalogs selected works from other publishing firms.

In addition to its comprehensive distribution services, Baker Book House has taken over the lists of several divisions of the former Gleneida Publishing Group, including Fleming H. Revell, Chosen Books, Spire Books, and Wynwood Books.

BAKER BOOK HOUSE

The publishing division of Baker Book House issues titles of general trade interest as well as a wide selection of books for ministers, students, schools, libraries, and church workers.

The Baker Interactive Books for Lively Education lineup gives a distinctive new voice and dimension to Bible storytelling. The authors, Jill and Stuart Briscoe, want this series to help young children experience with laughter the simple retelling of old stories, allowing imagination to refresh favorite events, using songs and simple dramas to promote understanding. Titles: *Jesus Makes a Major Comeback and Other Amazing Feats*; *Moses Takes a Road Trip and Other Famous Journeys*; *David Drops a Giant Problem and Other Fearless Heroes*; *Paul Hits the Beach and Other Wild Adventures*.

Highlighting the Baker program: *Here We Stand! A Call from Confessing Evangelicals* (edited by James Montgomery Boice and Benjamin E. Sasse); *The Indestructible Book: The Bible, Its Translators, and Their Sacrifices* by Ken Connolly; *Life in Christ* by John Stott; *So That's What a Christian Is! 12 Pictures of the Dynamic Christian Life* by Warren W. Wiersbe; *When Not to Borrow: Unconventional Financial Wisdom to Set Your Church Free* by Ray Bowman with Eddy Hall; *Behind the Stained Glass Windows: Money Dynamics in the Church* by John and Sylvia Ronsvalle; *Adding Cross to Crown: The Political Significance of Christ's Passion* by Mark A. Noll; *Ready, Set . . . Wait: Help for Life on Hold* by Karen Barber; *Good News for Women: A Biblical Picture of Gender Equality* by Rebecca Merrill Groothuis; *Explaining Your Faith* by Alister McGrath; *Precious in His Sight: Childhood and Children in the Bible* by Ray B. Zuck.

FLEMING H. REVELL
CHOSEN BOOKS
SPIRE BOOKS

This Baker wing specializes in spiritually oriented works for the popular religious audience, including a wide range of fiction. Offerings from the Revell program include the Treasury of Helen Steiner Rice line of inspirational titles (including the Precious Moments series). The Chosen Books imprint produces evangelical Christian books for personal growth and enrichment. Spire accents an inspirational list of personal stories told through autobiography and memoir.

From Revell: *Pillow Talk: The Intimate Marriage from A to Z* by Karen Scalf Linamen; *The Climb of Your Life* by Ken Jones; *Give & Take: Creating Marital Compatibility* by Willard F. Harley, Jr.; *Trauma: The Pain That Stays* by Robert M. Hicks; *The Messie Motivator: New Strategies to Restoring Order in Your Life and Home* by Sandra Felton; *Men's Secret Wars* by Patrick A. Means.

Chosen titles include: *The River Is Here: Receiving and Sustaining the Blessing of Revival* by Melinda Fish; *Receiving the Power: Preparing the Way for the Holy Spirit* by Zeb Bradford Long and Douglas McMurry.

On the Spire roster: *Safer Than a Known Way* by Pamela Rosewell Moore; *The Compulsive Woman* by Sandra Simpson LeSourd; *Say Yes to Tomorrow* by Dale Evans Rogers with Floyd W. Thatcher; *Please, Somebody Love Me!* by Jillian Ryan and Joseph A. Ryan.

WYNWOOD PRESS

Wynwood Press lists primarily nonfiction in self-awareness and self-improvement. The Wynwood Press program currently produces occasional new titles only. Wynwood's extensive backlist includes cookbooks, works on language and lexicography, as well as select fiction titles. (Wynwood was the original publisher of John Grisham's first novel, *A Time to Kill*.)

Query letters and SASEs should be directed to:

Jane Schrier, Adult Fiction Acquisitions Editor

Paul Engle, Professional Books Acquisitions Editor

Allan Fisher, Director of Publications

Bill Petersen, Senior Acquisitions Editor

Dan Van't Kerkhoff, General Trade Acquisitions Editor

Jim Weaver, Academic and Reference Books Acquisitions Editor

BEAR & COMPANY PUBLISHING

P.O. Box 2860
Santa Fe, NM 87504
505-983-5968
fax: 505-989-8386

Bear & Company publishes a wide array of titles in historical and contemporary spiritual traditions, healing, and energetic medicine. Bear's list in health and medicine accents revolutionary techniques that incorporate such elements as emotion, intuition, channeling, herbs, and crystals.

Conceived over a kitchen table in the fall of 1979, Bear & Company (founded formally in 1980) originally highlighted titles in creation spirituality. The publisher has built a substantial backlist in this field (including Matthew Fox's *Original Blessing: A*

Primer in Creation Spirituality)—and publishes works exhibiting an increasingly diverse spectrum of thought.

A natural outgrowth of the original Bear & Company approach is a remarkable lineup in Native American spirituality, including works that expand the interpretation of pre-Columbian traditions into the contemporary arena. Bear's benchmark title in this area is *The Mayan Factor: Path Beyond Technology* by José Argüelles.

The house insignia—a rambling bear under a full moon—marks a roster of thoughtful, vivid, and evocative explorations into who we are and where we came from, and the destiny of the species, as illuminated by the company's trade slogan: "Books to celebrate and heal the Earth."

The evolving seasonal booklist demonstrates that artistry continues to waft from the Bear & Company kitchen: *Medicine of the Cherokee: The Way of Right Relationship* by J. T. Garrett and Michael Garrett; *Therapeutic Touch Inner Workbook: Ventures in Transpersonal Healing* by Dolores Krieger, Ph.D., R.N.; *Transformation Through Bodywork: Using Touch Therapies for Inner Peace* by Dan Menkin; *Embracing Death: Riding Life's Transitions into Power and Freedom* by Angela Browne-Miller; *Toltecs of the New Millennium* by Victor Sanchez.

A Bear hallmark is the divination series, which features illustrated books and sets of cards. Packages include: *Contact Cards: An Extraterrestrial Divination System* by Kim Carlsberg and Darryl Anka; *The Mayan Oracle: Return Path to the Stars* by Ariel Spilsbury and Michael Bryner (illustrations by Donna Kiddie); *Inner Child Cards: A Journey into Fairy Tales, Myth & Nature* by Isha Lerner and Mark Lerner (illustrated by Christopher Guilfoil); *Medicine Cards: The Discovery of Power Through the Ways of Animals* by Jamie Sams and David Carson (illustrations by Angela Werneke).

From Bear's bestselling backlist: *Beyond My Wildest Dreams: Diary of a UFO Abductee* by Kim Carlsberg; *The Trickster, Magician & Grieving Man: Reconnecting Men with the Earth* by Glen A. Mazis; *The Woman with the Alabaster Jar: Mary Magdalen and the Holy Grail* by Margaret Starbird; *Journey to the Four Directions: Teachings of the Feathered Serpent* by Jim Berenholtz; *Dolphins, ETs & Angels: Adventures Among Spiritual Intelligences* by Timothy Wyllie; *Bringers of the Dawn: Teachings from the Pleiadians* by Barbara Marciniak; *Gift of Power: The Life and Teachings of a Lakota Medicine Man* by Archie Fire Lame Deer and Richard Erdoes; *Liquid Light of Sex: Understanding Your Key Life Passages* by Barbara Hand Clow; *The Earth Chronicles* (series) by Zecharia Sitchin.

Bear & Company distributes its list via a network that includes several distribution services and wholesalers.

Query letters and SASEs should be directed to:

Barbara Hand Clow, Editorial Director

BETHANY HOUSE PUBLISHERS

11300 Hampshire Avenue South
Minneapolis, MN 55438
612-829-2500
fax: 612-829-2768

Bethany House Publishers (founded in 1956) issues hardcover and trade paperback titles in evangelical Christian fiction (with an accent on historicals) and nonfiction, as well as a powerful youth lineup. Areas of Bethany House nonfiction interest include devotional works, relationships and family, and Biblical reference.

Bethany's fiction authors include such best-selling names as Janette Oke, Judith Pella, and Gilbert Morris. The program accents titles with American prairie and Western themes, historical romances, and works with contemporary settings; the house also offers boxed series sets. Among Bethany fiction features are the series by the father/daughter writing team Lynn Morris and Gilbert Morris.

The house's trade credo is: "God's light shining through good books." Bethany's traditional devotion to bookmaking is evident in its enduring backlist.

Nonfiction from Bethany: *What if I Married the Wrong Person?* by Dr. Richard E. Mattheson and Janis Long Harris; *Shattering Our Assumptions: Who Is Today's Christian Woman?* by Miriam Neff and Debra K. Klingsporn; *How a Man Handles Conflict at Work* by Paul Tomlinson; *How a Man Prays for His Family* by Dr. John W. Yates II; *Families That Play Together Stay Together! Fun and Healthy TV-Free Ideas* by Cameron and Donna Partow; *The New Absolutes and How They Are Eroding Moral Character, Families, and Society* by William D. Watkins; *The Embrace of God: Seeing Beyond Imperfect Parents to Glimpse a Nurturing Heavenly Father* by Dr. M. Lloyd Erickson; *Reclaiming Intimacy in Your Marriage: A Plan for Facing Life's Ebb and Flow Together* by Robert and Debra Bruce; *The Soul at Rest: A Journey into Contemplative Prayer* by Tricia McCary Rhodes; *Glimpses: Seeing God in Everyday Life* by Annie Herring; *LifeKeys: Discovering Who You are, Why You Are Here, What You Do Best* by Jane A. G. Kise; David Stark, and Sandra Krebs Hirsh; *The Roman Catholic Controversy: What Draws and Divides Evangelicals* by James R. White.

Overview of Bethany adult fiction: *The Braxtons of Miracle Springs* by Michael Phillips; *Close to a Father's Heart* by Neva Coyle (Summerwind series); *Return to Harmony* by Janette Oke and T. Davis Bunn; *The Fires of Autumn* by Robert Funderburk (a Dylan St. John novel); *Nana's Gift* by Janette Oke; *The Penny Whistle* by B. J. Hoff; *Tread Upon the Lion* by Gilbert Morris (the Liberty Bell series); *A New Day Rising* by Lauraine Snelling; *Secret Place of Thunder* by Lynn Morris and Gilbert Morris (Cheney Duvall, M.D. series); *The Music Box* by T. Davis Bunn; *Heart of Valor* by Alan Morris (Guardians of the North Series); *The Oyster Pirates* by Jim Walker (the Wells Fargo Trail series); *White Nights, Red Morning* by Judith Pella (the Russians series); *The Emerald Flame* by Patricia Hickman (Land of the Far Horizons Series).

Nonfiction for youth and young adults: *Hero Tales: A Family Treasury of True Stories from the Lives of Christian Heroes* by Dave and Neta Jackson; *Hot Topics, Tough Questions: Honest Answers to Your Hardest Questions* by Bill Myers.

Youth and young-adult fiction: *In Too Deep* by Patricia Rushford (Jennie McGrady Mysteries); *Faded Dreams* by Judy Baer (Live from Brentwood High series); *Mirror of Dreams* by Yvonne Lehman (White Dove Romances); *The Mystery of the Silly Goose*, *The Mystery of the Copycat Clown*, and *The Mystery of the Honeybees' Secret* by Elspeth Campbell Murphy (Three Cousins Detective Club series); *A Light in the Castle* by Robert Elmber (Young Underground series); *Midnight Rescue* by Lois Walfrid Johnson (The Riverboat Adventures series); *Out of the Blue* by Lauraine Snelling (High Hurdles series); *House of Secrets* by Beverly Lewis (SummerHill

Secrets series); *Mandie and the Courtroom Battle* by Lois Gladys Leppard (Mandie Books Mysteries).

Backpack Mysteries is a series for early readers. Written for readers ready for their first books divided into chapters, these books are packed with surprise twists and lasting lessons. Titles: *Too Many Treasures* and *Big Island Search* by Mary Carpenter Reid.

Portraits is a series of contemporary romance novels from bestselling Christian authors; the line provides inspiring stories of love combined with mystery, intrigue, and page-turning suspense. Titles: *Masquerade* by B. J. Hoff; *Stillpoint* by Marily Kok; *Blind Faith* by Judith Pella.

Bethany House distributes to the trade through Ingram, Baker & Taylor, and other wholesalers.

In accord with its current acquisitions policy, Bethany House is not considering unsolicited manuscripts or proposals. Query letters and SASEs should be directed to:

Gary Johnson, Publisher

BROADMAN & HOLMAN PUBLISHERS

127 Ninth Avenue North
Nashville, TN 37234
615-251-2000

Broadman & Holman is a division of the Southern Baptist Convention that publishes books for a mainstream religious trade readership as well as the professional religious market. The house publishes a frontlist keyed to contemporary social, cultural, and religious interests, along with an array of inspirational and self-improvement titles, textbooks, and historical views of the Baptist church and theology, as well as works for younger readers. Broadman & Holman's catalog also lists audiovisual materials, as well as liturgical and other church-related supplies. Broadman & Holman represents the merger of Broadman Press (founded in 1891) and Holman Bible Publishers.

Broadman & Holman books: *The Father Connection: Ten Qualities of the Heart That Empower Your Children to Make Right Choices* by John McDowell; *The Financially Confident Woman* by Mary Hunt; *Moral Earthquakes and Secret Faults: Protecting Yourself from Minor Moral Lapses That Lead to Major Disaster* by O. S. Hawkins; *The Moral of the Story: Timeless Tales to Cherish and Share* (edited by Jerry Newcombe); *Ultimate Warriors: Dare to Shake Your World for Christ* by Tom Sirotnak with Ken Walker; *Intentional Integrity: Aligning Your Life with God's Values* by Millard N. Macadam; *Keeping Life in Perspective: Sharpening Your Sense of What's Important* by Jim Henry with Marilyn Jeffcoat; *Sharpening Your People Skills: Ten Tools for Success in Any Relationship* by William J. Diehm; *The 25 Most Common Problems in Business (And How Jesus Solved Them)* by Jim Zabloski; *Take the Stand: Because You're the Best Christian Somebody Knows* by Charles B. Graham; *The Plans of His Heart: Understanding How You Fit into God's Perfect Will* by Chip Ricks; *You Can Raise a Well-Mannered Child* by June Hines Moore; *Trading Your Worry for Wonder: A Woman's Guide to Overcoming Anxiety* by Cheri Fuller; *Devotion Explosion: What To Do When Your Quiet Time Becomes Too Quiet* by Stephen Schwambach.

Broadman & Holman distributes its own list.

Query letters and SASEs should be directed to:

Vicki Crumpton, Acquisitions Editor

General religious topics, trade books on Christian living.

John Landers, Project Editor

Richard P. Rosenbaum, Jr., Editorial Director

Kenneth H. Stephens, Publisher

Janis Whipple, Project Editor

Devotional, juvenile, inspirational material.

Trent Butler, Editor

Reference books and Bibles.

BUDDHA ROSE PUBLICATIONS

Box 548

Hermosa Beach, CA 90254

310-543-9673

Buddha Rose Publications (founded in 1989) is a subsidiary of Buddha Rose International. The press produces a variety of print materials ancillary to its book-publishing program. The Buddhist Books imprint publishes works that explore and enlighten from the Buddhist perspective.

The publisher's list is extremely selective; interested authors might to well to familiarize themselves with the house list; by all means please query (with a brief letter and SASE) initially.

Buddha Rose handles its own distribution.

Query letters and SASEs should be directed to:

Scott Shaw, President and Editor-in-Chief

Elliott Sebastian, Editor

CHARIOT/VICTOR PUBLISHING
CHARIOT FAMILY PUBLISHING
VICTOR BOOKS
SCRIPTURE PRESS
LION PUBLISHING

4050 Lee Vance View

Colorado Springs, CO 80918

719-536-3271

fax: 719-536-3269

Chariot/Victor produces mainstream Christian religious titles in books and other media. Divisions include: Chariot Books & Multimedia for Children, Victor Books & Multimedia for Adults, Lion Publishing, Rainfall Toys & Gifts.

Chariot/Victor Publishing (a division of Cook Communications) marks the merger (in July of 1996) of Chariot Family Publishing and Scripture Press Publications/Victor Books, along with the operation's relocation from Illinois to Colorado.

The house mission is to assist in the spiritual development of people by producing and distributing consumer-driven, centrist Christian products that foster saving faith; increase understanding of the Bible; and promote the application of Christian values in everyday life.

Chariot/Victor products are prayerfully crafted to fit their prime audience. They are inspirational, fun, creative, and provide sound Christian education. They are easy and simple for parents, teachers and others to use effectively. The nature of the house product and its marketing will encourage end-users to link to the strong foundational support of local church ministries.

Chariot/Victor markets lines that target broad sectors of the market: youth (primarily from the Chariot Family Publishing division), adult (mainly Victor Books), educational (Scripture Press), and general religious trade (Lion Publishing).

Chariot/Victor distribution utilizes a network of field representatives and services that includes its own in-house catalog and marketing operations.

Chariot Family Publishing

Chariot produces a strong list of titles with a religious orientation in the publishing areas of juveniles, poetry, inspirational and devotional, reference (most of them works for young readers), and Sunday school curriculum, as well as works for a general religious readership. Chariot markets a line of illustrated Bibles and illustrated inspirational and devotional readings. Chariot Family Publishing was operated as a division of Cook Communications (formerly David C. Cook Publishing—"Serving His Church since 1875").

As the publishers of Chariot note: We have been called to Christ to foster the spiritual development of children. That is why first, through Chariot and Rainfall, we focus on training children in and through the family. We exist to help parents evangelize and disciple their children as a part of everyday life as commanded in Deuteronomy 6:5–9. We will facilitate family discipleship by providing an organized Christian growth program of market-sensitive, exemplary products.

Chariot Children's Books offers a wide range of reading materials for ages birth to teen. Rainfall Toys offers gift and educational items that are inspirational and fun— toys, games, and gift products for ages birth to teen.

Chariot imprint LifeJourney Books cover selected fiction and nonfiction for adults. LifeJourney fiction is strong in the area of frontier adventure, historical romance, and mystery genres. Nonfiction from LifeJourney accents the personal-growth category.

Chariot book titles: *365 Children's Prayers* (compiled by Carol Watson); *Adam Raccoon Parables for Little Kids* by Glen Keane (illustrated by the author); *The Baby*

Bible Stories About Jesus by Robin Currie; *Bumper the Dinosaur* by Mary Hollingsworth; *Discovering Oceans, Lakes, Ponds & Puddles* by Jean Ashford Frame (illustrated by Scott Holladay); *Who Made the Morning?* by Jan Godfrey and Kathleen Crawford (illustrated by Jane Cope).

VICTOR BOOKS
SCRIPTURE PRESS PUBLICATIONS

Victor Books and Scripture Press Publications (founded in 1934) offer a wide range of books keyed to spiritual, religious, philosophical, and social topics for the adult, as well as educational materials and supplies. The Scripture Press list features a Bible-based orientation, with many titles offering a mainstream evangelical Christian perspective.

Categories of publishing interest include family, men's studies, women's studies, books of the Bible, Bible characters, groupbuilder resources, and general topics. The Victor Books imprint marks the trade-directed portion of the program. Rainfall is the imprint that marks games and gifts for adults. Scripture covers the Christian educational market and distributes the closely allied line from Accent Publications.

The Victor product line meets various personal needs of the market. Victor reaches evangelicals with the purpose of aiding the intended audience in their spiritual formation. Rainfall adult products facilitate fun learning of Bible truths through adult group and family interaction with such items as games, puzzles, and activities.

Titles from Victor: *Money: How Much Is Enough?* by James and Martha Reapsome; *The Top Ten Ways to Make Your Wife Crazy* by Hans and Donna Finzel; *Tuned-Up Parenting* by Karen Dockrey; *Shepherding the Church into the 21st Century* by Joseph M. Stowell III; *The Prophecy Knowledge Handbook* by John Walvoord; *Management: A Biblical Approach* by Myron D. Rush; *Letters from a Skeptic* by Gregory A. Boyd and Edward K. Boyd; *How to Save Your Kids from Ruin* by Jerry Johnston; *How to Get It Right After You've Gotten It Wrong* by Gary J. Oliver; *Healing Meditations for Life* by David Seamands; *Healing the Dysfunctional Church Family* by David Mains; *Cults, World Religions, and the Occult* by Kenneth Boa; *101 Days in the Epistles with Oswald Chambers* (edited by James R. Adair and Harry Verploegh).

LION PUBLISHING

Lion Publishing produces works for the religious trade and serious general trade markets. Seeker products (Lion books for children and adults) is the house's primary line.

Through the Lion imprint the publisher strives to reach the spiritually inquisitive or "seeker" directly or through outreach gift giving. Such books do not presuppose any prior Christian or biblical understanding. Instead, seeker adult and children's books facilitate the spiritual development process, primarily at pre-evangelism and evangelism levels.

SCRIPTURE PRESS PUBLICATIONS

4050 Lee Vance View
P.O. Box 36640
Colorado Springs, CO 80918-3664
800-323-9409

The Scripture Press Publications division catalogs Sunday school curriculum for early childhood, primary, middle, junior, young teen, high school, and adult classes.

ACCENT PUBLICATIONS

4050 Lee Vance View
P.O. Box 36640
Colorado Springs, CO 80936
800-525-5550

For over half a century Accent Publications has been committed to local churches. Accent has developed and is constantly improving a full range of curriculum materials to help make the Sunday school enjoyable and spiritually rewarding for teachers and students alike.

Query letters and SASEs should be directed to:

Julie Smith, Managing Editor

CONTINUUM PUBLISHING GROUP

(See Directory of United States Publishers)

CROSSROAD PUBLISHING COMPANY

370 Lexington Avenue
New York, NY 10017-6550
212-532-3650
fax: 212-532-4922
800-395-0690

Crossroad Publishing Company (founded in 1980) publishes scholarly and general-interest titles in religion, philosophy, spirituality, and personal improvement. Crossroad offers books in spirituality, religion, and counseling for general and popular religious markets. The Crossroad Herder imprint publishes books in theology, religious studies, and religious education for professionals and active members of Catholic and mainline Protestant churches.

Crossroad and sibling imprint Crossroad Herder (formerly Herder & Herder) is a United States–based wing of the international firm Verlag Herder (founded in 1798). The programs of Crossroad and Crossroad Herder offer books by some of the most distinguished authors in the United States and abroad in the fields of theology, biblical studies, spirituality, religious education, women's studies, world religions, psychology, and counseling. Crossroad supports a strong backlist.

Crossroad and Continuum, now two completely separate entities sharing the same address, were corporate affiliates within the Crossroad/Continuum Publishing Group from 1980 through the early 1990s. Even through the dual-house years, each publisher retained its distinct identity. (For Continuum, please see the entry in the directory of United States Publishers.)

Crossroad is an entrepreneurial house of modest size, with a tightly focused program that takes advantage of diverse marketing channels—as such, this publisher provides an excellent environment for authors looking for personalized and long-term publishing relationships.

Frontlist titles: *Still by Your Side: A True Story of Love and Grief, Faith and Miracles* by Marjorie Holmes; *Prayers for Lovers* by William Cleary; *Gift of the Red Bird: A Spiritual Encounter* by Paula D'Arcy; *The Complete Guide to Prayer-Walking: A Simple Path to Body-and-Soul Fitness* by Linus Mundy; *101 Ways to Nourish Your Soul* by Mitch Finley; *Quantum Theology* by Diarmuid O'Murchu; *The Great Apparitions of Mary: An Examination of the Twenty-Two Supranormal Appearances* by Ingo Swann; *In Love Abiding: Responding to the Dying and Bereaved* by Christine Chapman; *Dear Heart, Come Home: The Path of Midlife Spirituality* by Joyce Rupp; *Seeds of Peace: Contemplation and Non-Violence* by William H. Shannon; *Living with God . . . In Good Times and Bad* by John Carmody; *Hidden Women of the Gospels* by Kathy Coffey; *Against an Infinite Horizon: The Finger of God in Our Everyday Lives* by Ronald Rolheiser.

Selections from the backlist: *Caring for Elderly Parents* by Ruth Whybrow; *Let Someone Hold You* by Paul Morrissey; *Parables and the Enneagram* by Clarence Thompson; *The Zen Teachings of Jesus* by Kenneth S. Leong; *Medicine Wheels: Native American Vehicles of Healing* by Roy I. Wilson; *In the Courts of the Lord: A Gay Priest's Story* by James Ferry.

An ongoing Crossroad line is the Adult Christian Education Program, which issues series titles in scripture study, theology and church history, Christian living, and world religious traditions.

Crossroad has sponsored the Crossword Women's Studies Award and the Crossroad Counseling Book Award, both of which bestow publication under the house imprimatur. (Details are available upon request from the publisher.)

Crossroad distributes via Spring Arbor Distributing.

CROSSROAD HERDER

Books published under the Crossroad Herder imprint mark the cutting edge of theology. Each volume presents fresh perspectives on a topic of interest, expands discussion on an issue of concern, and is accessible to the theologian and interested readers alike. Titles: *An American Emmaus: Faith and Sacrament in the American Culture* by Regis A. Duffy; *The Future Church of 140 B.C.E.: A Hidden Revolution* by Bernard J. Lee; *The Struggle for Theology's Soul: Contesting Scripture in Theology* by William A. Thompson; *Raising Abel: The Recovery of the Eschatological Imagination* by James Alison; *Living in the Margins: Intentional Communities and the Art of Interpretation* by Terry Veling.

Backlist Crossroad Herder titles: *The Girard Reader* by René Girard (edited by James G. Williams); *Resurrection from the Underground: Feodor Dostoevsky* by René Girard (translated by James G. Williams); *Wrestling with God: Religious Life in Search of Its Soul* by Barbara Fiand; *Finding God in All Things* (edited by Michael J. Himes and Stephen J. Pope); *The Growth of Mysticism: Gregory the Great Through the 12th Century* by Bernard McGinn.

Query letters and SASEs should be directed to:

Michael Leach, Publisher

Bob Heller, Editor

CROSSWAY BOOKS
1300 Crescent Boulevard
Wheaton, IL 60187
630-682-4300

Crossway produces a small seasonal list of books with a Christian perspective aimed at both the religious and general audience, including issue-oriented nonfiction, evangelical works, inspiration, self-awareness, and fiction. Crossway also issues a line of audiobooks. Crossway Books (founded in 1938) is a division of Good News Publishers.

From the Crossway nonfiction list: *A Woman's Walk with God: A Daily Guide for Prayer and Spiritual Growth* by Sheila Cragg; *Ten Secrets for a Successful Family* by Adrian Rogers; *God in the Dark* by Os Guiness; *No More Excuses: Be the Man God Made You to Be* by Tony Evans; *Telling the Truth: How to Revitalize Christian Journalism* by Marvin Olasky.

Representative Crossway fiction: *Code of the West* by Stephen Bly; *Fated Genes* by Harry Lee Krauss, Jr.; *The Gathering Storm* by W. E. Davis; *Wells of Glory* by Mary McReynolds.

Sample children's books: *Annie Henry and the Secret Mission* by Susan Olasky; *Children of the King* by Max Lucado; *Hattie Marshall and the Dangerous Fire* by Debra Smith.

Crossway handles its own distribution.

Query letters and SASEs should be directed to:

Leonard G. Goss, Editorial Director

Dharma Publishing

2425 Hillside Avenue
Berkeley, CA 94704
510-548-5407
fax: 510-548-2230

Mailing address:
2910 San Pablo Avenue
Berkeley, CA 94702
800-873-4276

Dharma Publishing is a specialist house active in a variety of formats. Dharma publishes trade paperbacks and journals; distribution includes subscription and mail order. Areas of interest include art, history, biography, literature, philosophy, psychology, spiritual, scholarly, cosmology, and juveniles.

Established by Tarthang Tulku in 1971, Dharma Publishing's founding purpose was twofold: to preserve Tibetan texts and art, and to lay the foundation for Dharma education in the West. Incorporated as a nonprofit organization in 1975, Dharma Publishing and Press have continued to rely on a small staff of Dharma students and volunteers to accomplish their goals. All profit from sales of books and art is dedicated to the production of more books and sacred art.

Dharma's Tibetan Translation series develops appreciation of the Buddha and the qualities of enlightenment, and also deepens understanding of the science of consciousness, the nature of the Bodhisattva, and the Vajrayana.

The Nyingma Psychology series is written for individuals coping with life in modern society. Books in this series offer ways to relieve anxiety, cultivate creative aspects of mind, and transform every situation into an opportunity for self-knowledge and insight. This series includes Dharma's most popular books on the development of awareness and spiritual satisfaction in daily life and work: *Gesture of Balance*, *Skillful Means*, and *Mastering Successful Work* by Tarthang Tulku.

Dharma's Time, Space, and Knowledge series stimulates a dynamic inquiry into knowledge. Free from doctrine and dogma, these books offer a forum for discovering the nature of mind and all phenomena.

The Crystal Mirror series is designed to introduce Westerners to the Dharma. Each volume explores a particular aspect of the development of Buddhism from the time of the Buddha to the present.

Dharma's Art, History, and Culture series offers the reader a broad view of Tibetan Buddhist culture.

The Jataka Series for Children presents the profoundly moving stories of the Buddha's previous lives adapted for a young audience. Conveying universal values of generosity, integrity, and compassion, these tales encourage ethical, caring action and provide uplifting, positive models for young people.

Dharma titles: *Masters of the Nyingma Lineage* (introduction by Tarthang Tulku); *Path of Heroes: Birth of Enlightenment* by Zhechen Gyaltsab; *Wisdom of Buddha: The Samdhinirmocana Sutra* (translated by John Powers); *The Voice of the Buddha* (translated by Gwendolyn Bays); *Tibet in Pictures* by Li Gotami Govinda; *Skillful Means: Patterns for Success* by Tarthang Tulku; *Tibetan Buddhism in Western Perspective* by Herbert V. Guenther.

Dharma Publishing reflects the Odiyan style of Dharma, a form of Buddhism that practices a blend of spiritual concerns with independence, individual responsibility, and down-to-earth knowledge. The publishing house considers projects from sectarians only, and rarely publishes books from outside writers.

Query letters and SASEs should be directed to:

Tarthang Tulku, President and Editor

DIMENSIONS FOR LIVING
(see Abingdon Press)

DISCIPLESHIP RESOURCES
1908 Grand Avenue
Nashville, TN 37212
615-340-7068

Mailing address:
P.O. Box 840
Nashville, TN 37202-0840

Discipleship Resources (founded in 1951) is the publishing component of the General Board of Discipleship, one of the major program boards of the United Methodist Church. Areas of publishing interest encompass United Methodist history, doctrine, and theology, as well as Bible study, Christian education, ethnic church concerns, evangelism, ministry of the laity, stewardship, United Methodist men, and worship.

Discipleship Resources issues a varied inventory including books, booklets, manuals, audiovisuals, packets, and supplies directed to local church members and leaders, lay and clergy, men and women, children, youth, and adults—as well as to district and conference leaders and others serving the congregation. Some resources guide the leader of an area of work or particular program, while others are aimed toward individual study and enrichment.

Titles from Discipleship Resources: *Living Our Beliefs: The United Methodist Way* by Kenneth L. Carder; *Faith-Sharing: Dynamic Christian Witnessing by Invitation* by George E. Morris and H. Eddie Fox; *Aging: God's Challenge to Church and Synagogue* by Richard H. Gentzler, Jr. and Donald F. Clingan; *Postmoderns: The Beliefs, Hopes, and Fears of Young Americans (1965–1981)* by Craig Kennet Miller; *Designing a Single Adult Ministry* by William J. Cox; *24 Effective Ideas for the Small Membership Church* by Steven M. Murray.

Writers who wish to submit materials to Discipleship Resources for publishing consideration may acquire editorial guidelines upon request from the publisher. The guide includes versatile tips that are broadly applicable to manuscript preparation in general.

Discipleship Resources handles its own sales and distribution.

Query letters and SASEs should be directed to:

Alan K. Waltz, Managing Editor

WILLIAM B. EERDMANS PUBLISHING COMPANY

255 Jefferson Avenue SE
Grand Rapids, MI 49503
616-459-4591

Eerdmans publishes books of general interest; religious, academic, and theological works; books for young readers; regional history and American religious history. The Eerdmans publishing reach offers a Christian handle on such areas as anthropology, biblical studies, biography, African American studies, church administration, music, philosophy, psychology, science, social issues, current and historical theology, and women's interests.

The Eerdmans catalog also highlights general reference works, such as Bible commentaries and theological dictionaries, as well as titles in Old and New Testament studies.

William B. Eerdmans Publishing Company (founded in 1911) is one of the largest independent nondenominational Christian religious publishers in the United States.

On the Eerdmans list: *A Gallery of Reflections: The Nativity of Christ* by Richard Harries; *The Man Who Created Narnia: The Story of C. S. Lewis* by Michael Coren; *Beyond Chaos: Living The Christian Family in a World Like Ours* by Chris William Erdman; *Understanding New Religious Movements* by John A. Saliba; *People of the Book: Christian Identity and Literary Culture* by David Lyle Jeffrey; *The Epistle to the Romans* by Douglas Moo; *Faces of Latin American Protestantism* by José Miguez Bonino; *The Church for Others: Protestant Theology in Communist East Germany* by Gregory Baum; *The Trinity in a Pluralistic Age* (edited by Kevin J. Vanhoozer); *Practical Praying* by Linette Martin; *Why Believe? Reason and Mystery As Pointers to God* by C. Stephen Evans; *Between Noon and Three: Romance, Law, and the Outrage of Grace* by Robert Farrar Capon; *Adultery and Grace: The Ultimate Scandal* by C. Welton Gaddy; *Charles G. Finney and the Spirit of American Evangelicalism* by Charles E. Hambrick-Stowe; *Patterns of Discipleship in the New Testament* (edited by Richard N. Longnecker); *Pure Kingdom: Jesus' Vision of God* by Bruce Chilton; *Celtic Women: Women in Celtic Society and Literature* by Peter Berresford Ellis; *The Dead Sea Scrolls Translated: The Qumran Texts in English* by Florentino Garcia Martinez; *Sworn on the Altar of God: A Religious Biography of Thomas Jefferson* by Edwin S. Gaustad.

A special Eerdmans project is the beautifully produced *The Leningrad Codex: A Facsimile Edition* (Astrid B. Beck, managing editor; David Noel Freedman, general editor; James A. Sanders, publication editor).

EERDMANS BOOKS FOR YOUNG READERS

Eerdmans Books for Young Readers issues a variety of nonfiction and fiction works, including several successful series as well as individual titles. From Eerdmans Books for Young Readers: *Only a Star* by Margery Facklam (illustrated by Nancy Carpenter); *Morning Has Broken* (based on the hymn inspired by Psalm 118:24, and the popular song by Cat Stevens) (written by Eleanor Farjean; illustrated by Tim Ladwig); *Ten Christmas Sheep* by Nancy White Carlstrom (illustrated by Cynthia Fisher); *Merry Birthday, Nora Noel* by Ann Dixon (illustrated by Mark Graham).

As a companion to the Women of Spirit books (ages 10–14), Eerdmans has introduced the Men of Spirit series. Each book depicts the life of an exemplary individual who excelled in his chosen field while maintaining a deep and abiding commitment to the Christian faith. Title: *Thomas Merton: Poet, Prophet, Priest* by Jennifer Fisher Bryant. Women of Spirit titles: *Dorothy Day: Friend to the Forgotten* by Deborah Kent; *Maria Mitchell: The Soul of an Astronomer* by Beatrice Gormley; *Lucretia Mott: A Guiding Light* by Jennifer Fisher Bryant.

William B. Eerdmans Publishing Company distributes its own list with the assistance of regional sales representatives.

Query letters and SASEs should be directed to:

Jon Pott, Editor-in-Chief

Amy Eerdmans, Children's Book Editor

Charles van Hof, Managing Editor

FELDHEIM PUBLISHERS

200 Airport Executive Park
Nanuet, NY 10954
914-356-2282

Feldheim Publishers (founded in 1954) is among the leading houses in areas of publishing activity that include works of contemporary authors in the field of Orthodox Jewish thought, translations from Hebrew of Jewish classical works, dictionaries and general reference works, textbooks, and guides for sabbaths and festivals, as well as literature for readers ages three and up (Young Readers Division). The Feldheim publishing program is expanding, and the house releases an increasing number of new titles each season. Feldheim retains a comprehensive backlist.

From Feldheim: *Maalos Hatorah* by Avraham ben Shlomo Zalman; *The Rebbe: The Story of Rabbi Esriel Hildesheimer* by J. A. Sinason; *Chochmo U'mussar* by Rav Shlomo Breuer; *Writing It Right* by Chaya Kushnir (workbook designed to prepare children to write Hebrew script); *A Midrash and a Ma'aseh* by Hanoch Teller; *Eretz Ha-tzvi* by Rabbi Tzvi Teichman; *Lying for Truth: Understanding Yaakov's Deception of Esav; Memo to Self: Songs of Jewish Living* (poetry) by Ruth Lewis.

Feldheim Publishers handles its own distribution as well as offers books of additional publishers such as American Yisroel Chai Press and Targum Press.

Query letters and SASEs should be directed to:

Yitzchak Feldheim, President

FRIENDSHIP PRESS

475 Riverside Drive
New York, NY 10115
212-870-2383

The Friendship list encompasses religious books as well as mainstream trade titles in the public-interest realm that address contemporary topics including: cultural pluralism, the media, global awareness, health and wholeness, technology and the environment, human rights, and world peace. Friendship also produces ecumenical religious, spiritual, inspirational, and educational program materials intended for the use of adults, youths, and children. The house also offers several lines of videos, maps, notecards, and informational posters.

Friendship Press was established in 1902 as a missionary education movement in the United States and Canada. Now part of the National Council of the Churches of Christ USA, Friendship Press is a leading ecumenical publisher of educational materials for schools and parishes.

Titles from Friendship Press: *Welcome the Child: A Child Advocacy Guide for Churches* by Shannon P. Daley and Kathleen A. Guy; *We Belong Together: The Churches in Solidarity with Women* (edited by Sarah Cunningham); *Torch in the Night: Worship Resources from South Africa* by Anne Hope; *The Indian Awakening in Latin America* (edited by Yves Materne); *The Caribbean: Culture of Resistance, Spirit of Hope* (edited by Oscar Bolioli); *Remembering the Future: The Challenge of the Churches in Europe* (edited by Robert C. Lodwick); *Keeping Covenant with the Poor: Study Guide on Poverty in North America* by Nancy A. Carter; *Justice and the Intifada* (edited by Kathy Bergen, David Neuhaus, and Ghassan Rubeiz); *Haiku, Origami, and More: Worship and Study Resources from Japan* by Judith May Newton and Mayumi Tabuchi; *Angle of Vision: Christians and the Middle East* by Charles A. Kimball.

Friendship Press publishes a limited number of new titles per season—most of which are commissioned additions to the house's ongoing curriculum series. Friendship is, however, open to considering manuscripts by authors written from an embracing global cultural perspective.

Friendship Press distributes its own list.

Query letters and SASEs should be directed to:

Susan C. Winslow, Senior Editor

Roger Burgess, Executive Director

GLENEIDA PUBLISHING GROUP

(see Baker Book House and Liguori Publications)

GOSPEL LIGHT PUBLICATIONS
REGAL BOOKS

2300 Knoll Drive
Ventura, CA 93003
805-644-9721

Gospel Light accents titles in general religious interest, religious education, and juveniles; the house also offers video and audio selections. Regal Books (founded in 1933), a division of Gospel Light Publications, specializes in resources for evangelism, discipleship, and Christian education.

The publisher's mission is to equip every Christian, their church, their community, and their world with the good news of Jesus Christ. The Gospel Light/Regal trade motto is "Bright ideas to help you grow."

Gospel Light/Regal Books highlights: *Drugproof Your Kids* by Stephen Arterburn and Jim Burns; *Helping Others Find Freedom in Christ: Connecting People in God Through Discipleship Counseling* by Neil T. Anderson; *Pastors of Promise* by Jack Hayford; *Secrets of a Lasting Marriage: Building a Love That Will Last Forever* by H. Norman Wright.

On the Regal list of children's and youth books: *How to Be a Christian Without Being Religious* by Fritz Ritenour; *Busting Free: Helping Youth Discover Their Identity in Christ* by Neil T. Anderson and Dave Park; *What Hollywood Won't Tell You About Love, Sex, and Dating* by Susie Shellenberger and Greg Johnson.

Gospel Light oversees its own distribution.

Unsolicited manuscripts are not accepted.

Query letters and SASEs should be directed to:

Kyle Duncan, Acquisitions

HARPER SAN FRANCISCO

353 Sacramento Street, Suite 500
San Francisco, CA 94111-3653
415-477-4400
fax: 415-477-4444
http://www.harpercollins.com (World Wide Web)

Harper San Francisco produces books in a variety of general trade and religious specialist areas: psychology, self-awareness, and self-help; inspiration and meditation;

writing, journaling, and creativity; gender studies and the field of sexual identity and expression; spirituality worldwide (historical traditions and contemporary trends); Judaica; Gnosticism; the historical Jesus; gift books; parenting; wellness and recovery; health and fitness; alternative therapies; biography; society and culture; ethics and philosophy; science; environment and nature; Native American studies; spiritual journeys; mysticism; witchcraft and the occult; mythology; Celtic studies; music; and cookbooks. In addition, the publisher offers occasional works of fiction and books with themes of mainstream-readership interest.

HSF focuses on books that inspire and nurture the mind, body, and spirit; explore the essential religious, spiritual, and philosophical questions; present the rich and diverse array of cultures and their wisdom traditions; and support readers in their ongoing personal discovery and enrichment.

It is the policy of Harper San Francisco to publish books that represent important religious groupings, express well-articulated thought, combine intellectual competence and felicitous style, add to the wealth of religious literature irrespective of creedal origin, and aid the cause of religion without proselytizing for any particular sect.

HSF has featured works by Martin Luther King, Jr., Norman Vincent Peale, the Dalai Lama of Tibet, C. S. Lewis, Matthew Fox, and Melodie Beattie. The house is also represented by the Hazelden imprint (for selected books copublished with Hazelden Educational Materials) and is corporately affiliated with the editorially independent Zondervan subsidiary of HarperCollins (see separate Hazelden and Zondervan listings).

HarperEdge is an HSF imprint for which plans are to take full advantage of the house's West Coast presence to issue titles that spotlight the interface between culture and technology. A Pillow Book is the tag for a line of HSF works that embrace the varieties of sexual experience.

Harper San Francisco is a division of the international HarperCollins corporate family of publishers. Harper San Francisco is an imprint of HarperCollins Adult Trade Division (which includes imprints emanating from the HarperCollins New York offices; see HarperCollins in the directory of U.S. publishers). Harper San Francisco benefits directly from core HarperCollins marketing and sales power, and retains its editorial independence and identity.

Frontlist trade books from Harper San Francisco: *Mars and Venus in Love: Inspiring and Heartfelt Stories of Relationships That Work* by John Gray, Ph.D.; *By the River Piedra I Sat Down and Wept* by Paul Coelho (translated by Alan R. Clarke); *Mystic Cats: A Celebration of Cat Magic and Feline Charm* by Roni Jay (illustrated by Lorraine Harrison); *Seven Hundred Kisses: A Yellow Silk Book of Erotic Writing* (edited and with an introduction by Lily Pond).

Works of discovery and awareness: *Romancing the Shadow: A Guide to Finding Gold in the Dark Side* by Connie Zweig, Ph.D. and Steve Wolf, Ph.D.; *Living Life on Purpose: A Guide to Creating a Life of Success and Significance* by Greg Anderson; *The Knitting Sutra: Craft as a Spiritual Practice* by Susan Gordon Lydon; *A Call to Joy: Making Life a Spiritual Adventure* by Matthew Kelly; *Your Sixth Sense: Activating Your Psychic Potential* by Belleruth Naparstek; *The Masters of the Spirit: A Golf Fable* by Anne Kinsman Fisher; *Leap Over a Wall: Earthy Spirituality for Everyday*

Christians by Eugene H. Peterson; *The Power Behind Positive Thinking: Unlocking Your Spiritual Potential* by Eric Fellman.

Inspiration and devotional works: *Lamp unto My Feet: A Verse-a-Day Devotional* by Art Toalston; *Between Heaven and Earth: Prayers and Reflections That Celebrate an Intimate God* by Ken Gire; *Streams of Living Water: Celebrating the Great Traditions of Christian Faith* by Richard J. Foster; *Promises to Keep: Daily Devotions for Men Seeking Integrity* by Nick Harrison; *Little X: Growing Up in the Nation of Islam* by Sonsyrea Tate; *Finding God on the A Train: A Journey into Prayer* by Rick Hamlin; *Living the Message: Daily Reflections* by Eugene H. Peterson; *Between the Dreaming and the Coming True: The Road Home to God* by Robert Benson; *On My Own at 107: Reflections on Life Without Bessie* by Sarah L. Delany with Amy Hill Hearth.

Titles of academic interest and books for the religious and popular trade: *Facing East: A Pilgrim's Journey into the Mysteries of Orthodoxy* by Frederica Mathewes-Green; *Liberating the Gospels: Reading the Bible with Jewish Eyes, Freeing Jesus from 2,000 Years of Misunderstanding* by John Shelby Spong; *The Dead Sea Scrolls: A New Translation* by Michael Wise, Martin Abegg, Jr., and Edward Cook; *The Moral Vision of the New Testament: Community, Cross, New Creation, A Contemporary Introduction to New Testament Ethics* by Richard B. Hays; *The Essential Gay Mystics* (edited by Andrew Harvey); *Martyrs: Contemporary Writers on Modern Lives of Faith* (edited by Susan Bergman).

A special HSF set is *The Music of Silence: Entering the Sacred Space of Monastic Experience* by David Steindl-Rast with Sharon Lebell (packaged with CD of Benedictine Monk music).

The house invites prospective authors to correspond first via a brief query letter describing the essential character of the projected work, along with author qualifications and any previous books or professional credentials. Detailed guidelines for submissions are available upon request from the editorial department.

Harper San Francisco handles distribution through independent fulfillment offices; the house direct-mail catalog incorporates an extensive backlist. Harper San Francisco titles are also available through the offices of the parent company, HarperCollins Publishers.

HARPEREDGE

Harper San Francisco proudly unveiled the HarperEdge imprint in 1997. HarperEdge explores the convergence of technology and culture, bridging the apparent gap between everyday lives and the dynamic realm of cyberspace. Embracing the concept that all of us are affected in myriad ways by emerging technologies, HarperEdge publishes books that cover a wide range of subjects—from politics to psychology to pop culture. Each book, in its own way, makes this high-tech realm accessible—and exciting—to everyone.

On the cusp at HarperEdge: *The Conscious Universe: The Scientific Truth of Psychic Phenomena* by Dean Radin, Ph.D.; *What Will Be: How the New Role of Information Will Change Our Lives* by Michael Dertouzos (foreword by Bill Gates); *Design for Dying* by Timothy Leary with David Prince; *Data Smog: Surviving the Information Glut* by David Shenk; *The Soul of Cyberspace* by Jeff Zaleski.

Venturesome fiction: *Ecstasy Club* (love story, allegory, and cyberthriller) by cyber-pundit extraordinaire Douglas Rushkoff energizes the interface of alternative subcultures and avant-garde technology to syncretize a new storytelling tradition.

Query letters and SASEs should be directed to:

Lisa Bach, Editor
Popular psychology and self-help; women's studies/feminist spirituality; gay and lesbian studies; alternative spirituality and inspiration. Projects include *A Course in Love* by Joan Gattuso, *Chasing Grace* by Martha Manning, *Prayers of the Saints* by Woodeene Koenig-Bricker, and *The Optimystic's Handbook* by Terry Lynn Taylor and Mary Beth Crain.

Kevin Bentley, Associate Editor
Gay and lesbian spirituality, memoir, and general nonfiction, popular, psychology, personal growth; writing; alternative/New Age; packaged projects and paperback reprints in all Harper San Francisco publishing areas. Projects include *Revelations for a New Millennium* by Andrew Ramer; *Sex Between Men* by Douglas Sadownick; and *Totems* by Brad Steiger.

Clayton Carlson, Senior Vice President
Acquires consistent with house list.

Mark Chimsky, Executive Editor
Religious studies; popular spirituality; psychology, sexuality; gay and lesbian studies; popular culture. Projects include *Honest to Jesus* by Robert Funk; *A Commentary on the Torah* by Richard Elliott Friedman; and *The Dead Sea Scrolls: A New Translation* by Michael Wise, Martin Abegg, Jr., and Edward Cook.

Thomas Grady, Executive Editor
World religions, Christian spirituality and mysticism, alternative spirituality; psychology and personal growth. Projects include *The Essential Rumi* by Coleman Barks; *The Faithful Gardener* by Clarissa Pinkola Estés; and *The Joy of Living and Dying in Peace* by the Dalai Lama.

Patricia Klein, Senior Editor
Books on all aspects of Christian life, ranging across the entire spectrum of the Christian tradition from conservative Evangelical to progressive Catholic, including (but not limited to) spirituality, devotion, personal growth, spiritual renewal, family life, Christian thought and teaching, the Bible. Projects include *Glimpses of Grace: Daily Thoughts and Reflections* by Madeleine L'Engle; *Streams of Living Water* by Richard Foster; and *The Power Behind Positive Thinking* by Eric Fellman.

John V. Loudon, Executive Editor
Religious studies, psychology/personal growth, inspiration, Eastern religions, Jewish and Christian spirituality. Books include *By the River Piedra I Sat Down and Wept* by Paulo Coelho; *The Real Jesus* by Luke Timothy Johnson; and *Entering the Circle* by Olga Kharatidi.

Caroline Pincus, Editor
Psychology/self-help; Jewish spirituality; alternative and complementary health; lesbian and gay studies; multicultural studies. Titles include *Prayer Is Good Medicine* by

Larry Dossey; *Everyday Sacred* by Sue Bender; *Journey to the Heart* by Melodie Beattie; and *Suzanne White's Guide to Love* by Suzanne White.

Susan Reich, Vice President and Publishing Director
Acquires in areas consistent with house list.

HARVEST HOUSE PUBLISHERS

1075 Arrowsmith
Eugene, OR 97402-9197
541-343-0123

Harvest House produces religious-oriented nonfiction and fiction, Bible study and theological thought, and educational and devotional resources. Harvest House frontlist titles address topics of current interest, often with widespread implications on the social-religious front. Subjects include media, technology, politics; parenting, youth, relationships, and the family; Christian living and contemporary values; cults and the occult; personal awareness, inspiration, and spiritual growth; Christian history and heritage; and humor.

The publisher's nondenominational list features many works that offer an Evangelical Christian perspective and includes a number of notably individualist author voices. Harvest House publishes books in hardcover, trade paperback, and mass-market paperback editions.

The house issues a number of strong lines directed toward the children's-and-youth market (please see separate subentry below). Harvest House also produces books in the Spanish language, as well as audiobooks, calendars, and daily planners.

Harvest House Publishers (founded in 1974) holds the following credo for books and other product lines: "Helping people grow spiritually strong."

Nonfiction titles: *The Common Made Holy: Being Conformed to the Image of God* by Neil Anderson; *The Total Christian Guy* by Phil Callaway; *Living Above Your Circumstances: Real Victory Over Disappointment, Depression & Stress* by Bob George; *Promising Waters: Stories of Fishing and Following Jesus* by Jim Grassi; *Men of the Promise: Becoming a Man of Courageous Faith* by Ed Hindson; *If Mama Ain't Happy, Ain't Nobody Happy! Making the Choice to Rejoice* by Lindsey O'Connor; *The Marriage Maker: The Holy Spirit and the Hidden Power of Becoming One* by John and Teri Neider; *The Master's Degree: Majoring in Your Marriage* by Frank and Bunny Wilson; *A Strong Delusion: Confronting the "Gay Christian" Movement* by Joe Dallas; *Jesus in an Age of Controversy* by Douglas Groothuis; *In Defense of the Faith: Biblical Answers to Challenging Questions* by Dave Hunt.

Special Harvest House project: *Simpler Times* by Thomas Kinkade, an artist renowned for light-infused paintings of nostalgic, heartwarming scenes, combines his visual talents with thoughtful narrative in this exquisitely designed gift book. More than 20 full-color paintings are accompanied by Thomas Kinkade's thoughts on living in a complex age, keeping perspective, and creating balance.

Fiction from Harvest House includes mainstream novels with a religious accent; historical adventure tales; Bible-based stories; books geared toward a women's readership (including romances); occult thrillers; mystery and suspense fiction; and futuristic works.

Biblical and historical fiction from Harvest House: *Israel, My Beloved* by Kay Arthur; *Before Night Falls* by Mary An Minatra; *Under the Southern Moon* by Virginia Gaffney; *Whispers of Moonlight* by Lori Wick; *Conquered Heart* by Lisa Samson.

Harvest House manages its own distributional network.

HARVEST HOUSE BOOKS FOR CHILDREN AND YOUNG ADULTS

Harvest House produces a selection of books directed toward a youthful readership, as well as titles of interest to teachers and parents. The solid list encompasses coloring books, picture books, storybooks, interactive books, joke books, general nonfiction, and novels (including a number of successful series).

On the Harvest House children's-and-youth list: *Dusty's Beary Tales: Building Character with Bible Virtues* by Ruthan Winans and Linda Lee; *Close Your Eyes So You Can See: Stories of Children in the Life of Jesus* by Michael Card; *Tricks, Stunts & Good Clean Fun* by Bob Phillips.

Query letters and SASEs should be directed to the **Manuscript Coordinator**.

HAZELDEN PUBLISHING GROUP

15251 Pleasant Valley Road
P.O. Box 176
Center City, MN 55012-0176
612-257-4010

Hazelden Publishing Group issues books for a general and professional readership in such areas as awareness, discovery, wholeness and transformation, meditation, recovery, personal and spiritual growth, self-help, spirituality, substance abuse, and compulsive behaviors. The house's backlist represents all areas of the Hazelden publishing program.

The Hazelden publications and marketing vision encompasses books, pamphlets, audiocassettes and videocassettes, computer software, calendars, organizers, and books for young readers, along with a gift line.

Hazelden: A Mission in Motion. When Hazelden opened its doors nearly 50 years ago, the mission seemed simple: to rehabilitate clients and restore self-worth and dignity to their lives. Hazelden still commits to this mission as a multidimensional organization involved in public policy, research, education, evaluation, and many other areas of chemical dependency. Hazelden has become a respected leader in the chemical-dependency field and the premier publisher of bibliotherapy. As a pioneer in addiction research and education, Hazelden's clinical expertise is reflected in educational materials that cover a wide range of topics in the treatment of chemical dependency and other additions. Core to the success of the treatment process, Hazelden materials interact with clients. This matrix of materials reinforces important information to clients. Most of all, these materials are a concrete way for clients to retain the concepts they learn in treatment.

Hazelden was established as a publishing operation (in 1954, as Hazelden Educational Materials) with the hardcover release of *Twenty-Four Hours a Day* by Rich W (still in print in hardcover and paperback editions). Hazelden is a division of the Hazelden Foundation, which also operates a network of recovery centers. The publisher has a major concentration in materials related to the 12-Step approach.

In early 1994, Hazelden purchased CompCare and Parkside, two former niche publishers (both with strong backlists) in areas consistent with Hazelden's publishing range—particularly in treatment and recovery titles, as well as the broader general-interest trade arena. Hazelden also bought PIA (Psychiatric Institute of America), a publisher with similar scope. The titles of these publishers have been folded into the Hazelden list, thereby augmenting Hazelden's preeminence in this particular publishing arena.

In addition to the aforementioned *Twenty-Four Hours a Day,* Hazelden's best-selling trade entrants include *Codependent No More* and *The Language of Letting Go* (both by Melody Beattie), and *Each Day a New Beginning.*

From Hazelden: *Twelve Step Sponsorship: A Sponsor's Guide to How It Works* by Hamilton B; *Fountain House: Portraits of Lives Reclaimed from Mental Illness* by Mary Flannery and Mark Glickman; *The Golden Ghetto: The Psychology of Affluence* by Jessie H. O'Neill; *Consuming Confessions: The Quest for Self-Discovery, Intimacy, and Redemption* by Sharon Mymer, Ph.D.; *The Thin Books: Strategies & Meditations for Fat-Free, Guilt-Free, Binge-Free Living* by Jeane Eddy Westin; *Accepting Ourselves & Others: A Journey into Recovery from Addictive and Compulsive Behaviors for Gays, Lesbians, and Bisexuals* by Sheppard B. Kominars, Ph.D. and Kathryn D. Kominars, Ph.D.; *Listen to the Drum: Blackwolf Shares His Medicine* by Blackwolf Jones, M.S., C.A.S. and Gina Jones; *Keep Quit! A Motivational Guide to a Life Without Smoking* by Terry Rustin, M.D.; *Pathways from the Culture of Addiction to the Culture of Recovery: A Travel Guide for Addiction Professionals* (revised edition) by William L. White, M.A.; *Addictive Personality: Understanding the Addictive Process and Compulsive Behavior* (revised edition) by Craig Nakken.

Representing the Hazelden children's program: *The Cat at the Door and Other Stories to Live By: Affirmations for Children* by Anne D. Mather and Louise B. Weldon (illustrated by Lyn Martin); *Making the Most of Today: Daily Readings for Young People on Self-Awareness, Creativity, and Self-Esteem* by Pamela Espeland and Rosemary Wallner; *Starry Night* (written and illustrated by David Spohn).

Hazelden publications appear in the trade book market through projects sponsored conjointly with Harper San Francisco. Hazelden also furnishes its titles to the bookstore trade directly, and has made inroads into the gift-distribution world. Additional marketing avenues for Hazelden trade titles include the house's direct-to-the-consumer mail-order business. Hazelden books are popular items worldwide, with a foreign distribution network that includes Russia and Canada.

Other areas to which Hazelden markets include: Structured care (Hazelden develops and markets print, audio, and visual materials for treatment centers, hospitals, and professional markets); prevention, education, and professional training (the publisher accesses the markets of primary and secondary schools, counselor-training programs, and community prevention and treatment programs); and corrections (the publisher addresses the needs of county, state, and federal corrections facilities).

Hazelden books and series are available to the trade via Hazelden's own distributional services, and through Harper San Francisco.

Query letters and SASEs should be directed to the **Editorial Department** or to:

Betty Christiansen, Associate Editor

HEBREW PUBLISHING COMPANY

P.O. Box 157
Rockaway Beach, NY 11693
718-945-3000

Hebrew Publishing Company (established in 1901) offers a wide range of titles in such categories as reference and dictionaries; religion, law, and thought; rabbinic literature; literature; history and biography; children's books; Hebrew language textbooks and Hebrew culture; Yiddish; Bible, Hebrew/English; Bible, English only; prayers and liturgy: daily, Hebrew only, and Hebrew/English; prayers and liturgy: sabbath, high holidays, and festivals; prayers and liturgy: memorial; prayers and liturgy: Purim; general prayers and liturgy; Hanukkah items; Haggadahs; educational materials; sermons and aids of the rabbi; and calendars. The house publishes a limited number of new titles and maintains an established backlist.

On the HPC list: *Acharon Hamohikanim (The Last of the Mohicans)* by James Fenimore Cooper; *Business Ethics in Jewish Law* (Jung/Levine); *Encyclopedia of Jewish Concepts* by Philip Birnbaum; *Rahel Varnhagen: The Life of a Jewess* by Hannah Arendt; *Torah and Tradition* by Orenstein and Frankel.

Hebrew Publishing Company oversees its own distribution, utilizing services of independent fulfillment and distribution firms.

Query letters and SASEs should be directed to:

Charles Lieber, Editor-in-Chief
Hebrew Union College Press
3101 Clifton Avenue
Cincinnati, OH 45220-2488
513-221-1875

Hebrew Union publishes scholarly Judaica, along with some frontlist titles of broader appeal. Within the Hebrew Union College scope are books representing a variety of divisions, institutions, and programs: Klau Library, Skirball Museum, *Kuntresim* (Hebrew texts copublished with Ben-Zion Dinur Center of the Hebrew University), the journals *Hebrew Union College Annual* and *American Jewish Archives*, and special-interest projects (such as books and videotapes) from HUC-UC Ethics Center.

Hebrew Union College Press (founded in 1921) publishes a select list of new titles covering a full range of its list, while tending a full backlist. HUC engages in copublishing projects with other institutions, including Harvard University Press, KTAV Publishing House, University of Alabama Press, and Yale University Press.

From Hebrew Union College Press: *"Your Voice Like a Ram's Horn": Themes and Texts in Traditional Jewish Preaching* by Marc Saperstein; *Karaite Separatism in Nineteenth-Century Russia* by Philip Miller; *Reason and Hope: Selections from the Jewish Writings of Hermann Cohen* (translated, edited, and with an introduction by Eva Jospe); *To Write the Lips of Sleepers: The Poetry of Amir Gilboa* by Warren Bargad; *The Merit of Our Mothers: A Bilingual Anthology of Jewish Women's Prayers* (compiled by Tracy Guren Klirs); *Jewish Lore in Manichaean Cosmogony: Studies in the Book of Giants Traditions* by John C. Reeves; *The Jews of Dynastic China: A Critical Bibliography* by Michael Pollak.

HUC welcomes the submission of scholarly manuscripts in all areas of Judaica. For further information, contact Professor Michael Meyer, Chair, Publications Committee, at the publisher's address.

Hebrew Union College Press is distributed by Behrman House.

Query letters and SASEs should be directed to:

Michael Meyer, Chair, Publications Committee

Barbara Selya, Managing Editor

HERALD PRESS

616 Walnut Avenue
Scottdale, PA 15683
412-887-8500
fax: 412-887-3111

Areas of Herald Press publishing interest include the family, cookbooks, biography and personal experience, fiction, peace and social concerns, devotional works, Bible study, Bible and theology, Church life and missions, Mennonite history and culture, songbooks, publications for younger readers, and non–English-language publications (primarily in Spanish). Herald Press (established in 1908) is the trade division of the Mennonite Publishing House, the official publishing agency of the Mennonite Church.

Herald Press releases a well-balanced variety of books for adults, young people, and children. The publisher's purpose is to produce books that witness to faith in Jesus Christ according to the Scriptures as interpreted in the Anabaptist/Mennonite tradition—to provide resources that are honest in presentation, clear in thought, stimulating in content, appropriate in appearance, superior in quality, and conducive to the spiritual growth of the reader.

Herald Press is committed to offer fresh models of understanding to replace worn paradigms and metaphors that can no longer effectively guide us through a changing world and church. To engage issues honestly and forthrightly, erring on the side of courage rather than blandness. To reach readers tired of platitudes, who plead with the church to be "real." To produce quality resources on urgent concerns emerging in such areas as contemporary social problems, peace and justice, missions and evangelism, family life, Bible study, church history, Christian ethics, and theology.

Herald Press's vision is to provide books that help individuals, churches, and denominations in the Christian faith community and beyond to address the daunting yet exciting challenges of the third millennium. Herald Press strives to make available to both the church and the world the best in thinking and spiritual leadership.

Titles from Herald: *Complete Evangelism: The Luke–Acts Model* by Pedrito U. Maynard-Reid; *Entrepreneurs in the Faith Community: Profiles of Mennonites in Business* (edited by Calvin Redekop and Benjamin W. Redekop); *God's Power, Jesus' Faith, and World Mission: A Study in Romans* by Steve Mosher; *Godward: Personal Stories of Grace* by Ted Koontz; *Meditations for New Parents* by Gerald and Sara Wenger Shenk; *Keeping Salvation Ethical: Mennonite and Amish Atonement Theology in the Late Nineteenth Century* by J. Denny Weaver; *Through Fire and Water: An Overview of Mennonite History* by Harry Loewen, Steven Nolt, Carol Kuerksen, and Elwood Yoder; *Peace Was in Their Hearts* by Richard C. Anderson; *Little Foxes That Spoil the Vine* by W. Barry Miller.

Herald fiction includes biblical novels and stories with an Amish farm life milieu. Some titles: *No Strange Fire* by Ted Wojatasik; *Abigail* and *Bathsheba* by James R. Shott; *Mandy* by Mary Christner Borntrager; *A Treasured Friendship* and *A Golden Sunbeam* by Carrie Bender.

HERALD PRESS PUBLICATIONS FOR YOUNG READERS

Children's books from Herald Press include stand-alone titles and series in fiction and nonfiction. Series for an audience of teens and adults include the Bible-based historical novels by James R. Schott under the banner People of the Promise; Mary Christner Borntrager's contemporary stories published as the Ellie's People line; and Carrie Bender's continuing epistolary family romance/saga *Miriam's Journal*.

Representative children's fiction: *The Crooked Tree* by Esther Bender; *The Flying Pie and Other Stories* by Susan Yoder Ackerman; *Summerville Days* by Carrie Bender (Whispering Brook series); *Dead Letters* by Susan Kimmel Wright (Dead-End Road Mysteries); *The Mystery of Sadler Marsh* by Kim D. Pritts (illustrations by Matthew Archambault).

Also: *More Little Stories for Little Children: A Worship Resource* by Donna McKee Rhodes; *Let's Make a Garden* by Tamara Awad; and the collage-illustrated creation story *And It Was Good* by Harold Horst Nofziger.

Writers may request editorial guidelines from the publisher—the pamphlet includes information on writing for journals of the Mennonite Publishing House.

Herald Press handles its own distribution, including trade fulfillment, direct mail, and its chain of Provident Bookstores.

Query letters and SASEs should be directed to:

David Garber, Editor

HORIZON PUBLISHERS

50 South 500 West
P.O. Box 490
Bountiful, UT 84011-0490
801-295-9451
fax: 801-295-0196
800-453-0812

Horizon Publishers (founded in 1971) is a smaller house that produces hardcover and paperback works with emphasis in the areas of religion, inspiration, health foods, self-sufficient living, music, marriage and family, children's activities, cross-stitch and needlework design and instruction, and general youth and adult fiction and nonfiction.

Horizon is a privately owned corporation with no official ecclesiastical ties; the major readership of the house's theologically oriented books is Latter-Day Saint (Mormon), and religious works that Horizon issues are compatible with that basic doctrinal perspective. A wide range of Horizon's publishing interests are encompassed within that purview—from books on doctrine and church history to children's religious teaching stories to religious music. The Horizon list includes religious humor, faith-promoting experiences, historical works, biographies of well-known leaders, doctrinal studies, and religious fiction. Horizon also produces a line of inspirational and doctrinal cassette tapes.

The house's pamphlet detailing guidelines for authors is filled with apt advice for all writers.

Representative of the Horizon list: *Alien Encounters: The Deception Menace* by James L. Thompson; *Briant Stringham and His People* by Nathaniel G. Stringham and Briant S. Hinkley; *How to Write Your Personal History* by Duane S. Crowther; *Journeys Beyond Life: True Accounts of Next-World Experiences* by Arvin S. Gibson; *Music Reading: Quick and Easy, A Singer's Guide* by Duane S. Crowther; *Amazing but True Mormon Stories* by Joan Oviatt; *Ancient American Indians: Their Origins, Civilizations & Old-World Connections* by Paul and Millie Chessman; *Mastering Management: Practical Procedures for Business Control* by A. Leslie Derbyshire; *The Black Powder Plainsman: A Beginner's Guide to Muzzleloading and Reenactment on the Great Plains* by Randy Smith; *Stalking Trophy Mule Deer* by Walt Prothero; *Dutch Oven Secrets* by Lynn Hopkins; *The Desert Shall Blossom: A Comprehensive Guide to Vegetable Gardening in the Mountain West* by David E. Whiting; *Retiring First Class* by Clint Combs and Larry Bradshaw.

Fiction titles: *Crescendo* by Terry J. Moyer; *Cracked Wheat for Christmas* by Ted C. Hindmarsh; *The Feather of the Owl* by Lee Dalton.

Family-oriented books: *Play with Me: Crafts for Preschoolers* by Barbara Miles; *God's Special Children: Helping the Handicapped Achieve* by Keith J. Karren and Sherril A. Hundley; *It Makes Cents: The Family Thrift Book* by Vi Judge.

Horizon Publishers handles its own distribution.

Query letters and SASEs should be directed to:

Jenny Anderson, Editorial Assistant

HUMANICS LTD.
(see Directory of United States Publishers)

INNER TRADITIONS INTERNATIONAL
One Park Street
Rochester, VT 05767
802-767-3174

Inner Traditions publishes across such subject areas as acupuncture, anthroposophy, aromatherapy, the arts, astrology, bodywork, cookbooks, crafts, cultural studies, earth studies, Egyptian studies, gemstones, health and healing, homeopathy, indigenous cultures, African-American traditions, inner traditions of the West and the East, myth and legend, massage, natural medicine, self-transformation, sacred sexuality, spirituality, and travel.

Inner Traditions International (founded in 1975) produces hardcover trade books and trade paperbacks, illustrated gift books, and mass-market paperback editions, as well as a line of audioworks and selected videotapes. The house also packages specialty items such as boxed sets and tarot decks.

Special imprints include Destiny Books, Destiny Recordings, Healing Arts Press, and Park Street Press. Inner Traditions en Español is a line published in the Spanish language. Inner Traditions India issues works aimed at the Indian market. The house has announced a forthcoming slate of multimedia titles in the works. Inner Traditions International publishes a medium-sized list each year and maintains a strong backlist.

The **Inner Traditions** imprint accents works that represent the spiritual, cultural, and mythic traditions of the world, focusing on inner wisdom and the perennial philosophies.

Inner Traditions imprint titles: *Sacred Woman, Sacred Dance: Awakening Spirituality Through Dance and Ritual* by Iris J. Stewart; *Mother and Child: Visions of Parenting from Indigenous Cultures* by Jan Reynolds; *Harmonic Experience: Tonal Harmony from Its Natural Origins to Its Modern Expression* by W. A. Mattieu.

Destiny Books are contemporary metaphysical titles for a popular audience with special emphasis on self-transformation, the occult, and psychological well-being. Destiny Recordings are cassettes and compact discs of spiritual and indigenous music traditions. Destiny Audio Editions include Inner Traditions books on tape as well as original spoken-word cassettes.

Destiny Books titles: *The Light and Shadow Tarot* by Brian Williams and Michael Gofferd; *The Healing Power of Gemstones: In Tantra, Ayurveda, and Astrology* by Harish Johari.

Healing Arts Press publishes works on alternative medicine and holistic health that combine contemporary thought and innovative research with the accumulated knowledge of the world's great healing traditions.

Healing Arts Press books: *Meals That Heal: A Nutraceutical Approach to Diet and Health* by Lisa Turner; *Chi Kung: The Chinese Art of Mastering Energy* by Yves Réquéna; *The Encyclopedia of Aromatherapy* by Chrissie Wildwood; *Hemp for Health: The Nutritional and Medicinal Uses of the World's Most Extraordinary Plant* by Chris Conrad; *The Estrogen Alternative: Natural Hormone Therapy with Botanical Progesterone* by Raquel Martin with John R. Lee, M.D. and Judi Gerstung, D.C.; *A Russian Herbal: Traditional Remedies for Health and Healing* by Igor Vilevich Zevin with Nathaniel Altman and Lilia Vasilevna Zevin; *The Whole Food Bible: How to Select and Prepare Safe, Healthful Foods* by Chris Kilham; *Herbal Teas for Health and Healing* by Ceres.

Park Street Press produces books on travel, psychology, consumer and environmental issues, archeology, women's and men's studies, and fine art.

Park Street Press titles: *Kava, Medicine Hunting in Paradise: The Pursuit of a Natural Alternative to Anti-Anxiety Drugs and Sleeping Pills* by Chris Kilham; *Women of the Golden Dawn: Rebels and Priestesses* by Mary K. Greer.

Inner Traditions en Español is the house's Spanish-language publishing program, in cooperation with Lasser Press of Mexico City. This line includes popular titles from a variety of Inner Tradition imprints.

Selections from the Inner Traditions en Español list: *Astrología Dinámica (Dynamic Astrology)* by John Townley; *El Cáñamo para la Salud (Hemp for Health)* by Chris Conrad.

Inner Traditions India is a series comprising selections from the Inner Traditions International list, along with projects that arise in India; these works are produced in India for the Indian market.

Kits and gift packages from Inner Traditions: *The Book of Doors Divination Deck* by Athon Veggi and Allison Davidson; *The Lakota Sioux Sweat Lodge Cards* by Chief Archie Fire Lame Deer and Helene Sarks; *Leela: The Game of Self-Knowledge* by Harish Johari.

Inner Traditions supervises its own distribution.

Query letters and SASEs should be directed to:

Rowan Jacobsen, Managing Editor

INNISFREE PRESS
136 Rumfort Road
Philadelphia, PA 19119
215-247-4085
800-367-5872

Innisfree is a creative publishing forum for books, tapes, and journaling programs that feature the areas of personal growth with spiritual and feminine dimensions. The editorial sphere encompasses self-discovery, relationships, cooking and nutrition, parenting and child development, writing and journaling, healing and inspiration, transition and renewal, Bible study, and meditation. Innisfree acquired LuraMedia in late 1996.

From the Innisfree list: *Silence: Making the Journey to Inner Quiet* by Barbara Erako-Taylor; *Spiritual Lemons: Biblical Women, Irreverent Laughter, and Righteous Rage* by Lyn Brakeman; *Success Redefined: Notes to a Working Woman* by Lori Giovannoni; *Raising Peaceful Children in a Violent World* by Nancy Lee Cecil with Patricia L. Roberts; *Rattling Those Dry Bones: Women Changing the Church* (edited by June Steffensen Hagen); *Keeper of the Night: A Portrait of Life in the Shadow of Death* by Lee Modjeska; *Nobody Owns Me: A Celibate Woman Discovers Her Sexual Power* by Francis B. Rothluebber; *Feeding the Whole Family: Down-to-Earth Cookbook and Whole Foods Guide* by Cynthia Lair; *Seven Times the Sun: Guiding Your Child Through the Rhythms of the Day* by Shea Darian; *Guerrillas of Grace: Prayers for the Battle* by Ted Loder (drawings by Ed Kerns).

LuraMedia, Inc. (founded in 1982) was known as a small house that undertook to select, design, produce, and distribute its list with care and flair; the publisher's stated goal was to provide materials that foster healing and hope, balance and justice. Effective November 15, 1996, LuraMedia was sold to Innisfree Press in Philadelphia, Pennsylvania, and the San Diego office of LuraMedia closed. LuraMedia books are available through the new company.

Innisfree distributes to the trade via Consortium.

Query letters and SASEs should be directed to:

Marcia Broucek, Publisher

INTERVARSITY PRESS

5206 Main Street
Box 1400
Downers Grove, IL 60515
708-964-5700
http://www.ivpress.com (World Wide Web)

InterVarsity Press publications embrace the main fields of Bible study guides, reference books, academic and theological books, popularly written and story-oriented books, and issue-oriented books of general interest to educated Christians. IVP produces lines for children and young adults in addition to its adult list.

Nonfiction categories in areas of contemporary religious interest include titles in self-improvement, spirituality, and interpersonal relations. IVP fiction focuses on fantasy and science fiction and includes titles in other popular mainstream categories (but no romance or historical novels). The house produces a solid list in humor.

InterVarsity Press (founded in 1954) is the publishing arm of InterVarsity Christian Fellowship of the USA. The press operates within IVCF's framework and publishes interdenominational books (in hardback and paperback) under the banner "for those who take their Christianity seriously."

Indicative of the InterVarsity Press nonfiction frontlist: *The Journey: A Spiritual Roadmap for Modern Pilgrims* by Peter Kreeft; *To Forgive Is Human: How to Put Your*

Past in the Past by Michael E. McCullough, Steven Sandage, and Everett L. Worthington, Jr.; *Praying Jesus' Way: A Guide for Beginners and Veterans* by Brian Dodd; *What on Earth Is the Church? An Exploration into New Testament Theology* by Kevin Giles; *The Battle of Beginnings: Why Neither Side Is Winning the Creation–Evolution Debate* by Del Ratzsch; *Woman of Influence: Ten Traits of Those Who Want to Make a Difference* by Pam Farrel; *When God Interrupts: Finding New Life Through Unwanted Change* by M. Craig Barnes; *Black Man's Religion* by Craig S. Keener and Glenn Usry; *Straight and Narrow? Compassion and Clarity in the Homosexuality Debate* by Thomas E. Schmidt.

On the InterVarsity fiction list: *A Time to Speak* by Linda Shands; *The Mystery of the Campus Crook* by John Bibee; *Stolen Identity* (suspense) by Brian Regrut.

The Saltshaker Books imprint underscores its mission of meeting the needs of mind and heart by addressing contemporary nuances of women's life. LifeGuide Bible Studies introduces new titles that focus on particular scriptural areas and specific books of the Bible.

That the InterVarsity Press list is intended for those who take their Christianity seriously certainly applies to the IVP approach to humor: The house issues a notable line of cartoon books: *Attack of the Zit Monster & Other Teenage Terrors* by Randy Glasbergen; *Murphy's Laws of Marriage* by Steve Dennie and Rob Suggs; *As the Church Turns* by Ed Koehler.

A full set of guidelines for manuscript submission to InterVarsity Press is available upon request from the publisher.

InterVarsity Press distributes its own list.

Query letters and SASEs should be directed to:

Andrew T. Le Peau, Editorial Director

JEWISH LIGHTS PUBLISHING

P.O. Box 237
Sunset Farm Offices, Route 4
Woodstock, VT 05091
802-457-4000

Jewish Lights Publishing shows a vigorous approach to titles relevant to Jewish tradition, theology, history, and contemporary culture—all within the trade motto "Words for the soul—made in Vermont." Jewish Lights offers books in hardcover, quality paperback, and gift editions.

Jewish Lights features authors at the forefront of spiritual thought. Each voice is unique, and each speaks in a way readers can hear. Jewish Lights books are judged as successful not only by whether they are beautiful and commercially successful, but the difference they make in their readers' lives.

Jewish Lights Publishing (founded in 1990), a division of LongHill Partners, Inc., describes itself as publishing books that reflect the Jewish wisdom tradition for people of all faiths and all backgrounds. Their books really focus on the issue of the quest for the self, seeking meaning in life. They are books that help you to understand who you are and who you might become as a Jewish person, or as a person who is part of a tradition that has its roots in the Judeo-Christian world. They deal with issues of personal growth. They deal with issues of religious inspiration.

Jewish Lights's principal goal is to stimulate thought and help all people learn about who the Jewish People are, where they come from, and what the future can be made to hold. While people of diverse Jewish heritage are the primary audience, Jewish Lights books speak to people in the Christian world as well and will broaden their understanding of Judaism and the roots of their own faith.

Jewish Lights seeks out materials about the unity and community of the Jewish People and the relevance of Judaism to everyday life. To help them in these efforts, respectful of the rich diversity of the Jewish Heritage, they have established an Advisory Board representing a broad range of Jewish perspectives. The Advisory Board helps seek out new material and provides insights into the publishing needs of the Jewish community.

The press publishes the award-winning Kushner Series: Classics of Modern Jewish Spirituality by Lawrence Kushner. A related special-edition project is *The Book of Letters: A Mystical Hebrew Alphabet* (designed by Lawrence Kushner).

From Jewish Lights: *How to Be a Perfect Stranger (Volume 1: Major Faiths in America): A Guide to Etiquette in Other People's Religious Ceremonies* (edited by Arthur J. Magida); *How to Be a Perfect Stranger (Volume 2: Other Faiths in America): A Guide to Etiquette in Other People's Religious Ceremonies* (edited by Stuart M. Matlins and Arthur J. Magida); *God & The Big Bank: Discovering Harmony Between Science & Spirituality* by Daniel C. Matt; *Minding the Temple of the Soul: Balancing Body, Mind & Soul Through Traditional Jewish Prayer, Movement and Meditation* by Dr. Tamar Frankiel and Judy Greenfeld; *Finding Joy: A Practical Spiritual Guide to Happiness* by Dannel I. Schwartz with Mark Hass; *Invisible Lines of Connection: Sacred Stories of the Ordinary* by Lawrence Kushner; *Bar/Bat Mitzvah Basics: A Practical Family Guide to Coming of Age Together* (edited by Cantor Helen Leneman); *Embracing the Covenant: Converts to Judaism Talk About Why & How* (edited by Rabbi Allan Berkowitz and Patti Moskovitz).

The Art of Jewish Living series from the Federation of Jewish Men's Clubs provides the following titles: *A Time to Mourn, A Time to Comfort: A Guide to Jewish Bereavement and Comfort*; *The Shabbat Seder*; and *Hanukkah* by Dr. Ron Wolfson.

The Jewish Thought Series from Israel's MOD Books is distributed exclusively by Jewish Lights. A part of Israel's Broadcast University Series, the books are written by leading experts and authors in their respective fields. Titles are published jointly by Tel Aviv University, the Chief Education office of the IDF, and IDF Radio. Selected series offerings: *Jerusalem in the 19th Century* by Yehoshua Ben-Arieh; *Jewish Reactions to the Holocaust* by Yehuda Bauer; *Lectures on the Philosophy of Spinoza* by Professor Yosef Ben-Shlomo; *The Spiritual History of the Dead Sea Sect* by David Flusser; *The World of the Aggadah* by Avigdor Shinan; *Human Rights in the Bible and Talmud* by Haim H. Cohn.

Children's titles and books for the family from Jewish Lights: *A Prayer for the Earth: The Story of Naamah, Noah's Wife* by Sandy Eisenberg Sasso (illustrated by Bethanne Andersen); *In God's Name* by Sandy Eisenberg Sasso (illustrations by

Phoebe Stone); *When a Grandparent Dies: A Child's Own Workbook for Dealing with Shiva and the Year Beyond* by Nechama Liss-Levenson; *The New Jewish Baby Book: A Guide to Choices for Today's Families* by Anita Diamant.

Jewish Lights Publishing handles its own distribution.

Query letters and SASEs should be directed to:

Stuart M. Matlins, Editor

THE JEWISH PUBLICATION SOCIETY

1930 Chestnut Street
21st Floor
Philadelphia, PA 19103-4599
215-564-5925
fax: 215-564-6640

The Jewish Publication Society specializes in hardcover and trade paperback books of Jewish interest, as well as works of general interest in the areas of history and culture, religious thought, graphically lavish gift and art books, and literature that includes historical as well as contemporary fiction and poetry. JPS publishes editions of traditional religious works (including the Torah) as well as relevant commentaries; the house also produces children's books for readers from preschool to young adult.

The Jewish Publication Society (founded in 1888) upholds a commitment to the English-speaking Jewish community by publishing works of exceptional scholarship, contemporary significance, and enduring value. The publisher traditionally assumes a demanding balancing act among the various denominations of Jewish institutional life, between academic and popular interests, between past and present visions of Judaism.

On the JPS frontlist: *What a Country! Dry Bones Looks at Israel* by Yaakov Kirschen (collection of cartoons); *Distant Sisters: The Women I Left Behind* by Judith Rotem; *Biblical Women Unbound: New Counter-Tales* by Normal Rosen; *Studies in Modern Theology and Prayer* by Jakob Petuchowski; *Preparing Your Heart for the High Holy Days: A Guided Journal* by Kerry M. Olitzky and Rachel T. Sabath; *From Jerusalem to the Edge of Heaven: Meditations on the Soul of Israel* by Ari Elon.

Indicative of JPS nonfiction: *The View from Jacob's Ladder: One Hundred Midrashim* by David Curzon; *In the Year 1096: The First Crusade and the Jews* by Robert Chazen; *Reclaiming the Dead Sea Scrolls* by Lawrence Schiffman; *On the Possibility of Jewish Mysticism in Our Time* by Gershom Scholem, *On Family and Feminism* by Blu Greenberg; *Blessings* (a prayer book) by Melanie Greenberg.

Works in the field of literature and the arts include *Genesis: The Beginning of Desire* by Avivah Gottlieb Zornberg; *Emma Lazarus in Her World: Life and Letters* by Bette Roth Young; *Shaking Eve's Tree: Short Stories of Jewish Women* (edited by Sharon Niederman); *Look to the Hills* (historical fiction of the American West) by Hazel Krantz; *A Jewish Bestiary: A Book of Fabulous Creatures Drawn from Hebraic Legend and Lore* (illustrated work) by Marc Podwall.

The Jewish Publication Society is a not-for-profit educational institution that distributes its own list and, through its book club, offers to its membership Judaica from other publishers as well.

THE JEWISH PUBLICATION SOCIETY CHILDREN'S BOOKS

The dynamic children's books branch of the Jewish Publication Society develops projects in four categories: preschool, primary, middle readers, and young adults. The kids' list encompasses picture books, storybooks, biographies, general nonfiction, and works with specific religious or cultural themes.

Representative titles: *The Kids' Catalog of Jewish Holidays* by David A. Adler; *Of Heroes, Hooks and Heirlooms* by Faye Silton; *Moe Berg: The Spy Behind Home Plate* by Vivian Grey; *Remarkable Jewish Women: Rebels, Rabbis, and Other Women from Biblical Times to the Present* by Emily Taitz and Sondra Henry; *David and Max* by Gary Provost and Gail Levine-Provost; *The Great Jewish Quiz Book* by Barbara Spector; a set of titles by Melanie Hope Greenberg: *Celebrations: Our Jewish Holidays* and *Blessings: Our Jewish Ceremonies.*

For readers of all ages, JPS offers *We Are Children Just the Same: Vedem, the Secret Magazine by the Boys of Terezin* (edited by Paul Wilson), a collection of excerpts from *Vedem*, a clandestine journal produced by youths imprisoned at Theresienstadt during the Holocaust.

Query letters and SASEs should be directed to:

Dr. Ellen Frankel, Editor in Chief

Bruce Black, Editor, Children's Books

KAR-BEN COPIES

6800 Tildenwood Lane
Rockville, MD 20852
301-984-8733
karben@aol.com (e-mail)
http://www.karben.com (World Wide Web)

Kar-Ben Copies offers an expansive Jewish library for young children, in addition to titles for adult and family readers, as well as teachers. The Kar-Ben list encompasses presentations keyed to high holidays, sabbath, culture and tradition, and general-interest concepts.

Kar-Ben's children's books are handsomely produced volumes that often incorporate fine illustrative work. The Kar-Ben catalog also highlights books especially for toddlers, as well as a reference line for youngsters (My Very Own Jewish Library). The house also offers audiocassettes and calendars.

Kar-Ben titles: *Kids Love Israel, Israel Loves Kids: A Travel Guide for Families* (revised edition) by Barbara Sofer; *Simchat Torah: A Family Celebration* by Judith Z.

Abrams; *Hanukkah, Oh Hanukkah* (illustrated by Miriam Sagasti); *A Costume for Noah: A Purim Story* by Susan Remick Topek; *Israel Fun for Little Hands* by Sally Springer (games, riddles, puzzles, and mazes introduce young children to favorite sites in Israel); *Jewish Holiday Games for Little Hands* by Ruth Esrig Brinn (illustrated by Sally Springer); *Sammy Spider's First Passover* by Sylvia A. Rouss (illustrated by Katherine Janus Kahn).

A special Kar-Ben line comprises book-and-cassette packages, with accompanying leader's guides for family services keyed to the high holidays (Selichot, Rosh Hashanah, and Yom Kippur). These works are written by Judith Z. Abrams, designed and illustrated by Katherine Janus Kahn, with original music by Frances T. Goldman.

Kar-Ben (founded in 1976) welcomes comments, kudos, and manuscripts.

Kar-Ben has its own expanded order-fulfillment facility; many Kar-Ben titles are also available through Baker & Taylor as well as other trade-book distributors.

Query letters and SASEs should be directed to:

Madeleine Wikler, Editor-in-Chief

H. J. KRAMER, INC.

P.O. Box 1082
Tiburon, CA 94920
415-435-5367
fax: 415-435-5364

Kramer covers spiritual life, interpersonal relationships, resources for good health, and self-awareness and guidance. The Starseed Press imprint publishes books for younger readers (see subentry below). Kramer books are finely produced editions in trade paperback and hardcover. The house typically issues a small number of new titles seasonally and sustains a strong backlist.

The books H. J. Kramer publishes are contributions to an emerging world based on cooperation rather than on competition, on affirmation of the human spirit rather than on self-doubt, and on the certainty that all humanity is connected. The goal of the publishers is to touch as many lives as possible with a message of hope for a better world.

H. J. Kramer, Inc. (founded in 1984 by Hal and Linda Kramer) holds a commitment to publish books that touch the heart, and open us to spirit. Kramer books, old and new, are intended to support the reader's personal vision. A number of Kramer books sell exceedingly well in the mainstream market and garner translation rights worldwide as well as domestic book-club sales.

From Kramer: *The Alchemy of Prayer: Rekindling Our Inner Life* by Terry Lynn Taylor; *Reclaiming Our Health: Exploding the Medical Myth and Embracing the Source of True Healing* by John Robbins; *Into a Timeless Realm: A Metaphysical Adventure* by Michael J. Roads; *Tara's Angels: One Family's Extraordinary Journey of Courage and Healing* by Kirk Moore; *The Laws of Spirit: Simple, Powerful Truths for Making Life Work* by Dan Millman.

The Earth Life series by Sanaya Roman, channel for Orin, is a course in learning to live with joy, sense energy, and grow spiritually. Titles include: *Living with Joy: Keys to Personal Power and Spiritual Transformation*; *Personal Power Through Awareness: A Guidebook for Sensitive People*; *Spiritual Growth: Being Your Higher Self*.

A Kramer hallmark is Dan Millman's renowned set of writings (including *Way of the Peaceful Warrior*) that, in addition to audiocassette rendering, has now branched into a children's series. Kramer has also published a number of works in José Silva's mind-control method.

Prospective authors please note: Kramer's list is selective and is, generally speaking, fully slated several publishing seasons in advance; Kramer and Starseed are thus essentially closed to unsolicited submissions.

H. J. Kramer's list is distributed to the trade by Publishers Group West, Bookpeople, and New Leaf Distributing Company.

STARSEED PRESS

Starseed Press children's books from H. J. Kramer are award-winning children's books that build self-esteem, inspire nonviolence, and encourage positive values. The imprint produces illustrated works slated for trade as well as educational markets.

Starseed books embody the principles of education through the power of story and incorporate myths, legends, fables, fairy tales, folklore, and original author visions into volumes of contemporary appeal.

Titles here: *Today I Am Lovable: 365 Positive Activities for Kids* by Diane Loomans; *The Lovables in the Kingdom of Self-Esteem* by Diane Loomans (illustrated by Kim Howard); *Dragon Soup* by Arlene Williams (illustrated by Sally J. Smith).

The Peaceful Warrior children's series by Dan Millman (illustrated by T. Taylor Bruce) includes these titles: *Secret of the Peaceful Warrior* and *Quest for the Crystal Castle*. The series adapts the characters, lessons, and spirit of Dan Millman's international bestseller *Way of the Peaceful Warrior*.

Backlist benchmarks include *The Land of the Blue Flower* by Frances Hodgson Burnett (author of *The Secret Garden* and *The Little Princess*) in an edition illustrated by Judith Ann Griffith.

Query letters and SASEs should be directed to:

Hal Kramer, President

Linda Kramer, Publisher

Jan Phillips, Acquisitions Editor

KTAV PUBLISHING HOUSE INC.

900 Jefferson Street
P.O. Box 6249
Hoboken, NJ 07030-7205
201-963-9524

KTAV Publishing House (founded in 1924) features books of Jewish interest, including scholarly Judaica, sermonica, textbooks, and books for a younger readership. KTAV also markets religious educational materials (including books), as well as gifts and decorative items. Many KTAV titles in the scholarly vein relate the history of Jewish thought and culture within the context of broader issues—some of global scope—and are of appeal to the interested general reader.

KTAV's catalog embraces the categories of Judaica, Biblica, Torah study, Jewish law, contemporary Halachic thought, sermonica, Jewish history, Jewish thought, contemporary Jewry, and Torah and science.

Titles from KTAV: *A Small Glimmer of Light: Reflections on the Book of Genesis* by Steven Saltzman; *Critical Jewish Issues: A Book for Teenagers* by Rabbi Ronald H. Isaacs; *Jewish Mourner's Handbook* by Rabbi Ron H. Isaacs and Rabbi Kerry M. Olitzky; *Finding the God of Noah: The Spiritual Journey of a Baptist Minister from Christianity to the Laws of Noah* by J. David Davis; *Understanding Jewish History I* by Sol Scharfstein; *The Guide to the Jewish Internet* by Michael Levin; *Prophetic Inspiration After the Prophets: Maimonides and Others* by Abraham J. Heschel; *Zen and Hasidism: The Similarities Between Two Spiritual Disciplines* by Harold Heifetz; *Torah Readings for Weekdays* (edited by Rabbi David H. Lincoln).

Representing KTAV's diverse historical and cultural perspective: *Voices in Exile: A Study in Sephardic Intellectual History* by Marc D. Angel; *Modern Medicine and Jewish Ethics* (in a revised and augmented edition) by Fred Rosner; *Roots and Boots: From Crypto-Jew in New Spain to Community Leader in the American Southwest* by Floyd S. Fierman; *The Jewish Woman in Time and Torah* by Eliezar Berkovits.

Of scholarly note: *The Metsudah Linear Chumash—Rashi: A New Linear Translation* (in five volumes) by Rabbi Avrohom Davis and Rabbi Abrohom Kleinkaufman: *Volume I: Bereshis*; *Volume II: Shemos*; *Volume III: Vayikro*; *Volume IV: Bamidbar*; *Volume V: Devarim*.

KTAV distributes its own list; in addition, the house distributes the books of Yeshiva University Press.

Query letters and SASEs should be directed to:

Bernard Scharfstein, President

LIGUORI PUBLICATIONS

Triumph Books
One Liguori Drive
Liguori, MO 63057-9999
314-464-2500

New York–area office:
333 Glen Head Road
Old Brookville, NY 11545
516-759-7402
http://www.liguori.org (World Wide Web)

Liguori Publications and its trade imprint Triumph Books represents a twofold approach to religious publishing. Liguori (run by Redemptionist priests) produces books and pamphlets focused on the needs of Catholic parishes and specialized religious-bookstore markets, and publishes *Liguorian* magazine. Triumph Books publishes for the mainstream religious-trade-book market. Under the rubric of Liguori Faithware, the publisher supplies computer resources for Catholics.

Liguori initiated its book program in 1968 and met with immediate success with *Good Old Plastic Jesus* by Earnest Larsen and *Keeping Your Balance in the Modern Church* by Hugh O'Connell.

Though Liguori, America's largest producer of Catholic publications, is assuredly a business, it is primarily a ministry. Through publications—in print and through electronic media—Liguori is able to reach people in ways that are not available in ordinary day-to-day ministry. Authors interested in Liguori or Triumph may request from the publisher a brochure covering submissions guidelines.

Liguori titles: *Living Advent: A Daily Companion to the Lectionary* by Julia Dugger; *Revisiting the Journey: Adult Faith-Sharing with the Catechism of the Catholic Church* (a Redemptorist Pastoral Publication); *The Light of the World* by David Fielding; *Two Voices: A Father and Son Discuss Family and Faith* by Jim Doyle and Brian Doyle; *Following Christ* by Daniel Lowery; *Never Stop Walking: The Life and Spirit of Saint Alphonsus Liguori* by Nancy Fearon; *We're Running Late: Teachable Moments for Working Mothers* by Kass P. Dotterweich.

Highlights from Liguori include *Mother Teresa: In My Own Words* by Mother Teresa; *Family Planning: A Guide for Exploring the Issues* by Charles and Elizabeth Balsam; *Sex and the Christian Teen* by Jim Auer.

Liguori's 1994 edition of *Catechism of the Catholic Church* (along with the Spanish-language *Catecismo de la Iglesia Católica*) rose to the coveted rank of number-one bestseller in the religious-books list.

From Liguori Faithware comes *How to Survive Being Married to a Catholic* (an interactive CD-ROM/book combination).

Liguori Publications promotes and markets through such vehicles as catalog mailings and listings in *Liguorian* magazine, circulates bookstore and parish newsletters, and utilizes fliers and self-mailers.

TRIUMPH BOOKS

Triumph Books emphasizes an ecumenical perspective in the religious trade market. Triumph reaches a wide readership through books in a variety of areas including psychology, spirituality, inspiration, awareness, theology, and Christian living.

Triumph Books asserts the impact of social and cultural developments on readers' values and religious faith, and reflects this stance in its selection of new titles. The publishing program accents topics of contemporary controversy and debate. Triumph was formerly part of Gleneida Publishing Group.

From Triumph: *Twelve Months of Monastery Soups* by Brother Victor-Antoine D'avila-Latourrette; *Where Does God Live? Questions and Answers for Parents and Children* by Rabbi Marc Gellman and Monsignor Thomas Hartman; *Divine Energy:*

God Beyond Us, Within Us, Among Us by Donal Dorr; *Life Doesn't Get Any Better Than This: The Holiness of Little Daily Dramas* by Robert A. Alper; *Short Prayers for the Long Day* (compiled by Giles and Melville Harcourt); *A Company of Women: Journey Through the Feminine Experience of Faith* (edited by Irene Mahoney); *Listen to the Desert: Secrets of Spiritual Maturity from the Desert Fathers and Mothers* by Gregory Mayers; *On Death: Wisdom and Consolation from the World's Great Writers* (compiled by Barry Ulanov); *Priesthood Imperiled: A Critical Examination of Ministry in the Catholic Church* by Bernard Haring, C.S.S.R.

Triumph offers a line of titles from the world-renowned guru J. P. Vaswani, including *The Good You Do Returns: A Book of Wisdom Stories*. A noteworthy Triumph edition is the popularly oriented classic, *Peace of Soul* by Fulton J. Sheen.

Query letters and SASEs should be directed to:

Rev. Thomas Santa, Publisher, Editor-in-Chief, Book and Pamphlet Department (Liguori, MO)

Anthony Chiffolo, Managing Editor, Triumph Books (Liguori, MO)

(Ms.) Pat Kossmann, Executive Editor (Old Brookville, NY)

Joan Marlowe Golan, Administrative Editor (Old Brookville, NY)

LLEWELLYN PUBLICATIONS

P.O. Box 64383
St. Paul, MN 55164-0383
612-291-1970
www.llewellyn.com/lwlpc@llewellyn.com (World Wide Web)

Traditional areas of Llewellyn publishing concentration include astrology, magick, the occult, self-improvement, self-development, spiritual science, alternative technologies, nature religions and lifestyles, spiritist and mystery religions, divination, phenomena, and tantra. These works are brought out under the lustrous Llewellyn logo: a crescent moon. Llewellyn's trade motto—"new worlds of mind and spirit"—indicates the publisher's openness to explore new territory.

Llewellyn Publications (established in 1897) is a venerable house with a historical emphasis on the practical aspects of what today may be termed New Age science— how it works, and how to do it.

Llewellyn catalogs a full stock of new seasonal releases along with a prolific backlist in hardcover, trade paper, and mass-market editions. Llewellyn also issues tarot decks and divination kits. The house's expanded program includes Spanish-language trade paperbacks.

On the Llewellyn list: *Entering the Summerland: Customs and Rituals of Transition into the Afterlife* by Edain McCoy; *Sacred Site of the West* by Bernyce Barlow; *The Angels' Message to Humanity: Ascension to Divine Union—Powerful Enochian Magick* by Gerald Schueler, Ph.D. and Betty Schueler, Ph.D.; *Predictions for a New Millennium* by Noel Tyl; *The Tarot of the Orishas* (created by Zolrak; illustrated by

Durkon); *The Sabbats: A New Approach to Living the Old Ways* by Edain McCoy; *The Once Unknown Familiar: Shamanic Paths to Unleash Your Animal Powers* by Timothy Roderick; *The Healing Earth Tarot* by Jyotie McKie and David McKie; *The Handbook of Celtic Astrology: The 13-Sign Lunar Zodiac of the Ancient Druids* by Helena Paterson; *The Grail Castle: Male Myths and Mysteries in the Celtic Tradition* by Kenneth Johnson and Marguerite Elsbeth; *Sexuality in the Horoscope* (edited by Noel Tyl); *Secrets of a Natural Menopause* by Edna Copeland Ryneveld; *How to Develop and Use Psychometry* by Ted Andrews; *Hawaiian Religion and Magic* by Scott Cunningham; *Faery Wicca* by Kisma K. Stepanich; *Egyptian Magick: Enter the Body of Light & Travel the Magickal Universe* by Betty Schueler; *Holistic Aromatherapy: Balance the Body and Soul with Essential Oils* by Ann Berwick; *A Kitchen Witch's Cookbook* by Patricia Telesco.

Llewellyn has produced a limited number of fiction titles. Among them: *Visions of Murder* by Florence Wagner McClain; *Lilith* by D. A. Heeley; *Cardinal's Sin: Psychic Defenders Uncover Evil in the Vatican* by Raymond Buckland; *Walker Between the Worlds* by Diane DesRochers; *The Holographic Dollhouse* by Charlotte Lawrence.

Llewellyn is a specialty house and looks for projects (books and audiotapes, as well as videos and computer software) that will have extended sales viability; Llewellyn is not geared toward academic or scholarly publishing and its products are aimed at general audiences without specialist knowledge or training. Authors may request the house's writers' guidelines, which contain valuable tips generally applicable to structuring and proposing publishing projects.

To request a copy of the Llewellyn Writers' Guidelines for book publication, send SASE to Nancy Mostad, Acquisitions Manager. Only writers who request and adhere to writers' guidelines will be considered for publication.

An aggressive marketer and promoter, Llewellyn publications and authors are given full house support, including the areas of arranging author interviews and appropriate advertising and subsidiary rights—often incorporated into the schedule is placement in Llewellyn's magazines (*New Times*) and primarily promotional venues (*New Worlds*). Llewellyn's marketing network encompasses distributional arrangements worldwide.

Query letters and SASEs should be directed to:

Nancy Mostad, Acquisitions Manager

LOTUS LIGHT PUBLICATIONS

P.O. Box 1008
Silver Lake, WI 53170
414-889-8501
fax: 414-889-8591
800-548-3824

Lotus Brands, Inc.
P.O. Box 325
Twin Lakes, WI 53181
800-824-6396

Lotus Light produces works in the fields of health, yoga, Native American and New Age metaphysics. In addition to books, Lotus Light produces video and audio materials, as well as incense and other related sideline materials such as essential oils, body-care products, charts, artwork, greeting cards, jewelry, chimes, and crystals.

Lotus Light Publications (founded in 1981) is a division of Lotus Brands, Inc. Lotus Light Enterprises, Inc. conducts business under the rubrics Lotus Light Natural Body Care, Blue Lotus Distributing, Wishing Well Video, Auro Trading Company, Ltd., and InterNatural. Lotus Light is a wholesale distributor of health and body-care merchandise to the health food trade nationwide, with primary emphasis on providing high-quality, natural products. Blue Lotus offers gifts and sidelines. Wishing Well has a large, well-rounded selection of videotapes.

On the Lotus Light list: *Ayurveda Secrets of Healing* by Maya Tiwari; *The Complete Reiki Handbook: Basic Introduction and Methods of Natural Application* by Walter Lubeck; *The Magic and Power of Lavender* by Maggie Tisserand and Monica Junemann; *Ayurvedic Cooking for Westerners* by Amadea Morningstar; *Aromatherapy: to Heal and Tend the Body* by Robert Tisserand; *New Eden: For People, Animals, Nature* by Michael W. Fox (illustrated by Susan Seddon Boulet); *Spirit Stones* by Douglas Brodoff; *Rainforest Remedies: One Hundred Healing Herbs of Belize* by Rosita Arvigo and Michael Balick; *Stargazer: A Native American Inquiry into Extraterrestrial Phenomena* by Gerald Hausman; *Secrets of Precious Stones* by Ursula Klinger Raatz; *Cosmo-Biological Birth Control* by Shalila Sharamon and Bodo Baginski.

Lotus Light publications distributes primarily through special product outlets such as health-food stores and spiritual-interest booksellers.

Query letters and SASEs should be directed to:

Niran Kar

LuraMedia, Inc.

(See listing for Innisfree Press)

Mesorah Publications, Ltd.

4401 Second Avenue
Brooklyn, NY 11232
718-921-9000

Mesorah Publications hosts a wide-ranging program that includes works of contemporary cultural and popular interest in addition to traditional Judaica, Bible study, liturgical materials, history, and juveniles. Mesorah also produces series on audiocassette. The Art Scroll Library series is produced with special attention to design and production.

Mesorah Publications, Ltd. (founded in 1976) publishes hardcover and paperback editions within a traditional approach, as noted by the publisher's trade motto: Mesorah Publications, helping preserve the heritage . . . one book at a time.

From Mesorah: *Encyclopedia of Biblical Personalities* by Yishai Chasidah; *Along the Maggid's Journey* and *The Maggid Speaks* by Rabbi Raysach J. Krohn; *Tomorrow May Be Too Late* by Chana Stavsky Rubin (historical novel); *The Jewish Action Reader* (an Orthodox Union Publication); *The Bostoner Rebbetzin Remembers* by Rebbetzin Raichel Horowitz of Boston; *Architect of Judaism for the Modern World* by Rabbi Samson Raphael Hirsch.

Mesorah catalogs books from such other houses as Orthodox Union, Shaar Press, Tamar Books, and NCSY Publications.

Query letters and SASEs should be directed to:

Abraham Biderman, Acquisitions Editor

MOODY PRESS

820 North LaSalle Boulevard
Chicago, IL 60610-3284
312-329-2101

In addition to general-interest religious titles (Bible-based interdenominational), Moody produces a list that includes Bibles, books for children and youths, novels, biographies, educational resources, and works for religious professionals. Moody's books are issued in clothbound editions, trade paper, and mass-market paperback. Moody also catalogs computer software, audiotapes, and videocassettes. Moody Press (founded in 1894) serves as the publishing ministry of Moody Bible Institute.

Moody produces a number of targeted and successful lines that encompass the spectrum of the house's publishing interests. This portion of the Moody program offers such series as Men of Integrity, Moody Acorns, Golden Oldies, Healing for the Heart, Quiet Time Books for Women, and Salt & Light Pocket Guides.

Representative Moody titles: *Are Christians Destroying America?: How to Restore a Decaying Culture* by Tony Evans; *Battle for a Generation: The Life-Changing Youth Ministry That Makes a Difference* by Ron Hutchcraft with Lisa Hutchcraft Whitmer; *Break Down the Walls: Experiencing Biblical Reconciliation and Unity in the Body of Christ* by Raleigh Washington and Glen Kehrein with Claude King; *First and Goal: NFL Players Talk About Football and Faith* by Dave Brannon; *Hope for the Separated: Wounded Marriages Can Be Healed* by Gary Chapman; *Hope When It Hurts: A Personal Testimony of How to Deal with the Impact of Cancer* by Larry Burkett with Mike Taylor; *A Passionate Commitment: Recapturing Your Sense of Purpose* by Crawford Loritts; *The Serpent of Paradise: The Incredible Story of How Satan's Rebellion Serves God's Purposes* by Erwin W. Lutzer; *Sound Mind Investing: A Step-by-Step Guide to Financial Stability and Growth As We Move Toward the Year 2000* by Austin Pryor; *Spiritual Disciplines Within the Church: Participating Fully in the Body of Christ* by Donald S. Whitney; *When the Going Gets Tough, the Tough Start Laughing* by Martha Bolton.

Northfield Publishing, an imprint of Moody Press, is a line of books for non-Christians in your life, those who are exploring the Christian faith, or acquaintances who identify themselves as Christians but may not be active in a local church. While remaining true to biblical principles, certain Christian wording and Scripture book references are eliminated to avoid reader confusion. Covering such areas as finances, relationships, and business, Northfield authors are professionals in their field who write with relevance and offer wide-ranging perspectives.

Some Northfield titles: *Five Love Languages: The How to Express Heartfelt Commitment to Your Mate* by Gary Chapman; *Reinventing Your Career: Surviving a Layoff and Creating New Opportunities* by Stephen P. Adams; *The Relaxed Parent: Helping Your Kids Do More As You Do Less* by Tim Smith.

Fiction from Moody includes historicals, high-tech espionage, and contemporary mysteries. Larry Burkett Products is a line of books and tapes accenting the social/financial sphere.

MOODY CHILDREN & YOUTH

Moody produces a variety of publications geared toward a younger readership, including picture books, biographies, Bible stories, read-aloud volumes, and gift editions. Moody Children & Youth series include Children's Bible Basics (authored by Carolyn Nystrom), Dallas O'Neil and the Baker Street Sports Club (by Jerry B. Jenkins), Patricia St. John Books (inspirational novels), and Sensitive Issues Books (by Carole Gift Page).

Query letters and SASEs should be directed to:

Jim Bell, Editorial Director

MOORINGS

As of spring 1996, Random House/Ballantine ceased publishing under the Moorings imprint.

MULTNOMAH PRESS

(See Questar Publishers)

THOMAS NELSON

501 Nelson Place
P.O. Box 141000
Nashville, TN 37214-1000
615-889-9000

Thomas Nelson (founded in 1961) produces Christian trade books in hardcover and trade paperback in the areas of health, inspiration, self-help, psychology, family concerns, parenting, contemporary issues and interest, and healing and recovery. Nelson also issues a line of titles for young readers (currently accenting the Tommy Nelson division). The house offers a strong, select list of adult and young-adult fiction. Thomas Nelson produces magazines and journals and is among the largest publishers of Bibles and scriptural commentary in the United States. Oliver-Nelson is a trade-oriented imprint.

Already among the major players in the religious-publishing arena, Nelson enjoys its current phase of corporate exuberance. The house bought Here's Life Publishers from Campus Crusade for Christ and expanded their evangelism and discipleship markets. Nelson addresses the growing Christian Spanish readership in the United States and abroad through their Editorial Caribe and Editorial Betania divisions (both acquired in 1994). Thomas Nelson also owns the editorially independent Word Publishing (see separate main entry in this directory). The overall corporate banner for the various divisions in this enterprise is NelsonWord Publishing Group.

Thomas Nelson's publishing philosophy: To grow through fairness and integrity in distinctive service to all. Thomas Nelson's purpose: To publish, produce, and market products that honor God and serve humanity and to enhance shareholder value.

Nonfiction titles from Thomas Nelson: *The God You're Looking For: Understanding Him and His Way Will Make a Radical Difference in Your Life* by Bill Hybels; *Day of Deception: Separating Truth from the Falsehoods That Threaten Our Society* by John Hagee; *The Success Journey: The Process of Living Your Dreams* by John C. Maxwell; *Let Faith Change Your Life* by Becky Tirabassi; *Advanced Nutritional Therapies* by Kenneth H. Cooper, M.D.; *The Magic of Teamwork: Proven Principles for Building a Winning Team* by Pat Williams; *Personal Coaching for Results: How to Mentor and Inspire Others to Amazing Growth* by Lou Tice; *How to Keep Your Kids on Your Team* by Charles Stanley; *Like a Rock: Becoming a Person of Character* by Andy Stanley; *Men and Sex: Discovering Greater Love, Passion, and Intimacy with Your Wife* by Clifford L. Penner, Ph.D. and Joyce J. Penner, M.N., R.N.; *Unveiled Hope: Eternal Encouragement from the Book of Revelation* by Scotty Smith and Michael Card; *Diamonds in the Dark: Scriptural Insights for Comfort and Encouragement* by Jack Graham; *Seeds of Destiny: Restoring Purpose to Everyday Life* by Arthur F. Miller, Jr. and William Hendricks; *A Place Called Home: A Spirituality for Anxious Times* by Harriet Crosby; *Spurgeon's Daily Treasures in the Psalms* (updated and edited by Roger Campbell); *Taking the Word to the World: 50 Years of the United Bible Societies* by Edwin H. Robertson.

Nelson fiction includes historical and contemporary novels, as well as futurist thrillers. Fiction from Nelson: *One False Move* by T. Davis Bunn; *The Hope Valley War* by Brock Thoene; *Dark Road to Daylight* by Gary E. Parker; *DeathStrand* by Maurice S. Rawlings, M.D. and Robert Liparulo; *The Pandora Project* by David Ward.

A noted Nelson project is a series of family-oriented works from Carolyn Coats and Pamela Smith. Titles include *Things Your Mother Told You but You Didn't Want to Hear*; *Things Your Dad Always Told You But You Didn't Want to Hear*; and *My Grandmother Always Said That.*

TOMMY NELSON

Tommy Nelson is a children's-publishing division geared toward the youngest readers up through young adults. Launched as the new home for the highly successful Word Kids! and Nelson Jr. product lines, the Tommy Nelson list features such bestselling authors as Max Lucado, Frank Peretti, and Bill Myers. Tommy Nelson is particularly strong in fiction and novelty items. Series include the Itty Bitty Books line.

Representative titles: *The Crippled Lamb* by Max Lucado; *The Legend of Annie Murphy* by Frank Peretti; *The Parable of the Sunflower* by Liz Curtis Biggs; *Whose Eyes Are These?* by Elizabeth Burman; *Cyber: The Pharaoh's Tomb* by Sigmund Brouwer; *God Loves You* (a pop-up book) by Vlasta Van Kempen.

Thomas Nelson handles its own distribution.

Query letters and SASEs should be sent to:

Curtis Lundgren, Acquisitions Editor

NEWCASTLE PUBLISHING COMPANY

P.O. Box 7589
Van Nuys, CA 91409
818-787-4378

Newcastle publishes in a broad range of areas that covers art therapy and journaling; self-help and psychology; health and nutrition; personal transformation and spirituality; numerology; palmistry; handwriting analysis; tarot books and decks; Celtic lore; mythology; education and child rearing; and how-to books for senior citizens and older adults, as well as selected general-interest occult nonfiction. Imprints include Forgotten Fantasy Library, the Living Well Collection, the Newcastle Tarot Library, and Greenbrier Books.

Newcastle Publishing Company (established in 1970) purveys paperback originals and reprints (catalogued under the banner "Quality books for the discerning reader").

Newcastle titles: *Tarot: The First Handbook for the Master* by Eileen Connolly, Ph.D.; *I've Got Your Number! How to Psychoanalyze Yourself and Your Friends* by Doris Webster and Mary A. Hopkins; *The Great Within* by Christian D. Larson; *The Symbolism of Color* by Ellen Conroy.

The Living Well Collection is especially written for older adult readers. Newcastle Publishing has developed an innovative and thought-provoking series of consumer guidebooks for the older adult. Written for the discerning mature adult with specific needs and concerns, these easy-to-read books provide the basics on everything from business to creativity. Titles: *Lambda Gray: A Practical, Emotional, and Spiritual Guide for Gays and Lesbians Who Are Growing Older* (compiled by Karen Westerberg Reyes); *Schemes & Scams: A Practical Guide for Outwitting Today's Con Artist for the 50+ Consumer* by Douglas P. Shadel and John T. (foreword by Walter Cronkite); *Outsmart Crime! 200 Creative Strategies for Baffling the Criminal Mind* by Doug Shadel and Al Ward; *Living Well: Answers to Life's Practical Mysteries* by Teresa

Herring; *Longer Life, More Joy: Techniques for Enhancing Health, Happiness, and Inner Vision* by Gay Gaer Luce, Ph.D.; *Your Personal Fitness Survey: A Guide to Your Current State of Health* by David Gamon and Kathleen O'Brien; *Blueprint for Success: The Complete Guide to Starting a Business After 50* by Albert Myers.

Newcastle is distributed by Baker and Taylor, Bookpeople, DeVorss & Company, Ingram, Indland Book Company, Moving Books, New Leaf Distribution, Pacific Pipeline, Samuel Webster, Inc., Summit University Press.

Query letters and SASEs should be directed to:

Al Saunders, President and Publisher

Gina Gross, Editor

NEW LEAF PRESS

P.O. Box 726
Green Forest, AR 72638
501-438-5288
fax: 501-438-5120
800-643-9535

Areas of New Leaf publishing include Christian living, ethics, prophecy and eschatology, biography, theology, applied Christianity, history, Bible study, family/home/marriage, friendship and love, education, evangelism, devotional works (including daily readings), humor, and fiction. Master Books is the house's imprint for its broad-interest titles. The house has a solid backlist.

New Leaf Press (founded in 1975) publishes primarily for the Christian religious market, with some trade-religious crossover titles. New Leaf produces in hardcover and paperback (trade paper and mass-market); many New Leaf books are priced economically.

On the New Leaf/Master Books list: *The Children's Illustrated Bible* (stories retold by Selina Hastings; illustrated by Eric Thomas); *A Bouquet from Heaven: Celebrating God's Magnificence Through His Gift of Wildflowers* (devotions by Melva Stephens Lard; paintings by Steve McGuire); *Hear the Rush of Angel Wings* by Joel and Jane French; *Mini-Moments for Leaders: Forty Bright Spots to Encourage Those in Leadership* by Robert Strand; *A Palace for the Antichrist* by Joseph Chambers; *Everything I Need to Know I Learned in Sunday School* by David Shibley; *Unshakable Man: A Stable Spiritual Force in the Home* by Ron Auch; *Life After Lucy: The True Story of* I Love Lucy's *Little Ricky* by Keith Thibodeaux with Audrey T. Hingley.

New Leaf titles for younger readers include *Columbus and Cortez, Conquerors for Christ* by John Eidsmoe.

New Leaf Press distributes its own list; New Leaf also provides distribution services for other publishers with related market outlooks.

Query letters and SASEs should be directed to:

Jim Fletcher, Editor

NUMATA CENTER

2620 Warring Street
Berkeley, CA 94704
510-843-4128
http://www.slip.net/~numata (World Wide Web)

Numata Center for Buddhist Translation and Research is a nonprofit organization established by Mr. Yehan Numata, founder of the Mitutoyo Corporation, international manufacturer of precision measuring instruments.

Numata has undertaken the translation and publication of the Chinese Buddhist canon, as well as additional works, in finely produced English-language editions.

Numata engages a variety of scholars and writers to participate in this landmark program, and the initial volumes have been received heartily by the library market, as well as specialty and trade booksellers.

Sample titles: *The Lotus Sutra* (translated by Kubo Tsugunari and Yuyama Akira); *The Summary of the Great Vehicle* (translated by John P. Keenan); *Letters of Master Rennyo* (translated by Minor Rogers); *Essentials of the Eight Traditions* (translated by Leo Pruden).

The BDK Tripitaka Translation Project covers the entire Buddhist Canon, translated by internationally known scholars, using the Taisho Edition of the Chinese Tripitaka. The First Series consists of 139 titles in 108 volumes.

Query letters and SASEs should be directed to:

Reverend Seishin Yamashita, President

Reverend Kiyoshi Yamashita, Director

PARAGON HOUSE PUBLISHERS
(See Directory of United States Publishers)

ORBIS BOOKS

Walsh Building
P.O. Box 308
Maryknoll, NY 10545-0308
914-941-7636

Orbis covers such topics as theology, global religious issues, social justice, interreligious matters, mission theology, spirituality, politics, ecology, and African-American studies. Orbis also offers audio and video products. Orbis Books (founded in 1970) is a division of Maryknoll Fathers and Brothers.

From the Orbis program: *Spirit of Fire: The Life and Vision of Teilhard de Chardin* by Ursula King; *The Hidden Heart of the Cosmos: Humanity and the New Story* by Brian

Swimme; *Were You There? Godforsakenness in Slave Religion* by David Emmanuel Goatley; *Martin Luther King: The Inconvenient Hero* by Vincent Harding; *Dialogue of Life: A Christian Among Allah's Poor* by Bob McCahill; *Apostle of Peace: Essays in Honor of Daniel Berrigan* (edited by John Dear); *John Paul II: the Encyclicals in Everyday Language* (edited by Joseph G. Donders); *Theology for Earth Community: A Field Guide* (edited by Dieter T. Hessel); *Women Healing Earth: Third-World Women on Ecology, Feminism, and Religion* (edited by Rosemary Radford Ruether); *Nonviolent Story: Narrative Conflict Resolution in the Gospel of Mark* by Robert R. Beck; *Divine Revolution: Salvation & Liberation in Catholic Thought* by Dean Brackley; *Compassionate Ministry: Theological Foundations* by Bryan P. Stone; *Fire and Water: Basic Issues in Asian Buddhism & Christianity* by Aloysius Pieris; *The Intercultural Challenge of Raimon Panikkar* (edited by Joseph Prabhu); *Jesus and the Other Names: Christian Mission & Global Responsibility* by Paul F. Knitter; *The Missionary Movement in Christian History: Studies in the Transmission of Faith* by Andrew F. Walls.

The History of Vatican II 1959–1965 (edited by Giuseppe Alberigo and Joseph Komonchak; translated by Matthew O'Connell) will be the definitive history of this pivotal event, from conception to conclusion. *The History* (in five volumes to be published over the next five years in editions in French, Spanish, Italian, German, and Portuguese as well as English) is written by an international group of experts under the general editorship of two of the world's leading church historians. This work will become an indispensable reference work for the most important event in the Roman Catholic Church in the 20th Century.

Forthcoming volumes in *The History of Vatican II: 1959–1965* include: 1997 Volume 2, *The First Period and First Intersession: Foundations;* 1998 Volume 3, *The Second Period and Second Intersession: Maturity;* 1999 Volume 4, *The Third Period and Third Intersession: Communion;* 2000 Volume 5, *The Fourth Period and Close of Vatican II: Transition.*

Orbis Books is distributed by Westminster/John Knox Press

Query letters and SASEs should be directed to:

Robert Ellsberg, Editor in Chief

PAULIST PRESS

997 Macarthur Boulevard
Mahwah, NJ 07430
201-825-7300
paulistp@usa.pipeline.com (e-mail)

Paulist Press publishes Roman Catholic as well as ecumenical titles in Bible study, biography, women's studies, spirituality, current issues, self-help and personal growth, Catholicism, liturgy, theology, philosophy, ethics, Jewish-Christian relations, world religions, youth ministry, and education, along with a selected list in fiction. The Paulist list ranges from popularly oriented traditionalist works to provocative frontiers of religious thought. In addition to books, Paulist offers a video and audio line.

Paulist Press (founded in 1866) is a publishing division of the Missionary Society of St. Paul the Apostle.

On the Paulist list: *Accepting the Troll Underneath the Bridge: Overcoming Our Self-Doubts* by Terry D. Cooper; *Christian Spirituality: Themes from the Tradition* by Lawrence S. Cunningham and Keith J. Egan; *Discovering Our Jewish Roots: A Simple Guide to Judiasm* by Anna Marie Erst; *Letting Go of Mother: How We Mesh with Our Mothers, What Works, What We Must Leave Behind* by James M. McMahon; *An Untimely Loss: A Passage to the Gentle Side of Grief* by Linda Zelenka; *Youth Ministry That Works: Practical Ideas for Working with Young People* by George Boran; *Along Your Desert Journey* by Robert M. Hamma; *My Life, My Choices: Key Issues for Young Adults* by Mary Ann Burkley Wojno; *The Parish in Catholic Tradition: History, Theology and Canon Law* by James A. Coriden; *People, Promise and Community: A Practical Guide to Creating and Sustaining Small Communities of Faith* by Harriet Burke, Bill Edens, Ken Maguire, and Maggie Stapp; *Understanding Christian Spirituality* by Michael Downey; *When Christians Gather: Issues in the Celebration of Eucharist* by Neil Darragh; *The Lawyer's Calling: Christian Faith and Legal Practice* by Joseph G. Allegretti.

Paulist Press distributes its own list and catalogues selected titles from other publishing houses.

Query letters and SASEs should be directed to:

Donald Brophy, Managing Editor

Pilgrim Press
United Church Press

700 Prospect Avenue East
Cleveland, OH 44115-1100
216-736-3700
fax: 216-736-3703
pilgrim@ucc.org (Pilgrim Press e-mail)
ucpress@ucc.org (United Church Press e-mail)

Pilgrim publishes general trade books (with cultural or religious themes), religious books, and curriculum aids. Pilgrim Press (founded in 1957) is the book-publishing banner of the publishing wing of the United Church of Christ. United Church Press is a Pilgrim imprint geared primarily toward the inspirational readership.

Pilgrim's trade motto: Publishing books that make a difference, that take a stand, that have the potential to change the way we are in the world. The Pilgrim Press and United Church Press—meaningful reading for today and tomorrow.

The house has a tradition of publishing books and other resources that challenge, encourage, and inspire, crafted in accordance with fine standards of content, design, and production.

Indicative of the Pilgrim list: *Reconciliation: The Ubuntu Theology of Desmond Tutu* by Michael Battle; *Defying the Darkness: Gay Theology in the Shadows* by J. Michael Clark; *To Liberate and Redeem: Moral Reflections on the Biblical Narrative* by Edward Leroy Long, Jr.; *Capital Punishment: A Reader* (edited by Glen H. Stassen); *The Face of a Man/The Face of a Woman: Images from Around the World* (two books of black-and-white photographs and prose by Ethan Hubbard); *Island Lighthouse Inn: A Chronicle* by Jeffrey Burke; *Water Bugs and Dragonflies: Explaining Death to Young Children* by Doris Stickney (illustrated by Gloria Claudia Ortiz).

The Pilgrim Library of World Religions is a series designed for both classroom and general use, written by authorities in each tradition. The series addresses how five great world religions—Judaism, Hinduism, Buddhism, Islam, and Christianity—approach a certain critical issue. Title: *God* (edited by Jacob Neusner). Projected titles include: *Evil and Suffering*; *Women, Death and Afterlife*; *Sacred Texts and Authority*. A representative title from Pilgrim Library of Ethics: *Abortion: A Reader* (edited by Lloyd Steffen).

United Church Press titles: *They Like to Never Quit Praisin' God: The Role of Celebration in Preaching* by Frank A. Thomas; *Writing with Light: Meditations for Caregivers in Word and Image* by Robert Merrill Eddy and Kathy Wonson Eddy; *My Rose: An African American Mother's Story of AIDS* by Geneva Bell; *I Witness: Dramatic Monologues from Hebrew Scriptures* by Ray Kostulias.

United Church Press has introduced a delightful and meaningful set of picture books for young children. The Word and Picture Books are the perfect "first Bible" books for infants and toddlers up to 4 years of age. Titles: *Come to Jesus*; *Jesus, a Special Baby*; *Jesus Goes Fishing*; *Breakfast at the Lake*; *Loving Shepherd*; *The First Church.*

Pilgrim/United Church Press oversees its own distribution.

Query letters and SASEs should be directed to:

Timothy Staveteig, Senior Editor

Lynne M. Deming, Publisher

Sidney Fowler, Curriculum Editor

QUESTAR PUBLISHERS
MULTNOMAH BOOKS

305 West Adams
P.O. Box 1720
Sisters, OR 97759
541-549-1144

Questar and Multnomah cover the major categories of Christian trade publishing in general nonfiction and fiction. The Questar list offers a Christian perspective for titles in self-awareness and improvement, spirituality, theology, and popular fiction.

Multnomah sets a contemporary tone with its list of works on Christian life and the family, inspirational and devotional items, gifts, and children's titles. Together, Questar and Multnomah share overlapping topical interests and present distinct, complementary approaches to Christian publishing.

QUESTAR PUBLISHERS

Questar features programs in Christian-oriented self-awareness and improvement, popular spirituality and theology, and selected works of fiction. Questar Publishers (founded in 1987) initially gained recognition for its Gold'n'Honey line of books for children. The house was started by Donald C. Jacobson, previously of Multnomah Press (which is now part of the Questar publishing family; see subentry below).

Frontlist Questar titles: *In the Company of Friends* by Brenda Hunter, Ph.D. and Holly Larson; *Designing a Woman's Life Bible Study* by Judith Couchman; *It Takes Commitment* by Chad Hennings (of the Dallas Cowboys); *You Can Lead a Bible Discussion Group* by Dr. Terry Powell. From the Questar backlist: *The Beginner's Bible* by Karen Henley.

Children's books (including Gold'n'Honey favorites): *Once Upon a Parable* by Mack Thomas (illustrated by Hilber Nelson); *The Nursery Bible Bedtime Book* by L. J. Sattgast (illustrated by Trish Tenud); *Songs and Rhymes for Wiggle Worms* by Mary Hollingsworth.

The Questar list is handled by the house's personal account representatives; titles can also be ordered through Spring Arbor.

MULTNOMAH BOOKS

Multnomah produces books and audiocassettes with a contemporary verve in Christian living and family enrichment, as well as lines of devotional titles, gift books, and children's books. Multnomah Books (now part of Questar) was founded in 1969 as Multnomah Press, a division of Multnomah School of the Bible.

Representative of the Multnomah list: *Butterworth Gets His Life Together* by Bill Butterworth; *The Cure for a Troubled Heart* by Ron Mehl; *Teaching to Change Lives* by Howard G. Hendricks; *Reaching the Heart of Your Teen* by Gary and Ann Marie Ezzo.

Multnomah offers a strong list of fiction, including contemporary and historical novels, romances, sagas, and thrillers. From Multnomah fiction: *Quiet Thunder* by Al Lacy (Book 6 of the Journeys of the Stranger series); *The President* by Parker Hudson; *Stonehaven* by Amanda MacLean; *The Call of the Green Bird* by Alberta Hawse.

Multnomah children's titles: *The Rhyme Bible: Read-Aloud Stories from the Old and New Testament* by L. J. Sattgast (illustrated by Toni Goff); *Quiet Times with God* by Mack Thomas (illustrated by Terri Steiger); *My Little Book of Big Bible Promises* by L. J. Sattgast (illustrated by Nan Brooks).

Query letters and SASEs should be directed to the **Editorial Department** or to:

Don Jacobson, President

Linda Bennett, Acquisitions

REGAL BOOKS

(See Gospel Light Publications)

ST. ANTHONY MESSENGER PRESS AND FRANCISCAN COMMUNICATIONS

1615 Republic Street
Cincinnati, OH 45210
513-241-5615
http://www.americancatholic.org (World Wide Web)

Areas of St. Anthony Messenger publishing interest include Catholic identity, family life, morality and ethics, parish ministry, pastoral ministry, prayer helps, sacraments, saints and Christian heroes, scripture, seasonal favorites, small-group resources, spirituality for every day, and youth ministry. The house produces books (hardcover and paperback, many in economically priced editions), magazines, audiotapes, and videocassettes as well as educational programs.

St. Anthony Messenger Press (founded in 1970) and Franciscan Communications publishes Catholic religious works and resources for parishes, schools, and individuals.

Titles from St. Anthony Messenger: *Jesus of the Gospels: Teacher, Storyteller, Friend, Messiah* by Arthur E. Zannoni; *Reading the Gospels with the Church: From Christmas Through Easter* by Raymond E. Brown, S.S.; *Jesus' Plan for a New World: The Sermon on the Mount* by Richard Rohr, O.F.M. with John Bookser Feister; *Lights: Revelations of God's Goodness* by Jack Wintz, O.F.M.; *Following Francis of Assisi: A Spirituality for Daily Living* by Patti Normile; *Journeys into Matthew: 18 Lessons of Exploration and Discovery* by Raymond Apicella; *Marriage and the Spirituality of Intimacy* by Leif Kehrwald; *God Is Close to the Brokenhearted: Good News for Those Who Are Depressed* by Rachael Callahan, C.S.C. and Rea McDonnell, S.S.N.D.

A special St. Anthony Messenger Press project is *A Retreat with . . .* , a series (edited by Gloria Hutchinson) that features the words of such historical figures as Thomas Merton, Gerard Manley Hopkins, and Hildegard of Bingen. Did you ever wonder what it would be like to make a retreat with some great holy person from history? Authors weave the mentor's own words into seven days of prayer, dialog, and deepening acquaintance. Selected titles: *A Retreat with Pope John XXIII: Opening the Windows to Wisdom* by Alfred McBride, O.Praem.; *A Retreat with Francis de Sales, Jane de Chantal and Axlred of Rievaulx: Befriending Each Other in God* by Wendy M. Wright; *A Retreat with Francis and Clare of Assisi: Following Our Pilgrim Hearts* by Murray Bodo, O.F.M. and Susan Saint Sing; *Retreat with Thomas Merton: Becoming Who We Are* by Antony Padovano.

St. Anthony Messenger Press also offers music CDs, computer software, videos and audiocassettes.

St. Anthony Messenger Press handles its own distribution.

Query letters and SASEs should be directed to:

Barbara Beckwith, Managing Editor

SCRIPTURE PRESS PUBLICATIONS/VICTOR BOOKS

(See Chariot/Victor Publishing)

SHAMBHALA PUBLICATIONS

Horticultural Hall
300 Massachusetts Avenue
Boston, MA 02115-4544
617-424-0030

Shambhala publishes hardcover and paperback titles in creativity, philosophy, psychology, medical arts and healing, mythology, folklore, religion, art, literature, cooking, martial arts, and cultural studies. Shambhala generally issues a modest list of new titles each year and tends a flourishing backlist; the house periodically updates some of its perennial sellers in revised editions.

The house packages a number of distinct lines including gift editions and special-interest imprints. Shambhala Dragon Editions accents the sacred teachings of Asian masters. Shambhala Centaur Editions offers classics of world literature in small-sized gift editions. The New Science Library concentrates on titles relating to science, technology, and the environment. Shambhala copublishes C. G. Jung Foundation Books with the C. G. Jung Foundation for Analytical Psychology. Shambhala Redstone Editions are fine boxed sets comprising books, postcards, games, art objects, and fold-outs. Shambhala Lion Editions are spoken-word audiotape cassette presentations. Little Barefoot Books features children's literature (much of it classic) in miniature illustrated editions.

Shambhala Publications is a foremost representative of the wave of publishers specializing in the arena of contemporary globalized spiritual and cultural interest. Since Shambhala's inception (the house was founded in 1969), the field has blossomed into a still-burgeoning readership, as underscored by the many smaller independent presses and large corporate houses that tend this market.

From Shambhala: *The Healing Power of Mind: Simple Meditation Exercises for Health, Well-Being, and Enlightenment* by Tulku Thondup; *The Eye of Spirit: An Integral Vision for a World Gone Slightly Mad* by Ken Wilber; *A Mapmaker's Dream: The Meditations of Fra Mauro, Cartographer to the Court of Venice* by James Cowan; *The Mysticism of Sound and Music: The Sufi Teaching of Hazrat Inayat Khan* by Hazrat Inayat Khan; *Subtle Sound: The Zen Teachings of Maurine Stuart* (edited by Roko Sherry Chayat); *The Posture of Meditation: A Practical Guide for Meditators of All Traditions* by Will Johnson; *The Art of the Warrior: Leadership and Strategy from the Chinese Military Classics* (translated by Ralph D. Sawyer); *The Kabbalah of Money: Insights on Livelihood, Business, and All Forms of Economic Behavior* by Rabbi Nilton Bonder.

Features from Shambhala's strong backlist: *Hard Travel to Sacred Places* by Rudolph Wurlitzer; *The Beat Book: Poems and Fiction from the Beat Generation* (compiled by Anne Waldman; foreword by Allen Ginsberg); *A Brief History of*

Everything by Ken Wilber; *The Erotic Spirit: An Anthology of Poems of Sensuality, Love, and Longing* (edited by Sam Hamill); *Spiritual Path, Sacred Place: Myth, Ritual, and Meaning in Architecture* by Thomas Barrie; *Awakening the Hidden Storyteller: How to Build a Storytelling Tradition in Your Family* by Robin Moore; *The Female Ancestors of Christ* by Ann Belford Ulanov; *The Forbidden Self: Symbolic Incest and the Journey Within* by John Perkins; *Same-Sex Love: And the Path to Wholeness* (edited by Robert H. Hopke, Karen Lofthus Carrington, and Scott Wirth).

Shambhala Redstone Editions offers special boxed: *José Guadalupe Posada: Mexican Popular Prints* (edited by Julian Rothstein); *A Gambling Box* (edited by Kate Pullinger); *Surrealist Games* (compiled by Alistair Brotchie; edited by Mel Gooding).

Little Barefoot titles include: *The Outlandish Adventures of Orpheus and the Underworld* by Paul Newham (illustrations by Elaine Cox); *The World Is Round* by Gertrude Stein (illustrations by Roberta Arenson); *The Brownies' Merry Adventures* by Palmer Cox (illustrated by the author).

Shambhala distributes to the trade via Random House. Shambhala services individual and special orders through its own house fulfillment department.

Query letters and SASEs should be directed to:

Nandini Lee, Editorial Assistant

Emily Hilburn Sell, Editor

Samuel Bercholz, President and Editor-in-Chief

SIGNATURE BOOKS

564 West 400 North
Salt Lake City, UT 84116-3411
801-531-1483
fax: 801-531-1488
800-356-5687

The Signature list emphasizes contemporary literature as well as scholarly works relevant to the Intermountain West. Signature Books (established in 1981) publishes subjects that range from outlaw biographies to speculative theology, from demographics to humor. In addition to a wide range of nonfiction, Signature publishes novels and collections of poetry. The common objective of the selections on Signature's roster is to provide alternatives to the institutional agendas that underlie many of the publications in the region.

Indicative of Signature nonfiction: *Canyon Interludes: Between White Water and Red Rock* by Paul W. Rea; *Mahonri Young: His Life and Art* by Thomas E. Toone; *God the Mother and Other Theological Essays* by Janice Merrill Allred; *Matters of Conscience: Conversations with Sterling M. McMurrin* by L. Jackson Newell; *The Essential James E. Talmage* (edited by James Harris; Classics in Mormon Thought series); *Digging in Cumorah: Reclaiming Book of Mormon Narrative* by Mark D. Thomas; *San Bernardino: The Rise and Fall of a California Community* by Edward

Leo Lyman; *The Mormon Hierarchy: Extensions of Power* by D. Michael Quinn; *Tending the Garden: Essays on Mormon Literature* (edited by Eugene England and Lavina Fielding Anderson).

Representative of Signature fiction and popular literature: *Special Living Lessons for Relief Society by Sister Fonda AlaMode* (humor) by Laurie Johnson; *Love Chains* (stories) by Margaret Blair Young; *My New Life* (memoirs) by Ron Molen; *Aspen Marooney* (fiction) by Levi S. Peterson; *on keeping things small* (poetry) by Marilyn Bushman-Carlton; *Secrets Keep: A Novel* (mystery thriller) by Linda Sillitoe.

Signature Publications oversees distribution of its titles via in-house ordering services and a national network of wholesalers.

Signature Books does not accept unsolicited manuscripts. Please address all written queries to Gary J. Bergera. Query letters and SASEs should be directed to:

Gary J. Bergera, Director

SWEDENBORG PUBLISHING HOUSE

P.O. Box 549
West Chester, PA 19381-0549
610-430-3222
fax: 610-430-7982
800-355-3222
http://www.swedenborg.com (World Wide Web)

Swedenborg Publishing produces books and videos relating to the theological works and insights of Emanuel Swedenborg (1688–1772), as well as a line of Swedenborg's complete theological works. Under the Chrysalis Books aegis, the house publishes the trade series Chrysalis Reader, which features stories, essays, poetry, and art that explores themes of spiritual development. Swedenborg Publishing House is part of Swedenborg Foundation, Inc. (founded in 1849).

Swedenborg publications for the general religious trade (under the Chrysalis imprint): *Conversations with Angels: What Swedenborg Heard in Heaven* (edited by Leonard Fox and Donald L. Rose; translated by David Gladish and Jonathan Rose). The Chrysalis Reader series, edited by Carol Lawson, features Swedenborgian thought alongside other spiritual traditions. Releases include: *The Power of Play: New Visions of Creativity* (an anthology of original stories, poetry, and essays with the theme of the power inherent in the experience of play). The Monograph series features *Swedenborg, Buddha of the North* by D. T. Suzuki.

New Translations series titles, such as *The Last Judgment in Retrospect* by Emanuel Swedenborg (edited and translated by George F. Dole), reflect the publisher's commitment to making Swedenborg readily accessible to today's readers.

Query letters and SASEs should be directed to:

Mary Lou Bertucci, Editor

Jeremy P. Tarcher, Inc.

(See listing under Putnam Berkley Publishing Group in directory of United States book publishers)

Triumph Books

(See Liguori Publications)

Tyndale House Publishers

351 Executive Drive
P.O. Box 80
Wheaton, IL 60189
630-668-8300
fax: 630-668-8905

Tyndale offers a comprehensive program in Christian living, devotional, inspirational, and general nonfiction, from a nondenominational evangelical perspective. Tyndale publishing interest also encompasses religious fiction. The house also offers a strong line of Bibles. Tyndale House Publishers (founded in 1962) produces hardcover, trade paperback, and mass-market paperback originals as well as reprints. Tyndale also catalogs audio and video products.

From Tyndale: *Sons of the Father: Healing the Father-Wound in Men Today* by Gordon Dalbey; *Walking with the Savior* by Max Lucado; *Men Read Newspapers, Not Minds . . . and Other Things I Wish I'd Known When I First Married* by Sandra P. Aldrich; *SoulShaping: Taking Care of Your Spiritual Life* by Douglas J. Rumford; *Hold Me Close* and *Keep Me Faithful* by Ruth Harms Calkin (prayer-poems); *365 Bible Promises for Hurting People* by Alice Chapin; *Experiencing God Together* by David Stoop, Ph.D.; *The Best Things Ever Said About Parenting* by Bill and Nancie Carmichael.

In a publishing partnership with the American Association of Christian Counselors, Tyndale offers books written by leading Christian counselors that integrate counseling principles and biblical theology as they offer authoritative analysis and research for the Professional Counseling Library. Titles: *Counseling Children Through the World of Play* by Daniel Sweeney, Ph.D.; *Psychology, Theology, and Spirituality in Christian Counseling* by Mark R. McMinn; *Counseling Through the Maze of Divorce* by George Ohlschlager; *Treating Sex Offenders* by Daniel Henderson; *Brief Counseling* by Gary J. Oliver; *Treating Victims of Sexual Abuse* by Diane Langberg.

Tyndale fiction includes mainstream novels as well as a number of inspirational romance series, including works set in Revolutionary War and Civil War milieus. The house is interested in Evangelical Christian–theme romance in other historical periods (including Regency), as well as those with a humorous twist.

The Tyndale program of books for children and young adults is in a transitional phase; currently the house is not interested in fiction geared for this younger age group.

Tyndale House oversees its own distribution.

Tyndale does not accept unsolicited manuscripts. For manuscript submissions, send SASE to the Manuscript Review Committee requesting a copy of the committee's writer's guidelines—and query first.

Query letters and SASEs should be directed to the **Editorial Department** or to:

Karen Ball, Senior Editor

UNION OF AMERICAN HEBREW CONGREGATIONS/UAHC PRESS
838 Fifth Avenue
New York, NY 10021-7064
212-249-0100

Union of American Hebrew Congregations/UAHC Press publishes in the areas of religion (Jewish), Reform Judaism, textbooks, audiovisual materials, social action, biography, and ceremonies. In trade categories, UAHC Press accents juvenile fiction and adult nonfiction books as well as titles in basic Judaism and inspirational works. The house catalogs books, audiocassettes, videotapes, and multimedia products.

The UAHC Press provides the highest quality in religious educational materials and has done so for well over a hundred years. The publications of the press are suitable for all ages, from preschool through adult, for use in both the classroom and at home. The publishers are committed to providing their readers with the foremost in materials and service, to be a continuing resource for books, publications, audiocassettes, videotapes, and multimedia.

Founded in 1873, UAHC Press is a division of Union of American Hebrew Congregations. The UAHC Press publishing program includes the *Reform Judaism* magazine.

Indicative of UAHC Press interest: *Judaism and Spiritual Ethics* by Niles E. Goldstein and Steven S. Mason; *Pirke Avot: A Modern Commentary on Jewish Ethics* (edited and translated by Leonard Kravitz and Kerry M. Olitzky); *The Book of the Jewish Year* by Stephen M. Wylen; *America: The Jewish Experience* by Sondra Leiman; *The Jewish Condition: Essays on Contemporary Judaism Honoring Rabbi Alexander M. Schindler* (edited by Alan Hirt-Manheimer); *A Congregation of Learners: Transforming the Synagogue into a Learning Community* by Isa Aron, Sara Lee, and Seymour Rossel.

Children's titles from UAHC: *Our Land of Israel* by Chaya M. Burstein (illustrated by the author); *Listen to the Trees: Jews and the Earth* by Molly Cone (illustrated by Roy Doty); *A Torah Commentary for Our Times* by Harvey J. Fields (illustrated by Gloria Carmi); *Sefer Ha-Aggadah: The Book of Legends for Young Readers* by

Seymour Rossel (illustrated by Judy Dick); *The Matzoh Ball Fairy* by Carla Heymsfeld (illustrated by Vlad Guzner).

UAHC Press handles its own distribution.

Query letters and SASEs should be directed to:

Aron Hirt-Manheimer, Acquisitions Editor, Trade

David Kasakove, UAHC Education Department
Textbooks, preschool through adult.

VEDANTA PRESS

1946 Vedanta Place
Hollywood, CA 90068-3996
213-465-7114
fax: 213-465-9568
800-816-2242
info@vedanta.org (e-mail)
http://www.vedanta.org (World Wide Web)

Vedanta publishing interest includes meditation, religions and philosophies, women's studies, devotional songs and poetry, biography, history, myth, and children's books. In addition to its list of titles imported from the East (primarily from Indian publishers), Vedanta's program embraces works of Western origin. The publisher catalogs titles from other publishers and also sells audiotapes and videotapes.

The house publishes books on the philosophy of Vedanta, with an aim to engage a wide variety of temperaments, using a broad spectrum of methods, in order to attain the realization of each individual personality's divinity within. Vedanta Press (founded in 1947) is a subsidiary of the Vedanta Society of Southern California.

Titles from the press: *Seeing God Everywhere: A Practical Guide to Spiritual Living* by Swami Shraddhananda; *Values: The Key to a Meaningful Life* (an anthology of articles printed in the magazine *Vedanta Kesari*); *Six Lighted Windows: Memories of Swamis in the West* by Swami Yogeshananda; *Women Saints: East and West* (edited by Swami Ghanananda and Sir John Stewart-Wallace); *Encountering God: A Spiritual Journey from Bozeman to Banares* by Diana Dick; *Learning the Sanskrit Alphabet* by Thomas Egenes.

Vedanta publishes many classic Vedic works in a variety of editions and translations. Among them: *Bhagavad Gita: The Song of God* (translated by Swami Prabhavananda and Christopher Isherwood; introduction by Aldous Huxley).

Vedanta Press handles its own distribution.

Vedanta's books originate in house, though the publisher is open to considering additional projects that may fall within its program. Vedanta does not wish to receive unsolicited manuscripts. Query letters and SASEs should be directed to:

Bob Adjemian, Manager

VICTOR BOOKS
(See Chariot/Victor Publishing)

WATERBROOK PRESS
220 Pine Street, Suite 106
Sisters, OR 97759
541-549-0773

WaterBrook Press publishes works with a Christian outlook in such categories as inspiration, fiction, marriage and family, popular theology, and practical Bible study.

WaterBrook Press is a new venture; the house is an autonomous subsidiary of Bantam Doubleday Dell Publishing Group (BDD), which is part of the German-based communications conglomerate Bertelsmann Publishing Group International.

BDD was already a Christian-market presence with its Doubleday religious imprint and through some of its Bantam hardcover and paperback inspiration/spirituality lines. Bertelsmann has success with its evangelical-Christian–oriented Crossings Book Club (initiated in 1993).

Dan Rich, WaterBrook head, was previously president and publisher at Questar (and has stints in at Word as well as Thomas Nelson). Former Questar comrades Steve Cobb and Doug Gabbert are onboard as WaterBrook vice presidents, as is editor Lisa Bergren.

Rich anticipates major growth ahead in the Christian book market, and foresees the possibility of increased mutual market penetration by all partners of the BDD operation in both religious and mainstream sectors.

WaterBrook Press has its own field sales force and tends the Christian Booksellers Association (CBA) market; trade distribution is through Bantam Doubleday Dell Publishing Group.

Query letters and SASEs should be directed to:

Thomas Womack, Senior Editor

Lisa Bergren, Executive Editor for Fiction

SAMUEL WEISER, INC.
P.O. Box 612
York Beach, ME 03910-0612
207-363-4393
fax: 207-363-5799
weiserbooks@ichange.com (e-mail)

Areas of Weiser publishing interest include self-transformation, alternative healing methods, meditation, metaphysics, consciousness, magic, astrology, tarot, astral projection, Kabbalah, earth religions, oriental philosophy and religions, Buddhism, t'ai chi, healing, and Tibetan studies.

The publisher has observed the many paths that lead to personal transformation, and strives to publish books to help many different people find the path that is right for them. Samuel Weiser, Inc. specializes in books relating to all facets of the secret and hidden teachings worldwide.

Frontlist Weiser titles characteristically revamp age-old themes into new and vibrant works of contemporary sensibility. In addition to new titles, Weiser publishes classic references and tracts in reprint; Weiser also offers a particularly distinguished selection of titles pertinent to the life and works of Aleister Crowley as well as a strong line of Gurdjieff studies. The house publishes in hardcover and paperback editions and maintains a thriving backlist. Samuel Weiser, Inc. was founded in 1955.

Representative Weiser titles: *The Sacred Magic of the Angels* by David Goddard; *Mithras: Mysteries and Initiation Rediscovered* by D. Jason Cooper; *The Magic Thread: Astrological Chart Interpretation Using Depth Psychology* by Richard Idemon; *Prana: The Secret of Yogic Healing* by Atreya; *Seasons of the Sun: Celebrations, Festivals & Observances* by Patricia Telesco; *Ojise: Messenger of the Yoruba Tradition* by Baba Ifa Karade; *Shaolin Nei Jin Qi Gong: Ancient Healing in the Modern World* by Peter Fenton, Ph.D.; *The Light of the Spirit: An Introductory Guide* by Mary Bassano; *Priestess: Woman as Sacred Celebrant* by Pamela Eakins, Ph.D.; *Handbook of T'ai Chi Ch'uan Exercises* by Zhang Fuxing; *Practical Solitary Magic* by Nancy B. Watson.

Samuel Weiser handles its own distribution and distributes selected titles from other houses; the Weiser distribution catalog lists titles from over 200 publishers. Weiser as well utilizes the services of several national trade distributors.

Query letters and SASEs should be directed to:

Eliot Stearns, Editor

WESTMINSTER/JOHN KNOX PRESS

100 Witherspoon Street
Louisville, KY 40202-1396
502-569-5000

Westminster/John Knox publishes general-interest religious trade books as well as academic and professional works in biblical studies, theology, philosophy, ethics, history, archaeology, personal growth, and pastoral counseling. Among Westminster/John Knox series are Literary Currents in Biblical Interpretation, Family Living in Pastoral Perspective, Gender and the Biblical Tradition, and The Presbyterian Presence: The Twentieth-Century Experience.

Westminster/John Knox Press represents the publications unit of the Presbyterian Church (USA). The house unites the former independents, Westminster Press and John Knox Press, which were originally founded as one entity in 1838, then separated into distinct enterprises, and again merged as W/JK following the reunion of the Northern and Southern Presbyterian Churches in 1983.

Selected titles from Westminster/John Knox: *The Religion Factor: An Introduction to How Religion Matters* (edited by William Scott Green and Jacob Neusner); *Westminster Dictionary of Theological Terms* by Donald K. McKim; *God's Self-Confident Daughters: Early Christianity and the Liberation of Women* by Anne Jensen (translated by O. C. Dean, Jr.); *Money Matters: Personal Giving in American Churches* by Dean R. Hoge, Charles Zech, Patrick McNamara, and Michael J. Donahue; *Redeeming Men: Religion and Masculinities* (edited by Stephen B. Boyd, W. Merle Longwood, and Mark W. Muesse); *New Testament Ethics: The Legacies of Jesus and Paul* by Frank J. Matera; *Portraits of Paul: An Archaeology of Ancient Personality* by Bruce J. Malina and Jerome H. Neyrey; *The Victorious Christ: A Study of the Book of Revelation* by C. Freeman Sleeper.

W/JK's Studies in the Family, Religion, & Culture series offers informed and responsible analyses of the state of the American family from a religious perspective, and provides practical assistance for the family's revitalization. Titles: *For the Love of Children: Genetic Technology and the Future of the Family* by Ted Peters; *Religion, Feminism, and the Family* (edited by Anne Carr and Mary Steward Van Leeuwen); *Faith Traditions and the Family* (edited by Phyllis D. Airhart and Margaret Lamberts Bendroth).

Westminster/John Knox distributes its list through Spring Arbor. The house also represents titles from other publishers, including Orbis Books, Pilgrim Press, Saint Andrew Press of Scotland, and Presbyterian Publishing Corporation.

Query letters and SASEs should be directed to:

Stephanie Egnotovich, Managing Editor

WISDOM PUBLICATIONS

199 Elm Street
Somerville, MA 02144
617-536-3358

Wisdom Publications centers on Buddhism, Tibet, and related East–West themes. The house offers books and tapes, as well as the journal *Tricycle: The Buddhist Review.* Wisdom Publications (founded in 1975) was initiated by Lama Thubten Yeshe around the time he established the international Foundation for the Preservation of the Mahayana Tradition (FMPT).

Wisdom Publications, a not-for-profit publisher, is dedicated to making available authentic Buddhist works for the benefit of all. The press publishes translations of the sutras and tantras, commentaries and teachings of past and contemporary Buddhist masters, and original works by the world's leading Buddhist scholars.

Wisdom titles are published in appreciation of Buddhism as a living philosophy and with the commitment to preserve and transmit important works from all the major Buddhist traditions. Wisdom products are distributed worldwide and have been translated into a dozen foreign languages.

Wisdom is the exclusive North American distributor of books published by the Pali Text Society of London, founded in 1881 as a resource for those interested in exploring the wisdom of the Pali scriptures, the sacred texts of Theravadan Buddhism.

On the Wisdom list: *The Good Heart: A Buddhist Perspective on the Teachings of Jesus* by The Dalai Lama (edited by Robert Kiely); *Mindfulness with Breathing: A Manual for Serious Beginners* by Ajahn Buddhadasa Bhikkhu (translated and edited by Venerable Santikaro Bhikkhu); *Luminous Mind: The Way of the Buddha* by Kala Rinpoche; *Perfect Conduct: Ascertaining the Three Vows* by Ngari Panchen (translated and annotated by Khenpo Gyurme Samdrub and Sangye Khandro); *The Warrior Song of King Gesar* by Douglas J. Penick; *Meditative States in Tibetan Buddhism* by Lati Rinbochay and Denma Locho Rinbochay (edited and annotated by Leah Zahler; translated by Leah Zahler and Jeffrey Hopkins); *The First Discourse of the Buddha* by the Venerable Dr. Rewata Khamma.

Wisdom publishes the celebrated Tibetan Art Calendar, containing 13 full-color reproductions of the world's finest Indo-Tibetan Thangka paintings accompanied by detailed iconographical descriptions.

Wisdom highlight: *The World of Tibetan Buddhism: An Overview of Its Philosophy and Practice* by the Dalai Lama (translated by Geshe Thupten; foreword by Richard Gere).

Wisdom Publications handles its own distribution.

Query letters and SASEs should be directed to:

Timothy J. McNeill, Publisher

WORD PUBLISHING

1501 LBJ Freeway, Suite 650
Dallas, TX 75234
214-488-9673

Word Publishing offers a list with a predominantly nondenominational Christian orientation. Word's field of interest encompasses biography, inspirational and spiritual works, contemporary issues, fiction, counseling and psychology, love and marriage, divorce, men, women, parenting and family living, singles, youth, music, evangelical and the mission, theology and doctrine, and Bibles and biblical studies. Word also accents series such as Contemporary Christian Counseling, Word Biblical Commentary, WordSoft Bible Software, and Communicator's Commentary. Word Music specializes in songbooks, choral arrangements, and musical performance resources.

Word Publishing produces hardcovers and trade paperbacks, as well as audiotapes and videotapes, computer software, and educational products. Word Publishing (founded in 1951) is a unit of the NelsonWord Publishing Group, a Division of Thomas Nelson, Inc. Word was previously a subsidiary of Capital Cities/ABC Inc.

The publisher's intonation is essentially academic and professional. However, Word's bestselling crossover titles for the religious-trade and general audiences provide the house with a strong public presence.

Word Publishing's mission statement in part says: . . . The goal of Word Publishing is to enrich the lives of consumers through exemplification, life-application and communication of the Christian gospel through various media: by sustaining a position of enabling, servant leadership to the evangelical community, by adopting and maintaining a leadership position as a publisher to the broader fellowship of believers and would-be believers . . . From disillusioned seekers to serious believers, we have before us a diverse population looking for real answers that will enable them to live with hope and joy rather than fear and despair. Perhaps more so than ever in Word's history, our commitment is to reach these people with quality products that are relevant, innovative, and life-changing.

Nonfiction from Word: *Love Must Be Tough: New Hope for Families in Crisis* by Dr. James Dobson; *Love Is Always Right* by Josh McDowell and Norm Geisler; *In the Grip of Grace* by Max Lucado; *An Uncommon Friend: The Authorized Biography of Ruth Bell Graham* by Patricia Cornwell; *In the Face of God: The Dangers & Delights of Spiritual Intimacy* by Michael S. Horton; *The Invisible Hand: Do All Things Really Work for Good?* by R. C. Sproul; *Hope Again: When Life Hurts and Dreams Fade* by Charles R. Swindoll; *Counseling Youth in Crisis Resource* by John McDowell; *2001: On the Edge of Eternity* by Jack Van Impe; *The Book of Uncommon Prayer* (compiled by Connie and Daniel Pollock); *Who Was Jesus: A Jewish Christian Dialogue* by Paul Copan; *Making Love Last Forever* by Gary Smalley.

On the Word fiction list: *The Shadows of Crazy Mountain* (a Sam Dodd Western mystery) by H. L. Richardson; *Shiloh's Choice* by Lee Roddy; *Wings of a Dove* by Beverly Bush Smith; *Blood Ties* by Sigmund Brouwer.

Highlight from Word Bibles: *The Everyday Study Bible*. This Bible is packed with thousands of reference notes and includes 260 thematic articles that address current issues and the most important people and ideas in the Bible, an exclusive chain-reference system, and a daily study plan.

Word Kids! has a publishing profile for younger readers similar to that of the adult division, with many of the same authors appearing here. Among them: *Paw Paw Chuck's Big Ideas in the Bible* by Charles R. Swindoll; and the Cooper Kids Adventure Series by Frank Peretti. Word Kids! is undergoing reorganization, with some titles and lines switched and redefined under Thomas Nelson's Tommy Nelson imprint (please see entry for Thomas Nelson in this directory).

From WordSoft Bible Software: an advanced Scriptural study system (which incorporates, among other features, text in Greek and Hebrew); simplified Bible search tools and databases; dictionaries; several software versions of the Bible.

Word Publishing oversees its own distribution.

In accord with current acquisitions policy, Word Publishing does not consider unsolicited manuscripts or proposals. All query letters and SASEs should be directed to:

Lynn Wheeler, Assistant to the Vice President, Trade Publishing

WYNWOOD PRESS

(See Baker Book House)

YESHIVA UNIVERSITY PRESS

500 West 185th Street
New York, NY 10033
212-960-5400

Yeshiva University Press (founded in 1960) produces a select list that includes original academic works as well as titles of mainstream reader interest; the house also produces scholarly Judaica in reprint editions.

Representing the Yeshiva University list: *A Treasury of Sephardic Laws and Customs* by Herbert C. Dobrinsky; *Ashkenaz: The German Jewish Heritage* (edited by Gertrude Hirschler); *Faith After the Holocaust* by Eliezer Berkovits; *Jewish Woman in Jewish Law* by Moshe Meiselman; *Modern Medicine and Jewish Ethics* by Fred Rosner; *The Renaissance of the Torah Jew* by Saul Bernstein.

Books from Yeshiva University Press are distributed through KTAV Publishing House.

Query letters and SASEs should be directed to the editorial offices of **KTAV Publishing House** (please see entry for KTAV in this section of the directory).

ZONDERVAN PUBLISHING HOUSE

5300 Patterson Avenue SE
Grand Rapids, MI 49530
616-698-6900
fax: 616-698-3439 (fax)
http://www.zondervan.com (World Wide Web)

Zondervan produces nonfiction books that address contemporary issues in spirituality, counseling, inspirational novels, juveniles, humor, Bibles, and Bible study guides. As well as books, Zondervan has entries in the form of computer software, audiotape, and videotape. Zondervan Publishing House (founded in 1931) is among the most potent publishers specializing in evangelical Christian titles.

As the publisher notes: In the everyday commerce of speech, words should be selected as carefully as treasured jewels. The right word at the right time uplifts, inspires, corrects, and instructs. Since 1931, through the power of words, Zondervan Publishing House has brought positive and redemptive change into the lives of people worldwide. Zondervan publishes their 2,000 bestselling and award-winning Bibles, books, audio books, videos, software, multimedia, and gift products to promote biblical principles and to meet the needs of people.

Zondervan's public persona includes eye-catching bookseller floor displays, posters, advertising schedules, and tie-ins via other media outlets including programming on the Zondervan Radio Network. Zondervan authors are among the most enterprising in this area of publishing. Zondervan's HarperCollins connection (the house has been an editorially independent subsidiary of HarperCollins since 1988) makes for a brawny marketing arm, and Zondervan's readership and distribution is extraordinary.

From Zondervan: *Matthew* by David Bauer (The NIV Application Commentary series); *Preparing Yourself for the Next Life* by Rita Bennett; *After Your Child Divorces* by Marjorie Lee Chandler; *Open Your Life to God* by Wesley L. Duewel; *Kindness of God* by Ken Gire; *Caring and Campaigning* by Ray Johnston; *Wake Up Your Dreams* by Walt Kallestad; *The Spiritual Lives of the Great Composers* by Patrick Kavanaugh; *Our Character, Our Future, Reclaiming America's Moral Destiny* by Alan Keyes; *Breakfast for the Heart: Meditations to Nourish Your Soul* by Diane M. Komp, M.D.; *Music as Medicine: Deforia Lane's Life of Music, Healing, and Faith* by Deforia Lane and Rob Wilkins; *Mother in the Middle: Searching for Peace in the Mommy Wars* by Deborah Shaw Lewis and Charmaine Crouse Yoest; *Ten Golden Rules for Financial Success* by Gary Moore; *The Ten Commandments of the Workplace and How to Break Them Every Day* by Perry Pascarella; *The American Family: Discovering the Values That Make Us Strong* by Dan Quayle and Diane Medved; *Reclaiming the Urban Family: How to Mobilize the Church as a Family Training Center* by Dr. Willie Richardson; *Miracle Answers to Prayer* by Quin Sherrer; *God's Outrageous Claims* by Lee Strobel; *Long Ago and Far Away: Story Sermons for Children* by John Timmer; *How to Love a Black Woman* by Clarence Walker.

HarperCollins handles Zondervan's distribution to the book trade.

Zondervan asks that interested authors write to request submissions guidelines before submitting manuscripts or other material. Query letters and SASEs should be directed to:

Scott W. Bolinder, Publisher, Trade Books

David Lambert, Editor
Youth books and fiction.

Sandy Vander Zeicht, Editor
Self-help and other nonfiction trade books.

Canadian Publishers

Canadian Book Publishing and the Canadian Market

Greg Ioannou

Canadian and United States writers who are considering submitting inquiries to Canadian publishers should keep a few important points in mind. In most cases, Canadian book publishers are looking for material of Canadian interest. However, this does not mean they are not interested in queries from writers who reside in or are native to other countries.

Indeed, there is a rich current in the Canadian publishing stream that features the Canadian experience from outlander or expatriate perspectives. Canadian reader interests are also keyed into a number of broader market sectors, such as North American pop culture or British Commonwealth concerns.

Appropriate queries (see the listings for these publishers) will be considered. Keep in mind the markets as well as the mandates of each house.

Publishing in Canada is markedly different from the industry in the United States. A large percentage of Canadian-owned publishing houses are small- to medium-sized, with net sales that may seem low to those accustomed to the standards of the U.S. marketplace. (Remember, the English-language Canadian market is only one-tenth the size of the United States market.)

Canada *is* a separate market, and some writers are able to sell the Canadian rights to their books separately from the U.S. rights. Before you sign a contract for "North American rights," consider whether your book would likely sell enough copies in Canada that it would be of interest to a Canadian publisher.

Don't just blithely sell the Canadian rights to a hockey book or a biography of a Canadian celebrity (such as Faye Wray or Neil Young or Peter Jennings) to a U.S. publisher for the blanket "foreign rights" or "world English-language rights" rate—the Canadian rights alone may be worth more than the U.S. or rest of the world-wide rights are!

The Canadian government directly subsidizes the book industry to help ensure that Canadian writers get their works published domestically and to keep the national market from being overwhelmed by the publishing giants to the south. The government grant system makes possible a greater independence on the part of Canadian-owned houses, which comprise the creative heart of publishing in Canada.

Never send an unsolicited manuscript to a Canadian publisher. Many Canadian publishers will send them back unopened because of a court ruling that forced Doubleday Canada to pay a writer thousands of dollars in compensation for losing the only copy of an unsolicited manuscript. Send query letters only!

It is a nice touch for American writers to remember that Canada is *not* part of the United States, so Canadian publishers cannot use U.S. stamps to return anything you send them. Use International Reply Coupons (available at any post office) instead.

BANTAM DOUBLEDAY DELL
BANTAM BOOKS CANADA
DOUBLEDAY CANADA LIMITED
CORGI
DELL
SEAL

105 Bond Street
Toronto, ON M5B 1Y3
416-340-0777

This publishing operation is the corporate cousin to the New York firm Bantam Doubleday Dell. Bantam Books Canada releases a significant frontlist of hardcover editions; the house also produces a large number of trade paperbacks (originals as well as reprints) and mass-market paperback editions (mainly reprints). Doubleday Canada is primarily a hardcover operation. Doubleday produces a broad list of commercial and literary fiction, children's titles, and range of nonfiction categories, including politics, history, autobiography, current affairs, arts, sports, travel, and cookbooks. Doubleday Canada has a strong Canadian orientation, and emphasizes Canadian authors.

Corgi, Dell, and Seal concentrate on trade and mass-market paperbacks. These houses all publish a solid selection of works by Canadian writers (particularly the McClelland-Bantam line), as well as authors from throughout the British Commonwealth nations.

Bantam Doubleday Dell Canada, which also includes allied imprints McClelland-Bantam and Delacorte, inhabits a historic office building in the heart of downtown Toronto. The component divisions share interlocking ownership and operate virtually as a single editorial entity.

Representative of the list: *Women and Ghosts* by Alison Lurie; *The Modern Canoe* by Ted Bissland and Stephen Pellerin; *The Canadian Patient's Book of Rights* by Lorne Rozovsky; *Exposure* by Evelyn Anthony; *Dead Meat* by Philip Kerr; *An Imaginative Experience* by Mary Wesley; *A Spanish Lover* by Joanna Trollope.

Bantam Doubleday Dell Seal Books Canada handles its own Canadian distribution; United States distribution is through Bantam Doubleday Dell order-processing department.

Queries with SASEs only—Doubleday accepts no unsolicited manuscripts. Query letters and SASEs from United States writers should be directed to the **New York office of Bantam** (see Bantam Doubleday Dell in Directory of United States Publishers).

DOUGLAS & MCINTYRE PUBLISHERS

1615 Venables Street
Vancouver, BC V5L 2H1
604-254-7191

Toronto office:
585 Bloor Street West
2nd Floor
Toronto, ON M6G 1K5
416-537-2501

Douglas & McIntyre Publishers (founded in 1964) offers a publishing program with Canadian emphasis—often with a specifically British Columbian inflection. The house produces hardcover and paperback books in both fiction and nonfiction. Nonfiction areas of interest include native art, current affairs, history, travel, and nature studies. Douglas & McIntyre fiction tends toward literary works, serious popular fiction, and tales of mystery and suspense.

Nonfiction titles: *Haida Art* by George F. MacDonald; *Cold as Charity: The Truth Behind the High Cost of Giving* by Walter Stewart; *Politically Speaking* by Judy Rebick and Kiké Roach; *HeartSmart Chinese Cooking* by Stephen Wong and The Heart & Stroke Foundation of Canada; *Working Dollars: The VanCity Savings Story* by Herschel Hardin; *Mike Harcourt: A Measure of Defiance* by Michael Harcourt with Wayne Skene; *The Immortal Beaver: The World's Greatest Bush Plane* by Sean Rossiter; *Bishop's: The Cookbook* by John Bishop; *Back to the Front: An Accidental Historian Walks the Trenches of World War I* by Stephen O'Shea; *Toni Cavelti: A Jeweller's Life* by Max Wyman.

Fiction and literary works: *Bachelor Brothers' Bedside Companion* by Bill Richardson (illustrated by Rose Cowles); *eye wuz here: 30 women writers under 30* (edited by Shannon Cooley); *The Lesser Blessed* by Richard Van Camp; *Let the Drums Be Your Heart: New Native Voices* (edited by Joel T. Maki) *Local Colour: Writers Discovering Canada* (edited by Carol Martin); *A Story as Sharp as a Knife: An Introduction to Classical Haida Literature* by Robert Bringhurst; *Notes from the Century Before: A Journal from British Columbia* by Edward Hoagland (illustrations by Claire Van Vliet).

The **Greystone Books** imprint offers travel guides, one-day getaways, regional histories, sports books (especially hockey), and titles in hiking, camping, and outdoor recreation. Representative titles from Greystone: *Cowgirls* by Candace Savage; *British Columbia: A Natural History* by Richard Cannings and Sydney Cannings; *Cold War: The Amazing Canada–Soviet Hockey Series of 1972* by Roy MacSkimming; *Hockey the NHL Way: The Basics* by Sean Rossiter; *The Nature of Shorebirds: Nomads of the Wetlands* by Harry Thurston; *The Nature of Penguins: Birds of Distinction* by Jonathan Chester; *Orca: Visions of the Killer Whale* by Peter Knudtson; *Courting Saskatchewan: A Celebration of Winter Feasts, Summer Loves and Rising Brookies* by David Carpenter; *Day Trips from Vancouver* by Jack Christie; *Fishing in the West* by David Carpenter; *52 Weekend Activities Around Vancouver* by Sue Lebrecht and Judi Lees.

Douglas & McIntyre handles its own distribution, as well as purveying books from additional houses and institutions including Canadian Museum of Civilization, the Mountaineers, the New Press, Sierra Club Books, and Thames and Hudson.

DOUGLAS & MCINTYRE CHILDREN'S DIVISION

Within its children's division, Douglas & McIntyre offers several special imprints. Groundwood Press publishes titles for preschoolers through young adults. Earthcare Books is an environmental series for middle-grade readers, which includes *For the Birds*, written by Canadian novelist Margaret Atwood. First Discovery is a series of nature books for toddlers and early readers. Rounding out Douglas & McIntyre's juveniles list are fiction for young adults, picture books, the Walker imprint's nonfiction and picture books (some of which are targeted for appeal to the entire family), and Meadow Mouse paperbacks.

On the list: *So You Love to Draw: Every Kid's Guide to Becoming an Artist* by Michael Seary (illustrated by Michel Bisson); *Jade and Iron: Latin American Tales from Two Cultures* (translated by Hugh Hazelton; edited by Patricia Aldana; illustrated by Luís Garay); *A Completely Different Place* by Perry Nodelman (fiction for ages 10–13); *Mary Margaret's Tree* by Blair Drawson (picture book for ages 3–6); *Beaver the Tailor: A How-to Picture Book* by Lars Klinting (for ages 5–7); *The Rooster's Gift* by Pam Conrad (illustrated by Eric Beddows) (picture book for ages 4–8); *Steel Drums and Ice Skates* by Dirk Mclean (illustrated by Ho Che Anderson) (picture book for ages 6–9); *Sarah and the People of Sand River* by W. D. Valgardson (illustrated by Ian Wallace) (picture book for ages 5–9); *Enchantment in the Garden* by Shirley Hughes (ages 8 and up).

Query letters and SASEs should be directed to **Acquisitions Editor**; correspondence will be redirected in house. The Toronto office handles fiction and children's books; the rest of the Douglas & McIntyre list is issued from the Vancouver office.

FIREFLY BOOKS

3680 Victoria Park Avenue
Willowdale, ON M2H 3K1
416-499-8412
800-387-5085

Firefly produces trade nonfiction in areas that include popular biography, popular science, lifestyles, the natural world, hobbies and crafts, gardening, food, sports, recreation, and health.

Representative of the Firefly list: *The Houseplant Encyclopedia* by Ingrud Jantra and Ursula Kruger; *The Tomato Handbook* by Jennifer Bennett; *Classic Quilts* by Ruth McKentdry; *Summer Weekend Cookbook* by Jane Rodmell; *Wild Waters: Canoeing North America's Wilderness Rivers* by James Raffan; *The Secret Lives of Birds* by Pierre Gingras; *Nature Photography* (National Audubon Society Guide) by Tim Fitzharris; *In Quest of the Big Fish* by Henry Waszuk and Italo Labignan; *The Complete Breast Book: Everything You Need to Know About Breast Disease* by June Engel; *Mike Tyson: The Release of Power* by Reg Gutteridge and Norman Giller.

Firefly Books handles its own distribution.

Query letters and SASEs should be directed to:

Lionel Koffler, President

FITZHENRY & WHITESIDE LTD.

195 Allstate Parkway
Markham, ON L3R 4T8
905-477-9700

Fitzhenry & Whiteside Ltd. (founded in 1966) specializes in trade nonfiction, producing books in both English and French languages. Fitzhenry & Whiteside issues a line of fiction and literary works, much of it showing a Canadian inclination. The firm also offers a textbook list.

Fitzhenry & Whiteside nonfiction titles range through Canadian history, architecture, biography, gardening, art (including puzzles and how-to), native studies, nature, and guides to collectibles and antiques. Fitzhenry & Whiteside also publishes a limited list of children's books, with emphasis on books for preschoolers and young schoolchildren. The house typically publishes a small number of new seasonal titles.

From Fitzhenry & Whiteside nonfiction: *Trees in Canada* by John Laird Farrar; *Toronto in Art: 150 Years Through Artists' Eyes* by Edith Firth; *Dr. Alan Brown: Portrait of a Tyrant* by B. Foster Kingsmill; *Contemporary Canadian Architecture: The Mainstream and Beyond* by William Bernstein and Ruth Cawker; *100 Best Restaurants of Canada: Canada's National Restaurant Guide to Fine Dining* by John McCann.

Fitzhenry & Whiteside fiction and literature: *Tuppence Ha' Penny Is a Nickel* by Francis X. Atherton; *The Poetry of Lucy Maude Montgomery* (selected by Kevin McCabe and John Ferns); *The Fitzhenry & Whiteside Fireside Book of Canadian Christmas* (edited by Patrick Crean).

On the children's list: *Ladybug Garden* (written and illustrated by Celia Godkin); also of interest: *Understanding and Appreciating Your Child's Art* by Mia Johnson; *Celebrating Canadian Women* by Greta Hofmann Nemiroff.

Fitzhenry & Whiteside Ltd. distributes its own list and provides distribution services in Canada for a number of United States publishers.

Query letters and SASEs should be directed to:

Robert Fitzhenry, Chairman
Adult trade books.

Sharon Fitzhenry, President

HARLEQUIN ENTERPRISES LIMITED
WORLDWIDE LIBRARY

225 Duncan Mill Road
Don Mills, ON M3B 3K9
416-445-5860

The Harlequin Enterprises home base in Ontario, Canada, issues the greater portion of Harlequin Books series, while the New York office issues several Harlequin series as well as the Silhouette list (please see listing for Harlequin Books in the directory of United States publishers and editors). Harlequin Enterprises Limited also publishes the Worldwide Library, which accents on titles in the mystery/suspense and thriller mode.

HARLEQUIN BOOKS

The Harlequin series of romance novels published in Canada, like their American counterparts, each stake out particular market-niche segments of reader interest within the overall categories of romance fiction and women's fiction.

The editorial acquisitions departments for Harlequin Romance and Harlequin Presents are located at the operation's United Kingdom offices (the address for which is listed below). Following are overviews of some of the editorial guidelines supplied to authors:

Mira Books is dedicated to mainstream single-title women's fiction in hardcover and mass-market paperback editions. Mira titles assume no particular genre designation, though the works are considered to be of interest to a primarily women's readership. Mira Books hosts a wide variety of authors and approaches.

Harlequin Temptation introduces strong, independent heroines and successful, sexy heroes who overcome conflict inherent to their heated relationships, and in the end decide to marry. The books in this series are known for their wit as well as emotional strength.

Harlequin Temptations are sensuous romances about choices . . . dilemmas . . . resolutions . . . and, above all, the fulfillment of love. The most highly charged and most sensual Harlequin series.

Harlequin Superromance is a line of longer, contemporary romance novels. Realistic stories with emotional depth and intensity . . . more involving plots . . . more complex characters. Superromance women are confident and independent, yet eager to share their lives.

Harlequin Superromances are the longest books of the Harlequin series (approximately 350 manuscript pages) and therefore require a more complex plot and at least one fully developed subplot. This series is generally mainstream in tone, with romance of course being the propelling theme. Love scenes may be explicit so long as they exhibit good taste.

Harlequin Regency Romances are set in England during the Regency period (1811 to 1820) and the writer should be able to provide accurate details of dress, speech, and customs of that historical period. These stories are in general lighthearted and lively, often feature elements of intrigue and adventure, and offer a minimum of sexual activity.

Detailed information is available upon request from the publisher. Harlequin will send prospective authors full editorial guidelines with suggested heroine and hero profiles, as well as information pertaining to manuscript length, setting, and sexual approach and content.

Make sure your query is clear as to which line it is intended for: Harlequin Romance, Harlequin Presents, Harlequin Temptation, Harlequin Superromance, or Harlequin Regency Romances. Query letters and SASEs should be directed to:

Brenda Chin, Assistant Editor
Harlequin Temptation.

Paula Eykelhof, Senior Editor
Harlequin Superromance.

Ilana Glaun, Assistant Editor
Mira Books.

Wendy Blake Kennish, Assistant Editor
Harlequin Superromance, Harlequin Temptation.

Dianne Moggy, Senior Editor and Editorial Coordinator
Mira Books.

Amy Moore, Associate Editor
Mira Books.

Jane Robson, Editor
Harlequin Superromance.

Susan Sheppard, Editor
Harlequin Temptation, Love and Laughter.

Zilla Soriano, Editor
Harlequin Superromance.

Maureen Stonehouse, Editor
Harlequin Regency Romances and Harlequin Superromances.

Birgit David Todd, Senior Editor
Harlequin Temptation.

Malle Vallick, Editor
Harlequin Temptation, Love and Laughter.

Marsha Zinberg, Senior Editor and Editorial Coordinator, Special Projects

HARLEQUIN MILLS & BOON
HARLEQUIN ROMANCE
HARLEQUIN PRESENTS
MILLS & BOON/HARLEQUIN ENTERPRISES LTD.

Eton House, 18-24 Paradise Road
Richmond, Surrey TW9 1SR
United Kingdom

Acquisitions Harlequin Romance and Harlequin Presents are through the United Kingdom offices. Query the offices to request a set of editorial guidelines supplied to prospective authors:

Harlequin Romance is the original line of romance fiction, the series that started it all—over 35 years ago. These are warm, contemporary novels, filled with compassion and sensitivity, written by world-famous authors.

Harlequin Presents is overall the bestselling Harlequin line, published in 16 different languages and sold in almost every country of the world. Heartwarming romance novels about bright, capable women who are taking charge of their own lives, set in exotic locales.

To query the U.K. divisions, write (and enclose SASE) in care of the **Editorial Department** (especially to request guidelines), or direct inquiries to the following individual editors:

Tessa Shapcott, Senior Editor
Harlequin Presents (contemporary romances).

Linda Fildew, Senior Editor
Harlequin Romance (contemporary romances).

Sheila Hodgson, Senior Editor
All Mills & Boon series.

Elizabeth Johnson, Senior Editor
Love on Call (medical romances).

Karen Stoecker, Editorial Director
All Mills & Boon series.

Samantha Bell, Editor
All Mills & Boon series.

Gillian Green, Editor
All Mills & Boon series.

Marysia Juszczakievicz, Editor
All Mills & Boon series.

WORLDWIDE LIBRARY
WORLDWIDE MYSTERY
GOLD EAGLE BOOKS

225 Duncan Mill Road
Don Mills, ON M3B 3K9
416-445-5860

The Worldwide Library division of Harlequin Enterprises hosts two major imprints, Worldwide Mystery and Gold Eagle Books. Worldwide Library emphasizes genre fiction in the categories of mystery and suspense, action-adventure, futuristic fiction, war drama, and post-holocaust thrillers. The house gives its titles (primarily mass-market paperbacks) solid marketing and promotional support.

The **Worldwide Mystery** imprint specializes in mainstream commercial mystery and detective fiction in reprint. This imprint has not been issuing previously unpublished, original fiction; however, Worldwide is not to be overlooked as a resource regarding potential reprint-rights sales in this field. The house generally keeps lines of popular writers' ongoing series in print for a number of seasons, sometimes indefinitely.

Titles in reprint at Worldwide: *Zero at the Bone* by Mary Willis Walker; *Time of Hope* by Susan B. Kelly; *The Hour of the Knife* by Sharon Zukowski; *Murder Takes Two* by Bernie Lee; *Hard Luck* by Barbara D'Amato; *A Fine Italian Hand* by Eric Wright.

Gold Eagle Books is known for a fast-and-furious slate of men's action and adventure series with paramilitary and future-world themes. Series include Deathlands, the Destroyer, the Executioner, and Stony Man. Gold Eagle also publishes Super Books keyed to the various series—longer novels with more fully developed plots. Prospective authors should be familiar with the guidelines and regular characters associated with each series.

Query letters and SASEs should be directed to:

(Mr.) Feroze Mohammed, Senior Editor and Editorial Coordinator
Gold Eagle Books.

Randall Toye, Editorial Director
Gold Eagle-Worldwide Library.

KEY PORTER BOOKS LTD.

70 The Esplanade, 3rd Floor
Toronto, ON M5E 1R2
416-862-7777

Key Porter Books Ltd. (founded in 1981) is a midsize house that publishes a primarily nonfiction list with a Canadian twist. Key Porter produces titles in current affairs, science and health, travel, the environment, ecology, politics, sports, and a solid line of money books and entrepreneurial guides. Windsor Books is a Key Porter division that specializes in travel guides. Key Porter also issues books for children and young adults. In addition, the house offers coffee-table and gift editions, as well as occasional fiction and literary works.

Frontlist Key Porter titles are provided full promotional support that spotlights targeted review venues, national media exposure, magazine advertising (including co-op arrangements), and foreign-rights sales. The house maintains a strong backlist.

Among Key Porter highlights: *The House Plant Encyclopedia* by Ingrid Jantra and Ursula Kruger; *Skate: 100 Years of Figure Skating* by Steve Milton (principal photographs by Barbara McCutcheon); *Rebel Daughter: An Autobiography* by Doris Anderson; *No Fat Chicks: How Women Are Brainwashed to Hate Their Bodies and Spend Their Money* by Terry Poulton; *The Fight for Canada* by Diane Francis; *Naming Rumpelstiltskin: Who Will Profit (and Who Will Lose) in the Workplace of the 21st*

Century by Ann Finlayson; *I Have Lived Here Since the World Began: An Illustrated History of Canada's Native People* by Arthur J. Ray (a joint venture with Lester Publishing); *Lord High Executioner: An Unashamed Look at Hangmen, Headsmen, and Their Kind* by Howard Engel; *Armed and Dangerous: Shopping Right and Staying Fit* by Wendy Buckland and Barb Nicoll, with John Lawrence Reynolds; *Throw Your Heart over the Fence: The Inspiring Story of the Famous People Players* by Diane Dupuy; *What Are We Going to Do Now? Helping Your Parents in Their Senior Years* by Dr. William Molloy; *The Future of Health Care in Canada* by Dr. Lawrence E. Bryan; *Women in the Know: How to Build a Strategy to Achieve Financial Success* by Janice Book; *Corporate Abuse: How "Lean and Mean" Robs People and Profits* by Marti Smye and Lesley Wright; *Goalies: Guardians of the Net* by Daniel Daignault (photographs by Denis Brodeur).

KEY PORTER KIDS

Key Porter Kids is an imprint that specializes in works for younger readers, including pop-ups, board books, storybooks, novels, and reference works. The house publishes science books for children under the imprint Greey de Pencier/Books from Owl. Some titles from this division are cross-cataloged with the house's core list.

Introducing Key Porter Kids Classic Horror Series: *The Hunchback of Notre Dame* by Victor Hugo (retold by Tim Wynne-Jones; illustrated by Bill Slavin)—this is the first volume in a new series that brings classics of the horror genre to younger children (ages 8 and up). Coming next year: Bram Stoker's *Dracula*.

Other titles: *The Story of Canada* by Janet Lunn and Christopher Moore, illustrated by Alan Daniel (a joint venture with Lester Publishing); *Songs for Survival: Songs and Chants from Tribal Peoples Around the World* (edited by Nikki Siegen-Smith; illustrated by Bernard Lodge); *Animal Hideaways* (text by Anita Ganeri; illustrations by Halli Verrinder); *Creepy Crawlies in 3-D!* by Rick and Susan Sammon (photography by David Burder); *How on Earth? A Question-and-Answer Book About How Our Planet Works* by Ronald Orenstein; *Anne of Green Gables* (pop-up dollhouse with dolls).

Key Porter handles its own distribution.

Query letters and SASEs should be directed to:

Susan Renouf, President and Editor-in-Chief

LESTER PUBLISHING LIMITED

56 The Esplanade
Toronto, ON M5E 1A7
416-862-7777

Lester Publishing Limited (founded in 1991) produces a compact list of trade nonfiction and fiction and offers lines in children's and young-adult books. Lester titles have garnered an admirable array of publishing awards.

Nonfiction from Lester: *I Have Lived Here Since the World Began: An Illustrated History of Canada's Native People* by Arthur J. Ray (a joint venture with Key Porter Books); *Way Down Deep in the Belly of the Beast: A Memoir of the Seventies* by Douglas Fetherling; *The Anxious Years: Politics in the Age of Mulroney and Chrétien* by Jeffrey Simpson; *Tarnished Brass: Greed and Corruption in the Canadian Military* by Scott Taylor and Brian Nolan.

Backlist hits: *North Star to Freedom: The Story of the Underground Railroad* by Gena K. Gorrell; *Bad Blood: The Tragedy of the Canadian Tainted Blood Scandal* by Vic Parsons; *Great Moments in Canadian Baseball* by Brian Kendall; *False God: How the Globalization Myth Has Impoverished Canada* by James Laxer.

Lester fiction and literature: *Truly Grim Tales* (stories) by Priscilla Galloway; *A Place Not at Home* (autobiographical novel) by Eva Wiseman; *The Animals' Waltz* (novel) by Cary Fagan; *The Rose Tree* (lyrical fiction) by Mary Walkin Keane.

Lester's list for children and young adults includes: *The Night Voyagers* (novel) by Donn Kushner; *The Sugaring-Off Party* (a picture book) by Jonathan London (illustrated by Gilles Pelletier); *Saying Good-Bye* (stories) by Linda Holeman.

Lester Publishing books are marketed and distributed to the trade by Key Porter Books.

Query letters and SASEs should be directed to:

Malcolm Lester, Publisher

Kathy Lowinger, Executive Editor

Janice Weaver, Assistant Editor

LITTLE, BROWN AND COMPANY CANADA LIMITED

148 Yorkville Avenue
Toronto, ON M5R 1C2
416-967-3888

Little, Brown and Company Canada Limited (founded in 1953) publishes original titles of Canadian interest as well as works for the wider English-speaking market. The house also purchases the Canadian rights to books published in the United States. When asked if they were interested in books by United States writers, Ann Ledden replied, "We would love to find a good new American writer." Little, Brown issues a seasonal list of new books in hardcover and trade paperback; the publisher maintains a substantial backlist.

On the Little, Brown fiction list: *Evening Class* by Maeve Binchy; *Angel Walk* by Katherine Govier; *Darkest England* by Christopher Hope; *The Potato Factory* by Bryce Courtenay; *Slow Emergencies* by Nancy Huston; *A Kiss Is Still a Kiss* by Barry Callaghan; *Next of Kin* by Joanna Trollope; *Every Woman Knows a Secret* by Rosie Thomas; *The Last Time I Saw Jane* by Kate Pullinger; *Bodies in Motion* (a Matthew Prior mystery) by Anthony Quogan; *The Hole That Must Be Filled* (stories) by Kenneth J. Harvey; *Theory of War* by Joan Brady; *A Suitable Boy* (a saga of India) by Vikram Seth.

Nonfiction from Little, Brown: *Invisible Darkness: The Strange Case of Paul Bernardo and Karla Homolka* by Stephen Williams; *Herbal Remedies in Pots* by Effie Romain and Sue Hawkey; *Casselmania: More Wacky Canadian Words and Sayings* by Bill Casselman; *The Battles of the Somme* by Martin Marix Evans; *Oh, Canadians!* by Gordon Snell (illustrated by Aislin); *Classic Fabrics* by Henrietta Spencer-Churchill; *Just a Minute: The Great Canadian Heritage Quiz Book* by Marsha Boulton; *The Daycare Handbook: A Parent's Guide to Finding and Keeping Quality Daycare in Canada* by Barbara Kaiser and Judy Sklar Rasminsky; *The People of the Pines: The Warriors and the Legacy of Oka* by Geoffrey York and Loreen Pindera.

Little, Brown and Company (Canada) Limited distributes its own list as well as for United Kingdom and Commonwealth-based publishers and smaller Canadian presses.

Query letters and SASEs should be directed to:

Kim McArthur, President

MACFARLANE WALTER & ROSS

37A Hazelton Avenue
Toronto, ON M5R 2E3
416-924-7595

Macfarlane Walter & Ross specialties include current events, futurist works, social trends, and sports; a good percentage of Macfarlane books evidence a marked humorous edge. MW&R emphasizes Canadiana, especially biographies, business, history, politics, travel, and culture; the house also boasts a hefty selection of literary fiction and criticism.

Macfarlane Walter & Ross (founded in 1988) typically publishes a small seasonal list that nonetheless covers a wide range of nonfiction. MW&R publishes original titles of Canadian interest and also buys the Canadian rights to books from United States publishers. The house supports a solid backlist.

Macfarlane Walter & Ross nonfiction and popular works: *The Divorce from Hell* by Wendy Dennis; *Ask Me Anything: Love, Sex, and Relationships in the '90s* by Rhona Raskin; *An Acre of Time: The Enduring Value of Place* by Phil Jenkins; *What to Listen for in Beethoven: An Introduction to the Composer and to Classical Music* by Robert Harris; *Toronto for Kids: The Complete Family Travel Guide to Attractions, Sites and Events* by Anne Holloway; *Frank Ogden's New Book: Roadmaps for the Future* by Frank Ogden (packaged with a CD-ROM version).

In the Macfarlane Walter & Ross literary and cultural lineup: *City to City* by Jan Morris; *A Fool in Paradise* and *The Good* Wine (a two-volume autobiography by artist Doris McCarthy); *Photographs That Changed the World* by Lorraine Monk; *The Gates of Paradise: The Anthology of Erotic Short Fiction* (edited by Alberto Manguel); and a full slate of titles by John McPhee.

Macfarlane Walter & Ross is distributed by Stoddart Publishing.

Query letters and SASEs should be directed to the **Acquisitions Editor**.

MACMILLAN CANADA

29 Birch Avenue
Toronto, ON M4V 1E2
416-963-8830

Macmillan Canada nonfiction subject areas include business, sports, biographies, politics, true crime, cookbooks, history, and general reference works with a Canadian flavor. Macmillan Canada publishes selected works of fiction geared to the literary and commercial mainstream, including mysteries, suspense, and thrillers. The company also produces a line of calendars. Macmillan Canada is especially strong in books with a Canadian connection.

Macmillan Canada is corporately affiliated with the British publisher Macmillan. The house is not connected with the United States–based Macmillan (which is part of Simon & Schuster).

Representative of Macmillan Canada nonfiction: *The Ultimate Book of Household Hints & Tips* by Cassandra Kent; *The Ontario Harvest Cookbook: An Exploration of Feasts and Flavours* by Anita Stewart and Julia Aitken; *Goin' the Distance: Canada's Boxing Heritage* by Murray Greig; *Feel Fantastic: Maye Musk's Good Health Clinic* by Maye Musk; *Big, Bold, and Beautiful: Living Large on a Small Planet* by Jackqueline Hope.

Fiction and literary works from Macmillan Canada: *Desert Kill* by Philip Gerard; *How to Start a Charter Airline* by Susan Haley; *Genetic Soldier* by George Turner.

On the children's list: *My Rainy Day Activity Book* and *The Children's Step-by-Step Cookbook* (both by Angela Wilkes); *Sharing the Secrets: Teach Your Child to Spell* by Ruth Scott and Sharon Siamon.

Macmillan Canada distributes its own list, and handles Canadian distribution for a number of international houses including IDG Books, Irwin Professional Publications, Microsoft Press, and William Morrow.

Query letters and SASEs should be directed to:

Shannon Potts, Editorial Assistant

McCLELLAND & STEWART

481 University Avenue, Suite 900
Toronto, ON M5G 2E9
416-598-1114

McClelland & Stewart (established in 1906) publishes a wide-ranging and respected program in fiction and nonfiction, with hardcover and trade paperback lines. The house trade motto—"the Canadian publishers"—signals the fine array of Canadian authors between McClelland & Stewart covers.

Trade nonfiction areas encompass general-interest works of topical interest in current events and public issues, lifestyle and travel, medicine, religion, history, memoirs and biography, true crime, and the arts. In fiction the McClelland & Stewart list includes mainstream and category titles as well as literary fiction. The house also publishes literary nonfiction and poetry. New Canadian Library is a paperback line covering Canada's literary tradition, past and present. McClelland & Stewart offers a line for young readers (on its own list as well as through the newly acquired Tundra Books division) and vends the Audio Renaissance series of book tapes.

McClelland & Stewart nonfiction books: *Driving Force: The McLaughlin Family and the Age of the Car* by Heather Robertson; *The Group of Seven: Art for a Nation* by Charles C. Hill; *Karen Kain, Movement Never Lies: An Autobiography* by Karen Kain with Stephen Godfrey and Penelope Reed Doob; *The Judas Kiss: The Undercover Life of Patrick Kelly* by Michael Harris; *Boys Don't Cry: The Struggle for Justice and Healing in Canada's Biggest Sex Abuse Scandal* by Darcy Henton with David McCann; *The Last Best Hope: How to Start and Grow Your Own Business* by Rod McQueen; *In School: Our Kids, Our Teachers, Our Classrooms* by Ken Dryden; *Nationalism Without Walls: The Unbearable Lightness of Being Canadian* by Richard Gwyn; *A Year in Figure Skating* by Beverley Smith (edited by Dan Diamond); *SCTV: Behind the Scenes* by Dave Thomas; *In the Crease: Goaltenders Look at Life in the NHL* by Dick Irvin; *Scams, Scandals, and Skulduggery: A Selection of the World's Most Outrageous Frauds* by Andreas Schroeder.

The Screech Owls series by Roy MacGregor is a line of adventure stories about hockey for young readers (ages 11–14) that combines drama on the ice and off. Titles: *Mystery at Lake Placid*; *The Night They Stole the Stanley Cup*; *The Screech Owls' Northern Adventure*; *Murder at Hockey Camp*.

McClelland & Stewart fiction and literary writing: *Tales from the Canadian Rockies* (edited by Brian Patton); *The Canadian Cowboy: Stories of Cows, Cowboys, and Cayuses* by Andy Russell (illustrations by Don Brestler); *For Those Who Hunt the Wounded Down* by David Adams Richards; *George Bowering Selected: Poems 1961–1992* (edited by Roy Miki).

The house publishes *The Canadian Writer's Market: An Extensive Guide for Freelance Writers* by Jem Bates and Adrian Waller.

McClelland & Stewart distributes its own titles and handles Canadian distribution for a number of international publishing firms, such as Atlantic Monthly Press, I. B. Tauris & Company, and St. Martin's Press.

Query letters and SASEs should be directed to the **Editorial Board**.

TUNDRA BOOKS

481 University Avenue, Suite 802
Toronto, Ontario M5G 2E9
416-598-4786

In the United States:
Tundra Books of Northern New York
P.O. Box 1030
Plattsburgh, NY 12901
416-598-4786

Tundra is a specialist in children's books, with a compact list of original, primarily illustrated titles. Tundra Books was recently purchased by McClelland & Stewart, long considered among Canada's leading publishers of Canadian literature, now celebrating its tenth decade of publishing excellence.

Tundra children's titles: *A Mountain Alphabet* by Margriet Ruurs (illustrated by Andrew Kiss); *The Fish Princess* by Irene Watts (illustrated by Steve Mennie); *The Basketball Player* by Roch Carrier (illustrated by Sheldon Cohen); *Houses of China* by Bonnie Shemie (illustrated by the author).

Query letters and SASEs should be directed to:

Kathy Lowinger, Editor in Chief

McGill–Queen's University Press

Montreal office:
McGill University
3430 McTavish Street
Montreal, QC H3A 1X9
514-398-3750

Kingston office:
Queen's University
Kingston, ON K7L 3N6
http://www.mcgill.ca/mqupress (World Wide Web)

McGill University is a participant in the Combined Online Catalogue Project of the Association of American University Presses. Book descriptions from all participating publishers can be searched by author, title, and Library of Congress subject keyword. The site can be accessed from our homepage or directly at:

http://www.press.uchicago.edu
http://aaup.princeton.edu
gopher://aaup.princeton.edu

Publications from McGill–Queen's University Press include works in architecture, biography, British studies, business history, Canadian history, Canadian politics, economics, environment, French history, housing policy, international history, Irish history, Judaica, literature and literary criticism, Loyalist history, native studies, philosophy, political economy, psychology, Quebec history, sociology, urban geography, women's studies, and general-interest works primarily in areas of current interest in international and cultural affairs. McGill–Queen's publishes no hard sciences.

McGill–Queen's University Press (founded in 1969) produces trade books with scholarly market crossover, as well as titles geared specifically for the academic market. The press is a conjoint publishing endeavor of Queen's University (Kingston) and McGill University (Montreal). Many McGill–Queen's books have a Canadian subject slant; in addition, the house is strong in a variety of fields in the international arena as well as the social sciences and humanities. McGill–Queen's publishes in the French and English languages.

On the McGill–Queen's list: *Marguerite Bourgeoys and Montreal, 1640–1665* by Patricia Simpson; *Foisted upon the Government? State Responsibilities, Family Obligations, and the Care of the Dependent Aged in Late 19th Century Ontario* by Edgar-André Montiguy; *Canada Enters the Nuclear Age: A Technical History of Atomic Energy of Canada Limited as Seen from its Research Laboratories* by E. Critoph et al.; *Degrees of Freedom: Canada and the United States in a Changing World* (edited by Keith Banting, George Hoberg, and Richard Simeon); *The Secession of Quebec and the Future of Canada* by Robert A. Young; *A Long Way from Home: The Tuberculosis Epidemic Among the Inuit* by Pat Sandiford Grygier; *Canada's Cold Environments* (edited by Hugh M. French and Olav Slyamaker); *The Glory of Ottawa: Canada's First Parliament Buildings* by Carolyn A. Young.

The McGill–Queen's literary purview embraces criticism, memoir, biography, and letters. Offerings here: *Lying About the Wolf: Essays in Culture and Education* by David Solway; *Aesthetics* by Colin Lyas; *African Exploits: The Diaries of William Stairs, 1887–1892* (edited by Roy MacLaren); *The Cassock and the Crown: Canada's Most Controversial Murder Trial* by Jean Monet; *Cold Comfort: My Love Affair with the Arctic* by Graham W. Rowley; *Mapping Our Selves: Canadian Women's Autobiography* by Helen M. Buss; *The Birth of Modernism: Ezra Pound, T. S. Eliot, W. B. Yeats, and the Occult* by Leon Surette; *Fear and Temptation: The Image of the Indigene in Canadian, Australian, and New Zealand Literatures* by Terry Goldie.

Distribution for McGill–Queen's University Press is handled by the University of Toronto Press.

Query letters and SASEs should be directed to:

Philip J. Cercone, Director of Press and Acquisitions Editor (Montreal)

Aurele Parisien, Editor (Montreal)

John Zucchi, Editor (Montreal)

Donald H. Akenson, Editor (Kingston)

Joan Harcourt, Editor (Kingston)

Roger Martin, Editor (Kingston)

NC PRESS LIMITED

345 Adelaide Street West
Toronto, ON M5V 1R5
416-593-6284

NC Press publishes a broad range of topics covering the spectrum of general trade interest in areas such as cooking, health, Canadian history, politics, poetry, art and performance, literature and literary criticism, folkways and lifeways, the natural world, self-help, and popular psychology.

NC Press Limited (incorporated in 1970) is a trade publisher of Canadian books dedicated to the social, political, economic, and spiritual health of the human community. This is a small press—currently publishing a frontlist of 6 to 10 new books each year—

with an expansive vision: "To make a difference." NC Press thus strives to present complex ideas in ways accessible to a wide readership. Among NC Press books are numerous literary-award winners. The press has served as agent for non-Canadian publishers and catalogs a substantial backlist.

In 1988 Gary Perly, president of Perly's Maps, purchased a majority interest in NC Press Limited; the house now produces the Perly's map and atlas series, which offers a strong line of urban atlases and street guides to such environs as Toronto, Montreal, and Quebec City.

NC Press nonfiction: *Ninety-Nine Days: The Ford Strike in Windsor in 1945* by Herb Colling; *Living and Learning with a Child Who Stutters: From a Parent's Point of View* by Lise G. Cloutier-Steele; *Eating Bitterness: A Vision Beyond Prison Walls* by Arthur Solomon; *A Woman in My Position: The Politics of Breast Implant Safety* by Linda Wilson with Dianne Brown.

Literary and works of cultural note: *Voices from the Odeyak* by Michael Posluns; *Folktales of French Canada* by Edith Fowke; *One Animal Among Many: Gaia, Goats and Garlic* by David Walter-Toews; *Images: Thirty Stories by Favorite Writers* (compiled and with paintings by Len Gibbs).

NC Press books are distributed via the publisher's network, which involves independent sales representatives worldwide and the fulfillment services of University of Toronto Press.

Query letters and SASEs should be directed to:

Caroline Walker, President and Publisher

PENGUIN BOOKS CANADA LIMITED

10 Alcorn Avenue, Suite 300
Toronto, ON M4V 3B2
416-925-2249

Penguin Books Canada Limited operates independently of its American affiliate Penguin USA. Founded in 1974, Penguin Canada's mandate is to publish Canadian authors; the house does so with fine style, covering a mother lode of original trade nonfiction as well as a golden seam of mainstream and category fiction and literary works.

Penguin Books also purveys via its catalog and distribution network featured titles from the parent company's various international divisions, including Penguin USA, Bloomsbury, Viking Australia, and Viking UK. Among Penguin Canada's offerings is a major concentration of works from British Commonwealth–based writers. The Viking Canada imprint hosts a select list of Canadian fiction and nonfiction. Penguin Puffin and Viking Kestrel are the house's juvenile imprints. Penguin Canada markets the Highbridge line of audiobooks.

From the Penguin Canada list: *The Windsor Castle: Official Guide* by Michael Joseph; *The Puck Starts Here: The Origin of Canada's Great Winter Game—Ice Hockey* by Garth Vaughn; *The Night Inside: A Vampire Thriller* by Nancy Baker;

Shakedown: How the Government Screws You from A to Z by James Bovard; *From Here to Paternity: An Intimate View of a Father's Day* by Jay Teitel; *Dead Silence: The Greatest Mystery in Arctic Discovery* by John Geiger and Owen Beattie.

A special Penguin Canada project comprises *The Sacred Earth* (a gift volume featuring the photography of Courtney Milne) and companion work *The Pilgrim's Guide to the Sacred Earth* (travel reference) by Sherrill Miller. Penguin also offers works by Mordechai Richler and Peter C. Newman, among other Canadian scribes.

Penguin Books Canada Limited utilizes the services of its own distribution center.

PENGUIN BOOKS CANADA BOOKS FOR YOUNG READERS

Penguin Books Canada publishes a full slate of books for young readers, which covers reading levels from preschool through young adult (with the focus of the program in the range of preschool through grade 6). The house produces easy-readers, lift-the-flap books, mini editions, giant books, board books, pop-up books, joke books, fiction, folklore, poetry, music, and plays as well as general nonfiction. Imprints include Puffin, Kestrel, and NAL Young Adult.

Young readers' titles from Penguin Books Canada: *Why Mosquitoes Buzz in People's Ears: A West African Tale* by Verna Aardema; *Rent a Genius* by Gillian Cross; *Nini at Carnival* by Errol Lloyd; *Just Too Cool* by Jamie Callan; *Coming to Tea* by Sarah Garland; *Elephant Pie* by Hilda Offen.

In accordance with its current acquisitions policy, Penguin Books Canada does not accept unsolicited manuscripts. Query letters and SASEs should be directed to:

Cynthia Good, Publisher

RANDOM HOUSE OF CANADA LIMITED

1265 Aerowood Drive
Mississauga, ON L4W 1B9
905-624-0672

Random House of Canada Limited produces a select list of trade nonfiction within a wide-ranging adult trade lineup. Nonfiction areas include popular topical interest and current events; enterprise journalism and narrative investigative stories; lifestyle and the arts; history, politics, biography, and memoirs; business and finance; general how-to and self help; and popular science. In fiction and literature Random House of Canada issues frontlist novels; outstanding mysteries, suspense tales, and thrillers; literary criticism and biography; and pop-cultural works.

Random House of Canada Limited (founded in 1944) is a subsidiary of Random House, Inc., the United States publisher. The house produces a list of new titles from its Canadian offices, with major concentration in books of appeal to the Canadian market.

Random House of Canada operates its own marketing network and handles Canadian distribution for the Random House U.S. divisional imprints and client companies, such as National Geographic Books, Prima Publishing, Shambhala Publications, and Sierra Club Books.

Query letters and SASEs should be directed to:

Douglas Pepper, Executive Editor

STODDART PUBLISHING COMPANY LTD.

34 Lesmill Road
Don Mills, ON M3B 2T6
416-445-3333

Stoddart Publishing maintains a hold on the mainstream of commercial publishing. Stoddart nonfiction categories include humor, history, military history, politics, biography, cooking, environment, nutrition, and business and consumer guides. Stoddart also publishes a solid fiction line that encompasses mainstream novels and genre categories including mysteries and thrillers. Stoddart Publishing (founded in 1984) is the trade-publishing arm of General Publishing Company. The house produces a wide range of titles with a Canadian orientation or by Canadian authors.

Nonfiction from Stoddart: *The Klondike Quest: A Photographic Essay* (compiled and with essays by Pierre Berton); *The Japan We Never Knew: A Journey of Discovery* by David Suzukki and Keibo Oiwa; *Gifts of Leadership: Team-Building Through Focus and Empathy* by Art Horn; *Boom, Bust & Echo: How to Profit from the Coming Demographic Shift* by David K. Foot with Daniel Stoffman; *The Instant Parent: 50 Quick, Effective Ways to Help Your Children* by Stanley Shapiro and Karen Skinullis with Richard Skinullis; *From the Cop Shop: Hilarious Tales from Our Men and Women of the Badge* by Peter V. MacDonald; *Money to Burn: Trudeau, Mulroney, and the Bankruptcy of Canada* by D'Arcy Jenish; *Contracting Your Own Home: A Step-by-Step Guide* (revised edition) by David Caldwell; *Freenet: Canadian On-line Access, the Free and Easy Way* by Pierre Bourque and Rosaleen Dickson.

Stoddart fiction and literature: *Sandman Blues* (novel) by Stéphane Bourguignon (translated by David Homel); *A Shriek in the Forest Night: Wilderness Encounters* by R. D. Lawrence; *The Third Illustrated Anthology of Erotica* (compiled and edited by Charlotte Hill and William Wallace).

Stoddart orchestrates its own distributional network worldwide, and handles distribution for books issued by a number of other houses, including Anansi, the Boston Mills Press, and Macfarlane Walter & Ross. In the United States, Stoddart distributes to the trade through General Distribution Services, Inc.

STODDART JUVENILES

Stoddart publishes a children's program with an emphasis on Canadian works. Stoddart's young-adult paperbacks list includes the Gemini and Junior Gemini lines. Stoddart Young Readers are for preschoolers through young adults, and include picture books, pop-up books, fairy tales, and science titles for young adults.

Query letters and SASEs should be directed to:

Don Bastian, Managing Editor

University of British Columbia Press

6344 Memorial Road
Vancouver, BC V6T 1Z2
604-822-3259

Categories of University of British Columbia Press interest include Canadian culture and history, political science, Asian studies, native studies with an accent on the Northwest Coast, Pacific Rim studies, global geography, fisheries and forestry, environmental studies, Northern studies, and Canadian sociology.

University of British Columbia Press (founded in 1971) publishes academic books, as well as general-interest works, with an emphasis on Canadian subjects.

On the University of British Columbia Press list: *Ancient People of the Arctic* by Robert McGhee; *The Private Eye: Observing Snow Geese* by Marcy Burns; *Life in Stone: A Natural History of British Columbia's Fossils* (edited by Rolf Ludvigsen); *Aboriginal and Treaty Rights in Canada: Essays on Law, Equality, and Respect for Difference* (edited by Michael Asch); *Treaty Talks in British Columbia: Negotiating a Mutually Beneficial Future* by Chris McKee; *The Resettlement of British Columbia: Essays on Colonialism and Geographical Change* by Cole Harris; *Politics, Policy, and Government in British Columbia* (edited by Ken Carty); *Clearcutting the Pacific Coast: Production, Science, and Regulation in the Douglas Fir Forests of Canada and the United States, 1880–1965* by Richard A. Rajala; *Qualities of Mercy: Justice, Punishment, and Discretion* (edited by Carolyn Strange).

University of British Columbia Press handles its own distribution.

Query letters and SASEs should be directed to:

Jean Wilson, Senior Editor

University of Toronto Press

10 Saint Mary Street, Suite 700
Toronto, ON M4Y 2W8
416-978-2239

University of Toronto Press publishes in a range of fields including history and politics; women's studies; health, family, and society; law and crime; economics; workplace communication; theory/culture; language, literature, semiotics, and drama; medieval studies; Renaissance studies; Erasmus; Italian-language studies; East European studies; classics; and nature. The list includes topical titles in Canadian studies, native studies, sociology, anthropology, urban studies, modern languages, and music, as well as travel and touring guides.

University of Toronto Press produces titles for the general trade as well as academic works. UTP issues a series of specialist journals of note including *Scholarly Publishing*. The house produces no original contemporary fiction or poetry.

Representing the University of Toronto nonfiction list: *Place Names of Atlantic Canada* by William B. Hamilton; *Born at the Right Time: A History of the Baby Boom Generation* by Doug Owram; *A History of Ukraine* by Paul R. Magocsi; *Glaucoma: A Patient's Guide to the Disease* by Graham E. Trope; *Profits and Politics: Beaverbrook and the Gilded Age of Canadian Finance* by Gregory P. Marchildon; *Bad Attitude/s on Trial: Pornography, Feminism, and the Butler Decision* by Brenda Cossman, Shannon Bell, Lise Gotell, and Becki Ross; *Gender and Political Discourse in Upper Canada* by Cecilia Morgan; *Mounties, Moose, and Moonshine: The Patterns and Context of Outport Crime* by Norman Okihiro; *Quest for Self-Knowledge: An Essay in Lonergan's Philosophy* by Joseph Flanagan; *City Lives and City Forms: Critical Research and Canadian Urbanism* (edited by Jon Caulfield and Linda Peake).

Publications in the arts and literature: *Power to Rise: The Story of the National Ballet of Canada* by James Neufeld; *Painting Place: The Life and Work of David B. Milne* by David P. Silcox; *Modern Furniture in Canada, 1920–1970* by Virginia Wright; *Fred Cumberland: Building the Victorian Dream* by Geoffrey Simmins; *Paths of Desire: Images of Exploration and Mapping in Canadian Women's Writings* by Marlene Goldman; *Allusion: A Literary Graft* by Allan H. Pasco; *Discoveries of the Other: Alliterity in the Work of Leonard Cohen, Hubert Aquin, Michael Ondaatje, and Nicole Brossard* by Winifred Siemerling; *The Logic of Ecstasy: Canadian Mystical Painting 1920–1940* by Ann Davis; *Northern Voices: Inuit Writing in English* (edited by Penny Petrone); *Sounding Differences: Conversations with Seventeen Canadian Women Writers* by Janice Williamson; *The Political Writings of Mary Wollstonecraft* (edited by Janet Todd).

University of Toronto Press oversees a distributional network encompassing offices and sales agents worldwide; the house handles titles from other book publishers as well as for institutions such as Royal Ontario Museum and Canadian Museum of Nature.

Query letters and SASEs should be directed to:

Joan Bulger, Editor
Art and classics, architecture.

Virgil Duff, Executive Editor
Social sciences, scholarly medical books, law and criminology, women's studies.

Gerald Hallowell, Editor
Canadian history and Canadian literature.

Ron Schoeffel, Senior House Editor
Romance languages, native languages, religion and theology, education, philosophy.

Kieran Simpson, Editor, Department of Directories

Suzanne Rancourt, Editor
Medieval studies, medieval and Old English Literature.

PART TWO

Insider's Directory
of Literary Agents

What Makes This Agent Directory Special?

JEFF HERMAN

No other listing of literary agents comes anywhere close to this one. We don't just tell you who the agents are and where to find them; we get the agents to actually talk to you and reveal a slice of their personalities. These surveys also reveal what each agent wants to represent (and doesn't want to); when and where they were born and educated; their career history; and their agenting track record. Memorize some of these tidbits and you can be something of a gossip.

About 200 exceptionally well-qualified agents are included in this listing. Each year I invite the 200+ members of the Association of Author Representatives, as well as a couple dozen excellent nonmember agents, to be in the book. As you might expect, many of the most successful agents are not overly hungry for unsolicited new submissions, and some of them therefore do not wish to participate. We listed no one against their wishes, and allowed all of our agent contributors to be as terse or expansive as they pleased.

There are surely many superb agents of whom I am not aware, and therefore didn't reach out to for inclusion. My staff and I have done our best to include only legitimate agents who can, and do, get the job done for their clients. Although we can't guarantee it, we trust that the surveys were answered accurately and honestly. Let us know if you discover otherwise.

AAA Literary Agency

Authors Adventure Assistance Literary Agency
P.O. Box 22121
San Diego, CA 92192
619-276-0308
mmaine@axnet.net (e-mail)

Agent: Mark Maine.

Born: March 16, 1958; San Diego, California.

Education: B.S., forensic science.

Career history: Law enforcement, multi-corporate president, and author.

Hobbies/personal interests: Flying and sailing.

Subjects/categories most enthusiastic about agenting: Anything fresh, exciting, and new. Something that draws the reader within its pages. Be it fiction or nonfiction, we are open to all categories. Surprise us with your own personal style and flair.

Subjects/categories not interested in agenting: We will generally not reject a specific category. We review each submission independently.

Best way for a prospective client to initiate contact: Send a 1-page query letter or synopsis with SASE to our P.O. box or a very brief description to our e-mail.

Reading-fee policy: No reading fee.

Client representation in the following categories: Nonfiction, 15%; Fiction, 60%; Children's, 20%; Textbooks, 5%.

Commission: 10% USA and international.

Number of titles sold during the past year: 12.

Approximate percentage of all submissions (from queries through manuscripts) that are rejected: 96%.

Representative titles sold:

The Untitled Boxer by Stephen Bradford (Melluso Films).

J.J. by Captain Jonathan Williams, USN (Magicworld Studios).

The Yellowtail Derby by Mike Reardon (Maritime Associates).

Description of the Client from Hell: A pushy, bothersome, arrogant, sniveling brat. One who thinks that, just because they have crafted a marketable piece of work, this somehow entitles them to bypass all common courtesies and professional etiquette.

Description of Dream Client: The dream client is one who meets all deadlines with time to spare, promptly keeps all appointments, submits new work every 6 months, is always receptive to suggestions, has a positive interpretation of all circumstances, and is always considerate and professional.

The most common mistakes potential clients make when soliciting an agent to represent them: Trying too hard to impress me, and not allowing their work to sell itself.

What writers can do to enhance their chances of getting an agent (besides being good writers): Be genuine, patient, and understanding of the volume of submissions we receive.

Why did you become an agent? I have a passion for negotiating creative projects.

What might you be doing if you weren't an agent? Sailing the world on a yacht with my family and exploring new lands.

Comments: An excuse is just the skin of a lie stuffed with reasons.

AEI

Atchity Editorial/Entertainment International
Motion Picture Production and Literary Management
9601 Wilshire Boulevard
Box 1202
Beverly Hills, CA 90210
213-932-0407
fax: 213-932-0321

New York office:
212-765-9592
212-581-0104
aeikja@lainet.com (e-mail)
http://www.lainet.com/~aeikja (World Wide Web)

Manager names: Kenneth Atchity, President; Chi-Li Wong, Partner and Vice President of Development and Production; Andrea McKeown, Executive Vice President, Editorial; Moira Coyne, Associate Manager; Mai-Ding Wong, Associate Manager; Sidney Kiwitt, business affairs (NY). Writer's Lifeline associates: David Angsten (senior editor), Paul Aratow, Monica Faulkner (senior editor), Sherry Gottlieb, Vicki Preminger, Ed Stackler.

Personal information pertaining to KEN ATCHITY:

Born: Eunice, Louisiana.

Education: B.A., Georgetown; Cambridge; Ph.D. in comparative literature, Yale.

Career history: Professor of comparative literature (classics, medieval, Renaissance), Occidental College (1970–1987); instructor, UCLA Writer's Program (1970–1987). Author of 13 books, including *A Writer's Time: A Guide to the Creative Process, from Vision Through Revision* (Norton), *The Mercury Transition: Career Change Through Entrepreneurship* (Longmeadow), and *Writing Treatments That Sell* (with Chi-Li Wong; Owl Books). Producer of 20 films for video, television, and theater, including *Champagne for Two* and *The Rose Café* (Cinemax-HBO), *Amityville: The Evil Escapes* (NBC), *Shadow of Obsession* (NBC), *Falling Over Backwards*, and *Meg* (Walt Disney Productions and Zide Films).

Hobbies/personal interests: Collecting autographed editions, pitchers; tennis; travel.

Subjects/categories most enthusiastic about managing: Nonfiction: Strong mainstream nonfiction, especially true and heroic stories with TV or film potential; business books, especially with entrepreneurial orientation; previously published books with solid sales records. Fiction: Mainstream commercial novels (action, horror, thrillers, suspense, mainstream romance, espionage, outstanding science fiction with strong characters) that can also be made into TV or feature films. Scripts: For TV: strong female leads. For film: All kinds, especially action, romantic comedy, thrillers, science fiction, and horror.

Subjects/categories not interested in managing: Drug-related; fundamental religious; category romance; category mystery or Western; poetry; children's; "interior" confessional fiction.

Best way for a prospective client to initiate contact: Query letter (with SASE) and 30–50 sample pages.

Reading-fee policy: No reading fee. $150 one-time fee charged against expenses, upon signing, to writers who have not yet previously published a book. AEI's Writers' Lifeline, an affiliated company, offers an analysis service with fees ranging from $250 to $650. We offer this service only to writers requesting specific feedback for their careers or seeking to enter our Lifeline consulting service for one-on-one coaching by editors trained in the methods outlined in *A Writer's Time*. The Writers Lifeline also offers re-writing and ghost-writing services.

Client representation in the following categories: Nonfiction 45%; fiction 45%; screenplays 10%.

Commission: 15% of all domestic sales, 25% foreign. If we exercise our option to executive produce a project for film or television, commission on dramatic rights sale is reduced.

Number of titles sold during the past year: 4.

Approximate percentage of all submissions (from queries to manuscripts) that are rejected: 95%.

Representative titles sold:
Fiction:
180 Seconds at Willow Park by Rick Lynch (New Line Pictures).
Megalodon by Steve Alten (Walt Disney Pictures and Doubleday Bantam; Literary Guild Main Selection).
Sign of the Watcher by Brett Bartlett (Propaganda Films).
Sins of the Mother, *Telephone Tag*, *Moral Obligations* by Cheryl Saban (Dove Books).
The Hong Kong Sanction by Mitch Rossi (Kensington/Pinnacle).
The Cruelest Lie by Milton Lyles (Dunhill House).
An Invitation to Sanctuary by George Klembith and Tammy Schwartz (Dunhill House).
Chokecherry Roots by Floyd Martinez (Arte Público).
Nonfiction:
Success Through Cashflow Reengineering by Jim Sagner (American Management Association).
The Rag Street Journal: A Guide to Thrift Shops in North America by Elizabeth Mason (Owl).
The Secret Castle by Carole S. Hughes (St. Martin's Press).
Anatomy of Deceit by Jerry M. Blaskovich (Barclay House).
Simply Heavenly: The Monastery Vegetarian Cookbook by Abbott George Burke (Macmillan).

Atchity's *Encyclopedia of American Folklore* (Random House).
Achieving Sexual Ecstasy by Amy Rosen (Barclay House).

Description of Client from Hell: He or she is so self-impressed it's impossible to provide constructive criticism; makes his package impossible to open, and provides return envelope too small to be used.

Description of the Dream Client: He or she comes in with an outstanding novel that's both *high concept* and *castable*, plus an outline for two more; and is delighted to take commercial direction on the writing and the career.

The most common mistakes potential clients make when soliciting an agent to represent them: The most costly and time-consuming mistake is remaining ignorant of where your work fits into the market, and of who your reader might be. Don't send kinds of work (romances, light mysteries, episodic scripts) we're specifically *not* looking for.

What writers can do to enhance their chances of getting an agent (besides being good writers): Be a great writer and a determined, optimistic client ready for an exciting, new lifelong career. And think *high concept*: Would this story make a blockbuster film?

Why did you become a manager? Nearly two decades of teaching comparative literature and creative writing at Occidental College and UCLA Writers Program, reviewing for the Los Angeles *Times* Book Review, and working with the dreams of creative people through DreamWorks (which I cofounded with Marsha Kinder) provided a natural foundation for this career. I made the transition from academic life through producing, but continued my publishing-consulting business by connecting my authors with agents. As I spent more and more time developing individuals' writing careers, as well as working directly with publishers in my search for film properties, it became obvious that literary management was the next step. True or fiction, what turns me on is a good story.

What might you be doing if you weren't a manager? If I weren't a literary manager, writer, and producer, I'd be doing the same thing and calling it something else.

Comments: Dream big. Don't let anyone define your dream for you. Risk it. The rewards in this new career are as endless as your imagination, and the risks, though real, are not greater than the risk of suffocating on a more secure career path. Begin by learning all you can about the business of writing, publishing, and producing, and recognizing that as far off and exalted as they may seem, the folks in these professions are as human as anyone else. We're enthusiasts, like you: Make us enthused!

ALTAIR LITERARY AGENCY

141 Fifth Avenue, Suite 8N
New York, NY 10010
212-505-3320

Agents: Nicholas Smith; Andrea Pedolsky.
 Born: Smith: 1952; St. Louis, Missouri. Pedolsky: 1951; New York, New York.

Education: Smith: Languages, Vassar, 1973–1974; Arts Management, SUNY/Purchase, 1985. Pedolsky: B.A., American Studies, CUNY/Queens College; M.S., Library Service, Columbia University.

Career history: Smith: Bookseller and bookstore manager, Scribner's, 1974–1976; Reference book editor and publisher (5 years); Marketing and sales manager, Kodansha/International, 1985–1986; Marketing, Bowker, 1986–1988; Director, New Product Development, T.E.N./Japan, 1990–1991; Literary agent, Intercultural Group, New York office, 1991–1993; independent agency, 1993–1995; cofounded Altair Literary Agency, 1996. Pedolsky: Editor, reference and professional books, Neal-Schuman Publishers, 1978–1988; Acquisitions editor, AMACOM Books, 1988–1993; Executive editor, Peterson's/Pacesetter books, 1994–1996; cofounded Altair Literary Agency, 1996.

Hobbies/personal interests: Smith: Music, photography, reading, travel, Japanese pottery. Pedolsky: Art, music, reading, walking, travel, old cities.

Subjects/categories most enthusiastic about agenting: Nonfiction: Series nonfiction, including contemporary issues, business, biography, spirituality; popular reference, culture, and science; art and science museum exhibit-related books; photography and illustrated books; history; health; relationships; travel; nature and the environment. Children's books: Author-illustrated books that tell a great story and have an underlying theme or lesson.

Subjects/categories not interested in agenting: Fiction (it's what we read when we are not at work).

Best way for a prospective client to initiate contact: A well-thought-out and composed query letter that will compel us to call and ask for the proposal and sample chapters. Also, include a bio/c.v. To ensure a response, include SASE.

Reading-fee policy: No reading fee.

Client representation in the following categories: Nonfiction, 98%; Children's, 2%.

Commission: 15% domestic, 20% foreign.

Approximate percentage of all submissions (from queries through manuscripts) that are rejected: 95%.

Representative titles sold:

Winning Strategies for Capital Formation by Linda Chandler (Irwin).

A Cheerful Note for Jack by Arlene Boehm (Roberts Rinehart).

CyberWriting by Joe Vitale (AMACOM Books).

Careers in Birth by Su Robotti and Maggie Inman (Wiley).

Myth, Magic, and Mystery: 100 Years of American Children's Book Illustration by M. Hearn, H.N.B. Clark, and T. Clark for the Chrysler Museum (Roberts Rinehart).

Shot on This Site by William Gordon (Carol/Citadel).

Women's Guide to Investment Basics by Marsha Bertrand (AMACOM Books).

Dictionary of the Performing Arts by F. L. Moore and M. Varchaver (Contemporary).

Dreams Are a Long Road by Aaron Levin (Artisan/Workman).

25 Words or Less by Emily Calvo and Larry Minsky (NTC/Contemporary).

Kids Eat New York by Elizabeth Carpenter and Sam Freund (Little Bookroom).

Small Business Guide to the Internet by Al Bredenberg (Nikkei BP/Japan).

The Complete Manager's Organizer by Lisa Davis (AMACOM Books).

Stumbling Toward Enlightenment by Geri Larkin (Ten Speed/Celestial Arts).

The Fortune Sellers by William Sherden (Wiley).

Beyond Competition by Harvey Robbins and Michael Finley (McGraw-Hill).

ISO 14000 Answer Book by Lawson, Sasseville, and Wilson (Wiley).

Description of the Client from Hell: Smith: The author who doesn't deliver on time or on what was agreed to, requires an unreasonable amount of hand-holding, and who expects *instant results*. Pedolsky: Luckily, there have not been many. Those that come to mind have little or no understanding of the book marketplace and whether their proposed book has a ready audience.

Description of Dream Client: The author who has a great and salable idea; has the knowledge, expertise, and background to support their proposal; understands the collaborative aspects of working with an agent; understands deadlines; and has a sense of humor.

The most common mistakes potential clients make when soliciting an agent to represent them: Failing to know the difference between enthusiasm and being bothersome; that evaluating query letters and proposals can take time. Not owning up to the fact that they have already submitted their proposal to other agents or publishers. Sending us material we do not represent.

What writers can do to enhance their chances of getting an agent (besides being good writers): Show us, through their query letter, proposal, and background information, that they are the best author(s) to write this book, that the ideas are fresh and new, and that there is a real market for their book.

Why did you become an agent? Smith: Three reasons: (1) Great respect for those who are able to use language in such a way that, no matter how great or small my interest in their topic, I can *see* what they are describing in words. (2) Working closely with authors and their books and the editors who also find their books compelling is the reason I enjoy coming to work day after day. (3) I love to bring people and projects together and then mediate the process to everyone's benefit. Pedolsky: Working as an editor for 20 years, I had to confine and align my acquiring efforts to a particular house's list. (I was also too often accused of being more worried about my authors than the company!) Being an agent has freed me up: I am now working with a wonderful variety of authors with unique voices and styles, who write on a broad range of topics. What Fun!

What might you be doing if you weren't an agent? Smith: Since I love what I do, I can't imagine doing anything else. Pedolsky: I'd probably find an agent and write another book.

MARCIA AMSTERDAM AGENCY

41 West 82nd Street, Suite 9A
New York, NY 10024
212-873-4945

Agent: Marcia Amsterdam.

  Education: B.A., English and journalism, Brooklyn College.

  Career history: Editor; agent (1960–present).

  Hobbies/personal interests: Reading, theatre, movies, art, travel, discovering wonderful new writers.

Subjects/categories most enthusiastic about agenting: An eclectic list of mainstream and category fiction and popular nonfiction. I enjoy medical and legal thrillers, character-driven science fiction, mysteries, horror, historical romance, contemporary women's fiction, and quality young-adult fiction.

Subjects/categories not interested in agenting: Children's books, poetry, short stories, technical books, thrillers about drug cartels.

Best way for a prospective client to initiate contact: A query letter (with SASE).

Reading-fee policy: No reading fee.

Client representation in the following categories: Nonfiction, 10%; Fiction, 90%.

Commission: 15% domestic; 20% on foreign sales and movie and television sales (split with subagents); 10% on screenplays.

Number of titles sold during the past year: A fair number.

Approximate percentage of all submissions (from queries through manuscripts) that are rejected: Alas, most.

Representative titles sold:

Free Fall (Dell).

Shanghai Star (Kensington).

Moses Goes to A Concert (Farrar Straus & Giroux)

Patrick Stewart: The Unauthorized Biography (Kensington).

The most common mistakes potential clients make when soliciting an agent to represent them: Spelling and grammar still count, as does a comfortable, legible typeface.

What writers can do to enhance their chances of getting an agent (besides being good writers)? A smartly written query letter that makes me smile, that asks a surprising question, that presents an original idea in an interesting voice.

Description of the Client from Hell: I wouldn't know. I've never had one.

Description of Dream Client: One who trusts the reader, is professional, adaptable, has a sense of humor, and has confidence in my judgment.

Why did you become an agent? When I was an editor, other editors often came to me for suggestions about books they were working on. I found that I enjoyed giving editorial and career advice. One editor said, *You keep selling my books. Why don't you become an agent?* So I did.

What might you be doing if you weren't an agent? Reading published books more, traveling more.

THE AUDACE LITERARY AGENCY

645 North Broadway, No. 18
Hastings, NY 10706
914-478-1553
914-681-0015
yente@panix.com
Joanmoran@aol.com

Agents: Rachel Levine, Joan Moran.

The following information pertains to RACHEL LEVINE:

Education: B.A., English/secondary education, SUNY Stonybrook; M.F.A. fiction, Brooklyn College.

Career history: Everything from sales, purchasing agent, teaching, computer programming, and training. Wrote copy for Macy's and was copy chief for a direct-mail house. Publishing: editorial assistant.

Hobbies/personal interests: Dancing, writing.

Subjects/categories most enthusiastic about agenting: I like *any* project that is well written, original, and professional.

Subjects/categories not interested in agenting: Poetry, academic materials, short-story collections, screenplays, teleplays, stage plays.

Best way for a prospective client to initiate contact: Send a query letter for nonfiction (or e-mail something like a query letter). For fiction, send me three chapters and a synopsis, so I know the full plot of the novel.

Reading-fee policy: No reading fee.

Client representation in the following categories: Nonfiction, 70%; adult fiction, 10%; children's fiction, 20%.

Commission: 15%.

Number of titles sold during the past year: 1 (we started the agency in late 1995).

Approximate percentage of all submissions (from queries through manuscripts) that are rejected: 90%–95%.

Representative titles sold:

Can I Pray with My Eyes Open? by Susan Taylor Brown (Hyperion Books for Children (spring 1998).

Description of the Client from Hell: The new (i.e., previously unpublished) writer with unrealistic expectations. We've had writers walk away from decent deals because they wanted more money when they had virtually no previous history publishing books. Writers who are intransigent about changing their work even when we are willing to work with them to produce a compelling proposal.

Description of Dream Client: The writer who has studied the craft, considers him- or herself a professional, and acts like one. The writer who is willing to *pay his or her dues* when starting out and isn't petulant about it.

The most common mistakes potential clients make when soliciting an agent to represent them: They phone us. If you're a writer, *write* to us! Show us what you've got!

What writers can do to enhance their chances of getting an agent (besides being good writers): Understand that we are running a business and behave professionally. Show us more than one project so that we know you are prolific. It happens that publishers often like the writing but not the subject. A writer with more than one project has better odds of getting published.

Why did you become an agent? It marries the two things I love: writing and business.

What might you be doing if you weren't an agent? Writing, writing, writing!

Comments: New writers have a great opportunity to work with us because we are a new agency and have to *grow our own* writers, so to speak. When we get a very talented, committed writer, we are willing to do extensive work with them to produce a professional, marketable *package*. What we ask in return is that the writer learn from us, follow our lead, and be willing to work hard. Since every human being has an opposable thumb, every human being can write. But being a *writer* isn't an anatomical description! Please study the *craft* of writing and then be open to learning about the *business* of writing as well.

The following information pertains to JOAN MORAN:
Education: Graduate, St. Peter's College (major: English; minor: art).
Career history: Always in sales; I started a small publisher (Stein & Day) then went to Dell, from Dell to Bantam Doubleday Dell, then onto Western Publishing; therefore, I have broad experience in many aspects of book publishing.
Hobbies/personal interests: Hiking, travel, music, cross-country skiing, rollerblading, reading, baking.
Subjects/categories most enthusiastic about agenting: Alternative/popular health, self-help, fitness, nutrition, children's.
Subjects/categories not interested in agenting: Science, textbooks, science fiction, poetry, plays, articles and journals, dramas.
Best way for a prospective client to initiate contact: Write a query letter (with SASE). No phone or fax.
Description of the Client from Hell: Unprofessional.
Description of Dream Client: Professional.
The most common mistakes potential clients make when soliciting an agent to represent them: Not including SASE or leaving a telephone number for me to contact them.
What writers can do to enhance their chances of getting an agent (besides being good writers): Send a focused cover letter, personal background information, and a well-thought-out proposal.

AUTHENTIC CREATIONS LITERARY AGENCY
911 Duluth Highway, Suite D3-241
Lawrenceville, GA 30243
770-339-3774

Agent: Mary Lee Laitsch.
  Born: Baraboo, Wisconsin.
  Education: B.S., Education, University of Wisconsin.
  Career history: Taught library science. Established my literary agency in 1995.
  Hobbies/personal interests: Family, reading, crafts, and sewing.
  Subjects/categories most enthusiastic about agenting: Fiction: Adventure, children's, fantasy, historical, murder mysteries, romance, science fiction, suspense, young adult, and, of course, literary fiction. Nonfiction: Business, cookbooks, crafts, how-to, humor, inspirational, political, sports, and women's issues.
  Subjects/categories not interested in agenting: Poorly crafted works.

Best way for a prospective client to initiate contact: Letter with SASE. It certainly helps if the letter has been proofread to eliminate mistakes. It makes me feel the manuscript will arrive the same way, with few or no errors.

Reading-fee policy: No reading fee.

Client representation in the following categories: Nonfiction, 30%; Fiction, 70%.

Commission: 15% domestic, 20% foreign.

Number of titles sold during the past year: 12.

Approximate percentage of all submissions (from queries through manuscripts) that are rejected: 90%.

Representative titles sold:

Since my husband is a lawyer and contributes to the agency by assisting in the negotiations with publishers and explanation of contractual terms with our clients, he prefers that we do not disclose this sensitive client information.

Description of the Client from Hell: We have clients from all over the world, but none of them, to our knowledge, comes from Hell. We attempt to treat all of our clients as the unique and talented artists they are, and in return expect them to respect our professional opinion in how to get their books published. So far this system has worked out well for us.

Description of Dream Client: A talented writer who has carefully proofread the manuscript before submitting it to us.

Why did you become an agent? I enjoy working with new writers to develop their initial works into publishable manuscripts.

What might you be doing if you weren't an agent? President of General Motors or a librarian. Probably a librarian because it would be a lot more fun.

Comments: Since we are still a relatively new agency, we are eager to work with new authors.

AUTHOR AUTHOR LITERARY AGENCY LTD.

12000 37th Street, SW
P.O. Box 34051
Calgary, AB T3C 3W2 Canada
403-242-0226 (telephone and fax)

Agent: Joan Rickard.

Born: Toronto, Ontario.

Education: Business instructor, Alberta Vocational College; editorial consultant; published author of numerous magazine articles and two books.

Career history: Agency is now in its fifth year.

Subjects/categories most enthusiastic about agenting: Fiction/nonfiction, adult and juvenile: novels, short story collections, scholarly, New Age.

Subjects/categories not interested in agenting: No poetry, screenplays, or magazine short stories/articles.

Best way for a prospective client to initiate contact: Submit entire manuscript proposal.

Reading-fee policy: No reading fee.

Client representation in the following categories: Nonfiction, 20%; Fiction, 65%; Children's, 10%, Textbooks, 5%.

Commission: 15% domestic (Canadian); 20% foreign (non-Canadian).

Number of titles sold during the past year: 3.

Approximate percentage of all submissions (from queries through manuscripts) that are rejected: 90%.

Representative titles sold:

Battling the Bulge by Roderick W. Dingwall, M.D. (Commonwealth).

Ice Break by Kim Kinrade (Commonwealth), national bestseller.

Why Elephants and Fleas Don't Sweat by Gideon Louw, Ph.D. (Detselig).

Description of the Client from Hell: The client from Hell is singularly self-focused, overbearing, and opinionated.

Description of Dream Client: Dream clients— most of my people—are mature and professional in outlook. Patience, in what is an excessively tight publishing market, and a sense of humor are helpful allies, too.

The most common mistakes potential clients make when soliciting an agent to represent them: Improperly presented proposals. There is an abundance of good reference books on the market or in libraries to teach writers the basic mechanics and techniques: proper formatting, spelling, punctuation, composition, etc. Good writing is the marriage of creative style and correct presentation. The former is an art, the latter a skill. In the least, both may be significantly improved if writers are willing to do their homework and study the craft before placing their proposal on agents' and publishers' desks.

What writers can do to enhance their chances of getting an agent (besides being good writers): Be courteous. Submit neatly presented/printed proposals. Submit rather than phone or fax your proposal. And, remember that unlike authors (who have only their own proposal(s) to think about), agents are busy folks trying to cram two hours into every one.

Why did you become an agent? I love the world of writing. With my experience as an editor and author, it was an obvious direction.

What might you be doing if you weren't an agent? Author and editorial consultant.

Comments: Study your chosen genre thoroughly to learn style/technique and what publishers are contracting. It is not agents' or publishers' jobs to teach creative writing courses, or revamp the mechanics of formatting, punctuation, and/or composition. Most will not, or will charge extra for this service. Please ensure manuscripts are properly formatted; double-spaced; standard print (11-, 11.5-, or 12-point). No dot matrix. Include a brief high-impact synopsis of your proposal (as seen on books' jackets) and bio. Each may be less than but not exceed 100 words (double-spaced). SASE or IRCs must be enclosed or manuscript/inquiries will not be returned. If a work is good enough and it appeals to a broad enough market that it is worth the publisher's investment of considerable dollars, with patience and perseverance it should, eventually, find its place on the market. Publishers are looking for material that is, in their opinion, very well written (although we all sometimes wonder about their choices), especially by authors with impressive portfolios, whose works are not so controversial that they detract rather than attract sales, yet are distinctive enough to separate themselves from what's already out there. Simple. Most writers believe their proposals to be above the crowd; some are even correct.

THE WENDY BECKER LITERARY AGENCY

530-F Grand Street, Suite 11-H
New York, NY 10002
212-228-5940 (telephone/fax)
dulf86a@prodigy.com (e-mail)

Agent: Wendy Becker.
   Education: B.S., Psychology, SUNY at Albany.
   Career history: Associate editor, McGraw-Hill. Editor, John Wiley & Sons. Agency begun 1994.
   Hobbies/personal interests: Reading (what else?), music/opera, travel.
   Subjects/categories most enthusiastic about agenting: Nonfiction (trade): business, biography, history, current events, parenting/psychology. Selective "genre" fiction: mystery, romance, science fiction.
   Subjects/categories not interested in agenting: Poetry, literary fiction, short stories, children's books, anything in the college market.
   Best way for a prospective client to initiate contact: Query letter (with SASE), to include outline, table of contents, author résumé, and up to three sample chapters. Do *not* call. Do *not* send complete manuscripts.
   Reading-fee policy: No reading fee.
   Client representation in the following categories: Nonfiction, 80%; Fiction, 20%.
   Commission: 15%.
   The most common mistakes potential clients make when soliciting an agent to represent them: Never approach an agent initially via telephone, because there is no way to properly evaluate an author without seeing his/her work.

BERMAN, BOALS AND FLYNN

225 Lafayette Street, Suite 1207
New York, NY 10012
212-966-0339

Agents: Lois Berman, Judy Boals, Jim Flynn.
   Career history: Agency is over 20 years old.
   Subjects/categories most enthusiastic about agenting: Dramatic and black comedies. (Works for theater and screen.)

Subjects/categories not interested in agenting: Works exhibiting extreme violence and/or that are abusive to anyone.

Best way for a prospective client to initiate contact: Query letter (with SASE), biography, current work available.

Representation: Dramatic only.

Commission: 10%.

Approximate percentage of all submissions (from queries to manuscripts) that are rejected: 98%.

The most common mistakes potential clients make when soliciting an agent to represent them: Too many phone calls. With no track record, claims a similarity in talent to well-established writers.

Description of Dream Client: Keeps writing, trying new things, grows.

Why did you become an agent? Love theater. Enjoy putting together creative people.

What might you be doing if you weren't an agent? Producing theater.

MEREDITH BERNSTEIN LITERARY AGENCY, INC.

2112 Broadway, Suite 503A
New York, NY 10023
212-799-1007
212-799-1145

Agents: Meredith Bernstein; Elizabeth Cavanaugh, associate.

Born: Bernstein: July 9, 1946; Hartford, Connecticut; Cavanaugh: October 16, 1962.

Education: Bernstein: B.A., University of Rochester, 1968; Cavanaugh: B.A., literature and creative writing, Ohio University, Athens, Ohio.

Career history: Bernstein: Many jobs before becoming an agent: freelance reader, story editor, and worked for another agency for 5 years before starting my own in 1981. Cavanaugh: Before working in publishing, held a number of positions that were "book" related, including working for a period as a librarian; began in publishing with the Bernstein agency in the mid-1980s, and was instrumental in the development of our foreign rights activity.

Hobbies/personal interests: Bernstein: I am a collector of vintage and contemporary costume jewelry and clothing, so fashion is a strong interest; sports of all kinds; almost any cultural event—I'm an avid theatergoer; spending time with friends; travel, adventure, and personal-growth work. Cavanaugh: I am interested in all forms of art and love museums, movies, dance, music (I studied the violin for 10 years), and, of course, reading. I am also an avid cook, love gardening, and am currently renovating a 70-year-old house. I am a strong environmentalist and love animals and nature, and enjoy camping, hiking, and canoeing.

Subjects/categories most enthusiastic about agenting: Bernstein: personal memoirs, women's issues, medical and psychological subjects, almost any strong *narrative* nonfiction; good novels; literary fiction; creative projects. Cavanaugh: narrative non-fiction, parenting, pop-science, general nonfiction, mysteries, literary fiction, mainstream fiction.

Subjects/categories not interested in agenting: Bernstein: Anything too technical, science fiction, children's books. Cavanaugh: science fiction, children's, poetry, or screenplays.

Best way for a prospective client to initiate contact: A query letter with SASE.

Reading-fee policy: No reading fee.

Client representation in the following categories: Nonfiction, 50%; Fiction, 50%.

Commission: 15% domestic; 20% on foreign sales (split with subagents).

Number of titles sold during the past year: Many!

Approximate percentage of all submissions (from queries through manuscripts) that are rejected: Unsure, but probably fairly high because we must truly believe in the projects we represent and, therefore, are selective about what we request to see.

Representative titles sold:

Bernstein:

Saving the Kingdom by Dr. Martin Goldstin (Knopf).

The Purina Encyclopedia of Feline Care by Amy Shojai (Ballantine).

The Purina Encyclopedia of Canine Care by Amy Shojai (Ballantine).

Pregnant Fathers by Jack Heinowitz (Andrews and McMeel).

Lost Wisdom of a Man's Life by Denis Boyles (HarperCollins).

Optimum Health by Dr. Stephen Sinatra (Bantam).

Cavanaugh:

Beyond the River by Wynema McGowan (Pinnacle), fiction.

All the Love in the World by Maggie Conroy (Kensington).

International Adoption Resource Book by Maggie Conroy (Birch Lane).

The Cannibal King by Marilyn Campbell (Onyx), fiction.

The most common mistakes potential clients make when soliciting an agent to represent them: Bernstein: Poor presentation, no SASE. Cavanaugh: Poorly re-searched projects (which includes not knowing the market in terms of what is already on the shelves for the type of book they are writing), sloppy presentation.

What writers can do to enhance their chances of getting an agent (besides being good writers): Bernstein: Be a great storyteller! Present a good idea. Be a person well versed in his/her field, well prepared and enthusiastic. Cavanaugh: Submit a clean, professional presentation with something fresh and new to say or with a unique voice in which to tell their tale.

Description of the Client from Hell: Bernstein: Pushy, demanding, inflexible, calls too much, sloppy presentation of material, egomaniacal. Cavanaugh: Someone who does not take a professional approach to their career and who does not appreciate the role of an agent.

Description of Dream Client: Bernstein: Professional, courteous, sees our relationship as teamwork, respects how hard I work for him/her. Cavanaugh: A great writer whose talent and passion for his/her work brings the project to life and who wants to work together to reach his/her potential.

Why did you become an agent? Bernstein: I was born to do this! Cavanaugh: As an agent, the diversity of projects I represent allows me to work within the creative process in *many* different genres and with many different publishers.

What might you be doing if you weren't an agent? Bernstein: I wouldn't mind running another creative business—fashion/public relations/maybe a store. Something that requires vision, sales ability, and gives visible results. Cavanaugh: It would most likely involve some aspect of books or publishing (maybe editing or even writing), or perhaps be as far afield as environmental science or catering.

PAM BERNSTEIN & ASSOCIATES INC.

790 Madison Avenue, Suite 310
New York, NY 10021
212-288-1700

Agent: Pam Bernstein.
  Career history: Director, foreign rights, William Morris Agency, 1978–1992.
  Hobbies/personal interests: Reading, skiing, sailing, horseback riding, cooking, gardening.
  Subjects/categories most enthusiastic about agenting: Nonfiction: adult, women's issues. Fiction: adult, women's. Also, espionage thrillers, health, medicine, self-improvement, spiritual.
  Subjects/categories not interested in agenting: Science fiction, horror, "coffee table" books.
  Best way for a prospective client to initiate contact: Query letter with an SASE.
  Reading-fee policy: No reading fee.
  Client representation in the following categories: Nonfiction, 60%; Fiction, 40%.
  Commission: 15%.
  Number of titles sold during the past year: 20.
  Approximate percentage of all submissions (from queries through manuscripts) that are rejected: 90%.
  Representative titles sold:
  Recovery of Sacred Psychology by Peter Rinehart (Addison-Wesley).
  A Jury of Her Peers by Jean Hanff Korlity (Crown).
  JobSmarts for 20-Somethings by Bradley Richardson (Vintage/Random House).
  The Virgin Homeowner by Janice Papolos (Norton).
  The Perfect Setting by Peri Wolfman and Charles Gold (Clarkson Potter).
  Tumbling by Diane Whetstone (William Morrow).
  Angry All the Time by Scott Wetzler (HarperCollins).
  Friends for Life: Mothers and Their Adult Daughters by Susan Jonas and Marilyn Nissenson (Morrow).

Description of the Client from Hell: The person with unrealistic dreams about his talent, his advance, and importance with his publisher. It takes time to build an author's career.

Description of the Dream Client: A warm, appreciative, talented writer who understands that we both have different roles in this relationship, and who respects the differences.

The most common mistakes potential clients make when soliciting an agent to represent them: Repeated phone calls, poorly typed letters.

What writers can do to enhance their chances of getting an agent (besides being good writers): Submit strong proposals, display organizational talents and clear thinking, and have impressive writing credentials.

Why did you become an agent? I love the creative process of working with authors—reading, selling, finding the right marriage of editor and author.

DANIEL BIAL AGENCY

41 West 83rd Street, Suite 5-C
New York, NY 10024
212-721-1786

Agent: Daniel Bial.

Education: B.A., English, Trinity College.

Career history: Editor for 15 years, including 10 years at HarperCollins. Founded agency in 1992.

Hobbies/personal interests: Travel, cooking, music, parenting.

Subjects/categories most enthusiastic about agenting: Nonfiction: popular reference, business, popular culture, science, history, humor, Judaica, sports, psychology, cooking. Fiction: quality fiction, mysteries.

Subjects/categories not interested in agenting: Nonfiction: academic treatises, crafts, gift books. Fiction: romances, horror, medical thrillers, children's books, poetry, novels by authors with no publishing credits.

Best way for a prospective client to initiate contact: Query letter with SASE.

Reading-fee policy: No reading fee.

Client representation in the following categories: Nonfiction, 90%; Fiction, 10%.

Commission: 15% domestic; 20% foreign.

Number of titles sold during the past year: 18.

The most common mistakes potential clients make when soliciting an agent to represent them: A surprising number of writers devote time in their query letter to telling me about their previous failures. They essentially reject themselves.

What writers can do to enhance their chances of getting an agent (besides being good writers): Savvy writers research their field and rate the competition's strengths and weaknesses. They highlight why their book is going to be new, different, better.

They explain why they are the best writer on the topic. And they display an enthusiasm that suggests it will survive all the ups and downs of the publishing process.

Description of the Client from Hell: Clients from Hell are almost always wrapped up in private grievances and needs. They talk when they should listen, try force when they should use tact, and get involved in personal gamesmanship when much of publishing calls for team play. They suspect the worst and often cause crises simply through their own closed-mindedness.

Description of Dream Client: Dream clients produce trim, tight, ready-to-sell material. They know the business and how to get ahead. They recognize the importance of marketing and that good intentions don't sell books—hard work does. They take pride in their work and their relationships.

Why did you become an agent? I became an agent for the same reason I first became an editor: because I loved the discovery of new authors and books, loved helping create a sellable project, and loved negotiating big advances. I switched desks because I wanted to be my own boss.

THE BLAKE GROUP

8609 Northeast Plaza Drive, Suite 300
Dallas, TX 76225
214-373-2221
214-361-7200
Visit us at our Web site: http://www.blakegroup.com.

Agents: Dr. Albert H. Halff, President; Mrs. Lee Halff, Consulting Editor; Hal Copeland, Marketing/PR Consultant.

Subjects/categories most enthusiastic about agenting: Virtually any fiction or nonfiction subject or category may be considered by the Blake Group.

Best way for a prospective client to initiate contact: Send us a strong query letter with two or three chapters. Persuade us to request your complete manuscript. Include some information about yourself and SASE. Mail is always preferred to fax or telephone calls.

Reading-fee policy: No fee.

Commission: 15% domestic; 20% foreign

Approximate percentage of all submissions (from queries through manuscripts) that are rejected: 85%

Representative titles sold: Our published clients include Edward Bradley, Betty Bunker, Paul Dempsey, Harold Durham, Elizabeth Dunn and Laura Hays, Te Edwards, Frank Goodwyn, Lloyd Hill, Peggy Hitchcock, Deanna Hudak and Rougeau, Linda McKenzie and son, Bonnie Neely, Pam Russell and Debbie Good, Charles Pugh, Lannon Reed, Pamela Sanchez, Maynard Smith, John Wright, and Julie Yarbrough.

Publisher sales include Algonquin Books, Augsburg Fortress, Ballantine, Harbinger House, Hazelden/Compcare, Holloway House, McFarland and Co., Pelican Publishing, Pendragon Press, Pilot Books, SRA/McGraw Hill, Texas A&M University Press, University of Pennsylvania Press, and Zebra Books.

BLASSINGAME–SPECTRUM CORPORATION
SPECTRUM LITERARY AGENCY

111 Eighth Avenue, Suite 1501
New York, NY 10011
212-691-7556

Agent: Lucienne Diver.

Education: Degree in English/writing and anthropology, summa cum laude, State University of New York, Pottsdam.

Hobbies/personal interests: Hobbies: reading, writing, painting, mandolin, theater. Personal interests: forensics, anthropology.

Subjects/categories most enthusiastic about agenting: Fantasy, science fiction, mysteries, et al. Whatever catches my interest.

Best way for a prospective client to initiate contact: Query letter with brief synopsis and SASE.

Reading-fee policy: No reading fee.

The most common mistakes potential clients make when soliciting an agent to represent them: The biggest turn-off is ego. An author convinced that his/her first novel will break all sales records the first week on the shelves is likely to be disappointed and difficult to work with.

One very basic mistake is the failure to include an SASE with a submission. Most agencies and publishing houses will not even look at material that does not come with a response envelope.

Many writers underestimate the importance of the cover letter, which is, after all, the first impression the reader gets.

What writers can do to enhance their chances of getting an agent (besides being good writers): Do the research necessary to target the right person and take time to polish.

Description of the Client from Hell: Has unrealistic expectations (first novel will break all sales records first week on the shelves and be made into a major motion picture grossing billions). It happens, but not daily.

Description of the Dream Client: Someone who has taken the time to learn something of the business, and who can make informed decisions.

Why did you become an agent? I can get *paid* to read books!!! I love books, was always excited by the prospect of a job in publishing, and I love working with intelligent, creative people.

What might you be doing if you weren't an agent? I considered going to graduate school for forensic anthropology. Publishing won out!

BROCK GANNON LITERARY AGENCY

172 Fairview Avenue
Cocoa, FL 32967
407-633-6217

Agent: Louise Peters.

Born: Over 21.

Education: B.S., Radford University.

Career history: Teacher, editor, agent.

Hobbies/personal interests: Sailing.

Subjects/categories most enthusiastic about agenting: Fiction.

Subjects/categories not interested in agenting: Open to all subjects.

Best way for a prospective client to initiate contact: Query or send complete manuscript.

Reading-fee policy: We only charge for postage, long distance calls, photocopying, etc. We *don't* critique, edit, evaluate, etc.

Client representation in the following categories: Fiction, 20%; Nonfiction, 70%; Children's/young adult, 10%.

Commission: 10%.

Number of titles sold during the past year: 2 (we're a new agency).

Approximate percentage of all submissions (from queries through manuscripts) that are rejected: 90%.

Representative titles sold:

New Jerusalem by Lang Marc.

The Black Man's Guide to Working in The White Man's World (General Publishing Group).

Description of the Client from Hell: Someone who calls often for no reason and consumes a great deal of time.

Description of Dream Client: A good writer.

The most common mistakes potential clients make when soliciting an agent to represent them: Sending inappropriate material. Not having the manuscript edited. Not having a cover letter. Not knowing the market for the book.

What writers can do to enhance their chances of getting an agent (besides being good writers): Follow directions.

Why did you become an agent? The written word can be a thing of beauty.

What might you be doing if you weren't an agent? Teaching.

Comments: I accept no censorship. When I have something to say, I say it and believe this is everyone's right.

ELIZABETH BROOME AGENCY

Box 507

Nye, MT 59061

405-328-6234 (telephone and fax)

agent@writeme.com (e-mail)

http://members.tripod.com/~beattitude/indx.htm/ (World Wide Web)

Agent: Elizabeth Broome Hardy.

Education: Master's degree (English), Duke University, 1971.

Career history: Manuscript editor and revisionist since 1981; worked with late father in his agency.

Hobbies/personal interests: Used to be knitting and crocheting—no time anymore.

Subjects/categories most enthusiastic about agenting: Specialize in Christian material. Also interested in true crime, exposé, "whistle-blowing."

Subjects/categories not interested in agenting: Will not consider occult, New Age, metaphysics.

Best way for a prospective client to initiate contact: E-mail or snail mail (with SASE).

Reading-fee policy: No reading fee.

Client representation in the following categories: Nonfiction, 35%; Fiction, 53%; Children's, 10%; Textbooks, 2%.

Commission: 10% U.S.; 15% Canadian; 20% elsewhere. (Considering a 5% raise.)

Number of titles sold during the past year: I'm brand new as an agent.

Approximate percentage of all submissions (from queries through manuscripts) that are rejected: 40%.

Representative titles sold: I'm brand new.

Description of the Client from Hell: The one who calls or e-mails every day to ask, "What's going on?" A client should let the agent do his *job* and not "bug" him. The one who wants you to help him write all his new material—who runs everything by you before he writes it.

Description of Dream Client: The one who sits back and lets me do my job, who trusts me to notify him of any developments (or lack thereof). I make it a policy to supply copies of correspondence (even standard "rejection slips") to clients.

The most common mistakes potential clients make when soliciting an agent to represent them: Approaching me as if I'm being interviewed for a job as an agent, implying that I may or may not be blessed with the privilege of busting my can to represent him. *Not!*

What writers can do to enhance their chances of getting an agent (besides being good writers): Express confidence in me as a part of the team—recognizing that, as his representative, I have an emotional and financial interest in *his* success, and that it is not beneficial to an agent to work *against* his client.

Why did you become an agent? My father did it for 30 years, and I worked with him for many of those years. He taught me what he knew. It's my natural niche.

What might you be doing if you weren't an agent? Writing novels of my own, if I had time.

Comments: Please realize that your agent is on your side. He is not your enemy.

When I accept a client for representation, I go forward as though I were representing *myself*. In a very real sense, that is exactly what I *am* doing.

ANDREA BROWN LITERARY AGENCY, INC.

P.O. Box 429
El Granada, CA 94018
415-728-1783

Agent: Andrea Brown.

Education: B.A., Journalism and English, Syracuse University.

Career history: Editorial assistant, Dell; editorial assistant, Random House; assistant editor (all children's books), Knopf; started agency in 1981.

Hobbies/personal interests: Golf, theatre, gardening, travel, my cats.

Subjects/categories most enthusiastic about agenting: Chapter books, funny middle-grade fiction, science, high-tech nonfiction.

Subjects/categories not interested in agenting: No general adult fiction or nonfiction. No rhyming picture books.

Best way for a prospective client to initiate contact with you: Query letter (with SASE) or phone-call query.

Reading-fee policy: No reading fee.

Client representation in the following categories: Children's, 95% (Nonfiction, 40%; Fiction, 60%).

Commission: 15% domestic; 20% foreign.

Number of titles sold during the past year: Too many to count.

Approximate percentage of all submissions (from queries through manuscripts) that are rejected: 95%.

Representative titles sold:
The Bully Brothers at the Beach (Scholastic).
One April Morning (Lothrop, Lee & Shephard).
Slime (Millbrook).

The most common mistakes potential clients make when soliciting an agent to represent them: Faxing queries. I hate that. Or long calls asking lots of questions before I'm even interested. And calling after I've said no already. Or re-sending with minor changes after we have rejected it. It closes the door on any future interest I may have in the writer.

What writers can do to enhance their chances of getting an agent (besides being good writers): Include your phone number on query letters. If I'm interested, it's easier to call the writer, and so many people just list their address.

Description of the Client from Hell: One who has to talk to his agent on a daily basis, always thinks his work is perfect as it is, and that the editor is always wrong.

Description of Dream Client: One who works hard and takes his career seriously, and respects that an agent has many clients to represent, but still remembers to mention that he appreciates the time and effort on his behalf.

Why did you become an agent? I loved publishing as a business and working with authors, but hated publishing houses and their attitudes about authors.

If you were not a happy and prosperous literary agent, what do you think you would be? Teaching or still being a book editor, or laying on my deck or beach.

Comments: Children's books are in a period of change and turmoil. The publishers have glutted the market, and now the authors are suffering as well, with cutbacks and cancellations. Writers must write terrific books that are also commercial. I worry about the quality of children's literature in the future, as publishers are forced to cut fiction and their midlist.

CURTIS BROWN LTD.

Ten Astor Place
New York, NY 10003
212-473-5400

Branch offices:
1750 Montgomery Street
San Francisco, CA 94111
415-954-8566

1235 Bay Street, Suite 400
Toronto, ON M5R 3K4 Canada
802-362-5165

Agents: Perry H. Knowlton, Chairman and CEO; Peter L. Ginsberg, President; Timothy F. Knowlton, COO. Books: Ellen Geiger, Peter L. Ginsberg, Emilie Jacobson, Ginger Knowlton, Perry H. Knowlton, Marilyn E. Marlow, Jennie McDonald, Laura Blake Peterson, Andrew Pope, Clyde Taylor, Jess Taylor, Maureen Walters, Mitchell S. Waters. Film, TV, and Multimedia Rights: Timothy Knowlton, Jess Taylor. Audio Rights: Christopher McKerrow. Translation Rights: Dave Barbor.

The following information pertains to PERRY KNOWLTON:

Born: Unknown. Some think I'm in my sixties, but I'm actually going to be 140 some time next year. I owe the unusually advanced age to the ingestion of yogurt since birth (my mother's suggestion). Some say that yogurt also stimulates the imagination.

Education: Prep school (Exeter); college (Princeton); no graduate schooling.

Career history: Teacher (English); editor (Scribner's); agent (Curtis Brown) 1959 to present day.

Hobbies/personal interests: Boating, dogs, cats, birds, collecting (various, but including money, also spending it)! Reading for pleasure (when there's time), genealogy (mine), children (mine, mostly), grandchildren (again mine, mostly).

Subjects/categories most enthusiastic about agenting: I find the question confusing.

Subjects/categories not interested in agenting: Poetry. I have represented poets in the past, but it's no longer possible economically.

Best way for a prospective client to initiate contact: The best way is to persuade a friend, who also happens to be a client of mine, to read the work and let me know what he or she thinks of it. Failing that, try the usual query-letter approach (return envelope, etc.). Keep in mind that on my next birthday I'll be 140 years old, so I'm trying to be as selective as possible.

Reading-fee policy: No reading fee.

Client representation in the following categories: Nonfiction, 49$^1/_2$%; Fiction, 49$^1/_2$%; Juvenile and young adult, 1%.

Commission: 15% domestic; 20% foreign.

Number of titles sold during the past year: A fair number.

Approximate percentage of all submissions (from queries through manuscripts) that are rejected: Approximately 98%.

Representative titles sold recently: This is a difficult one for me. What, for instance, does "recently" mean? Some of the books I've sold that don't yet have titles or publication dates, were sold to publishers that now belong to another publisher, and some of them were sold only a year or two back, others longer ago than that, and some to publishers whose names are no longer recognizable to the average writer. When asked, I tend to avoid listing the names of my authors for three reasons. The first is simply that I'm afraid of leaving out the name of an author who might resent its not being on the list; the second is the obverse side of that coin, fear of listing an author who'd rather not be listed; and the third is that I know there are hundreds of eager agents out there who have been waiting patiently for me to make this particular mistake so they can then have the opportunity to raid the pantry, so to speak, and slake their piranha-like hunger. After all, many of these people are my friends, and I'd hate to lose them. I refer to the agents, of course. My clients would never leave me.

A costly mistake a potential clients make when soliciting you to represent them: A letter whose last paragraph concludes with, "Just between you and *I*, you'll never regret taking me on."

What writers can do to enhance their chances of getting an agent (besides being good writers): My enthusiasm tingles when some young genius—talented, of course—says "Just between you and *me*, you're going to make a fortune through the representation of my work. I Guarantee it!"

Description of the Client from Hell: A client who decided to be an exception to the above.

Description of the Dream Client: Any one of my clients.

Why did you become an agent? I don't think about it very much at this stage of my long life, but I do know that I switched from the publishing side because, as an editor in the employ of a publisher, my conscience forced my loyalty towards my authors, not my employer, and I didn't like the schizoid position I found myself occupying. And that was a long time ago when I was at Scribner's, and Scribner's was owned and operated by a Scribner, a good man who was a friend of mine as well as my boss. I try not to think too much about what it would be like today.

What might you be doing if you weren't an agent? I might consider a life as a peregrine falcon or an eagle—a golden eagle, I think. Although I still enjoy a relatively full head of hair, the idea of that glistening white head on the bald eagle would seem a bit redundant.

The following information pertains to PETER L. GINSBERG:

Subjects/categories most enthusiastic about agenting: Nonfiction: history, business, biography, religion, current affairs. Fiction: mystery, literary.

Subjects/categories not interested in agenting: Science fiction, romance, how-to nonfiction.

Best way for a prospective client to initiate contact: Query letter (with SASE).

Client representation in the following categories: Nonfiction, 80%; Fiction, 20%.

Approximate percentage of all submissions (from queries through manuscripts) that are rejected: 95%.

Description of the Dream Client: Responsive, creative, enterprising, patient.

The following information pertains to ELLEN GEIGER:
Born: March 24; New York, New York.
Education: Graduate degrees in education and anthropology; broad eclectic interests.
Career history: Background in film production; was public television executive prior to becoming literary agent.
Hobbies/personal interests: Film, theater, pop culture, tennis, France, history, psychology, and others—too many to mention.
Subjects/categories most enthusiastic about agenting: Serious fiction and nonfiction, politics, social issues, history, biography, gender studies, psychology, pop culture, religion and spirituality, current affairs, health, self-help. Also commercial fiction—mysteries, thrillers, and big commercial women's novels.
Subjects/categories not interested in agenting: Romance, science fiction, children's, New Age.
Best way for a prospective client to initiate contact: Send query letter and sample chapters and/or outline (with SASE).
Reading-fee policy: No reading fee.
Client representation in the following categories: Nonfiction, 75%; Fiction, 25%.
Commission: 15%.
Approximate number of writers currently represented: 50.
Approximate percentage of all submissions (from queries through manuscripts) that are rejected: 95%.
Representative titles sold:
Asian Health Secrets by Letha Hadady (Crown).
Monkey Bridge by Lan Lao (Viking).
The Opera Lover's Guide to Europe by Carol Plantamura (Citadel).
Three in Love: The Menage a Trois from Ancient to Modern Times by Barbra and Michael Foster (Harper San Francisco).
Dreamworks: The Making of the New Studio by Greg Kilday (Dutton).
The Suitcase: Refugee Writing from Bosnia by Julie Mertus (University of California Press).
The most common mistakes potential clients make when soliciting an agent to represent them: Faxing a long proposal; calling every day or few days to check up; misspellings or sloppy writing errors in their proposal; sending something out that isn't their best effort.
What writers can do to enhance their chances of getting an agent (besides being good writers): Present a thoughtfully written letter and a good proposal or chapter outline, and/or an original idea (hard to find). Whatever you do, don't use a form letter to query an agent. If nonfiction, have some credentials that would quality you to write on the subject.
Description of the Client from Hell: Someone who can't be pleased, who is dissatisfied no matter what happens.
What might you be doing if you weren't an agent? I'd raise horses and live on a farm.
Comments: I'm very interested in cutting-edge issues—for example, sex, race, class, gender, health. I'm happier if I can meet the potential client to see if we would get along.

The following information pertains to EMILIE JACOBSON:

Subjects/categories most enthusiastic about agenting: General trade fiction and nonfiction. Some material for older children (no picture books).

Subjects/categories not interested in agenting: Technical and/or textbooks, poetry, science fiction, prizefighting.

Best way for a prospective client to initiate contact: Query letter (with SASE). Please, *not* by fax!

Reading-fee policy: No reading fee.

Commission: 15% domestic; 20% Canada/overseas.

Approximate percentage of all submissions (from queries through manuscripts) that are rejected: 97%.

Description of the Client from Hell: Eternal complainer, telephones constantly, delivers manuscript Christmas Eve so I can read it over the holiday. Alienates all editors.

Description of the Dream Client: Has confidence in my ability. Trusts me to be in touch when there is anything to report. Writes like an angel. Understands the publishing business.

The following information pertains to GINGER KNOWLTON:

Education: B.A., child development (minors in communication studies and English).

Career history: Preschool teacher and director; office manager of a bed-and-breakfast inn.

Hobbies/personal interests: Tennis, sailing, skiing, reading, playing, learning, gardening, golf.

Subjects/categories most enthusiastic about agenting: Middle-grade and young-adult fiction and nonfiction; historical fiction; anything superb.

Subjects/categories not interested in agenting: Pornography.

Best way for a prospective client to initiate contact: If it's a picture book, send the whole manuscript with a letter. If it's anything else, send the first 20 pages or a proposal with a letter. Of course, always include SASE.

Reading-fee policy: No reading fee.

Client representation in the following categories: Nonfiction, 5%; Fiction, 5%; Children's, 90%.

Commission: 15% domestic, 20% foreign.

Approximate percentage of all submissions (from queries through manuscripts) that are rejected: 98%.

The most common mistakes potential clients make when soliciting an agent to represent them: Form letters that begin "Dear Agent" or "Dear Editor" or "Dear Curtis Brown" or "Dear Mr. Brown"; grammatical and spelling errors in the query letter and/or the manuscript.

What writers can do to enhance their chances of getting an agent (besides being good writers): A professional approach, especially one with humor.

Description of the Client from Hell: Fortunately, I don't have firsthand experience with "Clients from Hell" so I don't want to jinx myself by describing one.

Description of the Dream Client: One who writes well, trusts me implicitly, and makes millions of dollars.

What might you be doing if you weren't an agent? Working with children if I still had to earn a living. If I had the luxury of not needing to work, I would play tennis 'til I drop, garden, and spend lots of time with my daughter and husband.

The following information pertains to JENNIE MCDONALD:

Born: July 16, 1960; San Jose, California.

Education: Radcliffe Publishing Program; B.A. with honors University of Oregon, University of London.

Career history: Agent since 1992 (McDonald & Associates, now Curtis Brown); rights director and editor at North Point Press; also worked at Jossey-Bass, St. Martin's Press, the Ecco Press, and in bookstores and as a teacher.

Hobbies/personal interests: Tennis, hiking, camping, birds, gardening.

Subjects/categories most enthusiastic about agenting: Nonfiction: Sports, science, child development, memoirs, women's issues, natural history. Fiction: Literary.

Subjects/categories not interested in agenting: Self-help, humor, romance.

Best way for a prospective client to initiate contact: Fiction: Query letter with SASE. Nonfiction: Proposal with SASE. Do not call to talk about your book. I will be eager to call you if I am interested in the work.

Reading-fee policy: No reading fee.

Client representation in the following categories: Nonfiction, 70%; Fiction, 29%; Children's, 1%.

Commission: 15%.

Number of titles sold during the past year: 15.

Approximate percentage of all submissions (from queries through manuscripts) that are rejected: 95%.

Representative titles sold:

Mother Nature by Sarah Blaffer Hardy (Pantheon).

Shooting from the Outside by Joan Ryan and Tara VanDerveer (Avon).

Does Jane Compute? Preserving our Daughters Place in the Cyber Revolution by Roberta Purger (Warner).

The House of Forgetting by Benjamin Alire Saenz (HarperCollins).

Description of the Client from Hell: The writer with a chip on his or her shoulder. Someone who calls all the time and is never happy. Someone who receives advice from 25 friends and calls to share it with me. I almost never have a client like this.

Description of Dream Client: A writer who writes, meets deadlines, is flexible, easy to communicate with, and professional. One with whom it is a pleasure to work. Most of my clients are like this.

The most common mistakes potential clients make when soliciting an agent to represent them: Some writers do not thoroughly research their idea (nonfiction) and/or the competition. Or they do not fully develop their idea. The other most common mistake is to expect a response within a week or so and call to say so. Authors forget to enclose postage too.

What writers can do to enhance their chances of getting an agent (besides being good writers): Thoroughly research their nonfiction project and be able to articulate what they hope to do with it. Share anecdotal information and put the book in context—historically, politically, socially. When it comes to fiction, all it takes is a strong story beautifully told—and luck.

Why did you become an agent? Because I love to talk, read, learn, and thrive on both the editorial process and deal making.

What might you be doing if you weren't an agent? I might be involved in the sciences—teaching and/or writing.

The following information pertains to LAURA BLAKE PETERSON:

Born: Not yesterday.

Education: B.A., English, Vassar College.

Career history: I served as an intern at Curtis Brown while I was still in college, began work at CB two weeks after graduation, and have been here ever since.

Hobbies/personal interests: Film, theater, reading, gardening, regional equestrian competitor, the outdoors.

Subjects/categories most enthusiastic about agenting: Anything outstanding. Nonfiction: history, biography, current affairs, health issues, satire. Fiction: Anything exceptionally written.

Subjects/categories not interested in agenting: Poetry, science fiction, and fantasy.

Best way for a prospective client to initiate contact: The best way is through a referral from either a client of mine or an editor with whom I work.

Reading-fee policy: No reading fee.

Client representation in the following categories: Nonfiction, 45%; Fiction, 45%; Children's, 10%.

Commission: 15% domestic; 20% foreign.

Approximate percentage of all submissions (from queries through manuscripts) that are rejected: 98%.

The most common mistakes potential clients make when soliciting an agent to represent them: Authors who call are unwelcome. Send an intelligent, professional query letter.

Description of the Dream Client: A talented writer who knows the idiosyncrasies of the publishing business yet nonetheless remains determined to be a part of it; a writer with the skills and patience to participate in an often frustrating and quirky industry.

Why did you become an agent? I have a great love of books, and I love fighting for the little guy.

What might you be doing if you weren't an agent? Teaching or riding horses.

The following information pertains to ANDREW POPE:

Born: January 20, 1971.

Education: A.B., English literature, University of Georgia.

Career history: Started in the business as assistant to the CEO of Curtis Brown (Perry Knowlton); moved up to agenthood a couple of years later.

Hobbies/personal interests: Reading, writing, drawing.

Subjects/categories most enthusiastic about agenting: Solid fiction—either literary or commercial. I like odd, quirky, dark, and humorous things. Southern fiction and short-story collections appeal to me as well. As far as nonfiction goes, I look for history, humor, and biography (especially literary) among other things.

Subjects/categories not interested in agenting: Horror, science fiction, children's books.

Best way for a prospective client to initiate contact: A simple, straightforward letter works best.

Reading fee policy: No reading fee.

Client representation in the following categories: Nonfiction, 40%; Fiction, 60%. **Commission:** 15%.

Approximate percentage of all submissions (from queries through manuscripts) that are rejected: 98%.

The most common mistakes potential clients make when soliciting an agent to represent them: Query letters that are riddled with misspellings and sixth-grade grammar fouls never fail to mystify me. Embarking on a career as a writer without learning to write a decent piece of mail strikes me as a rather costly mistake.

What writers can do to enhance their chances of getting an agent (besides being good writers)? That's a tough question.

Description of Dream Client: Patient, confident, realistic, ambitious, easy-going.

What might you be doing if you weren't an agent? Looking for one, I suppose.

The following information pertains to CLYDE TAYLOR:

Career history: More than 15 years in publishing before joining Curtis Brown in 1980.

Subjects/categories most enthusiastic about agenting: Nonfiction: history, politics, biography, law. Fiction: literary to commercial suspense and mystery. Almost anything else with story quality.

Subjects/categories not interested in agenting: Children's books, science fiction, romances, self-help.

Best way for a prospective client to initiate contact: Query letter with SASE and first 50 pages.

Reading-fee policy: No reading fee.

Client representation in the following categories: Nonfiction, 80%; Fiction, 20%. **Commission:** 15% domestic, 20% foreign.

Description of Dream Client: One whose work I always look forward to reading.

The following information pertains to JESS TAYLOR:
Born: March 11, 1960.

Education: B.A., English and American literature, Harvard; M.A., English and comparative literature, Columbia.

Career history: 7 years at Curtis Brown Ltd; TV/movie development before that.

Hobbies/personal interests: Fiction, Caravaggio paintings, odd rituals, independent movies, remote islands, and food.

Subjects/categories most enthusiastic about agenting: Suspense, psychological manipulation, intrigue, general malfeasance.

Subjects/categories not interested in agenting: Self-help, food, diet, and all the non-narrative categories.

Best way for a prospective client to initiate contact: With a recommendation from a writer I know, a friend, or an editor/producer; otherwise, with a letter describing a project as specifically and concisely as possible.

Client representation in the following categories: Nonfiction, 10%; Fiction, 80%; Children's, 10%. Or Deals: Film/TV, 85%; Publishing, 15%.

Approximate percentage of all submissions (from queries through manuscripts) that are rejected: 98%.

Description of the Client from Hell: Vague.

Description of the Dream Client: Focused.

What might you be doing if you weren't an agent? Editing trailers for movies; running a sleazy bar/restaurant in some third-world outpost.

The following information pertains to MAUREEN WALTERS:

Subjects/categories most enthusiastic about agenting: Women's fiction, mysteries and suspense, self-help nonfiction.

Subjects/categories not interested in agenting: Science fiction and fantasy.

Best way for a prospective client to initiate contact: Query letter (with SASE).

Reading-fee policy: No reading fee.

Client representation in the following categories: Nonfiction, 20%; Fiction, 70%; Children's, 10%.

Commission: 15%.

The following information pertains to MITCHELL S. WATERS:

Born: June 19, 1957.

Education: A.B.D., English literature, Fordham University; B.A., English literature, Fairleigh Dickinson University (1982).

Career history: Tennis instructor; college composition and literature instructor.

Hobbies/personal interests: Tennis, painting, music, acting, theatre (opera, ballet, dance in general), skating, film.

Subjects/categories most enthusiastic about agenting: Nonfiction: history, biography, current affairs, health, pop culture, gender studies, gay studies. Fiction: literary, mystery, gay, romance, young adult.

Subjects/categories not interested in agenting: Science fiction, poetry, picture books.

Best way for a prospective client to initiate contact: Query letter (with SASE).

Reading-fee policy: No reading fee.

Client representation in the following categories: Nonfiction, 45%; Fiction, 45%; Children's, 10%.

Commission: 15% domestic, 20% foreign.

Approximate percentage of all submissions (from queries through manuscripts) that are rejected: 98%.

The most common mistakes potential clients make when soliciting an agent to represent them: Sloppily written letters, no SASE, faxed submissions.

What writers can do to enhance their chances of getting an agent (besides being good writers): An elegantly written letter that shows they've done their homework about both their material and the agent they're approaching.

Why did you become an agent? I love books and being an advocate.

What might you be doing if you weren't an agent? Teaching literature.

THE BURNETT LITERARY AGENCY

154 Spring Creek Lane
Wilmington, NC 28405
910-686-9807
http://www.burnettweb.com/agency/index.html (World Wide Web)

Agent: Edmond W. Burnett.

    Career history: Started agency in 1996.

    Hobbies/personal interests: Reading, writing, fishing, boating, camping, the outdoors.

    Subjects/categories most enthusiastic about agenting: Science fiction, fantasy, action/adventure, historical fiction, thrillers, suspense, general/mainstream fiction.

    Subjects/categories not interested in agenting: Nonfiction, Children's, short stories, poetry, most horror, occult related, romance, erotica. I am not interested in representing novels that contain an excess of explicit sex, rape, or foul language.

    Best way for a prospective client to initiate contact: Query letter, brief synopsis, SASE (required for a reply), and your résumé or bio (please list previous publishing credits, if any). You may optionally include the first one or two chapters of your novel. Please do not query by phone.

    Reading-fee policy: No reading fee.

    Client representation in the following categories: Fiction, 100%.

    Commission: 15% domestic; 20% foreign.

    Number of titles sold during the past year: This is a new agency.

    Approximate percentage of all submissions (from queries through manuscripts) that are rejected: 95%.

    Description of Dream Client: A published novelist who comes to me with a fabulous manuscript and an outline for one or two more. One who is professional, courteous, and talented.

    What writers can do to enhance their chances of getting an agent (besides being good writers): Before you submit, polish your manuscript until it is absolutely perfect. Produce a professional and well-crafted query letter and synopsis. Make sure your material is in the correct, standard format. Always include SASE.

    Why did you become an agent? I love working with creative authors and the publishing industry in general.

    Comments: No matter what happens, keep writing!

SHEREE BYKOFSKY ASSOCIATES, INC.

11 East 47th Street
New York, NY 10017
212-308-1253

Agent: Sheree Bykofsky.

    Born: September, 1956; Queens, New York.

Education: B.A., State University of New York, Binghamton; M.A., Columbia University (English and comparative literature).

Career history: Executive editor/book producer, The Stonesong Press (1984–present); freelance editor/writer (1984–present); general manager/managing editor, Chiron Press, 1979–1984. Author of six books and co-executive editor of *The New York Public Library Desk Reference*.

Hobbies/personal interests: Tournament Scrabble, poker, racquetball, movies, bridge.

Subjects/categories most enthusiastic about agenting: Popular reference, adult nonfiction (hardcovers and trade paperbacks), quality fiction (highly selective).

Subjects/categories not interested in agenting: Genre romances, science fiction, Westerns, occult and supernatural, children's books.

Best way for a prospective client to initiate contact with you: Send a well-written, detailed query letter with SASE. Please, no phone calls.

Reading-fee policy: No reading fee.

Client representation in the following categories: Nonfiction, 80%; Fiction, 20%.

Commission: 15%.

Number of titles sold during the past year: 40.

Approximate percentage of all submissions (from queries through manuscripts) that are rejected: 90%.

Representative titles sold:

Ten Minute Life Lessons for Kids by Jamie Miller (HarperCollins).

Christmas Miracles: Magical Stories of Modern Day Miracles from the Season of Love compiled and edited by Jamie Miller, Laura Lewis, and Jennifer Basye Sander (Morrow).

Pilgrim Souls, edited by Elizabeth Powers, and Amy Mandelker (Norton).

How to Be an Advocate for Your Disabled Child by Katherine Graham (Norton).

The Secret History of Rock: The Most Influential Bands You've Never Heard by Roni Sarig (Billboard Books).

He Rents, She Rents by Laurie Viera and Richard Roeper (St. Martin's Press).

Keep What You Earn: Tax Saving Strategies for the Self-Employed by Henry A'im Fellman (Pocket).

Movie Time: A Chronological History of the Movies and the Movie Industry by Gene Brown (Macmillan/Prentice Hall).

Debt Free: Bankruptcy Without Guilt by James Caher and John Caher (Holt).

Handbook for the Soul, edited by Richard Carlson and Benjamin Shield (Little Brown).

Multicultural Manners by Norine Dresser (Wiley).

More Oral Sadism and the Vegetarian Personality by Glenn Ellenbogen (Brunner/Mazel).

The Parent's Dictionary by Merrill Furman (humor) (Contemporary).

Public Speaking for the Painfully Shy by Don Gabor (Crown).

Vital Touch: The Role of Touch in Infant Development, An Evolutionary Perspective by Sharon Heller (Holt).

The Executive Toolbox: 60 Power Breaks by James Joseph (Berkley).

All Aboard: The Comprehensive Guide to North American Train Travel by Jim Loomis (Prima).

Life's Little Frustration Book by G. Gaynor McTigue (St. Martin's).

Lavender Light: Meditations for Gay Men in Recovery by Adrian Milton (Perigee).

Jimmy Carter: A Prophet Scorned by Kenneth Morris (University of Georgia).

500 Things You Should Never Do by Ed Morrow (Contemporary).

The Hidden Face of Shyness by Frank Schneier and Lawrence Welkowitz (Avon).

No Human Involved by Barbara Seranella (fiction) (St. Martin's).

Men Are Lunatics and Women Are Nuts! by Ron Shwartz (Running Press).

The most common mistakes potential clients make when soliciting an agent to represent them: Excessive hubris, not explaining what the book is about, paranoia (we're not going to steal your idea), sloppy grammar, punctuation, and spelling.

What writers can do to enhance their chances of getting an agent (besides being good writers): I love a query letter that is as well written as the proposed book or a polished, perfect, professional proposal.

Description of the Client from Hell: I only take on an author if I feel we can work well together.

Description of Dream Client: One who is not only a talented writer but who is a professional in every sense—from writing the proposal to promoting the book. Also, one who appreciates my hard work on his/her behalf. So far, all of my clients have proven to be dream clients.

Why did you become an agent? It suits me, and I feel I have the talent and experience to do it well.

What might you be doing if you weren't an agent? Writing and editing.

Comments: In addition to being an agent, I am a book packager and author. This gives me *and my clients* a perspective that most agents do not have.

CAMBRIDGE LITERARY ASSOCIATES

Author's Representatives
150 Merrimac Street, Suite 301
Riverport Landing
Newburyport, MA 01950
508-499-0374

Agent: Michael Valentino.

Born: August 3, 1965; Somerville, Massachusetts.

Education: B.A., 1987; M.A., 1992 Harvard University.

Career history: Reporter/writer, *Commercial Record*; Reporter, Beacon Press; Freelance magazine writer; Freelance ghostwriter.

Hobbies/personal interests: Travel, biking, skiing, sailing, film.

Subjects/categories most enthusiastic about agenting: Priority: true life, novels, action/adventure.

Subjects/categories not interested in agenting: New Age.

Best way for a prospective client to initiate contact: Query letter.

Reading-fee policy: No reading fee.

Client representation in the following categories: Nonfiction, 20%; Fiction, 60%; Children's, 5%; Textbooks, 2%; Short Story, 13%.

Commission: 15% domestic, 20% foreign.

Number of titles sold during the past year: 18.

Approximate percentage of all submissions (from queries through manuscripts) that are rejected: 85–90%.

Representative titles sold:

Jitters by Linda Rentschler (Lifetime TV World Premiere, May 5, 1997).

Five Centuries of Italian American History (Executive Press).

Description of the Client from Hell: Unpublished and wants an advance on his first novel. This same type expects an auction and is disappointed if he doesn't get one.

Description of Dream Client: He/she writes well, is realistic about his/her chances, and appreciates every read.

The most common mistakes potential clients make when soliciting an agent to represent them: Vague and unprofessional query letters; no SASE; braggadocio by beginners.

What writers can do to enhance their chances of getting an agent (besides being good writers): Send a focused, detailed description of the book/screenplay with an SASE.

Why did you become an agent? Lifelong love of books and literature.

What might you be doing if you weren't an agent? Work as an editor for a publishing house.

Comments: We at Cambridge understand that we are dealing with something precious: *our client's dreams*, and we treat them accordingly.

MARIA CARVAINIS AGENCY, INC.

235 West End Avenue
New York, NY 10023
212-580-1559

Agent: Maria Carvainis.

Born: March 24, 1946; Brisbane, Australia.

Education: B.A., City College of New York, 1967; New York State Merit Scholar.

Career history: Established the agency in 1977 after more than 10 years in the publishing industry as a Senior Editor with Macmillan Publishing, Basic Books, Crown Publishing, and Avon Books.

Subjects/categories most enthusiastic about agenting: The agency represents both fiction and nonfiction with special interest in general fiction/mainstream, literary fiction, mystery and suspense, thrillers, fantasy, historical Regency, young adult and children's, category romance, political and film biographies, medicine, women's issues, business, finance, psychology, and popular science. The agency also considers screenplays from writers who have previously been professionally produced.

Subjects/categories not interested in agenting: Science fiction and screenplays from writers who have not previously been professionally produced.

Best way for a prospective client to initiate contact: Query first with a 1–2 page synopsis and a cover letter outlining previous writing history, if any, vividly illustrating what is special about the project. Enclose SASE.

Reading-fee policy: No reading fee.

Client representation in the following categories: Nonfiction, 25%; Fiction, 60%; Children's, 15%.

Commission: 15% domestic, 20% foreign.

Approximate percentage of all submissions (from queries through manuscripts) that are rejected: 99%.

Representative titles sold:

Fat Tuesday by Sandra Brown (Warner Books).

Sheer Gall by Michael Kahn (Dutton).

Silent Melody by Mary Balogh (Berkley).

Beyond Workplace 2000 by Joseph H. Boyett and Jimmie T. Boyett (Wiley & Sons).

Charmed by Catherine Hart (Kensington).

Impact: The Threat of Comets and Asteroids by Gerrit L. Verschuur (Oxford).

The most common mistakes potential clients make when soliciting an agent to represent them: Having me read material that does not represent a writer's best efforts. Not knowing what he/she is offering for sale and if it will realistically fit with a publisher's needs and readers' interests.

What writers can do to enhance their chances of getting an agent (besides being good writers): Be savvy about his/her particular writing talent or expertise for the marketplace. Have short-term and long-term career plans.

Why did you become an agent? I wanted to unequivocally represent the writer's interests and have the opportunity to make money, neither of which was the case while I was an editor.

What might you be doing if you weren't an agent? Reading, traveling, enjoying the performing arts, knitting, and gardening.

Martha Casselman, Literary Agent

P.O. Box 342
Calistoga, CA 94515
707-942-4341

Agent: Martha Casselman.

Born: June 8, 1935; New York City.

Education: B.A., English and education, Jackson College of Tufts University; attended Radcliffe Publishing Procedures Course.

Career history: Magazines, editorial assistant, copyeditor, editor (*Good Housekeeping*, *Show* magazine, *Holiday* magazine); freelance editor and reader (Book-of-the-Month Club, Viking, etc.)—in New York before move to California in 1976.

Hobbies/personal interests: Can you believe—reading? (Belongs to reading group).

Subjects/categories most enthusiastic about agenting: Food books, some nonfiction, other exciting books too wonderful to turn away.

Subjects/categories not interested in agenting: Poetry, textbooks, religion, all kids' books.

Best way for a prospective writer to initiate contact with you: Write brief letter (with SASE), and be straightforward about what other contacts are being made; make proposal/query so good it's impossible for me *not* to go after it (but expect long-distance return calls to be collect if you make a query by phone).

Reading-fee policy: No reading fee.

Client representation in the following categories: Nonfiction, 100%.

Commission: 15%, plus some copying, overnight mail expenses; 20% if using subagents.

Number of titles sold during the past year: Confidential.

Approximate percentage of all submissions (from queries through manuscripts) that are rejected: 99%.

Representative titles sold: Confidential.

The most common mistakes potential clients make when soliciting an agent to represent them: For nonfiction: not enough research on the market of books already in print.

What writers can do to enhance their chances of getting an agent (besides being good writers): Make your proposal *so* good (for nonfiction) that when I get an editor to take it to the publishing board, the editor could keel over in the hall and the proposal could sell itself to the editors at that meeting. Should have: excellence, excitement, and imagination—in the sample material, *not* the cover letter.

Description of the Client from Hell: The client signs a contract, then spends the next three years complaining about its clauses; also, the client who has something under submission from this office and then gets sweet-talked into accepting a contract without the agent's guidance.

What might you be doing if you weren't an agent? It changes. I can't remember *not* being an agent.

Comments: It's not getting any easier.

CASTIGLIA LITERARY AGENCY

1155 Camino Del Mar, Suite 510
Del Mar, CA 92014
619-753-4361

Agent: Julie Castiglia.

Education: Educated in England.

Career history: Published writer (3 titles), freelance editor (10 years), agent (last 11 years).

Hobbies/personal interests: Traveling, hiking, skiing, gardening, animals, decorative arts, books.

Subjects/categories most enthusiastic about agenting: Mainstream, literary and ethnic fiction. Nonfiction: psychology, science and health, biography, women's issues, niche books, contemporary issues.

Subjects/categories not interested in agenting: Horror and science fiction, contemporary genre romance.

Best way for a prospective client to initiate contact with you: A query letter, plus a one-page outline/or synopsis plus the first two chapters.

Reading-fee policy: No reading fee.

Client representation in the following categories: Nonfiction, 75%; Fiction, 25%.

Commission: 15% domestic; 20% foreign.

Number of titles sold during the past year: 20.

Approximate percentage of all submissions (from queries through manuscripts) that are rejected: 95%.

Representative titles sold:

Living with Your Dreams by Dean Hamer and Peter Copeland (Doubleday).

Jesus in Blue Jeans by Laurie Beth Jones (Hyperion).

Going Out in Style by Doug Keister and Xavier Cronin (Facts on File).

Remember the Time by Annette Reynolds (Bantam).

Grow Something Besides Old by Laurie Beth Jones (Simon & Schuster).

Cuttin' the Rug in the Moonlit Sky by Sharony Andrews Green (Doubleday).

Inside the Bungalow by Doug Keister and Paul Duchscher (Penguin).

Nitty Gritty Grammar by Edith Fine and Judith Josephson (Ten Speed).

Cooking with Jesus by Kitty Morse (Ten Speed).

Portfolio Management and Asset Allocation by Gordon Williamson (Macmillan).

Postpartum Depression by Shari Roan (Adams Media).

The most common mistakes potential clients make when soliciting an agent to represent them: Impoliteness, calling too often, talking too much.

What writers can do to enhance their chances of getting an agent (besides being good writers): Attitude, credentials, and obvious knowledge of publishing business.

Description of the Client from Hell: Loquacious, untrustworthy, grumpy, promises but does not perform, doesn't meet deadlines. Talks but doesn't write!!!

Description of Dream Client: Trustworthy, intelligent, hard-working—understands the business. All the clients I work with have become good friends. They trust my judgment and appreciate what I do for them—they are my dream clients.

Why did you become an agent? I've always loved books and knew the publishing business well, having sold my own three books and edited other writers' work. It was a natural step.

What might you be doing if you weren't an agent? Writing and traveling.

CISKE & DIETZ LITERARY AGENCY

N.E. Branch:
P.O. Box 163
Greenleaf, WI 54126
414-864-7702
EVRGREn39@aol.com (e-mail)

Milwaukee office:
10605 West Wabash Avenue
Milwaukee, WI 53224-2315
414-355-8915

Agents: Andrea Boeshaar (Milwaukee office); Patricia Dietz (N.E. Branch).

Born: Dietz: January 16, 1951.

Education: Boeshaar: English major, University of Wisconsin at Milwaukee; professional communication and business management, Alverno College. Dietz: Western Illinois University: English, Spanish, professional writing.

Career history: Boeshaar: 12 years writing experience; 5 years writing for Evangelical Christian market, 2 published novels, several published articles. Dietz: Editor, *Your Christian Connection* magazine; freelance writer.

Hobbies/personal interests: Dietz: Spending time with my family, writing, acting, directing, cycling/walking.

Subjects/categories most enthusiastic about agenting: Boeshaar: Inspirational (for the Evangelical Christian market only) which includes fiction, nonfiction, with a special interest in romance. Dietz: Suspense and mystery, Young Adult fiction, nonfiction (all types).

Subjects/categories not interested in agenting: Boeshaar: Anything that does not target the Evangelical Christian market, poetry, short stories. Dietz: Occult, New Age.

Best way for a prospective client to initiate contact: Boeshaar: Query letter (with SASE), brief outline, and first three chapters of manuscript. Dietz: Send a query letter or, for fiction, a partial including a cover letter, a synopsis, and the *first* ten pages of the manuscript. For nonfiction, a query or formal book proposal. No response without SASE.

Reading-fee policy: No reading fee.

Client Representation: Nonfiction, 30%; Fiction, 70%.

Commission: 15% domestic; 20% foreign.

Approximate percentage of all submissions (from queries through manuscripts) that are rejected: 98%.

Description of the Client from Hell: An inflexible person who expects the agent to be a full-time personal editor. The writer whose impatient demands and unrealistic expectations are high, and whose work output is low and slow.

Description of Dream Client: A reasonable person who is thoughtful of my time. My Dream Client studies the markets and knows the market or genre they are writing for. They spend time writing, rewriting, and polishing and are willing to keep rewriting until the material is ready. The bottom line here is, the manuscript quality sells the book. If you submit the best product, we can get the best sale!

The most common mistakes potential clients make when soliciting an agent to represent them: Boeshaar: Not including SASE. Sending randomly chosen chapters instead of the first three chapters. Dietz: Please avoid telephone or e-mail queries. Your query letter should focus on the specifics of the book submitted and the author's qualifications. Show me you can write with your query letter! Please don't submit manuscripts via certified or express mail. An author's most costly mistake, in my opinion, is to spend his/her time writing a book without studying the markets. Write to a specific market.

What writers can do to enhance their chances of getting an agent (besides being good writers): Boeshaar: Queries that sum up the book in one paragraph, including word length, setting, and clearly stating what it is: fiction, nonfiction, historical romance, etc., with SASE enclosed. Read what's being sold in the Christian market—get a feel for what's being published and make your work meet those standards (or exceed them!). Dietz: I love a query letter that sells the book so well, it sells the author before I ever see his/her qualifications. Use tight, powerful writing and strong specifics. Tell me what market you've targeted. Tell me why your book will sell. Make the presentation of your query, partial, or proposal as crisp and professional as possible. Be patient.

Why did you become an agent? Dietz: I love writing and can relate to an author's unique struggles. I've read avidly and analytically for many years. I love working with people.

What might you be doing if you weren't an agent? Boeshaar: Writing and serving the Lord in another capacity. Dietz: Dividing my time between my family and my own writing.

Comments: Dietz: Be patient. Be persistent. Be willing to rewrite and rewrite until you can pick up the best books in your chosen area and know your own writing surpasses them all. Fresh, tight, carefully crafted writing sells. If the manuscript doesn't compete, neither can the agent.

CONNIE CLAUSEN & ASSOCIATES LITERARY AGENCY

250 East 87th Street
New York, NY 10128
212-427-6135
fax: 212-996-7111

Agents: Connie Clausen, Founder; Stedman Mays, Principal Associate. Junior Associates: Kristina Richards, Danielle Chapman, Regan Graves.

Education: Mays: M.A. in English, University of Virginia.

Career history: Clausen: MGM Studios, Production Department and Head of Special Promotion; Senior Editor *Haire's Infant and Children's Review*; TV Spokeswoman: *Live Like a Millionaire* (co-host), the Colonial Airline show, Arm & Hammer, Vel, Beech-Nut (with Dr. Spock), Coca-Cola, Ponds, Gleem; Dramatic roles: *The Gambler* (Broadway), *Love of Life, Goodyear Theater, Danger,* and *Suspense* (all TV); Author of the autobiographical memoir *I Love You Honey, But the Season's Over*

(Holt) and various articles; Publicist, Publicity Director, Head of Marketing, and Vice President at Macmillan; Founder of Connie Clausen & Associates, 1976.

Subjects/categories most enthusiastic about agenting: (Mostly Nonfiction): memoirs, biography, autobiography, true stories, medical, health/nutrition, psychology, how-to, financial, women's issues, relationships, men's issues, parenting, spirituality, religion, history, true crime, fashion/beauty, style, humor, rights for books optioned for TV movies and feature films.

Subjects/categories not interested in agenting: We normally do not represent fiction.

Best way for a prospective client to initiate contact: A query letter (containing proposed book concept and author bio) or brief proposal (containing the following sections: Concept, Market Analysis, Competition, Publicity, Author's Credentials, and Outline), including SASE for return of materials.

Reading-fee policy: No fees.

Client representation in the following categories: Nonfiction, 100%.

Commission: 15%.

Approximate percentage of all submissions (from queries through manuscripts) that are rejected: 90%.

Representative titles sold:

Way Bandy: Designing Your Face by Way Bandy (Random House).

The Good Luck Book by Stefan Bechtel and Laurence Roy Stains (Workman).

The Practical Encyclopedia of Sexual Health by Stefan Bechtel (Rodale).

Born to Be Wild: Murder, Rape, and Deception—The True Story of a Biker's Ride of Terror by Barry Bowe (Warner Books).

The Way of the Scout by Tom Brown (Berkley).

Filling the Void: Six Steps from Loss to Fulfillment by Dorothy Bullitt (Rawson/Scribner).

Investment Basics for Women by Kathy Buys and Jonathan Berohn (Macmillan).

Healing the Child: A Mother's Story by Nancy Cain (Rawson/Scribner).

Big City Look: Achieving That Metropolitan Chic—No Matter Where You Live by Sherry Suib Cohen and Vincent Roppatte (HarperCollins).

Looking for the Other Side: The Extraordinary Adventures of a Skeptical Journalist as She Explores the Non-Material World by Sherry Suib Cohen (Clarkson Potter).

The Stuff of Heroes: The Eight Business Secrets of Extraordinary Battle Leaders by William Cohen, Ph.D. (Longstreet Press).

The Naked Civil Servant by Quentin Crisp (Penguin).

Resident Alien: The New York Diaries Quentin Crisp (Alyson).

A Flat Stomach ASAP: The Fastest Way to Perfect Abs—A Revolutionary New Program Combining Diet and Exercise by Ellington Darden, Ph.D. (Pocket Books).

Drawing Angels Near: Children Tell of Angels in Words and Pictures Mimi Doe and Garland Waller (Pocket Books).

Nurturing Your Child's Soul: 10 Principles of Spiritual Parenting by Mimi Doe and Marsha Walch, Ph.D. (HarperCollins).

The Rules: Time-Tested Secrets for Capturing the Heart of Mr. Right Ellen Fein and Scherrie Schneider (Warner Books).

The Rules II: More Rules to Live and Love By by Ellen Fein and Sherrie Schneider (Warner Books).

Pilaf, Risotto, and Other Ways with Rice Sada Fretz (Little, Brown)

What Men Really Want from Women: Inside the Mind and Heart of the Professional Man by Bradley Gerstman, Christopher Pizzo, and Richard Seldes (HarperCollins).

Price of Honor: Muslim Women Lift the Veil of Silence on the Islamic World by Jan Goodwin (Little, Brown and Penguin).

Eat to Win and *Eat to Succeed* by Robert Haas (HarperCollins).

Permanent Remissions: Life Extending Diet Strategies by Robert Haas (Pocket Books)

How to Talk So People Listen by Sonya Hamlin (HarperCollins).

Growing Myself: A Spiritual Journey through Gardening by Judith Handelsman (Dutton).

"I Love Him, But . . .": The Things Men Do That Drive Their Wives Crazy by Merry Bloch Jones (Workman)

"Please Don't Kiss Me at the Bus Stop!": Over 600 Things Parents Do that Drive Their Kids Crazy by Merry Bloch Jones (Andrews & McMell).

What the IRS Doesn't Want You to Know by Marilyn Kaplan and Naomi Weiss (Villard—revised annually).

Dancing Around the Volcano: Freeing Our Erotic Lives by Guy Kettelhack (Crown).

Shadows of the King: The Secret Bonds Between Gay Men and Their Fathers by Guy Kettelhack (Crown).

How to Write a Movie in 21 Days: The Inner Movie Method by Viki King (HarperCollins).

The Common Sense Kitchen Advisor by Deborah Krasner (Harper Collins)

The Pocket Doctor by Michael LaCombe, M.D. (Andrews & McMeel)

The Pocket Pediatrician by Michael LaCombe, M.D. (Andrews & McMeel)

The "Late Night with David Letterman" Book of Top Lists and *An Altogether New Book of Top Ten Lists from "Late Night with David Letterman"* by David Letterman and the "Late Night with David Letterman" Writers (Pocket Books).

Angels of Emergency: True Life Rescue Stories from America's Paramedics and EMTs by Dary Matera and Donna Theisen (HarperCollins).

Charlie and Me: Life after Helter Skelter by Dary Matera and Ed George (St. Martin's Press).

The Chiropractor's Health Book by Leonard McGill (Clarkson Potter)

Jackson Pollock: An American Saga by Steven Naifeh and Gregory White Smith (Clarkson Potter, awarded the Pulitzer Prize).

The Morman Murders: A True Story of Greed, Forgery, Deceit, and Death by Steven Naifeh and Gregory White Smith (Weidenfield and Onyx/Penguin).

Access 2 for Dummies by Scott Palmer (IDG Books)

How to Make Love to a Man by Alexandra Penney (Clarkson Potter).

Scavullo on Beauty by Scavullo (Random House).

Dharma Lion: A Biography of Allen Ginsberg by Michael Schumacher (St. Martin's Press).

Rejecting Mothers, Wounded Daughters by Ann Symonds (Rawson/Scribner).

Dumped!: A Survival Guide for the Women Who's Been Left by the Man She Loved by Andrea Thompson and Sally Warren (HarperCollins).

Your Thyroid: A Home Reference by Lawrence Wood, M.D., David Cooper, M.D., and E. Chester Ridgway, M.D. (Ballantine, now in its third edition).

Description of the Dream Client: An author who has read and digested Strunk and White; who has read a book or two about how to get published, about how to write a query letter and a proposal; who listens to constructive suggestions and revises accordingly.

It is also important for an author to be willing to promote the book aggressively with all their resources. Publishers look for authors skilled at generating publicity.

Why did you become an agent? Love publishing—learn with every book.

RUTH COHEN, INC.

P.O. Box 7626
Menlo Park, CA 94025
415-854-2054

Agent: Ruth Cohen.

Subjects/categories most enthusiastic about agenting: Women's fiction (contemporary "themes" of modern women), mysteries (different settings with fascinating characters), juvenile literature (quality picture books, middle-grade fiction/nonfiction, young-adults showing "special" writing skills).

Subjects/categories not interested in agenting: Films, poetry, books in verse, science fiction, Westerns, how-to books.

Best way for a prospective client to initiate contact: Send a query letter (with SASE), which also includes the opening 10 to 15 pages of the manuscript. Please, *no* unsolicited *full manuscripts.*

Reading-fee policy: No reading fee, except for foreign mailings and faxes.

Client representation in the following categories: Nonfiction, 5%; Fiction, 60%; Children's, 35%.

Commission: 15% domestic; 20% foreign.

Number of titles sold during the past year: 87.

Representative titles sold:

One Perfect Rose (Ballantine).

Slow Dance, Round Dance (Avon).

Sammy's Story.

What writers can do to enhance their chances of getting an agent (besides being good writers): Submit a well-written, well-crafted, well-disciplined manuscript.

Description of Client from Hell: There aren't really any clients from hell. There are clients who grow disappointed and who despair of the publishing world as it merges and alters and leaves fewer opportunities for new writers to succeed in work they love—writing.

Description of Dream Client: Clients who understand that our combined efforts generally will advance both our careers, and that patience and stamina are the preferred attributes for getting published well—now and always.

Comments: Keep trying—and keep trying to detach yourself from your own writing so that you can view it objectively. Then reassess, revise, rework, and resubmit.

RICHARD CURTIS ASSOCIATES, INC.

171 East 74th Street
New York, NY 10021
212-772-7363

Agent: Richard Curtis.

Born: June 23, 1937.

Education: B.A., American studies, Syracuse University; M.A., American studies, University of Wyoming.

Career history: Foreign rights manager, Scott Meredith Literary Agency (1959–1966); freelance author (1967–1975); started own agency (1975); incorporated Richard Curtis Associates, Inc. (1979); first president of Independent Literary Agents Association (1980); treasurer (1991–1995) and president (1995–1997) of Association of Authors' Representatives.

Hobbies/personal interests: Watercolor painting, softball, racquetball, classical music.

Subjects/categories most enthusiastic about agenting: Although best known for such categories as science fiction, thrillers, Westerns, and romance, I've become more and more interested in mainstream fiction, commercial nonfiction, and software/multimedia.

Subjects/categories not interested in agenting: See last question.

Best way for a prospective writer to initiate contact with you. One-page query letter plus no more than one-page synopsis of proposed submission. Must be accompanied by SASE or we won't reply. No faxed queries, no e-mail queries. No submission of material unless specifically requested. If requested, submission must be accompanied by SASE or we assume you don't want your submission back.

Reading-fee policy: No reading fee.

Client representation in the following categories: Nonfiction, 30%; Fiction, 70%.

Commission: 15% on basic sale to U.S. publisher; 15% on dramatic (movies, television, audio, multimedia); 20% on British and foreign publication rights.

Number of titles sold during the past year: Approximately 150.

Approximate percentage of all submissions (from queries through manuscripts) that are rejected: 99%.

Representative titles sold:

Ignition by Kevin Anderson and Doug Beason (Tor Books, Universal Pictures).

Blood Relations by Barbara Parker (Dutton/Penguin Publishers).

Exquisite Corpse by Poppy Z. Brite (Simon & Schuster).

The Crook Factory by Dan Simmons (Avon Books).

Two romance novels by Jennifer Blake (Harlequin/Mira).

Four Western novels by Matthew Braun (St. Martin's Paperbacks).

Two untitled novels by Megan Chance (HarperPaperbacks).

Three untitled novels by Dave Duncan (Avon Books).

Four novels by Greg Keyes (Del Rey Books).

The most common mistakes potential clients make when soliciting an agent to represent them: Phone queries instead of a letter. Want to see us before we've read material. Don't proofread their work.

What writers can do to enhance their chances of getting an agent (besides being good writers): Simple letter, well-described synopsis of work to be submitted.

Description of the Client from Hell: High PITA factor. PITA stands for *Pain In The Ass*. Divide commissions earned into time dealing with complaints.

Description of Dream Client: Low PITA factor.

Why did you become an agent? Love authors, love publishers, love books, love being in the middle.

What might you be if you weren't an agent? A pianist, an artist, a catcher for the New York Mets, a linebacker for the New York Giants, a volleyball player on a California beach, a psychotherapist, a rabbi, a playwright.

Comments: Anyone thinking of going into writing or publishing must become adept with a computer. The writer of tomorrow will create with images and sounds, like a one-person movie producer.

DH LITERARY, INC.

P.O. Box 990
Nyack, NY 10960
212-753-7942

Agent: David Hendin.

Born: December 16, 1945.

Education: B.S., biology, education, University of Missouri (1967); M.A., journalism, University of Missouri (1967).

Career history: United Feature Syndicate/United Media; senior vice president and chief operating officer of United Feature Syndicate; president and chief operating officer of World Almanac, Pharos Books (1970–1993). Author of 11 nonfiction books including *Death As a Fact of Life* (Norton, Warner), *The Life Givers* (Morrow), and coauthor of *The Genetic Connection* (Morrow, Signet).

Hobbies/personal interests: Archaeology.

Subjects/categories most enthusiastic about agenting: Strong nonfiction, inspirational and how-to nonfiction, medical and psychology nonfiction, women's interest nonfiction, thrillers and unusual mysteries, literary fiction. I also represent comic strips and columns for newspaper syndication (very selectively).

Subjects/categories not interested in agenting: Genre fiction, children's.

Best way for a prospective client to initiate contact: Query letter (with SASE) or one-page e-mail query.

Reading-fee policy: No reading fee.

Client representation in the following categories: Nonfiction, 75%; Fiction, 20%; Textbooks 5%.

Commission: 15%.

Number of titles sold during the past year: 24.

Approximate percentage of all submissions (from queries through manuscripts) that are rejected: 90%.

Representative titles sold:

Hug the Monster by David Smith and Sandy Leicester (Andrews and McMeel).

Miss Manners Rescues Civilization by Judith Martin (Crown).

Talking Tall by Jeff McQuain (Random House).

The Thin You Within You by Dr. Abraham Twerski (St. Martin's).

Norton Anthology of Rock'N'Roll by William McKeen and Dave Marsh (W. W. Norton).

Legend of St. Nicholas by R. O. Blechman (Stewart, Tabori & Chang).

Eating the Bear by Carole Fungaroli (Farrar Straus & Giroux).

His Promised Land: The Memoir of John P. Parker, Escaped Slave and Conductor on the Underground Railroad (W. W. Norton/Tri-Star for Jonathan Demme to direct).

The most common mistakes potential clients make when soliciting an agent to represent them: Send too much material before being asked; don't write a good query letter; don't enclose SASE; start the query by telling me they have 14 unpublished projects . . .

What writers can do to enhance their chances of getting an agent (besides being good writers)? Great ideas and superb query letters.

Description of the Client from Hell: I have no clients from hell.

Description of Dream Client: Great ideas, prompt delivery, at least a passing interest in the business side of publishing.

Why did you become an agent? I have been a newspaper columnist, book author, and president of a publishing company. Becoming an agent was the next logical extension of my professional life—not to mention that some of my best friends are writers!

What might you be doing if you weren't an agent? Excavating ruins in the Middle East or teaching journalism at a university (both of which I've done).

Comments: Writers—send me your fabulous ideas. I have a relatively small number of clients and love to work on projects I like.

DHS LITERARY, INC.

Twin Sixties Tower
6060 North Central Expressway, Suite 624
Dallas, TX 75206
214-363-4422
fax: 214-363-4423

Agent: David Hale Smith, President; Ashley A. Carroll.

The following information pertains to DAVID HALE SMITH:

Born: July 9, 1968.

Education: B.A., English, Kenyon College, 1990.

Career history: Copyeditor, one year, Southwest NewsWire, Inc., Dallas; assistant agent/agent, three years, Dupree/Miller & Associates, Dallas; founded DHS Literary Agency, March 1994.

Hobbies/personal interests: Reading, writing, camping, hiking, travel.

Subjects/categories most enthusiastic about agenting: Mainstream fiction: thrillers, suspense, mystery, and historical fiction; literary fiction; Westerns. Business nonfiction. Multicultural interests. Pop culture, music, film and television, technology. General nonfiction and gift books.

Subjects/categories not interested in agenting: Children's, young-adult, short stories, poetry.

Best way for a prospective client to initiate contact: Query with synopsis and SASE. Material sent without SASE will not be acknowledged or returned. Direct queries to V. Michele Lewis, Submissions Director.

Reading-fee policy: No reading fee.

Client representation in the following categories: Nonfiction, 50%; Fiction, 50%.

Commission: 15% domestic sales; 25% on foreign (via subagents).

Number of titles sold during the past year: About 30, including film options and rights sales.

Approximate percentage of all submissions (from queries through manuscripts) that are rejected: As a new agency, we are extremely selective. We reject 90%–95% of all submissions.

Representative titles sold:

A Flash of Red by Clay Harvey (Putnam).

Hollywood Hi-Fi by George Gimarc and Pat Reeder (St. Martin's).

Could You Love Me like My Cat? by Beth Fowler (Fireside/Simon & Schuster).

Kontum Diary by Paul Reed and Ted Schwarz (Summit).

The Babysitter's Companion by Mary Jayne Fogerty (Ten Speed/Tricycle).

Lone Star Song by Rick Koster (St. Martin's).

The *"Moving To"* Series by Bookworks (4-book deal) (Macmillan/Alpha Books).

The most common mistakes potential clients make when soliciting an agent to represent them: The biggest mistake I see people making is coming on too strong without backing up their claims of "sure-fire" success. I think that people *must* be aggressive to get noticed in this business—but if you're all style and no substance, it is a waste of everybody's time. Another common blunder I see is just a general lack of preparedness. Spend some time learning about the business, *before* contacting agents and publishers.

What writers can do to enhance their chances of getting an agent (besides being good writers): When someone says, "I've got something that will knock your socks off," and it *does*, that excites me.

There is nothing quite like the experience of reading a brilliant cover letter, and then tearing into an even better manuscript.

Description of the Client from Hell: Unprofessional people who think that once they have an agent, their role in placing and selling their work is finished. I had a client who made the mistake of thinking this agency was his personal secretarial and counseling firm, without ever realizing that all the time we spent talking to him and doing his busywork was time we couldn't spend selling his stuff. He is no longer a client.

Description of the Dream Client: A professional in every phase of the business, who believes that the agent-author relationship is a team endeavor. A successful publishing experience is the result of a collaborative effort. I work extremely hard for my clients—and I work even harder for those who make it easier for me to do my job by working *with* me, not against me.

Why did you become an agent? I have always loved books, reading good ones and talking about them with other people—that's the best part of the job. When I learned that agents get to see the good stuff even before the publishers do, that's where I wanted to be.

What might you be doing if you weren't an agent? I am in awe of good writers, and I have always wanted to be one. I know some pretty good stories, and I plan on taking a crack at writing them down someday.

I would also like to sail around the world with my family one day.

Comments: *Always* read the book first, then go see the movie!

The following information pertains to Ashley A. Carroll:
Born: June 30, 1972; Dallas, Texas
Education: Texas A&M University and Southwest Texas State University.
Career history: Before joining DHS Literary, Inc., worked as a literary agent with Dupree/Miller and Associates. Have secured publishing contracts for a variety of clients whose areas of specialization range from parenting to business to commercial fiction.

Hobbies/personal interests: Tennis, running, water skiing, reading, Epicurean delights, volunteer work for Girls, Inc.

Subjects/categories most enthusiastic about agenting: Mostly nonfiction. Interests include business; child guidance/parenting; communications, Internet/computer; cooking/foods/nutrition; health; crafts; gift books; how-to; humorous nonfiction; self-help; sports; travel; women's issues/studies; religious/spiritual; pop-culture; celebrity-driven books.

Client representation in the following categories: Nonfiction, 60%; Fiction, 40%.
Representative titles sold:
A Whisper of Black by Clay Harvey (Putnam).
Could You Love Me Like My God? by Beth Fowler (Simon & Schuster/Fireside).
The Vitality Factor by Elizabeth Somer, M.S., R.D. (Morrow).
A Woman's Faith by Mark McGarry (Carol Publishing).
Firebirds by Chuck Carlock (Bantam Books).
The 100 Best Freelance Careers by Kelly Reno (Arco/Macmillan).
Jesse James: A Biography by Marley Brant (Putnam Berkley).

Jim Donovan Literary

4515 Prentice, Suite 109
Dallas, TX 75206
214-826-1251

Agent: Jim Donovan.
   Born: December 6, 1954.
   Education: B.S., University of Texas.
   Career history: In books since 1981 as a bookstore manager; chain-store buyer; published writer (*Dallas: Shining Star of Texas*, 1994, Voyageur Press; *The Dallas Cowboys Encyclopedia*, 1966, Carol Publishing); freelance editor; and senior editor, Taylor Publishing, 6 years. Literary agent since 1993.
   Subjects/categories most enthusiastic about agenting: Any book with something fresh to say, whether it's fiction or nonfiction.
   Subjects/categories not interested in agenting: Children's, poetry, short stories, romance, religious, technical books, computer books.
   Best way for a prospective client to initiate contact: Query first with brief synopsis, first chapter (fiction), and SASE.
   Reading-fee policy: No reading fee.
   Client representation in the following categories: Nonfiction, 80%; Fiction, 20%.
   Commission: 15%.
   Number of titles sold during the past year: 13.
   Approximate percentage of all submissions (from queries through manuscripts) that are rejected: 97%.
   Representative titles sold:
Augusta by Curt Sampson (Villard).
Junction by Jim Dent (Ballantine).
Elvis, Hank and Me by Horace Logan (Oxford).
Inside the Dragon: The Jackie Chan Story by Clyde Gentry (Taylor).
   The most common mistakes potential clients make when soliciting an agent to represent them: The top ten query letter turnoffs: (1) Don't use a form letter that begins with "To whom it may concern" or "Dear editor." (2) Don't say your writing is better than bestselling writers'. (3) Don't mention your self-published books unless they've sold several thousand. (4) Don't refer to your "fiction novel." (5) Don't brag about how great or how funny your book is. (6) Don't quote rave reviews from your relatives, friends, or editors whom you've paid. (7) Don't tell the agent how you're positive your book will make both of you rich. (8) Don't say it's one of five novels you've finished. (9) Don't tell the editor that they'll be interested because it will make a great movie. (10) Don't ask for advice or suggestions (if you don't think it's ready, why should they?).
   What writers can do to enhance their chances of getting an agent (besides being good writers): Provide a clear, well-thought-out query letter or proposal that describes the book, and for nonfiction, why there's a need for it, how it does something better

than or different from the competition, and why the author is the perfect person to write the book.

What might you be doing if you weren't an agent? A publisher.

JANE DYSTEL LITERARY MANAGEMENT

One Union Square West, Suite 904
New York, NY 10003
212-627-9100

Agent: Jane Dystel.

Education: B.A., New York University. Attended, but did not graduate from Georgetown Law School.

Career history: Permissions editor at Bantam Books; managing & acquisitions editor at Grosset & Dunlap; Publisher of *World Almanac* and founder of *World Almanac* publications; partner at Acton and Dystel Inc.; partner at Acton, Dystel, Leone and Jaffe; founder and owner of Jane Dystel Literary Management.

Hobbies/personal interests: Golf, gardening, cooking, ice-skating, travel.

Subjects/categories most enthusiastic about agenting: Literary and commercial fiction; serious nonfiction; cookbooks.

Subjects/categories not interested in agenting: Genre fiction (i.e., romance, Westerns), poetry, children's books.

Best way for a prospective client to initiate contact: Submit a query letter accompanied by an outline and a couple of sample chapters (with SASE).

Reading-fee policy: No reading fee.

Client representation in the following categories: Nonfiction, 80%; Fiction, 20%.
Commission: 15%.

Number of titles sold during the past year: 80.

Approximate percentage of all submissions (from queries through manuscripts) that are rejected: 95%.

Representative titles sold:

The Sparrow by Mary Doria Russell.
Magic City by Jewell Parker Rhodes.
Cocolat by Alice Medrich.
The Man in the Box by Thomas Moran.
Ben & Jerry's: The Inside Scoop by Fred Lager.
The Price of a Child by Lorene Cary.
I Never Forget a Meal by Michael Tucker.
Tiger's Tail by Gus Lee.
The Splendid Table by Lynne Rossetto Kasper.
Guilty by Harold Rothwax.
Don't Pee on My Leg and Tell Me It's Raining by Judy Sheindlin and Josh Getlin.

Living the Simple Life by Elaine St. James.

What the Deaf Mute Heard by Dan Gearino.

The most common mistakes potential clients make when soliciting an agent to represent them: Flashy, self-important letters full of hype and cuteness. Authors who refer to their work as "fictional novels."

Most common and costly mistakes have to do with bad grammar, sloppy presentation, illegible material (exotic fonts or single spacing), and lack of proofreading.

What writers can do to enhance their chances of getting an agent (besides being good writers): Intelligent, well-written queries that show originality.

Description of the Client from Hell: Someone who calls incessantly wanting updates and hand-holding. Someone who whines about everything. Someone who is dishonest and unpleasant.

Description of the Dream Client: Someone who is talented and asks intelligent questions. Someone who is patient and understanding of the fact that selling books can be a slow process. Someone who takes rejection in his/her stride.

Why did you become an agent? Having worked in many other areas of publishing, it seemed like an exciting new field to explore. I was intrigued by the increasing importance of the agent-author relationship in the publishing world.

What might you be doing if you weren't an agent? I'd be in some area of law or public service.

Comments: People should read more and read better books.

ANN ELMO AGENCY, INC.

60 East 42nd Street
New York, NY 10165
212-661-2880

Agent: Lettie Lee.

Subjects/categories most enthusiastic about agenting: Romance, juvenile, nonfiction.

Subjects/categories not interested in agenting: Poetry.

Best way for a prospective client to initiate contact: Query letter.

Commission: 15%.

FIRST BOOKS, INC.

2040 North Milwaukee Avenue
Chicago, IL 60647
773-276-5911

Agent: Jeremy Solomon

Education: B.A., University of Wisconsin (1986); Graduate, Radcliffe Publishing Course (1987); studied film at NYU (1989); MBA, Wharton School at the University of Pennsylvania (1992).

Subjects/categories most enthusiastic about agenting: Agent all categories of trade fiction and nonfiction *except* romance and religious works.

Subjects/categories not interested in agenting: Romance and religious works.

Best way for a prospective client to initiate contact: Send query letter, with 50 pages and full SASE. All submissions must include FULL SASE—otherwise they are not considered.

Reading-fee policy: No reading fee.

Client representation in the following categories: Nonfiction, 60%; Fiction, 40%.

Commission: 15%.

Number of titles sold during the past year: Sold approximately 45 titles last year.

Approximate percentage of all submissions (from queries through manuscripts) that are rejected: Reject over 90% of all submissions.

Representative titles sold:

Wash Your Hair with Whipped Cream by Joey Green (Hyperion, 1997).

Secrets from the Search Firm Files by John Rau (McGraw-Hill, 1997).

Too Proud to Beg by John T. Olson (Andrews & McMeel, 1997).

Description of the Client from Hell: A Client from Hell is an unpleasant person who doesn't write.

Description of Dream Client: A Dream Client is one who writes well, is a dear to work with, and makes us a lot of money.

The most common mistakes potential clients make when soliciting an agent to represent them: Not including an SASE in their submission; being rude to us on the phone.

What writers can do to enhance their chances of getting an agent (besides being good writers): Be polite and include an SASE with their submission.

Why did you become an agent? To work with writers and to have my own business.

What might you be doing if you weren't an agent? A family practice physician.

JOYCE A. FLAHERTY, LITERARY AGENT

816 Lynda Court
St. Louis, MO 63122
314-966-3057

Agent: Joyce A. Flaherty (Member: AAR).

Education: University of Wisconsin, Madison; Webster University, St. Louis, B.A. and postgraduate work.

Career history: Journalist; executive director for nonprofit business organization; public relations consultant, which included publishing clients. Founded literary agency in June 1980.

Hobbies/personal interests: Reading and tracking books in bookstores.

Subjects/categories most enthusiastic about agenting: Commercial fiction: women's fiction, genre fiction, thrillers, psychology and suspense. Nonfiction: self-help or how-to for commercial publishing markets, investigative reporting and Americana. We are interested in a broad range of fiction and nonfiction.

Subjects/categories not interested in agenting: Science fiction, Westerns, erotica, children's books, poetry, collections of short stories or articles, syndicated materials, screenplays—except for the books sold.

Best way for a prospective client to initiate contact with you: Query first with brief synopsis, first chapter, and SASE.

Reading-fee policy: No reading fee.

Client representation in the following categories: Nonfiction, 20%; Fiction, 80%.

Commission: 15% domestic.

Number of titles sold during the past year: 55.

Representative titles sold:

McKenna's Bride by Judith E. French (Ballantine).

Gypsy Dance by Patt Bucheister (Bantam).

Scottish Magic by Howell, Kaye, Michaels, Piel (Kensington), 4-set collection.

The most common mistakes potential clients make when soliciting an agent to represent them: Queries don't give enough information that we need to evaluate the submission. Cover letters don't give word counts, phone number where the writer can be reached, doesn't include SASE.

What writers can do to enhance their chances of getting an agent (besides being good writers): Great letter, great first chapter, and wonderful commercial ideas that give a fresh, new slant or twist. Everything mentioned in the letter or proposal is pertinent.

Description of the Client from Hell: We have wonderful, professional clients.

Description of Dream Client: Turns in clean copy, always meets deadlines, pleasant-natured and great writing with fresh, commercial ideas.

Why did you become an agent? I have always loved books and have been interested in publishing and writers. It's such a fascinating business. Sometimes tough, but always a challenge.

What might you be if you weren't an agent? A bookstore owner.

Comments: It's been a tough market for new authors. The wholesale market seems to be consolidating. Yet new authors continue to appear on the shelves, and so I would advise authors to keep on searching for the right agent. Don't give up! Although at this time we have no unpublished book authors, we always look for special new talent.

THE FOGELMAN LITERARY AGENCY

7515 Greenville Avenue, Suite 712
Dallas, TX 75231
214-361-9956

Agents: Evan M. Fogelman, Linda M. Kruger.

Born: Fogelman: May 1, 1960.

Education: Fogelman: B.A. with honors (1982), Juris Doctor (1985), Tulane University; Stanford Publishing Course. Kruger: B.A,. media theory and criticism, University of Texas at Austin (1989).

Career history: Fogelman: Entertainment attorney, book reviewer, author publicist. Kruger: Production manager for a national advertising agency.

Hobbies/personal interests: Fogelman: poetry, opera, French bulldogs, step aerobics, laughter, literary theory and, of course, reading. Kruger: Exercising, movies, crafts, travel, dogs, cooking, reading.

Subjects/categories most enthusiastic about agenting: Fogelman: Women's fiction (both category and mainstream, including romance, mysteries); popular business, psychological self-help; nonfiction geared for the women's market; political biography; author biography. Kruger: All categories of romance. Our agency works primarily with published authors of the romance genre. However, I invite unpublished romance authors to query with an SASE. Nonfiction: subjects that target a female audience, pop culture, some self-help, mainly commercial nonfiction.

Subjects/categories not interested in agenting: Fogelman: Police procedurals, technothrillers, science fiction, fantasy, shoot-'em-up Westerns, cyberpunk novels, children's books, poetry, short stories. Kruger: Poetry, short stories, true Westerns, science fiction, historical fiction, action adventure, New Age, mysteries.

Best way for a prospective client to initiate contact with you: Fogelman: Query letter (with SASE). Kruger: A query letter with SASE will be responded to within five business days. Published authors are invited to call. No unsolicited material, please.

Reading-fee policy: No reading fee.

Client representation in the following categories: Fogelman: Nonfiction, 50%; Fiction, 50%; Kruger: Nonfiction, 30%; Fiction, 70%.

Commission: 15% domestic, including all agency-negotiated subsidiary-rights deals; 10% foreign.

Number of titles sold during the past year: 40+.

Approximate percentage of all submissions (from queries through manuscripts) that are rejected: Fogelman: 99.5%. Kruger: 99.5%.

Representative titles sold:

Fogelman:

The Healthy Traveler by Karon Karter (Carol).

Blue Ribbon by Jessie Gray (Berkley).

Country Music's Book of Lists by Ace Collins (St. Martin's Press).

Silent Partners by Crystal Stovall (Zebra).

Dr. Quinn, Medicine Woman by Teresa Warfield (Berkley).

Various Silhouette Desires by Anne Eames.

Two Historical Romances by Julie Beard (Berkley).

Two Historical Romances by Shirl Henke (St. Martin's Press).

One Contemporary Romance by Katherine Sutcliffe (Berkley).

Kruger:

A Reluctant Rogue by Pam McCutcheon (Harlequin).

Across the Rainbow by Victoria Chancellor (Leisure).

Devil and the Deep Blue Sea by Karen Leabo (Bantam).

Everybody's Hero by Martha Hix (Silhouette).

Holiday Hero by Hayley Gardner (Silhouette).

Kept by a Countess by Pat Cody (Leisure).

Wooing Wanda by Gwen Pemberton (Harlequin).
Two titles by Alice Duncan (Dell).
Three titles by Emma Craig (Leisure).
Two titles by Rachel Wilson (Berkley).
Two titles by Delia Parr (St. Martin's Press).
Two titles by Pamela Ingraham (Silhouette).

The most common mistakes potential clients make when soliciting an agent to represent them: Fogelman: Gratuitous hostility or scrupulous meanness, sloppiness, gimmicks, and uninformed impatience. Kruger: When a writer cannot tell me what type of a book he/she has written. One writer described his books as (and this is an actual quote): "a non-genre erotic contemporary mainstream men's fantasy action/adventure romantic sexual comedy novel, or, if you really need a category, call it Romance Novel, Male Division." In helping a writer categorize his/her book, I always ask one question: If you had one copy of your manuscript and you had to put it on one bookshelf at the bookstore, where would it go? Also, I hate unsolicited material.

What writers can do to enhance their chances of getting an agent (besides being good writers): Fogelman: Published authors who can plainly and informatively articulate what they want make me enthusiastic. Saying, "I want to write bestsellers" does nothing for me. Saying, "I know I need an editor who wants me to write bestsellers" sends me into an enthusiastic and delightful orbit—it's what the business is based on. Kruger: When a writer researches what I'm looking for and delivers, upon request, a professional, clean presentation of their work. Also, when writers are enthusiastic about their work, it catches my attention.

Description of the Client from Hell: Fogelman: Anyone who assumes the publishing business will reward him/her just for being intelligent. Kruger: A writer who does not realize that this is a creative, yet *professional* business. I don't want a client wrapped up in gossip or contests or anything that would distract him/her from his/her writing career.

Description of Dream Client: Fogelman: Someone who understands writing is a wonderful, difficult business that requires focus, ability to deal with rejection, and, most importantly, the devoted persistence to finish what he/she starts. Kruger: Someone who keeps the lines of communication open. This is a two-way relationship. As for the creative process, my dream client creates characters and then releases those characters to tell the story.

Why did you become an agent? Fogelman: I completely enjoy the crossroads of art and commerce. Kruger: There are many reasons I became an agent, but what keeps me in this business is the chance to work with such creative individuals. This is an exciting business, one unlike any other profession. The atmosphere of our agency is always entertaining and challenging. I wouldn't change a thing.

What might you be doing if you weren't an agent? Fogelman: Oil-well wildcatter. Kruger: Eating a lot of barbecue.

Comments: Fogelman: If you're reading this because you're writing, good. If you're reading this *instead* of writing, bad. Kruger: When sending a query, or a partial or completed manuscript to an agent or editor, put your best work first. This is the all-important first impression, so never send a *rough draft*. Believe in your writing, your work, proof and reproof, and never let your enthusiasm die. Best of luck!

FORTHWRITE LITERARY AGENCY

3579 East Foothill Boulevard, Suite 327
Pasadena, CA 91107
818-798-0793

Agent: Wendy Keller.
  Born: October 2, 1964.
  Education: Journalism, Arizona State University.
  Career history: Journalism and sales.
  Hobbies/personal interests: Mothering my daughter, epée fencing, reading, and gardening.
  Subjects/categories most enthusiastic about agenting: Business, self-help, pop psychology, how-to, health, computer, and consumer reference on a variety of subjects!
  Subjects/categories not interested in agenting: No fiction, true crime, poetry, syndicated, shorts, or cartoon books.
  Best way for a prospective client to initiate contact: (1) Get a referral from one of our satisfied editors or clients. (2) Have the credentials to write on your subject and say so in your query letter (with SASE!).
  Reading-fee policy: No reading fee.
  Client representation in the following categories: Nonfiction, 100%.
  Commission: 15% domestic; 20% foreign.
  Number of titles sold during the past year: 29.
  Approximate percentage of all submissions (from queries through manuscripts) that are rejected: 95–99%.
  Representative titles sold:
  The Entrepreneur's Handbook of Business Law by Sean Melvin, J.D. (Macmillan).
  Copyright Made Simple by Cheryl Besenjak (Career Press).
  Timeless Face: 90 Days to a Younger You by Ellae Elinwood (St. Martin's Press).
  The Creative Negotiator by Stephen Kozicki (Adams Media).
  Be the Person You Want to Be Using NLP by John J. Emerich, Jr. (Prima).
  Seven Secrets of a Blissful Childhood by Joyce Seyburn (Putnam/Berkley).
  The most common mistakes potential clients make when soliciting an agent to represent them: Calling for any reason other than to verify our address before a submission; telling us all their friends *loved* the book, so we should, too; claiming to be such a better writer than (insert famous name here). Read my section in *The Portable Writer's Conference* (Quill Driver Books, 1996) to find out more.
  What writers can do to enhance their chances of getting an agent (besides being good writers): Know your material, know the competition, and be able to market yourself and your book very well.
  Description of the Client from Hell: Eee! The client from Hell? Not many people "from hell" make it to "client" status. But the wannabes from hell are plentiful. They don't research their subject or their book's competition and therefore assume it's the only book in the world done the way they've done it. I could go on about the ones who send curses if we decline their manuscript, or people who call ten minutes after they

post their query letter to see if we've gotten it. But those poor folks just don't know any better or they would act like and become real authors.

Description of the Dream Client: Most of my clients are Dream Clients! They have valuable material, are well read in their niche, write well (or work well with a ghost!), can promote a book once it is published, and never, ever, ever ask for loans, to borrow my car, or call to whine about their publisher or editor!

Why did you become an agent? I *love* being an agent because there are those incredible moments when the book the world needs comes from a wonderful writer and is bought by a terrific, enthusiastic, creative editor. That synergy makes me high. I'm an agent because I'm addicted!

What might you be doing if you weren't an agent? I'd probably do book publicity, or own a small chain of independent book stores, or maybe rival Amazon.com on The Web.

Comments: What writers do is *so* important in the world! Books are created for one of four reasons: inform, inspire, educate, or entertain. Each of these is crucial to the advancement of civilization and the proliferation of knowledge. Writers have the power to change lives. Eudora Welty said, "Whatever our theme in writing, it is old and tried. Whatever our place, it has been visited by the stranger, it will never be new again. It is only the *vision* that can be new; but that is enough."

JEANNE FREDERICKS LITERARY AGENCY, INC.

221 Benedict Hill Road
New Canaan, CT 06840
203-972-3011

Agent: Jeanne Fredericks.

Born: April 19, 1950.

Education: B.A., Mount Holyoke College, 1972; Radcliffe Publishing Procedures Course; M.B.A., New York University Graduate School of Business Administration, 1979.

Career history: Assistant to editorial director and foreign/subsidiary rights director, Basic Books (1972–1974); managing editor and acquisitions editor, Macmillan (1974–1980); editorial director, Ziff-Davis Books (1980–1981); literary agent, Susan P. Urstadt Agency (1990–1996); acting director, Susan P. Urstadt Agency (1996–1997); established own agency, February 1997.

Hobbies/personal interests: Family activities, tennis, skiing, swimming, coaching soccer, reading, cooking, traveling, biking, gardening, casual entertaining, antiquing, and pets.

Subjects/categories most enthusiastic about agenting: Practical, popular reference by authorities, especially in health, sports, science, business, cooking, parenting, travel, antiques and decorative arts, education, gardening, women's issues, plus an occasional outstanding juvenile or novel.

Subjects/categories not interested in agenting: Horror, occult fiction, true crime; in juveniles, no formula characters.

Best way for a prospective client to initiate contact with you: Please query (with SASE) by mail, with outline, description of project, author biography, sample writing. No phone calls. No fax.

Reading-fee policy: No reading fee.

Client representation in the following categories: Nonfiction, 90%; Fiction, 5%; Children's, 5%.

Commission: 15% domestic.

Number of titles sold during the past year: 15.

Approximate percentage of all submissions (from queries through manuscripts) that are rejected: 95%.

Representative titles sold:

Native Gardens for the Prairie States by Andy and Sally Wasowski (University of Minnesota Press).

The Instant Budget Gardener by Maureen Gilmer (Viking).

Altitude Superguide to Colorado by Patrick Soran and Dan Klinglesmith (Altitude).

Leaves by Alice Vitale (Stewart, Tabori & Chang).

The Ornamental Kitchen Garden by Jan and Michael Gertley (Taunton).

Under Water with Ogden Nash illustrated by Katie Lee (Little Brown/Bulfinch).

Cooperstown by Kathleen Quigley (Simon & Schuster).

Retraining by Sharon Smith (Howell House).

How to Get the Home You Want by Carolyn Janik (Kiplinger).

The Art of French Vegetarian Cooking by Karen Hanson and Barbara Somers (Prima).

The Art of Italian Vegetarian Cooking by Sally Maraventano (Prima).

Whole Healing by Elliott Dacher, M.D. (Dutton).

What writers can do to enhance their chances of getting an agent (besides being good writers): Submit a complete, professional proposal. Be respectful of agent's time and other commitments. A good agent's first responsibility is to current clients.

Why did you become an agent? Love of books.

What might you be doing if you weren't a literary agent? A trade book publisher or a writer.

SAMUEL FRENCH, INC.

45 West 25th Street
New York , NY 10010
212-206-8990

History: Agency founded 1930; incorporated 1950.

Subjects/categories most enthusiastic about agenting: Plays and musicals.

Best way for a prospective client to initiate contact: By sending a complete manuscript.

Reading-fee policy: No reading fee.

Client representation in the following categories: Plays, musicals, and books on the theatre, 100%.

Number of titles sold during the past year: Annual publication of approximately 100 titles.

Approximate percentage of all submissions (from queries through manuscripts) that are rejected: Varies.

The most common mistakes potential clients make when soliciting an agent to represent them: Explaining the play.

What writers can do to enhance their chances of getting an agent (besides being good writers): Being good writers—isn't that enough?

SARAH JANE FREYMANN LITERARY AGENCY

59 West 71st Street, Suite 9B
New York, NY 10023
212-362-9277
fax: 212-501-8240

Agency was formerly known as Stepping Stone Literary Agency.

Agents: Sarah Jane Freymann, President; Katharine Sands, Associate; Steven Schwartz, Associate.

Personal information for SARAH JANE FREYMANN:

Born: London, England.

Education: Although educated mostly in New York, I went to a French school—the Lycée Francais—which is why I am fluent in many languages; and I traveled a great deal from a very early age.

Career history: My first job was with the United Nations; I also worked as a model, and as an editor.

Hobbies/personal interests: Spiritual paths and journeys with a special interest in those of women; adventures of all kinds which ultimately provide insight, growth, and a greater appreciation of our world; mind/body well-being, wondrous food shared with good friends and family; exercise; experiencing different cultures and lifestyles; opera; my daughter.

Subjects/categories most enthusiastic about agenting: Nonfiction: Spiritual, psychology, self-help; women's/men's issues; health (conventional and alternative); cookbooks; narrative nonfiction, travel, natural science, nature and environment, memoirs, biography; cutting-edge current events, multicultural issues, popular culture. Fiction: quality mainstream and literary fiction.

Subjects/categories not interested in agenting: Science fiction, fantasy, horror, genre romance, genre mysteries, screenplays, anything channeled.

Best way for a prospective client to initiate contact with you: Via a query letter (with SASE). Not by phone. Not by fax.

Reading-fee policy: No reading fee.

Client representation in the following categories: Nonfiction, 79%; Fiction, 19%; Children's, 2%.

Commission: 15%.

Approximate percentage of all submissions (from queries through manuscripts) that are rejected: 75%.

Representative titles sold:

Judging Time by Leslie Glass (Bantam Books), fiction.

A Place to Dream by Kathy Corey and Lynne Blackman (Warner).

Children of the "Troubles" : Our Lives in the Crossfire of Northern Ireland by Laurel Holliday (Pocket Books).

Reflections on a California Pool by Melba Levick and Cleo Baldon (Rizzoli).

The Seven Deadly Sins: A Handbook by Steven Schwartz (Macmillan).

Cooking Beyond Recipes by Pam Anderson.

Flavors Market Table Cookbook by Pamela Morgan and Michael McLaughlin (Viking/Penguin).

Owning It: Zen and the Art of Facing Life by Perle Besserman (Kodansha).

Just Listen: A Guide to Finding Your Own True Voice by Nancy O'Hara (Broadway).

One Continuous Mistake: Strategies for Writers by Gail Sher (Penguin/Arkana).

The Wisdom of Depression by Dr. Jonathan Zeuss (Harmony/Crown).

Encantado: Pink Dolphins of the Amazon by Sy Montgomery (Simon & Schuster).

Evita by Tomas de Elia and Juan Pablo Quieroz (Rizzoli).

The most common mistakes potential clients make when soliciting an agent to represent them: We do not keep an accounting of "costly mistakes"—we all make mistakes. I used to say, however, that nothing in particular turned us off. Experience has made me qualify that statement. I am "turned off" by writers who are arrogant and belligerent and by writers who invariably feel that the publisher is their enemy.

What writers can do to enhance their chances of getting an agent (besides being good writers): I want writers who are experts in their fields for nonfiction and willing to admit that they might need a coauthor if their writing skills are not well honed. I like to see a well-written proposal and 2–3 chapters. With fiction, we prefer writers who have been previously published. They need solid, well-honed writing skills, a great story, and a fresh "voice."

Description of the Client from Hell: I wouldn't know—we've never had one.

Description of Dream Client: One who not only writes beautifully, with passion and intelligence, but who is also a nice human being—a "mensch." Someone with a sense of humor. Someone who has the patience and willingness to rewrite and rework his or her material, if necessary. And last, but not least, a client who has the confidence not to call us too often and who realizes that, if we spend all our time talking to them on the phone, we won't have that time to spend selling their work.

Why did you become an agent? Probably in the genes. I'm a natural matchmaker and a physician's daughter. I like to think that, thanks to my intervention, this author and that publisher met, formed a relationship, and that I am the midwife to this wonderful book.

What might you be doing if you weren't an agent? An actress, a spiritual teacher, a marathon runner, a writer, an opera singer, the mother of 15 children, a 19th century explorer, a doctor, a filmmaker—all of which I may still do!

Comments: Life is all about feeling engaged and connected. I love being able to make that kind of heart and mind commitment to authors and to their work. That is what makes the *business* of selling books become the *joy* of selling books. Seeing my authors successfully, creatively, and happily published is my goal as an expert. I delight in the knowledge that, out of this relationship, something came into being that people can both benefit from and find enjoyment in.

SHERYL B. FULLERTON ASSOCIATES

1010 Church Street
San Francisco, CA 94114
415-824-8460

Agent: Sheryl Fullerton.

Born: March 24, 1948.

Education: B.A., English, University of Utah, Phi Beta Kappa, magna cum laude.

Career history: Production editor, Prentice Hall (college textbooks) (1971–1974); development editor, Wadsworth Publishing Company (college textbooks (1974–1978); acquisitions editor (music, sociology, religion, anthropology), Wadsworth (1979–1988); editorial manager, Wadsworth (1988–1993); literary agent (1994–present).

Hobbies/personal interests: Cooking, gardening, travel.

Subjects/categories most enthusiastic about agenting: Psychology, psychotherapy, business, management, social and cultural issues, popular culture, religion/spirituality, women's issues, gay and lesbian issues, health and wellness, current affairs, pop culture, selected reference, self-help and how-to.

Subjects/categories not interested in agenting: Science, technology, computers, nature/environment, fiction.

Best way for a prospective client to initiate contact: By mail—a strong query letter (with SASE) will get a prompt response. Prefer *not* to get calls or unsolicited manuscripts.

Reading-fee policy: No reading fee.

Client representation in the following categories: Nonfiction, 90%; Fiction, 5%; Textbooks, 5%.

Commission: 15% domestic, 20% foreign.

Number of titles sold during the past year: 10.

Approximate percentage of all submissions (from queries through manuscripts) that are rejected: 90%. I am willing to work with relatively inexperienced but talented authors who know that writing is a craft.

Representative titles sold:

Girls' Night Out by Chloe Atkins (St. Martin's Press).

The Fear Factor by Kay Gilley (Butterworth-Heinemann).

Crystal Diary by Frankie Hucklenbroich (Firebrand Books).

On Our Way: Everywoman's Guide to the Mid-Life Journey by Melene Smith and Naomi Lucks, with Margaret Cuthbert, M.D. (Prima Publishing).

Lessons from the Giants: Conversations with America's Greatest Entrepreneurs by Rama Dev Jager and Rafael Ortiz (Business McGraw-Hill).

From Where I Stand: Critical Perspectives on Multi-Cultural America by Larry Shinagawa, Deborah Woo, and James Gray (St. Martin's Press).

The most common mistakes potential clients make when soliciting an agent to represent them: No SASE, phoning rather than writing a strong query letter, not being up front about talking to other agents at the same time. Most costly mistake: Not doing their homework up front concerning the market for their book (e.g., competing books, bookselling realities). And not asking why a reader would pay money to read this book.

What writers can do to enhance their chances of getting an agent (besides being good writers)? A strong, well-written query letter accompanied by a realistic and enthusiastic proposal that indicates market savvy will get my attention every time.

Description of the Client from Hell: Ignorant, arrogant, and lazy person who expects to be handed success as a gift.

Description of Dream Client: Someone with: a great idea that has been checked against realities; passion and persistence; willingness to work and learn as a writer; personal credibility (does what she says she'll do); excellent writing skills and more than one book idea; strong connections (professional) that will help sell the book. (I represent mostly nonfiction authors.)

Why did you become an agent? I love working with authors and being part of the world of ideas. I also enjoy the autonomy of having my own business and working with and developing authors' careers.

What might you be doing if you weren't an agent? I would probably be an editor or an author myself—possibly writing on food/wine/restaurants (not really a surprise, considering I live in the *foodie* capital of the West).

Comments: Writers need to understand the realities of contemporary publishing and bookselling. The more educated they are and the more they understand the importance of selling and marketing themselves and their ideas, the more likely their chances of success. Get over the illusion that publishers are waiting eagerly for manuscripts—they are busy, skeptical, and harried—so the better job the agent and author do of making their decisions easier, the better the process works for everybody.

GARON-BROOKE ASSOCIATES

(See entry for Pinder Lane & Garon-Brooke Associates, Ltd.)

MAX GARTENBERG, LITERARY AGENT

521 Fifth Avenue, Suite 1700
New York, NY 10175
212-860-8451

Agent: Max Gartenberg.

Born: New York City.

Education: B.A., New York University; M.A., Brown University.

Career history: As an English major with a graduate degree, I drifted into college teaching, then realized that I wanted to be where the action was, not where it had been in the past. I was living in the Midwest when that lightning bolt struck—about the same time I had to go to New York on family business. The rest is commentary.

Subjects/categories most enthusiastic about agenting: Although I will occasionally take on a new novelist whose talent seems to me superior, fiction writers might be well advised to look elsewhere. I am most interested in solid nonfiction—books that present fresh and significant information or viewpoints—regardless of subject area, whether for trade, paperback, or reference.

Subjects/categories not interested in agenting: I am not interested in category fiction, novelty books, and personal memoirs.

Best way for a prospective client to initiate contact with you: With a one- or two-page, first-class letter describing any relevant background information, accompanied by an SASE if the writer wishes for any sort of reply. I usually don't read sample pages or chapters if these are included. And I am absolutely turned off by cold calls and faxed queries.

Reading-fee policy: No reading fee.

Commission: 15% on initial sale; thereafter 10% on sales in the U.S., 15–20% elsewhere.

Approximate percentage of all submissions (from queries through manuscripts) that are rejected: 95%.

Representative titles sold:

Sea Turtles: Their Life and Behavior by Ann and Jack Rudloe (Crown).

Escape Routes by David Roberts (The Mountaineers Books).

The Tao of Spycraft by Ralph D. Sawyer (Westview Press).

The Measured Man by Howard Owen (HarperCollins).

Description of the Client from Hell: The client who demands unceasing attention, who is never satisfied with the deal I bring him (he always has friends whose agents got twice as much), who delivers his manuscript late and in such disorder that the publisher rejects it and demands return of the advance—and who, on top of everything, blames me for the mess. This is not an imaginary character.

Description of Dream Client: A writing professional who can be counted on to produce a well-made, literate, enlightening, and enjoyable book with a minimum of *Sturm und Drang*. Fortunately, this is not an imaginary character, either.

The most common mistakes potential clients make when soliciting an agent to represent them: What most turns me off is a solicitation which tells me almost nothing about the writer or his material but requests detailed information about myself and my services, which is readily available in such books as the *Writer's Guide*.

What writers can do to enhance their chances of getting an agent (besides being good writers): A sense that the writer knows his subject, has reviewed the literature which has come before, and has written a book that is genuinely fresh and new.

Why did you become an agent? I love good books. They are the pillars of our civilization. It is a privilege to work with those who create them.

THE SEBASTIAN GIBSON AGENCY

Literary, Musical, and Performing Artist
Talent and Modeling Agency
125 Tahquitz Canyon Way, Suite 200
Palm Springs, CA 92262
619-322-2200
fax: 619-322-3857

Agent: Sebastian Gibson.

Born: December 8, 1950.

Education: B.A., cum laude, UCLA; L.L.B., magna cum laude, University College Cardiff, Great Britain; J.D., University of San Diego School of Law.

Career history: Author of two novels, six screenplays, the lyrics and music to a stage musical, and hundreds of copyrighted songs. Author of published legal articles in both the United States and England. Performed as a stage musician on tour in the U.S. and Europe, and in a national television special. Obtained law degrees in both the U.S. and Great Britain. Practiced law in San Diego for four years, subsequently in England and the Middle East, and in 1984 began the Law Offices of Sebastian Gibson in Palm Springs, California. Presently practice law and represent literary, entertainment clients, and models from law offices in Palm Springs, California, and Las Vegas, Nevada.

Hobbies/personal interests: Reading well-written books, traveling to book fairs, discovering new talent.

Subjects/categories most enthusiastic about agenting: All categories of fiction, particularly novels with interesting characters and well-woven plots. Especially interested in legal and psychological thrillers, historical novels, mystery/suspense and action/adventure or espionage with romance subplots and interesting twists, crime/police with humorous/gritty elements, medical dramas, women's fiction, sagas, and any well-written novel with unusual characters. Nonfiction with unusual approaches or written by celebrities, cookbooks or photography with a novel twist, humorous diet books, controversial issues, biographies, current affairs, "kiss and tell" books, and women's issues. Also children's, juvenile, young adult, stage plays, musicals, television scripts, and screenplays. What really gets us excited is when we read something fresh and new, with a genre all its own, or a story told in a way that has never been told before. If it grabs our imagination, it will grab the imagination of a publisher and the buying public as well.

Subjects/categories not interested in agenting: Poetry, textbooks, essays, short stories, how-to books, books in verse, computer, gardening, pornography, autobiographies by non-celebrities, drug recovery.

Best way for a prospective client to initiate contact: Fiction: Send query letter or book proposal with outline *and* three sample chapters or up to 50 pages with SASE. Proposals and sample chapters without postage will be trashed. No disks, please. Sample chapters should already be edited and without typographical errors or incorrect grammar.

Reading-fee policy: No reading fee as such. We do, however, request a bush-league, small potato, hardly worth mentioning but ever so popular contribution to our efforts of $10 per submission to pay for guard dogs to keep other agents away from our authors, to send those delightfully tacky pens and coasters that publishers like so much, and to pay for all those cocktails at the pools in Palm Springs and Las Vegas where we do our reading (eat your hearts out, you agents who winter in New York). Seriously, each year we receive more and more submissions, and to give each one the time they deserve increases our overhead dramatically.

Client representation in the following categories: Nonfiction, 30%; Fiction, 60%; Children's, 10%.

Commission: 10% domestic; 20% foreign (split with foreign agents).

Number of titles sold during the past year: Confidential, as some clients are represented by the Law Offices of Sebastian Gibson.

Approximate percentage of all submissions (from queries through manuscripts) that are rejected: 95%–98%.

Representative titles sold: Confidential, as some clients are represented by the Law Offices of Sebastian Gibson.

Description of the Client from Hell: We don't have any overdemanding clients with unrealistic expectations. Five years ago we buried them all alive in killer anthills in the desert.

Description of Dream Client: A bestselling author who leaves his or her present uncaring agent for the personal care our agency can provide.

The most common mistakes potential clients make when soliciting an agent to represent them: Sending first drafts, no SASE, incessant calls, autobiographies, and travel memoirs of trips to Orlando or Tijuana.

What writers can do to enhance their chances of getting an agent (besides being good writers): Bribes. Seriously, book proposals and manuscripts already well edited and thoughtfully and creatively written.

Why did you become an agent? With a background in music, literature, interests in Europe, and the law, it was a natural progression to add a literary, talent, and modeling agency to our law firm.

What might you be if you weren't an agent? Sipping piña coladas on a beach in Greece, far away from telephones, car phones, beepers, pagers, and computers.

Comments: The world needs more good books. An author with something to say that pulls on one's emotions and sparks one's interest can have a profound effect on others. Share your strength, your intellect, and don't be afraid to bare the soul of your characters, as long as it's done in an interesting way.

IRENE GOODMAN LITERARY AGENCY

521 Fifth Avenue
New York, NY 10175
212-682-1978
fax: 212-490-6502

Agent: Irene Goodman.
   Born: November 29, 1949; Detroit, Michigan.
   Education: B.A., University of Michigan, 1971; M.A., University of Michigan, 1973.
   Career history: Editorial assistant at T. Y. Crowell, 1975–1976; assistant at Kirby McCauley Agency, 1976–1978; established own agency in 1978.
   Hobbies/personal interests: Theatre, opera, cooking, Nantucket, the Berkshires, *Doonesbury*, figure-skating (watching, not doing), politics, movies, hanging out with small children, watching cooking shows on weird cable channels.
   Subjects/categories most enthusiastic about agenting: All types of women's fiction, romance novels, mysteries, biographies, some popular nonfiction.
   Subjects/categories not interested in agenting: Literature, esoteric nonfiction, technothrillers, macho genre books, psychobabble, feminist diatribes. I don't handle children's books because I like to leave something sacred.
   Best way for a prospective client to initiate contact with you: The very best way is through a referral by a client.
   Reading-fee policy: No reading fee.
   Client representation in the following categories: Nonfiction, 5%; Fiction, 95%.
   Commission: 15% until the author sells a book for $25,000 or more, or until the author brings in $50,000 in a calendar year, then the commission goes permanently to 10%.
   Number of titles sold during the past year: 56.
   Approximate percentage of all submissions (from queries through manuscripts) that are rejected: 98%.
   Representative titles sold:
   My Outlaw by Linda Lael Miller (Pocket).
   No Ordinary Princess by Pamela Morsi (Avon).
   This Matter of Marriage by Debbie Macumber (Mira)
   The most common mistakes potential clients make when soliciting an agent to represent them: The biggest problem is a general one and it concerns the sheer volume. No one I know in the business can seriously devote any real attention to the "slush pile," simply because there is too much of it. While I look at everything, I do it very rapidly, often giving only seconds to each piece. This means that I'm probably missing something in there that's good, but it still isn't worth it to me to spend the time. The odds are about one in a thousand, and that doesn't justify the time spent.
   What writers can do to enhance their chances of getting an agent (besides being good writers): People who find an appropriate way to separate themselves from the masses. This can mean outstanding quality, being useful and visible at a conference, or

getting referred by someone I know and respect. It definitely means having something that is salable as opposed to something that needs a lot of work or is completely off the mark or not what I represent.

Description of the Client from Hell: Someone who wants me to be mother, psychiatrist, best friend, sounding board, loan officer, editor, accountant, and lawyer—all rolled into one. I am none of those things in my work. What I am is an agent.

Description of Dream Client: I have several real dream clients. It is my privilege to work with them. Here's what they all have in common: They work hard, they don't whine, they have a terrific sense of humor, they are intelligent, they have lives and expect me to have one, and—oh, yes—they have talent. They are responsible for themselves, they know how to say thank you, they know how to laugh at themselves (and at me occasionally, when I deserve it), and they like to give people the benefit of the doubt. They enrich my life and give as much back to me as I give to them.

Why did you become an agent? I became an agent because it was my destiny. That sounds pompous, but consider this: I don't like working in large companies because I can't tolerate the politics. I like to be a part of a working community, but I also need to fly solo. Autonomy is stimulating to me; it motivates me to get things done. I love making deals, I love books, and I love having an equal partnership with a very talented author. Bureaucracy makes me crazy, and I love being in a position where I can cut through it.

What might you be doing if you weren't an agent? When I was in my 20s, I was considering two career options: pursuing an advanced degree in medieval studies and studying gourmet cooking in Paris. The third option was to come to New York and go into book publishing, which is obviously what I did.

ASHLEY GRAYSON LITERARY AGENCY

1342 18th Street
San Pedro, CA 90732
310-514-0267

Agents: Ashley Grayson, Carolyn Grayson, Dan Hooker.

The following information pertains to ASHLEY GRAYSON:
Education: B.S., physics.
Career history: Computer sales, management consultant, literary agent.
Subjects/categories most enthusiastic about agenting: Commercial and literary fiction, historical novels, suspense, thrillers, young adult, science fiction. I read widely and would be happy to have a top-of-category work in just about any area. I am the U.S. agent for a number of German publishers and am willing to read published books in German for possible sale in the U.S./UK markets. I am also the agent for a number of entertainment companies and Web sites who wish to spin their properties into books.

Subjects/categories not interested in agenting: I believe I can obtain an optimal business deal for virtually any book on any topic if one or more buyers can be identified. I am unlikely to be an effective crusader to locate a single publisher for narrow-focused works on politics, diet and health, and religion. Books from recognized leaders in these areas, however, are of interest.

Best way for a prospective client to initiate contact: Published authors can fax or call to discuss their needs. An intelligent query letter is the best way for an unpublished writer to apply.

Reading-fee policy: No reading fee.

Client representation in the following categories: Nonfiction, 15%; Fiction, 65%; Children's, 20%.

Commission: 15%, U.S. and Canada; 20%, international; 10%, film/TV plus sub-agent/legal fees.

Number of titles sold during the past year: More than 100.

Approximate percentage of all submissions (from queries through manuscripts) that are rejected: Greater than 95%.

Representative titles sold:

Mother of Storms by John Barnes (Tor).

Headcrash by Bruce Bethke (Warner).

Momentary Monsters by David Lubar (Scholastic).

Managing Microsoft's Internet Information Server by Baldwin and Thayer (Academic Press).

Description of the Client from Hell: Of course, we don't represent any clients from hell, but such a person is more interested in the celebrity of being an author than in actually writing books. Those who feel that grammar and spelling are for the *little people* to fix, who call after working hours, are late on delivery, or want to borrow money. Anyone who won't work on the next book until the first (or second) one sells. Anyone who calls up weekly and asks, "How about a book about (insert *the news event of the week*)—would that be worth a lot of money?" Any client who also wants to second-guess his/her agent.

Description of Dream Client: The dream client always has a few ideas simmering for the next book or two. S/he always listens to input and feedback, but ultimately decides what to do and how to do it because the client both respects the market and upholds his or her standards of art and technique. We seek productive authors with a proven audience whose works we can sell in multiple territories and across different media: books to film and TV.

The most common mistakes potential clients make when soliciting an agent to represent them: Unrealistic and outrageous claims for the quality of the work or the potential audience for the work are frequent. Errors of grammar in cover letters are surprisingly common.

What writers can do to enhance their chances of getting an agent (besides being good writers): A personal recommendation by a bestselling author never hurts. Really, mastery of the topic and craftsmanship in writing is key.

Why did you become an agent? I love to read books and sell new ideas. The real reason I became an agent is that Judy-Lynn Del Rey (the late founder of the Del Rey imprint at Random House) told me in 1976 that I should. She had great insight—I'm still having a great time.

What might you be doing if you weren't an agent? I would probably be running a software or net-based company.

Comments: Our international success is expanding our reputation as the agent's agents; we represent a number of European agents in the U.S./UK and U.S.-based agents in the rest of the world.

The following information pertains to CAROLYN GRAYSON:

Born: Los Angeles, California.

Education: B.A., English, Wellesley College; M.B.A., marketing, UCLA.

Career history: Market research analyst for several high-tech companies and advertising agency; consultant and managing editor for company producing market studies.

Hobbies/personal interests: Reading, gardening, travel, snorkeling, golf, investing, wine, cooking.

Subjects/categories most enthusiastic about agenting: Literary and commercial fiction. Women's fiction: mainstream, historical and contemporary romance; general audience: mystery, suspense, thrillers, crime and true crime, horror; children's and young adult fiction. Would like to take on more nonfiction: travel, gardening, cookbooks, health, some self-help, how-to, parenting, pop culture.

Subjects/categories not interested in agenting: Action/adventure, war books, poetry, novelty, personal experiences, biography/autobiography, New Age, psychic phenomena, textbooks, business and professional books, social issues, religion, screenplays.

Best way for a prospective client to initiate contact: By referral or query letter with synopsis and SASE.

Reading-fee policy: No reading fee.

Client representation in the following categories: Nonfiction, 10%; Fiction, 60%; Children's, 30%.

Commission: 15% domestic; 20% foreign.

Number of titles sold during the past year: Difficult to answer because we sell most of the foreign rights for clients' works ourselves, so we have sold some books six or more times in a year.

Approximate percentage of all submissions (from queries through manuscripts) that are rejected: 95%.

Representative titles sold:

Trapped by Carol Matas (Simon & Schuster Books for Young Readers), young adult fiction.

Contagion of Good by Carol Matas (Scholastic Canada), young-adult fiction.

Mary Louise Loses Her Manners by Diane Cuneo (Bantam Books for Young Readers), picture book.

Momentary Monsters by David Lubar (Rageot-Editeur, France), young-adult fiction, 4-book series.

The Listeners by Christopher Pike (Editions J'ai lu, France), horror.

Description of the Client from Hell: One who tries to do my job; calls three times a day; thinks she/he is my only client.

Description of Dream Client: One who keeps writing wonderful books; is in command of his or her craft; is willing to accept editorial advice, either from us and/or from editors; is creative, respectful, loyal, and dependable.

The most common mistakes potential clients make when soliciting an agent to represent them: Query letters that contain either too much hyperbole or not enough information to make a decision. Giving incomplete information regarding previous published works. Sending more than one query to our agency.

What writers can do to enhance their chances of getting an agent (besides being good writers): Show they understand their craft and the market and are professional.

Why did you become an agent? The joy of discovering new talent and seeing the books in print.

What might you be doing if you weren't an agent? Ad agency executive; landscape architect; interior designer; living on the beach in Hawaii.

Comments: We also represent several French and German publishers for U.S./UK rights and can read and speak French, German, and Spanish in the agency.

The following information pertains to DAN HOOKER:

Born: Los Angeles, California.

Education: B.A., Spanish, UCLA.

Career history: Several jobs before coming to agenting. Agenting the last 5 years. Published writer: about a dozen short stories and articles.

Hobbies/personal interests: Writing, reading, checking out bookstores wherever I go, sports, strange low-budget movies.

Subjects/categories most enthusiastic about agenting: Commercial fiction; mysteries; thrillers; suspense; hard science fiction; contemporary fantasy; horror; young adult and middle-grade; quality fiction by outstanding new voices.

Subjects/categories not interested in agenting: Epic fantasy, poetry, religion.

Why did you become an agent? As an aspiring writer, I wanted to learn about the publishing business, but I didn't want to move to New York to work in a publishing house. I found a good agency near my home, and they gave me a chance. Turned out I really liked agent stuff.

What might you be doing if you weren't an agent? Writing, which I do anyway, as time permits.

Comments: I always like to connect with talented new writers who aren't afraid to express their unique perspectives on this world of ours. Determination and a professional attitude are absolute requirements, too.

SANFORD J. GREENBURGER ASSOCIATES, INC.

55 Fifth Avenue
New York, NY 10003
212-206-5600
fax: 212-463-8718

Founded: 1932

Agents: Heide Lange, Vice President; Faith Hamlin; Beth Vesel; Theresa Park; Elyse Cheney; Daniel Mandel.

International Rights Agent: Christina Harcar.

Best way for a prospective client to initiate contact: Query letter with a SASE.
Reading-fee policy: No reading fee.
Client representation in the following categories: Nonfiction, 60%; Fiction, 40%.
Commission: 15% domestic; 20% international
Number of titles sold during the past year: Hundreds.

The following information pertains to HEIDE LANGE:
Born: July 21, 1949.
Education: B.A., Hunter College, CUNY.
Career history: I started working at the agency while attending college. As Sanford Greenburger's assistant, I was fortunate to learn the business from a "publishing gentleman" with an international reputation, and it's been my home for 28 years. My books have generally reflected my background, interests, and stages in life. Married, two children, I've handled general nonfiction, from art, which was my college major (*Drawing on the Right Side of the Brain* was my first bestseller), to relationships and sex (*The G Spot*), pregnancy and childbirth, parenting, women's health and other issues, current events, controversy, biographies, memoirs, journalism, some general reference, how-to, self improvement.
Hobbies/personal interests: Reading, gardening, bicycling, roller-blading and any other activities I can share with the family before our children are off to college (in a flash, it seems).
Subjects/categories most enthusiastic about agenting: See above and representative titles below, but basically, if an author is passionate about and experienced in the subject he or she is writing about, I'm prepared to be enticed by it.
Subjects/categories not interested in agenting: Category fiction, children's books.
Representative titles sold:
Let Me Hear Your Voice: A Family's Triumph over Autism by Catherine Maurice (Knopf).
Emotional Wisdom by Jean Grasso Fitzpatrick (Viking).
Raising Your Spirited Child by Mary Kurcinka (HarperCollins).
Swim with the Dolphins: How Women Can Succeed in Corporate America on Their Own Terms by Connie Glaser and Barbara Smalley (Warner).
The Multi-Orgasmic Man: How Any Man Can Experience Multiple Orgasms and Dramatically Enhance His Sexual Relationship by Mantak Chia and Douglas Abrams Arava (Harper San Francisco).
The Random House Word Menu by Stephen Glazier (Random House).
Life's Big Instruction Book: The Almanac of Indispensable Information by Carol Madigan and Ann Elwood (Warner).
Encyclopedia of the Renaissance edited by Paul Grendler (Scribner).
Lauren Groveman's Kitchen: Nurturing Foods for Family and Friends by Lauren Groveman (Chronicle).
Italian Food and Drink: An A to Z Guide by John Mariani (Broadway Books).
A Cold Stay in Hell: One Woman's Tale of Courage & Survival on Mount McKinley by Ruth Ann Kocour as told to Michael Hodgson (St. Martin's).
Rains All the Time: A Social History of Weather in the Pacific Northwest by David Laskin (Sasquatch Books).

Darwin's Orchestra: An Almanac of Nature in History and the Arts by Michael Sims (Holt).

Why did you become an agent? The fact that I love to read was really my entry into this business, and sometimes I still can't believe I can make money doing what I love. That, and the clients I can help to realize their dreams, makes this very gratifying work.

The following information pertains to FAITH HAMLIN:

Born: Pre-babyboomer.

Education: Boston University—speech therapy and psychology.

Career history: Parent to two children; bookstore buyer/manager; sales rep for several publishers; sales manager for Macmillan, Atheneum, Scribner, Free Press; agent for 10 years.

Subjects/categories most enthusiastic about agenting: Adults: Most nonfiction, especially health, medical, psychology, parenting, women's issues, sports, biography/autobiography, gay/lesbian, science, humor, the arts, and books by journalists. I look for people with strong credentials, a point of view, and excellent writing skills. Children's: Picture books, middle grade, young adult, commercial but not cartoon characters; illustrators and photographers who can also write text. With the flood of submissions I receive, I can consider only writers with a track record.

Subjects/categories not interested in agenting: Adult—fiction, except mysteries; Children's—no science fiction.

Representative titles sold:

Adult books:

Right-Brain Power by Jeffrey Freed and Laurie Parsons (Simon & Schuster).

The Moral Compass of the American Lawyer by Richard M. Zitrin and Carol A. Langford (Ballantine).

Emotional Fitness Conditioning by Ronald Berman, Ph.D. with Anita Weil Bell (Putnam).

Behind the Crystal Ball by Anthony Aveni (Times Books).

Wilder Times by Kevin Lally (Henry Holt).

Curse of Rocky Colavito by Terry Pluto (Simon & Schuster).

A Rocket at Heart by Rudy Tomjanovich and Robert Falkoff (Simon & Schuster).

Jackie Under My Skin by Wayne Koestenbaum (FSG/Plume).

Body in the Bog by Katherine Hall Page (William Morrow).

Raising a Thoughtful Teenager by Rabbi Ben Kamin (Dutton).

Maria Tallchief: Native American Dancer by Maria Tallchief and Larry Kaplan (Henry Holt).

Allegra Kent by Allegra Kent (St. Martin's Press).

Women's Crisis Handbook by Lauren Hartman (Houghton Mifflin).

Dr. Spock Biography by Thoman Maier (Harcourt Brace).

Songs for Myself by Jack Maguire (Jeremy Tarcher).

Prostate Cancer: A Guide for Women and the Men They Love by Sandra Haber, Barbara Wainrib, Jack Maguire.

It's About Time by Linda Sapadin and Jack Maguire (Penguin).

Dr. Mom's Breastfeeding Guide by Marianne Neifert, M.D. (Dutton)

Children's books:

Rodeo by Ken Robbins, (Henry Holt).

Thunder on the Plains by Ken Robbins (Scholastic).

Red Bird by Doreen Rappaport (Dial).

Wild Colorado by Richard Maurer (Crown).

Hostage by Ed Myers (Hyperion).

Christie and Company by Katherine Hall Page (Avon).

How They Sleep by Cor Hazelaar (FSG).

Do Your Ears Pop in Space? by Astronaut Mike Mullane (Wiley).

The following information pertains to BETH VESEL:

Education: B.A., English/political theory, UC Berkeley; graduate work in Comparative literature, UC Berkeley.

Career history: Senior agent, Greenburger Associates since August 1988; assistant to Gloria Loomis/Watkins Loomis, January 1985–August 1988; assistant, Little, Brown subsidiary rights/special sales, November 1983–December 1984.

Subjects/categories most enthusiastic about agenting: Serious psychology, psychology; cultural criticism; gender/gay/lesbian studies; extraordinary fiction.

Subjects/categories not interested in agenting: Self-help; genre fiction.

Best way for a prospective client to initiate contact: Through a current client or an editor with whom I work.

Reading-fee policy: No fees

Client representation in the following categories: Nonfiction, 70%; Fiction, 30%.

Commission: 15%

Number of titles sold during the past year: 12.

Approximate percentage of all submissions (from queries through manuscripts) that are rejected: 97%.

Representative titles sold:

Attending to Ritalin by Larry Diller (Bantam).

The Secret Language of Eating Disorders by Peggy Claude-Pierre (Times Books/Vintage).

Home Truths by Marjorie Garber (Simon & Schuster).

Denial by Keith Ablow (Pantheon).

Why did you become an agent? Because I love books and care about authors. I was once a writer myself.

What might you be doing if you weren't an agent? A writer.

The following information pertains to THERESA PARK:

Education: B.A., University of California, Santa Cruz; J.D., Harvard Law School.

Career history: Previously an attorney with Cooley Godward, L.L.P. (Palo Alto, CA); joined Sanford J. Greenburger Associates in 1994.

Subjects/categories most enthusiastic about agenting: Commercial fiction; serious nonfiction (including cultural studies, science, history, international issues, multicultural/cross-cultural issues, memoir, social narrative, serious psychology, law & business); literary fiction; Asian-American work; cookbooks.

Subjects/categories not interested in agenting: Science fiction, humor.

Approximate percentage of all submissions (from queries through manuscripts) that are rejected: 97%

Representative titles sold:

The Notebook by Nicholas Sparks (Warner Books).

Torchlight by Robert Louis Stevenson III (Putnam).

The Silent Cradle by Margaret Cuthbert (Pocket Books).

Counterparts by Gonzalo Lira (Putnam Berkley).

Blood Lines: From Ethnic Pride to Ethnic Cleansing by Vamik Volkan, M.D. (Farrar Straus & Giroux).

Remaking Eden: Playing God in a Brave New World by Lee Silver, Ph.D. (Avon Books).

Cooking with the Seasons: A Year in My Kitchen by Monique Hooker and Tracie Richardson (Henry Holt).

Why did you become an agent? I love books, I love to work with people, and I love to do deals! Also, with my background as a transactional lawyer, it seemed like the right area of publishing to get into. One of the best thing about being a lawyer was having clients—I enjoy getting to know people and working closely with them on their manuscripts and proposals; the personal rewards of watching a client's career blossom are the best part of my job.

What might you be if you weren't an agent? I don't know—I love being an agent so much that I can't imagine doing anything else right now.

The following information pertains to ELYSE CHENEY:

Born: December 23, 1967.

Education: University of Pennsylvania; B.A. in English literature.

Career history: Art curator; agent at Connie Clausen since 1992–1995.

Hobbies/personal interests: Tennis, politics, crime, women's issues.

Subjects/categories most enthusiastic about agenting: Thrillers, women's fiction, literary fiction, memoirs, narrative nonfiction, serious psychology, social issues, and academics with crossover potential.

Subjects/categories not interested in agenting: Science fiction, right-wing, children's.

Best way for a prospective client to initiate contact: Query letter with SASE.

Reading-fee policy: No reading fee.

Client representation in the following categories: Nonfiction, 65%; Fiction, 35%.

Commission: 15%.

Number of titles sold during the past year: 10.

Approximate percentage of all submissions (from queries through manuscripts) that are rejected: 95%.

Representative titles sold:

The Black Athlete by William C. Rhoden (Crown).

Needles by Andrea Dominick (Scribner).

Celebration by Andrew Ross (Ballantine).

Potted Gardens by Rebecca Cole (Clarkson Potter).

Webonomics: Nine Business Principles of the World Wide Web by Evan Schwartz (Broadway).

Description of the Client from Hell: Imperious and lazy.

The most common mistakes potential clients make when soliciting an agent to represent them: Handing in bad writing.

What writers can do to enhance their chances of getting an agent (besides being good writers): Be totally professional and submit great writing.

Why did you become an agent? I like reading, writing, editing, and selling. I like the entrepreneurial aspect of the profession.

The following information pertains to DANIEL MANDEL:

Education: B.S., Cornell University

Career history: Associate, Diane Cleaver, Inc.

Subjects/categories most enthusiastic about agenting: Fiction, new media, politics, popular culture.

Representative titles sold:

New York Diary by Daniel Drennan (Ballantine).

Creative Edge: 11 Creative Strategies for Making It in New Media by John Geirland, Ph.D. and Eve Sonesh-Kedar, Ph.D. (Free Press).

Guerrilla Girls' Bedside Companion to the History of Western Art by the Guerrilla Girls (Viking/Penguin).

What might you be if you weren't an agent? I would, of course, be a writer.

THE CHARLOTTE GUSAY LITERARY AGENCY

10532 Blythe Avenue
Los Angeles, CA 90064
310-559-0831

Agent: Charlotte Gusay.

Education: B.A. (English literature/theatre); M.A. (education).

Career history: Taught in secondary schools for several years. Interest in filmmaking developed. Founded (with partners) a documentary-film company in the early 1970s. Soon became interested in the fledgling audio-publishing business. Became the managing editor for the Center for Cassette Studies/Scanfax, producing audio programs, interviews, and documentaries.

In 1976 founded George Sand, Books in West Hollywood, one of the most prestigious and popular book shops in Los Angeles. It specialized in fiction and poetry, sponsored readings and events. Patronized by the Hollywood community's glitterati and literati, George Sand, Books was the place to go when looking for the "best" literature and quality books. It was here that the marketing of books was preeminent. It closed in 1987. Two years later the Charlotte Gusay Literary Agency was opened.

Hobbies/personal interests: Gardens and gardening, magazines (a magazine junkie), good fiction reading, anything French, anything Greek.

Subjects/categories most enthusiastic about agenting: I enjoy both fiction and nonfiction. Prefer commercial, mainstream—but quality—material. Especially like books that can be marketed as film material. Also material that is innovative, unusual, eclectic, nonsexist. Will consider literary fiction with crossover potential. TCGLA is a signatory to the Writers' Guild, and so represents screenplays and screenwriters selectively. I enjoy unusual children's books and illustrators but have begun to limit children's projects.

Subjects/categories not interested in agenting: Does not consider science fiction or horror, poetry or short stories (with few exceptions), or the romance genres per se.

Best way for a prospective client to initiate contact with you: Send one-page query (with SASE). Then if we request your material (book, proposal, whatever it is), note the following guidelines: **For Fiction:** Send approximately first 50 pages and a synopsis, along with your credentials (i.e., list of previous publications, and/or list of magazine articles, and/or any pertinent information, education and background). **For Nonfiction:** Send a proposal consisting of an overview, chapter outline, author biography, sample chapters, marketing and audience research, and survey of the competition. **Important note:** Material will not be returned without SASE. **Second Important Note:** Seduce me with humor and intelligence.

Reading-fee policy: No reading fee.

Client representation in the following categories: Nonfiction, 40%; Fiction, 15%; Children's, 10%; Books to film/screenplays, 35%.

Commission: 15% books; 10% screenplays.

Representative titles sold:

Ten Pearls of Wisdom: For Achieving Your Goals and Capturing Your Dreams (Kodansha Publishers).

Bukowski in the Bathtub (Little, Brown).

Walking in the Sacred Manner (Touchstone/Simon & Schuster).

A Garden Story (Faber & Faber/hardcover; Mercury House/paperback).

The Women Who Write the Movies (Birch Lane Press).

This Nervous Breakdown Is Driving Me Crazy (Dove Books).

Groucho Marx and Other Short Stories and Tall Tales: Selected Writings of Groucho Marx (Faber & Faber).

Love, Groucho: Letters from Groucho Marx to His Daughter Miriam Marx (Faber & Faber).

I'll Know What to Do: A Young People's Guide to Natural Disasters (Magination Press).

The History of Christmas (Dove Kids).

Entertainment rights:

Maiden Voyage (Villard Publishers).

The Fall Line (Kensington Publishing).

Carnival of Saints (Ballantine Books).

Dead Languages (Knopf, optioned by Sanford/Pillsbury).

Les Travailleurs de la Mer (screenplay based on Victor Hugo novel).

Drop-Off; *Big Fish*; *Drowned Man's Key* (St. Martin's, optioned by Warner Brothers).

Description of the Client from Hell: The one who does not understand the hard work we do for our clients. Or the one who refuses to build a career in a cumulative manner, but rather goes from one agent to the next and so on. Or the one who circulates his/her manuscript without cooperating with his agent. Or the one who thinks it all happens by magic. Or the one who does not understand the nuts and bolts of the business.

Description of the Dream Client: The one who cooperates. The one who appreciates how hard we work for our clients. The one who submits everything on time, in clean, edited, proofed, professional copies of manuscripts and professionally prepared proposals. The one who understands the crucial necessity of promoting his/her own books until the last one in the publisher's warehouse is gone. The one who works as hard on his/her bookselling campaign in tandem with the agent. The author/agent relationship, like a marriage, is a cooperative affair, and it is cumulative. The Dream Client will happily do absolutely whatever is necessary to reach the goal.

The most common mistakes potential clients make when soliciting an agent to represent them: Clients must understand the role of agents and that agents represent only the material they feel they can best handle. Potential clients must understand that any given agent may or may not be an editor, a sounding board, a proposal writer, or guidance counselor. Because of the enormous amount of submissions, queries, proposals, the agent most often has only the time to say yes or no to your project. Above all, when clients don't understand why in the world I can't respond to a multiple submission with regard to their "900-page novel" within a few days, all I can do is shake my head and wonder if that potential client realizes that I am human.

What writers can do to enhance their chances of getting an agent (besides being good writers): The first requisite is always that writers be courteous, respectful, and professional. Then they should be ready to describe their work or project in a few dynamite words and be knowledgeable about where and how their work fits into the trade market. Then I'm impressed and my enthusiasm begins to build.

Why did you become an agent? I became an agent because I know how to sell books and movies. Above all, I am knowledgeable, experienced, and I love agenting.

What might you be doing if you weren't an agent? I would write a book called *Zen and the Art of Gardening with a Black Thumb* (I'm kidding!). I would travel to Istanbul and become a foreign agent. I would finish all of Proust. I would re-read Jane Austen. Work on my French. Study Greek. Play the piano. Tap dance.

Comments: There is a curious mindset in the "literary milieu." Clients assume that agents should do their work for free. When, as it becomes necessary for various of life's services, authors pay their plumber, their mechanic, their babysitters, their gardeners, their dentists, *their lawyers.* Why do authors come to a professional agent and expect services to be gratis. (I do not charge reading fees.) So kindly ponder for a moment: how many 900-page novels am I able to read in any given week, and how shall I be paid for *my time?* What an odd and archaic business this is! Something's wrong with this picture. And the queries stack up, the reading pile grows, the frustration level rises. And then . . . And then I discover some wonderful writer, and I'm off and running with a new client, flush from the reward of discovery. I wish you, dear writers, all the best and everything you deserve. I'm on your side.

REECE HALSEY AGENCY

8733 Sunset Boulevard, Suite 101
Los Angeles, CA 90210
310-652-2409 (Halsey telephone)
fax: 310-652-7595
Note: Contact Dorris Halsey by referral only. All new submissions and SASEs should be directed to Kimberly Cameron.

Reece Halsey North:
98 Main Street, Suite 704
Tiburon, CA 94920
415-789-9177 (Cameron telephone/fax)

Agents: Dorris Halsey, Kimberley Cameron.

Education: Halsey: educated in France. Cameron: Marlborough School, Humboldt State University, Mount St. Mary's College.

Career history: Halsey: worked with her husband, Reece, who was head of the literary department at William Morris. They opened this office in 1957. Cameron: former publisher, Knightsbridge Publishing Company. Has been working with Dorris Halsey since 1993.

Hobbies/personal interests: Reading for the sheer pleasure of it.

Subjects/categories most enthusiastic about agenting: Literary fiction, writing that we feel is exceptional in its field.

Subjects/categories not interested in agenting: Children's fiction, poetry, cookbooks.

Best way for a prospective client to initiate contact with you: Ms. Halsey works with referrals only. Please send an SASE with all queries to Kimberley Cameron at Reece Halsey North.

Reading-fee policy: No reading fee.

Client representation in the following categories: It depends completely on the material we decide to represent. It changes often. The most accurate breakdown is: Nonfiction, 30%; Fiction, 70%.

Commission: 15% domestic; 20% foreign.

Number of titles sold during the past year: We don't feel this should be public information.

Approximate percentage of all submissions (from queries through manuscripts) that are rejected: 98%.

Representative titles sold: Dorris Halsey has the distinguished honor of representing the Aldous Huxley Estate. HarperCollins is publishing all his works, marking the centennial of his birth (1894–1963).

Dorris has sold many celebrity biographies, nonfiction works, and fiction to most major houses and smaller houses, including Knightsbridge.

The most common mistakes potential clients make when soliciting an agent to represent them: We are always impressed by politeness, in a well-written letter or otherwise. Their most costly mistake is using too many rhetorical adjectives to describe their own work.

What writers can do to enhance their chances of getting an agent (besides being good writers): Show patience, understanding, politeness, and trust.

Description of the Client from Hell: One who calls too often and asks, "What's new?"

Description of Dream Client: A *patient* author who understands the publishing business and knows what it takes to get a book sold.

Why did you become an agent? We both love books and what they have to teach us. We both understand how important and powerful the written word is, and appreciate what it takes to be a good writer.

What might you be doing if you weren't an agent? Reading.

Comments: This business, especially today, is all uphill. We work extremely hard at what we're doing, and the love of books is what keeps us going. I don't think many agents do what they do every day for the money. We feel an exceptional amount of responsibility for our authors, and I just wish they could see and hear what we do for them. We have the highest regard for the process of writing, and do the best we can with the material in our hands.

What more can one do?

JEANNE K. HANSON LITERARY AGENCY

5441 Woodcrest Drive
Edina, MN 55424
612-920-8819

Agent: Jeanne Hanson.

Born: August 12, 1944.

Education: B.A., Wellesley College (philosophy and English); M.A.T., Harvard University (English); M.A., University of Minnesota (journalism); Radcliffe publishing course (1984).

Career history: Teacher 2 years; journalist for 15 years; literary agent for 13 years.

Hobbies/personal interests: Reading, aerobic exercise of all kinds, talking, negotiating things in all aspects of life.

Subjects/categories most enthusiastic about agenting: Any kind of nonfiction book that a journalist might write—all my clients are journalists. For example, the following subjects are of interest: humor, business, travel, journalistic books, food, science, nature, health, psychology, self-help, illustrated books, pop reference, pop culture, thrillers, and so on!

Subjects/categories not interested in agenting: Commercial fiction (glitzy type), memoirs of any kind, category fiction.

Best way for a prospective client to initiate contact with you: A letter (with SASE).

Reading-fee policy: No reading fee.

Client representation in the following categories: Nonfiction, 97%; Fiction, 3%.

Commission: 15%.

Number of titles sold during the past year: 27.

Approximate percentage of all submissions (from queries through manuscripts) that are rejected: 98%.

Representative titles sold:

Three travel guides (Fielding).

Eating-disorders book (Simon & Schuster).

Humor book (Workman).

Business book (Viking Penguin).

Nature book (Morrow).

Pop reference book (Warner).

Nature book (NorthWord).

Sports book (Simon & Schuster).

Psychology book (Houghton Mifflin).

Science book (St. Martin's Press).

The most common mistakes potential clients make when soliciting an agent to represent them: Sending a query to multiple agents. Also, faking it by saying, "I got your name from someone who admired your work" or some such.

Description of the Client from Hell: Someone who approaches me for the first time by addressing the letter "Dear Sir" or "To whom it may concern." Someone who is rude. Also, someone who packages a proposal in such a way that it takes ten minutes to open.

Description of Dream Client: A superb journalist who comes to me out of the blue or via an existing client. Someone with an idea so "on-target" in the culture that I just gasp!

Why did you become an agent? Because I love books, love one-on-one interactions with people about ideas, and love negotiating and organizing.

What might you be doing if you weren't an agent? I guess being a journalist again.

Comments: Let's get those damn publishers to do a better job selling the books once the authors work so hard writing them!

THE HARDY AGENCY

3020 Bridgeway #204

Sausalito, CA 94965

415-380-9985

Agents: Anne Sheldon; Michael Vidor.

Born: Sheldon: 1958; California. Vidor: 1950; Michigan.

Education: Sheldon: West Valley College; San Jose State. Vidor: Western Michigan University; Wayne State University (1975): Communications, Sociology, Journalism.

Career history: Sheldon: Publisher, Enchante' Publishing; publishing and marketing consultant; co-founded The Hardy agency in 1990. Vidor: Former major market advertising account directory; certified bodyworker; publishing and marketing consultant; co-founded The Hardy Agency in 1990.

Hobbies/personal interests: Sheldon: Gardening, music, film, cooking, the great outdoors. Vidor: Sailing, athletics, outdoors, art, film, my children.

Subjects/categories most enthusiastic about agenting: Sheldon: Quality literary and contemporary fiction, innovative and progressive writing. Nonfiction in the categories of contemporary affairs, self-help, lifestyle and cooking, memoirs, history. Vidor: Contemporary and commercial fiction. Nonfiction in the categories of alternative health, New Age and spirituality, self-help, social issues and contemporary affairs, and biography and memoirs.

Subjects/categories not interested in agenting: Children's, romance, historical fiction, science fiction.

Best way for a prospective client to initiate contact: Query letter with one or two sample chapters.

Reading-fee policy: No reading fee.

Client representation in the following categories: Nonfiction, 60%; Fiction, 40%.

Commission: 15% domestic; 20% foreign; 20% film.

Number of titles sold during the past year: 6.

Approximate percentage of all submissions (from queries through manuscripts) that are rejected: 95%.

Representative titles sold:
The Book of Secrets by Robert Petro (HarperCollins).
Whiskey's Children by Jack Erdmann and Larry Kearney (Kensington).
Funerals for Horses by Catherine Ryan Hyde (Russian Hill).

Description of the Client from Hell: One who thinks writing is an easy way to make a living, they're looking for a fast buck so they can retire. The client from hell lacks appreciation and doesn't have a clear understanding of what we do on their behalf. One who doesn't know the market, or where they fit in it.

Description of Dream Client: One who has done the work, both from a writing and a marketing standpoint. In nonfiction, one who continues to become a recognized authority on their subject. In fiction, one who continues to write, master the art, and develop credibility.

The most common mistakes potential clients make when soliciting an agent to represent them: They convey a lack of objectivity about their work. Many don't have a clear understanding of the realities of the publishing business.

What writers can do to enhance their chances of getting an agent (besides being good writers): They should make sure the work is complete, polished, and proofread; never send a work in progress. They need to know what *finished* means, technically. They should be professional yet personable. They need to be proactive in their respective markets. Do the homework. Walk the talk.

Why did you become an agent? Initially, because of a love for books. I continue to do it because when I find a gem, there's nothing like it. Vidor: Love for the written word, masochistic tendencies, and a discerning eye.

What might you be doing if you weren't an agent? Sheldon: I'd be a landscape architect, or I'd live on the beach somewhere. Vidor: I'd be writing or reporting in the islands.

Comments: Don't work in a vacuum. Have objective people read your work and comment honestly. Don't just show it to people who will tell you what you want to hear. Support your own continuing education and be active in your own marketplace. Don't lament about the *garbage* that is published today, as nothing will cause you to be rejected more quickly. Treat the industry, and those in it, with respect. Be dedicated beyond all expectation, and realize that most people in this business are, as well.

CHADWICK ALLEN HARP, ESQUIRE

119 Lincoln Terrace
Jeffersonville, PA 19403
610-631-9795
wickmode@aol.com (e-mail)

Agent: Chadwick Allen Harp.

Born: March 24, 1969, Norristown, Pennsylvania.

Education: B.A. (history and philosophy), cum laude, The George Washington University, 1991; J.D., Dickinson School of Law, 1996.

Career history: My career history can be divided into the areas of writing, medicine, and law. Writing: My articles and essays have appeared in magazines and newspapers across the country, including *The Arizona Republic*, *The Cumberland County Sentinel*, *Cape Cod Life*, *The Minneapolis Star Tribune*, *The Montgomery Advertiser*, *Pennsylvania Heritage*, *The San Francisco Chronicle*, *The Tampa Tribune*, *The Tampa Times*, *The Washington Post*, and *The Washington Times*. Medicine: I spent five years serving in various administrative positions at the George Washington University Medical Center. Law: Since 1994, I have prepared tax returns and worked in the areas of estate planning and estate administration, tax law, and entertainment law.

Hobbies/personal interests: I enjoy writing, visiting with friends and family, traveling, and dining. I am a member of the Board of Directors of the Children's Aid Society of Montgomery County, Pennsylvania. I am interested in child welfare and child abuse issues and issues surrounding children and their families. Volunteering my time and talents is an important part of my life. I play golf as often as I can.

Subjects/categories most enthusiastic about agenting: I will consider all ideas and projects regardless of the genre or subject matter. I want to represent writers who have solid, professional writing skills and who can tell a story. Please proofread and polish everything that you write.

Subjects/categories not interested in agenting: I will consider all projects or ideas that are accompanied by solid, professional writing skills.

Best way for a prospective client to initiate contact: I prefer that prospective clients contact me by sending a query packet. The packet should include the following items. First, send me a 1–2 page cover letter describing your project, your ideas, and the status of the project. You may also wish to tell my why you believe that we will work well together and why you decided to send a query package to me. Second, include your resume, biography, or other document that will tell me about your background. Third, include the first 20–30 pages of the project and, if appropriate, the table of contents or a 1–2 page synopsis. I will respond to your query within 4–6 weeks. Always enclose a return envelope with sufficient postage.

It is worth stating that I expect a professionally prepared query packet. If you send me garbage, I will recycle it. I will not waste the time of Mike, my mailman, to return garbage to you.

Reading-fee policy: I do not charge a reading fee. I feel that charging a reading fee is unprofessional and unethical. My recycling policy allows me to separate quickly those projects I will and will not consider.

Client representation in the following categories: Nonfiction, 30%; Fiction, 30%; Textbooks, 20%; Children's, 20%.

Commission: I charge a 10% commission on all contracts I negotiate for a client. This includes any and all contracts, including, for example, book contracts for domestic or foreign sales, contracts for television or theatrical motion picture productions, and contracts concerning merchandising. To prevent our relationship from appearing or becoming adversarial, I prefer that oral understandings (not written words) establish and govern our respective duties, responsibilities, and obligations.

Number of titles sold during the past year: The basis of my professional relationships is confidentiality. I neither confirm nor deny who I do and do not represent. I do not discuss any aspect of my professional relationships. Therefore, I will not disclose the titles that I have sold during the past year.

Approximate percentage of all submissions (from queries through manuscripts) that are rejected: All the writers I represent began our relationship with a professionally prepared query packet. I will initiate a professional relationship with a new client in precisely the same manner. I reject 90% of the submissions that I receive.

Representative titles sold: Confidential.

Description of the Client from Hell: The client from hell forgets the limitations and the responsibilities of our respective roles. As an agent, my responsibility is to contact appropriate editors, to negotiate contracts and the terms thereof, to encourage the authors I represent, and to act as the advocate of my client. As a writer, your responsibility is to write with care and professionalism, to meet reasonable deadlines, and to listen to the advice of others. A client from hell breaches these duties or imposes others beyond our professional relationship. A client from hell acts unprofessionally. I will end my relationship with a client from hell.

Description of Dream Client: A dream client is a good writer who understands our respective duties and obligations. A dream client has a good sense of humor, is patient, works hard, listens to my counsel, and seeks to build our relationship based on trust and good faith. A dream client proofreads and polishes everything he or she writes.

The most common mistakes potential clients make when soliciting an agent to represent them: The most costly mistake a writer can make is a poor first impression. If a first impression is poor, it is very difficult to ameliorate my subsequent conduct. A poor impression is made when a writer sends me garbage or when a writer calls me without an invitation to do so. Here are some helpful things: Purchase good quality letterhead for your cover letters; send a polished, professionally prepared cover letter and manuscript; make sure all your printing is of laser quality. I will recycle all query packets—and not bother Mike the mailman—if they are prepared unprofessionally.

What writers can do to enhance their chances of getting an agent (besides being good writers): I am enthusiastic about fresh ideas presented by a writer who approaches the craft and our relationship in a professional manner. I am excited about discovering talent and helping an author during his or her career. Writers who are compassionate and sensitive, caring and kind, honest and thoughtful, passionate and brave are most likely to work well with me.

Why did you become an agent? I became an agent because I love discovering new talent. I love books—collecting them and reading them. As an agent, my responsibility is to find good projects and to help writers. My responsibility is to assume some of the administrative responsibilities involved with professional writing so that my client can concentrate on his or her craft.

What might you be if you weren't an agent? If I was not an agent, the time I spend doing so would be spent on other pursuits. I enjoy very much the time I spend as an agent. As an entrepreneurial, creative person with empathy and compassion, I understand the thoughts and concerns of authors. I know that many concerns do not involve money or contracts. And yet, I offer counsel in the administrative areas surrounding the wonderful world of writing. I feel a sense of accomplishment when I voluntarily assume some of the details of a writer's life so that he or she may focus time and energy upon writing.

HARRIS LITERARY AGENCY

P.O. Box 6023
San Diego, CA 92166
619-658-0600

Agent: Barbara J. Harris.

Born: Madison, Wisconsin.

Education: B.S., University of Wisconsin, Madison; M.A., San Diego State University.

Career history: Literary editor; speech/language pathologist; marketing director for a publishing company.

Hobbies/personal interests: Reading, running, sailing, golf, swimming, bicycling, and skiing.

Subjects/categories most enthusiastic about agenting: Mainstream fiction: thrillers, suspense, mystery, and humor. Nonfiction: Biography, adventure, and self-help.

Subjects/categories not interested in agenting: Poetry, textbooks, essays, short stories, how-to books, fantasies, children's stories, Westerns, erotica, horror, and science fiction.

Best way for a prospective client to initiate contact: Query letter with SASE.

Reading-fee policy: No reading fee.

Client representation in the following categories: Nonfiction, 10%; Fiction, 90%.

Commission: 15% domestic, 20% foreign (maximum of $250 in advance for expenses covering foreign submission costs—postage, photocopying, and long distance phone calls).

Number of titles sold during the past year: We are a new company. We are aggressive and expect to sell many excellent works in the coming year.

Approximate percentage of all submissions (from queries through manuscripts) that are rejected: 90–95%.

Representative titles sold: We are a new agency with contracts in progress.

Description of the Client from Hell: We do not tolerate this client, but if you insist: He/she calls for constant updates, ignores constructive advice, has unrealistic expectations, and demands instant attention and gratification.

Description of Dream Client: We do welcome this client with open arms: He/she is a team player who understands the game, accepts critique, is patient and cooperative, and is a creative writer.

The most common mistakes potential clients make when soliciting an agent to represent them: They do not follow our guidelines and have poorly written query letters and/or synopses.

What writers can do to enhance their chances of getting an agent (besides being good writers): They must make a good first impression—be concise, legible, and follow submission guidelines.

Why did you become an agent? Having been an editor for a number of years, I observed excellent material go unpublished and thought I could better serve authors by promoting their works to publishers.

What might you be doing if you weren't an agent? I would be sailing off into the sunset with a good book—one that I had published, of course!

Comments: Ralph Waldo Emerson wrote, "Talent alone cannot make a writer." I agree and, therefore, would like to add my advice: "Persevere."

JOHN HAWKINS & ASSOCIATES

71 West 23rd Street, Suite 1600
New York, NY 10010
212-807-7040

Agents: Moses Cardona; J. Warren Frazier; William Reiss; Elly Sidel; Anne Hawkins.

The following information pertains to MOSES CARDONA:

Born: October 8, 1966.

Education: B.S., Marketing, New York University (1988).

Career history: Bookkeeper/officer manager; foreign rights agent, literary agent (also handling agency's foreign rights and subsidiary rights).

Hobbies/personal interests: Tennis, roller-blading, jigsaw puzzles.

Subjects/categories most enthusiastic about agenting: Science fiction, horror-supernatural, fantasy, mysteries.

Subjects/categories not interested in agenting: Children's, military, poetry.

Best way for a prospective client to initiate contact: Query letter with a few sample chapters.

Reading-fee policy: No reading fee.

Commission: 15%

Why did you become an agent? I fell into the profession. A friend who was a client helped me find this position starting at the agency, and I grew through the years to appreciate this industry. I realized there were few Latino professionals and wanted to give a voice and presence to the world of publishing.

The following information pertains to J. WARREN FRAZIER:

Education: Princeton.

Subjects/categories most enthusiastic about agenting: Fiction: culture, mystery, literary. Nonfiction: biography, travel.

Subjects/categories not interested in agenting: Romance.

Best way for a prospective client to initiate contact:: Letter with personality, 1/2-page synopsis of book with first 3–4 chapters.

Reading-fee policy: No reading fee.

Client representation in the following categories: Nonfiction, 50%; Fiction, 50%.

Commission: 15%

Approximate percentage of all submissions (from queries through manuscripts) that are rejected: 95%.

What writers can do to enhance their chances of getting an agent (besides being good writers): Somebody whose letter shows both intelligence and a sense of humor.

The following information pertains to WILLIAM REISS:

Born: September 14, 1942.

Education: B.A., Kenyon College.

Career history: Freelance researcher; editorial assistant to Lombard Jones (a graphic designer and editor); encyclopedia editor, Funk & Wagnalls Standard Reference Library; literary agent.

Subjects/categories most enthusiastic about agenting: Biographies, nonfiction historical narratives, archaeology, science fiction and fantasy, mysteries and suspense, true-crime narrative, natural history, children's fiction, adult fiction.

Subjects/categories not interested in agenting: Romance novels, poetry, plays.

Best way for a prospective client to initiate contact: Telephone, or send a letter describing project with a few sample pages to provide a sense of writing style.

Reading-fee policy: No reading fee.

Commission: 15%

Representative titles sold:

Edith Wharton: An Extraordinary Life by Eleanor Dwight (Abrams).

Wicked by Gregory Maguire (ReganBooks/HarperCollins).

Walking Towards Walden by John Hanson Mitchell (Addison-Wesley).

Tiger, Tiger Burning Bright by Ron Koertge (Orchard Books).

The Lost Diaries of Frans Hals by Michael Kernan (St. Martin's).

The following information pertains to ELLY SIDEL:

Education: B.A., Bennington College.

Career history: I have had a long, varied career in publishing, film, and television, as well as raising two children as a single mom and working as a certified chemical-dependency counselor at Hazelden in Minnesota. Also vice president of movies and mini-series, Warner Brothers; television director of special projects, CBS Entertainment, New York; vice president of production, 20th Century Fox Film Corporation; senior editor, Bantam Books; manager of subsidiary rights, Bantam Books; etc.

Hobbies/personal interests: Reading; going to the ballet, movies, theatre; watching television, especially ice skating, cops, and *Seinfeld*; hanging out; playing with friends and family; walking; swimming; politics; travel.

Subjects/categories most enthusiastic about agenting: Literary and commercial fiction, narrative nonfiction, psychology (pop and otherwise), popular culture, women's issues, journalism.

Subjects/categories not interested in agenting: Cookbooks, children's, science fiction.

Best way for a prospective client to initiate contact: The very best way of contact is through a referral or a query letter (with SASE).

Reading-fee policy: No reading fee.

Commission: 15%

The most common mistakes potential clients make when soliciting an agent to represent them: Someone who is too pushy and aggressive and won't take no for an answer.

Description of the Client from Hell: Pushy, demanding, inflexible, argumentative, dumb person with unrealistic expectations.

Description of Dream Client: A talented, flexible, creative professional writer who understand that this is a process. Someone with a sense of humor and a Pulitzer Prize.

Why did you become an agent? Good way to integrate all of my professional and personal experience, use my contacts, work with ideas and smart, creative people, as well as earn a living.

What might you be doing if you weren't an agent? Travel around the world.

The following information pertains to ANNE HAWKINS:

Education: A.B., Bryn Mawr College.

Hobbies/personal interests: Music, gardening—almost any excuse to be outdoors.

Subjects/categories most enthusiastic about agenting: Literary and commercial fiction, including science fiction/fantasy and historical fiction; narrative nonfiction, especially women's issues; history; current affairs; and science.

Subjects/categories not interested in agenting: Horror, military, romance and juvenile fiction; how-to nonfiction.

Best way for a prospective client to initiate contact: Brief, well-written query letter, one-page synopsis, three or four sample chapters.

Reading-fee policy: No reading fee.

Commission: 15%.

Approximate percentage of all submissions (from queries through manuscripts) that are rejected: 90–95%.

The most common mistakes potential clients make when soliciting an agent to represent them: Long, rambling query letters and sample chapters containing grammatical, spelling, and usage errors.

What writers can do to enhance their chances of getting an agent (besides being good writers): A concise, well-written query letter that makes me believe that I would enjoy representing both the author and his/her work.

Why did you become an agent? I love to read, of course, and truly enjoy working with authors and others in the publishing industry.

HEACOCK LITERARY AGENCY, INC.

1523 Sixth Street, Suite 14
Santa Monica, CA 90401-2514
310-393-6227
fax: 310-451-8524
GraceBooks@aol.com (e-mail)

Agents: Rosalie Heacock, Robin Lea Henning.

Born: Heacock: Girard, Kansas; Henning: Manhasset, New York.

Education: Heacock: B.A., Fine Arts/English; M.A., humanities, California State University. Henning: B.A., University of California at Los Angeles.

Career history: Heacock: Editor, Green Hut Press; executive editor, Kids & Company; sole founder of the Shelley Muir Agency in 1973, which became the Heacock Literary Agency in 1978, the latter cofounded with James B. Heacock (b. 1924; d. 1994). Member: Association of Authors' Representatives, Author's Guild, Southern California Book Publicists.

Hobbies/personal interests: Heacock: Reading; all aspects of art; *en plein air* landscape painting (on site as opposed to studio painting), choral singing, hiking. Founding member, 1987, of the Plein Air Artists of the Santa Monica Mountains and Seashore.

Subjects/categories most enthusiastic about agenting: Well-written manuscripts on timely subjects, particularly books which make a contribution.

Subjects/categories not interested in agenting: Please, no scripts, young adult, science fiction, true crime, horror, books that would be better magazine articles (including bad-news books and other *downers*). We do not represent reprint efforts on out-of-print or self-published books.

Best way for a prospective client to initiate contact with you: Please, no multiple queries, telephone calls, or faxes. Just send us a well-written one–two page query letter that includes your writing experience, why you have written the book, and brief biographical data. It is the mark of a professional to accompany queries with a self-addressed stamped envelope (SASE). Letters without SASE cannot be answered. Mailed queries receive our first attention and are preferred to e-mail queries. However, should you wish to send e-mail, please do not attach files and do not include us in multiple queries.

Reading-fee policy: No reading fee.

Client representation in the following categories: Nonfiction, 92%; Fiction, 4%; Children's, 4%.

Commission: 15%.

Number of titles sold during the past year: 19.

Approximate percentage of all submissions (from queries through manuscripts) that are rejected: 90%.

Comments: One of our newly signed authors remarked, "When you write what you love, you receive your payment in the writing of it. Anything else is simply an added reward." Publication is believed to validate a writer's efforts and provide monetary compensation, but if this is the sole reason you are writing, there are easier ways to make money. There are not, however, easier ways to realize the joy of creation which is uniquely your own, or the inner excitement of crafting something to the best of your ability. Writing is a noble endeavor.

RICHARD HENSHAW GROUP

264 West 73rd Street
New York, NY 10023
212-721-4721

Agent: Rich Henshaw.

Born: September 18, 1964; New York, New York.

Education: B.A., Franklin and Marshall College.

Career history: Independent since 1995; 1987–1995 agent and director of foreign rights, Richard Curtis Associates; 1992–1995, partner in the Content Company, an agency specializing in new media.

Hobbies/personal interests: My family, books, cooking, wine, travel, skiing.

Subjects/categories most enthusiastic about agenting: Mainstream and genre fiction, including mysteries and thrillers, science fiction, fantasy, horror, historical, literary, and young adult. Nonfiction areas of interest are business, celebrity biography, computer, current events, health, history, how-to, movies, popular culture, popular reference, popular science, psychology, self-help, and sports. I am also interested in working with books that lends themselves to adaptation to CD-ROM and other new media formats.

Subjects/categories not interested in agenting: Fiction: category romance, Westerns, poetry, short stories. Nonfiction: coffee-table books, cookbooks, scholarly books.

Best way for a prospective client to initiate contact: Query letter and first 50 pages (with SASE) for fiction. Query letter (with SASE) for nonfiction. I also accept queries by e-mail, not to exceed one page. My Internet address is RHGagents@aol.com.

Reading-fee policy: No reading fee.

Client representation in the following categories: Nonfiction, 20%; Fiction, 80%.

Commission: 15% domestic; 20% foreign.

Number of titles sold during the past year: 15.

Approximate percentage of all submissions (from queries through manuscripts) that are rejected: 95%.

Representative titles sold:

Trick Me Twice by Stephen Solomita (Bantam).

Shaky Ground by Steve Brewer (St. Martin's Press).

You're Dead, David Borelli by Susan Brown (Atheneum).

Fade Away by Harlan Coben (Dell).

The Eternal Guardians (series) by Ronald Anthony Cross (Tor).

Breakup by Dana Stabenow (Putnam).

John Stanley's Creature Features Movie Guide by John Stanley (Berkley/Boulevard).

The Well-Trained Mind by Jessie Wise and Susan Wise Baure (W. W. Norton).

The most common mistakes potential clients make when soliciting an agent to represent them: No SASE. Unpolished manuscripts. Bound manuscripts. Slick queries that say little about the characters, plot, subject, or style of the work.

Description of the Client from Hell: Blames agent for all pitfalls in the publishing process. Never expresses gratitude or appreciation for a good job done.

Description of Dream Client: Informed, courteous, loyal, professional.

Why did you become an agent? Since I wrote my first (terrible) short story in college and attempted to market it, I've been fascinated by the creative process involved in writing and the manner in which books and other intellectual property is commercially exploited. I've always been an agent and I can't imagine doing anything else.

What might you be if you weren't an agent? I might start my own publishing company.

THE JEFF HERMAN AGENCY, INC.

140 Charles Street, Suite 15A
New York, NY 10014
212-941-0540

Agents: Jeff Herman; Deborah Levine Herman; Jamie M. Forbes.

The following information pertains to JEFF HERMAN:

Agent: Jeff Herman.

Born: December 17, 1958; Long Island, New York.

Education: Nursery school through college, Syracuse University, bachelor's, 1981.

Career history: First job: In-house publicity associate for a book publisher, followed by several years in corporate marketing, both on staff and as an independent consultant. Cleaned public toilets in late 1970s. Launched literary agency in late 1980s.

Hobbies/personal interests: Playing with my dogs and iguanas, daydreaming, leaving the office.

Subjects/categories most enthusiastic about agenting: This varies depending on the day, the time, whether I've eaten or not, and how well it was digested, and my wife's mood.

Subjects/categories not interested in agenting: Same answer as above.

Best way for a prospective client to initiate contact: Write me a really good letter. If there's no response, write me another really good letter.

Reading-fee policy: Nope, we don't charge fees.

Client representation in the following categories: Nonfiction, 90%; Fiction, 9%; Textbooks, 1%.

Commission: 15% domestic; 10% foreign if I use a subagent.

Number of titles sold during the past year: More than 40.

Approximate percentage of all submissions (from queries through manuscripts) that are rejected: 98%.

Representative titles sold:

Story Sense: How to Get the Edge That Will Get You Published by Gary Provost (deceased) and Peter Rubie (Writer's Digest Books).

Mexican Remedies: Homegrown Wisdom for Health & Healing by Annette Sandoval (Berkley).

Kiss-Off Corporate America: Alternatives for Disenchanted Young Professionals by Lisa Kivirist (Andrews and McMeel).

Black Roots: How to Trace Your Family Tree by Tony Burroughs (Simon & Schuster).

How to Get Rich with an 800 Number by Dial-A-Mattress (Regan Books).

Why the South Lost the Civil War by Wiley Sword (St. Martin's Press).

Description of the Client from Hell: Anyone who makes me fantasize about cleaning public toilets.

Description of Dream Client: One who doesn't own a phone.

The most common mistakes potential clients make when soliciting an agent to represent them: Showing themselves to be long-winded, egotistical, high-maintenance nags.

What writers can do to enhance their chances of getting an agent (besides being good writers): Somehow demonstrate that they can provide more than they will take and will contribute more solutions than problems.

Why did you become an agent? I was single at the time.

What might you be doing if you weren't an agent? Write books exposing the greatest conspiracies of the century.

Comments: Write your first draft with a pen on a legal pad. Primitive methods are the most honest and compelling. It will force you to *draw* your material with each stroke and will help to keep you humble and grounded.

The following information pertains to DEBORAH LEVINE HERMAN:

Agent: Deborah Levine Herman (formerly Adams).

Born: October 4, 1958; Port Jefferson, New York.

Education: Too much. B.A., Ohio State University, Master's of Journalism, Ohio State University Graduate School in a dual degree with the College of Law. Got Juris Doctorate, passed the bar, and have been in recovery ever since.

Career history: An assistant attorney general for Ohio, private litigator–civil matters, writer neophyte, rejection-letter expert (recipient), ghostwriter, book proposal/book doctor/literary agent/rejection-letter expert.

Hobbies/personal interests: My three children, low-brow entertainment, yard sales, antiques, flea markets, oil painting, karaoke, gossip magazines, celebrities.

Subjects/categories most enthusiastic about agenting: Popular culture, unique nonfiction. I like books that usher in the trends rather than trail behind.

Subjects/categories not interested in agenting: Anything pompous, judgmental, or boring. Autobiographies are difficult to place, but they can be used as the backdrop for exceptional projects. No matter how wonderful or tragic your life might be, it will take a lot for it to compete as straight autobiography.

Best way for a prospective client to initiate contact: Query letter sent to my attention through our Midwest Editorial office: 731 East Broad Street, 1st Floor, Columbus, OH 43205

Reading-fee policy: No. Nada. Nyet. Never.

Client representation in the following categories: Nonfiction, 95%.

Commission: 15%.

Description of the Client from Hell: Someone who views their writing as a destination and not a process. We can each be messengers of the greater light. The trick is to know when to get out of the way. There are no real Clients from Hell because, if they are too arrogant to accept direction, I send them back to the Universe for further polishing and education.

Description of Dream Client: Someone who listens to and finds his or her own inner voice. This is where the best writing is found. A person like this understands that time and space are not always what we want them to be. Sometimes the Universe has its own agenda.

The most common mistakes potential clients make when soliciting an agent to represent them: Asking me to sell myself to them. I'm too busy. Being rude or demanding on the phone. We all answer phones to cover each other. Those of you who try to get past our screening process by behaving like royalty might just find yourself talking to me and pitching yourself right into embarrassment. Another mistake is to try to pitch by phone unless we know you or are related to you. This is a hard-copy business; follow protocol.

What writers can do to enhance their chances of getting an agent (besides being good writers): Focus on writing from a business perspective. If no one would ever buy your book, how can we possibly sell it for you? If your project is well thought-out and commercially meaningful, you have as much chance as anyone else.

Why did you become an agent? To learn to become a writer. Then I married Jeff Herman to ensure representation. He still makes me put it in writing!

What might you be doing if you weren't an agent? God only knows.

JAMIE M. FORBES represents selected projects for the Jeff Herman Agency, Inc.:
Born: Chevy Chase, Maryland.

Education: Master's degree in psychology from the Graduate Faculty of Political and Social Science at the New School for Social Research (New York); bachelor of arts from Washington University (St. Louis).

Career history: Musician, metals broker, performance artist, sensory-evaluation consultant for the food industry. Worked for publishers and book packagers (both in-house corporate as well as freelance and consultant) in editorial capacities, project development, and publicity and promotion. Wrote dozens of hardcore flesh novels (under various pseudonyms—and anonymously). Reviewed manuscripts for literary agencies. Book doctor; ghostwriter.

Hobbies/personal interests: Sports that use blades, legs, projectiles, brains; food with delirious seasonings; books!

Special projects and services: There are many writers out there who may already have achieved a measure of publishing presence with little or no association with outside agents, editorial consultants, or researchers. There may come a point at which you wish to take your career to new heights. We're interested in creative growth and professional development for newer (meaning already published or with a contract offering from a publisher) as well as established authors. We can manage business aspects of your writing career—orchestrating ways to increase your marketable output (or at least decrease your personal workload) and sales of literary properties that may benefit from (hitherto unexplored) reprint or foreign-rights sales. Please send us a listing of your published books (or related projects, such as novelty merchandise items or multimedia products), plus a rundown of your current work.

Subjects/categories most enthusiastic about agenting: Investigative stories and critical works of penetrating force and high-interest reader appeal; incisive biographical interpretations of established celebrities or cult icons; astonishing new directions in health, nutrition, popular psychology, and awareness; on-field accounts from the political, financial/business, and military arenas. Imaginative works that flout conventional distinctions among fiction and nonfiction categories and are marketable *because* they are so compelling. Commercial fiction: trailblazing works from new voices with astounding points of view. Nothing less will get through to major print publication. This applies particularly to suspense fiction, which includes thrillers and mysteries—new writers automatically compete with the many powerhouse writers who dominate that particular turf. Literary writing: Commercial literary works embody (if not predict) rising cultural tides and show strong and dominant concept development (not necessarily action-heavy plotting).

Subjects/categories not interested in agenting: Whatever causes gag-reflex from market overexposure.

Best way for a prospective client to initiate contact: Query letter that sells the concept and demonstrates that the author knows how to excite editorial response (with SASE).

Reading-fee policy: No reading fee.

Client representation in the following categories: Fiction: 20%; nonfiction: 50%; calendars, games, puzzles, humor: 15%, the rest are creative and investigatory works that break the boundaries of traditional fictional forms or do not necessarily slot into nicely defined nonfiction categories.

Commission: 15% domestic; 10% on foreign sales (when going through the offices of a coagent, who gets another 10%).

Approximate percentage of all submissions (from queries through manuscripts) that are rejected: 99+%.

Description of the Client from Hell: Someone who attempts to impose capricious notions of what publishing *should* be onto an entire industry that could hardly care less about them.

Description of Dream Client: Superb word-stylist and exceptional market researcher who can make a reader's head dance—and induce publishers to cough up bounteous advances.

The most common mistakes potential clients make when soliciting an agent to represent them: Writers often (and perhaps unwittingly) undermine their own presentations in a number of ways. Among the most common: Flagrant knock-off of an over-published motif or cookie-cutter version of an established writer's signature approach—thus brandishing other writers' hard-won gold as if it's their lode to mine. Or the contrary approach of saying certain renowned writers bite—therefore their own work will blow everyone away instantly (and there's no backup by way of offering an outstanding original project). Rambling, virtually pointless queries.

What writers can do to enhance their chances of getting an agent (besides being good writers): Bring bankable book-publishing credits to the project. Acquire celebrity status in a field with marketable tie-ins to book publishing.

Failing the above high-profile classifications, show you have the potential to sell extremely well—so that publishers are convinced they must take a chance on you as a new author. Attractively packaged and well-organized presentations pinpoint your publicity, promotional, and marketing flair. Elements such as press clippings, interviews, reviews of previous work, lists of your previous publications, performances, workshops, seminars—these suggest to an agent or editor that you can draw an audience and that other media professionals share enthusiasm for the author's product.

Why did you become an agent? I want to rule Hell.

What might you be if you weren't an agent? Divine.

Comments: I'm looking for something that jazzes the reader's juices. Something scary can be good. Creative works and investigatory stories that confront terror, suspicion, and controversy are rewarded with precious return in book publishing as well as in virtually all media and entertainment avenues. People find such tales incredibly uplifting and fun. Tip: Invent the next sizzling true-life issue and portray it in a compelling, humanized manner.

Want a taste of life on the corporate side? Invest in publicly traded international communications entities and/or publishing firms. Buy stock in paper-manufacturing companies. Sit back, track your money for a few months. In your leisure time, contact freelance editors, book designers, typesetters, printers, and distributors—get a rough idea of the resources required to get a book to the marketplace (especially dig those paper prices). Research some advertising rates. Tote up approximate expenses for a projected 12-city tour. Then ask yourself: Would I publish my book?

ALICE HILTON LITERARY AGENCY

13131 Welby Way
North Hollywood, CA 91606
818-982-5423

Agent: Alice Hilton.
Born: November 10, 1925; Brooklyn, New York.
Education: M.A., American Literature, Columbia University, New York City.
Career history: Teacher, Literary Agent since 1977.

Hobbies/personal interests: Won poetry prize in college, was film critic for local paper (*Canyon Crier*) in 1960s.

Subjects/categories most enthusiastic about agenting: Category fiction, general fiction, how-to and other nonfiction and biographies. Also television scripts and feature length screenplays, children's literature and young adult.

Subjects/categories not interested in agenting: No poetry, stageplay scripts, inspirational writing, promotional schemes, short stories, or magazine/newspaper material. No pornography.

Best way for a prospective client to initiate contact: Query letter with brief description of project. Send SASE!

Reading-fee policy: Yes, contact for brochure.

Client representation in the following categories: Nonfiction, 20%; Fiction, 75%; Children's, 3%; Textbooks, 2%.

Commission: 10–15%, depending on project.

Number of titles sold during the past year: 6.

Approximate percentage of all submissions (from queries through manuscripts) that are rejected: 90%.

Representative titles sold:

Raw Food: Key to Longer Life by Larry Singer and Boris Isaacson (Tomorrow Now Press).

The Woman Inge by Audrey Langer (New Saga Press).

Description of the Client from Hell: No stalkers, please!

Description of Dream Client: Professional attitude, realistic expectations.

The most common mistakes potential clients make when soliciting an agent to represent them: Querying on unfinished manuscript, submitting material not in our areas of interest, submitting bizarre queries, manuscript printed with teeny or otherwise hard-to-read type fonts. Faxing lengthy queries.

What writers can do to enhance their chances of getting an agent (besides being good writers): Query as specified, send SASE, present manuscript clean, error free, nice open type font, easy-to-read size.

Why did you become an agent? I met and married an agent who has now passed on and discovered this was a way to work with my literary background and interests.

What might you be doing if you weren't an agent? Teach remedial reading, helping people write their autobiographies.

Comments: The love affair of the literary agent with his material helps to determine the success that may result.

HULL HOUSE LITERARY AGENCY

240 East 82nd Street
New York, NY 10028
212-988-0725
fax: 212-794-8758

Agent: David Stewart Hull; Lydia Mortimer, Associate.

The following information pertains to DAVID STEWART HULL:
Born: March 21, 1938; Oshkosh, Wisconsin.
Education: B.A., Dartmouth College, 1960; University of London, School of African and Oriental Studies, 1960–1962.
Career history: 1966–1968, East Coast story editor, MCA–Universal Pictures; 1968–1970, editor, Coward, McCann Publishers; 1970–1981, partner, vice president, James Brown Associates, Inc.; literary agency sold to Curtis Brown (UK) in 1978; 1981–1987, agent, Peter Lampack Agency, Inc.; 1987–present, president, Hull House Literary Agency.
Hobbies/personal interests: Collecting and researching American 19th-century painting. I have been a guest curator at the New-York Historical Society.
Subjects/categories most enthusiastic about agenting: Fiction: crime novels, commercial fiction—but will consider literary fiction. Nonfiction: biography, true crime, history (particularly military), books on arts.
Subjects/categories not interested in agenting: Juveniles, young adult, short stories, science fiction, Westerns, poetry, New Age, historical novels except those set in the U.S., screenplays/teleplays, humor.
Best way for a prospective client to initiate contact with you: Write a one-page letter outlining the project, also listing prior book-length publications, if any. All queries *must* be accompanied by an SASE.
Reading-fee policy: No reading fee.
Client representation in the following categories: Nonfiction, 40%; Fiction, 60%.
Commission: 15% domestic; 20% foreign (split with foreign agent).
Number of titles sold during the past year: We do not give out this information.
Approximate percentage of all submissions (from queries through manuscripts) that are rejected: Just for the hell of it, we kept a record of the number of query letters received during 1996. The total was 3,129! And during the first month of 1997, the number of queries increased by approximately 20% over last year's monthly figures.

From that appalling 1996 total, we asked to see about 10 manuscripts, and took on 3 for representation here. A couple of authors didn't reply to our request to see their manuscripts, which is bad manners. While it is understandable that multiple-agent queries might generate several requests from agents to see a manuscript, it is common courtesy to let an agent know that it is being reviewed or represented elsewhere.
Representative titles sold:
All the Dead Lie Down by Mary Willis Walker (Doubleday/Bantam).
The Time of the Wolf by William D. Blankenship (Donald I. Fine).
The most common mistakes potential clients make when soliciting an agent to represent them: Writing a letter with bad grammar! I am astonished at the misuse of apostrophes and inability to distinguish between *lie* and *lay*. (The last misuse of this was observed in a letter from a writer with a degree in English, which makes one wonder.) And I don't take too kindly to being addressed by my first name by writers unknown to me. While the fax machine is one of man's greatest inventions, sending a lengthy query letter by this method is certain to get my attention in a way you don't want.
What writers can do to enhance their chances of getting an agent (besides being good writers): Produce good writing on interesting subject matter.

Description of the Client from Hell: Over the last 25 years in this business, I have had remarkably little difficulty with my clients, but there have been a few exceptions. Not too long ago, an author disagreed with my recommendations on placing of a second novel and effectively sabotaged a most promising career. Disregarding the advice of an experienced agent is not a wise thing to do.

Description of Dream Client: A writer who understands the publishing process.

Why did you become an agent? My first two jobs in New York City involved dealing with agents, and it seemed to me that what they were doing was more interesting than my own work. So after considerable investigation, I became a partner in an existing agency, and eventually formed my own firm.

What might you be doing if you weren't an agent? I think I might have become a dealer in American painting.

Comments: This agency is always willing to consider the work of unpublished writers. While the majority of our clients have previously published book-length works, a number of them started with us without a publication history. We firmly believe in the encouragement of quality writing, and there is obviously a lot of it out there.

We are very active in the foreign-language sales of books by our clients. In one case, a book has been sold in 13 foreign languages including Bulgarian (a first for us). We also work closely with motion picture agents on the West Coast, and during the past year three books by our clients have been optioned for major sums.

We are painfully aware of the lack of traditional editorial functions at some publishing houses. We are always willing to give comments of a limited nature to clients on their manuscripts. If, in our opinion, a promising manuscript needs more editorial work than we can carry out on the agency level, we recommend a number of freelance editorial services which we know have benefited our other clients.

THE JETT LITERARY AGENCY

(See entry for The Snyder Literary Agency.)

JOY SCULPTURING LITERARY AGENCY

3 Golf Center, Suite 141
Hoffman Estates, IL 60195
847-310-0003
fax: 847-310-0893

Agent: Carol Joy Lippman.

Born: Los Angeles, California.

Education: Mesa Community College; Northern Michigan University (secondary education, English major).

Career history: Education for 30 years. Owned/operated three successful sales businesses including Christian bookstore.

Hobbies/personal interests: Reading, writing, cross-country skiing, health and religious pursuits.

Subjects/categories most enthusiastic about agenting: Fiction: Most categories. Nonfiction: Self-help, how-to, health, and religious categories.

Subjects/categories not interested in agenting: Horror, science fiction, New Age, excess sex and language.

Best way for a prospective client to initiate contact: Query letter describing your work or sample (20 pages) of your writing. Enclose SASE.

Reading-fee policy: No reading fee initially. Readers and editing services are available for fee if so contracted separately.

Client representation in the following categories: Nonfiction, 49%; Fiction, 51%.

Commission: 15% or individual editing and reading services available (fees available upon request).

Number of titles sold during the past year: 1. Have been in business less than one year.

Approximate percentage of all submissions (from queries through manuscripts) that are rejected: 89%.

Description of the Client from Hell: Depressed, negative, loser. I'm glad I have never had any.

Description of Dream Client: One who never gives up; who is willing to continue to learn and improve.

What writers can do to enhance their chances of getting an agent (besides being good writers): Contact me by mail.

Why did you become an agent? I saw a need. So many good writers do not know how to sell or do not have a passion for selling their work. They have put forth so much effort creating a gem and don't take the next step—getting it out to a publisher. I love to sell something I'm enthusiastic about. I have tenacity and persistence. I enjoy my work.

What might you be doing if you weren't an agent? I might be a college professor teaching journalism.

Comments: As our name implies, it is our desire to assist in sculpturing the ordinary writer into a literary success. We are willing to work with the authors to help them produce masterful quality writing. The word *eclat* comes to mind: "A Brilliant Success."

J. KELLOCK AND ASSOCIATES LTD.

11017 80th Avenue
Edmonton, AB T6G 0R2 Canada
403-433-0274

Agent: Joanne Kellock.

Education: B.A., honors English, University of Alberta; graduate studies, University of Alberta and Harvard/Radcliffe.

Career history: Sales representative, while still at university, for Penguin, Pan, Fontana, Van Nostrand Reinhold, Macmillan Canada (university text market). Bantam publicist: author promotion. Marketing manager: Government of Canada, National Museums of Canada, Ottawa, Ontario. Literary Agent full time since 1987.

Hobbies/personal interests: Classical music, collecting paintings and sculpture, cooking for guests only now.

Subjects/categories most enthusiastic about agenting: Literary fiction, all categories works for children, creative nonfiction, extraordinarily well-written commercial genre.

Subjects/categories not interested in agenting: Poetry, essays, short stories (unless from previously published writer), esoteric, New Age, texts.

Best way for a writer to initiate contact: Query letter—no initial telephone calls please.

Reading-fee policy: Yes, a fee is charged for previously unpublished writers, or published writers of, say, nonfiction, who have now written a novel or a work for children.

Fee Schedule: $140 U.S., for three chapters plus brief synopsis. If style works with subject or subject is something selling today, balance read free of charge. $100 U.S. for picture book for children.

Client representation in the following categories: Nonfiction, 30%; Fiction, 30%; Children's/young adult, 40%.

Commission: 15% North America; 20% foreign and UK unless subject is one I handle myself in UK, i.e., works for children, fiction, and some nonfiction.

Number of titles sold during the past year: 15.

Approximate percentage of all submissions (from queries through manuscripts) that are rejected: 90%.

Representative titles sold:

Campfire Tales by Andy Russell (McClelland & Stewart, Canada), Nonfiction.

Adventures in Pirate Cover by Martyn Godfrey (Avon Books, New York), 3-book series.

Emma's Eggs by Barbara Spurll (Stoddart Publishing, Canada), illustrations only.

Bird Song and *Shadow Dance* by Tololwa M. Mollel (Clarion Books, New York), picture books.

Mom, the School Flooded by Ken Rivard (Annick Press, Canada), picture book.

Kitiko's Journey by Tololwa Mollel (Stoddart Publishing, Canada), picture book.

Do You Want Fries with That? by Martyn Godfrey (Scholastic, Canada).

Why Just Me? Mass-market rights (Scholastic, Canada).

The most common mistakes potential clients make when soliciting an agent to represent them: Initial telephone query calls; cover letter carelessly written and mistake-ridden; manuscript carelessly written, filled with typos, spelling errors, grammar errors, and that old saw—errors in logic.

What writers can do to enhance their chances of getting an agent (besides being good writers): They are not guilty of any of the most common mistakes (see above question).

Description of the Client from Hell: Those who do not read the complete listing in Jeff Herman's *Writer's Guide to Book Editors, Publishers, and Literary Agents.*

Description of Dream Client: The client that presents me with a *knock-your-socks-off* novel or creative work of nonfiction. The client who behaves professionally and does not barrage me with letters, faxes, telephone calls soon after a submission. The client who always encloses SASE, plus necessary postage for responses to queries, toing and froing of material, or return of material, and knows (having read the complete listing), that first, I do require a fee from all previously unpublished writers—magazine, newspaper, periodical publications are not a book—and also knows that I cannot mail to the U.S. with U.S. postage.

Why did you become an agent? Evolution—it seems to me that anyone who starts out anywhere in the publishing industry, stays. Most of us seem to move around within the industry. I have a sincere love of literature.

What might you be doing if you weren't an agent? Running an art gallery or doing an honors degree in 17th century history; but I would rather be reading Jane Austen.

Comments: *Rather, I would ask, why is it everyone today thinks they can write a book? So, you want to write a novel, are you prepared to spend the next ten years of your life learning how?* (Quote from W. O. Mitchell, well-known Canadian novelist, from a workshop I attended on the novel.)

Natasha Kern Literary Agency, Inc.

P.O. Box 2908
Portland, OR 97208-2908
503-297-6190

Agent: Natasha Kern.
   Born: 1945; Lindsey, California.
   Education: University of North Carolina, Chapel Hill; Columbia University, New York; graduate work, New York University.
   Career history: Publicist and editor for New York publishers and acquisitions editor for New York agents prior to founding her own agency in 1986.
   Hobbies/personal interests: Activities involving my children and our Shiba Inu; gardening; travel; animals; yoga; shamanism; performing arts; history; and, of course, storytelling and reading.
   Subjects/categories most enthusiastic about agenting: Fiction: commercial and literary; mainstream women's; romances, historicals; thrillers and mysteries. Nonfiction: health, science, feminism, parenting, spirituality, psychology, self-help, business, gardening, current issues, gay topics, animals/nature, controversial subjects, and reference.
   Subjects/categories not interested in agenting: Fiction: Horror and science fiction, true crime, children's or young adult. Nonfiction: Sports, computers, technical, or scholarly.
   Best way for a prospective client to initiate contact with you: Query letter with SASE.
   Reading-fee policy: No reading fee.
   Client representation in the following categories: Nonfiction, 45%; Fiction, 55%.
   Commission: 15% domestic and film; 20% foreign.
   Number of titles sold during the past year: 41.

Approximate percentage of all submissions (from queries through manuscripts) that are rejected: 99% unsolicited; 85% solicited partials, proposals, and manuscripts. From 3,000 queries every year, approximately 10 writers are accepted for representation. Write a good query!

Representative titles sold:

Herbal Prescriptions: Gingko for Better Health by Don Brown (Prima).

Aphrodite's Daughters by Jalaja Bonheim (Simon & Schuster).

Extinct by Charles Wilson (St. Martin's Press/NBC).

Sons Without Fathers by Kennedy and Terdal (Carol Publishing).

Breast Cancer: What Your Doctor May Not Tell You by Steve Austin (Prima).

Barracuda, Final Bearing by Mike DiMercurio (Donald I. Fine/NAL).

Rosie O'Donnell by George Mair and Anna Green (Carol Publishing).

Between Love and Hate by Lois Gold (Penguin USA).

Patterns of Love by Robin Lee Hatcher (HarperCollins).

Mortal Fear by Greg Iles (Dutton/Signet).

River of Our Return by Gladys Smith (HarperCollins).

Lesbian Gulls and Gay Giraffes by Bruce Bagemihl (HarperCollins).

African American Women in Congress by Laverne Gill (Rutgers University Press).

Magic Spells by Christy Cohen (Bantam Books).

Dreams of an Eagle by Lori Handeland (Leisure Books).

The most common mistakes potential clients make when soliciting an agent to represent them: It does not appeal to me when writers tell me their mom, friends, or children love their book and their writing is better and will make more money than that of the current number-one bestselling author. Writers need to study how to write a great query letter; many elements are often missing, such as: length of manuscript, genre, if it is completed, publishing credits, etc. Also don't just say "here's a book I've written" and attach a ten-page synopsis—it won't get read. Obviously, errors in grammar or spelling are unacceptable. The worst are queries that are threatening, bizarre, obscene, plain weird, or arrive by fax. No SASE means no response.

What writers can do to enhance their chances of getting an agent (besides being good writers): In nonfiction, the author's passionate belief in the subject as well as expertise and a defined audience are very appealing. If there are writing problems, I will get them help in producing a book. In fiction, a wonderful, fresh authorial voice, a page-turning plot, character depth, well-structured chapters, and strong imaginative prose. The writing is everything in fiction.

Description of the Client from Hell: I do not have any clients like this. All of my clients are people I respect and admire as individuals as well as writers. They are committed to their own success, and I am committed to helping them to achieve it. They understand the complex tasks involved in agenting including sales, negotiations, editorial, arbitration, etc.

Description of Dream Client: One who participates in a mutually respectful business relationship, is clear about needs and goals, and communicates about career planning. If we know what you need and want, we can help you to achieve it. A dream client has a gift for language and storytelling, a commitment to a writing career, a desire to learn and grow, and a passion for excellence. How wonderful that so many of my clients are dream clients.

Why did you become an agent? When I left New York, I knew that I wanted to stay in publishing. However, editorial work was not sufficiently satisfying by itself. I knew I could acquire and develop salable properties and that my background gave me expertise in sales and running a company. I wanted to work with people long term and not just on a single project or phase of one. Plus, I had an entrepreneurial temperament, and experience negotiating big-money deals from raising venture capital for high-tech firms. When I developed literary projects for other agents that did not sell, I knew I could sell them myself—so I did. I've never regretted that decision. Agenting combined my love of books, my affinity for deal making, and my preference for trusting my own intuition. I sold 28 books the first year the agency was in business.

What might you be doing if you weren't an agent? I did everything else I ever wanted to do before becoming an agent. Agenting is truly a calling for me, and I would not be as happy doing anything else. It is a case of "do what you love (and are good at) and the money follows."

Comments: Believe in yourself and your own gifts. Keep in mind that the challenge for every writer is twofold—to have something to say and to have the mastery of the craft to say it well. Study and practice plotting, pacing, point of view, etc.—so you can express exactly what you want to say. Nothing is more important than being true to your own artistic vision and understanding the requirements of the medium you have chosen to express it, whether you are writing a symphony, a haiku, or a novel. Keep in mind that in imitating other writers you can only be second-rate at being them. Expressing your own inner thoughts, feelings, and stories in your own way is the only path to real success. Your world, your history, your experiences, your insights cannot be duplicated by anyone else. Bring us in to share your vision, your imagination. No one can do it better than you can, because the truth of your uniqueness is what you are here to offer everyone else. It is what moves us and takes us outside of our own lives when we read what you have written.

KIDDE, HOYT & PICARD

335 East 51st Street
New York, NY 10022
212-755-9461
fax: 212-223-2501

Agents: Kay Kidde; Laura Langlie, associate agent (telephone: 212-755-9465).

   Born: Kidde: August 30, 1930; Montclair, New Jersey. Langlie: January 21, 1964.

   Education: Kidde: Chatham Hall, Virginia (1948); B.A., Vassar College (1952). Langlie: University of Iowa.

   Career history: Kidde: Has taught, worked as editor, senior editor at NAL, Putnam/Coward McCann, Harcourt. Langlie: Assistant to the publisher at Carroll & Graf Publishers, Inc.; associate production manager at Kensington Publishing Corporation.

Hobbies/personal interests: Kidde: Published poet, writer; tennis, ocean swimming, sailing. Langlie: Theater-going, film-watching, cooking, and reading.

Subjects/categories most interested in agenting: Kidde: Mainstream/literary fiction, mainstream nonfiction, romantic fiction, mystery. Langlie: General nonfiction, biographies, mainstream/literary fiction, nature writing, mystery and suspense fiction, historical romances.

Subjects/categories not interested in agenting: Male adventure, porn, science fiction, young adult, juvenile, poetry, unpublished short stories.

Best way for a prospective client to initiate contact with you: Write a query letter (with SASE), preferably one to three pages, including a synopsis, past publishing credits, and other writing experience.

Reading-fee policy: No reading fee. Author is responsible for photocopying, some long-distance telephone and fax expenses, and postage expenses for manuscripts being returned to the author.

Client representation in the following categories: Nonfiction, 25%; Fiction, 75%.
Commission: 15% for new clients.

Number of titles sold during the past year: 15.

Approximate percentage of all submissions (from queries through manuscripts) that are rejected: 90%.

Representative titles sold:
Inside the Lie by Lelia Kelly (Kensington).
The Kindness of Strangers by Mike McIntyre (Berkley).
Flesh and Stone by Mark Miano (Kensington).
The Murder of Edgar Allen Poe by George Hatrary (Carroll & Graf).
Don't Talk to Strangers by Bethany Campbell (Bantam).
Mind Games by C. J. Koehler (Carroll & Graf).
The Judas Glass by Michael Cadnum (Carroll & Graf).
Hen Frigates by Joan Druett (Simon & Schuster).
The Rose of Rawlings by Patricia Cabot (St. Martin's Press).

The most common mistakes potential clients make when soliciting an agent to represent them: Kidde: Insistence; the coy, undisciplined, lack of straight presentation of selves. Langlie: An incomplete presentation of their book projects. Presumptuousness.

What writers can do to enhance their chances of getting an agent (besides being good writers): Kidde: Write a beautiful novel with agape in it. Langlie: Be original and get to know the market. Read!

Description of the Client from Hell: The prospective Client from Hell is one who is pushy, loud, not a stylist, unpublished.

Why did you become an agent? Kidde: Because I love good books. Langlie: I enjoy putting people together. I'm a good matchmaker in business.

What might you be doing if you weren't an agent? Kidde: Writing more. Langlie: Somehow, I'd be involved with authors and publishing. This always has been what I've wanted to do.

Comments: Go for good values, go for love, style and reality.

THE KIRKLAND LITERARY AGENCY, INC.

P.O. Box 50608
Amarillo, TX 79159-0608
806-356-0216
fax: 806-356-0452

Agent: Jean Price.

Career history: Member of AAR; President of Kirkland Literary Agency, Inc., business in operation since 1993.

Subjects/categories most enthusiastic about agenting: Novel-length fiction, specializing in romance, mainstream, and mystery.

Subjects/categories not interested in agenting: Poetry, short stories, short-story collections, screenplays, Westerns, children's, science fiction.

Best way for a prospective client to initiate contact: Query letter (with SASE).

Reading-fee policy: No reading fee.

Client representation in the following categories: Nonfiction, 1%; Fiction, 99%.

Commission: 15% domestic, 20% foreign.

Number of titles sold during the past year: Between 20–30.

Approximate percentage of all submissions (from queries through manuscripts) that are rejected: Extremely selective at this time.

Representative titles sold:

Home for the Holiday Series: Won't You be My Husband?; Mistletoe Bride; New Year's Wife by Linda Varner (Silhouette Romance).

Beckoning Shore by DeWanna Pace (Jove), historical.

Devil's Rim by Sam Brown (Walker & Company), Western.

Drawn to the Grave by Mary Ann Mitchell (Leisure), horror.

The Wedding Quilt by Lenora Nazworth (Steeple Hill), inspirational.

A Matter of Trust by Cheryl Wolverton (Steeple Hill), inspirational.

Circle in Time by Jean Walton (Robinson/Scarlet), time travel.

Wishes Come True by Kathleen Nance (Leisure), fantasy.

On Thin Ice by Eve Gaddy (Bantam), contemporary romance.

Cupid's Workshop by Sheridon Smythe (Jove), Our Town Historical.

The Beholding by Dia Hunter (Leisure), single-title historical.

The Tender Touch by Lynn Emery (Arabesque), multicultural.

Description of the Client from Hell: Frequent calls to whine about writer's block; unable to meet deadlines; thinks his/her writing is written in stone and is unwilling to work with editorial suggestions.

Description of Dream Client: Produces marketable material; calls or writes for business purposes rather than personal; keeps me informed of novel's completion date; takes editorial suggestions and revises accordingly; networks, keeps updated with his/her particular genre; more than a one-book wonder; meets deadlines before schedule.

The most common mistakes potential clients make when soliciting an agent to represent them: Sends manuscripts in categories we don't represent; rambles in the query about how so-and-so relative loved the project (we'll make up our own minds);

hand-written, white-out used, colored paper, too small type pitch to sustain reading for long periods of time (please use Courier 12 or equivalent).

What writers can do to enhance their chances of getting an agent (besides being good writers): Know your market; write toward a specific market; remember grammar, spelling, and format count. Be persistent. Because we might reject one of your projects doesn't mean we aren't willing to look at more. We appreciate writers who don't take it personally and keep trying. Editors do too!

Why did you become an agent? Went to writers' conferences for 10 years. Met industry officials. Formerly owned a marketing firm and decided to combine my marketing expertise with my love of reading.

What might you be doing if you weren't an agent? Good question. Who Knows? I prefer not to find out.

Comments: Like any job or career, study your craft. Know the market and network. Publication doesn't happen overnight, but you must write and *complete* projects. Remember that each book must be better than the last.

HARVEY KLINGER INC.

301 West 53 Street
New York, NY 10019
212-581-7068

Agents: Harvey Klinger; Laurie Liss, Associate; Carol McCleary, Associate.

The following information pertains to HARVEY KLINGER:
Born: April 1, 1951.
Education: B.A., New College; M.A., the Writing Seminars, Johns Hopkins University.
Career history: Began as Doubleday trainee; founded own agency in 1977.
Hobbies/personal interests: Travel, water sports, collecting, exercise, theater, my own country house.
Subjects/categories most enthusiastic about agenting: Mainstream and literary fiction. Nonfiction: psychology, self-improvement, important biography, science, current issues.
Subjects/categories not interested in agenting: Category romance, historicals, science fiction, fantasy, Westerns, computers, children's.
Best way for a prospective client to initiate contact: Query letter with brief description/synopsis (plus SASE). *Do not telephone*!
Reading-fee policy: No reading fee.
Client representation in the following categories: Nonfiction, 50%; Fiction, 50%.
Commission: 15% domestic; 25% foreign (subagent collects 10%).
Number of titles sold during the past year: 50+.
Approximate percentage of all submissions (from queries through manuscripts) that are rejected: 90%.
Representative titles sold:

Ask Barbara by Barbara DeAngelis (Delacorte).
Howard Hawks: The Grey Fox of Hollywood by Todd McCarthy (Grove/Atlantic).
Perfect Harmony by Barbara Wood (Little, Brown).
Runaway Child by Terry Kay (Morrow).
The Seduction Mystique by Ginie Sayles (Avon).
Starting Out in the Evening by Brian Morton (Crown).
Forever 39 by Karlis Ullis, M.D. (Simon & Schuster).

The most common mistakes potential clients make when soliciting an agent to represent them: Too many phone calls and faxes. Trying to sell themselves, rather than letting the material speak for itself.

What writers can do to enhance their chances of getting an agent (besides being good writers): Have been referred by people whose opinions I respect.

Description of the Client from Hell: Someone who *kvetches* all the time, but doesn't want to listen to constructive advice.

Description of the Dream Client: The opposite.

Why did you become an agent? To use both my creative and legal (I come from a family of lawyers) sides.

What might you be doing if you weren't an agent? At this point in time, I have no idea. Ask me again in ten years.

Comments: If you've truly got talent, *persevere*. Unfortunately, there's just not much great talent out there, especially among younger would-be writers who grew up on TV and video games, rather than the printed word. They think they know how to write; they don't!

LINDA KONNER LITERARY AGENCY

10 West 15th Street, Suite 1918
New York, NY 10011
212-691-3419

Agent: Linda Konner.

Born: Brooklyn, New York.

Education: B.A., Brooklyn College (major: modern languages); M.A.T., Fordham University (majors: sociology and urban education).

Career history: 1976–1981, editor at *Seventeen* magazine; 1981–1983, managing editor and, 1983–1985, editor in chief at *Weight Watchers Magazine*; 1985–1986, entertainment editor at *Redbook*; 1986–1993, entertainment editor at *Woman's World* magazine; 1996–present, literary agent. Author of 8 books.

Hobbies/personal interests: Movies, theater, travel, exploring New York City.

Subjects/categories most enthusiastic about agenting: Nonfiction only: especially health, self-help, fitness and nutrition, relationships, pop psychology, celebrities, how-to.

Subjects/categories not interested in agenting: Fiction, children's.

Best way for a prospective client to initiate contact: Send a brief query letter along with SASE.

Reading-fee policy: No reading fee.

Client representation in the following categories: Nonfiction, 100%.

Commission: 15% domestic, 25% foreign (my foreign rights subagent collects 15%).

Number of titles sold during the past year: About 10 (my first year).

Approximate percentage of all submissions (from queries through manuscripts) that are rejected: 75%.

Representative titles sold:

Kiss and Sell: The Making of a Supergroup by C. K. Lendt (Billboard Books).

Special Siblings by Mary McHugh (Hyperion).

Toxic Friends, Healthy Friends by Florence Isaacs (William Morrow).

How to Help Your Man Get Healthy (Without Being a Nag) by Maria Kassberg and Steven Jonas, M.D. (Avon).

Go Romance! The Single Woman's Guide to Flirting, Dating, and Finding Love Online by Lisa Skriloff and Jodie Gould (St. Martin's Press).

Description of the Client from Hell: Doesn't follow through. Says he/she will turn in a proposal promptly/do a rewrite promptly/come up with ideas for the next book but then never does. Shmoozes endlessly with me on the phone either out of loneliness or to get my help coming up with a new idea. Thinks that "fun" multicolored proposals with lots of (needless) visuals are great (they do not save an otherwise poor idea or poor writing).

Description of Dream Client: One who writes well and has a steady stream of good, commercial nonfiction ideas. Not afraid to think big. Has a sense of the marketplace—what's happening in the publishing world and what is likely to sell. Follows directions. Turns things around promptly. Keeps phone conversations brief and to the point. Appreciates the efforts I'm making on his/her behalf.

What writers can do to enhance their chances of getting an agent (besides being good writers): See description of a dream client.

Why did you become an agent? I wanted a change from book writing. Also, I had successfully sold and negotiated contracts for several books of my own and my friends' (often getting better deals for myself than my agents had gotten), and I enjoyed the process. Also, I had always had many more good book ideas than I ever had the time to write myself, and now I can see some of my ideas (such as *How to Help Your Man Get Healthy*) blossom into books written by other talented people who may be good writers but don't have a concrete book idea at the moment.

What might you be doing if you weren't an agent? Writing books, in particular, a book I can't sell for the life of me called *Apartners: Living Apart and Loving It* (my honey of 19 years and I are not married and don't live together).

BARBARA S. KOUTS, LITERARY AGENT

P.O. Box 560
Bellport, NY 11713
516-286-1278

Agent: Barbara S. Kouts.

> **Born:** October 24, 1936.

> **Education:** B.A., English, New York University; M.A., English, SUNY at Stony Brook.

> **Career history:** Freelance editorial work at book publishers and magazines; began working in literary agency 1980; founded own agency in 1991.

> **Hobbies/personal interests:** Walking, swimming, reading, bicycle riding, gardening, spending time with my family and friends.

> **Subjects/categories most enthusiastic about agenting:** Children's, literary novels, psychology, parenting, interpersonal relationships. Mysteries and fast-moving movie tie-in novels. Novels with depth in ideas and characters. Health, sports, and gardening.

> **Subjects/categories not interested in agenting:** Science fiction and romance novels. Mass-market children's books.

> **Best way for a prospective client to initiate contact:** Query letter and description of project (with SASE).

> **Reading-fee policy:** No reading fee (only photocopying expenses).

> **Client representation in the following categories:** Nonfiction, 20%; Fiction, 20%; Children's, 60%.

> **Commission:** 10%.

> **Number of titles sold during the past year:** Lost count!

> **Approximate percentage of all submissions (from queries through manuscripts) that are rejected:** 90% of new submissions and queries.

> **Representative titles sold:**

Dawn Land by Joseph Bruchac (Fulcrum Publishers).

The Faithful Friend by Robert Sans Souci (Simon & Schuster).

How to Get a Good Job in 30 Days by Hal Gieseking (Simon & Schuster).

Minty by Alan Schroeder.

> **The most common mistakes potential clients make when soliciting an agent to represent them:** Calling on the phone over and over again to find out about everything! Constantly! Sending sloppy and unprofessional work!

> **What writers can do to enhance their chances of getting an agent (besides being good writers):** They are professional in all aspects of their query letter and phone conversations. Real pros stand out!

> **Description of the Client from Hell:** Expecting much too much—instant reads, instant dollars, instant attention! A feeling of non-trust, quibbling over everything.

> **Description of the Dream Client:** Hard-working, reliable, consistent in writing, willing to rewrite and revise, kind and considerate. Upbeat and cheerful.

> **Why did you become an agent?** Great love of books! And good reads! I love to see a manuscript turn into a published book.

> **What might you be doing if you weren't an agent?** Working with books or writing in some other capacity. Getting a Ph.D. in English. Reading all the great classics!

> **Comments:** Keep on writing—never give up! "To one's own self be true." *Hakuna matata.*

IRENE KRAAS AGENCY

220 Copper Trail
Santa Fe, NM 87505
505-474-6216

Agent: Irene W. Kraas.

Born: August 16, is this necessary?

Education: B.A., psychology; M.Ed., educational psychology.

Career history: Career counselor; management consultant and trainer to business, universities, and government; literary agent (1990–present).

Hobbies/personal interests: Reading, hiking, and enjoying life.

Subjects/categories most enthusiastic about agenting: Fiction: especially science fiction, mysteries, and all genre and good literature.

Subjects/categories not interested in agenting: Poetry, young children's (I do young adult), most nonfiction, no category romances, or westerns.

Best way for a prospective client to initiate contact: Send me a short cover letter, the first 50 pages of a *completed* manuscript, and return postage. Please no query letters!!

Reading-fee policy: No reading fee.

Client representation in the following categories: Fiction, 100%; Young Adult, 30%.

Commission: 15%.

Number of titles sold during the past year: Varies from year to year.

Approximate percentage of all submissions (from queries through manuscripts) that are rejected: 95%.

Representative titles sold:

Breakaway by Kimberly Griffiths Little (Avon, 1997), young adult.

Enchanted Runner by Kimberly Griffiths Little (Avon, 1998), young adult.

Gramp's Song by Christopher Farran (Avon, 1998), young adult.

Seraphim Rising by Elisabeth DeVos (ROC, 1998).

Bone Wars by Brett Davis (Baen), 2 books.

Gabriel Hart by Linda George (Harlequin, 1998).

Spider Worlds by Duncan Long (HarperCollins).

Deathweave Series by Cary Osborne (Ace), 2 books.

Ty Merrick Series by Denise Vitola (Ace), 3 books.

The most common mistakes potential clients make when soliciting an agent to represent them: No cover letter or no return postage. Envelope too small. I can ignore everything if it's a great manuscript.

What writers can do to enhance their chances of getting an agent (besides being good writers)? I have to admit that I'm really only interested in the manuscript, so if the writer just sends the 50 pages and SASE, I'm a happy camper.

Description of the Client from Hell: I'll take the fifth, thanks.

Description of Dream Client: A great writer who trusts me to do the very best for them.

Why did you become an agent? I went from 20 years in business consulting to becoming the great American writer to agenting. I love using my business acumen in helping first authors get a break.

What might you be doing if you weren't an agent? I've done what I've wanted all along and this is the ultimate. However, if I had to choose, I would be a rich publisher and publish all those great books that I've had rejected!

PINDER LANE & GARON-BROOKE ASSOCIATES, LTD.

159 West 53rd Street, Suite 14-E
New York, NY 10019
212-489-0880
pinderl@interport.net (e-mail)

Agents: Dick Duane, Robert Thixton, Nancy Coffey. Vice President-Office Manager and Submissions Supervisor: Jean Free.

Career history: Duane: agent since 1960, co-owner; also packages feature films, movie tie-ins, extensive advertising background. Thixton: agent since 1975, co-owner. Coffey: Agent since 1992; previously editorial advisor to editor in chief at Putnam/Berkley Publishing; editorial director, Ballantine Books and Avon Books.

Subjects/categories most enthusiastic about agenting: In general, any intriguing well-written book, either fiction or nonfiction. Fiction: Commercial and literary fiction including thrillers, technothrillers, adventure, romance, science fiction/fantasy, and some young adult fiction. Nonfiction: personal lifestyle including cookbooks, pop culture, historical biographies, investigative reporting, and natural history.

Subjects/categories not interested in agenting: None.

Best way for a prospective client to initiate contact: A one-page query letter briefly stating the subject of the work and a short bio on the writer.

Reading-fee policy: No charge for requested material.

Client representation in the following categories: Nonfiction, 25%; Fiction, 75%.

Commission: 15% domestic; 30% foreign/translation sales.

Number of titles sold during the past year: 25.

Approximate percentage of all submissions (from queries through manuscripts) that are rejected: 95%.

Representative titles sold:

Newman by Richard Steinberg (Doubleday).

The Secret Castle by Carole Smith (St. Martin's Press).

Scenes from a Sistah by Lolita Files (Warner Books).

Wall Street's Dirty Little Secrets by J. Michael Pinson (Prentice Hall).

Cows by Sara Rath (Voyager Press).

Shattered Bone by Major Chris Stewart (M. Evans).

Reaper by Ben Mezrich (HarperCollins).

Protect & Defend by Eric Harry (HarperCollins).

A Desperate Man by Rosemary Rogers (Avon).

A Plaza Wedding by Lawrence Harvey (Villard).

Description of the Client from Hell: An author who calls asking why his or her book hasn't sold after a very short submission time. An author who does not know the state of the publishing industry, who does not do research "on the shelves" in book-stores. The market is very tough out there, and a writer should be as objectively tough on his/her manuscripts as publishers are when they respond to a submission.

Description of Dream Client: The author who listens to his or her agent concerning rewrites, editorial work, and knows the state of the publishing marketplace. An author who will rewrite and edit regardless of how many times it is required, knowing that it is critical to have the manuscript in the best possible shape before submitting it to pub-lishers. An author who understands that not all books are sold the "first-time out."

The most common mistakes potential clients make when soliciting an agent to represent them: Telling the agency that they are considering several other agencies and they will "let you know." Our agency doesn't audition and that type of potential client will not be signed. Any material submitted to our agency must be on an exclu-sive basis while we take the time to read and evaluate a manuscript.

What writers can do to enhance their chances of getting an agent (besides being good writers): They should listen to comments our agents have to make about their work without becoming defensive. A willingness to listen to suggestions in order to make a manuscript better and salable is the only attitude possible and is often *the* de-ciding factor in whether or not a client is signed.

Why did you become an agent? The agents at Pinder Lane & Garon-Brooke Associates, Ltd. have an enduring love of literature in all its forms. To be able to nur-ture a writer's career strikes us as the most desirable job anyone, anywhere, could have.

Comments: The future of book publishing will be so closely aligned to other media that agents will have to have expertise in all fields of films, television, Internet, elec-tronic, and other new media in order to negotiate the best contracts for their clients. Because our agents have cross-media experience in all areas of publishing, promotion, advertising, and other related fields, we feel Pinder Lane & Garon-Brook Associates, Ltd. is uniquely positioned as a literary/media agency for the publishing in the late 1990s and into the 21st century.

MICHAEL LARSEN/ELIZABETH POMADA LITERARY AGENTS

1029 Jones Street
San Francisco, CA 94109-5023
415-673-0939

Agents: Michael Larsen, Elizabeth Pomada.

Born: Larsen: January 8, 1941; New York, New York. Pomada: June 12, 1940; New York, New York.

Education: Larsen: City College of New York, 1965. Pomada: Cornell University, 1962.

Career history: Larsen: Worked at William Morrow, Bantam, and Pyramid (now Berkley). Pomada: Worked at Holt, David McKay, and the Dial Press. Started Northern California's oldest literary agency in 1972. Members of AAR. Larsen wrote *How to Write a Book Proposal* and *Literary Agents; What They Do, How They Do It, and How to Find and Work with the Right One for You.* Speak at writer's conferences and present seminars on writing proposals and "How to Make Yourself Irresistible to Any Agent or Publisher."

Hobbies/personal interests: Larsen: Reading books between covers without the phone ringing, movies, jazz and classical music, technology and other exciting aspects of the future, France, and the media. Pomada: France, traveling and writing about it, reading for pleasure.

Subjects/categories most enthusiastic about agenting: Nonfiction: Larsen: Business, technology, trends, visions of the future, how-to's, health, spirituality, architecture, belly-laugh humor, promotable illustrated books, new ideas with social or esthetic value that will interest the general public, and anything else that the major houses will buy because of the author's ability to promote the book. Pomada: Women's interests, travel, food, biographies, the arts, memoirs. Fiction: Commercial, literary, and genre (romance and mystery).

Subjects/categories not interested in agenting: Articles, short stories, poetry, scripts, young adult or children's books, textbooks. Also Westerns and hard-core science fiction unless they break out of the genre and sweep Elizabeth away. People don't want to spend money buying books to get depressed; don't sell a problem, sell a solution.

Best way for a prospective client to initiate contact with you: Fiction: After you have completed a novel and gotten feedback on it from people who know writing, please send the first 30 pages, a brief synopsis, SASE, and your daytime phone number. Nonfiction: Read Michael's book on proposals so you will know what editors need to see. Then send him your title and your promotion plans with SASE. If Michael feels that he can help you, he will advise you on how to make your proposal as salable as possible. For a free brochure, please send stamped, self-addressed #10 envelope.

Reading-fee policy: No reading fee.

Client representation in the following categories: Nonfiction, 70%; Fiction, 30%.

Commission: 15% domestic, which includes most normal expenses; 20% foreign.

Number of titles sold during the past year: 15–20.

Approximate percentage of all submissions (from queries through manuscripts) that are rejected: More than 90%.

Representative titles sold:

The Emerald Tablet: Message for the Millennium by Dennis Williams Hauck (Penguin).

El Cocodrillo's Cookbook: Over 100 High-Flavor Recipes Fused with a Caribbean and Latin American Kick by Marie Perucca-Ramirez and Julio J. Ramirez (Macmillan).

Drums of Silence by Jo Clayton (Tor).

A Faerie Glimmer: The Celtic Shaman's Journey by Francesca Duhie (HarperCollins).

Hidden Treasure: Where to Find It, How to Get It by Bill Yenne (Avon).

How to Get what You Deserve: Guerrilla Marketing Yourself by Jay Conrad Levinson, coauthor (Avon).

I'm Not as Old As I Used to Be by Frances Weaver, Seniors Editor, *The Today Show* (Hyperion).

Making Documentary and Reality Videos: A Practical Guide to Planning, Filming, and Editing Documentary Films and Reality Videos by Barry Hampe (Henry Holt).

Marketing Your Services for People Who Hate to Sell by Rick Crandall, Ph.D. (Contemporary).

The Family Business: Power Tools for Survival, Success, and Succession by Roger and Russell Allred (Berkley).

The Random House Writing Dictionary by Robert Masters (Random House).

Visionary Selling: Infiltrate Top Executive Levels, Align with Their Vision, Add Value with Ideas by Barbara Geraghty (Simon & Schuster).

Wild Child: My Friendship with Jim Morrison by Linda Ashcroft (Hodder & Stoughton, UK).

The Wit and Wisdom of Herb Caen edited and with an introduction by Barnaby Conrad (Chronicle).

Money for Writers: Over 800 Cash Awards, Grants, Prizes, Contests, Scholarships, Retreats, and More, edited by Diane Billot (Henry Holt).

The most common mistakes potential clients make when soliciting an agent to represent them: Contacting an agent before two things are in place: The proposal or manuscript is as well conceived and crafted as the author can make it, and especially for nonfiction, the list of things in descending order of importance that the author will do to give the book continuing national impact is as long and strong as possible. For selling most nonfiction to major houses, the promotion plan is eight times more important than the content.

Query letters addressed to "occupant." Not knowing about competitive nonfiction books. Not knowing who will walk into bookstores in 50 states more than a year from now and buy their books or why.

What writers can do to enhance their chances of getting an agent (besides being good writers): Know that we have written 13 books, been in business 25 years, and sold books to more than 100 publishers, and are available by phone during business hours. Be eager to work with us. Read the last four chapters of Michael's books on agents.

Description of the Client from Hell: The Nag. The writer with unrealistic expectations. The whiner who won't take responsibility for her own career. The know-it-all.

Description of Dream Client: Dream writers are grateful, faithful, creative in coming up with fresh ideas, conscientious in writing and rewriting, tireless in promoting, and patient. Also, they have a positive but realistic perspective on agenting and publishing, know their literary and financial goals, and are totally committed to developing their craft and career. They understand that, since they can leave us at any time, we want them to be satisfied with our efforts, become life-long friends, and inspire us to be Dream Agents.

Why did you become an agent? We became agents because we loved working with books and discovered that there were no publishing jobs available in California when we moved here, so we had to create our own jobs.

What might you be doing if you weren't an agent? If Michael was not an agent, he would be publishing and writing books that can help make the world a better place. He still believes that the right book can change the world. If Elizabeth was not an agent, she would be traveling the world and writing about it.

Comments: You can only write as well as you read. Read what you love to read and write what you love to read. What works for you in the books you love will work for your readers.

We like to handle books that we like, by people we like, and sell them to editors we like. We must find new writers to make a living. We love to get excited about new books and writers, and are as eager to find promising new writers as they are to be published.

Writing and selling a book are easy compared to making it successful. If you are writing nonfiction, your ability to promote your work will be a major factor in determining the editor, publisher, and deal you get for your books. To be a successful author published by a large house, you must be 100% committed to your career.

Writers are the most important people in publishing because they make it go. Now is the most exciting time ever to be alive and the best time to be a writer. The age of information is the age of the writer.

There are more agents, publishers, and formats for your books to be published in, more ways to get your books published, and more ways to promote and make money from them than ever. Be professional but relentless. Persistence rewards talent.

LEVANT & WALES LITERARY AGENCY, INC.

108 Hayes Street
Seattle, WA 98109
206-284-7114

Agent: Elizabeth Wales.
Born: March 30, 1952.
Education: B.A., Smith College; graduate work in English and American literature at Columbia University.
Career history: Worked in the trade sales departments at Oxford University Press and Viking Penguin; also worked in city government and served a term on the Seattle school board; also worked as a bookseller and publisher's representative.
Hobbies/personal interests: Reading, theater, cooking/eating, visual arts—all that Seattle has to offer in "the arts." Walking, hiking/backpacking, camping.
Subjects/categories most enthusiastic about agenting: Sponsors a wide range of narrative nonfiction titles: especially interested in projects that might be termed difficult or risky, or could have a progressive cultural or political impact. In fiction, looking for talented mainstream storytellers, both new and established. Especially interested in writers from the Northwest, Alaska, the West Coast, and what have become known as the Pacific Rim countries.
Subjects/categories not interested in agenting: Children's books, almost all genre projects (romance, historicals, true crime, horror, action/adventure).

Best way for a prospective client to initiate contact: Send query letter with writing sample(s) and a brief description of the book project with SASE to the agency for consideration.

Reading-fee policy: No reading fee.

Client representation in the following categories: Nonfiction, 80%; Fiction, 20%.

Commission: 15% domestic.

Number of titles sold during the past year: 14.

Approximate percentage of all submissions (from queries through manuscripts) that are rejected: Most of our projects and authors come from referrals, but several times a year we "discover" a beauty of a book from the submissions pile.

Representative titles sold:

Can I Get a Witness: Black Women Recovering from Depression by Julie A. Boyd (Dutton, 1998).

Birdgirl: An Athabaskan Indian Legend from Alaska by Velma Wellis (HarperCollins Publishers, 1997).

Animals As Teachers and Healers by Susan Chernek McElray (Ballantine, 1997).

A Long Way from St. Louis: Travel Memoirs by Colleen J. McElroy (Coffee House Press, 1997).

What writers can do to enhance their chances of getting an agent (besides being good writers): It's hard to miss writing talent. It stands out.

Why did you become an agent? For the adventure and the challenge; also, I am a generalist—interested in variety.

Comments: I am particularly interested in writers who are dedicated to writing, and/or who have a particularly compelling story to tell.

ELLEN LEVINE LITERARY AGENCY

15 East 26th Street, Suite 1801
New York, NY 10010-1505
212-889-0620
No phone queries accepted. Please query by letter.

Agents: Diana Finch, Louise Quayle.

The following information pertains to DIANE FINCH:

Born: September 16, 1954, Hanover, New Hampshire.

Education: B.A., Harvard University, 1976; M.A., University of Leeds, Leeds, England, 1977.

Career history: Sanford A. Greenburger Associates, assistant agent, 1981–1984; St. Martin's Press, assistant editor, 1978–1981. In addition to representing my own clients, I handle translation and magazine rights and attend the Frankfurt Book Fair annually, so I am always looking out for opportunities for my clients to be published in magazines and other countries.

Hobbies/personal interests: Sports, including skiing, soccer, and field hockey—as participant. Theater.

Subjects/categories most enthusiastic about agenting: Serious nonfiction.

Subjects/categories not interested in agenting: Romance fiction, mysteries.

Best way for a prospective client to initiate contact: By query letter with SASE.

Reading-fee policy: No reading fee.

Client representation in the following categories: Nonfiction, 50%; Fiction, 30%; Children's, 20%.

Commission: 15%.

Number of titles sold during the past year: 12 (not including foreign sales).

Approximate percentage of all submissions (from queries through manuscripts) that are rejected: 99%—I receive many queries.

Representative titles sold:

Going Part-Time by Cindy Tolliver (Avon).

Marketing Online by Marcia Yudhin (Plume).

Golf's Mental Hazards by Alan Shapiro, Ph.D. (Simon & Schuster).

When Black Couples Work Together by Anita Diggs and Vera Paster, Ph.D. (Kensington).

Circle of Stones: A Novel of Our Earliest Beginnings by Joan Lambert (Pocket Books).

Untitled nonfiction book on the John Muir Trail by Daniel Duane (Farrar Straus & Giroux).

The most common mistakes potential clients make when soliciting an agent to represent them: Writers who approach me about a number of unsold projects or who stress the marketing possibilities without equal attention to the content of their work turn me off.

What writers can do to enhance their chances of getting an agent (besides being good writers): They are recommended by writers or editors whose judgment I trust. They present polished material that is in final form. They write about their work in a clear and inspired way.

Description of the Client from Hell: I am delighted to say: currently none of mine. Perhaps someone who does not allow for the time it can take for an agent to give good feedback or collect correct information.

Description of the Dream Client: An inspired, intelligent writer who communicates their concerns to me clearly and stays involved in all aspects of writing and publishing.

Why did you become an agent? I was an editor first, and I became an agent to be 100% on the writer's side.

What might you be doing if you weren't an agent? Teaching or editing.

The following information pertains to LOUISE QUAYLE:

Born: July 15, 1961; New Hartford, New York.

Education: B.A., Stephens College. Readings in ethics and 19th-century and contemporary British women writers. St. Peters College, Oxford University.

Career history: McIntosh and Otis, Inc., assistant agent, 1991–1995; freelance editor, author, 1989–1990; Quarto Marketing (a book packager), editorial assistant, 1986–1988; *Open Places*, managing editor, 1984–1985.

Hobbies/personal interests: Aviation, sports (golf, swimming, softball), history, women's history.

Subjects/categories most enthusiastic about agenting: Literary fiction; serious nonfiction with a social, cultural, political slant; narrative history, particularly encompassing "marginalized" groups; science for the general reader.

Subjects/categories not interested in agenting: Anything that is racist, sexist, homophobic; romance, hard science fiction.

Best way for a prospective client to initiate contact: Query letter with SASE.

Reading-fee policy: No reading fee.

Client representation in the following categories: Nonfiction, 10%; Fiction, 85%; Children's, 5%.

Commission: 15% domestic, 20% UK and foreign.

Number of titles sold during the past year: 5.

Approximate percentage of all submissions (from queries through manuscripts) that are rejected: 90%.

Representative titles sold:
Mysterious Skin by Scott Heim (HarperCollins).
Audrey Hepburn's Neck by Alan Brown (Pocket Books).
On the Rocks: Earth Science for Everyone by John S. Dickey (John Wiley).
What is Marriage For? by E. J. Graff (Beacon Press).
The Inheritor's Handbook by Dan Rottenberg (Bloomberg Press).

Description of the Client from Hell: Someone who is unrealistic about what the market will bear, who insists on submitting unsalable work—but I guess I wouldn't represent that someone!

Description of Dream Client: Someone who is open to comments and suggestions, works efficiently, and delivers on time. I also like working with clients who ask questions and are actively involved in the publishing process, long after the editing is finished.

The most common mistakes potential clients make when soliciting an agent to represent them: The gimmicky and cute query letter, not saying enough about their own experience/background.

What writers can do to enhance their chances of getting an agent (besides being good writers): A neat, concise, and professional presentation.

Why did you become an agent? To bring new voices to readers; to be a writer's advocate.

What might you be doing if you weren't an agent? Camping on the Olympic Peninsula; teaching hard-to-reach teens.

Comments: I'm in it for language, a good story, promoting social responsibility, and I would hope my clients are too.

JAMES LEVINE COMMUNICATIONS, INC.
Creative Development and Business Representation
Literary and Multimedia Projects

330 Seventh Avenue, 14th Floor
New York, NY 10001
212-268-4846
fax: 212-465-8637

Agents: James A. Levine, Arielle Eckstut, Daniel Greenberg.

Born: Levine: April 20, 1946. Hailey: December 13, 1945. Greenberg: October 13, 1970.

Education: Levine: B.A., Amherst College; M.A. (C. Phil. in English literature), University of California at Berkeley; Ed.D., Harvard University. Eckstut: B.A., University of Chicago. Greenberg: B.A. (history), University of Wisconsin at Madison.

Career history: Levine: Spent much of my career doing what I do now: putting together ideas, people, and money; identifying, nurturing, and marketing talent; creating projects that make a difference. As an entrepreneur in the not-for-profit and academic sectors, including a decade as Vice President for Product Development at the Bank Street College of Education, I channeled people's expertise into a variety of media: print, software, video, and audio. Have also written 6 books, 2 software manuals, and over 60 articles for leading magazines. Eckstut: Pastry chef prior to becoming literary agent. Greenberg: Dutton Books, subsidiary rights; Roberto Sautachiara Literary Agency (Italian subagent).

Hobbies/personal interests: Levine: Jazz, sports (playing them), photography, travel, voracious reading. Eckstut: I'm a member of an improvisational theatre group. I also love to cook, bake, make art (I have a design background), and I'm an avid moviegoer. Greenberg: Sports, music, Italian cooking, Irish history.

Subjects/categories most enthusiastic about agenting: Levine: A very wide range, as long as it's well written, including psychology, business, parenting, narrative nonfiction, literary fiction, technology, medical, how-to, social issues. Eckstut: Narrative nonfiction, food (cookbooks and philosophy of), urban studies, psychology, health, gardening, science, social sciences, spirituality, religion, and literary fiction (adult and young-adult). Greenberg: Fiction, sports, history.

Subjects/categories not interested in agenting: Levine: Anything that's poorly written. Eckstut: Self-help, popular fiction, romance, children's, true crime, academic and professional books. Greenberg: Romances.

Best way for a prospective client to initiate contact with you: Query letter (with SASE), with outline, sample chapter, and credentials.

Reading-fee policy: No reading fee.

Client representation in the following categories: Nonfiction, 95%; Fiction, 5%; (Children's, 15% of all titles).

Commission: 15%.

Approximate percentage of all submissions (from queries through manuscripts) that are rejected: 98%.

Representative titles sold:

Inside the Tornado (HarperBusiness). *Business Week* bestseller.

Working Wounded by Bob Rosner (Warner).

All I Really Need to Know in Business I Learned at Microsoft by Julie Bick (Pocket).

Undercurrents: A Life Beneath the Surface by Martha Manning (Harper San Francisco).

Been There Haven't Done That by Tara McCarthy (Warner).

The Seeing Glass by Jacqueline Gorman (Riverhead).

Catherine, Called Birdie by Karen Cushman (Clarion), Newbery Honor Award.

The Midwife's Apprentice. (Clarion), Newbery Award winner.

Undoing Depression by Richard O'Connor (Little, Brown).

The Growth of the Mind by Stanley Greenspan (Addison-Wesley).

The Parent's Journal Guide to Raising Great Kids by Bobbi Connor (Bantam).

It's NOT Just a Phase by Susan Swedo, M.D. and Henrietta Leonard, M.D. (Golden Books Family Entertainment).

Energize Your Life by Bradford Keeney (Golden Books Family Entertainment).

A Gynecologist's Second Opinion by William Parker, M.D. (Plume).

How to Raise Low-Fat Kids in a High-Fat World by Judith Shaw (Chronicle).

366 Simply Delicious Dairy-Free Recipes by Robin Robertson (Plume).

Room Redux: A Decorator's Workbook by Joann Eckstut and Sheran James (Chronicle).

Read My Lips: An Illustrated History of Lipstick by Meg Cohen-Ragas and Karen Kozlowski (Chronicle).

The Genesis of Ethics by Burton Visotzky (Crown).

Poemcrazy: Freeing Your Life with Words by Susan Goldsmith Wooldridge (Clarkson Potter).

The most common mistakes potential clients make when soliciting an agent to represent them: Sends a whole manuscript, unsolicited, with no SASE (the only worse scenario is the person who keeps calling—wanting to know why they have not gotten their manuscript back). Insists they've written the next great American novel. Says their friends and family like it (not even *love* it!). Says their murder mystery is funny and cute! Gives no biography that says who they are or why they're qualified to write what they've written.

What writers can do to enhance their chances of getting an agent (besides being good writers): Levine: I love the challenge of working with smart people with great ideas. Eckstut: First: great writing. Second: great recipes. Greenberg: For fiction, any piece of solid writing interests me, no matter the genre. I also look at credentials and publishing history. I keep my eyes open for a sharp sense of humor.

Description of the Client from Hell: Calls all the time for unnecessary reasons; is rude, haughty, disorganized; takes for granted everything you do; and never once says thanks!

Description of Dream Client: Organized, thoughtful, easy to get along with, conscientious, reliable, cordial, and fun!

Why did you become an agent? Levine: I was an agent before I ever knew I was an agent. Eckstut: Pure luck. Greenberg: I enjoy working with talented and interesting people. There is also nothing quite as exciting as the huge deal!

What might you be doing if you weren't an agent? Levine: Writing and working in some other organizational setting to develop people's talent. Eckstut: Architect? Actor? Chef? Who knows!

Comments: We feel passionately about feeling passionately about the projects we take on.

KAREN LEWIS & COMPANY

P.O. Box 741623
Dallas, TX 75374-1623
214-342-3885
fax: 214-340-8857

Agent: Karen K. Lewis.
  Education: M.A., journalism.
  Subjects/categories most enthusiastic about agenting: Fiction: Literary and genre.
Nonfiction: self-help, psychology, health, women's issues.
  Subjects/categories not interested in agenting: Poetry, short stories, juveniles.
  Best way for a prospective client to initiate contact: Query letter (with SASE),
brief synopsis, and first chapter.
  Reading-fee policy: No reading fee. Charge for copies, overseas calls, and postage.
  Client representation in the following categories: Nonfiction, 40%; Fiction, 60%.
  Commission: 15% domestic, 20% foreign.
  **Approximate percentage of all submissions (from queries through manuscripts)
that are rejected:** 95%.
  Description of the Client from Hell: A writer who lacks the ability to judge his or
her own work objectively.
  Description of Dream Client: A client who is patient and looks for creative ways to
make positive things happen.
  Why did you become an agent? I love to read and work with promising writers.
  What might you be doing if you weren't an agent? College professor of literature.

THE LITERARY GROUP INTERNATIONAL

270 Lafayette Street, Suite 1505
New York, NY 10012
212-274-1616

Austin branch office:
1300 Guadalupe Street, Suite 208
Austin, TX 78701
HORNFISH@MAIL.UTEXAS.EDU (e-mail)
(Phone queries are not encouraged; please initiate contact in writing or electronically—
query only; no attachments.)

Agents: Scott Waxman, Jim Hornfischer

  The following information pertains to SCOTT WAXMAN (New York office):
  Born: June 19, 1967.
  Education: Fieldston High School, Bronx, New York; Cornell University (English
major).

Career history: Assistant editor at HarperCollins (1990–1993); agent, the Literary Group International (1993–present).

Hobbies/personal interests: Piano, golf, tennis, biking.

Subjects/categories most enthusiastic about agenting: Nonfiction only. Categories include: sports, Judeo-Christian subjects, African-American subjects, politics, memoirs, history.

Subjects/categories not interested in agenting: Investment, poetry, children's science.

Best way for a prospective client to initiate contact: Query letter (with SASE).

Reading-fee policy: No reading fee.

Client representation in the following categories: Nonfiction, 90%; Fiction, 10%.

Commission: 15%.

Number of titles sold during the past year: 25.

Approximate percentage of all submissions (from queries through manuscripts) that are rejected: 90%.

Representative titles sold:

How Sweet the Sound: My Life with God & Gospel by Cissy Houston (Doubleday).

Traces of Wisdom: Amish Women Reflect on Life's Simple Pleasures (Hyperion).

Lessons from St. Francis: A Monk's Guide to Daily Life by John Michael Talbot (Dutton).

The Life & Death of Emmett Till: A Mother's Story by Marie Till-Mobley (Dutton).

Raise the Church, Raise the Spirit! How a Small Black Church in Oklahoma Rose from the Ashes by Reverend Alfred Baldwin, Jr.

Description of the Client from Hell: One who won't trust my judgment and uses other people's poor advice to refute what I say.

Description of Dream Client: One with faith in my judgment, a wealth of great ideas, and strong contacts in their field.

The most common mistakes potential clients make when soliciting an agent to represent them: Don't like queries that try to shock. If the idea is good, I'll read it.

What makes you enthusiastic about the way some writers solicit you? A good, succinct query letter with solid sales points.

Why did you become an agent? I love books, I love talent, and I love making deals.

What might you be if you weren't an agent? Too terrifying to ponder.

The following information pertains to JIM HORNFISCHER (Austin branch office):

Born: November 18, 1965; Salem, Massachusetts.

Education: B.A., Colgate University (Phi Beta Kappa); M.B.A., University of Texas at Austin.

Career history: Editorial positions in the McGraw-Hill general books division (1987–1989) and the HarperCollins adult trade division (1989–1992). Agent, Literary Group International, (1993–present).

Hobbies/personal interests: Net surfing, travel, military history and hardware, chess, typography/graphic design, sports.

Subjects/categories most enthusiastic about agenting: Nonfiction: Biography and memoirs, narrative nonfiction, business/management, health/diet/fitness, general-interest science, medicine, history, politics, exposes, African-American, Native American and Hispanic issues, relationship guides, academic/professional writing for a general audience. Fiction: Quality mainstream and literary; distinctive, writerly prose.

Subjects/categories not interested in agenting: Romance and most genre fiction, poetry.

Best way for a prospective client to initiate contact: Nonfiction: Submit an overview, chapter summaries, author bio, three chapters, and SASE. Fiction: Submit a one-page synopsis, the first 30 pages of the finished manuscript, and SASE.

Reading-fee policy: No reading fee.

Client representation in the following categories: Nonfiction, 90%; Fiction, 10%.

Commission: 15%; 20% on foreign rights sales.

Approximate percentage of all submissions (from queries through manuscripts) that are rejected: The same parade-drenching number as the rest of them.

Representative titles sold:

Lady Bird Johnson by Jan Jarboe-Russell (Scribner/Lisa Drew).

Himpressions by Valerie Shaw (HarperCollins), a national bestseller in the self-published edition.

Selena! by Clint Richmond (Pocket), the four-week #1 New York Times bestseller.

The Martyring by Thomas Sullivan (Forge), literary suspense novel. The Chicago Tribune wrote: "One is convinced that an outsize performer is trying his wings—a John Barth or a John Irving, with a touch of William Gaddis and maybe a dash of Kurt Vonnegut."

Looking for Lost Bird by Yvette Melanson with Claire Safran (Avon hardcover). The singular story of an adopted Jewish woman from Queens who discovered she is a Navajo.

The Reckless Decade: America in the 1890s by H. W. Brands (St. Martin's/Thomas Dunne).

T.R.: The Romantic Journey of Theodore Roosevelt by H. W. Brands (Basic).

Ten Bad Choices That Mess Up Black Women's Lives by Gracie Cornish (Crown).

Convicted in the Womb: One Man's Journey from Prisoner to Peacemaker by Carl Upchurch (Bantam).

Rebel Private: Front and Rear by William A. Fletcher (Dutton).

Mother Knew Best: Wit and Wisdom from the Moms of Celebrities by Elsa and David Hornfischer (Penguin/Plume). The authors perceptively write: "When you have a son who is a literary agent, it is dangerous to suggest an idea for a book."

Father Knew Best: Wit and Wisdom from the Dads of Celebrities by Elsa and David Hornfischer (Penguin/Plume). And doubly so.

Good Days and Mad by Dick DeBartolo (Thunder's Mouth). *Mad* magazine's "Maddest Writer" on 30-plus years at America's favorite satirical magazine.

Luck by Nicholas Rescher (Farrar Straus & Giroux).

The Lost History of the Canine Race by Mary Elizabeth Thurston (Andrews and McMeel hardcover; Avon paperback), selection of the Book-of-the-Month Club.

Right Thinking: Conservative Common Sense Through the Ages by James D. Hornfischer (Pocket). The perfect gift for the conservative in your family (a plug for my own little book there).

Raising Safe Kids in an Unsafe World by Jan Wagner (Avon trade paper).

War's End: An Eyewitness Account of America's Last Atomic Mission by Major General Charles W. Sweeney, USAF (Avon hardcover).

The Assassination of the Black Male Image by Earl Ofari Hutchinson (Simon & Schuster).

Not Now Honey, I'm Watching the Game: What to Do When Sports Comes Between You and Your Mate by Kevin Quirk (Simon & Schuster).

Barbara Jordan: A Biography by Mary Beth Rogers (Bantam).

The most common mistakes potential clients make when soliciting an agent to represent them: Telephoning. Writers *write* (and reserve for relatives the need to reach out and touch someone). Dropping by the office and insisting on "just a moment of your time." Exhibiting mistrust of their parcel carrier by checking in repeatedly after submitting their work. Requiring me to audition for the role of their agent before I'm even remotely interested. Not enclosing return postage.

What writers can do to enhance their chances of getting an agent (besides being good writers): They grasp the rudiments of the business (though as creative artists they'd prefer not to bother), temper their ambition with patience and faith, and just write the lights out (the latter tending to mitigate failings in one or more of the former).

Description of Dream Client: Thinks big, drinks from glasses that are half-full, even his grocery lists are beautifully written, keeps an open ear for useful advice and invariable runs with it in brilliantly surprising ways.

Why did you become an agent? Making a good book happen is a joy second to none.

What might you be doing if you weren't an agent? Flying an F-16, playing first base for the Bosox, or writing a curmudgeonly column for a village weekly newspaper.

LOWENSTEIN-MOREL ASSOCIATES

121 West 27th Street, Suite 601
New York, NY 10001
212-206-1630
fax: 212-727-0280

Agent: Eileen Cope.

Education: Degrees in political science and journalism.

Career history: Editor with the Putnam Berkley Group.

Subjects/categories most enthusiastic about agenting: Areas of interest include literary and multi-cultural fiction, comparative religions, psychology, ethics, contemporary social issues, contemporary ethnic and cultural issues, Asian studies, history, anthropology, sexuality, politics, and the arts (particularly music, theatre, and art history).

Subjects/categories not interested in agenting: All category fiction, children's, young adult.

Best way for a prospective client to initiate contact: Please send a query letter and c.v. (with SASE).

Reading-fee policy: No reading fee.

Client representation in the following categories: Nonfiction, 80%; Fiction, 20%.
Commission: 15% domestic, 20% foreign.
Representative titles sold:
A partial listing of Eileen Cope's acquisitions and sales for 1996–1997 include:
Awakening The Buddha Within: Timeless Teachings for a Western World by Lama Surya Das (Broadway Books).
The Mozart Effect: Using the Power of Music to Heal the Body, Strengthen the Mind, and Unlock the Creative Spirit (Avon hardcover).
The Three-Day Energy Fast: Cleanse Your Body, Clear Your Mind, and Claim Your Spirit (HarperCollins).
A Radiant Life: Bringing Sacred Traditions and Spiritual Practices into Everyday Living (Harper San Francisco).
Black Feathers: Short Stories by Cecilia Tan (HarperCollins).
Fight the Power! Rap, Race, and Reality by Chuck D, foreword by Spike Lee (Delacorte).
Mama Knows Best: African-American Wives Tales, Myths, and Remedies for Mothers and Mothers-To-Be (Simon & Schuster).
Conscious Connections by Dr. Ron Taffel with Melinda Blau (Golden Books).
The Deadhead's Taping Compendium (Henry Holt).
The Dying Time: Choreographing Life's Final Act (Bell Tower).

LUKEMAN LITERARY MANAGEMENT LTD.

205 West 80th Street, Suite 4C
New York, NY 10024
212-874-5959

Agent: Noah Lukeman.
   Education: B.A., Brandeis; Higo Honors, English and creative writing, cum laude.
   Career history: Worked at William Morrow; Farrar Straus & Giroux; Steppingstones Press; Delphinium Books; and David Vigliano Agency.
   Subjects/categories most enthusiastic about agenting: Open to most categories.
   Subjects/categories not interested in agenting: Poetry, children's books, juvenile or young adult.
   Best way for a prospective client to initiate contact: Send in query letter, 10 sample pages, and an adequate SASE.
   Reading-fee policy: No reading fee.
   Client representation in the following categories: Nonfiction, 50%; Fiction, 50%.
   Commission: 15%
   Number of titles sold during the past year: 11 (in the last six months).
   Approximate percentage of all submissions (from queries through manuscripts) that are rejected: 90%
   Representative titles sold:
Clacum Navigation by Steve Lattimore (Houghton Mifflin), story collection.
Dark Hands by Donald Rawley (Avon Books), fiction.

Mothers Who Drive Their Daughters Crazy by Susan and Ed Cohen (Prima).

Searching for Mary Poppins: Childcare Chills and Nightmare Nannies by Troy Lederman (Dove).

Dogs and Their People by Steve Diner (Hyperion).

Dreaming Wildly: The Life and Work of James Rouse by David Dillon (Counterpoint), a biography.

The Fight Against Fat: 20 Years As a Weight Watchers Group Leader by Rosalie Kaufman with Daniel Myerson and Dioi Meller (Kensington).

The Power of Cartilage by Dr. Stephen Hold (Kensington).

The Second Commitment: Repairing the Mid-Marriage Crises by Dr. David Truman with Esmond Chovere (Carol Publishing).

Untitled novel by Steve Lattimore (Houghton Mifflin).

Description of the Client from Hell: Pushy, impatient, controlling.

Why did you become an agent? To help writers.

DONALD MAASS LITERARY AGENCY

157 West 57th Street, Suite 1003
New York, NY 10019
212-757-7755

Agent: Donald Maass; Jennifer Jackson.

Born: Maass: 1953, Columbus, Georgia; Jackson: 1971, Cambridge, New York.

Education: Maass: B.A., St. Lawrence University, 1975; Jackson: B.A., St. Lawrence University, 1993.

Career history: Maass: 1977–1978, editor, Dell Publishing; 1979; agent, Scott Meredith Literary Agency, Inc.; 1980, founded Donald Maass Literary Agency. Jackson: 1993–1994, editorial assistant; 1994–1995, assistant agent; 1995–1996, associate agent, 1996–present, agent, Donald Maass Literary Agency.

Hobbies/personal interests: Maass: Reading, theatre, sailing, squash, antiques, stock market. Jackson: Writing, book collecting, Web-page design, home brewing, hiking, camping.

Subjects/categories most enthusiastic about agenting: Maass: Fiction specialist. concentration in science fiction, fantasy, mystery, suspense, horror, frontier, mainstream, and literary. Jackson: Science fiction, fantasy, mystery, suspense, romance, women's fiction, horror, mainstream, and literary fiction. Genre-fiction related nonfiction.

Subjects/categories not interested in agenting: Maass: Pop psychology, how-to, true crime, humor/novelty, juvenile. Jackson: Nonfiction, juvenile.

Best way for a prospective client to initiate contact with you: Concise (one-page!) query letter that includes prior short-story, novel, article, and/or nonfiction book credits.

Reading-fee policy: No reading fee.

Client representation in the following categories: Nonfiction, 5%; Fiction, 95%.

Commission: 15% domestic; 20% foreign.

Number of titles sold during the past year: 75.

Approximate percentage of all submissions (from queries through manuscripts) that are rejected: 99%.

Representative titles sold:

The Silent Cry by Anne Perry (Fawcett Columbine).

Brunswick Gardens by Anne Perry (Fawcett Columbine).

Confluence by Paul McAuley (Morrow).

Flanders by Patricia Anthony (Berkley/Ace).

The White Tribunal by Paula Volsky (Bantam).

Blood Roses by Chelsea Quinn Yarbro (Tor).

Lost Days by Mike Moscoe (Berkley/ACE).

Kriegspiel by Eric T. Baker (NAL/ROC).

The Still by David Feintuch (Warner/Aspect).

The Seeds of Time by Kay Kenyon (Bantam).

The Players by Stephanie Cowell (W. W. Norton).

The Book of Night with Moon by Diane Duane (Warner/Aspect).

Don't Open This Book! edited by Marvin Kaye (Doubleday).

Dragons of Argonath by Christopher Rowley (NAL/ROC).

The most common mistakes potential clients make when soliciting an agent to represent them: One common turnoff: Query letters that try too hard. Keep it simple. Who are you? What have you got? What do you want in an agent? Avoid long summaries.

What writers can do to enhance their chances of getting an agent (besides being good writers): Display a professional manner, original ideas, great storytelling, and ambition coupled with realism about the business.

Description of Dream Client: Patient, passionate, dedicated to craft, writes for the joy of it, works well with others, enjoys the publishing game.

Why did you become an agent? Maass: I love books, and I believe that fiction matters. Jackson: With a book addiction and an abiding interest in the creative process, it seemed a natural step.

What might you be doing if you weren't an agent? Maass: Oh, Lord, it's too late to think about that now. Jackson: I'd probably be at home reading a big, fat paperback novel and baking chocolate-chip cookies (from scratch, of course).

Comments: Maass: Interested writers may want to read my book, *The Career Novelist,* published in 1996 by Heinemann. Jackson: Work hard, play hard, and keep submitting. Also, invite me to your writer's conferences—I'd love to meet you.

CAROL MANN AGENCY

55 Fifth Avenue

New York, NY 10003

212-206-5635

Agent: Carol Mann.

   Born: July 23, 1949; Cambridge, Massachusetts.

   Education: University High, Chicago; Smith College.

   Career history: Teacher, the Brearley School; educational marketing, Avon Books.

   Hobbies/personal interests: Tennis, film, social history.

Subjects/categories most enthusiastic about agenting: Fiction: Authors Paul Auster, Marita Golden. Nonfiction: history, psychology, health and fitness, alternative medicine, sociology, anthropology, political science, American social history, popular culture, biography, memoir, true crime.

Subjects/categories not interested in agenting: Any genre fiction (i.e. romance, historicals, mysteries, etc.), children's books and/or illustrated books.

Best way for a prospective client to initiate contact with you: With a query letter and SASE. No phone or fax queries. No unsolicited manuscripts (query first).

Reading-fee policy: No reading fee.

Client representation in the following categories: Nonfiction, 75%, Fiction 25%.

Commission: 15%.

Representative titles sold:

All God's Children: The Bosket Family and the American Tradition of Violence by Fox Butterfield (Knopf).

Gathering Storm by Morris Dees (HarperCollins).

The Good Marriage by Dr. Judith Wallerstein (Houghton Mifflin, Warner).

The Holistic Pediatrician by Dr. Kathi Kemper (HarperCollins).

Mr. Vertigo by Paul Auster (Viking).

When Work Disappears by William Julius Wilson.

Mastering the Zone by Barry Sears.

PBS: Behind the Screen by Larry Jarvik.

Description of Dream Client: For nonfiction: Someone who has extensive experience and credentials in their field and is willing to self-promote. For fiction: Stronger writers who have previously had their work published by a (big or small) trade house and/or in a serious literary journal, *Granta*, *Paris Review*, *Story*, etc.

Comments: If you want to write professionally (i.e., for a living), know your market, learn about the process, and be willing to self-promote as you would in any job.

MARCH TENTH, INC.

4 Myrtle Street
Haworth, NJ 07641
201-387-6551

Agent: Sandra Choron.

Education: B.A., Lehman College, New York.

Career history: As an editor, publisher, author, and book producer, I have had experience in all aspects of book publishing at both large (Dell) and small (Hawthorn) firms.

Hobbies/personal interests: Popular culture, music, folk art, painting, writing, spying on kids to find out what the next generation is *really* up to.

Subjects/categories most enthusiastic about agenting: Popular culture, history, commercial fiction, fine fiction, general nonfiction, music, self-help (those without credentials need not apply), biography, new trends, novelties.

Subjects/categories not interested in agenting: Genre fiction, technothrillers, politics, personal memoirs of people who never did anything interesting, special interest, picture books, short fiction, poetry.

Best way for a prospective client to initiate contact with you: Submit a query letter (with SASE).

Reading-fee policy: No reading fee.

Client representation in the following categories: Nonfiction, 98%; Fiction, 1%; Children's, 1%.

Commission: 15% domestic; 20% foreign or dramatic rights.

Number of titles sold during the past year: 20.

Approximate percentage of all submissions (from queries through manuscripts) that are rejected: 90%.

Representative titles sold:

If: Questions for the Game of Life (4 volumes) by James Saywell and Evelyn McFarlane (Villard).

All Area Access: A History of the Rock Concert Industry by Dave Marsh (Simon & Schuster).

Bruce Springsteen Lyrics by Bruce Springsteen (Avon).

Shock Value by John Waters (Thunder's Mouth/Marlowe).

Boldly Live As You've Never Lived Before by Richard Raben and Hiyaguha Cohen (Morrow/Avon).

Strong for Potatoes by Cynthia Thayer (St. Martin's Press), fiction.

The most common mistakes potential clients make when soliciting an agent to represent them: They fail to describe the project in a concise way. They fail to state their credentials. No SASE (these do not receive a reply). I don't like being hyped. Facts and sales ammunition are great, but if there are three exclamation points in your first paragraph, my shit-detector goes crazy!

What writers can do to enhance their chances of getting an agent (besides being good writers): Work on your promotability.

Description of the Client from Hell: Someone who is convinced that "everyone" will buy his book.

Description of Dream Client: Tall, dark . . .

What might you be doing if you weren't an agent? I'd be running a publishing company, specializing in the eclectic.

Comments: Publishing a book is an incredibly gratifying experience. It can also be unbelievably grueling. Enter at your own risk!

DENISE MARCIL LITERARY AGENCY, INC.
685 West End Avenue, 9C
New York, NY 10025
212-932-3110
fax: 212-932-3113

Agent: Denise Marcil.

Born: Troy, New York.

Education: B.A., Skidmore College (major: English; minor: art history).

Career history: Avon Books, editorial assistant; Simon & Schuster, assistant editor; literary agency president, 1977 to present.

Hobbies/personal interests: Entertaining, cooking, ballroom dancing, fly fishing, attending theater and ballet.

Subjects/categories most enthusiastic about agenting: Women's commercial fiction; thrillers; mainstream suspense; medical thrillers; popular reference nonfiction, especially by experts with national exposure in seminars, workshops, and speaking engagements; some business books; parenting; personal finance; health; popular psychology; and spirituality.

Subjects/categories not interested in agenting: Men's action adventure; science fiction/fantasy; young adult or children's; most serious narrative nonfiction. I take on very little literary fiction.

Best way for a prospective client to initiate contact with you: One-page query letter with SASE. Do not send sample material or manuscript.

Reading-fee policy: No reading fee.

Client representation in the following categories: Nonfiction, 25%; Fiction, 75%.

Number of titles sold during the past year: 70.

Approximate percentage of all submissions (from queries through manuscripts) that are rejected: 95%.

Representative titles sold:

The Pregnancy Book by Dr. William Sears and Martha Sears, R.N. (Little, Brown).

Lethal Practice by Dr. Peter Clement (Ballantine Publishing Group).

Making Waves by Catherine Todd (Avon Books).

The Connective Edge: Leading in an Independent World by Jean Lipman-Blumen (Jossey-Bass).

Fly Fishing: A Life in Midstream by Turhan Tirana (Kensington).

Finding Your Soul by Father Paul Keenan (Warner Books).

Night Scents by Carla Neggers (Pocket Books).

True Heart by Arnette Lamb (Pocket Books).

The most common mistakes potential clients make when soliciting an agent to represent them: When a potential author doesn't follow instructions for submitting material, that tells me I couldn't work with him or her. For example, if I ask for the first chapter or three chapters and I receive half the manuscript or the entire manuscript, I know I'm in trouble. Also, not including an SASE with a letter or SAS mailer with a manuscript is a serious mistake.

Potential clients who are pushy or arrogant are a turn-off.

Also, if a writer is submitting his or her work to more than one agent, this should be stated in the letter. There's nothing worse than taking the time to read something only to learn the author has already signed up with another agent. It's discourteous to the other agents.

What writers can do to enhance their chances of getting an agent (besides being good writers): Be courteous, honest, and ethical. Tell me their expectations and communicate openly and reasonably with me.

Description of the Client from Hell: Someone who fails to keep me informed of his needs or problems (or change of address), assuming I know what he wants or that he is dissatisfied. My office is set up with systems in place to serve authors efficiently. I consider an author unreasonable if he expects always to be the exception to the rule, and makes demands for services I don't normally render unless circumstances require.

Description of Dream Client: Someone who is aware of and appreciates the hard work I put in for him. He communicates openly and honestly and writes the best book he's capable of.

Why did you become an agent? Having worked as an editor, I realized that I could offer my clients the extra skill and service of editorial feedback in addition to selling their work and managing their careers. I love books, and my favorite part of this job is discovering new authors and selling their first books.

What might you be doing if you weren't an agent? Frankly, I can't imagine working in another field.

Comments: Authors should know that their agents are their advocates. For an author to view the author/agent relationship as adversarial can only hurt him.

MARGRET MCBRIDE LITERARY AGENCY

7744 Fay Avenue, Suite 201
La Jolla, CA 92037
619-454-1550
fax: 619-454-2156

Agents: Margret McBride, President; Winifred Golden, Vice President; Kim Sauer, Associate Agent; Mindy Riesenberg, Manager of Submissions.

Subjects/categories most enthusiastic about agenting: Mainstream fiction and nonfiction.

Subjects/categories not interested in agenting: Children's books, poetry, genre and category romance, scientific/professional (non-trade) books, textbooks, magazine articles.

Best way for a prospective client to initiate contact with you: Query letter with SASE.

Reading-fee policy: No reading fee.

Client representation in the following categories: Nonfiction, 75%; Fiction, 25%.

Commission: 15% domestic; 25% foreign.

Number of titles sold during the past year: 20.

Approximate percentage of all submissions (from queries through manuscripts) that are rejected: 97%.

Representative titles sold:
Do They Hear You When You Cry? By Fauziya Kasinga with Layli Miller Bashir (Dell), nonfiction.
The Unimaginable Life by Kenny and Julie Loggins (Avon), nonfiction.
The Color Code by Dr. Taylor Hartman (Scribner), nonfiction.
Gung Ho! by Ken Blanchard and Sheldon Bowles (Morrow), nonfiction/business.
Ain't Gonna Be the Same Fool Twice by April Sinclair (Hyperion), fiction.
The Golden Door Cookbook by Michel Stroot (Broadway), nonfiction.
The most common mistakes potential clients make when soliciting an agent to represent them: Calling to set up an appointment to meet, prior to submitting work. Verbal/telephone queries seldom work.

GERARD MCCAULEY AGENCY

P.O. Box 844
Katonah, NY 10536
914-232-5700

Agent: Gerard F. McCauley.
   Born: April 9, 1934.
   Education: B.A., University of Pittsburgh; graduate studies, Columbia University.
   Career history: Editor, college texts, Alfred A. Knopf; associate editor, trade texts, Little, Brown; literary agent, Curtis Brown Ltd.; Founded own agency in 1970.
   Hobbies/personal interests: Baseball, reading, golf, writing letters.
   Subjects/categories most enthusiastic about agenting: History, biography, general nonfiction.
   Subjects/categories not interested in agenting: Fiction, how-to books, business books.
   Best way for a prospective client to initiate contact: Recommendation by editor or another writer.
   Reading-fee policy: No reading fee.
   Client representation in the following categories: Nonfiction, 80%; Textbooks, 15%; Children's, 5%.
   Commission: 15%.
   Number of titles sold during the past year: 42.
   Approximate percentage of all submissions (from queries through manuscripts) that are rejected: 95%
   Representative titles sold:
Westward Migration by Walter Nugent (Knopf).
Sentimental Democracy by Andrew Burstein (Will and Wang).
Mission School by John Demos (Knopf).
Roosevelt and the Depression by Alonzo Hamby (Free Press).
United States American History by Harold Livesay (Norton).

The most common mistakes potential clients make when soliciting an agent to represent them: A phone call where portions of the proposal are read aloud. Any unsolicited manuscript sent Federal Express without SASE, which is sent to 50 editors and agents simultaneously.

What writers can do to enhance their chances of getting an agent (besides being good writers): Intelligent and well-written proposals.

Description of the Client from Hell: Evening and weekend calls. Needs response to 300-page manuscript within a week. Presents own proposals to editors without my knowledge. Suffers from writer's cramp as soon as contract is signed.

Description of the Dream Client: One who views relationship as a partnership, which is true of 90% of the clients I represent.

Why did you become an agent? I like writers.

What might you be doing if you weren't an agent? Editor or unemployed with the time to read the work of several novelists free of the distraction of reading unsolicited manuscripts.

Comments: Ninety percent of the writers submitting book proposals or manuscripts have little talent for writing, but the tenacity to type well.

McIntosh and Otis, Inc.

310 Madison Avenue
New York, NY 10017
212-687-7400

Agents: Renée Cho; Dorothy Markinko.

Career history: McIntosh and Otis, Inc. has the oldest juvenile department of any agency.

Subjects/categories most enthusiastic about agenting: We are looking for well-written, thoughtful books for children on all subjects from baby books to young-adult, fiction and nonfiction. We like to see the work of writers who are willing to take risks either in style, content, or subject matter. We are looking for material that is fresh, original, and special in some way.

Best way for a prospective client to initiate contact with you: For picture books, please send the whole manuscript. For older fiction or nonfiction, we prefer a query letter and sample chapter (include SASE).

Reading-fee policy: No reading fee.

Commission: 15%.

The most common mistakes potential clients make when soliciting an agent to represent them: We prefer short introductory or query letters. It is unnecessary to describe the plot of a picture book and to suggest marketing strategies or potential to sell us on the submission. The manuscript must speak for itself.

CLAUDIA MENZA LITERARY AGENCY

1170 Broadway, Room 807
New York, NY 10001
212-889-6850

Agents: Claudia Menza, Richard Derus, Shaan Liburd.

The following information pertains to CLAUDIA MENZA:

Career history: 1969–1973, assistant editor, Evergreen Review; 1973–1983, various titles, managing editor before leaving, Grove Press; 1983–present, president, Claudia Menza Literary Agency.

Subjects/categories most enthusiastic about agenting: African-American studies, African-American fiction, Avant Garde fiction, literary fiction, serious nonfiction, photography books, mysteries and thrillers.

Subjects/categories not interested in agenting: Romances, mainstream fiction (e.g., Danielle Steel, John Grisham), science fiction, pop culture, poetry, plays.

Best way for a prospective client to initiate contact: Query letter with SASE. No phone calls.

Reading-fee policy: No reading fee.

Client representation in the following categories: Nonfiction, 50%; Fiction, 40%; Children's, 10%.

Commission: 15% on all rights represented, except in case of a coagent's involvement when it's 20%. Coagents are used for film, dramatic, foreign rights. We do not reduce commissions.

Approximate percentage of all submissions (from queries through manuscripts) that are rejected: 70%.

Representative titles sold:

Book of African-American Lists edited by Barboza and Garlock (New York University Press).

Sam and the Tigers by Julius Lester (Dial Books for Young Readers).

Dark Eros edited by Reginald Martin (St. Martin's Press).

Naming the New World by Calvin Baker (A Wyatt Book).

Description of the Client from Hell: A constant nudge who calls three times a week for updates on a book's submission status.

Description of Dream Client: A client who sends *us* flowers when we get particularly stupid rejects of the client's book.

The most common mistakes potential clients make when soliciting an agent to represent them: Sending unrequested samples with query letters. Calling us to solicit interest in their manuscript. Calling us three times a week to see if we've read it yet, three weeks after sending us a manuscript. Not including SASE with submission—letters get filed, manuscripts are recycled, no phone calls are made.

What writers can do to enhance their chances of getting an agent (besides being good writers): Respect our time—if you are taking time away from our selling someone else's book, think what *they're* doing! Everyone, including Dickens and Faulkner, could have made their masterpieces shorter, more direct, and/or better without sacrificing either style or content. Accept criticism as helpful, even when you disagree. Try it the way you're asked to before rejecting the criticism. Remember, *it's not personal.*

Why did you become an agent? It's too hard to explain. As of now, what else would anyone sane *want* to do? It's a lot of fun.

What might you be doing if you weren't an agent? Being a publisher.

The following information pertains to RICHARD DERUS:

Career history: Book sales, 1974–1979; advertising coordinator, *The Daily Texan* newspaper, 1982–1987; production manager, various printing and publishing companies, 1987–1992; partner, Claudia Menza Literary Agency, 1992–present.

Subjects/categories most enthusiastic about agenting: Gay studies/fiction, literary fiction, history/biography, serious nonfiction, thrillers (with exceptions).

The following information pertains to SHAAN LIBURD:

Career history: This is my first publishing job.

Subjects/categories most enthusiastic about agenting: Screenplays/treatments for television, pop culture, literary fiction, children's books.

DORIS S. MICHAELS LITERARY AGENCY, INC.

One Lincoln Plaza, Suite 29R
20 West 64th Street
New York, NY 10023
212-769-2430

Agent: Doris S. Michaels.

Born: May 1955, Lodi, California.

Education: B.A., English and German literature, University of California at Santa Cruz; M.A.T., German and English, University of California at Berkeley; Certificate in Computer Technology, Columbia University; Certificate in Book and Magazine Publishing, Summer Publishing Institute, New York University.

Career history: Acquisitions editor for Prentice Hall, 1982–1984; technology consultant and trainer for PHINET and Prudential-Bache, 1984–1987; International Information Center manager for Union Bank of Switzerland based in Zurich, 1987–1992; independent literary agent based in NYC, 1994–present.

Hobbies/personal interests: Reading, music, especially listening to classical music and playing the violin. Sports, especially mountain biking, skiing, and swimming. Computers.

Subjects/categories most enthusiastic about agenting: Fiction: commercial fiction, literary fiction, women's fiction, novels with strong screen potential. Adult nonfiction (hardcovers and trade paperbacks): Biographies, business, classical music, sports, women's issues. Multimedia electronic works for computers.

Subjects/categories not interested in agenting: Science fiction, fantasy, mysteries, thrillers, romances, Westerns, occult and supernatural, horror stories, poetry, textbooks, religion, film scripts, cookbooks, diet books, short stories, articles, humor, professional manuals.

Best way for a prospective client to initiate contact: Query first with SASE. Please, no calls.

Reading-fee policy: No reading fee.

Client representation in the following categories: Nonfiction, 30%; Fiction, 70%.

Commission: 15%.

Number of titles sold during the past year: 20.

Approximate percentage of all submissions (from queries through manuscripts) that are rejected: 98%.

Representative titles sold:

All We Know of Heaven by Anna Tuttle Villegas (St. Martin's Press); ten international deals made by the agency in countries including Germany, France, Italy, Spain, Israel, Greece, and Korea.

The Neatest Little Guide to Stock Market Investing by Jason Kelly (Plume/Penguin USA).

Memories of the Mick by Maury Allen and Bob Olen (Taylor Publishing).

365 Reflections on Love and Friendship by Eva Shaw (Adams Media Corporation).

The most common mistakes potential clients make when soliciting an agent to represent them: They send an unprofessional query letter without an SASE. Nonfiction projects arrive without a clearly written proposal.

What writers can do to enhance their chances of getting an agent (besides being good writers): The writers who do their homework and check the market for the project create a much better impression. Only the best possible representation of the work should be sent.

Description of the Client from Hell: I only work with clients with whom I can develop a good working relationship.

Description of the Dream Client: Someone who has talent, understands the publishing process, appreciates the hard work I do, and listens carefully.

Why did you become an agent? I enjoy reading good fiction and the process of helping talented writers get published.

What might you be doing if you weren't an agent? Touring as a concert violinist.

Comments: Having lived and worked in Europe (Germany, Switzerland, and England) for over six years and being a first-generation American enables me to represent books that can appeal to a broader, more international market.

JEAN V. NAGGAR LITERARY AGENCY

216 East 75th Street, 1E
New York, NY 10021
212-794-1082

Agents: Jean V. Naggar, Anne Engel, Frances Kuffel.

The following information pertains to JEAN V. NAGGAR:

Education: B.A. with honors, London University.

Career history: Writer, editor, translator, book reviewer.

Hobbies/personal interests:. Parenting, reading, music, business, travel, cooking. Wide-ranging other interests that do not include sports and politics.

Subjects/categories most enthusiastic about agenting:. Fiction: strong, well-written mainstream fiction, literary fiction, contemporary, suspense, historical fiction, mysteries. Nonfiction: biography, literary autobiography or memoirs, science for the lay person, psychology, and sophisticated self-help.

Subjects/categories not interested in agenting: Sports, politics, category fiction, most science fiction, KGB/South American drug-cartel espionage.

Best way for a prospective client to initiate contact: Query letter.

Reading-fee policy: No reading fee.

Client representation in the following categories: Nonfiction, 45%; Fiction, 45%; Children's, 10%.

Commission: 15% domestic; 20% international.

Number of titles sold during the past year: 47.

Approximate percentage of all submissions (from queries through manuscripts) that are rejected: 96%.

Representative titles sold:

Seven Moves by Carol Anshaw (Harcourt Brace).

Imperfect Justice by Catherine Arnold (Dutton/Signet).

When the Joe-Pye Blooms by Homer Blakeslee (Ballantine).

Emotional Unavailability by Bryn Collins (Contemporary Books), nonfiction.

Pope Joan by Donna Woolfolk Cross (Crown).

The Daddy Clock by Judy Markey (Bantam).

Perfect Angel by Seth Margolis (Avon Books).

The Undertaker's Widow by Phillip Margolin (Doubleday/Bantam).

Angle of Impact by Bonnie MacDougal (Ballantine).

Virus, Ground Zero by Ed Regis (Pocket Books), nonfiction.

Lady Moses by Lucinda Roy (HarperCollins).

The Living Sea by Carl Safina (A Jack Macrae Book, Holt), nonfiction.

The most common mistakes potential clients make when soliciting an agent to represent them: Not doing any background research on agents *before* contacting; asking, *Do you want to see my work?* without describing it; calling every five minutes to *check up on things*—a sure precursor of the Client from Hell!

What writers can do to enhance their chances of getting an agent (besides being good writers)? Professional queries that identify and define reasons why I might want to read the book.

Description of the Client from Hell: An author who has chosen me as an agent but never quite trusts me.

Description of Dream Client: Talented, appreciative, intelligent, knowledgeable.

Why did you become an agent? I love reading and respect writers. I enjoy being an advocate for writers I respect.

The following information pertains to ANNE ENGEL:

Education: Bachelor of Laws, London University.

Career history: 20 years as an editor in British publishing houses.

Hobbies/personal interests: Looking at cities, cooking and entertaining.

Subjects/categories most enthusiastic about agenting: Science, biography.

Subjects/categories not interested in agenting: Fiction, children's books.

Best way for a prospective client to initiate contact: An enthusiastic, balanced letter.

Reading-fee policy: No reading fee.

Client representation in the following categories: Nonfiction, 100%.

Commission: 15% domestic; 20% international.

Representative titles sold:

The Universal Kitchen by Elizabeth Rozin (Viking).

Signs of Life by Robert Pollack (Houghton Mifflin).

Telling the Truth About History by J. Appleby et al. (Norton).

The following information pertains to FRANCES KUFFEL:

Born: 1956.

Education:. B.A., English, B.A., religious studies, University of Montana; M.F.A., creative writing, Cornell University.

Career history: Left Ph.D. program in English to get a life and have been with this agency ever since.

Hobbies/personal interests: Reading, history (especially World War II), biography, 19th century English novels, cooking and entertaining, writing.

Subjects/categories most enthusiastic about agenting: Literary fiction with a strong, probably masculine, storyline. Serious nonfiction: biography and history, women's studies, cultural studies.

Subjects/categories not interested in agenting: Espionage anything; genre books: science fiction, romance, fantasy, mystery, horror, Westerns.

Best way for a prospective client to initiate contact: Query letter.

Reading-fee policy: No reading fee.

Client representation in the following categories: Nonfiction, 33%; Fiction, 33%, Children's, 33%.

Commission: 15% domestic; 20% international.

Number of titles sold during the past year: 18.

Approximate percentage of all submissions (from queries through manuscripts) that are rejected: 98%.

Representative titles sold:

Easy by Phillip DePoy (Bell Books).

City of Trees by Fred Haefele (Baskerville).

Down on Ponce by Fred Willard (Longstreet Press).

Too Easy by Phillip DePoy (Dell Books).

Alligator Sue by Sharon Doucet (Darling Kindersley).

Vampires: A Field Guide to Emotional Predators by Daniel Rhodes and Barbara Cobb McMahon (Prometheus Books).

The most common mistakes potential clients make when soliciting an agent to represent them: Telling me in the query letter what their writing means, rather than what it's about; telling me how *strong, powerful, dynamic,* etc. their writing and story is; telling me how much other readers have loved it. Telling me about themselves at more length and before describing the plot of subject matter. Oh—and hearing from a wife about her husband's book!

What writers can do to enhance their chances of getting an agent (besides being good writers)? A writer who *briefly* conveys his or her storyline and prose style; subject matter that's different and makes *me* interested in something new.

Description of the Client from Hell: One who expects a phone call even when there is nothing to discuss; one who is unreasonable or suspicious about what I can achieve for them. A *loose pistol*—acting independently of my efforts and without telling me!

Description of Dream Client: One who has a sense of humor and a sense of reality about how long things take in publishing; one who trusts me to do my job; one who takes criticism of their work well, and quickly. A writer with very literary capabilities and a healthy dose of cynicism about precious writing for its own sake.

Why did you become an agent? I'm nuts about books, and in what other job can you be involved with everything from the goofiest projects and children's books to scholarship?

What might you be doing if you weren't an agent? Stand-up comic; adjunct professor in some grim little English department; secretary in an insurance office in Montana.

Comments: Stop whining and get a real job—the world does *not* owe you a living you can perform in your pajamas!

RUTH NATHAN LITERARY AGENCY

53 East 34th Street
New York, NY 10016
212-481-1185

Agent: Ruth Nathan.
  Born: New York City.
  Education: B.A., Radcliffe College.
  Career history: Theatrical producer, trade book publisher, story editor for film studios and independent producers.
  Hobbies/personal interests: Theater, film, history (especially medieval), cooking, travel.
  Subjects/categories most enthusiastic about agenting: Show biz, historical fiction (medieval), decorative arts, specialties in each field only.
  Subjects/categories not interested in agenting: Male adventure, romance, children's books, science fiction, fantasy, technothrillers, serious political material.
  Best way for a prospective client to initiate contact with you: No unsolicited manuscripts. Query letter essential as is SASE.
  Reading-fee policy: No reading fee.
  Client representation in the following categories: Nonfiction, 50%; Fiction, 50%.
  Commission: 15%.
  Number of titles sold during the past year: 4.

Approximate percentage of all submissions (from queries through manuscripts) that are rejected: 95%.

Representative titles sold:

King of Comedy (biography of Jerry Lewis) by Shawn Levy (St. Martin's).

No Good Deed and *Protocol for Murder* by Paul Nathan, mystery novels.

Book of Days by Stephen Rivelle (Carroll & Graf USA, Macmillan UK).

The most common mistakes potential clients make when soliciting an agent to represent them: Sending unsolicited work or misrepresenting material not researched.

What writers can do to enhance their chances of getting an agent (besides being good writers): Cooperate.

Description of the Client from Hell: Impatient, illiterate, ignorant, and deals with other agents at same time. I do not allow this!

Description of Dream Client: Civilized, modest, and above all, a *good* writer.

Why did you become an agent? Propinquity.

What might you be doing if you weren't an agent? Producing writing seminars with various colleges (will welcome inquiries about this).

Comments: Remember—I am selective and cranky!

New Brand Agency Group

A Division of Alter-Entertainment LLC

3801 West Hillsboro Boulevard, Suite B-102

Coconut Creek, FL 33073

954-725-6462

Agent: Eric D. Alterman.

Born: April 4, 1963.

Education: Undergraduate, Tufts University; Law School, Washington College of Law, American University.

Career history: Attorney, owner-operator of radio broadcasting company, legal and marketing consulting, literary agent.

Hobbies/personal interests: Guitar, golf, reading.

Subjects/categories most enthusiastic about agenting: Original and exciting contemporary fiction. Nonfiction that has an interesting or novel presentation of ideas relating to subject matter that will appeal to a wide audience. Thrillers, mysteries, romance, young adult novels.

Subjects/categories not interested in agenting: Hard-core science fiction and fantasy.

Best way for a prospective client to initiate contact: Send 50 pages, summary and SASE to our address. We'll get back to you within a few weeks.

Reading-fee policy: No reading fee.

Client representation in the following categories: Nonfiction, 50%; Fiction, 40%; Children's, 10%.

Commission: 15%.

Number of titles sold during the past year: 10.

Approximate percentage of all submissions (from queries through manuscripts) that are rejected: 90%.

Representative titles sold:

Multiple mystery novels by Rae Foley (Thorndike Press, Chivers Press).

The Complete Guide to Buying Your Shelter Dog.

The most common mistakes potential clients make when soliciting an agent to represent them: Writers should be sure to follow submission instructions. It is frustrating when no SASE is enclosed, etc. One of the biggest mistakes a new writer can make is submitting a hard-to-read manuscript (should be 12-point, double-spaced, clear printing, etc.).

What writers can do to enhance their chances of getting an agent (besides being good writers)? Strong, clear, confident letter with short, but comprehensive, summary of the manuscript.

Description of the Client from Hell: Doesn't take care in checking his/her manuscript for errors; doesn't include SASE with submissions; expects publishers to respond overnight; forgets my birthday.

Description of Dream Client: Polite bestselling author who remembers my birthday.

Why did you become an agent? At some point in her or his career, every lawyer must ask the question, *Is there some other way I might make a living?* I love working with new writers who have lots of energy and a drawer full of fresh ideas.

What might you be doing if you weren't an agent? I might be sitting around somewhere spending all day reading published books instead of unpublished books (it wouldn't be as fun).

Comments: Find an agent who seems to care about your work. There is no substitute for enthusiasm.

NEW ENGLAND PUBLISHING ASSOCIATES, INC.

P.O. Box 5
Chester, CT 06412
203-345-7323
fax: 203-345-3660

Agents: Elizabeth Frost-Knappman, President; Edward W. Knappman, Vice President; staff: Rebecca Barardy, Victoria Harlow, Ron Formica.

Born: EFK: October 1, 1943. EWK: November 17, 1943

Education: EFK: B.A., anthropology, George Washington University (1965); completed all coursework for an M.A. in this field. EWK: B.A., history, George Washington University (1965); M.S., journalism, Columbia University (1966).

Career history: EFK: Senior editor, William Morrow; senior editor, Doubleday; editor, William Collins & Sons (London); associate editor, Natural History Press. Author of *Women's Suffrage in America* and *Women's Rights on Trial* (with Kathryn

Cullen-Du Pont), *World Almanac of Presidential Quotations, ABC-CLIO History of Women's Progress in America, The Quotable Lawyer* (with D. Shraeger). EWK: Publisher of Facts On File; executive vice president of Facts On File. Editor of *Great World Trials, American Jobs Abroad* (with V. Harlow), and *Sex, Sin and Mayhem.*

Hobbies/personal interests: EFK: Writing in the area of women's history, singing, knitting, gardening, and tennis. EWK: Reading in the areas of history and politics and keeping up with computer developments.

Subjects/categories most enthusiastic about agenting: EFK: Women's subjects, biographies, true crime, literature. EWK: Reference, history, information, self-help, biographies.

Subjects/categories not interested in agenting: Personal memoirs, fiction, children's books, screenplays.

Best way for a prospective client to initiate contact with you: Send a well-thought-out proposal with a sample chapter and résumé.

Reading-fee policy: No reading fee.

Client representation in the following categories: Nonfiction, 90%.

Commission: 15%, unless coagents must be employed for dramatic or foreign rights.

Number of titles sold during the past year: 35.

Approximate percentage of all submissions (from queries through manuscripts) that are rejected: 90%.

Representative titles sold:
One-Minute Parliamentarian (HarperCollins).
When Your Child Hears a Different Drummer (Contemporary Books).
Questions and Answers About Adoption (Wiley).
Everything You've Heard About Investing Is Wrong (Random House).
100 Reasons to Keep Him, 100 Reasons to Dump Him (Crown).
The Prettiest Feather (Bantam).
Speaking of Love (Random House).
The Puzzle Club Mysteries (Concordia).
Susan Sontag (Norton).
Eudora Welty (Doubleday).
Women's Rights on Trial (Gale Research).
Elements of Expression (Holt).
Carey McWilliams (Crown).
Guide to Concise Writing (Writer's Digest).
Rebecca West: A Biography (Scribner).
Let's Hear It for the Girls (Viking Penguin).
The Summer House (St. Martin's Press).
Penguin Dictionary of English Usage (Penguin).
Back to Butler Creek (Random House).

The most common mistakes potential clients make when soliciting an agent to represent them: It's important to put in the time and effort to perfect a proposal. The key is to carefully research your competition, not just in the bookstores, but in the libraries, union catalog, and *Books in Print*.

What writers can do to enhance their chances of getting an agent (besides being good writers): Be friendly people who can sum up their book idea and why it's different with brevity. Writers must not mind revising proposals and working hard. Produce a well-crafted proposal that anticipates all the questions an editor or agent might ask: target audience, competition, qualifications for writing the book, the angle for the work, and how it is organized.

Description of the Client from Hell: There are no Clients from Hell, just people anxious to make a living from their writing.

Description of Dream Client: Professional, flexible about revisions, patient, friendly.

Why did you become an agent? After many years as an editor (EFK) and publisher (EWK), we needed to find a way to remain in the industry we loved while having our own business. Our combined literary agency, book-producing business, and consulting operations allow us to do this. What started as a small business in 1983 has grown to a good-sized one, with eight employees to serve clients.

What might you be doing if you weren't an agent? EFK: Writing books in the area of women's history. EWK: Publishing books from the concept stage to their marketing and distribution. Both of us might be traveling to various countries we have not yet visited.

Comments: We would suggest that authors persevere, and not get discouraged about their writing. Somewhere there is a publisher for your work, or a way to continue writing, even if a book publisher seems uninterested. Writers' groups and professional associations can be very helpful—as are friends who are writing professionally. A subscription to *Publishers Weekly* and regular visits to bookstores and libraries to see what is being published are indispensable. But always remember, it's a good idea to keep your day job.

ORIOLE LITERARY AGENCY

P.O. Box 1540
Alpine, CA 91903-1540
619-445-4735
fax: 619-445-6786

Agent: Steve Albrecht.

Born: February 22, 1963.

Education: B.A., English, University of San Diego; M.A., security management, Webster University.

Career history: 12 years as an author and 3 years as a literary agent.

Subjects/categories most enthusiastic about agenting: Business and management books.

Subjects/categories not interested in agenting: No books not related to business or management.

Best way for a prospective client to initiate contact with you: We accept one-page query letters or faxes. Please don't send writing samples, chapters, or complete manuscripts. You must include SASE to get your material answered.

Reading-fee policy: No reading fee.

Client representation in the following categories: Nonfiction, 100%.

Commission: 15%.

Approximate percentage of all submissions (from queries through manuscripts) that are rejected: We are very focused on business-related books. We reject everything else.

Representative titles sold:

We have good relationships with the top 15 business book publishers.

The most common mistakes potential clients make when soliciting an agent to represent them: Don't tell me, *We are both going to make lots of money* or *This will be an instant bestseller.*

What writers can do to enhance their chances of getting an agent (besides being good writers): Good clients go to the bookstores to see what is on the shelves (or not) in their fields.

Description of the Client from Hell: He or she won't take no for an answer.

Description of Dream Client: He or she writes salable proposals and demonstrates both writing competence and business experience.

Why did you become an agent? I love writing and the art of business.

O-SQUARED LITERARY AGENCY

13944 Cedar Road, Suite 113
University Heights, OH 44118
216-291-5800

Agent: Mary N. Oluonye.

Born: 1955; Cleveland, Ohio (half of life spent in Nigeria, the other half spent in the United States).

Education: B.S., Biology, University of Windsor, 1978. Paralegal certificate, Sawyer Business College, 1991.

Career history: Basically an entrepreneur. First job after college was as an administrative officer (student affairs department) at a major university in Nigeria. Have owned several businesses: home-based juvenile accessories company, home child day-care business; freelance proofreader; line and development editor for writers; paralegal; founded and was president of Adult and Child Care Services, which operated high-quality, state-licensed, child day-care centers. Currently business writer and consultant.

Hobbies/personal interests: Reading! Watching movies, when I have the time. Writing, research, meeting people, travel.

Subjects/categories most enthusiastic about agenting: Literary: Juvenile (quality picture books, middle-grade fiction/nonfiction, young adult); mainstream fiction; genre fiction; nonfiction (especially biographies); multicultural interests. Art: Book illustrators (book jackets); graphic designers. We want to see work that is well-written and has the ability to touch, inspire, and teach.

Best way for a prospective client to initiate contact: Writers: send an outline or proposal, 3 sample chapters, and a bio. Artists: send an outline or proposal, quality copies, photostats, and/or slides of your work, and a bio. *NEVER SEND ORIGINALS!!!* To ensure safety of your work, please send only copies of your art or writings. Always enclose a self-addressed stamped envelope (SASE) to ensure a prompt reply.

Client representation in the following categories: We are a new company and our goal is to establish an organization known for the high caliber of writers and artists we represent. O-Squared Literary Agency is currently seeking new and established writers and artists to work with. This is your invitation to be part of a company that's going places, a company committed to giving all the creative people we work with our very best.

What writers can do to enhance their chances of getting an agent (besides being good writers): *First impressions count!* Submit only your best work. When choosing an agent, do not undertake the task lightly. It is one of the most important decisions you will ever make in your career as a writer or artist. The O-Squared Literary Agency knows that the author-agent relationship is a 50/50 partnership. We have to be enthusiastic about the writers and artists we represent, and his or her work. These individuals must be just as enthusiastic about working with us. O-Squared Literary Agency provides in-depth, quality services, assuring top-notch assistance to everyone we work with.

Why did you become an agent? I am an entrepreneur. My business skills include detailed analysis, solid research, and taking risks. I would like to use my entrepreneurial/business skills to do those things that I truly love to do: read, write, proofread, edit. I enjoy talking to people about their ideas and find it extremely gratifying to help my clients achieve their goals (be it in business, writing, or art illustration).

Comments: It is a well-known fact that publishers and editors cannot possibly read all the unsolicited manuscripts they receive. Some companies do not accept unsolicited work, but those that do receive hundreds of manuscripts per day! That's where the literary agent comes in. Most publishers rely on qualified agents, like those at the O-Squared Literary Agency, to screen manuscripts and separate the *good* from the *bad and ugly*. This gives you, the qualified writers and artists we represent, a better opportunity to have your work considered by a variety of markets closed to unagented individuals.

OTITIS MEDIA LITERARY AGENCY

1926 Dupont Avenue South
Minneapolis, MN 55403
612-377-4918

Agents: B. R. Boylan, Melissa C. Banczak, Greg Boylan, Hannibal Harris, Ingrid DiLeonardo.

The following information pertains to B. R. BOYLAN:
Born: Chicago, Illinois.

Education: Loyola University, Chicago.

Career history: Author of 16 published books, nonfiction and fiction; editor, books and periodical publications; literary agent; stage director and producer; film producer; photographer; historian.

Hobbies/personal interests: Historical research, scenic and historic photography, opera and classical music, book collecting.

Subjects/categories most enthusiastic about agenting: Nonfiction: history, music, biography, satire, comedy, anthropology/archeology, true crime. Fiction: adventure, history, action, time-travel, multi-layered mystery, erotic, travel, crime, satire, and comedy.

Subjects/categories not interested in agenting: Children's books, self-help, poetry, academic treatises, science fiction, college textbooks, young adult, positivism, theology, coming of age, short stories, diatribes, new age, nutritional quackery, occult, outdoor, cookbooks.

Best way for a prospective client to initiate contact: We'll take a *brief* telephone call from an experienced pro who wants to know if we are interested in the manuscript or script he has written. But anyone without a professional track record should use the mails to send a query letter, which consists of a *brief* (3–4 sentences) synopsis of the story, along with a brief biography listing published or produced works, with names and dates essential. If nothing has been published commercially, a bit about their credits, training, classes, and personal interests. The first 25 pages of the work are *all* that we will accept. Unsolicited complete manuscripts rarely are read, and no SASE means nothing will be read or returned.

Reading-fee policy: No reading fee. We regard them as unethical.

Client representation in the following categories: Nonfiction, 10%; Fiction, 90%.

Commission: 15% domestic, 20% foreign.

Number of titles sold during the past year: Confidential.

Approximate percentage of all submissions (from queries through manuscripts) that are rejected: 90%.

Representative titles sold: Confidential.

The most common mistakes potential clients make when soliciting an agent to represent them: This is an easy one. The wannabe who insists he is a *writer* or an *author*, yet produces drivel. The wannabe who calls or writes us with a demand that we audition for him, manuscript and track record unseen, demanding to know the names of all the books and screenplays we have sold, for how much, and to whom. Requesting references from our contacts in film and publishing! Telling us what the real role of agent is: "You guys get rich off the money we make for you."

The most costly mistakes? Sending a query letter announcing they have written the next socko hit novel/screenplay, and inviting us to get rich with them. Another is the query letter that barely mentions the project but tells us what a splendid writer the author is and how he *loves to write!* That is a statement that clearly separates the amateurs from the professionals.

There is an overwhelming arrogance abroad now that is drilling empty heads with such slogans as "everyone has a story, and has the inalienable right to see that story in print," and "publishers are crooks, editors are their flunkies, and agents are the bottom feeders—all at the extent of the long-suffering writer."

What writers can do to enhance their chances of getting an agent (besides being good writers)? Be low-keyed and professional in contacting us, by phone, e-mail, or regular mail. Follow the instructions you get over the phone and, if you have problems with any of them, say so right away. Do not call the day after you've sent something us, nor harangue us with phone calls. We'll look at your proposal in turn and get back to you. If you haven't heard anything from us after, say, a month, then call and pleasantly remind us, which is guaranteed to get our butts twitching.

Description of the Client from Hell: Writers to whom we describe our submission guidelines, but who then ignore them blatantly, arguing that their work cannot be understood without reading it all. We don't have time to plow through every script and manuscript that rolls in. If it's worthwhile, we'll know by the fifth page, definitely by the tenth. Also, the beginners who ignore correct formats, refuse to revise or improve their proposals, call us constantly, expect an immediate reaction, or waste their query letter with references to their support/critique groups, assuring us that everyone who has read it just loves it and predicts a glowing future of success, fame, and lots of money.

Other clients from hell demand a written critique of the book from the editor who just said no, or demand a list of editors, publishers, and phone numbers, then drive the stake deeper into their hearts by calling that editor or producer and arguing. There is the writer who, if we express interest in a particular proposal, then inundates us with his 12 other unpublished novels, poetry, and screenplays. We are particularly turned off by the whiner who calls every day, wanting hand-holding or psychotherapy.

By far, the worst writer is the one who has just won 10th place in a screenplay writing summer camp, and who lunges for an agent. Somewhere, someone is churning a large pot of wannabe writers and telling them that as soon as they *finish* a manuscript, to start lining up an agent. Nothing is ever said to them about rewriting, editing, or having an uninvolved third party take a critical look at the manuscript.

Description of Dream Client: A good writer who moves from one project to the next, understanding the patience required to circulate and sell books. This client can accept rejection without help from his therapist, noting any specific remarks offered by the editor. The dream client does not second-guess us or the editors, based on what his relatives or friends tell him. The only writer we want to represent is the person who writes and rewrites, edits, and seeks out professional guidance.

Why did you become an agent? My years as a theatrical director, when I was pulling all the strings in order to produce the best possible performance, gave me a sense of overall responsibility for a good project. After suffering a brief burnout from doing too much writing, I found agenting a splendid way to regain a healthy perspective. I suddenly was overwhelmed with the good, the awful, and the pedestrian. I early on ran into the client from hell, followed shortly by the dream client, and was rolling. Agenting is a difficult packaging job, harder than almost anything I had tried before. As a result, my own writing enthusiasm returned with a whoosh, and I found myself enjoying that which I have always dreaded—selling.

What might you be doing if you weren't an agent? Photographing and leading historical expeditions. Running a theater, directing plays, musicals, and opera.

Comments: Unless you really are born with a *divine spark*, spare the world your turgid, egocentric, 10-book-series proposals. Even if you do well in a creative writing class does not mean you should rush out and get an agent. To be taken seriously, you're going to have to take your best work, hold it up for an unbiased opinion from someone who has nothing to gain from being kind to you. If it is critical and if you are sufficiently sharp to recognize a potential improvement, dig right in. That *divine spark* is rare and fickle. If you think you have it, you have to work like hell to haul it to the surface and then start to scrape and dig and chip and shine. The only sure definition of a writer is someone who cannot stand what he is doing while writing for publication, yet who is drawn back to the keyboard whenever he's away.

The following information pertains to MELISSA C. BANCZAK:

Born: April 23, 1964; California.

Education: B.A., social science, California State University, Sacramento.

Career history: Freelance writer; teacher for adult-literacy program.

Hobbies/personal interests: Machine knitting—it's a mind-numbing way to relax after a long day.

Subjects/categories most enthusiastic about agenting: Fiction: thrillers, mystery, action, adventure comedy. Nonfiction: history, biography, true crime.

Subjects/categories not interested in agenting: Romance, textbooks, poetry.

Best way for a prospective client to initiate contact: Please query through a letter.

Reading-fee policy: No reading fee.

Client representation in the following categories: Nonfiction, 5%; Fiction, 95%.

Commission: 15% domestic; 20% foreign.

Number of titles sold during the past year: Confidential.

Approximate percentage of all submissions (from queries through manuscripts) that are rejected: 98%.

Representative titles sold: Confidential.

Description of the Client from Hell: I've been spared so far.

Description of Dream Client: One who is patient with the process.

The most common mistakes potential clients make when soliciting an agent to represent them: They don't take the time to read our guidelines.

What writers can do to enhance their chances of getting an agent (besides being good writers): Pay close attention to our guidelines. Send me a query first, and then wait for me to contact you.

What might you be doing if you weren't an agent? Probably teaching.

THE RICHARD PARKS AGENCY

138 East 16th Street, Suite 5B
New York, NY 10003
212-254-9067

Agent: Richard Parks.

Education: B.A., Duke University; M.A., University of North Carolina.

Career history: Curtis Brown, Ltd. (1970–1978); United Artists Corporation (1978–1981); Alexander, Smith & Parks (1981–1988); The Richard Parks Agency (1989–present).

Best way for a prospective client to initiate contact with you: Fiction: by referral only. Nonfiction: By referral or query letter.

Reading-fee policy: No reading fee.

Client representation in the following categories: Nonfiction, 50%; Fiction, 50%.

Commission: 15% domestic, 20% foreign.

The most common mistakes potential clients make when soliciting an agent to represent them: No calls, e-mail, or faxed queries, please.

PEGASOS LITERARY AGENCY

269 South Beverly Drive, Suite 101
Beverly Hills, CA 90212
310-712-1218

Agent: Karen Stein.

Born: August 8, 1958; Fort Lauderdale, Florida.

Education: USC, M.B.A.

Career history: 1983–1987: Goldstein and Associates; involved in the acquisition of intellectual property; 1987–present: running my own literary agency.

Hobbies/personal interests: Traveling, horses, reading, gourmet food, movies, modern art, classical music, theater, charity work.

Subjects/categories most enthusiastic about agenting: Literary fiction with a strong story line; women's fiction, mysteries, contemporary, suspense; commercial fiction; serious nonfiction; popular psychology and self-help.

Subjects/categories not interested in agenting: Poetry; children's books; juveniles; academic books.

Best way for a prospective client to initiate contact: Query letter (with SASE) with a one-page synopsis.

Reading-fee policy: No reading fee. There is a $100 annual charge for photocopying, long-distance calls, and postage.

Client representation in the following categories: Nonfiction, 30%; Fiction, 70%.

Commission: 15%.

Number of titles sold during the past year: 25.

Approximate percentage of all submissions (from queries through manuscripts) that are rejected: 90%.

Representative titles sold:

Boogie in the Garden by Jon Carroll (Universal Publishing).

In the Shadow of Justice by Billie McCord (East West Publishing).

Why Marriage Doesn't Work in the '90s by Elaine Nash (Stirling Press).

Description of the Client from Hell: In my opinion, there aren't clients from hell—there are arrogant agents, however.

Description of Dream Client: All my clients have been angels from a dream.

The most common mistakes potential clients make when soliciting an agent to represent them: Forget the point of writing a query letter, call too often, forget to send a birthday card (just kidding).

What writers can do to enhance their chances of getting an agent (besides being good writers): "Brevity is a sister of talent."—Chekhov. I completely subscribe to this aphorism when reviewing my queries.

Why did you become an agent? My most favorite and rewarding occupation in the world.

What might you be doing if you weren't an agent? I would never trade being an agent for being anything else, so there's no point in asking.

Comments: New authors: Don't give up too soon. There's an advance at the end of the tunnel. Fresh voices, where are you?

PELHAM LITERARY AGENCY

2290 East Fremont Avenue, Suite C
Littleton, CO 80122
303-347-0623

Agent: Howard Pelham.

Born: February 21, 1927.

Education: Advanced degrees in English and social anthropology.

Career history: Teaching and writing. Published 15 Western novels.

Hobbies/personal interests: Reading and writing.

Subjects/categories most enthusiastic about agenting: Young adult, Western, genre fiction of all kinds.

Subjects/categories not interested in agenting: Film scripts.

Best way for a prospective client to initiate contact: Either by telephone or query by mail. Do not send manuscript before querying.

Reading-fee policy: No reading fee.

Client representation in the following categories: Nonfiction, 10%; Fiction, 90%.

Commission: 15%.

Number of titles sold during the past year: 2.

Approximate percentage of all submissions (from queries through manuscripts) that are rejected: 80% of the queries I respond to send me manuscript not ready to be submitted.

Representative titles sold:

Foreign Adoption by Barbara Bascomb and Carole McKelvey (Pocket Books).

Death of a Gunslinger by Howard Pelham (Thomas Bouregey, Inc.).

The most common mistakes potential clients make when soliciting an agent to represent them: Those who assume what they haven't written is a boon to the publishing business and set an advance figure before anyone bids on the manuscript.

Description of the Client from Hell: I haven't met one yet, but I don't like clients who send me manuscripts cold and then keep calling me about them before I have a chance to read them.

Description of the Dream Client: One who writes blockbuster bestsellers and is patient.

Why did you become an agent? I sold my own books for 15 years. The next natural step was to sell books by others.

What might you be doing if you weren't an agent? Writing.

PERKINS ASSOCIATES

5800 Arlington Avenue, Suite 18J
Riverdale, NY 10471
212-304-1607 (Peter Rubie)
718-543-5344 (Lori Perkins)
fax: 718-543-5354

Agents: Lori Perkins, Peter Rubie.

Born: Perkins: April 8, 1959; Rubie: May 3, 1950.

Education: Perkins: B.A., Journalism, New York University, 1980. Rubie: Journalism degree, NCTJ, England.

Career history: Perkins: Publisher and founder, *Uptown Dispatch*, an Upper Manhattan weekly; adjunct professor of journalism, New York University; agent with Barbara Lowenstein, 1986–1989. Rubie: Fleet Street newspapers (England); BBC radio news (England); fiction editor, Walker & Company (New York City); book doctor (New York City); literary agent; published novelist and nonfiction writer.

Hobbies/personal interests: Perkins: Parenting a 3^1/2-year-old, journal writing, modern art. Rubie: Movies, chess, politics/world affairs, music, science.

Subjects/categories most enthusiastic about agenting: Perkins: Pop culture, Hispanic culture and fiction, gay fiction and nonfiction. Rubie: Cutting-edge, well-characterized stories, and strong nonfiction.

Subjects/categories not interested in agenting: Perkins: Westerns, screenplays, short stories, poems, romance. Rubie: Westerns, romance, children's.

Best way for a prospective client to initiate contact with you: Perkins: Query letter (with SASE). Rubie: Query letter (with SASE) and proposal.

Reading-fee policy: No reading fee.

Client representation in the following categories: Perkins: Nonfiction, 80%; Fiction, 20%; Rubie: Nonfiction, 75%; Fiction, 25%.

Commission: 15% domestic; 20% foreign.

Number of titles sold during the past year: Perkins: 50; Rubie: 40.

Approximate percentage of all submissions (from queries through manuscripts) that are rejected: Perkins: 99%; Rubie: 95%.

Representative titles sold:
Perkins:
Death Wore a Smart Little Outfit by Orland Outland (Berkley).

Darkness and Light: The Authorized Biography of Dean Koontz by Katherine Ransland (HarperCollins).
Future Noir: The Making of Blade Runner by Paul Sammon (HarperCollins).
Termination Note by Lois Gresh and Robert Weinberg (Del Rey).
Rubie:
Finder by Greg Rucka (Bantam).
Sing the Warmth by Louis Marley (Berkley).
How to Keep Your Cool with Your Kids by Lok Makarowski (Perigee).
How the Tiger Lost Its Stripes by Cory Meacham (Harcourt Brace).

The most common mistakes potential clients make when soliciting an agent to represent them: Perkins: Too many projects to consider at once. Expects that once s/he has an agent, the book is sold. Rubie: Overly *cute* approach, putting form over substance, belligerent and aggressive, pleading and whining, unprofessional.

What writers can do to enhance their chances of getting an agent (besides being good writers): Perkins: They have researched the kind of books I do and know my abilities. Rubie: Strong, direct writing and story idea, simply but powerfully presented, and thorough professionalism.

Description of the Client from Hell: Perkins: Daily phone calls. A new project idea every day. Rubie: Unprofessional, unreal expectations, no knowledge of the publishing industry, calls every day for *news*, does not listen to advice, and a *control* freak.

Description of Dream Client: Perkins: Knows the market and how to present his/her material; takes editorial input well; has patience. Rubie: Calls every six weeks or so, works with agent as part of an effective team, responsive, responsible, thoroughly professional.

Why did you become an agent? Perkins: I love to read. Rubie: To help discover new talent and help further the careers of established writers. As a writer, I try to be the sort of agent *I* would like to have.

What might you be doing if you weren't an agent? Perkins: Running a newspaper. Rubie: Writing full time; music.

Comments: Perkins: I wish more writers considered themselves professionals and looked at their careers accordingly. What I'm looking for: Turn-of-the-millennium Judeo/Christian horror. Rubie: To understand my philosophy of writing, read my book *The Elements of Storytelling* (John Wiley, 1996).

JAMES PETER ASSOCIATES, INC.

P.O. Box 772
Tenafly, NJ 07670
201-568-0760
fax: 201-568-2959
bholtje@attmail.com (e-mail)

Agent: Bert Holtje
  Born: February 24, 1931.

Education: B.S.; M.A., experimental psychology.

Career history: Founded James Peter Associates, Inc., in 1971. Author of 27 published books.

Hobbies/personal interests: Amateur radio, W2TQS; used to play clarinet, sax, and bass; history and politics; used to fly.

Subjects/categories most enthusiastic about agenting: All nonfiction, but especially interested in: history, politics, current affairs, pop culture, health, general reference, business, science, biography.

Subjects/categories not interested in agenting: Fiction, children's and young adult books.

Best way for a prospective client to initiate contact with you: Query letter (with SASE) with brief outline and description.

Reading-fee policy: No reading fee. Member of AAR (Association of Authors' Representatives).

Client representation in the following categories: Nonfiction, 100%.

Commission: 15% domestic, 20% foreign.

Number of titles sold during the past year: 28.

Approximate percentage of all submissions (from queries through manuscripts) that are rejected: 70%.

Representative titles sold:

Trade and reference titles:

Balance of Power: Power and Politics from the Era of McCarthy to the Age of Gingrich by Jim Wright, former Speaker, United States House of Representatives (Turner Publishing).

No Holds Barred: The Strange Life and Crimes of John DuPont by Carol Turkington (Turner Publishing).

Women's Guide to Self-Protection: Protecting Yourself under the Law by Patricia Phillips, J.D. and George Mair (Macmillan).

The Coping Life Series by Frank Bruno, Ph.D. (Macmillan). Includes *Stop Worrying, Conquer Loneliness, Stop Procrastinating, Overcome Shyness, Defeat Depression, Get a Good Night's Sleep.*

Who Is Eleanor Rigby and 1,001 More Questions and Answers about the Beatles by Brandon Toropov (HarperCollins).

Great Cities to Get Started In by Sandra Gurvis (Macmillan).

The Complete Idiot's Guide to Getting the Job You Want by Marc Dorio (Macmillan).

The Complete Idiot's Guide to American History by Alan Axelrod (Macmillan).

The Complete Idiot's Guide to Wine by Philip Seldon (Macmillan).

The Art and Skill of Dealing with People by Brandon Toropov (Simon & Schuster).

Business books:

The Executive Assistant's Employment Almanac by Melba Duncan (McGraw-Hill).

The Business Communicator's Library by James Holtje (Simon & Schuster).

Talking It Out: The Supervisor's Instant Access Desk Reference by Ray Dreyfack (Prentice Hall).

The most common mistakes potential clients make when soliciting an agent to represent them: Writers who send material that we don't handle.

What writers can do to enhance their chances of getting an agent (besides being good writers): Their own enthusiasm coupled with a realistic notion of the potential of their books.

Description of the Client from Hell: The client who refuses to accept the realities of commercial publishing today.

Description of the Dream Client: A person with good ideas who can express them clearly, entertainingly, and with enthusiasm.

Why did you become an agent? I like writing. I am the author of 27 books. I like writers. And I like the give and take of negotiation.

What might you be doing if you weren't an agent? Be an architect.

PMA LITERARY AND FILM MANAGEMENT, INC.

132 West 22nd Street, 12th Floor
New York, NY 10011
212-929-1222

Agent: Peter Miller.

Born: August 15, 1948.

Education: A.S., Atlantic Community College; B.A., Monmouth College. Additional courses: MFA program, Rutgers University; NYU; and the New School.

Career history: Founded Writers House, a literary agency, 1972; founded the Peter Miller Agency, 1974; incorporated agency in 1981; founded PMA Literary and Film Management, Inc., 1992. Founded 21st Century Lion, Inc. (a production company) in 1996. Have now been in business for 25 years.

Hobbies/personal interests: Traveling, gourmet food and wine, reading, fishing, playing with my daughters (Liseanne and Margo).

Subjects/categories most enthusiastic about agenting: Action suspense fiction, history, serious journalism and current events, pop culture.

Best way for a prospective client to initiate contact with you: A query letter written to my attention detailing the essence of the book and why it is commercial, along with biography of the author.

Reading-fee policy: PMA does not have obligatory evaluation fee. However, if desired by an author, PMA has a non-obligatory evaluation and editorial service.

Client representation in the following categories: Nonfiction, 49%; Fiction, 50%; Children's, 1%.

Commission: 15% domestic; 10%–15% film rights; 20%–25% foreign.

Approximate percentage of all submissions (from queries through manuscripts) that are rejected: 90%–95% of all unsolicited manuscripts are rejected.

Representative titles sold:

The History of Mars by Susan Wright (Viking Studio).

Area 51 by Susan Wright (St. Martin's Press).

The Chieftains by John Glatt (St. Martin's U.S./Random House UK).

The Killer's Game by Jay Bonansinga (Simon & Schuster).

The Fifth Canon by Michael Eberhardt (Dutton).

Erotic Astrology by Olivia (Ballantine).

Ticket to Hell, Slave Girls by Wensley Clarkson (St. Martin's Press).

The Plaque Tales by Ann Benson (Delacorte).

Bitch Quotient by Chris Rogers (Bantam).

Untitled investment book by David Newman (Simon & Schuster).

The most common mistakes potential clients make when soliciting an agent to represent them: Many authors express a negative attitude towards agents and the publishing industry in general. What a way to win your potential agent's confidence!

What writers can do to enhance their chances of getting an agent (besides being good writers): Professional, well-thought-out query letter with polished synopsis and/or manuscript presentation.

Description of the Client from Hell: The client sends you a handwritten manuscript and calls you every day to see if you have read it.

Description of Dream Client: A client who trusts your judgment and lets you work for them. After all, I've been selling books for 25 years and have sold over 750, so I must be doing something right.

Why did you become an agent? It happened, and I'm glad it did because I think I'm good at it. I love my work.

What might you be doing if you weren't an agent? Be a publisher or film producer. Be an executive at a film studio.

Comments: Writers, write on!

SUSAN ANN PROTTER, LITERARY AGENT

110 West 40th Street, Suite 1408
New York, NY 10018
212-840-0480

Agent: Susan Ann Protter.

Education: B.A., 1961; M.A., NYU, 1965.

Career history: French teacher, Lawrence High School, Cedarhurst, New York, 1963–1964; publishing assistant, *Report Magazine*, New York, 1964–1965; associate director, subsidiary rights department, Harper & Row Publishers Inc., 1966–1970; consultant, Addison-Wesley Publishers, Reading, Massachusetts, 1970–1971; founded Susan Ann Protter agency, 1971.

Hobbies/personal interests: Sailing, film, opera, travel, languages.

Subjects/categories most enthusiastic about agenting: Fiction: thrillers, mysteries, science fiction. Nonfiction: women's health, parenting, popular psychology, true crime, medicine, biography, advice, how-to.

Subjects/categories not interested in agenting: Start Trek, Star Wars, romance, Westerns, children's books.

Best way for a prospective client to initiate contact: Query letter (with SASE).

Reading-fee policy: No reading fee.

Client representation in the following categories: Nonfiction, 45%; Fiction, 55%.
Commission: 15%.

Number of titles sold during the past year: 15.

Approximate percentage of all submissions (from queries through manuscripts) that are rejected: 96%.

Representative titles sold:

Freeware by Rudy Rucker (Avon).

Einstein's Bridge by John G. Cramer (Avon).

The Science Fiction Century edited by David G. Hartwell (BOMC and Tor).

Shadow Heart by Lynn Armistead McKee (Signet/Onyx).

Breastfeeding and the Working Mother, Revised Edition by Diane Mason and Diane Ingersol (St. Martin's Press).

Dr. Nightingale Dances with Lions by Lydia Adamson (Signet).

A Cat on Stage Right by Lydia Adamson (Dutton).

The Fifth Element by Terry Bisson (St. Martin's Press), novelization.

The Gift by Patrick O'Leary (Tor).

The most common mistakes potential clients make when soliciting an agent to represent them: Spend first paragraph of letter apologizing for taking up your time or tell you that they are unaware of the proper way to write a manuscript.

What writers can do to enhance their chances of getting an agent (besides being good writers): Be professional and be patient. Do your homework and tell us why your book is different and who the market is for such a book. Most importantly, get straight to the point in your query letter.

Description of the Client from Hell: Calls all the time and tells me how to run my business.

Description of the Dream Client: A creative, disciplined writer with an ability to write with a clear audience in mind, who takes editorial comments and criticism constructively and delivers on time.

Comments: Don't give up. Rewrite and then rewrite again.

RAINES & RAINES

71 Park Avenue
New York, NY 10016
212-684-5160

Agents: Theron Raines, Joan Raines, Keith Korman.

Best way for a prospective client to initiate contact: One-page letter (with SASE).

Reading-fee policy: No reading fee.

Commission: 15% domestic, 20% foreign.

Approximate percentage of all submissions (from queries through manuscripts) that are rejected: Most.

Representative titles sold:

The Uses of Enchantment and other books by Bruno Bettelheim.

Deliverance and other books by James Dickey.

The Shawl, Fame & Folly, Puttermesser, and other books by Cynthia Ozick.

The Detective, Die Hard, and other books by Roderick Thorp.

My Dog Skip and other books by Willie Morris.

The Destruction of the European Jews and other books by Raul Hilberg.

HELEN REES LITERARY AGENCY

308 Commonwealth Avenue
Boston, MA 02115
617-262-2401

Agent: Helen Rees.

Born: October 2, 1936.

Education: B.A., history, George Washington University.

Career history: Director of Office of Cultural Affairs, City of Boston (1978–1982); literary agent (1983–present).

Hobbies/personal interests: Horseback riding, opera, theatre, hiking.

Subjects/categories most enthusiastic about agenting: Literary fiction, history, psychology, business.

Subjects/categories not interested in agenting: Children's books, young adult, science fiction, poetry, cookbooks, gardening books, photography.

Best way for a prospective client to initiate contact with you: Query letter (with SASE) with three chapters and a synopsis.

Reading-fee policy: No reading fee.

Commission: 15% domestic; 20% foreign.

Number of titles sold during the past year: 14.

Approximate percentage of all submissions (from queries through manuscripts) that are rejected: 85%.

Representative titles sold:

The Advocate's Devil by Alan Dershowitz.

Bankruptcy 1995 by Harry Figgie.

Reengineering the Corporation by Michael Hammer and James Champy.

Thriving in Transition by Marcia Perkins-Reed.

The most common mistakes potential clients make when soliciting an agent to represent them: In a query letter, they unrealistically hype their material.

What writers can do to enhance their chances of getting an agent (besides being good writers): Produce an original idea and execute it well.

Description of the Client from Hell: Someone who sends a manuscript over and calls an hour later to see if I've read it.

Description of Dream Client: Someone who listens and is talented.

THE NAOMI REICHSTEIN LITERARY AGENCY

5031 Foothills Road, Room G
Lake Oswego, OR 97034
503-636-7575
fax: 503-636-3957
nreichstein@northwest.com (e-mail)

Agent: Naomi Wittes Reichstein.

Education: B.A., Harvard College.

Career history: Before opening agency, was British and Foreign Rights Manager at W. W. Norton & Company, Inc. While at Norton, was awarded an Editorial Fellowship by the Jerusalem International Book Fair of 1995. Previously, was Subsidiary Rights Supervisor at The Free Press and an associate agent at Mildred Marmur Associates Ltd.

Hobbies/personal interests: Classical music, opera, dance, art.

Subjects/categories most enthusiastic about agenting: Fiction and nonfiction for adults. Of particular interest are novels of quality and nonfiction in areas that include (but are not limited to) history, cultural studies and issues, travel, geography, the environment, science, music, the arts, architecture, memoirs, literature, psychology, women's issues, how-to, and humor. New writers, as well as published ones, are welcome.

Subjects/categories not interested in agenting: Science fiction, horror, category romance, children's books, young adult, individual articles or short stories, plays, or film or television scripts, poetry.

Best way for a prospective client to initiate contact: Query by mail with SASE or by e-mail to nreichstein@northwest.com. No phone calls or faxes.

Reading-fee policy: No reading fee.

Commission: 15% domestic; 20% on deals concluded outside the U.S.

Description of the Client from Hell: The Client from Hell undertakes many projects simultaneously and resists the agent's suggestions and advice to focus on a small number of strong, current projects. The client gives the agent sloppy proposals and manuscripts that the agent has to proofread and retype. The client then calls the agent several times a day, seven days a week, at work and at home to ask for updates on submissions even though the agent forwards editors' letters regularly. The client resents the agent's work on behalf of other clients. When disappointing news comes in, the client blames it on the agent and bad mouths the agent to editors and other writers. The client undercuts the efforts of the agent by entering into negotiations directly with the editor. The client is particularly abusive to the assistants of his or her agent and editor.

Description of Dream Client: The dream client writes beautifully and succinctly and in an organized fashion, has original, serious things to say about important issues, is well qualified by background to write about them, and can abide by deadlines. Recognizing that the agent has to put his or her best foot forward when approaching publishers, the client always presents manuscripts and proposals that are proofread, typed, double-spaced, and printed in an easily decipherable font and in dark ink. The client is personable, professional, and agreeable to work with. Rather than trying to churn out as much material as possible, the client writes selectively and understands how to self-edit but also welcomes suggestions. Savvy about the market, the client understands that even the best work can be difficult to sell and that the agent is doing his or her best, since a dutiful agent sends regular updates; the client never shoots the messenger. The client keeps the agent up to date in turn by sending copies of relevant articles he or she has written and notifying the agent of significant appearances made. If possible, the client retains a fax machine and an e-mail address for easy communication. The client is easy to reach. The client refers talented writers to the agent as other potential clients.

The most common mistakes potential clients make when soliciting an agent to represent them: Authors should query with a letter and SASE (I also welcome queries by e-mail) but *not* by fax or phone. A query should be legible, courteous, sober, and professional and, in one page, should summarize the contents of the book and the author's background and/or qualifications to write it. Authors should avoid gimmicks in queries and should not make exaggerated claims; they should address agents by last name. It's a mistake to follow up by phone too soon; agents receive many submissions and need time, in good faith, to review them. Authors shouldn't show up uninvited at agent's office or home to submit queries or manuscripts. Since agents owe the bulk of their time to the writers to whom they have already made commitments, querying authors should understand that agents may not have time to give general publishing advice or referrals.

JODY REIN BOOKS, INC.

7741 South Ash Court
Littleton, CO 80122
303-694-4430

Agent: Jody Rein.

Career history: Spent 13 years in publishing at Contemporary Books, Bantam Doubleday Dell, and Morrow/Avon Books. Incorporated Jody Rein Books in 1994.

Subjects/categories most enthusiastic about agenting: Very commercial nonfiction written by people who have both media contacts/experience and true expertise in their chosen subject matter. An amazing work of literary fiction by an award-winning short-story writer.

Subjects/categories not interested in agenting: Category fiction (mystery, romance, science fiction, horror, etc.), poetry, children's books.

Best way for a prospective client to initiate contact: A recommendation from someone I trust. A one-page query letter.

Reading-fee policy: No reading fee.

Client representation in the following categories: Nonfiction, 85%; Fiction, 15%.
Commission: 15%.

Number of titles sold during the past year: 11.

Approximate percentage of all submissions (from queries through manuscripts) that are rejected: 90%–95%.

Representative titles sold:

Twice Chosen: Reviving the Arts of Courage and Commitment by Wayne Brown (Golden Books adult division).

How to Raise Your Emotional Intelligence by Jeanne Segal, Ph.D. (Holt).

The Ten Greatest Gifts Our Children Gift to Us by Stephen Vannoy (Simon & Schuster).

Cancer Combat by Dean and Jessica King and Jonathan Pearlroth (Bantam).

A Woman's Guide to a Simpler Life by Andrea Van Steenhouse and Doris A. Fuller (Random House).

Description of the Client from Hell: Not someone I would do business with! (An author who expects a perfect publishing experience but doesn't expect to do any work on his own.)

Description of Dream Client: Someone with a fabulous idea and the requisite writing experience, life experience, education, and passion to pull it off. Plus media experience and contacts. Plus a real willingness to do whatever he or she can to work with the agent and publisher to make his or her book a bestseller. Plus respect for himself or herself, for the book, for the publisher, and for me.

The most common mistakes potential clients make when soliciting an agent to represent them: E-mail me; send me something I know nothing about; call me; say "I can write about anything!"; Say "Well, I don't really know if this has been done before . . . "

What writers can do to enhance their chances of getting an agent (besides being good writers): Do their homework. Know the market for the work. Write a thorough proposal or query letter. Convince me the idea is salable—convince me with concrete reasons (e.g. expertise of author, popularity of concept, knowledge of other books).

Why did you become an agent? I had been in the publishing business at the top levels for 13 years when I moved to Denver. I love this business. Being an agent was the only way to stay in the business, doing business with the top professionals in New York—and still live in the Rocky Mountains.

Comments: You can find good agents anywhere in the country, but make sure you protect yourself by doing adequate research. Ask the agent who wants to represent you if she has New York experience, how you would work together, and so on. But *don't* ask these questions until she has offered to represent you. If she doesn't want to sell your work, it doesn't matter what her experience is.

REMINGTON LITERARY ASSOCIATES, INC.

10131 Coors Road NW, Suite 12-886
Albuquerque, NM 87114
505-898-8305
fax: 505-890-0486

Agents: Kay Lewis Shaw (also known as "Happy" Shaw), President; Associate Agents: Denise Clegg, David Corwell; Karen South Moustafa; Jeffrey A. Poston. Screenplay and Teleplay Consultant: Rick Reichman.

The following information pertains to KAY LEWIS SHAW:

Born: December 11, 1948; Joanna, South Carolina.

Education: B.S., art education, University of Georgia (1972).

Career history: In the 1970s, I taught art in public schools and for a private museum in northern Georgia. After moving to New Mexico in 1978, I taught private art lessons. In 1982, I became a founding member of Southwest Writers Workshop and went on to serve as its treasurer (twice), vice president and president in 1987–1988. I began studying writing in 1982 and began teaching it professionally in 1988. I am now considered a master teacher of genre novel structure, and currently teach "Literature of New Mexico" for the University of New Mexico's Center on Aging's Elderhostel Programs.

Hobbies/personal interests: I love going to the movies and analyzing why they work or not. When I have the time, I like to read for pleasure, decorate, sew, create artwork, and collect blue-and-white china and wicker furniture. Currently, I also teach for UNM's Elderhostel Programs because I love teaching people from all over about the West and about our popular authors who have lived or still do live in New Mexico.

Subjects/categories most enthusiastic about agenting: I am currently taking clients on only in the series mystery category for adults and already published children's book illustrators and writers. I will also look at unpublished children's book texts, but prefer to review only artwork by illustrators who already have a track record or at least an art degree or some major recognition of their artwork.

Remington's other agents cover all areas of the market, except poetry collections and short-story collections. Screenplays and teleplays are read and evaluated by professional script consultant, Rick Reichman, author of *Formatting Your Screenplay* available from Writer's Digest Books. Script should be accompanied by SASE large enough to return the script to the author and must also include the $250 evaluation fee. If taken on for representation, the script is marketed by our Los Angeles associate.

Subjects/categories not interested in agenting: The agency does not represent autobiographical works by unknown writers. We also do not want material that has no clear market. You must know what category your work fits. Again, the agency does not represent adult poetry collections or adult short-story collections.

Best way for a prospective client to initiate contact: Please mail, *do not fax or phone us*, a professionally typed query letter addressed to me or one of the other agents. Please include SASE if you wish a response to your query. We also meet prospective clients at writers' conferences and through present client references.

A professional query is brief, 1–2 pages at the most. Tell us whether your book is fiction or nonfiction, if it is finished, and the approximate number of words. In case of fiction, give its category. In one short paragraph, briefly describe the main story element and main character's goal or problem. Please give your writing credits, if any, or important background on yourself in another paragraph. *Do not send any other material with a query letter*—no sample text pages, no synopsis, no personal pictures, or sample chapters.

Reading-fee policy: Absolutely! Due to the volume of queries and our client list, we can no longer evaluate anything for free. Critiques are 2–15 pages. We charge $75 for 75 pages of adult fiction or nonfiction (after reading the partial of 75 pages of adult fiction or nonfiction, if we wish to see the rest, we do not charge additional evaluation fees on the manuscript); $50 for children's and young adult novels under 200 pages; $25 for a picture book; $250 screenplay and teleplay evaluation by professional script consultant, Rick Reichman. Script evaluation is 12 pages plus 20 pages of line edit.

Client representation in the following categories: Nonfiction, 10%; Fiction, 60%; Children's, 40%.

Commission: 15% domestic; 20% foreign; 20% movie and other dramatic rights; and 20% electronic, CD-ROM, and audio rights.

Number of titles sold during the past year: Remington produces its own newsletter, updated throughout the year, which includes a current list of titles sold. To receive a copy, write us, requesting it, and include three 1st-class stamps to cover the postage.

Approximate percentage of all submissions (from queries through manuscripts) that are rejected: 90%.

Representative titles sold:

Please request our newsletter for a current list of titles sold (enclose three 1st-class stamps to cover postage).

The most common mistakes potential clients make when soliciting an agent to represent them: Besides telling me that they are wonderful writers and we are sure to make big bucks by taking them on as clients, the most common mistakes are: (1) They have never studied writing of any kind. (2) They know nothing about the type of writing they claim to be writing. They have never read a mystery, etc. but think they have written one. (3) They do not follow the rules, send unsolicited materials that we haven't requested and will not read. (4) They cannot take and do not want criticism on their work. They are just looking for someone to say it is perfect, that they are wonderful writers, and we can sell their work tomorrow, as is. (5) These people have the misguided perception that they will make an enormous amount of money on their first category novel advance, or for any manuscript in any area by an unknown or unpublished writer. (6) They do not realize there is a vast difference between owning the latest computer equipment and knowing how to write for a specific market. (7) They do not understand that this is a business and editors are looking for something they know the public will purchase. (8) They do not realize that an agent is also in business.

What writers can do to enhance their chances of getting an agent (besides being good writers): For heaven's sake, spend some money on your writing career. Buy books about writing and read them. Read in the area you want to publish in until you know what is selling there. Join writers' organizations. Get in a critique group, even if just by mail. Go to writers' conferences. Make contacts there with editors and agents and other writers. This business is just like other professions, and you increase your chances for success if you know what you are doing and do it well. Learn the craft, network, and know what it takes to get something published. If you want an agent or an editor to take a gamble on you, then make sure you put the best possible manuscript that you can create on their desks. No one is looking for potential any more; we have to have someone who can do the job and do it now. First drafts don't make it in this business. If you are not willing to do everything it takes to make your work shine, you've lost the game already.

Description of the Client from Hell: We quickly terminate any relationship with anyone who does not conduct business in a professional manner. There are simply too many people waiting in line in this business for anyone to behave in a rude or unprofessional manner. Publishing is a business for business people. It is not a not-for-profit charity. Finally, learn to accept criticism. Editors today are only looking for the most professional writers to work with. They expect their revision letters to be taken seriously. When compromise is necessary, be prepared to do it in a cheerful manner. Again, there are too many people waiting in line for any publishing slot today.

Description of Dream Client: All of our clients are now dream clients. They have no problem with revisions, criticism, or deadlines. The presentation of their materials is topnotch and in correct manuscript format. They only call us when they have something important to discuss, as they are too busy writing. If a situation comes up, they are willing to compromise. Dream clients never forget to say thank you to editors, agents, or anyone else who has helped them in any way with their manuscript or career.

Why did you become an agent? I've studied writing for over 14 years and have been teaching it professionally for 8 years. Becoming an agent seemed to be the next logical step.

What might you be doing if you weren't an agent? I would be a minister in the Church of Religious Science, or at least a practitioner, helping people to learn that life is a wonderful experience and how to turn negatives into positives. Or, I would be running a retreat center for creative people—writers and artists. Or, I would run a bookstore or an antique store. Or, I would be a bestselling author. Or, all of them.

Comments: To believe in yourself is not enough to make it in this business. Believing in yourself is not the same as knowing that you can write in a specific area of the market. Knowing means you have the knowledge and commitment to have learned the craft and gotten professional feedback, possibly by selling articles, short stories, etc. before trying to tackle the book market. Or you have gotten professional feedback from entering writing contests judged by editors and agents or published writers. If you aren't willing to do what it takes to reach professional status with your writing, why should anyone in the publishing business invest any time in reviewing or promoting material that clearly indicates the writer doesn't have a clue as to what a publisher will buy or the public will read? If you aren't willing to devote the time, energy, and money that it takes to create a professional writing career, go find something else that you love and devote your life to that. Not everyone is meant to be a brain surgeon or an accountant. The same is true of professional writers. This career isn't for everyone, even if you do know a little bit about it or have a great computer. Overnight successes in this business are rarer than the media would seem to indicate. Everyone wants to believe that they can become a bestselling author, and it is okay to believe. But like the lottery, the winners are going to be few and far between. If you want a steady career as a category writer of Westerns, romances, mysteries, science fiction, etc. that is possible. But don't expect the big money to come until after you've built up a following, which can take years.

The following information pertains to DAVID CORWELL:
Born: August 14, 1970; Albuquerque, New Mexico.
Education: B.A., English, University of New Mexico, 1995.

Career history: Have been an editor and copy editor for eight years now, and started my own freelance editing business in 1995. Currently a Contributing Editor for the *Sandoval Arts* magazine, a local arts and literary guide. Have worked as an office manager and bookseller for one of the major bookstore chains, and have been a member of the Horror Writer's Association and the Southwest Writer's Workshop since 1993.

Hobbies/personal interests: Love watching movies, particularly science fiction, fantasy, and horror. Am an avid book collector, Star Trek enthusiast, a fanatic TSR/White Wolf fan, and an ancient art (Egyptian, Mayan, Incan, etc.) replica hunter. And, of course, there's always reading and writing!

Subjects/categories most enthusiastic about agenting: I enjoy action and suspense in almost any category, but tend to concentrate on mysteries, science fiction (space operas, alternate worlds, near future, hard/soft science), especially Star Trek, fantasy (dark, epic, alternate history, sword and sorcery), and selective horror (supernatural, psychological, Gothic). I don't usually handle Westerns, but I'll take a look if a query or a book captures my interest.

Subjects/categories not interested in agenting: I cannot stand romance—send it to the agents in our agency who accept that category. Please don't send any contemporary fantasy, cyberpunk/splatterpunk horror, or any other horror written from the villain's point of view. I will not accept any work that is pornographic or violent in nature for its own sake.

Best way for a prospective client to initiate contact: Send a query letter *only*. Get my attention, sell me your book idea; I'll let you know if I want to see more, whether it be a partial, synopsis, or the entire manuscript. Please, no phone queries or other calls unless I specifically invite you to in my reply. I will always respond to queries, usually within 2–3 weeks. I also try to meet authors when I get out to conferences or workshops.

Description of the Client from Hell: A client from hell would be someone who submits materials that are not requested or materials in an improper format. He/she would not accept any criticism for manuscript improvement but would blame the agent when the book didn't sell. He/she would be untrusting, unprofessional, and rude, treating the agent more like a personal advisor than as a professional business consultant.

Description of Dream Client: A dream client would always approach me in a professional manner, whether it's through the mail or in person. He/she would fully understand that writing is a business, knowing that a lot of rewriting and polishing might be involved to produce a marketable manuscript. He/she would be willing to accept criticism, work hard, and understand that the journey toward publication is a team effort involving both writer and agent.

The most common mistakes potential clients make when soliciting an agent to represent them: I'm really turned off when a writer tells me that his/her book is the best that they've ever written or that his/her book is the best thing around since Stephen King, David Eddings—you get my drift. Incorrect manuscript submissions, especially those without a return SASE, are very annoying and usually brand the author as an amateur. Authors who have problems with constructive criticism, preferring to argue with their editor or agent rather than working to improve the overall quality of their manuscript, don't take the business of writing seriously, and ultimately harm their chances of ever being published.

What writers can do to enhance their chances of getting an agent (besides being good writers): I'm always excited to come across an author whose work shows remarkable skill and who realizes that the author-agent relationship is a professional partnership. Authors who know what they write (where their book would be shelved in a bookstore) and those with some sense of how they would market their work dramatically increase their chances for representation. I always welcome someone with the above traits, along with a pleasant demeanor and with a fervent desire to get published.

Why did you become an agent? I enjoy the process of discovery involved in every aspect of book publishing. Whether it's helping other writers to eventually fulfill their dreams of being published or riding the excitement over a potential bestseller, there is never a dull moment. Each book is as unique as its creator, and it's this constant variety that makes agenting a very satisfying vocation.

What might you be doing if you weren't an agent? I would spend more time with my writing and with my freelance editing business.

Comments: When submitting a query, don't try to impress me with flowery verbiage. You are trying to market your novel for representation, so get to the point and convince me that I would want to see your book. Always, always be professional in all your dealings with an agent or editor. Properly submitted material goes a long way to show that you mean business. Be open to criticism; though agent's have their personal opinions and preferences too, much of their advice focuses on sound market research and experience. Keep abreast of your market, particularly your audience, so that you don't write something that has already been done. And don't expect your agent to work miracles if your manuscript is not up to speed. You should only submit your work once it has been polished to the best of your ability.

The following information pertains to KAREN SOUTH MOUSTAFA:

Born: September 15, 1953; San Antonio, Texas.

Education: B.S., science; Ph.M., master's in business.

Career history: Healthcare administration for 24 years. Published writer-essayist.

Hobbies/personal interests: Reading and art.

Subjects/categories most enthusiastic about agenting: Mystery (no horror), fantasy, science fiction, suspense, all nonfiction.

Subjects/categories not interested in agenting: Horror.

Best way for a prospective client to initiate contact: Write and send a synopsis (2 pages) of story line and character change. This will show whether you have an ability to write clearly.

Description of the Client from Hell: Personality is important in marketing a book. If an author is rude to me, I would hesitate to have him/her appear for promotion—a big part of the author's job, after the book is written.

Description of Dream Client: Someone willing to discuss changes within the manuscript in a rational manner—describing pros and cons to reach a decision—based on his/her own vision of the story.

The most common mistakes potential clients make when soliciting an agent to represent them: Sending too much material before I'm ready for it.

What writers can do to enhance their chances of getting an agent (besides being good writers): Be clear about what you expect from me.

Why did you become an agent? I became frustrated that many good writers lacked the motivation or knowledge to sell their books. I know I can help.

What might you be doing if you weren't an agent? I can't imagine.

Comments: Keep writing and send me anything, except horror. I promise to give my honest opinion (remember, it's only an opinion) and do my best to sell your work if I believe in it.

The following information pertains to Jeffrey A. Poston:

Born: June 6, 1958.

Education: B.S.E.E., aerospace science and engineering.

Career history: 17-year Air Force career, retired as an officer and engineer. 12-year fiction writing/speaking career.

Hobbies/personal interests: Outdoor, nature activities such as camping and hiking are always personal favorites. I also enjoy volleyball, in-line skate racing, movies, reading, and writing.

Subjects/categories most enthusiastic about agenting: Fiction: I prefer action in almost any category but concentrate on Westerns, men/women's action-adventure, near-future science fiction and hard-core science fiction (especially Star Trek). Nonfiction: self-help, computer, men's health/awareness.

Subjects/categories not interested in agenting: Sorry, but romance makes me gag, although others in the agency accept that category.

Best way for a prospective client to initiate contact: Send a query letter with a brief (2-page maximum) description of work. For nonfiction, include credentials. But, please, don't call unless I invite you to on my reply. I *always* respond to queries, usually in 2–3 weeks.

The most common mistakes potential clients make when soliciting an agent to represent them: Some writers seem to expect the agent to be their private personal editor. They get too personal in what should *always* start out as a business relationship. Especially, never get so personal that you submit incomplete or unprofessional work. This wastes your money and my time and can even damage the relationship.

What writers can do to enhance their chances of getting an agent (besides being good writers)? When a writer realizes that I am first a businessman and also someone who can help them realize their goal of getting published, I really get excited, especially with new writers. It helps immensely when the writer realizes that agents aren't power-hungry, critical, writer bashers *only* looking for a bestseller.

Description of the Client from Hell: My Client from Hell falls into one of two categories: (1) He/she wants detailed critique/advice repeatedly at no charge. Or (2) he/she is unpublished, but can't accept criticism, preferring instead to defend every little word or counter every comment suggested that might make the work marketable. He/she wants an agent, then questions the agent's professionalism because that agent won't market the work *as-is*.

Description of Dream Client: The dream client *wants* to get published and gracefully accepts criticism, even though it may be painful. This client realizes that he/she is the creator while we (the agency) are the polishers. This client works the win-win scenario and is willing to do whatever is necessary to get published without sacrificing the integrity of their creation (or themselves).

Why did you become an agent? I have a personal mission to mentor people and help people achieve their goals. Of course, finding a potential bestseller helps a bit!

What might you be doing if you weren't an agent? If I weren't an agent, I would spend more time being a writer.

Comments: Remember, the writer's job is to create. The agent's job is to market. Try to consider objectively all comments by the agent to polish and improve your work. While every individual's opinions are unique, try to filter through the comments that are personal preferences of the agent and those that are based on sound judgment and experience. After all, the agents have their finger on the pulse of the publishing world—where you want your book to be. But, if you think you can write perfectly and don't want to rewrite, don't waste your time. Bestselling authors can get virtually any editor/agent/publisher they want, but they are all wise enough to accept professional critiques. Unless your agent proves to be incompetent, trust him/her and have faith in their judgment. Only then can he/she help you achieve your goal.

ANN RITTENBERG LITERARY AGENCY, INC.

14 Montgomery Place
Brooklyn, NY 11215
718-857-1460

Agent: Ann Rittenberg.
  Born: 1957; New York.
  Education: B.A., Eckerd College, 1979.
  Career history: 1980–1986, editor at Atheneum Publishers; 1987–1991, agent at Julian Buch Literary Agency; 1991–present, president of Ann Rittenberg Literary Agency.
  Subjects/categories most enthusiastic about agenting: Literary fiction, biography, cultural/social history, belles lettres, women's issues, gardening/flowers, nutrition.
  Subjects/categories not interested in agenting: Science fiction, romance, how-to, genre fiction.
  Best way for a prospective client to initiate contact: Write me a letter, briefly describe your work, your writing background, your education, tell me where you got my name, and enclose SASE.
  Reading-fee policy: No reading fee.
  Client representation in the following categories: Nonfiction, 50%; Fiction, 50%.
  Commission: 15% domestic, 20% foreign (10% subagent, 10% ARLA).
  Number of titles sold during the past year: 10.
  Approximate percentage of all submissions (from queries through manuscripts) that are rejected: 98%.
  Representative titles sold:
  Every Day by Elizabeth Richards (Pocket).

Bodies of Knowledge: A Season in the Anatomy Lab by Albert Howard Carter III (Picador).

Sacred by Dennis Lehave (Morrow).

The Poetry of Sight by Avis Berman and Clarkson Potter (Crown).

Altars in the Street by Melody Chavis (Harmony).

Description of the Client from Hell: One who calls twice before I've had a chance to return. One who calls every Monday at 9:01 a.m. or every Friday at 5:59 p.m. One who never revises his/her work. One who says "but I worked so hard on it." One who talks more about "marketing" than writing. One who never airs his/her worries or concerns.

Description of Dream Client: One who wants to make the manuscript great, no matter how much work it takes. One who follows through on ideas. One with persistence, tenacity, and determination. One who is simply wonderful, professional—a delight.

The most common mistakes potential clients make when soliciting an agent to represent them: They rabbit on about the vast potential market for the book. They write about weirdly named people doing sad esoteric things in obscure places. They fail to determine what kinds of books I actually do or do not represent.

What writers can do to enhance their chances of getting an agent (besides being good writers): Write with verve and an original voice. Write about the thing that most fascinates them in the world. Tell me a story.

Why did you become an agent? Because I wanted to be an advocate for authors. I like to sell, and I like to edit, and I like to work for myself.

What might you be doing if you weren't an agent? Writing literary criticism for scholarly journals, playing tennis and golf, and traveling for months at a time.

ROBINS & ASSOCIATES

727 Thorn Street
Mountain Home, AR 72653-3101
501-424-2191
cjrobins@centuryinter.net (e-mail)

Agent: Cris J. Baker-Robins.

Born: 1958; Michigan.

Education: Degree in business.

Career history: Former advertising agency founder/owner. Writer/editor and media producer.

Hobbies/personal interests: Computers, travel, reading.

Subjects/categories most enthusiastic about agenting: Science fiction/fantasy, strong mainstream fiction, children's work. New writers' work that has *potential*.

Subjects/categories not interested in agenting: Poetry, "grandma's stories," occult, porn of any kind.

Best way for a prospective client to initiate contact: E-mail or snail mail.

Reading-fee policy: We rarely charge reading fees.

Client representation in the following categories: Nonfiction, 5%; Fiction, 70%; Children's, 20%; Textbooks, 5%.

Commission: Negotiable, but within the 8%–20% range.

Number of titles sold during the past year: We just started in October of 1996. However, we are currently working on 8 sales before fall.

Approximate percentage of all submissions (from queries through manuscripts) that are rejected: 80%. Most authors are rejected because they failed to follow our guidelines.

Description of the Client from Hell: One whose talent is lacking, believes his/her mother's opinion is the most valued, and calls *every* day to remind us! This is usually a former client of another agency who has been burned before and is overly sensitive.

Description of Dream Client: One who understands that the process takes time, who is not afraid of making changes to improve their work, and gives us room to do our job. Most of our clients fall into this category because we are *very* selective of the people we represent. We take the time to build a trust bridge with our clients.

The most common mistakes potential clients make when soliciting an agent to represent them: They forget to listen and follow directions. We *never* ask for a full manuscript. Yet, writers feel they are "short changing" themselves if they don't send it all. There are reasons we set up guidelines—to make our lives and theirs easier.

What writers can do to enhance their chances of getting an agent (besides being good writers): Write a cover letter that makes us sit up and say, "Oh, my!" Then don't disappoint us with a manuscript that is written in pencil. We receive between 15–125 queries *every* day via e-mail. Each one is answered; however, not all receive requests for submission.

Why did you become an agent? Because there are a lot of new writers out there who deserve a break. They don't need editing scams or self-publishing outlets. They just need their work polished and published.

What might you be doing if you weren't an agent? Crime analyst—both involve research, sales, communications, and working with talented people.

Comments: Our guidelines are simple: submit a brief bio, an outline with approximate word count, and the first 10 pages of the actual work. We don't want to hear glowing praise from your local newspaper, clergy, or your mother. We do want to see work that has *potential*. We're willing to work with writers (new and old) to get their work into the market.

CAROL SUSAN ROTH, LITERARY REPRESENTATION

1824 Oak Creek Drive
Palo Alto, CA 94304
415-323-3795

Agent: Carol Susan Roth.

Born: October 22, 1947; New Brunswick, New Jersey.

Education: B.A., New York University; M.A., California Institute of Asian Studies; Professional Publishing Course, Stanford University.

Career history: Studied to be a psychotherapist and worked as a motivational trainer. More than a decade producing public author events (100+) and promoting best-selling authors (Scott Peck, Bernie Siegal, John Gray, etc.).

Hobbies/personal interests: Warm-water sailing, siddha yoga.

Subjects/categories most enthusiastic about agenting: Nonfiction only, specialty is spirituality, personal development/self-help, holistic health, "new" business.

Subjects/categories not interested in agenting: Any book written by an author unwilling or unable to commit time and money to its marketing and promotion.

Best way for a prospective client to initiate contact: I like getting a query, proposal, and marketing plan with SASE. Copies of promotional materials/workshop brochures/media kit most helpful.

Reading-fee policy: No reading fee. Consulting fee ($100/hour) if client wants proposal reworked.

Client representation in the following categories: Nonfiction, 100%.

Commission: 15% domestic.

Number of titles sold during the past year: Two submitted, two sold.

Representative titles sold:

Nature's Wisdom: Moving Gracefully Through Your Seasons of Change by Dr. Carol McClelland (Conari).

Stopping: How to Be Still When You Have to Keep Going by Dr. David J. Kundtz (Conari).

Description of the Client from Hell: An inexperienced author who thinks he knows more than his agent about marketing and representation.

Description of Dream Client: My clients! Hardworking, smart, and fun!

The most common mistakes potential clients make when soliciting an agent to represent them: Lack of objectivity about their work.

What writers can do to enhance their chances of getting an agent (besides being good writers): Be polite, cooperative, and enthusiastic.

Why did you become an agent? I promoted many authors on their way to the best-seller lists. One of my clients had a great self-published book that I thought I could sell. I didn't sell her book but sold the concept for the highest advance the publisher has ever paid! I like to think of myself as an *author's best friend*. I enjoy helping an author develop and promote her entire writing/teaching career.

What might you be doing if you weren't an agent? Book development, marketing strategy, and promotion for authors (which I also do now).

Comments: I want to make you a star if you have great work that serves humanity and this beautiful blue pearl Earth.

Pesha Rubinstein Literary Agency, Inc.

1392 Rugby Road
Teaneck, NJ 07666
201-862-1174
fax: 201-862-1180

Agent: Pesha Rubinstein.

Born: September 5, 1955.

Education: B.A., Bryn Mawr College.

Career history: 1990–present, independent agent; 1981–1990, editor, Zebra Books; 1980–1981, editor, Leisure Books; 1979–1980, assistant, Rolling Stone Press; 1978–1979, assistant, Simon & Schuster.

Hobbies/personal interests: My family, movies, the Tonight Show, and walking.

Subjects/categories most enthusiastic about agenting: Commercial fiction that is also literary; contemporary women's fiction.

Subjects/categories not interested in agenting: Men's adventure, Westerns, young adult fiction, poetry.

Best way for a prospective client to initiate contact with you: Query letter (with SASE) and first 10 pages of manuscript.

Reading-fee policy: No reading fee. Yes, photocopying reimbursement.

Client representation in the following categories: Fiction, 70%; Children's, 30%.

Commission: 15% domestic; 20% foreign.

Number of titles sold during the past year: 40.

Approximate percentage of all submissions (from queries through manuscripts) that are rejected: Unfortunately, I must reject most of what I read. However, I have gotten most of my clients just by reading the mail, and I encourage submissions.

Representative titles sold:

Subterranean by James Clemens (Avon).

Shakerag by Amy Littlesugar (Philomel).

Winning Rachel by Nikki Rivers (Silhouette).

The Fox Maiden illustrated by Tatsuro Kiuchi (Simon & Schuster).

Cheer Squad by Linda Joy Singleton (Avon Books for Young Readers).

Historical romances by Tanya Anne Crosby (Avon).

Historical romances by Karen Ranney (Avon).

Historical romances by Karyn Monk (Bantam).

Historical romances by Katherine Kincaid (Zebra).

The most common mistakes potential clients make when soliciting an agent to represent them: Some writers still submit manuscripts that are single-spaced and typed on both sides of the paper, and don't enclose SASE! Misspellings and poor grammar are big turnoffs. I cringe when I see "drug" as the past tense of "drag" and when "lay" and "lie" are used improperly.

What writers can do to enhance their chances of getting an agent (besides being good writers): *Being familiar with the market is essential.* If a query letter mentions books whose audiences the writer seeks, I find it helpful in determining whether I want to see a sample. *Networking* helps, but the writer should limit his number of online hours so he can get back to work!

Description of the Client from Hell: The one with horns and a tail.

Description of Dream Client: Prompt delivery of manuscript. One who accepts rather than fights constructive criticism. A client who understands that self-promotion is part of the writing process today.

Why did you become an agent? I need to be my own boss and there's nothing I love more than reading. Voilà! An agent is born!

What might you be doing if you weren't an agent? A tinker, a tailor, a soldier, a sailor . . .

Comments: An author's job is to write morning, noon, and oft at night. The down-side of the job: discouragement, rejection, blues, and lack of confidence. My advice to writers: Persist! Persist! From your task do not desist! Envision when Oprah's invitation makes you the world's literary sensation.

RUSSELL–SIMENAUER LITERARY AGENCY, INC.

P.O. Box 43267
Upper Montclair, NJ 07043
201-746-0539; 201-992-4198; 201-221-8067
fax: 201-746-0754

Agents: Jacqueline Simenauer, Margaret Russell.

Born: Simenauer: February 23, 1948. Russell: December 8, 1949.

Education: Simenauer: Fordham University. Russell: M.A., Columbia University.

Career history: Simenauer: Editor, World Wide Features, Inc.; president, Psychiatric Syndication Service, Inc.; freelance writer and coauthor: *Beyond the Male Myth* (Times Books); *Husbands and Wives* (Times Books); *Singles: The New Americans* (Simon & Schuster); *Not Tonight Dear* (Doubleday). Russell: Director of publicity, Ticknor & Fields; director of publicity, Basic Books; associate director of publicity, Simon and Schuster; coauthor *Nachemia: German and Jew in the Holocaust* (New Horizon Press).

Hobbies/personal interests: Simenauer: Cruising the world. Russell: Music, gardening.

Subjects/categories most enthusiastic about agenting: We like strong commercial nonfiction books that include medical, health, popular psychology, how-to/self-help, women's issues, spirituality, current issues, business, computers, reference.

Literary and mainstream commercial fiction. First novels welcome.

Subjects/categories not interested in agenting: Children's books, poetry, crafts, cookbooks.

Best way for a prospective client to initiate contact with you: By query letter (with SASE) with a good description of the book.

Reading-fee policy: No reading fee. We will read all material submitted to us free of charge. We do have a special Breakthrough Program for the first-time author who would like an in-depth critique of his/her work by our freelance editorial staff. There is a charge of $2 per page for this service, and it is *completely optional.*

Client representation in the following categories: Nonfiction, 98%; Fiction, 2%.

Commission: 15%

Number of titles sold during the past year: 25.

Approximate percentage of all submissions (from queries through manuscripts) that are rejected: 95%.

Representative titles sold:

The Benzo Blues by Edward Drummond, M.D. (NAL/Dutton).

The Joys of Fatherhood by Marcus J. Goldman, M.D. (Prima).

The Endometriosis Sourcebook by the Endometriosis Association (Contemporary Books).

The Healing Mind by Eileen Oster (Prima).

The Bride's Guide to Emotional Survival by Rita Bigel-Casher, Ph.D. (Prima).

The most common mistakes potential clients make when soliciting an agent to represent them: A hand-written, practically illegible query letter; a carelessly typed, single-spaced, and/or incomplete query or proposal; the handing down of a time limit, usually unviable, for the sale of his/her work to a publisher; the stipulation of daily updates on the status of the manuscript. These are all costly mistakes because we usually will not handle manuscripts under these circumstances.

What turns you on? Wit and warmth do wonders. The terrific presentation of ideas and excellent credentials do even bigger wonders.

Description of the Client from Hell: Arrogant writer who doesn't understand why his manuscript wasn't snapped up by a publisher yesterday, and who doesn't understand why agents "deserve" commission.

Description of Dream Client: We have lots of them!

Why did you become an agent? Simenauer: To paraphrase Douglas MacArthur, "Old Editors never die; they just become literary agents." Russell: Having been triple threats as publicist, editor, and author, I thought I would combine them and become formidable.

What might you be doing if you weren't an agent? Simenauer: An investment banker. Russell: A bed-and-breakfast host on Cape Cod.

Comments: Simenauer: Literary agents are more often than not yanked between the demands of the authors and the demands of the publishing houses, finding themselves rendering services *above and beyond*, which often goes unappreciated. That is when I think of becoming an investment banker. Russell: Any writer who doesn't love Mozart need not apply to the Russell-Simenauer Literary Agency.

RUSSELL & VOLKENING, INC.

50 West 29th Street, Suite 7E
New York, NY 10001
212-684-6050

Agents: Joseph Regal, Jennie Dunham.

The following information pertains to JOSEPH REGAL:
Education: English, magna cum laude, Columbia College.
Career history: Entire career spent with Russell & Volkening.
Hobbies/personal interests: Music (classical, jazz, hard rock, blues, etc.), sports (basketball, tennis, running), art, and, of course, books. Also interested in science, especially as it applies to the nature of time and the physics of our existence.
Subjects/categories most enthusiastic about agenting: Mainly interested in fiction, both literary and crime, but no romance or science fiction (which I like but do not agent). Also a fan of well-written nonfiction that tells me something about our

culture or another culture—exploration of who we are and what our future promises (or threatens).

Subjects/categories not interested in agenting: No romance or science fiction, no poetry (agents are more or less useless in that field); I also don't do screenplays or plays, though I do handle those rights if they stem from a book I represent.

Best way for a prospective client to initiate contact: Query letter (with SASE) and short description of the book.

Reading-fee policy: No reading fee. When we receive money for a client, we recover expenses we incur that specifically related to projects by the author. For example, we will recover the cost of sending copies of an author's books abroad to coagents or for photocopying.

Client representation in the following categories: Nonfiction, $33^1/3\%$; Fiction, $66^2/3\%$.

Commission: 10% domestic; 15% motion picture or other dramatic contracts; 20% foreign.

Number of titles sold during the past year: 10.

Approximate percentage of all submissions (from queries through manuscripts) that are rejected: 98%.

The most common mistakes potential clients make when soliciting an agent to represent them: I immediately stop reading if someone sends a query letter telling me they have written the next big bestseller. Also, if they have a long, profitable career ahead of them and seek a like-minded agent to act in synergy—well, who is seeking a dysfunctional, unprofitable relationship? I am also ever amazed at the number of query letters that arrive with typos. What kind of writer pays so little attention to his/her writing?

What writers can do to enhance their chances of getting an agent (besides being good writers): Many queries are clever, with multicolored paper clips or exciting stationery, et cetera, but in the end, the only thing that matters is the idea and the writing. If that is there and clearly presented, I am enthusiastic.

Description of the Client from Hell: There is no Client from Hell. I am straightforward with each client from the start; so far that has prevented any impossible expectations or enraging situations. It can be annoying when someone is not aware of the limitations of the agent's powers: If an editor does not want to buy the book, we cannot make him or her buy it.

Description of the Dream Client: Again, there is no Dream Client; we are all human and by and large rational creatures. I do prefer clients who are realistic about their writing and the market.

Why did you become an agent? I've always loved books, and in an agent's position I get to be more involved with every stage of the writing and development and publication than in any other job. It excites me to look for the next John Irving, or even to know that I have eased a writer's life and made them feel safe and comfortable.

What might you be doing if you weren't an agent? Selling vacuum cleaners door-to-door.

Comments: I would like to plug small agencies. (Here I admit that Russell & Volkening, founded in 1940, has only three agents). I can understand why writers would be attracted to bigger agencies—the lure of being at a place with 30 other bestselling authors, the lure of having legions of people working on various rights for you—but I strongly believe small agencies serve writers better. When I represent an author, I am involved with every aspect of his/her career. S/he is not a little fish in a big sea, nor are other people who may not like his/her book as much as I do working on various rights. When I make a commitment to a writer, it is more serious (and thus we choose more carefully) than if an agent with 50 other authors decides to try you and see how it goes. The relationship between author and agent is probably the most important in the business these days, and you should make sure that you have a communicative, honest, dedicated agent and that the connection is fulfilling.

The following information pertains to JENNIE DUNHAM:
Education: Princeton University (anthropology major).
Career history: Before getting my position at Russell & Volkening, I worked for John Brockman Associates and Mildred Marmur Associates. I have always been on the agency side of the business.
Hobbies/personal interests: Book arts and papermaking, movies, photography, Old English, language and linguistics, feminist/women's studies, travel, science, and religion.
Subjects/categories most enthusiastic about agenting: Quality fiction, nonfiction, children's.
Subjects/categories not interested in agenting: Romance, science fiction, poetry, horror, individual short stories.
Best way for a prospective client to initiate contact: Write a letter describing the project and the author's qualifications for the project and enclose the customary SASE for a response. Please do not send sample material unless requested. If the project seems as if I might be interested, I will request it.
Client representation in the following categories: Nonfiction, 40%; Fiction, 25%; Textbooks, 5%; Children's, 30%.
Approximate percentage of all submissions (from queries through manuscripts) that are rejected: The majority.
The most common mistakes potential clients make when soliciting an agent to represent them: In this day of computers, I think it's a mistake to send a form query letter without a specific person's name in the salutation. Also, sometimes writers address agents familiarly as if they knew them, which really should be reserved for people who do know them personally.
What writers can do to enhance their chances of getting an agent (besides being good writers): Professionalism, good writing, and good ideas.
Description of the Client from Hell: The client from hell is the exact opposite of the dream client—unproductive, unsuccessful, uninteresting, and unpleasant.
Description of the Dream Client: A client who is productive, successful, interesting, and pleasant is a good client.
Why did you become an agent? I collect books, and as an agent I like helping bring books to the world. I like the variety of book projects I handle as an agent. I receive great satisfaction in protecting authors by negotiating contracts for them. Ever since my first job as an agent, I knew that this is what I wanted for a career.

What might you be doing if you weren't an agent? Maybe I would be an anthropologist or a professor (English/folklore/communications). Maybe I would try to do business in a foreign country.

THE SAGALYN LITERARY AGENCY

4825 Bethesda Avenue, Suite 302
Bethesda, MD 20814
301-718-6440
fax: 301-718-6444

Agent: Raphael Sagalyn.

Subjects/categories most enthusiastic about agenting: Adult fiction and nonfiction.

Subjects/categories not interested in agenting: Cookbooks, children's, and poetry.

Best way for a prospective client to initiate contact: Send a cover letter, resume, and SASE. Please, no manuscripts, faxes, or telephone calls.

Representative titles sold:

The 500 Year Delta by Jim Taylor and Watts Wacker (HarperBusiness).

The Corner by Davis Simon (Broadway).

A Firing Offense by David Ignatius (Random).

The Invention That Changed the World: A History of Radar by Robert Buderi (Simon & Schuster).

The Moral Animal by Robert Wright (Pantheon).

Rising Ride: The Mississippi River Flood of 1927 by John Barry (Simon & Schuster).

The Second Curve by Dr. Ian Morrison (Ballantine).

Bowling Alone by Professor Robert D. Putnam (Simon & Schuster).

The Individualized Corporation by Christopher Bartlett and Sumantra Ghoshal (HarperBusiness).

VICTORIA SANDERS LITERARY AGENCY

241 Avenue of the Americas
New York, NY 10014
212-633-8811

Agent: Victoria Sanders.

Born: Hollywood, California.

Education: B.F.A., New York University, 1983; J.D., Benjamin N. Cardozo School of Law, 1988.

Career history: WNET/Channel 13 (PBS); Simon & Schuster Inc.; Carol Mann Agency; Charlotte Sheedy Agency; founded own agency in 1992.

Subjects/categories most enthusiastic about agenting: Fiction: literary and commercial. Nonfiction: history biography, politics, sociology, psychology. Special interests: African-American, Latin, women's, gay and lesbian work.

Subjects/categories not interested in agenting: Hard science, children's, textbooks.

Best way for a prospective client to initiate contact: Query letter with SASE.

Reading-fee policy: No reading fee.

Client representation in the following categories: Nonfiction, 50%; Fiction, 50%.

Commission: 15% straight; 20% if coagented foreign; 20% if coagented to film, TV (though I tend to handle my own, and then it's 15%).

Approximate percentage of all submissions (from queries through manuscripts) that are rejected: 90%.

Representative titles sold:

Sisters and Lovers by Connie Briscoe (HarperCollins), commercial novel.

Big Girls Don't Cry by Connie Briscoe (HarperCollins), commercial novel.

Bertice: The World According to Me by Dr. Bertice Berry (Scribner), inspirational memoir.

Flight of the Blackbird by Faye McDonald Smith (Scribner), commercial fiction.

He Say/She Say by Yolanda Joe (Doubleday), commercial fiction.

Caribe by Evangeline Blanco (Doubleday), literary fiction.

Featherbed Resistance: Selected Letters of Zora Neale Hurston edited by Dr. Carla Kaplan (Doubleday), nonfiction.

Straight from the Ghetto by Dr. Bertice Berry and Joan Coker, M.D. (St. Martin's Press), humor.

How to Stay Single Forever by Jenny Lombard (Warner Books), humor.

Grace the Table by Alexander Smalls (HarperCollins), cookbook/memoir.

The most common mistakes potential clients make when soliciting an agent to represent them: Don't query if you are unsure or hesitant about submitting without additional information on the agency or current clients.

What writers can do to enhance their chances of getting an agent (besides being good writers): The project is the most important part. A good novel or nonfiction project idea is always exciting.

Why did you become an agent? It's the best of both worlds. I get to read manuscripts and negotiate deals. I came from L.A. and film, and, after getting a law degree, realized that the best part of the entertainment business was in bridging the gap between the writer or artist and the producer or publisher. I love being the representative and friend of my clients.

What might you be doing if you weren't an agent? A producer.

HAROLD SCHMIDT LITERARY AGENCY

343 West 12th Street, Suite 1B
New York, NY 10014
212-727-7473

Agent: Harold Schmidt.

Born: Cincinnati, Ohio.

Education: University of Southern California, B.A., and graduate studies.

Career history: Creative Management Associates, 1974–1975; International Creative Management, 1975–1979; William Morris Agency, Inc., 1979–1983.

Subjects/categories not interested in agenting: Juveniles, romances.

Best way for a writer to initiate contact: Please send a query with SASE before submitting manuscript.

Reading-fee policy: No reading fee.

Client representation in the following categories: Nonfiction, 40%; Fiction, 60%.

Commission: 15% of domestic, dramatic; 20% on UK and foreign translation.

Approximate percentage of all submissions (from queries through manuscripts) that are rejected: 98%.

Representative titles sold:

The Gangster of Love by Jessica Hagedorn (Houghton Mifflin/Penguin).

The Dogs by Rebecca Brown (HarperCollins).

The King of Kings and I by Jaffe Cohen (HarperCollins San Francisco).

The Other World by John Wynne (City Lights).

Coming Out of Shame by Gershen Kaufman and Lev Raphael (Doubleday).

The most common mistakes potential clients make when soliciting an agent to represent them: Calling to pitch their work on the phone—please send a query letter instead. Faxed queries are also discouraged.

What writers can do to enhance their chances of getting an agent (besides being good writers): A detailed, carefully thought-out and professionally presented query letter is very important.

Description of the Client from Hell: A client with unrealistic expectations about his work and/or a client who is too impatient with the amount of time it takes to evaluate material, find a publisher, and negotiate an agreement.

What might you be doing if you weren't an agent? I am confident I would be involved with books and probably motion pictures in one capacity or another. And there's a part of me that has always wanted to own a used-book store.

SEBASTIAN LITERARY AGENCY

333 Kearny Street, Suite 708
San Francisco, CA 94108
415-391-2331

Agent: Laurie Harper.

Born: September 1954.

Education: Business and finance, with pre-law studies.

Career history: The literary agency was founded in 1985. It evolved simultaneously with the closing of my small Bay Area regional publishing company (Sebastian Publishing), which published gift books, selling to B. Dalton, Waldenbooks, and independents throughout the West Coast. After I placed books with other publishers for authors I could not publish, I discovered my strengths as an agent. I briefly experienced the author's side of publishing (very enlightening) by writing a media biography of a legendary radio personality (*Don Sherwood: The Life and Times of the World's Greatest Disc Jockey*, Prima Publishing, 1989), which enjoyed 12 weeks on the *San Francisco Chronicle*'s bestseller list. Prior to publishing, I was in banking (operations and lending) with a major California bank for 8 years.

Hobbies/personal interests: Apparently my real interests simply lie with people: who they are, what they are doing, where they have been, how they think . . . My insatiable curiosity is about how people live their lives, whether shown in books, film, the arts, or as discussed in local cafes. Being an agent is not only what I do, it's who I am in the sense that it reflects my true interests.

Subjects/categories most enthusiastic about agenting: Business (management, financial/investment, entrepreneurial, career issues, marketing and sales, human resource); biographies (historical, media-related, professional, or political; not family memoirs); consumer reference; health/nutrition; psychology/self-help; gift/inspirational; popular culture; social issues/current affairs; humor; sports.

Subjects/categories not interested in agenting: No fiction at this time. No poetry, children's or young adult, original screenplays, New Age, or scholarly.

Best way for a prospective client to initiate contact: *Please note that I am taking on few new clients at this time.* If, however, you absolutely, positively want me to review your proposal, send a query letter explaining the project, who you are, and why you are doing this book. Feel free to include the proposal, outline, and a sample chapter. And, of course, the SASE. I do not want phone calls unless the author has been referred to me by a client or colleague.

Reading-fee policy: No reading fee or *editorial* fee. I do charge my clients a $100 annual administration fee, which is a nominal contribution to phone and postage expenses incurred on their behalf, which I do not charge back. Once a client has earnings, the annual fee is rarely charged.

Client representation in the following categories: Nonfiction, 99%; Fiction, 1%.

Commission: 15% domestic; 20%–25% foreign translation licensing, depending on the territory/subagent; 20% dramatic/film licensing.

Number of titles sold during the past year: It usually averages 15–20.

Approximate percentage of all submissions (from queries through manuscripts) that are rejected: 95%. The majority of new clients come from referrals from my clients or industry professionals and colleagues. However, every submission is read and considered on its own merit.

Representative titles sold:

Good Intentions: The Nine Unconscious Mistakes of Nice People by Duke Robinson (Warner).

David Copperfield's Beyond Imagination created by Janet Berliner, coedited by Janet Berliner and David Copperfield (HarperCollins/Prism), 2-volume fiction anthology.

The Little Book of Big Profits by William Buchsbaum (Macmillan).

Index Mutual Funds by Jerry Tweddell and Jack Pierce (AMACOM).

Mothers Are Like Miracles by Janet Lanese (Fireside/Simon & Schuster).

The Food Lover's Guide to Type II Diabetes by Elaine Magee (John Wiley).

A Garden Full of Teapots by Michele Rivers (Cumberland House).

Holistic Pregnancy and Childbirth by James Marti (John Wiley).

Stock Car: Inside the Business of the Fastest Growing Sport by Robert Hagstrom, Jr. (John Wiley).

The Rebellious Body: Reclaim Your Life from Environmental Illness or Chronic Fatigue Syndrome by Janice Wittenberg (Plenum/Insight).

The most common mistakes potential clients make when soliciting an agent to represent them: It is a costly mistake to use anything other than the current year's re-source material when exploring potential agents. Too much changes in the constant motion of publishing and agencies to use last year's guide. It is also counterproductive to query without providing the agent sufficient orientation and information. We are reading the proposal cold. The author has to make it make sense; give it a proper frame-work. Demonstrate that you know the market for your book; what's been published, how your book fits into the scheme of things. You must answer the obvious questions: Who cares? Why? Are these book-buying people? How many are there? Can anyone find them? What do you specifically have to offer a publisher who would invest in this project? Publishing is, after all, first and foremost a business . . . not an endowment for the arts or for hobbyists.

What writers can do to enhance their chances of getting an agent (besides being good writers)? A solid, well-thought-out and well-written package that presents a pro-fessional, intelligent book and author. Even if I can't take that author, I will try to give the professional writer information or suggestions for other agents.

Description of the Client from Hell: The first thing has to be unrealistic expecta-tions; financial and promotional expectations that are simply not realistic for as-yet-unproven authors. For previously unpublished authors, it's understandable that they don't know the industry, but it is incumbent upon each prospective author to inform him/herself on the basics. Attend some conferences; do some reading; talk to other pub-lished authors. I'm happy to coach an author about strategy or problem solving, to help plan out a realistic publishing career path, but the agent can't be in charge of teaching Publishing 101. Another difficulty comes if the author expects the agent to perform miracles: We can't sell what isn't salable. It is the author's responsibility to consider and reflect upon the feedback given by agents and publishers, and to use that to im-prove the manuscript's potential for publication. I expect my clients to be mature pro-fessional adults, capable of approaching this process positively and constructively. No whining allowed.

Description of Dream Client: I fortunately have many. They can be described as committed; deeply thoughtful and caring about both the writing of their books and cul-tivating all the relationships inherent in a publishing *team*; honest and straightforward in their dealings; responsible in doing what they promise, when they promise it. This client is mindful and appreciative of the fact that the agent represents many clients and the editors have many authors, each of whom expect and deserve honest, focused, pro-ductive efforts to be made on their behalf. These clients make it all worthwhile, for everyone, and we go the extra mile for them.

Why did you become an agent? I love books—reading the learning, and I enjoy each of the diverse challenges of publishing. Books are fundamental to our society, and I take pride in being part of their contribution. There is enormous satisfaction from cre-ating a successful team—make the right match between author and publisher, negotiating a fair contract that promotes a successful venture, and assisting in every way to build long-lasting relationships.

What might you be doing if you weren't an agent? I would most likely be in contract law, perhaps working for the Authors Guild.

Comments: There is much that can be criticized and ridiculed in this industry. It's no secret that it isn't a well-run business, per se, or that there is precious little logic to it. But it is a constantly evolving business and each of us in it are charged with making our own contribution, as authors, agents, and publishers. It serves no constructive purpose to sit around bashing and trashing everything that goes wrong. I would like to see and hear more about what goes right and see a greater sharing of helpful information and experience. If you don't like the challenges of publishing, don't do it. If you enjoy the challenge, make a contribution to the best interests it serves. Don't worry about what everyone else does or doesn't do; do what you think is right and good.

THE SEYMOUR AGENCY

475 Miner Street Road
Canton, NY 13617
315-386-1831
fax: 315-386-1037

Agents: Mary Sue Seymour, Michael J. Seymour.

Birth: MSS: September 21, 1952. MJS: August 19, 1948.

Education: MSS: B.S., State University at Potsdam, New York; postgraduate work with Potsdam State, Ithaca College, Azusa Pacific College. MJS: B.S., Siena College, NY; M.S., St. Lawrence University; M.A., SUNY at Potsdam.

Career history: MSS: Taught 11 years in the public-school system; professional artist; currently teach part-time; freelance writer published in several national magazines. MJS: Taught over 20 years; columnist for newspaper group and regional editor for a magazine; Coast Guard captain—run fishing charter service seasonally.

Hobbies/personal interests: MSS: Piano, reading, alpine skiing, swimming, hiking, camping in the Adirondacks(!). MJS: Fishing, hunting—and then there's writing about fishing and hunting.

Subjects/categories most enthusiastic about agenting: Both agents: any women's fiction or romance; nonfiction proposals of any type; *any* quality fiction.

Materials not interested in agenting: Children's books, screenplays, short stories.

Best way for a prospective client to initiate contact with you: One to two-page query letter with first three chapters and three- to four-page synopsis. (Enclose SASE.)

Reading-fee policy: *No* reading fee, handling fee, management fee, or charge for office expenses (phone calls).

Client representation in the following categories: Nonfiction, 25%; Fiction, 75%.

Commission: 15% pre-published authors (commission for our published authors is negotiable); 20% foreign sales.

Number of titles sold during the past year: Several.

Approximate percentage of all submissions, from queries to manuscripts, that are rejected: 90%.

Representative titles sold:

Code Alpha by Joe Massucci (Leisure Books).

Flint Hills Journey by Cassandra Austin (Harlequin Historicals).

Whispers of the River by Tom Hron (Dutton Signet).

Whispers of the Mountain by Tom Hron (Dutton Signet).

Whispers of the Winds by Tom Hron (Dutton Signet).

Fool's Paradise by Tori Phillips (Harlequin Historicals).

Silent Knight by Tori Phillips (Harlequin Historicals).

Midsummer's Knight by Tori Phillips (Harlequin Historicals).

Taking Charge of our Lives by Jim Metcalf (Performance Development Training).

Bride Trilogy and one lead title by Tamara Leigh (Bantam).

Description of the Client from Hell: Never had one.

Description of Dream Client: A Dream Client is one who writes a lot, uses suggestions, is enthusiastic about her/his writing, appreciates what we try to do for him/her, and sends us a book we can sell.

The most common mistakes potential clients make when soliciting an agent to represent them: Unfocused queries, sending samplings of various chapters, faxing queries instead of enclosing SASE with correspondence.

What writers can do to enhance their chances of getting an agent (besides being good writers): A dynamic lead, dark print with easy-to-read type, focused query, realistic expectations, and professionalism.

Why did you become an agent? We are published authors and have had agency representation from three different agencies and left. We knew something about the profession, judged writing contests, and wanted to help those "almost" writers get started.

What might you be doing if you weren't an agent? MSS: giving private piano lessons; a professional watercolorist. MJS: teaching full-time.

Comments: Thousands of musicians are out of work in this country, but that doesn't diminish the quality of their music. Rejections don't diminish writers as people. Writing is a process. If you are willing to stay with it and endure the frustration of constant rewrites, you might make it. Not everyone gets a book published, but no one can accurately predict who will and who won't.

THE ROBERT E. SHEPARD AGENCY

4111 18th Street, Suite 3
San Francisco, CA 94114
415-255-1097
sfbiblio@well.com (e-mail)

Agent: Robert Shepard.
  Born: 1961, New Jersey.

Education: B.A. and M.A., English, University of Pennsylvania.

Career history: After writing speeches and doing research for a prominent professor of urban studies, I clawed my way into trade publishing, remaining at Addison-Wesley for nearly nine years. I spent time on the editorial, sales, and marketing sides of the business (ultimately in charge of a multimillion-dollar sales department), and later did some business consulting. But I missed my literary roots and am glad to be working with authors again.

Hobbies/personal interests: Hiking, biking, trains, and diagramming sentences.

Subjects/categories most enthusiastic about agenting: Nonfiction: especially subjects from the *social science* side of the aisle; current affairs, sociology, psychology, sexuality (especially gay/lesbian nonfiction), health, history, Judaica, biography, personal finance, business, and the *soft* side of science. But I regularly digress.

Subjects/categories not interested in agenting: I love fiction but do not represent it. In general, I stay away from works aimed solely at professional or academic audiences, and I'm extremely wary of collections and highly autobiographical works—although sometimes I can be convinced.

Best way for a prospective client to initiate contact: E-Mail (<sfbiblio@well.com>) is the best way. Otherwise, query letter (with SASE). Never call or fax. It won't speed consideration of your proposal.

Reading-fee policy: No reading fee.

Client representation in the following categories: Nonfiction, 100%; Fiction, 0%.

Commission: 15% domestic.

Number of titles sold during the past year: 10. We have deliberately kept the practice small in order to devote time to our clients. We are happy to see proposals from new authors (or published authors who are new to the trade side of publishing), provided that their credentials fit the work they are proposing.

Approximate percentage of all submissions (from queries through manuscripts) that are rejected: 98%.

Representative titles sold:

The Late Start Investor by John Wasik (Henry Holt).

New Men: The Making of Priests in the Heart of the Vatican by Brian Murphy (Grosset/Putnam).

The Rough Guide to Seattle by Richie Unterberger (Rough Guides).

The Healing Art of Tai Chi by Dr. Martin Lee (Sterling).

Wild and Outside: How a Renegade Minor League Revived the Spirit of Baseball by Stefan Fatsis (Walker).

Untitled book on personal finance by Jean Sherman Chatzky (Wiley).

The most common mistakes potential clients make when soliciting an agent to represent them: A big one is failing to share the proposal with a friend, another writer, or a trusted advisor before sending it out. Not to sound like the English teacher I sometimes think I should have been, but bad spelling and grammar spell doom. And a loyal ally can sometimes give you valuable feedback. I also dislike the classic proposal clichés: "There is no competition." "This is just like a Tracy Kidder/Peter Mayle/Martha Stewart/Tom Peters book."—etc. And I require SASE, but I hate to put that in the same league.

What writers can do to enhance their chances of getting an agent (besides being good writers)? Go to a good, independent bookstore. It's essential for authors to have some perspective on their work, and that means knowing all about books that are similar, or that an agent might mistake as being similar, and (in another vein) being able to talk about authors you respect whose work is in some ways akin to yours. There's nothing more helpful to me than a short overview that answers questions like these: Why did you write this book? What need does it fill? What audience do you envision? What are some books like yours, even if they are terrible (and say why)? Why are you the right person to write this book? What would you like your work to achieve that hasn't been achieved before? Browsing in bookstores, and buying and reading a few recent works, can be very helpful as you answer those questions. I recommend libraries, too, but it's essential to stay current.

Description of the Client from Hell: One who's good at selling an agent or editor on a book but doesn't want to actually write it. Writing is tough and an agent tries to help, but in the end the responsibility is the author's.

Description of Dream Client: One who is passionate about writing, passionate about his or her subject, and appreciative when things go right.

Why did you become an agent? I love books and believe they can and should still be central to our cultural life. But at a time when we're producing ever more titles, I think many of them are poorly crafted, in every sense. I see authors who still feel the creative urge but whose experiences in publishing have soured them to the whole enterprise, and I see editors who love what they do but feel overextended and underappreciated in the difficult business climate of the 1990s. In such an environment, I think an agent can be more than just someone who sells books, but rather one who can restore the health to some of those relationships that, for better or worse, are keys to the *business* of publishing. I try to create ongoing author-editor dialogues and play the role of moderator when it's helpful or necessary. When everything works, we can end up with books that are well written, well edited, and well marketed, and everyone can walk away ready and enthusiastic to do it again.

What might you be doing if you weren't an agent? It could go one of three ways: Either I would go back and get that Ph.D. and write papers on 19th-century authors who were extremely prominent in their day but paradoxically have become totally obscure (probably due to bad marketing), or I would be conducting a symphony orchestra, or I would be riding trains somewhere in an attempt to escape my job as publisher of a distinguished literary nonfiction house. I'm not picky.

LEE SHORE AGENCY, LTD.

Sterling Building
440 Friday Road
Pittsburgh, PA 15209
412-821-0440
800-898-7886 (for brochure and guidelines requests only)

LeeShore1@aol.com (e-mail)
http://www.olworld.com/olworld/m_1shore/ (World Wide Web) (use for instant access to brochure and guidelines)

Agent: Cynthia Sterling.

> **Born:** June 21, 1953; Johnstown, Pennsylvania.
>
> **Education:** University of Pittsburgh.
>
> **Career history:** Departmental assistant of nuclear medicine and cardiopulmonary functions; writing instructor.
>
> **Hobbies/personal interests:** Chairman for Sterling Foundation (nonprofit, tax exempt), which assists writers and artists; authoring and coauthoring on a variety of subjects; collecting art and antiques; gardening.
>
> **Subjects/categories most enthusiastic about agenting:** Trade, textbooks, scholarly, good fiction, both mass-market and genre; true stories.
>
> **Subjects/categories not interested in agenting:** Children's, poetry, plays, articles.
>
> **Best way for a prospective client to initiate contact with you:** Phone, personal letter with brief synopsis, stop by office (an appointment is necessary).
>
> **Reading-fee policy:** No fee for established authors. $125 evaluation fee for unpublished writers.
>
> **Client representation in the following categories:** Nonfiction, 34%; Fiction, 55%; Textbooks, 10%; Children's, 1%.
>
> **Commission:** 15% domestic; 20% foreign.
>
> **Number of titles sold during the past year:** 125.
>
> **Approximate percentage of all submissions (from queries through manuscripts) that are rejected:** 80%.
>
> **Representative titles sold:**
>
> *Stay Tuned . . .* by James E. Duffy (Dunhill).
>
> *The View from Rampart Street* by Mary Lou Widmer (Caramoor).
>
> *Hero's Journey in Literature* by Evans Lansing Smith (University Press of America).
>
> *Una's Song* by Megan Davidson (Zebra).
>
> *Hell's Creation* by John Russo (Ravenmor).
>
> *End the Pain* by Dr. Lynn Hawker and Terry Bicehouse (Zinn Publishing Group).
>
> *Getting Your Manuscript Sold* by Sterling and Davidson (Barclay).
>
> *The Rescue of Jennifer Lynn* (made-for-TV movie) (Benchmark Pictures).
>
> **The most common mistakes potential clients make when soliciting an agent to represent them:** Maybe it's that maturity thing, but around this agency we give all writers the benefit of the doubt. After all, not all the advice or information the writer receives from many sources is necessarily the way the real world works. Once in a while, I'll read to the staff a letter that is particularly off-base. We'll all shake our heads, then give the writer the same polite consideration we give all prospective clients.
>
> **What writers can do to enhance their chances of getting an agent (besides being good writers):** Have a professional approach with respect for my time and expertise—a rarity indeed.
>
> **Description of the Client from Hell:** Once upon a time I could give a vivid description of clients from both Heaven and Hell. After being in the business as long as I have,

meeting the people I've met, and traveling to various countries in pursuit of manu-scripts and education, I suppose I've grown a little wiser. Now I see my clients as people who, for their own set of reasons, act and react the way they do. I try to commu-nicate clearly both my praises and concerns regarding their attitude and listen to their concerns as well. After all, in the end, the client has the choice to seek representation elsewhere. I'm proud to say that most clients choose to stay with us.

Description of Dream Client: I would describe my dream client as being John Grisham, or Stephen King, or Tom Clancy, or any top-selling author of their caliber. If they're looking for an agent, I'm here. (I can dream, can't I?) Now, back to an obtain-able dream. A dream client is one who, first and foremost, can write; knows his audi-ence; is willing to learn rules and play by them; has a business side to them; can talk with (not to) their agent; understands that there are certain things in the industry that just *are* and cannot be changed, thereby making some points nonnegotiable; who is courteous, friendly, has a sense of humor, sends me expensive gifts, and realizes that I am the Queen . . . I just slid way back to la la land.

Why did you become an agent? My main purpose is to establish a writers' and artists' retreat. To do so, I needed to understand everything about writers, publishers, distributors, the art of writing, and running a business. The agent is like the hub in a wheel: As the wheel turns, each spoke brings in new information.

What might you be doing if you weren't an agent? I'd be an author full time, tak-ing another path to establish the writers' and artists' retreat.

Comments: Writing is a creative process, of course, but writing is also a craft. To learn that craft takes time, patience, and courage. The road to mastery is at least 10 years long, and most writers never become masters. But that does not mean you cannot get published at an earlier stage in your development. Remember, creativity without structure is chaos. So enjoy what you write, but work at your craft and know your audi-ence. Once you understand the conventions of writing—then you can experiment, cre-ate something new and different. If you are calling your work new and different just because you don't understand the conventions of writing, in the end (like a newspaper at the bottom of a bird cage) you'll have crap. Oops—I mean a mess.

MICHAEL SNELL LITERARY AGENCY

P.O. Box 1206
Truro, MA 02666-1206
508-349-3718

Agent: Michael Snell, President.

Born: August 16, 1945.

Education: B.A., DePauw University, Phi Beta Kappa.

Career history: Editor, Wadsworth Publishing Company (1967–1978); executive editor, Addison-Wesley (1978–1979); owner, Michael Snell Literary Agency (1979–present).

Hobbies/personal interests: Tennis, golf, shellfishing, fishing.

Subjects/categories most enthusiastic about agenting: Specialize in all types of business books, from low-level career, how-to, and self-help to sophisticated advanced professional and reference. Careers, management, leadership, small business, entrepreneurial, finance (personal and corporate), computer books (both trade and professional), and business technology. Popular psychology, especially how-to, self-help, and health/fitness. Pets and animals.

Subjects/categories not interested in agenting: New age, personal memoirs, poetry, non-commercial fiction and nonfiction, religion.

Best way for a prospective client to initiate contact with you: Send a one-page query letter (with SASE) outlining the topic and the author's credentials.

Reading-fee policy: No reading fee, except for added percentages for developmental editing and writing from author's advances and royalties, if and when agreed upon in advance of a publisher's contract. The publisher, not the author, pays these additional percentages according to the publisher's contract.

Client representation in the following categories: Nonfiction, 25%; Fiction, 25%; Textbooks, 25%; Children's, 25%.

Commission: 15% of advances and royalties.

Number of titles sold during the past year: 36.

Approximate percentage of all submissions (from queries through manuscripts) that are rejected: 90%.

Representative titles sold:

The Eleven Commandments of Wildly Successful Women by Pamela Gilberd (Macmillan Spectrum).

Body Learning by Virginia Whitelaw (Putnam Perigee).

Catperfect by Myrna Milani (Contemporary).

The Joy of Horses by Joy Roberts (Contemporary).

Marketing Strategies That Work by Barry Frig (Prentice Hall).

The Complete Idiot's Guide to Managing a Business by Hap Klopp and Brian Tarcy (Alpha).

The Complete Idiot's Guide to Football by Joe Thiesman and Brian Tarcy (Alpha).

From Book Idea to Bestseller by Michael Snell (Prima).

The Color-Blind Career by Ollie Stevenson and Dana Heubler (Peterson's).

60 Second Pain Relief by Peter Lehndorff and Brian Tarcy (New Horizons).

Digital Image Processing by Howard Burdick (McGraw-Hill).

Leadership IQ by Emmett Murphy (Wiley).

Heart Zone Training by Sally Edwards (Adams).

Bulletproofing Windows 95 by Glen Weadock (McGraw-Hill).

Advertising Methods That Work by Fred Hahn (Prentice Hall).

Analytical Tools for Financial Advisors by Ed McCrathy (Irwin).

Selling to Tough Customers by Josh Gordon (AMACOM).

Reinventing the Business Meeting by Ava Butler (McGraw-Hill).

Futuresex by Ken Maxwell (Plenum).

Vestpocket Guide to Business Writing by Deborah Dumaine (Prentice Hall).

Insider's Guide to Growing a Small Business by Pete Richman (Macmillan).

The Science Almanac by Ed Francis (Plenum).

Powerpoint Presentations by Glenn and Emily Weadock (IDG Books).

The most common mistakes potential clients make when soliciting an agent to represent them: The author who insists that her/his book will be an automatic bestseller but has not created a compelling proposal or manuscript. Many authors fail to analyze their market, their audience, and their competition fully enough. Authors who depend on friends, family, and amateurs for approval of their work but fail to obtain professional evaluation often live in a world of illusion and do not improve their work sufficiently. Others turn us off by acting as if they are considering hiring us, when the opposite is true: We are considering whether or not to invest valuable time, money, and expertise in advising them and helping them success.

What writers can do to enhance their chances of getting an agent (besides being good writers): We like writers who know their limitations with respect to understanding how publishing really works and who appreciate the need for joining with us in a partnership ruled by a clear division of labor, where they do their job (learning to develop winning material) and we do ours (providing developmental advice, marketing, and contract negotiation). We respond to brief query letters that get to the point about the topic and the author's background. A sense of humor, an eagerness to learn, a desire to affect people's lives in a positive and lasting way always help. Our hearts go out to *pragmatic idealists.*

Description of the Client from Hell: The expert on a subject who thinks she/he is an expert on publishing. The ambitious writer who will not listen to, and learn from, our 30 years of publishing experience. The author who is in a big hurry and cannot come to terms with the slow process of publishing a book. The author who wants so desperately to make money that she/he pays too little attention to shaping an excellent book proposal and manuscript that will appeal to editors and readers; those who write to make money seldom do, but those who write to change people's lives often do (and make money automatically).

Description of Dream Client: A person who knows a subject intimately, possesses professional credentials in that subject, and can write reasonably well. Someone who knows how to listen, learn, and take direction from publishing professionals. An author so committed to the subject that she/he will promote it tirelessly, regardless of the publisher's promotional budget. *A sense of humor.*

Why did you become an agent? A lifelong love of books, a belief that books can make a big difference in people's lives, and 13 years of working successfully as an editor/publisher. Bringing a book to market is like growing a garden or birthing a child: the harvest, the birth provides a deep satisfaction no amount of money can buy. We make a good living helping writers achieve both personal and financial satisfaction. The work gives us a perfect blend of idealism, lasting influence, and wealth creation.

What might you be doing if you weren't an agent? I suppose my impulse to grow and develop books could find a satisfying outlet in many fields, especially teaching or business. The art of turning an idea into a tangible product consumers find useful or uplifting applies not just to books but to everything from computers to farming. The joy of watching a student grow and develop could come from almost any educational endeavor, from software instruction to shaping bonsai trees.

Comments: We have grown increasingly weary of all the hype surrounding computers and the so-called information superhighway, because we believe that the *quality* of content will always be more important than the channel of distribution via which that content reaches people. We've published computer books since 1967, so we keep abreast of the field, but the quality of submitted material has declined while the quantity of material has skyrocketed. We continue to work hard to help writers generate the intellectual properties from which they can derive both personal satisfaction and income regardless of the means whereby their audience will obtain those properties.

Our advice to authors: Worry about content, worry about clear and concise and interesting communication, develop your subject matter and writing credentials, work with and learn from publishing professionals, and remain patient, perseverant, and humble as you do so. Your computer won't make you smarter. And electronic distribution of your work will not make it more creative, more useful, or even more valuable.

We keep stressing the old-fashioned qualities that make a book (or any sort of communication) valuable: work, work, work, learn, learn, learn, revise, revise, revise.

THE SNYDER LITERARY AGENCY

7123 East Jan Avenue
Mesa, AZ 85208
602-985-9400 (telephone and fax)

Agent: Dawn M. Snyder.
   Born: July 22, 1964; Baltimore, Maryland.
   Education: University of Maryland.
   Career history: Freelance writer for eight years; editor for several publishing houses and agents.
   Hobbies/personal interests: Traveling, writing, my husband, and my children.
   Subjects/categories most enthusiastic about agenting: Adult fiction and nonfiction, scripts, children's fiction with a message.
   Subjects/categories not interested in agenting: We are open to most subjects.
   Best way for a prospective client to initiate contact: Query letter with one-page synopsis and SASE.
   Reading-fee policy: No reading fee.
   Client representation in the following categories: Nonfiction, 50%; Fiction, 25%, Children's, 10%; Scripts, 15%.
   Commission: 15% on domestic sales; 20% on foreign sales.
   Description of the Client from Hell: Someone who constantly calls, is unrealistic in his expectations, and *knows* he has the next bestseller.
   Description of Dream Client: Professional, patient, understanding—all of which you must be in this business.
   The most common mistakes potential clients make when soliciting an agent to represent them: Sending manuscripts that have not been proofed. Watch spelling and grammatical errors!

What writers can do to enhance their chances of getting an agent (besides being good writers): Demonstrate professionalism—follow agency requirements.

Why did you become an agent? It was suggested to me by publishing houses and agents I edited for. I always admired the work of agents.

What might you be if you weren't an agent? Still writing for the corporate world.

ELYSE SOMMER, INC.

110-34 73rd Road
P.O. Box 751133
Forest Hills, NY 11375-8733
718-263-2668

Agent: Elyse Sommer.

Education: Graduate, major: journalism, minor: marketing, New York University.

Career history: Founded my own agency just four years out of college after a stint as a magazine editor. Agency has always been a one-person operation and remains.

Hobbies/personal interests: Reading, writing, computers, music, skiing.

Subjects/categories most enthusiastic about agenting: Nonfiction books: thoroughly researched, well thought-out, and organized.

Subjects/categories not interested in agenting: Science fiction, poetry, children's picture books.

Best way for a prospective client to initiate contact with you: A query letter that outlines your book, its stage of completion, your credentials, the nature of the submission (multiple or to me only), marketing history, if any. Since it's hard to judge a project from just a letter, a table of contents and writing sample (with SASE for its return) would be helpful.

Reading-fee policy: No reading fee.

Client representation in the following categories: Nonfiction, 80%.

Commission: 15% on manuscripts sold for an advance between $5,000 and $25,000; 10% on advances exceeding $25,000; 20% on advances under $5,000.

Number of titles sold during the past year: This is a small agency. We average a sale a month.

Approximate percentage of all submissions (from queries through manuscripts) that are rejected: As a one-person agent, I am highly selective in what I take on.

The most common mistakes potential clients make when soliciting an agent to represent them: *Fishing expedition* calls about a project on which the writer has done absolutely no work or proposals claiming to be unique when a quick search of the bookshelf or the Internet shows it has indeed been done (and usually better).

What writers can do to enhance their chances of getting an agent (besides being good writers). An interesting, lively style, and a proposal that anticipates questions.

Why did you become an agent? I loved books, and still do. I loved (and still do) seeing an idea turn into something that will entertain and inform many.

SOUTHEAST LITERARY AGENCY

P.O. Box 910
Sharpes, FL 32959
407-632-5019

Agent: Debbie Fine.
   Born: Over 21; New York City.
   Education: Hollins College.
   Career history: Magazine editor; major bookstore chain supervisor; lecturer.
   Subjects/categories most enthusiastic about agenting: Science fiction and most nonfiction works.
   Subjects/categories not interested in agenting: Novellas are very difficult to place.
   Best way for a prospective client to initiate contact: Send a marketing letter stating the genre and who will buy your book and why, as well as a synopsis and complete manuscript.
   Reading-fee policy: No reading fee.
   Client representation in the following categories: Nonfiction, 65%; Fiction, 29%; Children's, 4%; Textbooks, 2%.
   Commission: 10% domestic, 20% foreign.
   Number of titles sold during the past year: Brand new agency.
   Approximate percentage of all submissions (from queries through manuscripts) that are rejected: 90%.
   Representative titles sold:
   The Witness (Book World/Blue Star, Inc.).
   Description of the Client from Hell: Not sure yet, but I'll recognize them when I meet them.
   Description of Dream Client: Someone full of enthusiasm, knows who their market is, and doesn't call frequently to "check in."
   The most common mistakes potential clients make when soliciting an agent to represent them: Do not include self-addressed, stamped envelope and appropriate packaging with postage for manuscript return.
   What writers can do to enhance their chances of getting an agent (besides being good writers): Have a good marketing letter and synopsis that will "sell" their work to me and prospective editors.
   Why did you become an agent? I've always loved reading and the arts.
   Comments: Follow the guidelines of your agent and/or publisher. Send out your best work first. Be persistent but be patient. Frequent calls accomplish little and may work against you.

PHILIP G. SPITZER LITERARY AGENCY

50 Talmage Farm Lane
Easthampton, NY 11937
516-329-3650
fax: 516-329-3651

Agent: Philip Spitzer.

Born: August 6, 1939, New York City.

Education: M.A., New York University Graduate Institute of Book Publishing; M.A., French, University of Paris, France.

Career history: New York University Press, 1961–1962; McGraw-Hill Book Company, trade sales, sales promotion manager, art book department, 1963–1966; John Cushman Associates/Curtis Brown Ltd. Literary Agency, 1966–1969; Philip G. Spitzer Literary Agency, 1969–present.

Hobbies/personal interests: Sports, travel, etc.

Subjects/categories most enthusiastic about agenting: Fiction: literary and suspense. Quality nonfiction including sports, biography, current events.

Subjects/categories not interested in agenting: Most category fiction, most how-to.

Best way for a prospective client to initiate contact with you: Query letter (with SASE).

Reading-fee policy: No reading fee.

Client representation in the following categories: Nonfiction, 50%; Fiction, 50%.

Commission: 15% domestic; 20% foreign.

Number of titles sold during the past year: 30.

Approximate percentage of all submissions (from queries through manuscripts) that are rejected: 95%.

Representative titles sold:

Trunk Music by Michael Connelly (Little, Brown).

Cimarron Rose by James Lee Burke (Hyperion).

Dancing After Hours by Andre Dubus (Knopf).

The Blue Wall by Kenneth Abel (Delacorte).

Dark Witness: Why Black People Must Die by Ralph Wiley (Ballantine).

The Game of Their Lives by Geoffrey Douglas (Holt).

Bearing Secrets by Richard Barre (Walker).

The most common mistakes potential clients make when soliciting an agent to represent them: Telephoning is a mistake.

Description of the Client from Hell: Daily phone calls; impossible to satisfy; if book doesn't sell—either to publisher or subsequently in bookstores—agent is to blame.

Description of Dream Client: Informed; respectful; loyal.

Why did you become an agent? Best job I could find at the time. Started my own business because a publishing friend printed up stationery and business cards.

What might you be doing if you weren't an agent? Book sales representative.

STADLER LITERARY AGENCY

3202 East Greenway, Suite 1307-182
Phoenix, AZ 85032
602-569-2481
fax: 602-569-2265
bookwoma@sprunet.com (e-mail)

Agent: Rose Stadler.

Born: November 23, 1944.

Education: BSW, University of Minnesota, 1979; MSW, Arizona State University (May 1997).

Career history: 20+ years as a social worker; 14+ of those years as a Child Welfare Specialist involved with all areas of neglect and abuse with adoptions, foster care, and developmental disabilities. Statewide training officer. Certified counselor with the Arizona Board of Behavioral Health and Certified College Instructor. Taught social work at the undergraduate level for 5 years and taught (noncredit) fiction writing for 13 years at local community colleges. Presenter for national and local child-abuse prevention seminars.

Hobbies/personal interests: Writing, teaching both writing and social work, camping, photography.

Subjects/categories most enthusiastic about agenting: Fiction: historicals, literary fiction, mysteries, suspense, thrillers, children's literature, anything with movie potential. Nonfiction and social issues also interest me.

Subjects/categories not interested in agenting: Romance, science fiction, fantasy, short stories, war stories, high-tech or sports. I refuse to accept or handle pornography.

Best way for a prospective client to initiate contact: Query letter with sample chapters and SASE.

Reading-fee policy: No reading fee.

Client representation in the following categories: Fiction, 50%; Nonfiction, 50%.

Commission: 15% domestic; 20% foreign.

Number of titles sold during the past year: Since I'm the new kid on the block, I haven't actually sold anything as of this writing. *But*, I have seven authors who look like they might get publishing contracts and four others that are highly promising.

Approximate percentage of all submissions (from queries through manuscripts) that are rejected: Guesstimate: 75%.

What writers can do to enhance their chances of getting an agent (besides being good writers): I love a good laugh, and I love a well-written query letter. When I see professionalism, I respond as fast as I can. Good writing always gets my attention, but when a personal touch is added, it makes the writer a more than a piece of paper.

The most common mistakes potential clients make when soliciting an agent to represent them: Nothing beats a well-written query with adequate SASE, address, home phone number and daytime phone number. It bothers me when writers say, "I have this really great idea . . . and I want *you* to write it for me." A few things bother me about the way some people try to get my attention. One of them is dropping in with twenty pounds of manuscript that they want me to handle, right now! Another thing is poorly packaged manuscripts or boxes that fall apart in the mail.

I would strongly recommend that writers follow the rules of general business. Don't call in the middle of the night. Don't call collect. Don't "pop in" with manuscripts. Always enclose adequate SASE. Don't be rude, overbearing, or pushy. Don't send your grandmother to me on your behalf.

Being insulting or establishing an adversarial relationship with an agent is *not* a good way to do business. Not many, but a few writers think that if they insult their way to the top, they will publish faster. A lot of authors are temperamental and close to the edge, but being rude far outweighs the value of their work.

Description of the Client from Hell: The Client from Hell is a know-it-all who won't take criticism, won't rewrite, turns in sloppy work, won't get things back to me in a timely manner, then blames me for his or her deficits. The client from purgatory is one who forgets the SASE or just adds SASE to cover the cost of a #10 envelope, thinking that if he or she doesn't send the entire SASE, a rejection will not be forthcoming. Nail-biters, telephone callers, pacers bug me, but I can work around these impatient souls better than the know-it-alls.

Description of Dream Client: The ideal client is one who is takes his craft seriously, can take criticism, gets edits and rewrites done in a timely manner, and is pleasant to represent.

Why did you become an agent? I became an agent for several reasons: (1) I had taught fiction writing for 12+ years and have seen 106 of my former students experience the thrill of publication. (2) One of my students camped on my doorstep and begged me to represent him. (I was working full time as a social worker, going to school, teaching and trying to work on my own writing. It couldn't be done.) (3) I finally said, "Oh, all right." (4) A local newspaper picked up on my fly-by-the-seat-of-my-pants part-time job and two days later I had 187 phone calls. And (5) the most important reason of all, I've had my share of rejections, lost manuscripts, agents or publishers who let their dog sleep on my work. So I took a chance. I still love social work, but this combines the love of writing with my "people" skills.

What might you be if you weren't an agent? No doubt about it, I'd still be a social worker, dreaming about "someday."

Comments: To publishers, I would say: "Please give the new writer a chance. Everyone has to start somewhere. Sometimes an agent has to jump through the flaming hoops just to get thirty seconds of your time." To publishers I would also say this: "After a specific editor has accepted a proposal from me, it ends up in the 'unsolicited' slush pile? Why? Wouldn't it be easier to say 'no' at the onset and save us both the trouble?"

To aspiring authors, I would say: "Listen to what the experts have to say to you. Learn something and be willing to murder your darlings when necessary. Be persistent."

STEPPING STONE LITERARY AGENCY

(See entry for Sarah Jane Freymann Literary Agency)

GLORIA STERN AGENCY

2929 Buffalo Speedway, Suite 2111
Houston, TX 77098
713-963-8360

Agent: Gloria Stern.
   Born: New York, New York.

Education: Hunter College; Hans Hoffmann School of Fine Arts.

Career history: Published nonfiction book, 1975; five book clubs; National Press Association Award for Consumer Reporting Book Division; represented ASJA, 1975; started own agency, 1976.

Hobbies/personal interests: Travel, music, reading.

Subjects/categories most enthusiastic about agenting: Literary fiction, good popular fiction, biographies, history, women's issues, politics (by authorities), popular science, health, business, some self-help, literary memoir.

Subjects/categories not interested in agenting: Genre: science fiction, mystery, New Age, romance, fantasy. I cannot represent poetry or short stories by unpublished authors.

Best way for a prospective client to initiate contact: Send a letter consisting of a short, one-page description, including qualifications for chosen subject in nonfiction. For fiction, send a short outline, publication background, and one chapter. All prospective clients should send SASE or a large, stamped envelope for return of manuscript if desired.

Reading-fee policy: No reading fee.

Client representation in the following categories: Nonfiction, 85%; Fiction, 10%; Textbooks, 5%.

Commission: 15%.

Number of titles sold during the past year: 6.

Approximate percentage of all submissions (from queries through manuscripts) that are rejected: 90%.

Representative titles sold:

Faces of Feminism by Sheila Tobias (Westview/HarperCollins).

Sailing Safety by Jeremy Hood (Sheridan House).

Majoring in the Rest of Your Life by Carol Carter (Farrar Straus & Giroux).

Cultural History of Greenwich Village by Ross Wetzsteon (Random House).

Description of the Client from Hell: I don't have one.

Description of Dream Client: One who keeps communication going and completes the book moderately close to the deadline. Also knows how to promote book.

The most common mistakes potential clients make when soliciting an agent to represent them: Most common mistake is to send an unsolicited manuscript.

ROBIN STRAUS AGENCY, INC.

229 East 79th Street
New York, NY 10021
212-472-3282

Agent: Robin Straus.

Education: B.A., Wellesley College; M.B.A., New York University.

Career history: Little, Brown, editorial; Doubleday, subsidiary rights; Random House, subsidiary rights; Wallace & Sheil Agency, agent; Robin Straus Agency since 1983.

Subjects/categories most enthusiastic about agenting: General high-quality fiction and nonfiction.

Subjects/categories not interested in agenting: Science fiction, mysteries, romances, horror, *no screenplays.*

Best way for a prospective client to initiate contact: Letter, sample material, biographical information, and prior submission history—and SASE for *everything* sent.

Reading-fee policy: No reading fee.

Client representation in the following categories: Nonfiction, 65%; Fiction, 30%; Children's, 5%.

Commission: 15% domestic, 20% foreign.

Approximate percentage of all submissions (from queries through manuscripts) that are rejected: 99%.

Representative titles sold:

Authors represented include:

Thomas Flanagan (Dutton), fiction.

Andrew Hacker (Scribner), nonfiction.

J. G. Ballard (Farrar Straus & Giroux/St. Martin's Press), fiction.

Brian Aldiss (St. Martin's Press), fiction.

Frederick Turner (Holt), nonfiction.

James Villas (Morrow), cookbook.

David Burnham (Scribner), nonfiction.

Colum McCann (Metropolitan Books/Holt), fiction.

Theodore Zeldin (HarperCollins), nonfiction.

Colin Eisler (Bulfinch), nonfiction.

Thomas Lickona (Bantam), nonfiction.

Paul Preston (Basic), nonfiction.

Gustaw Herling (Viking), fiction and nonfiction.

The most common mistakes potential clients make when soliciting an agent to represent them: Faxing material or e-mailing.

What writers can do to enhance their chances of getting an agent (besides being good writers): Engaging query letter and sample writing. For nonfiction, professional proposal with solid market research or unique qualities, competition, etc. Good comments on their material from established writers.

ROSLYN TARG LITERARY AGENCY, INC.

105 West 13th Street
New York, NY 10011
212-206-9390
fax: 212-989-6233

Agent: Amy J. Browne

Susan Travis Literary Agency

1317 North San Fernando Boulevard, #175
Burbank, CA 91504
818-557-6538

Agent: Susan Travis.

Education: B.A., English Literature, University of California, Berkeley.

Career history: Prior to establishing my agency in 1995, I spent four years with the Margaret McBride Literary Agency, most recently as an associate agent. Before joining the McBride Agency, I worked in the managing editorial department of Ballantine Books, New York.

Subjects/categories most enthusiastic about agenting: I represent an even mix of fiction and nonfiction and truly enjoy working on both. For fiction, I am currently representing literary and mainstream fiction and am interested in reading just about anything, provided the writing is good and there is depth to the work. My nonfiction interests encompass a wide area. In the past, I've handled cookbooks, self-help/ psychology, health, and business. I would like to receive more nonfiction submissions for books targeted at a general audience, not those aimed at an exclusive or limited market.

Subjects/categories not interested in agenting: I do not represent children's or young-adult works, poetry or screenplays, and I do very little with science fiction and fantasy.

Best way for a prospective client to initiate contact: Fiction: A query letter that gives a brief synopsis or overview of the project and any pertinent information about the author. The letter should be concise. My interest is usually piqued more by a description of the underlying themes in a project rather than a blow-by-blow plot summary. The first 15–20 pages of the manuscript may be enclosed with the query.

Nonfiction: A query letter giving a brief overview of the project and a brief description of the author's credentials or expertise. Or, a complete proposal may be sent. If the manuscript is complete, the author should query first rather than sending the entire manuscript. *A SASE with correct postage must be enclosed for a reply and return of material.*

Reading-fee policy: No reading or marketing fees.

Client representation in the following categories: Nonfiction, 50%; Fiction, 50%.

Commission: 15% domestic, 20% foreign.

Approximate percentage of all submissions (from queries through manuscripts) that are rejected: 90%.

The most common mistakes potential clients make when soliciting an agent to represent them: Verbal/telephone queries seldom work. If an author is trying to market writing, then let the writing speak for itself. Authors have to make the effort to pitch their work using the written word. One of the most costly mistakes an author can make is to market work prematurely. I usually base decisions on an *as is* basis, not the hidden potential. Unpolished manuscripts can rarely compete with those by authors who have taken the extra time to polish their projects and make a professional submission.

What writers can do to enhance their chances of getting an agent (besides being good writers)? I'm looking for good writing, not gimmicks.

Description of Dream Client: Dream clients are those who are professional, business-like, yet friendly, who appreciate input and advice but don't require constant hand-holding.

SUSAN P. URSTADT INC. AGENCY
(See entry for Jeanne Fredericks Literary Agency)

THE RICHARD R. VALCOURT AGENCY, INC.
177 East 77th Street PPHC
New York, NY 10021
212-570-2340 (telephone/fax)

Agent: Richard R. Valcourt.
   Born: November 29, 1941, Fall River, Massachusetts.
   Education: B.A., Roger Williams College; M.A., New York University; A.B.D., City University Graduate School; L.L.B., LaSalle Extension University.
   Career history: Radio-television journalist (1961–1980); program administration, City University of New York (1980–1995); instructor, Department of Political Science, Hunter College (1981–1995); executive editor, International Journal of Intelligence (1986–present); founded Richard Valcourt Agency (1995).
   Hobbies/personal interests: Reading, films, baseball.
   Subjects/categories most enthusiastic about agenting: Nonfiction: government and politics; intelligence and other national security issues; military affairs; biography; political and social commentary; Judaica; some business. Fiction: a very limited amount of historical, political, and military fiction.
   Subjects/categories not interested in agenting: Now rejecting most fiction. Also, New Age, true crime, gardening, cooking, children's books, self-help, psychology, etc.
   Best way for a prospective client to initiate contact: Letter of inquiry (with SASE), brief biography, summary of material.
   Reading-fee policy: No reading fee. May charge for photocopying and phone calls if excessive.
   Client representation in the following categories: Nonfiction, 70%; Fiction, 30%.
   Commission: 15% domestic, 20% foreign.
   Approximate percentage of all submissions (from queries through manuscripts) that are rejected: 90%. In certain situations, I will work with the author to improve the manuscript instead of rejecting outright.
   Description of the Client from Hell: An overconfident author who is unwilling to respond to suggestions for improving a proposal or manuscript. Or an author who attempts to act as marketing specialist for own material. Or whose focus is more on the

work's potential as a movie than as a book. Or who calls or writes too frequently, indicating both impatience and a lack of understanding about the process.

Description of Dream Client: A good writer who, having conducted sufficient research, submits a professional manuscript and supporting materials, and patiently awaits the outcome of a frequently lengthy process.

The most common mistakes potential clients make when soliciting an agent to represent them: Sending unprofessional and incomplete materials; expecting immediate results; failing to inform me that they are querying several agents simultaneously (even when submitting a highly personalized query letter); failing to include SASE or additional postage for return of materials.

What writers can do to enhance their chances of getting an agent (besides being good writers)? Knowing their fields thoroughly; carefully thinking through the process of achieving publication; having realistic expectations; adhering to traditional business ethics and relationships.

Why did you become an agent? A lifelong love of books and the desire to help into print those authors whose works I have a personal wish to read.

What might you be doing if you weren't an agent? Running a small publishing house or editing a journal.

Comments: A solid book is as much a work of art as is a painting or other object. When an author's thoughts are conveyed to a reader through well-chosen words, the end result can be a timeless addition to literature and learning. That kind of book interests me as an agent.

THE VINES AGENCY, INC.

409 East 6th Street, No. 4
New York, NY 10009
212-777-5522
fax: 212-777-5978

Agent: James C. Vines.
Born: May 1, 1966; Huntsville, Alabama.
Education: Auburn University; New York University.
Career history: Raines & Raines, literary agent, 1989–1992; Virginia Barber Literary Agency, literary agent, 1993–1995; The Vines Agency, Inc., literary agent, 1995–present.
Subjects/categories most enthusiastic about agenting: Current events, pop culture, mainstream novels, graphic novels, music, suspense thrillers, film/television, celebrities, literary novels, comic novels, mystery novels.
Subjects/categories not interested in agenting: If it's well written, I want to see it.
Best way for a prospective client to initiate contact: Query with one-page letter describing the story, along with SASE.
Reading-fee policy: No reading fee.

Client representation in the following categories: Nonfiction, 49%; Fiction, 49%; Children's, 2%.

Commission: 15% domestic, 20% foreign.

Number of titles sold during the past year: 30.

Approximate percentage of all submissions (from queries through manuscripts) that are rejected: I reject 99% of the "over the transom" submissions I receive. The book must truly stand out.

Representative titles sold:

The Death and Life of Bobby Z by Don Winslow (Knopf).

Pest Control by Bill Fitzhugh (Avon).

Unbridled Power by Shelley Davis (HarperCollins).

Courage to Love by Barry Stopfel and Will Leckie (Doubleday).

Looking Great by Linda Dano (Putnam).

Rumble Tumble by Joe R. Lansdale (Warner Books).

Description of the Client from Hell: I do not represent hellish clients.

Description of Dream Client: See my list of authors under representative titles sold.

The most common mistakes potential clients make when soliciting an agent to represent them: Writing 12-page cover letters (single-spaced), sending chapters from the middle of the novel claiming "those are the best," and calling to see if I've had a chance to read the material yet.

What writers can do to enhance their chances of getting an agent (besides being good writers): A writer must make himself/herself relevant. Think about the national and international dialogue, think about our culture, and write something that relates to that. We don't want irrelevant books here.

Why did you become an agent? I love great authors and want to help them reach their goals.

What might you be doing if you weren't an agent? I am an agent because I can't be anything else.

Comments: Please don't write for the money, because if you *do* write for the money, you'll be intolerable once you finally get it.

JOHN A. WARE LITERARY AGENCY

392 Central Park West
New York, NY 10025

Agent: John A. Ware.

Born: May 21, 1942.

Education: B.A., philosophy, Cornell University; graduate work, English literature, Northwestern University.

Career history: Editor, eight years, Doubleday & Company; literary agent, one year, James Brown Associates/Curtis Brown Ltd.; founded John A. Ware Literary Agency in 1978.

Hobbies/personal interests: Music, choral singing and blues bands; running.

Subjects/categories most enthusiastic about agenting: Biography and history; investigative journalism *in re* social commentary and contemporary affairs; memoir and bird's eye views of phenomena; literary and suspense fiction; Americana and folklore; nature and science.

Subjects/categories not interested in agenting: Technothrillers and women's romances, men's action-adventure; how-to's, save the area of medicine and health; guidebooks and cookbooks; hard-core science fiction.

Best way for a prospective client to initiate contact: Query letter with SASE.

Reading-fee policy: No reading fee. Only for Xeroxing, authors' copies of galleys and books, and unusual mailing expenses.

Client representation in the following categories: Nonfiction, 80%; Fiction, 20%.

Commission: 15% on all sales, save foreign, which are 20%.

Approximate percentage of all submissions (from queries through manuscripts) that are rejected: 90%.

Representative titles sold:

Into Thin Air by Jon Krakauer (Villard/Random House).

Straight Through the Heart by Nancy Turner (Regan/HarperCollins), fiction.

My Mama's Waltz: A Book for Daughters of Alcoholic Mothers by Eleanor Agnew, Ph.D. and Sharon Robideaux (Pocket).

Ice in a Hot World by Jack Womack (Grove/Atlantic), fiction.

Denmark Vesey: A Biography by David Robertson (Knopf).

The Interceptor by Richard Herschlag (Ballantine), fiction.

What writers can do to enhance their chances of getting an agent (besides being good writers): Selectively, preferably one-on-one, rather than shopping among 20 agents (or so) via word processor and fax.

Description of the Client from Hell: Untrusting, and accordingly, nudging.

Description of the Dream Client: Professional at all aspects of his/her chosen writing area; trusting; in possession of a sense of humor.

Why did you become an agent? I like working with writers, editorially and otherwise, outside the corporate realms of meetings and red tape, inside of which I worked as an editor.

What might you be doing if you weren't an agent? Teaching philosophy or working as a sportswriter, or in some position in race relations.

Comments: In what remains of our genteel world of books, I would encourage a shoring up of the realm of common courtesy, returning phone calls, saying please and thank you, etc., etc.

JAMES WARREN LITERARY AGENCY

13131 Welby Way
North Hollywood, CA 91606
818-982-5423

Agent: Billie Johnson.

Born: 1947; Chicago, Illinois.

Education: B.S., Business, Cardinal Stritch University.

Career history: 25+ years as accountant and senior management executive.

Hobbies/personal interests: Writing, reading, stock market investing, and playing with my dogs!

Subjects/categories most enthusiastic about agenting: Full-length fiction, all genres and mainstream; specialized nonfiction, television and feature film screenplays.

Subjects/categories not interested in agenting: No children's or young adult stories, no poetry or inspirational writing, no textbooks.

Best way for a prospective client to initiate contact: Fiction: Query letter, brief synopsis, *first* 20 pages of manuscript, SASE. Nonfiction, send full proposal, outline, and 3 sample chapters.

Reading-fee policy: Yes, contact for brochure.

Client representation in the following categories: Nonfiction, 15%; Fiction, 80%; Textbooks, 5%.

Commission: 10–15%, project determines.

Number of titles sold during the past year: 5.

Approximate percentage of all submissions (from queries through manuscripts) that are rejected: 95%.

Representative titles sold:

Witty Words by Eileen Mason.

Madame President by Don Metz.

Description of the Client from Hell: Unrealistic expectations, phone calls at odd hours, showing up at office without an appointment.

Description of Dream Client: Well-written work, clean presentation, professional behavior.

The most common mistakes potential clients make when soliciting an agent to represent them: No SASE, hand-written letters, manuscript lousy with errors and typos.

What writers can do to enhance their chances of getting an agent (besides being good writers): Query per guidelines, include SASE, submit professional quality manuscript (clean, error free, nice size type). Educate yourself to the process!

Why did you become an agent? To make my avocation my vocation.

What might you be doing if you weren't an agent? A riverboat gambler!

Comments:

To submit is human,

To SASE, Divine!

WATERSIDE PRODUCTIONS, INC.

The Waterside Building
2191 San Elijo Avenue
Cardiff-by-the-Sea, CA 92007-1839
619-632-9190

Agents: David Fugate, Margot Maley, Matthew Wagner.

The following information pertains to DAVID FUGATE:

Education: B.A., literature, University of California at San Diego.

Career history: Been with Waterside Productions since 1994. Previously I worked at the Margret McBride Literary Agency.

Hobbies/personal interests: Travel, basketball, skiing, reading, and independent films.

Subjects/categories most enthusiastic about agenting: Computer books and compelling nonfiction in many areas, including pop culture, business, technology, sports, cyberculture, psychology, relationships, etc.

Subjects/categories not interested in agenting: New Age, children's, romance, poetry, short stories.

Best way for a prospective client to initiate contact: Query letter or proposal.

Reading-fee policy: No reading fee.

Client representation in the following categories: Nonfiction, 99%; Fiction, 1%.

Commission: 15% domestic, 20% film, 25% foreign.

Number of titles sold during the past year: 55.

Approximate percentage of all submissions (from queries through manuscripts) that are rejected: 95%.

Representative titles sold:

Mastering Visual Basic 5 by Evangelos Petroutsos (Sybex).

The Official Marimba Guide to Bongo by Danny Goodman (Sams).

Avatars! by Bruce Damer (Peachpit Press).

Mastering Java 1.1 by Steven Holzner (Sybex).

The State of the Net by Peter Clemente (McGraw-Hill Business).

The Shared Values that Make Companies Great by Rob Lebow and Bill Simon (Van Nostrand Reinhold).

The Schwa World Operations Manual by Bill Barker (Chronicle).

The most common mistakes potential clients make when soliciting an agent to represent them: Those who I can tell haven't researched their market thoroughly have little chance of success. I'm also turned off by anyone who wants to meet with me before showing me any of their materials.

What writers can do to enhance their chances of getting an agent (besides being good writers)? Those who have compelling, marketable ideas, who understand their audience and are willing to do what it takes to succeed. I'm especially impressed by authors who have taken the time to produce a quality proposal or treatment before they contact me.

Description of the Client from Hell: The client from hell is unprofessional; reactionary; isn't willing to put in the work to produce a quality book or proposal; fails to meet deadlines; and overestimates his or her value in the marketplace consistently.

Description of Dream Client: A talented writer who is professional, understands the business, meets deadlines, is easy to work with, has good relationships with his or her editor, and appreciates the value that a good agent can provide for their career.

Why did you become an agent? I like books and words and ideas.

What might you be doing if you weren't an agent? I would be the sixth man for some mediocre professional basketball team in Greece, or a nomadic ski bum, or a project-development person in Tarantino's production company, or on the editorial side of the publishing industry.

Comments: Check out our Web site at www.waterside.com for information about our authors, publishers we work with, and the Waterside Publishing Conference, held annually in San Diego.

The following information pertains to MARGOT MALEY:
Education: Literature, University of California at San Diego.
Career history: Literary agent, 5 years.
Hobbies/personal interests: Skiing, tennis, biking, cooking, reading.
Subjects/categories most enthusiastic about agenting: Computer books, sports books, business, and general nonfiction.
Subjects/categories not interested in agenting: Fiction, New Age, religious.
Best way for a prospective client to initiate contact: Through a query letter or a phone call.
Reading-fee policy: No reading fee.
Client representation in the following categories: Nonfiction, 100%.
Commission: 15%.
Number of titles sold during the past year: 65.
Approximate percentage of all submissions (from queries through manuscripts) that are rejected: 90%.
Representative titles sold:
A Dose of Sanity by Dr. Sydney Walker (John Wiley & Sons).
Take Charge Computing for Kids and Parents.
Cheapskate's Vacation Guide by Stephen Tannenbaum (Carol Publishing).
The most common mistakes potential clients make when soliciting an agent to represent them: A poorly written proposal or query letter or too many phone calls to *check on the status* of their proposal.
What writers can do to enhance their chances of getting an agent (besides being good writers)? Send a specifically addressed letter and proposal; be a writer who is professional and enthusiastic and has a great idea.
Description of the Client from Hell: A rude, arrogant, pushy, and impatient person who has completely unrealistic expectations.
Description of Dream Client: A great writer with good ideas who meets deadlines and is friendly and pleasant to deal with.
Why did you become an agent? Growing up I always seemed to have either a book or a phone in my hand.
What might you be doing if you weren't an agent? I would be leading safaris in East Africa.

The following information pertains to MATTHEW WAGNER:
Born: July 12, 1962.
Education: B.A., literature/creative writing, University of California at Santa Cruz.
Career history: I've been a library clerk, a book binder, a bookstore clerk and buyer. I've been a literary agent for 8 years.
Hobbies/personal interests: Yoga, tennis, golf, *lots* of reading.

Subjects/categories most enthusiastic about agenting: Computer books, Internet-specific programming titles, sports, culture and technology, general how-to, business, and management.

Subjects/categories not interested in agenting: Fiction, poetry, self-help.

Best way for a prospective client to initiate contact: Query letter.

Reading-fee policy: No reading fee.

Client representation in the following categories: Nonfiction, 95%; Text-books, 5%.

Commission: 15%.

Number of titles sold during the past year: 150.

Approximate percentage of all submissions (from queries through manuscripts) that are rejected: 90%.

Representative titles sold:

Parenting for Dummies (IDG).

Real Life Windows (IDG).

Free Throw (HarperCollins).

The Flexible Enterprise (Wiley).

Windows 95 for Dummies (IDG).

Netscape Publishing (Ventura).

The most common mistakes potential clients make when soliciting an agent to represent them: Telling me the book is sure to sell several million copies because the market is *everyone*. Insufficient market research.

What writers can do to enhance their chances of getting an agent (besides being good writers)? Professionalism and passion. Really great ideas. New wrinkles on old topics.

Description of the Client from Hell: Someone prone to projection who thinks he or she is always right.

Description of Dream Client: Professional, open-minded, creative, honest, and disciplined.

Why did you become an agent? Probably because I can talk *really* fast. Also, I love books and like dealing with writers and publishers. It helps to be on the cutting edge.

What might you be doing if you weren't an agent? Editor, publisher, or packager. I would love to run a bookstore someday.

WIESER & WIESER, INC.

118 East 25th Street
New York, NY 10010
212-260-0860

Agents: George J. Wieser, Olga B. Wieser, Jake Elwell.

Best way for a prospective client to initiate contact: Through a referral from someone we know well or by mail with a well-presented outline and opening 50 pages with SASE. Please no phone or faxed queries.

Reading-fee policy: No reading fee.

766 Insider's Directory of Literary Agents

Client representation in the following categories: Nonfiction, 45%; Fiction, 50%; Children's, 5%.

Commission: 15% domestic; 20% foreign.

Number of titles sold during the past year: 50.

Approximate percentage of all submissions (from queries through manuscripts) that are rejected: 97%.

Representative titles sold:

The Luckiest Girl in the World by Steven Levenkrom (Scribner).

Bonita Faye by Margaret Moseley (Harper).

Abra Cadaver by James N. Tucker (Dutton Signet).

Pandora's Clock by John J. Nance (Doubleday).

Modern Moonlighting by Roger Woodson (Contemporary).

Pilots Die Faster by C. W. Morton (St. Martin's Press).

War Breaker by Jim De Felice (Leisure).

Trail to Forever by Elizabeth Gregg (Topaz).

A King's Commander by Dewey Lambdin (Donald I. Fine).

The Good Cigar by H. Paul Jeffers and Kevin Gordon (Lyons & Burford).

Description of the Client from Hell: Pitches numerous, disparate ideas and expects reaction/action on all of them. Never is satisfied.

Description of Dream Client: Knowledgeable of the realities of publishing (good and bad). Appreciative, receptive to our input, resourceful and trustworthy.

The most common mistakes potential clients make when soliciting an agent to represent them: Showing material this is incomplete in planning or presentation. Pitches that try to shock or impress with *coolness*. We avoid faxed proposals, spiral (or otherwise) bound manuscripts and solicitations that include past rejection letters from agents and editors (yes, it happens!) like the plague.

What writers can do to enhance their chances of getting an agent (besides being good writers): Be professional. Learn the general rules of our industry and follow them. To that end, read *this* book cover to cover and Richard Curtis's books. Also, memorize the content of your neighborhood bookstore. *Know what sells.*

The following information pertains to GEORGE J. WEISER:

Education: B.A., Marietta College.

Career history: R.R. Bowker/Library Journal; Paramount Pictures: East Coast Story Editor; Agent since 1975.

Hobbies/personal interests: Golf, carpentry, reading.

Subjects/categories most enthusiastic about agenting: Action-adventure, mysteries, biography, cookbooks.

Subjects/categories not interested in agenting: Science fiction.

Why did you become an agent? Originally? I couldn't find another job.

What might you be doing if you weren't an agent? Playing golf.

The following information pertains to OLGA B. WIESER:

Career history: NYU Press; Agent since 1975.

Subjects/categories most enthusiastic about agenting: Well-written, challenging books of all kinds. Strong commercial and literary fiction; holistic, medical and psychological issues are of particular interest.

Subjects/categories not interested in agenting: Category romance; historicals.

Why did you become an agent? There's no job more rewarding, enriching, and exciting.

What might you be doing if you weren't an agent? Writing.

The following information pertains to JAKE ELWELL:

Born: July 23, 1964; Milton, Massachusetts.

Education: B.A., Lake Forest College.

Career history: House painter; high school English teacher; Weiser & Weiser: assistant 1989–1994; Agent, 1994–present.

Hobbies/personal interests: Antiques, book collecting, hockey, fishing, travel.

Subjects/categories most enthusiastic about agenting: Commercial fiction including mysteries, historicals, military, suspense, romance; the occasional Western or horror. Nonfiction backed by a strong author profile: history, true crime, biography, Americana, biography, pop medical.

Subjects/categories not interested in agenting: Science fiction, self-published books that did poorly.

Why did you become an agent? I like working in an entrepreneurial setting, and I love books. And there's nothing like playing a role in bringing a book to life.

What might you be doing if you weren't an agent? Teaching, traveling, trying to be a writer, painting houses.

RUTH WRESCHNER, AUTHORS' REPRESENTATIVE

10 West 74th Street
New York, NY 10023
212-877-2605

Agent: Ruth Wreschner.

Born: Frankfurt, Germany.

Education: B.A., McGill University, Montreal, Canada.

Career history: Assistant editor (medical division, 1973–1978) and executive assistant (science division, 1961–1973), John Wiley & Sons.

Hobbies/personal interests: Music (classical), art, travel, literature.

Subjects/categories most enthusiastic about agenting: Nonfiction: all areas, except erotica; special interest in popular medicine/psychology, parenting, business, health, science, biography, history. Fiction: primarily mainstream; secondary genre (mysteries, contemporary and historical romances, suspense/thrillers).

Subjects/categories not interested in agenting: Erotica and science fiction.

Best way for a prospective client to initiate contact with you: Nonfiction: Query letter (with SASE) containing detailed proposal. Fiction: Query letter (with SASE) containing brief synopsis; if I am interested, I will ask for sample chapters.

Reading-fee policy: No reading fee.

Client representation in the following categories: Nonfiction, 80%; Fiction, 20%. Children's: Nonfiction, 80%; Fiction, 20%.

Commission: 15% domestic; 20% foreign.

Number of titles sold during the past year: 12.

Approximate percentage of all submissions (from queries through manuscripts) that are rejected: 97%.

Representative titles sold:

Wall Street's Picks 1997 by Kirk Kazanjian (Dearborn).

How to Buy Mutual Funds for Free by Kirk Kazanjian (Dearborn).

The Eye Laser Miracle by Andrew Caster, M.D. (Ballantine).

Lady Semple's Secret by Shirley Kennedy (Ballantine).

What Is Your Company Worth? by Bruce Morgan (Van Nostrand).

The Best of Kentucky Cuisine by Linda Allison-Lewis (University Press of Kentucky).

Kinderlage, a book about the three youngest survivors of Auschwitz.

The most common mistakes potential clients make when soliciting an agent to represent them: Not including SASE with their queries. Their most costly mistakes might be to submit work in an unprofessional manner: sloppy, handwritten, without a cover letter.

What writers can do to enhance their chances of getting an agent (besides being good writers): Primarily their subject matter and credentials. And for fiction writers, it is all, of course, *on the page.* It is always a moment of ecstasy when a really exciting fiction arrives.

Description of the Client from Hell: People who are overly demanding of my time, particularly when they have totally unsalable work. Clients who go on relentless phone campaigns. *When I get an offer from a publisher, I call!*

Description of Dream Client: Someone who is pleasant and courteous to deal with, who trusts me, who submits a really professional proposal, and who meets deadlines and other obligations.

Why did you become an agent? I had worked in publishing for most of my career. I love the challenge, the people I meet, and, first and foremost, I love the written word.

What might you be doing if you weren't an agent? I honestly don't know. If I were *super rich*, I might devote time to charity (community work) and spend more time traveling than I have time to do now.

Comments: In fiction, *write with passion.* In nonfiction, you must be an acknowledged expert in the area in which you are writing. I cannot accept nonfiction clients in areas in which they have no expertise. For example, in popular medicine, you must be a physician (even if you have a collaborative writer) or in psychology you must be a psychologist; in business books, you must have the unique experience in the niche you are trying to fill.

WRITERS HOUSE

21 West 26th Street
New York, NY 10010
212-685-2400

Agents: Susan Ginsburg, Albert J. Zuckerman, Fran Lebowitz, Merrilee Heifetz, Amy Berkower, Susan Cohen.

Reading-fee policy: No reading fee.

Client representation: Agency as a whole has about 300 clients.

Commission: 15%.

Number of titles sold during the past year: Agency: More than 200.

Representative titles sold:

A Place Called Freedom by Ken Follett (Crown).

Blessing in Disguise by Eileen Goudge (Viking).

Green River Rising by Tim Willocks (Morrow).

The Select by F. Paul Wilson (Morrow).

Black Holes and Baby Universes by Stephen Hawking (Bantam).

The First Wives' Club by Olivia Goldsmith (Simon & Schuster).

Neverwhere by Neil Gaiman.

Other well-known clients are: Octavia E. Butler, Nora Roberts, Barbara Delinsky, Ridley Pearson, Michael Lewis, Ann Martin, Francine Pascal, James Howe, Bruce Sterling, Joan D. Vinge, Craig Thomas, Cynthia Voigt, Colin Wilson, Robin McKinley.

The following information pertains to SUSAN GINSBURG:

Born: New York.

Education: Yale University.

Career history: Editor-in-chief, Atheneum; executive editor, St. Martin's; executive editor, Simon & Schuster/Pocket Books.

Subjects/categories most enthusiastic about agenting: Fiction: commercial fiction of any type and literary fiction that is accessible. Nonfiction: broad range of topics chosen purely by interest and marketability. True crime, women's issues, science, biography/autobiography, cookbooks.

Subjects/categories not interested in agenting: Children's books, science fiction.

Best way for a prospective client to initiate contact: Through written correspondence—query letter (with SASE).

Client representation: 40–50 clients; Nonfiction, 60%; Fiction, 40%.

The following information pertains to ALBERT J. ZUCKERMAN:

Education: D.F.A., dramatic literature, Yale.

Career history:. Naval officer; foreign service officer, U.S. State Department; assistant professor of playwrighting, Yale Drama School; winner of Stanley Drama Prize for best new American play of 1964; author of two published novels and of *Writing the Blockbuster Novel*; writer for "The Edge of Night" on TV; Broadway producer.

Hobbies/personal interests: Helping writers; antique textiles and furniture.

Subjects/categories most enthusiastic about agenting: Fiction: wonderful novels of all kinds, especially those accessible and attractive to a large readership. Nonfiction: history, biography, narrative nonfiction.

Subjects/categories not interested in agenting: Scholarly, professional, screenplays.

Best way for a prospective client to initiate contact: An interesting, intelligent letter (with SASE).

Client representation: About 70 clients; Nonfiction, 33 1/3%; Fiction, 66 2/3%.

What writers can do to enhance their chances of getting an agent (besides being good writers): Be talented, study books that are having some success, and be willing to work their butts off.

The following information pertains to FRAN LEBOWITZ:
Born: Baltimore, Maryland.
Education: Franklin and Marshall College; University of Maryland.
Career history: Lowenstein Associates; William Morris Agency.
Hobbies/personal interests: Dangerous sports.
Subjects/categories most enthusiastic about agenting: Middle-grade and young-adult novels, popular-culture books, adult novels.

Subjects/categories not interested in agenting: Financial and self-help.

Best way for a prospective client to initiate contact: Letter (with SASE), a synopsis, and several sample chapters.

Client representation: Nonfiction, 20%; Fiction, 80%. Children's: 70%.

Number of titles sold during the past year: About 40.

Approximate percentage of all submissions (from queries through manuscripts) that are rejected: 99%.

The most common mistakes potential clients make when soliciting an agent to represent them: Calling the agency soon after sending a submission.

What writers can do to enhance their chances of getting an agent (besides being good writers): Writing a short cover letter with a strong hook.

The following information pertains to MERILEE HEIFETZ:
Education: B.A., Sarah Lawrence College.
Career history: Teaching writing to children, literary agent.
Hobbies/personal interests: Cooking, art, sports.
Subjects/categories most enthusiastic about agenting:. Fiction with an edge, distinctive mysteries, wonderful women's fiction, well-written but commercial fantasy; new technology.

Subjects/categories not interested in agenting: Men's adventure.

Best way for a prospective client to initiate contact: Letter (with SASE).

Client representation: Nonfiction, 10%; Fiction, 80%; Children's, 10%.

Number of titles sold during the past year: About 30.

Approximate percentage of all submissions (from queries through manuscripts) that are rejected: Unsolicited, 99%. Other, 75%.

The most common mistakes potential clients make when soliciting an agent to represent them: Harassing the agent.

Description of the Client from Hell: I don't have any.

Description of the Dream Client: Talented, professional, pleasant to deal with, prolific.

Why did you become an agent? I like reading and I like writers.

What might you be doing if you weren't an agent? Living in Italy.

THE ZACK COMPANY, INC.

Department JH
P.O. Box 247
Westfield, NJ 07091-0247
908-518-0318

Agent: Andrew Zack.

   Born: 1966, Massachusetts.

   Education: B.A., English and political science, University of Rochester, 1988.

   Career history: I began my publishing career on the retail side as the evening manager of an independent bookstore in Massachusetts. While attending the University of Rochester in Rochester, New York, I continued working on the retail side at the university's Barnes & Noble bookstore. Later, I served as an editor on several student publications, including two years as the managing editor of the university yearbook, *Interpres*. I graduated in 1988 with a B.A. and the summer following attended the Radcliffe Publishing Course at Harvard University, an intensive publishing "boot camp" led by numerous publishing veterans. In September of 1988, I began work at Simon & Schuster Trade Division as a foreign-rights assistant, where I worked with S&S's foreign subagents in the licensing of foreign editions. Not long thereafter, I moved to Warner Books as an editorial assistant. While there, I edited a number of titles and began acquiring on my own. I was substantively involved in the editing of several bestsellers, including the *Batman* movie tie-in and two *Headlines* titles by Jay Leno.

   I next worked at Donald I. Fine, Inc. as an assistant editor and rights associate. Within six months, I was promoted to associate editor and rights manager. I acquired numerous titles and also sold subsidiary rights to the entire Fine list, including serial, book club, reprint, large print, film and television. I also served as liaison with Fine's British and foreign subagents. The Berkley Publishing Group was my next home, having been recruited as an editor. I was eventually responsible for more than 40 titles and brought a number of first-time authors to the list. I left Berkley during a corporate downsizing and entered the world of freelance. As a freelance editor, I worked with a number of different clients, including several literary agencies, and major publishers such as The Berkley Publishing Group, Donald I. Fine, Inc., Avon Books, Dell Publishing, and Tom Doherty Associates. I also reviewed for *Kirkus* and the Book-of-the-Month Club. I became a literary agent in September of 1993, joining the then recently formed Scovil Chichak Galen Literary Agency as a full agent. I launched The Andrew Zack Literary Agency in March of 1996.

Hobbies/personal interests: Biking, movies, investing, computers, jazz, reading.

Subjects/categories most enthusiastic about agenting: History, particularly military history and intelligence services history; politics/current affairs; new media technology and issues; science and technology—how they affect society and business; narrative accounts of how big breakthroughs were achieved; new works that shatter old beliefs; natural science—geology, paleontology, biology, etc.; business—narrative accounts and management how-to; marketing; biography/autobiography; media-related (celebrity biography) and political; personal finance/investing; humor; narrative, topical and celebrity-related; commercial fiction (excluding *women's fiction*); thrillers in every shape and form—international, serial killer, scientific/technological/computer, medical, psychological, erotic, military, environmental, legal; mysteries and crime novels—less cozy, more hard-edged, but not necessarily hard-boiled; action novels in the David Morrell or Clive Cussler tradition.

Subjects/categories not interested in agenting: Women's fiction, romance novels, anything that is primarily aimed at women fiction readers; genre horror novels.

Best way for a prospective client to initiate contact: Nonfiction: query letter with résumé and a 2–3 page introduction to the project. Fiction: Query with history of previously published works, if any. Always include SASE for the return of any material.

Reading-fee policy: No reading fee.

Client representation in the following categories: Nonfiction, 35%; Fiction, 65%. (I want more nonfiction by leading authorities in their areas of expertise.)

Commission: 15% domestic, 20% foreign.

Approximate percentage of all submissions (from queries through manuscripts) that are rejected: 99.95%.

Representative titles sold:
New Lots by John Clarkson (Forge Books).
Blackbird Singing by Jay Amberg (Forge Books).
Straight Shooter by Captain Robert Gormly, retired, USN (Dutton).
Untitled *Instinct Series* novels 8, 9, and 10 by Robert W. Walker.
The Lost World by Alien Voices, Inc. (Simon & Schuster Audio), audio adaptation.

Description of the Client from Hell: The client from hell has probably published two or three, or maybe three or four, books. They are likely fiction, but might be nonfiction. He or she has "fired" his or her previous agent because his or her career is going nowhere and that is, of course, the agent's fault. He or she is looking for an agent who can "make things happen," and just to make sure those things happen, he or she calls a minimum of three or four times a week for updates. He or she regularly pitches ideas to his or her old editor, to the point where that editor calls me and asks me to stop my client from doing this constantly. The client is convinced that his or her ideas are future bestsellers and can't understand why no one agrees with him or her. He or she wants instant feedback from me or his editor and never once considers that I may have other clients or that the editor may have books on production schedules ahead of the client's. The client sends proposals via e-mail and doesn't understand why there isn't an instant response (the one downside to e-mail is that it creates a presumption that, because it's almost instantaneous in delivery, the reply to it should be instantaneous). Bottom line: the client from hell is the one who believes his or her needs outweigh everyone else's—his agent's, his editor's, his publicist's, and those of all of the other authors with whom those people may be working.

Description of Dream Client: The dream client acts like a professional. He or she prepared his material according to publishing standards. He or she keeps me updated on the progress of the work and on his or her career. He or she sends me an updated biography when something significant happens, copies of reviews of published books if they reach him or her before they get to my office. He or she calls with news, or faxes, or e-mails me with news, but generally is aware that time spent "chatting" is time that could be spent selling his or her works. And, of course, he or she is a *New York Times* bestselling author.

The most common mistakes potential clients make when soliciting an agent to represent them: Phoning instead of writing; having a poorly written synopsis; making repeated telephone calls to check on the status of their submissions; not sending SASE.

What writers can do to enhance their chances of getting an agent (besides being good writers)? Nonfiction writers have to be recognized experts in their subject areas, or proven journalists who have written with great success about a number of different subjects. Novelists should be, first and foremost, real *wordsmiths*. Understand *how* to write, not just type, a work of fiction. Then, know your marketplace. The combination of good writing and a commercial story will always sell.

Why did you become an agent? I had been in the publishing business as an editor and subsidiary rights salesperson for a number of years. I had the opportunity to move into representation with a start-up firm that held a lot of promise. It seemed to be the next, natural step in my career.

What might you be doing if you weren't an agent? I would likely still be an editor, or I might have gone to law school and pursued a career in entertainment law.

Comments: The agent/author relationship is a business partnership. The agent has his or her role and the author has his or her role. Neither is an *employee* of the other. Interestingly enough, I never hear about agents or authors *hiring* each other, but I hear about them firing one another all the time. Agents, obviously, are business people. Authors need to be business people too. Authors should do their best to be as informed as possible about the nature of the publishing business. They should subscribe to *Publishers Weekly*, or at least read it in the library every week. They should talk to their local independent bookseller (and if they *really* want to learn a few things, they should get a part-time job working in a bookstore). My best client is an *educated* client. I find the hardest thing about the agent/author relationship is communication. E-mail has become an important mode of communication for me. It's quick and easy and almost instantaneous as a form of communication. Authors should be able to ask their agents all the questions they want, and if an author's agent disagrees with that, it's time to find another agent. But authors also need to recognize that every minute spent on the phone with them is a minute that could be spent selling their projects. As long as an author understands the job he or she has and the job the agent has in the author/agent relationship, the business partnership will flourish and be profitable.

SUSAN ZECKENDORF ASSOCIATES, INC.

171 West 57th Street, Suite 11B
New York, NY 10019
212-245-2928

Agent: Susan Zeckendorf.

Born: New York City.

Education: B.A., Wellesley College; M.Ed., Columbia University Teachers College.

Career history: Counseling psychologist (1980–1988).

Hobbies/personal interests: Reading, music, film.

Subjects/categories most enthusiastic about agenting: Literary fiction, mysteries, thrillers, women's commercial fiction, social history, biography, music, psychology, science.

Subjects/categories not interested in agenting: Romance, science fiction, New Age.

Best way for a writer to initiate contact: Query letter (with SASE).

Reading-fee policy: No reading fee.

Client representation in the following categories: Nonfiction, 50%; Fiction, 50%.

Commission: 15%.

Approximate percentage of all submissions (from queries through manuscripts) that are rejected: 90%.

Representative titles sold:

Lethal Lessons by Karen Hanson Stuyck (Berkeley).

Fifth Avenue: The Best Address (A Social History) by Terry E. Patterson (Rizzoli).

The Woman Angler by Laurie Morrow (St. Martin's Press).

Shooting Sports for Women by Laurie Morrow (St. Martin's Press).

Dark Passions by Una-Mary Parker (Hodder Headline).

The Second Skin by Una-Mary Parker (Hodder Headline).

The most common mistakes potential clients make when soliciting an agent to represent them: Sending gimmicky letters. *Not* sending an SASE.

What writers can do to enhance their chances of getting an agent (besides being good writers): Submit a short query letter that is to the point—with an SASE.

Description of the Client from Hell: An unpublished writer who wants an auction and a six-figure advance for a mediocre project.

Description of Dream Client: Honest and considerate.

Why did you become an agent? Because I have great admiration and respect for those who have writing talent.

PART THREE

Insider Road Maps
to Your Success

Over the Transom and into Print

Maximizing Your Chances in the Battle of the UNs (Unagented/ Unsolicited Submissions)

JEFF HERMAN

Most major publishing houses claim to have policies that prevent them from even considering unagented/unsolicited submissions. *Unagented* means that the submission was not made by a literary agent. *Unsolicited* means that no one at the publisher asked for the submission.

It's possible that you, or people you know, have already run into this frustrating roadblock. You may also be familiar with the rumor that it's more difficult to get an agent than it is to get a publisher—or that no agent will even consider your work until you *have* a publisher. On the surface, these negatives make it seem that you would have a better shot at becoming a starting pitcher for the Yankees, or living out whatever your favorite improbable fantasy might be.

But, as you will soon learn, these so-called policies and practices are often more false than true. Especially if you develop creative ways to circumvent them.

I have dubbed the above obstacle course the Battle of the UNs. If you're presently unagented/unsolicited, you're one of the UNs. Welcome! You're in good company. Nobody is born published. There is no published author who wasn't at one time an UN. Thousands of new books are published each year, and thousands of people are needed to write them. You can be one of them.

In this chapter I'll show you how to win the Battle of the UNs. But first let me clarify an important distinction. When I use the word *win* here, I don't mean to say that you'll necessarily get your work published. What I mean is: You'll gain reasonable access to the powers-that-be for your work, and you'll learn how to increase the odds— dramatically—that your work will in fact be acquired.

Please be realistic. For every published writer, there are, at minimum, several thousand waiting in line to get published. "Many are called, but few are chosen."

It's completely within your power to maximize your chances of getting published. It's also within your power to minimize those chances. There are reasons why some highly talented people habitually underachieve, and those reasons can often be found within them. If you fail, fail, and fail, you should look within yourself for possible answers. What can you do to turn it around? If you find some answers, then you haven't failed at all, and the lessons you allow yourself to learn will lay the groundwork for success in this and in other endeavors.

Having an agent greatly increases the likelihood that you will be published. For one thing, on the procedural level, an established agent can usually obtain relatively rapid (and serious) consideration for his or her clients. One basic reason for this is that editors view agents as a valuable screening mechanism—that is, when a project crosses the editor's desk under an agent's letterhead, the editor knows it's undergone vetting from someone in the industry who is familiar with the applicable standards of quality and market considerations.

I usually recommend that unpublished writers first make every attempt to get an agent before they start going directly to the publishers. It's significantly easier to get an agent than it is to get a publisher—not the other way around. Most agents I know are always on the lookout for fresh talent. Finding and nurturing tomorrow's stars is one of our functions.

However, one of my reasons for writing and researching this book is to reveal to you that, as a potential author, not having an agent does not necessarily disqualify you from the game automatically. Before I show you ways to win the Battle of the UNs, I'd like you to have a fuller understanding of the system.

YOU ARE THE EDITOR

Imagine that you're an acquisitions editor at one of America's largest publishing firms in New York City. You have a master's degree from an Ivy League college and you, at least, think you're smarter than most other people. Yet you're earning a lot less money than most of the people who graduated with you. Your classmates have become lawyers, accountants, bankers, and so forth, and they all seem to own large, well-appointed apartments or homes—whereas you, if you fall out of bed, might land in the bathtub of your minuscule New York flat.

On the other hand, you love your job. For you, working in publishing is a dream come true. As in other industries and professions, much of your satisfaction comes from advancement—getting ahead.

To move up the career ladder, you'll have to acquire at least a few successful titles each year. To find these few good titles, you'll be competing with many editors from other publishers, and perhaps even with fellow editors within your own firm. As in any other business, the people who make the most money for the company will get the choice promotions and the highest salaries. Those who perform less impressively will tend to be passed over. (Of course, being a good editor and playing politics well are also important.)

There are two tried-and-true sources for the titles that publishers acquire: literary agents and direct solicitations.

Literary Agents

As an editor on the move, you'll cultivate relationships with many established literary agents. You'll want them to know what you like and what you don't like. And, by showing these agents you're disposed to acquiring new titles to build your position in the company, you'll encourage these agents to send you projects they think are right for you.

When you receive material from agents, you usually give it relatively fast consideration—especially if it's been submitted simultaneously to editors at other houses, which is usually the case. When something comes in from an agent, you know it's been screened and maybe even perfected. An established agent rarely wastes your time with shoddy or inappropriate material. They couldn't make a living that way because they'd quickly lose credibility with editors.

Direct Solicitations

If you're an ambitious editor, you won't just sit back passively and wait to see what the agents might bless you with. When you're resourceful, the opportunities are endless. Perhaps you'll contact your old American history professor and ask her to do a book showcasing her unique perspectives on the Civil War.

Or maybe you'll contact that young fresh fiction writer whose short story you just read in a leading literary journal. You might even try reaching that veteran United States senator who just got censured for sleeping with his young aides.

One place you'll tend *not* to use is the "slush pile." This is the room (more like a warehouse) where all the unagented/unsolicited submissions end up. Looking through the slush pile isn't a smart use of your limited time and energy. The chances that anything decent will be found there are much less than one percent. You have less-than-fond memories of your first year in the publishing business, when, as an editorial assistant (which was basically an underpaid secretarial job), one of your tasks was to shovel through the slush. Once in a great while, something promising could be found; but most of the stuff wasn't even close. At first, you were surprised by how unprofessional many of the submissions were. Many weren't addressed to anyone in particular; some looked as if they had been run over by Mack trucks; others were so poorly printed they were too painful for tired eyes to decipher—the list of failings is long.

No, the slush pile is the last place—or perhaps no place—to find titles for your list.

Now you can stop being an editor and go back to being whoever you really are. I wanted to show you why the system has evolved the way it has. Yes, though it's rational, it's cold and unfair; but these qualities aren't unique to publishing.

You're probably still wondering when I'm going to get to that promised modus operandi for winning the Battle of the UNs. Okay, we're there.

OUT OF THE SLUSH

The following steps are intended to keep you out of the infamous slush pile. Falling into the slush is like ending up in jail for contempt of court; it's like being an untouchable in India; it's like being Frank Burns on M*A*S*H. My point is that nobody likes the Slushables. They're everyone's scapegoat and nobody's ally.

Once your work is assigned to the slush pile, it's highly unlikely that it will receive effective access. Without access, there can be no acquisition. Without acquisition, there's no book.

Let's pretend that getting published is a board game. However, in this game you can control the dice. Here are several ways to play:

Get the Names!

If you submit to nobody, it will go to nobody. Sending it to "The Editors," "Gentlemen," or the CEO of a $100-million publishing house equals sending it to no one.

Use the directory in this book to get the names of the suitable contacts.

In addition to using this directory, there are two other proven ways to discover who the right editors may be:

1. Visit bookstores and seek out recent books that are in your category. Check the Acknowledgments section of each one. Many authors like to thank their editors here (and their agents). If the editor is acknowledged, you now have the name of someone who edits books like yours. (Remember to call to confirm that the editor still works at that publishing house).
2. Simply call the publisher and ask for the editorial department. More often than not, the phone will be answered by a young junior editor who will say something like "Editorial." Like people who answer phones everywhere, these people may sound as if they are asleep, or they may sound harried, or even as if they're making the most important declaration of their lives. Luckily for you, publishers plant few real secretaries or receptionists in their editorial departments, since it's constantly reconfirmed that rookie editors will do all that stuff for everyone else—and for a lot less money! Hence, real editors (although low in rank) can immediately be accessed.

Returning to the true point of this—once someone answers the phone, simply ask, "Who edits your business books?" (Or whatever your category is.) You can also ask who edited a specific and recent book that's similar to yours. Such easy but vital questions will bring forth quick and valuable answers. Ask enough times and you can build a list of contacts that competes with this book.

Don't Send Manuscripts Unless Invited to Do So!

Now that you're armed with these editors' names, don't abuse protocol (editors yell at *me* when you do—especially when they know where you've gotten their name). Initiate contact by sending a letter describing your work and encouraging the editor to request it. This letter, commonly referred to as a query letter, is in reality a sales pitch, or door-opener. (Please see the material in this book about query letters for a full overview of this important procedure.) In brief, the letter should be short (less than 1 ½ pages); easy to read and to the point; personalized; and well printed on good professional stationery. Say what you have, why it's hot, why you're a good prospect, and what's available for review upon request.

In addition to the letter, it's okay to include a résumé/bio that highlights any writing credits or relevant professional credentials; a brief summary (2–3 pages) if the book is nonfiction, or a brief synopsis if it's fiction; a photo, if you have a flattering one; and promotional materials. Be careful: At this stage your aim is merely to whet the editor's appetite; you don't want to cause information overload. Less is more.

Also include a self-addressed stamped envelope (SASE). This is an important courtesy; without it, you increase your chances of getting no response. Editors receive dozens of these letters every week. Having to address envelopes for all of them would be very time-consuming. And at 32 cents a pop, it's not worth doing. The SASE is generally intended to facilitate a response in the event of a negative decision. If the editor is intrigued by your letter, he may overlook the missing SASE and request to see your work—but don't count on it.

You may be wondering: If I have the editor's name, why not just send her my manuscript? Because you're flirting with the slush pile if you do. Even though you have the editor's previously secret name, you're still an UN; and UNs aren't treated kindly. An editor is inundated with reams of submissions, and her problem is finding good stuff to publish. If you send an unsolicited manuscript, you'll just be perceived as part of that problem. She'll assume you're just another slushy UN who needs to be sorted out of the way so she can go on looking for good stuff. A bad day for an editor is receiving a few trees' worth of UN manuscripts; it deepens her occupational neurosis.

On the other hand, a professional letter is quite manageable and is, at least, likely to be read. It may be screened initially by the editor's assistant, but will probably be passed upstairs if it shows promise.

If the editor is at all intrigued by your letter, she will request to see more material, and you will have earned the rank of being solicited. Even if your work is not ultimately acquired by this editor, you will have at least challenged and defeated the UNs' obstacle course by achieving quality consideration. Remember: Many people get published each year without the benefits of being agented or initially solicited.

It's okay, even smart, to query several editors simultaneously. This makes sense because some editors may take a very long time to respond, or, indeed, may never respond. Querying editors one at a time might take years. If more than one editor subsequently requests and begins considering your work, let each one know that it's not an exclusive. If an editor requests an exclusive, that's fine—but give him a time limit (4 weeks is fair).

Don't sell your work to a publisher before consulting everyone who's considering it and seeing if they're interested. If you do sell it, be sure to give immediate written and oral notification to everyone who's considering it that it's no longer available.

The query-letter stage isn't considered a submission. You only need to have follow-up communications with editors who have gone beyond the query stage, meaning those who have requested and received your work for acquisition consideration. If you don't hear back from an editor within 6 weeks of sending her your letter, it's safe to assume she's not interested in your work.

If you send multiple queries, don't send them to more than one editor at the same house at the same time. If you don't hear back from a particular editor within 6 weeks of your submission, it's probably safe to query another editor at that house. One editor's reject is another's paradise; that's how both good and bad books get published.

We've just covered a lot of important procedural ground; so don't be embarrassed if you think you've forgotten all of it. This book won't self-destruct (and now, presumably, you won't either).

Cold Calls Breed Cold Hearts

One more thing: It's best not to cold-call these editors. Don't call them to try to sell them your work. Don't call them to follow-up on query letters or submissions. Don't call them to try to change their minds.

Why? Do you like it when someone calls you in the middle of your favorite video to sell you land in the Nevada desert, near a popular nuclear test site?

Few people like uninvited and unscheduled sales calls. In some businesses, such as public relations, calling contacts is a necessary part of the process—but not in publishing. Furthermore, this business is based on hard copy. You may be the greatest oral storyteller since Uncle Remus, but if you can't write it effectively and engagingly, nobody is going to care. You'll end up soliciting their hostility. Of course, once they *are* interested in you on the basis of your hard copy, your oral and physical attributes may be of great importance to them.

On the other hand, some people are so skilled on the telephone that it's a lost opportunity for them not to make maximum use of it as a selling method. If you're one of these extremely rare and talented people, you should absolutely make use of whatever tools have proven to work best for you.

Everything I've said is my opinion. This is a subjective industry, so it's likely—no, it's for certain—that others will tell you differently. It's to your advantage to educate yourself to the fullest extent possible (read books, attend workshops, and so forth)—and in the end, to use your own best instincts about how to proceed. I'm confident that my suggestions are safe and sound; but I don't consider them to be the beginning and the end. The more you know, the simpler things become; the less you know, the more complex and confusing they are.

BREAKING THE RULES

Taken as a whole, this book provides a structure that can be considered a set of guidelines, if not hard-and-fast rules. Some people owe their success to breaking the rules and swimming upstream—and I can certainly respect that. Often such people don't even know they're breaking the rules; they're just naturally following their own unique orbits (and you'll find a few illustrations of this very phenomenon elsewhere in these essays). Trying to regulate such people can often be their downfall.

On one hand, most of us tend to run afoul when we stray from established norms of doing business; on the other hand, a few of us can't succeed any other way (Einstein could have written an essay about that). If you're one of those few, hats off to you! Perhaps we'll all learn something from your example.

Keep reading!

Write the Perfect Query Letter

DEBORAH LEVINE HERMAN

The query is a short letter of introduction to a publisher or agent, encouraging him or her to request to see your fiction manuscript or nonfiction book proposal. It is a vital tool, often neglected by writers. If done correctly, it can help you to avoid endless frustration and wasted effort. The query is the first hurdle of your individual marketing strategy. If you can leap over it successfully, you're well on your way to a sale.

The query letter is your calling card. For every book that makes it to the shelves, there are thousands of worthy manuscripts, proposals, and ideas knocked out of the running by poor presentation or inadequate marketing strategies. Don't forget that the book you want to sell is a product that must be packaged correctly to stand above the competition.

A query letter asks the prospective publisher or agent if she would like to see more about the proposed idea. If your book is fiction, you should indicate that a manuscript or sample chapters are available on request. If nonfiction, you should offer to send a proposal and, if you have them, sample chapters.

The query is your first contact with the prospective buyer of your book. To ensure that it's not your last, avoid common mistakes. The letter should be concise and well written. You shouldn't try to impress the reader with your mastery of all words over three syllables. Instead, concentrate on a clear and to-the-point presentation with no fluff. Think of the letter as an advertisement. You want to make a sale of a product, and you have very limited space and time in which to reach this goal.

The letter should be only one page long if possible. It will form the basis of a query package that will include supporting materials. Don't waste words in the letter describing material that can be included separately. Your goal is to pique the interest of an editor who has very little time and probably very little patience. You want to entice her to keep reading and ask you for more.

The query package can include a short résumé, media clippings, or other favorable documents. Do not get carried away, or your package will quickly come to resemble junk mail. Include a self-addressed stamped envelope (SASE) with enough postage to return your entire package. This will be particularly appreciated by smaller publishing houses and independent agents.

For fiction writers, a short (one- to five-page), double-spaced synopsis of the manuscript will be helpful and appropriate.

Do not waste money and defeat the purpose of the query by sending an unsolicited manuscript. Agents and editors may be turned off by receiving manuscripts of 1,000+ pages that were uninvited and not even remotely relevant to what they do.

The query follows a simple format (which can be reworked according to your individual preferences): (1) lead; (2) supporting material/persuasion; (3) biography; and (4) conclusion/pitch.

YOUR LEAD IS YOUR HOOK

The lead can either catch the editor's attention or turn him off completely. Some writers think getting someone's attention in a short space means having to do something dramatic. Editors appreciate cleverness, but too much contrived writing can work against you. Opt instead for clear conveyance of thoroughly developed ideas and get right to the point.

Of course, you don't want to be boring and stuffy in the interest of factual presentation. You'll need to determine what is most important about the book you're trying to sell, and write your letter accordingly.

You can begin with a lead similar to what you'd use to grab the reader in an article or a book chapter. You can use an anecdote, a statement of facts, a question, a comparison, or whatever you believe will be most powerful.

You may want to rely on the journalistic technique of the inverted pyramid. This means that you begin with the strongest material and save the details for later in the letter. Don't start slowly and expect to pick up momentum as you proceed. It will be too late.

Do not begin a query letter like this: "I have sent this idea to 20 agents/publishers, none of whom think it will work. I just know you'll be different, enlightened, and insightful, and will give it full consideration." There is no room for negatives in a sales pitch. Focus only on positives—unless you can turn negatives to your advantage.

Some writers make the mistake of writing about the book's potential in the first paragraph without ever stating its actual idea or theme. Remember, your letter may never be read beyond the lead; so make that first paragraph your hook.

Avoid bad jokes, clichés, unsubstantiated claims, and dictionary definitions. Don't be condescending; editors have egos, too, and have power over your destiny as a writer.

SUPPORTING MATERIAL: BE PERSUASIVE

If you are selling a nonfiction book, you may want to include a brief summary of hard evidence, gleaned from research, that will support the merit of your idea. This is where you convince the editor that your book should exist. This is more important for nonfiction than it is for fiction, where the style and storytelling ability are paramount. Nonfiction writers must focus on selling their topic and their credentials.

You should include a few lines showing the editor what the publishing house will gain from the project. Publishers are not charitable institutions; they want to know how they can get the greatest return on their investment. If you have brilliant marketing ideas, or know of a well-defined market for your book where sales will be guaranteed, include this rather than other descriptive material.

In rereading your letter, make sure you have shown that you understand your own idea thoroughly. If it appears half-baked, the editors won't want to invest time fleshing out your thoughts. Exude confidence so that the editor will have faith in your ability to carry out the job.

In nonfiction queries, you can include a separate table of contents and brief chapter abstracts. Otherwise, it can wait for the book proposal.

YOUR BIOGRAPHY IS NO PLACE FOR MODESTY

In the biographical portion of your letter, toot your own horn, but in a carefully calculated, persuasive fashion. Your story of winning the third-grade writing competition (it was then that you knew you wanted to be a world-famous writer!) should be saved for the documentary done on your life after you reach your goal.

In the query, all you want to include are the most important and relevant credentials that will support the sale of your book. You can include, as a separate part of the package, a résumé or biography that will elaborate further.

The separate résumé should list all relevant and recent experiences that support your ability to write the book. Unless you're fairly young, your listing of academic accomplishments should start after high school. Don't overlook hobbies or non-job-related activities if they correspond to your book story or topic. Those experiences are often more valuable than academic achievements.

Other information to include: any impressive print clippings about you; a list of your broadcast interviews and speaking appearances; and copies of articles and reviews about any books you may have written. This information can never hurt your chances and could make the difference in your favor.

There is no room for humility or modesty in the query letter and résumé. When corporations sell toothpaste, they list the product's best attributes and create excitement about the product. If you can't find some way to make yourself exciting as an author, you'd better rethink your career.

HERE'S THE PITCH

At the close of your letter, ask for the sale. This requires a positive and confident conclusion with such phrases as "I look forward to your speedy response." Such phrases as

"I hope" and "I think you will like my book" sound too insecure. This is the part of the letter where you go for the kill.

Be sure to thank the reader for his or her attention in your final sentence.

FINISHING TOUCHES

When you're finished, reread and edit your query letter. Cut out any extraneous information that dilutes the strength of your arguments. Make the letter as polished as possible so that the editor will be impressed with you as well as with your idea. Don't ruin your chances by appearing careless; make certain your letter is not peppered with typos and misspellings. If you don't show pride in your work, you'll create a self-fulfilling prophecy; the editor will take you no more seriously than you take yourself.

Aesthetics are important. If you were pitching a business deal to a corporation, you would want to present yourself in conservative dress, with an air of professionalism. In the writing business, you may never have face-to-face contact with the people who will determine your future. Therefore your query package is your representative.

If an editor receives a query letter on yellowed paper that looks as if it's been lying around for 20 years, he or she will wonder if the person sending the letter is a has-been or a never-was.

You should invest in a state-of-the-art letterhead—with a logo!—to create an impression of pride, confidence, and professionalism. White, cream, and ivory paper are all acceptable, but you should use only black ink for printing the letter. Anything else looks amateurish.

Don't sabotage yourself by letting your need for instant approval get the best of you. Don't call the editor. You have invited him or her to respond, so be patient. Then prepare yourself for possible rejection. It often takes many nos to get a yes.

One final note: This is a tough business for anyone—and it's especially so for greenhorns. Hang in there.

Query Tips

JEFF HERMAN

If you have spent any time at all in this business, the term *query letter* is probably as familiar to you as the back of your hand. Yet, no matter how many courses you've attended and books you've read about this important part of the process, you may still feel inadequate when you try to write one that sizzles. If it's any consolation, you're far from being alone in your uncertainties. The purpose of the query letter is to formally introduce your work and yourself to potential agents and editors. The immediate goal is to motivate them to promptly request a look at your work, or at least a portion of it.

In effect, the letter serves as the writer's first hurdle. It's a relatively painless way for agents and editors to screen out unwanted submissions without the added burden of having to manhandle a deluge of unwanted manuscripts. They are more relaxed if their in-boxes are filled with 50 unanswered queries, as opposed to 50 uninvited 1000-page manuscripts. The query is a very effective way to control the quality and quantity of the manuscripts that get into the office. And that's why you have to write good ones.

The term *query letter* is part of the lexicon and jargon of the publishing business. This term isn't used in any other industry. I assume it has ancient origins. I can conjure up the image of an English gentleman with a fluffy quill pen composing a most civilized letter to a prospective publisher for the purpose of asking for his work to be read and, perchance, published. Our environments may change, but the nature of our ambitions remain the same.

Let's get contemporary. Whenever you hear the term *query letter* you should say to yourself "pitch" or "sales" letter. Because that's what it is. You need the letter to sell.

QUERY LETTER TIPS

- *Don't be long-winded.* Agents/editors are receiving lots of these things, and they want to mow through them as swiftly as possible. Ideally, the letter should be a single page with short paragraphs. (I must admit I've seen good ones that are longer than a page.) If you lose your reader, you've lost your opportunity.

- *Get to the point; don't pontificate.* Too many letters go off on irrelevant detours, which makes it difficult for the agent/editor to determine what's actually for sale— other than the writer's soapbox.
- *Make your letter attractive.* When making a first impression, the subliminal impact of aesthetics cannot be overestimated. Use high-quality stationery and typeface. The essence of your words are paramount, but cheap paper and poor print quality will only diminish your impact.
- *Don't say anything negative about yourself or your attempts to get published.* Everyone appreciates victims when it's time to make charitable donations, but not when it's time to make a profit. It's better if you can make editors/agents think that you have to fight them off.

Q & A: More Query Letter Tips

Q: Why can't I bypass the query hurdle by simply submitting my manuscript?
A: You may—and no one can litigate against you. But if you submit an unsolicited manuscript to a publisher, it's more likely to end up in the so-called slush pile and may never get a fair reading. If sent to an agent, nothing negative may come of it. However, most agents prefer to receive a query first.

Sending unsolicited nonfiction book proposals is in the gray zone. Proposals are much more manageable than entire manuscripts, so editors/agents may not particularly mind. But you may want to avoid the expense of sending unwanted proposals. After all, the query is also an opportunity for you to screen out those who clearly have no interest in your subject. Also, you shouldn't be overly loose with your ideas and concepts.

These pointers, in combination with the other good information in this book and all the other available resources, should at least give you a solid background for creating a query letter that sizzles.

The Knockout Nonfiction Book Proposal

JEFF HERMAN

The nonfiction book proposal is as a sales brochure; viewed as such, and given its due and primary importance in the process of editorial acquisition and book publishing in general, mastery of proposal writing will give you more than a mere leg up: It will invariably make the difference between success and failure.

Before agents and publishers will accept a work of fiction (especially from a newer writer), they require a complete manuscript. However, nonfiction projects are different: A proposal alone can do the trick. This is what makes nonfiction writing a much less speculative and often more lucrative endeavor (relatively speaking) than fiction writing.

You may devote five years of long evenings to writing a 1,000-page fiction manuscript, only to receive a thick pile of computer-generated rejections. Clearly, writing nonfiction doesn't entail the same risks. On the other hand, writing fiction is often an emotionally driven endeavor in which rewards are gained though the act of writing, and are not necessarily based on rational, practical considerations. Interestingly, many successful nonfiction writers fantasize about being fiction writers.

Fiction writing, whether it be pulp or literary, is one of the most creative things a person can do. And there is a market for fiction: Millions of Americans read fiction voraciously. As is covered elsewhere in this book, the fiction market has a category structure through which agents and publishers can be approached.

Nevertheless, as an author, you should understand that writing nonfiction is the easier road to getting published.

As you'll learn, the proposal's structure, contents, and size can vary substantially, and it's up to you to decide the best format for your purposes. Still, the guidelines given below serve as excellent general parameters. In addition, a topnotch excellent model proposal is featured in the next chapter.

APPEARANCE COUNTS

- Your proposal should be printed in black ink on clean letter-sized (8 1/2" × 11") white paper.
- Avoid slick-surfaced computer paper. Be sure to type or print out your manuscript on bond paper—and to separate and trim the pages if they are generated from a fanfold tractor-fed printer.
- Letter-quality printing is by far the best. Make sure the ribbon or toner or ink cartridge is fresh and that all photocopies are dark and clear enough to be read easily. Be wary of old manual typewriters—have the proposal retyped on up-to-date equipment if necessary. Publishing is an image-driven business, and you will be judged, perhaps unconsciously, on the physical and aesthetic merits of your submission.
- Always double-space, or you can virtually guarantee reader antagonism—eyestrain makes people cranky.
- Make sure your proposal appears fresh and new and hasn't been dog-eared, marked-up, and abused by previous readers. No editor will be favorably disposed if she thinks that everyone else on the block has already sent you packing. You want editors to suppose that you have lots of other places you can go, not nowhere else to go.
- Contrary to common practice in other industries, editors prefer not to receive bound proposals. If an editor likes your proposal, she will want to photocopy it for her colleagues, and your binding will only be in the way. If you want to keep the material together and neat, it's best to use a paper clip; if it's a lengthy proposal, maybe it will work best to clip each section together separately.

THE TITLE PAGE

The title page should be the easiest part, but it can also be the most important, since, like your face when you meet someone, it's what is seen first.

Try to think of a title that's attractive and effectively communicates your book's concept. A descriptive subtitle, following a catchy title, can help to achieve both goals. It's very important that your title and subtitle relate to the book's subject, or an editor might make an inaccurate judgment about your book's focus and automatically dismiss it. For instance, if you're proposing a book about gardening, don't title it *The Greening of America*.

Examples of titles that have worked very well are:

How to Win Friends and Influence People by Dale Carnegie

Think and Grow Rich by Napoleon Hill

Baby and Child Care by Dr. Benjamin Spock

How to Swim with the Sharks Without Being Eaten Alive by Harvey Mackay

And, yes, there are notable exceptions: An improbable title that went on to become a perennial success is *What Color Is Your Parachute?* by Richard Bolles. Sure, you may gain freedom and confidence from such exceptional instances, and by all means let your imagination graze during the brainstorming stage. However, don't bet on the success of an arbitrarily conceived title that has nothing at all to do with the book's essential concept or reader appeal.

A title should be stimulating and, when appropriate, upbeat and optimistic. If your subject is an important historic or current event, the title should be dramatic. If a biography, the title should capture something personal (or even controversial) about the subject. Many good books have been handicapped by poorly conceived titles, and many poor books have been catapulted to success by good titles. A good title is good advertising. Procter & Gamble, for instance, spends thousands of worker-hours creating seductive names for its endless array of soap-based products.

The title you choose is referred to as the "working title." Most likely, the book will have a different title when published. There are two reasons for this: (1) A more appropriate and/or arresting title may evolve with time; and (2) the publisher has final contractual discretion over the title (as well as a lot of other things).

The title page should contain only the title; your name, address, and telephone number—and the name, address, and phone number of your agent, if you have one. The title page should be neatly and attractively spaced. Eye-catching and tasteful computer graphics and display-type fonts can contribute to the overall aesthetic appeal.

OVERVIEW

The overview portion of the proposal is a terse statement (one to three pages) of your overall concept and mission. It sets the stage for what's to follow. Short, concise paragraphs are usually best.

BIOGRAPHICAL SECTION

This is where you sell yourself. This section tells who you are and why you're the ideal person to write this book. You should highlight all your relevant experience, including media and public-speaking appearances, and list previous books and/or articles published by and/or about you. Self-flattery is appropriate—so long as you're telling the truth. Many writers prefer to slip into the third person here, to avoid the appearance of egomania.

MARKETING SECTION

This is where you justify the book's existence from a commercial perspective. Who will buy it? For instance, if you're proposing a book on sales, state the number of people who earn their livings through sales; point out that thousands of large and small companies are sales-dependent and spend large sums on sales training, and that all sales professionals are perpetually hungry for fresh, innovative sales books.

Don't just say something like "My book is for adult women and there are more than fifty million adult women in America." You have to be much more demographically sophisticated than that.

COMPETITION SECTION

To the uninitiated, this section may appear to be a set-up to self-destruction. However, if handled strategically, and assuming you have a fresh concept, this section wins you points rather than undermines your case.

The competition section is where you describe major published titles with concepts comparable to yours. If you're familiar with your subject, you'll probably know those titles by heart; you may have even read most or all of them. If you're not certain, check *Books in Print*—available in virtually every library—which catalogues all titles in print in every category under the sun. Don't list everything published on your subject—that could require a book in itself. Just describe the leading half-dozen titles or so (backlist classics as well as recent books) and *explain why yours will be different*.

Getting back to the sales-book example, there is no shortage of good sales books. There's a reason for that—there's a big market for sales books. You can turn that to your advantage by emphasizing what a substantial, insatiable demand there is for sales books. Your book will feed that demand with its unique and innovative sales-success program. Salespeople and companies dependent on sales are always looking for new ways to enhance sales skills (it's okay to reiterate key points).

PROMOTION SECTION

Here you suggest possible ways to promote and market the book. Sometimes this section is unnecessary. It depends on your subject and on what, if any, realistic promotional prospects exist.

If you're proposing a specialized academic book such as *The Mating Habits of Octopi*, the market is a relatively limited one, and elaborate promotions would be wasteful. But if you're proposing a popularly oriented relationship book along the lines of *The Endless Orgasm in One Easy Lesson*, the promotional possibilities are also endless. They would include most major electronic broadcast and print media outlets, advertising, maybe even some weird contests. You want to guide the publisher toward seeing realistic ways to publicize the book.

CHAPTER OUTLINE

This is the meat of the proposal. Here's where you finally tell what's going to be in the book. Each chapter should be tentatively titled and clearly abstracted. Some successful proposals have fewer than one hundred words per abstracted chapter; others have several hundred words per chapter. Sometimes the length varies from chapter to chapter. There are no hard-and-fast rules here; it's the dealer's choice. Sometimes less is more, at other times a too-brief outline inadequately represents the project.

At their best, the chapter abstracts read like mini-chapters—as opposed to stating "I will do . . . and I will show . . . " Visualize the trailer for a forthcoming movie; that's the tantalizing effect you want to create. Also, it's a good idea to preface the outline with a table of contents. This way, the editor can see your entire road map at the outset.

SAMPLE CHAPTERS

Sample chapters are optional. A strong, well-developed proposal will often be enough. However, especially if you're a first-time writer, one or more sample chapters will give you an opportunity to show your stuff, and help dissolve an editor's concerns about your ability to actually write the book, thereby increasing the odds that you'll receive an offer—and you'll probably increase the size of the advance, too.

Nonfiction writers are often wary of investing time to write sample chapters since they view the proposal as a way of avoiding speculative writing. This can be a short-sighted position, however, for a single sample chapter can make the difference between selling and not selling a marginal proposal. Occasionally a publisher will request that one or two sample chapters be written before making a decision about a particular project. If the publisher seems to have a real interest, writing the sample material is definitely worth the author's time, and the full package can then be shown to additional prospects too.

Many editors say that they look for reasons to reject books, and that being on the fence is a valid reason for rejecting a project. To be sure, there are cases where sample chapters have tilted a proposal on the verge of rejection right back onto the playing field!

Keep in mind that the publisher is speculating that you can and will write the book upon contract. A sample chapter will go far to reduce the publisher's concerns about your ability to deliver a quality work beyond the proposal stage.

WHAT ELSE?

There are a variety of materials you may wish to attach to the proposal to further bolster your cause. These include:

- Laudatory letters and comments about you.
- Laudatory publicity about you.
- A headshot (not if you look like the Fly, unless you're proposing a humor book or a nature book).
- Copies of published articles you've written.
- Videos of TV or speaking appearances.
- Any and all information that builds you up in a relevant way; but be organized about it—don't create a disheveled, unruly package.

LENGTH

The average proposal is probably between 15 and 30 double-spaced pages, and the typical sample chapter an additional 10 to 20 double-spaced pages. But sometimes proposals reach 100 pages, and sometimes they're 5 pages total. Extensive proposals are not a handicap.

Whatever it takes!

Note: Readers of *Writer's Guide* who wish to do more research on the topic of book proposals may be referred to *Write the Perfect Book Proposal: 10 Proposals That Sold and Why* by Jeff Herman and Deborah Adams (John Wiley & Sons). This work contains samples of successful book proposals along with commentary and coaching on techniques writers employ to develop book projects agents find salable—and publishers marketable.

Model Successful
Nonfiction Book Proposal

JEFF HERMAN

In this chapter is a genuine proposal that won a healthy book contract. It's excerpted from *Write the Perfect Book Proposal* by Jeff Herman and Deborah Adams (John Wiley & Sons), and includes an extensive critique of its strongest and weakest points. All in all, it's an excellent proposal and serves as a strong model.

The book is titled *Heart and Soul: A Psychological and Spiritual Guide to Preventing and Healing Heart Disease* and is written by Bruno Cortis, M.D. This project was sold to the Villard Books division of Random House. Every editor who saw this proposal offered sincere praise. Ironically, several of these editors regretted not being able to seek the book's acquisition. From the outset I was aware this might happen. The past few years have given us numerous unconventional health and healing books—many of which are excellent. Most publishers I approached felt that their health/spirituality quota was already full and that they would wind up competing with themselves if they acquired any more such titles.

Experienced agents and writers are familiar with the market-glut problem. In many popular categories it's almost endemic. If you're prepared for this reality from the outset, there are ways to pave your own road and bypass the competition. Dedicated agents, editors, and writers want to see important books published regardless of what the publishers' lists dictate. Further, it is not necessary for every publisher to want your book (though that is the proven way to maximize the advance). In the end, you need only the right publisher and a reasonable deal. Let's look at the title page from the book proposal.

HEART AND SOUL

(This is a good title. It conjures up dramatic images similar to a soulful blues melody. And it has everything to do with what this proposal is about. The subtitle is scientific and provides a clear direction for the patients.)

**Psychological and Spiritual Guide to
Preventing and Healing Heart Disease
by
Bruno Cortis, M.D.
Book Proposal**

**The Jeff Herman Agency, Inc.
140 Charles Street
Suite 15A
New York, NY 10014
telephone: 212-941-0540**

(The title page is sufficient overall. But it would have been better if the software had been available to create a more striking cover sheet. To a large degree, everything does initially get judged by its cover.)

OVERVIEW

(One minor improvement here would have been to shift the word "Overview" to the center of the page—or otherwise styling the typeface for such headings and subheadings throughout the proposal to make them stand out from the body text.)

Heart disease is the number-one killer of Americans over the age of 40. The very words can sound like a death sentence. Our heart, the most intimate part of our body, is under siege. Until now, most experts have advised victims of the disease, as well as those who would avoid it, to change avoidable risk factors, like smoking, and begin a spartan regimen of diet and exercise. But new research shows that risk factors and lifestyle are only part of the answer. In fact, it is becoming clear that for many patients, emotional, psychological, and even spiritual factors are at least as important, both in preventing disease and in healing an already damaged heart.

(This is a powerful lead paragraph. The author knows there are a lot of books out there about heart disease. The first paragraph of the overview immediately distinguishes this book proposal and draws attention to "new research." Anything that is potentially cutting edge is going to catch the eye of a prospective publisher.)

Like *Love, Medicine, and Miracles* by Bernie Siegel, which showed cancer patients how to take charge of their own disease and life, *Heart and Soul* will show potential and actual heart patients how to use inner resources to form a healthy relationship with their heart, actually healing circulatory disorders and preventing further damage.

(The preceding paragraph contains the central thesis for the project, and it is profoundly important. In retrospect, this could have worked exceedingly well as the first paragraph of the proposal, thereby immediately setting the table.) This is a clever comparison to a highly successful book. It indicates an untapped market that has already proven itself in a similar arena. Instead of merely making unsubstantiated claims based on the success of Dr. Siegel's work, the author shows what this book will do to merit the same type of attention.)

The author, Bruno Cortis, M.D., is a renowned cardiologist whose experience with hundreds of "exceptional heart patients" has taught him that there is much more to medicine than operations and pills.

(It is good to bring the author's credentials into the overview at this juncture. A comparison has been made with a highly successful and marketable doctor/author—which will immediately raise questions as to whether this author has similar potential. The author anticipates this line of editorial reasoning and here makes some strong statements.)

Dr. Cortis identifies three types of heart patients:

- Passive Patients, who are unwilling or unable to take responsibility for their condition. Instead, these patients blame outside forces, withdraw from social contacts, and bewail their fate. They may become deeply depressed, and tend to die very soon.
- Obedient Consumers, who are the "A" students of modern medicine. Following doctors' orders to the letter, these patients behave exactly as they are supposed to, placing their fates in the hands of the experts. These patients tend to die exactly when medicine predicts they will.
- Exceptional Heart Patients, who regard a diagnosis of heart disease as a challenge. Although they may have realistic fears for the future, these patients take full responsibility for their situation and actively contribute to their own recovery. While they may or may not follow doctors' orders, these patients tend to choose the therapy or combination of therapies that is best for them. They often live far beyond medical predictions.

(This is an exceptional overview—especially where it defines the three patient types.)

It is Dr. Cortis' aim in this book to show readers how to become exceptional heart patients, empowering them to take responsibility for their own health and well-being.

(The remaining paragraphs of this overview section show a highly focused and well-thought-out plan for the book. The writing collaborator on this project had to condense and assimilate boxes and boxes of material to produce this concise and to-the-point overview that leaves no questions unanswered. Although it took a great deal of effort for the writer to write such a good proposal, there is no struggle for the editor to understand exactly what is being proposed and what the book is going to be about.)

Although Dr. Cortis acknowledges the importance of exercise, stress management, and proper nutrition—the standard staples of cardiac treatment—he stresses that there is an even deeper level of human experience that is necessary in order to produce wellness. Unlike other books on heart disease, *Heart and Soul* does not prescribe the same strict diet and exercise program for everyone. Instead it takes a flexible approach, urging readers to create their own unique health plan by employing psychological and spiritual practices in combination with a variety of more traditional diet and exercise regimens.

While seemingly revolutionary, Dr. Cortis' message is simple: You can do much more for the health of your heart than you think you can. This is true whether you have no symptoms or risk factors whatsoever, if you have some symptoms or risk factors, or if you actually already have heart disease.

MARKET ANALYSIS

Heart and Soul could not be more timely. Of the 1 ½ million heart attacks suffered by Americans each year, nearly half occur between the ages of 40 and 65. Three fifths of these heart attacks are fatal. While these precise statistics may not be familiar to the millions of baby boomers now entering middle age, the national obsession with oat bran, low-fat foods, and exercising for health, shows that the members of the boomer generation are becoming increasingly aware of their own mortality.

(The writer would be well advised to ease off the use of the term baby boomer. It is so often used in book proposals that many editors are undoubtedly sick of it—and some have said so. It might have been better merely to describe the exceptional number of people in this pertinent age bracket—without attempting to sound trendy. Good use of facts, trends, and the public's receptivity to what some would characterize as an unorthodox treatment approach.)

This awareness of growing older, coupled with a widespread loss of faith in doctors and fear of overtechnologized medicine, combine to produce a market that is ready for a book emphasizing the spiritual component in healing, especially in reference to heart disease.

Most existing books on the market approach the subject from the physician's point of view, urging readers to follow doctor's orders to attain a healthy heart. There is very little emphasis in these books on the patient's own responsibility for wellness or the inner changes that must be made for the prescribed regimens to work. Among the best known recent books are:

(Not a big deal in this instance—but ordinarily it would be better to have identified this portion of the proposal as the competition section, and set it off under a separate heading.)

Healing Your Heart, by Herman Hellerstein, M.D., and Paul Perry (Simon and Schuster, 1990). Although this book, like most of the others, advocates proper nutrition, exercise, cessation of smoking and stress reduction as the road to a healthy heart, it fails to provide the motivation necessary to attain such changes in the reader's lifestyle. Without changes in thinking and behavior, readers of this and similar books will find it difficult, if not impossible, to follow the strict diet and exercise program recommended.

In *Heart Talk: Preventing and Coping with Silent and Painful Heart Disease* (Harcourt Brace Jovanovich, 1987), Dr. Peter F. Cohn and Dr. Joan K. Cohn address the dangers of "silent" (symptomless) heart disease. While informative, the book emphasizes only one manifestation of heart disease, and does not empower readers with the motivational tools needed to combat that disease.

(This section is termed the market analysis, which in this proposal actually departs from the approach of the typical marketing section of most proposals. Instead of telling the publisher how to sell the book, the writing collaborator (see the About the Authors section below) shows special insight into the target audience. The key is that this analysis is not merely a statement of the obvious. This type of in-depth analysis of the potential reader can be very persuasive.)

The Trusting Heart, by Redford Williams, M.D. (Times Books, 1989), demonstrates how hostility and anger can lead to heart disease while trust and forgiveness can contribute to wellness. While these are important points, the holistic treatment of heart disease must encompass other approaches as well. The author also fails to provide sufficient motivation for behavioral changes in the readers.

(The author does a good job of demonstrating the invaluable uniqueness of this particular project—especially important when compared with the strong list of competitors.)

The best book on preventing and curing heart disease is *Dr. Dean Ornish's Program for Reversing Heart Disease* (Random House, 1990). This highly successful book prescribes a very strict diet and exercise program for actually reversing certain types of coronary artery disease. This still-controversial approach is by far the best on the market; unfortunately, the material is presented in a dense, academic style not easily accessible to the lay reader. It also focuses on Dr. Ornish's program as the "only way to manage heart disease," excluding other, more synergistic methods.

(The writer collaborator directly analyzed the competition, highlighting the most relevant books on the market without listing each one directly. Although you do not want to present the editor with any unnecessary surprises, if there are too many similar books out in your particular subject area, you might want to use this approach. The writer confronts the heaviest competition directly by finding specific distinguishing factors that support the strength of her proposed project.)

APPROACH

Heart and Soul will be a 60,000- to 70,000-word book targeted to health-conscious members of the baby boom generation. Unlike other books on heart disease, it will focus on the "facts of the connection between the mind and the body as it relates to heart disease, showing readers how to use that connection to heal the heart. The book will be written in an informal but authoritative style, in Dr. Cortis' voice. It will begin with a discussion of heart disease and show how traditional medicine fails to prevent or cure it. Subsequent chapters will deal with the mind-body connection, and the role in healing of social support systems, self-esteem, and faith. In order to help readers reduce stress in their lives, Dr. Cortis shows how they can create their own "daily practice" that combines exercise, relaxation, meditation, and use of positive imagery. Throughout the book, he will present anecdotes that demonstrate how other Exceptional Heart Patients have overcome their disease and gone on to lead healthy and productive lives.

In addition to a thorough discussion of the causes and outcomes of coronary artery disease, the book will include tests and checklists that readers may use to gauge their progress, and exercises, ranging from the cerebral to the physical, that strengthen and help heal the heart. At the end of each chapter readers will be introduced to an essential "Heartskill" that will enable them to put the advice of the chapter into immediate practice.

Through example and encouragement *Heart and Soul* will offer readers a variety of strategies for coping with heart disease, to be taken at once or used in combination. Above all an accessible, practical book, *Heart and Soul* will present readers with a workable program for controlling their own heart disease and forming a healthy relationship with their hearts.

(This is a good summary statement of the book.)

ABOUT THE AUTHORS

Bruno Cortis, M.D., is an internationally trained cardiologist with more than 30 years' experience in research and practice. A pioneer of cardiovascular applications of lasers and angioscopy, a Diplomate of the American Board of Cardiology, contributor of more than 70 published professional papers, Dr. Cortis has long advocated the need for new dimensions of awareness in health and the healing arts. As a practicing physician and researcher, his open acknowledgment of individual spirituality as the core of health puts him on the cutting edge of those in traditional medicine who are beginning to create the medical arts practices of the future.

(This is a very good description of the author. The writing collaborator establishes Dr. Cortis as both an expert in his field and a compelling personality. All of this material is relevant to the ultimate success of the book.)

Dr. Cortis has been a speaker at conferences in South America, Japan, and Australia, as well as in Europe and the United States. His firm, Mind Your Health, is dedicated to the prevention of heart attack through the development of human potential. Dr. Cortis is the cofounder of the Exceptional Heart Patients program. The successful changes he has made in his own medical practice prove he is a man not only of vision and deeds, but an author whose beliefs spring from the truths of daily living.

(A formal vita follows in this proposal. It is best to lead off with a journalistic-style biography and follow up with a complete and formal resume—assuming, as in this case, the author's professional credentials are inseparable from the book.)

Kathryn Lance is the author of more than 30 books of nonfiction and fiction (see attached publications list for details). Her first book, *Running for Health and*

Beauty (1976), the first mass-market book on running for women, sold half a million copies. *The Setpoint Diet* (1985), ghosted for Dr. Gilbert A. Leveille, reached the New York *Times* bestseller list for several weeks. Ms. Lance has written widely on fitness, health, diet, and medicine.

(Though she wasn't mentioned on the title page, Lance is the collaborator. This brief bio and the following resume reveal a writer with virtually impeccable experience. Her participation served to ensure to editors that they could count on the delivery of a high-quality manuscript. Her bio sketch is also strong in its simplicity. Her writing credits are voluminous, but she does not use up space here with a comprehensive listing. Instead she showcases only credits that are relevant to the success of this particular project.

Comprehensive author resumes were also attached as addenda to the proposal package.)

HEART AND SOUL
by
Bruno Cortis, M.D.
Chapter Outline

(Creating a separate page (or pages) for the entire table of contents is a useful and easy technique to enable the editor to gain a holistic vision for the book before delving into the chapter abstracts. In retrospect, we should have had one here.)

(The following is an exceptional outline because it goes well beyond the lazy and stingy telegraph approach that many writers use, often to their own detriment. [Telegrams once were a popular means of communication that required the sender to pay by the word.] Here each abstract reads like a miniature sample chapter unto itself. It proves that the writers have a genuine command of their subject, a well-organized agenda, and superior skills for writing about it. Together they are a darn good team. Whatever legitimate reasons a publisher may have had for rejecting this proposal, it had nothing to do with its manifest editorial and conceptual merits. Some writers are reluctant to go this editorial distance on spec. However, if you believe in your project's viability and you want to maximize acquisition interest and the ultimate advance, you'll give the proposal everything you've got.)

Contents

Introduction: Beating the Odds: Exceptional Heart Patients
(See sample chapter.)

CHAPTER ONE. YOU AND YOUR HEART
Traditional medicine doesn't and can't "cure" heart disease. The recurrence rate of arterial blockage after angioplasty is 25%–35%, while a bypass operation only

bypasses the problem, but does not cure it. The author proposes a new way of look-ing at heart disease, one in which patients become responsible for the care and well-being of their hearts, in partnership with their physicians. Following a brief, understandable discussion of the physiology of heart disease and heart attack, fur-ther topics covered in this chapter include:

(This is a good technique for a chapter abstract. The writer organizes the structure as a listing of chapter topics and elaborates with a sample of the substance and writing ap-proach that will be incorporated into the book. The editor cannot, of course, be ex-pected to be an expert on the subject, but after reading this abstract will come away with a good sense of the quality of the chapter and the depth of its coverage.)

Heart disease as a message from your body. Many of us go through life neglect-ing our bodies' signals, ignoring symptoms until a crisis occurs. But the body talks to us and it is up to us to listen and try to understand the message. The heart bears the load of all our physical activity as well as our mental activity. Stress can affect the heart as well as any other body system. This section explores the warning signs of heart disease as "messages" we may receive from our hearts, what these mes-sages may mean, and what we can do in response to these messages.

Why medical tests and treatments are not enough. You, the patient, are ultimately responsible for your own health. Placing all faith in a doctor is a way of abdicating that responsibility. The physician is not a healer; rather, he or she sets the stage for the patient's body to heal itself. Disease is actually a manifestation of an imbalance within the body. Medical procedures can help temporarily, but the real solution lies in the patient's becoming aware of his own responsibility for health. This may in-volve changing diet, stopping smoking, learning to control the inner life.

(Although the abstracts are directed to the editor who reviews the proposal, the writer incorporates the voice to be used in the book by speaking directly to the reader. This is an effective way to incorporate her writing style into the chapter-by-chapter outline.)

Getting the best (while avoiding the worst) of modern medicine. In the author's view, the most important aspect of medicine is not the medication but the pa-tient/physician relationship. Unfortunately, this relationship is often cold, superfi-cial, professional. The patient goes into the medical pipeline, endures a number of tests, then comes out the other end with a diagnosis, which is like a flag he has to carry for life. This view of disease ignores the patient as the *main* component of the healing process. Readers are advised to work with their doctors to learn their own blood pressure, blood sugar, cholesterol level, and what these numbers mean. They are further advised how to enlist a team of support people to increase their own knowledge of the disease and learn to discover the self-healing mechanisms within.

How to assess your doctor. Ten questions a patient needs to ask in order to assure the best patient-doctor relationship.

Taking charge of your own medical care. Rather than being passive patients, readers are urged to directly confront their illness and the reasons for it, asking themselves: How can I find a cause at the deepest level? What have I learned from this disease? What is good about it? What have I learned about myself? Exceptional heart patients don't allow themselves to be overwhelmed by the disease; rather, they realize that it is most likely a temporary problem, most of the time self-limited, and that they have a power within to overcome it.

Seven keys to a healthy heart. Whether presently healthy or already ill of heart disease, there is a great deal readers can do to improve and maintain the health of their hearts. The most important component of such a plan is to have a commitment to a healthy heart. The author offers the following seven keys to a healthy heart: respect your body; take time to relax every day; accept, respect, and appreciate yourself; share your deepest feelings; establish life goals; nourish your spiritual self; love yourself and others unconditionally. Each of these aspects of heart care will be examined in detail in later chapters.

Heartskill #1: *Learning to take your own pulse.* The pulse is a wave of blood sent through the arteries each time the heart contracts; pulse rate therefore provides important information about cardiac function. The easiest place to measure the pulse is the wrist: place your index and middle finger over the underside of the opposite wrist. Press gently and firmly until you locate your pulse. Don't use your thumb to feel the pulse, because the thumb has a pulse of its own. Count the number of pulse beats in fifteen seconds, then multiply that by four for your heart rate.

This exercise will include charts so that readers can track and learn their own normal pulse range for resting and exercising, and be alerted to irregularities and changes that may require medical attention.

(The inclusion of this technique shows how specific and practical information will be included in the book—important for a nonfiction book proposal. Editors look for what are called the program aspects of a book, because they can be used in promotional settings—and may also be the basis for serial-rights sales to magazines.)

CHAPTER TWO. YOUR MIND AND YOUR HEART

This chapter begins to explore the connection between mind and body as it relates to heart disease. Early in the chapter readers will meet three Exceptional Heart Patients who overcame crushing diagnoses. These include Van, who overcame a heart attack (at age 48), two open heart surgeries, and "terminal" lung cancer. Through visualization techniques given him by the author, Van has fully recovered and is living a healthy and satisfying life. Goran, who had a family history of cardiomyopathy, drew on the support and love of his family to survive a heart transplant and has since gone on to win several championships in an Olympics contest for transplant patients. Elaine, who overcame both childhood cancer and severe heart disease, is, at the age of 24, happily married and a mother. The techniques used by these Exceptional Heart Patients will be discussed in the context of the mind-body connection.

(The authors do not save the good stuff for the book. If you have interesting case studies or anecdotes, include them in your abstracts: The more stimulating material you can include, the more you can intrigue your editor. In general, this chapter-by-chapter synopsis is exceptionally detailed in a simplified fashion, which is important for this type of book.)

How your doctor views heart disease: Risk factors v. symptoms. Traditional medicine views the risk factors for heart disease (smoking, high blood cholesterol, high blood pressure, diabetes, obesity, sedentary lifestyle, family history of heart disease, use of oral contraceptives) as indicators of the likelihood of developing illness. In contrast, the author presents these risk factors as *symptoms* of an underlying disease, and discusses ways to change them. Smoking, for example, is not the root of the problem, which is, rather, fear, tension, and stress. Smoking is just an outlet that the patient uses to get rid of these basic elements which he or she believes are uncontrollable. Likewise high cholesterol, which is viewed by the medical establishment as largely caused by poor diet, is also affected by stress. (In a study of rabbits on a high-cholesterol diet, narrowing of arteries was less in rabbits that were petted, even if the diet remained unhealthful.) Other elements besides the traditional "risk factors," such as hostility, have been shown to lead to high rates of heart disease.

A mind/body model of heart disease. It is not uncommon to hear stories like this: they were a very happy couple, married 52 years. Then, suddenly, the wife developed breast cancer and died. The husband, who had no previous symptoms of heart disease, had a heart attack and died two months later. All too often there is a very close relationship between a traumatic event and serious illness. Likewise, patients may often become depressed and literally will themselves to die. The other side of the coin is the innumerable patients who use a variety of techniques to enlist the mind-body connection in helping to overcome and even cure serious illnesses, including heart disease.

Rethinking your negative beliefs about heart disease. The first step in using the mind to help to heal the body is to rethink negative beliefs about heart disease. Modern studies have shown that stress plays a most important role in the creation of heart disease, influencing all of the "risk factors." Heart disease is actually a disease of self, caused by self, and is made worse by the belief that we are its "victims." Another negative and incorrect belief is that the possibilities for recovery are limited. The author asserts that these beliefs are untrue, and that for patients willing to learn from the experience, heart disease can be a path to recovery, self-improvement, and growth.

The healing personality: tapping into your body's healing powers. Although the notion of a "healing personality" may sound contradictory, the power of healing is awareness, which can be achieved by anyone. The author describes his own discovery of spirituality in medicine and the realization that ultimately the origin of disease is in the mind. This is why treating disease with medicine and surgery alone does not heal: because these methods ignore the natural healing powers of the body/mind. How does one develop a "healing personality"? The starting point is awareness of the spiritual power within. As the author states, in order to become healthy, one must become spiritual.

Writing your own script for a healthy heart. Before writing any script, one must set the stage, and in this case readers are urged to see a cardiologist or physician and have a thorough checkup. This checkup will evaluate the presence or absence of the "risk factors," and assess the health of other body organs as well. Once the scene is set, it is time to add in the other elements of a healthy heart, all of which will be explored in detail in the coming chapters.

Making a contract with your heart. We see obstacles only when we lose sight of our goals. How to make out (either mentally or on paper) a contract with one's heart that promises to take care of the heart. Each individual reader's contract will be somewhat different; for example, someone who is overweight might include in the contract the desire that in six months she would weigh so much. The point is to set realistic, achievable goals. Guidelines are provided for breaking larger goals down into small, easily achievable, steps. Creating goals for the future makes them a part of the present in the sense that it is today that we start pursuing them.

What to say when you talk to yourself. In the view of the author, the greatest source of stress in life is negative conversations we have with ourselves. These "conversations," which go on all the time without our even being aware of them, often include such negative suggestions as "When are you going to learn?" "Oh, no, you stupid idiot, you did it again!" When we put ourselves down we reinforce feelings of unworthiness and inadequacy, which leads to stress and illness. Guidelines are given for replacing such negative self-conversation with more positive self-talk, including messages of love and healing.

Heartskill #2: *Sending healing energy to your heart.* In this exercise, readers learn a simple meditation technique that will help them get in touch with their natural healing powers and begin to heal their hearts.

CHAPTER THREE. THE FRIENDSHIP FACTOR: PLUGGING INTO YOUR SOCIAL SUPPORT SYSTEM

Heart disease is not an isolated event, and the heart patient is not an isolated human being. Among the less medically obvious "risk factors" involved in coronary disease are social isolation. In this chapter the author discusses the importance of maintaining and strengthening all the social support aspects of the patient's life, including family, friendship, community, and sex. He shows how intimacy and connection can be used not just for comfort but as actual healing tools.

Sexual intimacy: the healing touch. Following a heart attack, many patients may lose confidence due to a fear of loss of attractiveness or fear of death. Citing recent studies, the author points out that there is a difference between making sex and making love. The desire for sex is a human need and is not limited to healthy people. Anybody who has had a heart problem still has sexual needs and ignoring them may be an additional cause of stress. Guidelines for when and how to resume sexual activity are offered. Other topics covered in this chapter include:

Keeping your loved ones healthy, and letting them keep you healthy
How you may be unwittingly pushing others out of your life
The art of nondefensive, nonreactive communication
Accepting your loved ones' feelings and your own
How to enlist the support of family and friends
Joining or starting your own support group
Heartskill #3: *Mapping your social support system*

CHAPTER FOUR. OPENING YOUR HEART: LEARNING TO MAKE FRIENDS WITH YOURSELF

In addition to enlisting the support of others, for complete healing it is necessary for the patient to literally become a friend to himself or herself. This may entail changing old ways of thinking and responding, as well as developing new, healthier ways of relating to time and other external stresses. In this chapter the author explores ways of changing Type A behavior, as well as proven techniques for dealing with life's daily hassles and upsets. An important section of the chapter shows readers how to love and cherish the "inner child," that part of the personality that needs to be loved, to be acknowledged, and to have fun. Equally important is the guilt that each of us carries within, and that can lead not only to unhealthy behaviors but also to actual stress. The author gives exercises for learning to discover and absolve the hidden guilts that keep each of us from realizing our true healthy potential. Topics covered in this chapter include:

A positive approach to negative emotions
Checking yourself out on Type A behavior: a self-test
Being assertive without being angry
Keeping your balance in the face of daily hassles and major setbacks
Making a friend of time
Identifying and healing your old childhood hurts
Letting go of hurts, regrets, resentments, and guilt
Forgiving yourself and making a new start
The trusting heart
Heartskill #4: *Forgiveness exercise*

CHAPTER FIVE. IDENTIFYING AND ELIMINATING STRESS IN YOUR LIFE

The science of psychoneuroimmunology is beginning to prove that the mind and body are not only connected, but inseparable. It has been demonstrated that changes in life often precede disease. Lab studies have shown that the amount of stress experienced by experimental animals can induce rapid growth of a tumor that would ordinarily be rejected. For heart patients, the fact of disease itself can become another inner stress factor that may worsen the disease and the quality of life. One out of five healthy persons is a "heart reactor," who has strong responses under stress that induce such unhealthful physiological changes as narrowing of the coronary arteries, hypertrophy of the heart muscle, and high blood pressure. In this chapter the author shows readers how to change stress-producing negative beliefs into constructive, rational beliefs that reduce stress. Included are guidelines to the five keys for controlling stress: diet, rest, exercise, attitude, and self-discipline.

Why you feel so stressed-out
Where does emotional stress come from and how does it affect your heart?
Your stress signal checklist
Staying in control
Calculating your heart-stress level at home and on the job
Stress management
Heartskill #5: *Mapping your stress hotspots*

CHAPTER SIX. YOUR FAITH AND YOUR HEART

As the author points out, there are few studies in the field of spirituality and medicine, because physicians, like most scientists, shy away from what is called "soft data." Soft data are anything outside the realm of physics, mathematics, etc.: the "exact sciences." As a physician, the author has grown ever more convinced of the body's natural healing power, which is evoked through mind and spirit. No matter how "spirit" is defined, whether in traditional religious terms or as a component of mind or personality, the truth is that in order to become healthy, it is necessary to become spiritual.

In a 10-month study of 393 coronary patients at San Francisco General Hospital, it was proven that the group who received outside prayer in addition to standard medical treatment did far better than those who received medical treatment alone. Those in the experimental group suffered fewer problems with congestive heart failure, pneumonia, cardiac arrests, and had a significantly lower mortality rate. This chapter explores the possible reasons for this startling result and illuminates the connection between spirit and health.

The difference between spirituality and religion. A discussion of the differences between traditional views of spirituality and the new holistic approach that sees mind, body, and spirit as intimately connected and interdependent.

Faith and heart disease. The healing personality is that of a person who takes care of his own body. He may also use such other "paramedical" means to get well as physical exercise, a proper diet, prayer, meditation, positive affirmations, and visualization techniques. The author surveys these techniques that have been used for centuries to contribute to the healing of a wide variety of diseases. Other topics exploring the connection between faith and a healthy heart include:

Tapping into your personal mythology
Forgiving yourself for heart disease
Keeping a psychological-spiritual journal
Heartskill #6: *Consulting your inner advisor*

CHAPTER SEVEN. PUTTING IT ALL TOGETHER: HOW TO DEVELOP YOUR OWN DAILY PRACTICE FOR A HEALTHY HEART

Daily Practice as defined by the author is a personalized program in which readers will choose from among the techniques offered in the book to create their own unique combination of mental and physical healing exercises. Each component of the daily practice is fully explained. The techniques range from the familiar—healthful diet and exercise—to the more spiritual, including prayer, meditation, and visualization. Included are examples of use of each of these techniques as practiced by Exceptional Heart Patients.

The benefits of daily practice
Meditation: how to do it your way
Stretching, yoga, and sensory awareness
Hearing with the mind's ear, seeing with the mind's eye
The psychological benefits of exercise
Healthy eating as a meditative practice
The healing powers of silent prayer
Creating your own visualization exercises
Creating your own guided-imagery tapes
Using other types of positive imagery
Heartskill #7: *Picking a practice that makes sense to you*

CHAPTER EIGHT. LEARNING TO SMELL THE FLOWERS

In our society, pleasure is often regarded as a selfish pursuit. We tend to feel that it is not as important as work. And yet the key element in health is not blood pressure, or cholesterol, or blood sugar; instead it is peace of mind and the ability to enjoy life. Indeed, this ability has been proven to prevent illness. In this chapter the author focuses on the ability to *live* in the moment, savoring all that life has to offer, from the simple physical pleasures of massage to the more profound pleasures of the spirit. Topics covered in this chapter include a discussion of Type B behavior, which can be learned. The secrets of this type of behavior include self-assurance, self-motivation, and the ability to relax in the face of pressures. The author shows how even the most confirmed Type A heart patient can, through self-knowledge, change outer-directed goals for inner ones, thus achieving the emotional and physical benefits of a Type B lifestyle. Other topics discussed in this chapter include:

Getting the most out of the present moment
Taking an inventory of life's pleasures
Counting down to relaxation
Hot baths, hot showers, hot tubs and saunas
Touching; feeding the skin's hunger for human touch
Pets, plants, and gardens as healing helpers
Heartskill #8: *Building islands of peace into your life*

CHAPTER NINE. CREATING YOUR FUTURE

The heart may be viewed in many different ways: as a mechanical pump, as the center of circulation, as the source of life. The author suggests viewing the heart above all as a spiritual organ, the center of love, and learning to figuratively fill it with love and peace. A *positive* result of heart disease is the sudden knowledge that one is not immortal, and the opportunity to plan for a more worthwhile, fulfilling life in the future. In this final chapter, Dr. Cortis offers guidelines for setting and achieving goals for health—of mind, body, and spirit. For each reader the goals, and the means to achieve them, will be different. But as the author points out, this is a journey that everyone must take, patients as well as doctors, readers as well as the author. No matter how different the paths we choose, we must realize that truly "our hearts are the same."

The Art of Happiness
Choosing your own path to contentment
Goals chosen by other exceptional heart patients
Developing specific action steps
Reinforcing and rethinking your life goals
Finding your own meaning in life and death
Heartskill #9: *Helping others to heal their hearts*

RECOMMENDED READING

APPENDIX I. FOR FRIENDS AND FAMILY: HOW TO SUPPORT AN EXCEPTIONAL HEART PATIENT

APPENDIX II. ON FINDING OR STARTING A SELF-HELP GROUP

APPENDIX III. ABOUT THE EXCEPTIONAL HEART PATIENT PROJECT

AUTHOR'S NOTES

ACKNOWLEDGMENTS

INDEX

(Appendixes are always a valuable bonus.)

(It is great to be able to include an actual endorsement in your proposal package. Quite often, writers state those from whom they intend to request endorsements—but do not actually have them lined up. Perhaps unnecessary to say, but valuable to reiterate, is that editors and agents are not overly impressed by such assertions. They do, however, nod with respect to those authors who demonstrate that they can deliver on their claims. The inclusion of at least one such blurb creates tremendous credibility.)

GERALD G. JAMPOLSKY, M.D.

Practice Limited to Psychiatry
Adults and Children
21 Main Street
Tiburon, California 94920
(415) 435-1622

April 1, 1998

Mr. Jeff Herman
The Jeff Herman Agency, Inc.
140 Charles Street, Suite 15A
New York, NY 10014

Dear Jeff:

You may use the following quote for Bruno's book:

> *"Dr. Bruno Cortis writes from the heart—for the heart. This is a much-needed and very important book."*

Gerald Jampolsky, M.D.
Coauthor of *Love Is the Answer*

With love and peace,

Jerry

Gerald Jampolsky, M.D.

(The author, Dr. Cortis, is very well connected in his field. He solicited promises from several prominent persons to provide cover endorsements like this one. Having these promises to provide such blurbs at the time I marketed the proposal further enhanced the agency's sales position.)

Rejected . . . Again

The Process and the Art of Perseverance

JEFF HERMAN

Trying to sell your writing is in many ways similar to perpetually applying for employment; it's likely you will run into many walls. And that can hurt. But even the Great Wall of China has a beginning and an end—for it's simply an external barrier erected for strategic purposes. In my experience, the most insurmountable walls are the ones in our own heads. Anything that is artificially crafted can and will be overcome by people who are resourceful and determined enough to do it.

Naturally, the reality of rejection cannot be completely circumvented. It is, however, constructive to envision each wall as a friendly challenge to your resourcefulness, determination, and strength. There are many people who got through the old Berlin Wall because for them it was a challenge and a symbol—a place to begin, not stop.

The world of publishing is a potentially hostile environment, especially for the writer. Our deepest aspirations can be put to rest without having achieved peace or satisfaction. But it is within each of us to learn about this special soil, and blossom to our fullest. No rejection is fatal until the writer walks away from the battle leaving the written work behind, undefended and unwanted.

WHY MOST REJECTION LETTERS ARE SO EMPTY

What may be most frustrating are the generic word-processed letters that say something like: "not right for us." Did the sender read any of your work? Did he or she have any personal opinions about it? Could she not have spared a few moments to share her thoughts?

As an agent, it's part of my job to reject the vast majority of the submissions I receive. And, with each rejection, I know I'm not making someone happy. On the other hand, I don't see spreading happiness as my exclusionary purpose. Like other agents and editors, I make liberal use of the generic rejection letter.

Here's why: Too much to do, too little time. There just isn't sufficient time to write customized, personal rejection letters. To be blunt about it, the rejection process isn't a profit center; it does consume valuable time that otherwise could be used to make profits. The exceptions to this rule are the excessive-fee-charging operations that make a handsome profit with each rejection.

In most instances, the rejection process is "giveaway" time for agents and editors since it takes us away from our essential responsibilities. Even if no personal comments are provided with the rejections, it can require many hours a week to process an ongoing stream of rejections. An understaffed literary agency or publishing house may feel that it's sufficiently generous simply to assign a paid employee the job of returning material as opposed to throwing it away. (And some publishers and literary agencies do in practice simply toss the greater portion of their unsolicited correspondence.) Agents and editors aren't Dear Abby, though many of us wish we had the time to be.

Therefore, your generic rejection means no more and no less than that particular agent/editor doesn't want to represent/publish you and (due to the volume of office correspondence and other pressing duties) is relaying this information to you in an automated, impersonal way. The contents of the letter alone will virtually never reveal any deeper meanings or secrets. To expect or demand more than this might be perceived as unfair by the agent/editor.

KNOW WHEN TO HOLD, KNOW WHEN TO FOLD

It's your job to persevere. It's your mission to proceed undaunted. And it's your option to determine the ways your judgment comes into play. Regardless of how many books about publishing you've read, or how many writers' conferences you've attended, it's up to no one but you to figure out how and when to change your strategy if you want to win at the book-publishing game.

If your initial query results are blanket rejects, then it may be time to back off, reflect, and revamp your query presentation or overall approach. If then there are still no takers, you may be advised to reconceive your project in light of its less-than-glamorous track record. Indeed, there might even come a time for you to use your experience and newfound knowledge of what does and doesn't grab attention from editors and agents—and move on to that bolder, more innovative idea you've been nurturing in the back of your brain.

AN AUTHENTIC SUCCESS STORY

Several years ago, two very successful, though unpublished, gentlemen came to see me with a nonfiction book project. My hunch was that it would make a lot of money. The writers were professional speakers and highly skilled salespeople, so I arranged for them to meet personally with several publishers, but to no avail.

All told, we got more than 20 rejections—the dominant reason being that editors thought the concept and material weak. Not ones to give up, and with a strong belief in their work and confidence in their ability to promote, the authors were ultimately able to sell the book for a nominal advance to a small Florida publishing house—and it was out there at last, published and in the marketplace.

As of this writing, *Chicken Soup for the Soul,* by Jack Canfield and Mark Victor Hansen, has sold millions of copies and has been a New York Times bestseller for a couple of years straight. Furthermore, this initial success has generated several best-selling sequels.

We all make mistakes, and the book rascals in New York are definitely no exception. Most importantly, Canfield and Hansen didn't take no for an answer. They instinctively understood that all those rejections were simply an uncomfortable part of a process that would eventually get them where they wanted to be. And that's the way it happened.

Whatever It Takes

A Relentless Approach to Selling Your Book

Jeff Herman

I once heard a very telling story about Jack Kerouac, one from which we can all learn something. Kerouac was a notorious literary figure who reached his professional peak in the 1950s. He's one of the icons of the Beat Generation and is perhaps best remembered for his irreverent and manic travel-memoir-as-novel *On the Road*.

SALES TALES FROM THE BEAT GENERATION

The story I heard begins when Kerouac was a young and struggling writer, ambitiously seeking to win his day in the sun. He was a charismatic man and had acquired many influential friends. One day Kerouac approached a friend who had access to a powerful publishing executive. Kerouac asked the friend to hand-deliver his new manuscript to the executive, with the advice that it be given prompt and careful consideration.

When the friend handed the manuscript to the executive, the executive took one glance and began to laugh. The executive explained that two other people had hand-delivered the very same manuscript to him within the last few weeks.

What this reveals is that Kerouac was a master operator. Not only did he manage to get his work into the right face, but he reinforced his odds by doing it redundantly. Some might say he was a manipulator, but his works were successfully published, and he did attain a measure of fame in his own day, which even now retains its luster.

. . . AND FROM THE BEATEN

I will now share a very different and more recent story. It starts in the 1940s, when a bestselling and Pulitzer Prize–winning young-adult book was published. Titled *The Yearling*, this work was made into an excellent movie starring Gregory Peck. The book continues to be a good backlist seller.

In the 1990s a writer in Florida, where *The Yearling*'s story takes place, performed an experiment. He converted the book into a raw double-spaced manuscript and changed the title and author's name—but the book's contents were not touched. He then submitted the entire manuscript to about 20 publishers on an unagented/unsolicited basis. I don't believe the submissions were addressed to any specific editors by name.

Eventually this writer received many form rejections, including one from the book's actual publisher. Several publishers never even responded. A small house in Florida did offer to publish the book.

What is glaringly revealed by this story? That even a Pulitzer Prize–winning novel will never see the light of day if the writer doesn't use his brain when it's time to sell the work.

How to Beat Yourself—And How Not To

People who are overly aggressive do get a bad rap. As an agent and as a person, I don't like being hounded by salespeople—whether they're hustling manuscripts or insurance policies. But there are effective ways to be heard and seen without being resented. Virtually anyone can scream loud enough to hurt people's ears. Only an artist understands the true magic of how to sell without abusing those who might buy. And each of us has the gift to become an artist in his or her own way.

Here's an example of what not to do:

It's late in the day and snowing. I'm at my desk, feeling a lot of work-related tension. I answer the phone. It's a first-time fiction writer. He's unflinchingly determined to speak endlessly about his work, which I have not yet read. I interrupt his meaningless flow to explain courteously that, while I will read his work, it's not a good time for me to talk to him. But he will not let me go; he's relentless. Which forces me to be rude and cold as I say "bye" and hang up. I then resent the thoughtless intrusion upon my space and time. And I may feel bad about being inhospitable to a stranger, whatever the provocation.

Clearly the above scenario does not demonstrate a good way to initiate a deal. I'm already prejudiced against this writer before reading his work.

Here's a more effective scenario:

Same conditions as before. I answer the telephone. The caller acknowledges that I must be busy, and asks for only 30 seconds of my time. I grant them. He then begins to compliment me; he's heard I'm one of the best, and so forth. I'm starting to like this conversation; I stop counting the seconds. Now he explains that he has an excellent manuscript that he is willing to give me the opportunity to read, and would be happy to send it right over. He then thanks me for my time and says good-bye. I hang up, feeling fine about the man; I'll give his manuscript some extra consideration.

In conclusion, relentless assertiveness is better than relentless passivity. But you want your style to be like Julie Andrews's singing voice in *The Sound of Music*, as opposed to a 100-decibel boombox on a stone floor.

The Literary Agency from A to Z

How Literary Agents Work

JEFF HERMAN

Literary agents are like stockbrokers, marketing or sales directors, or real-estate agents: They bring buyers and sellers together, help formulate successful deals, and receive a piece of the action (against the seller's end) for facilitating the partnership.

Specifically, literary agents snoop the field for talented writers, unearth marketable nonfiction book concepts, and discover superior fiction manuscripts to represent. Simultaneously, agents cultivate their relationships with publishers.

When an agent detects material she thinks she can sell to a publisher, she signs the writer as a client, works on the material with the writer to maximize its chances of selling, and then submits it to one or more appropriate editorial contacts.

The agent has the contacts. Many writers don't know the most likely publishers; even if the writers do have a good overview of the industry, and even some inside contacts, the typical agent knows many more players and also knows which editors like to see what material. And the agent may even be aware of finesse elements such as recent shifts in a publisher's acquisition strategy.

HOW AGENTS WORK FOR THEIR CLIENTS

A dynamic agent achieves the maximum exposure possible for the writer's material, which greatly enhances the odds that the material will be published—and on more favorable terms than a writer is likely to yield.

Having an agent gives the writer's material the type of access to the powers-that-be that it might otherwise never obtain. Publishers assume that material submitted by an agent has been screened and is much more likely to fit their needs than the random material swimming in the slush pile.

If and when a publisher makes an offer to publish the material, the agent acts on the author's behalf and negotiates the advance (the money paid up front), table of royalties, control of subsidiary rights, and many other important and marginal contract clauses that may prove to be important down the line. The agent acts as the writer's advocate with the publisher for as long as the book remains in print or licensing opportunities exist.

The agent knows the most effective methods for negotiating the best advance and other contract terms, and is likely to have more leverage with the publisher than the writer does.

There's more to a book contract than the advance-and-royalty schedule. There are several key clauses that you the writer may know little or nothing about but would accept with a cursory perusal in order to expedite the deal. Striving to close any kind of agreement can be intimidating if you don't know much about the territory; ignorance is a great disadvantage during a negotiation. An agent, however, understands every detail of the contract and knows where and how it should be modified or expanded in your favor.

Where appropriate, an agent acts to sell subsidiary rights after the book is sold to a publisher. These rights can include: serial rights, foreign rights, dramatic and movie rights, audio and video rights, and a range of syndication and licensing possibilities. Often, a dynamic agent will be more successful at selling the subsidiary rights than the publisher would be.

The Agent's Perspective

No agent sells every project she represents. Even though an author is signed on the basis of their work's marketability, agents know from experience that some projects with excellent potential are not necessarily quick-and-easy big-money sales. And, yes, each and every agent has at least on occasion been as bewildered as the author when a particularly promising package receives no takers. Some projects, especially fiction, may be marketed for a long time before a publisher is found (if ever).

The Author's Expectations

What's most important is that you the author feel sure the agent continues to believe in the project and is actively trying to sell it.

For his work, the agent receives a commission (usually 15%) against the writer's advance and all subsequent income relevant to the sold project.

Although this is an appreciable chunk of your work's income, the agent's involvement should end up netting you much more than you would have earned otherwise. The agent's power to round up several interested publishers to consider your work opens up the possibility that more than one house will make an offer for it, which means you'll be more likely to get a higher advance and also have more leverage regarding the various other contractual clauses.

The writer-agent relationship can become a rewarding business partnership. An agent can advise you objectively on the direction your writing career should take. Also, through her contacts, an agent may be able to get you book-writing assignments you would never have been offered on your own.

SCOUT FOR THE BEST AGENT FOR YOU

There are many ways to get an agent; your personal determination and acumen as a writer will be one of your most important assets. The best way to gain access to potential agents is by networking with fellow writers. Find out which agents they use, and what's being said about whom. Maybe some of your colleagues can introduce you to their agents, or at least allow you to drop their names when contacting their agents. Most agents will be receptive to a writer who has been referred by a current and valued client.

This book features a directory of literary agencies, including their addresses, the names of specific agents, and agents' specialty areas, along with some personal remarks and examples of recent titles sold to publishers.

QUERY FIRST

The universally accepted way to establish initial contact with an agent is to send a query letter. Agents tend to be less interested in—if not completely put off by—oral presentations. Be sure the letter is personalized: Nobody likes generic, photocopied letters that look like they're being sent to everyone.

Think of the query as a sales pitch. Describe the nature of your project and offer to send additional material—and enclose a self-addressed stamped envelope (SASE). Include all relevant information about yourself—along with a résumé if it's applicable. When querying about a nonfiction project, many agents won't mind receiving a complete proposal. But you might prefer to wait and see how the agent responds to the concept before sending the full proposal.

For queries about fiction projects, most agents prefer to receive story-concept sheets and/or plot synopses; if they like what they see, they'll request sample chapters or ask you to send the complete manuscript. Most agents won't consider manuscripts for incomplete works of fiction, essentially because few publishers are willing to do so.

If you enclose an SASE, most agents will respond to you, one way or another, within a reasonable period of time. If the agent asks to see your material, submit it promptly with a polite note stating that you'd like a response within 4 weeks on a nonfiction proposal, or 8 weeks on fiction material. If you haven't heard from the agent by that time, write or call to find out the status of your submission.

CIRCULATE WITH THE FLOW

You're entitled to circulate your material to more than one agent at a time, but you're obligated to let each agent know that such is the case. If and when you do sign with an agent, immediately notify other agents still considering your work that it's no longer available.

At least 200 literary agents are active in America, and their individual perceptions of what is and isn't marketable will vary widely—which is why a few or even several rejections should never deter writers who believe in themselves.

Buyer and Seller Reversal

When an agent eventually seeks to represent your work, it's time for her to begin selling herself to you. When you're seeking employment, you don't necessarily have to accept the first job offer you receive; likewise, you do not have to sign immediately with the first agent who wants you.

Do some checking before agreeing to work with a particular agent. If possible, meet the agent in person. A lot can be learned from in-person meetings that can't be gathered from telephone conversations. See what positive or negative information you can find out about the agent through your writers' network. Ask the agent for a client list and permission to call certain clients. Find out the agent's specialties.

Ask for a copy of the agent's standard contract.* Most agents today will want to codify your relationship with a written agreement; this should protect both parties equally. Make sure you're comfortable with everything in the agreement before signing it. Again, talking with fellow writers and reading books on the subject are excellent ways to deepen your understanding of industry practices.

When choosing an agent, follow your best instincts. Don't settle for anyone you don't perceive to be on the level, or who doesn't seem to be genuinely enthusiastic about you and your work.

Self-Representation: A Fool for a Client?

Agents aren't for everyone. In some instances, you may be better off on your own. Perhaps you actually do have sufficient editorial contacts and industry savvy to cut good deals by yourself. If so, what incentive do you have to share your income with an agent?

Of course, having an agent might provide you the intangible benefits of added prestige, save you the hassles of making submissions and negotiating deals, or act as a buffer through whom you can negotiate indirectly for tactical reasons.

You might also consider representing yourself if your books are so specialized that only a few publishers are potential candidates for them. Your contacts at such houses might be much stronger than any agent's could be.

Attorneys: Literary and Otherwise

Some entertainment/publishing attorneys can do everything an agent does, though there's no reason to believe they can necessarily do more. A major difference between the two is that the lawyer may charge you a set hourly fee or retainer, or any negotiated combination thereof, instead of an agency-type commission. In rare instances, writer-publisher disputes might need to be settled in a court of law, and a lawyer familiar with the industry then becomes a necessity.

---

* Please see sample agency contract in this book.

Bottom-Line Calculations

The pluses and minuses of having an agent should be calculated like any other business service you might retain—it should benefit you more than it costs you. Generally speaking, the only real cost of using an agent is the commission. Of course, using the wrong agent may end up causing you more deficits than benefits; but even then you may at least learn a valuable lesson for next time.

Your challenge is to seek and retain an agent who's right for you. You're 100% responsible for getting yourself represented, and at least 50% responsible for making the relationship work for both of you.

Points of Inquiry from the Writer's Side

Questions and Answers About Agents, Editors, and the Publishing Industry

Jeff Herman

In the course of my ongoing participation in publishing workshops, seminar presentations, and panels at writers' conferences, there are certain questions that arise time and again. Obviously, this implies widespread areas of interest and concern. Many of these oft-voiced requests for information zing straight to the heart of the world of book publishing. Indeed, these commonly raised points of inquiry touch upon matters of great importance to my own day-to-day work.

The following questions are asked from the gut and replied to in kind. In order to be of value to the author who wishes to benefit from an insider view, I answer these serious queries in unvarnished terms, dispensing with the usual sugarcoating in order to emphasize the message of openness and candor.

Q: Is it more difficult to get an agent than it is to get a publisher?
A: I believe it's substantially easier to get an agent than it is to get a publisher.

The primary reason for this is that no agent expects to sell 100% percent of the projects she chooses to represent. Not because any of these projects lack merit (though some of them may), but because only so many titles are published per year—and many excellent ones just won't make the cut. This is especially true for fiction by unknown or unpublished writers, or for nonfiction in saturated categories. As a result, many titles will be agented but never published.

Naturally, a successful agent prefers to represent projects that she feels are hot and that publishers will trample each other to acquire. But few if any agents have the luxury of representing such sure-bet projects exclusively. In fact, the majority of their projects may be less than "acquisition-guaranteed," even though they are of acquisition quality. The agent assumes that many of these projects will eventually be sold profitably, but probably doesn't expect all of them to be. Every experienced agent knows that some of the best cash cows were not easily sold.

Make no mistake—it's not easy to get a reputable agent. Most agents reject 98% of the opportunities that cross their desks. They accept for representation only material they believe can be sold to a publisher. That is, after all, the only way for them to earn income and maintain credibility with publishers. If an agent consistently represents what a publisher considers garbage, that will become her professional signature—and her undoing as an agent.

But don't despair. This is a subjective business, composed of autonomous human beings. One agent's reject can be another's gold mine. That's why even a large accumulation of rejections should never deter you as a writer. Some people get married young, and some get married later!

Q: Is there anything I can do to increase my odds of getting an agent?
A: Yes.

First consider the odds quoted in the previous answer. The typical agent is rejecting 98% of everything he sees. That means he's hungry for the hard-to-find 2% that keeps him in business. If you're not part of that 2%, he'll probably have no use for you or your project. Your challenge is to convince him that you're part of that select 2%.

Q: What do agents and editors want? What do they look for in a writer? What can I do to become that kind of writer?
A: Let's back up a step or two and figure out *why* agents want to represent certain projects and *why* editors want to buy. This industry preference has little to do with quality of writing as such.

Many highly talented writers never get published. Many mediocre writers do get published—and a number of them make a lot of money at it. There are reasons for this. The mediocre writers are doing things that more than compensate for their less-than-splendid writing. And the exceptional writers who nevertheless underachieve in the publishing arena are (regardless of their talents) most likely doing things that undermine their presentation, their potential, and, most importantly, their profitability in the eyes of the agents they contact.

In other words, being a good writer is just part of a complex equation. Despite all the criticism the educational system in the United States has received, America is exceedingly literate and has a mother lode of college graduates and postgraduates. Good, knowledgeable writers are a dime a dozen in this country. *Profitable* writers, however, are a rare species. And agents and editors obviously value them the most. Once more: Being an excellent writer and a financially successful writer don't necessarily coincide. Ideally, of course, you want to be both.

To maximize your success as a writer, you must do more than hone your ability to write; you must also learn the qualifiers and the disqualifiers for success. Obviously you wish to employ the former and avoid the latter. Publishing is a business, and agents tend to be the most acutely business-oriented of all the players. That's why they took the risk of going into business for themselves (most agents are self-employed).

If you wish, wear your artist's hat while you write. But you'd better acquire a business hat and wear it when it's time to sell. This subtle ability to change hats separates the minority of writers who get rich from the majority who do not. In my opinion, rich writers didn't get rich from their writing (no matter how good it is); they got rich by being good at business.

Many good but not-so-wealthy writers blame various internal or external factors for their self-perceived stagnation. My answer to them is: Don't blame anyone, especially yourself. To lay blame is an abdication of power. In effect, when you blame, you become a car with an empty gas tank, left to the elements. The remedy is to fill the tank yourself. Learn to view mistakes, whether they be yours or those of the people you relied upon, as inconvenient potholes—learning to move around them will make you an even better driver.

Observe all you can about those who are successful—not just in writing, but in all fields—and make their skills your skills. This is not to insist that making money is or should be your first priority. Your priorities, whatever they are, belong to you. But money is a widely acknowledged and sought-after emblem of success.

If an emphasis on personal gain turns you off, you may of course pursue other goals. Many successful people in business find the motivation to achieve their goals by focusing on altruistic concepts—such as creating maximum value for as many people as possible. Like magic, money often follows value even if it wasn't specifically sought. If you're unfortunate enough to make money you don't want, there's no need to despair: There are many worthy parties (including charities) that will gladly relieve you of this burden.

Here are specific ways to maximize your ability to get the agent you want:

- *Don't start off by asking what the agent can do for you.* You're a noncitizen until the agent has reason to believe that you may belong to that exclusive 2% club the agent wants to represent. It's a mistake to expect the agent to do anything to sell herself to you during that initial contact. You must first persuade her that you're someone who's going to make good money for her business. Once you've accomplished that, and the agent offers you representation, you're entitled to have the agent sell herself to you.
- *Act like a business.* As you're urged elsewhere in this book, get yourself a professional letterhead and state-of-the-art office equipment. While rarely fatal, cheap paper and poor-looking type will do nothing to help you—and in this business you need all the help you can give yourself.

  Virtually anyone—especially the intellectually arrogant—is apt to be strongly affected on a subliminal level by a product's packaging. People pay for the sizzle, not the steak. There is a reason why American companies spend billions packaging, naming, and advertising such seemingly simple products as soap. We would all save money if every bar of soap were put into a plain paper box and just labeled "Soap." In fact, the no-frills section does sell soap that way—for a lot less. But few people choose to buy it that way. Understand this human principle, without judging it, and use it when packaging yourself.

- Learn industry protocol. I never insist that people follow all the rules. As Thomas Jefferson wisely suggested, a revolution every so often can be a good thing. But you should at least know the rules before you break them—or before you do anything.

  For instance: Most agents say they don't like cold calls. I can't say I blame them. If my rejection rate is 98%, I'm not going to be enthusiastic about having my ear talked off by someone who is more than likely part of that 98%. Just like you, agents want to use their time as productively as possible. Too often, cold calls are verbal junk mail. This is especially true if you are a writer selling fiction; your hard copy is the foot you want to get through the door.

  Speaking for myself, most cold calls have a neutral effect on me (a few turn me off, and a few rouse my enthusiasm). I try to be courteous, because that's how I would want to be treated. I will allow the caller to say whatever he wants for about one minute before I take over to find out what, if anything, the person has in the way of hard copy. If he has some, I invite him to send it with an SASE. If he doesn't have any, I advise him to write some and then send it. Usually I don't remember much about what he said on the phone; I may not even remember that he called. But that doesn't matter; it's the hard copy that concerns me at first. This is the way it works with most agents. We produce books, not talk.

  An agent's time is an agent's money (and therefore his clients' money). So don't expect any quality access until the agent has reason to believe you're a potential 2 percenter. If you're the CEO of General Motors, for instance, and you want to write a book, then all you need to do is call the agent(s) of your choice and identify yourself; red carpets will quickly appear. But the vast majority of writers have to learn and follow the more formalized procedures.
- *As explained elsewhere in this book, view the query letter as a sales brochure.* The best ones are rarely more than 1½ pages long and state their case as briefly and efficiently as possible.

  Here are the most common query mistakes:
  1. Long, unfocused paragraphs.
  2. Pontificating about irrelevancies (at least matters that are irrelevant from the agent's perspective).
  3. Complaining about your tribulations as a writer. We all know it's a tough business, but nobody likes losers—least of all shrewd agents. Always be a winner when you're selling yourself, and you'll be more likely to win.

Most agents are hungry for that golden 2%, and they dedicate a great deal of time shoveling through mounds of material looking for it. You must be the first to believe that you are a 2 percenter, and then you must portray yourself that way to others. Reality begins in your own head, and is manifested primarily through your own actions—or lack thereof.

Every agent and editor has the power to reject your writing. But only you have the power to be—or not to be—a writer.

Q: Should I query only one agent at a time?

A: Some of my colleagues disagree with me here, but I recommend querying five to ten agents simultaneously, unless you already have your foot in the door with one. I suggest this because some agents will respond within 10 days, while others may take much longer, or never respond at all. Going agent by agent can eat up several months of valuable time before a relationship is consummated. And then your work still has to be sold to a publisher.

To speed up this process, it's smart to solicit several agents at a time, though you should be completely up front about it. If you go the multiple-submissions route, be sure to mention in your query letters to each agent that you are indeed making multiple submissions (though you needn't supply your agent list).

When an agent responds affirmatively to your query by requesting your proposal or manuscript, it's fine then to give the agent an exclusive reading. However, you should impose a reasonable time frame—for instance, 2 weeks for a nonfiction proposal and 4 weeks for a large manuscript. If it's a nonexclusive reading, make sure each agent knows that's what you want. And don't sign with an agent before talking to all the agents who are reading your work. (You have no obligation to communicate further with agents who do not respond affirmatively to your initial query.)

Most agents make multiple submissions to publishers, so they should be sensitive and respectful when writers have reason to use the same strategy agents have used with success.

Q: How do I know if my agent is working effectively for me? When might it be time to change agents?

A: As I remarked earlier, agents don't necessarily sell everything they represent, no matter how persistent and assertive they may be. In other words, the fact that your work is unsold doesn't automatically mean that your agent isn't doing his job. To the contrary, he may be doing the best job possible, and it may be incumbent upon you to be grateful for these speculative and uncompensated efforts.

Let's say 90 days pass and your work remains unsold. What you need to assess next is whether your agent is making active and proper attempts to sell your work.

Are you receiving copies of publisher rejection letters regarding your work? Generally, when an editor rejects projects submitted by an agent, the work will be returned within a few weeks, along with some brief comments explaining why the project was declined. (In case you're wondering, the agent doesn't have to include a SASE; the editors *want* agent submissions.) Copies of these rejection letters should be sent to you on a regular basis, as they are received by the agent. While no one expects you to enjoy these letters, they at least document that your agent is circulating your work.

If you have received many such rejection letters within these 90 days, it's hard to claim that your agent isn't trying. If you've received few or none, you might well call the agent for a status report. You should inquire as to where and when your work has been submitted, and what, if anything, the results of those submissions have been. In the end, you will have to use your own best judgment as to whether your agent is performing capably or giving you the run-around.

If it ever becomes obvious that your agent is no longer seriously trying to sell your work (or perhaps never was), you should initiate a frank discussion with the agent about what comes next. If the agent did go to bat for you, you should consider the strong possibility that your work is presently unmarketable, and act to preserve the agent relationship for your next project. Remember, if your work remains unsold, your agent has lost valuable time and has made no money.

If the evidence clearly shows that your agent has been nonperforming from day one, then your work has not been tested. You should consider withdrawing it and seek new representation.

Agent-hopping by authors is not rampant, but it's not uncommon either. Often the agent is just as eager as you—or more so—for the break-up to happen. One veteran colleague once told me that when he notices he hates to receive a certain client's phone calls, then it's time to find a graceful way to end the relationship.

The wisdom of agent-jumping must be assessed on a case-by-case basis. The evidence shows that many writers have prospered after switching, while others have entered limbo or even fallen far off their previous pace.

Before you decide to switch agents, you should focus on why you are unhappy with your current situation. It may be that if you appeal to your agent to discuss your specific frustrations—preferably in person, or at least by phone—many or all of them can be resolved, and your relationship will be given a fresh and prosperous start.

Agents are not mind readers. You only have one agent, but your agent has many clients. It is therefore mostly your responsibility as a writer client to communicate your concerns and expectations effectively to your agent. Your relationship may require only occasional adjustments, as opposed to a complete break-up.

Q: Who do agents really work for?
A: Themselves! Always have and always will.

True, agents serve their clients, but their own needs and interests always come first. Of course, this is the way it is in any business relationship (and in too many personal ones). You should never expect your lawyer, accountant, or stockbroker (and so on) to throw themselves into traffic to shield you from getting hit.

As long as the interests of the agent and the writer are in harmony, everything should work out well. However, on occasion the writer may have expectations that could be detrimental to the agent's own agenda (not to mention state of mind). Writers must never lose sight of the truth that publishers are the agent's most important customers. Only a foolish agent would intentionally do serious damage to her relationships with individual editors and publishing houses. It should be further noted that there is, therefore, a fine line that an agent will not cross when advocating for her clients.

Q: What do agents find unattractive about some clients?
A: Agents are individuals, so each will have his own intense dislikes. But, generally speaking, there is a certain range of qualities that can hamper any and all aspects of an agent's professional association with a client—qualities that often have similarly negative effects in realms other than publishing. Here's a litany of displeasing client types and their characteristics.

- *The Pest.* Nobody likes a nag, whether at home or at the office. A squeaky wheel may sometimes get the grease—not that anyone likes the effect—but more often they get the shaft.
- *The Complainer.* Some people can never be satisfied, only dissatisfied. It seems to be their mission in life to pass along their displeasure to others. These folks are never any fun—unless you're an ironic observer.
- *The BS Artist.* These clients believe everything even remotely connected with themselves is the greatest—for example, their fleeting ideas for books should win them millions of dollars up front. Of course, if they actually produce the goods, then the BS part of the term doesn't apply to them.
- *The Screw-Up.* These clients miss trains, planes, and deadlines. Their blunders can create major hassles for those who count on them.
- *The Sun God.* Some people believe they are more equal than others, and will behave accordingly. It's a real pleasure to see Sun Gods humbled.
- *The Liar.* Need I say more?

Sometimes these wicked traits combine, overlap, and reinforce themselves in one individual to create what an agent may rate as a veritable client from hell. Enough said on this subject for now, except that I would be remiss if I did not insist that no trade or professional class is immune to this nefarious syndrome—not even literary agents.

Q: How does someone become an agent?

A: For better or worse, anyone in America can declare themselves an agent—at any time. But what someone says and what they do are different things. Legitimate literary agents earn most or all of their income from commissions. The less-than-legitimate agencies most often depend on reading and management fees for their cash, with few if any actual book sales to their credit.

Most agents earn their stripes by working as editors for publishers. But that is by no means the only route, nor is it necessarily the most effective training ground. Good agents have emerged from a variety of environments and offer a broad range of exceptional credentials. What's most important is the mix of skills they bring to their agenting careers, such as: (1) Strong relationship skills—the ability to connect with people and earn their confidence. (2) Sales and marketing skills—the ability to get people to buy from them. (3) Persuasion and negotiating skills—the ability to get good results in their dealings. (4) An understanding of the book market and what publishers are buying. (5) An ability to manage many clients and projects at the same time.

Q: Who owns book publishing?

A: Many decades ago, book-publishing entities were customarily founded by individuals who had a passion for books. Though they obviously had to have business skills to make their houses survive and thrive, money was not necessarily their primary drive (at least not in the beginning), or they would have chosen more lucrative endeavors.

The vestiges of these pioneers can be found in the family names still extant in the corporate designations of most of today's publishing giants. But apart from the human-sounding names, these are very different companies today. Much of the industry is owned by multinational, multibillion-dollar conglomerates who have priorities other than the mere publication of books. The revenues from book operations are barely noticeable when compared with such mass-market endeavors as movies, TV/cable, music, magazines, sports teams, and character licensing. Stock prices must rise, and shareholders must be optimally satisfied for these firms to feel in any way stable.

Q: How does this type of ownership affect editors and the editorial-acquisition process?

A: This rampant corporate ownership translates into an environment in which book editors are pressured to make profitable choices if their careers are to prosper. At first look, that doesn't sound radical or wrongheaded, but a downside has indeed developed—editors are discouraged from taking risks for literary or artistic rationales that are ahead of the market curve, or even with an eye toward longer-term development and growth of a particular writer's readership.

The bottom line must be immediately appeased by every acquisition, or the nonperforming editor's career will crumble. The editor who acquires blockbusters that the culturally elite disdain is an editor who is a success. The editor whose books lose money but are universally praised by critics is an editor who has failed.

Of course, the above comparison is extreme. Most editors are not single-minded money-grubbers, and do their best to acquire meaningful books that also make commercial sense. Where the cut becomes most noticeable is for the thousands of talented fiction writers who will never write big money-makers. While slots still exist for them, large publishers are increasingly reluctant to subsidize and nurture these marginally profitable writers' careers. Commercially speaking, there are better ways to invest the firm's resources.

Q: What, if any, are a writer's alternatives?

A: Yes, the big kids are dominant on their own turf and intend to extend their claim to as much of book country as they can. But this isn't the end of the story. The heroes are the thousands of privately owned "Mom and Pop" presses from Maine to Alaska who only need to answer to themselves. Every year, small presses, new and old, make an important contribution to literate culture with books that large publishers won't touch. It's not uncommon for some of these books to become bestsellers. University presses also pump out important (and salesworthy) books that would not have been published in a rigidly commercial environment.

Q: Is there anything positive to say about the current situation?

A: I don't mean to imply that the corporate ownership of the bulk of the book industry is absolutely bad. Indeed, it has brought many benefits. Publishers are learning to take better advantage of state-of-the-art marketing techniques and technologies, and have more capital with which to do it. The parent entertainment and communications firms enable the mainstream commercial publishers to cash in on popular frenzies, as with dinosaur mania, the latest and most salacious scandals, fresh interest in the environment or fitness, or celebrity and other pop-culture tie-ins, such as *Gump* and *Madonna* books.

The emergence of superstores enables more books to be sold. The stores create very appealing environments that draw much more traffic than conventional old-style book-stores. Many people who hang out at the superstores were never before motivated to go book shopping. But once they're in one of these well-stocked stores—whether at the bookshelves, ensconced in a reading-seats, or perched in a steaming mug at an in-store cafe—they're likely to start spending.

The unfortunate part is that many small independent bookshops cannot compete with these new venues. However, many others are finding clever ways to hang on, by accenting special reader-interest areas or offering their own individual style of hospitality.

Q: How profitable is publishing?

A: One way to measure an industry's profitability is to look at the fortunes of those who work in it. By such a measure, the book business isn't very profitable, especially when compared to its 20th-century sisters in entertainment and information industries: movies, television, music, advertising, and computers. Most book editors require a two-income family if they wish to raise children comfortably in New York or buy a nice home. The vast majority of published authors rely upon their day jobs or spouse's earnings.

A handful of authors make annual incomes in the six and seven figures, but it's often the movie tie-ins that get them there, and in turn push even more book sales.

A fraction of book editors will climb the ranks to the point at which they can command six-figure incomes, but most never attain this plateau. Almost all of those writers just starting in the business earn barely above the poverty level for their initial publishing endeavors—if that.

A well-established literary agent can make a lot of money. The trick is to build a number of backlist books that cumulatively pay off healthy commissions twice a year, while constantly panning for the elusive big-advance books that promise short-term (and perhaps long-term) windfalls.

In many ways, the agents are the players best positioned to make the most money. As sole proprietors they're not constrained by committees and can move like lightning. When everything aligns just right, the agent holds all the cards by controlling access to the author (product) and the publisher (producer).

The publishing companies themselves appear at least adequately profitable, averaging about 5% to 10% return on revenues (according to their public balance sheets). The larger companies show revenues of between $1 billion and $2 billion, sometimes nudging higher.

These are not sums to sneeze at. But most of those sales derive from high-priced non-bookstore products like textbooks and professional books. Large and midsize publishers alike are dependent upon their cash-cow backlist books for much of their retail sales. These books entail virtually no risk or investment, since their customer base is essentially locked in for an indefinite period, and the publisher has long ago recouped the initial investment. Many backlist books are legacies from editors and business dynamics that current employees may know nothing about.

The real risk for the current regime is their *frontlist*, which is the current season's crop. Large houses invest tens of millions of dollars to acquire, manufacture, market and distribute anywhere from 50 to a few hundred "new" books. A small number of big-ticket individual titles will by themselves represent millions of dollars at risk. Most titles will represent less than $50,000 in risk on a pro-rata basis.

In practice, most of these frontlist titles will fail. The publisher will not recoup its investment and the title will not graduate to the exalted backlist status. But, like the fate of those innumerable turtle eggs laid in the lake, it's expected that enough spawn will survive to generate an overall profit and significant backlist annuities well into the future.

In the fairness of a broader picture, it is known that most motion pictures and television shows fail, as do most new consumer products (such as soap or soft drinks) that have engendered enormous research-and-development costs. It's the ones that hit—and hit big—that make the odds worth enduring for any industry.

Free Versus Fee

The Issue of Literary Agency Fees

JEFF HERMAN

Many literary agencies charge a fee to read unsolicited manuscripts, although the majority of well-established agencies don't charge such fees—yet.

There's a good deal of internal debate within the literary agency community about the ethics of charging reading fees, especially since many highly reputable agents have begun to charge relatively modest fees. Effective January 1, 1996, no members of the Association of Authors' Representatives are permitted to charge any kind of fees. While this addition to the organization's Canon of Ethics had an effect on only a fraction of its membership, it is too early to see whether the formerly fee-charging members put more stock in their fees or in their membership. (Fee-charging agencies, numbering a few hundred, are currently nonmembers of the AAR.)

Fees per se are a gray area, not necessarily right or wrong—though some *are* clearly wrong. The correctness of fee assessment must be judged on a case-by-case basis. How much is the fee? What's being provided in return for the fee? And, most importantly, what is the writer being led to believe he's getting for the fee?

FEES RANGE FROM $25 TO SEVERAL HUNDRED DOLLARS AND UP

When a reputable agency does charge a fee, it's usually modest—$50 to $100 for reading a complete manuscript. These agencies exonerate their fees by maintaining that they're merely breaking even on such charges, since the fees cover the costs of reading the manuscript cover-to-cover and providing a detailed and useful critique—even if the work is rejected (which it usually is).

It's morally incumbent upon these agencies to make it abundantly clear to the writer that payment of the fee guarantees only a fair reading and constructive comments, and does *not* mean that the writer will be offered representation. Better yet, these agencies might even reveal approximately what percentage of prospective writer-clients are in fact offered representation.

A much more controversial scenario involves agencies that charge writers hundreds of dollars for single readings, or into the thousands of dollars for what is portrayed as in-depth editorial feedback or additional literary services. It's obvious that among these agencies are those who reap significant profits simply by reading and, almost always, rejecting manuscripts written by often-vulnerable writers.

These agencies defend themselves by asserting that, even though they reject more than 95% of the manuscripts, their extensive critiques greatly enhance the writer's chances of success down the line. Many writers claim that the critiques from some of these firms, while indeed wordy, aren't overly useful. Attending a weekend writing workshop might well be a better use of the money—that's for the writer to decide.

Some fee-charging agencies require monthly or yearly retainers (typically running into at least several hundred dollars annually). The usual justification is that, particularly when handling new writers, the agency incurs enormous expenses and, in exchange for expending their efforts and skills on long-shot (but worthy) properties, they more than earn their money.

That may be—but how can a writer be sure there is honest application behind the operation, and not just perfunctory rendering of generic services? One eye-opening giveaway may be when, in response to a query for a nonfiction book or a short synopsis or chapter selection for a novel, a contract is almost instantly sent to the writer, along with a fee schedule.

Well, then: Get a friend to send in another copy of the same material (with only the author name and address changed) and watch what happens. Barring inadvertent office miscues, if there's a contract in the offing, there's another clue for you. Maybe even send in a sheaf of printed-out gibberish and see if that earns an offer of agent representation (in exchange for cash). If it does, it's time to say "Bingo!"—and time to move on in your search for an agent.

It should be noted that established, reputable literary agencies customarily bill their clients (or are reimbursed) for such amenities as manuscript copying, messenger service, and express correspondence and deliveries. But such fees are spelled out and agreed to in an agency-representation agreement, and there are no highly visible (or invisible) items (such as those sometimes termed "management fees") over and above the agency commission on sale of the author's literary properties.

Is the Critique Worth the Cash?

Many agents resent those agents who charge fees. They feel that the entire profession's image is negatively affected by such practices, and that it's wrong for agents to earn money from anything other than commissions.

Agents who do not charge reading fees are unlikely to spend much time reading and analyzing a manuscript once they've decided to reject it. The writer is likely to receive only a terse computer-generated rejection letter. It may sometimes appear that the manuscript hasn't even been read, since many agents do stop reading if the first few pages are a turn-off. On a bad-to-mediocre day, an agent may view all manuscripts as junk mail until proven otherwise.

It is therefore understandable that battle-weary writers are tempted by the siren song of fee-charging agencies. At least they promise to acknowledge that there's a living, breathing writer alive within you, and their customized comments on official stationery are like manna—yes it's just another rejection, but one with candy on top.

WHO CHARGES FOR WHAT— WITH NO GUARANTEES?

Just because someone charges for a service does not make him an impostor or knave. Conversely, just because someone is an excellent literary advisor with a string of impressive credits does not mean she will be able to turn your idea into a big-money plum—regardless of how well-honed the writing is.

This is a complicated issue, one that does not subscribe to cut-and-dried guidelines. Yes, there are combination editor/agents as well as editorial services that charge fees up front and have respectable, even estimable track records. The question for the potential client is how to separate the scamsters from the worthy professionals.

For that there is no easy answer. It is almost a given that, in order to be able to judge whether an editorial service is of topnotch commercial quality, the writer is probably superbly accomplished (on some level) already. Freelance editors, ghostwriters, and publishing consultants have been known to remark that their best and most appreciative clients are often those whose original writing ideas or other materials show the most professionalism to begin with.

Some flourishing freelance editors and book doctors (believe it or not) actually turn down a potential client's work (even if the editor isn't rich) unless they think the client's material has a solid shot at eventual publication. It may be in the consultant's best interest to concentrate on gigs that will earn that freelancer visible publishing credits and the prospect of happy referrals down the road—rather than glomming short-term bucks from someone who'll complain when their fantasy of literary glory is shot down in a shrapnel haze of computer-generated rejection sheets, regardless of how well the consultant has served the project.

One key here is that for the most part these freelance editors, literary advisors, book doctors, and publishing consultants do not represent themselves as literary agents per se. However, when these freelancers have a range of publishing contacts, they may be able to refer or recommend a project to an agent or publisher of their acquaintance. Again—it's a delicate task to weed out the riffraff from the respected professionals, and there can be no guarantees.

I will not pass judgment on the propriety of literary agencies that charge reading fees. But if I were a writer, I'd first try my luck with the many excellent agencies that don't charge anything.

For further insight into this issue, please read the chapter titled "The Literary Agent Trade Association," which includes the Association of Authors' Representatives Canon of Ethics.

A SAMPLE SEDUCTION . . .

The following is an actual pitch letter from a fee-charging agency with only the names and other identifying information changed. Such correspondence is typical of the alluring invitations writers often receive in response to their agent submissions. There's nothing illegal about this reverse solicitation, nor, in all fairness, should such a practice automatically be deemed morally reprehensible. It's possible that a worthwhile service is indeed being provided for the money requested. However, $1,650 (or $500 or $3,000) is real money.

If a writer chooses to explore this route, there are preliminary steps I strongly advise following:

1. Ask for references. You're being asked to shell out hundreds of dollars to a virtual stranger. Get to know those who would eat your money.
2. Ask for a list of titles sold. Find out whether the so-called agency actually has an agenting track record. Or is this particular operation just a high-priced reading service with an agency facade?
3. Better yet, call or write to non–fee-charging agents and ask them to recommend book doctors, collaborative writers, or editorial freelancers whom they use to shape and develop their own clients' works. This may be a better place to spend your money.

THE WE-CHARGE-A-FEE AGENCY
Candyland, USA 77777

April 1, 19§§

Ms. Desi Parrot
123 Hungry Street
Birdland, USA 00000

Dear Ms. Parrot:

I read with interest your letter of April 1, synopsis and excerpts from your novel, *The Child-Eater*, for which you are proposing agency representation. As you know, we specialize in this genre; from my experience, I can tell you that there is definite interest by publishers in novels like yours.

We believe that every writer can benefit from representation by a full-service literary agency in providing up-to-date information on editorial/media buying trends, associations with editors and producers, and in dealing with options, contract terms, advances, royalties and ancillary rights. The *odds against* publication by an unrepresented writer are considerable. We have the experience to identify markets for your writing, anticipate where problems are likely to arise, and work as an advocate for your ambitions and interests.

The first step towards representation and publication is a careful reading and market analysis of your material. This involves an evaluation of the literary and commercial prospects of your work by an experienced editor. If the material is immediately marketable, we will proceed to a representation contract and undertake to sell your work worldwide. If editing is needed, we will provide specific guidelines and unlimited consultative services to you in the revising or polishing of your work. Our goal is to help you become a *published* author.

If you have had minimal or no trade sales (i.e., book-length fiction), our consulting fee is $1,650.00. As you know, some agencies advertise free appraisals, but these "come-ons" mask the services of very high-priced editing services with little influence in the market. We *do not* charge monthly representation fees and your initial fee is refunded upon sale of the work. You may pay by check or money order, or by Visa, MasterCard or Discover; please include card number and expiration date and note that there is an additional five (5) percent charge for the use of credit cards. The fee is fully refundable upon sale of the manuscript.

We are accepting a limited number of new clients and look forward to reading your complete manuscript. Please read and sign the enclosed Material Submission Release Form. Once we make a sale for you, we will accept further material on our professional commission terms, eliminating all fees. Please drop me a line, Ms. Parrot, if I can answer any questions. I look forward to being of service to you with *The Child-Eater*.

Sincerely,

Doreem On

Doreem On,
President

Enclosed as an accompaniment to the letter on the previous page, this coupon reveals how some literary agents have come to employ modern marketing techniques to entice authors.

$150   **$150**

Fee-Reduction Certificate

This certificate entitles the author to a fee reduction of $150.00 from the standard consultation fee of $1,650.00. Please enclose this certificate with your manuscript and deduct $150.00 from your fee.

(Check or money order should be payable to "Doreem On.")

The manuscript must be submitted within sixty (60) days from this date.

Doreem On
_____   _____
FOR THE AGENCY   AUTHOR

April 1, 1988
_____   _____
DATE   TITLE

$150   **$150**

When the Deal Is Done

How to Thrive After Signing a Publishing Contract

Jeff Herman

Congratulations! You've sold your book to an established publishing house. You've gained entry to the elite club of published authors. You'll discover that your personal credibility is enhanced whenever this achievement is made known to others. It may also prove a powerful marketing vehicle for your business or professional practice.

Smell the roses while you can. Then wake up and smell the coffee. If your experience is like that of numerous other writers, once your book is actually published, there's a better-than-even chance you'll feel a bit of chagrin. Some of these doubts are apt to be outward expressions of your own inner uncertainties. Others are not self-inflicted misgivings—they are most assuredly ticked off by outside circumstances.

Among the most common author complaints are: (1) Neither you nor anyone you know can find the book anywhere. (2) The publisher doesn't appear to be doing anything to market the book. (3) You detest the title and the jacket. (4) No one at the publishing house is listening to you. In fact, you may feel that you don't even exist for them.

As a literary agent, I live through these frustrations with my clients every day, and I try to explain to them at the outset what the realities of the business are. But I never advocate abdication or pessimism. There are ways for every author to substantially remedy these endemic problems. In many cases this means first taking a deep breath, relaxing, and reaching down deep inside yourself to sort out the true source of your emotions. When this has been accomplished, it's time to breathe out, move out, and take charge.

What follows are practical means by which each of these four most common failures can be preempted. I'm not suggesting that you can compensate entirely for what may be a publisher's defaults; it's a tall order to remake a clinker after the fact. However, with lots of smarts and a little luck you can accomplish a great deal.

A PHILOSOPHY TO WRITE BY

Let me introduce a bit of philosophy that applies to the writer's life as well as it does to the lives of those who are not published. Many of you may be familiar with the themes popularized by psychotherapists, self-awareness gurus, and business motivators that assert the following: To be a victim is to be powerless—which means you don't have the ability to improve your situation. With that in mind, avoid becoming merely an author who only complains and who remains forever bitter.

No matter how seriously you believe your publisher is screwing up, don't fall into the victim trap. Instead, find positive ways to affect what is or is not happening for you.

Your publisher is like an indispensable employee whom you are not at liberty to fire. You don't have to work with this publisher the next time; but this time it's the only one you've got.

There are a handful of perennially bestselling writers, such as John Grisham, Anne Rice, Mary Higgins Clark, and Michael Crichton, whose book sales cover a large part of their publisher's expense sheet. These writers have perhaps earned the luxury of being very difficult, if they so choose (most of them are reportedly quite the opposite).

But the other 99.98% of writers are not so fortunately invested with the power to arbitrate. No matter how justified your stance and methods may be, if you become an author with whom everyone at the publishing house dreads to speak, you've lost the game.

The editors, publicists, and marketing personnel still have their jobs, and they see no reason to have you in their face. In other words: Always seek what's legitimately yours, but always try to do it in a way that might work *for* you, as opposed to making yourself persona non grata till the end of time.

ATTACKING PROBLEM NO. 1: NEITHER YOU NOR ANYONE YOU KNOW CAN FIND THE BOOK ANYWHERE

This can be the most painful failure. After all, what was the point of writing the book and going through the whole megillah of getting it published if it's virtually invisible?

Trade book distribution is a mysterious process, even for people in the business. Most bookstore sales are dominated by the large national and regional chains, such as Waldenbooks, B. Dalton, Barnes & Noble, and Crown. No shopping mall is complete without at least one of these stores. Publishers always have the chain stores in mind when they determine what to publish. Thankfully, there are also a few thousand independently owned shops throughout the country.

Thousands of new titles are published each year, and these books are added to the seemingly infinite number that are already in print. Considering the limitations of the existing retail channels, it should be no surprise that only a small fraction of all these books achieves a significant and enduring bookstore presence.

Each bookstore will dedicate most of its visual space to displaying healthy quantities of the titles they feel are safe sells: books by celebrities and well-established authors, or books that are being given extra-large printings and marketing budgets by their publishers, thereby promising to create demand.

The rest of the store will generally provide a liberal mix of titles, organized by subject or category. This is where the backlist titles reside and the lower-profile newer releases try to stake their claims. For instance, the business section will probably offer two dozen or so sales books. Most of the displayed titles will be by the biggest names in the genre, and their month-to-month sales probably remain strong, even if the book was first published several years ago.

In other words, there are probably hundreds of other sales books written in recent years that, as far as retail distribution is concerned, barely made it out of the womb. You see, the stores aren't out there to do you any favors. They are going to stock whatever titles they feel they can sell the most of. There are too many titles chasing too little space.

It's the job of the publisher's sales representative to lobby the chain and store buyers individually about the merits of her publisher's respective list. But here too the numbers can be numbing. The large houses publish many books each season, and it's not possible for the rep to do justice to each of them. Priority will be given to the relatively few titles that get the exceptional advances.

Because most advances are modest, and since the average book costs about $20,000 to produce, some publishers can afford to simply sow a large field of books and observe passively as some of them sprout. The many that don't bloom are soon forgotten, as a new harvest dominates the bureaucracy's energy. Every season, many very fine books are terminated by the publishing reaper. The wisdom and magic these books may have offered is thus sealed away, disclosed only to the few.

I have just covered a complicated process in a brief fashion. Nonetheless, the overall consequences for your book are in essence the same. Here, now, are a few things you may attempt in order to override such a stacked situation. However, these methods will not appeal to the shy or passive:

- Make direct contact with the publisher's sales representatives. Do to them what they do to the store buyers—sell 'em! Get them to like you and your book. Take the reps near you to lunch and ballgames. If you travel, do the same for local reps wherever you go.
- Make direct contact with the buyers at the national chains. If you're good enough to actually get this kind of access, you don't need to be told what to do next.
- Organize a national marketing program aimed at local bookstores throughout the country.

There's no law that says only your publisher has the right to market your book to the stores. (Of course, except in special cases, all orders must go through your publisher.) For the usual reasons, your publisher's first reaction may be "What the hell are you doing?" But that's okay; make them happy by showing them that your efforts work. It would be wise, however, to let the publisher in on your scheme up front.

If your publisher objects—which she may—you might choose to interpret those remarks as simply the admonitions they are, and then proceed to make money for all. This last observation leads to ways you can address the next question.

ATTACKING PROBLEM NO. 2: THE PUBLISHER DOESN'T APPEAR TO BE DOING ANYTHING TO MARKET THE BOOK

If it looks as if your publisher is doing nothing to promote your book, then it's probably true. Your mistake is being surprised and unprepared.

The vast majority of titles published receive little or no marketing attention from the publisher beyond catalog listings. The titles that get big advances are likely to get some support, since the publisher would like to justify the advance by creating a good seller.

Compared to those in other Fortune 500 industries, publishers' in-house marketing departments tend to be woefully understaffed, undertrained, and underpaid. Companies like Procter & Gamble will tap the finest business schools, pay competitive salaries, and strive to nurture marketing superstars. Book publishers don't do this.

As a result, adult trade book publishing has never been especially profitable, and countless sales probably go unmade. The sales volumes and profits for large, diversified publishers are mostly due to the lucrative—and captive—textbook trade. Adult trade sales aren't the reason that companies like Random House can generate more than $1 billion in annual revenues.

Here's what you can do:

Hire your own public relations firm to promote you and your book. Your publisher is likely to be grateful and cooperative. But you must communicate carefully with your publishing house.

Once your manuscript is completed, you should request a group meeting with your editor and people from the marketing, sales, and publicity departments. You should focus on what their marketing agenda will be. If you've decided to retain your own PR firm, this is the time to impress the people at your publishing house with your commitment, and pressure them to help pay for it. At the very least, the publisher should provide plenty of free books.

Beware of this common problem: Even if you do a national TV show, your book may not be abundantly available in bookstores that day—at least not everywhere. An obvious answer is setting up 800 numbers to fill orders, and it baffles me that publishers don't make wider use of them. There are many people watching *Oprah* who won't ever make it to the bookstore, but who would be willing to order then and there with a credit card. Infomercials have proven this.

Not all talk or interview shows will cooperate, but whenever possible you should try to have your publisher's 800 number (or yours) displayed as a purchasing method in

845

addition to the neighborhood bookstore. If you use your own number, make sure you can handle a potential flood.

If retaining a PR firm isn't realistic for you, then do your own media promotions. There are many good books in print about how to do your own PR. (A selection of relevant titles may be found in this volume's Suggested Resources section.)

ATTACKING PROBLEM NO. 3: YOU DETEST THE TITLE AND JACKET

Almost always, your publisher will have final contractual discretion over title, jacket design, and jacket copy. But that doesn't mean you can't be actively involved. In my opinion you had better be. Once your final manuscript is submitted, make it clear to your editor that you expect to see all prospective covers and titles. But simply trying to veto what the publisher comes up with won't be enough. You should try to counter the negatives with positive alternatives. You might even want to go as far as having your own prospective covers professionally created. If the publisher were to actually choose your version, the house might reimburse you.

At any rate, don't wait until it's after the fact to decide you don't like your cover, title, and so forth. It's like voting: Participate or shut up.

ATTACKING PROBLEM NO. 4: NO ONE AT THE PUBLISHING HOUSE SEEMS TO BE LISTENING TO YOU

This happens a lot—though I bet it happens to certain people in everything they do. The primary reasons for this situation are either (1) that the people you're trying to access are incompetent; (2) that you're not a priority for them; or (3) that they simply hate talking to you.

Here are a few things you might try to do about it:

- If the contact person is incompetent, what can he or she really accomplish for you anyway? It's probably best to find a way to work around this person, even if he begins to return your calls before you place them.
- The people you want access to may be just too busy to give you time. Screaming may be a temporary remedy, but eventually they'll go deaf again. Obviously their time is being spent somewhere. Thinking logically, how can you make it worthwhile for these people to spend more time on you? If being a pain in the neck is your best card, then perhaps you should play it. But there's no leverage like being valuable. In fact, it's likely that the somewhere else they're spending their time is with a very valuable author.
- Maybe someone just hates talking to you. That may be their problem. But, as many wise men and women have taught, allies are better than adversaries. And to convert an adversary is invaluable. Do it.

CONCLUSION

This essay may come across as cynical. But I want you to be realistic and be prepared. There are many publishing success stories out there, and many of them happened because the authors made them happen.

For every manuscript that is published, there are probably a few thousand that were rejected. To be published is a great accomplishment—and a great asset. If well tended, it can pay tremendous dividends.

Regardless of your publisher's commitment at the outset, if you can somehow generate sales momentum, the publisher will most likely join your march to success and allocate a substantial investment to ensure it. In turn, they may even assume all the credit. But so what? It's to your benefit.

Mastering Ghostwriting and Collaboration

GENE BUSNAR

If you're looking for a writing career with a never-ending source of opportunities, you might consider ghostwriting or collaborating on books. I've learned that there's an almost inexhaustible supply of would-be coauthors who are convinced that they're sitting on a bestseller—be it some kind of unique personal experience, a revolutionary new way of growing tulips, or a secret of the universe that's going to improve our lives.

Many of these unheralded giants are driven by an inflated sense of their own vision and self-importance. But, fortunately, quite a few potential collaborators actually do have commercially viable nonfiction book ideas. All they need is a professional writer to take care of a few "minor details," which can be paraphrased as follows:

- I have the ideas, but lack the writing skills.
- I don't have the time to write the book myself.
- I don't have an agent or book-publishing contacts.

Now, if these were the only reasons people needed collaborators or ghostwriters, this business would be a lot simpler. Anyone with a great story or a wonderful idea for a how-to book could hire a professional writer to put things in proper literary form. In theory, the book's content—its very soul—already exists, so the writer's job should be relatively simple.

Unfortunately, things usually don't turn out that way. Professional ghostwriters and collaborative writers are expected to know what book companies are buying at any given time, and to anticipate the inherent problems in a particular book idea—especially if it's being sold in proposal form.

A publisher or agent may come to you with a fully conceived project by an articulate, promotable coauthor. But this is relatively rare—especially when you are in the early stages of your career.

There have been times when I've had to reshape the idea, change the principal's voice and language around, and find a better title for the book. If you happen to possess these skills, coauthors shouldn't be all that hard to find. But first you have to get some publishing credits under your belt.

If you haven't yet published a book, try writing articles for magazines and local newspapers. But don't expect your first assignments to pay well. Think of them as vehicles that can propel you to a higher level.

It may be possible to short-circuit the steps most authors go through by coming up with an innovative book concept and putting together a proposal that indicates you can deliver the goods. But the skimpier and less relevant your credits, the more you'll be expected to prove before people will treat you with consideration—much less shell out some serious bucks for your effort.

Maybe you've heard inspirational stories of people who struck it rich on their first try. Such cases are rare. The vast majority of successful nonfiction writers work extremely hard at improving their craft and building their business—over the course of a number of projects and years.

For this chapter, I've chosen to focus mostly on the business aspects of collaboration and ghosting—since this is an area where many talented new writers need help. Frankly, I think it's ridiculous to enter such a difficult and competitive field unless you possess the necessary talent. So before you go any further, it might be worthwhile to take a few minutes to think about some of the issues on this talent-evaluation questionnaire:

Do You Have What It Takes?

1. What experience do you have (professional or otherwise) as a writer?
2. Have you ever received feedback about your writing from an agent or editor?
3. What was the thrust of that feedback?
4. Have you ever won any contests or received any writing awards? List them.
5. Have you worked with a teacher or mentor who encouraged you to pursue a professional writing career?
6. Are you open to constructive criticism of your writing?
7. Can you think of an instance where such criticism helped you to improve your writing?
8. Do your writing talents fit into a commercial category?
9. If not, are you willing to take steps to present them in more commercial ways?
10. What about your writing sets it apart from or makes it superior to that of your competitors?

If you honestly feel the talent is there, you may be off to a running start. But remember, even the greatest talent doesn't guarantee success.

It's a truism that many fine writers aren't good at business, but that's not surprising. Most people enter this field because they like to write—not because they expect to get rich.

If money is the primary motivation, you'd be better advised to seek out a career in law, copywriting, or any number of more financially lucrative fields. Still, if you're going to succeed—or at least survive—you'd better accept the fact that business and marketing skills are at least as important as literary talent. This is especially true in collaborative and ghostwriting work—fields that require a good deal of negotiation and personal interaction.

If you want to write just for pleasure, that's one thing. But the moment you decide to earn money at your craft, you become a business person. If you want to make it professionally, start thinking of yourself not just as a writer—but as someone who's in the *business* of writing. Here are four suggestions to help point your career in that direction:

1. Take a business-minded approach.
2. Present yourself powerfully.
3. Position yourself advantageously.
4. Price your services for profit.

TAKE A BUSINESS-MINDED APPROACH

Don't make the mistake of thinking that, because you're good, clients will find you. You've got lots of competitors out there who are aggressively pursuing work, so you can't afford to be too laid-back. It's part of your job to make potential clients aware of you. These include not only cowriters, but agents and editors who can direct projects your way.

Most successful nonfiction writers do all sorts of things to generate work and develop new contacts. No matter where you are in your career, you might want to consider devoting time and energy to the following activities:

- Join professional societies and attend their meetings.
- Associate with as many agents, editors, and potential collaborators as possible.
- Stay in touch with peers who have similar interests.
- Sign up for relevant courses, lectures, and seminars—especially those conducted by reputable people in your field.
- Read trade publications.
- Keep up with economic and other trends that influence our business.

In the final analysis, your success as a writer can hinge as much on how creative you are in your business as it does on your actual work. That's why it's essential that you understand and assume responsibility for the business side of your writing career as early in the game as possible.

PRESENT YOURSELF POWERFULLY

Whenever you submit a manuscript, proposal, or résumé to an editor, agent, or potential collaborator, it's essential to look at those presentation materials from the other person's point of view. When you present your work to people in a position to buy your services, you're selling yourself as well as the materials at hand.

Professionalism in your work and manner communicates that you are someone people ought to take seriously—even if they don't buy the immediate project. The creation of a professional image includes the following:

Looking Like a Pro

- Appropriate and well-organized materials.
- Dependability and promptness.
- A willingness to accept critical feedback.

Of all these factors, an openness to criticism and tolerance for rejection may be the most difficult. Here, especially, you need to get out of your own skin for a moment and imagine how you'd feel if you were an agent or an editor. One of the toughest things is telling other people that their work doesn't measure up—whatever the reason.

Criticism and rejection can be even more difficult when you're on the receiving end. Still, when you communicate a willingness to accept constructive criticism, you invite feedback that can help you make valuable refinements in your presentation. At the same time, you let people know that they're dealing with a confident professional—one who has a genuine interest in meeting their needs.

POSITION YOURSELF ADVANTAGEOUSLY

One key to presenting yourself professionally is giving potential clients a clear-cut picture of what you do. Since your potential clients have the option of choosing the writer who best fills their specific needs, it's your job to see to it that you occupy that particular niche in their minds. In advertising, this concept is called positioning. It's a principle that applies especially well to the business of writing.

Positioning saves your potential clients a good deal of time. You can assume that anyone who's in a position to give you paying work has certain requirements and categories in mind. It's your job to meet those criteria. If you don't, someone else will.

Many good writers are capable of collaborating or ghosting in a number of areas. Unfortunately, that's not what most agents and editors want to hear. Their lives are already too cluttered up with superfluous people and irrelevant information. If you try to hit them with all your credentials at once, they may find it difficult to remember anything about you.

Once you have an idea of what specific clients are looking for, you can present only the information that is most relevant. The best way to make that determination is to research potential clients before you approach them.

Let's say, for example, that you want to ghostwrite political autobiographies, and you're trying to interest an agent who specializes in that area. He asks you to send some samples of your work. How do you decide which materials to include and which ones to leave out?

As a rule, the best presentations are the most concise. That's why it's best to present potential clients with only those materials that relate to the job at hand. As you develop more of a relationship with agents and editors, you can make them aware of your other skills. But be careful not to overwhelm them with too much material.

If you tell an agent who perceives you as a political writer that you also have skills in the medical area, he may file that information away for future reference. But if a call for a medical writer comes in, he's most likely to go with someone who has positioned herself or himself primarily in that area.

Of course, there are exceptions to the rule. For example, the agent may not be able to get the medical writer he or she wants at that particular moment. The memory that you had some background in that area may surface—and suddenly your phone is ringing.

PRICE YOUR SERVICES FOR PROFIT

You may have never thought about it in this light, but in most professions, pricing is determined by positioning and perception rather than by any objective measure.

Have you ever wondered, for example, why your car mechanic charges $20 an hour, while your attorney can charge $200 an hour?

The reasons for this huge difference in pricing can't be measured in any real terms. But the fact is, nobody would pay $200 an hour to get their car fixed. And if an attorney asked for a mere $20 an hour, you'd probably question the guy's competence.

Unfortunately, pricing guidelines in the book-writing business are not nearly so well established as in lawyering or repairing cars. That's why it's essential to establish yourself as a business person who puts a high value on your hours.

Personally, I see no objective reason why the services of a good writer should be worth less than those of a mediocre attorney. But because writing is thought of as a glamour profession, people sometimes expect you to work for nothing—especially when you start out. Let them know that you're in this business for profit—not glamour.

I'll never forget how offended one celebrity became when I told him that I actually expected to be paid—and paid well—for working with him on his book proposal. This made a profound impression on me, and I've since made it a policy to regard people who take this attitude as a threat to my very survival.

In writing—as in any business—there are times when it may be worthwhile to accept a low-paying project. Just make sure that you have a clear idea of what's in it for you.

I've listed six compensating factors that can offset a low price. You may want to use them as negotiating points in deciding whether or not to accept a particular project:

What to Ask for When the Price Is Wrong

- The prominent appearance of your name on the cover and in all publicity for the book.
- A generous allowance for expenses and supplies.
- Greater creative freedom.
- A larger portion of the advance up front.
- A better deal on subsidiary or ancillary rights.
- A larger number of author's copies of the book.

Most writers take on work for a combination of three reasons: to make money; to be creative and expressive; and to build credibility—which will hopefully lead to making more money.

Once you accept these as the general business goals of collaboration and ghost-writing, it behooves you to look for projects that are fulfilling, well-paying, and career-enhancing.

If you can find a project that meets all three of these criteria, go for it. If a project allows you to achieve any two of these goals, it's certainly worth considering. One out of three would be a marginal call at best. But if the project doesn't satisfy any of these three tests, the decision is simple.

Forget it, and move on to something more rewarding.

The Youth Market
Books for Children and Young Adults

Jamie M. Forbes

Publishing programs geared toward children and young adults show splendid life in several important categories. Light reference and entertainingly educational nonfiction books are a traditionally strong area of sales across all age groups. There's vigorous interest in children's titles based on multicultural folktales, well told and finely illustrated. Mystery and horror are strong genres for ages ranging from the very earliest readers through young adults. Major publishers that are members of communications conglomerates have access to an array of licensed characters with built-in exposure to potential readers through television and film counterparts.

All this is by way of a major cautionary note: The market is tight for new talent, and it's tougher now for a greenhorn to break in. Established creators can be expected to protect their hard-won turf. Is everybody going to gang up and play meanie to all the new kids on the block? The rules of play may be changing, but this does not necessarily signal the game's over; it is, rather, a notice for the rookie players to pump up a notch and by all means keep hustling.

GOODBYE YELLOW BRICK ROAD

Everyone who's had a kid (or been one) believes they can write for the children's and young-adult market—or so it appears to editors and agents who are swamped with proposals they deem far off the mark. Though this scheme of visionary would-be-author unreality is not much different from the world of adult trade publishing (where it seems everyone has a how-to/inspirational book inside them, or a hook for a sizzling new thriller), it is an exceptionally excruciating phenomenon in the realm of kid's lit— it is immediately, abundantly clear when a prospective author has not done a bit of homework.

Publishers often have certain preferences for queries and submissions. Part of your homework is to find out from your target houses whether to include sample material with your query—and how much to include. Call the publisher and inquire about such protocols from someone in the editorial department—whatever information you have seen in print is subject to change, and requirements for individual series and lines are bound to vary.

If you have in mind an original series, it might be best to suggest this indirectly by first presenting a strong character whose escapades beg to be turned into a series, rather than stating your intent outright. Perhaps you can couch your ultimate goals somewhere in the presentation package subtly, without appearing bombastic or rude. As for novelizations and television/movie spinoffs—publishers often keep writers on tap for these projects; query the publisher and find out what you can do to become part of their crew.

Skip the trip down the yellow-brick road: If you want to write for children or young-adult readers, a nuts-and-bolts approach is called for at the outset. The routine of conceiving and structuring your work according to brutal publishing demands can be overbearing and numbing at first, and even confusing to the novice writer. However, as the guidelines are comprehended, they become a source of confidence that you're on the right track. Research in the field results in flights of insight that can guide the prospective author into shaping a proposal worthy of consideration rather than one that's ripe to hit the trashcan.

CHILDREN'S LITERATURE AS CORPORATE ENTERPRISE

In corporate-style children's publishing, many successful projects are now originated in house, or by those outside the company who can bring to bear considerable experience (and contacts) in writing, illustration, editing, design, manufacturing of product, and the marketing of same.

Many lines intended for children's and young-adult markets are handled by independent book packagers or book producers that specialize in this field. These typically small, entrepreneurial operations mastermind ideas, develop concepts (perhaps in tandem with their corporate clients), and commission work from artists, designers and writers. Many freelancers work through book packagers, rather than agents or publishers, with varying arrangements pertaining to compensation (flat fees, hourly rates, royalties) and author credit.

As a writer or illustrator for hire, you might not be an accredited author as such (at least when you start out), but you work for money, not on spec. In some established series with strict specifications or in start-up lines, it might not be much of a free-market atmosphere, but (and this part bears repeating) your creative labors are rewarded in currency, if not renown.

Children's publishing has traditionally been more open to unagented/unsolicited submissions than has the adult-publishing sphere; however, it is increasingly the case that acquisitions departments in major children's houses do not accept *any* unsolicited manuscripts directly from authors; all projects they consider are those that go through the screening process at literary agencies—and the agents whose author submissions get respect are themselves specialists in books for younger readers.

Not every agent listed in writer's-resource directories is skilled in addressing the nuances of the ever-changing children's/young-adult market. It behooves you, as a writer or illustrator, to seek out those agents who have expertise in this area and are open to new recruits.

In addition, it can be well worth your while (and worth your money) to avail yourself of the services of an independent editorial consultant with a solid background in children's publishing. Referrals to qualified professionals may be obtained through writers' organizations, editorial associations, or some of the more amiable literary agencies.

Aside from the major commercial publishers, there are numerous smaller and regional presses that have solid children's divisions or that specialize in works directed toward certain age groups. Check these guys out (there are a number of such publishers listed in the directories in this book); you might be surprised and gratified to know how open some of them are to new authors.

MARKETING BY DESIGN

No one in commercial publishing will let you forget that the primary objective is to circulate product—and create profit. As an artist or writer who wishes to participate financially in the publishing industry, please bear in mind at all times that you are in the research-and-development wing of what is essentially a manufacturing and marketing enterprise.

That means you, as an intelligent creator, must know your market and understand what it takes to reach your buyer. Apart from the niceties of promotion and distribution (to which your publishing overview should be attuned), knowledge of the special requirements of your selected area can make or break your project at the concept stage.

Illustrators must familiarize themselves with the prevailing conventions of books for young kids as they apply to the rendering of animals who dress up in clothing and speak, for the right mix of innocence and affection between young lovers who never kiss, for ways to portray action scenes in ways that are not overly scary.

Artists must also be experts in print technology, and be able to execute their designs expressively within the confines of layout requirements, with elements of shading, line, and color separation well defined in the backs of their minds before they begin their work.

For writers, there are particular sets of standards to be met in terms of readership level (such as vocabulary, sentence structure, and content). You've got one strong market made up of titles for tots who do not themselves read—here you want to write books that are inviting *to be read aloud to them.*

There is also the question of who is buying the book, and why. Obviously the adult caretaker is going to plunk down the bucks for products targeted at the youngest age groups. However, even here, the kids themselves have enormous input, gauged by their responses while browsing around children's sections (which, in some of the more lavish bookstores, are set up to resemble play areas).

Publishers design some children's lines to be read by younger readers on their own, because the kids themselves want to read them. Other series are keyed to the demands of the educational market, to be read in large part because they are assigned by teachers. Even though there is some sales overlap—school libraries represent an important market sector—the emphasis on individual creativity varies enormously within the overall readability guidelines.

Because the field is geared to specific age ranges, the actual makeup of each market-sector changes as readers progress through the various levels. This implies that children's publishers are wise to be aware of subtle cultural shifts that are sometimes much more slowly reflected in adult trade divisions. The trend toward books published in the Spanish language in addition to their English counterparts, as well as in bilingual Spanish/English editions, was evident in the arena of books for younger readers before the major commercial houses began to dance to that same tune.

In line with this view, children's books were multimedia affairs—in the tangibly physical sense—long before the advent of electronic versions. In order to tickle the fancy of admirably antic kids, children's books engage a variety of formats not strictly limited to type and pictures. Among established approaches are peek-a-board books, pop-up books, chunky-shaped books, cuddle-cloth books, mini-storybooks, glow-in-the-dark books with phosphorescent ink; books with puzzle-pages, ribbons, bows, and gilt; books boxed with wearable accessories, books in tandem with activity kits, and book-and-audio packages. Publishers construe such projects as unlikely to arise from the whimsical ideas and grandiose sheaves of notes that sometimes appear miraculously at writer's conferences.

In order to publish complex packages successfully, each element is handled by seasoned professionals. Of course artists and writers play important roles, but there is more variety of publishing skill, expertise, and expense involved in bringing these products out beautifully than there is when translating the words of adult literary masters into printed type, no matter how elegantly designed.

Children's-publishing houses make use of an array of personnel equipped with exquisite design skills, eagle editorial eyes, and consummate aesthetic sense; they require ingenious technicians familiar with the latest means of production and print, with a robust command of engineering concepts and manufacturing processes.

AIN'T NO PLAYPEN

At major publishing firms, there are fewer venues for the first-time writer or prospective illustrator, and an increasing emphasis placed on developing brand-name lines and series—particularly those with spinoff potential in other media, as well as into toyland and wearable apparel. If divisions and imprints with specialties in the arena of younger readers seem to be closing off the traditional avenues used by rookie talent to get to them, it's due to circumstances that have much to do with corporate consolidation at the larger houses, as well as insider advantages of personal contacts at smaller start-up operations.

Fun and games may be the end products of some children's and young-adult publishing projects, but getting to play in the first place is no lark for the aspiring writer and illustrator. As a personal pastime, many people enjoy composing sets of rhymes, developing story lines combined with pictures, or conceiving text-and-photographic layouts. With some copies of their creations printed and bound, these people are amply rewarded by the response of young readers in their personal circles.

If, however, you are determined to vie with the big kids in the publishing biz, it is essential to see the world of children's publishing up close as publishers view it—not in the golden light of far-off fantasies derived from half-forgotten images of childhood bliss. You are, at this level, in competition with all the others out there with the same dream. In order to get a toe in, you not only have to step out from the rest of the pack, you have to show accomplishment on the order of those with professional credentials. You may well have to master the requisite skills on your own, but there is a community of like-minded individuals and programs out there to assist you.

Be resourceful. This means literally taking advantage of the substantial resources at hand. That includes studying some of the many excellent books on the subject of writing for children and young adults, joining writers' groups, attending conferences, and making use of any and all networking connections you can negotiate. With a solid combination of refined skills, unflagging determination, and a growing mesh of contacts, you too can break through.

Novel Truths
Revealing the Secret World of Fiction

Jamie M. Forbes

You know you like it when you read it—but do you know what it is you've read? Maybe you like *this* writer (most of the time), or books from *that* publisher (some of the time), but never read any of *that* kind of stuff. Indeed, it might be said that you'd read even more than you already do if they published more of what you enjoy.

You know plenty of other people who feel just about the same way you do. Maybe you'd be mortified to find out that publishers view you as part of a specific market, the books that please you ideally seen in terms of categories, genres, brand-name authors, and high-identity imprints.

Wait a minute; back up a bit. You're not a number (how many books and what kind did you buy last year, ma'am?). You're an individual with personal tastes and a distinct style—give a babe a break once in a while! So long as you're asking what you can do about this state of affairs, guy—why don't you write a story about it? The kind others of your ilk will buy in droves.

What kind of book is that, bub?

A good one—just one hell of a novel.

You've got to do more than that to get it into print.

THE WAY OF THE WORD WARRIOR

Why classify your fiction in mercenary terms? As an accomplished writer, you've earned the right for the text to stand on its own. After all, you've got a riveting story complete with rich characters and exquisite atmosphere. Guess what: Regardless of how well honed a plot you've got, it's not enough. What, then, if anything, is gained by slapping on a label? It's certain that many folks suffer plenty in life from being pigeonholed, but remember: Life is tough, and writing is tougher.

Whether a novel is a heartfelt work of art or commercial calculation on the author's part, it finally does have to stand on its own, as an experience worthy of the reader's buck. However, in order to get to the reader, your work will be categorized for much the same reason any other product is packaged and named: A book is not a book until it's brought to the market ready to be bought.

MAP THE LITERARY LANDSCAPE

Browse through some of the bookseller superchains, take a peek into specialty bookstores: You will see that all books have to be someplace. And some are racked in a couple different places—certain popular fiction titles are also stocked in mystery or horror sections, or sometimes even under a sign bearing, of all things, the word *literature*.

All well and good, some writers may say. Booksellers and publishers are the marketing professionals; that's their game, and they can play it any way they want—so long as they do a good job selling books. Writers are the prose pros, and let's just leave it that way.

No chance.

For writers, bookselling is not a spectator sport. Nor should marketing be solely the province of publishers and booksellers. An author is in charge the instant the idea for a work springs forth. It quickly becomes apparent to fledgling writers that a marketing hook is as important in the initial query letter as it is in the finished book or promotional tour.

Writers are often advised to study the market (or markets), to gear their work for a particular slot, to learn how to position their work in the publishing emporium. Such stratagems sound sweet and dandy, but where to begin? One key to enlightenment is through the concept of category. Understanding how your novel fits within the category structure of contemporary fiction publishing may spell the difference between literary success and oblivion.

BE AWARE—AND GET THERE

Consider the following buzz terms: hard-boiled, cozy, psychological horror, vampire romance, contemporary Western, medical-legal thriller, spiritual adventure. Sound like anything you've written, by chance—or would choose to read? If so, lovely; if not, look around, there are plenty of other categories, genres, and subgenres to be found, each with its own special appeal, its own readership niche.

Though some classifications seem evident enough on the surface, plenty of pitfalls lurk underfoot. There are several different approaches to the horror story, and many forms of mysteries. Is *literary fiction* a category or simply a description, or is it both? Is a work categorized according to genre, or is genre fiction itself a category?

A customary breakdown of the fiction market describes three broad sectors that in practice do overlap. (1) There is category (or genre) fiction, wherein books are typified by genre or category (such as with detective fiction, horror, romance, suspense, thriller, or Western) and are marketed as such. (2) Commercial fiction (the high end of mainstream fiction) is expected to find a wide readership that supersedes or cuts across genres; the most marketable of these works are designated lead titles, or frontlist books (often literally placed at the front of the catalog listings). (3) Literary works are characterized by accomplishment in the art and craft of writing (or can be marketed as if they did), and may otherwise represent a genre (or not), have cult appeal (not limited to the academy), or even be considered commercial (when the author shows big sales).

You as writer can of course choose to write whatever you want, however you want—and by all means dream on during the idea stages. Nonetheless, please bear in mind that your chances of being published are incalculably greater if your work is seen clearly as having a conspicuous place in the category scheme of commercial publishing.

Booksellers and publishers are fond of pronouncements that put the market in perspective—their perspective. You may hear there is little crossover between the readership of horror and mystery; there is said to be more of a blend (but not much more) between aficionados of science fiction and avant-garde suspense. The evidence to support such claims may in actuality be scant, and your own anecdotal experience may seem to point out new and different readership trends.

However, publishers sign authors and sell books on the basis of what they have already sold successfully. If your work is a crossover piece, it's best to play it as commercially as possible, which by some definitions means watering down the specific genre attributes and pumping up your story with universal passions, intensifying the human interaction, and interlacing your plot elements with boffo schemes of fear and greed, intrigue and romance.

RIDDLE ME THIS: THE FICTION QUERY

Once you've got your product polished enough to hawk, you've need to find a place to sell it. Unless you're betting on internet distribution or planning to flog your own home-printed copies at the local flea market, your most likely venue is through the publishing establishment of editors and agents. You reach them, first of all, through the dreaded and ubiquitous query letter—with which publishing houses and literary agencies are deluged daily.

When you query an agent or editor, be sharp as a buccaneer's cutlass, and as stealthy as a sea-rover prowling for quarry. The initial aim of all paper pirates is to lure the reader to request the full manuscript. Make sure the dynamic appeal of your tale is portrayed in a conceptual hook of as few words as possible, up front, very likely in the opening sentence. The query lead whets the edge in order to make a breach in the impassive reader's defenses.

There are any number of ways to do this. Even the most obliquely suggested examples would undoubtedly result in an overwhelming tilt toward certain query approaches that have in the past proven to be eye-openers, and these techniques would quickly lose their edge—so you won't find any real recommendations here. You may choose to take a stand and be creative and original; or be pointed and precise. A fiction query is both a demonstration of writing agility and a business letter—it can work at either extreme or anywhere along the continuum.

Now that you've poked that opening, you're ready for the follow-through.

Embroider the opening gambit with a succinct depiction of the story's primary selling points. If you haven't done so in the lead, state how the work fits into the book-publishing industry's category structure and also what makes *this* piece so unique it screams to be published. Do it all in a sentence or two—regardless of how elaborate the actual story is.

Then you may highlight one or two further aspects of character, plot, or setting that accent the story's allure. Be careful: If this part of the query threatens to run more than two or three paragraphs, try to shave it down; the extra copy expended here risks diluting the impact (the material you cut might be used to better effect in a synopsis).

The space you save can be used to rattle off a few pertinent personal notes, such as prior publication, or special career or professional expertise brought to bear in the story. Writing tightly can allow a one-page query to pack more of a wallop than a glossy, brochure-sized writer's packet that contains diffuse credits and irrelevant fanfare.

RED FLAGS AND JOLLY ROGERS

Valid or not, certain approaches send out red flags in the eyes of agents and editors. Where original fiction is concerned, people in publishing tend not to be impressed by the invocation of big-money books or hugely popular movies with which an inquiring writer's work is to be compared. *So what?* is the unspoken response. *That's been done before, and done superbly. The market is saturated with good stuff already.* When your work is truly innovative, you've done yourself a grave disservice with a derivative presentation.

Likewise, citing topical societal motifs or current political fiascoes as if they existed intrinsically to sell a particular author's novel is inclined make a bad moon rise in a reader. Surely, finessing the context of contemporary culture can augment a book's appeal, but a query letter that runs far afield from the work at hand is apt to be read as preposterous posturing from a resounding blowhard. That's enough to make a reader suspect the manuscript is more of the same.

Don't get spooked by these protocols. Agents and editors are well aware that to get the big picture you have to read the whole story; they know that a query is in essence a sales pitch. They'll begin to appreciate your subtlety and breadth when they read the full piece (or get a taste in the sample chapters or short synopsis you enclose)—your query convinces them that their extra reading is likely to be worthwhile.

You as a writer can believe you oversimplify your story to the point of gross misrepresentation if you say your book is, for instance, a medical thriller (by god, it's about my *characters*!); but such a description shows the agent or editor you're not unfamiliar with such niceties as bookstores and book reviews: You indicate you are aware of industry dictates (however confining), and know a thing or two about positioning a product in the marketplace.

A final caveat: Don't advertise something that isn't there; your manuscript must be all you claim it to be—and more.

FOGGY NOTIONS AND PUBLIC DELUSIONS

Even that jaded someone in the corner office with the view, whose trenchant response can always be counted on—even that seasoned professional can be boggled by the occasional media blitzes and hefty cash figures bandied about the press. Such stories are newsworthy because they are rarities, not because they recount run-of-the-mill fiction-publishing rituals.

Research tip for new novelists: Check out *The Hottest State* (fiction) by Ethan Hawke, bought for what was widely reported as a $500,000 advance by Little, Brown (a house that retains the image of the Boston-based literary press it used to be, now re-located to New York as part of the Time-Warner multimedia establishment). This kind of money is pretty good (or at least borderline okay) for a first fiction from someone previously known mainly as an actor.

The tip? Get famous somewhere else first, then get a publisher to give you money—and please realize that the half-mil we're talking about speculatively is equivalent to peanuts in the typical successful-actor scheme of things. Over and above the sheer writing skills of the author, a publisher ascertains that a project like this offers uncommonly fertile ground for publicity across the board in virtually all mass-media arenas.

Likewise by way of Little, Brown, a cautionary note: Just because David Foster Wallace's visionary novel *Infinite Jest* checked in at over 1,000 published pages doesn't mean a first-timer should be shipping out 3,000-page manuscripts and expect editors and agents to jump like salmon on the run. Wallace had well over a decade of publishing credits behind him (even though your schnauzer might not have heard of him); publication of *Infinite Jest* was not remarkably visionary—by this point in the author's career, it was a remarkably ordinary business venture on the part of the publisher.

READERSHIP BASE: SAFE HAVEN OR STRANDED BY SUCCESS?

Calling your manuscript a literary sci-fi mystery thriller showcasing elements of sword-and-sorcery fantasy in an erotic action-adventure scenario may encompass your grand achievement very accurately. But such a description can also cover a work with lack of focus, unsteady vision, and terrifying scarcity of storytelling precision. A crossover concept, if it is not seen as highly commercial (regardless of the quality of writing), limits rather than expands potential appeal in the eyes of publishers, which equals no deal. (P.S.: The aforementioned work is likely one that can be presented more marketably as a science-fiction adventure.)

Be aware that, once published, authors, like their output, are classified by genre or category, and writers may encounter flak from editors and agents when they wish to break out of the mold their success in one arena has created. A way around this per-haps-enviable predicament is for a writer to use different pen names as brand names for certain series or lines, in much the same manner publishers devise special imprint names like Berkley Prime Crime, Warner Aspect, or Vintage Contemporaries.

Through genre-hopping, the writer may lose hard-won name recognition gained in one field and have to build a new readership virtually from the beginning—lower antic-ipated sales for a bankable author are a major reason for resistance from the publishing community, and low (if any) advances are an anticipated stance. The reverse is the case when a writer is moved from category classification to frontlist commercial status, for then the publisher is confident the writer is ready and able to break into a wider market and still retain an established readership base.

Your Own Compass

Navigating the literary seas can be treacherous indeed for the writer who is adrift; these are turbulent, murky waters, where fierce waves crash, whirlpools gyrate, and rocks await to dash your craft. In order to chart your course, it is provident to take out a map of the literary landscape before you begin your manuscript in earnest; compass your route to the marketplace during the initial stages of development, rather than after a complete draft, when major revisions (or an entirely new start) are required to bring your story into port rather than being tossed and forgotten on a forlorn beach.

If your premise and plot structure don't fit the established category format, you may be in for a real ordeal when trying to find a publisher, at least in the mainstream commercial arena. However, when the writing voice is strong, with sufficient resourcefulness and good fortune, a suitable publisher can be found.

Anne Rice's *Interview with the Vampire* didn't slide nicely into quaint horror formulas, and some might not classify it as proper literature; Knopf bought it, and millions of fans couldn't care less how her work is categorized. Did Tom Clancy invent the technothriller? Regardless of that subgenre's current popularity, it was Naval Institute Press, and not a commercial house, that initially brought out Clancy's *Hunt for Red October*. Did John Grisham break new legal-thriller ground with *The Firm*? (Grisham's first novel, *A Time to Kill*, was introduced by Wynwood, a primarily religious house.) James Redfield's *The Celestine Prophecy* would seem, on description, to be a defiantly uncategorizable mélange of genres—the book's commercial success shows how wise the writer was to follow through on his vision. Full-blooded romance in tandem with philosophical pursuits says rejection-slip wallpaper to many—to Robert James Waller it said: *Bridges of Madison County* and a full skein of subsequent bestsellers.

Books. Hooks. Premise and plot. That's a lot to think about when you start a new project. Once you begin, the whole shebang becomes internalized as you lose all trepidation and move along undaunted. It's downright glorious when you realize that, whether working in line with or in defiance of category guidelines, your writing is energized by your industry awareness.

Keep in mind that the sign on the spine of a paperback or the blurb on the back of a hardcover tells the bookseller where to rack the package. The prospective reader knows where to browse, look around, and pick up your book on the basis of its catchy title or snazzy design—if not yet on the basis of your burgeoning literary renown. This hungry book lover will then flip through the lush pages of your book and read here and there. The reader then is aware you are a writer with individuality and personal style (even though it is clearly being marketed as a category work). Next step: Head for the counter to buy your book.

For an unfettered treatment of the category structure of contemporary fiction publishing, please see Fiction Dictionary, *which follows.*

Fiction Dictionary

JAMIE M. FORBES

In book publishing, people describe works of fiction as they relate to categories, genres, and other market concepts, which, coming from the mouths of renowned industry figures, can make it sound as if there's a real system to what is actually a set of arbitrary terminology. Categories are customarily viewed as reflecting broad sectors of readership interest. Genres are either subcategories (classifications within categories) or types of stories that can pop up within more than one category—though *genre* and *category* are sometimes used interchangeably.

For instance, suspense fiction (as a broad category) includes the jeopardy story genre (typified by a particular premise that can just as easily turn up in a supernatural horror story). Or, again within the suspense fiction category, there's the police procedural (a subcategory of detective fiction, which is itself a subcategory of suspense that is often spoken of as a separate category). The police procedural can be discussed as a distinct genre with its own special attributes; and there are particular procedural genre types, such as those set in the small towns of the American plains or in a gritty urban environment. As a genre-story type, tales of small-town American life also surface in the context of categories as disparate as literary fiction, horror stories, Westerns, and contemporary and historical romance.

As we can see, all of this yakety-yak is an attempt to impose a sense of order onto what is certainly a muddy creative playing field.

The following listing of commonly used fiction descriptives gives an indication of the varieties of writing found within each category. This is not meant to be a strict taxonomy. Nor is it exhaustive. The definitions associated with each category or genre are fluid and personalized in usage, and can seem to vary with each author interview or critical treatise, with each spate of advertising copy or press release, or can shift during the course of a single editorial conference. One writer's "mystery" may be a particular editor's "suspense," which is then marketed to the public as a "thriller."

Then too, individual authors do come up with grand, original ideas that demand publication and thereby create new categories, or decline to submit to any such designation. But that's another story—maybe yours.

ACTION ADVENTURE

The action-oriented adventure novel is best typified in terms of premise and scenario trajectory. These stories often involve the orchestration of a journey that is essentially exploratory, revelatory, and (para)military. There is a quest element—a search for a treasure in whatever guise—in addition to a sense of pursuit that crosses over into thrillerdom. From one perspective, the action-adventure tale, in story concept if not explicit content, traces its descent from epic-heroic tradition.

In modern action-adventure we are in the territory of freebooters, commandos, and mercenaries—as well as suburbanites whose yen for experience of the good life, and whose very unawareness in the outback, takes them down dangerous trails. Some stories are stocked with an array of international terrorists, arms-smugglers, drug-dealers, and techno-pirates. Favorite settings include jungles, deserts, swamps, and mountains—any sort of badlands (don't rule out an urban environment) that can echo the perils that resound through the story's human dimension.

There can be two or more cadres with competing aims going for the supreme prize—and be sure to watch out for lots of betrayal and conflict among friends, as well as the hitherto unsuspected schemer among the amiably bonded crew.

Action-adventures were once thought of as exclusively men's stories. No more. Writers invented new ways to do it, and the field is now open.

COMMERCIAL FICTION

Commercial fiction is defined by sales figures—either projected (prior to publication, even before acquisition) or backhandedly through actual performance. Commercial properties are frontlist titles, featured prominently in a publisher's catalog and given good doses of publicity and promotion.

An agent or editor says a manuscript is commercial, and the question in response is apt to be: How so? Many books in different genres achieve bestseller potential after an author has established a broad-based readership and is provided marketing support from all resources the publisher commands.

Commercial fiction is not strictly defined by content or style; it is perhaps comparative rather than absolute. Commercial fiction is often glitzier, more stylishly of the mode in premise and setting; its characters strike the readers as more assuredly glamorous (regardless of how highbrow or lowlife).

A commercial work offers the publisher a special marketing angle, which changes from book to book or season to season—this year's kinky kick is next year's ho-hum. For a new writer in particular, to think commercially is to think ahead of the pack and not jump on the tail-end of a bandwagon that's already passed. If your premise has already played as a television miniseries, you're way too late.

Commercial works sometimes show elements of different categories, such as detective fiction or thrillers, and may cut across or combine genres to reach out toward a vast readership. Cross-genre books may thus have enticing hooks for the reading public at large; at the same time, when they defy category conventions they may not satisfy genre aficionados. If commercial fiction is appointed by vote of sales, most popular mysteries are commercial works, as are sophisticated bestselling sex-and-shopping oh-so-shocking wish-it-were-me escapades.

CRIME FICTION

Related to detective fiction and suspense novels, in subject matter and ambiance, are stories centered on criminal enterprise. Crime fiction includes lighthearted capers that are vehicles in story form for portrayal of amusingly devious aspirations at the core of the human norm. Crime stories can also be dark, black, *noir*, showing the primeval essence of tooth-and-nail that brews in more than a few souls.

Some of the players in crime stories may well be cops of one sort or another (and they are often as corrupt as the other characters), but detection per se is not necessarily the story's strong suit. It is just as likely that, in the hands of one of the genre's masters, the reader's lot will be cast (emotionally at least) in support of the outlaw characters' designs.

DETECTIVE FICTION

Varieties of detective fiction include police procedurals (with the focus on formal investigatory teamwork); hard-boiled, poached or soft-boiled (not quite so tough as hard-boiled); and the cozy (aka tea-cozy mysteries, manners mysteries, manor house mysteries).

Detectives are typically private or public pros; related professionals whose public image at least involves digging under the surface (reporters, journalists, computer hackers, art experts, psychotherapists, and university academics including archaeologists); or they may be rank amateurs who are interested or threatened via an initial plot turn that provides them with an opportunity (or the necessity) to assume an investigatory role.

The key here is that the detective story involves an ongoing process of discovery that forms the plot. Active pursuit of interlocking clues and other leads is essential—though sometimes an initial happenstance disclosure will do in order to kick off an otherwise tightly woven story.

The manifold denominations of modern detective fiction (also called mysteries, or stories or novels of detection) are widely considered to stem from the detective tales composed by the 19th-century American writer Edgar Allan Poe. Though mysterious tracks of atmosphere and imagery can be traced in the writings of French symbolists (Charles Baudelaire was a big fan of Poe), the first flowering of the form was in Britain, including such luminaries as Arthur Conan Doyle, Agatha Christie, and Dorothy L. Sayers. Indeed, in one common usage, a traditional mystery (or cozy) is a story in the mode initially established by British authors.

The other major tradition is the American-grown hard-boiled detective story, with roots in the tabloid culture of America's industrial growth and the associated institutions of yellow journalism, inspirational profiles of the gangster-tycoon lifestyle, and social-action exposés.

The field continues to expand with infusions of such elements as existentialist character conceits, the lucidity and lushness of magic-realists, and the ever-shifting sociopolitical insights that accrue from the growing global cultural exchange.

Occasionally detective fiction involves circumstances in which, strictly speaking, no crime has been committed. The plot revolves around parsing out events or situations that may be construed as strange, immoral, or unethical (and are certainly mysterious), but which are by no means considered illegal in all jurisdictions.

FANTASY FICTION

The category of fantasy fiction covers many of the story elements encountered in fables, folktales, and legends; the best of these works obtain the sweep of the epic and are touched by the power of myth. Some successful fantasy series are set within recognizable museum-quality frames, such as those of ancient Egypt or the Celtic world. Another strain of fantasy fiction takes place in almost-but-not-quite archeologically verifiable regions of the past or future, with barbarians, nomads, and jewel-like cities scattered across stretches of continental-sized domains of the author's imagination.

Fair game in this realm are romance, magic, and talking animals. Stories are for the most part adventurous, filled with passion, honor, vengeance—and *action*. A self-explanatory subgenre of fantasy fiction is termed sword-and-sorcery.

HORROR

Horror has been described as the simultaneous sense of fascination and terror, a basic attribute that can cover significant literary scope. Some successful horror writers are admired more for their portrayal of atmosphere than for attention to plot or character development. Other writers do well with the carefully paced zinger—that is, the threat-and-delivery of gore; in the hands of skilled practitioners, sometimes not much more is needed to produce truly terrifying effects.

The horror genre has undergone changes—there is overall less reliance on the religiously oriented supernatural, more utilization of medical and psychological concepts, more sociopolitical and cultural overtones, and a general recognition on the part of publishers that many horror aficionados seek more than slash-and-gore. Not that the readers aren't bloodthirsty—it is just that in order to satisfy the cravings of a discerning audience a writer must create an augmented reading experience.

The horror itself can be supernatural in nature, psychological, paranormal, or techno (sometimes given a medical-biological slant that verges on sci-fi), or can embody personified occult/cultic entities. In addition to tales of vampires, were-creatures, demons, and ghosts, horror has featured such characters as the elemental slasher/stalker (conceived with or without mythic content), a variety of psychologically tormented souls, and just plain folks given over to splatterhouse pastimes. Whatever the source of the horror, the tale is inherently more gripping and more profound when the horrific beast, force, or human foe has a mission, is a character with its own meaningful designs and insights—when something besides single-minded bloodlust is at play.

At times the horror premise is analogous to a story of detection (especially in the initial setup); often the horror plot assumes the outlines of the thriller (particularly where there is a complex chase near the end); and sometimes the horror-story scenario ascribes to action-adventure elements. However, rather than delineating a detailed process of discovery (as in a typical mystery) or a protracted hunt throughout (as in the thriller), the horror plot typically sets up a final fight to the finish (until the sequel) that, for all its pyrotechnics and chills, turns on something other than brute force.

LITERARY FICTION

The term *literary* describes works that feature the writer's art expressed at its most refined levels; literary fiction describes works of literature in such forms as the novel, novella, novelette, short story, and short-shorts (also known as flash fiction). In addition to these fictional formats, literary works include poetry, essays, letters, dramatic works, and superior writing in all nonfiction varieties covering such areas as travel, food, history, current affairs, and all sorts of narrative nonfiction as well as reference works.

Literary fiction can adhere to the confines of any and all genres and categories, or suit no such designation. A work of fiction that is depicted as literary can (and should) offer the reader a multidimensional experience. Literary can designate word selection and imagery that is careful or inspired, or that affects an articulated slovenliness. A literary character may be one who is examined in depth, or is sparsely sketched to trenchant effect. Literature can postulate philosophical or cultural insights, and portray fresh ideas in action. Literary works can feature exquisitely detailed texture or complete lack of sensory ambiance.

Structurally, literary fiction favors story and plot elements that are individualistic or astonishingly new rather than tried-and-true. In some cases the plot as such does not appear important, but beware of quick judgment in this regard: Plotting may be subtle, as in picking at underlying psychology or revelation of character. And the plot movement may take place in the reader's head, as the progressive emotional or intellectual response to the story, rather than demonstrated in external events portrayed on paper.

To say that a work is literary can imply seriousness. Nonetheless many serious works are not particularly sober, and literary reading should be a dynamic experience—pleasurably challenging, insightful, riveting, fun. A work that is stodgy and boring may not be literary at all, for it has not achieved the all-important aim of being fine reading.

Obviously, a book that is lacking with respect to engaging characters, consciousness of pace, and story development but features fancy wordplay and three-page sentences is hardly exemplary of literary mastery. Though such a work may serve as a guidepost of advanced writing techniques for a specialized professional audience, it is perhaps a more limited artifice than is a slice-and-dice strip-and-whip piece that successfully depicts human passion and offers a well-honed story.

Commercial literature, like commercial fiction in general, is essentially a back-definition; commercial literature indicates works of outstanding quality written by authors who sell well, as opposed to just plain literature, which includes writers and works whose readership appeal has not yet expanded beyond a small core. Non-commercial literary works are staples of the academic press and specialized houses, as well as selected imprints of major trade publishers.

When a literary author attracts a large readership, or manages to switch from the list of a tiny publisher to a mammoth house, the publisher might decide a particular project is ripe for a shot at the bigtime and slate the writer for substantial attention, accompanied by a grand advance. If you look closely, you'll note that literary authors who enter the commercial ranks are usually not just good writers: Commercial literary works tap into the cultural pulse, which surges through the editorial avenues into marketing, promotion, and sales support.

In day-to-day commercial publishing discourse, to call a piece of work literary simply means it is well written. As a category designation, literary fiction implies that a particular book does not truly abide by provisos of other market sectors—though if the work under discussion does flash some category hooks, it might be referred to in such catch-terms as a literary thriller or literary suspense.

MAINSTREAM FICTION

A mainstream work is one that can be expected to be at least reasonably popular to a fairly wide readership. In a whim of industry parlance, to various people in publishing the label mainstream signifies a work that is not particularly noteworthy on any count—it's a work of fiction that's not literary according to circumscribed tastes; and not something easily categorized with a targeted, predictable base of readership. Maybe not particularly profitable, either, especially if the publishing house is bent on creating bestsellers. A mainstream work may therefore be seen as a risky proposition rather than a relatively safe bet.

Let this be a cautionary note: In some publishing minds, a plain-and-simple mainstream book signifies midlist, which equals no sale. In a lot of publishing houses, midlist fiction, even if it's published, gets lost; many commercial trade houses won't publish titles they see as midlist (see **Midlist Fiction**).

A mainstream work may be a good read—but if that's all you can say about it, it's a mark against its prospects in the competitive arena. When a story is just a good story, the publisher doesn't have much of a sales slant to work with; in publishing terms that makes for a dismal enough prognosis for an editor or agent to pass.

If a manuscript has to sell on storytelling merits or general interest alone, it most likely won't sell to a major publisher at all. If mainstream fiction is what you've got, the writer is advised to return to the workshop and turn the opus into a polished piece with a stunning attitude that can be regarded as commercial, or redesign the story line into a category format such as mystery, suspense, or thriller. A mainstream mystery or mainstream thriller may contain characters who aren't too wacko and milieus that aren't overly esoteric. Such works are eminently marketable, but you might suppress the mainstream designation in your query and just call your work by its category or genre moniker.

If you've got the gifts and perseverance to complete a solid story, and you find yourself about to say it's a mainstream book and no more, you'll be further along faster if you work to avoid the midlist designation. Think commercially and write intrepidly.

Please note: Many editors and agents use the term *mainstream fiction* more or less synonymously with **Commercial Fiction** (see, please).

MIDLIST FICTION

Midlist books are essentially those that do not turn a more-than-marginal profit. That they show a profit at all might testify to how low the author's advance was (usually set so the publisher can show a profit based on projected sales). Midlist books may be category titles, literary works, or mainstream books that someone, somewhere believed had commercial potential (yet to be achieved).

The midlist is where no one wants to be: You get little if any promotion, few reviews, and no respect. Why publish this kind of book at all? Few publishers do. A midlist book was most likely not intended as such; the status is unacceptable unless the writer is being prepped for something bigger, and is expected to break through *soon*. When a writer or series stays midlist too long, they're gone—the publishers move on to more profitable use of their resources.

If the publishers don't want you, and the readers can't find you, you're better off going somewhere else too. (See **Commercial Fiction** or any of the other category designations.)

MYSTERY

Many people use the term *mystery* to refer to the detective story (see **Detective Fiction**). When folks speak of traditional mysteries, they often mean a story in the British cozy mold, which can be characterized—but not strictly defined—by an amateur sleuth (often female) as protagonist, a solve-the-puzzle story line, minimal body count (with all violence performed offstage), and a restrained approach to language and tone. Sometimes, however, a reference to traditional mysteries implies not only cozies but also includes stories of the American hard-boiled school, which are typified by a private eye (or a rogue cop), up-front violence as well as sex, and vernacular diction.

On the other hand, mysteries are seen by some to include all suspense fiction categories, thereby encompassing police procedurals, crime capers, thrillers, even going so far afield as horror and some fantasy fiction.

In the interests of clarity, if not precision, here we'll say simply that a mystery is a story in which something of utmost importance to the tale is unknown or covert at the outset and must be uncovered, solved, or revealed along the way. (See **Crime Fiction, Detective Fiction, Fantasy Fiction, Horror, Suspense Fiction,** and **Thriller.**)

ROMANCE FICTION

The power of love has always been a central theme in literature, as it has in all arts, in all life. For all its importance to the love story genre, the term *romance* does not pertain strictly to the love element. The field can trace its roots through European medieval romances that depicted knights-errant and women in distress, which were as much tales of spiritual quest, politics, and action as love stories. The Romantic movement of the nineteenth century was at its heart emblematic of the heightened energy lent to all elements of a story, from human passion, to setting, to material objects, to psychological ramifications of simple acts.

Thanks to the writers and readers of modern romances, they've come a long way from the days of unadulterated heart-stopping bodice-rippers with pampered, egocentric heroines who long for salvation through a man. Today's romance most often depicts independent, a full-blooded female figure in full partnership with her intended mate.

Modern romance fiction is most assuredly in essence a love story, fueled by the dynamics of human relationships. From this core, writers explore motifs of career and family, topical social concerns, detective work, psychological suspense, espionage, and horror, as well as historical period pieces (including European medieval, Regency, and romances set in the American West) and futuristic tales. Romance scenarios with same-sex lovers are highlighted throughout the ranks of vanguard and literary houses, though this theme is not a priority market at most trade publishers or romance-specialist presses.

Among commercial lead titles tapped for bestseller potential are those books that accentuate the appeal of romance within the larger tapestry of a fully orchestrated work. (See also **Women's Fiction**.)

Science Fiction

Take humankind's age-old longings for knowledge and enlightenment and add a huge helping of emergent technology, with the twist that science represents a metaphysical quest—there you have the setup for science fiction. Though the basic science fiction plot may resemble that of action-adventure tales, thrillers, or horror stories, the attraction for the reader is likely to be the intellectual or philosophical questions posed, in tandem with the space-age glitter within which it's set. In terms of character interaction, the story line should be strong enough to stand alone when stripped of its technological trimmings.

In the *future fiction* genre, the elements of science fiction are all in place, but the science tends to be soft-pedaled, and the story as a whole is character-based. In a further variation, the post-apocalyptic vision presents the aftermath of a cataclysm (either engendered by technology or natural in origin) that sets the survivors loose on a new course that demonstrates the often-disturbing vicissitudes of social and scientific evolution. Such scenarios are generally set in the not-too-distant future, are usually earth-based, or barely interstellar, with recognizable (but perhaps advanced) technology as the norm.

Purity of genre is at times fruitless to maintain or define. Is Mary Shelley's *Frankenstein* a science fiction tale or a horror story, or is it primarily a literary work? Is Jules Verne's *20,000 Leagues Under the Sea* science fiction or a technothriller—or a futuristic action-adventure?

Stories of extraterrestrial exploration, intergalactic warfare, and other exobiological encounters are almost certain to be placed within the science fiction category, until the day when such endeavors are considered elements of realism.

SUSPENSE FICTION

Suspense fiction embraces many literary idioms, with a wide range of genres and subdivisions categorized under the general rubric of suspense. Indeed, in broad terms, all novels contain suspense—that is, if the writer means for the reader to keep reading and reading, and reading on . . . way into the evening and beyond.

Suspense fiction has no precise formula that specifies certain character types tied to a particular plot template. It is perhaps most applicable for a writer to think of suspense as a story concept that stems from a basic premise of situational uncertainty. That is: Something horrible is going to happen! Let's read! Within suspense there is considerable latitude regarding conventions of style, voice, and structure. From new suspense writers, editors look for originality and invention and new literary terrain, rather than a copycat version of last season's breakout work.

However, that said, writers should note that editors and readers are looking for works in which virtually every word, every scene, every blip of dialog serves to heighten suspense. This means that all imagery—from the weather to social setting, to the food ingested by the characters—is chosen by the writer to induce a sense of unease. Each scene (save maybe the last one) is constructed to raise questions or leave something unresolved. Every sentence or paragraph contains a possible pitfall. A given conversational exchange demonstrates edgy elementals of interpersonal tension. Everything looks rosy in one scene? Gotcha! It's a setup to reveal later what hell lurks underneath. Tell me some good news? Characters often do just that, as a prelude to showing just how wrong things can get.

The *jeopardy* story (or, as is often the case, a *woman-in-jeopardy* story) reflects a premise rather than being a genre per se. A tale of jeopardy—a character under continuous, increasing threat and (often) eventual entrapment—can incorporate what is otherwise a psychological suspense novel, a medical thriller, an investigatory trajectory, or a slasher-stalker spree.

Additional subdivisions here include *romantic suspense* (in which a love relationship plays an essential or dominant role—see *Romance Fiction*); *erotic suspense* (which is not necessarily identical to neurotic suspense); and *psychological suspense* (see immediately below).

Psychological Suspense

When drifts of character, family history, or other psychodynamics are central to a suspense story's progress and resolution, the tale may aptly be typified as psychological. Sometimes superficial shticks or gimmicks suffice (such as when a person of a certain gender turns out to be cross-dressed—surprise!), but such spins work best when the suspense is tied to crucial issues the writer evokes in the characters' and readers' heads and then orchestrates skillfully throughout the story line.

There are, obviously, crossover elements at play here, and whether a particular work is presented as suspense, psychological suspense, or erotic suspense can be more of an advertising-copywriting decision than a determination on the part of editor or author.

THRILLER

The thriller category is exemplified more by plot structure than by attributes of character, content, or story milieu. A thriller embodies what is essentially an extended game of pursuit—a hunt, a chase, a flight worked fugue-like through endless variations.

At one point in the history of narrative art, thrillers were almost invariably spy stories, with international casts and locales, often set in a theater of war (hot or cold). With shifts in political agendas and technical achievement in the real world, the thriller formula has likewise evolved. Today's thriller may well involve espionage, which can be industrial or political, domestic or international. There are also thrillers that favor settings in the realms of medicine, the law, the natural environs, the human soul, and the laboratory; this trend has given rise to the respective genres of legal thriller, medical thriller, environmental thriller, thrillers with spiritual and mystical themes, and the technothriller—assuredly there are more to come.

The thriller story line can encompass elements of detection or romance, and certainly should be full of suspense; but these genre-specific sequences are customarily expositional devices, or may be one of many ambient factors employed to accentuate tension within the central thriller plot. When you see a dust jacket blurb that depicts a book as a mystery thriller, it likely connotes a work with a thriller plot trajectory that uses an investigatory or detective-work premise to prepare for the chase.

WESTERN FICTION

The tradition of Western fiction is characterized as much by its vision of the individualist ethic as it is by its conventional settings in the frontier milieu of the American West during the period from the 1860s to the 1890s, sometimes extending into the early 1900s. Though the image of the lone, free-spirited cowpoke with an internalized code of justice has been passed down along the pulp-paper trail, it has long been appreciated by historians that the life of the average itinerant ranchhand of the day was anything but glamorous, anything but independent.

Whatever the historical record, editors by and large believe readers don't want to hear about the lackluster aspects of saddle tramps and dust-busting ruffians. Nevertheless, there have been inroads by books that display the historically accurate notions that a good chunk of the Western scene was inhabited by women and men of African American heritage, by those with Latino cultural affinities, by Asian expatriates, and European immigrants for whom English was a second language, as well as a diversity of native peoples.

Apart from the traditional genre Western, authors are equipped for a resurgence in a variety of novels with Western settings, most notably in the fields of mystery, crime, action-adventure, suspense, and future fiction. Among the newer Western novels are those replete with offbeat, unheroic, and downright antiheroic protagonists; and the standardized big-sky landscape has been superseded by backdrops that go against the grain.

Family sagas have long included at least a generation or two who drift, fight, and homestead through the Western Frontier. In addition, a popular genre of historical romance is set in the American West (see *Romance Fiction*).

Many contemporary commercial novels are set in the Western U.S., often featuring plush resorts, urban and suburban terrain, as well as the remaining wide country. The wide variety of project ideas generated by writers, as well as the reader response to several successful ongoing mystery series with Western elements, indicates a lively interest out there.

WOMEN'S FICTION

When book publishers speak of women's fiction, they're not referring to a particular genre or story concept (even if they think they are). This category—if it is one—is basically a nod to the prevalence of fiction readers who are women. Women's fiction is a marketing concept. As an informal designation, women's fiction as a matter of course can be expected to feature strong female characters and, frequently, stories offered from a woman's perspective.

As for the writers of books in this category—many (if not most) are women, but certainly not all of them are; the same observation applies to readers. Men can and do read these works too—and many professional male writers calculate potential readership demographics (including gender) as they work out details of story and plot.

In essence, what we've got is storytelling that can appeal to a broad range of readers but may be promoted principally to the women's market. It makes it easier to focus the promotion and to pass along tips to the publisher's sales representatives.

Many women writers consider their work in abstract compositional terms, regardless of to whom it is marketed. Other women writers may be publicized as cultural pundits, perhaps as feminists, though they don't necessarily see their message as solely women-oriented. Are they women writers or simply writers? So long as sales go well, they may not even care.

Some women writers adopt the genderless pose of the literary renegade as they claw their way through dangerous domains of unseemly characterization, engage in breakthrough storytelling techniques, and explore emergent modes of love. (After all, how can a force of nature be characterized by sex?) Any and all of these female wordsmiths may find themselves publicized as women authors.

Romantic fiction constitutes one large sector of the women's market, for many of the conventions of romance tap into culturally significant areas of the love relationship of proven interest to women bookbuyers.

Descriptive genre phrases pop in and out of usage; some of them trip glibly from the tongue and are gone forevermore, while others represent established literary norms that endure: kitchen fiction, mom novels, family sagas, domestic dramas, historical romances, chick lit, lipstick fiction, erotic thrillers. When these popular titles are written and/or promoted in ways intended to pique the interest of women readers, whatever else they may be, they're automatically women's fiction.

The New Poetry
Barkers, Chargers, and Performance Artists

Jamie M. Forbes

Poetry has once again changed its face, and media moguls are on notice of an audience at the brink. Long out of grace in commercial book-publishing circles, poetry's current growth has been initially established in the realms of live performance, video, and audio presentations rather than print. What's this mean for the poet who wants a book contract? Too soon to tell for certain, but prospects look better than they have in a long spell.

WHY PUBLISHERS ARE AVERSE TO VERSE

Commercial publishers do not emphasize poetry due to one huge factor, and for a host of rationales related to that big one: Money. That is, poetry usually doesn't make much, if any, money for a publisher. Poetry programs from major publishers are often maintained as prestige lines that at best can be expected to break even or be marginally profitable.

When a book of poetry does render a hefty sum, publishers want to know why it does, in terms that translate into a successfully replicable marketing strategy. If a publisher deems it unlikely that a given type of work will sell profitably, why the hell buy it from the author in the first place?

It's not that publishers don't take chances. Publishers have found that breaking through with a work of nonfiction of high current interest by a first-time author, or a novel by a writer with a new voice in an established fiction category, while chancy, represent better bets—in large part because those markets are already strong. Poems from hitherto little-known poets have virtually no retailing presence, regardless of how good the work is, unless the author is in some manner promotable. An example of this line of reasoning occurs when the poet is a celebrity, a recognized name you can take to the bank—which is not to say a person necessarily renowned as a poet.

DEATH AND TRANSFIGURATION

During this century, through a quirk of literary fashion, the practice of poetry for a time resembled a cult of personality, wherein the poet's biography was essential to full appreciation of a personalized vision set within increasingly rarefied expression in verse. As formal poetry lost its universality and poets became less viable commodities, poetics—seen as academic and elitist—was the province of specialty publishers with restricted lists. At the same time, what had been a major cultural function of verse was taken over by popular literature (novels and short fictional forms), popular music, and other performance vehicles of mass appeal (including the movies, video, and modeling).

Lest you think poetry as a profession has dug its own way to cultural extinction, in a blink of the eye it's resurrected from within its original bardic tradition as a performance art, often in the context of music and movement. To those with a bookish inclination, it is enlightening to see today's poets stride forth as performers in their own right, go *mano a mano* with the masses and earn a widening audience. In the resultant ground swell, verse is reinvigorated and once again promotable; even book publishers are opening up their lists, albeit slowly, to the new field of contenders.

THE TRADITION THAT NEVER WAS

When discussing the tradition of academic poetry, we're in the realm of a perceptual figment. Bear in mind that the poet's assignation to the conservatory is an aberration, the theme of only a fragment of the twentieth century. For most of poetry's history it has been a popular form, practiced in public as well as in letters and print.

The meter and substance of verse were perhaps first derived from the settings of pasture and polis—poetry has always featured both pastoral and urban approaches, dealt with both the workaday world and refined pursuits. It is in no way surprising that the texture of today's most popular lyric formats is from the malls and the streets, the airports and the highways, with cadences resounding to the beat of found sounds—of music, electronics, and industry, of shoot-outs and party shouts.

In much the same way, writers of earlier generations warped their environments into poetic forms. Works from T. S. Eliot, Vachel Lindsay, Sylvia Plath, Allen Ginsberg, and Gregory Corso emanated from the milieus of the blues, Dixieland, swing, be-bop, and modern jazz. Now our poetics embrace the range of hardcore, grunge, techno, and hip-hop. Looking back over the timeline of a poet's career, the difference between an old master and a young bastard is who is speaking and when.

Virtuosos of verse appear in such guises as contributors to pop-culture fan magazines (in areas not queued primarily to poetry), in cyberspace exchanges, and in performance and poetry events (such as the slam circuit). In addition, the literary phase endures in the profusion of small and academic presses and literary journals, many with their own sponsored competitions.

WORDS WITH WINGS

Look over the rosters of trade publishing houses; there's poetry there. Every major publisher produces at least a few editions in the field, though they're rarely highlighted at the front of the catalog. The poetry book that does achieve the rank of lead title is most likely one with a commercial hook over and above that of its poetics. *The Book of Birth Poetry* edited by Charlotte Otten (Bantam) shows how a distinctive marketing angle that overlays a strong selection of poetic work can be positioned for a mainstream audience.

Poetry produced by commercial trade programs also includes point-of-purchase novelty volumes, often incorporating illustrations or other enticing trinkets such as posters, cards, or bubblegum gewgaws. This is not to decry the state. Some poets who take their unadorned words very seriously may look down on this notion; readers, however, are almost never dissuaded by such baubles—they simply see more reward to the package they are buying. Not so incidentally, word-and-picture packages are no less successful an approach when adopted by publishers in the fine arts or by literary presses—those projects are often among their biggest sellers. There's more than one way to fit your words with wings.

Devotees of straitlaced poetry publishing are sometimes resentful (not to say envious) of the relatively free rein occasionally given those who have not paid substantial poetic dues. Many bookbuyers, on the other hand, would be hard put to believe that a cloistered academic's synthetic poetic vision is automatically more riveting than the life experience at the heart of the volume *Always a Reckoning* by Jimmy Carter (issued through Times Books, with Random House audiobook spin-off). Even though Carter is without a master of fine arts degree in poetry and doesn't have much of a track record in literary magazines or poetry competitions, it is heartening to all poets that the man has acknowledged the practice of verse as worthy of one with his manifold global accomplishments.

Similarly, *Collected Poems* by John Updike (Knopf) might not have seen such high-profile publication if the author had not already achieved renown as a popular prose litterateur. In addition, Updike's volume may be seen in publishing terms as a lead-in to the house's slate of offerings by such respected versifiers as Cynthia Zarin, Mary Jo Salter, Carolyn Olds, John Hollander, and John Ashbery.

STATE-OF-THE-ART OR FALSE START?

The public declamation of verse enjoys a tradition that extends back to the earliest human gatherings, and onstage poetry performance continues unabated into the current age. Around the globe, poetry presentations, often in the form of competitions, are drawing many happy participants and listeners to cafés, bars, galleries, and salons.

One of the longest-running and most famed venues for this type of expression made it into book-length publication from a major house: *Aloud: Voices from the Nuyorican Poets Cafe*, an anthology edited by Miguel Algarín and Bob Holman (Henry Holt). Though it took the Nuyoricans two decades of enduring presence to gain the requisite level of public awareness and media clout to garner a commercial publishing contract, this publication signaled the breakout of renewed publisher attention. To wit: A poetry slam with a gay theme has been presented in print through the pages of *Gents, Bad Boys, and Barbarians*, edited by Rudy Kikel (Alyson Publications).

Popular poetry titles (those with niche or mass-market appeal) are now prominently and routinely displayed in a wide variety of bookstores—and there are more marquee poetry projects coming down the publishing pipeline.

Whether this revived interest in poetry is a flash-in-the-pan concept intended to cash in on fleeting public fancies or is indicative of a swelling, sustainable trend remains to be seen. The future of poetry publishing hinges on how poets and publishers seize the moment. Muddy marketing of sloppy product can surely kill the lights. One way poets can work to prevent such a dire fate is to ensure there's a more-than-adequate supply of fine verse from which publishers can select the best and the most potentially market-grabbing entrants.

POETS ANONYMOUS NO LONGER

How to make a publisher hunger for your verse? As with any school of industry, you want to work hard to research and develop your standout product. In this case, it means writing a lot of poetry, and then taking it to an audience. Enter competitions for written works and present yourself live and in-person at poetry slams. See what the response is and gear your ongoing poetic enterprise accordingly, to maximize your potential appeal. Get yourself published in literary journals and popular magazines. In short, make a name for yourself.

There are resources available for this line of endeavor. To name just a couple, which are updated periodically: Dustbooks offers *Directory of Poetry Publishers*; and Writer's Digest produces the volume *Poet's Market*. Familiarize yourself with the many niche publishers (well over a thousand in the United States alone) oriented toward such interests as multicultural, gender, and sociopolitical issues, in addition to humor, homespun, regional, religious, cowboy, splatterpunk, and aesthetic word-art, as well as mainline verse. Read these magazines and journals to gauge how your work fits in with what others are doing and to get a sense of what makes your work distinctive.

When you see your poetic output in this light, you'll know where and how to submit your work. Some publishers have extremely explicit and strict guidelines, whereas others are more free-spirited. Some editors like to see several pieces at once, others just one. (The response time is often measured in months—up to half a year or longer.) There are competitions you will want to be aware of, and theme-oriented editions of journals in the planning stages a year or more in advance, so watch for notices. *Be sure to enclose a self-addressed stamped envelope (the ubiquitous SASE) for return of your material.*

Cover letters should be as brief as possible. Provide a short, sweet encapsulation of your approach and appeal; list the poem(s) by title; slip in some bio material (including previous publications, awards, workshop or performance experience)—then over and out. If you haven't heard anything *after a few months*, feel free to query your submission's status via a short note and self-addressed stamped postcard.

Please be advised that many journals pay no money at all, and some of the best-known shell out a small honorarium at most—there's minimal remuneration in this publishing sector, but it does get your work out there.

Another avenue through which to access the public is covered by the publication from Poets & Writers titled *Author & Audience: A Readings and Workshops Guide*. In this arena you can hone your persona further. Some poets take an impresario approach and curate series of readings at bookstores, galleries, cafés, parks, or anywhere there's an open space. If they're the sort who can make themselves public point-persons, these carnival barkers are the ones listed as editors of books that include their own work in addition to that of their hard-charging star performers.

If you have a musical propensity, look real good, and your words work well as soundbursts, you might wish to team with a few other like-minded individuals and enter the fray in jazz, rock, hip-hop, or a musical approach of your own invention, and gain the opportunity to stake your claim to a cult following on which to build. The words of musically inclined writers as diverse as Jim Carroll, Leonard Cohen, and Patti Smith (all affirmed poets) are published in book form.

However you've done it, once you've achieved a recognizable identity, you (or your agent) can approach a commercial publisher with a skein of work and a proven record with many of the same attributes and sales venues available to the authors of business how-tos, self-help, and awareness titles (many of whom conduct workshops, appear at symposia, and are public speakers—that is, they're performance artists).

If your work and reputation is more suited to smaller literary houses, once you've had dozens of works published in recognized journals, you can select a representative package intended for book-length publication. Many literary and university presses sponsor poetry competitions in which the top prizes include publication—so check these out, especially if you're not yet published in book form.

Literary, not-for-profit operations have marketing considerations analogous to those found in the commercial trade, so your best shot, again, is to organize your work according to a definable style or theme that grabs hold of an area of reader interest and is sure to inspire catalog copy.

Another option for poets is publication in chapbook format—slimmer folios of work, most often in soft paper binding. Many small presses produce titles in this form, and every year individuals and groups of poets fund their own chapbook publications, often with the intent of getting a distribution deal through either a literary press or independent distribution service (and thus be available to the bookstore trade).

Yes, poetry is, as ever, changing and on the move. It behooves the creator to be inventive and indefatigable, and in the current environment to think in terms that are not bound by the antiquated vision of a book of verse. Performance is assuredly public; appearances on computer networks are by definition electronic publication; lyrics of pop music represent an established form of marketable verse. Think of a new way to do it, and you can be there first.

The Producer's Niche

Book Packagers and Superauthors—Creative Ways for Writers to Profit

JAMIE M. FORBES

Book producer. Sounds rather Hollywood to some—like a power-broking agent who packages film projects replete with star performers, name directors, and genius screenwriters. Indeed, book producers do the same thing as these major players in film production; the difference is they package books, not movies. And, again like those wheeler-dealers of the silver screen, the role of a book packager is to bring together the talent necessary (including writers) to carry through the vision at hand.

A LAND OF OPPORTUNITY OR JUST ANOTHER WRITER'S BLOCK?

The foregoing glitter masks the actual raw business talk about money and work and how a writer can get some of both—and, yes, there is much to be had. The good news begins just a bit further along. The bad part comes up immediately following, and will be over before you know it. As the benefits of hard knowledge begin to sink in, the potential dividends for writers who explore the book-producing field will become greatly apparent. And remember: On the playing fields of free enterprise, book producers are among the freest players.

To the writer who wants to jump-cut across the maze of agents, editors, and publishers and head straight toward successful publication (and who wouldn't?): Don't expect to approach a book producer cold with your original idea, have the producer beam at you gratefully, offer you a contract, a celebratory drink, and then handle all the hassles necessary to present you a juicy check. It's no bet. Don't hold your breath in anticipation. Don't even think of such a course as the last straw you grasp.

But don't screenwriters do that and sometimes the movie is made? And isn't book producing kind of like Hollywood fantasies, only in the book trade? Occasionally—so much so as to be a real rarity. All is not lost, however. With the explosion of unrealistic flights of fancy comes clear vision into the realms of actual potential for writers, including recognition of authorship and royalties to go with it.

Writers are essential to any book project, whether it is a traditionally written, conventionally published work or a complex volume representing the state of the book-making art—book producers package the entire gamut. With this in mind, be aware that a book producer is far more likely to pursue the initial developmental and creative work with people who are not writers who nevertheless do have ideas for books.

Why is that? No single answer applies, for the types of projects book producers carry out are extremely varied. For the purpose of considering book-production operations as fields of opportunities for writers, let's break down the atypical world of book producers into three broad categories and cite why it is unlikely that an outside writer be included on the ground floor of a given project, as well as note vital roles writers play along the way. At least one of these roles may surprise as well as inspire you.

First of all, these nonwriters with whom book producers work may be potential sponsors for the project—such as celebrity performers, athletes, politicians, or business leaders with a story to tell; or these sponsors may well be corporate entities (including nonprofit cultural or policy foundations in addition to commercial interests) with a lot of internal materials they'd like to see turned into a book. In these cases a book producer can hire a professional ghostwriter or coauthor, or commission someone who is credited full-fledged authorship to actually research and write the entire manuscript. We are talking about opportunities for writers here.

Second, book producers often work closely with publishing houses, for example to develop or expand a series or line of books, or compose a single specialty title the publisher wishes to farm out rather than do in house. In such instances the book producer interfaces with writers the same way that the sponsoring publisher would if the books were produced in the publishing house. More slots for wordsmiths to shoot for.

And the third reason a writer is not likely to be needed to ignite a project is that the book producer is often a writer too—this observation applies to one-person book-production firms as well as to people working within larger ensembles.

Someone who considers idea generation and project development as strong professional suits may wish to explore this field with an eye toward developing talents along this line; ultimately this person might consider whether it would be potentially advantageous to turn a trick packaging entire projects—in lieu of or perhaps in addition to unadorned literary pursuits.

A WORLD WHERE RULES ARE FEW

If you're still hazy about who, what, or where book producers are, and unable to circumscribe what it is book producers do, please know that the industry is right there with you. It's not that book producers as a group aren't anything you can describe—they are and will do almost anything imaginable in the book-publishing realm.

This shouldn't baffle anyone when industry definitions are far less than clear and may appear to be redefined throughout a given day; where skeptics speak of certain authors who are too busy to do any actual writing themselves; editors who do not have time to edit; publishers who have duties more pressing than the nuts-and-bolts of publishing. Someone must do all this scribbling, this editorial work; somehow the manu-script must be produced—otherwise there wouldn't be any books to have parties over.

With increasing frequency and success, book producers have stepped opportunely into publishing-industry gaps, staking claims to territory in the research-and-development area as well as any and all aspects of editing, design, production, and manufacture. Yes, book producers can do it all, which is why they defy typology.

Who Book Producers Are

Book producers usually comprise from one to several people on a full-time basis. As with other aspects of being a book producer, there are notable exceptions to this ac-count, and a few book producers offer positions to as many personnel as are employed by good-sized publishers. Regardless of core size, the book producer's staff can be ex-panded or contracted to embrace any number of freelancers and consultants as the pro-ject load demands.

What Book Producers Do

Simply put, book producers are service operations that undertake different tasks war-ranted as they perform functions otherwise typically rendered by book publishers, liter-ary agents, and authors. It is this shape-shifting aspect that gives book producers their flexibility and strength and that, perhaps more than anything else, accounts for their in-creasing vigor in the publishing marketplace—estimates run in the neighborhood of one out of every five to six books published in the United States being brought out through a book producer.

A book producer can take on the entire spectrum of editorial and production work—a process traditionally overseen by the publisher. Where the book producer almost in-variably bows out is in areas pertaining to marketing, sales, and distribution. Here too arise situations that belie the rule, as when the book producer works with the publisher to develop sales and marketing approaches, as well as to probe promotional venues and publicity angles. Careful now—too much of this sort of business and the book producer becomes just another publisher.

A book producer might as a matter of course try to reserve the rights to projects orig-inated by the producer in house. That is, subsidiary rights—ordinarily handled by either the publisher or literary agent—may be most profitably retained and purveyed by a skillful and active book producer (who is by far the most interested party in such schemes). These subrights can encompass territorial translation and reprint rights divvied up worldwide, serial rights, dramatic and screen rights, and electronic rights (including CD-ROM and multimedia adaptation).

Most definitely, book packagers function as their own brokers and managers. Book producers sell literary properties and deal with publishers on the same basis of person-to-person interaction and paperwork rituals as do those who go by the sobriquet of lit-erary agent.

Book producers are also the equivalent of superauthors. In addition to their roles as originators of book ideas and the writing capabilities of particular individuals, book producers are true authors of a project, providing editorial material either directly, indirectly, or a combination of both—as well as directing the entire creative team. In the case of complex works this can involve commissioning different writers for different sections, and hiring copyeditors, indexers, proofreaders, artists, designers, photographers, and production personnel.

Some book producers have a full-time staff to handle editing, production, research and development, and to attend such protocols as writing the project proposals. Other packagers do as much of the work as feasible personally; this is especially characteristic of small book-producer operations wherein, for instance, one of the associates is adept in layout and design and works with a partner who can write. Rather than having a staff as such (they may even perform their own office support, including filing and shipping duties), these producers utilize the services of freelancers on an as-needed basis.

Where Book Producers Are Located

Commercial publishers often operate from highly visible corporate headquarters in skyscrapers bearing their house logos or the banner of the communications conglomerate that owns them. Small presses can be veritable cottage industries, with components set up in basements, side rooms, and garages. As one might by now anticipate, where book producers are is a many-layered question with a multitiered response.

Often as not, a book producer does not inhabit a single place. There may be a homey den where the packager per se does anything but hibernate, or an entire suite of offices and production facilities. Members of a project team may be found in other offices, in other suites, in ateliers of artists and workshops of graphics consultants, as well as in studios of individual writers. Especially when equipped with electronic communications, members of these book-production teams are by no means confined to the same locality.

HOW BOOK PRODUCERS PACKAGE BOOKS

Book producers (alone or in league with a potential sponsoring participant) come up with the original idea for a publishing project, shape the proposal, sell the proposed work to the publisher, and supply the editorial and production talent to bring the project to fruition. How book producers package books might best be viewed from the vantage of how it is that book ideas come to be packaged.

Publishers are most certainly interested in a proposal that sets forth an easily categorized product. For commercial trade publishers, the most highly prized work is one that can be tightly marketed through mainstream bookstore chains, sell well on its merits as communicated via word of mouth and a smattering of reviews, be picked up by a specialty book club or two, and benefit cost-effectively from a modicum of advertising push and salesforce vigor. As entrepreneurs, book producers position their packages with those considerations in mind, just as any author is advised to do.

In many publishing deals, the chances for closure increase with the ability of the author or book-producer team to bring as much to the table as possible—especially in terms of elements that support the project's access to markets. The book producer, as the fulcrum for the project, is in position to orchestrate these elements.

To illustrate, let us conceive of a complex project, a series of international business guides that include sections offering travel tips; lifestyle reportage; cultural, political, and historical notes; practical business advice; and information keyed to contingencies such as healthcare and automobile emergencies. Lots of research here. Lots of writing. Jobs for photographers and designers too—these volumes will be lavish.

Lots of expenses.

The book producer fronts the coinage to cover the book proposal. That's part of the producer's act. As for the rest of the package—let's see how many beneficiaries we can bring in. There's the not-for-profit educational wing of a financial institution that would love to underwrite (in part) a high-profile top-quality project. How high profile is it? Since the financial institute is a potential player, there are corporate sponsorships in the works—as well as talk of a series geared to broadcast on noncommercial television.

The published books will of course point out the participation of those who gave goods and services—airlines, hotels, film companies, computer firms, sportswear outfitters, food and beverage councils, manufacturers of pharmaceuticals, windscreens, sunscreens, and weatherproof make-up. All sponsors benefit from publicity and promotional value.

If the public TV series goes blooey, let's try for an infomercial on cable and tailor the repositioned project more toward a for-profit home-study/seminar course (perhaps packaged with complementary audiotapes, videotapes, or computer software)—in which case the not-for-profiteer underwriter's got to walk. In either event, a major trade book publisher we know has already informally shown interest. If we go the infomercial route, a publisher with proven direct-mail sales expertise might prove an excellent partner.

WATCHWORDS AND BYLINES

As we have seen, there is no such thing as a typical packaged book. The book producer can be called on to coordinate complicated books, or can offer a publisher the straightforward advantages of expanded services—in which case the book producer becomes a virtual extended editorial staff through which a particular publisher can issue more books.

There are no givens as to what constitutes a book package or the deals book packagers make with publishers and writers. As Stephen R. Ettlinger, of Ettlinger Editorial Projects and president of American Book Producers Association, remarks: "What is the common denominator is that we make books happen. We turn ideas into books. We do that by assembling the creative team necessary—of which, of course, the writer is an element."

One should never forget that the publisher is the projected source for the book producer's money on any and all given projects. The book packager puts up money for proposals, but not beyond that. The basic agreement between a publisher and a book producer is similar to or identical with that drafted for an author-publisher contract.

What this implies is very important—agreements between book producers and writers can take any form that's appropriate for a given project.

Sometimes book producers have their own original projects that require expert writers in a given category. Which means lots of times the producer is the author, contractually and actually; or else the book producer will hire one or more writers. In such cases, book producers act essentially as editors. Some people write up the book proposals. Some write the books. Some have bylines. Some are ghosts. Sometimes the writing is work-for-hire, with other parties the copyright holders. Some writers get royalties—or what amounts contractually to equivalent compensation.

Some packaging projects are based on a flat fee to the book producer for a specified number of manufactured volumes—this means the book producer oversees the project through printing and binding. Other commissions can be keyed to anything from completed manuscript—edited, copyedited, and styled—or any other production stage up through electronic mechanicals. Occasionally book producers consult all the way into setting up the distribution end.

Deals with writers range from the book producer paying a writer a flat fee, to an hourly rate, to a contractually delineated even split of the royalties, to the idea that the book producer acts as a glorified agent with compensation at a slightly higher rate if the project was the packager's idea.

Of universal interest to writers is the question of who holds copyright—with implications regarding compensation in such areas as royalties and reprint rights. Regardless of the general run of cocktail chatter, at no point should anyone ever say definitively which parties should or shouldn't control the copyright without first examining the overall history of the project, and whether the writer's work has been commissioned under the auspices of a work-for-hire, as a coauthor, or as a sole writer. Again, there are no firm rules, only guidelines derived from experience. Who holds copyright? Perhaps the writer does, even if the book was the producer's original idea. In such instances royalties may still accrue to both book producer and author, with the breakdown provisional—depending on such eventualities as future sales.

THE WRITER'S APPROACH

For newer writers as well as veterans, there is the lush scenario that runs as follows: A timely referral to you personally when a book producer is in need of someone with your precise abilities and areas of expertise. Of course, you've worked hard to position yourself to accept just such a challenge, in many cases by means of more prosaic but equally time-honored techniques, including a cold first encounter.

The best way to approach a book producer cold is with a query letter and resume or page or so of sample writing; point out you are a writer available for hire—do some research beforehand to ascertain whether a particular producer pursues projects in your particular range, and target your queries accordingly.

This technique is not meant to be a last-gasp career saver: Your query and writer's kit most likely goes into the book producer's resource files for future reference; few book producers have tremendous volume (as compared with commercial publishers), but many book producers have a wide variety of projects they encounter as time goes on, whereas others have concentrated focus over a long haul (such as series novels or reference lines) that may necessitate calling in fresh troops—meaning you.

On the professional networking front, the American Book Producers Association (ABPA) offers an annual seminar (generally in October); this engagement is appropriate to attend if you want to become a book producer or wish to make contact with one regarding your skills as writer, designer, agent, or editor. The Association holds monthly luncheon meetings (often with guest speakers) that are open to the public and sometimes announced in *Publishers Weekly*.

The ABPA also maintains a freelancer database for use by book producers. Inquire at the ABPA office about how to send in information to be added to this database, as well as to obtain details regarding the aforementioned seminar and meetings, in addition to the Association's membership directory, which lists book producers' specialties, contact persons, and representative projects.

American Book Producers Association
160 Fifth Avenue, Suite 604
New York, NY 10010
212-645-2368

ESTABLISHING AND MAINTAINING A WORKING RELATIONSHIP

In the case of producers who specialize, once a writer gets a chance to give a best shot and comes up a winner, chances are excellent for that writer to establish ongoing or long-term associations. These book producers look for writers who have interests pertinent to the producer's scope and appreciate when a writer is particularly good at writing in these specialty areas—be they travel and lifestyle, fitness and health, or fiction for young adults. One manner of specialty can be standout excellence in a particular important ancillary task—gain notice as a book doctor or proposal writer and you have one big foot in the door.

If a writer is versatile—can also do research, edit, and copyedit, or do worthy writing in a number of fields—chances are good for developing a continuing relationship. That versatile publishing person is inherently valuable to versatile book producers, who, it may be expected, can place great value on others' adaptability.

In addition to specific professional prerequisites, an important aspect of initiating a relationship between a book producer and a writer is the anticipated texture of the working relationship. As is true in many endeavors, business and pleasure often run together. It makes a positive difference if a writer's presentation portrays a person with whom it is fun and easy to work, if the book producer and writer are indeed made for each other.

In order to sustain a working relationship, this impression of ease must always be backed up by performance reliability. This may entail the writer to be on call—to be available to come in for meetings or work in house. The writer should be equipped with such amenities as computer technology and communications facilities. The writer should be the sort who can achieve tight deadlines; who can work well as part of a team; who can share special expertise and use others' ideas effectively toward the project's ends; who, in short, can get things done under the gun, both within a structure or by dispensing with one, simultaneously if need be.

How do book producers choose a writer? Often a balancing act. "She's fast but not that good a writer. He's a good writer but not that fast." Which writer would you ask first? Depends on the nature of the project, of course.

In a previous life, Stephen Ettlinger was a picture editor. He asked a colleague to describe what a good picture was, and her response applies to writers as well as photographers: "For me a good picture is one that's on my desk before the deadline as opposed to one that isn't." All else—however fine the quality—can be useless if the work is not delivered on time.

Book producers cite other types of problems that can arise—as with writers who don't like answering machines or who ignore the basics of computer usage and have no back-ups available in the pinch.

Getting back to that essential literary imperative, money: Many of the worst eventualities can be avoided entirely when the writer has a thorough understanding of the financial arrangements among writer, book producer, and publisher. Expectations of financial return that were not set down in writing can be a personal and professional nightmare for both writer and producer. Again, if you were a book producer, which kind of writer would you choose?

Expanding the Writer's Envelope

As with hunting in any unknown territory, writers who hope to gain from an association with a book producer may heed the following. Explore the landscape thoroughly; stalk, watch, wait till you sight your quarry; and as you close in, be wary, wily, patient, and vigilant to your own interests.

Book publishing represents free enterprise at its best, especially in the sense that bookmaking tradition embodies the business ideals of imagination, creativity, resourcefulness, and quality—as well as teamwork in action. With regard to the process of developing and producing publishing product, the answers to many everyday questions about the industry may once have seemed pretty cut-and-dried, even if they were not always the obvious response. What is a writer's job? What does a publisher do?

In an era of increasing fluidity and change (both technological and entrepreneurial), opportunities abound in all arenas central and tangential to print publishing. Writers and allied professionals who like to get gritty playing with ideas and who have the bravado to do whatever it takes to make a product have an open field on which to play. To the usual round of questions has been added: Who or what is a book producer? And what do they do? The answers are up to you.

By way of inspiration, here's what someone else did. A writer named Paisley reached a level of success few writers achieve. Paisley has written, coauthored, collaborated on, and ghostwritten numerous articles, books, and corporate communications. Never one to be complacent, Paisley occasionally expressed to me a sense of stagnation even in light of these formidable accomplishments.

Along came another nonfiction book-collaboration assignment Paisley set to work on, this one commissioned by an entrepreneurial professional. As it happened, even with a glittery book-proposal package and stunning sample chapters, this particular project did not garner the type of offer from commercial publishers that impressed the author-entrepreneur sufficiently to give the go-ahead. Instead, after batting around a number of options (including accepting a publisher's small advance), the entrepreneur decided to pursue a glamorized version of self-publication by starting a small press—with one single title on its list.

The entrepreneur knew enough about publishing to recognize that such a project could likely be handled through a network of freelancers and consultants, with one person designated as project director. At this juncture, the one person in publishing the entrepreneur knew best (and trusted implicitly) was Paisley. Though coordinating this type of production was technically beyond the scope of Paisley's previous experience, the entrepreneur exuded the sort of confidence that proved contagious. As it happened, Paisley's contacts in the publishing industry were a solid base from which to work, and Paisley took the entrepreneur's book successfully through the writing and editorial phases, into production and manufacture, and was instrumental in working out a distribution deal through a firm that handled a group of small presses.

Voilá! Paisley is now a book packager (in addition to being a writer)—someone with experience in all phases of the publishing arts. Paisley can add many more diverse and remunerative credits to an already-glossy portfolio.

Should the varied roles book producers assume appeal to you—if ideas and their development and presentation are among your strong points, or if you manage projects outstandingly and find dealing with the business aspects of publishing invigorating—you might want to go the whole route. Package, produce—even write if you want to—and be a superauthor too.

Thanks go to Stephen R. Ettlinger, president of American Book Producers Association and president of Ettlinger Editorial Projects, for his gracious and much-appreciated interview input and research contributions that provided much of the information and resources utilized in the preparation of this essay.

Mirror, Mirror . . .

Self-Publishing and Vanity Publishing—Advantages and Differences

Jeff Herman

Achieving publication through the sale of an author's work to a major commercial trade publisher may not always be feasible, possible, or even the most desirable route into the literary marketplace for a given project. Some books may be excellent candidates for the list of a smaller press with artfully targeted audiences (such as business, religious, or literary house), while others fall naturally into the publishing sphere of the university press, or the array of independent scientific, professional, and scholarly publishers that cater to specialist interests.

Literary success is all about reaching the audience that best appreciates the work at hand; commercial success by definition is keyed to finding and selling to that primary readership economically, and expanding the readership base as cost-efficiently as possible.

Certain publishing options have special appeal to entrepreneurial authors—and others who, at least in theory, wish to control the outcome of their book to the greatest possible degree. Some authors wish to have final say over the creative and editorial content of the product; they prefer to oversee the means of production, manufacture, and distribution; and they plan to step lively as they orchestrate their own publicity and promotional endeavors. Assuming these various tasks, responsibilities, and risks should result in programs wherein the author-publisher stands to gain the greatest rate of financial return possible.

Such ventures, when appropriate, can be accomplished on the cheap; other projects may well justify the investment of money and labor of the same order that a publisher might put into a comparable project. Alternate publishing options are also available for those who wish to subsidize publication through firms that produce books and offer attendant publishing services more or less on order.

893

Self-publishing (often with the assistance of independent contractors and consultants) and publishing through the offices of a vanity press may sound similar in concept, but important distinctions must be recognized—these pertain as much to business practices of individual companies as they do to traditions associated with the author-as-self-publisher and the subsidy publisher.

VANITY PUBLISHING

Vanity publishing is more formally referred to as subsidy publishing (primarily in the promotional literature of its practitioners). In this context the term *subsidy* does not, of course, mean that the publication of a book is subsidized by a governmental or corporate agency, or funded by an arts or humanities council. Though this form of publishing does have many variations, in the strictest usage it is the author who subsidizes publication by paying the press to publish his or her book.

Vanity publishing is a controversial industry. Sometimes it's a perfectly legitimate means of seeing one's writings in print, and the author is fully satisfied with the results. However, there are many instances in which the author has misunderstood the process and is terribly disappointed—and in the hole for a lot of money.

Few conventional commercial publishers will engage in anything that smacks of vanity publishing. (*Note*: An author who promises to buy back many copies of a published book, and to spend a lot of his or her own money on marketing, can often induce even the most prestigious publishing house to publish a book that it would not otherwise have published.)

There are a number of companies, some quite large and well established, that function solely as vanity presses. Many of these publishers promote their services by means of a variety of outlets, including brochures sent through the mail to lists-of-the-likely, and classified as well as display advertisements in selected publications. *Writer's Digest* magazine is one of the more logical and frequently used advertising channels; and the classified section of the *New York Times Book Review* has over the years logged quite a roster of listings for vanity houses and allied services.

Know Exactly What Services Will Be Provided

In vanity or subsidy publishing, the way the arrangement often works is that the writer pays a flat fee to have a set number of books produced. Some subsidy publishers provide worthy editorial, production, design, marketing, and distribution assistance. Some make exaggerated claims regarding the value and caliber of these services—whereas others make no such claims at all, maintaining that these functions are the author's responsibility.

Over the years some practitioners of the vanity trade have discovered that they snag more customers when they can glibly deflect any discussion of the possible pitfalls of the process—even in response to a potential customer's direct questions. In addition, with increased volume and increasingly cheaper production costs (and standards), the profit margin is all that much higher. For the foregoing reasons, an uninformed and less-than-curious consumer is the vanity house's most valued customer.

In all cases, the more the writer knows about the publishing process in general—and is aware of the limited or nonexistent clout a vanity press has regarding book distribution—the better situated the author is to determine any advantages one particular subsidy publisher's program may have over another's, as well as how subsidy publishing stacks up against other available options, such as self-publishing.

Among several worst-case vanity press scenarios is one wherein the publisher simply prints the books and delivers them casually to the writer's doorstep—yours to do with as you please, thank you; we're out of it now—no marketing or distribution services provided. The writer could probably have engaged a printing house to do virtually the same thing for a fraction of the cost.

In another popular variation of the vanity-publishing approach, the contractual fee is set at a price that provides the publisher with a healthy profit even without the sale of so much as one copy of the published title—even though numerous (but decidedly perfunctory and ineffectual) promotion and marketing services are specified in the contract.

In this case, the publisher may have little motivation to promote or market a given published work. However, according to the terms of the agreement, the publisher will derive further income from any sales, even if the sales are really due to the successful independent marketing efforts of the paying writer.

Well within the bounds of everyday hard-nosed business practices perhaps, and a secure way to turn a profit if done right. So long as the vanity house's contractual obligations are met in full, the question here is rather the nature of the publisher's come-on. Visions of potential glamour and literary recognition that subsidy house brochures proclaim may not be dark and devious schemes to lure the naive (doesn't all advertising trade in similar notions?); however, such forms of hype appear calculated to offer shadows and gray areas in which hitherto obscure fantasies of the potential customer may feel free to take full beguiling shape.

If the writer knows up front exactly what he or she can and can't expect from the vanity publisher, then everything is square. But if the company has encouraged or knowingly allowed the writer to have unrealistic expectations, then a crime has been committed—morally and ethically at least, if not legally. Vanity publishers that grossly mislead writers while taking their money are guilty of fraud. In 1990, one of the largest vanity presses in the country lost a million-dollar class-action suit, and hundreds of hoodwinked writers were granted refunds.

Even so, most suits against vanity presses are based on the assertion of fraud in the execution of contractual services, and any rewards to the author clients are small potatoes compared with the kind of money conceivably involved if the complainant can prove a claim of fraud in the inducement of an agreement—a complaint that, no matter how heartfelt, is most difficult to substantiate.

Beware of Sharks!

The following correspondence is genuine, though all names and titles have been altered. My purpose for exposing these ever-so-slightly personalized form letters isn't to condemn or ridicule anyone. I simply wish to show how some subsidy publishers hook their clients. Again, as long as the writer truly understands the facts, no one has the right to cast any stones at this particular publishing option.

SHARK HOUSE PUBLISHERS

Mr. Bourne Bate
Brooklyn Bridge
East River, NY 00000

Dear Mr. Bate:

Your manuscript *A Fish's Life* is written from an unusual perspective and an urgent one. In these trying economic times which have created despair and anguish, one must give thought to opportunities, and this upbeat and enthusiastic book makes us realize that those opportunities are out there! My capsule critique: Meticulous aim! With a surgeon's precision we're taught how to work through everything from raising money to targeting areas. There is a sharp eye here for all of the nuances, studded with pointers and reasoning, making it a crucial blueprint.

What can I say about a book like this? It stopped me in my tracks. I guess all I can do is thank you for letting me have the opportunity to read it.

The editors that read this had a spontaneous tendency to feel that it was imbued with some very, very good electricity and would be something very special for our list and saw such potential with it that it was given top priority and pushed ahead of every other book in house. The further problem is that publishing being an extremely rugged business, editorial decisions have to be based on hard facts which sometimes hurt publishers as much as authors. Unfortunately, we just bought several new nonfiction pieces . . . yet, I hate to let this one get away. Publishing economics shouldn't have anything to do with a decision, but unfortunately it does and I was overruled at the editorial meeting.

Still I want you to know that this is a particularly viable book and one that I really would love to have for our list. Further, this might be picked up for magazine serialization or by book clubs because it is so different. Our book, *Enraptured* was serialized six times in *International Inquirer* and sold to Andorra. *The Devil Decided* sold well over 150,000 copies, and we have a movie option on it. *Far Away* serialized in *Places* magazine and *Cure Yourself* was taken by a major book club.

I really want this book for our list because it will fit into all the areas that we're active in. Therefore, I'm going to make a proposition for you to involve yourself with us. What would you think of the idea of doing this on a cooperative basis? Like many New York publishers these days, we find that sometimes investors are interested in the acquisition of literary properties through a technique which might be advantageous under our tax laws. There is no reason that the partial investor cannot be the writer, if they so choose. Tax advantages may accrue.

I'd be a liar if I promised you a best seller, but I can guarantee that nobody works as hard promoting a book as we do: nag paperback, book clubs, magazines, and foreign publishers with our zeal and enthusiasm. We do our PR work and take it seriously because this is where we're going to make the money in the long run. One of our authors hired a top publicist on his own for $50,000. He came limping back to us saying they didn't do the job that we did, and which we don't charge for. This made our office feel very proud of all our efforts.

I feel that your book deserves our efforts because it is something very special. Think about what I've written you, and I will hold the manuscript until I hear from you. I truly hope that we can get together because I really love this book and believe it is something we can generate some good action for vis-à-vis book clubs, foreign rights, etc., because it is outstanding and has tremendous potential.

Sincerely,

Eda U. Live

Eda U. Live
Executive Editor

The writer of *A Fish's Life* wrote back to Shark House (all names have been changed) and informed the vanity press that he did not want to pay any money to the publisher to have his book published. The vanity house responded with the following letter. This publisher has probably learned from experience that some exhausted writers will return to them with open wallets after fruitless pursuit of a conventional commercial publishing arrangement.

SHARK HOUSE PUBLISHERS

Mr. Bourne Bate
Brooklyn Bridge
East River, NY 00000

Dear Mr. Bate:

I have your letter in front of me and I want you to know that I think very highly of the book. Before I go any further, I want to tell you that it is a topnotch book and it hits the reader.

In order for us to do a proper job with a book, there is a great deal of PR work involved and this is very costly. To hire an outside agent to do a crackerjack job would cost you upwards of $50,000. Yet, here we do not charge for it because it is part of our promotion to propel a book into the marketplace and it is imperative that this be done. The author has to be booked on radio and TV, stores have to be notified, rights here and abroad have to be worked on, reviewers contacted, autograph parties, and myriad details.

In view of this, why did I ask you to help with the project? I think the above is self-explanatory especially when we are in the midst of a revolution between books and television. Publishers are gamblers vying for the same audience. Just because a publisher loves a book is no guarantee that the public is going to love it. In times when bookstores are more selective in the number of books they order, the best of us tremble at the thought of the money that we must put out in order to make a good book a reality.

Be that as it may, I have just come from another editorial meeting where I tried to re-open the case for us, but unfortunately, the earlier decision stands.

As a result, I have no choice but to return the manuscript with this letter. I would also like to tell you that you must do what the successful writers do. Keep sending it out. Someone will like it and someone will buy it.

I wish you every success. Live long and prosper.

Sincerely,

Eda U. Live

Eda U. Live
Executive Editor

SELF-PUBLISHING

Vanity publishing shouldn't be confused with self-publishing. If you can't find a commercial house to publish your book (or don't want them to), you can publish it yourself. In fact, many successful titles that eventually found their ways onto mainstream publishers' trade lists were initially self-published. As already mentioned, the basic production costs of doing it yourself should be much less than paying a vanity house essentially to "self-publish" it for you.

The key to the productiveness of this choice is the answer to the question: What will you do with the books after you've printed them?

It's exceptionally difficult (but not impossible) for a sole proprietor to achieve meaningful bookstore distribution—though you should at least check out the option of commissioning one of the regional or small press distribution services who send catalogs and offer representation on regional or nationwide basis.

On the other hand, if you're a born promoter who can achieve ample media visibility, or if you have an active seminar business, you can sell numerous copies of your book via back-of-the-room sales and 800 numbers.

Your per-unit profits will be many times greater than your per-unit royalties would have been if you'd used a commercial publisher. Once your up-front production costs have been met, your reprint costs can be very low (depending on quantity ordered); and the profit margin can be relatively astronomic if manufacturing volume can be matched closely to projected sales figures. As publishing houses well know, marketing and promotional efforts can entail the outlay of significant amounts of money, so discretion and prudence should be watchwords here.

If the author knows the intended audience well and has written a work geared to that familiar readership, that author may prove far more adept at reaching that readership than a given publishing house's expert but thinly spread staff would have been.

One more cautionary note about vanity houses is pertinent here: With publication under a vanity arrangement, even an ambitious author's promotional and marketing agenda may prove to be futile. Please realize that the names of the largest and most successful vanity presses are well known to booksellers and book reviewers. The jacket design and overall slack production quality of the typical vanity house's package is likely to draw snickers and sneers from industry professionals and may be more than subliminally noticeable even to casual browsers. If a bookstore were to stock such a shoddy item, it might reflect poorly on the quality of an outlet's other stock.

In a reverse-case scenario of name recognition, when faced with a volume issued under an ignominious vanity imprimatur, most bookstores or critics will have nothing to do with the work in question. If on close inspection the work is indeed worthy, it's too bad—it's all over already; a bookstore buyer or book reviewer won't even take it that far.

You're much better off with a well-packaged product under a newly minted name of your own devise that, though it may be unrecognized, at least has no one soured on it yet.

Self-publishing can be not only a boon in itself; it can be an asset with potential windfall ramifications. Successful self-publishers have licensed trade distribution rights to their books to major publishers in deals that have turned tidy profits for one and all.

The Literary Agent Trade Association

Jeff Herman

Literary agents, like attorneys and physicians, are practitioners of a line of work that requires a bit of special knowledge and mastery of certain techniques that may, at times, appear enigmatic, if not absolutely foreign to conventional wisdom. Unlike members of some august professions, such as the law or medicine, literary agents have no institutionalized industry trade groups to regulate who can and cannot practice legally. Thus anyone can declare himself to be a literary agent—even if he's incarcerated, since so much of the work is done by phone.

But the industry does have the Association of Authors' Representatives (AAR). The group was formed in October of 1991 through the merger of the Independent Literary Agents Association and the Society of Authors' Representatives.

The AAR has approximately 250 members. It has no policing or enforcement powers, other than the power to rule on membership status. To be a member of the AAR, the agent has to have met minimum professional performance standards, and must agree to adhere to a written code of professional practices. (Please see AAR Canon of Ethics and the organization's Television Packaging Disclosure Statement, both reprinted by permission below.)

It is unlikely that an illegitimate or discreditable agent would be able to gain membership to AAR. On the other hand, many perfectly qualified agents have, for a variety of reasons, opted not to join the AAR. An agent's nonmembership in the organization should never automatically be seen as a black mark against that agent.

The primary functions of the AAR are:

1. To serve as a formal and informal network for agents to share information.
2. To create a unified and forceful way for agents to advocate for their positions within the industry, which, in turn, generally benefits their clients.

3. To establish a code of ethics and standards for the agenting business. (As I've said, there is no enforcement power beyond granting or withholding membership.)

You may write to the AAR to obtain their membership list, brochure, and Canon of Ethics (include a check for $5 and SASE with 55¢ postage).

Association of Authors' Representatives, Inc.
Ten Astor Place, Third Floor
New York, NY 10003

CANON OF ETHICS

The following is the canon of ethics that all AAR members must agree, in writing, to uphold.

ASSOCIATION OF AUTHORS' REPRESENTATIVES, INC.
CANON OF ETHICS

1. The members of the Association of Authors' Representatives, Inc. are committed to the highest standard of conduct in the performance of their professional activities. While affirming the necessity and desirability of maintaining their full individuality and freedom of action, the members pledge themselves to loyal service to their clients' business and artistic needs, and will allow no conflicts of interest that would interfere with such service. They pledge their support to the Association itself and to the principles of honorable coexistence, directness, and honesty in their relationships with their co-members. They undertake never to mislead, deceive, dupe, defraud, or victimize their clients, other members of the Association, the general public, or any other person with whom they do business as a member of the association.

2. Members shall take responsible measures to protect the security and integrity of clients' funds. Members must maintain separate bank accounts for money due their clients so that there is no commingling of clients' and members' funds. Members shall deposit funds received on behalf of clients promptly upon receipt, and shall make payments of domestic earnings due clients promptly, but in no event later than ten business days after clearance. Revenues from foreign rights over $50 shall be paid to clients within ten business days after clearance. Sums under $50 shall be paid within a reasonable time of clearance. However, on stock and similar rights, statements of royalties and payments shall be made not later than the month following the member's receipt, each statement and payment to cover all royalties received to the 25th day of the previous calendar month. Payments for amateur rights shall be made not less frequently than every six months. A member's books of account must be open to the client at all times with respect to transactions concerning the client.

3. In addition to the compensation for agency services that is agreed upon between a member and a client, a member may, subject to the approval of the client, pass along charges incurred by the member on the client's behalf, such as copyright fees, manuscript retyping, photocopies, copies of books for use in the sale of other rights, long dis-

tance calls, special messenger fees, etc. Such charges shall only be made if the client has agreed to reimburse such expenses.

4. A member shall keep each client apprised of matters entrusted to the member and shall promptly furnish such information as the client may reasonably request.

5. Members shall not represent both buyer and seller in the same transaction. Except as provided in the next sentence, a member who represents a client in the grant of rights in any property owned or controlled by the client may not accept any compensation or other payment from the acquirer of such rights, including but not limited to so-called "packaging fees," it being understood that the member's compensation, if any, shall be derived solely from the client. Notwithstanding the foregoing, a member may accept (or participate in) a so-called "packaging fee" paid by an acquirer of television rights to a property owned or controlled by a client if the member: a) fully discloses to the client at the earliest practical time the possibility that the member may be offered such a "packaging fee" which the member may choose to accept; b) delivers to the clients at such time a copy of the Association's statement regarding packaging and packaging fees; and c) offers the client at such time the opportunity to arrange for other representation in the transaction. In no event shall the member accept (or participate in) both a packaging fee and compensation from the client with respect to the transaction. For transactions subject to Writers Guild of America (WGA) jurisdiction, the regulations of the WGA shall take precedence over the requirements of this paragraph.

6. Members may not receive a secret profit in connection with any transaction involving a client. If such profit is received, the member must promptly pay over the entire amount to the client.

7. Members shall treat their clients' financial affairs as private and confidential, except for information customarily disclosed to interested parties as part of the process of placing rights as required by law, or, if agreed with the client, for other purposes.

8. The AAR believes that the practice of literary agents charging clients or potential clients fees for reading and evaluating literary works (including outlines, proposals, and partial or complete manuscripts) is subject to serious abuse that reflects adversely on our profession. For this reason the AAR discourages that practice. New members and members who had not, before October 30, 1991, registered their intent to continue to charge reading fees shall not charge such fees. The term "reading fees" in the previous sentence includes any request for payment other than to cover the actual cost of returning materials. *Effective January 1, 1996, all AAR members shall be prohibited from directly or indirectly charging such fees or receiving any financial benefit from the charging of such fees by any other party.*

Until January 1, 1996, AAR members who, *in accordance with the registration provisions of the previous paragraph,* do charge such fees are required to comply with the following:

A. Before entering into any agreement whereby a fee is to be charged for reading and evaluating any work, the member must provide to the author a written statement that clearly sets forth (i) the nature and extent of the services to be rendered, including whether the work will be read in whole or in part and whether a written report is to be provided and, if so, the nature and extent of that report; (ii) whether the services are to be rendered by the member personally, and if not, a description of the professional background of the person who will render the services; (iii) the period of time within which the services will be rendered; (iv) under what circumstances, if any, the fee charged will be refunded to the author; (v) the amount of the fee, including any initial payment as well as any other payments that may be requested by the member for additional services, and how that fee was determined (e.g., hourly rate, length of work reviewed, length of report, or other measure); and (vi) that the rendering of such services shall not guarantee that the member will agree to represent the author or will render the work more salable to publishers.

B. Any member who charges fees for such services and who seeks or facilitates the member's inclusion in any published listing of literary agents shall, if the listing permits, indicate in that listing that the member charges such fees. Apart from such listings, members shall not solicit reading fee submissions.

C. The rendering of such services for a fee shall not constitute more than an incidental part of the member's professional activity.

Signature of AAR Member   *Date*

Please print or type your name here

TELEVISION PACKAGING DISCLOSURE STATEMENT

The following is the Television Packaging Disclosure Statement referred to in the AAR Canon above.

ASSOCIATION OF AUTHORS' REPRESENTATIVES, INC.
TELEVISION PACKAGING DISCLOSURE STATEMENT

The Association of Authors' Representatives requires all of its member agents to send this disclosure statement to their clients when the member agent is planning or expecting to share in a "packaging fee" from the sale of television rights in material represented by that agent. The purpose of this statement is to give such clients a general understanding of the issues raised by the practice of "packaging" in the television industry. This requirement does not apply, however, to deals which are subject to the jurisdiction of the Writers Guild of America.

Decades ago certain talent agencies working in the television industry established a practice of demanding a fee for their services, as opposed to a commission on their clients' income, when such agencies "attached" various elements (such as a screenwriter, director and star, almost all of whom are usually represented by that agency) to a particular property. This process is called "packaging" and the fees involved are called "packaging fees." The agencies pointed out that such projects were more likely to be produced as a result of their packaging efforts, which from our observation is certainly true, and therefore they were entitled to direct compensation for their services. Since most agencies don't take a commission on their clients' income if they receive a packaging fee (in many cases, primarily with clients who are members of various unions such as the Writers Guild of America, the Screen Actors Guild and the Directors Guild, the agencies are specifically prohibited from doing so), the packaging agents also argue that the process is beneficial to their clients because the client doesn't pay a commission to the agency. Obviously, one could argue that any services performed by an agency for the benefit of its clients' projects, including the process of "packaging" a project, are a logical extension of their services for such clients and that such agents are already compensated by their commission(s) on their clients' fees. Additionally, there is a potential conflict of interest since the agency would clearly have a financial incentive which is less closely allied with its clients' interests. For example, a packaging agent might choose to attach one of its directing clients to a particular project, in order to receive a packaging fee, rather than attach a more appropriate—perhaps even *better*—director who happens to be represented by another agency. As another example, the agent might not negotiate for the client as aggressively since the agent's compensation is not tied directly to the client's fees. This could be dangerous since the agent's potential participation in the packaging fee could create an incentive for the agent to grant concessions to a producer, for example, whose interests are directly at odds with the client's. On the other hand, the deals for each element of a package are often subject to especially close scrutiny, all the more so when a high profile actor, director or producer is involved, and most talent agents are particularly cautious about the possibility of conflicts of interest in packaging situations. As a result, the terms of each deal in a package, including that for the underlying rights, tend to be among the best possible.

Whatever the arguments (and there are many more on both sides of the issue), packaging has become a well-established practice in the television industry and packaging fees, often five to ten percent of the budget of the television movie, can be quite large, sometimes greater than the fee paid to the author of the underlying work (or the screenwriter, director, etc.). Additionally, the circumstances under which an agency might receive a packaging fee are less clearly defined than they were initially. In the early years after the networks and producers accepted the principle of packaging, a packaging agent was expected to provide at least three of the talent elements (e.g. screenwriter, producer and star) to be entitled to the packaging fee. Now it is possible for an agency to receive a packaging fee merely for representing the one element, say a very high profile actor or actress, who is the principal reason the project was scheduled for actual production (as opposed to development). The lines have become so blurred that it is possible for an agency to perform the majority of the "packaging" work only to find another agency demanding the packaging fee (or a large share of it) because of one "green-lighting" client. As a result, many of the talent agencies are also willing to pool their resources on particular projects and share the packaging fees. This practice of sharing packaging fees has been extended to literary agents as well.

Although the Association of Authors' Representatives has reservations about the practice of packaging as it has developed in the television industry, the AAR does recognize the reality of that practice in the television industry and realizes that there might be projects where an AAR member's participation in a packaging arrangement may be beneficial to the member's client.

Paragraph 5 of the AAR's Canon of Ethics contains the following language:

Members shall not represent both buyer and seller in the same transaction. Except as provided in the next sentence, a member who represents a client in the grant of rights in any property owned or controlled by the client may not accept any compensation or other payment from the acquirer of such rights, including but not limited to so-called "packaging fees," it being understood that the member's compensation, if any, shall be derived solely from the client. Notwithstanding the foregoing, a member may accept (or participate in" a so-called "packaging fee" paid by an acquirer of television rights to a property owned or controlled by a client if the member: a) fully discloses to the client at the earliest practical time the possibility that the member may be offered such a "packaging fee" which the member may choose to accept; b) delivers to the clients at such time a copy of the Association's statement regarding packaging and packaging fees; and c) offers the client at such time the opportunity to arrange for other representation in the transaction. In no event shall the member accept (or participate in) both a packaging fee and compensation from the client with respect to the transaction. For transactions subject to Writers Guild of America (WGA) jurisdiction, the regulations of the WGA shall take precedence over the requirements of this paragraph.

Clients of the members of the AAR are encouraged to explore fully with their agents all of the relevant factors of a potential package and the AAR members are expected to be as helpful as possible in answering their clients' questions and otherwise helping their clients reach a decision concerning the packaging of a particular project. Questions which such clients might wish to direct to their agents include:

- To whom was the material submitted and with what strategy?
- Was the material submitted to any other packaging agents?
- Are there any agencies, directors, stars, etc. who might be more appropriate?
- How large is the potential packaging fee?

The issues and potential conflicts of packaging are extremely complex. Each author should carefully weigh the specific details of the particular packaging arrangement. The AAR's Canon of Ethics and this statement have been developed by the AAR to help prevent questionable behavior by the members of the AAR on behalf of their clients and to provide some guidelines to help their clients understand the advantages and disadvantages of packaging. However, the AAR cannot prevent such behavior and this statement is not intended to be a comprehensive analysis of the practice of packaging in the television industry.

The Author–Agency Agreement

Jeff Herman

The author–agent relationship is a business relationship. Substantial sums and complex deals may be involved. It's to everyone's advantage to explicitly codify the rules and parameters of the relationship in a brief, plain-English agreement. It's true that the author–agent relationship can become unusually cozy. Still, there's no reason why even the best of friends can't have written business agreements without diminishing their mutual trust and affection. From at least one perspective, explicitly written agreements can be seen to go hand in hand with—and serve to underscore or amplify—existing bonds of confidence, faith, and friendship.

Some agents prefer oral understandings and handshakes, but most use a standard written agreement. It's unlikely that any two agencies will use the same agreement, but most agreements overlap each other closely in their intent and spirit.

There are several aspects of the author–agent arrangement covered by the typical agreement. Here are some of the major points of consideration, along with some key questions you might reflect on as you peruse the materials your prospective agent has submitted to you:

1. *Representation*

What precisely will the agency be representing? Will it be a per-project representation? Or will it include all future works as well? Will it automatically cover all non-book sales, such as magazine or newspaper articles? The extent of the representation should be spelled out so that there are no memory lapses or misunderstandings down the line.

2. *Agency Commission*

The agency will receive a commission for all sales it makes against the work's advance, and on any subsequent income derived from royalties and the licensing of various rights. According to a recent study by the Authors' Guild, most agencies charge new clients 15% for domestic sales. Many agencies charge 20%–30% for foreign sales, since the commission often has to be split with local subagents (the agent in the foreign country who actually expedites the sale).

3. *Duration and Potential Termination of the Agreement*

When does the agreement end? How can the author or agency act to terminate the agreement? What happens after it's terminated?

Are agency agreements negotiable? Probably. It's a case-by-case situation. Don't be afraid to question, or attempt to reword, some aspects of the agreement. It will be better if such discussions are held in a friendly manner, directly between you and the agent. As a cautionary note: it is a common observation that the involvement of third parties—especially lawyers—can backfire and ignite issues that are irrelevant to the traditional ground rules of the author–agent understanding. It's fine to consult a lawyer, but you should be the point person.

The following is the standard agreement that I use with my clients. It's provided for your reference. It's not the only way an agreement can be or should be.

SAMPLE LETTER OF AGREEMENT

This Letter of Agreement between THE JEFF HERMAN AGENCY, INC., ("Agency") and _____ ("Author"), entered into on (*date*), puts into effect the following terms and conditions:

REPRESENTATION

- The Agency is hereby exclusively authorized to seek a publisher for the Author's work, hereby referred to as the "Project," on a per-project basis. The terms and conditions of this Agreement will pertain to all Projects the Author explicitly authorizes the Agency to represent, through oral and written expression, and that the Agency agrees to represent. Separate Agreements will not be necessary for each single project, unless the terms and conditions differ from this Agreement.

COMMISSION

- If the Agency sells the Project to a publisher, the Agency will be the Agent-of-Record for the Project's income-producing duration and will irrevocably keep 15% of all the Author's income relevant to sold Project. The due Agency commission will also pertain to all of the Project's subsidiary rights sales, whether sold by the Agent, Author, or Publisher. In the event the agency uses a subagent to sell foreign or film rights, and the subagent is due a commission, the Agency commission for such will be 10%, and the subagent's commission will not be more than 10%.

All Project income will be paid by the publisher to the Agency. The Agency will pay the Author all due monies within a reasonable time, upon receipt and bank clearance, with full accounting provided. The Agency will not be required to return any legitimately received commissions should the Author–Publisher contract be terminated or if the Author's work is unacceptable to the Publisher. There will be an Agency Clause in the Author–Publisher contract stating the Agency's status, the wording of which shall be subject to Author approval. These terms will be binding on the Author's estate in the event of his/her demise.

EXPENSES

- The Agency will be entitled to receive reimbursement from the Author for the following specific expenses relevant to its representation of the Project: Manuscript/proposal copying costs; long-distance telephone calls and faxes between Author and Agency; necessary overnight deliveries and local messenger costs; postage and handling for manuscripts, foreign shipping and communications costs. An itemized accounting and records of all such items will be maintained by the Agency and will be shown to the Author. No significant expenses (in excess of $25.00) will be incurred without the Author's prior knowledge and consent. The Agency will have the option to either bill the Author for these expenses, regardless of whether or not the Project in question is sold to a publisher, or to charge such expenses against the Author's account.

PROJECT STATUS

- The Agency agrees to forward to the Author copies of all correspondence received from publishers in reference to the Author's Project(s).

REVISIONS

- This Agreement can be amended or expanded by attaching Rider(s) to it, if all parties to this agreement concur with the terms and conditions of the Rider(s) and sign them.

TERMINATION

- This Agreement can be terminated in writing by any party to it by writing to the other parties, at any time following its execution. However, the Agency shall remain entitled to due commissions which may result from Agency efforts implemented prior to the termination of this Agreement, and will remain entitled to all other due monies as stated in this Agreement. Termination of the Agency representation of one or more Author Projects will not imply termination of this Agreement, unless such is specifically requested in writing.

Signatures below by the parties named in this Agreement will indicate that all parties concur with the terms and conditions of this Agreement.

Signatures below by the parties named in this Agreement will indicate that all parties concur with the terms and conditions of this Agreement.

THE JEFF HERMAN AGENCY, INC.	AUTHOR
	Social Security No.:
	Date of birth:

Specific project(s) being represented at this time:

Q & A

Q: If you, Mr. Herman, were the writer, what are some of the key points that would most concern you about an agent's agreement?

A: If I were a writer, I would prefer to see the following incorporated into my agreement with the literary agency:

1. I would want the representation to be on a per-project basis. I would not want to be automatically obligated to be represented by the agent on my next project.
2. I would want a liberal termination procedure. If at any point after signing the agreement I change my mind, I want the ability to immediately end the relationship.

Of course, I realize that the agent will be entitled to his commission relevant to any deals I accept that result from his efforts on the project's behalf—even if the deal is consummated after my termination of the agent.

The Collaboration Agreement

JEFF HERMAN

Any book that is written by two or more writers is a collaborative effort. Such collaborative endeavors are predominately nonfiction works, though collaborative fiction is by no means unheard of (typically a novel featuring a celebrity author that is for the most part written by someone else, or two bestselling novelists looking to synergize their reader base). There are several reasons why a writer might choose to collaborate with another, as opposed to writing the book alone.

The most common reasons are:

- A person may have the essential expertise, professional status, and promotability to author a book, but may lack time, ability, and/or interest to do the actual writing. Therefore, retaining someone to do the writing is a sensible—even preferable—alternative.
- Some nonfiction projects, especially academic or professionally oriented ones, cover a broad range of material, and few individuals may have the requisite depth to write the book unilaterally. Therefore, two or more writers with complementary specializations may team up. For exceptionally technical books, such as medical texts, there can be several collaborators.

Many writers earn handsome incomes writing other people's books. When they are collaborative writers, their names are flashed along with the primary author of the project (and given second billing, usually preceded by "and," "with," or "as told to"). If they are true ghostwriters, they may well have the same level of input and involvement as collaborators, but will generally receive no public recognition for their work (other than perhaps a subtle pat on the back in the acknowledgments section).

WHAT ARE COLLABORATION AGREEMENTS?

As with any business relationship, it's wise for the collaborators to enter into a concise agreement (written in plain English) that spells out all the terms and conditions of the relationship—especially each party's respective responsibilities and financial benefits.

A collaboration agreement can run from 1 to more than 20 pages, depending on how much money is at issue and the complexity of the other variables. Most of the time we in the industry can keep these agreements down to an easy-to-read 2 pages. It's probably not necessary to go to the expense of retaining a lawyer for this task. If you have an agent, he can probably draw up an agreement for you, or at least show you several samples.

The following is a sample collaboration agreement that is similar to ones used by many of my clients.

(*Disclaimer*: This sample collaboration agreement is intended only as a reference guide.)

SAMPLE COLLABORATION AGREEMENT

This collaboration agreement (Agreement), entered into on [*date*], by and between John Doe (John) and Jane Deer (Jane), will put into effect the following terms and conditions, upon signing by both parties.

(1) Jane will collaborate with John in the writing of a book about [*subject or brief description goes here*].

(2) In consultation with John, Jane will prepare a nonfiction book proposal and sample chapter for the purpose of selling the book to a publisher.

(3) Jane and John will be jointly represented by [*name of literary agent/agency*].

(4) John will be the book's spokesperson. John's name will appear first on the cover and in all publicity, and his name will be more prominently displayed than Jane's.

(5) Following the sale of the project proposal to a publisher, if, for any reason, Jane does not wish to continue as a collaborator, she shall be entitled to [*monetary amount goes here*] against the book's first proceeds in consideration of her having written the successful proposal, and she will forfeit any future claims against the book and any connection thereto.

(6) Jane's and John's respective estates will be subject to the terms and conditions of this Agreement, in the event of either's demise.

(7) John agrees to indemnify and hold Jane harmless from any liability, claim, or legal action taken against her as a result of her participation in the book proposal or book. Such exoneration includes but is not limited to costs of defending claims including reasonable counsel fees. John agrees that any funds derived from sale of the proposal or book may be utilized to pay such claims.

(8) This Agreement can be amended or expanded by attaching riders to it, if such riders are signed by Jane and John.

(9) No other claims or representations are made by either party; both agree that this Agreement fully integrates their understanding. No other representations, promises or agreements are made except as may be in writing and signed by the party to be held responsible.

(10) Jane shall receive the first [*monetary amount goes here*] of the book's proceeds when sold to a publisher. John shall receive the next [*monetary amount goes here*]. All income thereafter shall be evenly received (50/50). All subsidiary rights income shall be split 50/50.

(11) John will own the book's copyright.

(12) John will be responsible for paying expenses relevant to the preparation of the proposal (photocopying; telephone; deliveries; travel, etc.). Upon the book's sale to a publisher and the receipt of the first part of the advance, John will be reimbursed for 50% of these expenses by Jane. John and Jane will equally split (50/50) costs relevant to writing the book following its sale to a publisher.

Jane Deer   John Doe

_____   _____

Q & A

Q: What about agent representation if it's a collaborative effort?
A: There are two possibilities:

1. *The same agent will represent both parties.* However, this requires the agent to be equal in her dealings with both parties. For instance, the agent should avoid tilting toward John while he's negotiating the collaboration agreement with Jane. What I do is provide both parties with accurate advice, and then step aside as they—hopefully—work things out between themselves and then come back to me with all issues resolved.

   More important: the agent should not "double-dip." In other words, my commission will only pertain to the work's income. I will not touch any money that one collaborator may pay to the other, even if such payments exceed the work's advance.

2. Some collaborations can be coagented. Each collaborator may already have a different agent. Or it may be felt that there will be a conflict of interest for the same agent to represent both parties

   When this happens, both agents will negotiate the collaboration agreement with each other in behalf of their respective clients. All parties will then work out a strategy to determine which agent is to be out front selling and negotiating the deal. Each agent will receive a commission only against her client's respective share.

As with any other business relationship, collaboration agreements generally have the best chance to produce a productive and successful outcome when they reasonably and realistically reflect the rights, responsibilities, special talents, and good interests of all involved parties.

Overcoming Writer's Roadblocks

Writer's Guide to a Wholesome Outlook and Sound Mind

JEFF HERMAN AND JAMIE M. FORBES

Trying to make it as a writer can drive anyone crazy, and may already have sent you over the edge. Regardless of your sanity rating, telling people you're a writer cuts you a lot of slack. They expect you to be a bit bizarre, if not an absolute miscreant.

You're already given a license to Nutsville, so it behooves you to use it. Yes, there are ways to play the game that can, at the very least, augment your inventiveness—and perhaps even amplify your cachet as a promotable personality.

We know that world-class athletes practice visualization techniques to enhance their performance mindset. Some teachers and counselors use specially designed systems of creative fantasy, role-play, artistic manipulation, and personal journals to search their clients' psyches and bring out the best that they can be.

Of course, we should say that the ideas provided are for entertainment or inspirational purposes only. This is, after all, the printed page, a medium that creates its own reality. Here are some scenarios to get your creative juices bubbling:

CREATIVE WAYS TO GAIN RICHES, FITNESS, FAME, AND LOVE

- Put wet cement into book-shaped boxes and send it to people who rejected your work, along with a cover note asking them to read your masterpiece. Change your pen name and *don't* remember to include an SASE. (You might also want to make a contribution to the U.S. Postal Service Hernia Fund, to protect your karma.)
- Cut out photos of models from *Cosmopolitan* or *GQ* magazines, and include them in your submission packages—don't say anything about them in your attached

correspondence. If and when editors and agents offer you contracts because they think you're a hunk/babe, who are they to complain? You told no lies. If you ever have to meet these editors or agents in person, you don't know what they're talking about.

- On the assumption that many in the effete trade of publishing come from landed gentry, threaten to surgically mutilate pedigreed livestock, tramp out crop circles visible from the country house, implant alien colonies underneath organic vineyards, and abduct extended aristocratic families en masse to other galaxies should certain editors reject you. Of course, government agents might pay you a surprise visit, and they are a notoriously humorless lot—you would be too if you were being tailed by all those black helicopters. (Although you can unnerve the entire New York editorial corps with such a campaign, various restraining orders might bar you from ever entering the city again. This could, however, prove an incomparable publicity hook, which can be parlayed into book and movie deals. You'll be the cream of TV talk shows — maybe even Court TV.)

- Change your name legally to resemble an established publishing author brand. Mix and match from first to last. Consider the pulse and flow of such names as Atwood, Chopra, Grisham, Oates, Rice, Rodman, Tan, Mosley, Walker, and Zelazny. These rhythms have subliminal power to evoke contractual echoes along Publishers' Row.

- Agents and editors are mercenary tramps anyway—so who's to say you couldn't do it better yourself? Beat the creeps at their own game: Send drab first drafts to the offices of various hotshot literary agencies and big-name publishers. You should soon accumulate plenty of rejection slips—many of them will be printed on official letterhead stationery.

  Produce computer mock-ups of these letterheads and compose notes that say thus-and-such literary agency wants you to sign with them. Write memos to other agencies saying that you'd rather sign with them, even though you have several fine offers already in hand (include copies of your forged notes from other agencies to buttress your case).

- If you don't sway a literary agency this way, all is by no means lost. Send your most calculatedly commercial manuscript around to a select group of renowned editors with a cover letter printed on the letterhead of the agency you feel is most impressive—be sure to insert your own telephone number (bill yourself under a snot-nosed alias, with the title "agent-at-large" or some such ritzy moniker that will lend credence to your "branch office" address).

  Wait for the offers to roll in. If they don't (or even if they do), remember you're already on the road to becoming a practiced trickster. As your newfound expertise bleeds into other notorious schemes, you may soon get a chance to prove your worth. As a highly respected jailhouse literary agent, you can negotiate book deals for other inmates.

- Put together a full-fledged press kit, complete with photographs, reviews, interviews, articles about you, and a tape of video clips. If these do not yet exist, invent an entire career for yourself and submit it as a book-proposal package—call it *How to Become a Celebrity in Seventeen Seconds* or say it's an avant-garde novel.

- Take a fancy lunch with someone you trust, then take a nap.
- Stop writing.
- Start writing.
- Eat well and prosper.

Glossary

A

abstract A brief sequential profile of chapters in a nonfiction book proposal (also called a **synopsis**); a point-by-point summary of an article or essay. In academic and technical journals abstracts often appear with (and may serve to preface) the articles themselves.

adaptation A rewrite or reworking of a piece for another medium, such as the adaptation of a novel for the screen. (*See* **screenplay**.)

advance Money paid (usually in installments) to an author by a publisher prior to publication. The advance is paid against royalties: If an author is given a $5,000 advance, for instance, the author will collect royalties only after the royalty moneys due exceed $5,000. A good contract protects the advance if it should exceed the royalties ultimately due from sales.

advance orders Orders received before a book's official publication date, and sometimes before actual completion of the book's production and manufacture.

agent The person who acts on behalf of the author to handle the sale of the author's literary properties. Good literary agents are as valuable to publishers as they are to writers; they select and present manuscripts appropriate for particular houses or of interest to particular acquisitions editors. Agents are paid on a percentage basis from the moneys due their author clients.

American Booksellers Association (ABA) The major trade organization for retail booksellers, chain and independent. The annual ABA convention and trade show offers a chance for publishers and distributors to display their wares to the industry at large, and provides an incomparable networking forum for booksellers, editors, agents, publicists, and authors.

American Society of Journalists and Authors (ASJA) A membership organization for professional writers. ASJA provides a forum for information exchange among writers and others in the publishing community, as well as networking opportunities. (*See* **Dial-a-Writer**.)

anthology A collection of stories, poems, essays, and/or selections from larger works (and so forth), usually carrying a unifying theme or concept; these selections may be written by different authors or by a single author. Anthologies are compiled as opposed to written; their editors (as opposed to authors) are responsible for securing the needed reprint rights for the material used, as well as supplying (or providing authors for) pertinent introductory or supplementary material and/or commentary.

attitude A contemporary colloquialism used to describe a characteristic temperament common among individuals who consider themselves superior. Attitude is rarely an esteemed attribute, whether in publishing or elsewhere.

auction Manuscripts a literary agent believes to be hot properties (such as possible bestsellers with strong subsidiary rights potential) will be offered for confidential bidding from multiple publishing houses. Likewise, the reprint, film, and other rights to a successful book may be auctioned off by the original publisher's subsidiary rights department or by the author's agent.

audio books Works produced for distribution on audio media, typically audiotape cassette or audio compact disk (CD). Audio books are usually spoken-word adaptations of works originally created and produced in print; these works sometimes feature the author's own voice; many are given dramatic readings by one or more actors, at times embellished with sound effects.

authorized biography A history of a person's life written with the authorization, cooperation, and, at times, participation of the subject or the subject's heirs.

author's copies/author's discount Author's copies are the free copies of their books the authors receive from the publisher; the exact number is stipulated in the contract, but it is usually at least 10 hardcovers. The author will be able to purchase additional copies of the book (usually at 40% discount from the retail price) and resell them at readings, lectures, and other public engagements. In cases where large quantities of books are bought, author discounts can go as high as 70%.

author tour A series of travel and promotional appearances by an author on behalf of the author's book.

autobiography A history of a person's life written by that same person, or, as is typical, composed conjointly with a collaborative writer ("as told to" or "with"; *see* **coauthor, collaboration**) or **ghostwriter**. Autobiographies by definition entail the authorization, cooperation, participation, and ultimate approval of the subject.

B

backlist The backlist comprises books published prior to the current season and still in print. Traditionally, at some publishing houses, such backlist titles represent the publisher's cash flow mainstays. Some backlist books continue to sell briskly; some remain bestsellers over several successive seasons; others sell slowly but surely through the years. Although many backlist titles may be difficult to find in bookstores that stock primarily current lists, they can be ordered either through a local bookseller or directly from the publisher.

backmatter   Elements of a book that follow the text proper. Backmatter may include the appendix, notes, glossary, bibliography and other references, list of resources, index, author biography, offerings of the author's and/or publisher's additional books and other related merchandise, and colophon.

bestseller   Based on sales or orders by bookstores, wholesalers, and distributors, best-sellers are those titles that move in the largest quantities. Lists of bestselling books can be local (as in metropolitan newspapers), regional (typically in geographically keyed trade or consumer periodicals), or national (as in *USA Today*, *Publishers Weekly*, or the *New York Times*), as well as international. Fiction and nonfiction are usually listed separately, as are hardcover and paperback classifications. Depending on the list's purview, additional industry-sector designations are used (such as how-to/self-improvement, religion and spirituality, business and finance); in addition, bestseller lists can be keyed to particular genre or specialty fields (such as bestseller lists for mysteries, science fiction, or romance novels, and for historical works, biography, or popular science titles)—and virtually any other marketing category at the discretion of whoever issues the bestseller list (for instance African-American interest, lesbian and gay topics, youth market).

bibliography   A list of books, articles, and other sources that have been used in the writing of the text in which the bibliography appears. Complex works may break the bibliography down into discrete subject areas or source categories, such as General History, Military History, War in the Twentieth Century, or Unionism and Pacifism.

binding   The materials that hold a book together (including the cover). Bindings are generally denoted as hardcover (featuring heavy cardboard covered with durable cloth and/or paper, and occasionally other materials) or paperback (using a pliable, resilient grade of paper, sometimes infused or laminated with other substances such as plastic). In the days when cloth was used lavishly, hardcover volumes were conventionally known as clothbound; and in the very old days, hardcover bindings sometimes featured tooled leather, silk, precious stones, and gold and silver leaf ornamentation.

biography   A history of a person's life. (*See* **authorized biography, autobiography, unauthorized biography**.)

blues (or bluelines)   Photographic proofs of the printing plates for a book. Blues are reviewed as a means to inspect the set type, layout, and design of the book's pages before it goes to press.

blurb   A piece of written copy or extracted quotation used for publicity and promotional purposes, as on a flyer, in a catalog, or in an advertisement (*See* **cover blurbs**).

book club   A book club is a book-marketing operation that ships selected titles to subscribing members on a regular basis, sometimes at greatly reduced prices. Sales of a work to book clubs are negotiated through the publisher's subsidiary rights department (in the case of a bestseller or other work that has gained acclaim, these rights can be auctioned off). Terms vary, but the split of royalties between author and publisher is often 50%/50%. Book club sales are seen as blessed events by author, agent, and publisher alike.

book contract   A legally binding document between author and publisher that sets the terms for the advance, royalties, subsidiary rights, advertising, promotion, publicity—plus a host of other contingencies and responsibilities. Writers should therefore be thoroughly familiar with the concepts and terminology of the standard book-publishing contract.

book distribution   The method of getting books from the publisher's warehouse into the reader's hands. Distribution is traditionally through bookstores, but can include such means as telemarketing and mail-order sales, as well as sales through a variety of special-interest outlets such as health-food or New Age venues, sports and fitness emporiums, or sex shops. Publishers use their own sales forces as well as independent salespeople, wholesalers, and distributors. Many large and some small publishers distribute for other publishers, which can be a good source of income. A publisher's distribution network is extremely important, because it not only makes possible the vast sales of a bestseller but also affects the visibility of the publisher's entire list of books.

book jacket   (*See* **dust jacket**.)

book producer or **book packager**   An individual or company that can assume many of the roles in the publishing process. A book packager or producer may conceive the idea for a book (most often nonfiction) or series, bring together the professionals (including the writer) needed to produce the book(s), sell the individual manuscript or series project to a publisher, take the project through to manufactured product—or perform any selection of those functions, as commissioned by the publisher or other client (such as a corporation producing a corporate history as a premium or giveaway for employees and customers). The book producer may negotiate separate contracts with the publisher and with the writers, editors, and illustrators who contribute to the book.

book review   A critical appraisal of a book (often reflecting a reviewer's personal opinion or recommendation) that evaluates such aspects as organization and writing style, possible market appeal, and cultural, political, or literary significance. Before the public reads book reviews in the local and national print media, important reviews have been published in such respected book-trade journals as *Publishers Weekly*, *Kirkus Reviews*, *Library Journal*, and *Booklist*. A gushing review from one of these journals will encourage booksellers to order the book; copies of these raves will be used for promotion and publicity purposes by the publisher and will encourage other book reviewers nationwide to review the book.

Books in Print   Listings, published by R. R. Bowker, of books currently in print; these yearly volumes (along with periodic supplements such as *Forthcoming Books in Print*) provide ordering information including titles, authors, ISBN numbers, prices, whether the book is available in hardcover or paperback, and publisher names. Intended for use by the book trade, *Books in Print* is also of great value to writers who are researching and market-researching their projects. Listings are provided alphabetically by author, title, and subject area.

bound galleys   Copies of uncorrected typesetter's page proofs or printouts of electronically produced mechanicals that are bound together as advance copies of the book (compare **galleys**). Bound galleys are sent to trade journals (*See* **book review**) as well as to a limited number of reviewers who work under long lead times.

bulk sales   The sale at a set discount of many copies of a single title (the greater the number of books, the larger the discount).

byline   The name of the author of a given piece, indicating credit for having written a book or article. Ghostwriters, by definition, do not receive bylines.

C

casing   Alternate term for binding (*See* **binding**).

category fiction   Also known as genre fiction. Category fiction falls into an established (or newly originated) marketing category (which can then be subdivided for more precise target marketing). Fiction categories include action-adventure (with such further designations as military, paramilitary, law enforcement, romantic, and martial arts); crime novels (with points of view that range from deadpan cool to visionary, including humorous capers as well as gritty urban sagas); mysteries or detective fiction (hard-boiled, soft-boiled, procedurals, cozies); romances (including historicals as well as contemporaries); horror (supernatural, psychological, or technological); thrillers (tales of espionage, crisis, and the chase), Westerns, science fiction, and fantasy. (*See* **fantasy fiction**, **horror**, **romance fiction**, **science fiction**, **suspense fiction**, and **thriller**.)

CD or **computer CD**   High-capacity compact disks for use by readers via computer technology. **CD-ROM** is a particular variety; the term is somewhere between an acronym and an abbreviation—CD-ROMs are compact computer disks with read-only memory, meaning the reader is not able to modify or duplicate the contents. Many CDs are issued with a variety of audiovisual as well as textual components. When produced by publishers, these are sometimes characterized as books in electronic format. (*See* **multimedia**.)

children's books   Books for children. As defined by the book-publishing industry, children are generally readers aged 17 and younger; many houses adhere to a fine but firm editorial distinction between titles intended for younger readers (under 12) and young adults (generally aged 12 to 17). Children's books (also called juveniles) are produced according to a number of categories (often typified by age ranges), each with particular requisites regarding such elements as readability ratings, length, and inclusion of graphic elements. Picture books are often for very young readers, with such designations as toddlers (who do not themselves read) and preschoolers (who may have some reading ability). Other classifications include easy storybooks (for younger school children); middle-grade books (for elementary to junior high school students); and young adult (abbreviated YA, for readers through age 17).

coauthor   One who shares authorship of a work. Coauthors all have bylines. Coauthors share royalties based on their contributions to the book. (Compare **ghostwriter**.)

collaboration   Writers can collaborate with professionals in any number of fields. Often a writer can collaborate in order to produce books outside the writer's own areas of formally credentialed expertise (for example, a writer with an interest in exercise and nutrition may collaborate with a sports doctor on a health book). Though the writer may be billed as a coauthor (*See* **coauthor**), the writer does not necessarily receive a byline (in which case the writer is a **ghostwriter**) Royalties are shared, based on respective contributions to the book (including expertise or promotional abilities as well as the actual writing).

colophon   Strictly speaking, a colophon is a publisher's logo; in bookmaking, the term may also refer to a listing of the materials used, as well as credits for the design, composition, and production of the book. Such colophons are sometimes included in the backmatter or as part of the copyright page.

commercial fiction   Fiction written to appeal to as broad-based a readership as possible.

concept   A general statement of the idea behind a book.

cool   A modern colloquial expression that indicates satisfaction or approval, or may signify the maintenance of calm within a whirlwind. A fat contract for a new author is definitely cool.

cooperative advertising (co-op)   An agreement between a publisher and a bookstore. The publisher's book is featured in an ad for the bookstore (sometimes in conjunction with an author appearance or other special book promotion); the publisher contributes to the cost of the ad, which is billed at a lower (retail advertising) rate.

copublishing   Joint publishing of a book, usually by a publisher and another corporate entity such as a foundation, a museum, or a smaller publisher. An author can copublish with the publisher by sharing the costs and decision making and, ultimately, the profits.

copyeditor   An editor, responsible for the final polishing of a manuscript, who reads primarily in terms of appropriate word usage and grammatical expression, with an eye toward clarity and coherence of the material as presented, factual errors and inconsistencies, spelling, and punctuation. (*See* **editor**.)

copyright   The legal proprietary right to reproduce, have reproduced, publish, and sell copies of literary, musical, and other artistic works. The rights to literary properties reside in the author from the time the work is produced—regardless of whether a formal copyright registration is obtained. However, for legal recourse in the event of plagiarism or other infringement, the work must be registered with the U.S. Copyright Office, and all copies of the work must bear the copyright notice. (*See* **work-for-hire**.)

cover blurbs   Favorable quotes from other writers, celebrities, or experts in a book's subject area, which appear on the dust jacket and are used to enhance the book's point-of-purchase appeal to the potential book-buying public.

crash   Coarse gauze fabric used in bookbinding to strengthen the spine and joints of a book.

curriculum vitae   (abbreviated **c.v.**) Latin expression meaning "course of life"—in other words, the **résumé** (which see).

D

deadline   In book publishing, this not-so-subtle synonym is used for the author's due date for delivery of the completed manuscript to the publisher. The deadline can be as much as a full year before official publication date, unless the book is being produced quickly to coincide with or follow up a particular event.

delivery   Submission of the completed manuscript to the editor or publisher.

Dial-a-Writer   Members of the American Society of Journalists and Authors may be listed with the organization's project-referral service, Dial-a-Writer, which can provide accomplished writers in most specialty fields and subjects.

direct marketing   Advertising that involves a "direct response" (which is an equivalent term) from a consumer—for instance an order form or coupon in a book-review section or in the back of a book, or mailings (direct-mail advertising) to a group presumed to hold a special interest in a particular book.

display titles   Books that are produced to be eye-catching to the casual shopper in a bookstore setting are termed display titles. Often rich with flamboyant cover art, these publications are intended to pique bookbuyer excitement about the store's stock in general. Many display titles are stacked on their own freestanding racks; sometimes broad tables are laden with these items. A book shelved with its front cover showing on racks along with diverse other titles is technically a display title. Promotional or **premium** titles are likely to be display items, as are mass-market paperbacks and hardbacks with enormous bestseller potential. Check your local bookstore and find a copy of this edition of *Writer's Guide*—if not already racked in display manner, please adjust the bookshelf so that the front cover is displayed poster-like to catch the browser's eye (that's what *we* do routinely).

distributor   An agent or business that buys books from a publisher to resell, at a higher cost, to wholesalers, retailers, or individuals. Distribution houses are often excellent marketing enterprises, with their own roster of sales representatives, publicity and promotion personnel, and house catalogs. Skillful use of distribution networks can give a small publisher considerable national visibility.

dramatic rights   Legal permission to adapt a work for the stage. These rights initially belong to the author but can be sold or assigned to another party by the author.

dust jacket (also **dustcover** or **book jacket**)   The wrapper that covers the binding of hardcover books, designed especially for the book by either the publisher's art department or a freelance artist. Dust jackets were originally conceived to protect the book during shipping, but now their function is primarily promotional—to entice the browser to actually reach out and pick up the volume (and maybe even open it up for a taste before buying)—by means of attractive graphics and sizzling promotional copy.

dust-jacket copy   Descriptions of books printed on the dust-jacket flaps. Dust-jacket copy may be written by the book's editor, but is often either recast or written by in-house copywriters or freelance specialists. Editors send advance copies (*see* **bound galleys**) to other writers, experts, and celebrities to solicit quotable praise that will also appear on the jacket. (*See* also **blurb**.)

E

editor   Editorial responsibilities and titles vary from house to house (often being less strictly defined in smaller houses). In general, the duties of the editor-in-chief or executive editor are primarily administrative: managing personnel, scheduling, budgeting, and defining the editorial personality of the firm or imprint. Senior editors and acquisitions editors acquire manuscripts (and authors), conceive project ideas and find writers to carry them out, and may oversee the writing and rewriting of manuscripts. Managing editors have editorial and production responsibilities, coordinating and scheduling the book through the various phases of production. Associate and assistant editors edit; they are involved in much of the rewriting and reshaping of the manuscript, and may also have acquisitions duties. Copyeditors read the manuscript and style its punctuation, grammar, spelling, headings and subheadings, and so forth. Editorial assistants, laden with extensive clerical duties and general office work, perform some editorial duties as well—often as springboards to senior editorial positions.

Editorial Freelancers Association (EFA)   This organization of independent professionals offers a referral service, through both its annotated membership directory and its job phone line, as a means for authors and publishers to connect with writers, collaborators, researchers, and a wide range of editorial experts covering virtually all general and specialist fields.

el-hi   Books for elementary and/or high schools.

endnotes   Explanatory notes and/or source citations that appear either at the end of individual chapters or at the end of a book's text; used primarily in scholarly or academically oriented works.

epilogue   The final segment of a book, which comes "after the end." In both fiction and nonfiction, an epilogue offers commentary or further information, but does not bear directly on the book's central design.

F

fantasy   Fantasy is fiction that features elements of magic, wizardry, supernatural feats, and entities that suspend conventions of realism in the literary arts. Fantasy can resemble prose versions of epics and rhymes, may be informed by mythic cycles or folkloric material derived from cultures worldwide. Fantasy fiction may be guided primarily by the author's own distinctive imagery and personalized archetypes. Fantasies that involve heroic-erotic roundelays of the death-dance are often referred to as the sword-and-sorcery subgenre.

film rights   Like **dramatic rights**, these belong to the author, who may sell or option them to someone in the film industry—a producer or director, for example (or sometimes a specialist broker of such properties)—who will then try to gather the other professionals and secure the financial backing needed to convert the book into a film. (*See* **screenplay**.)

footbands   (*See* **headbands**.)

footnotes   Explanatory notes and/or source citations that appear at the bottom of a page. Footnotes are rare in general-interest books, the preferred style being either to work such information into the text or to list informational sources in the bibliography.

foreign agents   Persons who work with their United States counterparts to acquire rights for books from the U.S. for publication abroad. They can also represent U.S. publishers directly.

foreign market   Any foreign entity—a publisher, broadcast medium, etc.—in a position to buy rights. Authors share royalties with whoever negotiates the deal, or keep 100% if they do their own negotiating.

foreign rights   Translation or reprint rights that can be sold abroad. Foreign rights belong to the author but can be sold either country-by-country or en masse as world rights. Often the U.S. publisher will own world rights, and the author will be entitled to anywhere from 50% to 85% of these revenues.

foreword   An introductory piece written by the author or by an expert in the given field (*see* **introduction**). A foreword by a celebrity or well-respected authority is a strong selling point for a prospective author or, after publication, for the book itself.

Frankfurt Book Fair   The largest international publishing exhibition—with five hundred years of tradition behind it. The fair takes place every October in Frankfurt, Germany. Thousands of publishers, agents, and writers from all over the world negotiate, network, and buy and sell rights.

Freedom of Information Act   Ensures the protection of the public's right to access to public records—except in cases violating the right to privacy, national security, or certain other instances. A related law, the Government in the Sunshine Act, stipulates that certain government agencies announce and open their meetings to the public.

freight passthrough   The bookseller's freight cost (the cost of getting the book from the publisher to the bookseller). It is added to the basic invoice price charged the bookseller by the publisher.

frontlist   New titles published in a given season by a publisher. Frontlist titles customarily receive priority exposure in the front of the sales catalog—as opposed to backlist titles (usually found at the back of the catalog), which are previously published titles still in print.

frontmatter   The frontmatter of a book includes the elements that precede the text of the work, such as the title page, copyright page, dedication, epigraph, table of contents, foreword, preface, acknowledgments, and introduction.

fulfillment house   A firm commissioned to fulfill orders for a publisher—services may include warehousing, shipping, receiving returns, and mail-order and direct-marketing functions. Although more common for magazine publishers, fulfillment houses also serve book publishers.

G

galleys   Printer's proofs (or copies of proofs) on sheets of paper, or printouts of the electronically produced setup of the book's interior—the author's last chance to check for typos and make (usually minimal) revisions or additions to the copy (*see* **bound galleys**).

genre fiction   (*See* **category fiction.**)

ghostwriter   A writer without a byline, often without the remuneration and recognition that credited authors receive. Ghostwriters often get flat fees for their work, but even without royalties, experienced ghosts can receive quite respectable sums.

glossary   An alphabetical listing of special terms as they are used in a particular subject area, often with more in-depth explanations than would customarily be provided by dictionary definitions.

H

hardcover   Books bound in a format that uses thick, sturdy, relatively stiff binding boards and a cover composed (usually) of cloth spine and finished binding paper. Hardcover books are conventionally wrapped in a dust jacket. (*See* **binding, dust jacket.**)

headbands   Thin strips of cloth (often colored or patterned) that adorn the top of a book's spine where the signatures are held together. The headbands conceal the glue or other binding materials and are said to offer some protection against accumulation of dust (when properly attached). Such bands, placed at the bottom of the spine, are known as footbands.

hook   A term denoting the distinctive concept or theme of a work that sets it apart—as being fresh, new, or different from others in its field. A hook can be an author's special point of view, often encapsulated in a catchy or provocative phrase intended to attract or pique the interest of a reader, editor, or agent. One specialized function of a hook is to articulate what might otherwise be seen as dry albeit significant subject matter (academic or scientific topics; number-crunching drudgery such as home bookkeeping) into an exciting, commercially attractive package.

horror   The horror classification denotes works that traffic in the bizarre, awful, and scary in order to entertain as well as explicate the darkness at the heart of the reader's soul. Horror subgenres may be typified according to the appearance of were-creatures, vampires, human-induced monsters, or naturally occurring life forms and spirit entities—or absence thereof. Horror fiction traditionally makes imaginative literary use of paranormal phenomena, occult elements, and psychological motifs. (*See* **category fiction**, **suspense fiction**.)

how-to books   An immensely popular category of books ranging from purely instructional (arts and crafts, for example) to motivational (popular psychology, self-awareness, self-improvement, inspirational) to get-rich-quick (such as in real estate or personal investment).

hypertext   Works in hypertext are meant to be more than words and other images. These productions (ingrained magnetically on computer diskette or CD) are conceived to take advantage of readers' and writers' propensities to seek out twists in narrative trajectories and to bushwhack from the main path of multifaceted reference topics. Hypertext books incorporate documents, graphics, sounds, and even blank slates upon which readers may compose their own variations on the authored components. The computer's capacities to afford such diversions can bring reader and hypertext literateur so close as to gain entry to each other's mind-sets—which is what good books have always done.

I

imprint   A separate line of product within a publishing house. Imprints run the gamut of complexity, from those composed of one or two series to those offering full-fledged and diversified lists. Imprints as well enjoy different gradations of autonomy from the parent company. An imprint may have its own editorial department (perhaps consisting of as few as one editor), or house acquisitions editors may assign particular titles for release on appropriate specialized imprints. An imprint may publish a certain kind of book (juvenile or paperback or travel books), or have its own personality (such as a literary or contemporary tone). An individual imprint's categories often overlap with other imprints or with the publisher's core list, but some imprints maintain a small-house feel within an otherwise enormous conglomerate. The imprint can offer the distinct advantages of a personalized editorial approach, while availing itself of the larger company's production, publicity, marketing, sales, and advertising resources.

index   An alphabetical directory at the end of a book that references names and subjects discussed in the book and the pages where such mentions can be found.

instant book   A book produced quickly to appear in bookstores as soon as possible after (for instance) a newsworthy event to which it is relevant.

international copyright   Rights secured for countries that are members of the International Copyright Convention (*see* entry below for **International Copyright Convention**) and respect the authority of the international copyright symbol, ©.

International Copyright Convention   Countries that are signatories to the various international copyright treaties. Some treaties are contingent upon certain conditions being met at the time of publication, so an author should inquire before publication into a particular country's laws.

introduction   Preliminary remarks pertaining to a piece. Like a foreword, an introduction can be written by the author or an appropriate authority on the subject. If a
book has both a foreword and an introduction, the foreword will be written by someone other than the author; the introduction will be more closely tied to the text and will
be written by the book's author. (*See* **foreword.**)

ISBN (International Standard Book Number)   A 10-digit number that is keyed to
and identifies the title and publisher of a book. It is used for ordering and cataloging
books and appears on all dust jackets, on the back cover of the book, and on the copyright page.

ISSN (International Standard Serial Number)   An 8-digit cataloging and ordering
number that identifies all U.S. and foreign periodicals.

J

juveniles   (*See* **children's books.**)

K

kill fee   A fee paid by a magazine when it cancels a commissioned article. The fee is
only a certain percentage of the agreed-on payment for the assignment (no more than
50%). Not all publishers pay kill fees; a writer should make sure to formalize such an
arrangement in advance. Kill fees are sometimes involved in work-for-hire projects in
book publishing.

L

lead   The crucial first few sentences, phrases, or words of anything—be it a query letter, book proposal, novel, news release, advertisement, or sales tip sheet. A successful
lead immediately hooks the reader, consumer, editor, or agent.

lead title   A frontlist book featured by the publisher during a given season—one the
publisher believes should do extremely well commercially. Lead titles are usually those
given the publisher's maximum promotional push.

letterhead   Business stationery and envelopes imprinted with the company's (or, in
such a case, the writer's) name, address, and logo—a convenience as well as an impressive asset for a freelance writer.

letterpress   A form of printing in which set type is inked, then impressed directly
onto the printing surface. Now used primarily for limited-run books-as-fine-art projects. (*See* **offset.**)

libel   Defamation of an individual or individuals in a published work, with malice
aforethought. In litigation, the falsity of the libelous statements or representations, as
well the intention of malice, has to be proved for there to be libel; in addition, financial
damages to the parties so libeled must be incurred as a result of the material in question

for there to be an assessment of the amount of damages to be awarded to a claimant. This is contrasted to slander, which is defamation through the spoken word.

Library of Congress   The largest library in the world is in Washington, D.C. As part of its many services, the LOC will supply a writer with up-to-date sources and bibliographies in all fields, from arts and humanities to science and technology. For details, write to the Library of Congress, Central Services Division, Washington, DC 20540.

Library of Congress Catalog Card Number   An identifying number issued by the Library of Congress to books it has accepted for its collection. The publication of those books, which are submitted by the publisher, are announced by the Library of Congress to libraries, which use Library of Congress numbers for their own ordering and cataloging purposes.

Literary Market Place (*LMP*)   An annual directory of the publishing industry that contains a comprehensive list of publishers, alphabetically and by category, with their addresses, phone numbers, some personnel, and the types of books they publish. Also included are various publishing-allied listings, such as literary agencies, writer's conferences and competitions, and editorial and distribution services. *LMP* is published by R. R. Bowker and is available in most public libraries.

literature   Written works of fiction and nonfiction in which compositional excellence and advancement in the art of writing are higher priorities than are considerations of profit or commercial appeal.

logo   A company or product identifier—for example, a representation of a company's initials or a drawing that is the exclusive property of that company. In publishing usage, a virtual equivalent to the trademark.

M

mainstream fiction   Nongenre fiction, excluding literary or avant-garde fiction, that appeals to a general readership.

marketing plan   The entire strategy for selling a book: its publicity, promotion, sales, and advertising.

mass-market paperback   Less-expensive smaller-format paperbacks that are sold from racks (in such venues as supermarkets, variety stores, drugstores, and specialty shops) as well as in bookstores. Also referred to as rack (or rack-sized) editions.

mechanicals   Typeset copy and art mounted on boards to be photocopied and printed. Also referred to as pasteups.

midlist books   Generally mainstream fiction and nonfiction books that traditionally formed the bulk of a publisher's list (nowadays often by default rather than intent). Midlist books are expected to be commercially viable but not explosive bestsellers— nor are they viewed as distinguished, critically respected books that can be scheduled for small print runs and aimed at select readerships. Agents may view such projects as a poor return for the effort, since they generally garner a low-end advance; editors and publishers (especially the sales force) may decry midlist works as being hard to market; prospective readers often find midlist books hard to buy in bookstores (they have short shelf lives). Hint for writers: Don't present your work as a midlist item.

multimedia   Presentations of sound and light, words in magnetically graven image—and any known combination thereof as well as nuances yet to come. Though computer CD is the dominant wrapper for these works, technological innovation is the hallmark of the electronic-publishing arena, and new formats will expand the creative and market potential. Multimedia books are publishing events; their advent suggests alternative avenues for authors as well as adaptational tie-ins with the world of print. Meanwhile, please stay tuned for virtual reality, artificial intelligence, and electronic end-user distribution of product.

multiple contract   A book contract that includes a provisional agreement for a future book or books. (*See* **option clause.**)

mystery stories or **mysteries** (*See* **suspense fiction.**)

N

net receipts   The amount of money a publisher actually receives for sales of a book: the retail price minus the bookseller's discount and/or other discount. The number of returned copies is factored in, bringing down even further the net amount received per book. Royalties are sometimes figured on these lower amounts rather than on the retail price of the book.

New Age   An eclectic category that encompasses health, medicine, philosophy, religion, and the occult—presented from an alternative or multicultural perspective. Although the term has achieved currency relatively recently, some publishers have been producing serious books in these categories for decades.

novella   A work of fiction falling in length between a short story and a novel.

O

offset (offset lithography)   A printing process that involves the transfer of wet ink from a (usually photosensitized) printing plate onto an intermediate surface (such as a rubber-coated cylinder) and then onto the paper. For commercial purposes, this method has replaced letterpress, whereby books were printed via direct impression of inked type on paper.

option clause/right of first refusal   In a book contract, a clause that stipulates that the publisher will have the exclusive right to consider and make an offer for the author's next book. However, the publisher is under no obligation to publish the book, and in most variations of the clause the author may, under certain circumstances, opt for publication elsewhere. (*See* **multiple contract.**)

outline   Used for both a book proposal and the actual writing and structuring of a book, an outline is a hierarchical listing of topics that provides the writer (and the proposal reader) with an overview of the ideas in a book in the order in which they are to be presented.

out-of-print books   Books no longer available from the publisher; rights usually revert to the author.

P

package   The package is the actual book; the physical product.

packager   (*See* **book producer**.)

page proof   The final typeset copy of the book, in page-layout form, before printing.

paperback   Books bound with a flexible, stress-resistant, paper covering material. (*See* **binding**.)

paperback originals   Books published, generally, in paperback editions only; sometimes the term refers to those books published simultaneously in hardcover and paperback. These books are often mass-market genre fiction (romances, Westerns, Gothics, mysteries, horror, and so forth) as well as contemporary literary fiction, cookbooks, humor, career books, self-improvement, and how-to books—the categories continue to expand.

pasteups   (*See* **mechanicals**.)

permissions   The right to quote or reprint published material, obtained by the author from the copyright holder.

picture book   A copiously illustrated book, often with very simple, limited text, intended for preschoolers and very young children.

plagiarism   The false presentation of someone else's writing as one's own. In the case of copyrighted work, plagiarism is illegal.

preface   An element of a book's frontmatter. In the preface, the author may discuss the purpose behind the format of the book, the type of research upon which it is based, its genesis, or underlying philosophy.

premium   Books sold at a reduced price as part of a special promotion. Premiums can thus be sold to a bookseller, who in turn sells them to the bookbuyer (as with a line of modestly priced art books). Alternately, such books may be produced as part of a broader marketing package. For instance, an organization may acquire a number of books (such as its own corporate history or biography of its founder) for use in personnel training and as giveaways to clients; or a nutrition/recipe book may be displayed along with a company's diet foods in non-bookstore outlets. (*See* **special sales**.)

press agent   (*See* **publicist**.)

press kit   A promotional package that includes a press release, tip sheet, author biography and photograph, reviews, and other pertinent information. The press kit can be put together by the publisher's publicity department or an independent publicist and sent with a review copy of the book to potential reviewers and to media professionals responsible for booking author appearances.

price   There are several prices pertaining to a single book: The invoice price is the amount the publisher charges the bookseller; the retail, cover, or list price is what the consumer pays.

printer's error (PE)   A typographical error made by the printer or typesetting facility, not by the publisher's staff. PEs are corrected at the printer's expense.

printing plate   A surface that bears a reproduction of the set type and artwork of a book, from which the pages are printed.

producer   (*See* **book producer**.)

proposal   A detailed presentation of the book's concept, used to gain the interest and services of an agent and to sell the project to a publisher.

public domain   Material that is uncopyrighted, whose copyright has expired, or is uncopyrightable. The last includes government publications, jokes, titles—and, it should be remembered, ideas.

publication date (or **pub date**)   A book's official date of publication, customarily set by the publisher to fall 6 weeks after completed bound books are delivered to the warehouse. The publication date is used to focus the promotional activities on behalf of the title—in order that books will have had time to be ordered, shipped, and be available in the stores to coincide with the appearance of advertising and publicity.

publicist (press agent)   The publicity professional who handles the press releases for new books and arranges the author's publicity tours and other promotional venues (such as interviews, speaking engagements, and book signings).

publisher's catalog   A seasonal sales catalog that lists and describes a publisher's new books; it is sent to all potential buyers, including individuals who request one. Catalogs range from the basic to the glitzy, and often include information on the author, on print quantity, and the amount of money slated to be spent on publicity and promotion.

publisher's discount   The percentage by which a publisher discounts the retail price of a book to a bookseller, often based in part on the number of copies purchased.

Publishers' Trade List Annual   A collection of current and backlist catalogs arranged alphabetically by publisher, available in many libraries.

Publishers Weekly (PW)   The publishing industry's chief trade journal. *PW* carries announcements of upcoming books, respected book reviews, interviews with authors and publishing-industry professionals, special reports on various book categories, and trade news (such as mergers, rights sales, and personnel changes).

Q

quality   In publishing parlance, the word *quality* in reference to a book category (such as quality fiction) or format (quality paperback) is a term of art—individual works or lines so described are presented as outstanding products.

query letter   A brief written presentation to an agent or editor designed to pitch both the writer and the book idea.

R

remainders   Unsold book stock. Remainders can include titles that have not sold as well as anticipated, in addition to unsold copies of later printings of bestsellers. These volumes are often remaindered—that is, remaining stock is purchased from the publisher at a huge discount and resold to the public.

reprint   A subsequent edition of material that is already in print, especially publication in a different format—the paperback reprint of a hardcover, for example.

résumé   A summary of an individual's career experience and education. When a résumé is sent to prospective agents or publishers, it should contain the author's vital publishing credits, specialty credentials, and pertinent personal experience. Also referred to as the curriculum vitae or, more simply, vita.

returns   Unsold books returned to a publisher by a bookstore, for which the store may receive full or partial credit (depending on the publisher's policy, the age of the book, and so on).

reversion-of-rights clause   In the book contract, a clause that states that if the book goes out of print or the publisher fails to reprint the book within a stipulated length of time, all rights revert to the author.

review copy   A free copy of a (usually) new book sent to print and electronic media that review books for their audiences.

romance fiction or **romance novels**   Modern or period love stories, always with happy endings, which range from the tepid to the torrid. Except for certain erotic-specialty lines, romances do not feature graphic sex. Often mistakenly pigeonholed by those who do not read them, romances and romance writers have been influential in the movement away from passive and coddled female fictional characters to the strong, active modern woman in a tale that reflects areas of topical social concern.

royalty   The percentage of the retail cost of a book that is paid to the author for each copy sold after the author's advance has been recouped. Some publishers structure royalties as a percentage payment against net receipts.

S

SASE (self-addressed stamped envelope)   It is customary for an author to enclose SASEs with query letters, with proposals, and with manuscript submissions. Many editors and agents do not reply if a writer has neglected to enclose an SASE with correspondence or submitted materials.

sales conference   A meeting of a publisher's editorial and sales departments and senior promotion and publicity staff members. A sales conference covers the upcoming season's new books, and marketing strategies are discussed. Sometimes sales conferences are the basis upon which proposed titles are bought or not.

sales representative (sales rep)   A member of the publisher's sales force or an independent contractor who, armed with a book catalog and order forms, visits bookstores in a certain territory to sell books to retailers.

satisfactory clause   In book contracts, a publisher will reserve the right to refuse publication of a manuscript that is not deemed satisfactory. Because the author may be forced to pay back the publisher's advance if the complete work is found to be unsatisfactory, in order to protect the author the specific criteria for publisher satisfaction should be set forth in the contract.

science fiction   Science fiction includes the hardcore, imaginatively embellished technological/scientific novel as well as fiction that is even slightly futuristic (often with an after-the-holocaust milieu—nuclear, environmental, extraterrestrial, genocidal). An element much valued by editors who acquire for the literary expression of this cross-media genre is the ability of the author to introduce elements that transcend and extend conventional insight.

science fiction/fantasy   A category fiction designation that actually collapses two genres into one (for bookseller-marketing reference, of course—though it drives some devotees of these separate fields of writing nuts). In addition, many editors and publishers specialize in both these genres and thus categorize their interests with catchphrases such as sci-fi/fantasy.

screenplay   A film script—either original or one based on material published previously in another form, such as a television docudrama based on a nonfiction book or a movie thriller based on a suspense novel. (Compare with **teleplay**.)

self-publishing   A publishing project wherein an author pays for the costs of manufacturing and selling his or her own book and retains all money from the book's sale. This is a risky venture but one that can be immensely profitable (especially when combined with an author's speaking engagements or imaginative marketing techniques); in addition, if successful, self-publication can lead to distribution or publication by a commercial publisher. Compare with **subsidy publishing**.

self-syndication   Management by writers or journalists of functions that are otherwise performed by syndicates specializing in such services. In self-syndication, it is the writer who manages copyrights, negotiates fees, and handles sales, billing, and other tasks involved in circulating journalistic pieces through newspapers, magazines, or other periodicals that pick up the author's column or run a series of articles.

serial rights   Reprint rights sold to periodicals. First serial rights include the right to publish the material before anyone else (generally before the book is released, or coinciding with the book's official publication)—either for the U.S., a specific country, or for a wider territory. Second serial rights cover material already published, either in a book or another periodical.

serialization   The reprinting of a book or part of a book in a newspaper or magazine. Serialization before (or perhaps simultaneously with) the publication of the book is called first serial. The first reprint after publication (either as a book or by another periodical) is called second serial.

series   Books published as a group either because of their related subject matter (such as a biographical series on modern artists or on World War II aircraft) and/or single authorship (a set of works by Djuna Barnes, a group of books about science and society, or a series of titles geared to a particular diet-and-fitness program). Special series lines can offer a ready-made niche for an industrious author or compiler/editor who is up to date on a publisher's program and has a brace of pertinent qualifications and/or contacts. In contemporary fiction, some genre works are published in series form (such as family sagas, detective series, fantasy cycles).

shelf life   The amount of time an unsold book remains on the bookstore shelf before the store manager pulls it to make room for newer incoming stock with greater (or at least untested) sales potential.

short story   A brief piece of fiction that is more pointed and more economically detailed as to character, situation, and plot than a novel. Published collections of short stories—whether by one or several authors—often revolve around a single theme, express related outlooks, or comprise variations within a genre.

signature   A group of book pages that have been printed together on one large sheet of paper that is then folded and cut in preparation for being bound, along with the book's other signatures, into the final volume.

simultaneous publication   The issuing at the same time of more than one edition of a work, such as in hardcover and trade paperback. Simultaneous releases can be expanded to include (though rarely) deluxe gift editions of a book as well as mass-market paper versions. Audio versions of books are most often timed to coincide with the release of the first print edition.

simultaneous (or multiple) submissions   The submission of the same material to more than one publisher at the same time. Although simultaneous submission is a common practice, publishers should always be made aware that it is being done. Multiple submissions by an author to several agents is, on the other hand, a practice that is sometimes not regarded with great favor by the agent.

slush pile   The morass of unsolicited manuscripts at a publishing house or literary agency, which may fester indefinitely awaiting (perhaps perfunctory) review. Some publishers or agencies do not maintain slush piles per se—unsolicited manuscripts are slated for instant or eventual return without review (if an SASE is included) or may otherwise be literally or figuratively pitched to the wind. Querying a targeted publisher or agent before submitting a manuscript is an excellent way of avoiding, or at least minimizing the possibility of, such an ignoble fate.

software Programs that run on a computer. Word-processing software includes programs that enable writers to compose, edit, store, and print material. Professional-quality software packages incorporate such amenities as databases that can feed the results of research electronically into the final manuscript, alphabetization and indexing functions, and capabilities for constructing tables and charts and adding graphics to the body of the manuscript. Software should be appropriate to both the demands of the work at hand and the requirements of the publisher (which may contract for a manuscript suitable for on-disk editing and electronic design, composition, and typesetting).

special sales Sales of a book to appropriate retailers other than bookstores (for example, wine guides to liquor stores). This classification also includes books sold as premiums (for example, to a convention group or a corporation) or for other promotional purposes. Depending on volume, per-unit costs can be very low, and the book can be custom-designed. (*See* **premiums**.)

spine That portion of the book's casing (or binding) that backs the bound page signatures and is visible when the volume is aligned on a bookshelf among other volumes.

stamping In book publishing, the stamp is the impression of ornamental type and images (such as a logo or monogram) on the book's binding. The stamping process involves using a die with raised or intaglioed surface to apply ink stamping or metallic-leaf stamping.

subsidiary rights The reprint, serial, movie and television, as well as audiotape and videotape rights deriving from a book. The division of profits between publisher and author from the sales of these rights is determined through negotiation. In more elaborately commercial projects, further details such as syndication of related articles and licensing of characters may ultimately be involved.

subsidy publishing A mode of publication wherein the author pays a publishing company to produce his or her work, which may thus appear superficially to have been published conventionally. Subsidy publishing (alias vanity publishing) is generally more expensive than self-publishing, because a successful subsidy house makes a profit on all its contracted functions, charging fees well beyond the publisher's basic costs for production and services.

suspense fiction Fiction within a number of genre categories that emphasize suspense as well as the usual (and sometimes unusual) literary techniques to keep the reader engaged. Suspense fiction encompasses novels of crime and detection (regularly referred to as mysteries—these include English-style cozies; American-style hard-boiled detective stories; dispassionate law-enforcement procedurals; crime stories); action-adventure; espionage novels; technothrillers; tales of psychological suspense; and horror. A celebrated aspect of suspense fiction's popular appeal—one that surely accounts for much of this broad category's sustained market vigor—is the interactive element: The reader may choose to challenge the tale itself by attempting to outwit the author and solve a crime before detectives do, figure out how best to defeat an all-powerful foe before the hero does, or parse out the elements of a conspiracy before the writer reveals the whole story.

syndicated column   Material published simultaneously in a number of newspapers or magazines. The author shares the income from syndication with the syndicate that negotiates the sale. (*See* **self-syndication**.)

syndication rights   (*See* **self-syndication, subsidiary rights**.)

synopsis   A summary in paragraph form, rather than in outline format. The synopsis is an important part of a book proposal. For fiction, the synopsis portrays the high points of story line and plot, succinctly and dramatically. In a nonfiction book proposal, the synopsis describes the thrust and content of the successive chapters (and/or parts) of the manuscript.

T

table of contents   A listing of a book's chapters and other sections (such as the front-matter, appendix, index, and bibliography) or of a magazine's articles and columns, in the order in which they appear; in published versions, the table of contents indicates the respective beginning page numbers.

tabloid   A smaller-than-standard-size newspaper (daily, weekly, or monthly). Traditionally, certain tabloids are distinguished by sensationalism of approach and content rather than by straightforward reportage of newsworthy events. In common parlance, *tabloid* is used to describe works in various media (including books) that cater to immoderate tastes (for example, tabloid exposé, tabloid television; the tabloidization of popular culture).

teleplay   A **screenplay** geared toward television production. Similar in overall concept to screenplays for the cinema, teleplays are nonetheless inherently concerned with such TV-loaded provisions as the physical dimensions of the smaller screen, and formal elements of pacing and structure keyed to stipulated program length and the placement of commercial advertising. Attention to these myriad television-specific demands are fundamental to the viability of a project.

terms   The financial conditions agreed to in a book contract.

theme   A general term for the underlying concept of a book. (*See* **hook**.)

thriller   A thriller is a novel of suspense with a plot structure that reinforces the elements of gamesmanship and the chase, with a sense of the hunt being paramount. Thrillers can be spy novels, tales of geopolitical crisis, legal thrillers, medical thrillers, technothrillers, domestic thrillers. The common thread is a growing sense of threat and the excitement of pursuit.

tip sheet   An information sheet on a single book that presents general publication information (publication date, editor, ISBN, etc.), a brief synopsis of the book, information on relevant other books (sometimes competing titles), and other pertinent marketing data such as author profile and advance blurbs. The tip sheet is given to the sales and publicity departments; a version of the tip sheet is also included in press kits.

title page   The page at the front of a book that lists the title, subtitle, author (and other contributors, such as translator or illustrator), as well as the publishing house and sometimes its logo.

trade books   Books distributed through the book trade—meaning bookstores and major book clubs—as opposed to, for example, mass-market paperbacks, which are often sold at magazine racks, newsstands, and supermarkets as well.

trade discount   The discount from the cover or list price that a publisher gives the bookseller. It is usually proportional to the number of books ordered (the larger the order, the greater the discount), and typically varies between 40% and 50%.

trade list   A catalog of all of a publisher's books in print, with ISBNs and order information. The trade list sometimes includes descriptions of the current season's new books.

trade (quality) paperbacks   Reprints or original titles published in paperback format, larger in dimension than mass-market paperbacks, and distributed through regular retail book channels. Trade paperbacks tend to be in the neighborhood of twice the price of an equivalent mass-market paperback version and about half to two-thirds the price of hardcover editions.

trade publishers   Publishers of books for a general readership—that is, nonprofessional, nonacademic books that are distributed primarily through bookstores.

translation rights   Rights sold either to a foreign agent or directly to a foreign publisher, either by the author's agent or by the original publisher.

treatment   In screenwriting, a full narrative description of the story, including sample dialogue.

U

unauthorized biography   A history of a person's life written without the consent or collaboration of the subject or the subject's survivors.

university press   A publishing house affiliated with a sponsoring university. The university press is generally nonprofit and subsidized by the respective university. Generally, university presses publish noncommercial scholarly nonfiction books written by academics, and their lists may include literary fiction, criticism, and poetry. Some university presses also specialize in titles of regional interest, and many acquire projects intended for commercial book-trade distribution.

unsolicited manuscript   A manuscript sent to an editor or agent without being requested by the editor/agent.

V

vanity press   A publisher that publishes books only at an author's expense—and will generally agree to publish virtually anything that is submitted and paid for. (See **subsidy publishing**.)

vita   Latin word for "life." A shortened equivalent term for *curriculum vitae* (*See* **résumé**).

W

word count   The number of words in a given document. When noted on a manuscript, the word count is usually rounded off to the nearest 100 words.

work-for-hire   Writing done for an employer, or writing commissioned by a publisher or book packager who retains ownership of, and all rights pertaining to, the written material.

Y

young-adult (YA) books   Books for readers generally between the ages of 12 and 17. Young-adult fiction often deals with issues of concern to contemporary teens.

young readers or **younger readers**   Publishing terminology for the range of publications that address the earliest readers. Sometimes a particular house's young-readers' program typifies books for those who do not yet read; which means these books have to hook the caretakers and parents who actually buy them. In certain quirky turns of everyday publishing parlance, *young readers* can mean anyone from embryos through young adults (and "young" means *you* when you want it to). This part may be confusing (as is often the case with publishing usage): Sometimes *younger adult* means only that the readership is allegedly hip, including those who would eschew kid's books as being inherently lame and those who are excruciatingly tapped into the current cultural pulse, regardless of cerebral or life-span quotient.

Z

zombie (or **zombi**)   In idiomatic usage, a zombie is a person whose conduct approximates that of an automaton. Harking back to the term's origins as a figure of speech for the resurrected dead or a reanimated cadaver, such folks are not customarily expected to exhibit an especially snazzy personality or be aware of too many things going on around them; hence some people in book-publishing circles may be characterized as zombies.

Suggested Resources

The American Heritage Dictionary of the English Language (third edition) (Boston: Houghton Mifflin, 1992; updated periodically). Among American dictionaries intended for traditional writing-desk use, *The American Heritage Dictionary* stands out as a careful, comprehensive, and entertaining resource. The practicality and charm of this reference volume is reflected in a fine balance of layout, design, and illustrations; combined with articulate definitions, usage notes, and rich with historical details of the American lexicon, *The American Heritage Dictionary* is a boon for professional American writers (as well as full-blooded dictionary hounds).

Appelbaum, Judith. *How to Get Happily Published* (fourth edition) (New York: Harper & Row, 1988; NAL, 1992). Beyond the mere how-to-get-published primer; sensible advice on generating ideas, putting them into words, and maintaining control over the editing, sales, and marketing of one's work.

Appelbaum, Judith, Nancy Evans, and Florence Janovic. *The Sensible Solutions How to Get Happily Published Handbook* (New York: Sensible Solutions, 1981). Worksheets and additional information for authors of trade books, designed to be used in conjunction with *How to Get Happily Published.*

Aronson, Charles N. *The Writer Publisher* (Arcade, NY: Charles Aronson, 1976). Fascinating, often-horrific, account of author's experience with a major vanity press; also details the travails of self-publishing. Long-out-of-print masterwork—look for it in used-book bins and specialty bookdealer catalogs.

The Associated Press. *The Associated Press Stylebook and Libel Manual* (Reading, MA: Addison-Wesley, 1994). Easy to use, set up in dictionary format; adroit quick-reference guide to contemporary journalistic and mainstream usage. Far from comprehensive, but addresses most frequently encountered day-to-day nuts-and-bolts writing considerations. Treatment of libel issues is a must-read for investigative and opinionative writing. Materials pertaining to gaining resources under the authority of the Freedom of Information Act provides essential background for projects in the public interest. Fully revised and updated edition is edited by Norm Goldstein.

The Association of American University Presses Directory (Chicago: University of Chicago Press, published annually). Detailed description of each AAUP member press with a summary of its publishing program, names and responsibilities of key staff, and requirements for submitting proposals and manuscripts.

Atchity, Kenneth J. *A Writer's Time: A Guide to the Creative Process, from Vision Through Revision* (second edition) (New York: Norton, 1995). Comprehensive handbook offers a stylish account of how to get in tune, stay attuned, and fine-tune your writing skills. Includes section on effective marketing for writers.

Atchity, Kenneth J., and Chi-Li Wong. *Writing Treatments That Sell: How to Create and Market Your Story Ideas to the Motion Picture and TV Industry* (New York: Owl Books, 1997). First book on the market to focus explicitly on the one selling tool that will get your ideas noticed—the all-important and oft-neglected treatment that cuts through the addled and overworked attention of producers and agents. Entertaining, sometimes breathtaking, and often brilliant advice—plus valuable resource listings.

Balkin, Richard. *How to Understand and Negotiate a Book Contract or Magazine Agreement* (Cincinnati: Writer's Digest Books, 1985). Essential reading for every writer who stands to make a sale. Author is an established agent.

Ballon, Rachel. *Blueprint for Writing: A Writer's Guide to Creativity, Craft, and Career* (Los Angeles: Lowell House, 1994). Whether it be a novel, story, or script, carefully crafted narratives require development of such basic elements as structure, plot, and character in order to create depth, focus—and entertainment value. This book helps the professional writer fine-tune a work and demystifies the writing process for rookies. Author is founder and director of the Writer's Center in Los Angeles.

Ballon, Rachel. *The Writer's Sourcebook: From Writing Blocks to Writing Blockbusters* (Los Angeles, CA: Lowell House, 1996). A first-stop resource for writers: information on developing the skills needed to achieve writing goals, including what to write and how to format it for publication. Author owns and operates The Writer's Center in Los Angeles.

Barzun, Jacques. *Simple & Direct: A Rhetoric for Writers* (revised edition) (Chicago: University of Chicago Press, 1994). Techniques to take a writer's craft to new heights of effectiveness and expressiveness, through diction, syntax, tone, meaning, composition, and revision. Exercises, model passages, and amusing examples of good style gone bad.

Bates, Jem, and Adrian Waller. *The Canadian Writer's Market: An Extensive Guide for Freelance Writers* (11th revised edition) (Toronto: McClelland & Stewart, 1994). Provides writers with resources keyed to the Canadian market in magazines and book publishing. Includes advice, strategies, and editorial guidelines for thriving in the professional marketplace; information pertaining to writing courses, prizes, and awards, as well as some crossover market listings for the United States industry.

Benedict, Elizabeth. *The Joy of Writing Sex* (Cincinnati, OH: Story Press, 1996). Author deftly covers all the issues head on—from dealing with "internal censors" to writing about sex in the age of AIDS. Focus is on crafting compelling, believable sex scenes that hinge not on the mechanics of sex, but on freshness of character, dialogue, mood, and plot. Instructions are supported with examples from the finest contemporary fiction.

Bernard, André (editor). *Rotten Rejections* (Wainscott, NY: Pushcart Press, 1990). Humorous and harrowing collection of literary rejection letters, to such recipients as William Faulkner, Gustave Flaubert, James Joyce, and Vladimir Nabokov. Fine inspiration for writers encountering rejection during any phase of their careers.

Bernstein, Theodore. *The Careful Writer: A Modern Guide to English Usage* (New York: Atheneum, 1965). Lively, accurate, and articulate classic. Mainstream and mass-market writers may view it as too high-toned a tome to grace their shelves, but this work nevertheless addresses their needs accessibly with observations they might well heed.

Bernstein, Theodore. *Miss Thistlebottom's Hobgoblins: The Careful Writer's Guide to the Taboos, Bugbears, and Outmoded Rules of English Usage* (New York: Simon & Schuster, 1984). More apt insights from the author of *The Careful Writer*.

Block, Lawrence. *Telling Lies for Fun and Profit: A Manual for Fiction Writers* (New York: William Morrow/Quill, 1981). Inside look at winning techniques and career strategies by an admired master of both. Introduction to the new edition is by Sue Grafton.

Bly, Robert W. *Secrets of a Freelance Editor* (revised edition) (New York: Owl Books, 1997). Popular and invaluable how-to focuses on lucrative but lesser-known commercial markets (ads, annual reports, brochures, catalogs, newsletters, direct-mail packages, audiovisual presentations, promotional pieces), where many high-paying writing projects and clients exist.

Bolker, Joan (editor). *The Writer's Home Companion: An Anthology of the World's Best Writing Advice, From Keats to Kunitz* (New York: Owl Books, 1997). A blue-chip collection of hard-earned wisdom from some of the most respected writers in recent literary history.

Borcherding, David H. (editor). *Romance Writer's Sourcebook: Where to Sell Your Manuscripts* (Cincinnati: Writer's Digest Books, updated periodically). Illuminating essays and valuable resources to guide writers of romances through the reaches of this vast sector of the fiction market.

Boston, Bruce O. (editor). *Stet! Tricks of the Trade for Writers and Editors* (Alexandria, VA: Editorial Experts, 1986). Supple, interactive collection of articles that sets the writer inside the heads of editors and publishers.

Boswell, John. *The Awful Truth About Publishing: Why They Always Reject Your Manuscript . . . And What You Can Do About It* (New York: Warner Books, 1986). A view from the other side—that is, the inside view from within the large publishing house.

Brown, Rita Mae. *Starting from Scratch: A Different Kind of Writer's Manual* (New York: Bantam, 1988). Courage, philosophy, and practical guidance for holding to and honing your writer's vision through the travails of publishing.

Browne, Renni, and Dave King. *Self-Editing for Fiction Writers* (New York: HarperCollins, 1993). Guidance in an often-overlooked area that is crucial for today's fiction writers. In an age when many editors are too overworked to do it for you, best believe you better know how to do it yourself.

Bunnin, Brad, and Peter Beren. *Author Law and Strategies: A Personal Guide for the Working Writer* (Berkeley: Nolo Press, 1984). The ins and outs of publishing laws, published by specialists in do-it-yourself legal guides.

Burack, Sylvia K. (editor). *The Writer's Handbook* (Boston: The Writer, updated annually). Includes over 100 chapters on all fields of writing for publication by leading writers, literary agents, and editors. Includes information on the business side of writing, plus 3,000-item listing of where to sell manuscripts. Ms. Burack is the editor of *The Writer*, the pioneer magazine for literary workers. For over 100 years, aspiring as well as experienced writers have looked to *The Writer* as a practical guide to instruct, inform, and inspire them as they work toward the goal of all writers—publication. (See listing in United States Publishers, The Writer, Inc.). Ms. Burack is also the author of *How to Write and Sell Mystery Fiction*.

Burgett, Gordon. *The Writer's Guide to Query Letters and Cover Letters* (Rocklin, CA: Prima, 1992). Sound and pointed advice, from an expert's perspective, on how to utilize the query and cover letter to sell your writing.

The Chicago Manual of Style (14th edition) (Chicago: University of Chicago Press, 1993). In matters of editorial style—punctuation, spelling, capitalization, issues of usage—this book provides traditional, conservative, and justifiable guidelines. This esteemed work is not, however, a handbook of grammar per se and does not offer writers ready tips for resolving day-to-day creative and compositional questions. The *Chicago Manual* is, rather, a professional reference work for the publishing and editing trades— and in this area it remains the American standard. Many commercial writers and editors characterize the *Chicago Manual* as intricate and arcane relative to their own reference demands.

Chittenden, Margaret. *How to Write Your Novel* (Boston, MA: The Writer, 1996). Novelist Chittenden discusses all elements of successful novel writing. Part I covers inspiration, plot and character, synopsis, point of view, and style. Part II covers the rough draft, transition and flashbacks, endings, revision, and marketing.

Clardy, Andrea Fleck. *Words to the Wise: A Writer's Guide to Feminist and Lesbian Periodicals & Publishers* (Ithaca, NY: Firebrand, 1993; updated periodically). Popular pamphlet-sized handbook lists more than 150 United States and Canadian book and periodical publishers, references for children's book and scholarly publishers, and submissions and payment policies—keyed to publishing enterprises that actively acquire women's words.

Collier, Oscar, with Frances Spatz Leighton. *How to Write and Sell Your First Nonfiction Book* (New York: St. Martin's, 1994). Practical, encouraging how-to from industry professionals. Topics include choosing a subject; targeting an audience; writing the proposal; researching effectively and conducting interviews; dealing with agents and editors; understanding contracts; marketing your book.

Curtis, Richard. *Beyond the Bestseller: A Literary Agent Takes You Inside the Book Business* (New York: NAL, 1989; Plume, 1990). Incisive and practical advice, from a literary agent who is also an accomplished writer.

Curtis, Richard. *How to Be Your Own Literary Agent: The Business of Getting Your Book Published* (Boston: Houghton Mifflin, 1984). Insights and how-to; a personal point of view from one who knows the ropes and shows them to you.

Davidson, Jeffrey P. *Marketing for the Home-Based Business* (Holbrook, MA: Bob Adams, 1991). For entrepreneurs of all stripes (including writers) who are based in their homes. Digs beneath the obvious and uncovers ways to project a professional image and transform your computer, telephone, and fax into a dynamic marketing staff.

Dotson, Edisol W. *Putting Out: The Essential Publishing Resource for Lesbian and Gay Writers* (Pittsburgh, PA: Cleis Press, 1995; updated periodically). Specialized reference tool lists book publishers, magazines, newspapers, newsletters, theater groups, and agents—all of them with an interest in publishing, producing, or agenting gay and lesbian writing. Includes nuts-and-bolts submissions guidelines, pertinent publishers' marketing budgets, publishers' selection policies. How-to essays cover project development, contracts, marketing.

Doubtfire, Diane. *Teach Yourself Creative Writing* (second edition) (Lincolnwood, IL: NTC Publishing Group, 1996). A practical guide for aspiring writers. Discusses short stories, articles, poetry, novels, and plays. Covers specialty areas such as writing for radio, television, and children's books. Author has many books to her credit and is a respected teacher of creative writing.

Dustbooks (editors). The renowned Small Press Information Library from Dustbooks includes four separate books: *The Directory of Small Press Editors & Publishers*; *Directory of Poetry Publishers*; *The International Directory of Little Magazines and Small Presses*; and *Small Press Record of Books in Print* (Paradise, CA: Dustbooks, all volumes published annually). This set of references, geared toward the literary arena, is produced by the publishers of the industry journal *Small Press Review*. These resources for market exploration also provide writers with editorial requirements and procedures for manuscript submission keyed to individual publishers and periodicals.

Elwood, Maren. *Characters Make Your Story* (Boston, MA: The Writer, Inc.). Original approach to the essence of good fiction writing—creating true-to-life characters—by a renowned critic and teacher. Vivid examples.

Frensham, Raymond G. *Teach Yourself Screenwriting* (Lincolnwood, IL: NTC Publishing Group, 1996). A script is the blueprint from which a movie or television show is made. Covers fundamentals of translating creative ideas into this challenging format.

Fry, Ronald W. (editor). *Book Publishing Career Directory* (Hawthorne, NJ: Career Press, published annually). Descriptions of various publishing jobs by those who actually do them, plus advice on securing those positions.

Gage, Diane, and Marcia Hibsch Coppess. *Get Published: Editors from the Nation's Top Magazines Tell You What They Want* (New York: Henry Holt, 1986). An extensive survey of dozens of national magazines—who they are and what they're looking for.

Gardner, John. *On Becoming a Novelist* (New York: Harper & Row, 1983). Sympathetic and enjoyable account of the education, art, and survival of the beginning writer.

Garrand, Timothy. *Writing for Multimedia: Entertainment, Education, Training, Advertising, and the World Wide Web* (Newton, MA: Focal Press, 1996). This is the first in-depth analysis of how to write informational programs and stories for multimedia. Successful existing CD-ROMs and World Wide Web programs are analyzed and documented with extensive script samples, flowcharts, and other writing material.

Goldberg, Natalie. *Wild Mind: Living the Writer's Life* (New York: Bantam, 1990). Enlightened counseling and illuminating exercises to get the most from, and into, your craft.

Goldberg, Natalie. *Writing Down the Bones: Freeing the Writer Within* (Boston: Shambhala Publications, 1986). Thought-provoking and practical advice on the art and technique of writing. The author is a Zen Buddhist and writing instructor.

Gross, Gerald (editor). *Editors on Editing: What Writers Need to Know About What Editors Do* (New York: Grove/Atlantic Monthly Press, 1993). Celebrated editor and book doctor Jerry Gross offers a revised and updated edition of this consummate resource classic. Covering virtually every area of trade publishing from the large commercial houses to the small literary presses, top editors offer astute, practical, and provocative discussions of the author/editor relationship. Includes valuable tips on how to prospect, delineates the editorial process, details what writers can do to benefit most from an editor's attention.

Harman, Eleanor, and Ian Montagnes (editors). *The Thesis and the Book* (Toronto: University of Toronto Press, 1976). Selection of articles about the revision of scholarly presentations into works of broader appeal. The discussion of the demands of specialist audiences versus those of a wider market is pertinent to the development of general nonfiction projects—especially those involving collaboration between writing professionals and academics.

Henderson, Bill. *The Publish-It-Yourself Handbook: Literary Tradition and How-to Without Commercial or Vanity Publishers* (New York: Norton/Pushcart, 1987). Eminently readable classic comprising tales—both inspirational and cautionary—by persons who have self-published.

Hensley, Dennis E. and Holly G. Miller. *Write on Target* (Boston, MA: The Writer, Inc., 1996). Five-phase program: write professionally, sell your material, and map out a plan for lifelong success as a writer. Includes exercises and lessons.

Herman, Jeff, and Deborah M. Adams. *Write the Perfect Book Proposal: 10 Proposals That Sold and Why* (New York: Wiley, 1993). Analysis of successful nonfiction book proposals with pointed and insightful commentary from a team of accomplished industry professionals—New York literary agent Jeff Herman and book-proposal doctor (and author) Deborah Adams. Doesn't just tell you how to do it—this book shows you in detail how it was done.

Hollywood Creative Directory (Santa Monica, CA: HCD; updated periodically). Resources available in print, on diskette, or on-line. HRD also publishes *Hollywood Financial Directory*, *Hollywood Distributors Directory*, *Hollywood Movie Music Directory*, *Hollywood Interactive Entertainment Directory*, and *Hollywood Agents & Managers Directory*—as well as other specialized reference and resource materials, including mailing lists and labels.

Horowitz, Lois. *Knowing Where to Look: The Ultimate Guide to Research* (Cincinnati: Writer's Digest Books, 1984). An invaluable tool for anyone who has to dig up elusive facts and figures.

Huddle, David. *The Writing Habit: Essays* (Layton, UT: Gibbs Smith, 1992). A serious, useful book on the literary craft. Much more than a how-to guide; provides practical, energetic, supportive advice and imaginative approach to learning tricks of the trade.

Hudson, Bob. *Christian Writer's Manual of Style* (Grand Rapids, MI: Zondervan, 1988). Valuable overview and helpful details pertaining to writing expression and stylistic conventions in the field of Christian writing; directed toward the academic and professional market as well as more general readership.

Jacobsohn, Rachel. *The Reading Group Handbook: Everything You Need to Know, From Choosing Members to Leading Discussions* (New York: Hyperion, 1994). Reading groups are proliferating and thriving nationwide; such fellowships are sponsored by bookstores as well as booklovers (including writers) as fun, stimulating, and interactive recreational venues through which (incidentally) to support our home industry. This handbook takes readers through the territory and provides a variety of resource listings.

Judson, Jerome. *On Being a Poet* (Cincinnati: Writer's Digest Books, 1984). A discussion of the art of poetry—both the author's and that of other poets.

Judson, Jerome. *The Poet's Handbook* (Cincinnati: Writer's Digest Books, 1980). The art and mechanics of writing poetry by "rule" and example. Also includes tips on getting published.

Jerome, Judson. *Poet's Market* (Cincinnati: Writer's Digest Books, published annually). Market-research resource for the poet.

Killian, Kristi, and Sheila Bender. *Writing in a Convertible with the Top Down* (New York: Warner Books, 1992). How to quit stalling, shift into creative gear, and speed successfully on your way through the all-terrain territory known as publishing country. Wealth of advice and inspiration—as lively and informal as it is pertinent.

Kilpatrick, James J. *The Writer's Art* (Kansas City, MO: Andrews, McMeel & Parker, 1984). An opinionated discussion of proper usage, style, and just plain good writing from one of the news business's most popular curmudgeons.

Kirby, David. *Writing Poetry: Where Poems Come From and How to Write Them* (Boston, MA: The Writer, 1997). Guide to writing all types of poems. Discusses subject matter, form, rhyme, meter, and provides an overview of today's poetry market.

Klauser, Henriette Anne. *Put Your Heart on Paper: Staying Connected in a Loose-Ends World* (New York: Bantam, 1995). How to communicate, create, and relate through the written word. Invaluable tales and techniques that apply equally to the writer's craft and everyday life.

Klauser, Henriette Anne. *Writing on Both Sides of the Brain: Breakthrough Techniques for People Who Write* (New York: Harper & Row, 1986). How to refrain from editing while you write; how to edit, mercilessly and creatively, what you've just written.

Kremer, John. *Book Publishing Resource Guide* (Fairfield, IA: Ad-Lib Publications, updated periodically). Comprehensive listings for book-marketing contacts and resources—contains a vast bibliography and references to other resource guides.

Kremer, John. *101 Ways to Market Your Books—For Publishers and Authors* (Fairfield, IA: Ad-Lib Publications, 1986). Sensible, innovative and inspiring advice on, first, producing the most marketable book possible, and then on marketing it as effectively as possible.

Lamott, Anne. *Bird by Bird: Some Instructions on Writing and Life* (New York: Pantheon, 1994). Breathtakingly evocative and insightful commentary on commitment, training, and craft, and what it means to be a writer.

Larsen, Michael. *How to Write a Book Proposal* (Cincinnati: Writer's Digest Books, 1985). A clear and no-nonsense—even inspiring—step-by-step guide to the book proposal. Author is West Coast–based literary agent and writer.

Levin, Martin P. *Be Your Own Literary Agent: The Ultimate Insider's Guide to Getting Published* (Berkeley, CA: Ten Speed Press, 1996). A prominent publishing insider (former executive at several big New York houses, now a respected literary lawyer) offers insights and hard-to-get knowledge every aspiring author yearns for—from pitching the book to finding the ideal editor, getting the most out of a contract, and getting the book produced right.

Literary Market Place (New York: R. R. Bowker; published annually). Hefty annual directory of the publishing industry, including publishing houses and their personnel, literary agencies, and writers' organizations and events, as well as research, writing, editing, and publishing services nationwide.

Litowinsky, Olga. *Writing and Publishing Books for Children in the 1990s: The Inside Story from the Editor's Desk* (New York: Walker & Company, 1992). A leading editor and literary agent elucidates the world of children's and young-adult publishing. Consummate advice on writing for young readers, and for avoiding the many pitfalls in this hard-to-break-into field.

Long, Duncan. *You Can Be an Information Writer* (Port Townsend, WA: Loompanics, 1991). Irreverent resource manual shows where opportunities and money are in the burgeoning market for technical documentation, specialist articles, topical investigative reports, up-to-the-minute how-to guides, and advertising. Section on research techniques demonstrates ways to shave time and pump up the bucks simultaneously.

Luey, Beth. *Handbook for Academic Authors* (revised edition) (New York: Cambridge University Press, 1990). This reference pinpoints key (and unsuspected) considerations important in the field of academic publishing; valuable information with strategic implications for players in the publish-or-perish game.

Maass, Donald. *The Career Novelist: A Literary Agent Offers Strategies for Success* (Portsmouth, NH: Heinemann, 1966). Straightforward approach to commercial viability and success as a writer of fiction. Remarkable insights into the current (and future) publishing climate as they apply to veteran wordsmiths and aspiring storytellers alike. In addition to being an established literary agent, Donald Maass is the author of numerous published novels.

Mann, Thomas. *A Guide to Library Research Methods* (New York: Oxford University Press, 1987). A practical guide to the most helpful, time-saving, and cost-effective information sources.

McCormack, Thomas. *The Fiction Editor* (New York: St. Martin's Press, 1988). How to fine-tune fiction; every bit as helpful for writers as it is for editors.

McInerny, Ralph. *Let's Write a Mystery*; *Let's Write a Novel*; and *Let's Write Short Stories* (Arlington, VA: Vandamere Press/Quodlibetal Features, 1993). Series of vivid instructional packages on the art and marketing of written works. Individual programs are geared to the areas of mystery writing; mainstream novels; and short fiction. Each title includes a set of audiotapes, tutorial lessons, a workbook, and drafts of unpublished writing in its respective field.

Miller, Casey, and Kate Swift. *The Handbook of Nonsexist Writing* (New York: Harper & Row, 1988). Guidelines for eliminating sexist terms and constructions from all writing. Niggling resisters to usage reformation still exist among professional scribblers— the printed word has shown, however, that to be lexically correct liberates writers to be both admirably exact and at their exhilaratingly expressive best.

Namanworth, Phillip, and Gene Busnar. *Working for Yourself* (New York: McGraw-Hill, 1986). Everything you need to know about the business and personal side of freelancing and being self-employed. Great tips applicable to orchestrating a writer's business and working life.

Norville, Barbara. *Writing the Modern Mystery* (Cincinnati: Writer's Digest, 1986). Excellent overview, from concept to completed work. A framework for development rather than specific how-to, but plenty of tips to aid the writer in following through on fresh ideas.

Oberlin, Loriann Hoff. *Writing for Money* (Cincinnati: Writer's Digest Books, 1995). How your writing talents can supplement your regular income or establish a self-employed career. Supportive guide that covers such fields as writing books and articles, reference writing, teaching courses and seminars, and serving commercial clients.

O'Cork, Shannon. *How to Write Mysteries* (Cincinnati: Writer's Digest Books, 1989). Original approach to detective and crime fiction, from concept through composition. Author O'Cork is among the prototype practitioners in this literary field.

O'Gara, Elaine. *Travel Writer's Markets: Where to Sell Your Travel Articles and Place Your Press Releases* (revised edition) (Boston: Harvard Common, 1993). A must for travel writers; provides an abundance of practical information, as useful for field-hardened veterans as it is revelatory for greenhorns. How to submit manuscripts and photographs; how to research your market.

Paludan, Eve. *Romance Writer's Pink Pages* (Rocklin, CA: Prima, updated periodically). Definitive resource for romance authors and writers of women's fiction. Includes information on marketing your work, publishing trends, networking, and more. Incisive commentary from writers, editors, and agents.

Parinello, Al. *On the Air: How to Get on Radio and TV Talk Shows and What to Do When You Get There* (Hawthorne, NJ: Career Press, 1991). Exciting guide to the electronic media and their use for promotional purposes. Ties in marketing aspects common to such diverse fields as seminars, social activism, and professional training and advancement— and is especially appropriate for authors devoted to the entrepreneurial spirit.

Parsons, Paul. *Getting Published: The Acquisition Process at University Presses* (Knoxville: University of Tennessee Press, 1989) Traces steps in manuscript acquisition from initial contact to final approval. Thoughtful and astonishing analysis of consideration procedures and strategies of all the players.

Polking, Kirk, and Leonard S. Meranus (editors). *Law and the Writer* (third edition) (Cincinnati: Writer's Digest Books, 1985). A collection of pieces addressing legal issues that concern writers and their works.

Polti, Georges. *The Thirty-Six Dramatic Situations* (Boston, MA: The Writer, Inc.). Classic guide to plotting for fiction writers and playwrights.

Powell, Walter W. *Getting Into Print: The Decision-Making Process in Scholarly Publishing* (Chicago: University of Chicago Press, 1985). An eye-opening, behind-the-scenes look at the operations of two scholarly presses.

Poynter, Dan. *The Self-Publishing Manual* (Santa Barbara, CA: Para Publishing, 1989). Informative and complete step-by-step how-to by the principal of one of the most successful one-person publishing firms.

Poynter, Dan, and Mindy Bingham. *Is There a Book Inside You? How to Successfully Author a Book Alone or Through a Collaborator* (Santa Barbara, CA: Para Publishing, 1985). A thought-provoking series of exercises to help you assess your publishing potential.

Preston, Elizabeth. *Preparing Your Manuscript* (Boston, MA: The Writer). Covers submissions formats for all types of manuscripts, plus important rules of grammar, spelling, punctuation, and capitalization.

Preston, Elizabeth, Ingrid Monke, and Elizabeth Bickford. *Preparing Your Manuscript* (Boston: The Writer, 1992). Contemporary guide to manuscript preparation; provides step-by-step advice for professional presentation of work for submission to editors, publishers, agents, television producers. Covers punctuation, spelling, indexing, along with examples of proper formats for poetry, prose, plays; also offers essential information on copyright, marketing, and mailing manuscripts.

Princeton Language Institute (editors). *The 21st Century Manual of Style* (New York: Dell/Laurel, 1993). Dictionary-style reference with a futuristic outlook. Concise presentation of where language and lexical expression are now, directions the lingo is going, and where you as a writer want to be.

The Prolific Writer's Magazine (Oradell, NJ: BSK Communications, published quarterly). Literary/trade publication that provides educationally enriching and entertaining articles, news, blurbs, profiles, interviews, and much more. Assistance and support for the talents of aspiring and professional writers.

Provost, Gary. *The Freelance Writer's Handbook* (New York: NAL/Mentor, 1982). Invaluable reference and resource guide, mainly for writers of short pieces.

Provost, Gary. *Make Your Words Work* (Cincinnati: Writer's Digest, 1990). Astute approach to methods of expression, style, pacing, and compositional problem-solving; applicable to nonfiction as well as fiction. Instructive exercises to deliver the most power with your writing.

Prues, Don (editor). *Guide to Literary Agents* (Cincinnati, OH: Writer's Digest Books; updated annually). Listings for more than 500 literary and script agents in the United States and Canada.

Rivers, William L. *Finding Facts: Interviewing, Observing, Using Reference Sources* (Englewood Cliffs, NJ: Prentice-Hall, 1975). A careful inquiry into the demanding research process and the difficulties involved in achieving objectivity.

Roberts, Ellen E. M. *The Children's Picture Book: How to Write It, How to Sell It* (Cincinnati: Writer's Digest Books, 1981). A wise and enthusiastic step-by-step guide by an established children's book editor and popular editorial consultant.

Ross, Marilyn, and Tom Ross. *Marketing Your Books: A Collection of Profit-Making Ideas for Authors and Publishers* (Buena Vista, CO: Communication Creativity, 1990). Fine-tuned, cost-effective, innovative promotional designs. Authors should note: This book accentuates the philosophy that a successful marketing strategy begins at the concept stage—before the book itself is written.

Ross, Tom, and Marilyn Ross. *The Complete Guide to Self-Publishing* (Buena Vista, CO: Communication Creativity, 1990). Up-to-date, step-by-step information and procedures that take your book from the idea stage through production, setting up your publishing business, and into the hands of consumers. Not just for entrepreneurs who self-publish—contains valuable tips for commercially published writers to maximize the success of their titles.

Rubens, Philip (editor). *Science and Technical Writing: A Manual of Style* (New York: Henry Holt, 1992). Comprehensive one-stop style guide for writers and editors in scientific and technical fields (including students). Addresses fundamental issues of style and usage, distinguishes between specialized terminology and technobabble, and provides guidelines for achieving communication with one's audience.

Rubie, Peter. *The Elements of Storytelling: How to Write Compelling Fiction* (New York: Wiley, 1996). Decisive, silver-tongued guide to the art and craft of novelistic writing. Holistic approach to creating enticing characters and plot, sharpening the pacing, developing a graceful style and powerful structure. The author is an accomplished literary agent, writer, and editor.

Saltzman, Joel. *If You're Writing, Let's Talk: A Step-by-Step Approach to Keep You Writing and Help You Finish* (Rocklin, CA: Prima Publishing, 1996). Wonderfully comic approach to the woes of the writing life. Offers not only solace, but genuine solutions to difficult problems: innovative and effective ways to grab the reader's attention, turn everyday life into great fiction, flesh out character and plot, and know when it's finished.

Schaeffer, Garry, and Dr. Tony Alessandra. *Publish and Flourish—A Consultant's Guide: How to Boost Visibility and Earnings Through a Publishing Strategy* (New York: Wiley, 1992). Publishing is a business—and also a great adjunct to one. This book shows entrepreneurs, consultants, and freelancers in all fields how to use a publishing program both as a marketing tool and as a profit-centered part of their own business careers.

Schwartz, Marilyn and the Task Force on Bias-Free Language of the Association of American University Presses. *Guidelines for Bias-Free Writing* (Bloomington, IN: Indiana University Press, 1995). A valuable reference on contemporary style that can be used as a writer's guide to producing hard-hitting prose without being in the least contrite.

Seidman, Michael. *From Printout to Published* (New York: Carroll & Graf, 1992). Engaging and unvarnished consideration of the writer-publisher interface all the way from first draft through finished book. Detailed discussions of manuscript submissions, working with agents, contract negotiation, gaining ample advances, editing, cover design, book marketing, promotion—and more. Authored by renowned and popular editor.

Seidman, Michael. *Living the Dream: An Outline for a Life in Fiction* (New York: Carroll & Graf, 1992). Sage and sound philosophy and tips-of-the-trade in the what-goes-around-comes-around world of fiction publishing.

Seuling, Barbara. *How to Write a Children's Book and Get It Published* (revised and expanded edition) (New York, Scribner, 1991). Filled with broad truths and subtle nuances to guide authors successfully through the domain of children's publishing.

Seymour-Smith, Martin. *Dictionary of Fictional Characters* (Boston: The Writer, 1992). Updated, reedited, and expanded from the earlier text of Freeman and Urquhart, this new version of a classic work is the definitive writer's reference guide to over 50,000 fictional characters from novels, short stories, poems, plays, and operas.

Spy magazine editors. *Spy Notes on McInerney's* Bright Lights, Big City, *Ellis's* Less Than Zero, *Janowitz's* Slaves of New York . . . *and All Those Other Hip Urban Novels of the 1980s* (New York: Dolphin/Doubleday, 1989). "Becoming the Literary Voice of a Generation" is an astonishing examination of just what it takes to get published and why you may be better off staying undiscovered.

Sterling, C. L. and M. G. Davidson. *Getting Your Manuscript Sold: Surefire Writing and Selling Strategies That Will Get Your Book Published* (New York: Barclay House/Zinn Communications, 1995). With a practical how-to orientation, this book asks pertinent questions about a writer's work and gives illuminating answers to help launch a writing career. Authors are agent Cynthia Sterling and editor Megan Davidson.

Sterling, C. L. and M. G. Davidson. *Writing Aerobics* (New York: Barclay House/Zinn Communications, 1996). Practical and zesty methods that bring into play the entire range of a writer's talent. Insightful observations and imagination-sparking exercises.

Strunk, William, Jr., and E. B. White. *The Elements of Style* (third edition) (New York: Macmillan, 1979). This highly respected, widely read, and well-loved classic is seen by some contemporary writers as sheer stuffed-shirt punditry. It is, however, a slim volume and doesn't take up much space or require much time to read—and modern writers may well find themselves adopting Strunk-and-White principles in spite of themselves.

Stuart, Sally E. (editor). *Christian Writer's Market* (Wheaton, IL: Harold Shaw Publishers, updated annually). Bursting with information about book and periodical publishers, new media opportunities, writers' conferences, and specialized editors and agents. This work is a grand tool for beginning and advanced writers, full-time freelancers, agents, editors, publicists, and writing classes. Computer-disk version available.

Tapply, William G. *The Elements of Mystery Fiction* (Boston, MA: The Writer, 1996). Prolific mystery writer and winner of the Scribner Crime Novel Award explores his craft in this practical handbook. Using examples from his own work and that of other celebrated mystery writers, the author discusses planning and writing successful mystery fiction.

Todd, Alden. *Finding Facts Fast* (Berkeley: Ten Speed Press, 1979). Details basic, intermediate, and advanced research techniques; hundreds of ideas for those stuck in a research dead-end.

Volunteer Lawyers for the Arts. *Pressing Business: An Organizational Manual for Independent Publishers* (New York: VLA, 1984). Delineates legal and business concepts applicable to smaller literary and not-for-profit publishing enterprises. Addresses issues writers should be aware of, since for practical (including tax) purposes they are part and parcel to the same industry.

Welty, Eudora. *One Writer's Beginnings* (New York: Warner Books, 1984). "Listening," "Learning to See," and "Finding a Voice"—three beautifully written essays (based on lectures given at Harvard) that trace Ms. Welty's influences and her growth as a young writer in the South.

Whitney, Phyllis A. *Guide to Fiction Writing* (Boston, MA: The Writer). Leading novelist Whitney advises how to write publishable fiction. Practical aspects of planning a novel, characterization, suspense, flashbacks, beginnings, and endings.

Williams, John Hartley and Martin Sweeney. *Teach Yourself Writing Poetry* (Lincolnwood, IL: NTC Publishing Group, 1996). Demystifies the process of writing poetry by explaining the basics of rhyme and imagery. Various poetic forms are explained, including the sonnet, haiku, and blank verse.

Wilson, James. *Freelance Writer's Handbook: The Real Story* (Port Townsend, WA, Loompanics, 1988). How to stalk a market; how to command your career; how to get the most money and not get ripped off; how to handle editors; the use of photography— and more. Blithely scathing resource depicts behind-the-scenes publishing machinations as well as dispenses a wealth of advice toward resolving other terrors (writer's block, rejection) part and parcel to the writer's terrain. How-to-do-it manual written by a pro who has done it.

Wisniewski, Mark. *Writing & Revising Your Fiction* (Boston: The Writer, 1996). Hows and whys of the do-or-die process of working your fiction ideas through to publishable form. Provides tested techniques for creating salable fiction. Covers characterization, plotting, point of view, setting, rough drafts, revision, and marketing. Author is an accomplished fiction writer, writing teacher, and workshop leader.

Words into Type (Englewood Cliffs, NJ: Prentice Hall, 1974). This esteemed professional reference for the publishing industry covers technical considerations of editing, copyediting, proofreading, and typographic style, which can and should be of tremendous value to writers during manuscript preparation. The insight into what goes on inside the publisher's shop lets the writer in on what to expect from the sometimes-enigmatic production sequence. This reference work is based on studies by Marjorie E. Skillin, Robert M. Gay, and other authorities.

Wray, Cheryl Sloan. *Writing for Magazines: A Beginner's Guide* (Lincolnwood, IL: NTC Publishing Group, 1996). Guidebook to fundamentals of being a magazine free-lancer, writing and getting your articles published. Author is widely published in a variety of magazines.

Writer's Market (Cincinnati: Writer's Digest Books, published annually). A directory of thousands of markets and outlets; best known for its listing of the hundreds of consumer and trade periodicals. Also includes book publishers, book packagers, greeting-card publishers, syndicates—and more. (In addition, Writer's Digest Books offers a catalog of specialist and generalist sourcebooks and guidebooks for writers covering virtually the entire publishing spectrum.)

Zinsser, William. *On Writing Well* (New York: Harper & Row, 1985). How to simplify nonfiction writing and deliver fresh, vigorous prose. An excellent book to keep on hand.

Zobel, Louise Purwin. *The Travel Writer's Handbook* (Chicago: Surrey Books, 1994). Veteran travel writer Louise Zobel explains the practical aspects of travel writing, from pre-trip research, to photography, to selling strategies. Includes the most marketable formats for travel writing.

Zuckerman, Albert. *Writing the Blockbuster Novel* (Cincinnati: Writer's Digest Books, 1993). Thorough and incisive book geared toward producing popular "big-book" fiction. Writer-agent author (with a skein of successful clients) provides expert dissection of compositional techniques, narrative structure, character attributes and development, importance of conflict—all keyed to instructional examples from bestselling novels.

Index